ENCYCLOPEDIA OF AFRICAN-AMERICAN POLITICS

Robert C. Smith

Facts On File, Inc.

For Lovanya Dejean
(1943–2001)

Encyclopedia of African-American Politics

Copyright © 2003 by Robert C. Smith

Facts On File, Inc.
132 West 31st Street
New York NY 10001

Library of Congress Cataloging-in-Publication Data

Smith, Robert C., 1947–
Encyclopedia of African American politics / Robert C. Smith.
p. cm.
Includes bibliographical references and index.
ISBN 0-8160-4475-9 (alk. paper)
1. African Americans—Politics and government—Encyclopedias. 2. African
Americans—History—Encyclopedias. I. Title.
E185 .S58155 2003
973'.0496073'003—dc21   2002075473

Facts On File books are available at special discounts when purchased in bulk
quantities for businesses, associations, institutions, or sales promotions. Please call our
Special Sales Department in New York at (212) 967-8800 or (800) 322-8755.
You can find Facts On File on the World Wide Web at http://www.factsonfile.com

Text design by Joan M. Toro
Cover design by Cathy Rincon
Illustrations by Sholto Ainslie

Printed in the United States of America

VB Hermitage 10 9 8 7 6 5 4 3 2 1

This book is printed on acid-free paper.

Contents

★

List of Entries

Acknowledgments

★──────────────────────────────────────

This work was prepared with the assistance of my wife, Scottie Smith. It is dedicated to the memory of her friend and colleague, Lavonya Dejean. Lavonya was an advocate and activist for the education of disadvantaged children. She coordinated a movement of parents in the West Contra Costa, California, Unified School District to develop comprehensive policies and procedures for parental involvement in education. Through her leadership, diverse groups of teachers, parents, and students were taught the necessity of understanding each others' cultures and the need for equity and equality in the education of all children.

I should like to thank Owen Lancer for conceiving of the project, for inviting me to undertake it, and for his assistance and the assistance of the staff of Facts On File for guiding it to completion.

Introduction

Knowledge of African-American politics is indispensable to understanding the origins and evolution of the American democracy. The presence of Africans as slaves exerted an important influence on the writing of the Declaration of Independence and the Constitution. In the declaration, the United States committed itself to the then-radical idea of universal freedom and equality for all men. In its Constitution, however, it denied freedom and equality to the enslaved Africans. Throughout its history, a large part of America's politics has been concerned with the resolution of this contradiction between the declaration's promise and the Constitution's reality.

This contradiction has been and is the central concern of African-American politics. In other words, African-American politics is a politics about freedom and equality.

Politics is about power. The essence of politics lies in the processes of gaining, maintaining, and using power.

Power can be understood as the capabilities of individuals or groups to impose their will in relationship to others. African-American politics then is about the power relationship between blacks and whites in the United States. Historically, this relationship has been characterized by whites gaining, maintaining, and using various power capabilities to subordinate blacks and deny them freedom and equality. Blacks, on the other hand, have sought to gain, maintain, and exercise power capabilities in order to alter their subordinate relationship to whites and to achieve freedom and equality.

African-American politics understood in this way is an enduringly fascinating phenomenon because of the asymmetrical power relationship between blacks and whites. Power, political scientists teach, is not a lump. Rather, it is constituted by a number of capabilities, bases, or sources. These power bases or sources are things that give individuals or groups the potential—if maintained and skillfully used—to exercise power, depending on time, place, and circumstance.

Time, place, and circumstance are important. Just as power is not a lump, it is also not fixed or static. Rather, power is a dynamic variable. Power bases between individuals and groups vary by time, place, and circumstance. In other words, no individual or group is at all times, in all places, and in all circumstances powerful or powerless. This variable, dynamic quality of power is important in understanding the fascinating character of African-American politics in the United States.

What are some of the important power bases in human relationships in general and specifically in the relationship between blacks and whites in the United States? Karl Marx contended that there was only one base of power in social relationships—money—or, more precisely, wealth in the form of income derived from the ownership of property. Max Weber, another great social thinker, argued that there were three bases of power. In addition to wealth derived from property, Weber said power might be exercised on the basis of party and status. By *status*, Weber means the honor or deference accorded to an individual or group on the basis of some ascribed or achieved attribute. Although persons can possess status on the basis of individual achievement of honor or deference, in ethnically or racially stratified societies, status can also be an ascribed group phenomenon. That is, an individual's status is linked not so much to personal deference or honor but to the deference accorded her or his group in the society.

By *party*, Weber means control of legislative authority or the government. In a democracy, ordinary individuals without wealth or status could aspire to power by aligning themselves with a party that has achieved dominance through its size and cohesion or solidarity in voting. *Party* in this sense constitutes three distinct power bases: the size and solidarity of its voter base, the control of legitimate authority as exercised by the government, and the use of violence or coercion as the ultimate base of a government's capacity to impose its will on the people.

In addition to the five power bases—wealth, status, party size and solidarity, authority, and violence—Weber identified charisma as a power base exercised by extraordinary individuals with a "gift of grace" that allows them to exercise power based on some unique attributes that distinguish them in word and deed from ordinary people. In many societies power is also exercised on the basis of religion—the belief in a supreme being and his earthly spokespeople. That is, the power of God or the gods can be invoked by individuals in order to realize their will in relationships that are characterized by religious beliefs. Although closely related in many societies to religion, morality or moral authority—the sense that one's behavior or the behavior of a relationship should be conducted in accordance with standards of right and wrong—can be understood as a distinct, discrete base of power. Finally, knowledge is also a base of power. In this context, knowledge can be institutional, such as that generated in universities and stored in libraries; practical or technical, such as in engineering, medicine, or weaponry; and propaganda or persuasive information as gathered and disseminated by various media.

In the development of African-American politics, whites acquired and maintained the several bases of power and used them to subordinate blacks and maintain control over them. Meanwhile, blacks have attempted to acquire bases of power in order to end their subordinate relationship. Historically, however, whites have monopolized virtually all of the bases of power. From this perspective, African-American politics is an oxymoron: a politics without power. And yet, since power is a variable, a politics without power is also an oxymoron. African-American politics is circumscribed by its exercise of relative power, which has varied by time, place, circumstance, and context. From the era of slavery to the present, this relative white-black power gap has been an abiding, defining feature of African-American politics. The ensuing tug-of-war is what makes African-American politics, in all of its manifestations, an enduringly fascinating phenomenon. It is the objective of this encyclopedia to provide its readers, many of whom will be students, with a broad, objective, analytical understanding of this interesting phenomenon in all of its manifestations from the nation's beginning to the present.

There are other encyclopedias and reference works on the African-American experience in the United States. This volume is different in that its approach is simultaneously both broader and narrower. It is narrower in the sense that its focus is on politics rather than the full range of the African-American experience and heritage. But it is also broader in the sense that it covers the full scope of politics and the basic concepts, institutions, and processes necessary for readers to learn about the breadth of the African-American experience in politics, which is a subject worthy of understanding in its own right. We hope that the reader will learn something about the impact of this unique black experience and its integral relationship to the political history and development of politics in the United States.

There is, of course, some overlap between the entries in this volume and other reference works. This work, however, is distinguished by its focus on the political dimensions of these overlapping topics. For example, slavery and the abolitionist movement or segregation and the Civil Rights movement are analyzed as political phenomena in terms of power, authority, leadership, institutions, coalitions, movements, political participation, and public policy.

Of the more than 400 entries in the volume, readers will find essays on the philosophical and historical background guiding the design of the U.S. Constitution and its specific effects on blacks; on slavery and its progeny; on African-American political thought; on the basic concepts, institutions, and processes of the U.S. government; on political culture, public opinion, and political socialization; on policy making and public policy; on African-American leadership, ideologies, organizations, and movements; on coalitions; on important political personalities and events; and on the concepts necessary to the study of race in the United States, including race itself, racism, white supremacy, ethnicity, minorities, oppression, and subordinate and superordinate groups.

As an aid to students, the essays are written clearly and objectively, with a minimum of jargon. Numerous cross references are included to guide readers to related entries, and many entries are followed by a list of suggestions for further reading and study. In addition, the material is illuminated by 70 illustrations and photographs. Finally, there is an appendix that includes a list of important documentary sources on black politics and a bibliography that includes more than 400 entries.

Note on Style: I use the terms *black* and *African American* interchangeably, having no preference for either and viewing each as a legitimate and accurate name for persons of African descent in the United States.

Further reading: H. H. Gerth and C. Wright Mills, eds., *From Max Weber: Essays in Sociology* (New York: Oxford University Press, 1946); Harold Lasswell and Abraham Kaplan, *Power and Society: A Framework for Political Inquiry* (New Haven, Conn.: Yale University Press, 1950); Gunnar Myrdal, *An American Dilemma: The Negro Problem and Modern Democracy* (New York: Harper & Row, 1944); Hanes Walton, *Invisible Politics: Black Political Behavior* (Albany: State University of New York Press, 1985); Hanes Walton and Robert C. Smith, *American Politics and the African American Quest for Universal Freedom* (New York: Longman, 2000).

A

abolitionist movement

The abolitionist movement was the first interracial SOCIAL MOVEMENT in the United States. The goal of the movement was to abolish or end SLAVERY. As early as the 1720s adherents of the Society of Friends (a Christian religious sect popularly known as the Quakers) published pamphlets opposing slavery, and during the revolutionary era individuals of the status of Benjamin Franklin and Abigail Adams (wife of John Adams, the second president) were outspoken opponents, but as a social movement, opposition to slavery can be traced to 1831, when WILLIAM LLOYD GARRISON organized the New England Anti-Slavery Society, and to 1833, when he formed the American Anti-Slavery Society.

The movement to abolish slavery was also the first broad-based COALITION between blacks and whites in the United States, resembling in its leadership, strategy, and tactics—and in its divisions—the 20th-century CIVIL RIGHTS MOVEMENT. The movement among whites was rooted in the revival in the NORTHERN STATES of Christian, evangelical religious fervor, which sought to end all forms of sin. Thus, it employed morality and religion as bases of power, arguing that slavery was both morally wrong and sinful. The abolitionists argued that slavery was sinful because it violated the teachings of Jesus and was morally wrong because it violated the NATURAL RIGHTS doctrine that was the philosophical foundation of the DECLARATION OF INDEPENDENCE and the CONSTITUTION. These two bases of power—morality and religion—were also important resources in the Civil Rights movement.

The geographical base of the movement was in the Northeast, especially New England. Among whites, its leaders were largely middle- to upper-middle-class reformers, including (for that era) a relatively large number of women who supported slavery's abolition as part of a general reform agenda of FREEDOM and EQUALITY for all persons. White abolitionists were Protestants, disproportionately Quakers, and generally women and men of ideas—that is,

clergymen, educators, and journalists. Although black abolitionist leaders were less frequently middle class, they too tended to be Protestants (often deeply religious), to live in the Northeast, and to be disproportionately clergymen, journalists, and lecturers.

As a movement, the abolitionists had relatively few resources. The authority of the federal government, the governments of the SOUTHERN STATES, and most of the states of the North were arrayed against it. The majority of the white population in its size and solidarity was against the movement. Southern whites were virtually monolithic in their opposition to abolition, and whites in the North were hostile or indifferent, with probably no more than 10 percent of Northern whites favoring unconditional emancipation of the slaves. The movement had relatively few supporters in the established church, in the CONGRESS, in the universities, in the mainstream press, or among the men of wealth and property who dominated the economy. Meanwhile African Americans, even the handful of so-called FREE NEGROES, were virtually without any bases of power.

Given this asymmetrical power relationship between the movement and its adversaries, its leaders were almost from the outset divided among themselves over strategy and tactics. First, some like Garrison were committed primarily to the use of morality—moral suasion—and nonviolence as the primary strategies of the movement. Although FREDERICK DOUGLASS, the principal black leader of the movement, was for a time committed to Garrison's approach, when it proved unsuccessful he eventually embraced political action in the form of support for THIRD PARTIES that were opposed to slavery or its extension beyond the South. Douglass also eventually embraced violent resistance and rebellion as tactics, but his embrace was a reluctant tactical shift. Others in the movement, such as JOHN BROWN, HENRY HIGHLAND GARNETT, and DAVID WALKER, embraced VIOLENCE as a fundamental strategy of the movement.

1

THE
AMERICAN
ANTI-SLAVERY
ALMANAC,
FOR
1839,

EMANCIPATION, RUIN—SLAVERY, SALVATION !!
A West India paper, in 1838, says : "Institutions undreamt of in the days of slavery, have been founded for agricultural, literary and scientific purposes. New villages and towns are rising in various parts of the island ; new streets and houses are daily being erected in the old ; and new churches and chapels are rearing their heads in almost every district of the colony. A heathen is now as rarely to be met with, as was a Christian ten years since. Hundreds of children are brought weekly to the baptismal font ; thousands are daily receiving the rudiments of education. The vices peculiar to slavery are gradually wearing away ; nightly orgies and licentious practices are fast falling into disuse ; concubinage is receding before matrimony, and the long night of superstition rapidly evanishing before the sun of Christianity."—" The West Indian," Spanish Town, Jamaica.

NEW YORK & BOSTON:

NEW YORK : S. W. BENEDICT.—BOSTON : ISAAC KNAPP.

The antislavery movement zealously spread the message of abolitionism through such publications as the *Anti-Slavery Almanac. (Library of Congress, Billy Graham Center)*

Garrison was also an uncompromising critic of the CONSTITUTION, viewing it as a slaveholder's document. (In 1854 he burned a copy of the Constitution, describing it as a "covenant with death" and "an agreement with Hell.") But Douglass and others interpreted the Constitution in a way that made it an antislavery document. (See *DRED SCOTT V. SANFORD* for Douglass's antislavery interpretation of the Constitution.)

There were also disagreements about the status of the slaves once they were emancipated. Although the movement as a whole was committed to abolition, many white abolitionists were white supremacists who believed in the inferiority of African peoples and rejected the idea of uni-

versal freedom and equality for all men. Some, black and white, favored colonialization—the voluntary or forced repatriation of the emancipated slaves to Africa, Latin America, or the Caribbean. Still others (the overwhelming majority of blacks for certain and perhaps a majority of whites) favored universal freedom and equality for all African Americans.

The movement was also divided on the issue of FEMINISM. Douglass and Garrison were feminists (advocates of equality for women), but many—perhaps most—abolitionists were not, and within the movement there was DISCRIMINATION against women. For example, women were not allowed to sign the Anti-Slavery Society's Declaration of Principles, to hold leadership positions, or to serve as antislavery lecturers. Because of this kind of discrimination, women—black and white—later formed their own, separate antislavery society. But many white female abolitionists were also white supremacists and racists who only embraced the antislavery coalition as part of a broad reform movement to advance the cause of women. When the freedom of women and the freedom of black men came into conflict in the RECONSTRUCTION era over the ratification of the FOURTEENTH and FIFTEENTH AMENDMENTs, the coalition between blacks and white women collapsed.

A final source of division in the movement that undermined its solidarity was the conflict between blacks and whites over its leadership and over whether blacks should form separate, racially exclusive, all-black organizations such as the NATIONAL NEGRO CONVENTION. Douglass was a major leader of the convention, while Garrison was strongly opposed to its formation. Given their higher status, greater resources, and to some extent because of white supremacist sentiments, whites exercised dominant leadership of the movement. Blacks eventually came to resent this. In words that anticipate STOKELY CARMICHAEL and other advocates in the BLACK POWER MOVEMENT during the 1960s, Douglass said, "The man who has *suffered* the wrong is the man to demand the redress—the man struck is the man to CRY OUT and he who has endured *the cruel pangs of slavery* is the man to *advocate liberty*. It is evident that we must be our own representatives and advocates, but peculiarly—not distinct from—but in connection with our white friends."

The abolitionist movement, given its small size and limited resources as well as its internal divisions and conflicts, did not directly cause the end of slavery. That came about as a result of the CIVIL WAR. ABRAHAM LINCOLN was not an abolitionist. He was a "Free Soiler," opposed to slavery on moral grounds but prepared to accept it as long as it was not extended beyond the South to the "free soil" of the North. Insofar as abolitionism was concerned, Lincoln described it as "dangerous radicalism." However, the abolitionist movement, along with the SLAVE REVOLTS, contributed to the atmosphere of crisis leading up to the Civil War. Given its limited size and solidarity, the movement relied mainly on the power bases of knowledge, morality, and religion.

Much of this knowledge was propaganda. That is, whether fact or fiction, it was information disseminated with the intent of altering PUBLIC OPINION. The movement and its leaders used all the available MEDIA of the 19th century. Dozens of newspapers were established, including Garrison's *Liberator* and Douglass's *North Star;* scores of antislavery pamphlets and tracts were disseminated, and antislavery-society lecturers traveled throughout the North. This was a difficult enterprise because the editors, lecturers, and clergymen were often the victims of various forms of POLITICAL REPRESSION. Abolitionist literature was frequently delayed or destroyed by the post office, lecturers were often harassed at public meetings, and sometimes they were attacked by mobs and injured or killed in RIOTS. Yet the movement endured for more than 30 years, increasing in MILITANCY as time passed.

Much of its propaganda was based on religion and morality. Theodore Weld, a deeply religious and learned man, in 1839 wrote *American Slavery As It Is,* a religious and moral tract on slavery that was a best-seller at the time and is considered one of the classics of antislavery literature. Similarly, Harriet Beecher Stowe's more famous *Uncle Tom's Cabin* was also a best-seller and filled with Christian and moral arguments about the evils of slavery. Although religion and morality were used by abolitionists, they were also used by proponents of slavery as components of the ideology of the WHITE SUPREMACY that they used to justify black subordination in the United States. Thus, the abolitionists used these bases of power also as a kind of countermobilization against the ideas of slave propagandists.

The PRESIDENCY and the JUDICIAL PROCESS were effectively closed to the abolitionists. However, they did engage in LOBBYING to influence Congress, but this was largely unsuccessful because of the movement's limited resources. But even these limited efforts to lobby Congress were dealt a major setback in 1831 when the House of Representatives adopted a GAG RULE that prohibited members from receiving or discussing petitions to abolish slavery.

Finally, the violence associated with the SLAVE REVOLTS contributed to the atmosphere of crisis leading up to the Civil War and Lincoln's EMANCIPATION PROCLAMATION. Most of the leaders of these revolts were slaves and not a formal part of the movement. However, John Brown was an abolitionist leader, and his raid at Harper's Ferry, Virginia, in 1859 can be seen as the movement's last desperate act. This act of desperation was opposed even by Douglass, but in its very desperation it shocked and alarmed the nation. This small group of interracial rebels, led by a white abolitionist seized by religious fervor, was an omen of the terrible war to come that at its end would result in the abolition of slavery.

The abolitionist movement was the first interracial coalition that challenged the American system of racial subordination as it manifested itself at that time in Southern slavery. Compared with its adversaries, abolitionism was a weak and relatively powerless movement, relying mainly on morality, knowledge, and religion as bases of power. It did not directly achieve its objectives, but it made a contribution to slavery's end. And in the 20th century it served as the model for the "new abolitionists" of the NAACP and the Civil Rights movement, which constituted the second major interracial coalition to challenge a system of racial domination in the United States.

Further reading: Herbert Aptheker, *Abolitionism: A Revolutionary Movement* (Boston: Twayne, 1989); James McPherson, *The Struggle for Equality: Abolitionists and Negro Movement in the Civil War and Reconstruction* (Princeton, N.J.: Princeton University Press, 1964); Benjamin Quarles, *Black Abolitionists* (New York: Oxford University Press, 1970).

accommodationism

Accommodationism is a strategy of African-American LEADERSHIP that is unwilling or unable to challenge a prevailing system of racial subordination. Thus, it accepts or "accommodates" the racial status quo as it exists at any given time and place. GUNNAR MYRDAL first introduced accommodationism as an analytic construct to study black leadership. In *AN AMERICAN DILEMMA* Myrdal constructed a typology of African-American leadership based on what he described as the two extreme strategies of behavior on the part of leaders of the subordinate African-American community: accommodation and PROTEST.

Accommodation required leaders to accept and not challenge or protest the system of racial subordination and SEGREGATION, what Myrdal referred to in 1944 as the "subordinated caste" status of blacks. Thus, leaders led only in the context of seeking only those changes or modifications in the conditions of blacks that did not upset or alter the caste system. Because of their relative lack of power in relationship to whites, Myrdal contended that accommodation was historically the "natural," "normal," or "realistic" relationship of black leadership to white society and its leadership. Changes in the conditions of the group were to be pursued quietly and incrementally so as not to upset whites and stimulate their resistance. Over time these quiet, slow changes would lead to gradual changes that would create a new status quo. But, this new status quo had to be achieved in a way so that whites would hardly recognize the changes before they were accomplished.

Protest and MILITANCY are alternative leadership strategies, although accommodation has historically been the dominant pattern of black leadership behavior. While there were protests and rebellions during SLAVERY, most enslaved Africans generally accommodated the system and sought to better their conditions within it rather than seeking to overthrow it. During slavery this strategy of accommodation was based on a realistic assessment of the efficacy of protest and rebellion, since they inevitably led to heightened OPPRESSION and POLITICAL REPRESSION.

Slavery was a near total system of domination and subordination, one in which whites monopolized all bases of power. This relationship changed briefly after the CIVIL WAR during the era of RECONSTRUCTION, during which blacks were able to acquire and use bases of power unavailable to them while enslaved. However, after the violent overthrow of Reconstruction, accommodation was personified by the leadership of BOOKER T. WASHINGTON and his famous "ATLANTA COMPROMISE" ADDRESS. In that speech, Washington advocated accommodationism, accepting the overthrow of Reconstruction and its denial of basic social and political FREEDOM in exchange for the opportunity for blacks to develop a separate, subordinate society without interference from whites. Given the VIOLENCE of post-Reconstruction oppression and political repression, Washington saw no realistic alternative to accommodation. Under these circumstances, accommodation rather than protest was the realistic core of African-American politics.

Booker T. Washington is probably the most powerful African-American leader in the entire history of the United States. But, because of his accommodationism, he is also the most controversial, viewed as the quintessential UNCLE TOM—a white-anointed leader who sells out the interests of the race. Yet, in all likelihood, Washington's accommodationism was the only realistic strategy for that time and circumstance, one where the white majority was willing to exercise all its power, including extreme violence to subordinate blacks. Washington's accommodationism therefore reflected the perception that blacks were unable to effectively protest the evolving system of white domination in the 1880s.

As an analytic construct, accommodationism versus protest or militancy has been used in some form by virtually all political scientists to classify or provide typologies of black leaders. Political scientists have also used terms like *conservative, moderate, traditionalist,* or *Uncle Tom,* but whatever the label, it refers to those black leaders who accept the existing system of subordination—whatever it is—and engage in gradual, incremental actions within its context or boundaries.

Studies of black leadership from the 1930s to the 1950s generally concluded that black leaders, especially in the SOUTHERN STATES but in the NORTHERN STATES as well, were accommodationist. However, during this period some scholars also observed a "rising spirit of protest" that emerged in the 1950s during the CIVIL RIGHTS MOVEMENT and gained ascendancy during the BLACK POWER MOVEMENT of the late 1960s and early 1970s.

As a result of the Civil Rights and Black Power movements, the post–Reconstruction era system of racial domination was abolished, formal FREEDOM and EQUALITY were established, and African-American leadership was incorporated or integrated into the new system. This new system retains at least remnants of WHITE SUPREMACY and RACISM and continues to relegate blacks as a group to a separate, unequal, and subordinate status in the United States. This POST–CIVIL RIGHTS ERA system of subordination, however, is not explicitly or legally racist, and it is characterized by growing class differences among blacks, resulting in a BLACK COMMUNITY that is more highly class stratified and with more diverse interests.

The CO-OPTATION or POLITICAL INCORPORATION of black leadership into the POLITICAL SYSTEM, the increasing CLASS STRATIFICATION, and the growing diversity of interests may be fomenting a new wave of accommodationism. Militancy and protest in the 1960s led to the end of the centuries-old system of subordination based explicitly on white supremacy and racism. They did not end, however, the SUBORDINATE GROUP status of the black community. For a time in the post–civil rights era, African-American leaders protested the economic and institutional structures underpinning this new system of subordination, but at the dawn of the 21st century, accommodationism rather than protest once again appeared to be the dominant strategy of black leaders. That is, contemporary black leaders appeared to accept the existing system of social, economic, and political arrangements, seeking only gradual, incremental adjustments to modify the conditions of blacks while eschewing a militant policy of protest.

This strategic shift toward accommodationism is partly a result of the incorporation and co-optation of middle-class black leaders into mainstream institutions and organizations. However, the argument might be made that because the civil rights era protest produced more results than accommodation, the relatively small degree of inclusion of middle-class blacks into mainstream institutions does not justify embracing the accommodationist imperatives of those institutions, especially given the distance blacks still have to go to achieve equality. Nevertheless, accommodationism was again paramount at the beginning of the 21st century, either because African-American leaders were unwilling to challenge the prevailing system of subordination or because, as historically has been the case, they felt they were unable to do so because they lacked the necessary bases of power. Thus, accommodationism became, as it had always been, the "realistic," "natural," "normal" course of black leadership behavior.

Further reading: Gunnar Myrdal, *An American Dilemma: The Negro Problem and Modern Democracy* (New York: Harper & Row, 1944), Chaps. 35–39; Ronald Walters and Robert C. Smith, *African American Leadership* (Albany: State University of New York Press, 1999), Chaps. 2–4.

Adams, John Quincy (1767–1848) *sixth president of the United States*

Most of the American presidents have been indifferent, ambivalent, or hostile to the African-American struggle for FREEDOM and EQUALITY. As president, John Quincy Adams was no different. Although he was morally opposed to SLAVERY, he subordinated his opposition to it to the cause of preservation of the Union and his wish to become president. However, after leaving the presidency, Adams (the son of the second U.S. president, John Adams) became the most outspoken and articulate opponent of slavery ever to hold the office of president.

Adams's election to the presidency in 1824 was one of the most controversial in American history. In a four-way race, Adams lost the popular vote to Andrew Jackson, receiving 31 percent to Jackson's 43 percent. The ELECTORAL COLLEGE vote, however, was somewhat closer—Jackson, 99; Adams, 84; William Crawford, 41; and Henry Clay, 37. The CONSTITUTION specifies that when no candidate for president receives a majority of the electoral college vote, the House of Representatives chooses the president from among the top-three contenders. When the House convened to make its decision, instead of choosing Jackson—the most popular candidate and the winner of both the popular and electoral vote—the House by a narrow margin elected Adams. Elected under these circumstances, Adams, although eminently qualified for the office (in addition to being the son of a former president, he was a Harvard professor and a former U.S. senator, diplomat, and secretary of state), did not have a particularly effective presidency and was defeated for reelection in 1828. Two years later he was elected to the House from Massachusetts.

While opposed to slavery in principle (as well as the more vulgar stereotypes of WHITE SUPREMACY), Adams was not committed to its abolition and was not sympathetic to the ABOLITIONIST MOVEMENT because he thought it threatened the preservation of the Union. In his first year in the House, Adams presented an antislavery petition at the request of his constituents. The presentation of the petition was not an act of courage or conscience, since such petitions were routinely presented, printed in the record, and referred to committee. However, partly in response to NAT TURNER's rebellion and the emergence of the abolitionist movement, the House in 1836 passed a GAG RULE requiring that all petitions to CONGRESS on the subject of SLAVERY be automatically tabled without being printed, referred to committee, or discussed or debated by the representatives. Members of the House violating the rule were subject to censure.

The gag rule outraged Adams, turning his tepid opposition to slavery into near fanatical opposition. In Adams's view, not only were the enslaved people denied freedom, but now they and whites were denied the elementary right guaranteed by the Constitution's First Amendment to petition the Congress. Thus, beginning in 1836, Adams became a leader in what was the nation's first great political struggle over African-American slavery. His status as a former president was an important resource in this struggle, but his struggle against the gag rule was a lonely one. Almost without allies, he was shunned by his colleagues in the House, threatened with assassination, and at one point was nearly censured when he submitted what House members thought was a petition from a group of Maryland slaves. Nevertheless, Adams persisted in speaking out, and in 1844 the rule was revoked.

Adams was not only the leader of one of the first antislavery political conflicts in Congress; he was also a leader in one of the first judicial conflicts involving slavery, a conflict that resulted in the SUPREME COURT's only antislavery decision in its history. In 1839, Joseph Cinque, an African, led a revolt on the Spanish slave ship *L'Amistad,* killing the captain and most of the crew. Cinque then ordered the ship, holding about 50 slaves, to sail to Africa. But the ship was seized by the U.S. Coast Guard, and Cinque and the others were arrested and charged with mutiny and murder. The abolitionist movement rallied to their cause, but a trial court in Connecticut convicted them and the conviction was upheld by a court of appeals. These decisions were then appealed to the Supreme Court, which heard arguments in 1841. Adams, in his 70s and nearly blind, argued the case on behalf of Cinque before the Court. Adams argued that *L'Amistad,* with its slave cargo, was bound for Cuba in violation of the Anglo-Spanish treaty of 1817, which prohibited the import of slaves into Cuba. Thus, Cinque and the others were, Adams argued, captured and enslaved in violation of international law, and therefore U.S. law should treat them as any other free persons escaping illegal servitude. The Supreme Court agreed, reversed the convictions, and ordered the release of Cinque and his fellow captives. Abolitionists raised funds, and Cinque and 32 others were returned to their homeland in Sierra Leone (the others had died while awaiting trial).

While he was elected to the presidency on dubious grounds, had an undistinguished term as president, and placed the preservation of the Union ahead of the freedom of the slaves, John Quincy Adams as a former president did more to advance the cause of African freedom than did most presidents while in office.

Further reading: Mary Hargreaves, *The Presidency of John Quincy Adams* (Lawrence: University Press of Kansas, 1985); Howard Jones, *Mutiny on the Amistad* (New York: Oxford, 1987); William Lee Miller, *Arguing about Slavery: The Great Battle in the United States Congress* (New York: Knopf, 1995); *Amistad,* dir. Steven Spielberg, prod. Steven Spielberg and Debbie Allen (Los Angeles: Dreamworks SKG, 1997).

Adarand Constructors Inc. v. Pena (1995)

Adarand v. Pena is one of a series of SUPREME COURT decisions in the 1990s questioning the constitutionality of AFFIRMATIVE ACTION programs and limiting their scope. This case involved a challenge to a provision of federal law that offered incentives to contractors working on federally funded highway projects if they hired as subcontractors firms owned by individuals from "socially and economically disadvantaged groups," which the law presumed included all racial minorities. In 1989 a construction company in Colorado awarded a subcontract to build a portion of a highway to a company owned by a Hispanic individual, although the lowest bid had been submitted by Adarand Contractors, a white-owned firm. Adarand sued in federal court, challenging both the preference granted minority-owned firms and the law's presumption that all minority-owned firms were controlled by individuals who were socially and economically disadvantaged. Adarand's case was dismissed by the District Court in Colorado and the Court of Appeals for the 10th Circuit.

The District and Appeals Courts rejected Adarand's claim on the basis of prior Supreme Court decisions (including *FULLILOVE V. KLUTZNICK*), which had allowed CONGRESS to provide preferences in awarding contracts to minority- and female-owned businesses as a means to remedy past DISCRIMINATION and assure fairness and equal opportunity in the allocation of government resources. In *Adarand* the Supreme Court virtually overruled *Fullilove* and other precedents that had allowed Congress to achieve the objectives of affirmative action by using racial or gender preferences. In their 5-4 decision, the justices did not explicitly declare preferences unconstitutional, but the opinion of the majority established a standard of review under the EQUAL PROTECTION CLAUSE of the FOURTEENTH AMENDMENT that made it much more difficult for the Congress to enact affirmative action programs in the future that would require or allow the use of race or gender in the allocation of government resources or benefits.

The impact of *Adarand* was almost immediate. Several months after the decision, President BILL CLINTON adopted modifications in affirmative action (which he termed "Mend it, don't end it") that significantly narrowed the number and scope of federal affirmative action programs. The president later ordered the suspension of all federal programs that reserved government contracts exclusively for minority- and women-owned firms.

affirmative action

Affirmative action and BUSING for purposes of DESEGREGATION of elementary and secondary schools are the two most controversial PUBLIC POLICY issues dealing with race since the end of the CIVIL RIGHTS MOVEMENT. Both raise novel and complex constitutional, legal, cultural, political, and policy questions. Both are deeply divisive, with white PUBLIC OPINION overwhelmingly hostile and black opinion divided and ambivalent. Because of the complexity of the issue of busing and because of the hostile character of white public opinion and the ambivalence of blacks, busing for purposes of school desegregation has for all intents and purposes been eliminated as a public policy in the United States. Whether affirmative action, for similar reasons, will suffer the same fate is one of the most important and interesting questions in American and African-American politics.

Origins of the Policy

Broadly defined, affirmative action is a set of policies and programs designed in the late 1960s and early 1970s to assure equal opportunities for African Americans (and subsequently women and other racial minorities) in access to education, employment, and government contracts. It is important to emphasize that, as public policy, affirmative action is a *set*—that is, a large number or a variety—of programs and policies rather than a single, all-encompassing policy or program. This diversity in programs and policies raises distinct philosophical, ideological, cultural, and political issues and involves different levels of controversy and public support.

The phrase *affirmative action* has been traced by the historian Hugh Davis Graham to the Wagner Act of 1935, which granted collective bargaining rights to organized workers in the United States. The phrase *affirmative action* as used in the context of this act defined the authority of the National Labor Relations Board to remedy an unfair labor practice. It required a company engaging in unfair labor practices to "cease and desist . . . and to take such affirmative action, including reinstatement of employees with or without back pay, as will effectuate the policies of this act." With respect to race, the phrase was first used by President JOHN F. KENNEDY in his Executive Order 10925 issued in 1961. This order required companies with government contracts to take "affirmative action to ensure that applicants are employed . . . without regard to their race, creed, color or national origins." These two innocuous and ambiguous words crafted by government bureaucrats to assure fairness in employment are the foundations of contemporary affirmative action policy.

President Kennedy's executive order was crafted by Vice President LYNDON B. JOHNSON, whom Kennedy had designated chair of the President's Committee on Equal Employment Opportunity, which was created by the executive order. Johnson appointed Hobart Taylor, an African-American protégé from Texas, as special counsel to the committee. In this capacity, Taylor claims he was responsible for inserting the words "affirmative action" into Kennedy's order. From the beginning, therefore, African Americans in the BUREAUCRACY have been intimately involved in the design of affirmative action.

President Lyndon Johnson's Howard University Address and the Beginnings of Affirmative Action

The innocuous and ambiguous phrase *affirmative action* was given its initial philosophical and conceptual underpinnings in President Johnson's 1965 address to HOWARD UNIVERSITY's graduating class. In his June 4, 1965, address to Howard's graduating class, the president signaled the end of the Civil Rights movement. He first recounted his work as leader of the Senate in passing the Civil Rights Acts of 1957 and 1960, his signing the previous year of the CIVIL RIGHTS ACT OF 1964, and his plans to soon sign the VOTING RIGHTS ACT OF 1965. But the president then noted that these legislative victories resulted in FREEDOM but not EQUALITY. Therefore, Johnson said the Civil Rights movement "is not the end. It is not even the beginning of the end. But, it is perhaps the end of the beginning." That beginning, Johnson said, was "freedom." Then, the president went on to articulate what was to become the main philosophical and conceptual justification for affirmative action public policies. He told the students:

> But freedom is not enough. You do not wipe away the scars of centuries by saying: Now you are free to go where you want, do as you desire, choose the leaders you please. You do not take a person who, for years, has been hobbled by chains and liberate him, bring him up to the starting line of a race and then say "you are free to compete with others" and still justly believe you have been completely fair. Thus, it is not enough just to open the gates of opportunity. All our citizens must have the ability to walk through those gates. This is the next and more profound state of the battle for civil rights. We seek not just freedom but opportunity—not just legal equity but human ability—not just equality as a right and a theory but equality as a fact and as a result.

In saying that freedom was not enough, the president was making the philosophical case that mere passage of civil rights laws would not in and of themselves create equality for African Americans because they had been "hobbled by chains." Thus, philosophically, some special, compensatory, remedial policies were necessary if equality for blacks was to be a "fact" rather than a "theory." Conceptually, the president linked the idea of freedom with "opportunity" and "results." That is, African Americans should not just be afforded the "right" to equality but the "ability" to achieve it. This results-oriented measure of opportunity is one of the principal justifications for race and gender preferences, goals and timetables, and QUOTAS.

In this address the president also appears to recognize the rights of blacks as a group, for he said, "For the task is to give 20 million Negroes the same chances as every other American . . . to pursue their happiness." This implied recognition of group rights is reinforced when later in the speech the president said that while there was a growing "middle class minority, . . . for the great majority of Negro Americans . . . the walls are rising and the gulf is widening." Thus, public policy should include policies and programs that would have the result or effect of narrowing the gap— the president said "gulf"—in education, employment, and income between the races.

In retrospect, President Johnson's speech has to be considered one of the most important ever given by an American president on the subject of race. It established, perhaps inadvertently, the philosophical and conceptual rationales for the bureaucracy to design and implement affirmative action as public policy. The speech established first the idea that merely ending RACISM and DISCRIMINATION and treating all persons the same without regard to race was not enough to overcome the effects of past racial discrimination. Second, it articulated the principle that fairness required that groups disadvantaged by past discrimination receive more than a theoretical opportunity to compete. Indeed, disadvantaged groups deserved compensatory or remedial policies to overcome or remedy the effects of past discrimination, thus making opportunity a reality. Finally, the speech set forth the idea that equality was to be measured by the results or effects of policies rather than their intent or stated purposes. Fairly soon after the president's address the CONGRESS, the bureaucracy, and the SUPREME COURT began to translate Johnson's ideas into public policy.

The Development of Public Policy

Major speeches by the president frequently serve as cues to the bureaucracy in policy development. Such appears to have been the case with President Johnson's Howard University address and the development of affirmative action policy. In September 1965, President Johnson issued Executive Order 11246, which, following Kennedy's order, required contractors to engage in affirmative action to assure equal employment opportunity. What affirmative action meant in terms of public policy, however, was left to the bureaucracy to define as it developed rules and regulations to implement Johnson's order as well as Title VII (which banned discrimination in employment on the basis of race and gender) of the recently passed 1964 Civil Rights Act.

The bureaucratic agency responsible for implementing Title VII is the EQUAL EMPLOYMENT OPPORTUNITY COMMISSION (EEOC), created by Congress in the Civil Rights Act of 1964. The agency responsible for implementing Executive Order 11246 was the OFFICE OF FEDERAL CONTRACT COMPLIANCE (OFCC), created in 1966 by the secretary of labor. In the Johnson administration, both of these agencies were headed by African Americans, Clifford Alexander at the EEOC and Edward Sylvester at OFCC. Perhaps acting on cues from President Johnson's address, these individuals defined nondiscrimination in employment in terms of results or effects rather than intentional discriminatory behavior on the part of the employer. In other words, they defined discrimination in terms of INSTITUTIONAL RACISM rather than INDIVIDUAL RACISM.

At EEOC, Alexander and his colleagues issued regulations that established that an employer could be found in violation of Title VII not only on the basis of overt, intentional acts of discrimination but also on the basis of statistical data that demonstrated that an employer's workforce was not constituted by an equitable number of blacks, based on their presence in the available labor market. That is, proof of nondiscrimination would be judged not merely on the basis of an employer's nondiscriminatory intent but on the actual composition of his workforce. If, for example, blacks were roughly 10 percent of the eligible or qualified workers in the employer's area, then blacks should constitute 10 percent of its employees in all job categories. If this was not the case, the burden of proof shifts to the employer to show that this statistical disparity or DISPARATE IMPACT was not a function of illegal discrimination. If this could not be demonstrated, then the EEOC would require the employer to develop an affirmative action plan with specific goals and timetables to eliminate the racial disparity.

Meanwhile, at the OFCC, Sylvester and his colleagues were proposing similar race-specific goals and timetables to enforce Executive Order 11246. However, before this work could be completed, President Johnson's term expired and RICHARD NIXON became president.

One of the ironies of the PRESIDENCY in the POST–CIVIL RIGHTS ERA and the issue of race is that Richard Nixon—a president who embraced an IDEOLOGY of CONSERVATISM and is the only post–civil rights era president who demonstrably was a WHITE SUPREMACIST—is also the president who established the most far-reaching antiracist public policy of the post–civil rights era.

In 1971, three years after Sylvester had failed, because of the expiration of Johnson's term, to establish a results or

effects mechanism to implement Executive Order 11246, the Nixon administration accomplished this objective. As in the Johnson administration, Nixon's policy was developed by African Americans in the bureaucracy—John Wilks, the new head of OFCC, and ARTHUR FLETCHER, an assistant secretary of labor. Fletcher and Wilks developed what was called the PHILADELPHIA PLAN, named for a strategy that was originally designed to deal with racial discrimination in employment in that city's construction industry. This plan, like EEOC's strategy to enforce Title VII, required a results test to determine compliance with affirmative action requirements for government contractors. Specifically, Executive Order 11246, as rewritten by Fletcher, required government contractors with (at that time) contracts of at least $50,000 and 50 or more employees to file with OFCC an affirmative action plan that would include (1) an analysis of all job categories to determine the underutilization of minorities ("underutilization" was defined as having fewer minorities in a particular job category than would be reasonably expected by their availability in the relevant labor force) and (2) a specific plan with goals and timetables to correct any identified underutilization.

Fletcher's Philadelphia Plan, as embodied in Nixon's executive order, was opposed by most labor unions and many liberals and Democrats in Congress, who contended that it used race as a criterion to determine the allocation of jobs and because goals and timetables were mere euphemisms for racial quotas. Although the House of Representatives voted to prohibit implementation of the executive order, it was upheld in the Senate and it became the model for affirmative action programs throughout the United States.

Affirmative Action and the Meanings of Racism
The historian Hugh Davis Graham calls the EEOC a "subversive bureaucracy" because of what he calls its "radical" redefinition of the meaning of racism and discrimination. What Alexander and his colleagues at EEOC and Fletcher and his colleagues at OFCC did was to introduce implicitly the concept of institutional racism into public policy debate in the United States. This concept was first developed in the book *Black Power* written by STOKELY CARMICHAEL and CHARLES HAMILTON. Institutional racism is the idea that an act could be identified as racist, not on the basis of its intent but on the basis of its results or effects on SUBORDINATE GROUPS. In other words, because of historical racism and contemporary institutional arrangements, an act can become racist in its consequences without the active, intentional behavior of individuals. Carmichael and Hamilton contrasted this type of racism with individual racism, which is defined as overt, intentional acts of invidious discrimination. In 1971 the Supreme Court implicitly adopted these definitions in

GRIGGS V. DUKE POWER when it distinguished between types of discrimination (the Court rarely uses the word *racism* in its opinions). What the Court calls DISPARATE TREATMENT is the judicial equivalent of individual racism, and what the Court calls "disparate impact" is the equivalent of institutional racism.

In two important ways, affirmative action also represented a radical departure from the tenets of classical LIBERALISM, especially its core principle of INDIVIDUALISM. It does so first by adopting RACE as an acceptable criterion of decision making in allocating values and resources. Second, it embraces the notion of group rights. For much of its history, the Civil Rights movement had rejected these ideas, but by the mid-1970s much of the LEADERSHIP of black America—to some extent reluctantly and ambivalently—had embraced these ideas as integral components of post–civil rights era public policy.

Affirmative Action and the Constitution

By the late 1970s affirmative action had been institutionalized in the United States and was applied more or less routinely in universities, large corporations, and STATE AND LOCAL GOVERNMENTS. As public policy, it allows governments and other institutions to take race (and gender and ethnic minority status) into account in order to give special considerations, preferences, or set-asides to individuals from historically disadvantaged groups. The purposes or justification for the policy vary, but they include one or some combination of the following: (1) to remedy or compensate the groups for past discrimination; (2) to enforce the antidiscrimination requirements of Title VII of the 1964 Civil Rights Act; (3) to create ethnic and gender diversity in education, employment, and government contracting; and (4) to bridge the disparities in education, employment, and income between white men *as a group* and minorities and women *as groups* to create equality in the long run. The fact that the policy permits the use of race in the decision-making process raises the question of whether this is constitutionally permissible or whether, as critics argue, the CONSTITUTION should be color-blind.

This question was first presented to the Supreme Court in *DeFunis v. Odegaard* in 1974. This case involved a challenge to the University of Washington's affirmative action program at its law school, which gave special consideration to minorities in its admission process. DeFunis, a white student who was denied admission, sued, claiming that the university's admission program was unconstitutional because it employed race in its selection process. But by the time the case reached the U.S. Supreme Court, DeFunis had applied for admission a second time, had been admitted to the law school, and was on the verge of graduation. Thus the Court declined to decide the case, declaring it moot. (The Court will quite often decline to

take or decide cases when there is no "controversy" or when its decision will not have a practical significance or consequence for the parties involved. In this case, since DeFunis was seeking a decision from the Court that would order his admission to a university from which he was about to graduate, any decision by the Court would have been irrelevant or moot.) Although Justice William Douglas in a written opinion argued that the Court should have decided the principle underlying the case (whether race could be used in the university's admission process) since it was of compelling and urgent national interest, the Court waited four more years until *BAKKE V. REGENTS OF THE UNIVERSITY OF CALIFORNIA* before it rendered its first of many judgments on affirmative action.

Two constitutional questions were before the Court in *Bakke.* First, the Court had to decide whether it was a violation of the EQUAL PROTECTION CLAUSE of the FOURTEENTH AMENDMENT for a state to take race into consideration in allocating resources, in this case admission to medical school. Second, if race was a constitutionally permissible decisional criterion, could the state use a numerical racial quota? (In *Bakke* this involved setting aside 16 of 100 slots in the medical school class for minorities only.) A deeply divided Court, issuing six separate opinions, held 5-4 that the answer to the first question was yes, the second no. Writing for a different majority on both questions, Justice Lewis Powell ruled that a state could use race in admissions decisions in order to achieve diversity in the composition of its student body, but that a fixed quota was both illegal (a violation of the Civil Rights Act of 1964) and unconstitutional (a violation of the equal protection clause).

Since *Bakke,* the Court has rendered more than a dozen decisions on affirmative action, and the principles of *Bakke* have been sustained, that is, affirmative action yes, quotas no. In two cases, *United States v. Paradise* (1987) and *Local 28 Sheet Metal Workers v. Equal Employment Opportunity Commission* (1986), the Court has permitted the use of quotas to enforce egregious violations of Title VII. In each of these cases, the Court has always been divided, and in its more recent cases, *ADARAND V. PENA* and *CROSON V. CITY OF RICHMOND,* the Court reversed prior cases and significantly narrowed the range and scope of permissible affirmative action programs. At the end of the 20th century, it appeared that a narrow five-person majority of the Court was prepared, if it received an appropriate case, to reverse *Bakke* and declare affirmative action unconstitutional, that is, to declare any consideration of race by a state in allocating resources a violation of the equal protection clause.

Affirmative Action and Public Philosophy

Affirmative action raises novel and difficult questions of public philosophy and has, since its inception, deeply divided the public. In terms of public philosophy, classical liberalism is committed to individualism, the idea that people should be treated as individuals and not as members of groups. This public philosophy constitutes the principles underlying both the DECLARATION OF INDEPENDENCE and the Constitution. And it was the purpose of the Civil Rights movement to vindicate these principles in terms of race. To make the nation live up to these principles was a part of the movement's moral appeal, an appeal couched in the liberal language of individualism, fairness, equality, equal opportunity, and nondiscrimination.

Thus, critics of affirmative action such as WARD CONNERLY—the African American who led the successful campaign in California to pass PROPOSITION 209, which abolished affirmative action race and gender preferences—often invoke the words of MARTIN LUTHER KING JR. in his famous "I HAVE A DREAM" SPEECH. King, the preeminent leader during the last years of the Civil Rights movement, in this the movement's template document, said, "I have a dream that one day this nation will rise up and live out the true meaning of its creed . . ." so that individuals will "not be judged by the color of their skin but by the content of their character."

Many Americans, black and white, are skeptical about or hostile to affirmative action because of their adherence to this liberal philosophy.

It is true that some whites likely oppose affirmative action because of racism and white supremacy, but others (including many blacks) may do so for reasons of political philosophy and principle.

In the Nixon and Johnson administrations, African Americans played important roles in the development and design of affirmative action; however, in the Carter administration an African American in a responsible position in the bureaucracy took the view that affirmative action was constitutionally impermissible. Wade McCree, the solicitor general, was responsible for drafting the administration's brief or opinion in the *Bakke* case. McCree, unlike Ward Connerly, a conservative, was a bona fide member of the liberal black leadership establishment. Yet in his initial draft brief, he wrote that affirmative action was unconstitutional because it violated the constitutional principle of individual rights. McCree's brief said, "We doubt that it is [ever] proper to use race to close any portion of the class for competition by members of all races" and "racial classifications favorable to minority groups are presumptively unconstitutional." It took the personal intervention of President JIMMY CARTER to persuade a reluctant McCree to reverse his brief so that it would support affirmative action, in spite of the fact that McCree was a part of the black leadership establishment that fervently supported the policy.

Of course, affirmative action can be defended by rejecting classical liberalism and individualism as inconsistent with the black quest for freedom and equality, as some philosophers and scholars have done. Or one can argue that affirmative action is simply a means to make liberal principles a reality for those long denied opportunities, not as individuals, but as groups, and not by whites as individuals but by whites as a group. This view has also been advanced by philosophers and scholars and was advanced by Justices THURGOOD MARSHALL and Harry Blackmun in *Bakke*. Justice Marshall wrote:

> While I applaud the judgment of the Court that a university may consider race in its admission process, it is more than a little ironic that, after several hundred years of class-based discrimination against Negroes, the Court is unwilling to hold that a class-based remedy for that discrimination is permissible. In declining to so hold, today's judgment ignores the fact that for several hundred years Negroes have been discriminated against not as individuals, but rather solely because of the color of their skins. It is unnecessary in 20th-century America to have individual Negroes demonstrate that they have been victims of racial discrimination; the racism of our society has been so pervasive that none, regardless of wealth or position, has managed to escape its impact.

And Justice Blackmun wrote:

> I suspect that it would be impossible to arrange an affirmative action program in a racially neutral way and have it successful. To ask that this be so is to demand the impossible. In order to get beyond racism, we must first take account of race. There is no other way. And in order to treat some persons equally, we must treat them differently. We cannot—we dare not—let the Equal Protection Clause perpetuate racial supremacy.

In the views of these justices and others, affirmative action is not a rejection of liberal principles but a means to their ends.

Affirmative Action and Public Opinion

Public support for affirmative action programs and policies depends on the type of program and policy. Polling began on the issue in the mid-1970s, and the polls have consistently shown that both whites and blacks are prepared to support affirmative action policies that do not involve preferences or quotas. A 1978 poll, for example, found that 91 percent of blacks and 71 percent of whites agreed with the statement: "After years of discrimination it is only fair to set up programs to ensure that women and minorities are given every chance to have equal opportunities in employment and education." And a 1980 poll found that 96 percent of blacks and 76 percent of whites supported the general proposition that "affirmative action programs that help blacks get ahead should be supported." However, when the type of affirmative action program is defined in terms of "preferences" for minorities or women, support declines dramatically among both blacks and whites. From 1970 to 1996, white support for affirmative action programs that include preferences has never exceeded 20 percent, while black support has rarely exceeded 50 percent. A 1984 poll found that only 10 percent of whites and 23 percent of blacks agreed with the statement: "To make up for past discrimination, women and minorities should be given preferential treatment in getting jobs and places in college as opposed to mainly considering ability as determined by test scores." And in 1996, when the public was asked whether because of past discrimination blacks should be given preference in hiring or promotion, only 10 percent of whites and 50 percent of blacks said yes.

There is therefore support among whites for the abstract or general principle of affirmative action to assure equal opportunities for minorities and women, but there is hardly any support for preferences as a tool to implement that principle. Among blacks, opinion is about equally divided. It is probable that some of the overwhelming opposition to affirmative action among whites is rooted in white supremacist and racist thinking, but some of it is also rooted in the American ideal of individualism and the related principle of meritocracy. Similarly, black opposition is probably also a reflection of their adherence to the idea of individual merit and achievement, which affirmative action appears to contradict.

Impact of Affirmative Action

It is difficult to measure the precise or specific impact of affirmative action on the educational, occupational, and income attainments of African Americans since its adoption in the late 1960s. Since the 1960s blacks have made substantial progress in each of these areas. However, it is difficult to trace this progress *directly* to affirmative action policies and programs. This is because a number of other developments occurred at the same time that may account for black progress, including growth in the national economy, the passage and implementation of the Civil Rights Act of 1964, and an overall decline in white supremacist thinking and racist practices.

Perhaps the clearest, direct evidence of affirmative action's direct impact is in the admission of black students to elite undergraduate colleges and to graduate and professional schools. This impact, however, is not so much a gain in black access to knowledge, which these students would have had access to without affirmative action, but rather access to education from institutions of higher status, which may mean access to higher-status occupations and higher incomes. Education at elite colleges and universities may

University of Cincinnati student Survi Parvatiyar gathers with several hundred other protesters, from a group calling themselves "By Any Means Necessary," to rally in favor of affirmative action on October 23, 2001, in downtown Cincinnati. *(Getty Images)*

also mean access to elite networks of power based on relationships established with the professors and students. Overall, black enrollment in college increased from about 5 percent in the 1950s to more than 10 percent in the 1990s, but much of this growth is probably only marginally affected by affirmative action.

There is some evidence that affirmative action resulted in specific although modest increases in the employment of blacks in companies covered by affirmative action, and that black entrepreneurs have benefited from access to government contracts as a result of affirmative action. Since affirmative action, blacks have also made gains in access to high-status occupations in the professions, in construction, and in corporate and state and local government workforces, some of which may be attributable to affirmative action. However, again it is difficult to separate the effects of affirmative action from other forces at work in the economy and society.

At best, one can conclude on the basis of the available research that affirmative action in the last 30 years has had some independent effects on the closing of the educational, occupational, and income gaps between blacks and whites, and it has therefore contributed to President Johnson's goal of equality as a matter of fact rather than theory.

The Future of Affirmative Action

The future of affirmative action, to the extent that some kind of racial or gender preference is necessary to its implementation, is in doubt. In the American DEMOCRACY it is not likely that a public policy opposed by 90 percent of the white majority can long continue. White women—the major beneficiaries of the policy since its inception—are as opposed to it as white men. And blacks—the group for which the policy was initially adopted—are deeply divided about its merits. In these circumstances, it is difficult to see how affirmative action can remain viable.

The voters of California in Proposition 209 in 1996 effectively abolished racial and gender preferences as a type of affirmative action. Two years later the voters in the state of Washington did the same thing. In its most recent series of decisions, a closely divided Supreme Court has significantly undermined affirmative action, as did President BILL CLINTON in his "Mend it, don't end it" reforms. However, in the Congress efforts to abolish affirmative action by legislation were defeated in 1997 by rather substantial margins: 58 to 37 in the Senate and 225 to 194 in the House. Continued congressional support in the 1990s, especially with conservative REPUBLICAN PARTY majorities in both the House and Senate, is an interesting phenomenon. Perhaps members of Congress expect and prefer the Supreme Court to eventually end affirmative action, because a decision by the Court, because of the principles of CONSTITUTIONALISM, would give the decision more legitimacy. Or perhaps the congressional majority believes that affirmative action is a necessary and appropriate policy to achieve equality, and therefore it is in the nation's interest and should be supported, public opinion notwithstanding. Or perhaps it is understood that abolition of affirmative action would increase blacks' ALIENATION from American society and its institutions and thereby contribute to racial divisions and foster the growth of RADICALISM and BLACK NATIONALISM.

During the debate on affirmative action after *Bakke*, the *New York Times* referred editorially to affirmative action as "Reparations, American Style." At the beginning of the 20th century, African-American leaders began to forcefully advocate for REPARATIONS, which is a much more radical and racially polarizing issue than affirmative action but one that would likely gain momentum among blacks if affirmative action were abolished.

Further reading: William Bowen and Derek Bok, *The Shape of the River: Long-Term Consequences of Consider-ing Race in College Admissions* (Princeton, N.J.: Princeton University Press, 1998); George Curry, ed., *The Affirmative Action Debate* (Reading, Mass.: Addison-Wesley, 1996; W. Avon Drake and Robert Holsworth, *Affirmative Action and the Stalled Quest for Black Progress* (Urbana: University of Illinois Press, 1996); Hugh Davis Graham, *The Civil Rights Era: Origins and Development of National Policy* (New York: Oxford University Press, 1990); Kathanne Greene, *Affirmative Action and Principles of Justice* (New York: Greenwood Press, 1989); Alan Sindler, *Bakke, DeFunis and Minority Admissions: The Quest for Equal Opportunity* (New York: Longman, 1978); John David Skrentny, *The Ironies of Affirmative Action: Politics, Culture and Justice in America* (Chicago: University of Chicago Press, 1996).

African American

African American is the name adopted in the late 1980s by elements of the black intelligentsia (intellectuals and political leaders) as the appropriate way to refer to persons of African descent in the United States.

Frequently in the United States persons of African ancestry have argued about what name they should be called, and occasionally new names have been adopted by the group. The most recent example of this is the proposed adoption of African American to replace BLACK. In 1988 at a Chicago meeting of national black leaders, Ramona Edelin of the National Urban Coalition persuaded the group to adopt the new name. At a press conference announcing the change, JESSE JACKSON, who had convened the meeting, said the name *African American* had "cultural integrity. It puts us in our proper historical context. Every ethnic group in this country has a reference to some land base, some historical cultural base. African Americans have hit that level of cultural maturity. There are Armenian Americans and Jewish Americans and Italian Americans; and with a degree of acceptance and reasonable pride, they connect their heritage to their mother country and where they are now." Jackson said the name *black* should now be rejected because it "does not describe our situation. In my household there are seven people and none of us have the same complexion. . . . We are of African heritage." Thus, African heritage rather than BLACKNESS becomes the basis of group identity.

Although some black intellectuals and others opposed the new name, unlike the adoption of *black* in the 1960s, the adoption of *African American* caused little controversy and was almost immediately embraced by virtually all of the black intelligentsia and white opinion makers and politicians. However, as with the change from "Negro" to "Black" in the 1960s, black PUBLIC OPINION did not follow the intelligentsia. A 1990 survey commissioned by the JOINT CENTER FOR POLITICAL AND ECONOMIC STUDIES found that 72 percent of blacks preferred *black,* 15 percent *African American,* 3 percent *Negro,* with the remainder giving no opinion or other names. It took several years of controversy and struggle before ordinary people accepted *black* in the 1960s, but unlike the 1980s, *black* was not accepted in isolation. Instead, the new name was accepted as part of the larger BLACK POWER MOVEMENT. Because no such movement is associated with *African American,* the new name's use may be limited to the intelligentsia and formal public discourse.

Ironically, *African American* was adopted coincident with the influx of a large number of immigrants from Africa. Some critics of the new name as a reference for native-born black Americans argue that *African American* should be used to refer to these new immigrants and to distinguish them from native-born blacks. But the use of *African American* to refer to African immigrants is also a misnomer because it conceals the enormous diversity among Africans. That is, immigrants from Africa tend to think of themselves not as African Americans but, rather, Ghanian, Kenyan, Nigerian, Senegalese, Ethiopian, or one of the other names that represent the ethnic and national diversity of the peoples of that vast continent.

See also MULTICULTURALISM and NAMES CONTROVERSY.

Further reading: Ruth Grant and Marion Orr, "Language, Race and Politics: From 'Black' to 'African American,'" *Politics and Society* 24 (1996): 137–52.

African-American politics, defined

African-American politics is but another manifestation of the universal power struggle between individuals and groups in the United States to realize or achieve their objectives. In a seminal article MACK H. JONES, an African-American political scientist on the faculty of ATLANTA UNIVERSITY, defined African-American politics as "essentially a power struggle between blacks and whites, with the latter trying to maintain their superordinate position vis-a-vis the former." In this article, Jones goes on to postulate that in order to distinguish black politics from other forms of group politics in the United States, one must add as a specifying condition "the stipulation that the ideological justification for the superordination of whites is the institutionalized belief in the inherent superiority of that group."

Theoretically, then, black politics involves an asymmetrical POWER relationship between two groups, one SUPERORDINATE and the other SUBORDINATE, with the former group trying to maintain the relationship and the latter trying to alter it. It should be clear to the student that this is a theoretical proposition, not an empirical one. That is, black politics (theoretically understood) assumes that whites as a group act toward blacks *as a group* so as to maintain the relationship of dominance, and that blacks *as a group* act toward whites to alter this relationship. This theoretical proposition does not suggest that empirically (as a matter of fact or in the real world) all whites and all blacks behave in the way specified theoretically. In other words, this definition is akin to what the sociologist Max Weber called an "Ideal Type," a theoretical concept that is primarily useful because it helps the social scientist to understand and explain the empirical world. In this sense, the definition is neither true nor false; rather, it is merely useful in scientific understanding and explanation. It is useful for understanding, research, and explanation to think of black politics in terms of superordinate and subordinate groups acting toward each other as groups.

In addition to the asymmetrical relationships of dominance and subordination, African-American politics in the United States is distinguished by white RACISM as a behavioral phenomenon and WHITE SUPREMACY as an ideological phenomenon. Blacks are subordinated to whites on the basis of their race (racism), and this subordination is justified on the basis of the IDEOLOGY that blacks are inherently inferior to whites (white supremacy).

Although in his formulation Jones does not explicitly call attention to VIOLENCE, it too in various manifestations is a distinguishing feature of African-American politics. The subordination or oppression of blacks in the United States was established and maintained on the basis of the exercise by whites of extraordinary violence beginning with the slave trade and SLAVERY. Although other bases of power were used by whites, ultimately the political relationship between the two groups was established and maintained on the basis of brute force.

All politics varies by time, place, circumstance, and context. But in all places, times, contexts, and circumstances, African-American politics has been about altering the superordinate-subordinate relationship. Thus, black politics in the revolutionary and antebellum eras was about altering and ending slavery so as to achieve the objective of FREEDOM. In the period after RECONSTRUCTION leading up to the CIVIL RIGHTS MOVEMENT, black politics was about regaining and exercising the freedom that had been lost. And in the POST–CIVIL RIGHTS ERA, black politics has been about the objective of INTEGRATION or EQUALITY. In each of these historical periods of the phenomenon's manifestations, blacks have sought whatever bases of power they could attain to achieve their objectives, and in each they have confronted in different manifestations or forms and in varying degrees racism, white supremacy, and violence.

See also FRANTZ FANON.

Further reading: Mack H. Jones, "A Frame of Reference for Black Politics" in *Black Political Life in the United States,* ed. Lenneal Henderson (New York: Chandler Publishers); Ira Katznelson, "Power in the Reformulation of Race Relations Research" in *Race, Change and Urban Society*, ed. Peter Orleans and William Ellis (Newbury Park, Calif.: Sage Publications, 1971); John Roucek, "Minority-Majority Relations in Their Power Aspects," *Phylon* 17 (1956): 24–30; Robert Staples, "Violence in Black America: The Political Implications," *Black World* 23 (May 1974): 17–32.

African-American studies

The historical roots of African-American studies—the systematic, interdisciplinary study of the experience of African peoples in the United States—can be traced to 1887 when W. E. B. DU BOIS at ATLANTA UNIVERSITY began a series of conferences that eventually evolved into a large-scale scientific project. And at a few of the HISTORICALLY BLACK COLLEGES AND UNIVERSITIES, systematic study of the black experience—especially history—was a standard part of the curriculum. However, the systematic study of the African-American experience at predominantly white American colleges and universities can be traced to the 1960s' BLACK POWER MOVEMENT and the outbreak of student activism associated with it.

In the 1967 book *BLACK POWER*, the authors STOKELY CARMICHAEL and CHARLES HAMILTON called for the establishment of black studies because, they wrote, "It is absolutely essential that people know their history, that they know their roots, and that they develop an awareness of their cultural heritage." Carmichael and Hamilton's call for black studies reflected the ideas of MALCOLM X, ideas that became a rallying cry for the increasing numbers of black students attending predominantly white campuses in the NORTHERN STATES in the late 1960s. These students established racially autonomous organizations on campus (usually called Black Student Unions) and began a movement to increase the numbers of black students and faculty on campus and to establish programs in African-American studies. Frequently, this movement involved PROTEST, strikes, and occasionally VIOLENCE, including a five-month student-faculty strike at San Francisco State University and a 36-hour demonstration by students armed with shotguns at Cornell University. As a result of these protests at predominantly white colleges and universities, as well as at some of the historically black colleges and universities, colleges and universities began to create courses and establish programs and departments in African-American studies. The first program established at a black campus was at HOWARD UNIVERSITY as a result of student protests led by NATHAN HARE, and the first program established at a predominantly white university was organized by Hare (after he was fired from Howard) at San Francisco State University.

Although estimates vary, from 1969 to 1972 between 500 and 800 full-fledged departments of African-American studies (usually called "black studies" at that time) were created on white campuses. (Many other colleges and universities for the first time began to hire black faculty to teach one or two classes, usually in history and literature.) Many of these early programs had radical cultural and political orientations rooted in the IDEOLOGY of BLACK NATIONALISM and the philosophy and the ethos of the BLACK POWER MOVEMENT. Consequently, they were strongly criticized by some campus administrators and faculty and black intellectuals and civil rights leaders. By the 1990s many of these more radical programs had been phased out, while others were allowed to wither away because of lack of interest or budget support. By the year 2000, estimates put the number of full-scale programs at about 300 to 400. These remaining programs have been more or less institutionalized. That is, they have become like traditional interdisciplinary programs and departments at American colleges and universities, leading critics such as Nathan Hare to describe them as "polka dot" rather than "black studies."

The several hundred African-American-studies programs that exist can be classified into two broad schools: traditionalist and AFROCENTRIC. Traditional programs, generally interdisciplinary and including white as well as black scholars, generally employ the paradigms and methodologies of the traditional disciplines in the study of the black experience. The Afrocentric school includes those programs that are generally separate, all-black departments with distinctive paradigms and methodologies, often Afrocentric. The majority of programs in African-American studies are traditional, and they frequently include a significant number of scholars (usually women) engaged in teaching and research on black FEMINISM.

African-American studies is an effort to acquire, maintain, and use systematic knowledge as a base of power in AFRICAN-AMERICAN POLITICS.

See also MOLEFI K. ASANTE.

Further reading: John W. Blassingame, ed., *New Perspectives on Black Studies* (Urbana: University of Illinois Press, 1971); Robert Harris, Darlene Clark, and Nellie McKay, *Three Essays: Black Studies in the United States* (New York: Ford Foundation, 1990).

African-American thought

The African-American political scientist MACK H. JONES argues that the political thought of a people grows out of what he calls their "anticipation and control needs." Anticipation and control needs, according to Jones, refer to a people's need for information that is useful for understanding their circumstances and developing prescriptions for moving toward their goals as posited in their worldview. A people's worldview, according to Jones, includes among other things "answers to the question: Who are we? Where did we come from? How did we get here? Where do we wish to go? What alternative strategies have been tried and what results were obtained and why? Who are our friends and enemies?" Jones is dealing here specifically with the African-American experience and its thought. However, what he says is true of all people and their philosophy and thought. Bertrand Russell, for example, writes in the preface to his *History of Western Philosophy,* "My purpose is to exhibit philosophy as an integral part of social and political life, not as the isolated speculations of remarkable individuals but as both an effect and cause of the character of the various communities in which different systems flourished." Similarly, George Sabine in the preface to his *A History of Political Theory* writes, " . . . theories of politics themselves are a part of politics. In other words, they do not refer to an external reality, but are produced as a normal part of the social motion in which politics itself has its being. . . . It can not be supposed that any political philosophy of the present or past can step out of the relationship in which it stands to the problems, the valuations, the habits or even the prejudices of its own time."

If Jones, Russell, and Sabine are correct African-American political thought, like that of any people, can only be understood in relationship to the real-world, concrete conditions and circumstances that give rise to it. In addition, African-American thought has been disproportionately produced by political activists rather than detached, unengaged philosophers. Also, African-American thought, like American political thought in general, tends, unlike European or Western philosophy, to be pragmatic, directed toward change or problem solving.

From its beginning in the colonial era African-American thought has focused on FREEDOM, deliverance, liberation, and EQUALITY. In an often-quoted letter written shortly after the CIVIL WAR, A. P. Taveau, a wealthy South Carolina rice planter, expressed surprise that his slaves deserted him as soon as the opportunity presented itself. Taveau wrote that he had believed that slaves were content, happy, and attached to their masters. But now he understood that blacks had for generations been "looking for the horse of universal freedom."

Taveau should not have been surprised. Given their circumstances and conditions, it would be virtually impossible for black political thought and behavior from the beginning not to be looking for this horse of universal freedom. Thus, any understanding of African-American political thought must analyze the concrete conditions and circumstances that gave rise to it.

The political thought of African Americans arises out of the conditions and circumstances of SLAVERY. In 1790,

three years after the CONSTITUTION was adopted, 92 percent of the African American population was enslaved, including 76 percent of the Southern population and 24 percent of the population of the North. By 1860 on the eve of the Civil War, not much had changed: 88 percent of African Americans nationally were slaves, including 83 percent in the SOUTHERN STATES and 17 percent in the NORTHERN STATES. Even Washington, the DISTRICT OF COLUMBIA, the nation's capital whose laws were made by CONGRESS, had a large slave population (81 percent in 1800), declining to 22 percent by 1860. The pervasiveness of slavery throughout the nation therefore resulted in freedom's emergence as a central idea in the thought of African Americans.

Even so-called FREE NEGROES were not fully free, since throughout the nation they were frequently denied the right to vote and access to job opportunities, housing, and many public places including restaurants and inns, not to mention the ever-present fear of being accused of being a runaway slave. Thus, nowhere in the United States did African Americans enjoy universal freedom. On the contrary, it was everywhere limited either completely through slavery or partially through restrictions on the civil and voting rights of so-called free Negroes. Indeed, the free Negroes should not be referred to as free but rather as Negroes who were not enslaved. This is important because although they were not slaves, the nonslave African Americans, as partially free persons, lived under circumstances and conditions that made freedom central to their thought and action.

The earliest expressions of the thought of African Americans are found in the numerous petitions submitted to Congress and the state legislatures and governors beginning in the Revolutionary era (1600s–1787). In these early petitions and in the subsequent speeches, pamphlets, and books that constitute the classical writings in African-American thought, blacks frequently invoked religion (specifically Christian teachings) and the philosophical principles of NATURAL RIGHTS and the SOCIAL CONTRACT to make arguments for freedom. An early example is an anonymous 1774 appeal to the governor and legislature of Massachusetts. It read in part:

> The petition of a Grate number of Blacks of this province who by divine permission are held in a state of slavery within the bowels of a free and Christian country. That your petitioners apprehend with other men a natural right to our freedoms without being deprived of them by our fellow men as we are freeborn people and have never forfeited this Blessing by any compact agreement whatever. . . . We therefore beg your excellency and Honors will give this its deer weight and considerations and that you will accordingly cause an act of the legisla-

ture to be passed that we may obtain our natural right to our freedoms and our children be set at lebety [*sic*].

In 1829 Robert Young published a brief document titled *The Ethiopian Manifesto Issued in Defense of the Black Man's Right To the Scale of Universal Freedom,* one of the earliest formal documents in black thought. It too is rooted in religion and natural rights and social-contract principles, as he proclaims that it is God's will that men be free and "I am myself a man, and as a man will live, or as a man die, for as I was born free of the will of God, so I do claim and purport to establish an alike universal freedom to every son and daughter descending from the black. . . ."

These ideas in the classical writings of blacks appear repeatedly in the writings and speeches of antebellum and civil rights–era thinkers and activists such as FREDERICK DOUGLASS's famous Fourth of July address and MARTIN LUTHER KING JR.'s even more famous "I HAVE A DREAM" SPEECH.

Classical black thought also often invoked the principles and language of the DECLARATION OF INDEPENDENCE and the Constitution, a practice also followed by Douglass in the 1850s and by King 100 years later. An early example of this pattern in black thought is *A Series of Letters by a Man of Color* written in 1813 by James Forten, a wealthy Philadelphia merchant and veteran of the Revolutionary War. He wrote, "We hold this truth to be self-evident, that God created all men equal, is one of the most prominent features of the Declaration of Independence, and that glorious fabric of collected wisdom, our noble Constitution. This idea embraces the Indian and the European, the Savage and the Saint, the Peruvian and the Laplander, the white man and the African, and whatever measures are adopted subversive of this inestimable privilege, are in direct violation of the letter and spirit of the Constitution."

In the foregoing passages, classical black thought is adopted from or derivative of classical American thought. Like the framers of the Declaration and the Constitution, black thinkers invoked ideas of natural rights, the social contract, and individual liberty as justifications for their quest for freedom. Unlike white Americans, however, the black idea of freedom was universal, including, as Forten wrote, "the Indian and the European, the Savage and the Saint, the Peruvian and the Laplander, the white man and the African." But in two ways, black thought from the beginning to the present has been distinctive. First, it has sought to vindicate the humanity of the African in the face of the dominant ideology of WHITE SUPREMACY. Second, it calls attention to the evil and hypocrisy of whites because of their OPPRESSION of the African.

The theme of African humanity is expressed forcefully in DAVID WALKER's 1827 appeal. Noting that many states had passed laws prohibiting interracial marriages, Walker scornfully wrote, "I wish candidly, however, before the Lord to be understood that I would not give a [pinch of snuff] to be married to any white person," and referring to THOMAS JEFFERSON's observation that the African's skin color was "unfortunate," Walker again wrote scornfully that "As though we are not thankful to our God for having made us as it pleased himself, as they (the whites) are having made them white." (Here Walker's thinking anticipates the 1960s BLACK POWER MOVEMENT with its emphasis on black pride, "black is beautiful," and "I am black and I am proud.") Finally, in an argument similar to that advanced by proponents of AFROCENTRICITY, Walker wrote that the "Sons of Africa or Ham are among whom learning originated and was carried to Greece, where it was refined." This valorization of Africa is also found in the writings of MARTIN DELANY and EDWARD WILMOT BLYDEN. In his seminal text, *The Condition, Elevation and Destiny of the Colored Race,* Delaney wrote:

> That the colored races have the highest traits of civilization will not be disputed. They are civil, peaceable and religious to a fault. In mathematics, sculpture and architecture, as arts, sciences, commerce and internal improvements as enterprises the white race may probably excel. But in languages, oratory, poetry, music, and painting, as arts and sciences and in ethics, metaphysics, theology and legal jurisprudence—in plain language, in the true principles of morals, correctness of thought, religion, and law or civil government, there is no doubt but the black race will instruct the world.

Delany and Walker's writings also contain early criticisms of whites as "evil" and as "devils" and hypocrites, ideas that are present in the modern era, especially in the thought of individuals in the tradition of BLACK NATIONALISM such as ELIJAH MUHAMMAD, MALCOLM X, and LOUIS FARRAKHAN. In the *Appeal,* Walker wrote " . . . that we, the Blacks or colored people, are treated more cruel by white Christians of America, than devils themselves ever treated a set of men, women and children on earth," and whites are "acting more like devils than accountable men." In his text Delany wrote, "We regret the necessity of stating the fact, but duty compels us to the task, that for more than two thousand years, the determined aim of whites has been to crush the colored races wherever found. With a determined will they have sought and pursued them in every quarter of the globe. The Anglo-Saxon has taken the lead in this work of universal subjugation. But the Anglo-American stands preeminent for deeds of injustice and acts of oppression, unparalleled, perhaps, in the annals of modern history."

The foundational elements of African-American thought include a focus on freedom, an emphasis on the principles of natural rights and the social contract, the defense of the humanity of the African people, the valorization of Africa, and the condemnation of whites for their oppression of Africans. These elements are rooted in the historical conditions and memories of African Americans, as well as the realities and perceptions of their modern situation. This thought is manifested politically in IDEOLOGY—fundamental differences between black intellectuals and leaders over how to acquire the power resources to achieve the generally agreed on objective of freedom for African peoples. In terms of ideology, some blacks embrace RADICALISM, others INTEGRATION, and still others black nationalism.

See also NEGRITUDE.

Further reading: Wilson J. Moses, *Classical Black Nationalism: From the American Revolution to Marcus Garvey* (New York: New York University Press, 1996); Sterling Stuckey, *The Ideological Origins of Black Nationalism* (Boston: Beacon Press, 1972).

African Blood Brotherhood

VIOLENCE was the major base of power exercised by whites in order to initially enslave Africans and subsequently to maintain their OPPRESSION or subordination. Violence in one form or another is an integral feature of the relationship between Europeans and Africans and is a defining attribute of AFRICAN-AMERICAN POLITICS. From the beginning of the black-white relationship in the United States, whites enjoyed a monopoly on legitimate force and violence as used by the government, as well as the illegitimate violence used by ordinary people. However, since the time of the SLAVE REVOLTS on the ships and on the plantations, blacks also have employed violence in their fights for FREEDOM. During the KU KLUX KLAN era of white terrorism after RECONSTRUCTION, there was occasional talk of blacks using organized violence as a form of resistance, but no organized group devoted to armed resistance to oppression emerged until the African Blood Brotherhood (ABB) was formed in 1919. The ABB was also one of the first black organizations to embrace RADICALISM and COMMUNISM as ideologies of the black freedom struggle. In its embrace of armed self-defense and radicalism, the ABB was the forerunner of the BLACK PANTHER PARTY of the 1960s.

The ABB (formally known as the African Blood Brotherhood for African Liberation and Redemption) was organized by Cyril Briggs and a small group of HARLEM-based African-American socialists and communists. Many of its organizers, like Briggs, were WEST INDIAN immigrants and were closely connected to the organization of another West Indian immigrant, MARCUS GARVEY and his UNIVERSAL NEGRO IMPROVEMENT ASSOCIATION. Members of both groups for a time sought a merger, but the ABB was a quasi-secret organization committed to SOCIALISM and communism, while Garvey's group was a mass-based organization committed to CAPITALISM. So, in the end, rather than merge, the two groups became rivals, and Briggs and Garvey engaged in bitter feuds and villifications, with each suing the other for libel.

The ABB achieved its greatest prominence in the aftermath of the Tulsa RIOTS of 1921, in which dozens of blacks and whites were killed and wounded in a series of armed confrontations. Tulsa officials and the national MEDIA blamed the ABB (which had a local unit in Tulsa) for the confrontation, and while it is unclear what its role was, the group hailed the confrontation in Tulsa as proof that blacks would fight to defend their rights. Membership in the group increased after the riots, and it began to attract a larger audience at its rallies. It also attracted increased attention from the JUSTICE DEPARTMENT and its Bureau of Investigation (the forerunner of the FBI), which had the group under surveillance since its inception.

The ABB was dissolved in 1924, and its membership was absorbed into the COMMUNIST PARTY. (Briggs continued to work in the party until his death at 69 in 1966.) In its five-year existence, the ABB published a newspaper, *The Crusader,* and raised to prominence the issue of the right of blacks to self-defense. Although its membership never exceeded several thousand (estimates range from a couple of hundred to several thousand) and it was not widely supported by ordinary blacks, who rejected its radicalism, the ABB is historically important because—in an era when LYNCHING and other forms of violence against blacks were ascendant—it, unlike other black organizations, asserted that blacks, like any other citizens, had a constitutional and human right to defend themselves. This idea was not to find organizational expression again until the 1950s and 1960s.

Further reading: Theodore Kornweibel, *Seeing Red: Federal Campaigns against Black Militancy, 1919–1925* (Bloomington: Indiana University Press, 1998); Mark Naison, *Communists in Harlem during the Depression* (Urbana: University of Illinois Press, 1983).

Afrocentricity (Afrocentrism)

Afrocentricity or Afrocentrism is an epistemology prominent in one school of AFRICAN-AMERICAN STUDIES. It asserts that Western civilization has its origins in the classical African civilizations, specifically Egypt (or "Kemet"), and that African paradigms, symbols, myths, and values should constitute the starting point or frame of reference for acquiring knowledge of the experience of African peoples wherever they are in the world. Although a number of scholars have contributed to the Afrocentric idea, two of its most influential advocates are RON KARENGA and MOLEFI K. ASANTE. Although not the dominant framework or approach in African-American studies, Afrocentrism is used in a number of programs, including the one at San Francisco State University, the birthplace in 1969 of the first modern black-studies department. In addition to its epistemological and pedagogical uses in black scholarship, Afrocentricity is also part of the larger movement of CULTURAL NATIONALISM, which in the United States seeks to accentuate African heritage and culture through the adoption of African names, fashions and dress (kente cloths, kufi hats, African beads), hair styles (braids, dreadlocks, Afros), food, music, and religiosity.

Critics (such as the white liberal historian Arthur Schlesinger Jr. and the liberal black scholar Henry Louis Gates Jr.) contend that Afrocentricity as a form of MULTICULTURALISM threatens to balkanize or divide the United States into distinctive ethnic communities, and that both as a pedagogy and as an expression of cultural nationalism it runs counter to classical LIBERALISM. Schlesinger argues that the pedagogy of Afrocentricity is in effect racist, writing, "If a kleagle of the Ku Klux Klan wanted to use the schools to disable and handicap black Americans, he could hardly come up with anything more effective than the Afrocentric curriculum." Meanwhile Asante contends that multiculturalism in education is a nonhierarchical approach to education that respects and celebrates a diversity of cultural perspectives and is a revolutionary challenge to the IDEOLOGY of WHITE SUPREMACY and the dominance of American culture and education by "Eurocentricity."

Further reading: Molefi K. Asante, *Kemet, Afrocentricity and Knowledge* (Trenton, N.J.: Africa World Press, 1991); Arthur Schlesinger Jr., *The Disuniting of America: Reflections on a Multicultural Society* (New York: W. W. Norton, 1991, 1998).

AIDS-HIV

During the early 1980s, acquired immunodeficiency syndrome (AIDS) and HIV (human immunodeficiency virus) became the most widely discussed health problem in the world. When HIV-AIDS first received national attention in 1981, it was generally regarded as a "gay disease" found almost exclusively among white male homosexuals. Therefore, it received little attention from the African-American MEDIA, from the BLACK CHURCH, or from CIVIL RIGHTS or political leaders. And even when it became clear that AIDS was not confined to white homosexuals, the black media and black leaders were reluctant to acknowledge its prevalence among blacks. This reluctance can be attributed to

the strong taboo against homosexuality in African-American CULTURE, generally, and to the power of African-American RELIGIOSITY, which strongly condemns homosexuality as sinful. Similarly, because the disease is also disproportionately transmitted among blacks through illegal, intravenous drug use and "promiscuous" sexual activity, there was also a religious and cultural reluctance to acknowledge AIDS's existence or to develop programs to deal with its causes and consequences.

By the early 1990s, however, this pattern of denial and neglect could not be sustained as the disease began to disproportionately impact the BLACK COMMUNITY. By the late 1990s it was undeniable that AIDS was an epidemic among blacks, with federal health agencies reporting that while blacks were only 12 percent of the population, they constituted 40 percent of those with AIDS, and among women 56 percent were black and among children 58 percent. (By the late 1990s AIDS also had reached epidemic proportions in Africa. Although only 13 percent of the world's population, it was estimated that perhaps as much as 70 percent of AIDS cases in the world were African.) The Harvard University AIDS Institute in 1996 reported that more African-Americans were infected with HIV than all other racial and ETHNIC GROUPS combined. In other words, AIDS was fast becoming the leading cause of death of blacks in the United States.

The epidemic proportions of the disease (and the fact that black celebrities such as basketball's Earvin "Magic" Johnson had become infected) finally led the black media and black church and political and civil rights leaders to start to pay attention to it and push for the development of educational and health policies and programs that would address its causes and consequences.

The AIDS epidemic also contributed to and reflected the deep sense of ALIENATION that is a central attribute of African-American culture. Polls conducted during the 1990s showed from half to two-thirds of blacks believed it was possible that AIDS was a man-made virus deliberately created by whites to harm or kill blacks. This view of AIDS as a conspiracy against blacks has been publicly supported by parts of the black nationalist community, including the NATION OF ISLAM and its leader LOUIS FARRAKHAN.

Further reading: Cathy Cohen, *The Boundaries of Blackness: AIDS and the Breakdown of Black Politics* (Chicago: University of Chicago Press, 1999).

Ali, Muhammad (Cassius Marcellus Clay) (1942–)
athlete, political activist

Three-time heavyweight champion of the world and a leading American Muslim, Muhammad Ali—originally named Cassius Clay—used his enormous status as an athlete as a base of power to confer legitimacy on and enhance the appeal of the NATION OF ISLAM, BLACK NATIONALISM, the BLACK POWER MOVEMENT, and opposition to the VIETNAM WAR.

Ali won the Olympic gold medal in 1960, and in 1964 he unexpectedly defeated Sonny Liston to become the heavyweight champion of the world. Shortly thereafter, under the guidance of MALCOLM X, he joined the Nation of Islam, changing his name from Cassius Clay to Muhammad Ali. Ali's decision to join the Nation of Islam (popularly referred to as the Black Muslims) sparked widespread criticisms from both black and white leaders and opinion makers because the Nation and its most prominent spokesman, Malcolm X, were viewed as radical, violence prone, antiwhite black separatists. Although he previously had been exempted from the military draft because of his failure to pass an aptitude test, in 1966 he was reclassified as eligible for military service and drafted into the army. He refused to be inducted, claiming exemption because he was a Muslim minister. He also did not think that blacks should fight in a "white man's war" in Vietnam when they did not have FREEDOM at home, famously saying "no Viet Cong ever called me nigger."

Muhammad Ali, formerly Cassius Clay, 1964 *(Library of Congress)*

Ali was tried and convicted for draft evasion and sentenced to five years in prison. Pending his appeal, he was allowed to remain free, but his title as heavyweight champion was taken away and his license to box was revoked. For the next five years, unable to practice his profession, Ali traveled the country as a Muslim minister, an advocate of black power, and an opponent of the Vietnam War.

In 1971 the SUPREME COURT reversed Ali's conviction; his right to box was reinstated; and he eventually twice regained the title of heavyweight champion. By the mid-1970s, Ali's status in American society had been transformed from that of a radical black nationalist extremist to an American icon. Hailed as one of the greatest athletes of all time (Ali in his characteristically boastful style referred to himself as "The Greatest"), Ali was feted by American presidents, sent on diplomatic missions, and hailed as a hero for his principled opposition to the war in Vietnam and for his courage in his religious convictions. At the 1996 Olympics in Atlanta, Ali, suffering from Parkinson's disease, was granted the honor of lighting the torch that opened the games.

Ali is important in AFRICAN-AMERICAN POLITICS because he used his status as a celebrity athlete to effect political change and become an influential leader during the 1960s. In 1975 he published his autobiography, *The Greatest: My Own Story.*

Further reading: David Remnick, *King of the World: Muhammad Ali and the Rise of an American Hero* (New York: Random House, 1998).

alienation

Alienation can be understood as attitudes that reflect a sense of isolation from society and its institutions: feelings of pessimism, cynicism, and a lack of trust in other individuals as well as the institutions of the society. That African Americans are more alienated than whites in the United States is a well-established conclusion in social-science research. Indeed, alienation in one form or another is a central component of African-American CULTURE in general and the POLITICAL CULTURE specifically. Classical sociological writings on alienation trace it to the development of industrial society and its dehumanizing impact on the working class. However, as FRANTZ FANON, among others, has shown, in an industrial society characterized by institutionalized RACISM and the IDEOLOGY of WHITE SUPREMACY, the problem of alienation is compounded. Its sources are twofold: race and class. Blacks are alienated as workers and as blacks. As Fanon described and analyzed it, black alienation is inherent in the processes of racial OPPRESSION because it relegates blacks to subordinate positions in both class and racial hierarchies.

Contemporary African-American culture is characterized by a relatively high degree of suspiciousness and cynicism about the motives of others; a relatively high degree of distrust in the government and its leaders; and a tendency to attribute problems of the BLACK COMMUNITY (such as AIDS and drugs) to conspiracies by whites. When they are reflected in the political culture, these tendencies tend to depress voting and other forms of POLITICAL PARTICIPATION, inculcate a cynical view of LEADERSHIP, and undermine group solidarity.

See also SUBORDINATE GROUP and SUPERORDINATE GROUP.

Further reading: Robert C. Smith and Richard Seltzer, *Race, Class and Culture: A Study in Afro-American Mass Opinion* (Albany, New York: SUNY Press, 1992).

Allen, Richard (1760–1831) *religious leader*

Richard Allen ranks as one of the greatest or most important African-American leaders in the history of the United States. This is so because he organized and led the first independent BLACK CHURCH, the most powerful institution or ORGANIZATION among blacks, blending the important power bases of size and solidarity and religion. The establishment of the African Methodist Episcopal (AME) Church by itself would make Allen a great leader, but he also organized the first independent black political organization—the NATIONAL BLACK POLITICAL CONVENTION—employing this time only the size and solidarity base.

Allen was born a slave in Philadelphia in 1760. Sometime in his early youth he underwent a religious conversion and, with the permission of his owner, traveled as a Methodist preacher. In 1780 the man who owned Allen allowed him to purchase his freedom by working at a variety of jobs, and by 1785 he had earned enough to pay the last installment on the $2,000 that his FREEDOM cost. While he was working for his freedom, Allen continued to preach when he could, but once he was out of bondage he, in effect, became a full-time minister, preaching throughout the Middle Atlantic region to blacks, whites, and occasionally Native Americans. In 1785 he was asked by the white elder of St. George's Church in Philadelphia to become the minister for the black members of the congregation. It was his ministry at St. George's that convinced Allen that blacks needed a separate church of their own where, as he put it in his autobiography, we could "worship God under our own vine and fig."

In 1794 Allen and 11 other black Methodists in Philadelphia formed Bethel African Church ("Mother Bethel," as it is called today). Although Allen had long been convinced of the need for an autonomous black church, the proximate cause of the formation of Bethel was when in 1792 or 1793 (the date is not certain) the black members of St. George's were told they could no longer sit in the pews as they normally did but instead had to sit upstairs in a newly constructed gallery. The black worshipers reluctantly agreed, but then they were ordered to sit at the back of the gallery. This they refused to do and walked out in protest. From this incident, the most important organization in black America has its origins.

The establishment of Mother Bethel as an autonomous black church under Allen's leadership led to a 20-year struggle with white Methodists who attempted to control the congregation's doctrines and property. Finally, in 1816 the Pennsylvania Supreme Court ruled that Bethel was legally independent and free to control its own affairs. Several months after the court's decision, black ministers from throughout the Middle Atlantic region convened in Philadelphia to unite their churches into the African Methodist Episcopal Church, with Allen as its first bishop. Now African Americans could develop their own version of Christianity while employing the resources of a united, autonomous church to develop their own community, including schools and mutual aid societies, and to work in the emerging ABOLITIONIST MOVEMENT.

In addition to his work as a clergyman, Allen was a businessman and political leader. He also was a writer, authoring several pamphlets attacking WHITE SUPREMACY, RACISM, and SLAVERY. In 1830 as racial DISCRIMINATION against FREE NEGROES in the North appeared to increase, Allen and other black leaders called for the convening in Philadelphia of the NATIONAL NEGRO CONVENTION in order to pool the resources of the race and develop a plan of action to defend its interests. Allen, then 70 years old, was elected president of the convention, which met periodically until 1864. Allen died a year later in 1831 having achieved recognition as the race's foremost religious and political leader.

See also LEADERSHIP.

Further reading: Carol George, *Segregated Sabbaths: Richard Allen and the Emergence of Independent Black Churches, 1760–1840* (New York: Oxford University Press, 1973); Clarence Walker, *A Rock in a Weary Place: The African Methodist Episcopal Church during the Civil War and Reconstruction* (Baton Rouge: Louisiana State University Press, 1982).

American Colonialization Society

The American Colonialization Society was formed in 1817 by prominent whites (including Supreme Court Justice Bushrod Washington) with the purpose of sending blacks back to Africa as an alternative to their emancipation and FREEDOM in the United States. Although its leaders did suggest that eventually slaves might be purchased for purposes of colonialization, the major purpose of the society was the return of the FREE NEGROES to Africa. It claimed that the free Negroes were inferior and living in terrible conditions of poverty and ignorance, and argued they would be better off if returned to Africa. The idea of colonialization received widespread support throughout the white community of the NORTHERN STATES and some support among black adherents of BACK-TO-AFRICA MOVEMENTS. But, generally, African-American leaders were opposed to the idea because it suggested blacks were inferior and could not succeed as free people in the United States. These leaders also argued that colonialization of free Negroes would only make SLAVERY more secure by removing its most effective opponents. They also argued that blacks were Americans by birth and entitled to CITIZENSHIP and EQUALITY in this country. Leaders of the ABOLITIONIST MOVEMENT in the 1830s also began to attack colonialization.

Colonialization was supported by all of the early American presidents and later by ABRAHAM LINCOLN. CONGRESS appropriated large sums to support it, and several thousand Africans were eventually settled in a colony in West Africa, which in 1847 became the independent Republic of LIBERIA. But ultimately the efforts of the society failed because most black people preferred freedom in the United States rather than going back to Africa.

American Dilemma, An

An American Dilemma is a classic, written by the Swedish economist GUNNAR MYRDAL. It is the most detailed and exhaustive study of the problem of race in the United States ever conducted. The book exerted a profound influence on social-science research on the problem of race, influenced SUPREME COURT decision making in *BROWN V. BOARD OF EDUCATION,* and helped shape the strategy of MARTIN LUTHER KING JR. in his LEADERSHIP of the CIVIL RIGHTS MOVEMENT. Like other great books that have helped to change the world, *An American Dilemma* is an excellent example of how knowledge was acquired and used as a base of power in AFRICAN-AMERICAN POLITICS.

In 1937 the Carnegie Corporation invited Myrdal, then a relatively unknown economist and member of the Swedish Parliament with no interest or experience in research on RACE, to become director of "a comprehensive study of the Negro in the United States, to be undertaken in a wholly objective and dispassionate way as a social phenomenon." Myrdal was selected rather than one of the many well-qualified white or black scholars of race because it was thought he would bring a tone of neutrality and objectivity to the study that would enhance its credibility. The study was inspired by liberal internationalist elements of the white POWER ELITE who, concerned about the United States's role in world affairs, saw a need to abolish legal DISCRIMINATION and SEGREGATION if the United States was to have credibility as leader of the "free world." As Myrdal wrote toward the end of *An American Dilemma,* "America, for its international prestige, power and future security, needs to demonstrate to the world that American Negroes can be satisfactorily integrated into its democracy." Familiar with the growing body of research that cast doubt on the IDEOLOGY of WHITE SUPREMACY as the justification for racial discrimination and SEGREGATION, the Carnegie Corporation thought that the most useful thing to do at that time was to present the facts to the American people as a first step in the long struggle to abolish legal distinctions based on race.

As proposed by Carnegie, the idea was to have Myrdal be responsible for the study as a whole but to provide him with the assistance of experts in the study of race in America. Myrdal assembled a distinguished team of black and white scholars, including RALPH BUNCHE and KENNETH CLARK. With ample time and money, these scholars examined virtually every aspect of the "Negro problem"—physiological, historical, psychological, cultural, economic, and political. When the work was published seven years later in 1944, it was immediately recognized as a classic. *An American Dilemma* reviewed, summarized, and confirmed widely accepted research and thus reinforced and legitimized its status as knowledge. In doing so, the two volumes served as a point of departure and established boundaries for subsequent research on race.

An American Dilemma was very important in undermining the scientific part of the ideology of white supremacy. In the introduction to Volume 1, Myrdal succinctly stated the thesis of his work. He wrote, "If the Negro was a 'failure' as he obviously was by every criterion that white society recognized as valid, then he was a failure because white America made him so." And then, noting the comprehensive character of his research, he continued, "All recent attempts to reach scientific explanations of why the Negroes are what they are and why they live as they do have regularly led to determinants on the white side of the race line." In other words, it was not, as the ideology of white supremacy would have it, the African-American's skull size, his genetically endowed intelligence, or the retention of his African cultural heritage that accounted for his "failure" in America. Rather, it was the environment of systematic OPPRESSION imposed and sustained by white people and the institutions of American society they controlled.

This view that "white racism" was the determinant or cause of black inequality in the United States was echoed a generation later in the KERNER REPORT in its investigations into the causes and remedies for the 1960s RIOTS.

Not only did *An American Dilemma* shape the development of research and knowledge on race, this knowledge influenced the reasoning of the Supreme Court in *Brown v. Board of Education* and the strategy employed by Martin Luther King Jr. in his use of the strategy of PROTEST during the final phase of the Civil Rights movement. In his opinion in *Brown*, Chief Justice EARL WARREN cited Myrdal's work in a footnote in order to make the case that there was no scientific basis for racism or ideas of black inferiority. And Myrdal's idea that the "Negro problem" in America was a "moral dilemma" that the nation had to confront was appropriated by King in his use of religion and morality as power bases in the Civil Rights movement.

Further reading: Walter Jackson, *Gunnar Myrdal and America's Conscience* (Chapel Hill: University of North Carolina Press, 1990); Ellen Lagemann, *The Politics of Knowledge: The Carnegie Corporation, Philanthropy and Public Policy* (Middletown, Conn.: Wesleyan University, 1989).

American Muslim Mission (American Muslim Society)

The American Muslim Mission (also known as the American Muslim Society) is a faction of the NATION OF ISLAM created by W. Deen Muhammad after the death of ELIJAH MUHAMMAD, the spiritual leader of the Nation. When Elijah Muhammad died in 1976, he designated his son, W. Deen Muhammad (then known as Wallace) as his successor. A charismatic religious group seldom survives without change after the death of its leader. However, the speed and radical nature of the changes in the Nation brought about by W. Deen Muhammad surprised both followers and observers of the group. He immediately repudiated the core principles of BLACK NATIONALISM in the Nation's IDEOLOGY, abandoned its theological understanding of whites as "devils," dismantled and sold the group's business enterprises, eliminated its paramilitia group the Fruit of Islam, and renounced the myth of creation underpinning the Nation's theology. The religious and moral codes of the Nation were modified, and the group formally embraced the orthodox teachings of the Koran and Islam, abandoning the Nation's proto-Islam. Finally, and perhaps most fundamentally, the group opened its membership to whites. In sum, the unorthodox, proto-Islamic, black nationalist Nation of Islam was in a few short years completely transformed into a thoroughly Americanized, mainstream, racially integrated, orthodox Muslim institution.

The American Muslim Mission has an estimated membership of 300,000 (mostly blacks), and in 1978 Saudi Arabia designated W. Deen Muhammad as the "sole trustee" for the distribution of funds for the propagation of Islam in the United States.

Shortly after W. Deen Muhammad radically transformed the Nation, LOUIS FARRAKHAN, the Nation's leading minister at the time of Elijah Muhammad's death, set about to reconstitute and revitalize the Nation on the basis of its original principles.

apartheid

Apartheid is the system of rigid racial SEGREGATION established by the government of South Africa in 1948. The word literally means separation of the races, but it also implied *brasskap*, the word among South Africans for white domination. Although apartheid in South Africa was frequently compared to the JIM CROW system of segregation established in the 1890s in the United States, the South African system was different. It was a more rigid system of OPPRESSION of blacks than was segregation in the United States. For example, in addition to denying blacks the right to vote, the right to use public accommodations, and the right to equal employment as was the case with blacks in the United States, blacks and other racial minorities in South Africa were denied the right to travel without a pass and were required to live outside of the cities in racially designated areas. (The whites reserved for themselves more than 85 percent of the land, although they were a small minority of the population.) Also, unlike in the United States, which was philosophically committed to the NATURAL RIGHTS doctrines of universal FREEDOM and EQUALITY for all men, the Republic of South Africa was founded on explicit racist principles of ethnic identity and hierarchy. Thus, Africans in South Africa could not readily draw on religion and morality as bases of power in the struggle against apartheid as Africans in America could in their struggle against segregation.

The system of segregation in the United States was formally abolished in the 1960s, but it was not formally dismantled in South Africa until the 1990s.

See also FOREIGN POLICY, RACISM, TRANSAFRICA, and WHITE SUPREMACY.

Further reading: Donald Culverson, *Contesting Apartheid: U.S. Activism, 1960–1987* (Boulder, Colo.: Westview Press, 1999); George Frederickson, *White Supremacy: A Comparative Study in American and South African History* (New York: Oxford University Press, 1981).

Aptheker, Herbert (1915–) *historian*

Herbert Aptheker is the most important historian and bibliophile of the black experience in the United States. He holds a Ph.D. in history from Columbia University, and he has authored more than 30 books on or related to black politics, including important studies of the SLAVE REVOLTS, the ABOLITIONIST MOVEMENT, and DAVID WALKER and NAT TURNER. A white scholar, Aptheker is a Marxist and a man with a passionate commitment to the use of knowledge in the black freedom struggle. Aptheker's work is sometimes referred to as polemical. He responds that knowledge is a weapon, that "History's potency is mighty," and that people suffering from OPPRESSION need knowledge for "identity and inspiration."

Aptheker's most important contribution to AFRICAN-AMERICAN STUDIES include his original studies in documentary history and his work as a literary executor of the papers of W. E. B. DU BOIS. His extensive efforts to document the black experience in politics in the United States resulted in the publication in the 1960s of a two-volume *Documentary History of the Negro People in the United States,* which included rare material from the 1600s to the early 20th century. It is an indispensable source for research and a classic of the genre. A close friend of Du Bois, Aptheker annotated Du Bois's publications and edited his correspondence, and Aptheker's work is an important reason why the writings and papers of Du Bois, the greatest scholar in African-American history, are available and accessible to students.

Asante, Molefi K. (1942–) *scholar*

Molefi K. Asante, a leading scholar of AFRICAN-AMERICAN STUDIES, has contributed perhaps more than any other scholar since the 1960s to the development and institutionalization of a distinctive AFROCENTRIC perspective in the study and teaching of the African-American experience in the United States. Asante established and for nearly 15 years chaired the African-American Studies Department at Temple University, for a time the largest such department in the country and one of only two that granted the Ph.D. The author or editor of more than 30 books and 200 articles, Asante for more than two decades edited the *Journal of Black Studies.* He received a Ph.D. in 1968 from UCLA in Communication Studies, but he now considers himself an "Africalogist," expert in the Afrocentric study of social phenomena.

Knowledge, Asante insists, is the indispensable base of power in AFRICAN-AMERICAN POLITICS. Therefore African-American studies is critically important, but he argues it should not be viewed, as it is at most colleges and universities, as simply an interdisciplinary collection of courses on the black experience. Rather, he sees it as a distinctive theoretical and methodological orientation based on Afrocentricity. In addition to advocating its primacy in higher education, Asante and others have also developed—and in several school districts partly implemented—Afrocentric curricula at the elementary and secondary levels. They argue that an Afrocentric curricula will increase the self-esteem, knowledge, and performance of black students and ultimately enhance the well-being and power of the entire BLACK COMMUNITY.

See also SCHOOLS AND EDUCATION.

assimilation

The term *assimilation* describes the processes by which a MINORITY or SUBORDINATE group gradually merges into or becomes a part of the society and culture of a majority or SUPERORDINATE group. The processes of assimilation may involve the minority group gradually acquiring the norms, values, and behavior patterns of the majority either in whole or in part (a process also sometimes referred to as acculturation). At an extreme, assimilation can involve the complete absorption and disappearance of the minority into the majority, including name changes, language, religious conversion, and high rates of intermarriage. In the United States, although the rate has varied depending on the group's ETHNICITY or national origins, most white immigrant groups who wished (some have not, such as the Amish) have found it relatively easy to assimilate into the majority Anglo-American society and culture while maintaining, to the extent they wished, some of the rituals and symbols distinctive to their ethnic cultures. Because of white RACISM and the IDEOLOGY of WHITE SUPREMACY, this has not been the case to the same extent for African Americans, Native Americans, and immigrants from Asia and Latin America. Also, there are greater cultural similarities between the dominant Anglo-American group and European immigrants, and they are all "white" or they can, if they wish, become white.

Historically, most African Americans have probably wished to assimilate into the American society and culture, and most have assimilated to some extent, since some degree of acculturation inevitably occurs when two cultures are in a sustained relationship. (The acculturation process here is reciprocal, since the dominant Anglo culture has also assimilated elements of African culture.) However, the ideology of white supremacy has been so pervasive and the practice of racism so tenacious that African Americans, whatever their wishes, have not been able to become fully assimilated. Moreover, many African Americans in the past and in the present have rejected assimilation or, in some cases, INTEGRATION, viewing it as requiring one to embrace WHITENESS while denying BLACKNESS or as a subterfuge for the maintenance of white supremacy.

See also MELTING POT, PLURALISM, and PLURAL SOCIETY.

Further reading: Nathan Glazer and Daniel P. Moynihan, *Beyond the Melting Pot* (Cambridge, Mass.: MIT Press, 1963, 1970); Milton Gordon, *Assimilation in American Life* (New York: Oxford University, 1964); Stanley Lieberson, *A Piece of the Pie: Black and White Immigrants since 1880* (Berkeley: University of California Press, 1980).

"Atlanta Compromise" address

The Atlanta Compromise was an informal agreement or "compromise" between the African-American community represented by BOOKER T. WASHINGTON and the white POWER ELITE of Northern capital and philanthropy and Southern agrarianism. The compromise was formalized by Washington in his famous 1895 address at the Atlanta Exposition. It called for blacks to temporarily give up the CIVIL RIGHTS and political freedoms they had recently acquired during RECONSTRUCTION in exchange for personal FREEDOM or autonomy and the right to work and the opportunity to develop their own separate economic, social, educational, and cultural institutions.

Washington proposed this compromise in the midst of the VIOLENCE and terrorism that led to the overthrow of Reconstruction, a period in U.S. history that one historian called the "nadir." During this period, blacks had hardly any effective power bases of their own and few allies among whites. Therefore, in Washington's view, compromise and ACCOMMODATIONISM was the only option available, since resistance was tantamount to genocide.

Washington argued that Reconstruction was a mistake because blacks were not ready for freedom and EQUALITY. Thus, they should be left to pursue (with the help of whites) a path of "separate but equal" development until through education, hard work, and property they would eventually earn freedom and equality, or what he called "full citizenship rights."

Booker T. Washington was the most powerful black leader of all time. He is also the most controversial. He is considered the paradigmatic accommodationist leader and the classic or prototype UNCLE TOM. At the time, however, his Atlanta Compromise was endorsed by W. E. B. DU BOIS, the paradigmatic PROTEST leader, and it was probably supported by a majority of the African-American people. There is also in Washington's compromise a powerful strain of BLACK NATIONALISM in terms of racial separatism in education, the economy, and community. The compromise in effect envisioned a PLURAL SOCIETY rather than ASSIMILATION or, in some versions, INTEGRATION. A vision of a plural society inspired the young MARCUS GARVEY, the 1920s black nationalist leader who originally came to the United States to visit Washington.

See also ISAIAH MONTGOMERY.

Atlanta University (Since 1988, Clark-Atlanta University)

Atlanta University was founded in 1865 as one of the handful of liberal arts HISTORICALLY BLACK COLLEGES AND UNIVERSITIES, in contrast to the predominantly agricultural, vocational, and technical schools established after the CIVIL WAR. Unlike TUSKEGEE INSTITUTE established by BOOKER T. WASHINGTON, Atlanta University and similar black liberal arts universities, including HOWARD UNIVERSITY, were created to provide a knowledge base for the BLACK COMMUNITY by training a TALENTED TENTH of the race. Also, Atlanta University and similar universities were conceived as institutions that would not only teach knowledge to students but would acquire knowledge through research and the training of others as scholars. W. E. B. DU BOIS, while on the faculty at Atlanta University, directed the first large-scale social-science research project on race, and for more than a decade he held a series of conferences and published volumes that are part of the foundation of modern AFRICAN-AMERICAN STUDIES. Over the years, the Atlanta University faculty included such distinguished scholars as E. Franklin Frazier, Whitney Young, Horace Mann Bond, SAMUEL DUBOIS COOK, and MACK H. JONES. With Howard University, Atlanta is one of two black universities that offers the Ph.D.

In 1988, because of financial difficulties, Atlanta University merged with its sister college, Clark, to become Clark-Atlanta University. The Atlanta University Center district includes five other colleges—Morehouse, Spellman, Morris Brown, Morehouse Medical School, and the Interdenominational Theological Center. Together these six institutions constitute one of the most comprehensive seats of African-American-generated knowledge in the United States.

B

back-to-Africa movements

Even before they arrived in the United States, many enslaved Africans wanted to go back to Africa, as evidenced by the many reported revolts on slave ships. Some of these SLAVE REVOLTS at sea were successful, and some Africans were able to take control of slave ships and return them to Africa. In the United States, Paul Cuffe, a wealthy Massachusetts businessman, was perhaps the first African American to systematically organize a back-to-Africa movement. SLAVERY in the SOUTHERN STATES and widespread DISCRIMINATION in the NORTHERN STATES (in Massachusetts, for example, blacks were denied the right to vote and to attend public schools) convinced Cuffe that Africans in the United States could never live in FREEDOM and EQUALITY and that they should return to Africa. Cuffe first sought congressional support for resettlement, and when this was unsuccessful in 1815 he used his own money to resettle a small number of blacks in what is now Sierra Leone.

After Cuffe, many major African-American leaders in the 19th and 20th centuries have supported back-to-Africa movements of one sort or another, including EDWARD WILMOT BLYDEN, MARTIN DELANY, ALEXANDER CRUMMELL, HENRY M. TURNER, W. E. B. DU BOIS, MARCUS GARVEY, MALCOLM X, STOKELY CARMICHAEL, and LOUIS FARRAKHAN. Some of these individuals supported a mass resettlement in Africa, while others supported the selective migration of an African-American TALENTED TENTH. Many wanted to return because they thought Africans could never be free in the United States. Others wished to resettle because Africa was their ancestral homeland and they wished to reconnect with their cultural heritage, while still others saw Africa as a backward, uncivilized continent and wanted to return as "civilizers," bringing the benefits of Christianity, CAPITALISM, and Western culture to the inferior, indigenous Africans.

Back-to-Africa movements were supported by the AMERICAN COLONIALIZATION SOCIETY and other racists and white supremacists, and by the 1830s these movements were opposed by most African-American leaders, who had come to see themselves as Americans and preferred to fight for freedom and equality in the United States rather than return to an Africa they had never seen and whose culture was a fading memory. Mass resettlement in any event was always impractical, and the selective resettlement of elite blacks raised the spectre of COLONIALISM and the exploitation of indigenous Africans by African Americans, which is to some extent what happened in LIBERIA.

Nevertheless, the idea of going back to Africa is an integral part of the African-American political tradition. It was a major animating force in the organization of the largest mass movement among blacks in United States history—Garvey's UNIVERSAL NEGRO IMPROVEMENT ASSOCIATION—and it is at the core of PAN-AFRICANISM. At the dawn of the 21st century there is little interest in mass back-to-Africa movements, but selective migration of members of the talented tenth is ongoing, especially to post-APARTHEID South Africa. And the NATION OF ISLAM's Louis Farrakhan has, since the MILLION MAN MARCH, routinely asked the U.S. government to release all blacks in prison for nonviolent offenses to the custody of the Nation of Islam for resettlement in Africa.

Baker, Ella Jo (1903–1986) *civil rights leader*

Ella Baker, although largely unheralded in the historiography and the popular imagination, was one of the most important and influential leaders of the CIVIL RIGHTS MOVEMENT. In all likelihood her important role in the movement is overlooked because she was a woman in a movement whose LEADERSHIP was dominated by men and by SEXISM. Baker, however, was in many ways the movement's indispensable woman, responsible for organizing and nurturing four major movement ORGANIZATIONS—the NAACP, the STUDENT NONVIOLENT COORDINATING COMMITTEE, the SOUTHERN CHRISTIAN LEADERSHIP CONFERENCE, and the MISSISSIPPI FREEDOM DEMOCRATIC PARTY.

Baker, the grandchild of slaves, was born in 1903 in Virginia. After attending Shaw University she moved to New York City, where she worked with various community, labor, consumer, and education groups, eventually becoming president of the New York City branch of the NAACP, the first woman to head this important chapter. Her work there caught the attention of the NAACP's national leaders in New York, and she was appointed national director of branches. In this post she traveled throughout the country organizing membership campaigns and establishing branches. In 1957 when MARTIN LUTHER KING JR. decided to organize the Southern Christian Leadership Conference (SCLC), Baker, at 52, became its first executive staff director. By all accounts, she was indispensable in developing the SCLC's bureaucracy and encouraging it to become, unlike the NAACP, a Southern-based, mass PROTEST organization. She served as SCLC staff director for two and a half years, and then she was indispensable in the formation of the Student Nonviolent Coordinating Committee (SNCC), the most radical of the civil rights organizations.

The spontaneous SIT-INS at Greensboro, North Carolina, lunch counters in February 1960 resulted in the rapid development of a sit-in movement involving thousands of students, black and white, throughout the United States. Realizing the potential of student activism, Baker organized a conference of student activists in April 1960. At this conference, held at Shaw University, Baker encouraged the students to form an independent civil rights organization. Baker's idea was opposed by NAACP and SCLC leaders, who wanted the students to affiliate as youth divisions of their organizations, but Baker prevailed and in 1961 SNCC was formed. Baker also was influential in persuading the students to adopt a nonhierarchical style of leadership and decision making and to involve themselves in grassroots work with the masses of rural blacks in the SOUTHERN STATES.

In 1963 Baker was a principal organizer of the Mississippi Freedom Democratic Party, an interracial party led by FANNIE LOU HAMER that challenged the seating of the all-white, racist, regular Mississippi Democratic delegation at the 1964 DEMOCRATIC PARTY Convention.

As important as her role was in establishing and nurturing important black organizations, Baker was also influential in encouraging a new style of leadership in the Civil Rights movement. She courageously challenged Dr. King and the leaders of the NAACP for their bureaucratic, hierarchical, conservative style of leadership, calling instead for what she called a group-centered, democratic leadership rooted in the masses of ordinary black people. And from the beginning of her career Baker worked with young people, encouraging them to lead by working independently of adults, whether in youth branches of the NAACP or in organizations like SNCC.

Further reading: Joanne Grant, *Ella Baker: Freedom Bound* (New York: John Wiley, 1998).

Baker v. Carr (1962)

Baker v. Carr is a landmark decision of the SUPREME COURT. Indeed, of the many landmark decisions of the Court during the tenure of EARL WARREN as chief justice, he said this decision was the most important because it helped to make the promise of the American DEMOCRACY more of a reality than it was before.

The case involved LITIGATION to compel the Tennessee Legislature to reapportion its state legislative districts on the basis of population, a requirement of the state's constitution that had been ignored for more than 60 years. In *Colegrove v. Green* (1946), the Supreme Court held that questions of reapportionment were "political" questions beyond the competence of the courts to adjudicate. *Baker* reversed this precedent and held that the federal courts had jurisdiction in such cases because malapportioned legislative districts might violate the EQUAL PROTECTION CLAUSE of the FOURTEENTH AMENDMENT. In subsequent decisions the Court did conclude that malapportioned districts violated the equal protection clause and required legislative districts (congressional, state, and local) to be drawn in such a way that they be "as nearly of equal population as is practicable" because, as Chief Justice Warren wrote in *Baker,* "legislators represent people, not trees." Thus, the constitutional principle of voting EQUALITY—"one person, one vote"—was established by *Baker.*

Prior to *Baker,* many states had drawn their state legislative and congressional districts with a bias in favor of rural areas at the expense of big cities. And since African Americans disproportionately live in cities, the bias was in effect also racial as well as urban. In Tennessee, for example, the smallest rural legislative district had a population of 3,400 while the largest urban district had 79,000. Yet each elected one member to the legislature. And in Georgia, although the average congressional district in 1960 had a population of 400,000, the largely urban and disproportionately black Atlanta district had a population of 823,000, while one rural district had a population of 272,000. Yet each district elected a single member of CONGRESS, meaning that votes in rural Georgia were valued at more than three times the votes in Atlanta. (Since the equal protection clause applies only to the states, the Supreme Court in *Wesberry v. Sanders* held that congressional districts' unequal populations violated the command of Article I, Section II, that congressmen be chosen "by the people of the several states.")

Baker led to the election of more members of Congress and state legislatures from urban and suburban areas, and along with the VOTING RIGHTS ACT OF 1965 led to the election of more blacks to state legislatures and to Congress. That is, with districts based on equality, blacks were able to maximize their size and solidarity to elect representatives of their own.

Bakke v. Regents of the University of California
(1978)

Bakke v. Regents of the University of California is the most important case dealing with race and CIVIL RIGHTS decided by the SUPREME COURT since *BROWN V. BOARD OF EDUCATION* (1954). In this case, a narrowly and deeply divided Court for the first time upheld the core principle of AFFIRMATIVE ACTION, stating that the government could, under some circumstances, take race into consideration in allocating benefits without violating the EQUAL PROTECTION CLAUSE of the FOURTEENTH AMENDMENT or the CIVIL RIGHTS ACT OF 1964.

In order to assure that its entering medical school class of 100 was representative of the state's ethnic diversity, the faculty of the University of California at Davis established an affirmative action program in which it filled 84 of the 100 class openings through the regular admissions process but set aside 16 positions to be filled through a special admission process for applicants who indicated that they wanted to be considered as "economically and/or educationally disadvantaged" and as members of specified ethnic minority groups (blacks, Latinos, Asian Americans, and Native Americans). Applicants to the affirmative action program were considered by a special admissions committee, a majority of whose members were always from minority groups. Although numerous disadvantaged whites applied for admission under the special program, none were admitted. And many of the minority students admitted had qualifying scores substantially lower than many whites who were rejected under the regular admissions process. Alan Bakke, a 34-year-old white engineer seeking to change careers, was one of those students. Indeed, Bakke was denied admission twice. Arguing that since his qualifying scores were higher than many of the minorities admitted under the special admission program, Bakke sued, charging that the university had denied him admission on the basis of his race through the use of QUOTAS for minorities.

A state trial court held that the university's affirmative action program constituted illegal DISCRIMINATION under Title VII of the 1964 Civil Rights Act, which prohibits the exclusion of persons from federally funded programs because of their race, and the equal protection clause of the Fourteenth Amendment as well as provisions of California's constitution. The trial court, however, refused to order Bakke's admission to the medical school because it concluded that he would not have been admitted even if there

was no affirmative action program. Bakke appealed to the California Supreme Court, which held that the university's program violated the equal protection clause because it used race as a decisional criterion. The court then ordered that the special admission program be dismantled and that Bakke be admitted, since the university had failed to prove that he would not have been admitted absent its affirmative action program. The regents of the university appealed this decision to the Supreme Court of the United States.

The case generated enormous press coverage and controversy, including PROTEST demonstrations by African Americans in front of the Supreme Court building in Washington. Polls indicated that PUBLIC OPINION was deeply divided, and these divisions were reflected in the opinions of a deeply divided Supreme Court. The nine justices issued six different opinions, but the opinion of Justice Lewis Powell, the Court's only Southerner, was controlling or decisive. That is, Powell's opinion ironically constituted the opinion of the Court. In a sense, he was a majority of one.

The Court's four more conservative justices held that Title VII of the 1964 Civil Rights Act (and by extension the equal protection clause of the Fourteenth Amendment) prohibited a state from ever using race to allocate benefits or resources and that the university's special admissions program violated Bakke's individual rights guaranteed by the CONSTITUTION. Under this judgment, Bakke was ordered admitted, and the university was ordered to cease using race in its admission decisions. The four more-liberal justices, including WILLIAM BRENNAN and THURGOOD MARSHALL, held that the university's use of race and a racial quota or set-aside was consistent with the Fourteenth Amendment's underlying purpose of achieving EQUALITY for the descendants of the slaves and therefore could not violate the equal protection clause or the Civil Rights Act of 1964. Justice Brennan wrote, "Davis's articulated purpose of remedying the effects of past societal discrimination is, under our cases, sufficiently important to justify race conscious admission programs where there is a sound basis for concluding that minority underrepresentation is substantial and chronic and that the handicap of past discrimination is impeding access of minorities to medical school."

In his opinion—again an opinion that constitutes the judgment of the Court—Justice Powell held that his conservative colleagues erred when they concluded that a state could never use race in allocating benefits. Rather, he wrote that a state has a "substantial interest that legitimately may be served . . . by the competitive consideration of race and ethnic origin" in its decisions. These legitimate interests, Powell concluded, can include remedying past discrimination and achieving diversity in the medical profession. However, Powell went on to write that a fixed racial quota violated the principle of INDIVIDUALISM that animates the Constitution in general and the Fourteenth

Amendment specifically. He wrote, "The guarantees of the Fourteenth Amendment extend to persons. Its language is explicit: No state shall deny to any person . . . the equal protection of the laws. It is settled beyond question that the rights created . . . by the Amendment are, by its terms, guaranteed to individuals. They are personal rights." In other words, African Americans could not be accorded rights or benefits because of their membership in a particular ethnic or racial group, nor could whites be denied benefits they were otherwise entitled to as individuals because of their race. Concluding that the university had not shown that Bakke was not denied admissions because of his race, Powell joined his conservative colleagues in ordering Bakke's admission to the university, where he was admitted and eventually was graduated.

For more than 20 years, Justice Powell's opinion in *Bakke* has remained the state of the law on affirmative action. A state may, as Powell wrote, take race into consideration in achieving diversity or remedying past discrimination, but quotas are not a constitutionally permissible means to achieve those ends. Although the Court's membership has changed significantly since *Bakke* was decided, it remained at century's end the law, although the Court was, as in *Bakke,* narrowly divided, with four conservative-leaning justices maintaining that the use of race is never permissible in allocative decisions, four liberal-leaning justices contending that it is permissible in pursuit of the broad goal of equality, and with Justice Sandra Day O'Connor replacing Justice Powell as the decisive swing vote.

Whether affirmative action can be maintained under these conditions is problematic. In the 1990s several five-to-four opinions authored by Justice O'Connor have significantly narrowed the constitutionally permissible use of race (see *ADARAND V. PENA, CROSON V. CITY OF RICHMOND,* and *SHAW V. RENO*) in affirmative action cases, and in *Hopwood v. Texas* (1996), the Court let stand a decision by the Fifth Circuit Court of Appeals (which covers Louisiana, Texas, and Mississippi) that explicitly overruled *Bakke* by declaring that race could never be used in admissions decisions in order to achieve diversity. The fate of affirmative action may hang on the IDEOLOGY of the president who makes the next appointments to the Supreme Court. A liberal-leaning president making two or three appointments could solidify affirmative action for a generation, while a conservative-leaning president and two or three conservative nominees could end the constitutional basis for affirmative action within several years.

Further reading: Joel Dreyfuss and Charles Lawrence, *The Bakke Case: The Politics of Inequality* (New York: Longman, 1979); Bernard Schwarz, *Behind Bakke: Affirmative Action and the Supreme Court* (New York: New York University Press, 1988).

balance of power

The balance of power is the idea, initially advanced by W. E. B. DU BOIS during the 1928 presidential election, that African Americans, although a minority in size, could under some circumstances use solidarity and become the balance of power that determined the outcome of PRESIDENTIAL ELECTIONS. Although Du Bois first made the balance-of-power argument in a 1928 article in the NAACP's *Crisis* magazine, the idea received its most systematic exposition in a 1948 book by Henry Lee Moon called *Balance of Power: The Negro Vote.* Moon, the NAACP's director of public relations, developed the idea in the context of presidential elections. However, it applies to any election (local, state, congressional, or presidential) in which the majority-white electorate is closely divided and the minority African-American electorate casts its vote as a unified bloc vote. In those circumstances, the solidarity of the black vote, despite its relatively small size, can determine the winner of an election.

The circumstance that allows the black vote to play this balance-of-power role in presidential elections came about as the result of the GREAT MIGRATION of rural blacks from the SOUTHERN STATES to the big cities of the Northeast and Midwest regions of the United States. The states in these regions are pivotal in electing the president because they have large populations and therefore large blocs of votes in the ELECTORAL COLLEGE that elects the president. A state's votes in the electoral college are cast on a "winner take all" basis, with the candidate winning the most votes getting all of a state's votes in the electoral college. Therefore, in an election where the white vote is evenly or narrowly divided, the black vote (or any cohesive minority vote) becomes the balance of power.

When Moon wrote in 1948, blacks in the Southern states were effectively denied the right to vote; therefore, the power of their vote could only play this role in the NORTHERN STATES. However, it is possible that, in the RECONSTRUCTION era, the black vote was the balance of power in the election of ULYSSES S. GRANT in 1872, and it was almost certainly the balance of power in the election of RUTHERFORD B. HAYES in 1876. In these elections, the white vote was narrowly divided, and Southern blacks cast a unified bloc of votes that may have determined the outcomes. After 1876 Southern blacks were gradually disenfranchised, and the black vote did not become a factor in presidential elections until their migration in mass numbers to the Northern states.

Since the election of President HARRY TRUMAN in 1948, the black vote has been the balance of power in the election of every DEMOCRATIC PARTY candidate for president except LYNDON JOHNSON in 1964. That is, in the elections of JOHN F. KENNEDY in 1960, JIMMY CARTER in 1976, and BILL CLINTON in 1992 and 1996, the white vote was either evenly divided or a majority voted for the REPUBLICAN PARTY. African Americans, by casting 75 percent or more of their votes for the Democratic candidate, determined the election outcomes.

Further reading: Henry Lee Moon, *Balance of Power: The Negro Vote* (New York: Doubleday, 1948); Ronald Walters, *Black Presidential Politics in America: A Strategic Approach* (Albany: State University of New York Press, 1988).

Baldwin, James (1924–1987) *novelist, playwright, essayist*

James Baldwin is one of the foremost examples of an African American who used art as a power base or weapon in AFRICAN-AMERICAN POLITICS. Born in HARLEM, the son of a preacher and steeped deeply in the ethos and rituals of African-American RELIGIOSITY, Baldwin in the 1960s became the literary voice of the CIVIL RIGHTS MOVEMENT. With the publication of his partly autobiographical novel *Go Tell It on the Mountain* in 1953, Baldwin began a rapid rise to fame as a writer. He then used his status as a celebrity to become a major interpreter of the black experience and an activist in the Civil Rights movement.

Although Baldwin saw himself primarily as a novelist, arguably his major contribution to black literature—and for certain his major contribution to black politics—was a series of highly personal, passionately written prophetic books of essays, including *Notes of a Native Son* (1961), *Nobody Knows My Name* (1961), and his most famous and influential book, *The Fire Next Time* (1963). What Baldwin did in his writings, lectures, and television appearances was to give white America a knowledge of the pain, rage, anger, and hatred of whites that constituted an important part of the black experience in the middle of the 20th century; and to cry out in Jeremiah-like fashion that if something was not done and done rapidly to end RACISM and WHITE SUPREMACY, the country would face the fires of violent black rebellion. In doing so, he educated a generation of whites, especially liberal whites, about the meaning of the black freedom struggle.

Baldwin was a homosexual, although never an activist in the GAY RIGHTS movement. However, his frank discussion of the subject in the early 1950s and 1960s in *Giovanni's Room* (1956) and *Another Country* (1962) drew criticism from within the BLACK COMMUNITY and made some civil rights leaders (including MARTIN LUTHER KING JR.) weary of his open participation in the movement.

Further reading: David Leeming, *James Baldwin: A Biography* (New York: Henry Holt, 1994).

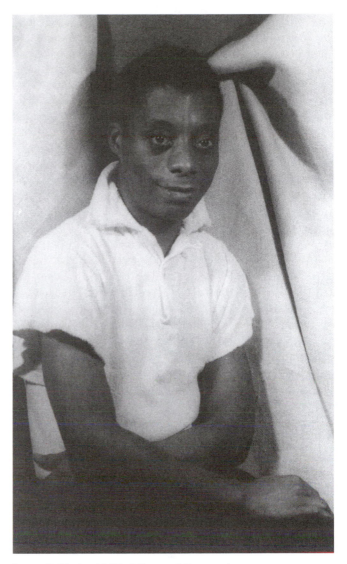

James Baldwin, 1955 *(Library of Congress)*

"Ballot or the Bullet" speech

The "Ballot or the Bullet" is MALCOLM X's most famous speech and, along with "Message to the Grassroots," is the fullest exposition of his IDEOLOGY after he left the NATION OF ISLAM.

Malcolm X was in many ways an intellectual—a man of ideas. However, he did not, for reasons of inclination and time, write. Thus, his major contribution to AFRICAN-AMERICAN THOUGHT was in a series of speeches and lectures he prepared and delivered at rallies, debates, and other forums. Many of these speeches and lectures were recorded on audiotapes, and after his death these tapes were widely distributed and are a principal means (along with his autobiography) by which his thought influenced the spread of BLACK NATIONALISM and the development of the BLACK POWER MOVEMENT after his death.

Malcolm X delivered the "Ballot or the Bullet" (his title for the speech) on several occasions, but it was given first in Cleveland, Ohio, on April 3, 1964, as part of a debate with Louis Lomax, an African-American journalist and scholar who espoused the ideologies of LIBERALISM and INTEGRATION then dominant in the CIVIL RIGHTS MOVEMENT. The speech was delivered less than a month after Malcolm had left the Nation of Islam and was his first effort to systematically formulate the ideology to guide the new movement he was attempting to create. Like any extemporaneous address, written without the time for extended reflection and revision, and delivered for its rhetorical as well as analytic effect, there are occasional errors in logical and grammatical composition. But the speech represents, in the context it was given, the best distillation of Malcolm's thought on RACISM, COLONIALISM, WHITE SUPREMACY, INTEGRATION, the Civil Rights movement and its leaders, as well as the COLD WAR and the THIRD WORLD. It is also a good exposition of his IDEOLOGY of black nationalism and his views on voting and VIOLENCE and reform and revolution in AFRICAN-AMERICAN POLITICS.

Two years after the speech and one year after Malcolm's death, the ideas expressed in the speech played an important role in the origins and development of the Black Power movement.

Bandung Conference

The Bandung Conference, convened in 1955 in Bandung, Indonesia, comprised 29 Asian and African nations, which met to discuss the problem of COLONIALISM and the self-determination of the colored peoples of the world. The idea of a THIRD WORLD of largely colored nations not aligned in the COLD WAR with either the Soviet Union or the United States was first advanced at Bandung. These 29 nations were nonwhite, and most had been subject to European colonialism. Therefore, they were strongly opposed to RACISM and WHITE SUPREMACY as it was practiced in the United States. The Communist People's Republic of China was expected to use the conference as a forum to attack the United States for hypocrisy in claiming that it was the leader of the "Free World" while continuing the OPPRESSION of its own Third World peoples, especially blacks. Although such attacks were muted at Bandung, Congressman ADAM CLAYTON POWELL JR. attended the conference in order to make a strong defense of America's record on CIVIL RIGHTS, calling attention in particular to the *BROWN V. BOARD OF EDUCATION* Supreme Court decision of the year before. W. E. B. DU BOIS was invited to the conference, but he was denied a passport. However, he sent a memorandum to the group condemning American racism as well as European colonialism.

Bandung signaled the emergence of the Third World as an actor in international relations in the cold war era. The struggle between the United States and the Soviet Union for the allegiance of Third World nations would become an important factor in the strategy of the CIVIL RIGHTS MOVEMENT.

Baraka, Imamu Amiri (Leroi Jones) (1934–) *poet, playwright, essayist*

Imamu Amiri Baraka is one of the most important intellectual and political leaders in POST–CIVIL RIGHTS ERA African-American politics. Born in Newark, New Jersey, as Leroi Jones, Baraka dropped out of HOWARD UNIVERSITY in the 1950s and moved to Greenwich Village, where he became a part of the left-liberal environment of the "beat" poets. He wrote several books of poetry during this time; an acclaimed play, *The Dutchman,* and *Blues People;* and an important book on black music. Later, Baraka moved uptown to HARLEM, where he established the Black Arts Repertory Theater and School, which became an important catalyst in the BLACK ARTS MOVEMENT. At this point Baraka was undergoing the first of many transformations in his IDEOLOGY, abandoning LIBERALISM and INTEGRATION and adopting a form of CULTURAL NATIONALISM. Baraka was not an activist in the CIVIL RIGHTS MOVEMENT, preferring to devote his energies to the disinterested creation of art. However, by the late 1960s he had abandoned this view of the role of the artist. Now, he claimed that it was the responsibility of the African-American artist and intellectual to use his knowledge and creative talents as a base of power in AFRICAN-AMERICAN POLITICS.

In the late 1960s Jones, having changed his name, returned to Newark, where he established the Committee for a Unified Newark, which played an important role in the election of Kenneth Gibson as the city's first black mayor. Later, he formed the Congress of African People to advance his new ideology of cultural nationalism. As a leading cultural nationalist, Baraka played an important role in developing a philosophical system called Kwaida, which inspired the creation of KWANZA, the African-American holiday developed and popularized by RON KARENGA.

By the early 1970s Baraka had again changed his ideology, this time to a variant of PAN-AFRICANISM. In 1972 he was the principal organizer and one of three coleaders of the NATIONAL BLACK POLITICAL CONVENTION, which was an effort to build race solidarity in politics and ultimately to form a political party that would unite all of the different ideological and political factions in the BLACK COMMUNITY. But in the midst of his leadership of the convention, Baraka again abruptly changed his ideology, this time to Marxism-Leninism or COMMUNISM. This abrupt turn to RADICALISM undermined the convention's solidarity and was a critical reason that it failed to live up to its promises.

Baraka was eventually dismissed from his leadership position in the convention. Subsequently, he joined the faculty of the State University of New York at Stony Brook as professor of AFRICAN-AMERICAN STUDIES and continued his writing and radical activism.

Further reading: Robert C. Smith, *We Have No Leaders: African Americans in the Post Civil Rights Era* (Albany: State University of New York Press, 1996), Chap. 2; Jerry Watts, *Amiri Baraka: The Politics and Art of a Black Intellectual* (New York: New York University Press, 2001); Komozi Woodward, *A Nation within a Nation: Amiri Baraka (Leroi Jones) and Black Power Politics* (Chapel Hill: University of North Carolina Press, 1999).

Bethune, Mary McLeod (1875–1955) *African-American leader*

Mary McLeod Bethune is the only woman ever to achieve the status as the recognized, preeminent leader of African Americans in the United States. From FREDERICK DOU-

GLASS in the 1840s to JESSE JACKSON in the 1990s, men have always been accorded the status as *the* leader of the BLACK COMMUNITY. But during the NEW DEAL era Bethune held this position for the first and only time. In a 2000 survey of black political scientists rating or ranking black leaders, Bethune was one of only three women on a list of the 12 greatest or most influential black leaders of all time. However, the other two—IDA B. WELLS-BARNETT and FANNIE LOU HAMER—were not accorded the status of preeminent leader during their times.

Bethune was born the 15th of 17 children to impoverished parents in Mayersville, South Carolina. She worked her way through school, graduating from Chicago's Moody Bible College in 1895. She worked for a while as a teacher and in 1915 established the Daytona School for Girls, which in 1927 merged with the Cookman Institute to become Bethune-Cookman College, one of the HISTORICALLY BLACK COLLEGES AND UNIVERSITIES. Her success as an educator and activist in the black woman's club move-

Mary McLeod Bethune, shown attending a Sunday chapel service at Bethune-Cookman College *(Library of Congress)*

ment led to an appointment as vice president of the URBAN LEAGUE. Later, she became president of the NATIONAL ASSOCIATION OF COLORED WOMEN, and in 1935 she founded the NATIONAL COUNCIL OF NEGRO WOMEN, an umbrella organization created to unite black women in solidarity and encourage their participation as women in civic, political, and social work activities.

Her educational work and civic activism on behalf of women, however, did not make her the preeminent black leader of her time. Rather, it was her work in the BUREAUCRACY in the administrations of FRANKLIN D. ROOSEVELT; her close relationship with his wife, Eleanor Roosevelt; and her leadership of the BLACK CABINET during the New Deal.

In 1935 President Roosevelt appointed Bethune as director of the Negro division of the National Youth Administration (NYA). In this position she joined about a dozen or so other African Americans who constituted an informal black cabinet that sought to work inside the bureaucracy to advance black interests during the Great Depression. In this position, she quietly and somewhat effectively worked to assure EQUALITY in NYA and other New Deal programs, although it was equality on the basis of SEGREGATION. While not always successful, Bethune was able to use her status (she was simultaneously president of the Council of Negro Women, head of NYA, and president of Bethune-Cookman) and her association with Mrs. Roosevelt to quietly engage in LOBBYING the president to provide African Americans in general, but especially women and young people, with more resources than they otherwise would have obtained during the New Deal. Her leadership was also important in bridging the factions within the black cabinet so that it exhibited greater solidarity in the presentation of issues to the Roosevelt administration.

Further reading: Rackham Holt, *Mary McLeod Bethune* (New York: Doubleday, 1974).

bigotry   See RACISM.

Bill of Rights

The Bill of Rights, the first 10 amendments to the CONSTITUTION, is the most democratic part of the document, granting or, more precisely, reserving to ordinary women and men fundamental rights as well as protection against arbitrary actions by the government. Philosophically, the Bill of Rights can be viewed as a partial codification of NATURAL RIGHTS, the rights of individuals that preexist governments, or as some of those rights of men that THOMAS JEFFERSON referred to in the DECLARATION OF INDEPEN-

DENCE as inalienable. However, when the Bill of Rights was adopted, these natural or inalienable rights did not apply to Africans in America. Ironically, the presence of African SLAVERY in the United States may have been among the reasons the framers of the Constitution failed to include a bill of rights for white Americans in the original Constitution. Equally ironic is the fact that the presence of African Americans eventually resulted in the application of the Bill of Rights (through the DUE PROCESS CLAUSE of the FOURTEENTH AMENDMENT) to all the people of the United States).

When the framers finished the Constitution, it did not include a bill of rights. Immediately, the framers were attacked by Thomas Jefferson, Patrick Henry, and other spokesmen for small farmers and working people who argued that without a bill of rights, the new government created by the Constitution would pose a threat to the rights and liberties of the people. This argument eventually became the most powerful case against approval of the Constitution. James Madison and Alexander Hamilton, among others, argued in response that a bill of rights was unnecessary because the government created by the Constitution was one of limited powers; that the Constitution contained elements of a bill of rights (citing provisions regarding a bill of attainder, ex post facto laws, habeas corpus, protections of private property); that the states under FEDERALISM were the repository of the peoples' rights; and that to enumerate a particular list or bill of rights would imply that those not listed were not protected. (This latter concern was addressed by the Ninth Amendment, which states that the list of rights in the Bill of Rights should not be interpreted to mean that the people did not retain other "unmentioned" rights).

Although the arguments of Hamilton and Madison have some merit in explaining the framers' refusal to include a bill of rights, the presence of slavery may also have influenced the decision because, as Charles Pinckney of South Carolina observed during the ratification debate, "Such bills generally began with declaring that all men are by nature free. Now we should make that declaration with very bad grace, when large parts of our property consists in men who are actually born slaves." (It is noteworthy that the Bill of Rights as proposed and adopted does not begin with a ringing declaration of the rights of men but, rather, with a series of legalistic prohibitions on the powers of CONGRESS).

The Bill of Rights became a part of the Constitution because, during the campaign for ratification, it became clear that without it several states might not approve the Constitution. Thus Madison and others promised that if the Constitution were ratified, among the first acts of the new Congress would be to propose a Bill of Rights. This promise was quickly kept. Congress proposed the Bill in

1789, and it was ratified two years later by the necessary three-fourths of the states. However, as a great charter of FREEDOM and EQUALITY it was undermined, limited by the SUPREME COURT in 1833 when it ruled in *Barron v. Baltimore* that its provisions applied only to the Congress or the federal government and not to STATE AND LOCAL GOVERNMENTS. Thus, under FEDERALISM, the states were free to ignore it. Contrary to the views of some scholars, the Supreme Court's interpretation of the scope of the Bill of Rights was probably correct in that its framers intended it as a limit only on the power of the federal government.

The Bill of Rights eventually was made applicable to the states through a process called "nationalization" or "incorporation." This came about as a result of the passage of the Fourteenth Amendment, adopted after the CIVIL WAR to secure freedom and equality for African Americans. It is through Supreme Court interpretation of this amendment (beginning in the early part of the 20th century) that the Bill of Rights was universalized. Thus, an amendment adopted to guarantee freedom to blacks is the basis for extending the freedom to all persons in the United States.

See also CIVIL LIBERTIES.

Further reading: Akil Reed Amar, *The Bill of Rights: Creation and Reconstruction* (New Haven, Conn.: Yale University Press, 1998); Leonard Levy, *Origins of the Bill of Rights* (New Haven, Conn.: Yale University Press, 1999).

Birmingham demonstrations

The PROTEST demonstrations led by Dr. MARTIN LUTHER KING JR. and the SOUTHERN CHRISTIAN LEADERSHIP CONFERENCE (SCLC) at Birmingham, Alabama, in 1963 led directly to the introduction by President JOHN F. KENNEDY of the CIVIL RIGHTS ACT OF 1964, which was enacted in the administration of LYNDON B. JOHNSON. This is because the VIOLENCE and disorders at Birmingham, in the mind of President Kennedy, threatened the stability of the POLITICAL SYSTEM and undermined the position of the United States in the COLD WAR.

Although nonviolence was the guiding principle and practice of King and his colleagues in SCLC, the strategy to some extent depended on a violent response by white supremacists and racists to be effective. The strategic purposes of the demonstrations, led by King after the MONTGOMERY BUS BOYCOTT, was to "demonstrate" to the nation and the world the nature of WHITE SUPREMACY and RACISM in the SOUTHERN STATES. This strategy was rooted in the philosophy of CIVIL DISOBEDIENCE and in the thesis of GUNNAR MYRDAL in *AN AMERICAN DILEMMA*. Myrdal's thesis held that most white Americans were committed to the equalitarian principles of the DECLARATION OF INDEPENDENCE, and if forced to choose between those principles and racism, they would choose to repudiate racism. Thus, the strategic purposes of the demonstrations were to force Americans to see racism on television and then choose. In effect, the strategy used peaceful protests by blacks as a means to invoke a violent response by Southern whites. This racist violence—transmitted by the MEDIA (especially television) to the nation and the world—would elicit the sympathy and support of whites in the NORTHERN STATES, resulting in a COALITION that would pressure the president and CONGRESS to enact laws altering the structure of Southern SEGREGATION.

In 1962 Dr. King led a series of demonstrations in Albany, Georgia. They failed, having no effect on segregation practices locally and, more importantly, no effect on the president and Congress. This is because Albany's police chief, Laurie Pritchett, apparently understood that King's strategy of protest required a violent response on the part of whites. Therefore, throughout the several weeks of the Albany demonstrations, the police not only did not respond violently but also protected the demonstrators from the threat of violence by white citizens. The result was episodic media coverage and consequently little pressure on the system. While the Albany protests failed in their larger strategic purposes, they were important in the lessons learned by SCLC and King. As the next target of demonstration, they deliberately chose Birmingham, Alabama, because of the reputation of its police chief and its white citizens for violent reaction to its local Civil Rights movement.

Birmingham—the state's largest city with a population of 300,000 (40 percent black)—had a national reputation for violent repression of the local CIVIL RIGHTS MOVEMENT. Its police commissioner, Eugene "Bull" Connor, had brutally broken up local civil rights meetings and had allowed a mob of whites in 1961 to brutally beat persons on the FREEDOM RIDES. And between 1957 and 1963, there were more than a dozen unsolved bombings in the BLACK COMMUNITY, earning the city the nickname "Bombingham." Thus the city was a fitting place to give King's strategy a good test.

The Reverend Fred Shuttlesworth, a member of SCLC and the leader of the local Civil Rights movement in Birmingham, invited King to bring the national movement to the city. King agreed, and after several weeks of careful planning, SCLC launched "Project C" (for "confrontation"), a systematic plan of attack on segregation in the city. In April the project was launched. By May more than 2,000 people had been jailed, including nearly 1,000 children. In a symbolic gesture, King had himself arrested on Good Friday. Placed in solitary confinement, King, writing on the margins of newspapers and scraps of toilet paper, wrote his famous "Letter from a Birmingham Jail," a modern classic of the civil disobedience literature that was first published as a pamphlet by the American Friends

Birmingham police arresting a young demonstrator *(Library of Congress)*

Service Committee and subsequently in dozens of magazines throughout the world.

The use of the children as demonstrators was the turning point in the Birmingham protests. Across the world, television and newspapers and magazines showed pictures of young children blasted with 100 pounds of pressure from fire hoses and being chased and attacked by vicious police dogs. Also, in May 1963 King's brother's home was bombed along with the Gaston Motel, where King was staying. As RIOTS took place in black neighborhoods, President Kennedy dispatched the U.S. Army to a nearby fort as a precautionary measure.

In the midst of the demonstrations in Birmingham, the state's governor, GEORGE WALLACE, on June 11 stood in the doorway of the University of Alabama to block the admission of two black students. This nationally televised confrontation led to the dispatch of the MILITARY to the campus and a speech later that evening by President Kennedy in which he said he was proposing comprehensive civil rights legislation. In the speech Kennedy said, "The fires of frustration and discord are busy in every city. Redress is sought in the street in demonstrations, parades and protest, which create tensions and threaten violence. We face, therefore, a moral crisis as a country and a people."

The president officially transmitted the legislation to Congress on June 19. He was murdered on November 22. The legislation he proposed was signed by President Johnson on July 2, 1964. One year later, King and SCLC led the SELMA DEMONSTRATIONS, which, like the Birmingham protests and the 1964 Civil Rights Act, led directly to the passage of the VOTING RIGHTS ACT OF 1964.

Further reading: Diane McWhorter, *Birmingham, Alabama: The Climactic Battle of the Civil Rights Revolution* (New York: Simon & Schuster, 2001).

Birth of a Nation, The

D. W. Griffith's *The Birth of a Nation* is a classic American movie, classic because of its then-unprecedented length (three hours), because of its innovative filmmaking techniques, and because it was the first of many stereotypical movies about blacks (portraying them as stupid, lazy, violent, and sexually obsessed) used to sustain RACISM and

WHITE SUPREMACY. A silent film, released in 1915, it is based on the novel *The Clansman* by Thomas Dixon. The novel and film recount the story of RECONSTRUCTION and portray the KU KLUX KLAN as heroes who redeemed the governments of the SOUTHERN STATES from ignorant and corrupt blacks. Although the film was profoundly racist and wrong in its depiction of Reconstruction, it was fairly faithful to what historians were writing and teaching on the subject at the time. Thus the movie is an example of the use of knowledge as a base of power to subordinate blacks. President WOODROW WILSON, a former professor of political science, viewed the film in the White House and described it as "history written with lightning" and said that he regretted that it was so "terribly true."

The film sparked powerful PROTEST from African Americans, including the recently formed NAACP. That the film openly justified LYNCHING and other forms of antiblack VIOLENCE at a time when such actions were widespread was particularly alarming to the NAACP, which warned that showing the movie could cause RIOTS. The NAACP's early protests against the film brought the new group to the attention of the MEDIA and the public, resulting in the deletion of some of the movie's more derogatory scenes. *Birth of a Nation* also established a precedent for the NAACP's concern about the stereotypical portrayal of blacks in movies. In response to the movie the NAACP initiated its first systematic LOBBYING campaign to get CONGRESS to enact antilynching legislation (see DYER ANTILYNCHING BILL).

Nevertheless, the movie was very popular and established a precedent for the negative portrayal of blacks in films, that is, when they were portrayed at all by Hollywood.

black

The term *black* is the name adopted by the African-American intelligentsia in the late 1960s as the appropriate way to refer to persons of African descent in the United States.

As part of the 1960s BLACK POWER MOVEMENT, the word *black* replaced *Negro* as the appropriate name for persons of African origins in the United States. The name *Negro* as early as the 1940s had been rejected by such ideologically diverse leaders as ELIJAH MUHAMMAD and ADAM CLAYTON POWELL JR. However, it was not until the 1960s Black Power movement that *Negro* was effectively replaced by *black* at both the elite and the mass levels.

In their book *BLACK POWER*, the authors STOKELY CARMICHAEL and CHARLES HAMILTON wrote, "There is a growing resentment of the word 'Negro' because this term is the invention of our oppressor; it's his image of us that it describes. Many blacks are now calling themselves African-Americans, Afro-Americans or black people because that is our image of ourselves." Carmichael and Hamilton's

views here are clearly a result of the growing influence of MALCOLM X on the thinking of the young activists in SNCC who started the Black Power movement. For example, the "basic unity program" issued by Malcolm's ORGANIZATION OF AFRO-AMERICAN UNITY in 1965 stated that the term "'Negro' is erroneously used and is degrading in the eyes of informed and self-respecting persons of African heritage. It denotes stereotyped and debased traits of character and classifies a whole segment of humanity on the basis of false information. From all intelligent viewpoints, it is a badge of slavery and helps to prolong and perpetuate oppression and discrimination. . . . In light of the historical meanings and current implications, all intelligent and informed Afro-Americans and Africans continue to reject its use in the noun form as well as a proper adjective. Its usage shall continue to be considered as unenlightened and objectionable or deliberately offensive whether in speech or writing. We accept the use of Afro-American, African, and Black man in reference to persons of African heritage. To every other part of mankind goes this measure of just respect. We do not desire more nor shall we accept less."

As Carmichael and Hamilton and the Organization of Afro-American Unity's statement indicate, a variety of alternatives to *Negro* were initially acceptable—AFRICAN AMERICAN, Afro-American, and black—but *black* eventually became the preferred choice in the 1960s. The word *black* was adopted because it had historically been a term of denigration institutionalized in the IDEOLOGY of WHITE SUPREMACY and internalized in the psyche of at least some blacks (see INTERNAL INFERIORIZATION). Thus, to use *black* was to simultaneously reject white supremacy and internal inferiorization while vindicating BLACKNESS and people whose skin color is black. For example, in the ideology of white supremacy, *black* is defined as ugly; in terms of the new consciousness being fostered by the advocates of black power, black would be understood as the opposite. The success of this campaign is evidenced by the popularity during the 1960s and 1970s of bumper stickers and other emblems declaring "Black Is Beautiful" and of James Brown's number-one record "I'm Black and I'm Proud." The second reason *black* was adopted rather than *African American* is that in the ideology of white supremacy, black elicits fear and loathing among whites, thus it was the appropriate name for expressing the movement's new MILITANCY, especially when the word *black* was linked with power.

It was a struggle in the late 1960s and early 1970s to have *black* replace *Negro,* and the successful imposition of the word was perhaps the Black Power movement's first major success. Despite the opposition of whites and many blacks, within two years of the MEREDITH MARCH that launched the Black Power movement, *black* was the preferred term among the black intelligentsia (intellectuals, students, and political leaders) and was gradually replacing *Negro* in the African-American MEDIA. Among whites, initially radicals and liberals began to use the term, but by 1968 even RICHARD NIXON used *black* in his campaign for president, using it to advance his notion of black CAPITALISM as the route to real black power. In 1970 the *New York Times* dropped use of the word *Negro* in favor of *black*, and the Associated Press revised its widely used stylebook, replacing *Negro* with *black*. These changes at the elite level soon transformed black PUBLIC OPINION. A 1968 poll by *Newsweek* found that 69 percent of blacks favored *Negro*, and only 6 percent *black;* by 1974 more than two-thirds favored *black*.

See also NAMES CONTROVERSY.

Further reading: Ben L. Martin, "From Negro to Black to African American: The Power of Names," *Political Science Quarterly* 106 (1991): 83–107.

black agendas

Throughout history the African-American LEADERSHIP has convened meetings, conventions, conferences, and congresses to develop agendas or programs and plans to achieve FREEDOM and EQUALITY. Agenda-setting is an important part of the PUBLIC POLICY process, representing the aggregation of the interests of the group in a consensus program that would unite it in solidarity around a common program and plan of action. The agendas then become the basis for developing strategies to bring pressure on the POLITICAL SYSTEM and a means of mobilizing resources and measuring progress.

One of the earliest black agendas was developed by FREDERICK DOUGLASS in an address at the NATIONAL NEGRO CONVENTION in 1864. The manifesto of the NIAGARA MOVEMENT developed by W. E. B. DU BOIS and WILLIAM MONROE TROTTER in 1905 constituted the agenda of the CIVIL RIGHTS MOVEMENT. In the POST–CIVIL RIGHTS ERA, black reform and radical agendas have been developed by groups such as the 1972 NATIONAL BLACK POLITICAL CONVENTION, the CONGRESSIONAL BLACK CAUCUS, the JOINT CENTER FOR POLITICAL AND ECONOMIC STUDIES, and the BLACK RADICAL CONGRESS.

These agendas constitute an important documentary record on the conditions of the BLACK COMMUNITY at various historical periods. They show how black leaders viewed those conditions and the various ideologies, policies, programs, strategies, and tactics that they proposed over the years to deal with the conditions of the RACE.

Black Arts movement

The Black Arts movement—like the name *black*, the concept of BLACKNESS, and organizations as different in ideology as

the BLACK PANTHER PARTY, and the CONGRESSIONAL BLACK CAUCUS—emerged out of the BLACK POWER MOVEMENT.

The Black Arts movement, like AFRICAN-AMERICAN STUDIES, employed knowledge as a base of power to advance the objectives of the Black Power movement. Like the HARLEM RENAISSANCE in relationship to the early CIVIL RIGHTS MOVEMENT, the Black Arts movement sought to develop an explicit connection between art and politics, viewing itself as the cultural vanguard of the movement. This connection between art and politics was made explicit in an influential essay by Larry Neal published in the summer of 1968 in the *Tulane Drama Review*. In this essay, which in a sense was the Black Arts movement's manifesto, Neal wrote:

> The Black Arts Movement is radically opposed to any concept of the artist that alienates him from his community. Black Art is the aesthetic and spiritual sister of the Black Power concept. As such, it envisions an art that speaks directly to the needs and aspirations of Black America. In order to perform this task, the Black Arts Movement proposes a radical reordering of the Western culture aesthetic. It proposes a separate symbolism, mythology, critique and iconology. The Black Arts and the Black Power concept both relate broadly to the Afro-American desire for self-determination and nationhood. Both concepts are nationalistic. One is concerned with the relationship between art and politics, the other with the art of politics.

This explicit connection between the arts and politics was on display in the 1960s and 1970s in virtually all genres (drama, poetry, jazz, rhythm and blues, creative writing, and visual arts) and all media (books, movies, journals, theater, and art galleries) on college campuses and in GHETTO neighborhoods. In many African-American communities new artistic organizations and institutions were established, including the Watts Writers Workshop in Los Angeles, Spirit House in Newark, the Negro Ensemble Company in New York, Broadside Press in Detroit, and the Black Scholar in Oakland, California. AMIRI BARAKA was probably the leading figure in the movement, articulating and advocating a variant of CULTURAL NATIONALISM in his poetry, criticism, and commentary. Other important figures include poets Sonia Sanchez and Haki Mudhabuti; playwright Ed Bullins; jazz performers Charles Mingus, Pharaoh Sanders, and Nina Simone; the historian HAROLD CRUSE; and popular artists like the "Last Poets" and CURTIS MAYFIELD.

It is difficult to measure or gauge the impact of art on politics, but there was in the 1960s and 1970s a reciprocal relationship between the MILITANCY in African-American arts and its expression in politics. And as militancy declined in politics, the Black Arts movement also declined. Indeed, several major figures in the Black Arts movement eventually came to reject the idea of black art as an "aesthetic and spiritual sister" of black politics, returning to the traditional view that the role of the artist is to stand at a distance from politics. They contended that to do otherwise risks compromising the integrity of one's art (a view held throughout his career by Ralph Ellison, author of the most acclaimed novel by an African American, *Invisible Man*). Nevertheless, the Black Arts movement's articulation of an AFRO-CENTRIC version of cultural nationalism continues to influence some African-American studies programs. Indeed, it was an inspiration for the development and commemoration of KWANZA, and some of RAP MUSIC's militant aesthetics can be traced to the Black Arts movement.

Further reading: Leroi Jones and Larry Neal, *Black Fire: An Anthology of African American Writing* (New York: William Morrow, 1968); Michael Schwarz, *Visions of a Liberated Future: Black Arts Movement Writings* (New York: Thunder's Mouth Press, 1989); Jerry Watts, *Heroism and the Black Intellectual: Ralph Ellison and the African American Intellectual* (Chapel Hill: University of North Carolina Press, 1994).

Black Cabinet

The Black Cabinet refers to the informal associations of blacks in the BUREAUCRACY during the administrations of several American presidents. The Black Cabinet is not to be confused with those persons who have actually served in the cabinets of American presidents. Rather, persons who served in the Black Cabinets held minor positions in the bureaucracy or served as "race relations" advisers to white cabinet members.

The Black Cabinet first emerged during the PRESIDENCY of William Howard Taft (1909–13). During Taft's administration, the half dozen or so black presidential appointees would gather informally to discuss the administration's race policies, patronage, and REPUBLICAN PARTY politics. Under the leadership of William Lewis, an assistant attorney general, the group called itself the black cabinet. Although President Taft met with the group on several occasions, it had little success in securing his support for anti-SEGREGATION and antilynching legislation. Instead, Taft actively pursued policies calculated to appease Southern white supremacists and racists. The defeat of Taft by WOODROW WILSON brought a quick end to the Black Cabinet, as Wilson promptly removed all black officeholders except those covered by civil service laws.

The institution reemerged in the 1930s during the administration of FRANKLIN D. ROOSEVELT. In the early days of the NEW DEAL, several white cabinet officers hired prominent African Americans as "racial advisers" to assist them on issues in their agencies related to RACE. Under the LEADERSHIP of MARY MCLEOD BETHUNE, these individuals constituted themselves as the "federal council" and held periodic meetings to develop strategies to assure equal access and participation by blacks in the various New Deal programs. Their activities resulted in modest increases in patronage, the start of efforts to desegregate the bureaucracy, and initiatives to increase opportunities for black employment in private industry. However, on the major issues of black concern—antilynching legislation and fair employment practices—the group's strategy of quiet behind-the-scenes LOBBYING had little impact on President Roosevelt's decision making. The president did issue Executive Order 8802 prohibiting DISCRIMINATION in defense industries, but this action was more a result of A. PHILIP RANDOLPH'S MARCH ON WASHINGTON MOVEMENT than the influence of the Black Cabinet.

Hardly any blacks were appointed to office during the presidencies of Dwight Eisenhower and HARRY TRUMAN. In the administrations of JOHN F. KENNEDY and LYNDON B. JOHNSON, black appointees did not organize themselves as a formal black cabinet with regular meetings, but LOUIS MARTIN would occasionally bring them together on an ad hoc basis to discuss civil rights and other issues related to race. Although President Johnson apparently encouraged these meetings, the group had little influence on the development of administration policies.

In the administration of RICHARD NIXON, black appointees once again organized as a black cabinet. The group, officially called "The Council of Black Appointees," met regularly and attempted to lobby the president on civil rights issues, but like its predecessor groups, it had little impact on presidential decision making. After the Nixon administration, black appointees did not organize formal black cabinets.

black church

W. E. B. DU BOIS described the black church as the "sole surviving social institution of the African fatherland." The church is and always has been the largest and potentially most powerful ORGANIZATION in the BLACK COMMUNITY. The source of its strength and its potential power is, as Du Bois suggested, rooted in African cultural survivals and in the RELIGIOSITY that is a core value in African-American CULTURE. A second source of its strength and potential power derives from the church's relative autonomy and independence from whites. Third, the church has size and solidarity. It has a larger membership than any secular black organization, and its members frequently exhibit solidarity in religious and nonreligious activities. Fourth, the church is a major agent of POLITICAL SOCIALIZATION in black America. Fifth, the church is and always has been an arena where blacks could practice politics. That is, the church was a haven where, independently of whites, the "struggle for power and the thirst for power could be satisfied" through service on church boards, participation in church elections, and in developing leadership and other civic skills. Finally, as a large and relatively autonomous institution, the church can serve as a base for political mobilization, as some churches did during the ABOLITION-IST MOVEMENT, the CIVIL RIGHTS MOVEMENT, and in various political campaigns such as JESSE JACKSON's for president.

However, the "black" church is a misnomer. The black church is not, like the Roman Catholic Church, a hierarchical, monolithic institution. Rather, it is more appropriate to refer to black "churches" rather than the "black church." In the United States there are approximately 60,000 black churches, more than 50,000 clergy, and a church membership of more than 17 million. These churches are organized into seven major denominations that, in turn, are organized in a COALITION called the Congress of National Black Churches. In addition to these Christian congregations, the NATION OF ISLAM, the AMERICAN MUSLIM MISSION, and other Islamic congregations play an important and growing role in black religious life.

In addition to political activism and mobilization, black churches have historically been involved in social and economic SELF-HELP (establishing mutual benefit societies, for example), and many black churches today are engaged in a variety of social and economic development activities that can include investment clubs; the development of black businesses; the construction of housing; the running of schools; job-training programs; and counseling and assistance on AIDS, alcohol and drug abuse, teenage pregnancy, and other social problems. These social and economic activities of some churches are increasing, sometimes with the support of the government and with guidance from leading church organizations such as the NATIONAL BAPTIST CONVENTION.

Because of the central role of religiosity in black culture, the role of church in black politics can be easily exaggerated. Most churches were not actively involved in the Civil Rights movement, nor were most actively involved in Jesse Jackson's presidential campaigns. Rather, most black churches (especially the smaller ones and those in the rural South) generally refrain from social and political activism, concentrating on their religious missions, devotional activities, and church governance. And while the church and religiosity tend to promote POLITICAL PARTICIPATION in a variety of ways, religiosity in African-American culture has always tended to work against RADICALISM. That is, the church historically has played a dual role in black politics, inculcating and encouraging the mainstream values of the POLITICAL SYSTEM while seeking system inclusion but discouraging MILITANCY and radicalism.

The black church, like other Western religious institutions on which it is partly based, is organized on principles of SEXISM, relegating women to a SUBORDINATE position by denying them (on doctrinal grounds) access to formal positions of LEADERSHIP in the clergy and other ecclesiastical posts. This is an increasing source of tension within some churches that may undermine the solidarity of the institution, since black church membership is disproportionately female. Since the 1970s, FEMINISM has become an important force in black politics, and its influence is likely to grow, which may make it difficult for churches to continue to maintain sexism in their doctrines and rituals. Yet within the churches, the traditional leadership and the congregants (including many women) oppose gender EQUALITY. But recognizing this gendered aspect of black church life, the African Methodist Episcopal Church in 2000 elected its first female bishop, Vashli McKenzie. Minister LOUIS FARRAKHAN also made history in 2000 by naming the first woman, Ava Muhammad, to head a Mosque of Islam anywhere in the world.

Further reading: Andrew Billingsly, *Mighty Like a River: The Black Church and Social Reform* (New York: Oxford University Press, 1999); Franklin E. Frazier, *The Negro Church in America* (New York: Schocken Books, 1963); C. Eric Lincoln and Lawrence Mamiya, *The BLack Church in America* (Durham, N.C.: Duke University Press, 1990).

black codes

The black codes were a system of OPPRESSION inaugurated in a series of laws passed by the SOUTHERN STATES after the abolition of SLAVERY. These laws were designed to effectively reenslave blacks by denying them the FREEDOM to travel, to make and enforce contracts, or to work in trades, crafts, or other forms of employment.

Although the laws that constituted the Black Codes varied from state to state (and within states), in general they all had the one prevailing purpose of maintaining the newly freed but nearly powerless African Americans as an oppressed SUBORDINATE GROUP. In some areas the black codes resembled aspects of South African APARTHEID in that blacks were forbidden access to certain jobs and denied the right to travel without a pass. One of the most effective mechanisms of subordination was the vagrancy laws that were used to force thousands of blacks into forced labor for the whites who had previously owned them. The codes were enforced by the authority and violence of STATE AND LOCAL GOVERNMENTS and by the informal violence of KU KLUX KLAN–like white-citizen vigilante groups.

The flagrant oppression of the emancipated slaves eventually caused the CONGRESS—over the objections of

President ANDREW JOHNSON—to enact a series of CIVIL RIGHTS laws to overturn the codes. Eventually, when these laws proved inadequate in the face of white resistance, Congress embarked on RECONSTRUCTION as a comprehensive program to assure African-American freedom and EQUALITY.

black community

The idea of a black or African-American community is central to the idea of black or AFRICAN-AMERICAN POLITICS in the United States. That is, black politics presupposes the existence of a relatively distinct SUPERORDINATE white community and a relatively distinct SUBORDINATE black community. If this is not the case, then theoretically African-American politics as a phenomenon has no meaning.

There is a black community in the United States. It is a historically constructed community of shared history and memory; psychologically and culturally bound; with relatively distinct economic and political interests; and with a geographic or spatial anchor in the nation's urban GHETTOS and the heavily populated rural "black belt" counties of the SOUTHERN STATES. The community is characterized by relatively autonomous religious, fraternal, educational, and MEDIA institutions; it has a relatively homogeneous view of its interests insofar as demands on the POLITICAL SYSTEM are concerned; and it exhibits very high solidarity in its VOTING BEHAVIOR.

In the POST–CIVIL RIGHTS ERA, this idea of community has been challenged by those who argue that because of increasing CLASS STRATIFICATION and because of the INTEGRATION of middle-class blacks into the larger American community, there is no discernible black community in the United States. Rather, it is argued that the idea of black community is a form of essentializing community on the basis of the myth of RACE or ETHNICITY. This view was argued by Justice Sandra Day O'Connor in her majority opinion in *SHAW V. RENO*, a case that invalidated the intentional creation of majority-black congressional districts in North Carolina. The district had been created pursuant to the VOTING RIGHTS ACT OF 1965. This act, as amended in 1982, implicitly recognized a black community of interests that merited REPRESENTATION of its own in CONGRESS and in state and local legislative bodies. In *Shaw*, O'Connor rejected this idea of a black community deserving of representation of its own, writing that it "reinforces the perception that members of the same racial group—regardless of their age, education, economic status or the community in which they live—think alike, share the same political interests and prefer the same candidates. We have rejected such perceptions elsewhere as impermissible racial stereotyping." The contemporary black community, like any other, is not monolithic, which is to say there are differences in interests and concerns based on age, gender, place of residence, religion, sexual orientation, and so on. However, these differences do not make the idea of community a stereotype or an essentialist myth any more than do, for example, similar differences in the United States undermine the idea of an American community. Indeed, the divisions between blacks and whites in America are much deeper than any divisions within black America. Yet both blacks and whites in the United States share a sense of being part of an American community.

Although at some point the African-American community may become "white" like the Irish-American community and cease to have distinctive community interests, that degree of ASSIMILATION is not yet observable with respect to African Americans at the beginning of the 21st century.

Further reading: Matthew Holden Jr., *The Politics of the Black "Nation"* (New York: Chandler Publishing, 1973).

black Muslims   See NATION OF ISLAM.

black nationalism

Black nationalism is the oldest tradition in AFRICAN-AMERICAN THOUGHT, and it is an integral tradition in which over the past 200 years African-American scholars and leaders have developed a set of ideas and doctrines that have a lot of continuity and that appear repeatedly in the thinking of persons as ideologically diverse as MARTIN DELANY and FREDERICK DOUGLASS, W. E. B. DU BOIS and MARCUS GARVEY, MARTIN LUTHER KING, JR. and MALCOLM X, and JESSE JACKSON and LOUIS FARRAKHAN. Black nationalism as an IDEOLOGY is often contrasted with RADICALISM and INTEGRATION. While this has some analytical and pedagogical value, in its broadest and most comprehensive conceptualization, black nationalism should be thought of as the "master ideology" in African-American thought and politics, having the capacity to encompass integration, contemporary LIBERALISM, CONSERVATISM, and RADICALISM.

Sterling Stuckey, who has written the most sophisticated studies of black nationalism, has shown that as a sentiment and later as a doctrine, black nationalism has its origins in the CULTURE that emerged during SLAVERY and that it emerges more as a result of African traditions of cultural autonomy and hegemony than any borrowing or adaptation from European theories or models. Because of the relatively greater degrees of FREEDOM of blacks in the NORTHERN STATES, nationalism as a doctrine first emerged there. However, its roots are in the slave culture in the SOUTHERN STATES, where the relative isolation from Europeans and the large and frequent infusions of Africans from the continent reinforced African consciousness and group solidarity. Indeed, until as late as the 19th century the slaves referred to themselves as Africans and probably did not consider themselves as Americans until after the CIVIL WAR.

How then is black nationalism as a political tradition—as a "master ideology"—to be properly defined and understood, and what are the core or fundamental elements of it as a system of African-American thought? Stuckey argues that its originators "emphasized the need for black people to rely primarily on themselves in vital areas of life—economic, political, religious, and intellectual—in order to effect their liberation." Bracey, Meier, and Rudwick write that "the concept of racial solidarity is essential to all forms of black nationalism." In this sense, they write, it has "no ideological or programmatic implications beyond the desire that black people organize themselves on the basis of their common color and oppressed condition to move in some way to alleviate their situation."

These definitions are quite broad and porous, allowing, without contradiction, the inclusion of diverse ideologies and programs. However, these broad formulations are exacting enough to *exclude* those individuals, ideologies, or programs that do not believe (1) that the condition or situation of blacks is a function of OPPRESSION, (2) that this oppression is a function of race or RACISM, or (3) that blacks, whatever the nature and source of their condition, should organize politically on the basis of race.

Black nationalism, then, is the broad tradition among African people in the United States that blacks as a group should unite in solidarity as a people to fight their *racially based* oppression in order to achieve freedom and EQUALITY. Given this understanding, the following can be identified as core or constituent elements of the tradition. First, there is an acute historical awareness or consciousness of oppression at the hands of whites as the source or cause of the condition of blacks. Second, there is a similar awareness or consciousness and appreciation of the persistence of group traits that distinguish African-American CULTURE from that of other groups in the United States, traits that survived the experience of slavery and that provide the cultural basis for group autonomy and solidarity in political behavior. Third, there is a PAN-AFRICANISM consciousness that posits bonds and obligations among African peoples everywhere. Fourth, there is a belief that the condition of blacks can only be altered as a result of SELF-HELP, self-reliance, and solidarity.

Thus, the tradition of black nationalism includes black separatists who believe that freedom and equality for blacks can only be achieved in a separate black homeland or nation or by a return to Africa. But the tradition also includes integrationists who believe that freedom and equality can be achieved within the boundaries of the United States.

Further reading: John Bracey, August Meier, and Elliot Rudwick, *Black Nationalism in America* (Indianapolis: Bobbs-Merrill, 1970); William J. Moses, *Classical Black Nationalism: From the Revolution to Marcus Garvey* (New York: New York University Press, 1996); Michael Dawson, *Black Visions: The Roots of Contemporary African American Political Ideologies* (Chicago: University of Chicago Press, 2002); Dean Robinson, *Black Nationalism in American Political Thought* (New York: Cambridge University Press, 2001); Robert C. Smith, "Ideology as the Enduring Dilemma of Black Politics," *Dilemmas of Black Politics*, ed. Georgia Persons (New York: HarperCollins, 1993), 211–24; Sterling Stuckey, *The Ideological Origins of Black Nationalism* (Boston: Beacon Press, 1972); ———, *Slave Culture: Foundations of Nationalist Thought* (New York: Oxford University Press, 1987).

blackness

Blackness is a problematic concept. That is, it is difficult to objectively define, and when defined it has multiple meanings. The specific idea of blackness, like the name BLACK, is a product of the 1960s BLACK POWER MOVEMENT, although it has some parallels with what was referred to as the "new Negro" or "race man" during the Civil Rights era. As it has been used since the 1960s, blackness is a boundary-maintenance concept that separates or distinguishes individuals on the basis of their presumed identification with the interests of the BLACK COMMUNITY. It has multiple dimensions or meanings—psychological, cultural, political, and ideological.

The psychological dimension requires a consciousness of one's identity as black, a rejection of the negative stereotypes that defined black as inferior, and an acceptance of alternative frames of reference that expresses pride in identification with one's African and African-American heritage.

The cultural dimension requires knowledge or involvement in the cultural life of the black community. However, given that there is disagreement as to what constitutes or distinguishes black CULTURE in the United States, it is difficult to give this dimension any fixed meaning. That is, what it means to be culturally black in the United States is amorphous and ambiguous, although there are certain values and rituals in RELIGION, MUSIC, and dance that over the years have been identified as at least partially distinctive black cultural attributes. But these are problematic and vary to a considerable extent by class, age, region, and residence (urban or rural).

The political dimension of blackness involves the psychological sense of identification with other blacks and the idea that one's fate is linked to other blacks, or to the black community. To be identified as politically black requires individuals to evaluate political issues in terms of their impact on the interests of the group, and to make political choices on the basis of whether they benefit or harm the group.

The ideological dimension of blackness is the most contentious. The African-American POLITICAL CULTURE is relatively homogeneous in terms of ideology. African-American PUBLIC OPINION is liberal, and African-American LEADERSHIP is liberal; therefore to be black is to embrace LIBERALISM. And because, since the 1960s, the DEMOCRATIC PARTY has been the more liberal of the two parties, to be black is to be Democratic in partisanship. To put this another way, since the 1960s, CONSERVATISM as it has been advanced by the REPUBLICAN PARTY is viewed in the black political culture as hostile to the interests of blacks, as "anti-black," and as the politically functional equivalent of RACISM. Thus, to be a black Republican or a black conservative is to be beyond the "boundaries of blackness."

This boundary-maintenance function of blackness ideologically can be seen in the reaction of most black intellectuals to the appointment of CLARENCE THOMAS, a conservative Republican, to the SUPREME COURT. An example is RONALD WALTERS, a leading interpreter of black politics in the MEDIA, who wrote in the *Washington Post* that Thomas was "estranged from his blackness." Blackness here is defined ideologically and politically, not necessarily culturally or psychologically.

Blackness in AFRICAN-AMERICAN POLITICS is a complex, ambiguous, and contentious, multidimensional concept. Theoretically, one can be black on one or more dimensions and not on others. For example, an individual African American could be psychologically or culturally black but politically and ideologically estranged from his or her blackness. Or the reverse could be the case. And a white American, while not psychologically black, could embrace blackness politically and ideologically. In the 1960s scholars of black leadership developed categories called "white Negroes" or "functional Negroes," white persons who identified so completely with the cause of CIVIL RIGHTS that they were viewed as Negro leaders or spokespersons. Similarly, a white person in the POST–CIVIL RIGHTS ERA who views issues on the basis of whether they advance the interests of blacks and is a liberal and a Democrat can be viewed politically and ideologically as having embraced blackness.

Black Panther Party

The Black Panther Party, while not the first ORGANIZATION of African Americans to employ VIOLENCE in the African-American struggle for FREEDOM and EQUALITY, historically is the most important. Before the Panthers, the AFRICAN BLOOD BROTHERHOOD, organized in 1919, advocated the use of violence by blacks to defend themselves against attacks by whites; in 1959 Robert Williams was removed as head of the Monroe, North Carolina, chapter of the NAACP because of his advocacy of defensive violence by blacks; and in the mid-1960s blacks in Bogalusa, Louisiana, organized the Deacons for Defense to defend civil rights workers from racist attacks. Thus, while nonviolence has always been the predominant strategy of African-American LEADERSHIP, there has always been a minority of blacks willing, as Robert Williams put it, "to meet violence with violence." The Black Panthers therefore are not unique in their advocacy of violence. Rather, their significance in AFRICAN-AMERICAN POLITICS is the widespread influence of the group in the late 1960s and its eventual embrace of aggressive, revolutionary violence rather than merely defensive violence as advocated by earlier African-American leaders and organizations.

The Black Panther Party for Self Defense was founded in 1966 by HUEY P. NEWTON and BOBBY SEALE, student activists at Oakland, California's, Merritt College. The group adopted its name and symbol, a black panther, from the Lowndes County, Alabama, Freedom Democratic Party, which used a black panther as its symbol. (The Lowndes County Party was founded in the early 1960s by SNCC to encourage blacks to register to vote and run for office.) As the full name of the party implies, it was originally founded as a self-defense organization (to defend blacks against police brutality and harassment). However, within two years it had transformed itself into a radical, revolutionary organization devoted to using violence as a base of power to overthrow the POLITICAL SYSTEM.

Aware that the police in Oakland and other American cities frequently harassed and brutalized blacks, Seale and Newton decided to organize armed patrols to monitor police encounters with blacks in San Francisco, Los Angeles, and Oakland. Their purpose was to observe the behavior of the police in order to discourage misconduct. (Their slogan to "observe and protect" was derived from the Los Angeles Police Department's motto "to serve and protect.") Although the Panthers did not intervene in the incidents they observed, the mere presence of armed black men monitoring their behavior alarmed the police, and soon a series of gun battles between the Panthers and the police occurred. Thereafter, the California legislature began considering legislation to ban the carrying of loaded guns in public. To PROTEST this legislation, 30 armed Panthers marched into the state capitol in Sacramento on May 2, 1967. This demonstration received widespread coverage in the MEDIA, and as a result the group almost overnight became nationally recognized. Occurring a year after the start of the BLACK POWER MOVEMENT, the image of armed black men dressed in black captured the imagination of young blacks across the country, and the MILITANCY of the incident led to rapid growth in party membership and chapters. From fewer than 100 members in Oakland, San Francisco, and Los Angeles in 1967, by late 1968 membership was estimated at 3,000 to 5,000 in more than 30 chapters throughout the United States.

Accompanying this rapid growth was an equally rapid change in the IDEOLOGY of the party as its leaders embraced RADICALISM and revolutionary violence. The revolutionary ideology of the Panthers was based on a varied and contradictory mix of ideas drawn from MALCOLM X, FRANTZ FANON, and orthodox marxism. On the basis of these ideas, Panther leaders argued that RACISM was caused by or was a by-product of CAPITALISM, and that the objectives of the party were the violent overthrow of the political system and the establishment in its place of a new, nonracist system based on SOCIALISM. The rapid growth of the armed, openly revolutionary Panthers occurred at the same time as a series of RIOTS by African Americans in the GHETTOS of the NORTHERN STATES. Also, there were a series of ongoing confrontations between the Panthers and

police, one of which resulted in the killing of an Oakland policeman in an incident involving Newton, which led to his arrest and jailing on murder charges. These developments caused alarm and fear in the nation's POWER ELITE.

In 1988 J. EDGAR HOOVER, the head of the FBI, declared that Panthers were the "greatest threat to the internal security of the United States" of all the radical groups then active. By this time, Hoover and the FBI had already developed COINTELPRO, a systematic program of POLITICAL REPRESSION. In 1968 this program made destruction of the Panthers its major priority, and by 1970 that goal had been largely accomplished. The group was in disarray, and its leaders were in jail, exile, or dead. The collapse of the Panthers was in part a result of political repression, but the group's own internal corruption and factional infighting were also contributing factors.

The Black Panther Party was the first mass-based revolutionary organization of African Americans. It openly advocated and to some modest extent actually used vio-

Black Panthers demonstrating in New York City *(New York Public Library)*

lence as a base of power to achieve freedom and equality. Adhering to an ideology that these objectives could not be achieved without socialism, the group set itself on a collision course with the core values of the political system. Given the system's disproportionate power, the group was inevitably destroyed, because no government that has the power will tolerate a violent challenge to its system.

Further reading: Charles E. Jones, *The Black Panther Party Reconsidered* (Baltimore, Md.: Black Classics Press, 1998); Hugh Pearson, *The Shadow of the Panther: Huey Newton and the Price of Black Power in America* (Reading, Mass.: Addison-Wesley, 1994).

Black Power movement

After the CIVIL RIGHTS MOVEMENT, the Black Power movement is the most important political phenomenon in the 20th-century history of AFRICAN-AMERICAN POLITICS. In its origins, evolution, and consequences, the movement known as black power had profound and enduring consequences on the cultural, ideological, and structural relationships between blacks and whites in the POST–CIVIL RIGHTS ERA. The Black Power movement also profoundly altered the internal ethos and ORGANIZATIONS of the BLACK COMMUNITY; shaped its identity, consciousness, and POLITICAL CULTURE; and for a brief time helped to give rise to genuinely revolutionary ideas and organizations. Also, together with the Civil Rights movement, black power served as an inspiration and model for SOCIAL MOVEMENTS among other Americans, including feminists, Latinos, and homosexuals. In doing this it contributed to the shift toward "identity politics" and an emphasis on MULTICULTURALISM in the United States. Finally, the book BLACK POWER: THE POLITICS OF LIBERATION IN AMERICA, the movement's manifesto, contributed to the development of a new understanding of RACISM and the conceptualization of INSTITUTIONAL RACISM as a form of the phenomenon.

Origins of the Movement

The phrase "black power" was first used by Richard Wright, the African-American novelist, in a 1950s book about African politics that used the phrase as the book's title. HARLEM's congressman ADAM CLAYTON POWELL had used the phrase in speeches in the early 1960s and a week before SNCC introduced the phrase during the MEREDITH MARCH in June 1966. Powell used "black power" as the theme of his address to HOWARD UNIVERSITY's graduating class, telling the students to seek "black power . . . an audacious black power . . . the power to build black institutions of splendid achievement." However, as a phrase that launched a movement, it has its origins in the Meredith march.

The Black Power movement, ironically, has its origins in the success of the Civil Rights movement. After a decade of intense PROTEST in the SOUTHERN STATES, the passage of the CIVIL RIGHTS ACT OF 1964 and the VOTING RIGHTS ACT OF 1965 granted to African Americans full civil and political rights. Thus, after five decades of LOBBYING, LITIGATION, and protest, the Civil Rights movement's agenda as outlined in the 1905 NIAGARA MOVEMENT had been achieved. However, in spite of the successes of the Civil Rights movement in getting laws passed, the day-to-day conditions of the average black outside of the South had hardly changed. Indeed, the economic conditions of blacks in the GHETTOS may have become worse during the 1960s, and blacks in the NORTHERN STATES already enjoyed many of the CIVIL RIGHTS won by the movement for blacks in the Southern states. The WATTS RIOT, which took place two weeks after the president signed the Voting Rights Act, was interpreted by many in SNCC as a signal that it was time for the Civil Rights movement to shift its attention from INDIVIDUAL RACISM in the South to institutional racism in the North and to the problem of black POVERTY throughout the country.

Scholars of the origin of black power generally agree that the following factors also played a role in its emergence: the rejection of the MISSISSIPPI FREEDOM DEMOCRATIC PARTY challenge at the 1964 Democratic National Convention; the growing influence of the writings of MALCOLM X and FRANTZ FANON within SNCC; and a growing disenchantment among blacks in SNCC with the role of whites in the movement. This latter is a critical proximate factor in the genesis of black power.

In 1966 SNCC's central committee voted to exclude whites from decision-making positions in the organization and to restrict their role to organizing in white communities. This to some extent reflected the rising influence of black nationalist sentiments in the organization. But more importantly, it reflected a felt need of the group's black leadership to effect a break with the liberal-labor elements of the civil rights COALITION and establish independent bases of black political action.

This concern emerged from three considerations. First, members of SNCC, black and white alike, felt a keen sense of betrayal by white liberals and labor because of their last-minute refusal to support the Mississippi Freedom Democratic Party challenge in the face of opposition from President LYNDON JOHNSON. Second, there was a view among some that whites exercised significant and perhaps distorting influence in the decision-making process of black civil rights organizations. And finally, it was argued that whites in important and visible leadership positions had a debilitating effect on the development of indigenous black LEADERSHIP.

It was these considerations that led STOKELY CARMICHAEL and his colleagues to argue that the Civil

Rights movement needed a change of orientation, in particular a break with the liberal-labor elements of the coalition and the development of independent black power. There was long and acrimonious debate within SNCC as to if, when, and how the break should be made. JOHN LEWIS's defeat as SNCC chairman by Carmichael in 1966, in effect, represented the resolution of the conflict in favor of those forces seeking to break with the established coalition and shift the emphasis to MILITANCY and BLACKNESS within the movement. After Carmichael's election, the question before the group was how and when to present the new orientation so as to obtain the maximum attention of the public. The Meredith march provided the answer.

There is some disagreement in the available scholarship as to precisely how the symbol black power came to be raised during the Meredith march. James Foreman, SNCC's executive secretary, reports that it was a spontaneous move on the part of himself and fellow SNCC staffers Willie Ricks, Ruby Robinson, and a few others who decided to take advantage of the presence of the news cameras at the march to make black power a "slogan of the masses." In his memoir, *The Making of Black Revolutionaries*, Foreman gives the following account of how the slogan came to be used on the March:

> "Hey Jim, I got an idea. I want to know what you think of it." It was Willie Ricks, the young SNCC field secretary who had acquired a reputation as a brilliant organizer of young people in Birmingham, Americus and other hot spots in the South. He had stopped in the Atlanta office on his way to Mississippi. The Meredith march on June 1966 was underway and Stokely Carmichael had asked Ricks to come over.
>
> "Suppose when I get over there to Mississippi and I'm speaking, I start hollering for 'black power' what do you think of that? Ricks asked. Would you back me up? You think it would scare people in SNCC"?
>
> "Black power—sure try it," I told him. Why not? After all, you'd only be shortening the phrase we are always using—power for poor black people. Black power is shorter, and means the same thing. Go on try it.
>
> And that is how the cry for black power came to be voiced.

While undoubtedly there was an element of spontaneity in the use of the slogan at the precise time of the march, other evidence tends to support the view that there was considerably more planning than the casual conversation of Ricks and Foreman would suggest. For example, the idea of black power was the product of many months of discussion and planning within SNCC. And MARTIN LUTHER KING's account of the use of black power on the Meredith march suggests that its use was not spontaneous but was

deliberately used by Carmichael and his colleagues because of its propaganda value. King quotes Carmichael as saying:

> How can you arouse people to unite around a program without a slogan as a rallying cry? Didn't the labor movement have slogans? Haven't we had slogans all along in the movement? What we need is a new slogan with "black" in it.

Agreeing that a new slogan might be necessary, King suggested such phrases as "black consciousness" or "black equality." He argued, "These phrases would be less vulnerable and would more accurately describe what we are about. The words 'black' and 'power' together give the impression that we are talking about black domination rather than black equality." Carmichael responded that neither would have the ready appeal and persuasive force of black power and concluded by saying, "Martin, I deliberately decided to raise this issue on the march in order to give it a national forum, and force you to take a stand for black power."

Whatever the precise origins of the use of the phrase during the Meredith march, the result was that an ambiguous, emotional, and provocative symbol was given a national audience. The news media now centered its attention on the apparent divisions in the movement symbolized by black power. The slogan was given frequent and emphatic repetition in scores of speeches and lectures by Carmichael and others and thus rapidly and dramatically captured the attention of the public. As one commentator said of the slogan in the summer of 1966, "It makes crowds roar, conversations sparkle and the television cameras click. It wins headlines. After all it made Stokely Carmichael a national figure overnight."

Reactions

The initial reaction of most American leaders, black and white, to the black power slogan was overwhelmingly hostile, as was the reporting and commentary in the MEDIA. Martin Luther King Jr., for example, called black power "racism in reverse," and ROY WILKINS, the head of the NAACP, was even harsher, describing black power as "a reverse Mississippi, a reverse Hitler, a reverse Ku Klux Klan." With the exception of SNCC's new leaders, the new leaders of CORE, and Congressman Adam Clayton Powell, hardly any other black leaders initially supported black power.

PUBLIC OPINION was also divided. In 1966 and 1967 polls indicated that the overwhelming majority of whites was opposed to black power. Those whites expressing an opinion said that black power represented "violence," "black domination," or efforts by blacks to "take over." Black public opinion was about evenly divided. Those who were favorable saw it as a call for black unity and an expression of a desire by blacks to get their fair share of society's resources, in other words, a quest for EQUALITY. Those blacks who were unfavorable saw black power as meaningless, simply a slogan or a form of empty symbolism. Nonetheless those blacks most likely to approve of black power were blacks in the Northern ghettos, while blacks in the rural South were least likely to approve. This regional difference in support was particularly pleasing to SNCC, since one of the aims of black power was to shift the focus of the Civil Rights movement from the rural South to the Northern ghettos.

To some extent, those who viewed black power as meaningless symbolism were correct. At the time it was articulated on the Meredith march, it had more symbolic meaning than substantive content. The slogan was ambiguous, perhaps deliberately so because ambiguity was itself a source of the slogan's power and vitality. Thus, black power was a dynamic symbol that could be given multiple meanings. And it was. Some defined black power as a militant version of the philosophy and program of BOOKER T. WASHINGTON; others defined it as a form of CULTURAL NATIONALISM; while still others saw in it a revival of RADICALISM and militancy. All these interpretations were to some extent accurate. However, the most basic and enduring meaning of black power was as a racialized version of the INTEREST GROUP politics that is a defining feature of the PLURALISM that is an important element of the American DEMOCRACY. This interest group understanding of black power was advanced by CHARLES HAMILTON in his writings and lectures in 1966 and 1967 and was the central theme of the book *Black Power* that he coauthored with Stokely Carmichael. But while Hamilton was defining black power in terms of nonviolent interest-group reform politics, Carmichael was defining it in terms of radicalism, SOCIALISM, and revolutionary PAN-AFRICANISM. Thus, for a time, black power meant reform and revolution; however, its lasting impact on American and African-American politics was reform and not revolution.

The Impact of Black Power on African-American Politics

Black power had multiple impacts on black politics. First, it increased racial-group consciousness and solidarity. As one group of political scientists wrote, as a "result of black power the appropriate dimension for understanding the political behavior of black citizens may have changed. Contemporary black leaders may have helped shape the political meaning of being black in ways black leaders two decades before could not. Certainly, racial identity is now the most useful prescriptive measure of the political choice of many citizens." Black power also led to a revival of cultural nationalism, as in the rise of the BLACK ARTS MOVE-

MENT, AFROCENTRICITY, and AFRICAN-AMERICAN STUDIES. It also, resulted in the creation of a large number of new racially exclusive or all-black organizations as well as the gradual displacement of whites from positions of leadership and influence in the traditional civil rights organizations such as the NAACP and the URBAN LEAGUE. Finally, the revolutionary or radical versions of black power—as manifested in Carmichael's rhetoric and writings, in the VIOLENCE of the 1960s RIOTS, and in the emergence of the BLACK PANTHER PARTY—led to two different, but in some ways complementary, responses of the POLITICAL SYSTEM.

The revolutionary and radical advocates of black power were repressed by the system. However, the perceived threat the radicals and revolutionaries posed to the system made the reform black-power advocates appear more reasonable, responsible, and moderate. Therefore, rather than POLITICAL REPRESSION, the response to these groups were political INCORPORATION and CO-OPTATION.

Poster showing John Carlos and Tommie Smith bowing their heads and raising their black-gloved fists in the air, a traditional symbol of black power, at the 1968 Summer Olympic Games in Mexico *(Library of Congress)*

Within a year of the Meredith march, white liberal elements of the POWER ELITE had embraced black power to the extent that it meant black consciousness, solidarity, and autonomous black interest groups working for reform within the system. The *New York Times* reported in 1967 on a survey that showed what it described as "significant support" for black power among white liberals "because they feel integration is impossible in the immediate future and favor instead building up Negro institutions." Also, most leaders of the traditional CIVIL RIGHTS organizations changed their attitudes and embraced the interest-group version of black power. In 1968 WHITNEY YOUNG of the Urban League, who in 1966 described black power as "black racism," now said he supported the concept "where it emphasized self-determination, self respect and participation and control of one's own community affairs."

Impact on American Politics

A major impact of black power was also felt in the white community. Partly in response to the radicalism and militancy of some black-power advocates and to the violence of the urban riots, white public opinion began to become more conservative on civil rights and other issues related to race. The increasing CONSERVATISM of whites on race and related issues helped to create a WHITE BACKLASH and build support for the openly racist PRESIDENTIAL CAMPAIGNS of GEORGE WALLACE and the subtly antiblack campaigns of RICHARD NIXON and RONALD REAGAN in their successful presidential bids.

Impact on Other Social Movements

The Civil Rights movement generally and the Black Power movement specifically had major influences on the development of social movements and interest groups among other SUBORDINATE GROUP who felt they were victims of DISCRIMINATION, racism, or OPPRESSION. The modern feminist movement to eliminate SEXISM and other forms of gender-based discrimination can be directly traced to the Civil Rights movement generally and to the participation of women in SNCC specifically. And many of the white women who launched the modern feminist movement in the late 1960s drew directly on their experiences in the Civil Rights movement, using it as an inspiration and model for strategy and tactics as they worked to build feminist consciousness, solidarity, and organization. Mexican Americans, Puerto Ricans, Native Americans, and Asian Americans also used black power as an inspiration and model for their movements. Later, homosexuals borrowed from black power to build the GAY RIGHTS MOVEMENT in the 1970s and 1980s, as did the elderly and other groups, including white Americans of eastern and southern European origins.

Black power, then, is responsible in a major way for the emergence of "identity politics" and multiculturalism in late-20th-century American politics. This kind of politics places emphasis on one's identity, consciousness, and solidarity based on gender, ETHNICITY, or sexual orientation instead of or in relationship with other broader identities such as social class or one's identity simply as an American.

Further reading: Joel Aberbach and Jack Walker, "The Meaning of Black Power: A Comparison of White and Black Interpretations of a Political Slogan," *American Political Science Review* 64 (1970): 332–64; Julius Lester, *Look Out Whitey!: Black Power Gonna Get Your Mama* (New York: Dial Press, 1968); Donald McCormack, "Stokely Carmichael and Pan Africanism: Back to Black Powers," *Journal of Politics* 35 (1973): 386–409; Robert C. Smith, "Black Power and the Transformation from Protest to Politics," *Political Science Quarterly* 96 (1981): 431–44.

Black Power: The Politics of Liberation in America 1967 book, manifesto of the Black Power movement

Black Power: The Politics of Liberation in America, a near classic, is one of the most important books in AFRICAN-AMERICAN POLITICS. It exerted a profound influence on the study of the subject and on its practice. Written by CHARLES HAMILTON and STOKELY CARMICHAEL, the book is a prime example of how knowledge can be used as a base of power in politics.

As an academic treatise, *Black Power* contributed significantly to theoretical understanding of African-American politics; demonstrated the limitations of PLURALISM and the MELTING POT as theories to explain black politics; clarified the concept of INTERNAL COLONIALISM as an alternative theory to explain black politics in the United States; introduced a new concept of RACISM and clarified its relationship to WHITE SUPREMACY as an IDEOLOGY; and introduced INDIVIDUAL RACISM and INSTITUTIONAL RACISM as new typologies of racism. Each of these contributions exercised important influences in study and research on African-American politics and contributed to establishing black politics as a recognized field of study in American political science.

The book, as the BLACK POWER MOVEMENT's manifesto, exerted an equally important influence on the practice of black politics. It helped to define new BLACK group consciousness and solidarity; to shift the direction of the CIVIL RIGHTS MOVEMENT away from a focus on JIM CROW–style SEGREGATION in the SOUTHERN STATES toward a concern with institutional racism and POVERTY in the NORTHERN STATES; developed a theory for the practice of black-white COALITION politics; and established the conceptual basis for understanding black power as a form of INTEREST GROUP politics. The book also articulated the case for the development of new strategies of autonomous or independent black political behavior and encouraged the formation of new, racially exclusive black ORGANIZATIONS.

In making these contributions to the academic study and practice of African-American politics, the volume along the way presents an interesting narrative of the work of SNCC in the Civil Rights movement and the origins and evolution of the MISSISSIPPI FREEDOM DEMOCRATIC PARTY. In 1992 a 25th-anniversary edition of the book with new afterwords by the authors was published.

Further reading: Stokely Carmichael (Kwame Turé) and Charles Hamilton, *Black Power: The Politics of Liberation in America,* 25th-anniversary edition (New York: Vintage Books, 1992).

Black Radical Congress

The Black Radical Congress was formed in June 1998 at a Chicago meeting of more than 2,000 African-American intellectuals, students, and community activists. Although at its initial meeting the group attracted a variety of individuals active in pursuing RADICALISM in AFRICAN-AMERICAN POLITICS, the congress was dominated by intellectuals such as MANNING MARABLE. As radicals, members of the congress expressed fundamental opposition to CAPITALISM. As blacks, members of the congress also opposed RACISM and WHITE SUPREMACY. The congress's "Statement of Principles," however, asserts that racism, class exploitation, and DISCRIMINATION based on gender and sexual orientation are so interconnected that one cannot effectively address the problems of race without also addressing problems of gender and sexuality as part of an overarching IDEOLOGY of radicalism that seeks the elimination of capitalism and its replacement with some form of SOCIALISM. This linking of black radicalism to the struggle for GAY RIGHTS and to a lesser extent FEMINISM is a product of compromises, as many in the congress preferred a form of black radicalism that focused only on the interconnection between racism and capitalism. After more than a year of intense discussion, the congress's leaders embraced the idea of a radical COALITION to include individuals from all groups who have been victims of discrimination or OPPRESSION. Minimal ideological agreement requires, however, that congress members link their particular group's struggle for FREEDOM to opposition to capitalism.

Further reading: The Freedom Agenda of the Black Radical Congress, www.blackradicalcongress.org.

Blair Education bill

A determination to acquire an education and knowledge has been an enduring feature of the black struggle for FREEDOM and EQUALITY in the United States. Even during SLAVERY, when the acquisition of knowledge was forbidden, blacks knew it was a base of power, and secretly and at great risk they tried to learn how to read and write. After emancipation, blacks largely embraced the struggle for education as a defining characteristic of their freedom and the fundamental basis for equality. Those opposed to black freedom and equality also understood that knowledge was a base of power, and therefore they resisted the education of blacks during slavery and thereafter. One of the most important cases of resistance to the education of blacks was the defeat of the Blair Education bill in the 1880s.

In 1880 the CENSUS showed that more than 70 percent of the black population, located mainly in the SOUTHERN STATES, was illiterate. This high rate of illiteracy in the Southern states was in part a result of the enforced ignorance of African Americans during slavery, but it also reflected the fact that the NORTHERN STATES spent much more on education per pupil than did the states of the South. To remedy this problem, in 1882 Senator Henry Blair of New Hampshire introduced a bill to provide grants to the states of more than $100 million over 10 years to be apportioned on the basis of a state's literacy rate. The bill also required the states to match the grants and to distribute the funds equally between black and white schools.

Although the legislation was proposed at a time of economic prosperity when the nation could afford it, in arguments similar to those made in the 1960s against the ELEMENTARY AND SECONDARY EDUCATION ACT, opponents claimed that the bill was unconstitutional. It was unconstitutional, they argued, because the CONGRESS lacked the authority to spend money on education and that federal aid to education violated the principles of FEDERALISM, states rights, and local control of schools. Some congressmen from Northern states also argued that the legislation was unfair because most of the taxes would be paid by their constituents while most of the money would be spent in the South and spent on the education of blacks rather than whites. Blair and other supporters of the bill responded that the CONSTITUTION's "general welfare" clause provided Congress's authority for the bill; that dealing with the country's race problem was more important than federalism and states rights; and that ignorance and illiteracy in the Southern states was a national problem that required the use of national resources, which inevitably transferred money from the richer to poorer states.

These arguments, however, did not persuade the House of Representatives, controlled by the DEMOCRATIC PARTY, which refused to consider the bill although it passed the Senate, controlled by the REPUBLICAN PARTY, three times between 1884 and 1890.

The Blair Education bill was supported by President BENJAMIN HARRISON and by many African-American leaders. Its defeat was one of the major failures of the post-RECONSTRUCTION era. If the bill had passed, and if black school children had received their fair share of the money, then the racially separate education in the South would have been more equal. This would have resulted in a more powerful BLACK COMMUNITY. Effective resistance to the idea of federal aid to education continued until the 1960s, when President LYNDON JOHNSON secured passage of the Elementary and Secondary Education Act as part of his GREAT SOCIETY reform program.

See also HISTORICALLY BLACK COLLEGES AND UNIVERSITIES and SCHOOLS AND EDUCATION.

Further reading: Daniel Crofts, "The Black Response to the Blair Education Bill," *Journal of Southern History* 34 (1971): 41–65; Allen Going, "The South and the Blair Education Bill," *Mississippi Valley Historical Review* 44 (1957): 269–90.

Blyden, Edward Wilmot (1832–1912) *scholar, pan-Africanist, Liberian politician, and diplomat*

Edward Wilmot Blyden, a major black intellectual who made important contributions to AFRICAN-AMERICAN THOUGHT, was born in 1832 on the WEST INDIAN island of St. Thomas. His parents were relatively privileged, which allowed him to be educated in local primary school and by a private tutor. In 1850 he emigrated to the United States to attend theological college but was refused admission at three universities. He was able, however, to receive informal training and mentoring from several prominent white Presbyterian ministers and missionaries. His failure to receive formal training frustrated and disillusioned him, and as a result of the FUGITIVE SLAVE ACT, Blyden, like many FREE NEGROES, feared he might be seized as a slave. Thus, he was persuaded by prominent whites in the AMERICAN COLONIALIZATION SOCIETY to emigrate to the independent African nation of LIBERIA.

In Liberia he attended school and eventually became an ordained minister. In a remarkable career, Blyden became a professor of classics and president of Liberia College, Liberian minister of interior, secretary of state, and the first ambassador in Europe from an African country (first to Britain and then France). He also ran unsuccessfully for president of Liberia.

An ardent advocate of PAN-AFRICANISM, Blyden sought to vindicate the "African personality" and unite the peoples of Africa into a single cultural community. His pan-Africanism, however, was rooted in the view that African civilizations were in many ways backward and required the civilizing influence of Western culture that would result from the influence of African-American immigrants. Thus, he frequently returned to the United States to encourage

BACK-TO-AFRICA MOVEMENTS. Like ALEXANDER CRUMMELL earlier, Blyden considered European COLONIALISM to have positive consequences for African development in that it brought the benefits of Western civilization and culture, although he also favored the retention of aspects of traditional African cultures.

Although a Christian clergyman, paradoxically, Blyden's major contribution to African-American thought was the publication in 1887 of his magnum opus, *Christianity, Islam and the Negro Race.* Originally written as a series of essays, when compiled into a single volume the work became a classic text in African-American thought. The thesis was controversial then, as it is now, because it contends that Christianity distorted the development of Africa and Africans, while Islam had helped to develop the "African personality" by building on traditional African cultures and acting as a force for solidarity in transcending tribal divisions. Blyden also wrote a major sociological study of African societies, *African Life and Customs*, in which he attempted to vindicate traditional African customs while encouraging the adoption of aspects of Western culture.

Blyden's thought, although contradictory in some respects, constitutes part of the intellectual foundation of pan-Africanism and the philosophy of NEGRITUDE, and it had important although indirect influence on the thought of MARCUS GARVEY, ELIJAH MUHAMMAD, and the NATION OF ISLAM.

Further reading: Hollis Lynch, *Edward Wilmot Blyden: Pan Negro Patriot* (London: Oxford University Press, 1967).

Brennan, William J. (1906–1997) *Supreme Court justice*

William J. Brennan was nominated to the SUPREME COURT by president Dwight Eisenhower in 1956. He retired in 1990. In his 34-year tenure, Justice Brennan became one of the most influential justices, known for his passionate and skillful advocacy of CIVIL RIGHTS and CIVIL LIBERTIES. Brennan viewed the CONSTITUTION as a "living" document, embodying the nation's aspirations to "social justice, brotherhood, dignity and rights for all persons." Thus, he argued that justices of the highest Court should not be bound by the so-called original intentions of the framers of the Constitution or its amendments. This "originalist" view, often advanced by conservative scholars and judges, Brennan wrote, was "arrogance cloaked as humility" because its proponents humbly claim to be merely following the intent of the framers while arrogantly claiming that they can know that intent.

Brennan authored a number of landmark opinions protecting civil liberties and civil rights, but his most important contributions in AFRICAN-AMERICAN POLITICS was in the area of AFFIRMATIVE ACTION and the death penalty. In the 1970s and 1980s he was the principal architect of the legal and constitutional principles upholding the validity of affirmative action, and his interpersonal skills and charisma allowed him to be an effective builder of COALITIONS on the Court that sustained affirmative action from the *Bakke* case in 1978 until his retirement in 1990. Brennan also consistently argued that the death penalty was unconstitutional "cruel and unusual" punishment in the language of the Constitution's Eighth Amendment. Brennan argued against the death penalty because it is administered in a racially discriminatory way or has a DISPARATE IMPACT on blacks, but also because, fundamentally, as he wrote, " . . . the fatal constitutional infirmity of capital punishment is that it treats members of the human race as non-humans, as objects to be toyed with and discarded. It is indeed cruel and unusual." In the mid 1970s Justice Brennan's views almost prevailed, as the Court came within one vote of abolishing the death penalty.

President Eisenhower is said to have remarked that the appointments of Brennan and Chief Justice EARL WARREN were among the worst mistakes of his presidency. But Brennan and Warren were among the best friends blacks ever had on the Court, and they are historically among the handful of whites in the POWER ELITE who used their authority to passionately advance the cause of African-American FREEDOM and EQUALITY.

See also BAKKE V. REGENTS OF THE UNIVERSITY OF CALIFORNIA.

Further reading: Kim Issac Fisler, *A Justice for All: William J. Brennan, Jr., and the Decisions That Transformed America* (New York: Simon & Schuster, 1993).

Brooke, Edward (1919–) *U.S. senator*

Edward Brooke was the first African American elected to the Senate by the vote of the people rather than a state legislature, becoming the first black senator since BLANCHE K. BRUCE was denied reelection by the Mississippi Legislature in 1880. Elected in 1966 from Massachusetts, Brooke served three terms before being defeated in 1984. Although a member of the REPUBLICAN PARTY, Brooke identified with the IDEOLOGY of contemporary LIBERALISM and, unlike CAROL MOSELEY-BRAUN, used his status as the Senate's only black member to forcefully articulate the interests of blacks although they constituted less than 3 percent of Massachusetts's population. Brooke played an important role in passage of the HUMPHREY-HAWKINS ACT and was a strong supporter of BUSING for purposes of school DESEGREGATION. Although Brooke had supported busing since his election, when the courts ordered Boston's

(the state's capital and largest city) schools to use busing to desegregate its schools, a WHITE BACKLASH developed, which contributed in part to his defeat in the next election.

Brotherhood of Sleeping Car Porters

The Brotherhood of Sleeping Car Porters was the first black union to be granted a charter by the American Federation of Labor (AFL), and for a time it was the most influential black trade union in the United States. During the 1930s and 1940s, it was one of the most important ORGANIZATIONS in AFRICAN-AMERICAN POLITICS.

The group was founded in 1925 and led until the 1960s by A. PHILIP RANDOLPH, the African-American journalist and socialist agitator. Although founded in 1925, the brotherhood did not obtain AFL recognition until 1935, and the Pullman Company, which monopolized the employment of black railroad workers, refused to recognize the union until 1937.

Blacks in the railroad industry were, because of RACISM, denied access to skilled jobs—engineers, conductors, firemen—and relegated to the low-skill, low-paid positions of porters. However, even in these positions they were denied membership in the all-white railroad unions because of the AFL's acceptance of SEGREGATION. Thus, there was a need for the brotherhood as a racially separate union to improve wages and working conditions of black workers.

Although the porters were not well paid, the job was considered, relatively speaking, a good one (in part because of the tips and the value of the experience of travel), and many porters were well educated and highly respected. This status frequently made them leaders in the BLACK COMMUNITY. Under Randolph's leadership, the brotherhood also became involved in the broader CIVIL RIGHTS MOVEMENT, spearheading the first MARCH ON WASHINGTON MOVEMENT in the 1940s. At its peak in the late 1940s, the organization had more than 100 locals and 1,000 members.

Further reading: William Harris, *Keeping the Faith: A. Philip Randolph, Milton P. Webster and the Brotherhood of Sleeping Car Porters* (Urbana: University of Illinois Press, 1977).

Brown, John (1800–1859) *abolitionist*

John Brown was a white activist in the ABOLITIONIST MOVEMENT whose opposition to SLAVERY was so deep, profound, and passionate that he turned to VIOLENCE in an attempted insurrection as the only means to end it and bring FREEDOM to the slaves. The abolitionist movement, as led by WILLIAM LLOYD GARRISON and FREDERICK DOUGLASS, generally opposed the use of violence as either morally wrong or strategically unwise. Brown, although not a major abolitionist leader, for a time accepted this tenet of the movement, but eventually he despaired and became convinced that it was the will of God that violence be used to purge the nation of the evil and sin that was slavery. Like many of the African Americans who led SLAVE REVOLTS, Brown was a deeply religious man. Thus religion constituted in his mind a base of power in the struggle to free the slaves.

Brown's plan involved seizing enough arms and ammunition from the government so as to permit the slaves to wage guerrilla war and, hopefully, eventually establish an independent, free state. He consulted Frederick Douglass and other abolitionist leaders, but they declined to join in his plan because, as Douglass told Brown, there was little chance for success. Douglass was correct. In October 1859 Brown and 18 other men—13 white, five black—attacked the federal arsenal at Harpers Ferry, Virginia. They were suppressed. Ten were killed, five escaped, and Brown and two of the blacks (John Copeland and Shields Green) were captured, tried, and hanged. The day of their executions was declared "martyrs' day" by black leaders, and black businesses were closed and black churches held memorial services. Copeland, one of the blacks hanged with Brown, on his way to the gallows said, "If I am dying for freedom, I could not die for a better cause. I had rather die than be a slave."

Brown's insurrection was, as Douglass told him, almost certainly doomed to fail given the government's disproportionate power in the form of violence. Nevertheless, Brown's raid was politically significant because it gave a sense of urgency and MILITANCY to the abolitionist movement, and it intensified and further polarized the sectional debate between North and South contributing to the sense of crisis that would result in the CIVIL WAR.

Further reading: Stephen Oates, *To Purge This Land with Blood: A Biography of John Brown* (Amherst: University of Massachusetts Press, 1984).

Brown, Ronald H. (1941–1996) *U.S. politician*

In 1989 Ronald Brown was elected chairman of the Democratic National Committee (DNC), becoming the first African American to head one of the two major political parties in the United States. The national committees of the Republican and Democratic Parties are constituted by representatives of the major groups and interests within the parties' COALITIONS. The committees are made up of 200 to 300 persons who are responsible for party policies in the interim between the conventions held every four years. The chairmen, elected by the committees, are responsible for managing the day-to-day operations of the parties as well as fund-raising, maintaining solidarity between the various factions within the coalition, and planning and coordinating congressional and presidential campaigns. The chair also serves as a chief spokesman for the party.

Both major parties are coalitions constituted by diverse groups, but the Democratic Party coalition is much more diverse than the Republican coalition. Thus, to lead it requires considerable bureaucratic and diplomatic skills. Ronald Brown is credited with bringing these skills to the post and helping in 1992 to elect BILL CLINTON as the first Democratic president in 12 years.

Brown was raised in HARLEM, where his father managed the famous Theresa Hotel, where many celebrities, black and white, often stayed or visited. Thus, throughout his adolescence, he often met and mingled with the elites of America, both black and white. This plus his education at elite, predominantly white prep schools and Middlebury College may have helped him as chair to bridge the racial divisions present within the party at the time of his election.

After graduating with a degree in political science in 1962, Brown served in the army (attaining the rank of captain) and in 1970 received a law degree from St. John's University. He then joined the staff of the URBAN LEAGUE, becoming the chief Washington lobbyist in 1973. It was this LOBBYING experience that brought Brown to the attention of Democratic Party elites in Washington. In 1980 Brown served as deputy campaign manager in the unsuccessful PRESIDENTIAL CAMPAIGN of Senator EDWARD M. KENNEDY. After Kennedy's defeat, he appointed Brown as chief counsel to the Senate Judiciary Committee (which Kennedy chaired), and later he became general counsel and staff director in the senator's office. Both of these appointments were firsts for African Americans. Brown then was appointed deputy chairman of the DNC, resigning in 1985 to become a partner in a prestigious Washington law firm. In 1988 he returned to national politics as a top aide in JESSE JACKSON's 1988 presidential campaign. Following Jackson's defeat, Brown was elected party chair in 1989.

Brown's candidacy was initially opposed by Southern conservative and Jewish factions in the party. (Southern conservatives opposed Brown because of his presumed LIBERALISM, and Jews disliked him because of his association with Jesse Jackson, who had allegedly made anti-Semitic comments during his 1984 presidential campaign.) Although clearly identified with the party's liberal faction, Brown promised that if elected he would be a conciliator and bring the various factions—racial, regional, ethnic, and ideological—together. With the overwhelming support of the committee's blacks (about one-third of the total membership), Brown was elected. In his speech accepting the chair, Brown said, "I did not run on the basis of my race, but I will not run away from it. I am proud of who I am . . . but the story of my chairmanship will not be about race. It will be about the races we win . . ." Clinton's 1992 election as a moderate, centrist Democrat is in part credited to Brown's leadership skills in persuading liberals to support Clinton in spite of his ideological moderation. In some ways, Brown's race and IDEOLOGY gave him the credibility to effectively help Clinton move the party in a more moderate direction without encountering opposition from blacks and liberals.

Clinton rewarded Brown by appointing him secretary of commerce, the first African American to hold this position in the cabinet. In April 1996 Brown was killed when a U.S. Air Force plane carrying him and other government officials and businesspeople on an official trade mission crashed into a mountain in Croatia.

Brown v. Board of Education of Topeka, Kansas
(1954)

Brown v. Board of Education of Topeka, Kansas is the most important CIVIL RIGHTS decision ever rendered by the SUPREME COURT and, along with the EMANCIPATION PROCLAMATION, the FOURTEENTH AMENDMENT, and the CIVIL RIGHTS ACT OF 1964, is one of the most important decisions by any of the three branches of the government of the United States in support of African-American FREEDOM and EQUALITY. *Brown's* significance is not in ending school SEGREGATION (it initially accomplished rather little of that) but, rather, its significance was its symbolism. The unanimous decision of the Court in 1954, overturning the principle of SEPARATE BUT EQUAL that it had promulgated in *PLESSY V. FERGUSON*, was a symbolic repudiation of RACISM and WHITE SUPREMACY. The Court in *Brown* declared segregation in schools a violation of the CONSTITUTION's principle of EQUALITY, and since CONSTITUTIONALISM is one of the core values of the POLITICAL SYSTEM, the Court in effect symbolically said that racism and white supremacy were "un-American."

Brown was the culmination of a strategy shift that began within the NAACP and the CIVIL RIGHTS MOVEMENT in the 1930s. From their inception in the 1900s, both the NAACP and the movement had relied on LOBBYING to pursue their objectives, but this strategy proved less than effective (see DYER ANTILYNCHING BILL). The NAACP therefore decided to shift its emphasis toward a strategy of LITIGATION. That is, rather than lobbying to get favorable laws passed by CONGRESS, the movement would seek favorable opinions from the Supreme Court. Litigation requires fewer resources than lobbying, and because of the importance of constitutionalism in the political system, favorable opinions by the Supreme Court might shape a more favorable climate of PUBLIC OPINION. In the long run, this then might make the strategy of lobbying more effective.

Not only was *Brown* the culmination of a strategy shift from lobbying to litigation, it was also the culmination of a series of cases brought by the NAACP attacking the *Plessy* doctrine of separate-but-equal educational opportunities for blacks and whites. WALTER WHITE was the NAACP's chief lobbyist, and THURGOOD MARSHALL, one of the greatest black leaders of all time, was the NAACP's chief litigator. Initially, Marshall and his colleagues focused on the "equal" rather than "separate" part of the *Plessy* doctrine, and on segregation in higher education rather than elementary and secondary education.

From the outset of the application of *Plessy* to education, the races were always separate but hardly ever equal, with spending on the education of whites many times greater than for blacks (see CUMMINGS V. BOARD OF EDUCATION). Thus, the NAACP would argue to the Court that it simply wished to have the Constitution obeyed. In other words, it would argue for equality but not INTEGRATION. Marshall and his colleagues also reasoned that while it would be more difficult and costly for the states to pay for equality in higher education, they might more readily integrate colleges and universities since white PUBLIC OPINION was thought to be less hostile to young adults going to school together than young children. This legal and political reasoning suggested an attack first at the level of graduate and professional education.

Knowledge was an important base of power in Marshall's work leading to *Brown*. Compared with lobbying, litigation requires fewer resources in terms of money (relatively speaking, that is, since the series of cases consolidated as *Brown* probably cost more than $100,000—no small amount for the NAACP at that time—and this figure does not include the free legal and research skills provided). Litigation requires mainly knowledge in the form of skilled legal talent systematically organized. In the 1930s CHARLES HAMILTON HOUSTON, dean of the HOWARD UNIVERSITY Law School and Marshall's teacher and mentor, transformed the institution into a civil rights training school and clearinghouse. The result was the training of a cadre of lawyers (including Marshall) committed to using knowledge of the Constitution in the cause of civil rights. With the formation of the NAACP LEGAL DEFENSE FUND as a separate organization headed by Marshall, this knowledge was mobilized in a systematic strategy to end racism in education.

The NAACP's attack on unequal educational opportunities at the graduate and professional levels had its first success in 1938 when, in *Missouri ex rel. Gaines v. Canada*, the Supreme Court invalidated Missouri's policy of excluding blacks from its law school and instead offering to pay for their attendance at out-of-state law schools. A year later in *Sweatt v. Painter* (1939), the Court found Texas's all-black law school was "inherently inferior" to its school for whites and ordered admission of blacks to the white school. And in

Newspaper headline announcing that the U.S. Supreme Court has abolished segregation in public schools *(Schomburg Center for Research in Black Culture)*

McLaurin v. Oklahoma State Regents (1950), the Court ruled that the state university's policy of segregating black students once admitted to its graduate school was unconstitutional. After these successes at the graduate level, the NAACP decided it was time to launch a direct attack on the doctrine of "separate but equal" by bringing a series of cases to the Court involving elementary and secondary schools. The result was *Brown.*

Brown was a consolidated opinion involving cases from Topeka, Kansas, three other states, and the DISTRICT OF COLUMBIA. The opinion for the unanimous Court was written by Chief Justice EARL WARREN. From the beginning of the cases, Warren had lobbied his colleagues for a unanimous opinion, which he would write, because he thought the legitimacy and acceptance of the decision would be greater if the Court spoke with one voice. *Brown* declared that the policy of separate but equal in elementary and secondary education was a violation of the EQUAL PROTECTION CLAUSE of the Fourteenth Amendment because, Warren wrote, even if spending and facilities were equal "separate educational facilities are inherently unequal."

(Because the District of Columbia is not covered by the equal protection clause, which applies only to the states, segregated schools there were declared a violation of the Fifth Amendment's DUE PROCESS CLAUSE.)

Two aspects of Warren's reasoning in the opinion require discussion because one was controversial at the time, and the other subsequently became controversial. The controversy involved Warren's assertion that racial segregation at the time of *Plessy* was based on the idea of black inferiority or white supremacy. In discussions with the other justices, Warren had insisted that segregation could only be justified on the basis of white supremacy, and he stated in the opinion that the idea of black inferiority was no longer supported by scientific knowledge: according to "modern authority . . . any language in *Plessy v. Ferguson* contrary to this finding is rejected." After this sentence, Warren added footnote 11, in which he cited the works of several social scientists including, among others, KENNETH CLARK and GUNNAR MYRDAL. This reasoning and footnote 11 immediately led critics, even many sympathetic to the decision, to label it a social science rather than a legal opinion. An example of this kind of criticism appeared the day after the decision was announced in a column in the *New York Times* by James Reston, one of the paper's most influential commentators. Titled "A Sociological Decision," the article contended that Warren's opinion was based more on sociology than constitutional law and legal precedent and that it "read more like an expert paper on sociology than a Supreme Court opinion." This kind of criticism of *Brown* was made frequently by constitutional scholars in the years following the opinion. However, as social-science knowledge was more frequently used in Court decisions on issues other than race, this kind of criticism gradually disappeared.

The second aspect of the opinion that is controversial is related also to Warren's use of social-science knowledge and footnote 1. In addition to declaring that segregation was premised on white supremacy, Warren also concluded that legally or officially sanctioned segregated schools resulted in INTERNAL INFERIORIZATION in black school children. Specifically, Warren wrote:

> Segregation of white and colored children in public schools has a detrimental effect upon the colored children. The impact is greater when it has the sanction of law; for the policy of separating the races is usually interpreted as denoting the inferiority of the Negro group. A sense of inferiority affects the motivation of the child to learn. Segregation with the sanction of law, therefore, had a tendency to [retard] the educational and mental development of Negro children and to deprive them of the benefits they would receive in a racially integrated school system.

This conclusion was based on the famous doll experiments conducted by Kenneth Clark and presented to the Court by the NAACP in its arguments. In subsequent years the scientific basis for Clark's conclusions were questioned, as well as the unstated premise that blacks could only receive an equal education in racially integrated environments.

Usually when the Supreme Court finds that the constitutionally protected rights of an individual have been violated, it will order the violation to cease "at once." However, in this case the Court did not do this. Instead, in what is called "*Brown II*" (*Brown v. Board of Education*) decided one year later, the Court said that states practicing racial segregation in schools need not stop at once or immediately but rather could do so slowly or with "all deliberate speed," to repeat the phrase Warren used in *Brown II*. The Court adopted this go-slow approach over the objections of the NAACP because Warren and his colleagues feared that an order for immediate DESEGREGATION of the schools would result in widespread resistance and VIOLENCE by Southern whites. The Court was correct, but so was the

NAACP, which argued for immediate desegregation. Despite the Court's effort to give the states time to adjust to and accept its decision, Southern whites and STATE AND LOCAL GOVERNMENTS nevertheless resisted, sometimes violently, requiring Presidents Eisenhower and Kennedy to use the army to enforce orders to desegregate schools in Little Rock, Arkansas, in 1957 and Oxford, Mississippi, in 1961.

The Court did not order the immediate desegregation of the schools until 14 years after *Brown II*, when in *Green v. New Kent County* (1968), Justice WILLIAM BRENNAN, writing for a unanimous Court, declared that school boards had an "affirmative duty" to eliminate segregated schools "root and branch . . . Now!"

While *Brown* did not lead to the dismantling of the separate and unequal schools for blacks and whites, it was the symbolic beginning of the process of ending legalized racism and segregation in the United States. The process was completed by the CONGRESS when it enacted the Civil Rights laws of the 1960s. But Warren and his colleagues did not wait for the Congress to act. Rather, they used *Brown* as a precedent to strike down segregation in public buildings, housing, transportation, and recreational facilities. In these areas, the Court merely cited *Brown* in a series of per curiam opinions (brief, unsigned opinions usually used by the Court when the issues raised in a case are clear and uncomplicated) to make the point categorically. As the Court put it in 1963, "It is no longer open to question that a state may not constitutionally require segregation of public facilities."

Further reading: Richard Kluger, *Simple Justice: The History of Brown v. Board of Education and Black America's Struggle for Equality* (New York: Vintage Books, 1975); Mark Tushnet, *The NAACP's Legal Strategy against Segregated Education, 1925–50* (Chapel Hill: University of North Carolina Press, 1987).

Bruce, Blanche K. (1841–1898) *U.S. senator*
Blanche K. Bruce was born in SLAVERY but escaped to FREEDOM in Kansas. Although he attended Oberlin College briefly, he was largely self-educated. After the CIVIL WAR, he settled in Mississippi and quickly rose to prominence as a businessman and politician, winning local elections as sheriff and tax collector. In 1874 he was elected by the Mississippi State Legislature to the Senate, where he served until 1880. A member of the REPUBLICAN PARTY, Bruce used his status as the Senate's only black to focus on CIVIL RIGHTS and other issues related to race, including efforts to integrate the BUREAUCRACY and prevent passage of the Chinese Exclusion Act of 1878. After the legislature refused to reelect him (it had been taken over by white

supremacists after the end of RECONSTRUCTION), he was appointed by President James Garfield to the office of registrar of the Treasury Department.

Bunche, Ralph (1904–1971) *scholar, diplomat*

Ralph Bunche was the first African American to receive a Ph.D. in political science from Harvard, the first head of the political science department at HOWARD UNIVERSITY, the first African-American president of the AMERICAN POLITICAL SCIENCE ASSOCIATION, and the first African American to win a Nobel Prize. Bunche was awarded the Nobel Peace Prize in 1950 for his negotiation of the first peace agreement between Israel and the Arab peoples in the Middle East. In 1955 he was appointed undersecretary-general of the UNITED NATIONS, which made him the highest-ranking American in the organization. His diplomatic skills at the United Nations were legendary, as he led peacemaking efforts in 1956 in the Suez area of the Middle East, the Congo in 1960, and Cyprus in 1964. One of the most prominent African Americans during the civil rights era, Bunche's

Ralph J. Bunche *(Library of Congress)*

status was unique in that, unlike other black leaders, it did not derive from his leadership on race issues.

Early in his career, however, Bunche played a major leadership role in the use of knowledge in black politics. His award-winning doctoral dissertation on COLONIALISM in West Africa led to his becoming head of the U.S. State Department's division dealing with colonial problems. From this post, he played a part in planning the organization of the United Nations Trusteeship Council, dealing with problems of colonialism. At Howard University he was instrumental in establishing the first political science department at a historically black college or university and the training of a first generation of black political scientists. He wrote long and detailed monographs on black politics for GUNNAR MYRDAL's project, parts of which were incorporated into *AN AMERICAN DILEMMA* and parts of which were published as articles in the *Journal of Negro Education.* In his early writings, Bunche embraced RADICALISM and SOCIALISM, urging black leaders to recognize that there was both a class and a race problem in America that required not just race solidarity but also a COALITION with the white working class. Finally, Bunche played an important role in the organization of the NATIONAL NEGRO CONGRESS, which for a time during the 1930s tried to implement his ideas about race and class solidarity.

During the height of the CIVIL RIGHTS MOVEMENT Bunche, while not actively involved, used his enormous status to speak out against RACISM and DISCRIMINATION. He participated in several PROTEST marches led by MARTIN LUTHER KING JR., and for more than 20 years until his death, he was a member of the NAACP's executive board. Near the end of his life, although ill and nearly blind, Bunche authored several important articles analyzing the WATTS RIOT and the BLACK POWER MOVEMENT. Although initially he attacked black power and BLACKNESS—what he described as "blackism"—as a racist and escapist philosophy, shortly before he died he changed his mind and partly embraced blackness and black power, linking them to the work he inspired at the 1930s National Negro Congress.

Further reading: Charles Henry, ed., *Ralph J. Bunche: Selected Speeches and Writings* (Ann Arbor: University of Michigan Press, 1995); Charles Henry, *Ralph Bunche: Model Negro or American Other* (New York: New York University Press, 1999).

bureaucracy

The bureaucracy is formally a part of the executive branch of the government of the United States, operating under the authority of presidents, governors, mayors, or other chief executives. However, because of its size, autonomy, and the complexity of issues in modern societies, it is also useful to think of the bureaucracy as a kind of fourth branch of government, along with the legislative, executive, and judicial.

The bureaucracy involves the exercise of power on the basis of knowledge organized rationally and hierarchically. The bureaucracy, in other words, is a system of bureaus and agencies that implement the PUBLIC POLICY of a government on a day-to-day basis using specialized knowledge, standardized procedures, and a specialization of duties and responsibilities. In addition to its central role in the implementation of policy, the bureaucracy is also involved in policy initiation and development. Thus, it frames government decisions at the beginning of the public-policy process, and at the end of the process it carries out those decisions. Therefore, if a group such as African Americans is to influence the development of government policies that serve its interests, participation in the bureaucracy is required, either in the overall bureaucracy or in the bureaus and agencies with the specific missions or purposes of serving or protecting those interests. For much of the history of the bureaucracy in the United States at both the federal level and in STATE AND LOCAL GOVERNMENTS, black participation has been limited.

Until RECONSTRUCTION, African Americans were totally excluded from the federal bureaucracy. During Reconstruction blacks were for a time appointed by presidents to minor posts in the bureaucracy, and in 1865 the CONGRESS created for the first time an agency in the bureaucracy, the FREEDMEN'S BUREAU, with the specific mission of serving and protecting the interests of African Americans. The end of Reconstruction for the most part brought an end to black participation in the bureaucracy, as relatively few blacks received presidential appointments and the Freedmen's Bureau was abolished.

The federal bureaucracy was fundamentally changed in 1883 when Congress passed the Civil Service Reform Act (often called the Pendleton Act). This act created a civil service system under which government employees are chosen on the basis of knowledge determined by merit examination. After qualifying and serving a probationary period, employees are then granted permanent tenure. Prior to the civil service system, federal employees were hired and fired on the basis of their loyalty and support of the president and his party. This system of patronage led to corruption and the hiring of people without knowledge in their areas of responsibilities. It also permitted widespread DISCRIMINATION on the basis of race. Thus, the new civil service system for the selection of most employees in the bureaucracy (initially the system covered only 10 percent of employees, but over the years it grew to cover virtually the entire bureaucracy) had the potential to create a more knowledgeable and less racially discriminatory system. For a time it did.

When the Pendleton Act was passed there were only 620 blacks in the federal bureaucracy. By 1893, as a result of the merit system, this number had increased 2,393. However, as black participation grew, the opposition of racists and white supremacists increased, and they pressured the Civil Service Commission to find ways to exclude African Americans from the bureaucracy. In 1914 during the presidency of WOODROW WILSON, the commission made photographs mandatory, which became an easy means to identify and exclude blacks who had qualified on the basis of examinations. The result of this kind of discrimination was a decline in the black presence in the bureaucracy. Moreover, President Wilson imposed JIM CROW–style SEGREGATION, forbidding blacks and whites from working in integrated settings, prohibiting blacks from supervising whites, and requiring separate toilets and eating facilities.

Although the percentage of blacks in the bureaucracy grew steadily after 1914 (approaching 10 percent by the 1940s), as a result of the discriminatory policies of the Wilson administration they were mainly employed in janitorial, clerical, and other lower-level positions. And they worked in segregated environments. Although a handful of blacks served in advisory positions in FRANKLIN D. ROOSEVELT's so-called BLACK CABINET, this situation did not change significantly until the presidencies of JOHN F. KENNEDY and LYNDON B. JOHNSON, who began to insist on nondiscrimination in federal employment. The CIVIL RIGHTS ACT OF 1964 banned discrimination in federal employment, and subsequently most federal agencies and bureaus adopted AFFIRMATIVE ACTION policies and programs to assure equal employment. As a result, the percentage of black civil servants had increased to more than 17 percent of the workforce by 2000. However, there is still a tendency to find blacks in lower- rather than senior-level positions. And blacks are underrepresented among officers in the MILITARY bureaucracy and in the State Department's FOREIGN POLICY bureaucracy. (In 2000 fewer than 3 percent of foreign service officers were black.)

The federal bureaucracy is a complex structure, which begins at the White House with its staff and bureaucracy and includes the executive office of the president (which includes presidential agencies like the Office of Management and Budget, the Council of Economic Advisors, and the so-called Drug Czar), the 14 cabinet departments, dozens of independent agencies without cabinet rank, and a number of independent regulatory commissions and boards. Nearly 2 million persons are employed in this complex structure (excluding uniformed military personnel and postal workers). The vast majority of these 2 million persons are civil servants, since a president has the authority to appoint only about 5,000 senior-level executives.

Since the Kennedy administration, most presidents have appointed at least a few blacks to some of these 5,000 positions, and Democratic presidents JIMMY CARTER and BILL CLINTON have appointed relatively large numbers as part of the "patronage" process in presidential politics that requires the distribution of important jobs on the basis, in part, of a group's contribution to the party's winning COALITION. The effectiveness of these high-level black appointees in representing black interests has varied depending on how they identified with and defined those interests, on the IDEOLOGY of the presidents who appointed them, and on their proximity and relationship to the president. In addition, whatever their inclinations, the bureaucratic process has its own constraints or imperatives that limit the extent to which any bureaucrat can represent the interests of any group.

Since the abolition of the Freedmen's Bureau in the 1880s, the Congress has created several agencies with specific race or civil rights missions, including the CIVIL RIGHTS DIVISION of the JUSTICE DEPARTMENT, the CIVIL RIGHTS COMMISSION, the EQUAL EMPLOYMENT OPPORTUNITY COMMISSION, and the OFFICE OF FEDERAL CONTRACT COMPLIANCE. Also, within each cabinet department and the independent agencies and commissions, there is usually an Office of Civil Rights with responsibilities for assuring equal employment within the agency and making certain that its programs are implemented on a nondiscriminatory basis.

Further reading: Desmond King, *Separate and Unequal: Black Americans and the U.S. Federal Government* (London: Oxford University Press, 1995); Samuel Krislov, *The Negro in Federal Employment: The Quest for Equal Opportunity* (Minneapolis: University of Minnesota Press, 1967); Robert C. Smith, "Black Appointed Officials: A Neglected Category of Political Participation Research," *Journal of Black Studies* 14 (1984): 369–88; Robert C. Smith, *We Have No Leaders: African Americans in the Post Civil Rights Era* (Albany: State University of New York Press, 1996), Chaps. 4–5; Hanes Walton, *When the Marching Stopped: The Politics of Civil Rights Regulatory Agencies* (Albany: State University of New York Press, 1988).

busing

The transportation of school children by buses for purposes of ending SEGREGATION in elementary and secondary schools or to implement the requirements of *BROWN V. BOARD OF EDUCATION* was one of the most controversial POST–CIVIL RIGHTS ERA issues of PUBLIC POLICY. Until it was effectively stopped by the SUPREME COURT in a series of cases beginning with *MILLIKEN V. BRADLEY* in 1974, white PUBLIC OPINION was overwhelmingly opposed to busing, and black public opinion was divided and ambivalent. The issue of busing was an important factor in the manifestation of the WHITE BACKLASH in the late 1960s and 1970s, help-

ing to build support among whites for the racially conservative presidential campaigns of GEORGE WALLACE, RICHARD NIXON, and RONALD REAGAN. The CONGRESS, in a direct attack on CONSTITUTIONALISM, almost passed legislation that would have taken away the authority of the courts to use busing as a means of protecting the constitutional rights of black school children. And throughout the "great school bus controversy," the evidence was never clear that busing did very much to improve the educational performance of black school children.

Busing has its origins in a decision by a unanimous Supreme Court in 1971 that required the Charlotte-Mecklenburg, North Carolina, school district to adopt a plan to bus black and white kids so that a rough racial balance would exist in each of the district's schools (see *SWANN V. CHARLOTTE-MECKLENBURG*). Although the Court said the CONSTITUTION did not require that there be a racial balance in every school, it did say that pupils of all grades should be assigned in such a way that, as nearly as practicable, the various schools at various grade levels would have about the same proportion of black and white kids. The purpose of this QUOTA system, the Court said, was to eliminate "root and branch" all vestiges of segregation in the district so that there would be neither black nor white schools, just schools. The Court's rationale for using busing was not to achieve INTEGRATION but rather to end unconstitutional dual school systems immediately—"at once"—and to require thereafter only unitary systems. However, many supporters and critics of *Swann* viewed the Court's ruling as standing for the proposition that the EQUAL PROTECTION CLAUSE required integrated rather than merely desegregated schools.

This view of the Court's interpretation of the Constitution was reinforced three years later in the case of *KEYES V. DENVER SCHOOL DISTRICT NO. 1* (1973), the first decision of the Court dealing with school segregation in the NORTHERN STATES. In this case, the Court held that although the Denver, Colorado, district had never maintained de jure or legal segregation, it had for years practiced de facto segregation by deliberately creating racially separate and unequal schools through a strategy of locating schools and drawing boundary lines in such a way as to place most blacks in separate schools and then providing those schools with fewer resources. Based on this finding, the Court ordered, as it had in *Swann,* that Denver bus black and white students to achieve a racial balance or quota in all its schools. The principles of the *Keyes* case were soon applied to school districts throughout the country, leading to a huge political controversy and eventually a decision by the Court to reverse its position and begin slowly to put an end to busing for purposes of school desegregation.

Busing was overwhelmingly opposed by whites (in the range of 75 to 80 percent), and polls showed that it enjoyed no more than 50 percent support among blacks. In many cities busing led to mass PROTEST by whites, boycotts, VIOLENCE, and WHITE FLIGHT to private or suburban schools. REPUBLICAN PARTY presidential candidates made busing a major issue in their campaigns, and members of Congress, liberal and conservative, North and South, began to introduce legislation to prohibit the Courts from ordering busing for purposes of school desegregation. Presidents RICHARD NIXON and Gerald Ford proposed similar legislation, and in 1974 the House overwhelmingly passed such a bill. In addition to prohibiting any future court-ordered busing (beyond the school's nearest or next nearest to the student's home), the House legislation also required the courts to reopen all existing cases that did not comply with this prohibition. The Senate in a narrow vote (47 to 46) rejected the House bill but adopted a resolution that in effect suggested to the courts that busing should be limited to cases where it was the only means available to guarantee black children their constitutional rights to an equal, nonsegregated education.

Several weeks after the Senate vote, the Supreme Court in *Milliken v. Bradley* (1974) appeared to take the Senate's suggestion, setting in motion a series of cases that ultimately resulted in the virtual end of busing. In *Milliken v. Bradley* the Court overturned a lower-court order that required busing between largely black Detroit and its surrounding largely white suburbs. The Court majority agreed that Detroit-area schools were unconstitutionally segregated but concluded that cross-district busing between city and suburb was not required to comply with the principles of *Brown.* In an angry dissenting opinion, Justice THURGOOD MARSHALL accused his colleagues of bowing to political pressure and of being unwilling to enforce the constitutional rights of black school children because busing was unpopular with the white majority. After the *Milliken* decision, a pattern was established in which lower courts declined to order cross-district busing and eventually began to dismantle busing within districts. Symbolically, busing's end can be seen in the Court's reversal of its busing orders in *Keyes* and *Swann.*

In 1995 a federal judge in Denver allowed the school district to abandon its 20-year busing program, even though the schools were more segregated than when the *Keyes* decision had been handed down in 1973. And in 2001 the 4th Circuit Court of Appeals ordered the Charlotte-Mecklenburg district to abandon its 30-year-old busing program. The Court concluded that while segregation was likely to increase when busing was discontinued, it was no longer constitutionally required because "all the vestiges of past discrimination" had been eradicated since *Swann.*

Urban school systems cannot be desegregated on the basis of busing within cities because of white flight to the suburbs or to private schools. And within-city busing tends to accelerate white flight. For example, before busing began in Boston in 1971, 60 percent of the district's students were

Satirical cartoon showing President Richard Nixon as a bus driver *(Library of Congress)*

white, but 30 years later only 18 percent were white. In a sense, then, busing—instead of achieving integration in Boston and elsewhere—achieved the opposite result, since studies show that de facto segregation is more prevalent in the late 1990s than it was in the 1970s. The only remedy to this situation is cross-district busing between city and suburbs, but the Supreme Court contends that this remedy is not constitutionally required. Thus, a half century after *Brown v. Board of Education,* most African-American children still attend schools that are separate and unequal.

Throughout the busing controversy, most Americans, black and white, overwhelmingly agreed that it was more important to improve schools in black neighborhoods than to bus black kids to white neighborhoods. This was especially the view of African Americans who adhered to BLACK NATIONALISM or CULTURAL NATIONALISM. At the 1972 NATIONAL BLACK POLITICAL CONVENTION, these nationalist forces, over the objections of liberals and integrationists, forced the adoption of a resolution condemning "forced busing" as "bankrupt" because "it is based on the false notion that black children are unable to learn unless they are in the same setting as whites." Instead of busing, the resolution proposed "black community control of our school system and a guarantee of an equal share of money." Mainstream African-American CIVIL RIGHTS leaders led by KENNETH CLARK argued throughout the 1970s and later that a racially separate education could not be equal, and that if black children attended racially separate schools they would always be isolated and treated unequally. Thus EQUALITY in education required racially mixed schools.

Both sides in this debate appear to have been at least partially correct. Evidence from studies of the performance of black children bused to white schools shows that performance did not markedly improve. The evidence also indicates that blacks attending racially identifiable schools receive an education that is not only separate but unequal.

See also SCHOOLS AND EDUCATION.

Further reading: Nicolaus Mills, *The Great School Bus Controversy* (New York: Teachers College Press, 1973); Gary Orfield, *Must We Bus?: Segregation and National Policy* (Washington, D.C.: Brookings Institution, 1978); ———, *Dismantling Desegregation: The Quiet Reversal of Brown v. Board of Education* (New York: Norton, 1996).

C

capitalism

Capitalism along with DEMOCRACY and CONSTITUTIONAL-ISM is one of the three core values of the POLITICAL SYSTEM in the United States. Capitalism is also based on INDIVID-UALISM, a core value of the American culture, and capitalism in the United States has been widely accepted in theory and practice since the American Revolution. However, among African-American leaders and thinkers, there has always been a powerful anticapitalist IDEOLOGY, and important individuals have embraced various forms of RAD-ICALISM, SOCIALISM, and COMMUNISM as alternatives to capitalism's hegemony in the culture and political system. Contemporary black PUBLIC OPINION also shows, compared with white opinion, a greater inclination to support socialist programs and policies. African-American skepticism toward capitalism is related to two factors, the first historical, the second theoretical. Historically, the skepticism of blacks toward capitalism is because, for much of their history, they were, through the practice of RACISM and WHITE SUPREMACY, virtually excluded from participation in the workings of American capitalism. Indeed, as slaves African Americans *were* capital. Theoretically, many African-American intellectuals have argued that racial OPPRESSION is a function or by-product of capitalism. Thus, in this view, in order to end race oppression it is necessary to end or at least modify capitalism.

Capitalism is an economic system based on the private ownership of the means of production (land, mines, factories, etc.); the production of goods and services for profit; a market economy based on supply and demand; and the principle of laissez-faire. This principle rejects government control and regulation of the economy while emphasizing individual initiative, the market, and the "invisible hand" of natural economic laws to regulate the production and distribution of goods and services. In the 20th century, most capitalist systems became mixed economies in which governments may own some parts of the means of production and where there is some government intervention in

and regulation of the market, a relatively high rate of taxation, and a fairly extensive WELFARE STATE. The United States, however, is the purest or most laissez-faire capitalist system in the world. The government of the United States owns virtually none of the means of production. And compared with other capitalist countries, the government intervenes in and regulates the market less; taxes on income and wealth are less; and the United States has a less expansive and generous welfare state.

Black Capitalism

Although many important African-American intellectuals (W. E. B. DU BOIS, PAUL ROBESON, AMIRI BARAKA, and ANGELA DAVIS) and political leaders (A. PHILIP RANDOLPH, BAYARD RUSTIN, MARTIN LUTHER KING JR., and MALCOLM X) have embraced socialism or communism to some degree—and African-American public opinion tends to favor some socialist ideas—most blacks, leaders and ordinary persons, support the core values of capitalism, including individualism, private property, the market economy, and production for profit. That is, historically most blacks have not rejected capitalism; rather, they have rejected racist exclusion from participation in the system.

During SLAVERY, rather than being allowed to accumulate capital, most blacks *were* capital, constituting in their persons the property that was a major source of the wealth of the white Southern capitalist class. A few small-business enterprises were established by FREE NEGROES (usually service and craft enterprises) during slavery, and during RECONSTRUCTION these enterprises for a time expanded. But because of racism and POLITICAL REPRES-SION, very few blacks could accumulate the wealth necessary for investment. After Reconstruction, BOOKER T. WASHINGTON encouraged an economic version of BLACK NATIONALISM or SELF-HELP, which led to the establishment of black businesses, banks, and insurance companies to serve the needs of the increasingly segregated black consumer market. Generally, these were small "mom and pop" personal-service enterprises such as beauty and barber shops, restaurants, taverns, and mortuaries. After the GREAT MIGRATION to the NORTHERN STATES, the segregated GHETTOS led to the creation of a larger black consumer market, and these small enterprises expanded and others developed, such as hotels, stores, nightclubs, and newspaper and recording companies. Black entrepreneurs like Madam C. J. Walker (reportedly the first African-American female millionaire) also developed enterprises to cater to the special hair-care and cosmetic needs of blacks, and John Johnson created a number of magazines that met the needs of blacks for an alternative MEDIA in popular magazines. Finally, black nationalist organizations such as MARCUS GARVEY's UNIVERSAL NEGRO IMPROVEMENT ASSOCIATION and ELIJAH MUHAMMAD's NATION OF ISLAM established business enterprises. However, the lack of access to capital (loans from banks or other financial institutions) and the segregated, relatively impoverished ghetto market limited the development and expansion of these enterprises.

The POST–CIVIL RIGHTS ERA further handicapped the development of black business enterprises as INTEGRATION led to a decline of the segregated market for many black businesses, and white businesses began to compete for the black consumer dollar. Black hotels, restaurants, and nightclubs closed, and many successful black cosmetic and recording companies (including the highly successful Motown recording company) were purchased by large white corporations. In 1968 President RICHARD NIXON advocated "black capitalism" as a means of incorporating blacks into the economy, and subsequently AFFIRMATIVE ACTION "set-asides" were established to provide black businesses with preferential access to small-business loans and government contracts. These programs, however, soon came under attack, and many were abolished during the presidency of BILL CLINTON. However, even with these programs, black businesses remained marginal to American capitalism. According to *Black Enterprise* (the African-American business magazine established in 1970), in the late 1990s there were 800,000 black-owned businesses in the United States, and these firms generated about $71 billion in revenue and employed approximately 700,000 people. These 800,000 businesses only made up 4 percent of the more than 20 million nonfarm businesses in the nation and accounted for a mere 0.4 percent of the $18.6 trillion of all business revenues in the United States. Thus, most black-owned enterprises are small, with few employees and modest receipts. Blacks have experienced only modest success in gaining entry into mainstream, white-dominated corporate America. Very few blacks, for example, have served on *Fortune* magazine's top 1,000 corporate boards or as their chief executive officers. Also, the black petit bourgeosie is relatively small and has decreased in size during the post–civil rights era, as African Americans increasingly do not own the small "mom and pop" enterprises that serve black communities.

African Americans in general are not anticapitalist, but generally they have not been very numerous or effective capitalists. This lack of success is not because of their rejection of capitalism's theory and practice but, rather, because racism has largely excluded them from the nation's mainstream capital and consumer markets. A black capital market (where large sums of money can be borrowed) does not exist, and while the black consumer market (disposable income after taxes) is relatively large ($572 billion out of a U.S. total of $7.1 trillion), black businesses are not able to effectively compete with white ones in an economy that is nationally and globally integrated.

Black Wealth

Wealth is not only the base of capitalism, it is capital. And it is also an important base of power in the political system. African Americans have relatively little wealth or capital and, except for a handful of athletes and entertainers, relatively few means of obtaining wealth. And the wealth of the wealthiest athlete or entertainer pales into insignificance when compared with the wealth of the wealthiest entrepreneur. For example, Oprah Winfrey, the talk-show host, in the late 1990s was reportedly the wealthiest African American in the United States. Her wealth was estimated at $675 million, but the wealthiest American—the computer entrepreneur Bill Gates—had an estimated worth in excess of $60 billion. Strikingly, Gates's wealth alone is about five times the total wealth of the entire BLACK COMMUNITY.

The wealth gap between black and white Americans is larger than the gap in income. Median family income for blacks in the late 1990s was about $23,000 compared with $37,000 for whites, a significant gap, with black income only 62 percent of white income. However, the gap in wealth (the total value of all assets including homes, cars, stocks, bonds, and saving accounts) is much greater. According to a report by the Federal Reserve Board released in 1999, the median net wealth of white families was $94,900, compared with $16,400 for nonwhite families. (The Federal Reserve combines data for all nonwhite groups without calculating details for blacks separately.) Black wealth is based almost entirely on home ownership rather than stocks or bonds. In the late 1990s 48 percent of whites owned stocks that accounted for 21 percent of their wealth, while only 10.4 percent of blacks owned stocks that accounted for less than 10 percent of their wealth. For households earning more than $75,000 annually, 67 percent of blacks owned stock compared with 81 percent of whites. Land is also an important source of wealth. At the start of the 20th century, blacks owned more than 15 million acres of land in the SOUTHERN STATES. At the century's end they owned little more than 1 million acres. The decline of black ownership can be traced to a number of factors, including the great migration of blacks to the Northern States, which resulted in the sale of land to whites. But there was also widespread theft of black land by whites through the legal processes of STATE AND LOCAL GOVERNMENTs and through VIOLENCE and intimidation. (The KU KLUX KLAN would frequently attack black owners, and occasionally LYNCHING or the threat of lynching would be used to drive blacks off the land.)

Finally, wealth in the United States tends to be inherited. In 1994 a survey by the University of Michigan found that whites were three times more likely to have inherited wealth in the last five years than blacks. And of those families that had an inheritance, the average for whites was $74,000 compared with $33,000 for blacks. Home ownership is the main source for building wealth in the black community, but only 47 percent of blacks compared with 72 percent of whites owned homes, and the value or equity in the homes owned by blacks was much less than for whites.

Capitalism is a core value of the United States and, arguably, one of the foundations of the nation's enormous wealth. However, because blacks were for so long treated as capital and then thereafter denied access to the nation's capital and consumer markets, "black" capitalism is inconsequential. Capitalism is also the foundation for the lack of EQUALITY between black and white Americans. This foundation is deeply entrenched and self-perpetuating. Therefore, without a redistribution of wealth, African Americans will not likely ever achieve equality with whites in terms of capital and wealth.

See also ADARAND V. PENA, CROSON V. CITY OF RICHMOND, and REPARATIONS.

Further reading: John Sibley Bulter, *Entrepreneurship and Self-Help among Black Americans* (Albany: State University of New York Press, 1991); Theodore Cross, *Black Capitalism* (New York: Athenaeum, 1971); Melvin Oliver and Thomas Shapiro, *Black Wealth/White Wealth: A New Perspective on Racial Equality* (New York: Routledge, 1995).

Carmichael, Stokely (Kwame Turé) (1941–1998)
civil rights leader, black-power advocate, pan-Africanist, socialist

In his development and articulation of the symbol and concept of black power near the end of the CIVIL RIGHTS MOVEMENT in the 1960s, Stokely Carmichael redefined AFRICAN-AMERICAN POLITICS in the United States. As a result of his efforts from 1966 to 1969, African Americans became more conscious of their racial identity, developed a greater sense of group solidarity, and established the princi-

ple that blacks should lead and control their own ORGANIZATIONS. For a time, these developments signaled a shift toward MILITANCY and RADICALISM in African-American politics, but the long-term, enduring or structural consequences of Carmichael's articulation of black power was its impact on the INCORPORATION or CO-OPTATION of African Americans as an INTEREST GROUP into the POLITICAL SYSTEM.

Carmichael was born in Trinidad, a WEST INDIAN island, but he was raised in New York City, where he was graduated from the prestigious Bronx High School of Science. As a student at HOWARD UNIVERSITY, he became active in the Civil Rights movement, subsequently dropping out of college to become a full-time SNCC (STUDENT NONVIOLENT COORDINATING COMMITTEE) organizer in

Stokely Carmichael addressing an audience, 1966 *(Library of Congress)*

the rural South. In SNCC Carmichael became legendary for his skill in organizing poor blacks and for his daring and courage in confronting the often violent forces arrayed against the movement in the small, isolated towns and villages of Alabama and Mississippi. In 1966 he defeated JOHN LEWIS in election for SNCC chair, and shortly thereafter he used his new position to start the BLACK POWER MOVEMENT. As the Black Power movement gained popularity, it was increasingly accepted by the white POWER ELITE and the established black LEADERSHIP as an appropriate strategy for black incorporation into the political system. Viewing incorporation into the system as a form of co-optation that could not result in the "liberation" or FREEDOM of African Americans, Carmichael became increasingly militant and radical, joining briefly the BLACK PANTHER PARTY and then forming his own organization, the All African Peoples Revolutionary Party, based on the principles of SOCIALISM and PAN-AFRICANISM.

In 1968 Carmichael moved to Guinea, a West African nation, changed his name to Kwame Turé (after Kwame Nkrumah of Ghana and Sekou Toure of Guinea, two leading African statesmen and leaders of the movement against African COLONIALISM), and spent the remaining years of his life traveling between the United States and Africa as an advocate of Pan-Africanism and socialist revolution. His ultimate objective was a version of Pan-Africanism that would unite all the nations of Africa into a single, socialist country, which he believed was indispensable to the freedom of Africans in America and throughout the world. He died in 1998 of prostate cancer (which he alleged he had been infected with by American intelligence agencies) and was buried outside Conakry, the capital of Guinea. In the last decades of his life Carmichael was not an important force in African-American politics, but in his second decade he helped to transform it.

See also BLACK, BLACKNESS, *BLACK POWER: THE POLITICS OF LIBERATION*.

Further reading: "Kwame Ture/Stokely Carmichael: A Tribute to a Life of Struggle," *The Black Scholar* Special Memorial Issue 27 (Fall/Winter 1998).

Carter, Jimmy   *39th president of the United States*

Jimmy Carter, the 39th president of the United States, was the first DEMOCRATIC PARTY president of the POST–CIVIL RIGHTS ERA. Elected in 1976 after one term as governor of Georgia, Carter was an unexpected choice. But his nomination by the Democratic Party reflected the party's gradual shift from traditional NEW DEAL–GREAT SOCIETY-style LIBERALISM, toward a more moderate, centrist IDEOLOGY. After the overwhelming defeat of the liberal George McGovern, the Democratic Party nominee in 1972, many

party leaders came to the conclusion that a liberal could not win the presidency because liberals had become identified with the WELFARE STATE and "special" INTEREST GROUPS such as African Americans. Thus Carter became the first of a series of Democratic nominees for president in the post–civil rights era to run as a nontraditional, moderate "new Democrat." Although African Americans, leaders and voters, tend to be disproportionately liberal and supporters of the welfare state, they were strong supporters of Carter in his quest for the nomination and in his close race with Gerald Ford in the general election.

As president, Carter appointed a large number of blacks to the BUREAUCRACY and the federal courts, but his rather conservative PUBLIC POLICY initiatives on the budget, welfare, urban policy, and the HUMPHREY-HAWKINS ACT created conflict with the CONGRESSIONAL BLACK CAUCUS and other African-American leaders. Carter's tepid support of the Humphrey-Hawkins Act—legislation designed to create a full-employment economy—was a particular source of strain between black leaders and the president. Thus, as the president's first term came to an end, his level of support among black voters had fallen to the same low level as it had among whites. However, unlike whites, most blacks continued to support the president, giving him near 90 percent of their vote in his unsuccessful race against the conservative RONALD REAGAN in 1980. The election and PRESIDENCY of Jimmy Carter represented a shift of the Democratic Party away from liberalism and, therefore, away from the interests of blacks who constitute the most liberal constituency in the party's COALITION. Nevertheless, black leaders and voters continued to support Carter and the Democrats because the conservative REPUBLICAN PARTY was not a viable alternative. Thus, the logic of the TWO-PARTY SYSTEM denied African Americans an effective choice in the 1980 election. Carter's presidency thus established the basic structure for the relationship between the Democratic Party and black voters in post–civil rights era presidential elections, a structure in which one party (the Democratic) can take black voters for granted and the other (the Republican) can ignore them.

See also BILL CLINTON and THIRD PARTIES.

Census, U.S.

The CONSTITUTION (Article I, Section 2) requires that a census, enumeration, or counting of the POPULATION of the United States occur every 10 years. The principal constitutional purpose of the census is to "reapportion" or redistribute the seats in the House of Representatives among the states on the basis of population changes. In addition to this constitutional purpose, the census collects a vast amount of information about virtually every relevant characteristic of the population; thus it provides the most comprehensive and accurate statistical data on the population. These data are then used to allocate various government benefits, such as assistance to poor people or areas. Thus the decennial census is an important tool of PUBLIC POL-ICY because it is used to allocate POWER in the POLITICAL SYSTEM (seats in the House of Representatives and votes in the ELECTORAL COLLEGE) and to allocate benefits and resources throughout the society.

However, the Census Bureau (that part of the BUREAU-CRACY responsible for conducting the census) routinely undercounts blacks and other racial minorities. In 1990 the bureau reported that it failed to count 4.6 percent of the African-American population and 5.2 percent of the Latino population. This means those groups and the cities and states where they lived lost political power and economic resources. After the 1990 undercount, the bureau concluded that it could adjust for the undercount in the enumeration (enumeration requires that persons who fail to return the census questionnaire by mail be interviewed in person or by a census worker) by statistical sampling. That is, it could statistically locate, count, and include the persons not counted in the actual enumeration. However, the SUPREME COURT concluded that federal law mandated an actual enumeration for purposes of reapportioning seats in the House of Representatives, although a statistically adjusted count could be used for purposes of allocating resources and by STATE AND LOCAL GOVERNMENTS for purposes of "redistricting" (the creation of congressional and other legislative districts within state and local jurisdictions). Thus, the 2000 census included for the first time two figures on the size of the population: the actual enumeration and a statistically adjusted figure based on sampling. Although statistical experts declared that the 2000 census was probably the most accurate ever, there was nevertheless an estimated undercount that missed 1.2 percent of the overall population compared with 1.6 percent in 1990. It is estimated that 2.1 percent of blacks were missed in 2000 compared with 4.6 percent in 1990, and 2.9 percent of Latinos compared with 5.2 percent in 1990. (These percentages translate into about 3.3 million uncounted persons.)

The Census and Race

The first census conducted in the United States in 1790 established the social or political meaning of RACE. The meaning established was a peculiar one, recognizing three races: "Negro," white, and Indian. However, any person of any African or "Negro" ancestry was defined as "Negro." Thus, the 1790 census enumerators were given the following instructions:

A person of mixed white and Negro blood should be returned as a Negro, no matter how small the percentage of Negro blood. Both black and mulatto persons are to be returned as Negroes, without distinction. A person of mixed Indian and Negro blood should be returned as Negro. . . . Mixtures of non-white races should be reported according to the race of the father, except that Negro Indian should be reported as Negro.

This meant that the United States, unlike other multiracial nations, at its origins refused to recognize a mixed or multiracial category; one was either BLACK, white, or red. Thus, individuals who in physical appearance were "white" but who were known to have any black ancestors were declared "black." This definition of race is unique to the United States.

As the United States became more ethnically diverse after the 1960s, this 1790 classification of Americans into just three "races" became inadequate. So in 1977, the Office of Management and Budget (OMB, the agency within the bureaucracy responsible for developing racial categories) issued Statistical Policy Directive No. 15 defining the meaning of race for purposes of public policy. According to this directive, there are four "races" in the United States: black, white, American Indian or Alaskan native, and Asian or Pacific Islander. To determine ethnic identification, black and white respondents are asked to check "Hispanic origin" or "not of Hispanic origin," in effect creating a fifth "race"—Latino. These five categories are used by the Census Bureau and all other government agencies that collect statistical data.

In the 1990s this definition of race was challenged by many Americans, especially the growing number of biracial or mixed-race couples and their children. They demanded that the government create a "mixed" or "multiracial" category. (A mulatto or mixed-race category was added in the 1850 census but dropped in 1920.) Although polls indicated that this new category was supported by a majority of blacks, it was opposed by most black leaders, who contended that a mixed-race category would result in a loss of political power and would undermine AFFIRMATIVE ACTION and lead to increased DISCRIMINATION and stigmatization of African Americans who are "black." (In 1990 there were about 964,000 black-white marriages, about 7 percent of all marriages among African Americans.) The Office of Management and Budget considered adoption of a multiracial category for the 2000 census but rejected it because it concluded that a new category would "add to racial tensions and further fragmentation of our population." However, for the 2000 census individuals were allowed to check more than one race on the census questionnaire. So, the 2000 census included the traditional definition of who is black as well as those persons who elected to select any other racial categories. Ninety-eight percent of Americans selected a single race, and 2 percent—6.8 million persons—selected a second race, including 1.7 million blacks (about half of the blacks who selected a second race reported they were white). This 1.7 million (25 percent of those who selected multiple categories) represents 4 percent of the "all-inclusive" black population or the population combining single- and mixed-race blacks. The all-inclusive figure is about 5 percent higher than the black figure, and adding the two together increases the black population percentage from 12.3 to 12.9 percent of the nation's population (from 34,658,190 to 36,419,434). The OMB decided that those blacks (and other minorities) who selected white would be assigned—following the practice of the first census—to the black category. However, it left ambiguous how those blacks who selected another minority group would be categorized. Thus, the compromise on meaning of race for the 2000 census likely creates as many problems as it resolves and is likely to be revisited before the next census, especially as the number of mixed-race marriages or relationships increases and as the nation becomes more ethnically diverse. But one thing is clear: The meaning of race in America will continue to be determined more by politics than biology.

See also MULTICULTURALISM.

Further reading: F. James Davis, *Who Is Black: One Nation's Definition* (University Park: Pennsylvania State University Press, 1991); Melissa Nobles, *Shades of Citizenship: Race and the Census in Modern Politics* (Palo Alto, Calif.: Stanford University Press, 2000); Peter Skerry, *Counting on the Census: Race, Group Identity and the Evasion of Politics* (Washington, D.C.: Brookings Institution, 2000); Jon Michael Spencer, *The New Colored People: The Mixed Race Movement in America* (New York: New York University Press, 1997).

Chisholm, Shirley (1924–   ) politician

Shirley Chisholm, the daughter of WEST INDIAN immigrants, was the first black woman elected to CONGRESS, and she is also the first black woman to seek the presidential nomination of one of the two major parties. Chisholm was elected to the House of Representatives in 1968 from Bedford-Stuyvesant, Brooklyn's black GHETTO. She defeated JAMES FARMER, the head of CORE during the early 1960s and one of the major leaders of the PROTEST phase of the CIVIL RIGHTS MOVEMENT. Farmer, the REPUBLICAN and Liberal Party nominee, ran a quasi-militant Black Power–style campaign while Chisholm, the DEMOCRATIC PARTY nominee, touted her independence from the Brooklyn political establishment (she titled her autobiography *Unbought and Unbossed*) and relied on a corps of women volunteers to spread her message in a district where women constituted 60 percent of the voters. Chisholm, then a member of the New York State Legislature, easily defeated Farmer with 66 percent of the vote.

In Washington, Chisholm joined several other blacks elected to the House in 1968, but her charisma and her status as the first and at that time only black woman in Congress enhanced her position as a national leader, since she was viewed as a leader in the BLACK COMMUNITY as well as a leader in the then-emerging feminist or women's liberation movement. Thus, unlike most newly elected members of the House, she frequently lectured throughout the country at colleges and universities and before women's groups. It was this national exposure that led Chisholm to run for president in 1972, just four years after her election to Congress.

In her memoir of her PRESIDENTIAL CAMPAIGN, *The Good Fight*, Chisholm describes its origins by writing, "Running for President was not my idea originally. It was a number of college students who started me thinking about it, against what I first thought was my better judgment.... A young man at a southern college asked why didn't I run.... I said I am black, I am a woman.... He said, Don't worry, we will be voting soon and we will support you.... The germ of the decision began there." At the time, however, that Chisholm was considering running for president, virtually the entire black LEADERSHIP was holding meetings looking toward the convening of a NATIONAL BLACK POLITICAL CONVENTION in 1972. A major purpose of the meetings and the convention was to decide on black strategy for participation in the 1972 presidential campaigns, with the specific purpose of deciding whether a black should run for president. When Chisholm abruptly announced her candidacy in the midst of these convention deliberations, it was immediately opposed by most black leaders, who said that she had broken the bonds of solidarity the convention was seeking to establish. Chisholm's critics in the African-American community also said her candidacy was more a feminist than a black campaign. Chisholm's response was to accuse her largely male critics of SEXISM, and in remarks that would later influence the development of black feminist politics, she said she had faced more DISCRIMINATION in politics because of gender than because of race, quipping, "If anyone thinks white men are sexist, let them check out black men."

When the Black Political Convention convened in March 1972, it declined to endorse Chisholm's candidacy (or any other), leading her once again to suggest sexism as a motive. Although she was an active campaigner, participating in most of the primaries and caucuses and in the debates, her candidacy gained little support among blacks or women. George McGovern won the 1972 Democratic Party nomination in a close contest with HUBERT HUMPHREY. Chisholm won fewer than 500,000 votes and fewer than 100 out of more than 3,000 convention delegates.

In 1982 Congresswoman Chisholm declined to seek reelection, although she had risen to a position of national stature in the House Democratic Party Caucus and was a member of the powerful House Rules Committee. In her retirement she remained active in feminist and black politics, participating in the founding of the National Women's Political Caucus and the NATIONAL POLITICAL CONGRESS OF BLACK WOMEN.

See also FEMINISM.

citizen diplomacy

The CONSTITUTION as interpreted by the SUPREME COURT places complete authority to conduct diplomacy in the PRESIDENCY. However, ever since George Logan in the administration of George Washington attempted to negotiate better relations between the United States and France in 1798, American citizens have engaged in diplomacy. (The CONGRESS responded to Logan's efforts by passing the "Logan Act" prohibiting unauthorized diplomatic activities by private citizens but the act has never been enforced.) African Americans have engaged in citizen diplomacy at least since Paul Cuffe in 1815 arranged for the settlement of 38 African Americans in Sierra Leone.

Citizen diplomacy involves the efforts of private citizens, with or without the authorization of the president, to have meetings with foreign leaders or others in order to advance the interests of their constituents or to pursue personal objectives in FOREIGN POLICY. Diplomatic initiatives by African-American citizens have involved both types of efforts: personal objectives and group interests.

In 1859 MARTIN DELANY and ALEXANDER CRUMMELL traveled to Nigeria and successfully negotiated a treaty on behalf of black Americans with a Yoruba king. The treaty provided for the settlement of blacks on unused tribal lands in exchange for the use of their knowledge in the development of the area. Although no blacks settled in the area, Delany was pleased that for the first time an agreement had been reached between black Americans and an African leader. He later gave a report on his expedition at the International Statistics Congress in London, which was published as the Official Report of the Niger Valley Exploration Party.

In the 1830s and 1840s FREDERICK DOUGLASS and other black abolitionists traveled to Europe to seek support for the antiSLAVERY cause. In the 1890s IDA B. WELLS-BARNETT traveled to Europe seeking support for the anti-LYNCHING cause. W. E. B. DU BOIS, WILLIAM MONROE TROTTER, and others traveled to the Paris Peace Conference on behalf of the colonized peoples of Africa, and Du Bois and the NAACP continued their anti-COLONIALISM activities at the founding of the UNITED NATIONS in 1945. Du Bois and PAUL ROBESON also traveled to the Soviet Union, met with its leaders, and condemned the United States position in the COLD WAR. In 1955 Congressman

ADAM CLAYTON POWELL attended the BANDUNG CONFERENCE of leaders of the emerging THIRD WORLD. In the 1960s MALCOLM X met with several African and Arab heads of state in efforts to forge links between the black struggle in the United States against RACISM and WHITE SUPREMACY and the struggles in Africa and the Middle East against colonialism and imperialism. Malcolm also sought the support of these leaders in bringing charges against the United States at the United Nations for violating the HUMAN RIGHTS of African Americans. And in the 1980s and 1990s LOUIS FARRAKHAN of the NATION OF ISLAM traveled throughout the Third World meeting with heads of state and religious leaders.

Most of these activities by African-American citizen diplomats were criticized by officials of the government, but the Logan Act was never used to prosecute them. However, many of them did face various forms of POLITICAL REPRESSION. Du Bois was indicted for failure to register as an agent of a foreign power and, along with Paul Robeson, was stripped of his passport and denied the right to travel outside the United States. And the activities of Malcolm X were carefully monitored by U.S. intelligence agencies.

In the 1980s JESSE JACKSON was perhaps the most prominent citizen diplomat in the United States. His activities, however, were not directed at advancing the interests of blacks. Instead, he pursued personal and political objectives, negotiating the release of American military persons held captive in Syria and Yugoslavia, arranging the release of political prisoners held in Cuba, and attempting to negotiate peace agreements in Central America. Jackson's diplomatic forays were generally opposed by the government, but since he was generally successful, he was applauded rather than prosecuted. And in the 1990s Jackson's citizen diplomacy received official recognition when President BILL CLINTON appointed him a special envoy to Africa, where he sought to negotiate peace agreements between warring factions in Sierra Leone and LIBERIA and to help other African nations move toward democratic government.

Further reading: Karin Stanford, *Beyond the Boundaries: Reverend Jesse Jackson in International Affairs* (Albany: State University of New York Press, 1997).

citizenship

Citizenship—the legal allegiance of an individual to a nation and his or her entitlement to the protections and privileges of its laws—in the United States was initially limited by RACISM and by the principles of FEDERALISM. Prior to the adoption of the CONSTITUTION, each state regulated citizenship, and five of the 13 states granted citizenship to FREE NEGROES. However, in the *DRED SCOTT* case the

SUPREME COURT ruled that while a state could confer citizenship on Africans, it was limited to that particular state and did not under the Constitution make that person a citizen of the United States or any other state. The only way Africans could become citizens of the United States, the Court said, was by an act of CONGRESS. But in the more than a dozen naturalization acts passed by Congress between 1790 and 1854, citizenship was always limited to "free white persons," leaving blacks and other people of color in an anomalous position: noncitizens in most states: citizens in some states, but only in those states; and the citizen of no nation at all. Thus, blacks in the United States were literally a people without a country, legally owing allegiance to no nation and therefore not entitled to the protection and privileges of any law. This was the purpose of Chief Justice Roger B. Taney's opinion in *Dred Scott:* to declare that blacks were without the protection of the Constitution and laws of the United States.

The adoption of the FOURTEENTH AMENDMENT after the CIVIL WAR changed the anomalous citizenship status of blacks and other people of color. In its first sentence, the amendment reads, "All persons born or naturalized in the United States, and subject to the jurisdiction thereof, are citizens of the United States and of the State wherein they reside." (In spite of this language, in *Elks v. Walkins* the Supreme Court in 1884 ruled that although born in the United States, Indians were not citizens because they owed their allegiance to their tribes and thus were no more citizens that the children of ambassadors born in the United States. It was not until 1924 that Congress conferred citizenship on the Native Americans.) As a result of the Fourteenth Amendment, citizenship in the United States is based on jus soli—place of birth—meaning that even the children of foreign tourists or illegal immigrants born in the United States are citizens. This contrasts with most other countries, where citizenship is based on jus sanguinis—the citizenship of the parent—no matter where the child is born.

City of Richmond v. J. A. Croson   See CROSON, J. A., *CITY OF RICHMOND V.*

civic culture

The civic culture is a subset of a broader POLITICAL CULTURE. It is a specific component of the political culture that deals with the relative presence or absence of civic attitudes among nations or among groups within a nation. These attitudes include knowledge and interest in politics, trust in government and its officials, and political "efficacy" or the sense that an individual has that she or he can effectively influence the government. Political knowledge, interest in politics, political trust, and political efficacy, then, are constituent elements of a nation's or group's civic culture. It is assumed that these civic attitudes have some influence on the behavioral components of the civic culture, such as POLITICAL PARTICIPATION and VOTING BEHAVIOR.

In the United States blacks and whites have relatively distinct civic cultures, although in most respects the distinctiveness is a result of the relatively large social class differences among the groups. That is, civic attitudes (and behavior) in the United States and elsewhere tend to be a function of social class rather than ETHNICITY. That is, middle-class persons of whatever nation or ethnic group tend to exhibit civic attitudes more so than lower-class persons of whatever ethnic background. And since blacks, compared with whites, are disproportionately lower class, one would expect that the black civic culture would mirror these class differences. In general, this is the case. African Americans have lower levels of knowledge and interest in politics, higher levels of distrust of the government and its officials, and they evaluate the performance of the government less positively. They also feel less efficacious, feeling they can have little or no influence on government decision making.

For the most part, however, these differences disappear when one takes into account class differences. Among both blacks and whites, knowledge of politics, interest in politics, and political efficacy are class-based phenomena, with lower-class persons (black and white) having less knowledge and interest in politics and less political efficacy. Further, middle-class blacks in knowledge, interest, and efficacy resemble more their white class counterparts than they do other blacks. This relationship among class, race, and civic attitudes holds whether social class is measured by education, occupation, or income. Thus, for these attitudes, there is not a distinctive African-American civic culture. This is not the case, however, for political trust. Blacks at all class levels display a relatively low level of trust in government, while among whites distrust in government tends to be found more among the lower class. Thus, lack of trust in government tends to be a distinctive characteristic of the African-American civic culture, reflecting deeper currents in black political culture and the CULTURE generally.

See also ALIENATION.

Further reading: Robert C. Smith and Richard Seltzer, *Race, Class and Culture: A Study in Afro-American Mass Opinion* (Albany: State University of New York Press, 1992).

civil disobedience

Civil disobedience is the refusal to obey laws, usually because they are considered unjust and illegitimate or immoral, as a form of PROTEST. Individuals and groups practicing civil disobedience frequently use morality as a base of power. It is a form of protest in which individuals willingly accept punishment, including social ostracism and prison, for their behavior. Civil disobedience was a principal strategy during the protest phase of the CIVIL RIGHTS MOVEMENT during the 1950s and 1960s, used especially by MARTIN LUTHER KING JR.

Henry David Thoreau, the 19th-century American writer, provided the intellectual and strategic argument for civil disobedience in his essay "Civil Disobedience." In it he wrote, "It is not desirable to cultivate a respect for the law, so much as for the right. . . . unjust laws exist; shall we be content to obey them, or shall we endeavor to amend them, and obey them until we have succeeded or shall we transgress them at once . . . if it [government] is of such nature that it requires you to be the agent of injustice to another, then, I say break the law . . . what I have to do is to see . . . that I do not tend myself to do the wrong which I condemn."

Mohandas Gandhi read Thoreau's essay and used it in the development of "Satyagraha," the philosophy of conflict and resistance he used to bring about the end of British COLONIALISM in India. Martin Luther King Jr. studied both Thoreau and Gandhi and used their theories, along with principles drawn from black RELIGIOSITY, to develop his strategy of resistance to racial SEGREGATION.

civil liberties

Civil liberties are those rights protected from arbitrary interference by a government. In the American political tradition, civil liberties can be understood as NATURAL RIGHTS based on the idea that the rights of individuals come not from the generosity of the government but by the grace of God. They are a form of the "inalienable" rights granted by the Creator that THOMAS JEFFERSON referred to in the DECLARATION OF INDEPENDENCE. In the SOCIAL-CONTRACT THEORY that is the underlying philosophical basis of the United States government, the idea is that when "men" decided to create a government and give it limited authority to rule, they retained for themselves their natural rights. Civil liberties, then, are the protection of natural rights or of those rights necessary to secure or preserve natural rights. These rights are found in the CONSTITUTION in general and in the BILL OF RIGHTS specifically.

Africans in the United States, however, were not part of the social contract that created the government. Rather, on the basis of the IDEOLOGY of WHITE SUPREMACY, they were excluded from the contract—the Constitution—and therefore denied their inalienable rights to life, liberty, and property and treated as part of the natural rights of white men to own them as their property. Thus, they had no civil liberties. As Chief Justice Roger B. Taney put it in the DRED SCOTT case, Africans under the Constitution had only those rights that the white men who held the power and the government might choose to grant them. It is out of the Constitution's initial denial of civil liberties to Africans that the idea of CIVIL RIGHTS emerges historically in the United States. Civil rights in this historical context can be seen as government- rather than God-given rights. Civil rights, then, historically are positive acts by the government designed to confer civil liberties or natural rights on individuals previously denied them, and to protect those individuals in the exercise of those rights from individuals and STATE AND LOCAL GOVERNMENTs that might abridge them. Civil rights in the United States first take the form of the RECONSTRUCTION-era THIRTEENTH, FOURTEENTH, and FIFTEENTH AMENDMENTs. These amendments (along with the Nineteenth granting women the right to vote) constitute the civil rights amendments to the Constitution, as Amendments One through Nine constitute the civil liberties amendments. After these civil rights amendments were ratified, CONGRESS adopted civil rights laws designed to protect individuals from arbitrary DISCRIMINATION by governments, corporations, and individuals on account of RACE or other characteristics deemed irrelevant to equal access to social values and resources.

civil rights

Civil rights are positive acts by the U.S. government and STATE AND LOCAL GOVERNMENTs in the form of amendments to the CONSTITUTION or statutes or laws passed by CONGRESS or state and local legislative bodies. These amendments or laws are designed to confer rights on individuals previously denied them and to protect those individuals from arbitrary DISCRIMINATION by governments, businesses, and individuals. These rights are not considered NATURAL RIGHTS or CIVIL LIBERTIES; rather, they are rights that governments may choose to grant to individuals in discrete categories or groups. Civil rights have their origins in the RECONSTRUCTION-era amendments to the Constitution conferring civil liberties or natural rights on blacks. Congress later passed a series of laws in the late 19th and 20th centuries prohibiting discrimination on the basis of RACE, religion, and ethnic origins. The basic or organic civil rights law in the United States is the CIVIL RIGHTS ACT OF 1964, which has since been amended or extended by other laws.

In addition to race, gender, religion, and ETHNICITY, Congress or state and local governments can confer rights on any discrete group of individuals. For example, in 1991 Congress passed the Americans with Disabilities Act conferring rights on and prohibiting discrimination against individuals with disabilities (defined as having, having had, or perceived as having a physical or mental impairment that limits in a substantial way one or more major life activity) in employment, public accommodations, transportation, public service, and telecommunications. (The Act requires that "reasonable accommodations" to the disabled be made by institutions unless such accommodations result in "undue hardships.") The Congress included HIV-AIDS as a disability, but it has declined to amend the Civil Rights Act to prohibit discrimination against homosexuals (see GAY RIGHTS). However, many state and local governments have laws banning discrimination against gays and lesbians, and several have considered conferring civil rights—and prohibiting discrimination—on the basis of obesity.

Civil Rights Act of 1964

The Civil Rights Act of 1964 is the organic or basic civil rights statute in the United States. Although other CIVIL RIGHTS laws were passed before and after the 1964 act, it, as amended, is the basic law that protects individuals against arbitrary and invidious DISCRIMINATION.

Proposed in 1963 by JOHN F. KENNEDY in response to the BIRMINGHAM DEMONSTRATIONS led by MARTIN LUTHER KING JR., the law was enacted under the PRESIDENCY of LYNDON B. JOHNSON. The legislation was enacted after the longest FILIBUSTER (six months) in Senate history. Along with the VOTING RIGHTS ACT OF 1965, the 1964 law is the most important legislative achievement of the CIVIL RIGHTS MOVEMENT. The act forbids discrimination based on RACE, color, religion, gender, ETHNICITY, or national origins in the allocation of values and resources in virtually all aspects of American life. (The sale and rental of housing was not covered by the 1964 act but was prohibited by the Civil Rights Act of 1968). The 1964 act includes several major provisions or "titles," including prohibitions on discrimination in voting, public accommodations, and employment. Other titles extend the life and authority of the CIVIL RIGHTS COMMISSION; authorize the federal government to engage in LITIGATION to desegregate public facilities and schools; provide for the withholding of federal funds from programs operating in a discriminatory way; and establish a Community Relations Service within the BUREAUCRACY to resolve civil rights problems at the local level. The act's prohibition on discrimination in voting was not effective, so

President Lyndon Johnson signs the Civil Rights Act of 1964 as Martin Luther King Jr. looks on. *(Johnson Library)*

one year later Dr. King led the SELMA DEMONSTRATIONS that resulted in passage of the Voting Rights Act of 1965. In 1968, after the murder of Dr. King and the RIOTS that followed, CONGRESS enacted the Civil Rights Act of 1968 (referred to as the "Fair Housing Act"), which prohibited discrimination in the sale or rental of housing. Together, these three pieces of legislation abolished the legal basis for intentional discrimination or INDIVIDUAL RACISM in the United States and completed the agenda of the Civil Rights movement as it was articulated by the NIAGARA MOVEMENT in 1905.

Further reading: Robert Loevy, *The Civil Rights Act of 1964: The Passage of the Law That Ended Racial Segregation* (Albany: State University of New York Press, 1997); Robert Mann, *The Walls of Jericho: Lyndon Johnson, Hubert Humphrey, Richard Russell and the Struggle for Civil Rights* (New York: Harcourt Brace, 1996); Charles Whelan and Barbara Whelan, *The Longest Debate: A Legislative History of the 1964 Civil Rights Act* (Cabin John, Md.: Seven Locks Press, 1985).

civil rights cases of 1883

The civil rights cases of 1883 are among the most important decisions ever made by the SUPREME COURT dealing with the African-American struggle for FREEDOM and EQUALITY. In this case, the Court made it clear for the first time that it would not use the RECONSTRUCTION amendments to the CONSTITUTION to dismantle RACISM and WHITE SUPREMACY. Although the 1896 *PLESSY V. FERGUSON* case is better known, it is the civil rights cases that first gave the imprimatur of CONSTITUTIONALISM to SEPARATE BUT EQUAL and JIM CROW–style SEGREGATION. The cases (three from separate parts of the country: New York, San Francisco, and Memphis) challenged the constitutionality of the Civil Rights Act of 1875. In the act, CONGRESS prohibited racial DISCRIMINATION in access to public accommodations such as inns, theaters, and cafes. Congress based its authority to do so on the EQUAL PROTECTION CLAUSE of the FOURTEENTH AMENDMENT and the THIRTEENTH AMENDMENT's prohibition of conditions that imposed a "badge of servitude" upon blacks. In an eight to one decision, the Court ruled that the 1875 act was unconstitutional. In his opinion for the Court, Justice Joseph Bradley concluded that the equal protection clause prohibited discrimination by STATE AND LOCAL GOVERNMENTS, not private businesses. Therefore, Congress lacked the authority to compel INTEGRATION of privately owned public places contrary to the wishes of their owners. Bradley also concluded that while being denied access to an inn or theater because of one's race might be "obnoxious," it was not "in any sense, incidents or elements of slavery." Much more so than *Plessy*

v. Ferguson, the decision in the civil rights cases caused a national furor. Bishop HENRY M. TURNER, for example, called it a "barbarous decision" that absolved the allegiance of blacks to the United States. In the CIVIL RIGHTS ACT OF 1964, Congress once again prohibited discrimination in places of public accommodation, basing its authority this time on the COMMERCE CLAUSE, which the Supreme Court upheld in *HEART OF ATLANTA MOTEL V. UNITED STATES*.

Civil Rights Commission, U.S.

The Commission on Civil Rights established by the Civil Rights Act of 1957 is one of several parts of the BUREAUCRACY with an explicit CIVIL RIGHTS or race-related mission (see also CIVIL RIGHTS DIVISION, EQUAL EMPLOYMENT OPPORTUNITY COMMISSION, and OFFICE OF FEDERAL CONTRACT COMPLIANCE). Originally the commission was a bipartisan (including members of the two major parties) agency of six members appointed by the president with Senate approval. However, in 1983 its membership changed to eight persons, four appointed by the president and four appointed by the leaders of the two houses of CONGRESS. With the 1983 changes, the president was also prohibited from dismissing commission members without cause. These changes came about because President RONALD REAGAN attempted to dismiss two commissioners who were critical of his administration's civil rights policies. President Reagan also appointed as chairman Clarence Pendleton, an African American who was very critical of BUSING and AFFIRMATIVE ACTION. Since busing and affirmative action were policies strongly supported by the black LEADERSHIP, this made the commission very controversial. Prior to these developments, the commission had generally been noncontroversial, supported by presidents and leaders of both political parties, and its investigative and fact-finding reports were generally well received by the press and political leaders.

The commission's main mission is to combat RACISM and DISCRIMINATION by using knowledge and information as power bases. It conducts investigations, issue reports, and serves as a clearinghouse for information on discrimination against blacks, other racial minorities, the elderly, the handicapped, and women. President Reagan disapproved of the generally liberal inclinations of the commission's reports and recommendations and sought, through his appointments, to change its ideological direction. As a result, the commission's solidarity was undermined as it became increasingly divided between liberals and conservatives. President Reagan also proposed large cuts in the commission's budget. As a result it had to cut back its work, and the work that was done became less influential because the commission had lost status in the eyes of the MEDIA and the bipartisan political community.

Civil Rights Division, Department of Justice

The Civil Rights Division (CRD) of the DEPARTMENT OF JUSTICE is the agency within the federal BUREAUCRACY with the primary responsibility for enforcing the nation's CIVIL RIGHTS laws. When the CRD was created by the Civil Rights Act of 1957, its mandate was limited to enforcing laws banning racial DISCRIMINATION in voting and to the enforcement of certain RECONSTRUCTION-era statutes. When the CIVIL RIGHTS ACTS OF 1964, the VOTING RIGHTS ACT OF 1965, and the Civil Rights Act of 1968 were enacted, the mandate of CRD was greatly expanded. As a result of these three new statutes the CRD had expanded responsibilities in the area of assuring nondiscrimination in voting and in the drawing of legislative and congressional district lines to ensure equitable minority REPRESENTATION in CONGRESS and in STATE AND LOCAL GOVERNMENTS. In addition to voting rights and representation, the 1964 and 1968 laws require CRD to enforce nondiscrimination on the basis of race, religion, and gender in education, employment, housing, public accommodations, access to credit, and in programs receiving federal grants. Subsequent laws passed in the 1970s and 1980s further expanded CRD's mandate to include discrimination based on immigration status, disability, age, family status, access to abortion clinics, and the determination of eligibility for REPARATIONS payments to individuals of Japanese ancestry. In carrying out these responsibilities, the division can sue private individuals and companies and state and local governments.

The rapid growth of the division's responsibilities since 1957 reflect the expanding understanding of civil rights in the United States since the success of the CIVIL RIGHTS MOVEMENT, which inspired other groups to demand protection from discrimination. However, the expansion of the groups entitled to protection and of the areas requiring protection (such as access to credit) creates problems for the division in terms of priorities in the allocation of its resources. When the CRD was established, it had only 17 employees. In 2000 it had more than 500 and a budget of more than $70 million. Yet, given its wide-ranging responsibilities, the division has experienced difficulty in delivering justice to all the groups and remedying all the types of discrimination its mandates cover.

Since the administration of RONALD REAGAN there has been controversy about the leadership of the division. Like the other major divisions of the Department of Justice, CRD is headed by an assistant attorney general who is appointed by the president with Senate approval. Until Reagan, these appointments were noncontroversial, generally supported by liberals and conservatives and DEMO-CRATIC and REPUBLICAN PARTY leaders. Reagan's CONSERVATISM in general—and with respect to civil rights specifically—changed the direction of the CRD, and since then the appointment of its head has often been the source of bitter ideological and partisan disputes.

President Reagan nominated William Bradford Reynolds to head the division. Reynolds decreased the number of suits brought by the division, preferring, he said, persuasion rather than LITIGATION. Reynolds also radically altered the division's approach to litigation, declining to file "class action" suits to address evidence of INSTITUTIONAL RACISM based on statistical evidence of DISPARATE IMPACT. (Such cases, if successful, usually require some kind of AFFIRMATIVE ACTION plan as a remedy.) Instead, Reynolds ordered the division's attorneys to focus on cases of INDIVIDUAL RACISM or DISPARATE TREATMENT, where the remedy is limited only to the individual victims of discrimination. Reynolds's approach was opposed by many of the career attorneys in the division, most civil rights leaders, and liberal Democrats in CONGRESS. The result was a divided CRD, persistent criticism of Reynolds (when Reagan tried to promote him to associate attorney general, the Democratically controlled Senate declined to approve the nomination), and ideological and partisan conflicts over the way to enforce civil rights laws.

Since the Reagan administration, there has been continuing conflict over the division's leadership. In both the George W. Bush and BILL CLINTON administrations, the Senate declined to approve nominees to head the division because of disagreements about their approach or strategy of enforcement. Twice in Clinton's administration, the Senate refused to approve his nominees, forcing the president to withdraw the nomination of Lani Guinier, an African-American law professor, and to give Bill Lann Lee, a Chinese-American attorney for the NAACP, a "recess" or temporary appointment.

These conflicts over the leadership of CRD reflect deeper conflicts over the nature and degree of RACISM and discrimination in the POST–CIVIL RIGHTS ERA and the appropriate ways to use the law to combat these phenomena. It is likely that these deeper conflicts will inhibit the development of a consistent and continuous approach to the enforcement of the nation's many and varied civil rights laws. Continuity and consistency is a vital part of effective law enforcement.

See also CIVIL RIGHTS COMMISSION and *SHAW V. RENO*.

Further reading: Brian K. Lansberg, *Enforcing Civil Rights: Race Discrimination and the U.S. Department of Justice* (Lawrence: University Press of Kansas, 1998); Raymond Wolters, *Right Turn: William Bradford Reynolds, the Reagan Administration and Black Civil Rights* (New Brunswick, N.J.: Transaction, 1996).

Civil Rights movement

The Civil Rights movement marks one of the great transformations in American history, preceded in importance perhaps only by the American Revolution and the CIVIL

WAR. This movement for African-American FREEDOM and EQUALITY not only secured these rights for blacks legally but also inspired and served as a model for SOCIAL MOVEMENTS among many other groups (women, other racial and ethnic minorities, homosexuals, and the disabled) in fighting for these rights. In many ways, the Civil Rights movement's success can be said to have sparked a "rights revolution" in the United States as well as other parts of the world. From its beginning, the movement for CIVIL RIGHTS relied on a variety of power bases—morality, religion, solidarity, charisma—in a broad COALITION with liberal whites (especially Jewish Americans) and parts of the labor movement and the religious community. In the power bases used and the coalition it assembled, the Civil Rights movement has its origins in and is a legacy of the 19th-century ABOLITIONIST MOVEMENT.

It is difficult for historians and social scientists to identify in a precise or exact way the origins of a social movement. But, with respect to the Civil Rights movement, one thing is clear: It did not begin in the 1950s with ROSA PARKS, the MONTGOMERY BUS BOYCOTT, or MARTIN LUTHER KING JR. The erroneous view that the movement has its beginnings in the 1950s has been advanced in both scholarly works and in the popular MEDIA, including the widely acclaimed and viewed Public Broadcasting System documentary *Eyes on the Prize: America's Civil Rights Years, 1954–1965.*

The origins of the movement can be traced to the organizing in 1890 of the National Afro-American League. Founded on the initiative of T. Thomas Fortune, a well-known black journalist, this organization of black intellectuals adopted a six-point BLACK AGENDA for civil rights, which included demands for antiLYNCHING legislation, equality in funding for public education for blacks and whites, and an end to DISCRIMINATION on railroad cars and in other public accommodations like hotels and theaters. The origins of the movement can also be traced to the organizing of the NIAGARA MOVEMENT in 1905 by W. E. B. DU BOIS, WILLIAM MONROE TROTTER, and other members of the TALENTED TENTH. Du Bois and Trotter were among the leaders of the Afro-American League, and its agenda—the Niagara manifesto—adopted much of the civil rights program of the league. Finally, the origins of the movement can be traced to the founding in 1909 of the NAACP. Whatever the date, organization, or individuals involved, the historical question is: When did the national black LEADERSHIP break with the ACCOMMODATIONISM of BOOKER T. WASHINGTON and embrace a civil rights agenda of social, political, and civil equality and freedom?

The Afro-American League and the Niagara movement represented the earliest organized civil rights initiatives. Du Bois in *THE SOULS OF BLACK FOLK,* published in 1903, had laid the intellectual foundations for the Civil Rights movement, and the formation of the NAACP, an interracial coalition, provided a centralized organizational vehicle for the movement. Thus, by the early 1900s the black Civil Rights movement was underway. Although the influence of Booker Washington's accommodationism was to continue for some time, the formation of the NAACP represented the beginnings of a consensus among black intellectuals and church and civic leaders around the basic goals and strategies of the Civil Rights movement as sketched out in the Afro-American League's agenda and the Niagara manifesto.

The Civil Rights movement, as it unfolded from the early 1900s to the late 1960s, can be divided into three phases—LOBBYING, LITIGATION, and PROTEST—based on the principal strategy it employed. In the first phase, the NAACP developed a campaign of education, propaganda, and lobbying to shape a favorable climate of PUBLIC OPINION on the issue of blacks and their civil rights. This phase, from roughly 1910 to the mid-1930s, also saw the NAACP engage in several lobbying campaigns in CONGRESS, including an unsuccessful 40-year effort to secure federal antilynching legislation (see DYER ANTILYNCHING BILL) and successful efforts to defeat immigration legislation prohibiting the entry of persons of African descent. With organized labor, the NAACP also played an important role in defeating the nomination of an allegedly antiblack, antilabor judge to the SUPREME COURT.

In the litigation phase, from the 1930s to the 1950s, the NAACP sought to secure the rights of blacks in a series of important court cases in a number of areas. These culminated in the invalidation of the WHITE PRIMARY in 1944 and the SEPARATE BUT EQUAL doctrine in the 1954 *BROWN V. BOARD OF EDUCATION* school desegregation cases.

The movement's final protest phase (1955–65)—involving boycotts, SIT-INS, and mass demonstrations—is the focus of much of the civil rights literature. Certainly this is the most dramatic phase of the movement and, in terms of its impact on PUBLIC POLICY, the most effective. Yet in terms of historical development, it is but a stream in the flow of a mighty river that crested in the 1960s. National-policy elites had responded to aspects of the civil rights agenda earlier in a series of court decisions, in FRANKLIN ROOSEVELT's executive order banning discrimination in war industries (issued in response to A. PHILIP RANDOLPH's threat of a mass MARCH ON WASHINGTON), and HARRY TRUMAN's order desegregating the armed forces. In general, however, the American government's response to the demand for civil rights before the 1960s can be characterized as neglect. The POWER ELITE from the 1900s to the 1960s essentially ignored blacks and their concerns, and it would have likely continued to do so if blacks had not broken with the routine politics of lobbying, litigation, and political partisanship and taken to the streets. That is, the

Leaders of the Civil Rights movement meet with government officials at the White House, June 22, 1963. *(Kennedy Library)*

American POLITICAL SYSTEM tends to respond to power and pressure, and until the 1960s blacks did not bring sufficient power and pressure to force the system to act.

After the Montgomery bus boycott, the movement's strategy shifted to mass protest. The NAACP was displaced as the leading organization in the movement by new mass-based protest organizations, such as SCLC and SNCC. The routine bureaucratic leadership of the NAACP's ROY WILKINS gave way to the charismatic leadership of MARTIN LUTHER KING JR. The NAACP and the URBAN LEAGUE continued to play a role in lobbying and litigation, but clearly it was the mass protests that caused President JOHN F. KENNEDY to act. Kennedy, like ABRAHAM LINCOLN a century earlier, was the reluctant race reformer. He had promised during the 1960 PRESIDENTIAL CAMPAIGN to propose comprehensive legislation as well as vigorous executive action, but once in office he hesitated. The BIRMINGHAM DEMONSTRATIONS led by Dr. King in 1963 forced the reluctant president to reorder his priorities and make civil

rights the principal item on his domestic agenda. Thus in June 1963, in a nationwide television address, Kennedy declared that the problem of civil rights was a "moral issue" of the highest national urgency and that the time had come to act and take the issue from the streets and into the Congress. Kennedy also said the VIOLENCE and disorders in Birmingham and elsewhere threatened system stability. Shortly thereafter, he proposed what was to become the CIVIL RIGHTS ACT OF 1964. This pattern of national-policy elites responding to protest in the streets rather than to routine lobbying and litigation also characterized enactment of the other major civil rights acts of the era—the VOTING RIGHTS ACT OF 1965 in response to the SELMA DEMONSTRATIONS and the Fair Housing Act of 1968 in response to the RIOTS following the assassination of Martin Luther King Jr.

The Civil Rights movement came to an end in the late 1960s after more than a half century of lobbying, litigation, and protest. Two theoretical points can be made about the political system's responses to the movement's demands. First, the responses were slow and mainly involved symbolism, with substantive civil rights laws coming only when protests, violence, and disorders threatened or were perceived by elements of the power elite to threaten system maintenance and stability. Second, while responding with positive civil rights laws in the 1960s, the system also responded simultaneously with CO-OPTATION and POLITICAL REPRESSION.

Further reading: Douglas McAdams, *Political Process and the Development of Black Insurgency, 1930–1970* (Chicago: University of Chicago Press, 1982); Aldon Morris, *The Origins of the Civil Rights Movement* (New York: Free Press, 1984); Charles Payne, *I've Got the Light of Freedom: The Organizing Tradition in the Mississippi Freedom Struggle* (Berkeley: University of California Press, 1995).

Civil War

A result of the Civil War (1861–65) was the emancipation of African Americans held in SLAVERY and a promise, long delayed, of FREEDOM and EQUALITY for them and their descendants. That was the result of the war, but historians still debate its causes: whether it was caused by the SOUTHERN STATES' pursuit of the states' rights to leave the union, by the NORTHERN STATES' insistence that the union of the states was perpetual and indissoluble, by economic rivalry between the agrarian South and the emerging industrial North, or by some combination of these factors. Hardly any historian, however, has concluded that the origins or purposes of the war were to secure the freedom of African Americans.

In his second inaugural address, President ABRAHAM LINCOLN said that slavery, which he described as a "peculiar" and "powerful" interest, was "somehow the cause of the war." However, President Lincoln did not propose the abolition of slavery as a war aim. Indeed, he signed what would have become, if ratified, the first Thirteenth Amendment that, unlike the second THIRTEENTH AMENDMENT (which abolished slavery), would have guaranteed its existence perpetually or as long as any Southern state would have wished to maintain it. The Southern states rejected the amendment and seceded from the Union. Then, as Lincoln said in the second inaugural, " . . . the war came."

Throughout the war, Lincoln said its purpose was not to free the slaves but to preserve the union of the states. And for this purpose, Lincoln said he would use any means necessary, including freeing none, some, or all of the slaves. As the war progressed, Lincoln eventually came to the conclusion that in order to win the war and preserve the Union it was necessary to promise freedom to some of the slaves. But, in using his authority to issue the EMANCIPATION PROCLAMATION, Lincoln said over and over again that it was done out of "military necessity" in order to win the war and restore the Union. As part of this military necessity, Lincoln reluctantly agreed to allow the arming and training of blacks as soldiers and sailors in the war.

The Civil War was the bloodiest in American history, involving the death of more than 500,000 Americans, black and white, North and South. Near its end, Lincoln sought to redefine the origins and purposes of the war in his GETTYSBURG ADDRESS, saying that the war had given rise to a "new birth of freedom." But while supporting the abolition of slavery, even at the war's end Lincoln could not bring himself to support—indeed, he opposed—full equality and freedom for the slaves or their descendants.

Like THOMAS JEFFERSON before him, Lincoln thought that slavery was morally wrong and an offense against God. And echoing Jefferson, who said, "I tremble for my country when I consider that God is Just," Lincoln concluded his second inaugural (which, with the Gettysburg Address, is his most important statement on the war's meaning) with the following historical-moral analysis:

> If we shall suppose that American slavery is one of those offenses which, in the providence of God, must needs come, but which, having continued through His appointed time, He now wills to remove, and that He gives to both North and South this terrible war as the woe due to those by whom the offense came, shall we discern therein any departure from those divine attributes which the believers in a living God always ascribe to Him?

Clark, Kenneth (1914–) *scholar*

Kenneth Clark was born in the Panama Canal Zone. At age five he moved to HARLEM, where he was educated in the public schools. He received a B.A. and M.A. from HOWARD UNIVERSITY and a Ph.D. from Columbia University. While at Howard he met Mamie Phillips, who became his wife and lifelong collaborator and colleague. At Howard they began studying INTERNAL INFERIORIZATION, that is, the effect of WHITE SUPREMACY and RACISM on the identity and psychological well-being of DISTRICT OF COLUMBIA schoolchildren.

Clark's early career included an appointment to the faculty of City College of New York, a research position at the Office of War Information, and work with GUNNAR MYRDAL on *AN AMERICAN DILEMMA*. In 1946 the Clarks, based on their studies of the pathological consequences of racism, established the Northside Center for Child Development.

As a part of their research on the psychological damage caused by racism, the Clarks developed the famous "doll tests." Black children in the early school ages were shown four identical dolls, two black and two white, and were asked to identify them racially and to indicate which doll was best, which was nice, which was bad, and which they would prefer to play with. The tests, administered to children in varying communities around the country, showed that a majority of the children rejected the black doll and expressed a preference for the white doll. For the Clarks, these tests were indisputable evidence of the negative effects of racism on the personality and psychological development of black children. As a result of this research, Clark was asked to prepare a report on the problems of minority youth for the White House Mid-Century Conference on Youth held in 1950. This report, published in revised form as *Prejudice and Your Child* (1955), summarized the results of the doll tests and related research and brought the young Clark to the attention of the NAACP, which was preparing to challenge the law requiring segregation in the nation's schools.

Clark's work for the NAACP played a major role in the SUPREME COURT's 1954 decision BROWN V. BOARD OF EDUCATION, which declared school SEGREGATION unconstitutional. In his testimony in several of the trials and in the social-science brief submitted to the Court, Clark and his colleagues argued that segregation tended to create in black children feelings of inferiority, self-rejection, and loss of self-esteem, which affected negatively their ability to learn. The influence of Clark on the Court's decision is apparent in the unanimous opinion written by Chief Justice EARL WARREN. The chief justice wrote:

> The policy of separating the races is usually interpreted as denoting the inferiority of the Negro group. A sense of inferiority affects the motivation of the child to learn. Segregation with the sanction of law, therefore, has a tendency to retard the educational and mental development of Negro children. . . .

To support this central finding of the *Brown* decision, the chief justice cited (in footnote 11) several social-science studies, the first being Clark's *Effects of Prejudice and Discrimination on Personality Development*.

As a result of his work on the *Brown* case, Clark in subsequent years became a leading advocate of school INTEGRATION and an intellectual leader of the CIVIL RIGHTS MOVEMENT, while continuing his research on the effects of racism and urging the application of social-science research to the resolution of the nation's race problems. In 1966 he authored *Dark Ghetto*, a prizewinning study of the dynamics of racial OPPRESSION and the resulting pathologies of the American GHETTO. Clark was also instrumental in the establishment of the JOINT CENTER FOR POLITICAL AND ECONOMIC STUDIES, an institution devoted to making social-science knowledge relevant to the Civil Rights movement and to the process of social change.

Throughout his career, Clark has been a leading advocate of integration, strongly opposing BLACK NATIONALISM in most of its forms and the 1960s BLACK POWER MOVEMENT. By integration, Clark means the abolition of racially distinctive communities, neighborhoods, schools, and other institutions based on race. He has also consistently opposed AFFIRMATIVE ACTION, where it takes the form of racial preferences or QUOTAS, while supporting it to the extent that it involves eliminating racism, or segregation and DISCRIMINATION on the basis of RACE. But, if affirmative action involves preferences or quotas for blacks on the basis of race, Clark is adamant: "I don't believe in preferential treatment. To me that is a form of racism."

Late in his career, Clark was a visiting professor at Harvard, Columbia, and the University of California, Berkeley, and a member of the board of trustees of Howard University. In 1966 he was appointed to the New York State Board of Regents, the first African American to serve on the state's highest education decision-making body. In a 1995 interview, Clark told the *New York Times* he would be an integrationist until his last day because nothing else would achieve EQUALITY.

See also PUBLIC INTELLECTUALS.

Further reading: Nat Hentoff, "The Integrationist," *New Yorker,* 23 August 1982.

class stratification

Class divisions or stratifications in the BLACK COMMUNITY historically have been highly skewed because of the existence of a large economically depressed lower class and a small, isolated, underemployed middle class. This skewed class structure has its roots in SLAVERY and in the early years of RECONSTRUCTION. Therefore, class analysis in black America must always be undertaken in a different way than in white America.

A class, according to the sociologist Max Weber, can be understood as a group of people who have in common specific causal components of their life chances insofar as the components affect access to opportunities for income in a marketplace. For Weber, like Karl Marx, property or lack of property is the basic component in class analysis, but under CAPITALISM most persons are propertyless, therefore their class situation or income is determined by their labor. This is true for the masses of all Americans, but especially for black Americans because, although some white Americans were able to acquire property (in the form of the ownership of farms, factories, mines, and the other basic productive resources of the society), most blacks for much of America's history were property. And when they ceased to be property after the CIVIL WAR, they found it very difficult to acquire wealth or property. Therefore, no authentic bourgeois or capitalist class emerged among black Americans in the United States. Thus, analysis of class in the black community is skewed because there is no bourgeois or capitalist class, rather only a class of workers stratified by occupation and income. Occupation and income are the basic causal components used to distinguish social class, but in modern, postindustrial societies like the United States, occupations and income are determined to a large extent by education. Therefore, educational attainments are also useful in class analysis.

Analysis and understanding of the modern class structure of black America must begin with developments since the 1960s. The American economy grew rapidly in the period after World War II, and while blacks shared in this prosperity, they could not do so fully until the CIVIL RIGHTS ACTS OF 1964 brought an end to legal DISCRIMINATION in education, employment, and pay.

The black class structure in the POST–CIVIL RIGHTS ERA is less skewed and resembles somewhat more the class structure of white America. However, there is still no black bourgeoisie in the United States. There are a few wealthy black athletes and entertainers and a few wealthy entrepreneurs, but taken as a whole, they own a minuscule percentage of the nation's capital or wealth and own or control none of the basic means of production in finance, industrial corporations, banks, utilities, communications, and transportation. This is illustrated by the annual list of the highest-paid Americans and the much longer lists of the wealthiest Americans. On the list of the Americans with the highest income, there are usually several black athletes and entertainers, but lists of the wealthiest rarely, if ever, include a black person. Thus, the black "upper class" is based almost entirely on income derived from highly paid labor rather than wealth derived from ownership of productive enterprises.

For most blacks, their class position is determined almost entirely by their education, occupation, and income. Using these criteria the black community can be divided into three strata of roughly equal size: a stable black middle class, a solid working class, and a class of poor people.

The black middle class has grown substantially since the 1960s, and the percentage of poor blacks has declined. In the early 1960s, about 9 to 12 percent of blacks were middle class, while more than half the black population was classified as poor. At the end of the 20th century about one-third of blacks are middle class and about 25 percent are classified as poor. In contrast, more than two-thirds of whites are middle class and less than 10 percent are classified as poor. Thus, while the post–civil rights era black class structure resembles somewhat more the white class structure, it is only *somewhat* more, since the white middle class is at least twice as large as the black middle class, and the percentage of blacks who are poor is twice as large as the percentage of whites in POVERTY.

In education, 1993 census data indicated 23 percent of adult whites had been graduated from college compared with 13 percent of blacks, about 25 percent of whites were employed in professional and technical occupations compared with about 15 percent of blacks, and white median family income was $39,310 compared with $21,500 for blacks. Income data may be the best criterion to use in stratifying individuals by class, since it is the basic determinant of an individual's life chances in a market economy. The median family income data show that for every dollar a white family earns, a black family earns about 55 cents, down from 61 cents in 1969.

The relative sizes of the three class strata in black America vary with the state of the economy. That is, there is some movement between the working class and the poor and to some extent between the middle class and the working class, depending on the level of growth and employment in the economy. For example, during the presidency of BILL CLINTON in the 1990s, the economy grew at unprecedented rates. As a result, the percentage of blacks in poverty declined from 31 to 22 percent, and the size of the middle class, measured by median family income, increased. Inevitably, when the economy declines the percentage of poor blacks will increase and the middle class will shrink.

In the post–civil rights era some scholars, most notably WILLIAM WILSON, have posited the existence of a fourth class or stratum in black America, a so-called black UNDERCLASS. The idea of a black underclass as a substratum of those blacks who are poor has been largely discredited and abandoned. But a central theme in underclass analysis is the disproportionately large size of the number of single-parent families and their relationship to poverty. More than 90 percent of single-parent families are female-parent families. In the early 1990s, 54 percent of black families were single parent compared with 21 percent of whites. And almost 50 percent of black single-female-parent families were poor, while only 12 percent of black two-parent families were poor. (Fourteen percent of white single-parent families were poor, 6 percent of male-parent families.) Thus, the black class structure is gendered, but not just in terms of its relationship to gender and poverty but also, increasingly in the post–civil rights era, in terms of gender and the middle class. Although the percentage of black men and women holding college degrees is roughly the same, more than two-thirds of the blacks enrolled in college and in graduate and professional schools in the late 1990s were women. In part because of the disproportionate incarceration of young black men, this gendered trend in class is likely to continue for some time.

See also CRIMINAL JUSTICE SYSTEM and FEMINISM.

Clinton, Bill (1946–   ) *42nd president of the United*
   States

In the manner in which he was elected, and in the manner in which he governed, Bill Clinton, the 42nd president of the United States, transformed the IDEOLOGY of the DEMOCRATIC PARTY and its relationship to modern LIBER-ALISM. Clinton's presidency also affected the relationship between African Americans—the Democratic Party's core liberal voting bloc—and the party and the relationship between African-American LEADERSHIP and the PRESI-DENCY in the POST–CIVIL RIGHTS ERA.

Like JIMMY CARTER, the first post–civil rights era Democratic president, Clinton ran for office on the assumption that an ideological liberal could not be elected president. This has been the conventional wisdom among the elites of politics and the MEDIA since the defeat of George McGovern in 1972. However, it gained added credibility with the election and landslide reelection of RONALD REAGAN in 1980 and 1984. In winning the presidency, Reagan campaigned on the traditional ideology of CONSERVATISM, attacking core liberal principles about the role of government, taxes, and the WELFARE STATE. Reagan's PRESIDENTIAL CAMPAIGNS also included specific attacks on those components of modern liberalism identified with the African-American struggle for FREEDOM and EQUALITY, including AFFIRMATIVE ACTION, welfare for poor women and children, the GREAT SOCIETY, and the WAR ON POVERTY. Running on these antiliberal themes, Reagan decisively defeated President Carter in 1980 and won reelection in a landslide (carrying 49 of 50 states) in 1984, defeating Walter Mondale, Carter's vice president. Running on similar conservative themes, George Bush, Reagan's vice president, decisively defeated Massachusetts governor Michael Dukakis in 1988. Both Mondale and Dukakis were identified with the Democratic Party's modern liberal tradition.

Reagan and Bush both won by attracting traditional white Democratic voters in the SOUTHERN STATES and in the suburbs of the NORTHERN STATES. These voters, who came to be called "Reagan Democrats," were said to have voted Republican because they associated the Democratic Party with "special interest groups," especially blacks but also feminists and homosexuals. Leading Democratic Party pollsters reported after the elections of 1984 and 1988 that these Reagan Democrats had turned against their party because of WHITE BACKLASH, specifically because of the party's perceived identification with African Americans. Stanley Greenberg (Clinton's 1992 pollster), for example, in a 1984 study for the Democratic Party reported that the reason that the Reagan Democrats had turned against the Democrats was because of their "distaste for blacks" and because of their association of the party with "them." Greenberg wrote:

These white Democratic defectors express a profound distaste for blacks, a sentiment that pervades almost everything they think about government and politics. . . . Blacks constitute the explanation for their vulnerability and for almost everything that has gone wrong in their lives, not being black is what constitutes being middle class, not living with blacks is what makes a neighborhood a decent place to live. These sentiments have important implications for Democrats, as virtually all progressive [liberal] symbols have been redefined in racial and pejorative terms.

Implicit in Greenberg's report was the notion that if the party was to win the presidency, it would have to distance itself—at least symbolically—from blacks and their interests. Further, it would have to present itself—again at least symbolically—as the party of the white middle class.

The implicit theme in Greenberg's 1984 study was made explicit in several other internal party studies and in a best-selling book by Thomas and Mary Edsal, two *Washington Post* reporters. The Edsals argued in *Chain Reaction: The Impact of Race, Rights and Taxes on American Politics* (1992) that the Democratic Party should deemphasize issues of RACISM, POVERTY, CIVIL RIGHTS, and affirmative action and instead focus on the concerns of the middle class in terms of lower taxes, opposition to QUOTAS, and a tough approach to welfare and crime. (Crime and welfare for poor women and their children in the post–civil rights era are issues or problems identified with blacks, because blacks are disproportionately recipients of welfare and persons accused of crimes.)

The analysis of the Edsals (candidate Clinton said he read their book and found it useful) reads almost like the script for Clinton's 1992 campaign. For example, Clinton promised to "end welfare as we know it" by limiting assistance to poor women and their children to two years; opposed affirmative action quotas; and took a strong position on crime, including becoming the first Democratic Party nominee in the post–civil rights era to support the death penalty. In spite of these positions, Clinton won the overwhelming support of black leaders and voters in both the primaries and in the general election.

Perhaps Clinton received the support of blacks in 1992 because, while running a campaign that in its symbolism distanced itself from African-American issues, he embraced other traditional liberal positions, proposing national health insurance, a major item on the agenda of modern liberalism and which, if enacted by the CONGRESS, would represent the largest expansion of the welfare state since the Great Society. Clinton also became the first candidate for president to fully support civil rights for homosexuals, and he supported full reproductive rights for women.

A girl holds a fan with a portrait of President Bill Clinton at a reception in the Harlem section of New York to celebrate Clinton's first day in his new Harlem offices. *(Mario Tama/Getty Images)*

As president, Clinton appointed a larger number of blacks to the BUREAUCRACY and the federal courts than any previous president, including four of 14 cabinet heads. Clinton also effectively used symbolism in his relationship to African Americans, including inviting blacks to the White House for state dinners; visiting Africa and hosting African heads of state; awarding the Presidential Medal of Freedom to prominent African Americans; and having a black man, VERNON JORDAN, as a highly visible golfing buddy and confidant. But in terms of PUBLIC POLICY, Clinton supported the abolition of federally guaranteed welfare for poor women and their children, even though this legislation was vigorously opposed by virtually the entire black LEADERSHIP. He also signed what the CONGRESSIONAL BLACK CAUCUS described as a draconian crime bill; supported an expansion of the death penalty; and while upholding the core principles of affirmative action, he presided over the dismantling of scores of affirmative action programs throughout the federal government.

After impeachment (on allegations of perjury and obstruction of justice in relationship to his sexual miscon-

duct with a White House intern), the historical legacy of the Clinton presidency is likely to be the unprecedented growth of the economy. This economic growth and prosperity led to a substantial reduction in African-American unemployment and poverty during the 1990s. However, unemployment and poverty rates remained more than twice as high among blacks as whites, and there was relatively little aggregate growth in the economy and in employment in the urban GHETTO (less then 15 percent of the more than 20 million new jobs created during Clinton's presidency were located in the central cities). The administration, however, did not propose policies or programs to deal with the racial disparities in employment, poverty, and prosperity, preferring instead to rely on encouraging private market initiatives and investments as proposed by the REPUBLICAN PARTY in Congress.

Although Clinton's public-policy record was not liberal and his positions on welfare and crime were opposed by most black leaders, African-American PUBLIC OPINION and the African-American leadership remained strongly supportive of the president throughout his tenure in office and especially during the efforts of the Republican congressional majority to impeach and remove him from office. In contrast, when Jimmy Carter—the previous centrist Democratic president—left office, he confronted PROTEST from black leaders, and his standing in the polls was very low among blacks. When Carter left office, only 30 percent of blacks approved of his performance in office; when Clinton left office, his performance was approved by more than 70 percent of blacks. Indeed, Clinton was more popular among blacks than any president has been since polling began.

The legacy of the Clinton presidency for AFRICAN-AMERICAN POLITICS was the emergence of a new style of ACCOMMODATIONISM. That is, African-American leaders, while liberal, can accept the view that a liberal (especially one identified with the cause of blacks) in the post–civil rights era cannot win the presidency, and therefore it is necessary to accept or accommodate the movement of the Democratic Party in a more conservative direction in general and on race specifically. When President Carter attempted to shift the party in a more conservative direction, blacks engaged in PROTEST, including twice supporting JESSE JACKSON as a liberal, protest candidate for the Democratic nomination. However, when Clinton much more effectively did the same thing, there was accommodationism instead of protest. This shift can be explained by two developments during the Clinton presidency. First, unlike the Carter years, during most of Clinton's presidency the Republican Party controlled both houses of Congress (in the House for the first time in 40 years). This development raised real fears among blacks that if a Democratic president was challenged and lost, Republican CONSERVATISM would dominate all branches of the federal government for the first time in the post–civil rights era. *Any* Democratic president was seen as preferable to this alternative.

The second development was the acceptance of the likelihood that a traditional Democratic liberal can not in the foreseeable future win the presidency, and therefore accommodationism is the "normal" or "natural" response of blacks to this situation. Related to this acceptance is the accommodationist imperative not to protest but, rather, to seek gradual, incremental changes within the context of the TWO-PARTY SYSTEM. This is because to protest risks upsetting enough whites—"Reagan Democrats"—to cause their defection to the Republicans. Gradual modifications or incremental changes in policies that rely on market rather than government solutions are accepted or accommodated. Over time, it can only be hoped that these gradual adjustments will result in greater EQUALITY between blacks and whites.

Further reading: Hine, Darlene Clark, and Pero Dagbovie, eds. *African Americans and the Clinton Presidency Reconsidered* (Urbana: University of Illinois Press, 2003); Kenneth O'Reilly, *Nixon's Piano: Presidents and Racial Politics from Washington to Clinton* (New York: Free Press, 1995), Chap. 10; Robert C. Smith, *We Have No Leaders: African Americans in the Post Civil Rights Era* (Albany: State University of New York Press, 1996), Chap. 10; Hanes Walton, *Reelection: William Jefferson Clinton as a Native Son Presidential Candidate* (New York: Columbia University Press, 2000).

Coalition of Black Trade Unionists

The Coalition of Black Trade Unionists (CBTU) is the major national-level ORGANIZATION representing the interests of black workers in the councils of organized labor and in AFRICAN-AMERICAN POLITICS. A COALITION of blacks from more than 40 different international and national unions, it was formed in 1972 by five black labor leaders to PROTEST the failure of the LEADERSHIP of the AFL-CIO—the dominant white labor organization in the United States—to support the DEMOCRATIC PARTY presidential nominee George McGovern. The AFL-CIO leaders refused to support McGovern because of his unwavering commitment to LIBERALISM, his support for AFFIRMATIVE ACTION, and his opposition to the VIETNAM WAR. Since African-American workers were strong supporters of McGovern, black labor leaders argued that the AFL-CIO had ignored their interests and in effect were contributing to the reelection of RICHARD NIXON, the REPUBLICAN PARTY candidate who was opposed by most blacks. The black labor leaders were also upset that no blacks were on the executive council of the AFL-CIO that made the decision. (Since CBTU's founding, it has worked to increase the representation of women and minorities on the executive council. In 2000, they held 13 of the 51 council seats.) From its founding in 1972 until the beginning of the 21st century, CBTU was led by William Lucy, the international secretary of the American Federation of State, County and Municipal Employees, which made him the highest-ranking black in the labor movement. The CBTU, after 30 years, is the oldest black labor organization in African-American history.

See also BROTHERHOOD OF SLEEPING CAR PORTERS.

coalitions

As a SUBORDINATE, MINORITY GROUP in the United States, African Americans must rely on coalitions to achieve many of their political objectives. Although the word *coalition* has many definitions or shades of meaning, put simply, a coalition involves two persons or groups bringing their resources or power bases together to achieve a common purpose. When a group can achieve its objectives alone, it might choose not to join a coalition.

Historically, as blacks have sought FREEDOM and EQUALITY in the United States, coalitions have always been necessary. However, blacks often have not been able to find coalition partners among whites, and they have been forced to go it alone. BLACK NATIONALISM as a philosophy has always been skeptical about the possibility of forming durable coalitions with whites, but even those blacks who in principle accept the idea of interracial coalitions have also embraced a go-it-alone strategy when white coalition partners cannot be found or when such coalitions do not endure.

Historically, blacks have participated in two types of coalitions: rights based and material based. Rights-based coalitions, like the ABOLITIONIST MOVEMENT and the CIVIL RIGHTS MOVEMENT, seek to achieve basic CIVIL RIGHTS or HUMAN RIGHTS, while material-based coalitions like JESSE JACKSON's RAINBOW COALITION or FRANKLIN D. ROOSEVELT's NEW DEAL coalition seek access to economic benefits such as education, employment, or health care. From the founding of the nation until the end of the 20th century, blacks have formed coalitions with virtually all elements of the American community: conservatives, liberals, and radicals; poor and middle- and upper-class whites; Quakers, Jews, Protestants, and Catholics; white women; and rural and urban whites. In the POST–CIVIL RIGHTS ERA, blacks have also attempted to form coalitions with Latinos, Asian Americans, and homosexuals. While some of these coalitions have resulted in important gains in terms of rights and benefits, others have been undermined by the forces of RACISM and WHITE SUPREMACY.

See also LEADERSHIP CONFERENCE ON CIVIL RIGHTS, MULTICULTURALISM, and POPULISM.

Further reading: Robert Allen, *The Reluctant Reformers: Reform Movements in the United States* (Washington, D.C.: Howard University Press, 1993); Ralph Gomes and Linda Williams, "Coalition Politics: Past, Present and Future" in *From Exclusion to Inclusion: The Long Struggle for Black Political Power,* ed. Ralph Gomes and Linda Williams (Westport, Conn.: Praeger, 1992); Hanes Walton and Robert C. Smith, *American Politics and the African American Quest for Universal Freedom* (New York: Longman, 2000), Chap. 7.

COINTELPRO

COINTELPRO is the acronym for counterintelligence programs used by the FBI (Federal Bureau of Investigation) for a series of secret activities of intelligence gathering, surveillance, and POLITICAL REPRESSION directed against various groups the FBI perceived as threats to the POLITICAL SYSTEM's prevailing values and structures. Although the FBI since its inception has been involved in various forms of political repression designed to protect the

political, economic, social, and racial status quo from dissident groups, COINTELPRO started in the 1950s when J. EDGAR HOOVER, the FBI director, directed the bureau to begin surveillance and repression of the COMMUNIST PARTY and other individuals and groups committed to RADICALISM. In the 1960s the targets of COINTELPRO were expanded to include "white hate groups" such as the KU KLUX KLAN and what the FBI called "black nationalist hate groups," and various "new left" student groups involved in PROTEST against the VIETNAM WAR. Although the FBI described its African-American targets as "black nationalist hate groups," in reality the targets included virtually all African-American groups involved in the CIVIL RIGHTS MOVEMENT, including in particular MARTIN LUTHER KING JR. Its other targets included SNCC, the NATION OF ISLAM, the REPUBLIC OF NEW AFRICA, and the BLACK PANTHER PARTY. During the period of its operation (the FBI said the program was formally stopped in 1971 because of fear of public exposure) 2,370 separate counterintelligence actions were taken against targeted groups, most of which were against African-American groups or individuals.

In its investigations of COINTELPRO, the U.S. Senate determined that the tactics used were "adopted wholesale from wartime counterintelligence." Indeed, William Sullivan, the associate bureau director said, "This is a rough, tough, dirty business, and dangerous. . . . It was dangerous at the time. No holds were barred. . . . We have used [these techniques] against Soviet agents. They have used [them] against us. . . . [The same methods were] brought home against any organization which we targeted. We did not differentiate. This is a rough, tough business." In effect, the FBI defined those involved in the African-American freedom struggle, whatever their IDEOLOGY, as "enemies" and treated them as it treated enemies during times of war. For example, the FBI spied on Dr. King and spread malicious gossip throughout the world about his sex life; it attempted to have him removed as leader of the movement and replaced by a person of its choosing (see SAMUEL PIERCE); and failing that, it attempted to force him to commit suicide or face exposure as a "pervert" and "hypocrite." (Most of Dr. King's colleagues in the movement and members of his family believe that the FBI was involved in his assassination, although none of the investigations of the assassination has produced evidence of bureau involvement.) In its report on its investigation of COINTELPRO, the Senate concluded that "many of the techniques would be intolerable in a democratic society even if all of the targets had been involved in violent activity, but COINTELPRO went far beyond that. The unexpressed major premise of the programs was that the law enforcement agency has the duty to do whatever is necessary to combat perceived threats to the existing social and political order." The Senate concluded that the FBI in unleashing COIN-

TELPRO had become a BUREAUCRACY beyond the effective control of the PRESIDENCY and CONGRESS. However David Garrow, a political scientist who carefully studied COINTELPRO and its repression of Dr. King and the Civil Rights movement, argues that the Senate's conclusion is not correct. Granting that the FBI had unprecedented authority and autonomy under Hoover, even so, Garrow concludes the presidents and members of Congress in Hoover's time were mostly white men of narrow conservative values, and Garrow contends that the FBI faithfully represented these same American values and was not an out-of-control bureaucracy. Rather, he writes, "The Bureau was not a renegade institution secretly operating outside parameters of American values, but a virtually representative bureaucracy that loyally served to protect the established order against adversary challenges."

Further reading: David Garrow, *The FBI and Martin Luther King, Jr.* (New York: Penguin Books, 1983); U.S. Senate, *Supplementary Detailed Staff Reports on Intelligence Activities and the Rights of Americans, Book III,* Final Report of the Select Committee to Study Government Operations with Respect to Intelligence Activities, 94th Cong., April 1976.

cold war

The cold war—the post–World War II struggle between the Union of Soviet Socialist Republics (USSR), and its allies, and the United States and its allies for world hegemony or domination—exerted major influences on the CIVIL RIGHTS MOVEMENT, PAN-AFRICANISM, and black MILITANCY and RADICALISM between 1947 and the late 1960s. In some ways the cold war was simply a manifestation of a classic, great-power conflict in international relations between Russia, the dominant power of the East, and America, the dominant power of the West. However, this classic big-power conflict was defined as (or became) an ideological conflict between COMMUNISM and CAPITALISM. It was the understanding of the cold war as an ideological struggle rather than as a mere big-power conflict that was the source of its potent influence on post-war American politics generally and on AFRICAN-AMERICAN POLITICS specifically. As an ideological conflict, the cold war was not simply a struggle between two great powers for hegemony but a struggle between the "free world" of democratic capitalism and the "unfree world" of totalitarian communism. In other words, it was a struggle between good and evil.

The cold war's origins can be traced to the famous "Iron Curtain" speech by Winston Churchill, the World War II British prime minister. In this speech, delivered by the former British leader in Fulton, Missouri, in 1946, Churchill declared that an "Iron Curtain" had descended across Europe, dividing the Soviet-led bloc of communist nations from the rest of Western Europe. He then called upon the United States to lead an alliance to resist the expansion of communism in Europe and to maintain order throughout the rest of the world. In his call for a "fraternal association of the English speaking peoples" to maintain world order, Churchill was seeking American support not only to resist communism in Europe but to maintain COLONIALISM in Africa and the rest of what was soon to be called the THIRD WORLD. At this time, much of the African-American LEADERSHIP and MEDIA were committed to ending COLONIALISM in Africa and the Third World, and they saw Churchill's speech and his call for a grand alliance of the West as an attempt to use the threat of communism to persuade the United States to support the maintenance of colonialism. Consequently, virtually the entire African-American leadership and media attacked Churchill and his idea of a Western alliance against the USSR and the fundamental premises of what was to become the cold war.

The attacks by black critics on Churchill and the cold war were frequently harsh. The *Chicago Defender* declared that "Churchill's cry that Russia is threatening world peace through an expansion of Communism is only a smokescreen to hide white supremacy and rule by oppression." And J. A. Rogers, a black journalist writing in the *Pittsburgh Courier,* said of Churchill and his speech that " . . . though he spouts democracy, he is a fascist at heart. Imperialism and Jim Crow are fascism." Most black leaders were more restrained in their criticisms, but at the outset of the cold war almost all black leaders and ORGANIZATIONS expressed opposition, including WALTER WHITE and W. E. B. DU BOIS of the NAACP and the leaders of the URBAN LEAGUE, the NATIONAL COUNCIL OF NEGRO WOMEN, and the NATIONAL NEGRO CONGRESS. The opposition of mainstream black leadership and media to the cold war was based on the premise that anticolonialism rather than anticommunism should be the priority of U.S. postwar FOREIGN POLICY and that the cold war was a subterfuge to maintain European colonialism in Africa and Asia. But some black leaders were also sympathetic to communism and radicalism and viewed the USSR as an ally in the struggle against WHITE SUPREMACY and RACISM at home and abroad. Prominent among such leaders and organizations were Du Bois, PAUL ROBESON, and the COUNCIL ON AFRICAN AFFAIRS.

Following Churchill's speech, President HARRY TRUMAN mobilized the resources of the United States to fight the cold war, creating a national-security apparatus at home (including a large standing army for the first time in American history) and a series of alliances in Europe, Asia, and the Middle East designed to stop the spread of communism. The United States also embarked on the Marshall Plan to rebuild Western Europe. At the founding of the UNITED NATIONS, the United States supported the European powers in their efforts to maintain their colonies in Africa and Asia, despite the opposition of Du Bois, MARY MCLEOD BETHUNE, and other black leaders who attended the United Nations founding meeting in San Francisco. U.S. foreign policy thus defined communism rather than colonialism as the main enemy in the Third World.

Although most African-American leaders at first opposed Truman's cold war initiatives, as the policy was consolidated there was an abrupt transformation in their attitudes so that by 1947 mainstream black leaders, organizations, and media joined in the anticommunism cold war consensus that was to dominate U.S. foreign policy until the VIETNAM WAR. In doing so, they largely abandoned pan-Africanism and solidarity with Third World peoples in their struggles against colonialism.

Several reasons account for this abrupt transformation in African-American leadership attitudes toward the cold war. (Not much is known about black PUBLIC OPINION on the cold war, since very few polls were taken.) First, a consensus quickly developed in support of Truman's cold war policies, a consensus that united liberals and conservatives, Democrats and Republicans. Thus, opposition to the cold war was increasingly defined as "disloyalty," as "anti-American," and as "giving aid and comfort to the enemy." Thus, African-American leaders became afraid of losing the support of important white liberal allies who were an important part of the civil rights COALITION and of being labeled "Red" (subversives who supported the communist enemy). This fear was intensified because of the strong anti–cold war stance of the American COMMUNIST PARTY, which mainstream black leaders did not wish to be associated with, and fear was heightened later by the climate of POLITICAL REPRESSION ushered in by the emergence of MCCARTHYISM. A second reason for the shift was a realistic sense that the USSR might be using Western racism and white supremacy and colonialism as subterfuges to advance its interests in hegemony in the Third World as well as its interests in revolution in the United States. Thus, these mainstream leaders came to see anticommunism as the appropriate strategy to defend American capitalism and DEMOCRACY at home and abroad. Walter White, head of the NAACP, for example, said that Russian imperialism was as bad as Western imperialism and that the triumph of Russia in the cold war would "mean the loss of manpower, raw materials and markets, without which the industrial West could not survive." Thus, the NAACP muted its criticism of U.S. support for colonialism, and its convention resolutions after 1948 began to consistently support the cold war, including the Marshall Plan, NATO (the organization of the Western military alliance), and the Korean War.

The NAACP also began to see and use the cold war as a resource that could be leveraged in the struggle against racism and white supremacy at home. For example, in its resolutions supporting the cold war, the NAACP consistently pointed to the use by the Russians at the United Nations and elsewhere of American racism as a weapon to advance their interests in the Third World. By noting that the Third World was nonwhite, African-American leaders and media contended that DESEGREGATION and EQUALITY at home were not only in the interests of African Americans, but they were also a "cold war imperative" if the United States was to win the support and gain access to the raw materials and markets of the Third World. For as long as blacks were denied equality at home, the Russians could and did point to the hypocrisy of the leader of the "free world" talking of FREEDOM while denying it to its colored or Third World minority. This strategic use of the cold war by the NAACP was to some extent effective, as President Truman used the cold war competition as part of the justification for his proposed CIVIL RIGHTS legislation in 1948, and it was used by the U.S. government in its brief filed with the SUPREME COURT in the *BROWN V. BOARD OF EDUCATION* case.

Not all black leaders, however, embraced the cold war consensus after 1947. Local NAACP chapters for a time continued to PROTEST, and radical leaders such as Du Bois and Paul Robeson and the Council on African Affairs continued their opposition to the cold war and colonialism. Du Bois and Robeson to some extent embraced Russia and communism as potential allies in the black freedom struggle in the United States and in the Third World. Because of their principled opposition both Du Bois and Robeson were subjects of various forms of political repression, including revocation of their passports and, in Du Bois's case, being fired by the NAACP for the second time and exile abroad, and, in Robeson's case, denial of the right to perform on stage and in concerts and exile at home. The adherence of most black leaders to the cold war consensus endured until it was shattered by the opposition of MALCOLM X, MARTIN LUTHER KING JR., MUHAMMAD ALI, and SNCC to the Vietnam War.

Further reading: Mary Dudziak, *Cold War Civil Rights: Race and the Image of American Democracy* (Princeton, N.J.: Princeton University Press, 2000); James Roark, "American Black Leaders: The Response to Colonialism and the Cold War, 1943–53," in *The African American Voice in U.S. Foreign Policy since World War II*, ed. Michael L. Krenn (New York: Garland, 1999); Mark Solomon, "Black Critics of Colonialism and the Cold War" in *The African American Voice in US Foreign Policy since World War II*, ed. Michael L. Krenn (New York: Garland, 1999).

Colfax massacre

VIOLENCE has frequently been employed as a base of power by whites to subordinate blacks and maintain their

OPPRESSION and as a method of POLITICAL REPRESSION when blacks resisted their subordination and oppression and fought for their FREEDOM. The massacre at Colfax, Louisiana, in 1873 is one of the most egregious examples of violent political repression in the whole of the African-American experience in the United States. Although not completely unique in the annals of black history, the massacre at Colfax is important because it indicated that the RECONSTRUCTION-era POLITICAL SYSTEM would not protect African Americans in the exercise of their VOTING RIGHTS, nor would it punish those whites who used violence to stop blacks from engaging in POLITICAL PARTICIPATION by voting and holding office. The symbolism of the massacre and its aftermath also suggested to blacks the futility of trying to resist violent repression by whites and helped to usher in the era of ACCOMMODATIONISM represented by the leadership of BOOKER T. WASHINGTON.

In 1872 Colfax—the county seat of Grant Parish, Louisiana (in Louisiana counties are called parishes)—was the site of a bitterly contested election for sheriff. At the time, Louisiana was also the site of an equally bitter dispute over control of its state government, including the legislature and the governor's office. In the 1872 election, a WHITE SUPREMACIST member of the DEMOCRATIC PARTY and a black-supported white REPUBLICAN PARTY member both claimed to have won the governorship. Louisiana at the time was one of the SOUTHERN STATES under the supervision of the U.S. Army. Because of the controversy, a judge ordered the U.S. marshall to seize the building in which the legislature met and hold it for the supporters of the Republicans. Meanwhile, as the dispute continued at the state level, in Grant and other parishes there were similar disputes by claimants to local offices. In Grant itself, an African-American Republican, Dan Shaw, claimed that he had been elected sheriff, but he was challenged by a white Democrat named Columbus Nash. In the course of the dispute, Shaw and his supporters occupied the courthouse, which was then surrounded by Nash and his supporters, who proceeded to burn the building, killing many inside and then hunting others down and killing them. Estimates vary, but somewhere between 150 and 280 blacks were killed, and one white was killed and two wounded.

News of the massacre, what one writer called the "apocalypse at Colfax," became a national sensation and was widely reported in Europe. When the army arrived in Colfax three days later, it arrested nine men under the Enforcement Act of 1870 and charged them with conspiracy and murder in order to deprive blacks of their rights to participate in the political process. After two trials, three of the men were convicted of multiple counts of conspiracy but acquitted of murder, and the others were acquitted of all charges. The three convicted men faced large fines and up to 10 years in prison. They appealed their convictions to the SUPREME COURT of the United States.

The Supreme Court in *Cruikshank v. the United States* (1876) reversed the convictions, declaring that under the principles of FEDERALISM it was the responsibility of the states to punish murder and that the Enforcement Act passed pursuant to CONGRESS's authority to enforce the rights and privileges guaranteed to blacks by the FOURTEENTH AMENDMENT did not give Congress the right to punish crimes traditionally left under federalism to the states. The Court also held that the Fourteenth Amendment did not prohibit action by individuals but rather by the states and that the murders at Colfax had been the work of private citizens and not officials of Louisiana. Finally, Chief Justice Morrison Waite, rather disingenuously, concluded that even if Congress had the authority to punish the abuse of blacks seeking to exercise their political rights, it was first necessary to prove that race was the motive in the massacre, which he said was not mentioned, let alone proven in the charges against the men.

It was clear to everyone, however, except Chief Justice Waite and his colleagues, that race was the motive. Indeed, shortly after the Court's decision the *Shreveport Times* in Louisiana published an editorial celebrating it by remarking about the "summary and wholesome lesson the Negroes have been taught in Grant Parish . . . by the white men of Grant." Several years after the massacre, whites in Colfax raised funds and placed a plaque on the Grant Parish Court House bearing the following inscription: "On this site occurred the Colfax riot in which three white men and 150 Negroes were slain. This event on April 13, 1873, marked the end of carpetbag misrule in the South."

The inscription was correct. The massacre at Colfax did represent one of the beginnings of the end of Reconstruction or what Southerners referred to as "carpetbag rule" in the South. For it signaled to blacks in a most graphic way that they could not defend themselves against the overwhelming violence of whites bent on their repression and oppression. And *Cruikshank* signaled that CONSTITUTIONALISM and its principles of federalism would be used to prevent the federal government from protecting them or punishing those who openly used violence as a method of political repression. *Cruikshank* was not effectively reversed until the 1960s.

colonialism

Colonialism is a system of domination or OPPRESSION in which one nation controls the economy and political process of a geographically distinct social or political entity. Frequently, the colonized area is inhabited by people of a different ETHNICITY or racial background, and usually the land, labor, and natural resources of the area are exploited for the benefit of the colonial power. Also, the political process of the area is dominated by the external nation as a result of the disproportionate POWER relationships that characterize the interactions between the peoples as SUPERORDINATE and SUBORDINATE groups.

In the modern world, the nations of western Europe colonized much of the rest of the world in most of Asia, Africa, the Americas, and the islands of the sea. (Between 1400 and 1900, 80 percent of the globe came under European domination.) European colonialization of Africa emerged after the Atlantic trade introduced SLAVERY into the colonies of the Americas, and indeed it may be that slavery was a necessary precondition for colonialism, since it may have contributed to the inability of African societies to resist. In any event, the colonialization of Africa and the enslavement of the Africans emerge out of the same historical processes of European expansion and exploitation of the peoples of the world. Both slavery and colonialism are products of the disproportionate power—technological and military—of the European compared with the nonwhite peoples. And both processes were based on the IDEOLOGY of WHITE SUPREMACY and RACISM and involved the use of extraordinary VIOLENCE as a means to impose relationships of domination—socially, economically, culturally, and politically. Thus, in some analyses the oppression of Africans in the United States is viewed as a form or as a manifestation of INTERNAL COLONIALISM.

In one of the most egregious cases of the violence and exploitation of European colonial rule, King Leopold of Belgium turned the Congo in central Africa into his personal fiefdom. For nearly 30 years he used extraordinary violence to turn that vast land into a huge forced-labor camp. In what is sometimes referred to as the "Congo holocaust," between 1885 and 1908 more than 10 million people died as a result of beatings (Congolese laborers were routinely beaten if they failed to meet their assigned quotas of ivory or rubber), exhaustion, starvation, or disease.

The leaders of Europe formally divided the societies and peoples of Africa among themselves at a conference in Berlin in 1884, with important colonies granted to France, Britain, Belgium, and Portugal. This system began to fall apart in the 1960s as African peoples intensified their struggles for independence. The African independence struggles have their roots, in part, in the philosophy of PAN-AFRICANISM developed by African Americans.

color stratification

The BLACK COMMUNITY in the United States, like the white community, is divided or stratified on the basis of class (see CLASS STRATIFICATION), but unlike the white community, the black community in the United States (and most communities of African peoples throughout the world) is also divided or stratified on the basis of skin color.

Historically, slave society in the United States was organized externally and, to some extent, internally on the basis of skin color differences among the African Americans. Persons with lighter skin color or who most resembled whites in appearance (because they were the offspring of slave owners and slave women) were accorded greater privileges—socially, economically, and politically—by the external white society and also internally within the slave community. (Rewards for runaway light-skinned slaves or mulattoes were generally much higher than for those who were dark.) The privileges granted to those with lighter skins over time resulted in their constituting a disproportionately large part of the middle and upper classes and of the LEADERSHIP of black America. Although no exact correlation between color and class can be established, GUNNAR MYRDAL concluded that at the time of the EMANCIPATION PROCLAMATION "what there was in the Negro of 'family background,' tradition of freedom, education and property ownership was mostly in the hands of mulattos. . . . They became the political leaders of the freedmen during Reconstruction, as well as their teachers, professionals and leaders." Many of the black leaders of the ABOLITIONIST MOVEMENT are usually described as persons of mixed race, and almost all of the black congressmen during RECONSTRUCTION were of mixed race, as were most of the leaders of the CIVIL RIGHTS MOVEMENT.

In contemporary black society, skin color still has its privileges. The white "gatekeepers" who control access to opportunities in America apparently still engage in DISCRIMINATION against darker-skinned blacks. And there is still color consciousness and discrimination within the black community. Studies in the 1960s and 1980s show that a higher proportion of African Americans who are high-school dropouts, unemployed, employed in low-status jobs, and who live in the GHETTO are dark skinned. A 1994 study conducted in Los Angeles, for example, concluded that being African American and dark skinned reduced the likelihood of finding a job by 52 percent after taking into account other relevant variables.

While skin color still makes a difference in social and economic status, its political consequences are less clear. Among whites, a 1993 study found that voters are more favorably disposed to light-skinned African-American candidates than to those with darker complexions, and in the black community there has always been some tension between the color-conscious mulatto black leadership and the masses of ordinary black people, and some of that tension persists into the early 21st century. There also has been occasional conflict based on skin color between lighter- and darker-skinned leaders (as, for example, famously between the light-skinned W. E. B. DU BOIS and the darker MARCUS GARVEY in the 1920s). However, little of that is observed among POST–CIVIL RIGHTS ERA black leaders. In terms of

IDEOLOGY and PUBLIC OPINION, blacks of all shades of color tend to adhere to modern LIBERALISM, but studies have shown that darker-skinned blacks tend to lean more toward elements of the philosophy of BLACK NATIONALISM and may express more overt hostility toward whites.

See also INTERNAL INFERIORIZATION.

Further reading: Kathy Russell, Midge Wilson, and Ronald Hall, *The Color Complex: The Politics of Skin Color among African Americans* (New York: Harcourt Brace Jovanovich, 1992); H. E. Ransford, "Skin Color, Life Chances and Anti-White Attitudes," *Social Problems* 18 (1970): 164–72; Richard Seltzer and Robert C. Smith, "Skin Color Differences in the Afro-American Community," *Journal of Black Studies* 21 (1991): 279–86.

commerce clause, U.S. Constitution

The CONSTITUTION of the United States limits the legislative or lawmaking power of CONGRESS. That is, Congress is not granted plenary authority to pass laws on any subject it wishes. Rather, its authority is limited by Article I's first sentence, which reads "All legislative powers herein granted" are vested in the Congress. The legislative powers "herein granted" are then listed in Article I, Section 8, which are referred to as the "delegated powers." All laws passed by Congress are supposed to be based on some language in Section 8. Otherwise, Congress lacks the authority to legislate, and the power to do so is, under the principle of FEDERALISM, "reserved to the states" unless the Constitution prohibits the states from acting.

Until the NEW DEAL, this notion of limited congressional legislative authority severely limited the power of Congress to address pressing problems in areas involving regulation of the economy, CIVIL RIGHTS, and the development of the modern WELFARE STATE. During the New Deal, FRANKLIN D. ROOSEVELT used the commerce clause in Section 8 (which grants Congress the Authority to "regulate commerce . . . among the several states") as the basis for many of the laws enacted regulating the economy and creating the welfare state. The SUPREME COURT initially held these laws unconstitutional. However, President Roosevelt's "court packing" plan of 1939 (in which he sought unsuccessfully to increase the size of the Court so that he could appoint justices sympathetic to his views) prompted the Court to change its decisions, and for the next half century the Court allowed the Congress to use the commerce clause as an almost plenary grant of power to legislate on any activity that it wished as long as it could show that it had some effect (direct or indirect) on interstate commerce (the movement of goods, services, and people across state lines).

The CIVIL RIGHTS ACT OF 1964 and all subsequent modern civil rights legislation are based on the commerce clause. Modern civil rights legislation is based on Congress's authority to regulate the movement of goods and services in interstate commerce rather than its more majestic power to enforce the EQUAL PROTECTION CLAUSE of the FOURTEENTH AMENDMENT. The reason for this is that in the CIVIL RIGHTS CASES OF 1883, the Supreme Court ruled that the equal protection clause only prohibited DISCRIMINATION by the states. Rather than challenge this 1880s precedent, the administrations of JOHN F. KENNEDY and LYNDON B. JOHNSON chose to base the civil rights legislation of the 1960s on the commerce clause, arguing that racial discrimination interfered with interstate commerce. Supreme Court Justice William O. Douglas argued at the time that this was a mistake and that the precedent of the civil rights cases of 1883 should be overturned. Writing a concurring opinion in *HEART OF ATLANTA V. UNITED STATES* Douglas wrote:

> I am reluctant to . . . rest solely on the Commerce Clause. My reluctance is not due to any conviction that Congress lacks the power to regulate commerce in the interest of human rights. It is rather my belief that the right of the people to be free of state action that discriminates against them because of race . . . occupies a more protected place in our constitutional system then does the movement of cattle, fruit, steel and coal across state lines. Hence, I would prefer to rest on the assertion of legislative power contained in Section 5 of the Fourteenth Amendment which states "The Congress shall have the power to enforce, by appropriate legislation, the provisions of this article"—a power which the Court concedes was exercised at least in part.

Douglas's reluctance to base the civil rights, or what he called HUMAN RIGHTS, of Americans on commerce rather than the Fourteenth Amendment's command of EQUALITY may turn out to have been prescient, since the Supreme Court in the late 1990s substantially restricted the Congress's use of the commerce cause in the area of civil rights and economic regulations.

With the appointment of CLARENCE THOMAS in 1991, the Supreme Court for the first time since the New Deal had a conservative majority, although a narrow one of only five justices. But with this narrow majority, the Court appeared to return to its pre–New Deal commerce clause jurisprudence. In 1995 in *United States v. Lopez*, the five-person conservative majority declared unconstitutional a law enacted by Congress that prohibited the possession of a gun near a school. This was the first time since the New Deal that the Court had invalidated an act of Congress based on the commerce clause. One year later in *Seminole Tribe v. Florida*, the Court held that individuals could not sue a state to enforce federal rights based on the commerce clause. Subsequently, the Court ruled several other commerce-clause-based laws unconstitutional, including ones involving age discrimination, minimum wages, and violence against women. (The violence against women's case is *United States v. Morrison* et al., decided in 2000.) And the Court agreed to decide whether individuals could sue to compel the states to obey the Americans with Disabilities Act (which prohibits discrimination on the bases of a variety of disabilities).

In each of these cases the Court has held that the activity (violence against women, for example) did not sufficiently affect interstate commerce or that, because of federalism, the states were immune from suits by individuals if the law is based on the commerce clause, because states can only be sued by individuals on the basis of laws based on the Fourteenth Amendment. Under this reasoning, civil rights laws in the United States are caught in a classic "Catch 22." For civil rights laws to be enforced against the states, they must be based on the Fourteenth Amendment, but if they are to be enforced against individuals and businesses, they must be based on the commerce clause. But, if they are based on the commerce clause, the states can violate them with impunity.

The commerce clause since the New Deal has been the constitutional basis for the modern welfare state and modern civil rights law, At the end of the 20th century, its use was challenged by a Supreme Court committed to CONSERVATISM and the principles of federalism.

communism

Communism is a broad social, economic, and political philosophy based on the principles that a society's means of production or its wealth in the form of productive property should be owned by all the people and administered on their behalf by the government in order to achieve an equalitarian society. Although Plato and other Western philosophers advocated communism in some forms, as have certain Christian sects, modern communism is based primarily on the writings of Karl Marx and V. I. Lenin. Thus, communism as an IDEOLOGY is also known as marxism or Leninism. Marx's theory postulated the inevitable collapse of CAPITALISM and the emergence of communism as a result of the "internal contradictions" of capitalism and the emergence of a class-conscious "proletariat" (working class). This class-conscious proletariat would essentially use its size and solidarity in a revolt against the bourgeoisie and establish a "dictatorship of the proletariat," which in turn would create a classless society, at which time the state or the government would "wither away." Lenin's contribution to communism was the development of a theory and strategy that resulted in the establishment in 1917 of the first communist state in Russia. In modified form, Lenin's

theory and strategy were employed by other successful communist revolutionaries in the establishment of communism, including Mao Tse-tung in China, Ho Chi Minh in Vietnam, and Fidel Castro in Cuba.

Communism as a philosophy and as the ideology of the USSR and other communist states is antithetical to capitalism, which is one of the core values of the American POLITICAL SYSTEM. From the end of World War II to the collapse of Soviet communism in the 1990s, the United States waged a COLD WAR to prevent the spread of communism and to foster its collapse abroad, while at home adherents of communism were defined as subversive and "un-American" and were subject to POLITICAL REPRESSION in various forms. Nevertheless, an influential stratum of black LEADERSHIP in the United States has been enamored of communism, including W. E. B. DU BOIS, PAUL ROBESON, AMIRI BARAKA, and ANGELA DAVIS. And to some extent MARTIN LUTHER KING JR. and MALCOLM X, while not adherents of communism, were in their last years flirting with SOCIALISM as an alternative to capitalism, and BAYARD RUSTIN, RONALD DELLUMS, and A. PHILIP RANDOLPH openly embraced socialism. Why have so many talented black individuals in leadership positions embraced RADICALISM in the forms of socialism and communism, given their antisystemic character, their definition as subversive and anti-American, and the near inevitability of political repression? Because in one way or another they all came to the conclusion that FREEDOM and EQUALITY for African Americans could not be achieved under capitalism. Also, the COMMUNIST PARTY in the United States historically was a strong supporter of CIVIL RIGHTS.

Communist Party

Although the Communist Party of the United States of America (CPUSA) never had a major influence on American politics, at its peak during the Great Depression it probably did as much to advance the cause of African-American FREEDOM and EQUALITY as any predominantly white group that blacks have joined. The success of the communist revolution in Russia in 1917 inspired the creation of communist parties throughout the world, and in 1919 the CPUSA was organized.

A major reason that communist and socialist parties have had relatively little influence on American politics is because Americans for a variety of reasons have rejected RADICALISM, but it is also true that radical socialists and communists have had to endure POLITICAL REPRESSION in various forms. From its formation until the 1970s, the CPUSA faced continued repression. In the 1920s its foreign-born members were subject to arrest and deportation; in the 1940s many of its leaders were jailed; the McCarran-Walter Act of the 1950s made membership in the party a crime and required its members to register with the federal government; and during the era of MCCARTHYISM party members were harassed and prohibited from holding a variety of jobs in education, labor unions, and in the arts. The major reason for the repression of the party was its adherence to Marxism-Leninism and advocacy of revolution. However, throughout its history the CPUSA was closely identified with the cause of racial justice, and this too was a reason for its repression, since the FBI and the U.S. Army viewed the CIVIL RIGHTS MOVEMENT as a threat to the internal security and stability of the POLITICAL SYSTEM.

The CPUSA at its 1922 convention adopted the principle of complete equality for African Americans and openly recruited blacks to join the party and participate in its leadership. However, the party's position on race was not determined by its American members but, rather, was dictated from Russia through its control of the Communist International. Following the Communist International position, the CPUSA adopted a rigid IDEOLOGY of BLACK NATIONALISM, which promoted a separate black nation-state as the only route to freedom for African Americans in the United States. The embrace of this extreme form of black nationalism as well as the party's commitment to COMMUNISM alienated it from mainstream black PUBLIC OPINION and the mainstream leadership of the Civil Rights movement, both of which tended to be anticommunist and antiblack separatism. Thus, although a number of black intellectuals, artists, and working people joined the party, it was never a major influence in AFRICAN-AMERICAN POLITICS.

The party achieved its greatest prominence and success among blacks in its defense during the 1930s of the "Scottsboro boys" (nine young black men accused of raping two white women in Alabama). The Scottsboro case became an international example of racial injustice in the United States and was used by lawyers affiliated with the party to eventually win a SUPREME COURT decision overturning the conviction of the men.

In the 1960s the Supreme Court, under the leadership of EARL WARREN, declared most of the laws used to repress the CPUSA unconstitutional. As a result, the party became more involved in politics, taking an active role in the Civil Rights and anti–VIETNAM WAR movements. In the late 1960s it took the lead in supporting ANGELA DAVIS, an African-American scholar who was fired from a teaching post at UCLA because of her membership in the party. In 1968 an African-American woman, Charlene Mitchell, was the party's nominee for president of the United States. After the collapse of the Soviet Union and the end of the COLD WAR in 1991, the CPUSA's already small membership declined and its always marginal role in American and African-American politics became even more marginal.

Further reading: Robin Kelly, *The Hammer and Hoe: Alabama Communists during the Great Depression* (Chapel Hill: University of North Carolina Press, 1990); Mark Naison, *Communists in Harlem during the Depression* (New York: Grove Press, 1983).

community control

Community control is a concept advanced by some African-American leaders in the late 1960s that called for the establishment of autonomous black communities within the geographic boundaries of major American cities. The concept is partly rooted in the philosophy of BLACK NATIONALISM and was forcefully advocated by MALCOLM X in the years prior to his death. Malcolm consistently argued that the philosophy of black nationalism required that blacks control the economy, culture, and politics of the BLACK COMMUNITY. The concept was also advanced by activists in the BLACK POWER MOVEMENT and was a part of the WAR ON POVERTY's Community Action Program, which required "maximum feasible participation" of persons from the neighborhoods in the design and implementation of community-based antipoverty programs.

Community-control advocates based the concept on the idea that there exists a distinctive black community in American cities, but it was not an autonomous community since decision making for it was controlled by whites who did not live within its geographic boundaries. Thus, CORE, for example, in its program called for the recognition of the autonomy of urban black communities, the allocation of an equitable share of city revenues to them, and the establishment of all-black governance and administrative structures that would manage the internal institutions of the community, including schools, libraries, police, and social-service bureaucracies. It was also envisioned that African Americans would develop autonomous economic and cultural institutions. The idea of community control was opposed by white liberals, who viewed it as a recognition of group rights and therefore a violation of the core liberal principle of INDIVIDUALISM, and it was opposed by African-American adherents of INTEGRATION because it constituted a form of racial separatism or an acceptance of SEGREGATION. Community control in the view of these critics would turn the GHETTOS into SUBORDINATE "Bantustans," akin to the separate homelands for blacks under the South African system of APARTHEID.

In the late 1960s several community-control initiatives were started, including a controversial experiment in New York City where blacks were granted authority to control a predominantly black school district in the Ocean Hill–Brownsville section of Brooklyn. The Ocean Hill–Brownsville experiment resulted in rancorous conflict between blacks and Jews over the hiring and firing of teachers and administrators. Ultimately the experiment was terminated and used as a case study in the weaknesses of the concept of community control.

Since the 1970s the demand for community control has declined in part because the election of blacks as mayors and to city councils and school boards in most major American cities gave blacks at least nominal control of the political institutions and bureaucracies that governed the black community. The failure of the experiment in Ocean Hill–Brownsville appeared to confirm the concerns of liberal critics of the concept. Also, the War on Poverty's Community Action Program was terminated. Finally, the broader urban political systems became more accessible to African Americans. There is, however, continuing support for the concept in black PUBLIC OPINION, particularly in terms of schools and the police. A survey conducted in the early 1990s found that 81 percent of blacks supported some degree of independent control over those institutions that most directly affect their own communities.

See also PLURALISM, PLURAL SOCIETY, and URBAN POLITICS.

Further reading: Alan Altshuter, *Community Control: The Black Demand for Participation in Large American Cities* (New York: Pegasus, 1970).

Compromise of 1877

The Compromise of 1877 is generally thought of as the event that brought an end to RECONSTRUCTION and began the era of SEGREGATION and JIM CROW that would characterize black-white relations in the SOUTHERN STATES until the 1960s.

The compromise relates to the disputed election for president in 1876 between the REPUBLICAN PARTY's candidate, RUTHERFORD B. HAYES, and the DEMOCRATIC PARTY candidate, Samuel Tilden. In the popular vote, Hayes lost to Tilden by a margin of 48 to 51 percent, and the ELECTORAL COLLEGE votes from three Southern states—South Carolina, Louisiana, and Florida—were in dispute. These states were the only ones in the South still under the control of Reconstruction governments and the supervision of the U.S. Army. The disputed elections involved not only the electoral votes of the three states for president but also control of their STATE AND LOCAL GOVERNMENTs. With both the Democrats and the Republicans claiming victory and organizing separate governments in each state, the prospect for violent conflict between the two parties seemed imminent unless the army intervened. To avoid this and secure his election, Hayes in the compromise agreed that in exchange for the disputed votes (which gave him an electoral college victory of 185 to 184 over Tilden) from the three states he would, once elected, withdraw the army from the states and permit the white supremacists and racists in the Democratic Party in those states (and throughout the South) to govern their affairs without fed-

eral intervention. Hayes also promised to assist the region in economic development and extracted from the representatives of the states a promise to respect the civil and political rights of African Americans. This promise, however, was not kept, for after the withdrawal of the army, a long campaign of VIOLENCE and POLITICAL REPRESSION was set in motion, resulting eventually in the almost total disenfranchisement of blacks and the imposition of a rigid system of segregation and OPPRESSION.

The Compromise of 1877, however, represents only the symbolic end to Reconstruction, since by the time of the compromise, white elite and mass opinion in the NORTHERN STATES had come to the view that it was time to withdraw the army from the South and bring Reconstruction to an end. In a sense the 1877 compromise represents the emergence of a first WHITE BACKLASH, a phenomenon in which whites grow tired of the divisive conflicts and struggles over black EQUALITY and seek a return to normalcy, even if this return to normalcy involves sacrificing the rights of African Americans. The compromise also represents the beginnings of the powerful CONSERVATIVE COALITION of Northern conservative Republicans and Southern Democrats, which blocked or substantially watered down CIVIL RIGHTS and WELFARE STATE legislation until the 1960s and 1970s.

Further reading: C. Vann Woodward, *Reunion and Reaction: The Compromise of 1877 and the End of Reconstruction* (Garden City, N.J.: Doubleday Anchor, 1956).

Congress

The SEPARATION OF POWERS, along with FEDERALISM, constitutes the distinguishing structural features of the government of the United States as established by the CONSTITUTION. Under the Constitution, the Congress is the supreme or first branch of government. It is granted the sole authority to legislate, to raise taxes, to appropriate or spend money, to raise and support the military, to declare war, and to regulate commerce and the currency. The Congress also has the authority to create the federal BUREAUCRACY, and the Senate has the authority to approve treaties and appointments to the bureaucracy and the federal courts. And through the process of impeachment, the Congress has the authority to remove from office the president and other officers of the government.

Representation of Blacks in the Congress

The vast legislative and related powers are conferred on Congress because it, rather than the PRESIDENCY or the SUPREME COURT, is suppose to be the branch of the government that represents the people. REPRESENTATION is central to legislative legitimacy and DEMOCRACY. As the

English philosopher John Stuart Mill put it in his 1869 book, *Considerations on Representative Government:*

> In a really equal democracy, every or any section would be represented, not disproportionately but proportionately. A majority of electors would always have a majority of the representatives but a minority of electors would always have a minority of representatives, man for man, they would be fully represented as the majority; unless they are, there is not equal government, but government of inequality and privilege: one part of the people rule over the rest. There is a part whose fair and equal share and influence in representation is withheld from them contrary to the principle of democracy, which professes equality at its very root and foundation.

Historically, the Congress has lacked legitimacy because it has failed to provide EQUALITY in representation to African Americans. Until the RECONSTRUCTION era, African Americans were completely denied representation in Congress, although the THREE-FIFTHS CLAUSE of the Constitution included blacks as a basis for providing representation to the whites in the SOUTHERN STATES who enslaved them. From 1787, the year of the first Congress, until 1870, no African American served in the Congress.

Joseph H. Rainey of South Carolina was elected to the U.S. House of Representatives in 1870. He was the first black American to serve in the House. *(Library of Congress)*

At the end of the 20th century 102 blacks had served: 98 in the House and four in the Senate. (A little more than 11,000 persons had served in the Congress by the end of the 20th century.) From the 1870s to 1891 blacks averaged two representatives in the House, and in the next decade there was only one black congressman to represent the nation's more than 8 million black citizens. In 1901 GEORGE WHITE became the last Reconstruction-era black member of the House. From 1901 to 1929 no blacks served in Congress. In 1928 Oscar Depriest was elected from Chicago, and in 1944 ADAM CLAYTON POWELL was elected from HARLEM. The elections of Depriest and Powell from NORTHERN STATES represent the political consequences of the GREAT MIGRATION. Until the POST–CIVIL RIGHTS ERA, only five blacks served in the House. Then in 1969 and again in 1992 there was a fairly rapid rise in black representation in the House, reaching an all-time high of 39 in 1993. This represents 9 percent of the 440 members of the House (including the five nonvoting members from the U.S. territories and the DISTRICT OF COLUMBIA), which, while not representing equality in representation (which would be, given the black proportion of the population, about 12 percent), is the largest black delegation ever to sit in Congress.

The growth in black representation in the House is a function of several factors: the size and solidarity of the black electorate concentrated in the big-city GHETTOS; the Supreme Court's "one person, one vote" principle established in *BAKER V. CARR;* and the implementation of the VOTING RIGHTS ACT OF 1965. However, these gains in black representation are jeopardized by the Supreme Court's decision in *SHAW V. RENO* (and related cases), which suggested that many of the districts represented by blacks may have been created in an unconstitutional way because they were deliberately created to have black-population majorities. Because of RACISM and WHITE SUPREMACY, it has been very difficult for blacks to be elected to the House from districts without a black majority or a majority minority (blacks and Latinos). Of the 98 blacks who have served in the House, only five (about 4 percent) have been elected from districts with an initial white majority.

In the Senate's more than 200-year history, only four blacks have served; BLANCHE K. BRUCE and HIRAM REVELS in the Reconstruction era and EDWARD BROOKE and CAROL MOSELEY-BRAUN in the post–civil rights era. It has been difficult for blacks to win Senate seats because senators are elected on a statewide basis, because no state has a black majority, and because whites are reluctant to vote for blacks.

In basing representation on geography rather than people (with each state—no matter its population—having two senators), the Senate is a particularly egregious case of a violation of John Stuart Mill's principle of equality in representation. WOODROW WILSON, the 21st president but also a political scientist, described the Senate as a "blemish" on the American democracy because of its unrepresentative character in his classic book *Congressional Government*. James Madison, the Constitution's principal author, favored a Senate based on the representation of the people, but his idea was rejected on the basis of federalism and the principle of the equality of representation of the states. This means, to use the words of Chief Justice EARL WARREN in *Baker v. Carr*, that senators represent "trees not people." (Under the Constitution as originally adopted, senators were selected by state legislatures rather than the people, a situation that did not change until the adoption of the Seventeenth Amendment in 1913.) If the Senate were based on the "one person, one vote" principle of *Baker v. Carr* (which it cannot be because Article V of the Constitution prohibits any change in representation in the Senate unless it is consented to by every state, an unlikely possibility), then the American people in general and African Americans in particular would have more equal and democratic representation. However, as things are and probably always will be (given the Fifth Article), the Senate is an extraordinarily unrepresentative body. For example, the smallest states with a combined population of less than 20 million have 20 percent of the votes in the Senate, while California—a state with a population of 30 million—has only 2 percent. Or, to put it another way, the 10 largest states with a combined population of more than 130 million have the same proportionate representation in the Senate as the 10 smallest states with their combined population of less than 20 million. The unrepresentative character of the Senate impacts all Americans, but it has a disproportionate impact on the representation of blacks. This is so, first, because the Senate overrepresents whites. In the 10 smallest-population states, the average white population is 90 percent while in the 10 largest-population states it is only 70 percent. Second, since there is no state with a black majority, it is very difficult for blacks to win election to the Senate. Indeed, since 1920, when senators were elected by the people of the states for the first time, only two blacks have been elected. Third, even when blacks are able to win election to the Senate from majority-white states, they have to represent the interests of the white majority rather than the BLACK COMMUNITY. In contrast, if the one-person, one-vote principle and the principles of the Voting Rights Act prior to *Shaw v. Reno* were applied to the election of senators, and if the country were divided into 100 senatorial districts with a population of approximately 2.8 million persons each, then instead of no black senators, there would probably be nine to 12 black senators from majority-black senatorial districts. These senators could then, like their counterparts in the senates of the states and in the U.S. House, represent the interests of blacks. But, alas,

the Constitution effectively can never be amended to make this change. The underrepresentation of blacks in the Senate is therefore constitutionally frozen.

Representation of Black Interests in the Congress

While the Congress does not, never has, and probably never will proportionately or descriptively represent blacks, it has from time to time substantively represented their interests. From 1787 to the 1860s, the Congress represented the interests of the slaveholders, although in 1808 (the earliest year permitted by the Constitution) it did abolish the slave trade, and earlier in 1787, in the Northwest Ordinance Act, it prohibited SLAVERY in the territories of the upper Midwest. But throughout the period leading up to the CIVIL WAR, the Congress ignored the ABOLITIONIST MOVEMENT and its demand for FREEDOM for the enslaved African. Indeed, from 1835 to 1844 the House imposed a GAG RULE prohibiting the receipt or debate of petitions by slaves for freedom. After the Civil War, in the Reconstruction era, the Congress was for a time dominated by the so-called RADICAL REPUBLICANS, who led it in responding for the first time to black demands for freedom and equality.

Between 1866 and 1875 Congress passed three CIVIL RIGHTS acts, three civil rights enforcement acts, and three civil rights amendments to the Constitution. Together, these acts and amendments abolished slavery and guaranteed freedom and equality. However, the Supreme Court either declared these acts unconstitutional or, through its interpretation, rendered them unenforceable. Thus, from the 1880s until the 1960s, blacks were effectively denied freedom and equality, as a system of rigid JIM CROW–style of SEGREGATION was imposed in the Southern states and a less rigid, more flexible system of subordination was imposed in the Northern states. During this period from the 1880s until the 1960s, the Congress was dominated by the CONSERVATIVE COALITION of Southern Democrats and Northern Republicans that first emerged in the COMPROMISE OF 1877. This coalition used its control of the Congress—especially its committees and the FILIBUSTER in the Senate—to block consideration of effective civil rights legislation until the 1960s.

In 1957 and 1960, Congress passed civil rights laws for the first time since Reconstruction. These laws, however, were largely symbolic, having little impact on racism in the North or South. As a direct result of the PROTEST of the CIVIL RIGHTS MOVEMENT, the Congress passed the CIVIL RIGHTS ACT OF 1964, the VOTING RIGHTS ACT OF 1965, and the Fair Housing Act of 1968. In the post–civil rights era, the Congress passed additional civil rights bills, including the Civil Rights Restoration Act of 1988 and the Civil Rights Act of 1991. The 1988 and 1991 acts were passed because of Supreme Court decisions that undermined the effectiveness of the laws passed in the 1960s. In the late

1990s the Congress rejected attempts to abolish AFFIRMA-TIVE ACTION in higher education and government contracting.

Blacks in the Power Structure of the House

In the late 20th century, African-American members of the House constituted an important bloc of votes within the House Democratic Party Caucus. Organized as the CONGRESSIONAL BLACK CAUCUS, the group tends to maintain solidarity in its voting behavior and has considerable seniority. Since leadership of House committees and subcommittees is based on seniority (the member of the majority party that is most senior in terms of length of service on a committee becomes chair), blacks chair many important committees and subcommittees when the Democratic Party has a majority of the members of the House. (Of the 39 blacks in the House in 2000, all except one was a Democrat.) These leadership positions on committees allow blacks to play important roles in shaping the party's agenda in the House. However, black House members tend to be liberal in their IDEOLOGY, and the House tends to be moderate or conservative, which means that blacks have relatively little power in overall House decision making. And of course blacks have no influence in the Senate, since it tends to have only one or two black members at most, and usually none.

Two African Americans have served in formal leadership positions in the House. In the 1980s, Congressman WILLIAM GRAY served as chair of the powerful Budget Committee, and he later became House majority whip, the number-three leadership position in the body. And in 1990, Congressman J. C. WATTS, the lone black Republican, became chair of the Republican Party Conference, the number-four leadership position.

Congressional Black Caucus

The Congressional Black Caucus is the most important ORGANIZATION to come out of the BLACK POWER MOVEMENT of the late 1960s. Among other things, this movement called for racial solidarity in politics and autonomous or all-black organizations. In 1968 the first post–Black Power group of congresspersons was elected. Younger and more activist and movement-oriented than their colleagues, this new group in 1969 sparked the formation of the caucus as a racially exclusive organization that would represent the collective interests of blacks in Congress. The more senior members of the black congressional delegation were apprehensive and reluctant to form a black caucus because of concern about the reactions of their white colleagues and because of its separatist or black nationalist implications. Congressman AUGUSTUS HAWKINS, for example, consistently argued that the group should not be racially exclusive but open to all who shared its objectives. Congressman Charles Rangel described the reaction of the House leadership to the formation of the caucus as "somewhat leery" and noted that, among most House members, "There is no question there was a great deal of resentment. Some people felt that color should not be something that binds a group; that we are all Americans and there was no need for one ethnic group to bind." In general, however, the leadership took a wait-and-see attitude toward the group after assurances from Congressman CHARLES DIGGS and other senior members that the group was "responsible" and not some militant Black Power clique that would subvert the decorum and integrity of the House.

The caucus first came to national attention as a result of its boycott of President RICHARD NIXON's 1971 State of the Union address. The boycott was undertaken to PROTEST the president's refusal to meet with the group. After the boycott, the president reluctantly agreed to the meeting, informing the caucus through Senator EDWARD BROOKE that he would see members after a face-saving period of a couple of months so as not to appear to be reacting to the boycott.

The boycott and subsequent meeting with the president brought the heretofore obscure group to the attention of the press and public. There were scores of generally laudatory articles in the black MEDIA and considerable attention in the national press (the *New York Times* suggested the group was assuming the leadership of blacks nationally, filling the void left by the death of MARTIN LUTHER KING JR.), including a *Newsweek* cover story and an invitation to appear on NBC's prestigious *Meet the Press* television interview program. By granting the caucus an audience the president, reluctantly to be sure, conferred legitimacy on the caucus as a black-power group in the Congress.

As a black-power organization, the caucus fairly quickly gained legitimacy and respectability in Congress and the broader policy process, but its organization on a racially exclusive basis continues to pose, as Congressman Hawkins warned from the outset, a series of dilemmas in terms of racial solidarity as an organizing principle in American politics. In 1975 Congressman Fortney Stark of California applied for caucus membership. A white liberal Democrat with a voting record indistinguishable from the caucus, Stark said he wished to join the caucus because it "represents the problems and struggles not only of blacks but of all poor and underprivileged people." After what then–caucus chairman Rangel described as a long and agonizing discussion, the caucus rejected Stark's application. The caucus explained its rejection in terms of symbolism, saying in a press release, "Essentially, the Caucus symbolizes black political development in this country. We feel maintaining this symbolism is critical at this juncture." Yet in 1990 the caucus accepted for membership Congressman Gary Franks, an extremely conservative black Republican elected from a white suburban Connecticut district who, judged by his voting record, is hostile to the aspirations of blacks and poor people. Indeed, several of his colleagues in the caucus publicly denounced Franks as a "traitor to the race" and an UNCLE TOM. Thus, fidelity to an all-embracing principle of race solidarity ironically undermined caucus solidarity. Congressman J. C. WATTS, a conservative black Republican from a majority-white district in Oklahoma, refused to join the caucus when he was elected in 1994.

When the caucus was formed, its members and some observers saw it not as just another organization of legislators but as an institution that would organize and represent in Washington the interests of the national BLACK COMMUNITY. The death of Dr. King, the shift of movement strategy from protest to electoral politics, and the perception that organizations like the NAACP and the URBAN LEAGUE had lost their viability led members of the caucus to argue that, as the "highest body of black elected officials," they had both the experience and the legitimacy to act as the principal spokesgroup for blacks in national politics. Through a series of hearings and conferences in the early 1970s, the caucus sought to develop a new POST–CIVIL RIGHTS ERA BLACK AGENDA and gain recognition (from the president, the Congress, and the media) for itself and its agenda as representing the basic demands of black America. This role of the caucus was never accepted by all members of the group (senior members such as Congressman Hawkins were particularly wary of the caucus attempting to function beyond a narrow legislative role) and was rejected outright by the traditional civil rights organizations as well as the then-influential radical and black nationalist elements of the LEADERSHIP in the community. Rejection of this national leadership role for the caucus was one of the factors that led to the calling of the NATIONAL BLACK POLITICAL CONVENTION in 1972. It was argued that the caucus was too narrowly based to legitimately represent the diversity of interests and ideologies in the black community. By the mid-1970s the caucus had abandoned its goal of trying to be the leading political organization for blacks, focusing instead on its symbolic representational role in Congress. The caucus's representational role is likely to remain largely symbolic because it is a relatively small group (39 of 440) and it is relatively liberal in a House that is relatively conservative.

Further reading: John Berg, *Unequal Struggle: Class, Gender, Race and Power in the U.S. Congress* (Boulder, Colo.: Westview Press, 1994); Robert Singh, *The Congressional Black Caucus: Racial Politics in Congress* (Thousand Oaks, Calif.: Sage Publications, 1998).

Congress of Racial Equality (CORE)

The Congress of Racial Equality (CORE) was one of the most important ORGANIZATIONS during the 1960s PROTEST phase of the CIVIL RIGHTS MOVEMENT. CORE has its origins in the Fellowship of Reconciliation (FOR), a pacifist organization committed to using CIVIL DISOBEDIENCE to solve social problems. JAMES FARMER, a Fellowship staff member, in 1942 organized the Chicago Committee on Racial Equality, dedicated to the use of civil disobedience to fight racial DISCRIMINATION. Two years later, CORE was formed as a national CIVIL RIGHTS organization. Like the STUDENT NONVIOLENT COORDINATING COMMITTEE (SNCC), CORE was an interracial COALITION of black and white young people committed to nonviolent direct action to achieve racial EQUALITY and INTEGRATION.

CORE is best known for the 1960s FREEDOM RIDES. As early as 1947 CORE had participated in FOR's "journey of reconciliation," which involved blacks and whites riding together on buses traveling through the SOUTHERN STATES in order to force compliance with a 1946 SUPREME COURT decision that held that SEGREGATION on buses in interstate commerce was unconstitutional. These Freedom Rides in the 1940s had little effect, but they were a model for the more successful 1960s Freedom Rides led by James Farmer, CORE's chair. In addition to the Freedom Rides, CORE participated in the SIT-INS and voter-registration campaigns during the 1960s. The 1964 murders of three of its workers—two whites (Michael Schwerner and Andrew Goodman) and a black (James Chaney)—became one of the most celebrated stories in the history of the modern Civil Rights movement and was the subject of television docudramas, documentaries, and the movie *Mississippi Burning.*

Like SNCC, the BLACK POWER MOVEMENT had a profound influence on CORE. In the late 1960s CORE abandoned nonviolence, excluded whites from its membership, and embraced BLACK NATIONALISM and COMMUNITY CONTROL as its ideological and political program. Then in the 1980s, under the autocratic leadership of Roy Innis, CORE embraced RONALD REAGAN and CONSERVATISM. Although its remnants continued into the 21st century in several American cities, it has not been a relevant force in AFRICAN-AMERICAN POLITICS since the 1980s.

Further reading: Charles Jones, "From Protest to Black Conservatism: The Demise of the Congress of Racial Equality," in *Black Political Organizations in the Post-Civil Rights Era,* ed. Ollie Johnson and Karin Stanford (New Brunswick, N.J.: Rutgers State University Press, 2002);

Dr. Martin Luther King Jr. addressing CORE demonstrators who are protesting the seating of the Mississippi delegation during the Democratic National Conference, Atlantic City, New Jersey, 1964 *(Library of Congress)*

August Meier and Elliot Rudwick, *CORE: A Study in the Civil Rights Movement* (New York: Oxford University Press, 1973).

Connerly, Ward (1939–) *businessman, opponent of affirmative action*

Ward Connerly, a California businessman and member of the University of California's Board of Regents, is nationally recognized as one of the leading opponents of AFFIRMATIVE ACTION in the United States and its most visible African-American opponent. Connerly came to national attention in 1995 when, as a member of the Board of Regents of the University of California, he led a majority of the regents in voting to end the university's use of racial and gender preferences in its admissions, hiring, and contracting poli-

cies. In 1996 Connerly became chair of the California Civil Rights Initiative, which successfully obtained more than 1 million signatures to place PROPOSITION 209 on the ballot in California. This proposition, an amendment to the state's constitution, abolished affirmative-action gender and ethnic preferences in all public policies and programs throughout the state. The following year Connerly supported a similar successful proposition in the state of Washington.

Connerly adheres to the IDEOLOGY of CONSERVATISM, arguing that affirmative action contradicts conservative principles as well as the principle of INDIVIDUALISM, which is at the core of classical LIBERALISM. Connerly also contends that the POST–CIVIL RIGHTS ERA African-American LEADERSHIP has betrayed the philosophical principles of the CIVIL RIGHTS MOVEMENT and MARTIN LUTHER KING JR.'s "dream" of a society in which individuals would be judged by the "content of their character rather than the color of their skin." Connerly also rejects the idea of BLACKNESS and BLACK COMMUNITY, favoring a version of INTEGRATION in which blacks, like other Americans, would merge into a MELTING POT.

Because he has used his race to advance opposition to affirmative action, Connerly has been referred to by some black leaders and in the black MEDIA as an UNCLE TOM who betrays the interests of the black community. Although Connerly obviously rejects the label *Uncle Tom,* in his memoir he does cast himself as a latter-day version of BOOKER T. WASHINGTON based on his belief in individual initiative and SELF-HELP.

Further reading: Ward Connerly, *Creating Equal: My Fight against Racial Preferences* (San Francisco, Calif.: Encounter Books, 2000).

conservatism

Conservatism is the political IDEOLOGY that, along with modern LIBERALISM, has dominated American politics throughout much of the nation's history. Although, like liberalism, it has no precise definition, conservatism since the classic writings of the English philosopher Edmund Burke has generally been understood as a set of beliefs that gives primacy to social and political stability, tending toward defense of the status quo and traditional values against major and abrupt social, economic, cultural, or political changes. In general, modern conservatives also tend to oppose extensive government regulation of the economy, heavy and progressive taxation, and the WELFARE STATE. Conservatives also tend to embrace FEDERALISM and therefore prefer STATE AND LOCAL GOVERNMENT activities over those of the federal government. If these are core values of conservatism, then—except perhaps for the emphasis on traditional values—it is an ideology that African Americans have historically found difficult to embrace. This is because the conditions of blacks in the United States have always cried out for major changes in the status quo, government intervention and regulation of the society and the economy, and the exercise of power by the federal government rather than state and local governments. Because they have historically been disproportionately poor, African Americans have also tended to favor relatively high and progressive taxation and an expansive welfare state. Finally, because conservatives embrace the status quo and federalism, they have tended to oppose federal CIVIL RIGHTS legislation. Thus, given the core principles of conservatism, it would be virtually impossible for most blacks to rationally embrace conservatism as an ideology relevant to their interests.

Ideological values or ideas notwithstanding, historically the black interest in FREEDOM and EQUALITY has always been advanced by liberal or nonconservative PUBLIC POLICY. Blacks have made major advances in their struggle for racial justice in three historical periods, each associated with liberalism. The first was the CIVIL WAR and RECONSTRUCTION era. The EMANCIPATION PROCLAMATION and the enactment of the THIRTEENTH, FOURTEENTH, and FIFTEENTH AMENDMENTs and the civil rights acts pursuant to them first rooted black thought in the liberal ideology. It was a liberal, interventionist federal government that emancipated blacks and established constitutional principles and procedures designed to secure their citizenship rights against hostile state governments and private persons and groups. Also, during this period the federal government established the FREEDMEN'S BUREAU (the first government social-welfare agency), which sought to raise the social and economic status of the former slaves. The second period was the NEW DEAL. Although FRANKLIN D. ROOSEVELT's New Deal scrupulously avoided a frontal assault on the civil rights issue, its social-welfare initiatives in employment, housing, cash assistance, and agricultural supports served further to anchor black opinion in the liberal ideology. In the third and final period of the 1960s, liberal Democratic administrations under JOHN KENNEDY and LYNDON JOHNSON secured passage of three major civil rights acts and launched the GREAT SOCIETY and the WAR ON POVERTY. The CIVIL RIGHTS ACTS of the 1960s were quintessentially liberal in that they involved federal intervention in the government of the SOUTHERN STATES to secure black civil and political rights and in the economy and society of all states to secure nondiscrimination in access to education, employment, and housing. The Great Society concept was also classically liberal, involving an array of spending programs that improved blacks' access to employment, housing, health care, education, legal services, and their capacity to participate more effectively in the political process. The War on Poverty is also associated with a significant reduction in the percentage of blacks living in poverty, and it had a dramatic impact on the growth and development of the black middle class. This last period, especially, explains the extreme and homogeneous profile of liberal black public opinion, particularly on issues of the economy and spending on social welfare. And since, in the American TWO-PARTY SYSTEM, the DEMOCRATIC PARTY is more liberal than the REPUBLICAN PARTY, blacks are also overwhelmingly Democratic in partisanship and VOTING BEHAVIOR.

Black Conservatives

On a visit to the Soviet Union in the 1930s Kelly Miller, a HOWARD UNIVERSITY professor, observed that in the United States some blacks were conservatives. His astonished Soviet hosts replied "Why? What do they have to conserve?" But, whether they had anything to conserve or not, some blacks have embraced conservatism. To some extent the ideology of BOOKER T. WASHINGTON can be described as conservative, but Washington's thought was more pragmatic ACCOMMODATIONISM than ideological conservatism. Still, there have been a handful of black intellectuals and leaders who have honestly embraced conservative ideas. But until the election of RONALD REAGAN, black conservatives were largely invisible in AFRICAN-AMERICAN POLITICS.

When Reagan was elected president in 1980, the conservative movement in the United States deliberately sought to create a black conservative LEADERSHIP group as an alternative to the liberal black leadership establishment. This effort to create an alternative black leadership was part of a larger effort by the conservative movement to bring about a revolution in the contextual basis of political and policy debate in the United States. White conservatives understood that in order to accomplish this objective, they would have to create a visible alternative to the liberal black leadership establishment. This process got under way in the early 1980s, and by the mid-1990s it was complete in the sense that a full-fledged black conservative leadership network had been consolidated. This network consists of a number of well-publicized PUBLIC INTELLECTUALS (THOMAS SOWELL, Walter Williams, Glenn Loury, and Shelby Steele) and several THINK TANKS, journals, radio talk shows, and political forums. While there have been relatively few black conservative ELECTED OFFICIALS (all elected from majority-white constituencies), the Reagan and George Bush administrations skillfully used their appointments to the BUREAUCRACY to create and sustain a black conservative leadership of government officials, the most notable example being Supreme Court Justice CLARENCE THOMAS.

Critics contend that these black conservatives are "manufactured" leaders, without significant support in African American mass opinion or any organizational presence in the community. While these criticisms are largely correct, these individuals have been influential in moving the debate on RACE and public policy in a conservative direction. For example, a principal line of argument of conservative theorists, black and white, is that the problems of the black UNDERCLASS are not structural or systemic but individual and communal, reflecting a lack of morality and individual responsibility. By the early 1990s, due in part to the influence of black conservative intellectuals, these ideas had come to dominate in Washington political and policy circles.

Black conservatives in America do not have a mass constituency in the black community or linkages with institutions indigenous to black America. Nor have they sought to build such a constituency or such linkages. Rather, their role is not to lead black people but to lead PUBLIC OPINION about black people.

See also CO-OPTATION, BARRY GOLDWATER, POLITICAL INCORPORATION, and RONALD REAGAN.

Further reading: J. Conti and B. Stetson, *Challenging the Civil Rights Establishment: Profiles of a New Black Vanguard* (Westport, Conn.: Praeger, 1989); Mack Jones, "The Political Thought of the New Black Conservatives," in *Readings in American Politics,* (Dubuque, Iowa: Kendall/Hunt, 1987); Martin Kilson, "Anatomy of Black Conservatism," *Transition* 59 (1993): 4–9; Clinton Rossiter, *Conservatism in America* (New York: Vintage Books, 1955); Gayle Tate and Lewis Randolph, eds., *Dimensions of Black Conservatism in the United States* (New York: Palgrave, 2002).

conservative coalition

The conservative coalition is the COALITION of conservative Northern Republicans and Southern, conservative WHITE SUPREMACIST Democrats in CONGRESS that blocked enactment of effective CIVIL RIGHTS legislation from the 1880s until the 1960s. This coalition also blocked or significantly compromised or watered down NEW DEAL legislation, and it is among the factors important in the failure of the United States to develop a comprehensive WELFARE STATE with universal benefits and coverage for all citizens. The coalition has its origins in the COMPROMISE OF 1877, which allowed African Americans in the SOUTHERN STATES to be subordinated socially, economically, and politically. This compromise between white supremacists and racist Southern political leaders and Northern white conservative, business-oriented political leaders sowed the seeds of an alliance that would come to full fruition between the 1930s and 1960s. Although many of FRANKLIN D. ROOSEVELT's NEW DEAL reforms were supported by a core of Southern Democrats in Congress, by the late 1930s Democratic members of Congress were increasingly abandoning their party on social and economic reform issues in order to vote with Northern, conservative Republicans. And while the REPUBLICAN PARTY continued to have a core of racial liberals or progressives, increasingly many of its members began to vote or otherwise support Southern members of the DEMOCRATIC PARTY on civil rights or race-related issues. During this period, African-American voters in the Northern states began to shift their allegiance to the Democratic Party in response to its social-welfare programs, and when the Democrats in 1948 adopted a civil rights platform the black vote became even more Democratic in its leanings. This development strengthened the conservative coalition in Congress, and thereafter it effectively blocked most of President HARRY TRUMAN's civil rights and social-welfare initiatives.

The coalition was able to prevent the passage of major civil rights and social welfare legislation from the late 1930s to the mid-1960s through its control of important committees in the Congress and through the use—or more frequently the threat of using—the FILIBUSTER in the Senate. In 1964 its power to block civil rights legislation was broken when the Senate ended a six-month filibuster and passed the CIVIL RIGHTS ACT OF 1964. The coalition's gridlock on social-welfare legislation was broken when President LYNDON B. JOHNSON won a landslide victory in 1964, which resulted in the defeat of a large number of Northern Republicans in the House and Senate. This paved the way for the passage of President Johnson's GREAT SOCIETY, which represented the biggest expansion of the welfare state since the New Deal.

These PUBLIC POLICY defeats on civil rights and social welfare were followed by a transformation in the regional basis of the coalition and a significant decline in its power. As a result of the implementation of the VOTING RIGHTS ACT OF 1965, blacks in the Southern states began to vote on a large scale for the first time since RECONSTRUCTION. The black vote since the 1970s has led to the election of moderate, less-conservative Democratic members of Congress who are less inclined to form coalitions on race and, to some extent, on social-welfare issues with conservative Republicans. However, the increasing identification of the Democratic Party with the interests of blacks and black voter support for the Democrats led the majority of Southern whites to switch their allegiance to the Republican Party. From the Compromise of 1877, to the 1960s, the 11 Southern states sent only Democrats to Congress. But by the year 2000, Republicans controlled 15 of the region's 22 Senate seats and 71 of its 125 House seats. This partisan transformation of the regional basis of the conservative coalition—from Southern Democrats to Southern Republicans—makes it very difficult to reconstitute the power of the coalition. This means that on most issues, if conservatives were to prevail in the Congress, they had to go it alone with Republican votes only because most Northern Democrats were liberal and there were relatively few Southern Democrats, and those few—because of the power of the black vote—tended to be less conservative than in the past.

See also SOUTHERN STRATEGY and WHITE BACKLASH.

Constitution, U.S.

The Constitution is the "organic" or fundamental law of the United States. It establishes the government, distributes governmental powers among various entities, and establishes the relationships between these entities and the people. The Constitution is a philosophically informed document rooted in the SOCIAL-CONTRACT THEORY and the doctrine of NATURAL RIGHTS. The social-contract theory and natural rights doctrine also informed the writings of the DECLARATION OF INDEPENDENCE. Africans in America were excluded from the social contract that established the Constitution, and the government established by the Constitution denied them

their natural rights. Thus, there has always been a conflict and a tension between the Constitution, CONSTITUTIONALISM, and AFRICAN-AMERICAN POLITICS because the organic law of the nation was based on RACISM and WHITE SUPREMACY. Although FREDERICK DOUGLASS, among others, argued that the Constitution was not a racist, white-supremacist document, in *DRED SCOTT* the SUPREME COURT declared that it was. Therefore, in order for blacks to achieve FREEDOM and EQUALITY, the Constitution had to be changed. But FEDERALISM and the SEPARATION OF POWERS—the two major structural features of the Constitution—make constitutional change very difficult. The Constitution itself, therefore, has frequently been a roadblock on the African-American path to freedom and equality.

Origins of the Constitution and African Americans

It is useful to begin analysis of the Constitution with a look at the men who gathered in Philadelphia in the summer of 1787. In a famous and still controversial book, Charles Beard in 1913 in *An Economic Interpretation of the Constitution* argued that the framers of the Constitution were an unrepresentative minority of wealthy property owners who drafted a Constitution that was undemocratic, written more to protect their economic interests than to make possible rule by democratic majorities. Analysis of the backgrounds of the 55 persons who participated in the writing of the Constitution clearly shows that they were an elite group, unrepresentative of the broad masses of the people. First, no women were at Philadelphia, no African or Native Americans, and no small farmers, workers, or mechanics. Rather, the framers were white, middle-aged, relatively well educated (one-third had some college education compared with less than 1 percent of the population at that time) white Anglo-Saxon Protestants. Fifty-five percent of the delegates were Southerners, and 15 percent owned slaves. Relatively speaking, 15 percent is not a large number. However, while there were few slaveholders at the gathering in Philadelphia, in each of the thirteen colonies (except Massachusetts, which abolished slavery in the 1780s) slavery was present. Thus, even those delegates that did not have a direct economic interest in SLAVERY nevertheless represented constituents that participated in the institution. In addition, many of those who did not own slaves had investments in shipping that prospered by transporting slaves. Clearly, then, slavery was a concern of the framers either as a result of personal ownership, constituent ownership, or economic interests.

While the Constitution was a philosophically informed document, its framers were not philosophers. Rather, they were practical politicians and men of affairs, and as in all politics they were men with distinct interests. In what is generally a sympathetic portrayal of the framers, the historian William Freehling writes, "If the Founding Fathers unquestionably dreamed of universal freedom, their ideological posture was weighed down equally with conceptions of priorities, profits and prejudices that would long make the dream utopian." The first or principal priority of the framers was the formation and preservation of the Union of the United States. This priority was thought indispensable to the priority of profit, that is, to the economic and commercial success of the nation. And as Freehling goes on to say, their concern with profits grew out of their preoccupation with property, and slaves as property were crucial. Thus "It made the slaves' right to freedom no more 'natural' than the master's right to property." It was this crucial nexus among profits, property, and slavery that led the men at Philadelphia to turn the idea of freedom for all men into a utopian dream.

Structural Principles of the Constitution and Their Impact on African Americans

In designing the Constitution the framers were guided by two overarching and interrelated principles: that the first object of government was the protection of private property, and that the power of government had to be limited in order to avoid tyranny. These two principles are interrelated because a government of unlimited powers could itself become a threat to private property, thereby undermining one of its core purposes. These two principles gave rise to what is the most important contributions of the framers to the art and practice of government, the idea of the "checks and balances" or the SEPARATION OF POWERS of the government into distinct parts or branches.

In perhaps the most famous of the *Federalist Papers (No. 10)*, James Madison argued that the first object or purpose of government was the protection of the rights of property. How does government carry out its first object in a DEMOCRACY? The problem confronting the framers stated simply was this: In a democratic, capitalist society where only a minority has property but a majority has the right to vote, the majority can use its voting rights to threaten the property rights of the minority. To avoid this danger while preserving what Madison called the "spirit and form" of democracy was the principal objective of the framers in designing the Constitution.

How is this objective attained? The principal means is through the separation of powers. Again, Madison is useful to quote. Writing in *Federalist Paper No. 47* he argued that "no political truth is certainly of greater intrinsic value or stamped with the authority of more enlightened patrons of liberty than that . . . the accumulation of all powers, legislative, executive and judiciary, in the same hands . . . may justly be pronounced the very definition of tyranny." It was not, however, the mere separation of powers of the government into four distinct parts (including the two parts of the Congress). In addition, the Constitution allowed the people, the voters, to directly elect only one of the four parts—the

House of Representatives, the least powerful of the four. The limited power of the House in the system of separation of powers is based on the idea that the popular branch of government should not be allowed full POWER because it might use it to enact laws attacking property rights.

In addition to the separation of powers, other checks on the ability of the government to act quickly in a way that might threaten liberty or property are the complicated amendment process, the limited grant of legislative power to the Congress, and federalism.

Article V specifies two ways to amend the Constitution. The first method requires a two-thirds majority of both houses of Congress and ratification or approval by three-fourths of the states. Or, alternatively, a convention called by two-thirds of the states can propose amendments, but these too must be ratified by three-fourths of the states. (This latter method has never been used to amend the Constitution.) This is a long, complicated, and tedious process. Consequently, although over 17,000 amendments have been proposed in the Congress, only 27 (17 if one excludes the BILL OF RIGHTS) have been adopted. Unlike the British Parliament or other European legislatures, the American Congress is not granted a general or plenary power to legislate. Rather, according to the first sentence of Article I, Congress's power to legislate is limited to those "herein granted" (see COMMERCE CLAUSE).

The framers of the Constitution deliberately designed a conservative, status quo–oriented government. Thus, what is referred to as "gridlock" in 20th-century Washington where nothing seems to get done (other than endless talk) is entirely consistent with what the framers intended. What Alexander Hamilton said in the *Federalist Papers (No. 70)* about the presidential veto can be said of the entire American political system:

> They will consider every institution calculated to restrain the excess of lawmaking and to keep things in the same state in which they happen to be at any given period, as more likely to do good than harm, because it is favorable to greater stability in the system of legislation. The major injury which may possibly be done by defeating a few good laws will be amply compensated by the advantage of preventing a number of bad ones.

In setting up this system of government, Donald Robinson in *Slavery in the Structure of American Politics* writes that "tensions about slavery were prominent among the forces that maintained the resolve to develop the country without strong direction from Washington." In limiting the power of the federal government in Washington, the framers simultaneously limited its power to liberate the slaves and, subsequently, to guarantee their freedom and equality.

African Americans, however, given their status first as slaves and subsequently as a poor, oppressed minority, have always found the status quo unacceptable and instead favored and favor today rapid, indeed radical change in the status quo. Thus, the Constitution and CONSTITUTIONAL-ISM have frequently been at war with their aspirations.

African Americans in the Constitution

As far as we can tell from the records of the federal convention, slavery was not the subject of much debate at the convention. Certainly its morality was never at issue, although there were several passionate opponents of slavery at the convention, including Benjamin Franklin, president of the Pennsylvania Society for Promoting the Abolition of Slavery. But neither Franklin nor any other delegate proposed abolition at Philadelphia, knowing that to do so would destroy any possibility of union. Hence, slavery was simply just another of the issues (like how the small and large states were to be represented in the Congress) that had to be compromised in order to accomplish the objective of forming the union.

Slavery is dealt with explicitly in four places in the Constitution, although the words *slave* and *slavery* are never used. It was James Madison, generally considered the "Father of the Constitution," who insisted that all explicit references to slavery be excluded. Madison is also the author of the most important and infamous of the clauses dealing with slavery, the THREE-FIFTHS CLAUSE.

The other clauses dealing explicitly with slavery include Article I, Section 9, paragraph 1, prohibiting the Congress from stopping the slave trade before 1808 and limiting any tax on imported slaves to $10; Article V's prohibition of any amendment to the Constitution that would alter the 1808 date or rate of taxation on imported slaves; and Article IV, Section 2, paragraph 2, creating the FUGITIVE SLAVE CLAUSE requiring the NORTHERN STATES to return slaves who escaped to freedom back to their bondage in the South. As far as we know, neither of these provisions caused much controversy at the convention, although the fugitive slave clause in Article IV initially would have required that escaped slaves be "delivered up as criminals," but this was modified to relieve the states of this obligation. Although these racist provisions of the Constitution have been rendered inoperative by subsequent amendments, they remain in the text of the document. This is because there has never been a second constitutional convention—representing all the people—to revise the document and remove the racially offensive clauses.

The framers, while committed to freedom, had a limited, nonuniversal vision of it: freedom for some—the some who were white men with property, including property in other men, women, and children. Professor Robinson cautions that "one wants to be fair to the framers, and above all to avoid blaming them as individuals for the sins of the culture, in which we all share. We must be careful not to imply that they should have done better unless we are prepared to show how better provisions might have been achieved politically." But, Robinson continues, "At the same time, we must be lucid in recognizing the terrible mistakes made at the founding. In the end the framers failed on their own terms."

Further reading: Charles Beard, *An Economic Interpretation of the Constitution* (New York: Free Press, 1913, 1965); Robert Brown, *Charles Beard and the Constitution: A Critical Analysis of an Economic Interpretation of the Constitution* (New York: W. W. Norton, 1965); Don Fehrenbacher, *The Slaveholding Republic: An Account of the United States Government's Relations to Slavery* (New York: Oxford University Press, 2000); William, Freehling, "The Founding Fathers and Slavery," *American Historical Review* 77 (1972): 81–93; Donald Robinson, *Slavery in the Structure of American Politics* (New York: Harcourt Brace Jovanovich, 1971).

constitutionalism

The United States has more than a written CONSTITUTION. It has an IDEOLOGY of constitutionalism: a set of beliefs that words written in 1787 in the Constitution should govern the behavior of men and women in the 20th century. This ideology venerates the Constitution and treats the men who wrote it, generally referred to as the "Founding Fathers," as demigods. President WOODROW WILSON in his book *Congressional Government* writing of American constitutionalism described it as "an undiscriminating and almost blind worship" and that "the divine right of Kings never ran a more prosperous course than this unquestioned prerogative of the Constitution to receive universal homage."

While many other countries have written constitutions, none except the United States has an ideology of constitutionalism. This ideology holds that the Constitution is a timeless document and should not be altered or changed except in the most extreme or urgent circumstances. Consequently, the U.S. Constitution has been changed relatively few times. If one excludes the BILL OF RIGHTS (because it was adopted as part of the organic or original document), then the Constitution has been changed only 17 times. Of these 17 amendments, two—the 18th and 21st—effectively cancel each other, since the former established a prohibition on the use of alcohol and the latter repealed it. Of the remaining 15 amendments, six (11, 12, 20, 22, 25, and 27) are minor, technical changes dealing with such things as balloting for president and vice president, presidential term limits, presidential disability and succession, and changing the dates when the newly elected CONGRESS and president take office. And the rest either alter the racist, sexist character of the original Constitution (13, 14, 15, and 19) or open the political process to full democratic participation (17, 23, 24, and 26) by abolishing the poll tax, granting 18-year-olds the right to vote, granting citizens of the DISTRICT OF COLUMBIA the right to vote for president, and providing for popular election of members of the Senate. Thus, the Sixteenth Amendment providing Congress the authority to tax income constitutes the only major substantive change in the Constitution (see the THREE-FIFTHS CLAUSE). The FOURTEENTH AMENDMENT is by far the most important change or amendment to the Constitution and was originally adopted to end RACISM and provide for the FREEDOM and EQUALITY of African Americans.

This historical continuity is a source of the Constitution's dynamism as an ideology or belief system. But, although the Constitution has not been frequently amended or formally changed, it has been frequently changed through SUPREME COURT interpretation. These interpretations by the Court also contribute to the dynamism of constitutionalism.

Constitutionalism, then, is along with CAPITALISM and DEMOCRACY one of the defining or core values of the American POLITICAL SYSTEM. To call a law or a PUBLIC POLICY unconstitutional is to brand it as not simply wrong or misguided but as antisystem, as un-American, or even as immoral. Constitutionalism therefore requires support for Supreme Court decisions interpreting the Constitution, even if one disagrees with them, because to do otherwise undermines the system. Constitutionalism understood in this way has sometimes advantaged African Americans in their struggle for freedom and equality, as in the case of BROWN V. BOARD OF EDUCATION, but more frequently it has disadvantaged them.

convention movements

Since RICHARD ALLEN organized the first NATIONAL NEGRO CONVENTION in the 1830s, African Americans have periodically come together in national congresses or conventions to discuss common problems and develop organizations, programs, and strategies to advance the interests of the BLACK COMMUNITY as a whole. These attempts have frequently involved efforts to unite the group in solidarity and develop a BLACK AGENDA in which all blacks, whatever their IDEOLOGY, social class, or other organizational affiliations could embrace. These efforts, which include the 1930s NATIONAL NEGRO CONGRESS and the 1970s NATIONAL BLACK POLITICAL CONVENTION, are based on the premise that an oppressed people must unite if they are effectively to fight for their FREEDOM. These efforts are also premised on the notion that divisions in class and ideology within the

black community can be transcended and that an encompassing group solidarity on a black agenda and program of action can be established. Historically, while solidarity in these conventions has been established and black agendas have been developed, the solidarity has been difficult to maintain, and the conventions have failed to become permanent features of AFRICAN-AMERICAN POLITICS or, in most cases, even to last for a long period of time. Always, the conventions have failed to endure because of deep ideological, class, or organizational differences within the black community, differences in the long run that could not be overcome by appeals to racial solidarity.

Cook, Samuel Du Bois (1928–   ) scholar

Samuel Du Bois Cook played an important role in the development of AFRICAN-AMERICAN POLITICS as a field of study in political science. During the late 1960s, as program officer in higher education at the Ford Foundation, he was instrumental in facilitating the award of major grants to HOWARD UNIVERSITY and ATLANTA UNIVERSITY. These grants permitted Atlanta University to establish a Ph. D. program in political science and Howard to expand its then fledgling program. These two universities are the only HISTORICALLY BLACK COLLEGES AND UNIVERSITIES that offer the Ph.D., and they are primarily responsible for the development of epistemological and theoretical foundations of the modern study of African-American politics. Together these two universities have graduated more Ph.D.s in political science than any other two universities in the United States.

Cook was born in Griffin, Georgia, and received a B.A. from Morehouse College and a Ph.D. from the Ohio State University. From 1956 to 1966 he was professor and chair of the political science department at Atlanta University. In 1971 he was appointed to the political science faculty at Duke University, becoming the first African American to hold a faculty appointment in political science at a predominantly white university in the SOUTHERN STATES. He also was the first black president of the Southern Political Science Association, and in 1975 he was named president of Dillard University, a historically black institution in New Orleans. Cook, who has a longstanding interest in improving black-Jewish relations in the United States, in 1996 was appointed to the U.S. Holocaust Memorial Council.

See also RALPH BUNCHE, MACK H. JONES, NATIONAL CONFERENCE OF BLACK POLITICAL SCIENTISTS, JEWEL PRESTAGE, RONALD WALTERS, and HANES WALTON.

co-optation

Co-optation is the process of absorbing, incorporating, or integrating new groups into the leadership structure of a

POLITICAL SYSTEM. This process has also been labeled POLITICAL INCORPORATION and INTEGRATION. Among social scientists there are no clear-cut distinctions among co-optation, integration, and incorporation. The three concepts are all used by different social scientists to describe the same phenomenon, that is, a group previously excluded from participation in a political system and its processes is brought into the system. If the previously excluded group is brought into the system because through PROTEST, RIOTS, or other forms of antisystemic activities it is perceived as posing a threat to the system's stability or maintenance, then it is labeled co-optation.

But if the group is included as part of the normal, evolutionary adjustment of a DEMOCRACY to the claims of new groups for inclusion, then the phenomenon is called incorporation. In addition to distinguishing the phenomenon on the basis of why it occurred—as a natural adjustment of democratic societies to the claims of a new group for inclusion or in response to disruptive activities by an aggrieved group—co-optation can be distinguished from incorporation or integration on the basis of the substantive impact on the group's interests. If inclusion or integration into the system of a group's leaders results in relatively few gains or benefits for the group, then it may be viewed negatively as co-optation—a "sellout"—because the group gains relatively little while its leaders, because they are part of the system, are unable to effectively protest. However, if inclusion in the system results in gains for the group as a result of its leaders "working within the system" to advance its interests, then it is referred to positively as incorporation or integration.

Since the late 1960s black leaders have been absorbed or integrated into the U.S. political system. They have been elected and appointed to important public offices, been integrated into the BUREAUCRACY, and have created new system-oriented organizations, most notably the CONGRESSIONAL BLACK CAUCUS. Whether this represents incorporation (a positive development) or co-optation (a negative development) depends on whether this development has allowed the black LEADERSHIP in the POST–CIVIL RIGHTS ERA to effectively advance the interests of the BLACK COMMUNITY or whether it has required them to sacrifice those interests as the cost of their inclusion within the system. This is an empirical question on which social scientists have not yet come to an agreement because the facts are ambiguous and open to varying interpretations, with some scholars saying that at the end of the 20th century it is too early to know.

See also ACCOMMODATIONISM and BILL CLINTON.

Further reading: Frances Fox Piven and Richard Cloward, *Poor Peoples Movement: Why They Succeed, Why They Fail* (New York: Vintage Books, 1977); Robert C. Smith, *We Have No Leaders: African Americans in the Post Civil Rights Era* (Albany: State University of New York Press, 1996).

CORE See CONGRESS OF RACIAL EQUALITY.

Council on African Affairs

The Council on African Affairs (CAA) was founded in the 1930s as an ORGANIZATION devoted to antiCOLONIALISM in Africa. Among its leaders were W. E. B. DU BOIS and PAUL ROBESON. A forerunner of TRANSAFRICA, CAA was not a mass organization but an elite group of intellectuals and activists that sought to use knowledge as the basis for LOBBYING the government to oppose the policies of the European colonial powers in Africa after the end of the Second World War. The CAA conducted research, published pamphlets and reports, and held conferences and rallies to influence government officials, the MEDIA, and PUBLIC OPINION. As the COLD WAR developed, the United States allied itself with the European powers in efforts to maintain colonialism in Africa and elsewhere in the THIRD WORLD. The CAA allied itself with the Soviet Union and COMMUNISM. Du Bois, Robeson, and other CAA leaders embraced communism because they saw Russia and China as allies in the struggle for African freedom, while the United States and CAPITALISM were viewed as hostile to the anticolonial struggle. The NAACP and other established black organizations refused to support CAA in its embrace of communism, and CAA and its leaders became the targets of various forms of POLITICAL REPRESSION.

In 1948 the DEPARTMENT OF JUSTICE placed CAA on its list of "subversive" organizations; Du Bois was indicted; and Robeson was denied his passport and the right to practice his craft as an entertainer. In the 1950s, during the era of MCCARTHYISM, the CAA ceased operation. It lacked resources; its leaders were politically repressed; it enjoyed little support in PUBLIC OPINION, black or white; and the established or mainstream black LEADERSHIP rejected it because of its RADICALISM.

The CAA was for a time the most important organization devoted to organizing support for decolonialization in Africa, but its embrace of radicalism in the midst of the cold war anticommunism consensus ultimately led to its repression and dissolution.

criminal justice system

The JUDICIAL PROCESS for determining the innocence or guilt of persons accused of crimes is one of the major manifestations of the power of a POLITICAL SYSTEM. In the SOCIAL-CONTRACT THEORY that constitutes the philosophical basis of the American government, the creation of a fair and impartial judicial process was one of the main reasons men agreed to create government in the first place. But, in probably no area of American life—not voting, officeholding, education, health, housing, or employment—have African Americans suffered DISCRIMINATION to a greater extent than in the area of crime and punishment. There have been many reports, articles, and books documenting the systematic history of RACISM in America's judicial process, a history that leads many blacks to view the legal system with suspicion and distrust.

These many studies have shown that historically crime rates for blacks have been disproportionately high; that the BLACK COMMUNITY has not received adequate police protection; that blacks have been disproportionately victimized by crime; that police officers have consistently engaged in patterns of misconduct, maltreatment, brutality, and murder; that blacks have not received "due process" or fair trials; and that blacks have been punished much more severely for comparable crimes than whites. Also, in the 20th century, African-American political leaders have been victimized by a historic pattern of POLITICAL REPRESSION, surveillance, provocations, and repression by police, intelligence, and military authorities.

These historical patterns manifest themselves in contemporary circumstances. First, at the close of the 20th century blacks continue to exhibit disproportionately high rates of crime and to be disproportionately victims of crime. In any selected year, the FBI Uniform Crime Reports indicate that although only about 12 percent of the population is African American, they are arrested for about 40 percent of the murders, rapes, and other crimes of VIOLENCE. And most of the people killed, raped, and assaulted by blacks are other blacks. In other words, during all periods for which systematic data are available, blacks have been overrepresented both as victims and offenders.

In many parts of the country, black communities still receive inadequate police services and protection. And blacks continue to be mistreated, brutalized, beaten, and killed by the police. In the aftermath of the worldwide televised beating of RODNEY KING by the Los Angeles police in 1991, the NAACP in collaboration with the Harvard Law School Criminal Justice Institute and the Monroe Trotter Institute of the University of Massachusetts conducted a study of police-community relations in America. The report concluded: "The beating of Rodney King is part of a long and shameful history of racially motivated brutality and degradation that continues to find expression in powerful places." Data from the Police Foundation show that during the 1980s, 78 percent of those killed and 80 percent of the nonfatally shot were minorities.

Allegations of abuse or misconduct by police or other law-enforcement agencies are rarely prosecuted by the JUS-TICE DEPARTMENT. The Associated Press (AP) analyzed computer records of all 1.4 million cases considered by the department between 1992 and 1996 and reviewed other department documents obtained through the Freedom of Information Act. The AP found that in 96 percent of the roughly 2,000 civil rights criminal cases referred each year, federal prosecutors took no action. This compares with prosecutions in 90 percent of immigration cases referred and 75 percent of drug cases. Overall, the Justice Department prosecutes in about half of all criminal matters referred to it, leading the AP to conclude that "civil rights crimes are the department's lowest prosecutorial priority."

After the Rodney King case, a 1993 study of reports of police brutality in 15 major daily newspapers between January 1990 and May 1992 found that the majority of the victims of police brutality were black. Of 131 such victims reported during this period, 87 percent were black, 10 percent were Latino, and 3 percent were white. In contrast, 93 percent of the officers involved were white, suggesting a national pattern of misconduct by white police officers toward black citizens.

Congressman John Conyers, the senior black on the House Judiciary Committee, estimates that 72 percent of the car drivers stopped by the police are black. Their offense of "DWB"—driving while black—is an offense from which no black is immune. As Congressman Conyers remarked on the House floor: "There are virtually no African-American males—including Congressmen, actors, athletes, and office workers—who have not been stopped at one time or another for an alleged traffic violation, namely driving while black." According to a 1999 Gallup poll (of 2,006 Americans, including 1,001 blacks and 934 whites), 56 percent of whites and 77 percent of blacks believe that "racial profiling" is widespread, that is, that police officers stop motorists of certain racial or ethnic groups because they believe these groups are more likely to commit certain types of crimes. Moreover, 57 percent of black respondents indicated that they believe they had been stopped by the police "just because of their race," a figure that rises to 72 percent among blacks aged 18 to 34.

As was the case with the Los Angeles RIOTS of 1992 (after the police officers who were videotaped beating Rodney King were acquitted by a nearly all-white jury), most of the major riots of the 1960s were touched off by encounters with the police. The 1969 "Report of the National Advisory Commission on Civil Disorders" (the so-called KERNER REPORT) found that police misconduct was the leading grievance of urban blacks against local authorities and frequently was a precipitant cause of the riots. The commission found that grievances against the police were greater in intensity than was concern about discrimination in housing, employment, or education.

Blacks continue to be punished in a disproportionately harsh manner compared with whites and other minorities. Historically, prosecutors are more likely to pursue full prosecutions, file more-severe charges, and seek more stringent penalties in cases involving minority defendants, particularly where the victims are white.

The United States imprisons more people than any other country in the world except Russia—in 1998 about 2 million people, almost twice the number of 1985. Nearly 40 percent of these people are African Americans. Furthermore, in 1995 more than 32 percent of young black men (20–29-year-olds) were in jail or prison or were on parole or probation, compared with only 7 percent of young white men. And, astonishingly, the percentage of young black women in jail (5 percent) is almost as large as that for white men (7 percent) (only 1.5 percent of white women are jailed). Some of this disproportionately high rate of black incarceration is due to the fact that young black men who are poor commit more crimes than whites, but also important is racial discrimination in the criminal justice system and unfairness in punishment for use of illegal drugs. In 1995, the *Nashville Tennesseean* analyzed all 1992–93 convictions in all federal district courts in the United States. The study found that criminal sentences for blacks were up to 40 percent longer than those of white criminals in some courts and that blacks are less likely than whites to get a break on their sentences. This disparity existed in all parts of the country, but it was highest in the West (California) and lowest in the South. And it was only a disparity for blacks, as Hispanics received the same sentences for the same crime as whites. (There were too few Asian Americans to make a comparison.)

There is also clear statistical evidence that the death penalty is imposed in a racially discriminatory manner. In *McClesky v. Kemp* (1987), the SUPREME COURT was presented with statistical data showing that race influences death sentencing. Using the state of Georgia as a case study, more than 2,000 murders in the state were analyzed during the 1970s. Among other things, it was found that a black was about 22 times as likely to be sentenced to die for killing a white than for killing a black. Hearing this evidence, Justice Lewis Powell, writing for the Court's majority to uphold the Georgia death penalty law, said that the evidence at best indicated "a statistical discrepancy that correlates with race" and that "apparent disparities in sentencing are an inevitable part of criminal justice." Powell wrote that to rule in favor of the black defendant would mean "we would soon be faced with similar claims as to other types of penalty." In other words, Justice Powell agreed that perhaps there is racial discrimination in imposition of the death penalty but, also, that there is discrimination in all types of sentencing. Thus, to strike down the death penalty as discriminatory would mean that sentencing in all types of cases could be challenged.

War On Drugs

For much of the 20th century the U.S. government has proscribed or prohibited the use of a variety of mind-altering drugs, including heroin, cocaine, and marijuana. As the use of these and other proscribed drugs increased in the 1960s, law-enforcement authorities intensified their efforts to suppress their use as President RICHARD NIXON launched what he called a "war on drugs." The drug war was escalated in the 1980s during the PRESIDENCY of RONALD REAGAN when a new drug called crack cocaine became widely available. This inexpensive (compared with powdered cocaine), highly addictive derivative of powdered cocaine resulted in an explosion of crack addiction and drug-related gang violence. This was followed by the passage of draconian drug laws and the jailing of large numbers of black men and, increasingly, black women. This led many blacks to describe the war on drugs as a war on blacks. Also, for many years there has been widespread belief in the black community that the government itself—most frequently and specifically the Central Intelligence Agency (CIA)—has been responsible for the widespread availability of drugs in black neighborhoods. This view of government involvement in drug trafficking in the black community was seemingly confirmed when in 1996 the *San Jose Mercury News* published a three-part investigative report by its correspondent Gary Webb. The report strongly suggested that the CIA was indeed responsible for the manufacture and distribution of crack cocaine by Los Angeles street gangs, as a means to finance a war the CIA was waging in the Central American nation of Nicaragua. After denials by CIA leaders and extensive criticisms by other major newspapers, the *San Jose Mercury News* reexamined Webb's story and concluded that parts of it were "oversimplification" and that there was no "proof" that "top CIA officials" knew that money from Los Angeles drug dealers was going to finance the war in Nicaragua. The newspaper's reexamination did not conclude that there was not CIA involvement but only that there was not sufficient evidence to conclude that the leaders of the agency knew about it. However, Webb, who subsequently resigned from the paper, continued to stand by his story and later went on to write a book documenting its central assertions in greater detail. (Several months later an internal CIA investigation of Webb's allegations found, as expected, no evidence linking the CIA to drug trafficking.) Whatever the truth about CIA involvement in the drug trade, it is nevertheless widely believed among African Americans; a 1997 poll found that 73 percent of blacks compared with 16 percent of whites said it was probably true that the CIA has been involved in importing cocaine for distribution in the black community.

While the government may not be involved in drug trafficking and the war on drugs may not be a war on blacks, the manner in which the criminal justice system enforces the drug laws is not racially neutral or color-blind. Rather, there is a large racially DISPARATE IMPACT, which strongly suggests that the war on drugs constitutes a form of INSTI-TUTIONAL RACISM. The statistics on the racially disparate impact of the drug war are powerful data for the case for institutional racism. While blacks and whites have similar rates of illegal drug use, blacks are likely to be treated differently than whites at each step in the criminal justice system. Blacks are more likely to be arrested for drug offenses, more likely to be convicted, more likely to be imprisoned, and more likely to receive longer sentences. For example, according to estimates by the federal government, in 1998 49 percent of crack users were white and 34 percent black, but 85 percent of those convicted were black and only 6 percent were white. Overall, from the mid-1980s to the 1990s, black incarceration for drug use went up 700 percent compared with 300 percent for whites.

Federal and state laws also discriminate against sellers of crack cocaine, who tend to be disproportionately black compared with sellers of powdered cocaine, who tend to be disproportionately white. Possession of five grams of crack cocaine requires a five-year minimum sentence, but in order to get that sentence for powdered cocaine, one would have to possess 500 grams (a disparity of 100 to 1). In 1989 the Minnesota State Supreme Court declared these kinds of racial disparities an unconstitutional form of racial discrimination under its state constitution. But the federal courts and most state courts have not accepted the reasoning of the Minnesota court, finding instead that the racial disparities notwithstanding, there was a rational basis for treating crack and powdered cocaine differently (because crack is allegedly more addictive and dangerous). This disparate treatment is also supported by leaders of both of the major political parties, and in 1995 the House of Representatives overwhelmingly defeated a bill offered by the CONGRESSIONAL BLACK CAUCUS that would have equalized sentences for the two drugs. Drug addiction and its criminalization (rather than treating it as a medical problem requiring treatment and rehabilitation) have major impacts on social disorganization in the GHETTO and on the increasingly asymmetrical class relationship between males and females in the black community.

Crime, Punishment, and Voting Rights

Under the CONSTITUTION and its FEDERALISM principle, each state sets its own qualifications for voting, except no state can deny the right to vote on the basis of race, religion, gender, age (18), or for failure to pay a poll tax. The states also have the authority to deny or revoke the right to vote for persons convicted of crimes. In the POST–CIVIL RIGHTS ERA, this has resulted in the denial of VOTING RIGHTS to a large segment of the black community. The

laws on the right of felons to vote vary from state to state. In three states—Massachusetts, Maine, and Vermont—felons are allowed to vote even while in prison, but in many states, especially SOUTHERN STATES, felons are denied the right to vote even after they have served their sentences and, in some states, for life. In Mississippi, the state with the largest percentage black population, it requires a two-thirds vote of both houses of the state legislature to restore a felon's voting rights. Given the disproportionate rates of felony convictions for black men, felony disenfranchisement has a major impact on their voting rights. In Alabama 32 percent of black men are ineligible to vote because of felony convictions, 31 percent in Florida, and 29 percent in Mississippi. Nationwide, 1.5 million black men are denied the right to vote because of criminal records; this represents 13 percent of black men compared with just 2 percent of white men. In 1999 the CONGRESSIONAL BLACK CAUCUS, led by Congressman John Conyers, proposed legislation that would restore felony voting rights in federal elections for the president and CONGRESS. However, it was opposed by many who contend that it is unconstitutional because it intrudes on the right of the states to establish voter qualifications. And in 2000, Massachusetts considered changing its law to deny voting rights to felons.

Crime and inequities and disparities in the criminal justice system at the end of the 20th-century disenfranchise more blacks today than did the poll tax prior to its abolition in 1964. And hardly any blacks have confidence in the fairness of the criminal justice system. A poll conducted by the *New York Times* in 1992 in the aftermath of the Rodney King verdict found only 9 percent of blacks agreeing with the statement, "Blacks and other minorities receive equal treatment as whites in the criminal justice system."

Further reading: David Cole, *No Equal Justice: Race and Class in the American Criminal Justice System* (New York: Free Press, 1999); Human Rights Watch, *Punishment and Prejudice: Racial Disparities in the War on Drugs,* www.lrw.org/reports/2000/usa; Randal Kennedy, *Race, Crime and Law* (New York: Pantheon, 1997); Mark Mauer, *Young Black Men and the Criminal Justice System* (Washington, D.C.: The Sentencing Project, 1995).

City of Richmond v. J. A. Croson (1989)

City of Richmond v. J. A. Croson is one of a line of SUPREME COURT decisions limiting the scope of AFFIRMATIVE ACTION programs. In 1983 the City of Richmond, Virginia, established an affirmative action program that set aside 30 percent of its construction subcontracts for minority-owned businesses, which were defined to include firms owned by blacks, Eskimos and Aleuts, Latinos, and Asian Americans. The purpose of the program was to remedy past DISCRIMINATION against minorities in awarding of city contracts. It was based on a similar program established by Congress in 1977 and approved by the Supreme Court in *FULLILOVE V. KLUTZNICK.* Specifically, the city program followed the congressional model by including in its coverage all of the nation's racial minorities, although hardly any nonblack minorities lived in Richmond. The 30 percent figure was based on the Congress's set-aside target of 10 percent, which represented a midway point between the percentage of contracts awarded to minorities and the city's minority population. Almost as soon as the program was adopted, it was challenged by J. A. Croson, Inc., a white-owned construction firm.

The city's program was upheld by the trial court and by the Fourth Circuit Court of Appeals. But in a five-to-four decision the Supreme Court declared the program unconstitutional, ruling that it violated the EQUAL PROTECTION CLAUSE of the FOURTEENTH AMENDMENT. Writing for the majority, Justice Sandra Day O'Connor said that Congress as a coequal branch of the government had the authority to establish such contract set-asides, but STATE AND LOCAL GOVERNMENTs were prohibited from doing so unless the plans were "narrowly tailored" to meet identified discriminatory practices. In her opinion, O'Connor wrote that affirmative action programs at the state and local level should be subjected to "strict scrutiny," which is a judicial procedure or standard for assessing programs using racial classifications that is very difficult to meet. In one of his many angry dissents during his last years on the Court, Justice THURGOOD MARSHALL rejected the strict-scrutiny standard and went on to describe his colleagues' overturning of the Richmond program as a "deliberate and giant step backward in this country's affirmative action jurisprudence" that assumes "racial discrimination is largely a phenomenon of the past, and that government bodies need no longer preoccupy themselves with rectifying racial injustice."

Although O'Connor indicated in *Croson* that Congress had the authority to establish targeted set-aside programs, six years later in *ADARAND V. PENA* she reversed herself and held Congress to the same high standard of scrutiny as state and local governments. The results of *Croson* and *Adarand* were a sharp decline in the number of government contracts awarded to minority-owned businesses.

Crummell, Alexander (1819–1898) *clergyman, scholar, founder of American Negro Academy*

Alexander Crummell, a clergyman and scholar, made important contributions to PAN-AFRICANISM and BLACK NATIONALISM in AFRICAN-AMERICAN THOUGHT. Born in 1819 in New York City to relatively privileged parents, Crummell was well educated, receiving a bachelor's degree from Queen's college in Cambridge, England, in 1853.

Upon graduation he emigrated to LIBERIA, where he spent the next 20 years working as a clergyman and member of the faculty of Monrovia College. Early in his career Crummell, like EDWARD WILMOT BLYDEN and many other black leaders, was opposed to the AMERICAN COLONIALIZATION SOCIETY and BACK-TO-AFRICA MOVEMENTS and their plans for black immigration to Africa, but he later changed his views and became a strong supporter of the selective migration of educated African Americans to Africa.

Crummell saw indigenous African civilizations as backward, and he believed that SLAVERY was God's will so that some Africans would gain the benefits of Christianity and Western culture. These "enlightened" blacks could then return to Africa as "civilizers." Crummell was probably of pure African ancestry, and throughout his career in Liberia he was in nearly constant conflict with the color-conscious mulatto elites, who he believed exercised disproportionate power in African and African-American communities. As part of his black nationalist approach, Crummell—notwithstanding his negative views of African cultures—embraced a kind of NEGRITUDE: a strong belief in the value of racial purity. Crummell also believed that FREEDOM and EQUALITY for blacks probably could not be achieved in the United States and, therefore, that a return to the African "fatherland" might be necessary.

In part because of the black-mulatto conflict, Crummell in 1873 returned to the United States, where in 1880 he established and became pastor of St. Luke's Church, which became a congregation of the DISTRICT OF COLUMBIA's middle-class elite. In 1894 he established the American Negro Academy, which although poorly funded became a forum for the exchange of ideas among black intellectuals, influencing the scholarship of the young W. E. B. DU BOIS. Indeed, it is likely that Du Bois's notion of the TALENTED TENTH was directly influenced by Crummell and the academy. In his classic *THE SOULS OF BLACK FOLK,* Du Bois included an essay called "Of Alexander Crummell" in which he wrote, "He did his work—he did it nobly and well; and yet I sorrow that here he worked alone, with so little human sympathy. His name to-day, in this broad land, means little, and comes to fifty million ears laden with no sense of memory or emulation. And herein lies the tragedy of the age: not that men are poor—all men know something of poverty; not that men are wicked—who is good? not that men are ignorant—what is truth? Nay, but that men know so little of men."

Further reading: W. E. B. Du Bois, "Of Alexander Crummell," in *The Souls of Black Folk* (New York: Fawcett Publications, 1903, 1961); William Moses, *Alexander Crummell: A Study of Civilization and Discontent* (New York: Oxford University Press, 1989); Alfred Moss, *The American Negro Academy: Voice of the Talented Tenth* (Baton Rouge: Louisiana State University Press, 1981).

Cruse, Harold (1916–) *scholar*

Harold Cruse is one of the most influential black intellectuals of the POST–CIVIL RIGHTS ERA. His influence is based primarily on the publication in 1967 of *The Crisis of the Negro Intellectual,* a scathing critique of the black intelligentsia that played a major role in the debate over the future of AFRICAN-AMERICAN POLITICS in the post–civil rights era.

Cruse was born in Petersburg, Virginia. After serving in World War II, he moved to HARLEM, where he became active in radical politics and, for a time, a member of the COMMUNIST PARTY. *The Crisis of the Negro Intellectual* is based in part on Cruse's experiences in Harlem's radical politics. Arguing that knowledge is an indispensable base of power in the struggles of oppressed peoples, Cruse indicts the black intelligentsia for its failure to develop a philosophical stance independent of white intellectuals, especially white radical and Jewish intellectuals. The consequence of this failure, Cruse argued, was that blacks as a group had failed to develop group POWER because its intellectuals had failed to root their ideas in the experiences and conditions—the CULTURE—of the group.

Cruse's IDEOLOGY of BLACK NATIONALISM rejects INTEGRATION and INDIVIDUALISM because, as he wrote in *The Crisis:*

> . . . America, which idealizes the rights of the individual above everything else, is in reality a nation dominated by the social power of groups, classes, in-groups, cliques—both ethnic and religious. The individual in America has few rights that are not backed up by the political, economic and social power of one group or another. Hence, the individual Negro has, proportionately, very few rights indeed because his ethnic group (whether or not he actually identifies with it) has very little political, economic or social power (beyond moral grounds) to wield. Thus, it can be seen that those Negroes, and there are very many of them, who have accepted the full essence of the Great American Ideal of individualism are in serious trouble trying to function in America.

Cruse's embrace of black nationalism is based on his belief that the BLACK COMMUNITY is a separate community and is likely to remain so because of the tenacity of RACISM and WHITE SUPREMACY. Therefore, rather then pursue what he believes is the "fantasy of integration," the black intelligentsia or TALENTED TENTH should embrace nationalism and seek to build a PLURAL SOCIETY in America, because an integrated one is not possible. Creation of this plural society in his view required the systematic reorganization of black economic, cultural, and political resources into autonomous institutions. Cruse's analysis in *The Crisis*

was especially concerned with culture, proposing that blacks should control the cultural institutions—publishing, the mass MEDIA, theaters, recording, and distribution outlets—that produces their creative work as the basis upon which to lay the foundations of an autonomous black community. In this sense, Cruse's nationalism is a variant or a form of CULTURAL NATIONALISM.

After publication of *The Crisis* in 1967, a series of his earlier essays was published as *Rebellion or Revolution,* and his *Plural but Equal: Blacks and Minorities in America's Plural Society* was published in 1987. A frequent contributor to black journals, Cruse also lectured throughout the United States from the 1970s to the late 1990s. Professor emeritus of history and AFRICAN-AMERICAN STUDIES at the University of Michigan, Cruse is one of the few scholars with only a high school education to be appointed to the faculty of a major research university. The appointment was made in recognition of the landmark importance of *The Crisis of the Negro Intellectual* as a contribution to knowledge.

Further reading: Center for Afro-American and African Studies, University of Michigan, Ann Arbor, *Voices "Commemorative Issue: 25th Anniversary of the Publication of Harold Cruse's The Crisis of the Negro Intellectual"* 9 (1994).

culture

Understanding African-American culture and its relationship to AFRICAN-AMERICAN POLITICS, its POLITICAL CULTURE, the CULTURE OF POVERTY, and the CIVIC CULTURE is one of the most difficult and complex tasks in AFRICAN-AMERICAN STUDIES. For a long time many students of the African-American experience contended that Americans of African descent were a people whose cultural heritage had been destroyed by SLAVERY and that African Americans were not a distinctive cultural group. Instead, they were wholly American, "exaggerated Americans" in GUNNAR MYRDAL's language. This view was forcefully rejected by new African-American studies scholarship in the 1960s. As MATTHEW HOLDEN JR. in *The Politics of the Black "Nation"* put it, "Since culture is behavior learned in cohorts, it follows that when two groups are separated by legal or behavioral frontiers over any significant time, some tendency toward cultural difference must develop. . . . The obverse is also true, at the same time, if they coexist within the same linguistic, economic, or political system, they must develop significant commonalities." Holden's formulation is useful because it calls attention to the fact that blacks are culturally American and share cultural commonalities with whites, but blacks also are BLACK and thus also share as a group certain "partially distinctive attributes" that constitute a black culture. The problem, then, is to identify those partially distinctive attributes that constitute black culture and shape contemporary black attitudes and behavior.

When referring to African-American culture, the concern is with shared values, beliefs, rituals, myths, and behaviors that constitute the meanings of a way of life. To constitute a culture, these shared attributes have to be relatively stable over time and to some extent they must cut across class, region, or other divisions so as to encompass the group as a whole. The identification of these shared attributes that distinguish black Americans in the United States has always been a difficult, complex problem in research. However, since the 1960s a considerable body of scholarship and research has come about that identifies several of these partially distinctive attributes that constitute elements of the black culture.

First, there is ample evidence of racial group consciousness, identity, and a sense of "linked fate" among blacks. Related to this race group consciousness and sense of linked fate, African-American culture is marked by a deep historical consciousness and "long memory" of slavery and racial OPPRESSION. This memory and consciousness gives rise to varying degrees of hostility and wariness toward whites and suspiciousness about their motives in their interactions with blacks.

Another distinctive feature of the culture is RELIGIOSITY, an "Africanized Christianity." MUSIC, dance, and oratory are also features of the rituals of the culture. Like the rituals of black Christianity, these features are clearly rooted in African heritage and culture. A wish for FREEDOM and a wish for resistance or defiance of whites are also deep and profound cultural values, represented in black folklore as the tradition of the "bad nigger" or the "crazy nigger" who defied the oppression of whites at all cost, even with his life, in order to be free. A final component of black culture that is widely accepted by scholars is cynicism, suspiciousness, and ALIENATION. This component likely arises out of the history of oppression, one of whose distinguishing marks is an exploitative, subordinate environment in which one's life chances are manipulable and manipulated by others, black and white. This cynical attribute, this sense of always needing to be aware of the possibility of betrayal, is part of the historical legacy of blacks in their experiences with whites. MARTIN LUTHER KING JR. expressed this in his "I HAVE A DREAM" SPEECH when he said, "America has given the Negro people a bad check; it has come back marked insufficient funds." This attribute is also a feature of culture that structures black-on-black interactions. In the long memory of blacks, it is recalled that many SLAVE REVOLTS were betrayed by blacks; thus a relative suspiciousness of the motives of other blacks as well as whites is an aspect of the culture. FREDERICK DOUGLASS expressed this attribute when he wrote, "The motto which I adopted when I started from slavery was this—'Trust no man.' I saw in every white man an enemy, and in almost every colored a cause for distrust." Douglass's motto is frequently found in black folklore, as in the *Brer Rabbit* stories, and it is an abiding motif of the blues, the foundation of black secular music. In the contemporary BLACK COMMUNITY, blacks are frequently heard to say that "blacks don't trust each other" as an explanation for some perceived failure in solidarity or SELF-HELP.

While other components or attributes of black culture can be identified, the foregoing are supported by substantial historical, ethnographic, and social-science research and therefore represent a kind of scholarly consensus on the phenomenon.

cultural nationalism

Cultural nationalism is an IDEOLOGY that seeks either to construct a program or strategy in AFRICAN-AMERICAN POLITICS on the basis of attributes of African-American CULTURE or, alternatively, to discover or manufacture a culture on which a political program and strategy might be developed. In terms of the latter, RON KARENGA, for example, has advanced the idea that the principles of Kwaida (and the celebration of KWANZA)—which he contends derive from traditional African civilizations—might, if embraced by blacks, become the basis of a black politics based on cultural nationalism. Similarly, adherents of AFROCENTRICITY such as MOLEFI K. ASANTE see it as a possible basis for a culturally nationalist politics. Cultural nationalism in the first sense seeks to use the materials of black folk culture and the creativity of black artists and intellectuals as the base for political movements and organizations. The HARLEM RENAISSANCE of the 1920s and 1930s and the BLACK ARTS MOVEMENT of the 1960s are examples of this kind of cultural nationalism. Cultural nationalism of the second type—one that seeks to construct a culture for African Americans based on allegedly African cultural traditions and rituals—is more problematic, since cultures evolve and either they exist or they do not, which means cultures are rarely, if indeed ever, successfully manufactured.

See also HAROLD CRUSE.

culture of poverty

A culture of poverty is a way of living that emerges among poor people in a situation of long-term, persistent unemployment or underemployment and where the WELFARE STATE is poorly developed, therefore providing relatively little assistance to unemployed men. The culture develops as an adaptation in the behavior—although not necessarily in the values or attitudes—of the people to this situation. Once adopted, the culture of poverty can achieve stability and persistence as it is passed down from generation to generation.

The culture-of-poverty concept was first introduced into social-science research on poverty by Oscar Lewis in a series of books published in the late 1950s and early 1960s. Unlike most scholars of poverty, who tend to be economists or sociologists, Lewis was an anthropologist who employed enthnographic methods in field studies of poverty in Mexican and Puerto Rican communities. A culture of poverty (more precisely a "subculture," since it is always part of a larger "mainstream" or autonomous culture), passed down from one generation to the next, emerges according to Lewis in societies organized on the principles of CAPITAL-ISM and which exhibit high CLASS STRATIFICATION and few or none of the characteristics of a highly developed welfare state. The culture occurs in any group of people who, over time, experience high rates of unemployment or poorly paid subemployment. Its characteristics include those things in the 1980s that came to be associated with the so-called UNDERCLASS in the black GHETTO, including female-headed households, a high incidence of substance abuse, communal VIOLENCE, exaggerated masculinity, and relatively conflict-ridden relationships between the sexes. Although Lewis's studies focused on Latinos, he explicitly formulated the concept in universalistic terms that cut across national, ethnic, or urban-rural differences. The common characteristic of a poverty subculture is long-term, persistent unemployment in a society or culture that does not provide alternatives to the market that would permit individuals (especially men) to sustain themselves and their families. When these families are residentially segregated, the result is a community or neighborhood characterized by high levels of social disorganization.

Lewis's ideas generated enormous controversy, largely because of some spurious scientific studies that suggested that since there was a *culture* of poverty, the culture rather than the poverty must be the cause of the poverty. This line of reasoning, which became very influential in policy circles in the United States in the 1980s and 1990s, contends that the culture of poverty is not rooted in the larger economy and society but, rather, in psychological processes (such as the inability to defer gratification) among some people that cause them to engage in behavior that will keep them poor. Despite the fact that these psychological processes are obscure and perhaps unknowable, the common wisdom is that they are what give rise to the culture. This psychological view is fundamentally contrary to Lewis's understanding, which views the culture of poverty as an adaptation of the poor to their marginal position in a highly individualistic, capitalist system. Lewis was so convinced of the culture of poverty's roots in capitalist structures that in 1969 he and a team of researchers went to Cuba to study directly the effects of the transition from capitalism to SOCIALISM

on poverty and the culture of the poor. Unfortunately, he was unable to complete his studies because he was ordered to leave Cuba within a year, and many of his papers were confiscated. Shortly after leaving Cuba, Lewis died of a heart attack, but his wife and other colleagues prepared a book based on his year of research. Although tentative, this work (*Four Men: An Oral History of Cuba*) does suggest that transition to socialism was having some effects on the behaviors associated with the culture of poverty.

Athough Lewis clearly rooted the culture of poverty in structural features of capitalism, implying that change in the culture required change in these features, he also noted some likely tendency toward self-perpetuation as a result of the socialization process. Thus, he recognized the possibility that some children growing up in the culture might be unable to adapt their behavior to take advantage of new opportunities brought about by beneficial changes in those structural features.

Further reading: Oscar Lewis, *Five Families* (New York: Basic Books, 1959); ———, *The Children of Sanchez* (New York: Random House, 1961); ———, *La Vida* (New York: Random House, 1966); ———, *Four Men: An Oral History of Cuba* (Urbana: University of Illinois Press, 1978); Charles Valentine, *Culture and Poverty* (Chicago: University of Chicago Press, 1968).

Cummings v. Board of Education (1899)

In *Cummings v. Board of Education*, decided three years after *PLESSY V. FERGUSON*, the SUPREME COURT refused to apply the equal part of the SEPARATE BUT EQUAL doctrine announced in *Plessy* to the education of black children in Richmond County, Georgia. The county school board levied a tax of two and two-tenths cents per $100 on all property owners, black and white, to support three high schools, two for whites and one for blacks. When the school board faced a budget shortfall, it closed the black high school while maintaining the two schools for whites (one for girls, one for boys). J. A. Cummings and two other black parents sued, alleging that the actions of the school board violated the EQUAL PROTECTION CLAUSE of the FOURTEENTH AMENDMENT because they were taxed to pay for the high school education of white children while their children were denied one. The parents claimed that this violated the "equal" part of the "separate but equal" doctrine expressed in *Plessy*. The county court of Richmond agreed and ordered the school board to provide EQUALITY in facilities for high school education for all children. The school board appealed, and the Georgia supreme court reversed the decision of the county court. Cummings then appealed to the U.S. Supreme Court, which agreed with the decision of Georgia's supreme court.

The opinion of the Supreme Court, ironically, was written by Justice John Marshall Harlan, the lone dissenter in *Plessy,* who in that case declared that the Constitution was "color blind." Harlan based his decision in *Cummings* on the principles of FEDERALISM, writing that there was no Fourteenth Amendment equal-protection issue because "the education of the people in the schools maintained by state taxation is a matter belonging to the respective states, and any interference on the part of Federal authority with the management of such schools cannot be justified except in the case of a clear and unmistakable disregard of the rights secured by the [Constitution]." And since there was no right in the CONSTITUTION to be the equal beneficiary of tax expenditures in education, the Richmond County school board did not violate the principles of the equal protection clause or *Plessy.*

African Americans were willing at this time to accept racially separate schools if they were to some degree equal. But *Cummings* stood for the proposition that inequality in education would mean not only racial SEGREGATION but racial inequality and subordination. Black parents could be constitutionally required to pay for the higher education of whites in a county that provided only an elementary education for black children. *Cummings* thus established for five generations the precedent that blacks could be constitutionally denied equal access to knowledge, a major base of power for any people, but especially an oppressed people.

See also SCHOOLS AND EDUCATION.

D

Davis, Angela (1944–) *scholar, radical activist*
Angela Davis is an example of the tendency in the BLACK COMMUNITY for many of its intellectuals to embrace RADICALISM. Born in Birmingham, Alabama, in a prosperous family, Davis was likely introduced to radical ideas while a student at Elizabeth Irwin High School in Greenwich Village, New York. In 1965 she was graduated from Brandeis University and went abroad to do graduate work in philosophy at the Sorbonne in France and Goethe University in Germany. But in 1967 she abruptly left Europe to return to the United States, saying that "my commitment to the struggle being waged by my people was something far more important than a doctoral dissertation." In Los Angeles she joined the local chapter of the STUDENT NONVIOLENT COORDINATING COMMITTEE (SNCC), but soon became disillusioned with the group because she viewed its black-power philosophy as too narrow and too hostile to whites and to COMMUNISM. In 1968 she joined the COMMUNIST PARTY, becoming a member of its all-black Che Lumumba Collective. Meanwhile, she was completing a master's degree at the University of California at San Diego under the famed Marxist professor Herbert Marcuse, and in 1969 she was hired as a philosophy instructor at the University of California at Los Angeles (UCLA). When her membership in the Communist Party became known, the California governor RONALD REAGAN insisted that she be fired. The faculty of the university resisted on the basis that adherence to communism should not disqualify a qualified philosopher from teaching. However, Governor Reagan convened a meeting of the university's governing board, which voted not to renew her contract because of her membership in the Communist Party.

Although she lost her job at UCLA, the controversy made her an international celebrity, a status that she used to advance the causes of MILITANCY and radicalism in African-American politics. (She wore her hair in a large "natural" or "Afro" as a symbol of this militancy.) In addition to her work in the Communist Party, Davis became active in what she called "prison solidarity work." As a result of this work, she met the "Soledad Brothers," three black convicts accused of killing a guard at Soledad State Prison. She developed an especially close relationship with Jonathan Jackson, one of the brothers. In 1971 Jackson was involved in the shooting of four people (including a judge) at the Marin County Courthouse. Davis was accused of supplying Jackson with the gun used in the killing, but before she could be arrested she went underground. Labeled by President RICHARD NIXON a "terrorist" and placed on the FBI's 10-most-wanted list, after two months she was captured. Jailed for 16 months before bail was posted, in 1972 she was found not guilty of all the charges, which included murder, kidnapping, and conspiracy.

After the trial, Davis resumed her radical activism and prison solidarity work. She also resumed her intellectual work, teaching for a time at Moscow University in the Soviet Union and Havana University in Cuba. She was also visiting professor at several American universities. In addition to her teaching, she wrote her memoir and several books on race, gender, and class oppression. She also embraced radical FEMINISM and activism in the GAY RIGHTS MOVEMENT. In 1980 and 1984 she was the Communist Party candidate for vice president of the United States, but in the 1990s she became disenchanted with the party, in part because of its failure to develop programs to address RACISM and SEXISM, and left it to join a group called the Committee of Correspondence. In an ironic twist, in 1995 Davis rejoined the faculty of the University of California—this time at the Santa Cruz rather than Los Angeles campus—as a presidential scholar, one of the university's highest honors. In 1988 she wrote *Angela Davis: An Autobiography.*

Further reading: Angela Davis, *Women, Race and Class* (New York: Random House, 1981).

Dawson, William L. (1886–1970) *politician*
William Dawson's election to CONGRESS in 1942 represented the emergence of tendencies that would dominate electoral

politics in the BLACK COMMUNITY throughout the 20th century. During the RECONSTRUCTION era the 22 blacks who served in Congress were elected as representatives from rural areas in the SOUTHERN STATES, and they were all members of the REPUBLICAN PARTY. Dawson was elected from Chicago and was a member of the DEMOCRATIC PARTY. After Dawson's election in 1942, no black would be elected to the Congress from the rural South until 1992, and no black Republican would be elected to the House until 1990.

The first tendency in black politics represented by Dawson's election was the nearly total disenfranchisement of black voters in the Southern states. After South Carolina's GEORGE WHITE, the last Reconstruction-era black congressman, was defeated in 1901, it would take more than seven decades before another black, ANDREW YOUNG of Georgia, would be elected to Congress from the Southern states. The second tendency reflected in the election of Dawson is the gradual shift of the base of black POWER in electoral politics to the NORTHERN STATES as a result of the GREAT MIGRATION. This migration of blacks from the rural South to the big cities of the North and South and their concentration in the GHETTOS was the basis of the election of every black to the Congress until 1992. The third tendency represented by Dawson's election was the change in the partisan allegiance of black voters from the Republican to the Democratic Party, a shift that came about in response to the NEW DEAL social-welfare reforms initiated by FRANKLIN D. ROOSEVELT. Since Dawson's election, the three black Republicans elected to the Congress have been elected from districts with a majority of white rather than black voters. In other words, since Dawson's election it has been virtually impossible for a black Republican to win election to Congress (or any other elective office) from a district where a majority of voters are African American.

Dawson was not the first black elected to Congress from the Northern states, nor was he the first black Democrat. The first Northern black elected to Congress was Oscar DePriest in 1928, also from Chicago. Elected from a majority-black district centered in the city's southside ghetto, DePriest—as the first black member of Congress in a generation—became a celebrity and was viewed by many as the representative of the entire black community. However, he did not live up to these expectations, rarely introducing legislation and voting against New Deal welfare legislation. After three terms he was defeated by Arthur Mitchell, the first black Democrat elected to Congress. Mitchell was more active than DePriest in representing black interests, supporting the New Deal and introducing antilynching bills and legislation to desegregate interstate transportation. After eight years Mitchell resigned and was succeeded by Dawson, who served for 28 years until his death in 1970.

William Dawson was born in 1886 in Albany, Georgia. He was graduated from Fisk University, one of the leading HISTORICALLY BLACK COLLEGES AND UNIVERSITIES. After graduation from law school he moved to Chicago to practice law and enter politics. Dawson's career in politics represents another important tendency in 20th-century black politics, which is the inclination of black elected officials to subordinate the interests of the race to the needs of the "political machines" that dominated URBAN POLITICS in the United States until the 1970s. Throughout his long career in Congress, Dawson was a loyal "organization man" who rarely spoke out on race issues. Instead, Dawson focused on patronage and its use in building and maintaining an efficient organization that could deliver a reliable black vote to the Democratic Party in local, state, and national elections. Even during the PROTEST phase of the CIVIL RIGHTS MOVEMENT during the 1960s, Dawson remained silent. Dawson even voted against legislation introduced by ADAM CLAYTON POWELL, his black colleague from HARLEM, prohibiting recipients of federal funds from practicing racial DISCRIMINATION and SEGREGATION.

In 1949 Dawson became chairman of the House Committee on Government Operations, becoming the first black to chair a congressional committee. The committee was one of the largest and most powerful in the House, with a large budget and staff and wide jurisdiction to investigate and legislate. Yet, Dawson employed only two blacks out of a staff of 50 and never used the committee's broad jurisdiction to investigate or legislate on CIVIL RIGHTS or other issues of concern to blacks. Because of this, Dawson was referred to as an UNCLE TOM during the 1950s and 1960s, and his ACCOMMODATIONISM was frequently contrasted with the MILITANCY of his Harlem colleague ADAM CLAYTON POWELL. However, because of his control of the political machine in the Chicago ghetto, Dawson was able to defeat all challengers, usually by large margins.

Further reading: James Q. Wilson, "Two Negro Politicians," *Midwest Political Science Review* 4(1960): 365–79.

Declaration of Independence
The Declaration of Independence is the nation's founding document, justifying the invention of America. Rooted in the philosophical principles of SOCIAL-CONTRACT THEORY and NATURAL RIGHTS, the declaration appears to commit the nation to EQUALITY, since in it THOMAS JEFFERSON wrote, "We hold these truths to be self-evident, that all men are created equal, that they are endowed by their Creator with certain unalienable Rights, that among these are Life, Liberty and the pursuit of Happiness." Given this self-evident equality of men (note that the word is *men*, not *men and women* or simply *persons*) and their God-given rights to

liberty or FREEDOM—a right that is inalienable, meaning it can not be surrendered and ought not be taken away—the obvious question is how can one simultaneously support SLAVERY, the taking of the liberty or freedom of millions of men, women, and children. Logically and rationally—the framers of the declaration and the CONSTITUTION were quintessentially rational men of the Enlightenment—one could not except by either denying the humanity of the slaves or by claiming that Jefferson's words did not mean what they plainly said. Both explanations were used in justifying the enslavement of African peoples. It was argued by some that Jefferson really did not mean men when he wrote all men were created equal, while others denied African humanity by suggesting that black men were not really men or at least not fully or completely men.

After voting to declare independence from England, the Continental Congress appointed a committee of five men to draft a document setting forth the reasons for the revolution. Jefferson and John Adams were asked by the other members of the committee to write the document that was to become the declaration, and Adams turned the actual writing over to Jefferson because he said Jefferson's writing was characterized by a "peculiar felicitousness of expression." The declaration, however, is not the work of Jefferson alone. Rather, it was substantially revised by members of the Continental Congress, who deleted about one-fourth of Jefferson's original draft. Jefferson was extremely displeased by the revisions and deletions, and for the remaining 50 years of his life he angrily contended that the Congress had "mangled" his manuscript.

Most of the substantive changes or deletions in Jefferson's draft—including the most famous—focused on the long list of charges against King George III. Most historians think that the charges against the king in the declaration as finally approved are exaggerated and, in any event, they are misplaced, since many of the actions complained of were decisions of the Parliament rather than the king. The king, however, made a more convenient target than the anonymous, amorphous Parliament.

The most famous of the passages deleted from Jefferson's draft was the condemnation of the king for engaging in the African slave trade. Jefferson had written:

He has waged cruel war against human nature itself, violating its most sacred rights of life and liberty in the persons of a distant people who never offended him, captivating and carrying them into slavery in another hemisphere, or to incur miserable death in their transportation thither. This piratical warfare, the opprobrium of infidel powers, is the warfare of the Christian king of Great Britain. Determined to keep open a market where men should be bought and sold, he has prostituted his negative for suppressing every legislative attempt to prohibit or to restrain this execrable commerce. And that this assemblage of horrors might want no fact of distinguished die, he is now exciting those very people to rise in arms among us, and to purchase that liberty of which he has deprived them, by murdering the people upon whom he also obtruded them: thus paying off former crimes committed against the liberties of one people, with crimes which he urges them to commit against the lives of another.

This passage, which was to be the climax of the charges against the king, was clearly an exaggeration and a disingenuous one, since the colonists themselves (including Jefferson) had enthusiastically engaged in slave trading and, as was made clear to Jefferson, they had no intention of abandoning it after independence. Jefferson recalls that "the clause too, reprobating the enslaving of the inhabitants of Africa, was struck out in compliance to South Carolina and Georgia, who had never attempted to restrain the importation of slaves and who still wished to continue it." Not only was there opposition to the passage from the Southern slave owners but, more tellingly, as Jefferson went on to say "our northern brethren also I believe felt a little tender under these censures; for tho' their people have few slaves themselves yet they have been pretty considerable carriers of them." In other words, virtually all of the leading white men in America, Northerner and Southerner, slave owner and non-slave-owner, had economic interests in the perpetuation of slavery. This was because a good part of the new nation's wealth and prosperity was based on the slave economy. To be consistent, one might have thought that the Continental Congress would also have deleted the phrase on the equality of men and their inherent right to liberty. They did not, apparently seeing no inconsistency either because the words did not mean what they said or because Africans, for them, were not men.

There has always been controversy about what Jefferson meant by the words "all men are created equal." As early as 1776 Rufus Choate, speaking for Southern slaveholders, said that Jefferson did not mean what he said. Rather, the word *men* referred only to nobles and Englishmen, who were no better than ordinary American freemen. "If he meant more," Choate said, it was because Jefferson was "unduly influenced by the French school of thought." (Jefferson was frequently accused of being influenced by Jean-Jacques Rousseau, who, when declaring the equality of man, said that slavery was absolutely impermissible in civil society.) On the eve of the Civil War, Chief Justice Roger B. Taney in his opinion in the *DRED SCOTT* case said that, on the surface, the words *all men are created equal* applied to blacks. Yet he concluded that "it is too clear for dispute that the enslaved African race were not intended to be included, and formed no part of the people who framed and adopted the declaration." Similarly, during his famous debates with ABRAHAM LINCOLN, Stephen Douglas argued that the phrase simply meant that Americans were not inferior to Englishmen as citizens. In the 20th century, conservative scholars such as Wilmore Kendal have argued that the word *men* in the declaration referred to property holders or to the nations of the world but not to men as such, writing that "The Declaration of Independence does not commit us to equality as a national goal." And as Daniel Boorstin, the former librarian of Congress and author of the celebrated *The Americans: The Democratic Experience,* writes, "We have repeated that 'all men are created equal' without daring to discover what it meant and without realizing that probably to none of the men who spoke it did it mean what we would like it to mean."

Jefferson, however, apparently meant *men* when he wrote men, and in his *Notes on Virginia,* written several years after the declaration, he strongly condemned slavery as an "unremitting despotism" that violated the natural rights of the enslaved persons. However, Jefferson, while believing that all men were created equal and that blacks were men, also believed that African men were inferior and not equal to European men. This notion of the inferiority of Africans—of their being less than fully human—was written into the Constitution in the infamous THREE-FIFTHS CLAUSE.

See also WHITE SUPREMACY.

Further reading: Carl Becker, *The Declaration of Independence: A Study in the History of an Idea* (New York: Vintage Books, 1922, 1970).

Delany, Martin R. (1812–1885) *writer, lecturer, and army officer*

Martin R. Delany is often referred to as the father of BLACK NATIONALISM. Historians confer this title on Delany largely because of his 1854 publication *The Condition, Elevation, Emigration, and Destiny of the Colored People of the United States,* which is considered the earliest systematic statement of black nationalist principles (the phrase "nation within a nation" to refer to African Americans was first used in this work) and is a seminal contribution to AFRICAN-AMERICAN THOUGHT. Delany is also important in the black nationalist tradition because, along with ALEXANDER CRUMMELL, he led an expedition to Africa and signed a treaty with a Yoruba king to provide for the settlement of African Americans on unused tribal lands. And throughout the 1850s Delany organized several emigration conventions; "The Political Destiny of the Colored Race" was originally prepared as a report to a convention organized to consider the feasibility of black emigration to Africa or elsewhere.

Delany was born in Virginia in 1812. He always claimed that his parents were descendants of African royalty and that he was of pure African ancestry. (Delany had a lifelong commitment to racial purity, which resulted in sometimes antagonistic relationships with mixed-race, or mulatto, colleagues.) Delany received his early education in a Pittsburgh, Pennsylvania, school run by the Reverend Lewis Woodson, an influential nationalist thinker also referred to by some as the father of black nationalism. He studied medicine under several doctors in Pittsburgh and attended Harvard Medical School briefly until protests by white students forced his withdrawal. Although he was a qualified physician, Delany's real interests were writing and politics. He wrote a novel *Blake* about a revolution to overthrow SLAVERY, and he was an important leader in the ABOLITIONIST MOVEMENT and the founder and editor of *The Mystery,* a black newspaper. *The Mystery* folded after four years, at which time he joined FREDERICK DOUGLASS as coeditor of his newspaper, *The North Star.* His collaboration with Douglass lasted only a short time, as Delany became increasingly disillusioned with the prospects for FREEDOM and EQUALITY in the United States and turned toward emigration. Several years after publication of "The Political Destiny," he left for Africa to explore emigration possibilities.

He returned to the United States on the eve of the CIVIL WAR. Believing that the war would bring freedom to the slaves, Delany urged the use of black soldiers and eventually became a full-time recruiter for blacks and was appointed by President ABRAHAM LINCOLN a major in the Union army, becoming the first African American to be commissioned as a field officer. Delany was dispatched to South Carolina to recruit blacks for a regiment he hoped to command, but before he could do so the war ended. Delany remained in South Carolina during RECONSTRUCTION, where he worked with the FREEDMEN'S BUREAU and became active in REPUBLICAN PARTY politics, serving on the party's executive committee and receiving an appointment as county jury commissioner. Soon, however, Delany became disillusioned with the Republican Party's Reconstruction policies, especially with what he saw as the paternalistic attitude of Northern whites toward South Carolina blacks. Thus, like a handful of other black leaders during Reconstruction, Delany argued that the Republican-dominated Reconstruction governments in the SOUTHERN STATES were corrupt and condescending toward blacks, and that the natural allies of blacks were the elite Southern plantation owners and businessmen. In effect, Delany was calling for a COALITION between the former slaves and their slave masters in a new DEMOCRATIC PARTY. As a result, he was widely condemned in South Carolina and throughout the nation as an UNCLE TOM.

When Reconstruction came to an end after the COMPROMISE OF 1877, Delany, once again disillusioned about the prospects for freedom and equality in the United States, turned to emigration and the development of plans for blacks to settle in LIBERIA. Moving from South Carolina to Wilberforce, Ohio, in 1880, Delany wrote another book dealing with issues of race and nationalism, *Principia of Ethnology: The Origins of Races with an Archeological Compendium of Ethiopian and Egyptian Civilization. Principia* is one of the earliest texts in AFROCENTRISM. In it he argues that Ethiopian and Egyptian civilizations were the earliest and highest and constitute the basis on which Greek and Roman civilizations emerged. Thus, nearly a century before the work of Afrocentric scholars like MOLEFI K. ASANTE valorized African civilization and culture, Delany wrote, "The African branch of this family is that which was the earliest developed, taking first strides in the progress of the highest known to the world, and for this cause, if no other, it may be regarded as the oldest race of man, having doubtless centuries prior to the others, reared imperishable monuments of their superior attainments." Delany died in 1885. In part because of his embrace of the white supremacist Democratic Party during Reconstruction, Delany's legacy was ignored until the 1960s BLACK POWER MOVEMENT and the development of AFRICAN-AMERICAN STUDIES led to a revival of interest in black nationalism and a new appreciation of Delany's contribution to its development.

See also BACK-TO-AFRICA MOVEMENTS and CITIZEN DIPLOMACY.

Further reading: Victor Ullman, *Martin R. Delany: The Beginnings of Black Nationalism* (Boston: Beacon Press, 1971).

Dellums, Ronald (1935–) *politician*

Ronald Dellums, elected to the House of Representatives in 1970, was the first African American elected to the House from a majority-white district. Dellums was elected from Berkeley, California, the most self-consciously radical congressional district in the United States. Dellums was first elected to the Berkeley City Council in 1967 and three years later to the House. In both elections a COALITION of blacks (the district was about 25 percent black in 1970), students, and upper-income liberal voters provided the basis of Dellums's electoral majority. The 1970 election was in a sense a referendum on the VIETNAM WAR. The incumbent, a liberal Democrat, opposed the war, but his opposition was viewed by many in Berkeley as too moderate and cautious. Dellums's RADICALISM and MILITANCY on the war and other issues garnered him 55 percent of the vote in the Democratic primary and 57 percent in the general election. He began his tenure in CONGRESS with a reputation as a militant "peacenik" and radical reformer.

Dellums lived up to this reputation. One of only two members of the House to openly embrace SOCIALISM as an IDEOLOGY, Dellums became a leader in efforts to get Congress to end the war, and once the war ended he became a militant opponent of military spending and an advocate of an expansion of the WELFARE STATE. In pursuit of these goals, Dellums went directly into the "lion's den" by seeking to become a member of the Armed Services Committee. Although his appointment to the committee was opposed by the conservative leadership of the committee, in his second term he was elected and became the leading spokesman for the CONGRESSIONAL BLACK CAUCUS on military issues.

Outside of Congress, Dellums worked to build a progressive coalition, working with the Democratic Socialists of America, the NATIONAL BLACK POLITICAL CONVENTION, and with CIVIL RIGHTS, peace, and environmental groups. An advocate of FEMINISM, Dellums worked closely with black and white women's groups and was an early supporter of JESSE JACKSON and his RAINBOW COALITION and Jackson's 1984 and 1988 presidential campaigns. In his work in CONGRESS and beyond, Dellums developed a national following as a spokesman for peace and FULL EMPLOYMENT to be pursued through a multiethnic and multiclass coalition.

After 20 years in the House, Dellums had become a senior and respected member, which was reflected in his election in 1993 as the chairman of the Armed Services Committee. Thus, the man who had once led antiwar demonstrations on the steps of the Capitol building and whose appointment to the committee was initially blocked because of his radicalism was now leader of the committee in charge of the military. On assuming the chair, Dellums continued to argue for major cuts in the military budget, but he abruptly resigned from the House in 1995 in order to head an organization devoted to fighting the AIDS-HIV epidemic in Africa. In 2000 he published his memoirs, *Lying Down with Lions: A Public Life from the Streets of Oakland to the Halls of Power.*

democracy

Democracy, along with CONSTITUTIONALISM and CAPITALISM, is one of the three core values of the American POLITICAL SYSTEM. The term is derived from the Greek word for "people" (*demos*) and for "authority" (*krotos*), and it is generally understood to mean a system of government where ultimate political authority rests with the people. In the 20th century, democracy in the Western world is understood to require at a minimum (1) regularly scheduled elections in which all citizens of a certain age are eligible to vote, (2) a fair count of the votes, (3) control of the government passing to the individuals or parties who win a majority of the votes, and (4) the losers accepting the outcome of the election as legitimate. Finally, democracy is thought to require a free and competitive press so that the candidates and parties can openly present their views to the voters. While the majority generally rules in a democracy, minority rights are protected and EQUALITY is guaranteed to all citizens in terms of formal POLITICAL PARTICIPATION. These are the general or formal characteristics of political systems described as democratic. In the United States, these general characteristics are structured by constitutionalism, which limits majority rule, and the SEPARATION OF POWERS, which allows the voters to directly elect only parts of the government. Democracy in America is also characterized by a high degree of PLURALISM, in which INTEREST GROUPS mobilize voters during elections and seek to influence PUBLIC POLICY after elections, and a POWER ELITE that exercises disproportionate POWER on certain issues.

Understood in this way, African Americans have and have always had an ambivalent relationship to the American democracy. First, for most of the country's history, African Americans were denied VOTING RIGHTS. It was not until the late 1960s, after passage of the VOTING RIGHTS ACT OF 1965, that African Americans throughout the United States were fully and completely allowed to vote. Second, until the 1960s, black interest groups were by and large excluded from effective participation in the structure of pluralism that characterizes the democracy, and relatively few blacks are found in the nation's power elite. Thus, democracy in America until the late 1960s was largely a sham for blacks because the influence of RACISM and WHITE SUPREMACY effectively undermined the application of its principles.

However, even when democracy in America is faithful to its principles, African Americans can still be disadvantaged by what James Madison in "Federalist Paper No. 10" and Alexis de Tocqueville in DEMOCRACY IN AMERICA described as "the tyranny of the majority." This is because blacks are a relatively small minority in a system where whites constitute the overwhelming majority, and from time to time this white majority may be hostile to the interests of blacks. Thus, on some issues, at some times, even if the American democracy completely lives up to its formal principles, it can disadvantage blacks if their candidates, interests, and policy preferences are contrary to those of the white majority. This problem is not unique to blacks as a minority in the United States, but because they are a historically oppressed and stigmatized minority, it may be more acute for blacks. That is, on some issues, at some times, blacks may constitute a permanent minority unable to advance their interests because of a permanent, hostile white majority. It was Tocqueville's pessimistic conclusion in *Democracy in America* that the more democratic the American political system became, the less likely were the possibilities of INTEGRATION and equality for African Americans.

Further reading: Lani Guinier, *The Tyranny of the Majority: Fundamental Fairness in Representative Democracy* (New York: Free Press, 1994).

Democracy in America

Democracy in America is widely considered the single most influential book on the subject of the American democracy and one of the most important ever written on the subject of DEMOCRACY in general. It was written by Alexis de Tocqueville, a 19th-century French writer and statesman who came to the United States in 1831 to study the prison system. With a colleague, Gustave de Beaumont, Tocqueville traveled throughout the United States, and after the two men returned to France they wrote up their findings on the prison system. Tocqueville then wrote *Democracy in America,* his most famous work published in two volumes in 1835–40. The book is a thorough and wide-ranging study of the origins and operations of the American democracy, with perceptive chapters on the CONSTITUTION, FEDERALISM, POLITICAL PARTIES, PUBLIC OPINION, and the POLITICAL CULTURE. Tocqueville generally admired the American democracy, but he was also critical. For example, he argued that public opinion in the United States could become tyrannical and that majority rule could become as oppressive as rule by a dictator. In addition to chapters on the American culture and American institutions, Tocqueville included in Volume I a chapter (23) on "The Present and Probable Future Conditions of the Three Races That Inhabit the Territory of the United States."

Of the Europeans, Tocqueville wrote they were "superior in intelligence, power and enjoyment . . . the man preeminently." Of the blacks and Indians, he wrote that European OPPRESSION has "at one stroke deprived the descendants of the Africans of almost all the privileges of humanity" and "has been no less fatal to the Indians . . . but its effects are different. . . . The Europeans having dispersed the Indian tribes and driven them to a wandering life, full of inexpressible suffering." Tocqueville thought the Indians would be exterminated, in his words they were "doomed to perish" by the time the European reached the Pacific Ocean. The Africans, he thought, however, were so "interwoven" with the Europeans that they were unlikely to be able to either "separate entirely or combine." Therefore, he wrote, "The most formidable of all the ills that threaten the future of the union arises from the presence of the black population on its territory." He described SLAVERY in the SOUTHERN STATES as a system of "unparalleled atrocities," atrocities so bad that "the laws of humanity have been totally perverted." Comparing slavery in the ancient world with that in America, he said the ancient slaveholders only attempted to keep the bodies of slaves in bondage, but the Americans have employed their despotism and their violence "against the human mind." In the end, Tocqueville believed that slavery would not survive in America because it was both unjust and uneconomical under CAPITALISM. He was uncertain, however, as to how its end would come. Perhaps, he speculated, through a "most horrible" CIVIL WAR or perhaps through SLAVE REVOLTS.

However it ended, Tocqueville was equally convinced that the end of slavery would not result in FREEDOM and EQUALITY for the Africans because WHITE SUPREMACY appeared to him to be greater in the NORTHERN STATES, where slavery had already been abolished; because the African's skin color would mark him and his descendants forever with the badge of inferiority; and because of the American democracy itself. In concluding his discussion of the future of black-white relations in America, Tocqueville wrote that he did not think equality between blacks and whites would be achieved in any country, but he wrote it would be most difficult to achieve in America because "as long as . . . democracy remains at the head of affairs, no one will undertake so difficult a task; and it may be foreseen that the freer the white population of the United States becomes, the more isolated it will remain."

Democratic Party

The Democratic Party is one of the two parties that constitute the TWO-PARTY SYSTEM in the United States. Although there have been and continue to be THIRD PARTIES in the United States, throughout most of the country's history, there have been only two parties with a realistic chance of winning seats in CONGRESS, votes in the ELECTORAL COLLEGE, or offices in STATE AND LOCAL GOVERNMENTS. This makes the United States unique among the nations of the world, since virtually every other modern DEMOCRACY has a multiparty system.

The roots of the Democratic Party go back to the election of THOMAS JEFFERSON, but it was formally organized in the 1820s, which makes it the oldest political party in the world. Throughout the 19th century the Democratic Party was the more conservative of the two major parties. It opposed social reforms, supported the principles of FEDERALISM, and opposed a strong, activist central government. The party's traditional base of support was among whites in the SOUTHERN STATES; therefore it supported SLAVERY during the 19th century and SEGREGATION in the 20th century. In the NORTHERN STATES the party's support was mainly among Irish and German immigrants. The handful of African Americans who could vote during this period supported the Whig Party or third parties.

With the election of ABRAHAM LINCOLN in 1860 the REPUBLICAN PARTY replaced the Whigs as the second party in the two-party system. After the CIVIL WAR during RECONSTRUCTION, almost all African Americans became Republicans. As FREDERICK DOUGLASS put it, "The Republican Party is the deck, all else the sea." This was because the Democratic Party was identified with RACISM and WHITE SUPREMACY, while the Republican Party during the Civil War had secured the FREEDOM of the slaves and passed laws and amendments to the CONSTITUTION to secure CIVIL RIGHTS for the freed slaves. From 1868 to 1888, black voters in the Southern states were the BALANCE OF POWER in the election of Republican presidents, governors, legislatures, and local officials. Although the right to vote was taken away from most Southern blacks after the COMPROMISE OF 1877, the few who could vote continued to support the Republican Party.

Black allegiance to the Republican Party begin to shift as a result of the GREAT MIGRATION and the NEW DEAL. As blacks left the South and settled in the cities of the Northern states, they found they could constitute the balance of power in the election of mayors and other city offices. Although most Northern blacks continued to vote Republican, gradually the Democratic Party political machines that dominated URBAN POLITICS began to offer programs and patronage to attract black voters because it was the only way it could win. But the major reason for the shift of blacks to the Democrats was the election in 1932 of FRANKLIN D. ROOSEVELT and the appeal of his New Deal programs. In 1932 most blacks had voted for Republican Herbert Hoover, but in 1936 most voted for Roosevelt, and since 1936 a majority of blacks have always voted for the Democratic candidate for president. Because of the continued dominance of the Southern states at Democratic conventions and their influence in the electoral college, Roosevelt refused to support CIVIL RIGHTS legislation, but his WELFARE STATE programs were enough to attract a majority of black votes, although the Republican Party during this period was more liberal on civil rights. In 1948 President HARRY TRUMAN, recognizing the pivotal role the black vote could play in his election, adopted a civil rights program, and the Democratic Party platform adopted a civil rights plank for the first time ever. The embrace of civil rights in 1948 was a decisive factor in Truman's election, although it led to a walkout by Southern delegates at the convention and a third-party presidential campaign by Southern white supremacists led by Governor Strom Thurmond of South Carolina.

By the election of 1948 the two major parties had essentially reversed their 19th-century positions on reform and RACE. The Democratic Party was now the party of reform and a strong, activist central government, while the Republican Party had become the antireform party and the party of states' rights and federalism. This transformation in the positions of the parties was completed in the election of 1964 between Republican BARRY GOLDWATER and Democrat LYNDON B. JOHNSON. As late as 1960 in the election between JOHN F. KENNEDY and RICHARD NIXON, Nixon, the Republican candidate, received about 25 percent of the black vote. Four years later, Goldwater, who had opposed the CIVIL RIGHTS ACT OF 1964 (Nixon supported it) and President Johnson's GREAT SOCIETY reforms, received about 6 percent of the black vote while carrying the anti–civil rights white vote, including five Southern states. After 1964, for African Americans the Democratic Party became the deck and all else the sea. Since 1964 the black vote has averaged 88 percent for the Democratic Party in national elections, compared with an average of 43 percent among white voters. And whereas whites in the Southern states use to be the most reliable base of support for the Democrats, they are since 1964 the most reliable bloc of votes for the Republicans.

Since the 1970s blacks have become the most reliable part of the Democratic Party COALITION, generally casting 90 percent of their vote for the party in national elections and constituting about one-fifth of the party's total national vote. The result has been increased black participation and influence in party affairs. From 1868 to 1936 there were no black delegates at Democratic national conventions; from 1948 to 1968 the average number of black delegates at the conventions was 3 percent. However, since 1972 the percent of black delegates at the conventions has been approximately 18 percent. Blacks hold more than 20 percent of seats on the Democratic National Committee, the party's governing body, and in 1989 RONALD BROWN was elected party chairman, becoming the first African American to head one of the two major parties.

The transformation of the Democratic Party into the party of reform civil rights and modern LIBERALISM—and the increased presence and influence of blacks in party affairs—began to be perceived as a liability by some party leaders in the 1970s. These leaders contended that the party's liberalism generally and its racial liberalism in particular were making it difficult for Democratic candidates to win the PRESIDENCY. Especially after the election of RONALD REAGAN in 1980, Democratic Party leaders and most commentators in the MEDIA began to say and write that the Democratic Party was too liberal and too "BLACK." Thus, by the 1990s, the party had moved in a more conservative direction on civil rights and the welfare state.

See also JIMMY CARTER and BILL CLINTON.

Further reading: Hanes Walton, "Democrats and African Americans" in *Democrats and the American Idea,* ed. Peter Kover (Washington, D.C.: Center for National Policy Press, 1992).

deracialization

Deracialization is the name for a POST–CIVIL RIGHTS ERA political and PUBLIC-POLICY strategy designed to facilitate the election of African Americans to offices in majority-white constituencies and to advance public policies that serve the interests of blacks without PROTEST and without specifically focusing on race or CIVIL RIGHTS. As a strategy, deracialization has been advocated by leading African-American intellectuals, including BAYARD RUSTIN, CHARLES HAMILTON, and WILLIAM J. WILSON, as a means to gain support for BLACK policy objectives, once the goals of the CIVIL RIGHTS MOVEMENT had been achieved with the passage of the civil rights laws of the 1960s. These laws were race-specific and they were enacted after protests by blacks. In the post–civil rights era Rustin, Hamilton, and Wilson, among others, argued that a focus on race-specific issues was not strategically useful in advancing the post–civil rights era BLACK AGENDA and that protests as they were used during the Civil Rights movement would not work in the new era. The main objective of the post–civil rights era black agenda was the development of policies to deal with the problems of joblessness and POVERTY in the GHETTOS.

To deal with these problems, Rustin in an influential essay titled "From Protest to Politics: The Future of the Civil Rights Movement," published in 1965, called for an end to a focus on issues of race and an end to protests. Instead, the movement should focus on "full employment" as the centerpiece of a comprehensive strategy to attack poverty in America, and the strategy should rely on voting and LOBBYING, rather than protests, in a COALITION with white liberals, labor, and religious groups that could become the governing majority in national elections. In 1973 Charles Hamilton wrote an article that advanced similar arguments about the relationship between FULL EMPLOYMENT, voting, lobbying, coalition politics, and the new black agenda, as did William J. Wilson in his influential writings on the black UNDERCLASS in the 1980s. Before his death in 1968, MARTIN LUTHER KING JR. had also called for a shift in the movement's agenda toward a focus on full employment as a means to attack poverty in America, but unlike Rustin (a major adviser to King), he favored the continued use of protest to achieve this new objective through the POOR PEOPLE'S CAMPAIGN. After King's death, the deracialization strategy advocated first by Rustin in 1965 became the dominant public-policy approach of African-American LEADERSHIP. The use of this strategy led in 1978 to passage of the HUMPHREY-HAWKINS ACT, which committed the government to a full-employment policy. This act, however, was mere symbolism because, as it was written, it included no programmatic means to fulfill the commitment. Nevertheless, deracialization remained the dominant public-policy strategy of African-American leaders.

Deracialization is also the strategy employed by black candidates to win offices in majority-white constituencies, such as when DOUGLAS WILDER was elected governor of Virginia in 1989 (the first and only black elected governor of one of the states) or when CAROL MOSELEY-BRAUN was elected to the U.S. Senate from Illinois in 1992. The essence of this electoral version of the deracialization strategy is that black candidates try to deemphasize their race (deracialize) and those issues (such as AFFIRMATIVE ACTION) that may be viewed as dealing explicitly with race while emphasizing issues such as health care or abortion rights that transcend or are irrelevant to race. Some black candidates have used deracialized strategies while running for offices in majority-black constituencies, but they are most often used by black candidates running in places where whites constitute the majority. As an electoral strategy, deracialization is viewed as the only realistic approach that black candidates can take if they wish to represent constituencies where blacks are not a majority. But, like its public-policy counterpart, the benefits of this electoral strategy to the BLACK COMMUNITY may be largely symbolic—seeing a black face in high places—since once elected under the circumstances required by deracialization, the candidate is reluctant to pursue policies of direct or specific concern to the interests of blacks and, indeed, sometimes may have to pursue policies adverse to those interests.

Further reading: Charles Hamilton, "Deracialization: An Examination of a Political Strategy," *First World* 1(1977): 3–5; Joseph McCormick and Charles Jones, "The Conceptualization of Deracialization" in *Dilemmas of Black Politics* ed. Georgia Persons (New York: Harper Collins, 1993); Robert Starks, "A Commentary and Response to Exploring the Meaning of Deracialization," *Urban Affairs Quarterly* 27(1991): 216–22; William Wilson, "Race Neutral Programs and the Democratic Coalition," *The American Prospect* 1(1990): 74–81.

desegregation

Desegregation is a process or technique to end SEGREGATION in the institutions of American society, including education, housing, recreational facilities, the military, and so on. It involves the removal of legal barriers to inclusion or participation based on ethnic or racial DISCRIMINATION. It is not to be confused with INTEGRATION, which may require the achievement of ethnic or racial diversity or EQUALITY in the institutions of society. Desegregation only requires the elimination of formal, legal barriers to inclusion or participation. Thus, a neighborhood or school may be desegregated—that is, there are no legal or formal barriers to inclusion—but not integrated in the sense that all ethnic or racial groups live in the neighborhood or attend the school. Since BROWN V. BOARD OF EDUCATION and the CIVIL RIGHTS ACT OF 1964, the law in the United States has required desegregation but not necessarily integration. In legal language, de jure segregation (segregation by law) is prohibited while de facto (segregation in fact) is not. Thus, for example, many African-American school children attend desegregated schools that in fact are segregated or virtually all black, and conversely many white school children attend desegregated schools that are in fact segregated or all white (see SCHOOLS AND EDUCATION and BUSING).

Diggs, Charles (1922–1998) *politician*

Charles Diggs was elected to the House of Representatives in 1955 from Detroit, Michigan, the third city in the NORTHERN STATES to send an African American to CONGRESS, after Chicago and New York. Diggs used his status as one of a handful of black congressmen in the 1950s and early 1960s to actively support the CIVIL RIGHTS MOVEMENT through speeches on the House floor and participation in PROTEST activities in the SOUTHERN STATES. In the POST–CIVIL RIGHTS ERA he became the dean (most senior member) of the black congressional delegation after ADAM CLAYTON POWELL left the House in 1970. In 1969 he was among the founders and the first chairman of the CONGRESSIONAL BLACK CAUCUS, and in 1972 he was one of three co-conveners and leaders of the NATIONAL BLACK POLITICAL CONVENTION. In the House, Diggs became chairman of the Subcommittee on Africa of the House Foreign Affairs Committee. In this position he became the Congress's recognized expert on African affairs, traveling frequently to the continent and using his authority as subcommittee chair to oppose the APARTHEID regime in South Africa and to impose sanctions on the white supremacist regime in Rhodesia. Because of his foreign-policy expertise, President RICHARD NIXON appointed Diggs to the American delegation to the UNITED NATIONS, but he soon resigned to protest the failure of the United States to vote in favor of sanctions on South Africa. His interest in Africa led him to convene with Georgia congressman ANDREW YOUNG during a conference in 1976, which resulted in the formation of TRANSAFRICA, the African-American INTEREST GROUP that engages in LOBBYING on issues related to U.S. foreign policy toward Africa and the Caribbean.

In 1973 Diggs became chairman of the House Committee on the DISTRICT OF COLUMBIA—the third black to chair a House committee—the committee responsible for legislating for the majority-black District of Columbia (Washington, D.C.). Previously, the Committee on the District was chaired by Southern white supremacists who blocked efforts to give the District "home rule," the right to elect its own local government. Under Diggs's leadership, the committee quickly reported out a home-rule bill, and it was passed by Congress in 1974.

In 1980 Diggs resigned from the Congress after he was convicted of taking $60,000 in kickbacks from his staff. He died in 1998.

discrimination

Discrimination in ordinary usage involves "discriminating" or distinguishing among individuals on the basis of some attribute or characteristic such as race, gender, or age. In this ordinary sense, discrimination is part of everyday life in the sense that people discriminate or express preferences for people they like or would prefer to associate with. Discrimination can also involve prejudice or stereotyping—the judging of individuals categorically rather than as individuals. When distinctions are made among individuals categorically (on the basis of gender or ethnicity, for examples) and it is invidious—with the intent or purpose to harm or damage—then it can become illegal discrimination as a matter of PUBLIC POLICY. The CIVIL RIGHTS ACT OF 1964 and the EQUAL PROTECTION CLAUSE of the FOURTEENTH AMENDMENT do not prohibit discrimination per se, but they can prohibit invidious, categorical discrimination on the basis of race, gender, religion, ETHNICITY, or disability. Invidious categorical discrimination is prohibited only in the public sphere (in access to voting or public accommodations, employment, housing, health care, etc.) but not in private activities such as the choice of friends, mates, or house guests. Nondiscrimination in the public sphere does not necessarily mean that individuals of the same category are treated the same. Rather, it requires that the differential treatment not be invidious or harmful.

disparate impact

Disparate impact is the term employed by the courts in the United States to evaluate policies and practices that, while not discriminatory in intent or purpose, can be judged discriminatory because they have a disproportionate or "disparate" negative or harmful impact on ETHNIC minorities or women. This legal concept is akin to what some social scientists refer to as INSTITUTIONAL RACISM. It was first enunciated by the SUPREME COURT in the employment DISCRIMINATION case of *GRIGGS V. DUKE POWER*.

See also DISPARATE TREATMENT.

disparate treatment

Disparate treatment is the term used by the courts of the United States to refer to actions by individuals or activities by institutions that have as their purpose invidious DISCRIMINATION on account of gender or ETHNIC minority status. Disparate treatment is sometimes referred to by social scientists as INDIVIDUAL RACISM, which is contrasted with INSTITUTIONAL RACISM, where the discrimination against women or minorities occurs without institutional purpose or individual intent.

See also DISPARATE IMPACT.

District of Columbia (Washington, D.C.) *U.S. capital, majority-black city*

The District of Columbia is the legal, formal name for the capital of the United States, Washington, D.C. (District of Columbia). The CONSTITUTION provided that a district (not exceeding 10 miles square) given to the CONGRESS by one or more of the states would become the "seat of government" of the new nation, and it provides the Congress with the authority to "exercise exclusive legislation in all cases whatsoever over such district." This constitutional arrangement was put into place on the basis of the principle of FEDERALISM, which suggests that the capital of the country should not be under the control or jurisdiction of any state. Rather, the capital of the United States should be controlled by all the people of the United States. Although the idea of placing the capital city of a federal republic in a separate district started in the United States, it has become a model for several other countries, including Brazil, Mexico, India, and Nigeria. While this arrangement can be defended on principles of federalism, it means that the residents of these cities may be denied basic rights enjoyed by other citizens, including being subject to taxation and military conscription without representation in the national Congress.

The District of Columbia was established in 1800 on land ceded to the federal government by Maryland and Virginia. The Virginia portion was returned to the state in 1846. Since Virginia and Maryland both had large black populations, Washington from its beginning has had a large African-American presence. (Part of the survey for the city was completed by the African-American scientist and mathematician Benjamin Banneker.) The population of 14,000 in 1800 included 4,000 blacks (22 percent), of which 80 percent were held in SLAVERY and 20 percent were FREE NEGROES. Because it was the nation's capital, the city was a kind of magnet for the TALENTED TENTH, who established businesses and educational and religious institutions. The city also became a center of activity of the ABOLITIONIST MOVEMENT. In 1835 and 1836 RIOTS occurred as white mobs attacked free blacks and alleged abolitionists. Tensions between blacks and whites also led to riots in 1919 and again in 1968 after the murder of MARTIN LUTHER KING JR.

Two years after the CIVIL WAR started, Congress abolished slavery in the District, which led to increased black migration to the city. This migration continued after the war, and several important black leaders settled in the city, including FREDERICK DOUGLASS, BLANCHE K. BRUCE, and ALEXANDER CRUMMELL. Important black religious, educational, and charitable organizations were established, including HOWARD UNIVERSITY. In 1864 Senator CHARLES SUMNER sponsored legislation granting black men the right to vote. In 1868, Jenks Bowen was elected mayor. Bowen is considered by some historians to have been black, while others contend he was merely sympathetic to blacks. Whatever the case, in 1871, in part as a reaction to the growing political power of blacks in the city, Congress took away the right of the citizens to elect their government and established a government appointed by the president and Congress. From 1871 to 1961, this appointed government was composed exclusively of white men, and usually the committees in Congress that supervised the District government were dominated by Southern racists and white supremacists.

By 1960, African Americans constituted a majority of the city's population. Due to the pressures of the CIVIL RIGHTS MOVEMENT, calls for reform that would restore the CITIZENSHIP rights of District residents became widespread. In 1961 the TWENTY-THIRD AMENDMENT granting residents VOTING RIGHTS in presidential elections was approved. In 1967 President LYNDON B. JOHNSON bypassed a hostile Congress and issued an executive order reorganizing the city's government. Under Johnson's reorganization plan, the city was governed by an appointed mayor/commissioner and council. Walter Washington, an African American, was appointed mayor, and five of the nine council members were black. In 1968, Congress allowed the city to elect its school board, and in 1970 the city was allowed to elect a nonvoting delegate to the House of Representatives. In 1974, the Congress, led by Congressman CHARLES DIGGS, approved a limited "home rule" charter providing for the election of a mayor and council. Congress, however, retained authority to approve the city's budget and rescind or veto legislation approved by the mayor and council.

Although the 1974 legislation provided for limited home rule, District residents have continued to push for complete home rule by seeking admission to the Union as a state, using the slogan "no taxation without representation." In 1978, LOBBYING by District officials persuaded the Congress to adopt a constitutional amendment granting full voting representation in the House and Senate, but it was approved by only 16 of the necessary 38 states. In 1993 the House rejected by a margin of 277-153 the District's application for statehood. In 2000, District residents initiated LITIGATION in federal court seeking an order directing the Congress to grant full voting representation in the House and Senate. The SUPREME COURT dismissed the suit, holding that the Constitution only provides for voting representation in Congress for persons living in states.

The significance of statehood for the District in terms of AFRICAN-AMERICAN POLITICS is that it would virtually guarantee the REPRESENTATION of blacks in the U.S. Senate, just as the Twenty-Third Amendment guarantees black representation in the ELECTORAL COLLEGE. This is one reason it is not likely to be approved, since conservatives and the REPUBLICAN PARTY are not likely to provide the votes needed to approve an amendment that would almost assure the election of two liberal DEMOCRATIC PARTY African-American senators. Other reasons that statehood is not likely to be granted are the District government's record of mismanagement and corruption since home rule was granted and the fact that statehood would violate the federalism principle that the federal capital should not be a part of any state, let alone a state itself.

Further reading: Constance Green, *The Secret City: A History of Race Relations in the Nation's Capitol* (Princeton N.J.: Princeton University Press, 1967); Charles Harris, *Congress and the Governance of the Nation's Capital* (Washington, D.C.: Georgetown University Press, 1995).

Douglass, Frederick (1817–1895) *leader, lecturer, journalist, abolitionist, diplomat*
Frederick Douglass, an escaped slave, was the recognized leader of black people in the United States from the 1840s until his death in 1895. He was the first person to achieve this status of preeminence. During his LEADERSHIP Douglass occupied a position like MARTIN LUTHER KING JR. during the CIVIL RIGHTS ERA, BOOKER T. WASHINGTON during the post-RECONSTRUCTION era, and JESSE JACKSON during the POST–CIVIL RIGHTS ERA. In a poll of black political scientists, Douglass ranked number four on a list of the 12 greatest African-American leaders of all time.

Douglass was born Frederick Bailey in 1817 or 1818 in Talbot County, Maryland, the child of an enslaved woman and an unknown white man. At an early age Douglass learned to read and became rebellious. At age 17 he was sent to a "slavebreaker," a man who specialized in breaking the spirit of independent and rebellious slaves. After six months of beatings by the slavebreaker, Douglass fought back, after which (he wrote in his autobiography) he was never beaten again. He described the fight with the slavebreaker as the "turning point" of his life as a slave. Before it, he said, he was "nothing," but afterward "I was a man." In 1883 Douglass escaped from SLAVERY, married a FREE NEGRO from Baltimore, changed his name from Bailey to Douglass, and moved to New Bedford, Massachusetts, where he became active in the ABOLITIONIST MOVEMENT led by WILLIAM LLOYD GARRISON. His eloquent and erudite lectures about his experiences as a slave made him a popular speaker on the abolitionist lecture circuit. However, his words were so learned and powerful that many began to doubt whether he had ever been a slave. Thus, in 1845 he published the first of his autobiographies, *Narrative of the Life of Frederick Douglass.* Widely read at the time, this book is now considered a classic in African-American literature. The success of the book, however, raised fears that his former slave master might recognize him and seek to return him to captivity under the FUGITIVE SLAVE ACT. Thus, he left for England, where he spent two years lecturing against slavery until his FREEDOM was purchased.

Like Martin Luther King Jr., Douglass was a gifted orator. In 1847 he also began to publish a newspaper, *The North Star* (later Frederick Douglass's *Weekly* and *Monthly*). His work as an orator and journalist is what led to his recognition as the preeminent black leader of the abolitionist movement and the preeminent leader of the BLACK COMMUNITY. Although William Lloyd Garrison, the preeminent white leader of the movement, had recruited Douglass, they soon became bitter rivals over movement strategy and leadership. Garrison believed in nonviolent "moral suasion," viewed the CONSTITUTION as unalterably racist, and was opposed to any form of participation in the established political process. Douglass, on the other hand, supported in principle the right of the slaves to use VIOLENCE to resist their OPPRESSION; interpreted the Constitution to be in part an antislavery document; and engaged in the political process by supporting antislavery THIRD PARTIES, such as the Liberty and Free Soil Parties. Many of Douglass's conflicts with Garrison and the whites in the abolitionist movement anticipate the conflicts between blacks and whites during the CIVIL RIGHTS MOVEMENT of the 1960s, conflicts that eventually resulted in the BLACK POWER MOVEMENT. Like the 1960s black-power advocates. Douglass raised questions about the role of white leadership and who should be part of "the generalship of the movement." Douglass argued, "The man who has *suffered* the wrong is the man to demand the redress—the man struck is the man to CRY OUT and he who has endured the *cruel pangs of slavery* is the man to advocate liberty. It is evident that we must be our own representatives and advocates, but peculiarly—not distinct from—but in connection with our friends." Following on this principle, Douglass—over the objections of Garrison—became a leader in the all-black NATIONAL NEGRO CONVENTIONS that met periodically from the 1840s to the 1860s. Although Douglass was in principle not opposed to the use of violence in the struggle against slavery, he vigorously opposed HENRY HIGHLAND GARNETT's address to the slaves calling for SLAVE REVOLTS and refused to join in his friend JOHN BROWN's attack at Harper's Ferry because he thought it had little chance of success. Nevertheless, since Douglass knew of Brown's plan, it led to allegations that he was part of Brown's conspiracy, forcing him to flee the country for six months to avoid possible arrest.

Douglass supported ABRAHAM LINCOLN in the 1860 presidential election, and once Lincoln became president he frequently and forcefully urged Lincoln to turn the war into a crusade against slavery rather than merely a war to preserve the Union, as was Lincoln's original goal. When Lincoln issued the EMANCIPATION PROCLAMATION, Douglass called on Lincoln to recruit black soldiers and subsequently organized two Massachusetts regiments. After the war during RECONSTRUCTION, Douglass's stature as the preeminent black leader was enhanced, as he was appointed to several posts in the BUREAUCRACY, including U.S. marshall for the DISTRICT OF COLUMBIA and minister to HAITI.

In addition to his leadership in the abolitionist movement, Douglass was an early supporter of FEMINISM and a close friend of white feminist leaders such as Susan B. Anthony. The masthead of his newspaper read "Right is of no sex, the truth is of no color." In 1872 he was the vice presidential candidate on the Equal Rights Party ticket with Victoria Claflin Woodhull, the first woman to run for president. However, Douglass broke with the white-led feminist move-

Frederick Douglass *(Library of Congress)*

ment over adoption of the FIFTEENTH AMENDMENT, which granted black men the right to vote. Leading feminists opposed the amendment unless women were included, and some said that it would permit black men, their "inferiors," more rights than white women. Douglass made a passionate rebuttal to these arguments. He wrote:

> I must say that I do not see how anyone can pretend that there is the same urgency in giving the ballot to the woman as the Negro. With us the matter is a question of life and death . . . When women are dragged from their houses and hung on lamp posts; when their children are torn from their arms and their brains dashed on the pavement; when they are the object of insult and outrage at every turn; when they are in danger of having their homes burnt down over their heads; when their children are not allowed to enter schools; then they will have an urgency to the ballot equal to our own.

Douglass was also passionately committed to INTEGRATION, ideologically and personally. He consistently opposed the various BACK-TO-AFRICA emigration plans of leaders such as MARTIN DELANY. It was his view until his death that the integration of Africans into American society on the basis of freedom and EQUALITY was not only desirable but possible. He was also personally committed to integration. Thus, when his wife died, he married his young secretary, a white woman. He was criticized by many blacks for this decision, but he unequivocally rejected the idea that marriage should be based on race and defended his actions as symbolic of a lifelong commitment to racial integration.

When Douglass died in 1895 at age 77, he was one of the most famous men in America, recognized for the literary contributions of his three autobiographies, his mastery of oratory, his leadership in the abolitionist and feminist movements, and his contributions late in his life as a political leader and diplomat.

Further reading: William McFeely, *Frederick Douglass* (New York: W. W. Norton, 1991).

Dred Scott v. Sanford (1857)

Dred Scott v. Sanford is one of the most important decisions dealing with the FREEDOM of African Americans ever made by the SUPREME COURT. It is also one of the most important decisions in the history of the Court, since it was then only the second time in its history that it used its authority to declare an act of CONGRESS unconstitutional. Historically, *Dred Scott* is also considered one of the worst decisions of the Court because while it was intended to resolve the issue of SLAVERY it instead was a contributing factor to the onset of the CIVIL WAR.

Dred Scott was born into slavery in Virginia in 1795. Scott's owner at the time of the case lived in Missouri, a slave state. However, he had lived for two years in Illinois, where slavery was illegal, and as an army officer he had served in the Wisconsin Territory, where slavery was prohibited by the Missouri Compromise adopted by Congress in 1820. Because he had lived in these free areas, Scott—with the assistance of lawyers provided by the ABOLITIONIST MOVEMENT—sued for his freedom, claiming that he became free in Illinois and Wisconsin and therefore remained free in Missouri. The Supreme Court of Missouri rejected Scott's claim, and he appealed to the U.S. Supreme Court, which upheld the decision of the Missouri court.

In his opinion for the Court's seven-to-two majority, Chief Justice Roger B. Taney wrote, "The question is simply this: can a Negro, whose ancestors were imported into this country, and sold as slaves, become a member of the political community formed and brought into existence by the Constitution of the United States, and as such become entitled to all the rights, and privileges, and immunities, guaranteed by that instrument to the citizen? One of which rights is the privilege of suing in a court of the United States in the cases specified in the Constitution." The answer to this simple question was no, because Taney wrote that the slaves were not intended to be included under the meaning of "citizen" in the CONSTITUTION. Therefore, Scott could claim none of the rights and privileges provided under the Constitution, including the right of LITIGATION in the federal courts. Under the normal procedures of the Court, Taney should have ended his opinion with this declaration and dismissed Scott's suit on the grounds that he lacked what is called "standing to sue." However, Taney went on to write an extended opinion that is one of the most racist and white supremacist in the Court's history. He wrote that the word "men" in the DECLARATION OF INDEPENDENCE (where it is declared that "all men are created equal") did not apply to the enslaved African because "for more than a century they had been regarded as beings of an inferior order and altogether unfit to associate with the white race, either in social or political relations; and so far inferior that they had no rights which the white man was bound to respect; and that the Negro might justly and lawfully be reduced to slavery for his own benefit." Taney then ignited a political firestorm that would help to precipitate the Civil War by declaring that the owners of slaves could take their property anyplace in the country they wished. Therefore the Missouri Compromise prohibiting slavery in the Northern Territories was unconstitutional. This declaration helped to cause the Civil War because, in effect, it denied Congress the authority to limit the expansion of slavery. The acceptance of slavery in the SOUTHERN STATES while limiting its expansion in the North was the position of ABRAHAM LINCOLN and the emerging

REPUBLICAN PARTY, as well as PUBLIC OPINION in the NORTHERN STATES.

Taney's opinion confirmed the view of abolitionist leaders like WILLIAM LLOYD GARRISON that the Constitution was inherently racist and white supremacist, and therefore did not deserve the respect of Americans. FREDERICK DOUGLASS, in a speech shortly after the decision, described Taney's opinion as "devilish," as an incarnation of "wolfishness," and as a "demonical judgment." Nevertheless Douglass disagreed with the Garrison view that the Constitution was inherently racist and proslavery. In his speech, he cited several provisions of the Constitution that could be interpreted as antislavery (including the Fifth Amendment's DUE PROCESS CLAUSE) and concluded, "Thus, the very essence of the whole slave code is in open violation of a fundamental provision of the Constitution, and is an open and flagrant violation of all objects set forth in the Constitution." Douglass's efforts to view the Constitution as an antislavery document were valiant and intellectually interesting, but was almost certainly incorrect. Taney and Garrison were almost certainly correct in their conclusion that the framers of the Constitution did not intend to include Africans under its protections because, as Taney wrote, they were "an article of property" who "had been excluded from civilized governments and the family of nations and doomed to slavery."

Drugs, War on   See CRIMINAL JUSTICE SYSTEM.

Du Bois, W. E. B. (1868–1963) *scholar, leader, lecturer, statesman, journalist, historian*

In a 2000 poll of African-American political scientists asked to select and rank the greatest African-American leaders of all time, W. E. B. Du Bois ranked No. 2 behind only MARTIN LUTHER KING JR. Du Bois's greatness as a leader of African Americans is based mainly on his intellectual work, although he was also an active participant in many important organizations and movements. Yet his contributions in the arena of thought and ideas are sui generis; he is the most important intellectual in African-American history and one of two or three major American intellectuals of the 20th century.

Leadership by intellect and ideas has always been difficult in American culture, but Du Bois did it, achieving in the early 20th century an eminence and status unrivaled by any other public figure. In his autobiography, *Dusk of Dawn: An Essay toward an Autobiography of a Race Concept* (1940), written at the halfway point in his career, Du Bois wrote that his "was a leadership solely of ideas." This is an understatement. Du Bois's leadership was not solely of ideas; rather, he was a unique combination of scholar, political organizer, and statesman, but he was not exaggerating or boasting when he wrote in the closing chapter of *Dusk of Dawn* ". . . In the period from 1910 to 1930, I was a main factor in revolutionizing the attitude of the American Negro toward caste. My stinging hammer blows made Negroes aware of themselves, confident in their possibilities and determined in self-assertion. So much so that today common slogans among the Negro people are taken bodily from the words of my mouth." As an intellectual and political organizer Du Bois played a major role in structuring the conditions for the development of the NAACP (National Association for the Advancement of Colored People). As the only African American among the founding leaders of the NAACP, Du Bois—through his editorship of *The Crisis,* the association's magazine—gave intellectual direction to its work and thereby defined the conceptual issues around which the NAACP struggled and grew. Similarly, he played a dominant role in defining the principles and themes around which PAN-AFRICANISM developed in the 20th century. He played a crucial role in defining the conceptual boundaries of the BLACK NATIONALISM–INTEGRATIONism debate that dominates the history of AFRICAN-AMERICAN POLITICS. At the same time, his creative historical and sociological studies helped to set the highest standards of scholarship for research on race issues, and he almost single-handedly created *Phylon,* the first interdisciplinary journal of scholarship and research on the African-American experience. As a consequence, scholarship in AFRICAN-AMERICAN STUDIES owes more to him alone than any other group of scholars. Finally, it was Du Bois in a famous 1903 address who made famous and influential the idea of the TALENTED TENTH or the best educated of the race who would provide LEADERSHIP for the masses of the BLACK COMMUNITY.

Du Bois was born on February 23, 1868, in Great Barrington, Massachusetts. He died 95 years later in the West African country of Ghana on the eve of the 1963 MARCH ON WASHINGTON. In these 95 years, Du Bois's life was one of extraordinary scholarship and political leadership, a life that at one point or another embraced every tendency in African-American thought—integration, black nationalism, and finally SOCIALISM and COMMUNISM. Du Bois was graduated from Fisk University, a historically black university in Nashville, Tennessee, in 1888. In 1895 he became the first African American to receive a Ph.D. from Harvard. (He came within a couple of months of earning a second Ph.D. from the University of Berlin.) His doctoral dissertation, *The Suppression of the African Slave Trade to the United State, 1638–1870,* was the first volume published in Harvard's Historical Studies series. He later went on to publish 15 other books on politics and race, three historical novels, two autobiographies, and numerous essays and works of fiction and poetry. While a professor at ATLANTA UNIVERSITY Du Bois directed the first large-scale social-science research project on the problem of race in the United States. Among his more important books are *Black Reconstruction in America,* a massive study showing that RECONSTRUCTION was one of the finest efforts in American history to achieve democracy; *The Philadelphia Negro: A Social Study,* the first sociological analysis of an urban community; and *THE SOULS OF BLACK FOLK,* his classic analysis of the psychological, cultural, and sociopolitical underpinnings of the African-American experience.

In addition to his life of the mind and scholarship, Du Bois was an extraordinary political leader. From the death of BOOKER T. WASHINGTON in 1915 until the mid 1930s, Du Bois was probably the most influential African-American leader. Early in his career Du Bois remarked, "We face a condition, not a theory." Therefore, any philosophy, ideology, or strategy that gave promise of altering the oppressed conditions of the race should be embraced. And as the conditions of African Americans changed, so did the thought of Du Bois. Early in his career, in his famous "Conservation of Races" essay, Du Bois appears to embrace black nationalism and separate development as a means to conserve the distinctive CULTURE of the group. Later, in

the face of Booker Washington's ACCOMMODATIONISM to the SEGREGATION and racial OPPRESSION that emerged after the end of Reconstruction, Du Bois embraced integration, organizing in 1905 the NIAGARA MOVEMENT as a forum for MILITANCY and PROTEST for CIVIL RIGHTS. In organizing the Niagara movement and authoring its manifesto, Du Bois became the "father" of the CIVIL RIGHTS MOVEMENT. Four years later in 1909, Du Bois was the only black among the leaders of the NAACP. Until the 1930s he edited *The Crisis,* using it as a forum to attack WHITE SUPREMACY and RACISM and espouse the causes of EQUALITY and FREEDOM. Watching the deteriorating conditions of blacks during the depression, Du Bois once again embraced black nationalism, arguing that blacks should develop a system of self-segregation and SELF-HELP in a separate "group economy" of producers and cooperative consumers. Charging that the NAACP had become too identified with the concerns of middle-class blacks, in 1934 Du Bois resigned from the association and his editorship of *The Crisis.* Du Bois expressed his interest in black nationalism also in terms of Pan-Africanism—the idea that the African people everywhere share a common culture and interest. In 1900 he organized the first Pan-African conference in London, which brought together African leaders and intellectuals from Africa, the United States, and the Caribbean. He was a principal leader of the four other Pan-African conferences held between 1912 and 1927. And at the end of World War I and again at the end of World War II, Du Bois attended the peace conferences urging that the European powers develop plans to free their African colonies. Du Bois briefly joined the Socialist Party in 1912 and continued to flirt with socialist ideas thereafter. However, during the 1950s he apparently came to the conclusion that justice for blacks and working people could not be achieved under CAPITALISM, and so in 1956 he joined the COMMUNIST PARTY and shortly thereafter moved to Ghana. The last years of his life were spent opposing the role of the United States in the COLD WAR, supporting THIRD WORLD solidarity, and editing the *Encyclopedia Africana,* a project funded and supported by the Ghana Academy of Sciences.

In his long career Du Bois embraced every possible solution to the problem of race—scholarship and protest, integration and nationalism, liberalism and communism, Pan-Africanism and international solidarity—and in doing so his prescient voice inspired generations in the struggle against global exploitation throughout the world.

W. E. B. Du Bois *(Library of Congress)*

Further reading: Gerald Horne, *Black and Red: W. E. B. DuBois and the American Response to the Cold War, 1944–1963* (Albany: State University of New York Press, 1986); David L. Lewis, *W. E. B. DuBois: Biography of a Race, 1868–1919* (New York: Henry Holt, 1993); David L. Lewis, *W. E. B. DuBois: The Fight for Equality and the*

American Century, 1919–1963 (New York: Henry Holt, 2000).

due process clauses, U.S. Constitution

The due process clauses in the United States CONSTITU-TION commit the federal and STATE AND LOCAL GOVERN-MENTS to fundamental fairness in their treatment of all persons within their jurisdictions. The Fifth Amendment to the Constitution provides that no person may be "deprived of life, liberty or property without due process of law." Until the 20th century, the Fifth Amendment's due process clause was interpreted by the SUPREME COURT as applying to or placing limits only on actions by the federal government. Thus in 1868 the clause was made a part of the FOURTEENTH AMENDMENT. Then, beginning in the 1920s and continuing through the 1960s, the Supreme Court used the Fourteenth Amendment's due process clause to apply provisions of the BILL OF RIGHTS to state and local governments. This use of the Fourteenth Amendment's due process clause in relationship to the states points to the significance of the presence of African Americans in expanding FREEDOM for all Americans, because the original purpose of the Fourteenth Amendment was to secure fair treatment and EQUALITY for the newly freed slaves in the SOUTHERN STATES.

The concept of due process has no precise constitutional or legal meanings, but it is generally understood to require governments to treat persons fairly or nonarbitrarily. In the course of LITIGATION over the years, the courts have identified two types of due process: procedural and substantive. Procedural due process involves fairness in trials or the JUDICIAL PROCESS generally, including the rights to hearings, to a lawyer, and to fair and impartial judges and juries. Substantive due process is more complex and controversial. It involves the courts striking down laws deemed unfair, unreasonable, or beyond the scope of any legitimate government purpose. Early in the 20th century the Supreme Court used substantive due process to prevent the states from passing various labor and welfare laws, claiming that such laws arbitrarily violated the "liberty" of businesses. Since the NEW DEAL, the courts have been reluctant to use substantive due process to strike down state social and welfare laws. But the Court did use the Fifth Amendment's due process clause to strike down school SEGREGATION in the DISTRICT OF COLUMBIA on substantive grounds. In the opinion of Chief Justice EARL WARREN in *BROWN V. BOARD OF EDUCATION,* "segregation in public education is not reasonably related to any proper government objective, and thus it imposes on Negro children of the District of Columbia a burden that constitutes an arbitrary deprivation of their liberty in violation of the Due Process Clause." Since *Brown,* substantive process has also been used in cases involving the rights of parents, the mentally ill, and the recipients of welfare benefits.

Dyer antilynching bill

The Dyer antilynching bill—introduced first in 1918 by Congressman Leonidas Dyer, a member of the REPUBLICAN PARTY from St. Louis, Missouri—was the prototype or model for antilynching bills introduced in CONGRESS and supported by the NAACP until the 1950s. Dyer's bill became the legislative basis for mobilizing opposition to LYNCHING, which was the primary form of VIOLENCE used by whites to maintain the OPPRESSION of blacks from the RECONSTRUCTION era to the end of the CIVIL RIGHTS MOVEMENT.

Between the 1980s and 1940s, lynching was an abomination, involving thousands of ritualistic and sadistic murders of blacks by mobs of whites that sometimes included women and children as victims and perpetrators. The lynching of blacks gave rise to various forms of PROTEST, LOBBYING, and LITIGATION and was responsible for the emergence of IDA B. WELLS-BARNETT to a position of national leadership among African Americans.

Legally, lynching was simple murder for the purposes of oppression and POLITICAL REPRESSION. Under the CONSTITUTION's principle of FEDERALISM, the responsibility for arrest and prosecution for murder is left to the states. Congressman Dyer introduced his legislation to make lynching a federal crime because it was clear that the authorities in the SOUTHERN STATES would not enforce the laws of murder against whites who lynched blacks, and sometimes the authorities themselves were involved in lynchings. Congressman Dyer's legislation defined killing by a mob of three or more persons acting without legal authority as a federal crime subject to prosecution in the federal courts. The legislation was based on the FOURTEENTH AMENDMENT'S EQUAL PROTECTION CLAUSE and was designed to protect persons from lynching when the states defaulted on their duties. The legislation provided for fines and imprisonment of local authorities who failed to apprehend and prosecute lynchers and required counties where lynchings occurred to pay restitution to the victims' heirs.

Congressman Dyer (whose St. Louis district had a large black population) was one of the few members of Congress willing to work with the newly organized NAACP on its CIVIL RIGHTS agenda, and lynching became the principal concern of the civil rights agenda and of Congressman Dyer. But Congress never passed an antilynching law. Some members of Congress from the NORTHERN STATES opposed Dyer's and similar bills on grounds of CONSTITUTIONALISM, claiming that the legislation violated principles of federalism and states rights. Meanwhile, all members of Congress from the Southern states opposed the legislation because of their adherence to RACISM and WHITE SUPREMACY. Antilynching bills passed the House in 1922, 1937, and 1940, but they were defeated each time in the Senate by a FILIBUSTER or the threat of a filibuster.

Lynchings began to decline in the late 1940s and early 1950s, making the need for the legislation less urgent, and the successes of the Civil Rights movement in the 1960s provided new protections for African Americans, including a 1968 law making it a federal crime to injure or kill a person seeking to exercise federally protected rights. After 1970, most authorities in the Southern states began to enforce the laws when blacks were murdered.

E

elected officials

Elected officials in the United States exercise power on the basis of authority—the legitimate, recognized right to make and enforce laws that govern the nation. All persons with authority of this kind are either elected directly or indirectly by the people, or they are appointed to office by persons who have been elected. Thus, to hold an elected office is to be in position to exercise considerable power in the United States.

Since 1970, the JOINT CENTER FOR POLITICAL AND ECONOMIC STUDIES has compiled data on the number of black elected officials in the United States and their distribution by category of office and region of the country. Near the end of the CIVIL RIGHTS MOVEMENT when the VOTING RIGHTS ACT was passed in 1965, there were an estimated 500 black elected officials out of a total of about 500,000. For several years after the Voting Rights Act was passed, the number of black elected officials grew rapidly, but by the end of the century this growth had come to an end. Between 1970 and 1989 the number of blacks holding elected office grew by 657 percent, from 1,469 to 7,226. Since then, the rate of growth has slowed and then essentially stopped. At the end of the 20th century blacks held approximately 9,000 elected offices, or 1.7 percent of the total compared with their 12 percent of the population. Thus, African Americans are substantially underrepresented in elective office, and it appears that this is not likely to change in the foreseeable future. That is, while there may be fluctuations, no projection on black elected officials predicts their number will double by the year 2025, for example, which still would only represent 3.4 percent of the total. And because of the way the SUPREME COURT interpreted the Voting Rights Act in *SHAW V. RENO*, it is possible that even this small number of black elected officials could decline rather than grow in the future.

A variety of reasons account for this minuscule level of black REPRESENTATION in elective offices, including lower levels of black registration and voting, which is usually attributable to their lower social class status. The decline in the number of majority-black constituencies is also a factor, since it is very difficult for blacks to win elections in places where they are not a majority. In many rural areas of the SOUTHERN STATES, blacks have not been able to win offices even in places where they constitute a majority because of low voter registration and lingering fears of white economic and social intimidation. Certain structural features of the electoral system also inhibit the election of blacks, features such as single-member congressional districting; the apportionment of U.S. Senate seats by states, rather than by population; the use by STATE AND LOCAL GOVERNMENTs of multimember and at-large election systems; and racial gerrymandering (the creation of large electoral districts where whites constitute the majority, enabling them to determine who is elected although blacks might constitute majorities in smaller districts). A major reason, however, is that white voters have been reluctant to vote for black candidates, and whites are the majority in most of the constituencies that elect persons to office.

A majority of blacks elected to office (more than 75 percent) hold relatively minor town council or school board positions in the rural South or in the cities of the Northeast and Midwest. Relatively few are represented in county or statewide elective executive, legislative, or administrative positions; none are in the U.S. Senate; and only one black, DOUGLAS WILDER, has ever been elected governor of one of the 50 states. It is only in the U.S. House of Representatives that blacks hold a reasonable number of offices in relationship to the proportion of the population: 39 members or 9 percent of the House in 2000. This number, however, may decline as a result of *Shaw v. Reno*.

See also VOTING BEHAVIOR.

Further reading: Theresa Chambliss, "The Growth and Significance of African American Elected Officials," in *From Exclusion to Inclusion: The Long Struggle for African American Political Power*, ed. Ralph C. Gomes and Linda

Williams (Westport, Conn.: Greenwood Press, 1995); John Conyers and Walter Wallace, *Black Elected Officials: A Study of Black Americans Holding Government Office* (New York: Russell Sage, 1976).

electoral college

The electoral college is the mechanism used to elect the president of the United States. In the American DEMOCRACY, a person is elected president not on the basis of winning a majority of the votes of the people but rather on the basis of winning a majority of votes in the electoral college. The electoral college is actually 51 electoral colleges representing the states and the DISTRICT OF COLUMBIA. Each state is granted as many electoral college votes as it has members of CONGRESS, which means that each state and the District of Columbia has at least three electors (based on two senators and a minimum of one member of the House). In all of the states except Maine and Nebraska, the electoral college votes of a state are based on the principle of "winner take all"; that is, the candidate who wins most of the votes of the people of a state (even if it is less than a majority in a multicandidate race) receives all of the state's electoral votes. Thus, a hypothetical candidate running in California who receive 39 percent of the vote in a four-person race would receive 100 percent of the state's 55 electoral votes. This system of choosing the president means that a loser can become the winner. That is—as has happened four times—a person can lose a majority of the votes of the people but nevertheless become president by winning a majority of the electoral votes. This undemocratic system of choosing the president is rooted in SLAVERY and was part of the several compromises the framers of the CONSTITUTION made to accommodate the interests of slaveholders, which undermined the interests of blacks and compromised the principle of democracy. Indeed, Donald Robinson in *Slavery in the Structure of American Politics* concludes, "The disenfranchisement of the slaves was, in fact, the decisive consideration against the popular election of the president."

The framers of the Constitution confronted three alternatives in considering how the president might be chosen. The first was election by the CONGRESS. This alternative was rejected because it violates the principle of the SEPARATION OF POWERS. The second alternative of election by the legislatures of the states was rejected because it would have violated the principle of an independent federal government. The last and most obvious and most democratic method was popular election by the people. This alternative was rejected because some of the framers felt that the people would not be educated or informed enough to make a good choice. However, election by the people would also have disadvantaged the slaveholding SOUTHERN STATES. James Madison, who at first favored election by the people, changed his mind in favor of the electoral college because he said election by the people "would gravely disadvantage the South since their slaves of course could not vote." The electoral college compromise not only did not disadvantage the Southern states, it gave them a bonus by allowing them to count their slaves in determining electoral votes on the basis of the THREE-FIFTHS CLAUSE used to allocate seats in the House of Representatives. In its earliest years of operation, the electoral college did work to the advantage of the South, as four of the first five presidents elected in the first 30 years were slave owners from Virginia.

The electoral college also represented other compromises that undermined principles of democracy. While it gave the states with the largest population the larger share of electoral votes, it gave the smaller states a two-seat bonus based on their senators. It left the manner of choosing the electors up to the states, except that they were prohibited from holding any federal office (including being members of Congress) and from meeting together as a group. (The electors meet separately on the same day in each state's capital.) The electors can be chosen in any manner the state legislature determines—by the legislature itself, by appointment of the governor, or by the voters—and once selected, they are free to vote for anyone they wish (as long as the person meets the constitutional qualifications of age, native-born citizenship, and residence), even if the person is not running as a candidate. The states are also free to determine the allocation of the electoral votes, whether winner take all on a statewide basis or proportionally by congressional districts. Early on, the politicians in most states saw the advantage of winner take all in maintenance of the TWO-PARTY SYSTEM and adopted it, but it was not until the 1840s that all of the states allowed the people to choose the electors in direct elections.

Four times the electoral college has resulted in a loser becoming the winner. In 1828 Andrew Jackson won most of the votes of the people and most (but not a majority) of the electoral college votes in a four-man race but lost the presidency to JOHN Q. ADAMS. In 1876 Samuel J. Tilden won the popular vote majority, but in the COMPROMISE OF 1877 the PRESIDENCY was won by RUTHERFORD B. HAYES by a one-vote margin in the electoral college. In 1888 Grover Cleveland narrowly won the popular vote, but BENJAMIN HARRISON won the electoral college by a large margin. And in 2000 Albert Gore won the election by a margin of 500,000 votes but lost the electoral college by a one-vote margin to George W. Bush. In three ironies of history, the elections of 1876, 1888, and 2000 involved allegations of suppression of the black vote in several Southern states. Also, in the elections of 1876 and 1888, race or CIVIL RIGHTS were issues.

Although the electoral college is rooted in slavery and RACISM, it is unclear whether its abolition in favor of choice by direct vote of the people would advantage or disadvantage African Americans in presidential elections. Although the small states where few blacks live have a bonus in the electoral college, it is the large states of the Northeast and Midwest that decide presidential elections. African Americans are disproportionately represented in these states. Therefore, in close elections they may constitute the BALANCE OF POWER in determining the winner. But blacks are also concentrated in the nation's largest cities throughout the country, and theoretically a candidate could also win the presidency by mobilizing large majorities in these cities. Thus, it is not clear whether abolition of the electoral college in favor of popular democracy would help or hinder AFRICAN-AMERICAN POLITICS.

One reform that would help the BLACK COMMUNITY in a two-party system, where one party tends to take the black vote for granted while the other ignores it, would be abolition of the winner-take-all system in favor of proportional allocation (where a candidate's electoral vote in a state would be determined on the basis of her percentage or proportion of the popular vote). A proportional system would facilitate the emergence of THIRD PARTIES with a realistic chance of getting a share of political power in the form of electoral college votes. As a cohesive minority, blacks might see their POWER enhanced in this kind of system.

Whatever the advantages reform in the electoral college might have for African Americans or others, reform is not likely. This is the case even though a majority of Americans in polls indicate support for abolition of the electoral college and replacing it with popular election. This is not likely to happen, however, because such a change would require a constitutional amendment, which requires the approval of three-fourths of the states. Given the bonus that small states have in the electoral college, they have an incentive and the votes to block any amendment. While reform of the winner-take-all system does not require a constitutional amendment, but rather simple acts by the legislatures, it too is unlikely to happen. This is because the legislatures of the states are controlled by the DEMOCRATIC and REPUBLICAN PARTIES and they are not likely to eliminate the winner-take-all system because they wish to maintain their control of the two-party system. Thus, unless there is massive grassroots mobilization and PROTEST, the electoral college is not likely to be altered.

Elementary and Secondary Education Act

The Elementary and Secondary Education Act enacted in 1965 was part of President LYNDON B. JOHNSON's program of GREAT SOCIETY reforms. It is the first program enacted by CONGRESS that provides general assistance from the federal government to local school districts for elementary and secondary education. Title I of the act established a program of compensatory educational expenditures for children from low-income families. It is based on a formula that provides aid on the basis of the number of children from low-income families in a school district. Since African-American families tend to be disproportionately low income, the Elementary and Secondary Education Act is indirectly the principal federal PUBLIC POLICY to improve the educational opportunities of black school children.

The BLAIR EDUCATION BILL proposed during the RECONSTRUCTION era was the first of numerous efforts to pass legislation to provide federal assistance to STATE AND LOCAL GOVERNMENTs for the education of poor children. However, these efforts failed largely because it was argued that such assistance violated the principle of FEDERALISM under which education is a responsibility of the states and their local school districts. This objection and others were overcome in the 1960s in part because of the success of the CIVIL RIGHTS MOVEMENT in challenging the principle of federalism as it related to SEGREGATION in education and other areas of American life. As a result, the nation committed itself to EQUALITY of educational opportunities for all children.

Although the federal assistance to local school districts represents less than 10 percent of their budgets, this small amount of money is nevertheless very important because it involves the federal government in setting local educational policies. The federal government has used the assistance it provides as leverage to compel obedience to the *BROWN V. BOARD OF EDUCATION* school DESEGREGATION decision and to enforce gender equality and the equal treatment of handicapped persons. Although the act did not result in closing the educational gap between poor African-American students and middle-class white students, it is important as a symbolic commitment to do so, and it provides the federal government with some leverage to fulfill that commitment.

See also SCHOOLS AND EDUCATION.

Emancipation Proclamation

The Emancipation Proclamation was issued by President ABRAHAM LINCOLN on January 1, 1863. While the proclamation itself liberated relatively free slaves, it set in motion a process that led to the abolition of SLAVERY and the granting of some FREEDOM to African Americans.

From the moment the CIVIL WAR started, Lincoln repeatedly made it clear that the war's objective was to preserve the union of the states. That is, his objective as president was to compel the rebellious SOUTHERN STATES to rejoin the NORTHERN STATES in a united country where, if they wished, they could continue slavery as long as they wished. To make this objective unambiguous, Lincoln

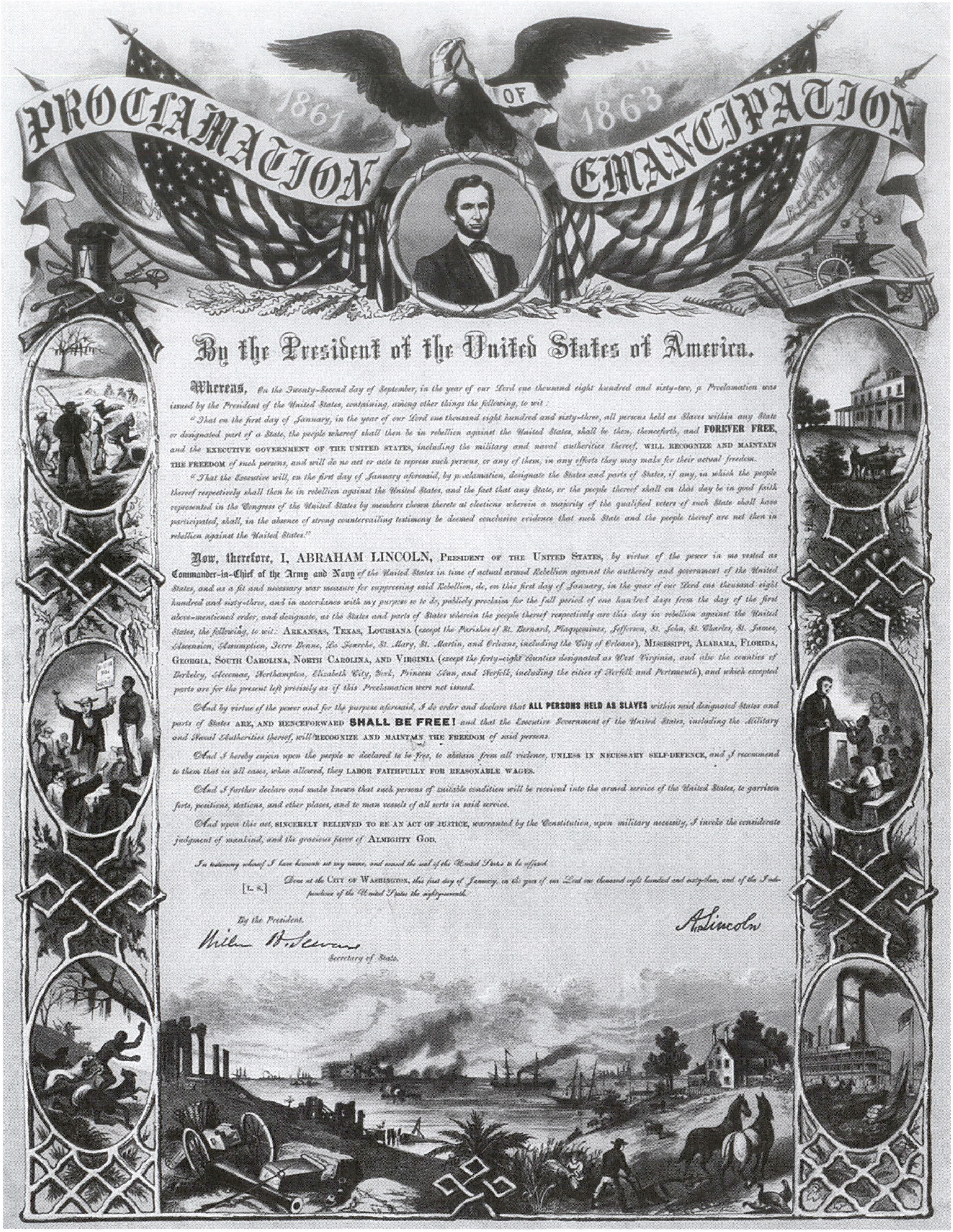

PROCLAMATION OF EMANCIPATION

1861 1863

By the President of the United States of America.

Whereas, *On the Twenty-Second day of September, in the year of our Lord one thousand eight hundred and sixty-two, a Proclamation was issued by the President of the United States, containing, among other things the following, to wit:*

"That on the first day of January, in the year of our Lord one thousand eight hundred and sixty-three, all persons held as Slaves within any State or designated part of a State, the people whereof shall then be in rebellion against the United States, shall be then, thenceforth, and **FOREVER FREE,** *and the* EXECUTIVE GOVERNMENT OF THE UNITED STATES, *including the military and naval authorities thereof,* WILL RECOGNIZE AND MAINTAIN THE FREEDOM *of such persons, and will do no act or acts to repress such persons, or any of them, in any efforts they may make for their actual freedom.*

"That the Executive will, on the first day of January aforesaid, by proclamation, designate the States and parts of States, if any, in which the people thereof respectively shall then be in rebellion against the United States, and the fact that any State, or the people thereof shall on that day be in good faith represented in the Congress of the United States by members chosen thereto at elections wherein a majority of the qualified voters of such State shall have participated, shall, in the absence of strong countervailing testimony be deemed conclusive evidence that such State and the people thereof are not then in rebellion against the United States."

Now, therefore, I, ABRAHAM LINCOLN, PRESIDENT OF THE UNITED STATES, *by virtue of the power in me vested as* **Commander-in-Chief of the Army and Navy** *of the United States in time of actual armed Rebellion against the authority and government of the United States, and as a fit and necessary war measure for suppressing said Rebellion, do, on this first day of January, in the year of our Lord one thousand eight hundred and sixty-three, and in accordance with my purpose so to do, publicly proclaim for the full period of one hundred days from the day of the first above-mentioned order, and designate, as the States and parts of States wherein the people thereof respectively are this day in rebellion against the United States, the following, to wit:* ARKANSAS, TEXAS, LOUISIANA *(except the Parishes of St. Bernard, Plaquemines, Jefferson, St. John, St. Charles, St. James, Ascension, Assumption, Terre Bonne, La Fourche, St. Mary, St. Martin, and Orleans, including the City of Orleans),* MISSISSIPPI, ALABAMA, FLORIDA, GEORGIA, SOUTH CAROLINA, NORTH CAROLINA, AND VIRGINIA *(except the forty-eight counties designated as West Virginia, and also the counties of Berkeley, Accomac, Northampton, Elizabeth City, York, Princess Ann, and Norfolk, including the cities of Norfolk and Portsmouth), and which excepted parts are for the present left precisely as if this Proclamation were not issued.*

And by virtue of the power and for the purpose aforesaid, I do order and declare that **ALL PERSONS HELD AS SLAVES** *within said designated States and parts of States* ARE, AND HENCEFORWARD **SHALL BE FREE!** *and that the Executive Government of the United States, including the Military and Naval Authorities thereof, will* RECOGNIZE AND MAINTAIN THE FREEDOM *of said persons.*

And I hereby enjoin upon the people so declared to be free, to abstain from all violence, UNLESS IN NECESSARY SELF-DEFENCE, *and I recommend to them that in all cases, when allowed, they* LABOR FAITHFULLY FOR REASONABLE WAGES.

And I further declare and make known that such persons of suitable condition will be received into the armed service of the United States, to garrison forts, positions, stations, and other places, and to man vessels of all sorts in said service.

And upon this act, SINCERELY BELIEVED TO BE AN ACT OF JUSTICE, *warranted by the Constitution, upon military necessity, I invoke the considerate judgment of mankind, and the gracious favor of* ALMIGHTY GOD.

In testimony whereof I have hereunto set my name, and caused the seal of the United States to be affixed.

[L. S.] *Done at the* CITY OF WASHINGTON, *this first day of January, in the year of our Lord one thousand eight hundred and sixty-three, and of the Independence of the United States the eighty-seventh.*

By the President.

William H. Seward

Secretary of State.

A. Lincoln

Proclamation of Emancipation *(Library of Congress)*

signed the first THIRTEENTH AMENDMENT, which, if it had been ratified, would have locked slavery into the CONSTITUTION forever. Lincoln saw what he described as his "official duty" as president to save the Union and not either to save or destroy slavery. As he wrote in a famous 1862 letter to Horace Greeley, a former congressman and liberal reform leader, "If I could save the union without freeing any slave I would do it, and if I could save it by freeing some and leaving others alone I would also do that—whatever I do about slavery and the colored race I do because I believe it helps to save the union. . . ." As the war progressed, Lincoln slowly and reluctantly came to the conclusion that in order to win the war and save the Union it was necessary to promise freedom to some of the slaves. He reached this conclusion because of increasing pressure from the RADICAL REPUBLICANS in CONGRESS and because he thought freeing the slaves and subsequently arming them would help bring the war to a speedier conclusion. There were also diplomatic reasons for the decision. Britain and France might have been considering extending diplomatic recognition to the government of the Southern states, and Lincoln thought that turning war into a crusade against slavery would forestall their actions by appealing to the antislavery sentiments in those countries. Thus, for political, diplomatic, and military reasons, in the summer of 1862 he decided to issue a proclamation of emancipation.

On September 22, 1862, Lincoln issued what is generally referred to as the "preliminary" Emancipation Proclamation. In this two-paragraph executive order, Lincoln's ambivalence on the issues of slavery, union, and the war is apparent because in it he told the South that if it ceased rebellion and returned to the Union, he would ask Congress to compensate them if they promised to gradually free their slaves. If they refused this offer and did not return to the Union by January 1, 1863, then the slaves in those states "shall then henceforward and forever be free." Lincoln's ambivalence was again on display in December 1862 when he proposed a constitutional amendment providing for gradual, compensated emancipation (any state freeing its slaves before 1900 would be compensated by the federal government) and the colonialization of the newly freed Africans in Africa or the Caribbean. The South rejected this proposal, so on January 1, 1863, Lincoln issued the final proclamation.

Of all the American presidents, Lincoln was the most gifted in the use of language, as shown in the moral eloquence and urgency of the GETTYSBURG ADDRESS and his second inaugural address. Yet, the proclamation has what the historian Richard Hoftstader called "all the moral grandeur of a bill of lading." That is, it was a deliberately dry, uninspiring, legalistic document. Using his authority as commander in chief of the army and navy, Lincoln declared the proclamation a war measure, "a fit and necessary mea-

sure for suppressing said rebellion." The proclamation applied only to those parts of the South in rebellion; specifically exempting slaveholding Union states such as Maryland and those parts of the South controlled by the Union army (such as New Orleans). Thus, in effect, Lincoln freed the slaves where he had no power to do so and left in slavery those where he had the power to free them. This led the *London Spectator* to scorn the proclamation as asserting "not that a human being cannot justly own another, but that he cannot own him unless he is loyal to the United States."

Although the proclamation on the day it was issued did not free a single slave, it set in motion a process that led to their liberation. As the Union army occupied rebellious parts of the South, slaves were freed, and eventually with Lincoln's strong support the second Thirteenth Amendment abolishing slavery throughout the United States was adopted in 1865.

Further reading: John Hope Franklin, *The Emancipation Proclamation* (Garden City, N.Y.: Doubleday, 1963).

Equal Employment Opportunity Commission

The Equal Employment Opportunity Commission (EEOC) was established by the CIVIL RIGHTS ACT OF 1964. The EEOC is one of the handful of agencies in the federal BUREAUCRACY with a specific race or CIVIL RIGHTS mission. The mission or responsibility of EEOC as established in 1964 is to investigate DISCRIMINATION in employment by employers, employment agencies, and unions based on race, religion, national origin, or gender. (The mission of the commission has been expanded since 1964 to cover discrimination based on age and disability.) Although the EEOC was established in 1964, its roots can be traced to the PROTEST and the MARCH ON WASHINGTON MOVEMENT by A. PHILIP RANDOLPH in 1941. Randolph's protest and threatened march forced President FRANKLIN D. ROOSEVELT to issue an executive order establishing a Fair Employment Practices Committee (FEPC) to enforce nondiscrimination in employment in businesses with defense contracts. Although the FEPC was not very effective in enforcing nondiscrimination, the CONGRESS in 1945 nevertheless abolished the committee. Repeated efforts to reestablish it failed due to the use of the FILIBUSTER in the Senate. Therefore, presidents from HARRY TRUMAN to JOHN F. KENNEDY used executive orders to establish committees on fair employment within the federal government and by businesses with government contracts. These committees, without congressional authority, had only modest effects on the employment of blacks by the federal government and hardly any on black employment by private companies. The pressures generated by the CIVIL RIGHTS

MOVEMENT finally resulted in the reemergence of FEPC as part of the 1964 Civil Rights Act.

The EEOC consists of five members, including the chair, appointed for five-year terms by the president with the approval of the Senate. In 2000 the commission had a budget of about $300 million and about 3,000 employees. Generally, the commission stresses persuasion and conciliation to achieve its objectives, although since 1972 it has had the authority to initiate LITIGATION if conciliation fails. The commission has issued a series of Uniform Guidelines on Employment Selection Procedures governing hiring and promotion standards for U.S. businesses and Guidelines on Affirmative Action explaining how employers can develop AFFIRMATIVE ACTION plans that employ numerical goals and timetables without violating the law or the CONSTITUTION.

equality

Equality and FREEDOM are core values in AFRICAN-AMERICAN POLITICS, its prime animating force, and its principal objectives. Equality is also a core value of the American DEMOCRACY, rooted in its philosophy of NATURAL RIGHTS and eloquently stated by THOMAS JEFFERSON in the DECLARATION OF INDEPENDENCE. The very nature of African-American politics, and the enduring dilemma of the American democracy is that while proclaiming equality for men, Jefferson and the other founders of America denied it to the Africans in America. While the Declaration of Independence proclaimed equality, the CONSTITUTION did not, and it was not until after the CIVIL WAR and the adoption of the FOURTEENTH AMENDMENT that the Constitution was amended to formally commit the nation to equality.

Equality as a concept is not clearly defined philosophically, constitutionally, or by social scientists. It is generally agreed that equality does not necessarily or always require that individuals or groups be treated identically or the same. Rather, it requires that differential treatment of individuals or groups not be invidious.

In the United States, equality usually refers to equality of opportunity and equality under the law. That is, each individual should have the same opportunity to pursue his or her natural rights to life, liberty, and property, and each person should have equal or the same opportunity to vote and participate in the political process. The idea of equality of opportunity is contrasted with the idea of equality of results or equalitarianism, which is the notion that societies should be structured in a way such that individuals enjoy equality of results or more or less identical access to education, employment, housing, health care, and social security. Because INDIVIDUALISM is also a core value in the United States, the idea of equality of results is generally rejected in favor of equality of opportunity. African Ameri-

cans tend, however, to support equality of results or at least the principle of equalitarianism. Studies of PUBLIC OPINION have consistently shown that blacks are more likely than whites to support the idea that the government should reduce inequality between individuals in America by seeing to it that all persons have access to decent jobs, education, health care, and housing. For many African Americans, equality defined in terms of results is the essence of INTEGRATION.

Because individualism is such an important value in American culture, equality is defined in terms of individuals rather than groups. For example, although the EQUAL PROTECTION CLAUSE was put in the Constitution to protect the rights of the newly freed slaves as a group, its actual language refers to persons or individuals. And the SUPREME COURT has consistently interpreted the clause's commitment to equality as a commitment to equality for individuals and not groups. This understanding of equality is at variance with the idea in African-American politics that blacks should be entitled to certain opportunities such as REPRESENTATION in CONGRESS or access to employment as a group rather than as individuals.

See also AFFIRMATIVE ACTION and QUOTAS.

equal protection clause, U.S. Constitution

The equal protection clause of the FOURTEENTH AMENDMENT is the only provision of the CONSTITUTION committing the nation explicitly to EQUALITY, although the SUPREME COURT has interpreted the DUE PROCESS CLAUSES as implicitly recognizing a commitment to equality. The Fourteenth Amendment's equal protection clause is a limited, narrow guarantee of equality, however, protecting persons only from actions by STATE AND LOCAL GOVERNMENTS that deny persons "equal protection of the law." It does not apply to actions by private corporations or individuals who may deny equality to persons on the basis of race, religion, gender, or ETHNICITY. This limited or narrow reach of the clause was stated by the Supreme Court in its 1883 Civil Rights cases, in which it ruled that CONGRESS could not prohibit racial DISCRIMINATION in hotels and other public accommodations based on race because the clause applied only to actions by state governments or their local entities. The Court reaffirmed this narrow reading of the clause as late as 1999 in *United States v. Morrison, et al.*, a case involving Congress's power to protect the victims of gender-motivated violence.

The equal protection clause as interpreted by the Supreme Court does not require that persons be treated the same by the states but, rather, that the difference in treatment of persons must not be arbitrary or unreasonable. However, when the differential treatment of persons is based on race, the Court has held that it must be given "the most rigid scrutiny." In practice, this means that a law passed by a state based on race is presumed to be unconstitutional unless the state can provide "compelling justifications." In other words, the state must prove that the use of race is necessary to achieve a permissible government purpose or objective and that it is virtually the only way the purpose or objective can be achieved. This standard of "strict scrutiny" was used by the Supreme Court to strike down state-imposed racial SEGREGATION in the schools in *BROWN V. BOARD OF EDUCATION* and in other state facilities in the 1950s and 1960s, and in the 1980s and 1990s to strike down state AFFIRMATIVE ACTION programs.

Although the equal protection clause was put in the Constitution after the CIVIL WAR to provide equality to the newly freed slaves, over the years it has been used as a kind of "equal rights amendment for all persons," including women, immigrants, the elderly, the poor, and homosexuals. The clause was also used by the Supreme Court to protect VOTING RIGHTS and REPRESENTATION in the case of *BAKER V. CARR*. The clause was also used in 2000 in *Bush v. Gore,* the case in which the Supreme Court stopped a recount of the votes in Florida that might have given Gore, the DEMOCRATIC PARTY candidate, enough votes to win the PRESIDENCY. The five-to-four Supreme Court majority held that different standards used by Florida counties in the recount violated Bush's right to equal protection of the law. This use of the clause is somewhat ironic, since there were widespread charges of suppression and failure to count the votes of African Americans, who voted by a margin of nine to one for Gore. If the Court had not stopped the recount, Gore might have won Florida and been elected president. But the Court stopped the recount by using the very clause placed in the Constitution to protect the rights of African Americans.

ethnicity (ethnic group)

Ethnicity is a basis for identifying or classifying individuals into groups or collectivities based on some shared characteristic that distinguishes or is believed to distinguish them from other groups in a society. Generally, members of the group have one or more characteristics that is consciously understood as the essence of their group distinctiveness. These characteristics may include race, religion, region or geographic area, language, tribal or national origins, or some combination of these. Individuals belonging to a particular ethnic group usually have some sense of shared ancestry and a real or imagined sense of a shared historical past and culture.

In the United States, ethnic groups based on RACE or color are often distinguished from those based on other characteristics, such as religion, language, or national origins. Thus, one refers to racial and ethnic minorities. For example, one refers to four "races"—"white" (European American), "black" (African American), "red" (Native American, or Indian), and "yellow" (Asian American)—and then to multiple ethnic groups within each race. Among whites, one distinguishes among Italian, Irish, and Jewish Americans, for example, based on religion, language, and national origins; among Asian Americans language and national origins are used to distinguish among Japanese, Korean, and Chinese Americans; distinctions are made among native Americans based on tribal affiliations such as Arapaho, Pawnee, and Hopi; and among African Americans, distinctions are made on the basis of national origins such as WEST INDIANS and Nigerian Americans. Although both social and natural scientists generally view the use of race in this way as inappropriate, it remains a part of ordinary and official discourse.

Also, in the United States, ethnicity or ethnic group has been used by the SUPERORDINATE GROUP—white Anglo-Saxon Protestants—to label SUBORDINATE GROUPS as ethnic minorities. But as African-American political scientist MATTHEW HOLDEN JR. writes, "It is superficial and inaccurate to simultaneously define 'Italo-Americans' as ethnics but Anglo-protestants as nonethnics. Each is as 'ethnic' as the other. Moreover . . . there is an explicit snobbery in the ordinary use of the term 'ethnic,' for it somehow implies that 'ethnics' are merely those white people who somehow deviate from the 'normal' cultural-political standards of the Anglo-protestant population." This "snobbish" and inaccurate use of ethnicity persists in the United States. For example, during the 1980s some supporters of President RONALD REAGAN were referred to as "ethnic" Democrats, meaning persons of Italian, Polish, and Irish national origins.

Both major strands of Western sociological theory—the radical one derived mainly from Karl Marx and the liberal one derived mainly from Max Weber—contend that in advanced industrial societies, ethnicity should gradually disappear as a basis of individual identification, to be replaced by social class identities. In the United States as well as other industrial societies, this has not occurred. Although ASSIMILATION is an important factor in the United States and other modern societies, ethnic identities also persist, suggesting that ethnicity may be a fundamental base of social organization, one that may be as important, if not more important, for some persons than their social class identity.

See also CENSUS.

Further reading: Nathan Glazer and Daniel P. Moynihan, *Ethnicity: Theory and Experience* (Cambridge, Mass.: Harvard University Press, 1975); Andrew Greeley, *Ethnicity in the United States* (New York: John Wiley & Sons, 1974).

Evers, Medgar (1925–1963) *civil rights leader*

Of all the SOUTHERN STATES, Mississippi—in the pervasiveness and VIOLENCE of its OPPRESSION of its huge black population, the largest of any state—was, as one historian wrote, in a "class by itself." MARTIN LUTHER KING JR. in his "I HAVE A DREAM" address called it a "desert state, sweltering with the heat of oppression." Thus, to fight for CIVIL RIGHTS in Mississippi was a dangerous endeavor. This is what Medgar Evers did for most of his adult life until he was murdered in the driveway of his home in 1963.

Evers was born and raised in Mississippi and attended Alcorn A & M, a historically black university in the state. After serving in the army during World War II, he returned to Mississippi, where he and his brother in 1946 registered to vote by facing down a hostile white mob. In 1954 he applied to the all-white university of Mississippi law school. After his application was rejected, he became the NAACP's first field secretary in the state. In this post from 1955 until his murder in 1963, he traveled throughout the state organizing local chapters and encouraging blacks to register to vote. He played an important role in the admission of JAMES MEREDITH to the University of Mississippi and organizing SIT-INS in the state's capital. He lived constantly under the threat of death, and on June 17, 1963, Byron de la Beckwith, a white supremacist and racist, shot and killed him. The assassination occurred the day after President JOHN F. KENNEDY's nationally televised address calling for racial reconciliation and proposing what would become the CIVIL RIGHTS ACT OF 1964. Beckwith was tried twice for the murder in the 1960s, but the juries could not reach a verdict. However, in 1994 he was finally convicted and sentenced to life in prison. In the POST–CIVIL RIGHTS ERA Evers's brother Charles was elected mayor of Fayette, Mississippi, thus becoming in 1969 the first black to head a multiracial Southern town since RECONSTRUCTION. Medgar Evers's wife, Myrlie, in the 1990s served as chair of the NAACP's national board.

Medgar Evers *(Library of Congress)*

executive orders

An executive order is a rule or regulation issued by the president, a governor, or a mayor to implement provisions of the law or, in the case of the president, the CONSTITUTION. They may involve narrow administrative rules and regulations or they may involve broad and general rules that have the same legal effect as a law passed by CONGRESS or a state or local legislative body. Although the legislative power is vested exclusively in the Congress, presidents since ABRAHAM LINCOLN have claimed the right to issue directives of broad and general application that have the same legal effect as a law passed by Congress. Presidents trace their authority to engage in this kind of quasi-legislative activity to the general grant of the "executive power" to the PRESIDENCY and to the command of Article II of the Constitution that "he shall take care that the laws be faithfully executed." The SUPREME COURT has upheld this board interpretation of presidential power by holding that executive orders have the full force of the law unless they conflict with a specific provision of the Constitution or of the law. Presidents use executive orders to establish policies when Congress refuses to do so.

Presidents have frequently employed executive orders in the development of CIVIL RIGHTS policy when Congress has refused to act. The first executive order dealing with civil rights or race was Lincoln's EMANCIPATION PROCLAMATION. (In addition to the general grant of executive power, Lincoln based his authority to issue the proclamation on his commander in chief powers.) In the 20th century, all American presidents since FRANKLIN D. ROOSEVELT have used executive orders to prohibit employment DISCRIMINATION in the federal government and discrimination by businesses with government contracts. President HARRY TRUMAN in 1948 used an executive order to require DESEGREGATION and nondiscrimination in the armed forces. President JOHN F. KENNEDY used an executive order in 1962 to prohibit discrimination in federally assisted housing, and in 1971 President RICHARD NIXON used an executive order to establish the basic program and guidelines for AFFIRMATIVE ACTION. Although executive orders are an easy way for presidents to go around Congress and establish PUBLIC POLICY, Congress can overturn such orders any time it wishes, and the orders also can be revoked by subsequent presidents.

Further reading: Kenneth Mayer, *With the Stroke of a Pen: Executive Orders and Presidential Power* (Princeton, N. J.: Princeton University Press, 2001); Ruth Morgan, *The President and Civil Rights: Policy Making by Executive Order* (New York: St. Martin's Press, 1970).

F

Fanon, Frantz (1925–1961) *scholar*

Frantz Fanon made a major contribution to theoretical understanding of the nature and consequences of European COLONIALISM and the OPPRESSION of THIRD WORLD peoples. Fanon was also a dedicated revolutionary, working actively in the Algerian war for independence from France. Indeed, his revolutionary activism informed his theoretical writings. Because of this extraordinary combination of revolutionary theorizing and activism, Fanon is sometimes referred to as "The Marx of the Third World," comparing his influence on revolutionary thought in the Third World to Karl Marx's influence on revolutionary theory and activism in Europe. Although his writings were based on his research and experiences in Africa, they provide critical insight into the history, psychology, and politics of RACISM and WHITE SUPREMACY in the United States and profoundly influenced many African-American political activists in the 1960s, including STOKELY CARMICHAEL, HUEY NEWTON, and AMIRI BARAKA. Fanon's life and writings were also a source of influence and inspiration for the BLACK POWER MOVEMENT and the BLACK PANTHER PARTY.

Fanon was born in 1925 to a middle-class family on the small French-controlled Caribbean island of Martinique. Gifted in French language and culture, he attended a prestigious French school on the island, where he was taught by Aimé Césaire, a communist leader, poet, and founder of the NEGRITUDE literary movement. When the Nazis defeated France during World War II and took over Martinique, Fanon left the island to join French anti-Nazi forces in Europe, where he participated in the invasion of southern Europe and won an award for heroism. Returning home, he worked in Césaire's successful COMMUNIST PARTY candidacy for a seat in the French Parliament. In 1947, he went to France to study medicine and psychiatry at the University of Lyons. There he became involved in RADICALISM and African and WEST INDIAN student politics; he edited a student newspaper, read philosophy, and wrote three plays. In 1952, he completed his medical studies and

began an internship at a small French hospital. A year later at age 27 he published his first book, *Black Skin, White Mask*, a brilliant study of INTERNAL INFERIORIZATION as an inevitable consequence of the oppression of people of color by whites. This work has been widely read throughout the Third World and is considered a classic in the psychology of racial oppression. After publication of the book, Fanon became a close friend of leading French intellectuals of the time, including the leading scholar of FEMINISM Simone de Beauvoir and the famed existentialist philosopher Jean Paul Sartre, who wrote the introduction to his second book, *The Wretched of the Earth*.

In 1953, Fanon became the head of a psychiatric hospital in Algeria, the French colony in North Africa. A year later, the Algerian war for independence began, and Fanon became involved by secretly providing medical supplies and training material to the FLN, the Algerian revolutionary organization. Fanon's hospital duties required him to provide psychiatric care to the Algerian victims of torture and their French torturers. This experience led him to conclude that colonial society was insane rather than his patients, and thus as a trained psychiatrist he could not merely treat the symptoms of disease in his patients while ignoring the causes in the society. Thus, in 1955 he wrote a letter of protest and resigned from the hospital and became a full-time revolutionary, editing the FLN's newspaper, running clandestine medical centers, and spying. By 1959 he had become an international spokesman for the FLN, and in 1960 he was appointed its ambassador to Ghana, but later in the year he was diagnosed with leukemia. Although he had survived three French assassination attempts, he would die of the leukemia within a year. Once he learned of the diagnosis, Fanon devoted himself to completing *The Wretched of the Earth* while also seeking treatment first in the African nation of Tunisia and then in the Soviet Union. On the advice of his Soviet doctors, Fanon in late 1961 came to the United States for treatment. However, the American CIA (Central Intelligence Agency) questioned him for eight days in a hotel room before providing medical care. Although he was eventually admitted to a hospital, he died in December 1961 while reviewing the final page proofs of *The Wretched of the Earth.* He was 36. At his request, he was secretly flown to Algeria, where he was buried with full military honors in FLN-held territory.

Fanon published four books in his short life, including *A Dying Colonialism,* an account of the resistance of ordinary people during the Algerian revolution, and *Toward the African Revolution,* a collection of his newspaper articles and essays published after his death. However, the books on which his reputation as theoretician of the oppressed and their revolutionary resistance rests are *Black Skin, White Mask* and *The Wretched of the Earth.*

Black Skin, White Mask is a study of ALIENATION, which for Fanon is central to the analysis of racial oppression in colonial societies or societies organized on the basis of racism and white supremacy. In such societies individuals are not only alienated from their color and traditional community but, Fanon argued, most importantly, from their very sense of being as black people. Under CAPITALISM, alienation is mainly a function of a worker's alienation from his labor, but in a racist, capitalist system a black person is alienated from his skin color as well as his labor. For Fanon, skin-color alienation is clearly the more crucial of the two, since as he put it, the white worker did not confront "the dilemma, turn white or disappear." As a psychiatrist, Fanon was well equipped to deal with this aspect of racial oppression. *Black Skin, White Mask* offers both a diagnosis of the problem and solutions that would result in disalienation. For Fanon, the solutions required not just changes in individual black people but also revolutionary changes in the structures of racially oppressive societies. Thus, he wrote,

> As a psychoanalyst, I should help my patient become conscious of his unconscious and abandon his attempts at a hallucinatory whitening, but also to act in the direction of a change in the social structure. In other words, the black man should no longer be confronted by the dilemma turn white or disappear, but he should be able to take cognizance of a possibility of existence. In still other words, if society makes difficulties for him because of his color, my objective will not be that of dissuading him from it by advising him to 'keep his place'; on the contrary, my objective, once his motivation has been brought into consciousness, will be to put him in a position to choose action or passivity with respect to the real source of his conflict—that is the social structure.

The Wretched of the Earth, written in just two months, is a significant contribution because of its advocacy of the use of VIOLENCE by oppressed people to secure their FREEDOM and because of its critique of African or BLACK NATIONALISM. Violence for Fanon was indispensable in the process of ending colonialism in Africa. To understand his insistence on the "absolute necessity" of violence, one has to understand that, for Fanon, violence is more than a mere political method to force the removal of the European oppressor. It is also a vital means for black psychological and social freedom. Fanon writes that "violence" is man re-creating himself: "The native cures himself through the force of arms." Fanon implies that if violence is not used in the revolutionary process, the African cannot become fully free; rather, he would remain psychologically an oppressed personality in a neocolonial system. And the inner violence within the oppressed personality—brought about by colonialism—if not used in a revolutionary way would inevitably, he felt, find expression in tribal wars and other forms of communal violence. This is because the function of violence in the context of colonialism is only incidentally political; its function is also psychological. Fanon in *The Wretched of the Earth* concluded that "the native's weapon is proof of his humanity. For in the first days of the revolt you must kill—to shoot down a white man is to kill two birds with one stone, to destroy an oppressor and the man he oppresses at the same time."

On black nationalism, Fanon was ambivalent. Although he was an advocate of black or African nationalism, believing it could be used as a means of mass mobilization and as a way to combat alienation and internal inferiorization, he was also fearful that it could easily become chauvinistic and dangerous to international or interracial solidarity and to the development of SOCIALISM. That is, he thought black leaders in Africa (and by extension the United States) might manipulate symbols of nationalism and racial pride in order to conceal or mask the exploitation of the interests of black people, a phenomenon that has characterized the leadership of some African nationalists in postcolonial Africa and some black nationalist leaders in the United States.

Although Fanon died at a very early age, his revolutionary activism helped Algeria to win independence from France in early 1962, and his revolutionary writings inspired and continues to inspire political activism throughout the Third World as well as in the United States. The Black Panther Party in the United States in the 1960s and the South African black consciousness movement against APARTHEID in the 1970s, for examples, were influenced and shaped by Fanon's writings.

Further reading: Dennis Forsythe, "Frantz Fanon: The Marx of the Third World," *Phylon* 34 (1973): 19–34; Irene Gendzier, *Frantz Fanon: A Critical Study* (London: Wildwood House, 1973); Robert C. Smith, "Beyond Marx: Fanon and the Concept of Colonial Violence," *Black World* 22 (1973): 23–33.

Farmer, James (1920–1999) *civil rights leader*

James Farmer was one of the major leaders of the 1960s PROTEST phase of the CIVIL RIGHTS MOVEMENT. Farmer was born in Marshall, Texas, in 1920. He received his undergraduate education at Wiley College, one of the HISTORICALLY BLACK COLLEGES AND UNIVERSITIES, and graduate training in divinity from HOWARD UNIVERSITY. In 1942 Farmer was among the founders of CORE (CONGRESS OF RACIAL EQUALITY) in Chicago, where he led SIT-INS protesting SEGREGATION in public facilities. In the 1960s he organized and led FREEDOM RIDES to desegregate buses traveling through the SOUTHERN STATES. He also led voter-registration campaigns in the South with MARTIN LUTHER KING JR. and JOHN LEWIS. Farmer was one of three major leaders of protest ORGANIZATIONs during the Civil Rights movement. After leading CORE to prominence during the early 1960s, Farmer resigned from the organization in 1966 because he disagreed with its embrace of the BLACK POWER MOVEMENT. In 1968 he ran for CONGRESS from New York but was defeated by SHIRLEY CHISHOLM. In 1969 President RICHARD NIXON appointed him to the federal BUREAUCRACY as an assistant secretary in the Department of Health, Education and Welfare. His former colleagues in the Civil Rights movement criticized him for accepting the appointment and not speaking out against what they saw as Nixon's anti–civil rights positions on BUSING for purposes of school DESEGREGATION. After a year, Farmer resigned his post and subsequently indicated that he had serious disagreements with President Nixon but did not feel he could speak out while serving in the administration. After leaving the administration, Farmer briefly established a THINK TANK on minority politics, lectured at colleges and universities about the civil rights movement, and wrote his memoirs, *Lay Bare the Soul: An Autobiography of the Civil Rights Movement* (1985).

Farrakhan, Louis (1933–) *nationalist leader*

Minister Louis Farrakhan, the spiritual leader of the NATION OF ISLAM, is the most influential POST–CIVIL RIGHTS ERA advocate of BLACK NATIONALISM and one of the most influential individuals in the post–civil rights era LEADERSHIP of the BLACK COMMUNITY. Farrakhan is also a deeply divisive leader, viewed by the vast majority of whites and about one-third of blacks as a racist bigot. In a 1995 poll only 4 percent of whites had a favorable opinion of him compared with 39 percent of blacks. These opinions on Farrakhan are based on a poll conducted in October 1995 after he led the MILLION MAN MARCH, the largest mass PROTEST demonstration in the DISTRICT OF COLUMBIA in the history of the United States.

Farrakhan was born in New York City to parents of WEST INDIAN origins. He grew up in Boston and attended Winston Salem Teachers College in North Carolina, but instead of pursuing teaching as a career, he became a nightclub singer. In 1955 Farrakhan abandoned his singing career after he was recruited by MALCOLM X into the NATION OF ISLAM. Farrakhan, who was born Louis Eugene Walcott, changed his name to Farrakhan after he became the minister in charge of the Nation's Boston mosque. In 1963 Malcolm X became involved in a dispute with ELIJAH MUHAMMAD, the founder of the Nation, and was suspended from the organization. A year later Malcolm left the Nation to form his own organization, the ORGANIZATION OF AFRO-AMERICAN UNITY. Although Malcolm had recruited him into the Nation and was his mentor, Farrakhan harshly criticized Malcolm for leaving the Nation, implying in one article in the group's newspaper that he should be killed. In 1965 Malcolm was murdered, and three members of the Nation of Islam were convicted of killing him. Farrakhan never faced any charges related to the murder and consistently denied any involvement, but in later years he conceded that his inflammatory rhetoric might have helped to create the "atmosphere" that led to the murder.

After Malcolm's death, Farrakhan was appointed to succeed him as head of the influential HARLEM mosque and chief national spokesman for the Nation of Islam. Like Malcolm, Farrakhan used his charisma and tremendous oratorical skills to effectively spread the Nation of Islam's message. When Elijah Muhammad died in 1976, Farrakhan, as the organization's best-known minister and its national spokesman, probably expected to succeed Muhammad as leader of the group. However, the elder Muhammad had designated his son, Wallace Muhammad, as his successor. Almost immediately upon assuming leadership, Wallace began to repudiate the core nationalist ideological and religious principles of the Nation of Islam, and he soon transformed it into a thoroughly Americanized mainstream, orthodox Islamic institution. When these radical changes in the Nation of Islam were inaugurated, Farrakhan, while displeased, remained silent. However, after traveling to Africa and several Islamic countries, Farrakhan returned to the United States, disassociated himself from Wallace's reforms, and set about to rebuild the Nation of Islam on the original principles of Elijah Muhammad.

Farrakhan based his strategy to rebuild the Nation first on an appeal to the black-nationalist tradition among the original followers of the Nation who were dissatisfied with Wallace's INTEGRATION. Second, he sought to recruit new adherent from among the lower middle class and young people of all classes who were alienated from the traditional religious, civil rights, and political leadership of the black community. Third, he sought, while retaining the fundamental tenets of the original doctrine of the Nation, to move it toward the mainstream of black political life by

Louis Farrakhan addressing a crowd gathered for the Million Family March, October 16, 2000, on Capitol Hill, Washington, D.C. *(Alex Wong/Newsmakers)*

attempting to form COALITIONS with the BLACK CHURCH on business enterprises and solving social problems. He also attempted to broaden the base of the group to attract middle-class blacks. To accomplish this, he to some extent modified or downplayed some of the Nation's more controversial tenets, such as the notion of whites as devils. Finally, Farrakhan abandoned the long-held tradition of the Nation of nonvoting and nonparticipation in American politics.

In 1983 Farrakhan led members of the Nation of Islam for the first time in registering blacks to vote, and in 1983 he endorsed the candidacy of Harold Washington, an African American, for mayor of Chicago. In 1984 he endorsed JESSE JACKSON when he sought the DEMOCRATIC PARTY nomination for president. In the course of Jackson's campaign, Farrakhan attacked a black reporter who had revealed that in private conversations Jackson sometimes referred to Jews in derogatory language, and later Farrakhan himself referred to Judaism as a "dirty" religion. Both of these events received extensive coverage in both the black and the white MEDIA, and as a result Farrakhan became much better known, becoming by the 1990s the second-most-recognized black American leader. The success of the Million Man March further enhanced his status and gave him international stature as a religious and political leader.

Although hardly any whites held a favorable view of him and he is viewed unfavorably by many blacks as well, his uncompromising rhetorical MILITANCY against RACISM and WHITE SUPREMACY and his emphasis on black solidarity and SELF-HELP continued to appeal to many blacks of all ages and classes. And the Nation of Islam under his leadership is the only national black ORGANIZATION with an indigenous mass base, operating independently of white financial contributions.

See also AMERICAN MUSLIM MISSION.

Further reading: Mattias Gardell, *In the Name of Elijah Muhammad: Louis Farrakhan and the Nation of Islam* (Durham, N.C.: Duke University Press, 1996).

FBI (Federal Bureau of Investigation)

The Federal Bureau of Investigation, the FBI, is the principal investigative and domestic security agency within the federal BUREAUCRACY. A part of the JUSTICE DEPARTMENT, it is the responsibility of the bureau to investigate violations of federal criminal laws such as bank robbery and kidnapping and to enforce certain civil laws such as those relating to CIVIL RIGHTS. The FBI is also the government's principal domestic intelligence agency, charged with investigating threats to the internal security of the POLITICAL SYSTEM. In this latter role, throughout much of its history, the FBI has been a major instrument in the POLITICAL REPRESSION of the African-American CIVIL RIGHTS MOVEMENT.

The Bureau of Investigation was formed in 1908 (it was renamed the FBI in 1935), and under the directorship of J. EDGAR HOOVER, who headed it from 1924 until his death in 1972, the bureau devoted much of its vast resources to repression of real or imagined threats to the internal security of the political system. In Hoover's view, such threats included virtually any challenges to the status quo of CAPITALISM, RACISM, and WHITE SUPREMACY. Thus, the FBI spied on and attempted to disrupt efforts by working-class Americans to organize trade unions, and it actively repressed all forms of RADICALISM, SOCIALISM, COMMUNISM, and left-wing MILITANCY.

The FBI under Hoover viewed the Civil Rights movement as the embodiment of militancy and a threat to national security because it was viewed as communist-inspired and committed to racial EQUALITY, which threatened the status quo of racism and white supremacy. Thus, from the 1920s to the 1960s, the FBI—using an extensive network of undercover agents and informants—engaged in surveillance and disruption of every black leader and organization, whether they were moderate like the NAACP and URBAN LEAGUE or militant like the AFRICAN BLOOD BROTHERHOOD and the BLACK PANTHER PARTY. This is because the bureau defined any challenge to the status quo of racial OPPRESSION as subversive and a threat to domestic security. The list of African-American leaders targeted by Hoover's FBI from the 1920s to the 1960s reads like a who's who of black LEADERSHIP, including, among others, W. E. B. DU BOIS, A. PHILIP RANDOLPH, MARCUS GARVEY, PAUL ROBESON, IDA B. WELLS-BARNETT, ELIJAH MUHAMMAD, MALCOLM X, ADAM CLAYTON POWELL, STOKELY CARMICHAEL, and MARTIN LUTHER KING JR. While engaging in repression of the Civil Rights movement, Hoover claimed that the FBI, because of FEDERALISM, lacked the authority to investigate LYNCHINGS and the violations of the rights of civil rights workers in the SOUTHERN STATES. During the 1960s, this led MARTIN LUTHER KING JR. to raise questions about the bureau's commitment to equal enforcement of the law. King's comments resulted in increased animus toward him by Hoover and the FBI, leading Hoover to call King "the most notorious liar" in America and to intensify the bureau's efforts to destroy his effectiveness as a leader of the movement and replace him with an individual of their own choice (see SAMUEL PIERCE).

After Hoover's death, investigations by CONGRESS and the MEDIA revealed the extent of the bureau's illegal activities and its violations of the CIVIL LIBERTIES and civil rights of the American people. As a result, Congress required its committees in both the House and Senate to more closely monitor the bureau and placed a 10-year term limit on its director. Because of these reforms, it is believed that the FBI since the 1970s has posed less of a threat to the individual rights of Americans and is no longer engaged in the widespread surveillance and repression of dissident movements. However, since it is a secret, intelligence-gathering organization, this can never be known for certain.

See also COINTELPRO.

Further reading: Kenneth O'Reilly, *Racial Matters: The FBI's Secret File on Black America* (New York: Free Press, 1989); Sanford Ungar, *FBI: An Uncensored Look behind the Walls* (Boston: Little, Brown, 1975).

federalism

Federalism and the SEPARATION OF POWERS, the two most important features in the structural design of the U.S. government, were both compromises designed as "checks and balances" on the exercise of POWER and as mechanisms to provide security for the institution of SLAVERY. It is a system of government in which power is divided by a CONSTITUTION between a central or "federal" government and state or regional government subdivisions. Both levels or divisions of government derive their authority from the Constitution, which cannot generally be changed without the consent of both governments, and both governments have independent authority to exercise power within the areas of authority granted by the Constitution. (By contrast, a "unitary" government grants all power and authority to the central government, and whatever powers regional or local

governments exercise are derived from and can be taken away by the central government.) Most of the nations of the world have unitary governments. Of the approximately 180 nations in the UNITED NATIONS, about 17 are federal, mostly large countries like Canada, Nigeria, Mexico, India, and Australia but also the small nation of Switzerland. And the governments of the 50 states in the United States are unitary.

Since the United States is a large country, federalism may be the ideal form of government, but federalism emerged as one of the compromises necessary to form the union of the states. At the time of the adoption of the Constitution, each of the 13 states retained independent power under the Articles of Confederation—a form of government referred to as "confederal"—and were reluctant to relinquish all of their powers to a central, unitary government. Therefore, federalism was a check on the complete exercise of power by a central government. The slaveholding SOUTHERN STATES also opposed a unitary government because they feared it could use its unlimited powers to regulate or abolish slavery. Thus, federalism was one of those constitutional compromises, like the separation of powers, the ELECTORAL COLLEGE, and the THREE-FIFTHS CLAUSE, that in part are a part of the Constitution because of the tensions at the constitutional convention about slavery.

The Tenth Amendment, the last of the BILL OF RIGHTS, establishes federalism. The Amendment "delegates" or gives some powers to the federal government, prohibits the states from exercising certain powers, and leaves or "reserves" all other powers to the states. The major powers delegated to the federal government were limited to regulating commerce and the currency, conducting diplomacy, and waging war. Almost everything else was to be done by the states, including the all-important "police powers." The police powers—the authority to pass laws regulating the health, safety, welfare, and morals of the people—is the vast power inherent in the very origins and purposes of government. It provides the basis for most of the laws that exist in a country, and it provides the basis for governments to provide education, health care, and other social services. It is also the basis for criminal and civil laws.

It is clear that the framers of the Constitution intended the states to exercise most of the powers of government, including virtually all of those relating to the day-to-day lives of the people. Over the years, however, power has shifted to the federal government. This shift of power away from the states has occurred in three distinct periods in American history, two of which are directly related to the presence of African Americans and their struggles for FREEDOM and EQUALITY. The first period was the RECONSTRUCTION era, the second was the NEW DEAL, and the third was during the 1960s with the CIVIL RIGHTS MOVEMENT and the GREAT SOCIETY social welfare programs. Of most importance in the power shift was the adoption during Reconstruction of the FOURTEENTH AMENDMENT. The major purpose of the amendment was to compel the states to guarantee freedom and equality to African Americans, but since its adoption it has become one of the two major bases for the expansion of federal power.

Federalism historically has worked to disadvantage blacks in their struggles for freedom and equality, but it has some advantages. It allows for the retention of local customs and traditions; it allows for the exercise of power by MINORITY GROUPS in state and local governments; it facilitates innovation and experimentation in PUBLIC POLICY by the states; and it allows individuals dissatisfied with their government's policies in one state to move to another that may have more satisfactory policies. As RONALD REAGAN, a strong advocate of federalism, used to say, it allows Americans to "vote with their feet." But for African Americans, federalism's disadvantages outweigh its benefits. As William Riker, a leading scholar on federalism, has written, "Federalism may have more to do with destroying freedom than encouraging it [because] the main beneficiaries throughout American history have been southern whites, who have been given the freedom to oppress Negroes first as slaves and later as a depressed caste." Riker concludes, "If in the United States one disapproves of racism, one should disapprove of federalism."

African Americans during slavery took advantage of federalism to escape to freedom in the nonslave NORTHERN STATES, and from the 1920s to the 1950s millions did so during the GREAT MIGRATION in order to flee SEGREGATION in the Southern states. Federalism in the POST–CIVIL RIGHTS ERA has allowed blacks as a minority group to exercise some power in URBAN POLITICS. But, on balance, Riker is correct; federalism has been and is hostile to black interests. Historically, it was used to maintain slavery and segregation; to depress black voting and other forms of POLITICAL PARTICIPATION; to block enactment of beneficial educational and welfare legislation such as the BLAIR EDUCATION BILL and the ELEMENTARY AND SECONDARY EDUCATION ACT; to distort in racially unfair ways the development of the WELFARE STATE during the New Deal; and to protect LYNCHING and other forms of VIOLENCE against blacks from effective prosecution. And while in the post–civil rights era blacks have been able to exercise some degree of power in STATE AND LOCAL GOVERNMENTS and in urban politics, they are far more effective and powerful in pursuing their interests at the federal level than they are at the state and local levels.

In general, the African-American LEADERSHIP and African-American PUBLIC OPINION are and always have been skeptical if not hostile to federalism and states rights, favoring instead a powerful and active federal government. The general trend in American politics from the New Deal

in the 1930s until the election of Ronald Reagan in the 1980s was toward centralization of power at the federal level. The election of Reagan interrupted this trend to some extent, and the appointments to the SUPREME COURT by Republican presidents since the 1980s created a pro-federalism, states-rights majority that also interrupted the trend toward the centralization of power.

See also COMMERCE CLAUSE.

Further reading: William Riker, *Federalism: Origins, Operations and Significance* (Boston: Little, Brown, 1964).

feminism

Feminism, the IDEOLOGY of gender EQUALITY and FREEDOM, has historically been an ambivalent phenomenon in the BLACK COMMUNITY and in AFRICAN-AMERICAN POLITICS. This is because African-American women historically have faced the double burden of OPPRESSION on the basis of RACISM and DISCRIMINATION on the basis of SEXISM. This double burden creates the dilemma of choosing whether elimination of racism or sexism should be the main focus of the struggles of black women, and to what extent black women should identify with and form COALITIONS with white women, who frequently are as racist and WHITE SUPREMACIST in their thinking as white men. Also, historically in the United States the struggle for women's rights and the struggle for the rights of blacks have been symbiotic and conflictual.

The earliest movement for women's rights originated from the activism of white women in the ABOLITIONIST MOVEMENT. However, these largely middle to upper-class women tended to view sexism as equal or more important than racism. The modern feminist movement that originated in the late 1960s and early 1970s also has its roots in black movements for freedom, specifically in the activism of middle-class white women in the PROTEST phase of the CIVIL RIGHTS MOVEMENT during the 1960s. The modern movement for women's liberation also drew on the BLACK POWER MOVEMENT for parts of its MILITANCY in rhetoric, strategies, and organizing principles. But, as during the abolitionist movement, tensions emerged as these middle-class white women also tended to see sexism as equal to or more important than racism.

Early feminists supported the abolition of SLAVERY as part of a general moral stance in favor of freedom for all persons. And FREDERICK DOUGLASS and many black abolitionists were strong supporters of women's rights. Thus, these two movements formed the basis for a coalition of equality for all persons without regard to race or gender. Yet, this coalition in the end fell apart for several reasons. First, unlike Douglass, many abolitionists, black and white, discriminated against women, refusing, for example, to allow women to sign the Anti-Slavery Society's Declaration of Principles, to hold leadership positions in the group, or to serve as antislavery lecturers. (Women, black and white, later formed their own National Female Anti-Slavery Society.) Second, many white feminists were white supremacists who embraced abolition as part of a strategy to advance the cause of women's rights, but except for gender equality, these white feminists generally held the same views about blacks as white men. The key issue in the collapse of the black-feminist coalition was black suffrage—whether black men should be granted the right to vote before white women. This issue first emerged with the adoption of the FOURTEENTH AMENDMENT, which for the first time included the word *male* in the CONSTITUTION. Feminist leaders felt deeply betrayed by this development, but the decisive break in the coalition came with adoption of the FIFTEENTH AMENDMENT, which granted the vote to black men. Leading white feminists opposed the amendment unless it included women, arguing it would permit black men—their "inferiors"—more rights than white women. A few black women feminist abolitionists also opposed the Fifteenth Amendment, most notably SOJOURNER TRUTH, who argued that its adoption would simply further empower black men to oppress black women. But most blacks, women and men, supported the amendment, and the result was that the feminist movement severed its tenuous coalition with blacks and became largely a movement of white women to get the vote and the other rights and privileges of WHITENESS in a racist society.

When women were granted the right to vote with the adoption of the Nineteenth Amendment in 1920, most African Americans who lived in the SOUTHERN STATES had been effectively denied that right. The white women who led the suffrage movement in general did not protest the disenfranchisement of black men, and some of them embraced it by arguing that giving the vote to white women, while denying it to blacks, would strengthen white supremacy. The ambivalence or opposition of many white feminist leaders to the right of blacks to vote led W. E. B. DU BOIS, an ardent feminist and supporter of the Nineteenth Amendment, to conclude, "The Negro race has suffered more from the antipathy and narrowness of women both North and South than from any other single source." Nevertheless, with few exceptions, most African Americans, whether male or female, supported VOTING RIGHTS for women. Despite this support, prominent black woman suffragists such as MARY CHURCH TERRELL and IDA B. WELLS-BARNETT had to fight SEGREGATION and discrimination within the movement.

Although they had to contend with sexism, women played important roles in the start of the Civil Rights movement. Although no women were among the 29 persons who drafted the NIAGARA MOVEMENT manifesto that launched the movement in 1905, approximately one-third of the signers of the call that led to the creation of the NAACP were women, including Mary Church Terrell and Ida B. Wells-Barnett. However, while active in the movement from its beginning in the 1900s to its end in the 1960s, women played largely supportive, behind-the-scenes "intermediary" rather than leadership roles. While some of these women were critical to the success of the movement and its organizations, no woman ever headed one of the "big five" (NAACP, URBAN LEAGUE, SNCC, CORE, and SCLC) civil rights ORGANIZATIONS. Ida B. Wells-Barnett emerged as the preeminent leader of the antiLYNCHING crusade in the 20th century; MARY MCLEOD BETHUNE was the recognized leader of the black community during the NEW DEAL era; and FANNIE LOU HAMER played an important role during the 1960s in founding and leading the MISSISSIPPI FREEDOM DEMOCRATIC PARTY. But in general, leadership of the Civil Rights movement and of the black community generally was and remains male. This is because black men, like white men, have generally held traditional sexist views about the subordinate roles of women, although historically there has always been greater acceptance in the black community and among black men of nontraditional roles for women. And as HOWARD UNIVERSITY sociologist E. Franklin Frazier wrote in *The Negro Family in the United States,* "The spirit of subordination to masculine authority" was never as strong among black as white women.

The modern movement for the liberation of women in America has been traced in part to the experiences of white, middle-class women active in the Civil Rights movement during the 1960s. Ironically, the seeds of modern feminism were planted in SNCC, the most radical of the movement organizations. Because of its RADICALISM, SNCC was organized in a less hierarchical way than the other civil rights organizations, which made possible a greater degree of female leadership. But it was this openness to greater degrees of female leadership that fueled demands within SNCC for really equalitarian gender relationships. Thus, in what might be viewed as one of the first manifestos of modern feminism, in 1964 white women at a SNCC retreat presented an unsigned paper criticizing "male supremacism" and sexism within the group. The paper contended that male supremacy and sexism could be as damaging to women as white supremacy and racism was to blacks. The men in SNCC, black and white, rejected the paper and even ridiculed it, with STOKELY CARMICHAEL famously quipping, "The only position for women in SNCC is prone." But the black women also rejected the concerns of the white women in part because they rejected the view that racism and white supremacy and sexism and male supremacy were equivalent, and in part because of sexual tensions over relationships between the black men and white women in SNCC.

The passage of the CIVIL RIGHTS ACT OF 1964 also helped to spark the modern feminist movement. Although this act was mainly concerned with prohibiting race discrimination, a Southern congressman—Howard Smith of Virginia—in an effort to defeat the act proposed that "sex" be added to the part of it dealing with employment discrimination. Smith thought that adding sex to the legislation would make the whole idea of equality in employment seem silly. Smith miscalculated. The inclusion of sex discrimination was opposed by black civil rights leaders (as well as white labor leaders) because they saw it as a threat to jobs for black men (the family "bread winner"). However, with the backing of President LYNDON B. JOHNSON, the amendment was adopted. The inclusion of sex as part of the nation's basic civil rights law provided the legal basis for women's equality. In 1966 the National Organization for Women (NOW), patterned after the NAACP, was established, and the modern movement of feminism was on its way to quickly becoming a major force in American politics.

African-American leaders, male and female, were initially skeptical if not hostile to this new movement of mainly middle-class white women. (Although NOW elected a black president, Eileen Hernandez, four years after its founding, it remained in its leadership, membership, and policies largely an organization of middle-class white women.) Several factors account for this skepticism and hostility. First, the movement of solidarity for women's rights was becoming prominent at the very time the movement for black rights was dividing and in decline. Thus, the rise of the women's movement was seen as coming at the expense of a declining black movement. Second, virtually all blacks rejected in the 1960s—as Frederick Douglass had in the 1860s—the attempt to compare the sex-based discrimination faced by women with the racially based oppression faced by blacks. As the African-American political scientist Linda Larue put it, "to compare the conditions of white women to that of blacks was like comparing the conditions of someone who suffered rope burns with someone who had been hanged." And black women thought white women were as racist as white men. As the novelist Toni Morrison wrote, "Black women look at white women and see the enemy, for they know that racism is not confined to white men and that there are more white women than white men in this country." Finally, while mainstream black liberal and integrationist leaders were muted in their comments, the then very influential black nationalist elements of African-American LEADERSHIP was openly and vociferously hostile. Ministers in the NATION OF ISLAM, including LOUIS FARRAKHAN, and influential figures such as AMIRI BARAKA and RON KARENGA openly called for reaffirmation of the subordinate place of women in black culture and society.

By the 1970s, however, a shift in attitudes toward feminism was apparent in the black community among both men and women, a shift that reflected an embrace of the major tenets of the new feminist agenda. The roots, however, of a black feminism go back to the antebellum era in the writings and activism of women like MARIA W. STEWART and Sojourner Truth, and to the late 19th-century writings of women like Anna Julia Cooper, whose 1892 book *A Voice from the South* is an important early work in the development of a distinctive black feminist thought. Black feminism is also rooted in the activities of the black club movement among women. These activities led to the formation in 1896 of the NATIONAL ASSOCIATION OF COLORED WOMEN and later the NATIONAL COUNCIL OF NEGRO WOMEN. The National Association of Colored Women, organized a decade before the NAACP, was the first national black ORGANIZATION to deal with race issues, and the National Council of Negro Women led by DOROTHY HEIGHT dealt with women's issues as well as broader issues of CIVIL RIGHTS during the 1950s and 1960s.

In the 1970s, however, it was clearly the feminist movement among white women that revitalized the ideology among black women, in spite of the skepticism and even hostility of many black women to the middle-class-dominated white feminist movement. The success of the Civil Rights movement in removing the obvious barriers to racial equality allowed for a renewed focus on gender equality among black women. SHIRLEY CHISHOLM's election as the first black woman in CONGRESS in 1968 and her 1972 campaign for the PRESIDENCY were important symbolically in inspiring black female political activism. Finally the SUPREME COURT's 1972 decision in *Roe v. Wade* legalizing abortion was a catalyst to action, since the decision was opposed by virtually the entire male-dominated black leadership establishment, including the NAACP and the Urban League. The NATIONAL BLACK POLITICAL CONVENTION in 1972 rejected a resolution supporting legal abortions; leading black nationalists denounced the decision as genocidal; and JESSE JACKSON equated *Roe v. Wade* with the *DRED SCOTT* decision. Indeed, of the major black organizations, only the BLACK PANTHER PARTY endorsed *Roe* and a woman's right to choose an abortion.

In 1973 black women formed the National Black Feminist Organization, which advocated a specifically BLACK AGENDA of gender equality. In 1974 radical black feminists and lesbians formed the Combahee River Collective (taking its name from a campaign led by HARRIET TUBMAN that freed several hundred slaves), which issued a manifesto defining itself as a group of black women "struggling against racial, sexual, heterosexual and class oppression." (This group is heavily influenced by the writings of Audre Lorde, a young black lesbian feminist and political activist who saw sexuality as an important part of black feminism. See her 1992 book *Zami: A New Spelling of My Name*.) In 1984 politically active black women formed the NATIONAL

POLITICAL CONGRESS OF BLACK WOMEN in order to pursue a distinctive gendered role in African-American politics, focusing on issues and the election and appointment of black women to office.

Feminism is not a monolithic force in black politics, however. Rather, there are divisions among black feminists based on ideology, and there are differences based on class, sexual orientation, age, and marital status. Ideologically, there is a liberal feminism that focuses on issues like abortion rights (since *Roe v. Wade*, the right to an abortion has become widely accepted in the black community, supported in PUBLIC OPINION and by almost all black leaders and organizations), equal employment and pay, health and child care, violence against women, and the full inclusion of women in the political process. Radical feminists support these liberal objectives but also focus on the perceived interrelationships among racism, sexism, heterosexism, and CAPITALISM. Thus, unlike liberal feminists, they tend to advocate SOCIALISM and GAY RIGHTS. Liberal feminists tend to be advocates of traditional marriage and the strengthening of the traditional family, while the radicals often see marriage and the traditional family as patriarchal structures that inevitably oppress women. These ideological differences are to some extent rooted in and related to age, sexual orientation, social class, and marital status.

Although black women in America face the double burden of race and gender discrimination, in the POST–CIVIL RIGHTS ERA they are far outpacing black men in educational and occupational attainments. In almost every area of education from completing high school and college to advanced degrees in the professions (law, medicine, and business) and doctorates, black women are outperforming men, and black women exceed black men in executive, administrative, managerial, and professional occupations. This type of gender differential in education and occupations is unique to the black community among all the ETHNIC GROUPS in the United States. Indeed, it is unprecedented in the history of the world. Historically, white men have always been more willing to accept black women than black men, and recent studies suggest that this historic bias continues as white employers express a strong preference for black women (of whatever class) over black men. This bias is reinforced by AFFIRMATIVE ACTION. These educational and occupational attainments mean that in the 21st century, women are poised to exercise power in a way unprecedented for an ethnic community. This suggests the prospects for increased gender tensions in black politics if black men are unwilling to yield their traditional dominance of the leadership.

The black community has always been more receptive to leadership by women than has the white community, and black men have been more receptive to leadership by women. Thus, black women constitute one-third of black ELECTED OFFICIALS and about one-fifth of blacks in Congress (compared with about 10 percent among whites), but few black women have ever selected to head one of the major civil rights organizations, and traditionally they have been excluded from leadership of the BLACK CHURCH. The black community's CULTURE historically exhibited more-traditional attitudes toward the role of women and their suitability for public roles as compared with their family responsibilities. Public opinion studies in the 1970s confirmed these traditional attitudes among black men and women. However, studies conducted in the 1990s show that black attitudes are converging with those of whites, although both black men and women are still somewhat more likely to embrace traditional ideas about the role of women, for example, that a married woman with children should not work if her husband is capable of supporting the family. But there is not a significant gender gap on these issues. Nor is there a significant gender gap in the black community on PUBLIC POLICY issues, ideology, partisanship, or VOTING BEHAVIOR, unlike among whites, where since the 1980s there has been a growing gender gap between white men and women. The absence of a significant gender gap in black politics provides a basis for long-term gender solidarity in the black community.

Further reading: Patricia Hill Collins, *Black Feminist Thought* (New York: Routledge, 1991); Sara Evans, *Personal Politics: The Roots of Women's Liberation in the Civil Rights Movement and the New Left* (New York: Vintage Books, 1979); Paula Giddings, *When and Where I Enter: The Impact of Black Women on Race and Sex in America* (New York: William Morrow, 1984); Michelle Newman, *White Women's Rights: The Racial Origins of Feminism in the United States* (New York: Oxford University Press, 1999); Belinda Robnet, *How Long? How Long?: African American Women in the Civil Rights Movement* (New York: Oxford University Press, 1997).

Fifteenth Amendment, U.S. Constitution

The Fifteenth Amendment prohibits the states from denying a person who is male the right to vote because of "race, color or previous condition of servitude." Adopted in 1870 five years after the CIVIL WAR, the purpose of the amendment was to confer VOTING RIGHTS on the enslaved Africans freed by the THIRTEENTH AMENDMENT. Under the CONSTITUTION's principle of FEDERALISM, qualifications to vote in both federal and state elections are established by the legislatures of each state. It was thought by many that the FOURTEENTH AMENDMENT would compel the SOUTHERN STATES to confer voting rights on black men, since it included a provision providing for reduction in a state's representation in the House of Representatives if it denied voting rights to any 21-year-old male (excluding Indians). However, this provision was ignored by the states and was never enforced by the CONGRESS, hence the need two years later for the Fifteenth Amendment explicitly guaranteeing black *men* the right to vote.

Although the amendment was directed toward the voting rights of blacks in the Southern states, it was equally important for blacks in the NORTHERN STATES. From the adoption of the Constitution in 1787 to the end of the Civil War in 1865, only six Northern states permitted FREE NEGROES to vote. Indeed, during this period white male voters in many Northern states in referendum after referendum rejected suffrage for black men, usually by large margins. In New York, for example, referenda on black voting rights were held in 1846, 1860, and 1869, and each time a majority of the white men who voted refused to allow

black men to vote. Thus, the Fifteenth Amendment was necessary for black suffrage in the North as well as the South, but its major impact was in the South, since that is where more than 90 percent of African Americans lived.

For a brief period during RECONSTRUCTION, the amendment worked, as black men voted, ran for office, and were elected. Black votes also served as the BALANCE OF POWER in the election of whites to Congress, to STATE AND LOCAL GOVERNMENT offices, and to the PRESIDENCY. This period of black voting was brief, however, since after the COMPROMISE OF 1877 the Southern states adopted an amazing series of roadblocks to black voting, including literacy tests, poll taxes, "grandfather clauses" (allowing whites otherwise disqualified by literacy or tax requirements to vote if their grandfathers had voted), and the WHITE PRIMARY. When these techniques did not work, eco-

One of several commemorative prints marking the enactment on March 30, 1870, of the Fifteenth Amendment and showing the parade celebrating it, which was held in Baltimore on May 19 of the same year *(Library of Congress)*

nomic intimidation (such as losing one's job or crop loans if one voted or attempted to register to vote) and KU KLUX KLAN terrorism and VIOLENCE were employed. As a result, between the early 1890s and 1900s, 95 percent of the African-American electorate in the Southern states was disenfranchised. Although the Fifteenth Amendment gave Congress the authority to enforce black voting rights with "appropriate legislation," it did not exercise this authority until the SELMA DEMONSTRATIONS led by MARTIN LUTHER KING JR. in 1965 pressured it to enact the VOTING RIGHTS ACT OF 1965. Thus, it would take almost 100 years for the promise of the Fifteenth Amendment to be fully realized throughout the United States.

Further reading: William Gillette, *The Right to Vote: Politics and the Passage of the Fifteenth Amendment* (Baltimore: Johns Hopkins University Press, 1969).

filibuster

The filibuster is a parliamentary technique used in the Senate of the United States that allows a minority of the senators to defeat a bill by filibustering or "talking a bill to death." Rule 22 of the Senate provides for unlimited debate, which permits senators to speak on a bill for as long as they wish. If enough senators exercise this right of unlimited debate, they can prevent a vote on a bill they know would otherwise pass. Until 1975, in order to stop a filibuster (by invoking "cloture" in the language of the Senate), a two-thirds vote of the Senate was required. Since 1975, cloture has required the support of three-fifths of the Senate (60 of the 100 members). This means that 40 senators can prevent a vote on a bill that might otherwise pass or, alternatively, on controversial legislation it takes 60 rather than 51 of the 100 senators to pass a bill.

The purpose of the filibuster is to allow for full debate on the merits of bills and to protect minority interests from the domination of popular majorities. While the filibuster has only infrequently served the purpose of full debate on the merits of issues (since senators frequently give long, often irrelevant speeches), it has served the second purpose of protecting minority interests. However, the minority interests the filibuster has historically protected have not been ethnic or racial minorities; rather, it has served those minorities who wished to maintain RACISM and WHITE SUPREMACY. For most of the history of its use, the filibuster was used by DEMOCRATIC PARTY senators from the SOUTHERN STATES in a CONSERVATIVE COALITION with some Northern REPUBLICAN PARTY senators to block CIVIL RIGHTS legislation. A filibuster or threat of filibuster was used to block antiLYNCHING legislation that was supported by a majority in CONGRESS, and from the 1890s until the 1960s the filibuster was used to block or significantly water

down civil rights legislation. Indeed, from the 1900s until the 1960s, the filibuster was rarely used for any other purpose. (The conservative coalition did use the threat of filibustering to significantly water down NEW DEAL legislation and to make sure the WELFARE STATE was not established on the basis of racial EQUALITY.)

The one-man record for filibustering is held by South Carolina senator Strom Thurmond, who spoke for more than 24 hours against the Civil Rights Act of 1957. In 1964 there was a six-month filibuster in an unsuccessful attempt to block passage of the CIVIL RIGHTS ACT OF 1964. One year later, a filibuster was employed to delay passage of the VOTING RIGHTS ACT OF 1965. Since the 1960s, the filibuster has not been used against civil rights legislation. Instead, it has been used to delay or block all kinds of legislation. Thus, from the 1900s to the 1960s, there were usually only one or two filibusters a year, nearly always by Southern senators to block civil rights bills. Since the 1970s, the average number of filibusters per year has exceeded 20 (in 1995–97 there were 50 filibusters), and they have been used by senators from all parts of the country on all kinds of issues.

The filibuster, like the Senate itself, is one of several institutional features of the POLITICAL SYSTEM and in the CONSTITUTION that are at odds with the principles of DEMOCRACY. And like most of these features, the filibuster has often been used to protect either minorities of wealth and property or minorities hostile to the African-American interest in equality and FREEDOM.

See also ELECTORAL COLLEGE, FEDERALISM, SUPREME COURT, and TWO-PARTY SYSTEM.

Fletcher, Arthur, Jr. (1924–) *U.S. government official*

Arthur Fletcher Jr., an assistant secretary of labor in the administration of RICHARD NIXON, was principally responsible for the design and implementation of the PHILADELPHIA PLAN, which became the model for AFFIRMATIVE ACTION programs in the United States.

Born in 1924 in Phoenix, Arizona, Fletcher moved to the state of Washington, where he became active in REPUBLICAN PARTY politics, running unsuccessfully for lieutenant governor in 1968. As one of the highest-ranking blacks in the BUREAUCRACY during the Nixon administration, Fletcher was a leader in organizing black appointees to advocate for the interests of blacks within the administration. In 1971 Fletcher resigned as assistant secretary of labor and was appointed a delegate to the UNITED NATIONS. In 1973 he became director of the United Negro College Fund, which raises funds for HISTORICALLY BLACK COLLEGES AND UNIVERSITIES. Over the years, Fletcher remained a staunch advocate of affirmative action (calling it "his baby") and a

Republican Party activist. As affirmative action became increasingly controversial in the 1980s and 1990s and the Republican Party dropped its support for it, Fletcher briefly considered running for the party's presidential nomination in 1996 in order to defend "his baby." However, he ultimately declined to run, recognizing that as a liberal in a party that now stood strongly for CONSERVATISM he would find little support in terms of money or votes.

foreign policy

Even before the United States became an independent nation, its foreign policy or relations with other nations of the world was related to and influenced by the presence of African Americans. SLAVERY and the slave trade made this inevitable. In the emerging nation's first foreign-policy statement to the world—the DECLARATION OF INDEPENDENCE—THOMAS JEFFERSON had wished to declare the slave trade as one of the grounds for separation from England, and during the Revolutionary War both England and the United States sought the allegiance of African Americans and their service as soldiers. Since then, blacks have been involved in the country's foreign policy in a variety of ways, beginning first perhaps with the BACK-TO-AFRICA MOVEMENTS and then as official and citizen diplomats, as participants in and dissenters from its wars, as participants in the peace conferences following the two world wars, at the founding of the UNITED NATIONS, and by PROTEST and LOBBYING to influence foreign policy toward Africa and the Caribbean. The presence of blacks was also an important factor in shaping the CIVIL RIGHTS policies of the United States during the COLD WAR, and African-American opposition to COLONIALISM and the influence of PAN-AFRICANISM and THIRD WORLD solidarity has shaped how elements of the black LEADERSHIP have responded to American foreign policy since the earliest days of the nation.

Perhaps the earliest involvement of African Americans in foreign policy was the back-to-Africa movements that started in the 1800s. These movements have appeared periodically since then and have involved important African-American leaders, including EDWARD WILMOT BLYDEN, MARTIN DELANY, ALEXANDER CRUMMELL, HENRY TURNER, and MARCUS GARVEY. While these initiatives never led to large-scale settlement of blacks in Africa, they resulted in the signing of a treaty with an African tribal king, the emigration of several thousand blacks to African nations, and the establishment of LIBERIA. In Liberia and the nearby West African nation of Sierra Leone, members of the TALENTED TENTH played roles in education and diplomacy. These efforts also led to the building of a Pan-African consciousness.

For much of its history, the foreign-policy BUREAUCRACY of the United States was almost the exclusive preserve of white men, but as early as the 1870s several blacks, including HENRY HIGHLAND GARNETT and FREDERICK DOUGLASS, were appointed to diplomatic posts in HAITI and Liberia. However, it was not until 1962 in the administration of JOHN F. KENNEDY that an African American, CARL ROWAN, was appointed ambassador to a European nation (Finland). Rowan later became director of the United States Information Agency (the government's international information and propaganda agency) under President LYNDON B. JOHNSON. In this post, Rowan became the first black to sit on the National Security Council, the highest foreign-policy decision-making body in the government. ANDREW YOUNG was appointed ambassador to the United Nations during the administration of JIMMY CARTER, and when he was fired he was replaced by Donald McHenry, who was also black. In 1987 in the administration of RONALD REAGAN, Gen. COLIN POWELL was named the National Security Advisor, and in 2001 Powell was appointed by President George W. Bush as the secretary of state, the highest position in the foreign-policy bureaucracy. Bush also appointed Condoleezza Rice, a black political scientist, as the national security adviser. In spite of these high-level appointments, the foreign-policy bureaucracy remained largely the preserve of whites. In 2000 only 2.7 percent of U.S. diplomats were black.

In their service in the foreign-policy bureaucracy, African Americans tended to follow the policy guidelines of the president, but black diplomats in Liberia and Haiti tried to use their positions to advance the interests of those nations, such as their efforts to prevent European powers from encroaching on Liberia's territory. At the United Nations, Andrew Young was an outspoken advocate of the policy interests of Africa and was eventually fired because of his support for the Palestinians in the Arab-Israeli conflict in the Middle East.

Although blacks have infrequently been official diplomats, they often engaged in CITIZEN DIPLOMACY, where they sought to advance African interests and to seek the support of African leaders for African-American interests. African-American leaders, including W. E. B. DU BOIS and WILLIAM MONROE TROTTER, attended the peace conference after World War I to argue for the easing of colonialism in Africa and other parts of the Third World.

Blacks have served in all of the nation's wars since the CIVIL WAR, but they also have been at the forefront of PROTEST against many of those wars. Frederick Douglass as early as 1848 was a scathing critic of the Mexican-American War, accusing the United States of "robbing Mexico of the most important and valuable of her territory." African-American leaders such as Bishop Alexander Walters of the National African American Council also expressed opposition to the Spanish-American War, especially the annexation of the Philippines. Viewing the war against the

Filipinos as a manifestation of American colonialism and WHITE SUPREMACY, Bishop Walters wrote that "had the Filipinos been white and fought as brave as they have, the war would have ended and their independence granted a long time ago." Although Du Bois in the NAACP's *Crisis Magazine* called for blacks to "Close Ranks" in full support of World War I, his position was denounced by William Monroe Trotter and A. PHILIP RANDOLPH, who exposed the hypocrisy of a nation fighting to "make the world safe for democracy" while practicing RACISM, JIM CROW, and SEGREGATION at home. ELIJAH MUHAMMAD expressed sympathy for the Japanese and was jailed for refusing to submit to the draft, but most black leaders did close ranks during World War II because they viewed fascism as a global manifestation of racism and white supremacy. Black support for the United States in World War II was enhanced when Italy invaded Ethiopia, which then was one of only two independent African nations. The invasion of Ethiopia galvanized the foreign-policy involvement of the BLACK COMMUNITY more than any other event before or since. The entire black leadership was mobilized; the black MEDIA was scathing in its reporting and editorials; pro-Ethiopian demonstrations and protests were held in most major cities (sometimes leading to violent clashes between Italian and African Americans); and blacks boycotted Italian-made products and sent money and medical supplies to the Ethiopian resistance. The Ethiopian protests led directly to the formation of the COUNCIL ON AFRICAN AFFAIRS, the first national black lobby group on Africa. After the war, African-American leaders including Du Bois, WALTER WHITE, RALPH BUNCHE, and MARY MCLEOD BETHUNE were present at the founding of the United Nations, where they supported the UNIVERSAL DECLARATION OF HUMAN RIGHTS and an end to colonialism. Later, Du Bois and others expressed support for Third World solidarity at the BANDUNG CONFERENCE.

Although African-American leaders were at first opposed to the cold war, the pressures of MCCARTHYISM eventually led most mainstream black leaders to support it. However, others such as Du Bois and PAUL ROBESON became prominent cold war critics. And even those blacks who supported the cold war tried to use it as a weapon in the CIVIL RIGHTS MOVEMENT by arguing that racism and white supremacy at home undermined the struggle against COMMUNISM abroad. This view was echoed by Secretary of State Dean Acheson, who was quoted in the U.S. government's brief in *BROWN V. BOARD OF EDUCATION* as concluding that "racial discrimination in the United States remains a source of constant embarrassment to this government in the day-to-day conduct of its foreign relations, jeopardizing the effective maintenance of our moral leadership of the free and democratic nations of the world."

The leaders of SNCC as well as MALCOLM X, MUHAMMAD ALI, and MARTIN LUTHER KING JR. were in the forefront of the opposition to the VIETNAM WAR during the 1960s. Since Vietnam, the African-American leadership has opposed all of America's wars, including the invasions of Grenada and Panama, air attacks on Libya and Syria, and the war against the revolutionary government in Nicaragua. African-American leaders also opposed the Persian Gulf War in the early 1990s, with all except one member of the CONGRESSIONAL BLACK CAUCUS voting against it and JESSE JACKSON taking a leading role in an emergent peace movement. It appears that since the end of the Vietnam War and the cold war, black leaders as well as black PUBLIC OPINION have embraced a "Third World perspective" on foreign policy, leading to opposition to U.S. wars because they have tended to be waged against Third World peoples. Related to this perspective, black leaders continue to support the Palestinian cause in the Middle East conflict and opposed the boycott against communist Cuba. Whenever Fidel Castro, the Cuban leader, visited the United Nations in New York, he was always accorded a hero's welcome by the HARLEM community's religious, civic, and political leaders.

With the formation of TRANSAFRICA in 1977, African Americans created an institutionalized LOBBYING capability to influence U.S. foreign policy on African and Caribbean issues. Protest demonstrations and lobbying by TransAfrica led to the imposition of sanctions by the United States on the white supremacist and APARTHEID regimes in Rhodesia and South Africa, which contributed to their collapse. TransAfrica and the Congressional Black Caucus also pressured President BILL CLINTON to occupy Haiti in order to restore to office its elected president who had been overthrown in a military coup. And in the Clinton administration, blacks in Congress and in the bureaucracy were instrumental in developing a comprehensive U.S. foreign policy toward Africa, focusing on trade, democratization of the continent's scores of dictatorial regimes, and assistance in the fight against the AIDS-HIV pandemic. Because of the concern of blacks, Clinton became the first American president to make state visits to several African nations. He also appointed Jesse Jackson as his special ambassador on African affairs. Clinton administration Africa policy initiatives were continued by Secretary of State Powell in the George W. Bush administration.

Further reading: Erol Henderson, *AfroCentrism and World Politics* (Westport, Conn.: Praeger, 1995); Charles Henry, ed., *Foreign Policy and the Black International Interest* (Albany: State University of New York Press, 2000); Michael Krenn, *Black Diplomacy: African Americans and the State Department* (Armonk, N.Y.: M. E. Sharpe, 1998); Michael Krenn, *The African American Voice in U.S. Foreign Policy since World War II* (New York: Garland, 1999); Jake Miller, *The Black Presence in American Foreign Affairs* (Washington, D.C.: Howard University

Press, 1978); Plummer, Brenda Gayle, *Window on Freedom: Race, Civil Rights and U.S. Foreign Policy* (Chapel Hill: University of North Carolina Press, 2003); Elliot Skinner, *African Americans and U.S. Policy toward Africa, 1850–1924*, Vol. 1 (Washington, D.C.: Howard University Press, 1992).

forty acres and a mule

Forty acres and a mule is the earliest expression of the idea of REPARATIONS in the United States. After the CIVIL WAR, Senator CHARLES SUMNER and Congressman THADDEUS STEVENS proposed legislation to confiscate the lands of the slaveholders, divide them into small plots of land, and give them to the former slaves as compensation or reparations for SLAVERY and as a means to punish the slaveholders for treason. Although they did not specify the size of the plots (nor mention a mule), the idea of forty acres and a mule as reparations has its origins in this kind of idea as the economic basis for RECONSTRUCTION. The Sumner-Stevens bill was not passed by CONGRESS, but in an 1865 bill to reauthorize the FREEDMEN'S BUREAU, Congress included a provision granting blacks 40 acres of abandoned land in the SOUTHERN STATES. President ANDREW JOHNSON vetoed the bill, claiming that the 40-acres provision violated the DUE PROCESS CLAUSE of the CONSTITUTION because it deprived persons of their property without compensation or due process.

Although the bill was never passed by Congress, several thousand blacks did get some land after the Civil War as a result of General William Sherman's Field Order No. 15. In January 1865, Gen. Sherman issued special Field Order No. 15 setting aside 400,000 acres of land off the South Carolina coast for the exclusive settlement of blacks. Sherman's order specified that each family receive 40 acres and the loan of an army mule (which is probably where the phrase "forty acres and a mule" originates). As a result some 40,000 blacks were settled on more than 400,000 acres. However, more than half of this land was eventually restored to its owners, and thousands of black families were evicted. In the end, probably no more than 3,000 black families actually kept the land Sherman's order promised.

Fourteenth Amendment, U.S. Constitution

The Fourteenth Amendment was adopted in 1868 after the CIVIL WAR in order to secure the FREEDOM and EQUALITY of African Americans, especially in the SOUTHERN STATES. One of three amendments adopted during RECONSTRUCTION, it is by far the most revolutionary in terms of changing the structural basis of the CONSTITUTION. JOEL SPINGARN, a founder of the NAACP, called it the "noblest result" of the Civil War. The historians Fred Friendly and

Martha Elliot in *The Constitution: That Delicate Balance* wrote, "It was as if Congress had held a second constitutional convention and created a federal government of vastly expanded proportions," and the political scientists HANES WALTON JR. and Robert C. Smith, in their textbook *American Politics and the African American Quest for Universal Freedom,* describe the amendment as "The American Charter of Universal Freedom."

The amendment was approved by the CONGRESS in 1866 and was ratified by the necessary number of states in 1868 (ratification was a condition for the readmission of some Southern states to the Union). The amendment was very controversial, and the debate on it in the Congress and in the states was intense. Indeed, it might not have been approved if ratification had not been made a condition for the reentry of several states to the Union. Much of the opposition was based on RACISM and WHITE SUPREMACY, with critics in both the North and the South arguing that it guaranteed equality to the "inferior races," not just blacks but Native Americans and the Chinese. Opposition was also rooted in support for the principle of FEDERALISM, which opponents argued, correctly, the amendment undermined.

The Fourteenth Amendment, containing five sections, is one of the longest in the Constitution. Section 1, discussed in detail below, is by far the most important. Section 2 required that if black males (or any male except an Indian) were denied the right to vote, a state's representation in the House of Representatives would be reduced proportionately. This section was included because the THIRTEENTH AMENDMENT in effect repealed the THREE-FIFTHS CLAUSE, the result of which enhanced the representation of the Southern states in the House and in the ELECTORAL COLLEGE. But if these states denied the vote to blacks—as it was thought they might—then the result of freedom for the slaves would be to increase the POWER of their former masters. This section therefore was potentially very important as a means to guarantee black voting rights, but it was never enforced, leading two years later to adoption of the FIFTEENTH AMENDMENT explicitly prohibiting denial of VOTING RIGHTS to black men. However, even when this amendment was violated, Congress never used its power to reduce the representation of the Southern states in the House. Ironically, then, the Constitutional guarantee of voting rights for black men for almost 100 years increased the power of the white men who denied black men the right to vote. As late as 1966 the STUDENT NONVIOLENT COORDINATING COMMITTEE and the MISSISSIPPI FREEDOM DEMOCRATIC PARTY tried to use Section 2 to reduce the size of the Mississippi delegation to the House, but like all previous attempts, this effort was defeated.

Section 3 disqualified former leaders of the Confederacy from holding federal office. The purpose of this section was to punish these men for their treason in waging war against the United States, but this too was only enforced for a brief period of time. Section 4 absolved the U.S. government of the debts of the Confederacy, and Section 5 gave the Congress the authority to enforce the provisions of the amendment with "appropriate legislation."

Section 1 is divided into four clauses. The first confers CITIZENSHIP on all persons born or naturalized in the United States, thereby overturning the DRED SCOTT case, which had denied citizenship to blacks. The second clause prohibits the states from denying the "privileges and immunities" of U.S. citizenship to its citizens. This privileges and immunities clause is historically the most disputed part of the amendment. The dispute concerns whether it was intended to incorporate or nationalize the BILL OF RIGHTS, that is, whether its authors intended the privileges and immunities to mean those rights listed in the Bill of Rights. Although the two principal authors of the amendment (Representative Jonathan Bingham and Senator Jacob Howard) said during the debates that the clause would compel the states to comply with the Bill of Rights, there is still no agreement about this among scholars who have studied the history of the amendment's adoption and ratification. Some historians argue that it was *clearly* the intent of the clause to nationalize the Bill of Rights, while others are just as certain that this was not the clause's purpose. There are, as Professor William Nelson writes in *The Fourteenth Amendment: From Political Principle to Judicial Doctrine,* volumes of research to support each side, concluding that there is an "impasse in scholarship" on the issue. Thus, Professor Nelson concludes we do not know for sure, and perhaps never will, what was the intent of the privileges and immunities clause. The SUPREME COURT historically has also been divided on the intent of the clause. Immediately after its adoption, the Court took the view that it did not make the Bill of Rights applicable to the states. In the SLAUGHTERHOUSE CASES, the first heard by the Court under the Fourteenth Amendment, a majority of the justices rejected the argument that the clause incorporated the Bill of Rights. Although three justices dissented, this case in effect rendered the privileges and immunities clause a nullity.

The DUE PROCESS CLAUSE is the third clause in Section 1. While it can be read as simply restating the procedural fairness requirements of the Constitution's Fifth Amendment's due process clause, beginning in the early 20th century the Supreme Court used it instead of the privileges and immunities clause to nationalize the Bill of Rights.

The EQUAL PROTECTION CLAUSE is Section 1's final clause. This clause is the only part of the Constitution that explicitly commits the nation to equality. However, like the privileges and immunities clause, it was undermined by early Supreme Court cases interpreting it. In the CIVIL RIGHTS CASES OF 1883, the Court held that the clause only prohibited DISCRIMINATION by the states and not by private individuals or businesses. Thus, it could not be used to ban discrimination in public accommodations such as hotels or theaters. And in 1896 in *PLESSY V. FERGUSON,* the Court continued its narrow reading of the clause by declaring that racial SEGREGATION did not violate equal protection. The Court repudiated its *Plessy* interpretation of the clause in *BROWN V. BOARD OF EDUCATION* in 1954, but its ruling in the 1883 civil rights cases remains law, reaffirmed in 2000 by the Supreme Court in a case overturning the Violence Against Women's Act. At the end of the 20th century, the Supreme Court appeared to significantly narrow Congress's authority to enforce the clause. In addition to overturning the Violence Against Women's Act, in a 2001 case the Court, in a 5-4 judgment, declared in *Board of Trustees of the University of Alabama et al. v. Garrett et al.* a portion of the Americans with Disabilities Act unconstitutional.

The Fourteenth Amendment was enacted primarily to protect the rights of African Americans. In the slaughterhouse cases, Justice Samuel Miller said the amendment's one overriding purpose was to secure freedom for the blacks who had been previously oppressed by the whites, and Justice Edward White was even more emphatic in declaring that the amendment was so "clearly for that race . . . that a strong case would be necessary for its application to any other." In spite of this, however, the amendment has been used to secure the rights of *all* persons in the United States, including corporations defined by law as "artificial persons." (Until the NEW DEAL, the amendment's due process clause was used more frequently to protect the liberty of corporations than the freedom of black people.) This is because while the manifest purpose of the amendment was to protect the rights of black people, it is written in classical LIBERALISM's language of INDIVIDUALISM, of "persons" rather than groups. Thus, it is the great charter of universal freedom. But, ironically, this means that an amendment put in the Constitution because of the presence of blacks and to protect their interests can be used to undermine those very interests that led to its adoption in the first place.

See also AFFIRMATIVE ACTION and *SHAW V. RENO.*

Further reading: William Nelson, *The Fourteenth Amendment: From Political Principle to Judicial Doctrine* (Cambridge, Mass.: Harvard University Press, 1988).

Franklin, John Hope (1915–   ) *scholar*

John Hope Franklin is frequently referred to as the "Dean of African-American historians." His seminal *From Slavery to Freedom: A History of Negro Americans,* first published in 1948, is now a classic and is considered the standard work on the subject.

Born in Tulsa, Oklahoma, Franklin was graduated from Fisk University in 1935, one of the HISTORICALLY BLACK COLLEGES AND UNIVERSITIES, and received his Ph.D. from Harvard in 1941. After teaching at HOWARD UNIVERSITY and other places, in 1956 he became the first African American to head a history department at a white university, first at Brooklyn College and then at the University of Chicago. Franklin was also the first African-American president of the American Historical Association. He conducted research for the NAACP on the origins and purposes of the FOURTEENTH AMENDMENT for use in its brief in *BROWN V. BOARD OF EDUCATION*. In addition to *From Slavery to Freedom,* Franklin authored many other books on black history. In 1997 Franklin headed a presidential advisory board appointed by BILL CLINTON to study race and ethnic relations in the United States. Although acknowledging that MULTICULTURALISM was an increasing force in America, Franklin insisted that race—the black-white dynamic—was still the central cleavage in America and likely always would be.

Freedmen's Bureau

The Bureau of Refugees, Freedmen and Abandoned Lands, better known as the Freedmen's Bureau, was established in 1865 and was the first social-welfare BUREAUCRACY established by the U.S. government. Advocated by the RADICAL REPUBLICANS in CONGRESS at the end of the CIVIL WAR, its purposes were to address problems of the refugees displaced by the war; to provide social, educational, and medical benefits to the newly freed slaves; to provide for their settlement and cultivation of abandoned lands; and to make sure they received fair wages for their work. The bill creating the bureau was opposed by conservative Republicans and Southern Democrats who saw it as an unconstitutional violation of the principle of FEDERALISM, and as unwise PUBLIC POLICY because the provision of social welfare violated the principle of INDIVIDUALISM. But, with the support of ABRAHAM LINCOLN, the bureau was created as a temporary, one-year agency within the War Department. However, it was given no public funds, having to rely instead on donations and monies from the rent of abandoned lands it controlled in the SOUTHERN STATES. President Lincoln selected Gen. Oliver O. Howard (for whom HOWARD UNIVERSITY is named) to head the bureau, but before he could make the appointment, Lincoln was killed. ANDREW JOHNSON, who was bitterly opposed to the bureau, appointed Howard but then sought to eliminate the bureau after its first year. President Johnson vetoed the first effort to extend the life of the bureau, but after a long and bitter struggle the Congress overrode his veto and extended the bureau for six years.

Although it was never adequately funded or staffed, historians agree that the bureau in its seven years of operation did a good job of relieving suffering among both blacks and whites in the immediate aftermath of the war. It distributed millions of dollars in food rations, established an extensive hospital system, and in what was perhaps its greatest achievement, established or supported a network of schools and universities, including Howard and ATLANTA UNIVERSITIES. The bureau also tried to distribute abandoned lands to freedmen in 40-acre plots that they could lease and eventually buy (see FORTY ACRES AND A MULE). But President Johnson blocked most of these efforts, even forcing the return of some land leased to former slaves. Thus, blacks were denied the opportunity to become small farmers and forced to return to work for their former owners as sharecroppers. The bureau then tried to regulate this system of labor and assure fair wages. However, in its short life it was not able to prevent the entrenchment of a system of sharecropping that was almost as exploitative of black labor as was slavery. (This system lasted in many of the Southern states until the 1950s.) Yet, as a result of the bureau's efforts, thousands of blacks did become landowners. Thus, the bureau's work was not a complete failure, especially when one takes into account its brief existence and the powerful opposition to its plans to redistribute land.

Despite efforts by the Radical Republicans in Congress to extend the life of the bureau, it was dissolved in 1872. As a social-welfare agency serving mainly African Americans, the bureau was never popular, and since it challenged principles of federalism, individualism, and CAPITALISM (through its efforts to assure fair wages and working conditions for plantation labor, it interfered with employer-employee relations), it was relatively easy for its opponents to kill the agency. Critics also charged the bureau with corruption, inefficiency, and racial favoritism. It was also argued that the bureau's programs made blacks dependent on handouts and thus undermined individual initiative and SELF-HELP. These charges against the Freedmen's Bureau in the 1860s were similar to charges raised against the GREAT SOCIETY's welfare programs during the 1960s, especially those targeted to help African Americans.

freedom

Freedom and EQUALITY are the fundamental aims of AFRICAN-AMERICAN POLITICS. Freedom is also an important theme in AFRICAN-AMERICAN THOUGHT. For example, one of the earliest published works in black thought is an essay by Robert Young published in 1829 called "The Ethiopian Manifesto Issued in Defense of the Blackman's Rights in the Scale of Universal Freedom." The idea and the ethos of freedom are also rooted in black CULTURE as it is expressed in RELIGIOSITY and MUSIC. C. Eric Lincoln and Lawrence Mamiya in their *The Black Church in the African American Experience* write, "A major aspect of black Christian belief is found in the importance given to the word 'freedom.' Throughout black history the term 'freedom' has found deep religious resonance in the lives and hopes of African Americans. . . . In song, word and deed freedom has always been the superlative value of the black cosmos." As Lincoln and Mamiya suggest, freedom has been a recurring theme in black music in spirituals, jazz, and rhythm and blues. In the 1960s, "Freedom Songs"—a type of music related to but different from spirituals, blues, or traditional protest songs—became an important part of the CIVIL RIGHTS MOVEMENT. The Civil Rights movement along with the ABOLITIONIST MOVEMENT are two of the most important freedom movements in the history of the United States. Both of these movements involved COALITIONS with whites, and while they were movements mainly for the freedom of blacks, their outcomes expanded freedom for all Americans, leading the historian HERBERT APTHEKER to write, "The Negro people have fought like tigers for freedom, and in doing so have enhanced the freedom struggles of all other people." It is one of the ironies of American history that while the slaveholding American founders eloquently articulated the idea of freedom, it has been the enslaved Africans and their descendants who have fought most militantly to make the idea a reality.

However, it must not be overlooked, as JOHN HOPE FRANKLIN has written, "that the concept of freedom that emerged bordered on licentiousness . . . it was a freedom to destroy freedom, the freedom of some to exploit the rights of others. It was, indeed, a concept with little or no social responsibility. If, then, a man was determined to be free, who was there to tell him that he was not entitled to enslave others." This bastardized notion of freedom has always been rejected in African-American thought and politics. Instead, African Americans have always had a vision of what the political scientists HANES WALTON JR. and Robert C. Smith refer to as "Universal freedom." This universal vision obviously rejects the freedom to enslave (more precisely the POWER to enslave) because African-American thought and politics have their origins in the struggle against SLAVERY.

The first component of the African-American vision of universal freedom is rooted in NATURAL RIGHTS, those rights or freedoms inherent in one's humanity, or what THOMAS JEFFERSON referred to in the DECLARATION OF INDEPENDENCE as life, liberty, and the pursuit of happiness. The vision also encompasses *personal freedom,* the rights of individuals to do as they wish within the limits of others to do the same or to the extent it does not interfere with the freedom of others. The vision also includes CIVIL RIGHTS, which encompasses NONDISCRIMINATION and equal treatment under the law. It also includes civic or *political freedom,* encompassing the right to vote and participate fully in governing the society. Universal freedom also includes *social freedom,* involving the right to choose one's own personal, religious, and fraternal associates. Finally, the African-American vision of universal freedom includes a vision of economic freedom involving the right of access to education, health care, employment, and housing (see EQUALITY and HUMAN RIGHTS).

From the early writings of Robert Young to the writings of W. E. B. DU BOIS and from the speeches of FREDERICK DOUGLASS to those of MARTIN LUTHER KING JR., one finds the idea of freedom as a recurring theme. Freedom, however, is ultimately linked to power. That is, the more power a group possesses, the more capable it is of achieving freedom for itself or denying it to others. And since African Americans are and always have been a relatively powerless group, their vision of universal freedom has in practice been limited by the superior power of whites.

Further reading: Richard King, *Civil Rights and the Idea of Freedom* (New York: Oxford University Press, 1992); Orlando Patterson, "The Unholy Trinity: Freedom, Slavery and the American Constitution," *Social Research* 54 (1987): 556–59; Hanes Walton Jr. and Robert C. Smith, *American Politics and the African American Quest for Universal Freedom* (New York: Longman, 2000).

Freedom Rides

The Freedom Rides—along with the SIT-INS, the 1963 MARCH ON WASHINGTON, the BIRMINGHAM DEMONSTRATIONS, and the SELMA DEMONSTRATIONS—are among the pivotal PROTEST events of the CIVIL RIGHTS MOVEMENT. The Freedom Rides involved black and white activists riding buses together in the SOUTHERN STATES in order to protest SEGREGATION on interstate buses and bus terminals. Although the SUPREME COURT as early as 1946 had outlawed segregation on buses traveling across state lines, black travelers in the Southern states were in 1961 still required to sit at the back of the bus and use separate ticket counters, waiting rooms, restaurants and restrooms. Thus in May 1961, CORE (CONGRESS OF RACIAL EQUALITY), under the leadership of JAMES FARMER, decided to send an interracial group of riders on buses starting in the DISTRICT OF COLUMBIA and ending in New Orleans. At several cities in Mississippi and Alabama, the riders were attacked by white mobs who brutally beat them using chains and baseball bats. On one ride, the bus itself was burned. When members of CORE could not continue the rides because of the beatings or because they were jailed, SNCC (STUDENT NONVIOLENT COORDINATING COMMITTEE) sent a group of riders who were also beaten and jailed.

Freedom Riders, sponsored by the Congress of Racial Equality, gather outside a burning bus in Anniston, Alabama, 1961. *(Library of Congress)*

This VIOLENCE led to condemnation of the United States throughout the world, forcing President JOHN F. KENNEDY to send U.S. marshals to protect the riders. On December 1, 1961, under pressure from the president, the Interstate Commerce Commission ordered an end to all segregation on interstate buses and bus terminals. Such segregation continued, however, in many parts of the South until the middle of the 1960s. But the Freedom Rides are important because they were part of the mounting pressures that eventually resulted in passage of the CIVIL RIGHTS ACT OF 1964.

free Negroes

Free Negroes is the term used during SLAVERY to refer to African Americans who were not enslaved. Although these persons were not slaves, they also were not fully free, since everywhere they lived their FREEDOM was abridged or limited. At the time of the first CENSUS in 1790 there were 750,000 blacks in the United States (19 percent of the population), and 59,000 or 9 percent of blacks were not enslaved. Some of these persons were "free" because they had never been enslaved, others because they had purchased their freedom, while still others had escaped from slavery or had been freed by their owners. By 1860 there were about 500,000 blacks who were not slaves, out of a population of about 4 million Africans. They generally lived in urban areas of both the North and the South. The restrictions on their freedom were greater of course in the SOUTHERN STATES, but even in the NORTHERN STATES they were generally denied the vote and were excluded from public accommodations and from the full range of occupations. Aside from DISCRIMINATION, they faced the ever-present danger of being kidnapped and sold into slavery, a danger that became especially acute after CONGRESS passed the Fugitive Slave Act in 1850.

Although not fully free, the blacks who were not slaves clearly had greater social and economic opportunities than the enslaved, and they used these opportunities to build the infrastructure of the BLACK COMMUNITY, including religious, educational, SELF-HELP, business, cultural, and MEDIA institutions. From this group a tiny middle class emerged, as did the black LEADERSHIP of the ABOLITIONIST MOVEMENT.

fugitive slave clause, U.S. Constitution

Article IV, Section 2 of the CONSTITUTION is the fugitive slave clause. It required that the nonslave NORTHERN STATES return escaped or "fugitive" slaves to their bondage in the slaveholding SOUTHERN STATES. This constitutional protection for SLAVERY was a compromise, since the initial draft of the clause was much harsher, requiring that escaped slaves be held as criminals. Although the clause was in the Constitution, it did not prevent blacks from escaping enslavement, as in the famous Underground Railroad organized by HARRIET TUBMAN. Therefore, in 1850 Congress passed the Fugitive Slave Act requiring the states of the North not only to return but to actively seek out and capture escaped slaves. This law dramatically escalated conflict over slavery because it led to the development and growth of slave catching as a business. As slave catchers roamed the North looking for alleged escapees, the FREEDOM of the FREE NEGROES was jeopardized, as many were falsely accused of being slaves. This was one of the factors leading to the call of the first NATIONAL NEGRO CONVENTION (to consider proposals for emigration to Canada). It also resulted in increased MILITANCY in the ABOLITIONIST MOVEMENT.

Full Employment and Balanced Growth Act of 1978

The Full Employment and Balanced Growth Act of 1978 is the official title of the HUMPHREY-HAWKINS ACT.

See also FULL EMPLOYMENT, AUGUSTUS HAWKINS, and HUBERT HUMPHREY.

full employment

Full employment is the concept that PUBLIC POLICY in the United States should require the government to see to it that all adults willing, able, and seeking employment should be guaranteed a job at a reasonable wage. The idea, which has its origins in the NEW DEAL, requires that the government manage the economy in such a way that private businesses will produce full employment, but if this was not possible then the government itself would act as the "employer of last resort." Technically, full employment is defined as an economy where there are always more jobs at fair wages than there are unemployed persons who can be expected to take them. In practice, however, it has always been defined by policy makers in the United States as some arbitrary level of unemployment—in the post–World War II era usually a 4

percent unemployment rate. Since African Americans have always been more likely to face unemployment than whites (since World War II, black joblessness has generally been twice the rate of whites), full-employment policies have been strongly supported by the black LEADERSHIP and by black PUBLIC OPINION. During the New Deal, the NAACP and the URBAN LEAGUE supported full employment, as did leaders such as A. PHILIP RANDOLPH and RALPH BUNCHE. In the POST–CIVIL RIGHTS ERA, full employment became the priority item on the BLACK AGENDA, supported by all the major black interest groups and the CONGRESSIONAL BLACK CAUCUS. It was also advocated by leading black intellectuals such as BAYARD RUSTIN, CHARLES HAMILTON, and WILLIAM J. WILSON. At the time of his death in 1968, MARTIN LUTHER KING JR. was planning to lead the POOR PEOPLES CAMPAIGN, one of whose major objectives was a federal law guaranteeing full employment. And in the 1970s African-American congressman AUGUSTUS HAWKINS was the principal author and cosponsor with HUBERT HUMPHREY of the HUMPHREY-HAWKINS ACT, legislation enacted by CONGRESS in 1978 that was supposed to guarantee full employment.

While full employment has been on the black agenda in the United States since the New Deal, most economists contend that it is not possible to have full employment under CAPITALISM. Thus, whenever the issue has been debated in Congress, it has been attacked, defeated, or undermined by critics labeling it as SOCIALISM. After World War II Congress enacted the Employment Act of 1946 (after deleting the word "full" from the title), and in 1978 it enacted the FULL EMPLOYMENT AND BALANCED GROWTH ACT. Both of these acts, however, were symbolic gestures because by the time they were passed, they had been so watered down that they could have little impact on creating jobs for the jobless.

Fullilove v. Klutznick (1980)

Fullilove v. Klutznick is one of the early SUPREME COURT decisions upholding the principles of AFFIRMATIVE ACTION in the awarding of government contracts to minority-owned businesses. In 1977 CONGRESS required that 10 percent of federal funds used in local public works projects be set aside for the purchase of goods or services from minority-owned businesses. Fullilove, a white-owned business, sued arguing that the 10 percent set-aside violated the DUE PROCESS CLAUSE of the Fifth Amendment. The Supreme Court in a six-to-three judgment upheld the set-asides, holding that it was a reasonable and limited use of RACE and ETHNICITY to achieve the Congress's "compelling interest" in eradicating the continuing effects of RACISM or past DISCRIMINATION in the awarding of federal contracts. The Court held that Congress's authority under the COMMERCE CLAUSE or Section 5 of the FOURTEENTH AMEND-

MENT was an ample basis in the CONSTITUTION for it to establish affirmative action set-asides. The dissenting justices concluded that set-aside programs were unconstitutional because racial classifications were too "pernicious" to permit their use except under the most exacting circumstances where there was a direct connection between the discrimination and the remedy.

Fullilove is an important case because it established the precedent for the constitutional legitimacy of affirmative action in the economy. It subsequently became the model for similar federal programs in STATE AND LOCAL GOVERNMENT. These precedents, however, were virtually overturned a decade later in CITY OF RICHMOND V. CROSON and ADARAND V. PENA.

G

gag rule

In 1837 the DEMOCRATIC PARTY in CONGRESS secured passage of the following resolution: "All petitions, memorials, resolutions or papers relating in any way or to any extent to the subject of slavery shall, without either being printed or referred, be laid on the table and that no further action whatever shall be had thereon." This gag rule effectively forbade members of the House of Representatives from discussing the issue of SLAVERY, under penalty of censure. As the ABOLITIONIST MOVEMENT led by WILLIAM LLOYD GARRISON gained strength, the number of petitions or "prayers" to Congress to ban slavery increased, resulting in various efforts at POLITICAL REPRESSION. In addition to the gag rule, postmasters were urged to monitor the mail and censor or remove abolitionist or other antislavery material. These efforts at repression of the antislavery movement intensified after NAT TURNER's bloody slave revolt in 1831. It was in the context of this increasing MILITANCY of antislavery forces that Congressman James Hammond of South Carolina proposed the gag rule. Hammond argued that since slavery was protected by the CONSTITUTION, the receipt of petitions for its abolition violated the rights of slaveholders and provided tactical support to the abolitionists. Opponents of the rule, led by former President JOHN Q. ADAMS, now a member of the House, argued that the rule not only violated the rights of enslaved persons but the free speech and petition rights of all Americans that are contained in the First Amendment of the BILL OF RIGHTS. In 1844, largely on the strength of Adams's work, the gag rule was revoked, as Northern Democrats broke ranks with their Southern counterparts and joined the Whig Party in voting against the rule. Although relatively short-lived, the gag rule was the forerunner of much more sophisticated efforts at political repression of African-American movements for FREEDOM and EQUALITY.

See also COINTELPRO, FBI, J. EDGAR HOOVER, POLITICAL REPRESSION.

Garnett, Henry Highland (1815–1881) *abolitionist, clergyman, and diplomat*

Henry Highland Garnett was an important African-American leader of the ABOLITIONIST MOVEMENT, probably the most important black leader in the movement after FREDERICK DOUGLASS. Indeed, Garnett and Douglass, in their different styles of abolitionist leadership during the 1840s, established patterns that defined and structured the character of LEADERSHIP in black America until the end of the 20th century. Douglass represented the moderate style or type of leadership, one that relies on COALITIONS with whites, morality, CONSTITUTIONALISM, nonviolent PROTEST, and voting and elections. This style of leadership was subsequently followed by W. E. B. DU BOIS, MARTIN LUTHER KING JR., and JESSE JACKSON. Garnett on the other hand represents MILITANCY as a leadership style or type, contending that the victims of OPPRESSION must free themselves "by any means necessary," including VIOLENCE. Garnett's style of leadership was subsequently followed by MALCOLM X, STOKELY CARMICHAEL, HUEY NEWTON, and BOBBY SEALE. Douglass's leadership also foreshadowed the IDEOLOGY of INTEGRATION that characterized the leadership of Du Bois, King, and Jesse Jackson, while Garnett's leadership characterizes the philosophy of BLACK NATIONALISM seen in the leadership of MARCUS GARVEY, Malcolm X, and Stokely Carmichael.

Garnett was born in 1815 in Maryland. At the age of nine he and his father escaped from SLAVERY and moved to New York City. He attended several schools in the city and became a close friend and colleague of ALEXANDER CRUMMELL and other young black activists. As a young man he became active in the abolitionist movement and remained active even after he became an ordained minister and pastor of a BLACK CHURCH in Troy, New York. Garnett is most famous for his 1843 "Address to the Slaves of the United States" delivered at a meeting of the NATIONAL NEGRO CONVENTION in Buffalo, New York. In this address, which anticipates the logic and rhetoric of Malcolm X's 1964 "BAL-

LOT OR THE BULLET" SPEECH, Garnett called for a general strike by the slaves as a means to overthrow the institution, and if this failed, he advocated armed rebellion. In preparing the address, Garnett was influenced by his study of DAVID WALKER's 1829 "Appeal to the Citizens of the Colored World," a powerful black nationalist manifesto that also called for SLAVE REVOLTS. (Garnett was so impressed by Walker's life and work that he visited Walker's widow in Boston in 1848 and republished the "Appeal" along with his own "Address to the Slaves" in a single volume.)

In his "Address to the Slaves," Garnett said, "You had better all die—*die immediately,* than live as slaves and entail your wretchedness upon your posterity. If you would be free in this generation, here is your only hope. . . . But, you are a patient people, you act as though you were made for the special use of these devils. . . . Brethren, arise, arise! Strike for your lives and liberties. Let your motto be resistance! Resistance! Resistance!" Garnett had wished his address to be adopted as the official manifesto of the convention, and it came within one vote of adoption. Only the strong opposition of Douglass, who argued that "moral suasion" should be given a little more time, led to its rejection. The rejection of the address at the convention by a single vote indicated, however, the extent of RADICALISM and militancy among black leaders and brought pressure on Douglass to move in a more militant direction.

Although his address was rejected, Garnett had nevertheless planned to go into the SOUTHERN STATES to foment rebellion, but his health would not permit it. (One of his legs had been amputated.) In addition to his advocacy of militancy and violence, Garnett was active in BACK-TO-AFRICA MOVEMENTS, favoring the emigration of blacks to Africa and the establishment of independent African nations. After the CIVIL WAR Garnett worked briefly in the FREEDMEN'S BUREAU, and in 1865 he became the first black clergyman to deliver a sermon to members of CONGRESS. In 1881 he was appointed minister to LIBERIA. A year later he died and was buried there.

Further reading: Earl Ofari Hutchinson, *Let Your Motto Be Resistance: The Life and Thought of Henry Highland Garnett* (Boston: Beacon Press, 1972).

Garrison, William Lloyd (1805–1879) *abolitionist*

William Lloyd Garrison, a deeply religious man, was the preeminent leader of the ABOLITIONIST MOVEMENT. A white man born in 1805 in Massachusetts, Garrison was a printer by trade but in 1829 he joined the struggle against SLAVERY by becoming a partner in the publication of a Baltimore antislavery newspaper. Garrison employed morality and religion as bases of power in the struggle against slavery. Believing that slavery was morally wrong and a viola-

tion of Christian teachings, Garrison was also a pacifist who believed that slavery should only be ended by "moral suasion." He therefore opposed VIOLENCE as well as voting in elections.

Early in his career his agitation against slavery led a slave trader to sue him for libel. Found guilty and unable to pay the fine, Garrison was jailed. After his release from prison, he moved from Baltimore to Boston, where in 1831 he established *The Liberator,* the most influential of antislavery newspapers. A year later he organized the New England Anti-Slavery Society and played a leading role in organizing the American Anti-Slavery Society, which he was president of from 1843 until the end of the CIVIL WAR.

In the history of the African-American struggle for FREEDOM and EQUALITY there have always been some whites so deeply committed to the cause that in a sense they became "black." JOHN BROWN was one such person, CHARLES SUMNER was another, and so was Garrison. A sense of Garrison's MILITANCY can be seen in the following quote from the first issue of *The Liberator:* "Let southern oppressors tremble . . . let northern apologists tremble, let all enemies of the persecuted blacks tremble. . . . urge me not to use moderation in a cause like the present. I am in earnest—I will not equivocate—I will not excuse—and I will be heard!" Rhetoric of this kind in Garrison's writing and lectures led to numerous assassination attempts, and the state of Georgia posted a $500 bounty for his arrest and conviction. As the recognized leader of the abolitionist movement, Garrison was "all on fire" in his passion for his ideas, and therefore he was often a source of dissension within the movement. At a time when SEXISM was the order of the day, Garrison embraced FEMINISM and urged equal participation for women in the movement and society generally. Garrison was also convinced that the CONSTITUTION was an immoral, proslavery document and therefore that it was immoral to participate in elections established by it. In 1848 he publicly burned the Constitution, describing it as a "covenant with death and an agreement with hell." This view of the Constitution resulted in conflict with FREDERICK DOUGLASS, the preeminent African-American leader, who argued that the Constitution was not inherently proslavery. Garrison and Douglass also clashed over the organization of the all-black NATIONAL NEGRO CONVENTION, which Garrison opposed because of his belief in INTEGRATION and because he thought the convention undermined the solidarity of the abolitionist movement. Seeing little possibility of ending slavery in the SOUTHERN STATES, Garrison eventually proposed the secession of the nonslave states, using as his motto "no union with slaveholders." This position also caused divisions within the movement, but when ABRAHAM LINCOLN was elected president, Garrison ceased to advocate separation and instead urged that the Civil War be fought to free the slaves as well as maintain the Union. With the issuing of the EMANCIPATION PROCLAMATION and the adoption of the THIRTEENTH AMENDMENT, Garrison said that his work was done. He immediately ceased publication of *The Liberator* and urged abolition of the antislavery societies. However, he continued his activism in other reform causes, including Indian rights, women's suffrage, and efforts to prohibit the sale of alcohol and tobacco. He died in New York City in 1879.

Further reading: Henry Mayer, *All on Fire: William Lloyd Garrison and the Abolition of Slavery* (New York: St. Martin's Press, 1998).

Garvey, Marcus M. (1887–1940) *nationalist leader*
Marcus Moziah Garvey is one of the most influential leaders of African peoples in the history of the world. In a 2000 poll of African-American political scientists, Garvey ranked fifth on a list of the 12 greatest African-American leaders of all time. Garvey is important as a leader for several reasons. The first is his contribution to the philosophy, cosmology, and practice of BLACK NATIONALISM. Garvey's black nationalism is rooted in the tradition and work of EDWARD WILMOT BLYDEN, HENRY HIGHLAND GARNETT, MARTIN DELANY, and HENRY M. TURNER, but Garvey made distinctive philosophical and practical contributions in his own right. Garvey is also important because of his distinctive contributions to PAN-AFRICANISM. His contributions to Pan-Africanism are rooted in the work of others, but he also made unique contributions. Garvey's contributions to black nationalism and Pan-Africanism are unique because, unlike the contributions of others to these traditions in AFRICAN-AMERICAN THOUGHT, Garvey not only contributed intellectually but organizationally, establishing an international organization that at its peak was the largest ORGANIZATION in the African world. Garvey's influence as an African-American leader is reflected in the development of the NATION OF ISLAM and the BLACK POWER MOVEMENT, and in the IDEOLOGY and styles of leadership of ELIJAH MUHAMMAD, MALCOLM X, STOKELY CARMICHAEL, and LOUIS FARRAKHAN. (The Rastafarian movement in Jamaica is also rooted in Garvey's philosophy.)

Garvey was born in 1887 on the WEST INDIAN island of Jamaica. After leaving school at the age of 14, he moved briefly to Costa Rica and subsequently traveled and worked throughout Central America and Europe. In 1913 he settled in England, attended classes at the University of London, and became associated with Duse Muhammad Ali, a black nationalist who edited a Pan-Africanist journal. In 1914 Garvey boarded a ship to return to Jamaica. On the voyage he claimed he encountered a passenger returning from missionary work in Africa who, in graphic detail, described the abuse of Africans by the Europeans who lived there. As a result of this conversation, Garvey claimed that he had a vision that led him to organize the UNIVERSAL NEGRO IMPROVEMENT ASSOCIATION (UNIA). In the vision Garvey claimed:

> I asked "where is the black man's government?" "Where is his king and his kingdom?" "Where is his president, his country, and his ambassador, his army, his navy, his men of big affairs?" I could not find them. . . . My brain was afire. There was a world of thought to conquer. . . . All day and the following night I pondered over the subject matter of that conversation, and at midnight, lying flat on my back, the vision and thought came to me that I should name the organization the Universal Negro Improvement Association and African Communities (Imperial) League. Such a name I thought could embrace the purpose of all black humanity.

Back home in Jamaica he started UNIA, based on the philosophy of SELF-HELP and industrial education then being advocated by BOOKER T. WASHINGTON in the United States (Garvey had been influenced by reading Washington's autobiography, *Up from Slavery*). In 1916 he traveled to the United States hoping to visit Washington's TUSKEGEE INSTITUTE, lecture, and raise money for UNIA. Settling in HARLEM, Garvey became well known for his street-corner speeches. Ironically his first formal speech was arranged by A. PHILIP RANDOLPH, who later became one of his most outspoken adversaries. Garvey quickly developed a following and in 1918 established UNIA's headquarters in Harlem. There he developed his brand of black nationalism, focusing on core principles of BLACKNESS, pride in black heritage and culture, opposition to European COLONIALISM in Africa, and a BACK-TO-AFRICA movement with the long-term goal of establishing a United States of Africa under his leadership. His charisma and organizing skills led to the UNIA's rapid growth. Within a year it had chapters throughout the United States, as well as in 22 countries in Latin America, the Caribbean, England, Canada, and West Africa. By 1920 its membership was estimated in the millions, and the UNIA included farms, factories, a quasi-military structure, independent educational institutions, the Universal African Orthodox Church, and perhaps most importantly, the Black Star Steamship Line. Garvey's weekly newspaper, *The Negro World,* for a time became the most widely read publication among African peoples in the world. In August 1920 more than 25,000 people gathered in New York's Madison Square Garden for the UNIA's first convention. The convention adopted a "Declaration of Rights of the Negro Peoples of the World," an anthem, a flag (red, black, and green), and elected Garvey president-general of UNIA and provisional president of Africa. A UNIA delegation was dispatched to LIBERIA to develop plans for the emigration of its members.

The rapid emergence of UNIA as the largest Pan-African organization in the world and Garvey's charismatic leadership of it alarmed authorities in both the United States and England, as well as established African-American leaders and organizations including W. E. B. DU BOIS and the NAACP and A. Philip Randolph. Garvey was also involved in factional disputes with the militant AFRICAN BLOOD BROTH-ERHOOD. American authorities were alarmed because of fears that the size of Garvey's following and the UNIA's MIL-ITANCY might pose a threat to the stability of the POLITICAL SYSTEM. British authorities were concerned that the spread of his ideas about the liberation of Africa from European colonial rule might threaten their hold on their African colonies. (Garvey popularized the slogan "Africa for the Africans.") As a result, Garvey and the UNIA were among the first targets of POLITICAL REPRESSION by J. EDGAR HOOVER and the FBI. Garvey's ideas and his popularity alarmed mainstream African-American leaders because they posed a threat to the hegemony of INTEGRATION in the BLACK COMMUNITY, threatened to siphon off support from their organizations, and because Garvey was viewed by many of these TALENTED TENTH leaders as an unlettered demagogue who exploited the vulnerabilities of the masses of blacks hungry for any program that gave promise of relieving their OPPRESSION. Du Bois and Garvey became particularly bitter adversaries, attacking each other on ideological grounds as well as on petty matters such as each other's skin color (Garvey was dark, Du Bois light) and Garvey's ETHNICITY. (Du Bois claimed that a recent immigrant of West Indian origins could not understand the problems of native-born blacks.) These established black leaders also viewed Garvey's grandiose plans for the unification of all of Africa under his leadership as utter fantasy; but the proverbial straw that broke the camel's back was Garvey's meeting with—and attempting to form an alliance with—the grand dragon of the KU KLUX KLAN.

Eventually these forces—British imperialism, the FBI, and African-American leaders—joined to destroy Garvey and the UNIA. Garvey, however, contributed to the destruction through his authoritarian, arrogant, egotistical, and often incompetent leadership. In 1921 the United States indicted him and several of his associates on charges of mail fraud in connection with the sale of stock in the Black Star Steamship Line. His associates were found not guilty, but Garvey was convicted and given the maximum sentence of five years in prison. The actual conviction was for using the U.S. mails to defraud one man of a mere $25. Garvey's second wife, Amy Jacques Garvey, and UNIA members immediately started a petition campaign to secure his release. After serving two years he was granted a presidential pardon, but a condition of the pardon was his

Marcus Garvey *(Library of Congress)*

immediate deportation from the United States. Upon returning to Jamaica, Garvey attempted to continue UNIA's work but found it difficult in the relative isolation of his homeland. He subsequently ran for office in Jamaica and briefly published two magazines. In 1933 he moved to London, where he attempted to revive UNIA, but again he met with little success. In 1940 he had a stroke and died at age 53, having never set foot on the African continent he had sought to liberate and lead.

Further reading: Edmund Croson, *Black Moses: The Story of Marcus Garvey and the Universal Negro Improvement Association* (Madison: University of Wisconsin Press, 1969); Amy Jacques Garvey and E. U. Essien-Odom, *The Philosophy and Opinions of Marcus Garvey* (London: CASS, 1977); Tony Martin, *The Ideological and Organizational Struggles of Marcus Garvey and the Universal Negro Improvement Association* (Westport, Conn.: Greenwood Press, 1976).

gay rights movement

The SOCIAL MOVEMENT for gay rights in the United States—the abolition of DISCRIMINATION based on sexual preference or orientation—has some parallels with the African-American CIVIL RIGHTS MOVEMENT and the BLACK POWER MOVEMENT. Despite these parallels, the gay rights movement historically has not had widespread support in the BLACK COMMUNITY; African-American gays and lesbians were not active in the movement until the 1990s. The lack of support for gay rights is rooted in the community's RELIGIOSITY and cultural traditions and in the skepticism or opposition of many African Americans to the efforts by gay and lesbian activists to compare discrimination on the basis of sexuality to the OPPRESSION of blacks on the basis of RACE.

Despite the traditional cultural and religious taboo against homosexuality in the black community, several of the leading figures in the HARLEM RENAISSANCE were homosexual or bisexual, as was JAMES BALDWIN, the literary interpreter of the Civil Rights movement, and BAYARD RUSTIN, the movement's principal strategist. However, MARTIN LUTHER KING JR. and the SOUTHERN CHRISTIAN LEADERSHIP CONFERENCE had strained relations with Baldwin and Rustin because of their acknowledged homosexuality, and ROY WILKINS and the NAACP prevented Baldwin from speaking at the 1963 MARCH ON WASHINGTON and stopped Rustin, who had planned the march, from holding the formal title of march director. Yet the gay rights movement parallels the Civil Rights movement and the Black Power movement, both of which served as inspirations and models for the gay rights movement that emerged in the late 1960s and 1970s. African-American gays were participants in the so-called Stonewall Rebellion in New York City in 1969, which, like the MONTGOMERY BUS BOYCOTT and the Civil Rights movement, is often seen as the starting point of the modern gay rights movement. (Stonewall refers to a near-riotous rebellion by gays in response to police harassment at the Stonewall Inn in Greenwich Village in New York City.) In spite of these parallels, during the 1960s the BLACK PANTHER PARTY was the only major black organization to support homosexual rights, while they were strongly opposed by the leaders of the BLACK CHURCH, the major civil rights organizations, and the NATION OF ISLAM.

In the 1980s and 1990s, black gays and lesbians formed several national organizations and became more visible and vigorous in advancing the parallels between racism and heterosexism. The AIDS-HIV epidemic among African Americans reinforced this activism. Increasingly, black advocates of RADICALISM and FEMINISM in the 1980s embraced gay rights, as in the writings of ANGELA DAVIS and the manifesto of the BLACK RADICAL CONGRESS, which declared that there was an inescapable connection among RACISM, SEXISM, heterosexism, and CAPITALISM. And in the late 1990s the traditional civil rights organizations and the CONGRESSIONAL BLACK CAUCUS endorsed legislation prohibiting discrimination on the basis of sexual preference or orientation. African-American PUBLIC OPINION also shifted in a more tolerant direction toward homosexuality. However, the traditional religious and cultural ethos proscribing homosexuality remained potent forces in the black community, and traditional black leaders rejected attempts to view racism and heterosexism as equivalent. For example, Gen. COLIN POWELL in opposing President BILL CLINTON's efforts to ban discrimination against gays in the MILITARY strongly rejected the attempt by the president to compare discrimination against gays to past discrimination against blacks in the military. And leading members of the Congressional Black Caucus, while supporting a ban on discrimination against gays in employment, indicated a preference for separate legislation to accomplish this objective rather than simply including gays and lesbians as protected groups covered by the CIVIL RIGHTS ACT OF 1964, as was done with women.

Gettysburg Address

The Gettysburg Address, delivered by President ABRAHAM LINCOLN in 1863, is one of the most important documents in the African-American struggle for FREEDOM and EQUALITY. It, along with MARTIN LUTHER KING JR.'s 1963 "I HAVE A DREAM" SPEECH, is also one of the most familiar speeches in American history. Both speeches, delivered 100 years apart, are important documents in defining and interpreting the nature and meaning of freedom in the American DEMOCRACY. It is not, for example, an accident that King, speaking at the Lincoln's Memorial in Washington, began his speech in 1963 by invoking Lincoln's language at Gettysburg. King was acutely aware of the historical connection between his words about freedom in 1963 and Lincoln's in 1863.

In 1863 President Lincoln was asked to deliver "a few appropriate remarks" at the dedication of the cemetery on a portion of bloody Gettysburg battlefield. Speaking for only three minutes, Lincoln used his address to redefine the meaning of the CIVIL WAR. Throughout his presidency Lincoln had insisted that the purpose of the war was merely to preserve the Union; however, at Gettysburg he said the purpose of the war was to vindicate the DECLARATION OF INDEPENDENCE's proposition about the equality of men. Although the question of whether THOMAS JEFFERSON had meant to include African Americans in his proposition about equality had long been debated, Lincoln throughout his career had always argued that the proposition included *all* men, including Africans, because in his philosophical view *all* men were entitled to the NATURAL RIGHTS of life, liberty, and property. Thus, the war had, against Lincoln's wishes, given rise to a "new birth of freedom." To some, Lincoln's words are disingenuous since when he spoke them he was not committed politically to the full emancipation or freedom of the enslaved African and certainly not to their equality. However, in this instance the words of Lincoln came to have more significance historically than his deeds, because they became a part of the rhetoric of freedom and in doing so helped to make it a reality. Thus the Gettysburg Address, unlike the EMANCIPATION PROCLAMATION, should be read and understood as a philosophical rather than a political document. At Gettysburg, Lincoln also said that the government of the United States was of, by, and for the people. This was a reaffirmation of another long-held Lincoln philosophical view controversial in his time and subsequently: that the government of the United States was created by the people of the United States, not the states themselves. In doing so he rejected the view of the leaders of the SOUTHERN STATES, who argued that the United States was a collection of sovereign states rather than a single nation. In Lincoln's view, the Civil War settled this question for all time, although some leaders of the South raised it anew during the 1960s as part of their resistance to federal enforcement of CIVIL RIGHTS laws.

See also FEDERALISM.

Further reading: Garry Wills, *Lincoln at Gettysburg: The Words that Remade America* (New York: Touchstone, 1992).

ghetto

A ghetto is an area of a city where members of a MINORITY GROUP live because of social, economic, political, or legal constraints. The term was first used to refer to areas of European cities where members of the Jewish ETHNIC GROUP lived or were required to live. In the United States the term generally refers to areas of American cities where African Americans are required to live because of the constraints of RACISM and WHITE SUPREMACY, enforced by social, economic, political, or legal mechanisms. Until the POST–CIVIL RIGHTS ERA, African Americans of all social classes were generally confined to ghettos. Since the 1970s—as a result of social, economic, legal, and political changes brought about by the CIVIL RIGHTS MOVEMENT—the ghettos have generally become places in cities where African Americans and some immigrant minorities live because of the constraints of racism and POVERTY.

As the GREAT MIGRATION of blacks out of rural areas of the SOUTHERN STATES to the cities of the South and the NORTHERN STATES accelerated after the world wars, blacks were usually confined to ghettos. Unlike European immigrant groups who tended to live together on the basis of choice or on the basis of the location of employment, the black migrants—whatever their preferences or wherever their jobs—were forced to live together on the basis of

their RACE. Generally, they were required to live in areas that had few manufacturing jobs and were characterized by old, deteriorating housing inhabited by earlier waves of European immigrants who had moved to more desirable areas of the cities in terms of jobs and housing. Blacks, even those who could afford it, were denied this kind of mobility. Although the SUPREME COURT in 1917 in *Buchannan v. Warley* prohibited cities from legally requiring residential SEGREGATION on the basis of race, such segregation was established and maintained by a variety of other mechanisms. These mechanisms included DISCRIMINATION by realtors and landlords in the sale and rental of housing; "restrictive covenants" in which owners of houses agreed not to sell to blacks; and occasional RIOTS and other forms of VIOLENCE by whites against blacks who did move into "white" neighborhoods.

These informal exclusionary practices were reenforced by the housing policies and programs of the NEW DEAL. The New Deal's housing policies, like its WELFARE STATE policies, generally were racially discriminatory. The Housing Act of 1937, for example, required the selection of tenants and the location of public housing projects on the basis of race. And the Federal Housing Administration used its "FHA" mortgage loans to "redline" areas where blacks lived, that is, to literally draw a red line around areas where loans would not be approved. Thus, as a result of PUBLIC POLICY, the ghettos were maintained and sustained legally and politically. Blacks could not get access to decent housing in "white" neighborhoods and were usually denied access to loans to build decent houses in the neighborhoods in which they were forced to live. (It is estimated that between 1937 and 1960, less than 2 percent of FHA loans went to African Americans.) Thus, the black ghettos were created and maintained as places for the OPPRESSION and exploitation of African Americans—Northern urban analogues to the plantations of the rural South.

From their creation in the late 19th century to the 1970s, the ghettos of America constituted the geographical or spatial anchor of the BLACK COMMUNITY. Because they were the places of residence of all classes of blacks, they provided a geography for race consciousness and solidarity, for the development of black CAPITALISM, and for the exercise of political power through the election of blacks to CONGRESS and to offices in STATE AND LOCAL GOVERNMENT. The ghettos also provided the geography for the nurturing of black CULTURE, and since the black middle and upper classes lived in relative proximity to poor and working-class blacks, the ghettos provided an opportunity for the TALENTED TENTH to exercise grassroots LEADERSHIP and SELF-HELP.

The CIVIL RIGHTS laws of the 1960s banning discrimination in employment, in the sale and rental of housing, and in mortgage loans (in 1948 the SUPREME COURT in

Shelly v. Kramer outlawed the enforcement of restrictive covenants) undermined the class cohesiveness of the ghettos as middle-class blacks took advantage of these opportunities to move out of the ghettos. Although middle-class blacks left the inner-city ghettos, they did not move into "white" neighborhoods in the cities or suburbs, most often moving instead to more affluent but still largely black areas of the cities or suburbs that were abandoned by whites as they moved out of the cities or to more-distant suburbs. Thus, in the POST–CIVIL RIGHTS ERA, middle-class blacks who left the ghettos generally still lived apart from middle-class whites. At the end of the 20th century it was estimated that in the typical large city in America, more than 80 percent of blacks would have to move in order to achieve residential INTEGRATION, meaning that middle-class blacks tend to be more separated from middle-class whites than from poor blacks. Some of this isolation of middle-class blacks from their white counterparts may be a matter of choice, but some of it is a function of still-widespread discrimination in mortgage lending and the sale and rental of housing.

The mobility of the black middle class since the 1970s, however, left the ghettos increasingly a place where poor minorities (immigrant Hispanic minorities, but mainly blacks) are forced to live because of the constraints of racism and poverty. WILLIAM J. WILSON, in his influential studies of ghetto poverty, concluded that the isolation of the black poor from the middle class is a major contributing factor to the rise and persistence of an urban UNDERCLASS. Although Wilson may overstate the importance of the isolation factor, the late-20th-century ghetto is disproportionately constituted by poor blacks who are either low-wage workers, unemployed, or on welfare. The housing tends to be old and somewhat dilapidated; well-paying jobs tend to be scarce; the schools are poorly funded and staffed; retail and service businesses tend to be few; and rates of crime and alcohol and drug abuse tend to be high. Thus, ghettos tend to be places to avoid unless one is forced to live or work in them.

In the 1960s there were public-policy initiatives to reconstruct the ghettos and integrate them and their inhabitants into mainstream urban life. By the 1980s, however, the federal government had by and large abandoned these initiatives, leaving the ghettos as sites for the isolation, subordination, and exploitation of poor minorities.

Further reading: Kenneth Clark, *Dark Ghetto* (New York: Harper & Row, 1965); Ulf Hannerz, *Soulside: Studies in Ghetto Culture and Community* (New York: Columbia University Press, 1969); Douglass Massey and Nancy Denton, *American Apartheid: Segregation and the Making of the Underclass* (Cambridge, Mass.: Harvard University Press, 1993); Alan Spear, "The Origins of the Urban Ghetto, 1870–1915," in *Key Issues in the Afro-American Experience,* ed. Nathan Huggins, M. Kilson, and D. Fox (New York: Harcourt Brace and Jovanovich, 1971).

globalization

Globalization is generally understood to refer to an economic process in which products and services move relatively freely across national boundaries. It is a process inherent in CAPITALISM. As early as their 1848 classic *The Communist Manifesto,* Karl Marx and Frederick Engels wrote that capitalism creates a "universal inter-dependence of nations" because " . . . the need of a constantly expanding market for its product chases the bourgeoisie over the whole surface of the globe. . . . It compels all nations, on pain of extinction, to adapt the bourgeois mode of production . . . to become bourgeois themselves. In a word, it creates a world after its own image." Thus, globalization is not a new phenomenon. What was new was the speed of the process in the late 20th century that Marx and Engels described in 1848.

The rapid growth of knowledge, technological changes, and the computer accelerated the process of globalization in the last decades of the 20th century, and this has had an impact on the lives of THIRD WORLD peoples. Global transactions in products and services and capital and information created enormous wealth in the United States, Europe, and Japan, while most nations in Africa, Latin America, and Asia became increasingly poorer, burdened by low-wage labor, crushing debt, and a virtually nonexistent WELFARE STATE. This process was accompanied by vast migrations of peoples of the Third World to the cities of their countries and to the cities of the United States and western Europe. A result of these patterns of internal and external migration was the creation of a global UNDERCLASS as the problems of long-term unemployment, family instability, drugs, crime, and the AIDS-HIV epidemic increasingly characterized cities throughout the globe. At the same time, MULTICULTURALISM increasingly shaped the cities of the United States and western Europe. The processes of globalization also made problems of RACISM and SEXISM global issues, leading the UNITED NATIONS to call international conferences dealing with both in addition to its traditional concerns with Third World POVERTY and debt.

As the world's major economic power, the United States through its monetary and trade policies and its dominance of international economic and political institutions played a major role in shaping the global economy. In Africa and other parts of the Third World, the United States has generally used its power to keep wages low and the welfare state modest on the assumption that high wages and generous welfare systems discourage capital investments and business activity. While largely white labor, environmental, and radical groups formed COALITIONS to PROTEST the role of the United States in the global economy, African-American LEADERSHIP and ORGANIZATIONS were not a part of these coalitions and generally have been silent on issues of globalization except for a narrow focus on African trade and the AIDS epidemic in Africa.

Further reading: Charles Green, ed., *Globalization and Survival in the Black Diaspora* (Albany: State University of New York Press, 1997).

Goldwater, Barry (1909–1998) *U.S. senator*

Barry Goldwater played a major role in shifting the REPUBLICAN PARTY toward CONSERVATISM and hostility to CIVIL RIGHTS in the POST–CIVIL RIGHTS ERA. Elected to the U.S. Senate from Arizona in 1952, in 1964 he won the Republican nomination for president. Although he was defeated (losing by more than 16 million votes) in a landslide by LYNDON B. JOHNSON, his ideas and strategies became the basis of the Republican Party's embrace of conservatism and its rise to power in the late 20th century. Goldwater was fervently committed to the IDEOLOGY of conservatism, but the post–World War II Republican Party was a COALITION of liberals, moderates, and conservatives who generally supported civil rights and accepted the basic principles and programs of FRANKLIN D. ROOSEVELT's reforms embodied in the NEW DEAL and the WELFARE STATE. Goldwater challenged these principles and programs, denouncing as SOCIALISM such landmark New Deal programs as social security, public housing, and labor's right to organize and bargain collectively. Goldwater also opposed the GREAT SOCIETY reforms enacted by President Lyndon Johnson, including medical insurance for the elderly and poor, the WAR ON POVERTY, and the ELEMENTARY AND SECONDARY EDUCATION ACT. Goldwater also opposed the CIVIL RIGHTS ACT OF 1964 and the VOTING RIGHTS ACT OF 1965, arguing that both violated principles of FEDERALISM.

Although Goldwater lost the 1964 election, the conservative forces he represented won control of the Republican Party, defeating its more liberal and moderate factions and paving the way for the election of RONALD REAGAN, a Goldwater protégé, in 1980. (Reagan received his first national political exposure in a televised speech for Goldwater in 1964.) From ABRAHAM LINCOLN in 1860 until Goldwater in 1964, the Republican Party was the more liberal or activist of the two major parties on issues of RACE and civil rights. After Goldwater, it became the more conservative party on race as it embraced Goldwater's SOUTHERN STRATEGY of appealing to the votes of Democratic whites in the SOUTHERN STATES who had opposed the CIVIL RIGHTS MOVEMENT and the civil rights laws of the

1960s. Because of his opposition to the Civil Rights Act of 1964, Goldwater won four Southern states while losing everywhere else in the country except his home state of Arizona. But, unlike RICHARD NIXON, who in 1960 received approximately one-third of the black vote, Goldwater four years later received less than 10 percent. Since 1964 this electoral pattern has remained basically unchanged: The Republican Party receives the overwhelming majority of the Southern white vote, and the DEMOCRATIC PARTY receives the overwhelming majority of the black vote. More so than any other individual, Goldwater is responsible for this transformation in the racial ideology and constituencies of the TWO-PARTY SYSTEM. After his defeat for the PRESIDENCY in 1964, Goldwater returned to the Senate, where he served until his retirement in 1986. Although Goldwater was a principled conservative whose opposition to civil rights was not based on RACISM or WHITE SUPREMACY, his legacy is the transformation of the Party of Lincoln into the party whose core ideas and strategies are indifferent to African-American FREEDOM and EQUALITY.

See also GEORGE WALLACE and WHITE BACKLASH.

Further reading: Rick Perlstein, *Before the Storm: Barry Goldwater and the Unmaking of the American Consensus* (New York: Hill and Wang, 2001).

Grant, Ulysses S. (1822–1885) *18th president of the United States*

Ulysses S. Grant is one of the more antiracist, pro–CIVIL RIGHTS persons to occupy the PRESIDENCY. Elected in 1872 to succeed ANDREW JOHNSON, one of the more RACIST and WHITE SUPREMACIST of the American presidents, Grant served as president during the height of RECONSTRUCTION. In his early months in office, Grant took a moderate, conciliatory attitude toward whites in the SOUTHERN STATES, but when they turned toward VIOLENCE and POLITICAL REPRESSION of black leaders and voters, Grant supported CONGRESS's enactment of three Enforcement Acts to provide federal protection for civil rights and authority for the president to use the army to enforce those rights. Three civil rights bills were passed during Grant's two terms, and the FOURTEENTH AMENDMENT and the FIFTEENTH AMENDMENT were adopted. Grant was also the first president to appoint a number of blacks to the BUREAUCRACY. Of Grant, FREDERICK DOUGLASS observed that he never exhibited "vulgar prejudices of any sort." (Grant owned one slave but early on freed him.)

Although Grant was as sympathetic to the interests of blacks as any American president except LYNDON B. JOHNSON, when he left office most blacks had been driven from the voter rolls and from political office, and most of the

Southern STATE AND LOCAL GOVERNMENTS were in the hands of racists and white supremacists who were starting a new system of race OPPRESSION based on SEGREGATION. Grant lamented these developments but could do little to stop them because the army he might have used to protect the rights of blacks was small and underfunded, and Congress and white PUBLIC OPINION in the NORTHERN STATES were reluctant to increase its size or support its use to enforce the rights of blacks. Historians have generally concluded that Grant was a superb supreme commander of the army during the CIVIL WAR but an incompetent president. Indeed, historians generally rank Grant among the worst of the American presidents. However, in terms of the interests of African Americans, he is among the best. Although he failed to protect the newly won FREEDOM of African Americans, he was committed to doing so and did as well perhaps as the situation at the time allowed.

See also WHITE BACKLASH.

Further reading: Jean Edward Smith, *Grant* (New York: Simon & Schuster, 2000).

Gray, William H. (1941–   ) *congressman*

William H. Gray III, elected to the House of Representatives in 1978, rose rapidly through the power structure of the DEMOCRATIC PARTY in the House to become one of the most influential African Americans ever to serve in CONGRESS; he was elected as chairman of the powerful House Budget Committee in 1982 and in 1989 as majority whip, the third-ranking position in the House leadership structure.

Like ADAM CLAYTON POWELL and many other black ELECTED OFFICIALS, Gray's route to office was through the BLACK CHURCH. Prior to his election to Congress, Gray served as pastor of Bright Hope Baptist Church, one of Philadelphia's largest and most influential congregations. Indeed, throughout his tenure as a congressman from Philadelphia, Gray continued to serve as pastor, preaching most Sundays. In the House, Gray quickly developed a reputation as a knowledgeable and articulate legislator, able to represent the interests of blacks as a leading member of the CONGRESSIONAL BLACK CAUCUS but also able to build COALITIONS across racial, regional, and ideological lines to represent the interests of the Democratic Party in the House as a whole. Within four years of his election these skills earned Gray the respect and admiration of his colleagues, who in 1984 elected him to chair the House Budget Committee. Gray's leadership of the committee showcased his coalition-building skills, as he produced moderate, middle-of-the-road budgets that compromised differences between liberals like himself and Democratic Party conservatives from the SOUTHERN STATES. His leadership of the committee meant, however, that he could not support the budgets of the Congressional Black Caucus as he had done prior to becoming budget committee chair. In fact, as chair, Gray ended up voting for budgets that as a member of the Congressional Black Caucus he would have opposed. This, for many of Gray's black colleagues, raised concerns about CO-OPTATION of a leader unwilling or unable to use his position of power to advance the interests of his constituent group. In response to allegations that as budget chair he failed to represent the interests of blacks, Gray said, "It's not an issue of being black. The issue is I'm chairman of the Budget Committee, a Democrat. I build a consensus. I walk out with a budget. Now, do I vote against my own budget? . . . That doesn't make a lot of sense. It's not a problem of race. It's what happens to any member of Congress who gets elevated to a position of leadership." Although Gray's response did not satisfy some of his black colleagues, it did apparently please his colleagues in the Democratic Party Caucus, because in 1989 he was elected majority whip. The post of majority whip is the third-ranking position in the leadership of the House and second in line of succession to become Speaker of the House. Although Gray had a very good chance to become the first black Speaker, in 1991 he abruptly resigned to become president of the United Negro College Fund, a group that raises and distributes funds for HISTORICALLY BLACK COLLEGES AND UNIVERSITIES.

Great Migration

At the end of the CIVIL WAR, more than 90 percent of African Americans lived in rural areas of the SOUTHERN STATES. By 1960 almost half the black POPULATION lived in the NORTHERN STATES, and almost 80 percent lived in cities. This transformation of the geographic or spatial anchor of the BLACK COMMUNITY from the nation's most rural people to one of its most urban represents the greatest mass migration in the history of the United States.

At the end of RECONSTRUCTION in the 1870s there was a resurgence of RACISM, WHITE SUPREMACY, POLITICAL REPRESSION, and KU KLUX KLAN–inspired VIOLENCE and LYNCHINGS. As a result, some blacks left the South for the North. Moses "Pap" Singleton, for example, is credited with leading thousands of blacks out of the South in what is sometimes referred to as the "Exodus of 1879," and thousands also migrated to Indian Territory in Oklahoma, where they established all-black towns and communities, wishfully thinking that Oklahoma (or parts of it) might become an all-black state. But, as late as 1910 more than 80 percent of blacks still lived in rural areas of the South. Then, in spite of the opposition of BOOKER T. WASHINGTON, then the preeminent leader of blacks, the great migration began.

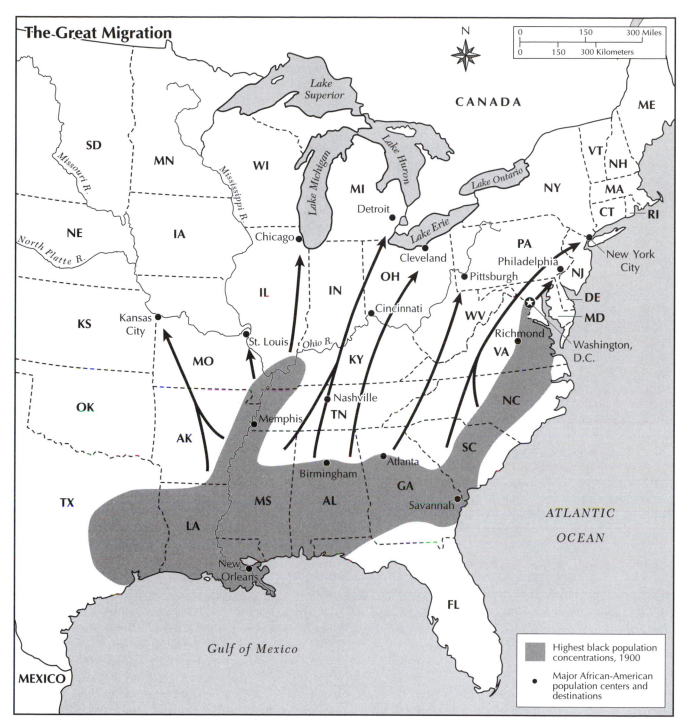

Great Migration, 1901–45 *(Facts On File)*

Several factors account for this mass movement of peoples. First, the cotton economy in which so many blacks worked collapsed. This caused many blacks to move North or to Southern cities in search of work. Second, the Northern industrial economy was growing rapidly, and CONGRESS was moving to restrict the flow of immigrants from Europe.

Thus, there was a labor shortage in the North that could be met by the unemployed black labor in the South. Third, in addition to the economic opportunities, the North provided a relative degree of FREEDOM and EQUALITY compared with the rigid JIM CROW system of SEGREGATION in the South. Fourth, the African-American MEDIA in the

North urged black migration. (The *Chicago Defender* was banned in parts of the South because of this.) As a result of these factors, it is estimated that more than 1 million blacks moved to Northern cities, while tens of thousands moved to Southern cities.

Although Southern blacks might have seen the North as a kind of promised land of freedom and equality, in the Northern cities they faced DISCRIMINATION and tensions with whites over jobs and housing. These tensions led to dozens of RIOTS by whites and ultimately to the formation of the big-city GHETTO. Although ghettoized, urban life facilitated the development of modern, urban black CAPITALISM and CULTURE; the growth of a middle class of business people and professionals; the emergence of CIVIL RIGHTS and other ORGANIZATIONS; and eventually the emergence of the black vote as a BALANCE OF POWER in state, local, and national elections, resulting for the first time since Reconstruction in the election of blacks to Congress and STATE AND LOCAL GOVERNMENT offices.

The Great Depression of the 1930s slowed the first great migration, but a second wave started in the 1940s, and between 1940 and 1960 an estimated 1 million more blacks left the South. By 1970 the great migration had come to an end due to the effects of the CIVIL RIGHTS MOVEMENT on ending blatant Southern racism and segregation. At the same time, economic opportunities were expanding in the South and declining in the North. By the mid-1970s, a reverse pattern of migration was underway as more blacks left the North for the South than the South for the North. This pattern continued modestly throughout the remainder of the 20th century. By 2000 about 53 percent of blacks lived in the Southern states and 80 percent in urban areas.

Further reading: Neil Flingstein, *Going North: Migration of Blacks and Whites from the South, 1900–1950* (New York: Academic Press, 1981); Nicholas Lemann, *The Promised Land: The Great Black Migration and How It Changed America* (New York: Knopf, 1991).

Great Society

The Great Society is the term used by President LYNDON B. JOHNSON to refer to a variety of reform policies and programs instituted in the 1960s. These reforms represented the largest expansion of the American WELFARE STATE since it was created by FRANKLIN D. ROOSEVELT as part of the NEW DEAL. The programs instituted as the Great Society include medical insurance for the elderly and the poor, the ELEMENTARY AND SECONDARY EDUCATION ACT, Head Start, the Jobs Corps and various job training programs, federal loans and grants for college education, legal assistance and services for the poor, and the WAR ON POVERTY.

In some ways, these reforms represented the unfinished agenda of modern LIBERALISM left over from the administrations of Franklin Roosevelt and HARRY TRUMAN. However, the war on poverty was an outgrowth and response to the CIVIL RIGHTS MOVEMENT.

The Great Society was strongly criticized by conservatives such as BARRY GOLDWATER in the 1960s and later by RONALD REAGAN in the 1970s and 1980s. Generally, conservatives contended that the Great Society programs were wasteful and ineffective. Studies, however, indicate that these programs were associated with substantial reductions in POVERTY; remarkable increases in access to health care by the elderly and poor; improved access by the poor to legal services; and increased POLITICAL PARTICIPATION by groups previously excluded, especially African Americans.

Griggs v. Duke Power Co. (1971)

Griggs v. Duke Power Co. (1971) is the seminal case in the SUPREME COURT's treatment of RACISM in the POST–CIVIL RIGHTS ERA. In this case the Court for the first time distinguished between INDIVIDUAL RACISM and INSTITUTIONAL RACISM, although the Court did not use those terms, preferring instead the legal concepts DISPARATE TREATMENT and DISPARATE IMPACT. The case deals with employment DISCRIMINATION.

Until the 1960s, Duke Power Co. engaged in overt, direct individual racism by prohibiting blacks from holding any job except those in the low-wage, low-skill labor category. When CONGRESS enacted Title VII of the CIVIL RIGHTS ACT OF 1964 prohibiting employment discrimination, Duke Power abandoned its overtly racist policy and in its place introduced a high school diploma and successful completion of two general intelligence tests as requirements to transfer to any nonlaborer job category or for initial hiring in such categories. Neither the test nor the high school diploma had been "validated" by the company, that is, shown to be related to performing a particular job or categories of jobs. Indeed, the evidence presented at the trial showed that whites in nonlaborer jobs who had not taken the test or graduated from high school received satisfactory job-performance evaluations, suggesting that neither of the new requirements was related to or predictive of job performance. However, the tests resulted in a 58 percent pass rate by whites, but only a 6 percent rate among blacks, and while 54 percent of white men in North Carolina (the state where the company was located) had graduated from high school, only 12 percent of black males had received a comparable level of schooling. The test and diploma requirements thus constituted a form of institutional racism, allowing Duke Power to continue to relegate most blacks to the lowest job categories in a manner almost as effective as when it practiced individual racism.

In a unanimous decision the Supreme Court struck down the new requirements. Writing for the Court, Chief Justice Warren Burger concluded that blacks had long received an inferior education and that this caused their disproportionately low high school graduation rates and performance on the tests. And since neither the tests nor the diploma requirements had been validated, the Court held that under Title VII, such procedures and requirements, although nonracist on their face or even in their intent, nevertheless were racist in their effects or consequences because they had a disparate impact on the employment opportunities of African Americans. The Court's clear recognition of institutional racism in *Griggs* was a landmark in CIVIL RIGHTS jurisprudence that had potentially important implications for restructuring institutionally racist practices in employment as well as other institutional arenas, but shortly thereafter the Court began to back away from the *Griggs* principles, and in 1989 in WARDS COVE V. ANTONIO, a divided Court completely repudiated them. Although the Congress in the Civil Rights Act of 1991 attempted to restore those principles, the legislation was so confusing, contradictory, and complex that the Court could ignore its mandate.

H

Haiti

Haiti, a nation that shares the WEST INDIAN island of Hispaniola with the Dominican Republic, is the oldest independent black republic in the world. Although a small and poor country, Haiti is important in the historical consciousness of African peoples and in AFRICAN-AMERICAN POLITICS. This is because it achieved its independence as a result of the first successful SLAVE REVOLT in the Western Hemisphere. The Haitian Revolution, then, is an example of the effective use by Africans of VIOLENCE in the struggle against WHITE SUPREMACY, COLONIALISM, and racial OPPRESSION. It inspired African Americans in the United States while alarming and frightening whites.

During the French Revolution, perhaps inspired by its emphasis on the rights of man, the mixed-race mulattoes in Haiti, who were free but lacked political rights, petitioned the French government for full FREEDOM and EQUALITY. (Although they were not fully free, most mulattoes supported SLAVERY and some owned black slaves.) The French government granted their request, but the French authorities on the island refused to abide by it and, as a result, the mulattoes led a revolt that was quickly and brutally suppressed. However, in 1791 the enslaved blacks, under the leadership of Toussaint Louverture, began a rebellion against both the whites and the mulattoes. Eventually organizing an army larger than the one that fought the British during the American Revolution, Toussaint led a long, bloody rebellion against both French and British forces, and, later, against mulatto forces. Between 1791 and independence in 1804 nearly 200,000 blacks died, as did thousands of mulattoes and as many as 100,000 French and British soldiers. During the course of the war Toussaint was captured and imprisoned, dying in 1803. His successor, Jean-Jacques Dessalines, defeated the French and on January 1, 1804, Haiti declared its independence and Dessalines was eventually crowned emperor.

Throughout the Haitian Revolution the United States supported the French and British. President George Washington provided money and arms and THOMAS JEFFERSON, fearing that African Americans would be galvanized by the rebellion, spent virtually his entire presidency trying to block any contact or flow of information between Haiti and the United States. After independence, Jefferson refused to recognize the new government (the United States did not formally recognize the Haitian government until the presidency of ABRAHAM LINCOLN during the 1860s), referring to Toussaint's army as "cannibals" and refusing to acknowledge that Haitian revolutionaries had the same right to fight for freedom as American revolutionaries. In 1805, Jefferson persuaded the CONGRESS to formally abolish all trade between the United States and Haiti, which effectively destroyed its emergent economy.

The Haitian revolution was led by Africans, and many initial leaders of the government were black. However, by the 1820s mulattoes had consolidated power, and in an extreme example of the negative effects of COLOR STRATIFICATION, some mulatto leaders instituted a pattern of POLITICAL REPRESSION and economic exploitation of the black Haitian majority. In 1915 in response to RIOTS and disorders by the black majority, President WOODROW WILSON sent in the marines to restore order. American puppet and other regimes were eventually followed by the brutal Duvaliers (François "Papa Doc" and Jean-Claude "Baby Doc"), who remained in power until 1986, when "Baby Doc" was finally forced into exile. In 1990 Jean-Bertrand Aristide, a black reform-minded former Catholic priest, was elected president, but the Haitian army ousted him a year later. The army then instituted a campaign of brutal repression, which led the UNITED NATIONS to impose an embargo. When the embargo failed to result in the army's withdrawal from power, the African-American LEADERSHIP, led by the CONGRESSIONAL BLACK CAUCUS and TRANSAFRICA, pressured President BILL CLINTON to threaten an American invasion. This threat forced the Haitian army to capitulate, and in 1994 the exiled President Aristide was returned to office.

At the end of the 20th century, Haiti—the first black nation to gain its independence from white colonial rule—was the poorest nation in the Western Hemisphere, leading many whites to assert, as Thomas Jefferson did in the 1800s, that this was proof that Africans could not govern themselves. This assertion, however, ignores the fact that the Haitian economy was initially decimated by Jefferson's 1804 trade embargo, reenforced by almost two centuries of brutally repressive regimes supported and maintained by a U.S. government unwilling to allow Haiti to become an example of a prosperous and democratic black-led government that came to power by using revolutionary violence to overthrow white rule.

Further reading: Plummer, Brenda Gayle. *Haiti and the United States* (Athens: University of Georgia Press, 1992).

Hamer, Fannie Lou (1917–1977) *civil rights leader*
Fannie Lou Hamer, a Mississippi sharecropper, is recognized as one of the most important African-American leaders in the history of the United States; she was rated 10th by African-American political scientists in a 2000 poll identifying the greatest black leaders in history. Political scientists in the poll described her as a "true grassroots leader" of the CIVIL RIGHTS MOVEMENT and as a woman who "with remarkable courage provided a moral light; a moral standard for the civil rights movement."

Born in rural Mississippi, the youngest of 20 children, Hamer spent most of her life working as a sharecropper. In 1962 her life was changed forever when she was inspired at a CIVIL RIGHTS rally to attempt to register to vote. For this she was fired and ordered to leave the plantation where she and her husband lived and worked. At this point she started to work in the Civil Rights movement. ROBERT MOSES of the STUDENT NONVIOLENT COORDINATING COMMITTEE (SNCC) recognized her charismatic presence, her inspiring oratory, and her powerful use of MUSIC, and he helped to facilitate her emergence as a grassroots leader in SNCC's voter-registration campaigns. Arrested and beaten in 1963 (she sustained permanent injuries to her kidney as a result), in 1964 Hamer was a cofounder of the MISSISSIPPI FREEDOM DEMOCRATIC PARTY (MFDP), an interracial COALITION that challenged the seating of the racist, all-white regular Mississippi delegation to the DEMOCRATIC PARTY's 1964 national convention. At the convention, Hamer recounted in vivid detail on national television the atrocities committed against blacks who tried to register and vote in Mississippi. Her pleas, however, to oust the all-white Mississippi delegation and replace it with MFDP delegates were rejected on the basis of direct instructions from President LYNDON B. JOHNSON. As a compromise, the MFDP was offered two honorary "at large" convention seats, which it rejected despite the pleas of MARTIN LUTHER KING JR.

Fannie Lou Hamer (carrying sign) *(Library of Congress)*

and white liberal leaders like HUBERT HUMPHREY. In rejecting the compromise Hamer said, "We did not come all this way for no two seats," as she led a PROTEST demonstration on the convention floor. After the convention, Hamer returned to Mississippi where she ran unsuccessfully for the CONGRESS. Her work in the movement demonstrated the capacity of ordinary people, poor and unlettered, to exercise LEADERSHIP, which Hamer continued to do until her death in 1977 at the age of 59.

Further reading: Chana Kai Lee, *For Freedom's Sake: The Life of Fannie Lou Hamer* (Urbana: University of Illinois Press, 2000); Kay Mills, *This Little Light of Mine: The Life of Fannie Lou Hamer* (New York: Dutton, 1993).

Hamilton, Charles V. (1929–) *scholar*
Charles Hamilton coauthored *BLACK POWER: THE POLITICS OF LIBERATION IN AMERICA*, the manifesto of the 1960s

BLACK POWER MOVEMENT with STOKELY CARMICHAEL. As a political scientist on the faculty of TUSKEGEE UNIVERSITY, the historically black university that was the headquarters of BOOKER T. WASHINGTON, Hamilton became active in the CIVIL RIGHTS MOVEMENT. While serving as an adviser to the STUDENT NONVIOLENT COORDINATING COMMITTEE (SNCC), he became acquainted with Carmichael and subsequently joined him to write *Black Power*. After writing the book Hamilton joined the political science faculty at Columbia University and became one of the nation's most influential scholars of black power and AFRICAN-AMERICAN POLITICS.

In his lectures and writings on black power Hamilton, in contrast to Carmichael, interpreted the movement as a moderate, nonthreatening form of INTEREST GROUP politics, similar to that practiced by European ETHNIC GROUPS during earlier periods of American history. Thus, contrary to Carmichael, who interpreted black power as a radical, revolutionary challenge to the POLITICAL SYSTEM, Hamilton saw it as well within the tradition of American PLURALISM. By the early 1970s Hamilton's reform interpretation had been adopted by the black LEADERSHIP establishment and accepted by the POWER ELITE. In an important way Hamilton was influential in helping to shift black power away from RADICALISM toward POLITICAL INCORPORATION or CO-OPTATION into the routines of U.S. politics. He was also the first black political scientist to advocate DERACIALIZATION as a strategy for POST–CIVIL RIGHTS ERA black politics, and to propose FULL EMPLOYMENT as the priority PUBLIC POLICY item on the post–Civil Rights BLACK AGENDA. In addition to his writings in the MEDIA and his public lectures, Hamilton published several important scholarly articles and books, including a biography of ADAM CLAYTON POWELL and *The Dual Agenda: Race and Social Policies of Civil Rights Organizations*, a critical study of the role of black interest groups during the NEW DEAL and the role of RACISM in shaping the development of the American WELFARE STATE. He earned his undergraduate degree from Roosevelt University, a law degree from Loyola University, and a Ph.D. from the University of Chicago.

Hare, Nathan (1934–   ) *scholar*

Nathan Hare, as much as any other scholar, is responsible for the development of AFRICAN-AMERICAN STUDIES as an academic discipline during the 1960s. Hare, a sociologist, earned his undergraduate degree from Langston University, a historically black university, and a Ph.D. from the University of Chicago. Recruited to the faculty of HOWARD UNIVERSITY in 1961 during the BLACK POWER MOVEMENT, Hare was among the faculty who joined students in PROTESTS to transform Howard into a "black" university, that is, a university explicitly committed in its research,

scholarship, teaching, and service to the use of knowledge to advance the struggle against racial OPPRESSION. (Part of the students' demands was the creation at Howard, for the first time, of an academic department in African-American studies.) Because of conflicts with the administration, Hare left Howard in 1967 and a year later was asked by student activists at San Francisco State University to become head of the first modern African-American studies department at a predominantly white university in the United States. The students recruited Hare because of his reputation for MILITANCY and because of his commitment to BLACK NATIONALISM as an integral part of the philosophy of African-American studies. Hare's vision of black studies involved a new approach to scholarship and pedagogy, one that "united the academy and the street" in a way that would make higher education directly relevant to the needs of the GHETTO by making community involvement an integral component of the curriculum. After several years of repeated clashes with administrators and faculty, including a five-month strike, Hare resigned and started publishing *The Black Scholar*, which became a leading journal of black-studies scholarship and militancy and RADICALISM in black politics.

Although a founder of modern African-American studies, Hare has consistently expressed disappointment with its direction. He contends that the discipline has either been co-opted by traditional academics who practice what he calls "polka dot studies" or has been rendered irrelevant by AFROCENTRISM, which Hare describes as "a museum approach" to black studies, focusing on the alleged past glories of ancient Africa while ignoring the grim realities of the BLACK COMMUNITY.

See also MOLEFI K. ASANTE and CO-OPTATION.

Harlem

Harlem, located roughly between 110th and 155th streets in northern Manhattan, is the most famous and influential black GHETTO in the United States. Harlem's reputation derives in part from its location in New York City, which is the most important and influential city in the United States. Sometimes referred to as the "Mecca of the Negro" and as the "RACE capital of America," Harlem is historically important as a place of African-American race consciousness, CULTURE, MEDIA, and MUSIC and as a place for nurturing important black ORGANIZATIONS and distinctive types and styles of black LEADERSHIP.

Harlem started as an affluent white suburb of New York City, but when housing prices collapsed at the beginning of the 20th century, Phillip Payton, owner of the Afro-American Realty Company and a protégé of BOOKER T. WASHINGTON, began to purchase and lease apartments in Harlem to BLACK migrants from the WEST INDIAN islands and the

SOUTHERN STATES. As a result of the first wave of the GREAT MIGRATION, by the 1930s Harlem had a black population of nearly 200,000, almost two-thirds of New York's black population. A BLACK COMMUNITY including persons of all social classes developed in Harlem, with a fairly large and prosperous middle-upper class living in neighborhoods like Striver's Row. This concentration of a socially, economically, and ethnically diverse population of African peoples in the nation's largest and most cosmopolitan city led to the development of the HARLEM RENAISSANCE, a literary and cultural movement that coincided with and contributed to the emerging CIVIL RIGHTS MOVEMENT. In the 1920s the SCHOMBURG CENTER FOR RESEARCH IN BLACK CULTURE, with its important repository of documents on the African-American experience, became the Harlem branch of the New York City Public Library. Many of Harlem's nightclubs and theaters (such as the Cotton Club, the Savoy Ballroom, and the Apollo Theater) became showcases for African-American music, dance, and nightlife. Several important congregations of the BLACK CHURCH were located in Harlem, and important elements of the black media were edited and published there. The philosophy of BLACK NATIONALISM found a home on Harlem's street corners, providing platforms for the emergence of MARCUS GARVEY and MALCOLM X as national leaders. And Harlem provided the geography for new and different styles of political leadership, as evidenced by the emergence of J. RAYMOND JONES and ADAM CLAYTON POWELL JR.

Although Harlem started as a fairly prosperous and economically diverse community, the Great Depression of the 1930s precipitated a slow decline and the emergence of the problems of persistent POVERTY, crime, and substance abuse typical of American ghettos. The depression also saw the COMMUNIST PARTY playing a major role in organizing the unemployed and fighting RACISM. In 1935 and again in 1943 there were major RIOTS in Harlem, involving widespread injuries and property damage. Harlem never fully recovered from the depression, and after World War II middle-class blacks began to leave the area; housing and schools deteriorated; and the community's literary, cultural, and political institutions declined. While Harlem is no longer the mecca that it was in the 1920s and 1930s, it remains an important place in the historical consciousness of black people throughout the world. Symbolic of its continuing significance was the decision by President BILL CLINTON to locate his post-presidential office there, which fueled hopes that the ongoing plans to redevelop and revitalize the community might come to fruition.

Further reading: James Weldon Johnson, *Black Manhattan* (Salem, N.H.: Ayer Co., 1930, 1988); Gilbert Osofsky, *Harlem: The Making of a Ghetto, 1890–1930* (New York: Harper & Row, 1966).

Harlem Renaissance

The Harlem Renaissance is a literary-cultural movement that blossomed in HARLEM between the late 1920s and 1930s. Although the renaissance is best known as the first cultural movement to give authentic expression to that African-American experience and to display artistic pride in BLACKNESS, it like the BLACK ARTS MOVEMENT of the 1960s also had a political dimension as it emerged at about the same time that the CIVIL RIGHTS MOVEMENT was beginning to have an impact on African Americans and American politics. Indeed, the relationship between the renaissance and the emerging Civil Rights movement was to some extent symbiotic, what one historian describes as a "civil rights arts movement." That is, it was a cultural movement that used art to express the Civil Rights movement's goals of FREEDOM and EQUALITY. Although the renaissance marked the first time that white, mainstream institutions published the poetry and fiction of black writers and gave them a national audience, these writers were also supported and published in *The Crisis* and *Opportunity*,

Langston Hughes *(Library of Congress)*

respective journals of the NAACP and the URBAN LEAGUE, the two major civil rights organizations. Alan Locke's *The New Negro*, the classic anthology that defined the aesthetics of the movement's literature, was the product of a dinner hosted by the Urban League to honor young black writers and introduce them to New York's white literary establishment. JAMES WELDON JOHNSON, an early renaissance writer, later became the first African American to head the NAACP, and undoubtedly many renaissance artists were inspired by MARCUS GARVEY's espousal of his brand of BLACK NATIONALISM, which emphasized pride in racial heritage.

Yet despite this symbiotic relationship between art and politics, the Harlem Renaissance was primarily a cultural movement in which artists (mainly writers, but there were related contributions in drama, jazz, blues, and paintings) were committed primarily to giving expression to the African-American experience in their art whatever, if any, its impact on politics, civil rights, or race pride. The idea of "art for art's sake" whatever its political consequences, led eventually to conflicts between some of the artists and some black political leaders, including W. E. B. DU BOIS and WALTER WHITE. Du Bois, for example, insisted that the idea of art for art's sake or the purity of the artist and his craft was nonsense, since he saw all art as political. As he wrote in 1926, "I do not give a damn for any art that is not used for political propaganda." Du Bois was also critical of writings that exploited what he called the "squalor of black life" and appealed to the prurient sensibilities of white readers interested in reading stereotypical portrayals of black "licentiousness." Generally, black renaissance writers rejected demands that their work be explicitly celebratory or propagandistic, a view expressed forcefully in a famous essay by Langston Hughes, "The Negro Artist and the Racial Mountain," published in 1926 in the white liberal journal *The Nation*. Hughes wrote:

> We younger negro artists who create now intend to express our individual dark-skinned selves without fear or shame. If white people are pleased we are glad. If they are not, it doesn't matter. We know we are beautiful. And ugly too. The tom-tom cries and the tom-tom laughs. If colored people are pleased we are glad. If not, their displeasure doesn't matter either. We build our temples for tomorrow, strong as we know how and we stand on top of the mountain, free within ourselves.

The renaissance is generally considered to have come to an end in the late 1930s, in large part as a result of the depression and the economic decline of Harlem. Despite its brief history, it had a major impact on African-American art and politics, influencing the NEGRITUDE movement in Africa and the Caribbean during the 1940s and 1950s and the Black Arts movement during the 1960s. The seminal debate between Du Bois and Hughes about the role of art in politics reverberated in the 1960s and again in the 1990s debate about the role of RAP MUSIC in African-American CULTURE and politics.

Further reading: Huggins, Nathan, *The Harlem Renaissance* (New York: Oxford University, 1971); David Levering Lewis, *When Harlem Was in Vogue* (New York: Knopf, 1981).

Harris, Patricia Roberts (1924–1985) *U.S. government official*

Patricia Roberts Harris was the first black woman to serve in the cabinet, appointed by President JIMMY CARTER first as secretary of the HOUSING AND URBAN DEVELOPMENT Department (HUD) and later as secretary of the Department of Health, Education and Welfare. Harris was also the first black woman to head an American embassy, appointed ambassador to Luxembourg by President LYNDON B. JOHNSON in 1965. A graduate of HOWARD UNIVERSITY (where she later was briefly dean of its law school), Harris had a long career of CIVIL RIGHTS activism prior to entering the BUREAUCRACY, working with the NAACP and serving on the board of directors of its LEGAL DEFENSE FUND. She was also an active member of the DEMOCRATIC PARTY, serving in positions of leadership at its national committee and at its conventions. In 1986 she ran unsuccessfully for mayor of the DISTRICT OF COLUMBIA. Harris was one of the few black Americans in the POWER ELITE—a partner in a powerful Washington, D.C., law firm and a member of the boards of the Chase Manhattan Bank, IBM, and Scott Paper Co. (Her appointment in 1971 to the Scott Paper board was the first for a black woman at a major corporation.)

Harrison, Benjamin (1833–1901) *22nd president of the United States*

Benjamin Harrison, the 22nd president, is one of the handful of the American presidents who have been generally sympathetic to the African-American struggle for FREEDOM and EQUALITY (see the PRESIDENCY). Elected in 1888, Harrison is one of four presidents elected by winning a majority in the ELECTORAL COLLEGE while losing the popular vote. Although he lost the popular vote, Harrison contended that his election was fair and legitimate because he would have won the popular vote if the black vote in the SOUTHERN STATES had not been suppressed. Harrison was the last president until HARRY TRUMAN in 1948 to advocate a CIVIL RIGHTS agenda, suggesting first the use of the COMMERCE CLAUSE to pass civil rights legislation and then a constitutional amendment to overturn the SUPREME COURT's decisions in the CIVIL RIGHTS CASES OF 1883. Harrison also supported legislation to enforce African-American VOTING RIGHTS in the South and proposals to make LYNCHING a federal crime. He appointed blacks to the BUREAUCRACY and supported the BLAIR EDUCATION BILL. None of the civil rights initiatives were passed by CONGRESS, and he was defeated in the next election in 1892 by Grover Cleveland, the man he had defeated four years earlier.

Hatcher, Richard (1933–) *politician*

In 1967 Richard Hatcher was elected mayor of Gary, Indiana, becoming (along with CARL STOKES) one of the first blacks elected mayor of a major American city. Hatcher's was a bitter and racially divisive election. Opposed by the white-dominated local DEMOCRATIC PARTY political machine and most white voters, Hatcher's election represented the beginnings of a pattern in URBAN POLITICS, with blacks being elected as mayors of major American cities as they became majority or near-majority black. Hatcher's election was marked by charges of vote fraud and harassment, requiring the presence of the FBI and a federal court order to assure a fair election. In the end Hatcher defeated his opponent Joseph Radigan by a narrow margin, 39,330 to 37,941. Immediately upon election, Hatcher faced a WHITE BACKLASH from the city's white establishment and voters along with a series of crises involving racial tensions, a strike by garbage collectors, a school boycott, and RIOTS in the aftermath of the 1968 assassination of MARTIN LUTHER KING JR. In his first term, white businesses (including U.S. Steel, the city's major employer) and residents began to flee the city; tax revenues declined; and rates of POVERTY and crime increased. After 20 years in office, Hatcher was defeated for reelection by Thomas Barnes, an African American.

When Hatcher took office in 1967, Gary was a reasonably prosperous city with a black population of about 40 percent. When he left office the entire city was essentially a GHETTO with a population more than 80 percent black and hyper-rates of poverty, crime, and drug abuse, and deteriorating schools and housing. Critics blamed Hatcher for Gary's rapid decline during his tenure, accusing him of running a corrupt, wasteful, and inefficient government. While there may have been some truth to these allegations, RACISM and WHITE SUPREMACY also contributed to Gary's decline as white residents and businesses withdrew from the city rather than live under a government headed by an African-American mayor committed to the empowerment of blacks.

While serving as mayor, Hatcher with AMIRI BARAKA and CHARLES DIGGS convened the 1972 NATIONAL BLACK POLITICAL CONVENTION, where he worked, unsuccessfully, to build a COALITION between radical and mainstream black leaders. He was also the first chair of the board of TRANSAFRICA. In 1978 President JIMMY CARTER offered Hatcher a position as a senior White House adviser, but he declined, preferring to continue as mayor. In 1988 he served as senior adviser in JESSE JACKSON's 1988 PRESIDENTIAL CAMPAIGN and then returned to Gary to practice law.

Hawkins, Augustus (1907–) *congressman*

Augustus Hawkins, elected to the CONGRESS in 1962, was the first African American elected to the House of Representatives from California. Pior to his election to the U.S. House, Hawkins had served in the California State Legislature for 28 years, for most of that time as its only black member. Hawkins was committed to the IDEOLOGY of LIBERALISM, rejecting BLACK NATIONALISM and MILITANCY in favor of INTEGRATIONism and COALITION-building across racial and ideological lines. This led him to oppose the establishment of the racially separate CONGRESSIONAL BLACK CAUCUS and the convening in 1972 of the NATIONAL BLACK POLITICAL CONVENTION. (Like WALTER WHITE, Hawkins in physical appearance was indistinguishable from a white man.) In Congress, Hawkins's moderate style of LEADERSHIP was instrumental in securing passage in 1978 of the HUMPHREY-HAWKINS ACT, legislation designed to achieve FULL EMPLOYMENT. As chair of the House Subcommittee on Employment Opportunities, he held a series of hearings on the problem of joblessness and on the need to address it with legislation. He also convened academic experts on the subject; wrote articles and papers; authored the first draft of the act; persuaded HUBERT HUMPHREY to cosponsor it in the Senate; helped to build coalitions for the act in Congress and among black, labor, liberal, and religious INTEREST GROUPS; and managed the negotiations with President JIMMY CARTER and congressional leaders that finally resulted in a compromise version of the Humphrey-Hawkins legislation. Although he expressed disappointment that the legislation was compromised and watered down from his original draft and did not achieve its goal of full employment, the act remains the only piece of legislation that bears the name of a black member of Congress. Hawkins retired from the House in 1990 after following in the path of ADAM CLAYTON POWELL JR. by becoming the second African American to chair the House Committee on Education and Labor.

Hayes, Rutherford B. (1822–1893) *19th president of the United States*

Rutherford B. Hayes's election to the PRESIDENCY in 1876 represents the symbolic end of RECONSTRUCTION. Hayes's election and presidency also represent the emergence of the CONSERVATIVE COALITION of Southern, WHITE-SUPREMACIST Democrats and Northern conservative Republicans who dominated the CONGRESS on CIVIL RIGHTS and WELFARE STATE issues until the 1960s.

Hayes was the second president to win the office while losing a majority of the vote. In the COMPROMISE OF 1877, Hayes was awarded a majority of the votes in the ELECTORAL COLLEGE after he promised to withdraw the army from the SOUTHERN STATES, thus effectively ending Reconstruction. Within two months of taking office he kept his promise and ordered federal troops in Louisiana and South Carolina to withdraw their protection of African Americans and the Reconstruction governments they were supporting. Hayes's actions were largely symbolic, because Reconstruction had largely come to an end with the withdrawal of most federal troops during the presidency of ULYSSES S. GRANT. Yet the symbolism of Hayes's quick action in withdrawing the troops was very important because it signaled to the nation the finality of Reconstruction and the end of any effort by the federal government to intervene to protect blacks from VIOLENCE, terrorism, and POLITICAL REPRESSION. The liberal magazine *The Nation* concluded at the time of Hayes's decision that "the Negro will disappear from the field of national politics. Henceforth, the nation, as a nation, will have nothing to do with him."

Historians continue to debate the significance of the Hayes presidency and the end of Reconstruction. Hayes apparently was not a RACIST, was sympathetic to black interests, and wished that Southern whites would treat blacks fairly. But in the face of a WHITE BACKLASH in PUBLIC OPINION and in Congress, Hayes apparently felt he had no choice but to withdraw the remaining federal troops from the South. Thus Hayes presided over the final demise of the Reconstruction policies that had offered African Americans the hope of FREEDOM and EQUALITY—a demise that was almost complete by the time of his election.

Further reading: Rayford Logan, *The Betrayal of the Negro: From Rutherford B. Hayes to Woodrow Wilson* (New York: Collier Books, 1965).

Heart of Atlanta Motel v. United States (1964)

Heart of Atlanta Motel v. United States (1964) is the seminal case by the SUPREME COURT establishing the right of the CONGRESS to use the COMMERCE CLAUSE to regulate the behavior of businesses in the interest of CIVIL RIGHTS. The decision prohibits DISCRIMINATION against individuals through actions that might impede or distort the movement of persons, products, or services across state lines. In its unanimous opinion, the Court was clear in its assertion of Congress's power to regulate commerce for moral purposes, including HUMAN RIGHTS. It held that the commerce clause was "specific and plenary" and that the only standards or questions were whether Congress had a ratio-

nal basis to conclude that racial discrimination by motels affected commerce and whether, if it had such a basis, the means selected to eliminate the "evil" were reasonable and appropriate. Concluding that the public-accommodations section of the CIVIL RIGHTS ACT OF 1964 met both standards, the Court said the motel had no right under the CONSTITUTION to engage in racial discrimination in its choice of patrons. (The owners of the Heart of Atlanta Motel had argued that they had been deprived of the rights of liberty and property guaranteed by the Fifth Amendment's DUE PROCESS CLAUSE.)

Justice William O. Douglas, while agreeing with the use of the commerce clause in this case, in a prescient concurring opinion wrote that he would have preferred to base the decision on the FOURTEENTH AMENDMENT's EQUAL PROTECTION CLAUSE. He reasoned that the right of persons to travel from state to state "occupies a more protected position in our constitutional system than does the movement of cattle, fruit, steel and coal across state lines." He also believed that a decision based on the Fourteenth Amendment "would have a more settling effect, making unnecessary litigation over whether a particular restaurant or inn is within the Commerce definition . . . and put an end to all obstructionist strategies and finally close one bitter chapter in American history." Justice Douglas's opinion was prescient because, 30 years later, the Supreme Court began to interpret the commerce clause to require particular definitions of commerce that undermined the civil rights of women and the disabled, thus threatening to undermine the basic decision in *Heart of Atlanta*.

See also FEDERALISM.

Height, Dorothy (1912–) *civil rights leader*

Dorothy Height was elected president of the NATIONAL COUNCIL OF NEGRO WOMEN (NCNW), the leading ORGANIZATION of women in AFRICAN-AMERICAN POLITICS, in 1957 and served in that position until she retired in 1999.

Born in Richmond, Virginia, Height earned graduate and undergraduate degrees from New York University and shortly thereafter joined the staff of the Young Women's Christian Association (YWCA) in HARLEM. While serving as assistant director of the Harlem YWCA, she met MARY MCLEOD BETHUNE, the founder and president of NCNW. As a result of this encounter, Height became an NCNW volunteer while continuing to work with the YWCA. In 1947 she was elected president of the Delta Sigma Theta sorority, and 10 years later she was elected president of NCNW. As NCNW president, Height was the only woman among the so-called big-six leaders of the CIVIL RIGHTS MOVEMENT during the 1960s, which included ROY WILKINS of the NAACP, WHITNEY YOUNG of the URBAN LEAGUE, JAMES FARMER of THE CONGRESS OF RACIAL EQUALITY,

JOHN LEWIS of the STUDENT NONVIOLENT COORDINATING COMMITTEE, and MARTIN LUTHER KING JR. of the SOUTHERN CHRISTIAN LEADERSHIP CONFERENCE. Although she was occasionally included in the deliberations of the leaders and in their formal meetings with the president and the leaders of CONGRESS, because of SEXISM her role was symbolic and peripheral. Perhaps the most egregious example of the sexist treatment of Height by her colleagues is that, of the big-six leaders, she was the only one denied an opportunity to speak at the historic 1963 MARCH ON WASHINGTON, where Dr. King gave the famous "I HAVE A DREAM" SPEECH. (No woman was allowed to speak at the march.) Although she did not protest at the time, years later in a 1996 interview, Height lamented the exclusion of women from visible leadership roles during the Civil Rights movement and from the established structure of black LEADERSHIP generally:

> I think it is important for African-American women to get credit for what we do, and to acknowledge that we are doing it well and to see ourselves as victorious and not forget women like FANNIE LOU HAMER and IDA B. WELLS-BARNETT. Any entity, even the political bodies and the churches, that is oppressive to women, we should withdraw our support from

Although not known as an advocate of FEMINISM, NCNW has since its inception supported gender as well as racial EQUALITY. In the 1990s it established the Dorothy Height Leadership Institute (to train black women in leadership skills) and the National Center for African American Women (to serve as a clearinghouse on issues of importance to African-American women and families).

Highlander Folk School

The Highlander Folk School is an example of an organization that used systematic knowledge as a base of POWER to assist African Americans in their struggle for FREEDOM and EQUALITY. Founded in 1932 by Myles Horton and Don West, the school was initially a training center for union organizers, but in the 1950s it shifted to CIVIL RIGHTS and quickly became a major center for recruiting and training workers in the CIVIL RIGHTS MOVEMENT. The center always focused on developing indigenous or grassroots leadership, arguing that the victims of OPPRESSION were best suited to lead the struggle against it. Located in rural Tennessee, Highlander was one of the few places in the SOUTHERN STATES where blacks and whites could interact freely. In the late 1950s and early 1960s it was a place of training for the STUDENT NONVIOLENT COORDINATING COMMITTEE (SNCC) and the SOUTHERN CHRISTIAN LEADERSHIP CONFERENCE (SCLC) staff and volunteers, including ROSA PARKS and ELLA BAKER. In 1957 MARTIN LUTHER

KING JR. addressed a training session at the school and the lyrics for "WE SHALL OVERCOME" were refined as the movement's anthem at Highlander. Although the school included Eleanor Roosevelt, the wife of FRANKLIN D. ROOSEVELT, among other high-status persons on its board, the FBI suggested that it was a "front" for the COMMUNIST PARTY and engaged in an ongoing pattern of POLITICAL REPRESSION. The group was also harassed by the KU KLUX KLAN, and in 1962 its charter was revoked and its property seized by the government of Tennessee. Highlander temporarily turned its training program over to SCLC, but in 1971 it returned to Tennessee renamed the Highlander Research and Education Center.

See also THINK TANKS.

Further reading: John Glen, *Highlander: No Ordinary School* (Lexington: University of Kentucky Press, 1988).

historically black colleges and universities

Historically black colleges and universities (HBCUs) are institutions established in the United States to educate African Americans. Knowledge is a very important base of POWER for a SUBORDINATE GROUP in its struggle for FREEDOM and EQUALITY. African Americans have always known this and sought to acquire knowledge, and whites bent on the OPPRESSION of blacks have always known this and have attempted to deny blacks access to education. In the totalitarian system of oppression that was American SLAVERY, enslaved persons were denied even the right to read, and those caught attempting to do so were severely punished. Nevertheless, many took the risk, and the earliest efforts at education for blacks can be traced to the secret reading groups that existed on many plantations in the SOUTHERN STATES. After the CIVIL WAR, African Americans exhibited what one historian describes as a "seemingly unquenchable thirst for education," viewing it as "central to the meaning of freedom." Thus, the establishment of schools of all kinds in all places was a major project of blacks during RECONSTRUCTION.

Although a few blacks attended white universities in the NORTHERN STATES prior to the Civil War, most such places excluded blacks. In response to this, the first of the historically black colleges was established in the North in 1837, now known as Cheyney University in Pennsylvania. But this institution and a couple of others established before the Civil War were little more than high schools. The real development of black higher education came in two waves, during and after Reconstruction. In the first wave religious institutions, black and white, established several HBCUs. The white American Missionary Association and the American Baptist Home Mission started several colleges, among them several prestigious institutions such as Fisk University in Tennessee and Morehouse and Spellman Universities in Atlanta. The African Methodist Episcopal Church also established or supported several HBCUs, including Morris Brown in Atlanta and Wilburforce in Ohio. And the CONGRESS, acting through the FREEDMEN'S BUREAU, established HOWARD UNIVERSITY in 1867. The second wave of HBCUs were created by Southern state governments. After the SUPREME COURT in PLESSY V. FERGUSON allowed the states to establish SEGREGATION in education, the states were required by Congress in the 1890 Morrill Act to create colleges for African Americans. These colleges, however, were for many years colleges in name only, since because of inadequate funding they were able to offer little more than a high school curriculum. It was well into the 20th century before most of the Southern states, fearing pressures toward DESEGREGATION of their white universities, began to provide enough funds for these institutions to offer something resembling a college education.

From the beginning, the higher education of blacks has been marked by conflicts and tensions regarding its purpose, the role of black administrators and faculty, and the role of the universities in the political struggles of African Americans. The first conflict was the classic dispute between BOOKER T. WASHINGTON and W. E. B. DU BOIS. Washington, using TUSKEGEE INSTITUTE as the model, argued that blacks should have an agricultural and mechanical curriculum to prepare them for the jobs available to them. Du Bois, using his alma mater Fisk as a model, argued that a TALENTED TENTH of African Americans should be educated in the liberal arts. Because Washington's ideas were supported by Northern white philanthropy and Southern state governments, agricultural, technical, and mechanical education dominated black college curricula until the 1930s. At the beginning of black higher education there were few blacks qualified to teach and administer at the colleges. But even as blacks became qualified, there was resistance at many institutions to hiring them as faculty and administrators, leading to student PROTEST. These protests and the MILITANCY of elements of the Talented Tenth eventually led to the hiring of blacks to teach and run black colleges, but it took a long time for this to happen. Howard University, for example, did not get its first black president until 1936, and most HBCUs still have sizable white faculty. Because most black colleges were funded by whites, who often were racists and white supremacists, POLITICAL REPRESSION of faculty and students who challenged RACISM and WHITE SUPREMACY was widespread. Although students in the 1950s and 1960s played an important role in the CIVIL RIGHTS MOVEMENT, they often did so at considerable risk, as they were frequently expelled or punished in other ways for their activism. Finally, the curricula of the HBCUs tended to be Eurocentric, ignoring African and African-American history and CULTURE. In the 1930s scholars such as Du Bois and CARTER G. WOODSON were harshly critical of the Eurocentrism and the political irrelevancy of HBCU curricula, but the curricula did not fundamentally change at most HBCUs until the emergence of AFRICAN-AMERICAN STUDIES in the late 1960s.

In spite of their historic limitations in terms of funding, curriculum, and staffing, HBCUs were the principal sources of black knowledge acquisition until the 1960s, and their teachers and students were important resources in the Civil Rights and BLACK POWER MOVEMENTS. They trained a Talented Tenth and provided the educational underpinnings for the emergence of the black middle class. At the end of the 20th century as a result of the Civil Rights movement, blacks are less reliant on HBCUs for knowledge acquisition. Most black students now attend predominantly white universities; the most talented black faculty often teach at white universities; and both public and private HBCUs tend to be poorly funded compared with white universities. (For example, Howard University, the best-endowed HBCU, has an endowment of about $150 million, a pittance compared with Harvard, the best-endowed American university at $7 billion.) Finally, because of the CIVIL RIGHTS ACT OF 1964, state-supported HBCUs in the Southern states were required to desegregate and admit white students. While most remain overwhelmingly black, some black educators fear that the pressures to desegregate may eventually result in the disappearance of HBCUs as distinctive institutions (blacks are now a minority of students at several HBCUs). In addition, some Southern states are under pressures to close HBCUs or merge them with predominantly white institutions in order to save money and avoid duplication. The long-term future of the 100 or so remaining HBCUs is unclear. These institutions have their origins in racism and white supremacy, but in spite of this most African Americans have pride in them, view them as important parts of the infrastructure of the BLACK COMMUNITY, and wish to preserve them as racially distinctive places of knowledge acquisition.

Holden, Matthew, Jr. (1931–) *scholar*

Matthew Holden Jr. is one of the most influential African-American political scientists in the United States. The scope of his research and scholarship is broad, spanning the fields of decision-making theory, public administration, the BUREAUCRACY, URBAN POLITICS, the PRESIDENCY, as well as the politics of RACE and ETHNICITY. But it is generally agreed that his most significant contribution to political science and the study of AFRICAN-AMERICAN POLITICS was his publication in 1973 of two books, *The Politics of the Black "Nation"* and *The White Man's Burden*. (Both books were also published together in a single volume under the title *The Divisible Republic.*) *The Politics of the Black "Nation"* is regarded by many as the best study of African-American politics written by an academic political scientist, and its impact on the study and teaching of the subject is rivaled only by HAROLD CRUSE's *The Crisis of the Negro Intellectual* and STOKELY CARMICHAEL and CHARLES HAMILTON's book *Black Power: The Politics of Liberation.* *The White Man's Burden* also made important contributions to the study of black politics, including analyses of INSTITUTIONAL RACISM, WHITE SUPREMACY, the SOUTHERN STRATEGY, and the strategic position of the TWO-PARTY SYSTEM on race in the POST–CIVIL RIGHTS ERA. But *The Politics of the Black "Nation"* is the more widely read and influential of the two volumes, with important chapters on CLASS STRATIFICATION, CULTURE, IDEOLOGY, LEADERSHIP, and ORGANIZATION. The book is built on the theoretical foundation of INTERNAL COLONIALISM, with Holden contending that the POLITICAL SYSTEM in the United States includes two "sociocultural nations locked into each other in a relationship which has been historically 'imperial,'" with the word *imperial* conveying the sense that the white "nation" has been dominant or SUPERORDINATE over the black "nation." Although Holden's work constitutes a seminal contribution to scholarship on black politics, it is also a work with a clearly stated ideological vision. Holden believed that INTEGRATION is the only "rational" ideology for African Americans, rejecting RADICALISM and most forms of BLACK NATIONALISM as either undesirable, unachieveable, or both. In many ways *The Politics of the Black "Nation"* is the most systematic and cogent exposition of integration as an ideology that one can find in African-American literature.

Holden was born in Mound Bayou, Mississippi, the all-black town founded by ISAIAH T. MONTGOMERY, the archetypal example of the "clientage" or UNCLE TOM-type leadership Holden writes about. (As a young man Holden had the opportunity to meet and "talk politics" with WILLIAM DAWSON, another black leader often referred to as an Uncle Tom.) He received an undergraduate degree from Roosevelt University and the Ph.D. from Northwestern University. In addition to teaching and research, Holden briefly served in the bureaucracy, appointed by President JIMMY CARTER to the Federal Energy Regulatory Commission. After leaving the commission, he was appointed to an endowed chair at the University of Virginia. In 2000 he was elected president of the American Political Science Association, becoming the third African American to hold the position in the 100-year history of the association.

See also RALPH BUNCHE.

Further reading: Joseph P. McCormick, ed., "A Retrospective on Matthew Holden, Jr.'s, *The Politics of the Black 'Nation,'" National Political Science Review* 8 (2001): 1–71.

Hoover, Edgar, J. (1895–1972) *U.S. government official*

J. Edgar Hoover, who directed the FBI, the nation's principal investigative and internal security BUREAUCRACY, for 48 years, is one of the most important persons in the 20th-century history of AFRICAN-AMERICAN POLITICS. He is important because he almost single-mindedly used the resources of the FBI for more than 40 years in a systematic campaign of POLITICAL REPRESSION of virtually every national African-American SOCIAL MOVEMENT, ORGANIZATION, and leader in the struggle for FREEDOM and EQUALITY. Apparently a person who believed in WHITE SUPREMACY and RACISM (in private he often used crude racial stereotypes to refer to blacks), Hoover viewed any challenge from blacks as a threat to the POLITICAL SYSTEM. He therefore used the FBI to spy on, disrupt, distort, or destroy any person or group that challenged racism and white supremacy. Defining the mission of the FBI as the protection of the political system's core values, he acted as if he believed those core values included racism as well as CAPITALISM, DEMOCRACY, and CONSTITUTIONALISM. Thus, from the start of his leadership of the bureau, he used it to repress RADICALISM, SOCIALISM, COMMUNISM, as well as the CIVIL RIGHTS MOVEMENT.

Hoover's targets for repression included moderate groups like the NAACP and URBAN LEAGUE, radical groups like the AFRICAN BLOOD BROTHERHOOD and the BLACK PANTHER PARTY, and black nationalist groups like the UNIVERSAL NEGRO IMPROVEMENT ASSOCIATION and the NATION OF ISLAM. The leaders targeted reads like a who's who list of 20th-century black leaders, including W. E. B. DU BOIS, MARCUS GARVEY, A. PHILIP RANDOLPH, ELIJAH MUHAMMAD, ADAM CLAYTON POWELL JR., MALCOLM X., MARTIN LUTHER KING JR., HUEY NEWTON, BAYARD RUSTIN, and STOKELY CARMICHAEL. Almost all black-owned MEDIA were targeted, as were leading congregations and pastors of the BLACK CHURCH.

The methods of repression used included surveillance and wiretaps; the planting of informants and agents provocateurs to disrupt and sow dissension within organizations; spreading false stories and gossip about prominent leaders; and harassment and false arrest. All of these methods of repression have been documented by historians and by the CONGRESS in its investigations of COINTELPRO. And while there is no documentary or other direct evidence to support it, most of Martin Luther King Jr.'s colleagues in SCLC and members of his family believe that the FBI either participated in the assassination of Dr. King or at least was aware of the conspiracy to kill him, allowed it to take place, and permitted the conspirators to escape arrest and prosecution. Meanwhile, while vigorously repressing the black movement, Hoover was reluctant to investigate white terrorists such as the KU KLUX KLAN, citing principles of FEDERALISM that prevented the bureau from interfering with law enforcement by STATE AND LOCAL GOVERNMENTS.

In American popular culture a mythology developed about Hoover's FBI. The bureau was viewed as an efficient police organization, and Hoover was portrayed as its gallant leader. This image of Hoover and the bureau was popularized in radio and television programs depicting the FBI capturing gangsters such as Bonnie and Clyde and John Dillinger and preventing spying and subversion by Japanese and German agents during World War II. Hoover did organize the bureau into an efficient police organization and was responsible for many innovative techniques and procedures in law enforcement, but his legacy in African-American politics is the destabilization and distortion of the capability and motives of black leaders and organizations.

Further reading: Theodore Kornweibel, *Seeing Red: Federal Campaigns against Black Militancy, 1919–1925* (Bloomington: Indiana University Press, 1998); Kenneth O'Reilly, *"Racial Matters": The FBI's Secret File on Black America* (New York: Free Press, 1989); Sanford Ungar, *FBI: An Uncensored Look behind the Walls* (Boston: Little, Brown, 1975).

Housing and Urban Development (HUD), U.S. Department of

The Department of Housing and Urban Development (HUD), established in 1965, is the principal agency in the BUREAUCRACY with responsibilities for housing and community development. Traditionally, it is also considered the department with primary responsibilities for dealing with problems of RACE and POVERTY as they are manifested in the GHETTOS of the United States. President JOHN F. KENNEDY first proposed creating HUD in 1961, but the CONGRESS refused to act because of the opposition of the CONSERVATIVE COALITION, which generally was not sympathetic to urban concerns and therefore did not wish to see such concerns elevated to cabinet status. RACISM and WHITE SUPREMACY were also factors in the opposition, since Kennedy had indicated his intention to appoint an African American, ROBERT WEAVER, to head the new department, making him the first black in the cabinet. After Kennedy's assassination, HUD was established during the administration of LYNDON B. JOHNSON, who appointed Weaver its first secretary. Reflecting its role as a department concerned with issues of race and MINORITY GROUPS, of its 12 secretaries since 1965, five have been racial minorities (three blacks, two Latinos), more than any other cabinet department in the history of the United States.

See also PATRICIA ROBERTS HARRIS and SAMUEL PIERCE.

Houston, Charles (1895–1950) *scholar*

Charles Hamilton Houston played a leading role in the research and scholarship that led to the strategy employed by the NAACP to end SEGREGATION in the United States, and as dean of the HOWARD UNIVERSITY law school he trained THURGOOD MARSHALL and a cadre of other black lawyers who implemented the strategy in BROWN V. BOARD OF EDUCATION. Born in the DISTRICT OF COLUMBIA, Houston was graduated Phi Beta Kappa from Amherst and received his law degree from Harvard. At age 34 he became dean of Howard's law school. Immediately, he set about to reform the law school by raising its standards of admission and graduation and hiring more-qualified faculty. The purpose of the reforms was to make the law school into a CIVIL RIGHTS laboratory and clearinghouse with the avowed purpose of using LITIGATION as a strategy to achieve racial EQUALITY. In addition to his teaching and research, Houston briefly served as an NAACP counsel, where he played a role in developing its strategy and in persuading it to hire his student Thurgood Marshall.

Further reading: Genna Rae MacNiel, *Groundwork: Charles Hamilton Houston and the Struggle for Civil Rights* (College Park, Md.: University of Maryland Press, 1983).

Howard University

Howard University, established in 1867 under the auspices of the FREEDMEN'S BUREAU (and named in honor of General Oliver O. Howard, the bureau's first director), is preeminent among the nation's HISTORICALLY BLACK COLLEGES AND UNIVERSITIES. Howard is the nation's only comprehensive research university, offering the Ph.D. in most of the arts and sciences as well as professional degrees in law, medicine, dentistry, theology, and business. The university is unique among colleges and universities because it is one of only two (the other is Gallaudet College for the deaf) chartered and funded by CONGRESS. Located in the DISTRICT OF COLUMBIA, Howard was always seen as a place to train the TALENTED TENTH, and until the success of the CIVIL RIGHTS MOVEMENT in the 1960s, it was home to the best and brightest African-American scholars and students. Its law school, under the leadership of CHARLES HOUSTON, trained THURGOOD MARSHALL and a cadre of black lawyers and served as a laboratory and clearinghouse for LITIGATION on CIVIL RIGHTS. Its political science department, founded by RALPH BUNCHE, trained a first generation of African-American political scientists and offers the only comprehensive graduate curriculum in AFRICAN-AMERICAN POLITICS in the United States. The Moorland-Spingarn Research Center at Howard rivals the SCHOMBURG CENTER FOR RESEARCH IN BLACK CULTURE in HARLEM as the largest repository of papers and documents on the African-American experience.

In part because of its location in the nation's capital and its preeminence, the university has always attracted a diverse student body, including students from Africa and the WEST INDIAN islands. It has also been a politically conscious and active university, with students and faculty organizing early PROTESTS against SEGREGATION in the city and LYNCHING throughout the country. Its faculty, under the leadership of Ralph Bunche, helped to organize the NATIONAL NEGRO CONGRESS in the 1930s; the university was used as a recruiting and training place for the SIT-INS and for SNCC volunteers; its faculty, led by RONALD WALTERS, helped to plan and staff the 1972 NATIONAL BLACK POLITICAL CONVENTION; and its faculty and students worked as advisers and staff to the CONGRESSIONAL BLACK CAUCUS and in JESSE JACKSON's two PRESIDENTIAL CAMPAIGNS. The university has also sponsored research and held conferences and symposia on most of the social, economic, and political issues of importance to the BLACK COMMUNITY. In the POST–CIVIL RIGHTS ERA, Howard, like most historically black colleges and universities, faced competition from predominantly white universities for the best and brightest black faculty and students. And because of its relatively small endowment, it is not in a good competitive position with elite white universities. But because of its historical legacy, its location in Washington, and the continuing allure of BLACKNESS, it is likely to remain the capstone of black education in the United States.

Further reading: Rayford Logan, *Howard University: The First Hundred Years, 1867–1967* (Washington, D.C.: Howard University Press, 1969).

human rights

Human rights is the concept that the rights of individuals are not derived from governments but, rather, are inherent in the humanity of all persons and therefore transcend CIVIL RIGHTS and national boundaries. This concept is to some extent rooted in the NATURAL RIGHTS doctrine that is the philosophical underpinnings of the DECLARATION OF INDEPENDENCE. But it is broader than this doctrine because, as codified in the UNITED NATIONS' 1948 UNIVERSAL DECLARATION OF HUMAN RIGHTS, it includes not merely natural rights but economic, social, and cultural rights as well as specific guarantees to be free from DISCRIMINATION on the basis of race or gender. African American leaders including W. E. B. DU BOIS, WALTER WHITE, and MARY MCLEOD BETHUNE were vigorous supporters of the United Nations' 1948 declaration, and even before its adoption, the NATIONAL NEGRO CONGRESS in 1947 and Du Bois and others in 1948 filed a petition with the United Nations (UN) asking it to intervene to dismantle SEGREGATION because it violated the human rights of African Americans. In 1955 Congressman CHARLES DIGGS wrote RALPH BUNCHE asking about the feasibility of submitting a

resolution charging the United States with violating the human rights of blacks. The year before his death in 1965, MALCOLM X was seeking the support of African leaders for a human-rights petition on behalf of blacks in the United States. In 2000, the LEADERSHIP CONFERENCE ON CIVIL RIGHTS presented a petition to the UN high commissioner on human rights asking for consideration of continuing racial discrimination in the United States as an agenda item of the 2001 UN-sponsored World Conference Against Racism. Human rights in the context of GLOBALIZATION allows African-American leaders to take problems of racism beyond the confines of the United States and its CONSTITUTION to the global community and its Universal Declaration of Human Rights.

Humphrey, Hubert H. (1911–1978) *U.S. senator, 38th vice president of the United States*
Hubert H. Humphrey—U.S. senator from Minnesota from 1948 to 1965, vice president of the United States from 1965 to 1969, and U.S. senator again from 1970 to 1978—was one of the most powerful advocates of CIVIL RIGHTS ever to serve in CONGRESS. Even before becoming a senator, while serving as mayor of Minneapolis, Humphrey embraced the cause of civil rights and racial EQUALITY. In a famous speech at the DEMOCRATIC PARTY's 1948 National Convention, Humphrey said, "The time has come for the Democratic Party to get out of the shadow of states' rights and walk forthrightly into the bright sunshine of human rights." In part as a result of the influence of this speech, the Democratic Party under the leadership of HARRY TRUMAN for the first time in its history adopted a civil rights agenda.

Elected to the Senate in 1948, Humphrey passionately embraced the cause of civil rights throughout the 1950s. Perhaps the Senate's leading advocate of LIBERALISM in the 1950s and 1960s, Humphrey was also a passionate supporter of the WELFARE STATE. Defeated by JOHN F. KENNEDY for the Democratic presidential nomination in 1960, in 1961 he became the deputy leader of the Democrats in the Senate. In 1964 he managed the debate that led to the end of a six-month FILIBUSTER by SOUTHERN STATE senators and to the passage of the CIVIL RIGHTS ACT OF 1964, thus fulfilling the pledge of his 1948 speech.

In part because of Humphrey's work on civil rights, President LYNDON B. JOHNSON selected him as his vice presidential candidate in the 1964 election. After Johnson declined to run in 1968, Humphrey won the Democratic nomination for president but was defeated in a close election by RICHARD NIXON. Humphrey lost in part because of white liberals who were disenchanted with his support of the VIETNAM WAR, although he was strongly supported by black leaders and voters. After leaving the vice presidency, Humphrey returned to the Senate. In the 1970s he joined with African-American congressman AUGUSTUS HAWKINS to sponsor the HUMPHREY-HAWKINS ACT. Although he died before the act was passed, he was succeeded by his wife, Muriel, who gained support for the legislation in part as a memorial to her husband. (The Humphrey-Hawkins Act is the only act of Congress that carries the senator's name.)

Further reading: Timothy Thurber, *The Politics of Equality: Hubert H. Humphrey and the African American Freedom Struggle* (New York: Columbia University Press, 1999).

Humphrey-Hawkins Act

The Humphrey-Hawkins Act is the informal designation used to refer to the Full Employment and Balanced Growth Act passed by CONGRESS in 1978. (The designation refers to Senator HUBERT HUMPHREY and Congressman AUGUSTUS HAWKINS, the legislation's sponsors.) The purpose of the act was to move the United States toward FULL EMPLOY-MENT, which became the principal item on the BLACK AGENDA of POST–CIVIL RIGHTS ERA black LEADERSHIP.

Full employment became the principal item on the black agenda in the late 1960s and early 1970s at the end of the CIVIL RIGHTS MOVEMENT, although it had been a concern of black leaders since the NEW DEAL. The 1963 MARCH ON WASHINGTON, where MARTIN LUTHER KING JR. delivered his "I HAVE A DREAM" SPEECH, was officially called a march for "Jobs and Freedom." However, the demand for jobs had to take second place to the demand for FREEDOM or basic CIVIL RIGHTS, which were achieved with the passage of the CIVIL RIGHTS ACT OF 1964 and the VOTING RIGHTS ACT OF 1965. But the problem of jobless-ness was clearly a major concern in the BLACK COMMUNITY, especially in the big city GHETTOS of the NORTHERN STATES, where blacks already had basic civil rights. Since the end of the depression, blacks have never experienced full employment (defined generally as 4 percent of the adult labor force). Rather, in the post–World War II era, black unemployment has been twice that of whites, usually at or above 10 percent of the adult labor force. It was there-fore almost inevitable that African-American leaders would turn to jobs—full employment guaranteed by the federal government—as their dominant concern.

At the time of his death in 1968, Martin Luther King Jr. was planning to lead the POOR PEOPLE'S CAMPAIGN in the DISTRICT OF COLUMBIA. This campaign was envisioned as a multiracial COALITION of poor peoples and their allies who would demand that the federal government guaran-tee all Americans a job or an income. After King's death, the Poor Peoples Campaign took place under the leader-ship of his associates, including JESSE JACKSON, but it did not result in any actions by the Congress. The issue of full employment, however, remained a priority in the writings of leading intellectuals such as CHARLES HAMILTON and BAYARD RUSTIN. In the early 1970s the CONGRESSIONAL BLACK CAUCUS adopted full employment as the lead item on its legislative agenda, and Congressman Augustus Hawkins drafted a bill, held hearings, and began to assem-ble a broad coalition of INTEREST GROUPS of blacks and lib-eral, labor, and religious groups.

A similar coalition had attempted to pass full-employment legislation a generation earlier, but by the time the bill was passed as the Employment Act of 1946, it offered only a symbolic commitment to full employ-ment, since the provision stipulating a guaranteed job had been deleted. Critics of the 1946 act included leading businessmen, newspapers, and economists, who argued that full employment was only possible under SOCIALISM. They characterized the legislation as "un-American," "utopian," and an affront to free-market CAPITALISM. The critics also argued that full employment would result in "runaway inflation."

Similar criticisms were aimed at the legislation intro-duced by Congressman Hawkins and Senator Hubert Humphrey in the 1970s. The original Humphrey-Hawkins bill, like the 1946 legislation, established the legal right to work for American citizens, and it required the Congress to create public-sector jobs for individuals who could not find employment in the private economy. But, as in 1946, when the legislation was signed in 1978 by President JIMMY CARTER, the provisions creating a legal right to work had been deleted, making it little more than a symbolic act. In the years following its passage, it did little to address the problem of persistent joblessness in the black community. It is symbolically significant, however, as the only piece of legislation that bears the name of an African-American congressman.

I

ideology

Ideology in Western political thought and in American political science is not defined in a single way. However, it is generally understood as a set of interrelated ideas used to justify the maintenance of an existing POLITICAL SYSTEM or as a set of interrelated ideas used to transform or alter an existing social or political system. Sophisticated ideologies developed by intellectuals and political leaders often include some conception of history and its relationship to the need for system maintenance or transformation. In a narrow sense, ideology is also related to ideas about the role, size, and purposes of government in the economy and society. In a broader sense, one can think of WHITE SUPREMACY as an ideology or a set of ideas used to justify SLAVERY, RACISM, COLONIALISM, and other forms of racially based OPPRESSION, while ideologies of BLACK NATIONALISM are sets of ideas used to justify the black struggle against oppression and to achieve FREEDOM and EQUALITY. In a broader sense, contemporary LIBERALISM and CONSERVATISM can also both be viewed as ideologies used to justify the existing social, economic, and political systems in the United States, while RADICALISM, SOCIALISM, and COMMUNISM can be viewed as ideas used to justify the transformation of these systems.

Further reading: Michael Dawson, *Black Visions: The Roots of Contemporary African American Political Ideologies* (Chicago: University of Chicago Press, 2001); Mack Jones, "Scientific Method, Value Judgments and the Black Predicament in the US," *Review of Black Political Economy* 7 (1976): 4–18; Willard Mullins, "On the Concept of Ideology in Political Science," *American Political Science Review* 66 (1972): 458–72; Robert C. Smith, "Ideology as the Enduring Dilemma of Black Politics," in *Dilemmas of Black Politics*, ed. Georgia Persons (New York: Harper Collins, 1993): 211–24.

"I Have a Dream" speech

The "I Have a Dream" speech by MARTIN LUTHER KING JR. at the close of the 1963 MARCH ON WASHINGTON is one of the most famous speeches in American history, comparable in its significance and familiarity with ABRAHAM LINCOLN's 1863 GETTYSBURG ADDRESS. In AFRICAN-AMERICAN THOUGHT the "I Have a Dream" speech ranks with FREDERICK DOUGLASS's 1852 4th of July Address, BOOKER T. WASHINGTON's 1895 "ATLANTA COMPROMISE" ADDRESS, and MALCOLM X's 1964 "BALLOT OR THE BULLET" SPEECH. Each of these speeches at the time they were delivered represented important statements about the sentiments of the BLACK COMMUNITY and constitute important documents in African-American thought.

The "I Have a Dream" address was delivered by King at the Lincoln Memorial in the DISTRICT OF COLUMBIA on August 28, 1963, before an audience of 250,000, at that time the largest PROTEST demonstration in the history of the United States. It came at a turning point in the CIVIL RIGHTS MOVEMENT. The BIRMINGHAM DEMONSTRATIONS in April 1963 had resulted in the introduction by JOHN F. KENNEDY of what a year later would become the CIVIL RIGHTS ACT OF 1964. On the verge of the movement's greatest success, King's address defined the movement's meaning in the context of the historical experience of the OPPRESSION of African Americans by placing their long struggle for FREEDOM and EQUALITY in the tradition of the nation's commitment to those values. In this sense, the speech is quintessentially both black and American.

As the Civil Rights movement's preeminent leader—King was introduced by A. PHILIP RANDOLPH as the "moral leader of the nation"—and its best orator, march planners unanimously agreed that King should give the closing address. But like the other leaders who spoke, he was limited to seven minutes. Although King had known for some time that he was going to deliver the address before a national audience of millions (since the march was televised live on the national television networks), he did not

Martin Luther King Jr. delivering his "I Have a Dream" speech at the March on Washington, August 1963 *(National Archives)*

write the speech until the night before. In a sense, however, he had been preparing for this historic moment in hundreds of speeches delivered since 1955. He began the speech by invoking the NATURAL RIGHTS doctrine articulated, he said, by the "magnificent words" of THOMAS JEFFERSON in the DECLARATION OF INDEPENDENCE and in Lincoln's EMANCIPATION PROCLAMATION. Arguing that these documents were "promissory notes" guaranteeing freedom to all Americans, King said America had given the Negro people a "bad check," one that had come back marked "insufficient funds." The purpose of the Civil Rights movement and the march was, he said to "cash this check." At this point, he recounted the searing history of blacks during SLAVERY and the 100 years since its end, and declared that "NOW!" was the time to make real the promises of the American DEMOCRACY. Aware that critics like MALCOLM X had dismissed the march, claiming it had been co-opted by the Kennedy administration, King invoked a tone of MILITANCY as he celebrated the courage of those struggling for freedom in the SOUTHERN STATES. He also promised continued disruption of the nation's stability until the movement's demands were satisfied. Also, mindful of the criticisms of Malcolm X and others about the role of whites in the movement and at the march, King rejected the allegations of CO-OPTATION while at the same time insisting on the indispensability of COALITIONS with what he called our "white brothers" in a struggle that he said would inevitably triumph. At this point, King departed from his written text and began, as he later said, to preach. This extemporaneous preaching became the most famous and memorable part of the speech, the part where he invoked over and over again the "I Have a Dream" refrain, ending with the words of what he called an old Negro spiritual "Free at last, free at last! Thank God Almighty, we are free at last!" The speech, which lasted 17 rather than the allotted seven minutes, was soon recognized as a classic in American oratory and as the template of the Civil Rights movement.

Widely reprinted and distributed on records and tapes, King's "I Have a Dream" speech and Lincoln's Gettysburg Address are the best-known and the most frequently recited speeches in American history. Interestingly, although delivered by different men with different purposes at different times, they are both integral to the African-American quest for freedom in the United States.

individualism

Although, as HAROLD CRUSE has pointed out, American society and politics are based on the exercise of power by groups, individualism is a core value in the philosophy of classical LIBERALISM that is the basis of the American political tradition, enshrined in both the DECLARATION OF INDEPENDENCE and the CONSTITUTION. Individualism is also central to the dynamism of CAPITALISM in the United States. In *DEMOCRACY IN AMERICA* Tocqueville identified individualism as one of the stable principles of the American DEMOCRACY, predisposing each citizen to withdraw into the "circles of family and friends" and leaving the "greater society to look out for itself." Studies in PUBLIC OPINION have documented the centrality of individualism in American culture. And comparative studies have shown that individualism is a much more important value in American CULTURE than it is in the rest of the Western world, predisposing Americans to think that it is the responsibility of the individual rather than the society or the government to deal with problems such as POVERTY. This value is an underlying reason for the late development and the relative stinginess of the American WELFARE STATE.

Although African Americans share the general cultural value of individualism, they are as a group more committed to communal values or an ethic of social responsibility. African Americans also understand that their OPPRESSION in the United States is based on their status as members of a group rather than as individuals, and therefore they have tended to embrace group-based rather than individually based remedies such as REPARATIONS and AFFIRMATIVE ACTION, remedies that many whites tend to reject in part because they are seen as violating the principles of individualism. And in the POST–CIVIL RIGHTS ERA, scholars of RACISM refer to "modern racism" or the "new racism" or contemporary WHITE SUPREMACY as phenomena directly linked to individualism. That is, many whites in the late 20th century exhibit hostility toward blacks and oppose programs to help them achieve EQUALITY because they view blacks as a *group* that is unwilling to adhere to principles of individualism in terms of individual initiative and hard work, or, in a word, blacks are said to exhibit a "lack of individual motivation." One scholar summarizes this research by writing "white Americans resist equality in the name of self-reliance, achievement, individual initiative, and they do so not because the value of individualism provides a socially acceptable pretext, but because it provides an integral component of the new racism." Thus, individualism as an American value may operate to impede the achievement of equality for African Americans.

See also LIBERALISM.

individual racism

RACISM can take two forms. Individual racism is when a person, acting individually or as part of an institution, intentionally takes the race of another individual or individuals into consideration in order to engage in invidious DISCRIMINATION or acts of subordination. Individual racism is contrasted with INSTITUTIONAL RACISM, where the discrimination or subordination occurs as a result of institutional practices without intentional racist acts on the part of any individual. STOKELY CARMICHAEL and CHARLES HAMILTON introduced this twofold classification of racism in their 1967 book *BLACK POWER: THE POLITICS OF LIBERATION*, and it has been employed by scholars of racism and the courts of the United States since that time. When the courts refer to individual racism, they use the term DISPARATE TREATMENT, while institutional racism is referred to as DISPARATE IMPACT. Examples of individual racism would include a police officer, a realtor, a banker, an educator, a doctor, or any other person in a position of POWER vis-à-vis others taking race into consideration to invidiously discriminate. Since the passage of the CIVIL RIGHTS ACT OF 1964 and related legislation, virtually all forms of individual racism have been illegal.

institutional racism

Institutional racism is a form or type of RACISM that originates in and is practiced by institutions in the society rather than by individuals. It is observed when the practices or patterns of institutions have the effect, result, or consequence of discriminating against or subordinating an individual or group on the basis of race. It is contrasted with INDIVIDUAL RACISM, which is observed when an individual intentionally takes into account the race of another individual or group and takes actions intended to discriminate or subordinate. STOKELY CARMICHAEL and CHARLES HAMILTON developed this way of classifying racism in their 1967 book BLACK POWER: THE POLITICS OF LIBERATION IN AMERICA. Prior to their book, the standard social science model of racism focused on legally mandated or intentional racism or SEGREGATION or the racist acts of individuals. This model influenced the CIVIL RIGHTS MOVEMENT, which assumed that once individual racism or segregation were made unlawful, and once individual attitudes and behavior changed to correspond with the law, racism would wither away. The concept of institutional racism as articulated in Carmichael and Hamilton's book suggested that racism might manifest itself not simply in racist laws or the racist acts of individuals, but it might stem also from institutional practices, seemingly neutral or nonracist in character, but which nevertheless result in systematically negative results or outcomes for blacks.

Scholars since Carmichael and Hamilton have used the concept in a variety of ways but there is one point of agreement: institutional racism is to be understood in terms not of the purposes or intent of institutional policies or practices but in terms of their consequences or results. The SUPREME COURT, in its POST–CIVIL RIGHTS ERA jurisprudence on racism, adopted this focus on the results or consequences of institutional practices in its use of the legal concept of DISPARATE IMPACT starting in GRIGGS V. DUKE POWER. While there is often an ambiguous quality in the evidence, empirical studies by social scientists since the 1960s have demonstrated the existence of institutional racism in education and employment, in the sale and rental of housing, in access to loans, in health care (including certain surgical procedures such as organ transplants and coronary-bypass procedures), in the purchase of consumer goods, and in the CRIMINAL JUSTICE SYSTEM. However, the Supreme Court in its cases since *Griggs v. Duke Power* has been slowly stepping back from recognizing institutional racism.

See also WARDS COVE V. ANTONIO.

Further reading: Joe R. Feagin, *Racist America: Roots, Current Realities and Future Reparations* (New York: Routledge, 2000); Robert C. Smith, *Racism in the Post Civil Rights Era: Now You See It, Now You Don't* (Albany: State University of New York Press, 1995).

integration

Integration, like BLACKNESS, is a contested concept in the study of AFRICAN-AMERICAN POLITICS. That is, it has multiple, controversial meanings. As MALCOLM X wrote in his autobiography, "The word has no meaning. I ask you: in the racial sense in which it is used so much today, whatever 'integration' is supposed to mean, can it be precisely defined?" The word can be precisely defined, but the problem is that it has multiple definitions and uses.

The word was hardly known in black politics before the 1950s, when it came into wide use during the PROTEST phase of the CIVIL RIGHTS MOVEMENT led by MARTIN LUTHER KING JR. As King and others used integration, it meant EQUALITY, which was the term used to define the objectives of the movement since its inception with the NIAGARA MOVEMENT in 1905. But in the 1950s integration was also used interchangeably with EQUALITY to define the goal of the movement. Integration during this period was also related to DESEGREGATION, which is a technique or process of ending SEGREGATION and achieving entry into places or institutions from which African Americans were historically excluded because of RACISM and WHITE SUPREMACY. Integration was also defined, however, not merely as a technique or process of desegregation but as a form of ASSIMILATION, in which African Americans would gradually abandon their CULTURE and heritage and embrace mainstream culture or the MELTING POT. This assimilationist concept of integration also envisioned a kind of random dispersal or integration of blacks into "white" neighborhoods and institutions. Ultimately, integration understood in this way would gradually result in the disappearance of a spatially, culturally, and institutionally distinctive BLACK COMMUNITY. In this meaning of integration, INDIVIDUALISM is the dominant value, that is, the United States becomes a nation of individuals who are Americans and nothing else. A final meaning of integration is as an IDEOLOGY, integrationism, that rejects BLACK NATIONALISM in favor of incorporation or integration into American society. This ideological meaning of integration, while not assimilationist, is also not nationalist in the sense that nationalism embraces some forms of separatism or withdrawal from participation in American institutions.

If integration is defined as equality or as a technique to end segregation, then it is widely accepted throughout the African-American community. MATTHEW HOLDEN JR., whose 1973 book *The Politics of the Black "Nation"* contains the most systematic exposition of integration and integrationism, defines integration or an integrated society as one where RACE does not determine the distribution of material well-being or psychic self-esteem to any significant degree. Again, this is a meaning or definition of integration that virtually all blacks have always aspired toward. However, this meaning of integration is also used by RONALD WALTERS to define the objective or aspiration of black nationalism, which contributes to the confusion or lack of clarity about its meaning. If integration, however, is defined as assimilation or dispersal, then it is widely rejected in the black community. Of this meaning of integration, Malcolm X said black people reject it because "they don't want to be dispersed, because they have racial pride, because they prefer to live together, or because dispersal could be a method of dividing Negroes physically and reducing their ability to defend their common interest against whites, whose good intentions they have little reason to believe in." Similarly STOKELY CARMICHAEL and CHARLES HAMILTON in *BLACK POWER: THE POLITICS OF LIBERATION* rejected integration because they saw it as based on the ideology of white supremacy and INTERNAL INFERIORIZATION, writing that integration "is based on the complete acceptance of the fact that in order to have a decent house or education, black people must move into a white neighborhood or send their children to a white school. This reinforces, among both black and white, the idea that 'white' is automatically superior and 'black' by definition is inferior. For this reason 'integration' is a subterfuge for the maintenance of white supremacy. . . . The fact is that integration, as traditionally articulated, would abolish the black community."

As an ideology, integrationism is rejected by advocates of RADICALISM and some versions of black nationalism. Unlike radicalism and black nationalism, integrationism lacks a tradition of ideas, doctrines, and myths that have been passed down from generation to generation. There is, for example, neither a "founding father" like MARTIN DELANY is to black nationalism nor a classical doctrinal statement such as EDWARD WILMOT BLYDEN's *Christianity, Islam and the Negro Race,* which is in the black nationalist tradition. Rather, integrationism as an ideology tends to be ad hoc and pragmatic, without systematic attention to problems of historical consciousness or internal consistency or coherence. Thus, it is difficult to identify the core ideas of integrationism. However, a fundamental difference between integrationism and radical and black nationalist ideologies is that integrationists believe that the American POLITICAL SYSTEM, except for RACISM and WHITE SUPREMACY, is fundamentally sound. Therefore, strategies and programs for ending racism and white supremacy must, given the fundamental soundness of the system, be moderate and consistent with maintenance of the system's stability. Integrationism also assumes that racism and white supremacy are not fundamental or core values of the sys-

tem but, rather, are contrary to the system's values and therefore are subject to change within the boundaries of CAPITALISM, CONSTITUTIONALISM, and DEMOCRACY. Finally, while emphasizing the importance of black solidarity, integrationists also believe that interracial COALITIONS and cooperation are essential components of AFRICAN-AMERICAN POLITICS.

interest groups

Interest groups are an important and integral feature of the American DEMOCRACY, which is structured on the basis of PLURALISM. The United States as a pluralist democracy functions on the basis of individuals joining together in groups to articulate their interests, however they are defined, to decision makers in the POLITICAL SYSTEM. Although INDIVIDUALISM is an important part of the American political tradition and culture, POWER in America, as HAROLD CRUSE so forcefully argues, is exercised on the basis of organized groups, with individuals coming together around some common interest or concern. In order for interest groups to emerge, individuals must have some consciousness that they have some interests in common with other similarly situated individuals and sufficient solidarity to form ORGANIZATIONS to express or articulate those interests.

Almost from the beginning of American history the African peoples developed a consciousness, solidarity, and organizations on the basis of RACE, having a common interest as individuals in ending their OPPRESSION on the basis of their membership in a group defined by RACISM and WHITE SUPREMACY. From SLAVERY in the 18th century until the 21st century, ending race oppression has been the overriding interest that has bound all African Americans in consciousness, solidarity, and organization in a struggle for FREEDOM and EQUALITY. Although as individuals they may have had other interests, ending race oppression has been the all-pervading one. Thus, blacks from all walks of life have formed interest groups to pursue the interest of the race as well as their narrower interests as black farmers, workers, entrepreneurs, professionals, or women. These include general CIVIL RIGHTS organizations such as the NAACP and the URBAN LEAGUE, women's organizations such as the NATIONAL COUNCIL OF NEGRO WOMEN, professional organizations like the National Medical and Bar Associations (organizations of black lawyers and doctors), and labor groups like the BROTHERHOOD OF SLEEPING CAR PORTERS and the COALITION OF BLACK TRADE UNIONISTS. Compared with similar interest-group organizations among whites, the black organizations have less power and have been less effective in advancing their interests. Nevertheless, these organizations, taken as a whole, have provided continuity and predictability in AFRICAN-AMERICAN POLITICS and have generally helped to advance the interest of the race in freedom and equality.

internal colonialism

Internal colonialism is a theory developed in the 1960s to explain the OPPRESSION or subordination of African Americans in the United States. The theory sought to establish parallels between the processes and patterns of COLONIALISM in the THIRD WORLD and what had happened to blacks within the United States. HAROLD CRUSE as early as 1962 used the concept of "domestic colonialism" to describe the relationship between whites and African Americans, and in his research on HARLEM, KENNETH CLARK described its relationship to the larger white society as essentially colonial. The colonial analogy received its most influential exposition in 1967 in STOKELY CARMICHAEL and CHARLES HAMILTON's book, *BLACK POWER: THE POLITICS OF LIBERATION.* As a result of the influence of Carmichael and Hamilton's book and the MILITANCY inspired by the BLACK POWER MOVEMENT, many scholars, black and white, began to use the theory in their research on RACE in the United States, and the BLACK PANTHER PARTY in its program claimed that the GHETTOS constituted domestic colonies for which it was prepared to wage a war of liberation similar to those fought by Third World countries like Algeria against European domination.

While the internal colonialism concept was popular among militant and radical black scholars, it was rejected by most scholars of black politics, who contended that colonialism *necessarily* involves the exploitation and domination of a geographically distinct territory and its people by people from another country. While recognizing that the analogy was not exact, scholars using it contended that there were enough parallels or "common core elements" between overseas and domestic colonialism to make it useful in studying the relationship between whites and blacks in the United States. The most important of these common core elements linking internal and overseas colonialism is that both involved RACISM as a principle of domination and WHITE SUPREMACY as an IDEOLOGY. In addition, both overseas and domestic colonialism involve economic exploitation, political domination, and the denigration and transformation of the indigenous CULTUREs of colonized peoples.

Whatever the relative merits of internal colonialism as a theory in studying black politics, it became prominent in the context of militancy in politics, and as that militancy declined after the 1960s and 1970s, so did the popularity of the internal colonialism theory.

Further reading: Robert Blauner, "Internal Colonialism and Ghetto Revolt," *Social Problems* 16 (Spring 1969): 398–408.

internal inferiorization

Internal inferiorization is the process by which oppressed people over time accept or "internalize" the notion of their inferiority and display patterns of self-hatred and low self-esteem. Students of the European OPPRESSION of Africans and African Americans have long contended that it resulted in internal inferiorization. That is, it is suggested that the oppression of blacks by whites on the basis of the institutionalization of the IDEOLOGY of WHITE SUPREMACY necessarily results in the development among some, if not all, blacks of at least some feelings of inferiority. The key variable is institutionalization—through the church, MEDIA, schools, and popular culture—of the notion of black inferiority so that it consequently comes to exercise a pervasive and continuous influence, conscious and unconscious, on the psyche of blacks. An essential component of the institutionalization of the ideology of white supremacy is the denigration of blackness. Thus, it is common to read in the literature on race in the United States observations such as the following: "White Americans have devalued black skin color. Blackness in general has been associated with discouragement, despair, depression, coldness, the unknown, the haunting shadow and nightmare." And "the American Negro has long adopted this negative blackness concept. For several reasons he identified with the white ego ideal. Thus, for decades within the American black culture the owner of a black skin resigned himself to the fact that he was negative, inferior and less attractive." FRANTZ FANON referred to this inferiority complex among Africans as "the outcome of a double process—primarily economic and social. Subsequently, the internalization—or better the epidermalization—of inferiority." KENNETH CLARK documented it among African Americans in the famous doll experiments with school children, and many other scholars have shown its manifestations among black adults in such things as negative stereotypes about Africans and African Americans, light-skin-color preference in mates and friends, and intragroup VIOLENCE—what Fanon referred to in Africa as the phenomenon of "niggers killing niggers on Saturday night" and what is referred to in the United States as "black on black crime." And MALCOLM X frequently referred to it in his speeches and in his autobiography, writing that "Negroes hated themselves, hated how they looked, hated their hair, most of all hated Africa." Frequently he said that blacks had no respect for the ability or accomplishments of other blacks except perhaps in entertainment "to play some horn, make you feel good but in serious things . . . no."

Although there is ample historical, theoretical, scientific, and anecdotal evidence to confirm the existence of internal inferiorization in the black communities of the world, in the POST–CIVIL RIGHTS ERA some black psychologists have challenged the pervasiveness of the phenomenon in the United States. What this new scholarship seems to show is not a lack of evidence of widespread internal inferiorization but, rather, that the evidence is not always conclusive or unambiguous and that evidence of negative images toward blacks as a group does not necessarily translate into an *individual* sense of inferiority or low self-esteem. Thus, while the institutional mechanisms of society exert their influence, human beings naturally reject their own denigration or inferiorization however powerful and pervasive its institutionalization. Thus, it may be that some blacks feel ambivalent about their BLACKNESS; what W. E. B. DU BOIS in *THE SOULS OF BLACK FOLK* referred to as a "peculiar sensation," a "double consciousness"; this "sense of always looking at one's self through the eyes of others, of measuring one's soul by the tape of a world that looks on in amused contempt and pity." In addition, the successes of the CIVIL RIGHTS MOVEMENT and the BLACK POWER MOVEMENT as well as the BLACK ARTS MOVEMENT are thought to have resulted in a rise in both individual and collective self-esteem in the post–civil rights era BLACK COMMUNITY.

Several studies have documented the extent of these changes. Kenneth Clark in a study published in *Ebony Magazine* in 1980 found evidence of a more positive race identification in terms of a decline in light-skin-color preference and a decrease in the importance of skin color in mate selection. Yet the study concluded "an unfortunately high percentage (41 percent) indicated either ambivalence or rejection of traditional black features." Other studies show similar results, that is, endorsement of the idea of positive identification with blackness but with some ambivalence. Developments during the 1960s probably resulted in a long-lasting decline in internal inferiorization, but there remains a degree of ambiguity or ambivalence among some, if not all, blacks, which is probably to be expected, since the culture constantly bombards blacks with messages that "white is beautiful" and is to be emulated. This decline in internal inferiorization has important consequences for AFRICAN-AMERICAN POLITICS. It is frequently said that the most pernicious effect of RACISM is not material but psychological. SLAVERY and its legacies shackled not only the bodies of blacks but their minds as well. Consequently, the black struggle for FREEDOM has always been twofold: to battle the material or structural basis of oppression and its psychological or mental consequences. The two struggles are interrelated, with an almost chicken-and-egg quality as to which comes first. Before an effective struggle can be waged against the material basis one must fight to remove the psychological barriers that inhibit the struggle against the material. Thus, one must "free the minds" before one can "free the bodies." Yet, it may be that a precondition for psychological freedom is some measure of material freedom, since psychic self-esteem is related to material well being.

Further reading: Kenneth Clark and Mamie Clark, "What Do Blacks Think of Themselves," *Ebony* November 1980: 176–82; William Cross, *Shades of Blackness: Diversity in African American Identity* (Philadelphia: Temple University Press, 1991); Frantz Fanon, *Black Skin, White Mask: The Experiences of a Black Man in a White World* (New York: Grove Press, 1967).

J

Jackson, Jesse (1941–) *activist*

Jesse Louis Jackson is the preeminent African American leader of the POST–CIVIL RIGHTS ERA. Beginning as a student activist in the early 1960s, Jackson became an associate of MARTIN LUTHER KING JR., and after King's murder he sought to become his successor as the nation's preeminent African-American leader. By the 1970s he had achieved that objective by using a combination of charisma, oratorical and mobilizing skills, and access to the MEDIA. In a 2000 poll of African-American political scientists rating or ranking the greatest African-American leaders of all time, Jackson ranked seventh on a list of 12 and was the only then-living person on the list.

Jackson was born in Greenville, South Carolina, and attended North Carolina Agricultural and Technical College, one of the HISTORICALLY BLACK COLLEGES AND UNIVERSITIES. (He received an athletic scholarship to play football at the University of Illinois but left, he later said, because he was denied the opportunity to play quarterback because he was black.) At the age of 22 he led PROTEST demonstrations against SEGREGATION at lunch counters in Greensboro, North Carolina. Later, he helped to organize a student CIVIL RIGHTS group, the North Carolina Intercollegiate Council on Human Rights. Shortly thereafter, he joined the staff of Dr. King's SOUTHERN CHRISTIAN LEADERSHIP CONFERENCE (SCLC). Although King was surrounded by a very able staff, Jackson clearly impressed him as a dynamic young leader, and King soon appointed him to head SCLC's Chicago chapter, where Jackson was living while attending divinity school. In Chicago he started Operation Breadbasket, an ORGANIZATION that led highly visible and successful boycotts against some of the city's leading stores and businesses. The purpose of the boycotts—modeled on the work of Rev. LEON SULLIVAN in Philadelphia—was to protest DISCRIMINATION in employment and contracting. Often the boycotts resulted in employment opportunities for black workers and contracts for black entrepreneurs. Operation Bread-

basket became SCLC's most successful initiative in the NORTHERN STATES, suggesting itself as a model as Dr. King considered shifting the focus of the CIVIL RIGHTS MOVEMENT from the SOUTHERN STATES to the GHETTOS after passage of the CIVIL RIGHTS ACT OF 1964 and the VOTING RIGHTS ACT OF 1965. Jackson was with King at the time of his assassination in Memphis in 1968. Although others present at the assassination dispute it, Jackson claimed that he cradled the dying King in his arms on the balcony of the Lorraine motel where he was shot. This dispute about Jackson's actions at the time of King's murder was the beginning of differences between King's associates in SCLC and Jackson that eventually led to his suspension and then resignation from the organization. Another source of early differences was Jackson's appearance on national television a day after the assassination in clothing that he claimed bore King's bloodstains. At the time of the assassination, King was planning to lead the POOR PEOPLE'S CAMPAIGN in the DISTRICT OF COLUMBIA. Although King's designated successor—Ralph Abernathy, SCLC's vice president—was nominally in charge of the campaign, it was Jackson who gained national media attention as the leader with the charismatic authority to become King's successor as the preeminent African-American leader.

After the Poor Peoples Campaign, Jackson asked for a higher position within SCLC but was turned down by the group's board of directors. Returning to Chicago to run Operation Breadbasket, Jackson was recognized as the city's preeminent black leader as Operation Breadbasket's protests and related activities (including "Black Expo," an exposition of black business and cultural accomplishments) became highly successful. In 1971 the SCLC board asked Jackson to move Operation Breadbasket to Atlanta, the group's national headquarters; Jackson refused. Later the board suspended Jackson for 60 days because of a conflict about the management of SCLC's Breadbasket funds. Rather than accept the suspension, Jackson resigned and created OPERATION PUSH (People United to Save Humanity). Naming himself president of Operation PUSH, Jackson continued the Breadbasket activities, expanding them to include political organizing and mobilization. He also established PUSH-EXCEL to encourage high performance by black schoolchildren and traveled the country preaching moral responsibility (especially in terms of teenage sex and drug abuse) and SELF-HELP.

While continuing his activities as protest and moral leader, Jackson in 1972 made his first venture into national politics by leading an alternate Illinois delegation to the DEMOCRATIC PARTY's national convention. Charging that the regular delegation (headed by Chicago's powerful mayor, Richard Daley) excluded minorities, women, and young people, Jackson was able to oust it and replace it with the alternate delegation, which he cochaired. This initial foray into national party politics made Jackson not only a protest and moral leader but also an important Democratic Party leader. In 1984 and 1988 he elevated his stature as a party leader by waging two PRESIDENTIAL CAMPAIGNS under the banner of the RAINBOW COALITION. Although he did not come close to winning the Democratic nomination, he created a COALITION of blacks, other minorities, and liberal whites and established himself as the leading African American in the Democratic Party and one of the party's leading spokesmen for LIBERALISM. By the late 1980s PUBLIC OPINION polls showed that among both blacks and whites, Jackson had achieved in the post–civil rights era the status held by Martin Luther King Jr. as the most influential black leader in the United States. Except for LOUIS FARRAKHAN, other black leaders in these polls received so little support as to be virtually unknown to the public.

As the 20th century came to a close, Jackson was the nation's major protest leader, leading marches and demonstrations in causes that included not only civil rights but workers rights, women's rights, and the environment. He was also a leading practitioner of CITIZEN DIPLOMACY, successfully negotiating the release of American prisoners of war and hostages in Syria, Cuba, and Yugoslavia. During the 1990s Jackson moved into the economic arena, establishing the "Wall Street Project" to facilitate the access of blacks and other minorities to investment capital, credit, and opportunities for contracts from and positions in the hierarchies of major American corporations. Jackson's role as Democratic Party leader and his increasing identification with Wall Street and black CAPITALISM reflected a shift away from protest toward ACCOMMODATIONISM. Early in 2001 the tabloid media revealed that Jackson had fathered a child out of wedlock with a member of his staff (who had written a book about his citizen diplomacy). This revelation diminished his authority as a moral leader and led to allegations of financial irregularities regarding his organizations' payments to his mistress and their child. Subsequent investigations by the media did not reveal major irregularities in Jackson's

Jesse Jackson *(Wong/Newsmakers)*

organizations' finances, but they did show a pattern of crony capitalism in which Jackson used his influence with corporations to obtain business opportunities for his relatives and friends. While these allegations diminished his stature as a moral and political leader, they did not alter his standing as one of the most influential leaders of African Americans in the history of the United States.

Further reading: Marshall Frady, *Jesse: The Life and Pilgrimage of Jesse Jackson* (New York: Random House, 1996); Lorenzo Morris, ed., *The Social and Political Implications of the 1984 Jesse Jackson Presidential Campaign* (Westport, Conn.: Praeger, 1990); Adolph Reed, *The Jesse Jackson Phenomenon* (New Haven, Conn.: Yale University Press, 1986).

Jefferson, Thomas (1743–1826) *third president of the United States*

Thomas Jefferson—author of the DECLARATION OF INDEPENDENCE, third president of the United States, and probably the most intellectually gifted man to occupy the PRESIDENCY (at a White House dinner honoring American winners of the Nobel Prize, President JOHN F. KENNEDY quipped that the dinner was the greatest assembly of intellect ever to gather at the White House with the exception of when Thomas Jefferson dined alone)—was the living embodiment of the hypocrisy that is at the foundation of the American DEMOCRACY. Jefferson's hypocrisy, and the hypocrisy of the American democracy that he helped to establish, is found in the nation's founding document, the Declaration of Independence, which Jefferson wrote. The declaration declares that "all men are created equal" and endowed by their creator with certain "unalienable" (inalienable) rights (meaning they can not be surrendered and ought not be taken), among which is liberty or FREEDOM. Yet Jefferson not only personally deprived hundreds of people of African descent of their liberty but supported the institution of SLAVERY, which deprived millions of this inalienable right. It was argued by some at the time of the declaration in 1776, and by others thereafter, that Jefferson did not literally mean *men* when he wrote the declaration, and therefore he did not mean to include the enslaved Africans when he used the word. However, in the famous last paragraph of Jefferson's draft (which was deleted by his colleagues), he condemned the British king for the slave trade, writing that King George was "determined to keep open a market where MEN should be bought and sold. . . ." This would seem to suggest that he really meant men. We know that he was selected to write the declaration because he was careful and skillful in the uses of words. Therefore it is difficult to believe that he would have stated a claim for the EQUALITY of all men in the first paragraph and then specifically define men (in all capitals) to include the enslaved Africans in the last paragraph without logically meaning to include the enslaved Africans as men. It was of course easy for Jefferson to condemn the king in faraway London for the slave *trade,* while not proposing the abolition of *slavery* in the United States or freeing his own slaves. It was a skillful propaganda technique to express moral outrage at the slave trade as a final justification for independence from the evil British king, but it was also blatantly hypocritical. In any event, in writing the declaration Jefferson showed himself to be a manipulative and unprincipled person, his towering intellect notwithstanding.

In addition to his hypocrisy in writing the declaration while owning slaves and supporting slavery, Jefferson in his *Notes On Virginia* also articulated one of the first systematic "scientific" arguments by an American intellectual for the IDEOLOGY of WHITE SUPREMACY as a justification for RACISM and as a rationale for his opposition to equality for Africans in the United States. In the *Notes* Jefferson defended slavery as necessary to meet the labor needs of the plantation economy, but he nevertheless saw it as evil and unjust, writing, "The whole commerce between master and slave is a perpetual exercise of the most boisterous passions, the most unremitting despotism on the one part, and degrading submission on the other." And in a famous passage that would be echoed by ABRAHAM LINCOLN during the CIVIL WAR, Jefferson suggested that God would surely punish America: "Indeed, I tremble for my country when I reflect that God is just; that his justice cannot sleep forever. . . . The almighty has no attribute which can take side with us in such a contest." But since slavery was a necessary evil, he could not call for its immediate abolition. Rather, he called for its gradual abolition as soon as the enslaved Africans could be deported and replaced by free white labor from Europe. Anticipating the inevitable question of why not simply free the slaves and integrate them into American society, thereby saving the money involved in deporting the Africans and transporting the whites, he wrote that "deep rooted prejudices entertained by whites, ten thousand recollections by the blacks of injuries they have sustained, the real distinctions which nature has made and many other circumstances" made the INTEGRATION of blacks and whites impossible. Indeed, Jefferson believed that if the races were not separated, VIOLENCE (what he called "convulsions") would probably occur, ending in the "extermination of one or the other race." Jefferson, however, was not content to base his arguments against integration on these practical grounds. Rather, he wanted to base his conclusions on scientific "facts" and "empirical observations." Thus, he offered one of the first of many "scientific proofs" of black inferiority. His proofs included the "facts" that blacks were uglier than whites, that they had a "strong and disagreeable odor," and that black men were more sexually aggressive or, as he put it, more "ardent after their female." (In the late 1990s DNA evidence provided near-conclusive scientific proof that Jefferson fathered children by Sally Hemings, a young enslaved girl.) The ultimate basis for his conclusion of black inferiority, however, was based on intelligence, and in his view, blacks were "inferior in faculties of reason and imagination." Jefferson noted that some might argue these alleged differences in intelligence might be a result of the harsh conditions of slavery, but he rejected this explanation, concluding that it was their "nature" not their "condition" that produced the differences.

Jefferson was of course a product of his times, when virtually all Europeans shared his racist and white supremacist views. What makes Jefferson extraordinarily different and interesting is that he was a man of extraordinary intellect who was asked, because of his intellect and erudition, to write the nation's founding document enshrining freedom and equality as its highest principles, yet he betrayed those principles in both his public and private lives. His contradictions and hypocrisies thus embody the nation's.

Further reading: Joseph Ellis, *American Sphinx: The Character of Thomas Jefferson* (New York: Knopf, 1997).

Jim Crow

Jim Crow is a term used to refer to the widespread practice of racial SEGREGATION instituted in the SOUTHERN STATES after the end of RECONSTRUCTION. The precise origins of the term as a reference for racial segregation is not known, but it may be related to the minstrel songs done by whites in blackface that became popular during the early years of segregation.

See also *PLESSY V. FERGUSON.*

Further reading: Vann C. Woodward, *The Strange Career of Jim Crow* (New York: Oxford University Press, 1966).

Johnson, Andrew (1808–1875) *17th president of the United States*

Of the men who have served as president of the United States, Andrew Johnson, from the perspective of the African-American struggle for FREEDOM and EQUALITY, is the worst. Arguably, his time in the PRESIDENCY did more to retard the advance of freedom and equality than any of his predecessors or successors. Or to put this another way, if a man less racist and white supremacist and less arrogant and stubborn than Johnson had become the 17th president, the long struggle for black freedom after the CIVIL WAR would have started out in a better way for blacks and for the nation.

Andrew Johnson succeeded to the presidency after the assassination of ABRAHAM LINCOLN in April 1865. Johnson at that time was in his first months as vice president, having been selected as Lincoln's running mate to bring regional and political balance to the 1864 presidential ticket. Born in poverty in Tennessee, Johnson had served two terms as governor and was elected to the Senate in 1857. A member of the DEMOCRATIC PARTY, Johnson had refused to join the secessionists in his state, and this loyalty to the Union made him an attractive candidate for vice president as Lincoln sought to build a "unionist" COALITION between the REPUBLICAN PARTY in the NORTHERN STATES and moderate Democrats in the SOUTHERN STATES. Johnson also had a reputation as a politician who stood up for the rights of poor people against the interests of the rich and powerful. But he was also devoted to RACISM and WHITE SUPREMACY.

A former slaveholder, he was a strong supporter of SLAVERY but thought it could best be maintained by the Southern states remaining in the Union. Johnson was a rabid white supremacist who believed that blacks were inherently inferior to whites and unworthy of living in "civilized" society except as slaves or subordinates to whites. He also believed strongly in the principle of FEDERALISM or "states' rights." He also wished to be elected president in 1868 in his own right. Finally, he was an arrogant and stubborn man. These factors in combination led to Johnson's becoming the worst president for black people in American history.

When Johnson became president, plans for RECONSTRUCTION were not settled. Lincoln's views were not clear at the time of his death, although he apparently leaned toward deportation of the slaves once they were freed. But it was left to Johnson to develop plans to deal with the status of the soon-to-be-freed slaves as well as plans for the return of the rebellious states to the Union. Given his racist and white supremacist views, he adopted a lenient policy toward the rebellious whites in the South. In May 1865 he started what is called the period of "Presidential Reconstruction," issuing proclamations pardoning all Southern whites except Confederate leaders and wealthy plantation owners (later he gave most of these individuals pardons as well), appointing provisional governors in the Southern states, and allowing the states to reenter the union and manage their own affairs without federal interference. The only requirements for reentry were repudiation of SLAVERY and secession and abrogation of the Confederate debt. Insofar as African Americans were concerned, their status was to be left up to their former slave masters, who controlled the newly formed STATE AND LOCAL GOVERNMENTS. Immediately these new governments enacted the BLACK CODES and allowed whites to use VIOLENCE and other forms of intimidation against the blacks in an effort to keep them in a status close to slavery. The RADICAL REPUBLICANS in CONGRESS, led by THADDEUS STEVENS and CHARLES SUMNER, immediately attempted to overturn Johnson's policies; however, more-conservative Republicans supported him until he vetoed a bill extending the life of the FREEDMEN'S BUREAU. Johnson had led the conservative Republicans in Congress to believe that he would sign the bill, but he reneged on the promise in an effort to appeal to white Southerners and conservative Democrats in the North as the basis to build a coalition that would elect him president in 1868. Subsequently, he vetoed a CIVIL RIGHTS bill establishing black CITIZENSHIP and legal equality. This caused the conservative and moderate Republicans in Congress to join the Radical Republicans in ending Presidential Reconstruction and imposing "Congressional Reconstruction." In vetoing the Civil Rights bill Johnson was blunt in his defense of racism and white supremacy, saying the bill would "place every spay-footed, bandy-shanked, thick lipped, flatnosed, wooly-haired, ebony-colored Negro in the country on an equal footing with the poor white man."

Congressional Reconstruction placed the Southern states under military rule, enacted the Civil Rights bill over Johnson's veto, and made ratification of the FOURTEENTH AMENDMENT a condition of the readmission of the Southern states to the Union. Congress also passed the Tenure of Office Act to curtail the president's power to interfere with the implementation of its plans. When Johnson violated the act by attempting to dismiss the secretary of war, the House of Representatives passed a resolution of impeachment. In the Senate trial in 1868 he came within one vote of the necessary two-thirds required for conviction and removal from office. Although he continued as president until the end of the term in 1869, all the while trying to pass legislation and figure out a strategy to run for president, his power in the presidency was essentially finished after impeachment, although not his career in politics. Upon returning to Tennessee, he was elected to the U.S. Senate.

For African Americans, Johnson was the wrong man in the wrong office at the wrong time. He was an arrogant and stubborn man unwilling to compromise with moderate and conservative Republicans; he was stubbornly committed to federalism at a time when it was clearly a subterfuge for the reenslavement of blacks; and he was a rabid white supremacist and a racist at a time when the country was prepared, however grudgingly, to begin to move toward equality.

Further reading: Albert Castel, *The Presidency of Andrew Johnson* (Lawrence: University Press of Kansas Press, 1979).

Johnson, James Weldon (1871–1938) *author, diplomat*

James Weldon Johnson was the first African American to head the NAACP, becoming its executive secretary in 1920. Much of the credit for the NAACP's growth and development into the most effective CIVIL RIGHTS organization in the United States is due to Johnson's leadership during the 1920s and his choice of WALTER WHITE as his assistant and successor.

Born in Jacksonville, Florida, Johnson was graduated from ATLANTA UNIVERSITY. A lawyer, journalist, writer, and lyricist, Johnson wrote more than 200 songs, the most famous of which "Lift Every Voice and Sing" is generally referred to as the NEGRO NATIONAL ANTHEM. Among his most important books are *The Autobiography of an Ex-Colored Man* and his 1963 study of HARLEM, *Black Manhattan*. As a result of his support of Theodore Roosevelt's 1904 campaign for pres-

ident (he wrote a song during the campaign called "You're All Right Teddy"), he was appointed to the diplomatic BUREAUCRACY, first as consul to Venezuela and later to Nicaragua. In 1916 JOEL E. SPINGARN asked Johnson to become the NAACP's field secretary, putting him in charge of organizing the association's branches. Johnson viewed energetic local branches as the cornerstone of the NAACP's struggle against SEGREGATION and DISCRIMINATION, and his efforts as field secretary were instrumental in establishing the importance of the branches and in increasing their size and membership. Johnson was also strongly committed to INTEGRATION as an IDEOLOGY. He therefore worked to make sure that the NAACP was—at the national level and, where possible, at the branches as well—an interracial COALITION of blacks and whites. When John Shillady, the NAACP's executive secretary, was badly beaten by a white mob in Austin, Texas, in 1919, Johnson was appointed by the board in 1920 to succeed him. This began the transition of the NAACP from a white- to a black-led ORGANIZATION and to increased reliance on a paid professional staff rather than volunteers. Johnson's organizational and diplomatic skills had started to turn the NAACP into a respected LOBBYING force by the time he left office in 1930. In addition,

James Weldon Johnson *(Library of Congress)*

Johnson led the group in its support of the DYER ANTI-LYNCHING BILL and planned the famous Silent March against LYNCHING in New York City in 1917. He also helped to organize opposition to the American occupation of HAITI. His choice of Walter White as his successor was an important contribution, since while White was not popular with many of the staff, especially W. E. B. DU BOIS, he became a strong-willed and effective leader who in his quarter-century as executive secretary, building on Johnson's legacy, made the NAACP the most important organization in AFRICAN-AMERICAN POLITICS.

In 1930 Johnson retired from the NAACP to become a professor of literature at Fisk University, one of the HISTORICALLY BLACK COLLEGES AND UNIVERSITIES. From there he helped to shape the ethos and understanding of the HARLEM RENAISSANCE. Although most of his important literary contributions came before the renaissance, in them he had explored the racial themes important to renaissance writers, and many viewed him as a kind of elder statesman of the movement. At the time of his death in a car accident, he was widely recognized as both a literary and civil rights leader. In 1933 he published his memoirs, *Along the Way: The Autobiography of James Weldon Johnson*.

Further reading: Eugene Levy, *James Weldon Johnson: Black Leader, Black Voice* (Chicago: University of Chicago Press, 1973).

Johnson, Lyndon B. (1908–1973) *36th president of the United States*

Ironically, the worst and best presidents for African Americans in their struggle for FREEDOM and EQUALITY were both named Johnson. And both succeeded assassinated predecessors who, almost 100 years apart, had reluctantly committed themselves to the cause of black freedom or equality. ANDREW JOHNSON, who succeeded the murdered ABRAHAM LINCOLN in 1865, was the worst president for blacks, and Lyndon B. Johnson, who succeeded the murdered JOHN F. KENNEDY, was the best.

Lyndon Johnson was born and reared in the West Texas hill country and was elected to the Senate in 1948. Although an avid supporter of FRANKLIN D. ROOSEVELT and the NEW DEAL, Johnson, coming from Texas, the largest of the SOUTHERN STATES, was ambivalent about CIVIL RIGHTS, since it was difficult for a supporter of civil rights to win statewide office in Texas. Yet Johnson was never known in Texas as a racist or white supremacist, and he was not an outspoken advocate of the SEGREGATION then legally enforced in Texas. And while serving as the DEMOCRATIC PARTY leader in the Senate during the 1950s, he was responsible for passing in 1957 and 1960 the first

civil rights acts since RECONSTRUCTION. These bills, however, were widely viewed as weak compromises negotiated by Johnson in order to simply get a bill, any bill, passed. Thus, black leaders were wary when Kennedy in 1960 selected Johnson as his running mate, and they were concerned when he became president in 1963 after the president's assassination. But as president, Johnson became the most passionate and powerful advocate of black freedom and equality ever to occupy the PRESIDENCY. Using his knowledge of the workings of CONGRESS and his legendary persuasive skills, Johnson in three short years did more to advance freedom and equality than virtually all his predecessors combined. Less than a year after taking office he signed the CIVIL RIGHTS ACT OF 1964. A year later he signed the VOTING RIGHTS ACT OF 1965, and in 1968 he signed the Fair Housing Act. These three acts together brought racial segregation and legal RACISM to an end. In 1964 Johnson started the WAR ON POVERTY, a series of programs implicitly designed to attack the widespread POVERTY among blacks; and he also started the GREAT SOCIETY program, which was the largest expansion of the WELFARE STATE since the New Deal. In a 1965 speech at HOWARD UNIVERSITY, Johnson provided the philosophical rationale and the programmatic cues for AFFIRMATIVE ACTION, and later that year he signed the ELEMENTARY AND SECONDARY EDUCATION ACT, which was designed to target the improvement of education for poor and minority students. President Johnson also appointed many blacks to the BUREAUCRACY, including ROBERT WEAVER as the first black in the cabinet and THURGOOD MARSHALL as the first black on the SUPREME COURT.

In pushing through the civil rights reforms of the 1960s, Johnson was building on the legacy of President Kennedy and responding to the mounting PROTESTS of the CIVIL RIGHTS MOVEMENT, which he viewed as a threat to the stability of the POLITICAL SYSTEM; but he went far beyond what the political situation at the time required. Johnson's embrace of civil rights and social reform was passionate (in his 1965 address to Congress proposing the Voting Rights Act of 1965, he closed by invoking "We Shall Overcome," the anthem of the Civil Rights movement), which was not predicted or predictable by his personal or political backgrounds. Johnson knew his support for civil rights was risky in terms of his personal future and the future of the DEMOCRATIC PARTY. (When he signed the Civil Rights Act of 1964 he told his aides "We've lost the South for a generation.") Nevertheless, he acted and acted boldly, and in doing so he became the greatest president insofar as the rights of blacks are concerned. And if it had not been for the tragedy of the VIETNAM WAR, he would rank among the greatest of all the American presidents for all of the American people, not just African Americans.

Further reading: Vaughn Barnet, *The Presidency of Lyndon B. Johnson* (Lawrence: University of Kansas Press, 1997); Mark Stern, *Calculating Visions: Kennedy, Johnson and Civil Rights* (New Brunswick, N.J.: Rutgers University Press, 1992).

Joint Center for Political and Economic Studies

As the CIVIL RIGHTS MOVEMENT drew to a close and black politics began its shift from movement-style PROTEST to routine INTEREST-GROUP policies, it was early recognized that African Americans needed their own THINK TANK. KENNETH CLARK in a 1965 essay on the major civil rights ORGANIZATIONS concluded that they lacked a "research capacity," and this was a critical shortcoming because "major decisions must now reflect painstaking, difficult and time consuming staff work based on fact finding, intelligence and continuing critical analysis of data and strategies." Similarly, the African-American political scientist MATTHEW HOLDEN JR. wrote that "black politics urgently requires its own think tank" because "it is urgent to develop some institutional capacity which bring more penetrating analysis and knowledge into alliance with political purpose." The Joint Center for Political and Economic Studies was founded in 1969 to meet this need for research and analysis identified by Clark and Holden. It was called the "Joint" Center because it was initially a collaborative endeavor with HOWARD UNIVERSITY.

The Joint Center's early projects included the collection and dissemination of data on the rapidly growing number of black ELECTED OFFICIALS (eventually this became its annual *Roster of Black Elected Officials*); the publication of a monthly newsletter; and the provision of technical training, workshops, and a publication for black elected officials on electoral strategy, implementation of the VOTING RIGHTS ACT OF 1965, local government personnel and budgeting practices, as well as information on the preparation of proposals for various federal grants. Most of these workshops and publications were directed at the new group of blacks being elected to office in the rural parts of the SOUTHERN STATES. The center also from the outset encouraged black elected officials to form caucuses and was instrumental in creation of the National Coalition on Black Voter Participation.

In 1972 Eddie Williams became president of the center. Williams set about to broaden the center's work beyond educational and technical assistance and research support for black elected officials. Williams also sought to diversify the center's board and staff and to broaden the base of its financial support. The result was that the center became a national research organization in the tradition of Brookings and the American Enterprise Institute, rather than simply a technical and institutional support resource for black elected officials.

Although its budget was modest compared with other Washington think tanks, the center did a remarkable job in facilitating the institutionalization of black politics, guiding its transformation from protest to interest-group politics. Its studies of the growth and development of black elected officials, its work on the implementation of the Voting Rights Act, its work on the development of a consensus BLACK AGENDA, and its monthly newsletter, *Focus*, made the Joint Center the recognized, authoritative source on black politics in the POST–CIVIL RIGHTS ERA.

Jones, Mack H. (1937–) *scholar*

Mack H. Jones, one of the leading black political scientists in the United States, made important contributions to the development of AFRICAN-AMERICAN POLITICS as a field of study in political science and to the training and professional development of black political scientists in the POST–CIVIL RIGHTS ERA. Jones also contributed to the development of a distinctive epistemological and theoretical alternative to the traditional study of the politics of RACE. He received the Ph.D. in political science from the University of Illinois in 1968, at the height of the BLACK POWER MOVEMENT. Earlier he had done undergraduate studies at Southern University in Baton Rouge, Louisiana, the largest of the HISTORICALLY BLACK COLLEGES AND UNIVERSITIES. However, he was graduated from Texas Southern University, another black college, after being expelled from Southern because of his participation in the SIT-INS and other forms of PROTEST during the CIVIL RIGHTS MOVEMENT. After receiving the Ph.D. he joined the faculty at ATLANTA UNIVERSITY, where he served as professor and chair of the political science department from 1967 to 1985 and as distinguished professor in the department from 1994 to 2002. While he has taught at other historically black colleges, including HOWARD UNIVERSITY, Jones made his major contributions while on the faculty at Atlanta, where he was instrumental in developing the Ph.D. program. Influenced by the Black Power movement's philosophy calling for the development of knowledge relevant to the struggle for liberation from race-based OPPRESSION, Jones developed at Atlanta a distinctive "Afrocentric" curriculum. This alternative curriculum was based on the assumption that the traditional theories, epistemologies, methodologies, and graduate courses in political science were geared toward maintenance of the POLITICAL SYSTEM. And since that system acted toward blacks in a manner that maintained their oppression, a political science geared to its maintenance could not be relevant to black (or white, for that matter) political scientists working for black liberation. Thus, there was a need for a "black" political science, that is, a political science geared toward the eradication of RACISM, WHITE SUPREMACY, and the race-based inequalities generated by

CAPITALISM. The curriculum at Atlanta was organized on the basis of these assumptions.

Jones wrote a series of important epistemological and theoretical papers that helped to influence the way a generation of black political scientists taught and conducted research on black politics at universities throughout the United States, but especially at the historically black colleges, where many Atlanta University graduates are employed. Jones also was the founding president of the NATIONAL CONFERENCE OF BLACK POLITICAL SCIENTISTS (NCOBPS), the professional association of black political scientists established in 1970. He argued that black political scientists needed their own professional ORGANIZATION, separate and distinct from the largely white American Political Science Association, because it, like the political science discipline, was devoted mainly to maintenance of the white-dominated political system. Thus, NCOBPS was needed, he wrote, for those scholars "who see the full liberation of black Americans as the ultimate objective to be served by their work."

See also AFROCENTRISM.

Further reading: Mack H. Jones, "A Frame of Reference for Black Politics," in *Black Political Life in the United States,* ed. Lenneal Henderson (New York: Chandler Publisher, 1972); Mack H. Jones, "Political Science and the Black Political Experience: Issues in Epistemology and Relevance," *National Political Science Review* 3 (1992): 25–40; Earl Picard, ed., "Essays in Honor of Mack Jones," *National Political Science Review* 9 (2002): 4–19.

Jones, Raymond J. (1899–) *politician*

In 1963 J. Raymond Jones was elected chairman of the New York County (Manhattan) DEMOCRATIC PARTY Committee, generally referred to as "Tammany Hall." His election represented the first time an African American had become leader of a county party committee (the basic building block of state and national party organizations) of one of the parties in the TWO-PARTY SYSTEM. It also represented the beginnings of an important transition in URBAN POLITICS that in the next decade would result in a shift of power from European immigrant ETHNIC GROUPS to African Americans and their election as mayors throughout the United States. Jones, a WEST INDIAN immigrant, came to the United States in 1918. When he arrived he settled in HARLEM and became an active member of MARCUS GARVEY'S UNIVERSAL NEGRO IMPROVEMENT ASSOCIATION. It was during his association with Garvey's ORGANIZATION that Jones began to see the potential of the black vote as a BALANCE OF POWER in New York City elections. With the decline of Garvey's black nationalist movement, Jones and his associates started to organize independent black Democratic Party clubs, and from these clubs the POLITICAL INCORPORATION of blacks into the party began to take place in the 1930s. From this beginning Jones rose slowly through the party hierarchy to become party leader in HARLEM by the 1950s and in 1963 the county leader. During this period he developed a reputation as a skillful political operative, referred to by friends and adversaries as the "Harlem Fox." An early supporter of LYNDON B. JOHNSON for the presidency, Jones played an important behind-the-scenes role with President Johnson in making certain that ADAM CLAYTON POWELL JR. would become chairman of the House Education and Labor Committee in spite of the opposition of most Democrats in CONGRESS from the SOUTHERN STATES. Active in Democratic Party politics from the HARLEM RENAISSANCE until the end of the CIVIL RIGHTS MOVEMENT, Jones was an important player in the gradual emergence of African Americans as a key part of the Democratic Party COALITION. In 1968 he retired as party chairman and returned to his native Virgin Islands.

Further reading: John C. Walter, *The Harlem Fox: J. Raymond Jones and Tammany Hall, 1920–1970* (New York: State University of New York Press, 1989).

Jordan, Vernon (1935–) *lawyer, civil rights leader*

Vernon Jordan was appointed the fifth head of the URBAN LEAGUE in 1961, succeeding WHITNEY YOUNG as executive director. Prior to his appointment at the Urban League, Jordan was head of the Georgia field office of the NAACP, director of the Voter Education Project (an organization that sponsored voter registration campaigns in the SOUTHERN STATES), and president of the United Negro College Fund. As director of the league, Jordan continued its emphasis on social services and SELF-HELP while expanding its LOBBYING activities and increasing its capacity to function as a THINK TANK on POVERTY and CIVIL RIGHTS issues. While leading the league Jordan became one of the most recognized persons in the black LEADERSHIP structure, lecturing widely, writing a syndicated column, and appearing frequently in the MEDIA. In May 1980 he was shot and wounded by a gunman outside of a motel in Fort Wayne, Indiana. Shortly after he recovered from the assassination attempt Jordan left the league and became a partner in an influential Washington law firm. A longtime friend of BILL CLINTON, when Clinton became president Jordan served as his confidant and close personal adviser. In 2000 he became a senior managing director of Lazard Frères, the Wall Street investment firm, while remaining counsel at the Washington law firm. As a partner in one of the nation's leading law firms, a director of a major investment house, and member of nearly a dozen corporate boards, Jordan was among the most influential African

Americans in the POWER ELITE. In 2001 he wrote *Vernon Can Read,* a memoir covering his life through his years as head of the Urban League.

judicial process

The judicial process in the United States—the institutions and procedures used to determine the guilt or innocence of individuals charged with crimes and to settle disputes between individuals, groups, corporations, and governments—is structured by the principle of FEDERALISM. Like the federalism principle in general, federalism in the judicial process has generally worked to the disadvantage of African Americans seeking due process or fairness in the courts. The source of this disadvantage or unfairness is rooted in federalism's multiple judicial institutions and procedures—one in each of the 50 states and then an overlapping federal one for the entire United States. Historically this has meant that justice for blacks has depended on where they lived, and since for a long time they lived in the SOUTHERN STATES where RACISM and WHITE SUPREMACY were pervasive, it was very difficult for them to obtain fairness in the judicial process. Thus, crimes such as LYNCHINGS frequently went unpunished, and African Americans were often deprived of their liberty and property by racist state judges and juries. And even when a case was tried before federal judges and juries, racism was frequently also present, since through a practice called "senatorial courtesy," federal judges in the states tend to be informally selected by the senators from those states rather than the president. Thus, Southern federal judges were often as racist and white supremacist as the state judges. And it was not until 1986 in *Batson v. Kentucky* that the SUPREME COURT ruled definitively that blacks could not be systematically excluded from juries. In the 1960s through a process called the nationalization of the BILL OF RIGHTS, the Supreme Court incrementally used the FOURTEENTH AMENDMENT to create national or uniform procedures that all courts had to comply with in criminal cases, including standards for searches and seizures, the right against self-incrimination, the right to a lawyer, and the right to be free from "cruel and unusual punishment." Yet, these standards are unevenly applied in the courts of the states, resulting in a demonstrated lack of EQUALITY in the CRIMINAL JUSTICE SYSTEM.

The organization of the judicial process on the basis of federalism also has limited the election or appointment of blacks as prosecutors and judges. Although blacks and other minorities constituted about 14 percent of federal judges at the end of the presidency of BILL CLINTON, they constituted a much smaller proportion of the many more state judges. The first black federal judge was not appointed until 1949 by President HARRY TRUMAN, and the first black federal judge in the SOUTHERN STATES was not seated until the late 1970s during the presidency of JIMMY CARTER.

Justice Department, United States

The Department of Justice, created in 1870 during RECONSTRUCTION, is the principal law-enforcement agency within the federal BUREAUCRACY. Headed by the attorney general, a senior member of the president's cabinet, the department oversees the investigation and prosecution of all federal crimes and the handling of LITIGATION involving the United States. Since its inception, the enforcement of CIVIL RIGHTS has been a major responsibility of the department, although it did not take the responsibility seriously in a systematic way until the creation of its CIVIL RIGHTS DIVISION in 1957. Although no African American has served as attorney general, two have served as deputy attorney general, three as solicitor general (the number-three post in the department and the individual responsible for arguing cases for the government before the SUPREME COURT), two have headed the Criminal Division, and three have headed the Civil Rights Division. The FBI also is part of the Justice Department, but it tends to operate in a quasi-independent manner.

Karenga, Ron (1943–) *activist, scholar*

Ron Karenga was one of the leading activists during the 1960s BLACK POWER MOVEMENT and later a leading scholar of AFROCENTRISM in AFRICAN-AMERICAN STUDIES. Philosophically, Karenga adheres to BLACK NATIONALISM, a distinctive variant of CULTURAL NATIONALISM that calls on blacks in America to foster a distinctive CULTURE based on African traditions rather than European or "white" values. His name (he was born Ronald Everett) Karenga is derived from African traditions (meaning "keeper of tradition"), and based on his understanding of those traditions in the late 1960s he created KWANZA as an African-American holiday celebrated at Christmas. He also founded and led the Los Angeles–based ORGANIZATION "US" (as opposed to them, the whites), which attempted to advance his cultural nationalist program, including Kwanza. US and Karenga during the late 1960s were involved in a series of ideological clashes with the BLACK PANTHER PARTY and its leaders HUEY NEWTON and BOBBY SEALE. In 1969 one of those clashes led to the killing of two members of the Panthers on the campus of UCLA. Although it was later learned that the confrontation at UCLA may have been partly provoked by the FBI as part of its COINTELPRO program of POLITICAL REPRESSION, three members of US were convicted of murder and imprisoned. Karenga himself was imprisoned in 1971 for assaulting two female members of US who allegedly were conspiring to undermine his leadership of the organization. After his release from prison, he earned a Ph.D. (earlier he had graduated with a B.A. and M.A. in political science from UCLA), conducted extensive research on ancient African civilizations, and published two widely used textbooks in African-American studies. In the 1990s he became head of the black studies department at California State University, Long Beach.

Although a controversial figure, Karenga exerted a major influence on AMIRI BARAKA, before Baraka embraced COMMUNISM, as well as on the 1960s BLACK ARTS MOVEMENT. And Kwanza is commemorated by millions of African Americans.

Kennedy, Edward M. (1932–) *U.S. senator*

Like THADDEUS STEVENS and CHARLES SUMNER during RECONSTRUCTION and HUBERT HUMPHREY during the CIVIL RIGHTS MOVEMENT, Edward Kennedy was the leading member of CONGRESS on issues of CIVIL RIGHTS and in the cause of LIBERALISM during the POST–CIVIL RIGHTS ERA. Kennedy was elected to the Senate in 1962 to take the seat vacated by his brother JOHN F. KENNEDY when he became president. Throughout his more than four decades in the Senate, he has been a leader on every civil rights bill from the CIVIL RIGHTS ACT OF 1964 to the Civil Rights Act of 1991.

After the assassination of his brother Robert Kennedy in 1968 (Robert Kennedy served as attorney general in his brother's cabinet, was elected to the Senate in 1964, and was running for the DEMOCRATIC PARTY's presidential nomination at the time of his murder), Kennedy seemed to make the cause of the poor and racial minorities his cause. As the Senate's most famous member and as a skilled and passionate legislator, he also was the leader in Congress for the minimum wage, national health insurance, GAY RIGHTS, and FEMINISM. In 1980 he challenged President JIMMY CARTER for renomination, charging that Carter had abandoned the cause of liberalism. After he lost to Carter, Kennedy in the Senate became a leading opponent of the conservative civil rights and welfare policies of President RONALD REAGAN. Although his efforts to succeed his brother in the presidency were unsuccessful, history will show that he was one of the 20th century's great senators and one who did as much as anyone who has served in the Congress to advance the causes of African-American FREEDOM and EQUALITY.

Further reading: Adam Clymer, *Edward M. Kennedy: A Biography* (New York: Morrow, 1999).

Kennedy, John F. (1917–1963) *35th president of the United States*

John F. Kennedy, the 35th president of the United States, was the first American president to declare unambiguously that the problem of CIVIL RIGHTS and EQUALITY for blacks was a moral issue. In what was the most important statement on race by an American president since ABRAHAM LINCOLN issued the EMANCIPATION PROCLAMATION in September 1863, Kennedy in June 1963—in words much more eloquent and passionate than Lincoln's—declared that the principle of racial equality was "as old as the scriptures . . . and as clear as the American Constitution." This statement was made by Kennedy in a nationally broadcast speech on the evening after the JUSTICE DEPARTMENT had successfully overcome Governor GEORGE WALLACE's efforts to block the DESEGREGATION of the University of Alabama. Almost on the spur of the moment, Kennedy decided to give a speech on civil rights. Revising the hurriedly prepared text as he went on the air, he frequently spoke spontaneously, but the address went farther than any offered by his predecessors in supporting the cause of African-American FREEDOM and equality. Describing in detail the injustices facing blacks, Kennedy said they were "shameful" and asked whites to ponder who among them would be willing to have the color of their skin changed and "stand in the Negro's place." Although the bill had not yet been prepared by his staff, Kennedy told the nation he was sending to CONGRESS comprehensive legislation to eradicate SEGREGATION and racial DISCRIMINATION in the United States.

Although the black vote in 1960 constituted the BALANCE OF POWER in Kennedy's narrow victory over RICHARD NIXON, he had not in his Senate career or during the presidential campaign been a strong supporter of civil rights, unlike, for example, HUBERT HUMPHREY. Once he was elected president, he decided to postpone sending comprehensive civil rights legislation to Congress until after his anticipated reelection in 1964. Kennedy decided to delay because, first, he had other issues—tax cuts, medicare, trade—that were more important to him than civil rights, and he worried that the CONSERVATIVE COALITION in Congress would block these priorities if he also embraced civil rights. Second, he believed that even if he proposed a civil rights bill that it would not pass, and therefore to do so would be merely a symbolic gesture that might jeopardize his other priorities as well as his chances for renomination and reelection in 1964. Calculating that he would be reelected by a wide margin in 1964, the delay in proposing a civil rights bill would enhance its chances for passage, Kennedy reasoned, and would not jeopardize his political future.

The BIRMINGHAM DEMONSTRATIONS led by MARTIN LUTHER KING JR. dramatically altered these calculations. First, the demonstrations resulted in the activation of powerful elements of the Democratic Party COALITION—labor, liberal, and religious groups—that served to counterbalance the power of the conservative coalition. Second, the televised VIOLENCE and POLITICAL REPRESSION of the CIVIL RIGHTS MOVEMENT at Birmingham, in Kennedy's view, undermined the American position in the COLD WAR struggle against the spread of COMMUNISM in the THIRD WORLD. Finally, and most critically, Kennedy believed the demonstrations at Birmingham and elsewhere threatened the stability of the POLITICAL SYSTEM. Thus, it was time to act now to avoid further violence and disorders. So, in 1963 he made his speech and proposed what was to become the CIVIL RIGHTS ACT OF 1964.

Although Kennedy procrastinated in submitting civil rights legislation until forced by circumstances, earlier in his administration he had taken several symbolic actions designed to demonstrate his commitment to civil rights. First, he directed his brother Robert Kennedy, the attorney general, to investigate and prosecute violations of existing civil rights laws. Second, he appointed almost 40 blacks to the federal BUREAUCRACY, almost as many as all of his predecessors combined. Third, he issued EXECUTIVE ORDERS prohibiting discrimination in federally assisted housing and establishing an early version of AFFIRMATIVE ACTION. Finally, Kennedy was the first American president to invite African Americans on a regular basis to White House dinners and social events. Although he was reluctant to become engaged, when the circumstances in 1963 forced him to act, he became the most eloquent and one of the two or three most effective presidents in the cause of civil rights. His assassination in Dallas, Texas, during the course of the debate on his civil rights bill made him in the eyes of many blacks a martyr in the cause of their freedom.

Further reading: Carl Brauer, *John F. Kennedy and the Second Reconstruction* (New York: Columbia University Press, 1977).

Kerner Report (National Advisory Commission on Civil Disorders)

The Kerner Report is the informal name for the report of the seven-person National Advisory Commission on Civil Disorders appointed by President LYNDON B. JOHNSON to investigate the causes of and solutions to the RIOTS that occurred in the 1960s in the GHETTOS of the NORTHERN STATES. Beginning with the WATTS RIOT in 1965, African Americans rioted every year until 1968 in what came to be referred to as the "long hot summers" of VIOLENCE and rebellion. These occurred at the same time as the rising MILITANCY of the BLACK POWER MOVEMENT and the creation of the BLACK PANTHER PARTY, so there was concern that these developments taken together might pose a threat to the stability of the POLITICAL SYSTEM. As a result, President Johnson appointed the commission. It was headed by the governor of Illinois, Otto Kerner (hence the commission and its report's informal name), and it included two African Americans, ROY WILKINS of the NAACP and Senator EDWARD BROOKE. One of the first persons to testify before the commission was KENNETH CLARK, who told it that he questioned the usefulness of the commission since there had been previous riot commissions and reports but they had what he called an "*Alice-in-Wonderland* quality with the same moving picture reshown over and over again, the same analysis, the same recommendations and the same inaction." Although the findings of the Kerner Report were somewhat surprising, in general Clark's skepticism was well founded. The surprise in the report was its unexpected conclusion that the riots were caused by "white racism" rather than by communist agitators, black-power militants, criminals, or other forces internal to the BLACK COMMUNITY. Instead, the Commission concluded that "what white Americans have never fully understood—but what the Negro can never forget—is that white society is deeply implicated in the ghetto. White institutions created it, white institutions maintain it, and white society condones it." The commission then recommended a series of immediate reforms in education, employment, welfare, and housing to keep the nation from moving more and more "toward two societies, one black, one white—separate and unequal." It also recommended an end to stereotypical coverage of blacks in the MEDIA and the hiring of more black reporters.

Although the commission's findings and conclusions blaming the riots on WHITE SUPREMACY and RACISM were surprising, the fate of its recommendations were not, because as Kenneth Clark predicted they were ignored. President Johnson—facing increasing CONSERVATISM in the CONGRESS, a growing WHITE BACKLASH, and the pressures of the VIETNAM WAR—accepted the report but declined to propose implementation of its recommendations. The leaders of the Congress also ignored the report, as they were more interested in passing laws to suppress the riots and toughen the punishments for crimes in general. The Kerner Report is therefore a useful historical document, but a 1989 study by the National Academy of Science found little change since the Kerner Report, concluding that as a result of continuing DISCRIMINATION, blacks remained "separated from the mainstream of national life."

Further reading: *Report of the National Advisory Commission on Civil Disorders* (New York: Bantam, 1968).

Keyes, Alan (1951–) *author, government official*
In 1996 and 2000 Alan Keyes ran for the REPUBLICAN PARTY nomination for president. In 1972 SHIRLEY CHISHOLM ran for the DEMOCRATIC PARTY's nomination, as did JESSE JACKSON in 1984 and 1988, but Keyes was the first African American to seek the nomination of the Republican Party. Like Chisholm and Jackson, Keyes had little chance of getting the nomination but ran in order to use the PRESIDENTIAL CAMPAIGN as a forum to gain national attention for himself and his ideas. But, unlike Jackson and Chisholm, who embraced the IDEOLOGY of LIBERALISM, Keyes embraced CONSERVATISM. Indeed, in both 1996 and 2000 Keyes was widely viewed as the most conservative of all the candidates seeking the Republican nomination. In both campaigns, Keyes emphasized moral issues such as opposition to abortion, FEMINISM, and GAY RIGHTS, but he also opposed AFFIRMATIVE ACTION and the WELFARE STATE.

Keyes received his undergraduate degree and his Ph.D. in political science from Harvard. He then spent a decade working in the federal BUREAUCRACY, first in the State Department and then in the administration of RONALD REAGAN, where he was ambassador to the UNITED NATIONS' Economic and Social Council. After leaving the government, Keyes hosted a national radio talk program and twice ran unsuccessfully for the U.S. Senate from Maryland. In his two campaigns for the presidency Keyes raised relatively little money, was generally ignored by the MEDIA, and received less than 3 percent of the vote.

Keyes v. School District No. 1, Denver, Colorado *(1973)*

Keyes v. School District No. 1, Denver, Colorado is the first decision by the SUPREME COURT applying the principles of *BROWN V. BOARD OF EDUCATION* to school districts in the NORTHERN STATES. It was also the first decision of the Court requiring BUSING for the purposes of school DESEGREGATION in school districts outside of the SOUTHERN STATES. In *Keyes*, the Court ruled that even if a school district had never practiced de jure (legal) SEGREGATION, it could violate the principles of *Brown* by practicing de facto segregation, that is, segregation in practice or in fact. In the 7-1 decision (because he was from Colorado, Justice Byron White recused himself), the Court ruled that although Denver had never maintained de jure segregation, it had deliberately created a separate and unequal school system through a strategy of locating schools and drawing boundary lines in such a way as to place blacks in separate schools with the oldest books and the least-experienced teachers. The Court then ordered, as it had in *SWANN V. CHARLOTTE-MECKLENBURG*, that Denver bus black and white children in order to achieve racial balance in all of its schools. The principles of the *Keyes* case were soon applied nationwide, leading to an enormous controversy and eventually a decision by the Court to reverse its position and began to put an end to school busing.

See also *MILIKEN V. BRADLEY*.

King, Martin Luther, Jr. (1929–1968) *civil rights leader*

Martin Luther King Jr. is universally recognized as the greatest leader in the history of the African-American struggle for FREEDOM and EQUALITY. In a survey of African-American political scientists conducted in 2000, he was ranked the greatest or most important leader, that is, the individual who had the "greatest impact on the well being or destiny of the African people in the United States." King is also universally recognized as one of the greatest American leaders of all time, ranking with George Washington, ABRAHAM LINCOLN, and FRANKLIN D. ROOSEVELT as individuals who had decisive influences on the course of American history. His "I HAVE A DREAM" SPEECH is among the most celebrated and familiar in American history, and his birthday is one of only three celebrated as a national holiday, the other two being Jesus Christ and Christopher Columbus. King's significance as a leader relates to his leading the CIVIL RIGHTS MOVEMENT, which with the American Revolution and the CIVIL WAR is one of the great transformative events in American history, to its successful conclusion in the 1960s. King did not lead or direct the movement away from the course established by W. E. B. DU BOIS, WILLIAM MONROE TROTTER, and their colleagues in the NIAGARA MOVEMENT in 1905, and his work was built on foundations established by leaders of the NAACP, including JOEL E. SPINGARN, JAMES WELDON JOHNSON, WALTER WHITE, and THURGOOD MARSHALL. But his creative use of mass PROTEST and CIVIL DISOBEDIENCE was a decisive force in breaking the back of WHITE SUPREMACY, RACISM, and SEGREGATION in the SOUTHERN STATES.

King was born in Atlanta, Georgia, in 1929. His father was pastor of a leading BLACK CHURCH in the city (King's grandfather and great-grandfather were also preachers), and so he grew up in the relatively prosperous circumstances of the "black bourgeoisie." After graduating from Morehouse College, the elite historically black college for black men, he attended seminary and later earned a Ph.D. in philosophy from Boston University. After completing the Ph.D. at the age of 25, he became pastor of the Dexter Avenue Baptist Church, a prominent congregation in Montgomery, Alabama. A year later, after ROSA PARKS's refusal to give up her seat on a bus led to the MONTGOMERY BUS BOYCOTT, King became the boycott's leader. The success of the boycott instantly made King a national leader of the Civil Rights movement. In 1957 he created the SOUTHERN CHRISTIAN LEADERSHIP CONFERENCE (SCLC) and began to develop a systematic strategy of nonviolent protests designed to eradicate segregation in the Southern states. A decade later, this part of King's work was essentially complete—the BIRMINGHAM DEMONSTRATIONS led by him in 1963 resulted in passage of the CIVIL RIGHTS ACT OF 1964, and the SELMA DEMONSTRATIONS he led in 1965 resulted in passage of the VOTING RIGHTS ACT OF 1965. These two acts of CONGRESS and the Fair Housing Act of 1968, which was passed in the wake of the RIOTS following King's assassination, effectively ended legal segregation in the United States. Thus, King's leadership was directly related to passage of two of the three major CIVIL RIGHTS laws in the United States and indirectly to passage of the third. Two weeks after President LYNDON B. JOHNSON signed the Voting Rights Act, the WATTS RIOT took place, and one year later the BLACK POWER MOVEMENT got its start on the MEREDITH MARCH, led by King and STOKELY CARMICHAEL. These two events precipitated a change in the focus of King's work as well as increased MILITANCY in both his program and strategies.

The Watts riot forced King to change the focus of his work from INDIVIDUAL RACISM and segregation in the Southern states to problems of INSTITUTIONAL RACISM and POVERTY in the GHETTOS of the NORTHERN STATES. In effect, the riot in Watts and riots in subsequent cities until 1968 forced the problem of the UNDERCLASS on to the BLACK AGENDA, signaling that laws against legal segregation had little relevance to blacks outside of the South, since for the most part they already enjoyed civil rights. The Black Power movement, with its emphasis on principles of BLACK NATIONALISM and its embrace of VIOLENCE as a strategy, required King to rethink the approaches he had used since the Montgomery bus boycott. At the same time, King began to feel compelled to speak out against the VIETNAM WAR: first, because he thought the war was morally wrong, and second, because he thought it was draining money and attention away from the WAR ON POVERTY. His receipt of the Nobel Peace Prize in 1964 deepened his opposition to the war, as did his growing sense of solidarity with the peoples of the THIRD WORLD. These circumstances led King increasingly toward militancy and RADICALISM. First, in his private deliberations and then increasingly in his speeches and sermons, he begin to sharpen his critique of CAPITALISM and express admiration for democratic SOCIALISM as it was practiced in countries like Sweden. King's critique of capitalism became more powerful in the late 1960s, although it was not a new view on his part, since in the early 1950s he preached sermons expressing skepticism about what he termed capitalism's excesses. (See, for example, the 1956 sermon "Paul's Letter to American Christians.") King's confrontation with the poverty of the ghettos and the rural South led him to focus on the economy, joblessness, and FULL EMPLOYMENT. Thus, at the time of his death he was—against the advice of many of his staff, including BAYARD RUSTIN and JESSE JACKSON—planning to lead the POOR PEOPLE'S CAMPAIGN in the DISTRICT OF COLUMBIA, where he would challenge an underpinning of capitalism by demanding either a guaranteed job or income for all Americans.

King initially rejected the Black Power movement, but by the time of his death he had changed his mind and begun to embrace BLACKNESS and the movement's ideas about racial solidarity and organization and pride in black heritage and CULTURE. This, however, like King's views on capitalism and socialism, was not a wholly new departure. Although committed to INTEGRATION throughout his career, it was integration as EQUALITY rather than as the ASSIMILATION of individual blacks or the BLACK COMMUNITY into the MELTING POT. For example, King throughout his public life emphasized core black nationalist principles such as race group consciousness and solidarity as well as independent or autonomous black ORGANIZATION (especially the black church and black colleges). King was also deeply rooted in black culture and skillfully used its RELIGIOSITY and MUSIC to advance the movement. Still, he never became racially chauvinistic or separatist, believing throughout in the Christian ethic of the brotherhood of man and what he called the "beloved community." King also thought that multiracial COALITIONS were indispensable in AFRICAN-AMERICAN POLITICS, and he was unalterably opposed on philosophical and strategic grounds to the use of VIOLENCE. Throughout the last years of his life, King repeatedly stated that he would resist the use of violence, even if he was the last black man in America to do so. King's opposition to violence as a political method was strategic (he did not think it would work for blacks in the United States), but it was mainly philosophical and religious. This philosophical and religious commitment to nonviolence eventually reinforced his militant opposition to the Vietnam War, antagonizing his senior colleagues in the movement, including ROY WILKINS of the NAACP and WHITNEY YOUNG of the URBAN LEAGUE.

King's evolving militancy—his leading role in protest against the war in Vietnam, his embrace of some of the principles of the Black Power movement, his planned Poor Peoples campaign, and his increasing attacks on capitalism and Western imperialism—angered President Lyndon B. Johnson, J. EDGAR HOOVER, and other high-level persons in the POWER ELITE, including those in the mainstream MEDIA, who increasingly began to see him as a threat to the POLITICAL SYSTEM's stability. This led the FBI and the army to intensify their campaign of POLITICAL REPRESSION against him, a campaign that began in 1947, when King was a boy of 18. The army opened its surveillance file on King in 1947, photographing him as he left a meeting allegedly organized by a member of the COMMUNIST PARTY. As the COINTELPRO campaign to destroy his effectiveness as a leader intensified, King became dispirited and worried, exclaiming at one point to his aides, "They [the highest authorities in the government] are trying to break me." Although his spirit waned for a time, they did not break him. Indeed, his passionate commitment to the causes of

Martin Luther King Jr. at a New York press conference, 1961 *(Library of Congress)*

peace and economic and racial justice intensified in the last year of his life. In 1968 he was murdered in Memphis, Tennessee, where he was preparing to lead a protest campaign for better wages and working conditions for striking African-American garbage workers.

Martin Luther King Jr. richly deserves his ranking as the greatest black leader of all time. He was an extraordinary leader who came to believe that he had been chosen by God to play the role he played in history. At the remarkably early age of 25, he had the presence to use multiple bases of power—knowledge in strategic thinking, tactical planning, religion, morality, and charisma—to consolidate a movement of race solidarity while mobilizing a multiracial coalition that achieved the objectives of black people. W. E. B. Du Bois is the only leader of blacks to rival King in preeminence. Du Bois's leadership, however, spanned seven decades, while King's was a little more than one.

Further reading: Taylor Branch, *Parting the Waters: America in the King Years, 1954–1963* (New York: Simon & Schuster, 1988); Claybourne Carson, ed., *The Autobiography of Martin Luther King, Jr.* (New York: Warner Brothers, 1998); David Garrow, *Bearing the Cross: Martin*

Luther King, Jr. and the Southern Christian Leadership Conference (New York: Morrow, 1986).

King, Rodney (1965–) *victim of police violence*
In the late 20th century Rodney King, an unemployed black construction worker, became a symbol of police VIOLENCE and misconduct in the BLACK COMMUNITY, of black ALIENATION from the CRIMINAL JUSTICE SYSTEM, and of the deep cleavage that divides black and white PUBLIC OPINION on police procedures and the JUDICIAL PROCESS. In May 1991, King failed to yield to Los Angeles police (because, he later said, that he feared a traffic violation might result in revocation of his parole) and was chased by the Los Angeles police and the California Highway Patrol. When his car was finally stopped, several white officers began to "beat him to death," in the words of one of the officers. Of the 20 officers at the scene, at least three beat King, hitting him between 53 and 56 times while he lay defenseless on the ground. At least one officer stomped on his head; the right socket in one of his eyes was broken; and bones were broken in the base of his skull. The beating occurred in full view of residents of a nearby apartment complex, from which one resident videotaped the incident. After the beating, King was arrested. While taking him to jail, the officers bragged, boasted, laughed, joked, and made racist slurs about King and the beating, all of which was picked up on police radio transmitters. As a result of the beating, King was left permanently disabled and psychologically traumatized. Four of the 20 officers were charged with assault and the use of deadly force. Tried by a jury of 10 whites, one Asian, and one Hispanic, three of the officers were acquitted and one was found guilty of one count of the use of excessive force. On the afternoon of the verdict, RIOTS broke out in the GHETTOS of Los Angeles. The riots lasted three days, resulting in 52 deaths, 2,500 injuries, and an estimated $1 billion in property damage. It took the dispatch of the U.S. Army to finally suppress the rebellion.

Shortly after the verdict and the riot, several polls were conducted by the national MEDIA to gauge black and white opinion on the beating, the verdict, and the riot. The polls attempted to examine opinion on these issues in the context of opinions in general about the criminal justice system in the United States. A *Washington Post* poll of a representative sample of the nation found that 54 percent of whites and 12 percent of blacks thought the police treated blacks and whites equally. Results for the criminal justice system were similar, with 52 percent of whites stating that blacks received equal treatment in the criminal justice system, a view held by only 9 percent of blacks. In contrast to these significant opinion differences between the races about the criminal justice system, there was little difference between blacks and whites about the verdict: 93 percent of whites and 99 percent of blacks disagreed with it. However, 81 percent of blacks agreed with the statement that the verdict showed blacks could not get justice in the United States, a view shared by only 27 percent of whites. Opinion on the riot also divided along racial lines, with 82 percent of blacks but only 44 percent of whites agreeing with the statement that only violent demonstrations or riots get the attention of the government.

After the riots, the JUSTICE DEPARTMENT indicted the four officers on federal charges of violating King's CIVIL RIGHTS. Two of the four were found guilty and sentenced to 30 months in prison. In a civil suit against the city of Los Angeles, King was awarded $3.8 million in compensatory damages for his injuries.

Ku Klux Klan

The Ku Klux Klan (KKK) is the best known of the several white terrorist groups that emerged in the SOUTHERN STATES during and after RECONSTRUCTION. These groups used LYNCHING and other forms of VIOLENCE to intimidate the BLACK COMMUNITY from exercising the economic, civil, and political rights conferred on it after the CIVIL WAR. Although the Klan initially operated only in the Southern states, as the GREAT MIGRATION of blacks to the NORTHERN STATES got underway in the 20th century, the Klan expanded northward. Various organizations have used "KKK" as their name, but the original group was founded in Pulaski, Tennessee, in 1865 by several former Confederate army generals. Beginning as a fraternal organization, the Klan quickly turned to terrorism against the blacks and whites who were running the Reconstruction governments. Usually clothed in white robes or sheets and pointed hoods, the Klan burned crosses to intimidate people and resorted to beatings, torture, and murder as methods of repression.

CONGRESS passed several laws designed to suppress the Klan and similar groups, and President ULYSSES S. GRANT for a time used the army to disarm and arrest hundreds of Klansmen, but after the army was withdrawn as part of the COMPROMISE OF 1877 the Klan in collaboration with authorities in the Southern STATE AND LOCAL GOVERNMENTS effectively imposed their domination on the African-American community. The Klan then faded away but never completely disappeared as, from time to time in various parts of the country, different groups adopted the name and practices of the original KKK. In the 1920s it expanded its activities into the Northern states and its targets to include Catholics, Jews, and Communists. At the height of the PROTEST phase of the CIVIL RIGHTS MOVEMENT during the 1950s and 1960s the Klan intensified its terrorist activities, and rarely were its members arrested or prosecuted for their crimes. It was only near the end of the

Civil Rights movement in the mid-1960s that the FBI and the JUSTICE DEPARTMENT effectively suppressed the Klan's terrorist activities. Various Klan "Klaverns" or chapters continued to engage in parades, marches, and other symbolic activities in defense of RACISM and WHITE SUPREMACY; however, they posed little threat to the black community. And in the POST–CIVIL RIGHTS ERA, several Klansmen were finally arrested and prosecuted for crimes committed during the 1960s, including the men who bombed a BLACK CHURCH during the BIRMINGHAM DEMONSTRATIONS in 1963 and who murdered MEDGAR EVERS in 1963.

Kwanza (Kwanzaa)

Kwanza is the African-American holiday, celebrated for seven days in late December, created by RON KARENGA in 1966. An expression originally of a militant form of CULTURAL NATIONALISM, the holiday was created by Karenga in Los Angeles a year after the WATTS RIOT in an effort to establish a tradition in African-American CULTURE based on African values. It was conceived as an alternative to Christmas and its commercialization and commodification by market CAPITALISM. Kwanza—meaning "first fruits" in the African language of Swahili—is a blend of rituals and traditions drawn from Karenga's understanding of African traditions. It is based on the seven principles of "Nguzo Saba" or a black value system that includes (in the English translation from Swahili): unity, self-determination, work and responsibility, cooperative economics, purpose, creativity, and faith. It is celebrated over a seven-day period during which persons light a candle affirming each principle. Gifts exchanged during the holiday were supposed to be creative rather than commercial, thus providing an alternative to traditional Christmas buying and offering the BLACK COMMUNITY an alternative to the exploitation inherent in what Karenga saw as the decadence of America's celebration of Christmas. As Kwanza has evolved, however, it too has become commercialized and commodified, with products related to its celebration sold in major stores and malls. Thus, it has lost much of its authenticity and significance as an expression of MILITANCY in AFRICAN-AMERICAN POLITICS. Celebrated in some manner by an estimated 20 million African Americans in the United States and elsewhere, it has been incorporated into mainstream American culture, including schools and the MEDIA. Ironically, as Kwanza became more popular, it became more like the Christmas holiday it was intended to replace, and as a consequence of its success it lost whatever capacity it might have had to foster a distinctive African-American value system.

See also AFROCENTRISM.

L

Langston, John Mercer (1829–1897) *government official*

John Mercer Langston is credited with being the first BLACK who became an ELECTED OFFICIAL in the United States, elected town clerk of Oberlin, Ohio, in 1855. Later he served briefly in the CONGRESS and was recognized during RECONSTRUCTION as the African-American leader second in importance only to FREDERICK DOUGLASS. Historically, as an elected official and member of Congress, Langston's leadership is comparable to that of ADAM CLAYTON POWELL JR., who served in Congress during the era of the CIVIL RIGHTS MOVEMENT.

Langston was born a FREE NEGRO in Virginia in 1829. His father was a white slaveholder, married to a woman of mixed African and Indian ancestry. When his father died, he left Langston a substantial inheritance, which he used to get an extensive education and, through investments in real estate, a substantial fortune. After receiving degrees in education and theology from Oberlin College in 1850, Langston aspired to become a lawyer. But Ohio law prohibited blacks from practicing law. However, after studying law with a white attorney, the Ohio authorities ruled that Langston's light skin entitled him to the rights and privileges of white men, and he was admitted to the bar in 1854 as the state's first black attorney. Quickly building a reputation as a skillful lawyer, Langston was eventually placed in charge of Oberlin's legal affairs, was elected to the town council, and played an important role in shaping Oberlin's public education system. Prior to his political successes in Oberlin, Langston was active in PROTEST politics in Ohio, working in the ABOLITIONIST MOVEMENT and in the state's chapter of the NATIONAL NEGRO CONVENTION. At this stage of his work he exhibited a MILITANCY that expressed itself in support of emigration and BLACK NATIONALISM. He supported black nationalism and emigration in the early 1850s because he, like MARTIN DELANY, said he believed that the forces of RACISM and WHITE SUPREMACY were unlikely to ever fundamentally change, and therefore FREEDOM and EQUALITY for Africans were impossible in the United States. But as his professional and political aspirations in Oberlin were fulfilled, Langston changed his mind and embraced the IDEOLOGY of INTEGRATIONism, writing that black Americans could some day hope for "liberation" in the land of their birth.

After the CIVIL WAR Langston joined the staff of the FREEDMEN'S BUREAU, where he traveled throughout the SOUTHERN STATES encouraging POLITICAL PARTICIPATION by the former slaves in Reconstruction government and politics. After his travels through the Southern states, he joined the faculty of HOWARD UNIVERSITY, where he became dean of the law school and acting president. His application, however, to become Howard's first black president was rejected because of his race. Angry and bitter, Langston and the entire law faculty resigned in protest. From 1864 to 1868 he was president of the National Equal Rights League. Founded at the 1864 National Negro Convention, the league was an early precursor of the NAACP. He was also active in REPUBLICAN PARTY politics, working in the PRESIDENTIAL CAMPAIGNS of ULYSSES S. GRANT and RUTHERFORD B. HAYES and helping CHARLES SUMNER to draft the Civil Rights Act of 1875. Hayes appointed Langston to the diplomatic BUREAUCRACY as minister to HAITI for eight years. When he returned to the United States he ran for the Congress from a heavily black congressional district in Virginia. Although he won the election, through fraud and corruption the seat was awarded to his white DEMOCRATIC PARTY opponent. It took Langston almost two years and thousands of dollars before he was able to successfully challenge the election and take his seat in the House of Representatives. By this time, he had only three months left in his two-year term, and he was defeated in his bid for election to a second term. Although he served in Congress for only three months, he was outspoken in the cause of CIVIL RIGHTS, making speeches and introducing bills and a constitutional amendment to protect black voting rights in the Southern states. After leaving

Congress, Langston continued his activism in Republican Party politics and the practice of law. In 1894, three years before his death, he wrote his autobiography, *From the Virginia Plantation to the National Capital.*

leadership

Leadership is one of the most important resources in politics. Leadership is probably more important in AFRICAN-AMERICAN politics than in American politics generally because the BLACK COMMUNITY, as an oppressed MINORITY GROUP, has much less POWER than the dominant white majority group. Therefore, effective leadership and leaders have always been important resources in the struggle for the FREEDOM and EQUALITY of black people in America because it is a resource that can be produced out of the indigenous CULTURE and institutions—especially the BLACK CHURCH—of the community. Yet, the task of effectively leading the black community is an extraordinarily difficult one for two distinct although interrelated reasons. First, black leadership must operate in an environment where the dominant POWER bases in the society—political, economic, social, and cultural—are controlled by whites, who have tended to be hostile to the aspirations of blacks. This means that "white leaders" often have more influence on the destiny of the black community than black leaders. This creates the second difficulty, which is that black leaders must first understand the interests and aspirations of the black community and then mobilize its relatively meager resources for purposes of its internal growth and development and for purposes of influencing the decisions of whites, who have an overwhelming impact on those internal processes of development and growth.

Despite the critical importance of leadership in politics in general and in studies of African-American leadership specifically, the concept does not have a widely accepted definition. Rather, the concept of leadership has been defined generally, and in studies of African-American leadership specifically, in a variety of ways. In general, however, leaders are understood as persons who exercise some influence on the definition of the interests and objectives of a group and on the means or strategies used to pursue those objectives. Given this broad definition, African-American leaders can be classified as internal and external. The first can be understood as an individual whose primary concerns are dealing with the internal aspirations, objectives, and strategies of the black community in terms of its cultural and institutional development; such persons might lead religious, fraternal, or cultural groups within the community. The second type of African-American leader would be one whose primary concern is the articulation of the interests and aspirations of the black community in its external relationships to whites or to the POLITICAL SYS-

TEM. Examples here would be the leaders of CIVIL RIGHTS organizations or black ELECTED OFFICIALS who represent BLACK constituencies. Of course both types of leadership—the internal and external—can overlap. For example, an individual could be both a church leader and the leader of a civil rights organization, as were MARTIN LUTHER KING JR. and ADAM CLAYTON POWELL JR., who was a church leader and an elected member of CONGRESS representing HARLEM. In addition to these broad ways of classifying or distinguishing black leaders, political scientists have also classified leadership in black America on the basis of ACCOMMODATIONISM versus PROTEST; MILITANCY versus UNCLE TOM; and on the basis of IDEOLOGY, including CONSERVATISM, LIBERALISM, RADICALISM, INTEGRATIONISM, and BLACK NATIONALISM.

Historical Development

African-American leadership as a structured phenomenon emerged in the antebellum era (circa 1820–30) among the FREE NEGROES in the NORTHERN STATES, who established an infrastructure of black churches, fraternal associations, small businesses, newspapers, and SELF-HELP societies. These early ORGANIZATIONS constituted the base from which African Americans participated in BACK-TO-AFRICA MOVEMENTS, the ABOLITIONIST MOVEMENT, and the CONVENTION MOVEMENT, with the first NATIONAL NEGRO CONGRESS meeting in 1830 under the leadership of RICHARD ALLEN, the founder of the independent black church. Other important leaders during this formative period leading up to the CIVIL WAR included FREDERICK DOUGLASS, HENRY HIGHLAND GARNETT, EDWARD WILMOT BLYDEN, and MARTIN DELANY. Operating outside this more formal structure, individuals like HARRIET TUBMAN and SOJOURNER TRUTH played significant roles in the antislavery crusades, as did NAT TURNER and others who led SLAVE REVOLTS. Once slavery was abolished, the antebellum leadership consolidated during RECONSTRUCTION under the charismatic leadership of Douglass and expanded to include such elected officials as BLANCHE K. BRUCE, HIRAM REVELS, and JOHN MERCER LANGSTON, who served in the Congress.

At the end of Reconstruction, black elected officials all but disappeared from African-American leadership as it came to be dominated by educators, preachers, and journalists. The preeminent leader during this period was BOOKER T. WASHINGTON, who for a time exercised near-dictatorial leadership in black America. Washington's approach to leadership during this period focused on internal community development and accommodationism, but as early as 1890 a civil rights protest organization, the National Afro-American League, was created by, among others, T. Thomas Fortune, a well-known newspaper editor. The league did not last very long, but it was one of the early precursors of the NAACP, which was established in 1909 as a result of the groundwork laid by W. E. B. DU BOIS and WILLIAM MONROE TROTTER in the NIAGARA MOVEMENT, which began in 1905. And in the 1890s the black women's club movement started, leading in 1896 to the establishment of the NATIONAL ASSOCIATION OF COLORED WOMEN led by MARY CHURCH TERRELL and IDA B. WELLS-BARNETT.

By the 1930s the modern structure of the black leadership establishment was in place, including the NAACP and the URBAN LEAGUE as the principal civil rights organizations, the leading black churches, the black MEDIA, and groups such as A. PHILIP RANDOLPH's labor organization the BROTHERHOOD OF SLEEPING CAR PORTERS and MARY MCLEOD BETHUNE's federation of women's groups, the NATIONAL COUNCIL OF NEGRO WOMEN. This structure of black leadership constituted the black establishment, or a power elite, that dominated African-American politics throughout the 20th century and into the 21st. The ideology of this elite or establishment was generally based on some variant of liberalism and the use of such tactics as LOBBYING, LITIGATION, and peaceful protest. As the CIVIL RIGHTS MOVEMENT developed, this establishment expanded to include groups like Martin Luther King's SOUTHERN CHRISTIAN LEADERSHIP CONFERENCE, the STUDENT NONVIOLENT COORDINATING COMMITTEE, and the CONGRESS OF RACIAL EQUALITY. In the POST–CIVIL RIGHTS ERA, it expanded to include black elected officials, most prominently the CONGRESSIONAL BLACK CAUCUS but also the mayors of major American cities. These periodic expansions of the leadership establishment, however, did not alter its fundamental ideological, strategic, or social characteristics. Since the 1930s it has been liberal and integrationist ideologically; moderate and conventional in political strategies and tactics; and constituted by middle-class men, although women and lower-class persons have always constituted a larger proportion of the black power elite than its white counterpart.

Although the black leadership establishment has been hegemonic or dominant, it has since the 1920s faced periodic and powerful challenges from leaders and groups favoring radicalism and variants of black nationalism, including MARCUS GARVEY and the UNIVERSAL NEGRO IMPROVEMENT ASSOCIATION in the 1920s; ELIJAH MUHAMMAD, MALCOLM X, and the NATION OF ISLAM in the 1950s and early 1960s; and STOKELY CARMICHAEL, HUEY NEWTON, and BOBBY SEALE and the BLACK POWER MOVEMENT and the BLACK PANTHER PARTY in the late 1960s and early 1970s.

Until the Black Power movement, the black leadership establishment always included a fairly large number of whites. In the Abolitionist movement of the 19th century, in Booker Washington's accommodationism, and in the 20th century Civil Rights movement, "white interracialists" have been important "Negro leaders." Generally these were upper-status persons (in the 20th century, also disproportionately Jewish) from philanthropic groups and labor, liberal, and religious groups who constituted the COALITION that enacted the civil rights laws of the 1960s. While these white leaders in the black establishment brought resources to the group, they also tended to exercise disproportionate influence in determining ideology and strategy, and for this reason the advocates of black power in the 1960s called for exclusively black African-American leadership. The result was a decline in interracialism in black leadership. However, white philanthropy continues to play an important role in financing black leadership.

Great Leaders in African-American History

In studying leadership in the American government, scholars since the 1940s have asked panels of historians and political scientists to rank or rate the American presidents from the greatest or best to the worst. Although the use of this "ratings game" in evaluating the American presidents has been criticized by some as subjective and impressionistic, these studies, in the half century they have been conducted, have yielded some interesting and useful insights on the nature of leadership in the PRESIDENCY.

In 2000 this methodology was used for the first time in studying African-American leadership when a panel of 46 African-American political scientists selected from the membership roster of the NATIONAL CONFERENCE OF BLACK POLITICAL SCIENTISTS selected the greatest African-American leaders of all time. Specifically, the panel was asked to select or list "in rank order the five African Americans who, in your historical judgment, have had the greatest impact, for good or ill, on the well being and destinies of the African people in the United States." The table below lists the 10 greatest leaders as selected by the panel. (The fifth and 10th persons were mentioned by the same number of panelists. Thus, the table includes 12 rather than 10 persons.) The table includes data on the frequency of mentions, the number of times the individual was ranked first and fifth, and each individual's mean score. In addition to the 12 persons listed in the table, the panelists mentioned 21 other persons at least once (Harriet Tubman was mentioned four times, and Elijah Muhammad, ELLA BAKER, and LOUIS FARRAKHAN were mentioned three times). Although, like the panel studies of presidential leadership, this list is to some extent subjective, it nevertheless provides some useful impressions of how African-American political scientists view the phenomenon of leadership as it has developed historically in the black community. Of the 12 individuals listed as the greatest black leaders of all time, all except two—Douglass and Washington—are 20th-century leaders, although Washington's leadership carries over into the 20th from the 19th century. Three women are on the list of great leaders; eight of the 12 were college edu-

Rank	Leader	Frequency[1]	Rank by No. 1[2]	Mean Score[3]
	THE NCOBPS PANEL: THE TEN GREATEST AFRICAN-AMERICAN LEADERS*			
1	Martin Luther King Jr.	42	21(3/5)	1.9
2	W. E. B. Du Bois	33	7(2/5)	2.4
3	Malcolm X	19	3(1/5)	3.0
4	Frederick Douglass	18	3(5/5)	2.6
5	Booker T. Washington	13	2(5/5)	2.7
5	Marcus Garvey	13	2(1/5)	3.1
6	Thurgood Marshall	12	2(1/5)	3.0
7	Jesse Jackson	8	0(4/5)	4.1
8	Ida B. Wells-Barnett	7	0(1/5)	3.2
9	Mary McLeod Bethune	6	0(4/5)	4.6
10	Fannie Lou Hamer	5	1(0)	2.6
10	Adam Clayton Powell Jr.	5	0(4/5)	4.6

[1]*Frequency represents the number of times the individual was mentioned by panelists. The fifth and 10th persons were mentioned by the same number of panelists. Thus, the list includes 12 rather than 10 persons.*

[2]*Rank by No. 1 represents the number of times the individual was ranked first. The figures in parentheses represent the number of times the individual was ranked fifth.*

[3]*Mean score calculated by summing the rankings of the individual (1–5) and dividing by the number of mentions.*

Adapted from Robert C. Smith "Rating Black Leaders," National Political Science Review 8 (2001): 124–38.

cated (including four with advanced degrees); four were clergymen; five were leaders of civil rights organizations; four edited important newspapers or journals; and there is one elected and one appointed official. (THURGOOD MARSHALL, the appointed official, achieved his leadership greatness as head of the LEGAL DEFENSE FUND prior to his appointments to the BUREAUCRACY and the SUPREME COURT.) Finally, two ideological black nationalists, Garvey and Malcolm X, are on the list.

Several additional generalizations about African-American politics and leadership are suggested by this ranking of leaders. First, blacks appear to have made their greatest progress toward freedom and equality in the 20th century. Second, the leadership of black America has been drawn disproportionately from the TALENTED TENTH. Third, although often overlooked, women have played leadership roles. Finally, clergymen, educators, and orators have played major roles and elected officials near inconsequential ones, although it is worth noting that the only then-living person on the list, JESSE JACKSON, was noted by the panel for his leadership in the transition from militancy and protest to elections and party politics.

Leadership in the 21st Century

At the beginning of the 21st century, African-American leadership continues to operate in a context where it has relatively few resources but enormous demands from a black community that still has a long way to go to achieve equality. The leadership at the beginning of the century also still confronts the dynamic tension between accommodationism and protest identified by GUNNAR MYRDAL in *AN AMERICAN DILEMMA*, although in the post–civil rights era accommodationism has been dominant while protest has withered away or become largely symbolic.

Relative powerlessness and the dynamic tension between accommodation and protest have always been characteristics of black leadership, but in the 21st century, black leadership is likely to confront several new situations. The first concerns the role of women, who have traditionally played intermediary leadership roles. But in the 21st century women are poised to play a larger role because of changing attitudes among women about their roles and because they constitute a growing proportion of the "talented tenth" from which leaders are normally recruited. However, because of SEXISM and the forces of tradition and stereotypical thinking, the men who dominate most black organizations may be unwilling to share preeminent leadership roles with women, which could result in gender tensions and conflicts. Second, historically African-American leaders have defined the struggle for equality as a binary black-white conflict, but in the 21st century it is likely to become multiracial as a result of the growing size and influence of the new ETHNIC GROUPS of "color" from Asia and Latin America. This new MULTICULTURALISM presents black leaders with possibilities for both conflict and coalitions as the new immigrants also struggle for equality. Finally, in the 21st century, African Americans who are leaders of America rather than of the black community are likely to become increasingly prominent. Prior to the successes of the Civil Rights movement, blacks who wished to be leaders were confined to leading within the black community. Increasingly, black leadership will become binary; that is, although many blacks will continue to see leading blacks as the primary focus of their work, others will seek to lead America as mayors, governors, judges, and generals (as examples, DOUGLAS WILDER, COLIN POWELL, WILLIAM GRAY, J. C. WATT, CLARENCE THOMAS). Blacks generally want to see blacks in leadership positions throughout America. This was a major goal of the Civil Rights movement, the integration of blacks into all facets of American life. Yet to effectively lead America requires transcending the interests of blacks and embracing the interests of the nation as a whole, which may conflict with the narrow or specific interests of blacks. When a black obtains a leadership position in America, there is a possibility of CO-OPTATION, thus creating tensions and conflicts with those blacks leading blacks, including allegations by the latter that the former are UNCLE TOMS.

Further reading: Lerone Bennett, "The Black Establishment" in *The Negro Mood and Other Essays* (New York: Ballentine Books, 1964); John Hope Franklin and August Meier, eds., *Black Leaders of the Twentieth Century* (Urbana: University of Illinois, 1982); Leon Litwack and August Meier, *Black Leaders of the Nineteenth Century* (Urbana: University of Illinois Press, 1988); Belinda Robert, *How Long? How Long?: African American Women in the Civil Rights Movement* (New York: Oxford University Press, 1997); Robert C. Smith, "Rating Black Leaders," *National Political Science Review* 8 (2001): 124–38; Ronald Walters and Cedric Johnson, *Bibliography of African American Leadership: An Annotated Guide* (Westport, Conn.: Greenwood Press, 2000); Ronald Walters and Robert C. Smith, *African American Leadership* (Albany: State University of New York Press, 1999).

Leadership Conference on Civil Rights

The Leadership Conference on Civil Rights (LCCR) is the oldest and largest COALITION of INTEREST GROUPS devoted to the cause of CIVIL RIGHTS. It was founded in 1949 by A. PHILIP RANDOLPH, the African-American labor leader; ROY WILKINS, then the assistant director of the NAACP; and Arnold Aronson, a Jewish labor leader. Initially it was a coalition of about 40 black, labor, Jewish, and other religious groups whose major objective was the passage of legislation to secure the civil rights of blacks, especially in the SOUTHERN STATES. The LCCR and the NAACP were the principal groups LOBBYING for civil rights during the 1950s and 1960s. (During this time CLARENCE MITCHELL, head of the NAACP's Washington office, was also head of

LCCR.) The success of the CIVIL RIGHTS MOVEMENT served as a model for other groups facing various forms of DISCRIMINATION. These groups—women, Latinos, Asian Americans, gays, the disabled—joined LCCR in the 1960s, 1970s, and 1980s, expanding its membership from about 40 groups in 1949 to more than 150 in 2000. While in 1949 black ORGANIZATIONS were a majority of LCCR, in 2000 fewer than one-third were black. The expansion of LCCR has increased its resources, but inevitably it has also led to periodic tensions and conflicts along lines of ETHNICITY, gender, and sexuality. However, as a broad-based coalition, it reflects the realities of MULTICULTURALISM in the struggle for EQUALITY in the United States.

Legal Defense Fund

The Legal Defense Fund (LDF) was established in 1939 by the NAACP as the legal arm of the CIVIL RIGHTS MOVEMENT. Until the 1990s the official name of the organization was the NAACP Legal Defense and Educational Fund, although legally it was separate and distinct from the NAACP. (It was established as a separate organization from the parent NAACP so that it could get tax-exempt contributions.) The LDF used LITIGATION rather than LOBBYING or PROTEST to pursue CIVIL RIGHTS. Under the leadership of THURGOOD MARSHALL, it developed a systematic strategy to use the CONSTITUTION and CONSTITUTIONALISM, particularly the FOURTEENTH AMENDMENT and its EQUAL PROTECTION CLAUSE, to destroy the legal foundations of RACISM and SEGREGATION. Although it won a significant number of cases in the 1940s, its most important victory was the historic 1954 *BROWN V. BOARD OF EDUCATION* case in which the SUPREME COURT declared the doctrine of "separate but equal" in education unconstitutional. The success of LDF in *Brown* led other groups—women, Latinos, Asian Americans, gays—to develop strategies and organizations of litigation to pursue their rights. As a result, civil rights was expanded to include the elderly, the disabled, language minorities, and immigrants.

The NAACP created the LDF in 1939 because it was relatively powerless in lobbying CONGRESS. In the POST–CIVIL RIGHTS ERA, the NAACP and other black ORGANIZATIONS were somewhat more influential in lobbying Congress while the Supreme Court has become less sympathetic to civil rights. Thus the LDF and litigation are less important than they were from the 1940s to the 1980s. However, in 1970 LDF successfully litigated *GRIGGS V. DUKE POWER*, the landmark employment discrimination case that established judicial recognition of INSTITUTIONAL RACISM. In the 1970s and 1980s the fund also sought abolition of the death penalty as a violation of the "cruel and unusual punishment" clause of the Eighth Amendment of the BILL OF RIGHTS and because it was racially discriminatory. Although the Court refused to declare the death penalty unconstitutional, in *Coker v. Georgia* (1977) LDF did persuade it to declare capital punishment unconstitutional in rape cases. In 1979 in a dispute over strategy and fund-raising with the NAACP, the LDF was required to delete NAACP from its official name and refer to itself simply as the Legal Defense Fund.

Lewis, John (1940–   ) *civil rights leader, congressman*

John Lewis was one of the principal leaders of the PROTEST phase of the CIVIL RIGHTS MOVEMENT during the 1960s. A sharecropper's son from Alabama, Lewis was a founding member of the STUDENT NONVIOLENT COORDINATING COMMITTEE (SNCC) and served as its chair from 1963 until 1966. As chair, he was one of the so-called big-six leaders of the Civil Rights movement. At the age of 18 he met MARTIN LUTHER KING JR. and thereafter he was involved in every major civil rights protest of the 1960s. He led SIT-INS at lunch counters, was one of the early participants in the FREEDOM RIDES, and led the first of the SELMA DEMONSTRATIONS. At Selma, Lewis was brutally beaten, as he was on several other occasions during his leadership of SNCC. Jailed more than 40 times, Lewis was widely admired for his decency, determination, and courage.

When SNCC in 1966 started the BLACK POWER MOVEMENT, Lewis was defeated as chair by STOKELY CARMICHAEL. He subsequently resigned from the group because he felt the principles of the Black Power movement violated the Civil Rights movement's principles of interracialism and nonviolence. After leaving SNCC Lewis became director of the Voter Education Project in Atlanta, Georgia, which was responsible for the registration of black voters in the SOUTHERN STATES. During the administration of JIMMY CARTER, Lewis served in the BUREAUCRACY as director of ACTION, the agency responsible for coordinating voluntary activities by citizens at the local level. In 1977 he ran for CONGRESS from Atlanta to replace ANDREW YOUNG, who had resigned to become ambassador to the UNITED NATIONS. He was defeated in 1977, but in 1986 he was elected as the second African-American congressman from Georgia.

During the early 1960s Lewis was known for his MILITANCY. Indeed, his proposed speech at the 1963 MARCH ON WASHINGTON was thought to be so militant in tone that the organizers required him to revise it; otherwise he would not have been allowed to speak. However, as the movement turned toward black-power RADICALISM in the late 1960s, Lewis remained steadfast in his philosophy of nonviolence and interracialism. In the Congress, Lewis earned a reputation for moderation and COALITION building across racial lines. While deeply committed to LIBERALISM and the DEMOCRATIC PARTY, he was widely respected for his calm demeanor and his ability to work across ideological and party lines. A genuine hero of the Civil Rights movement, Lewis in 1990 became one of the leading members of the Democratic Party in the House of Representatives.

liberalism

Liberalism as a philosophy and as an IDEOLOGY occupies an ambivalent place in AFRICAN-AMERICAN POLITICS. In order to understand this ambivalence, one has to distinguish between *classical liberalism* as a political *philosophy* and *contemporary liberalism* as an *ideology*.

As a political philosophy, classical liberalism is hegemonic in the United States, bridging differences between the ideologies of liberalism and CONSERVATISM in contemporary American politics. Classical liberalism is rooted in the SOCIAL-CONTRACT THEORY and NATURAL RIGHTS doctrine of John Locke, who is frequently referred to as the philosophical father of the American DEMOCRACY because of the influence of his ideas on the DECLARATION OF INDEPENDENCE and the CONSTITUTION. At the core of classical liberalism as a political philosophy is INDIVIDUALISM, the belief that each individual should have the FREEDOM or liberty to do as he or she wishes (so long as they refrain from harming others) without interference by the government. The liberal philosophy also generally supports private property, limited government, CONSTITUTIONALISM, CAPITALISM, and CIVIL LIBERTIES, although not necessarily CIVIL RIGHTS. Classical liberalism supports civil liberties but not necessarily civil rights because it is fundamentally concerned with individual autonomy and freedom, which might encompass the freedom of individuals to engage in DISCRIMINATION. Indeed, BARRY GOLDWATER and RONALD REAGAN opposed the CIVIL RIGHTS ACT OF 1964 partly on the classical liberal principle that individuals had the liberty or freedom to discriminate on the basis of race if they wished, particularly if the discrimination involved use of their property.

Classical liberalism has an ambivalent relationship to African-American politics first because, as individuals, African Americans were excluded because of RACISM and WHITE SUPREMACY from the social contract that created the American democracy. However, even after they were included as a result of adoption of the THIRTEENTH AMENDMENT and the FOURTEENTH AMENDMENT, the ambivalence remained, primarily because of the primacy the philosophy gives to individualism. This is because African-American politics is not and never has been primarily concerned with individualism or individual rights. Rather, as a *group* of individuals historically oppressed and subordinated on the basis of their *group* membership, African Americans have always given primacy to *group rights* rather than the rights of individuals. African-American politics also has tended to resist the idea of the ASSIMILA-

TION of individual blacks, preferring instead to maintain the autonomy and integrity of the CULTURE and institutions of a BLACK COMMUNITY. Also, the classical liberal principles of constitutionalism and capitalism and the sanctity of private property have always had less support, especially among black intellectuals, because these principles have from time to time been viewed as adverse to the interests of blacks as a community. Finally, classical liberal principles—individualism especially—have been used as the philosophical basis for opposition to civil rights laws and policies designed to benefit blacks as a group, including FORTY ACRES AND A MULE, AFFIRMATIVE ACTION, and REPARATIONS.

If blacks have been skeptical or hostile to classical liberalism as a philosophy, they have been enthusiastic about contemporary or modern liberalism as an ideology. Indeed, African Americans are and probably always have been the most ideologically liberal group in the United States. Liberalism as an ideology can be distinguished from conservatism on the basis of four criteria. First, liberalism tends to promote intervention by the government in the society and economy in order to foster social change. Second, modern liberalism tends to be hostile to FEDERALISM or states rights, preferring intervention by the federal government in the affairs of the states as well as the society and economy. Third, liberalism since FRANKLIN D. ROOSEVELT and the NEW DEAL has advanced the cause of an expanding WELFARE STATE. Finally, the liberal ideology tends to favor policies and programs that foster EQUALITY. Looked at in terms of these criteria, it would be virtually impossible for blacks, given their history and circumstance, to be other than liberal. This is because intervention by the government in the society and economy in the form of various civil rights laws has been indispensable in meliorating their OPPRESSION. Intervention by the federal government in the affairs of the states has also been important because, historically, federalism was used by the SOUTHERN STATES to maintain SLAVERY and SEGREGATION. Because of their disproportionate POVERTY, blacks have seen an expansive welfare state as in their interests, and a principal goal of black politics has always been equality.

African Americans as an INTEREST GROUP and their ORGANIZATIONS and LEADERSHIP have been strong supporters of liberal principles and programs, from the CIVIL WAR and RECONSTRUCTION in the 1860s to the New Deal in the 1930s and to the GREAT SOCIETY during the 1960s. Studies of PUBLIC OPINION have also shown consistent support for liberal programs among ordinary blacks, especially when their views are compared with whites. One group of scholars in the 1970s found that 85 percent of blacks identify with liberalism as an ideology compared with less than one-third of whites. African-American public opinion is, for example, strongly supportive of the welfare state, with two-thirds to three-fourths of blacks compared with about one-third of whites agreeing with the statement that it is the responsibility of the government to see to it that all Americans have access to decent jobs, health care, education, and housing. Seventy-three percent of blacks (compared with 44 percent of whites) in a 1996 poll agreed that it was the government's responsibility to reduce income inequality between the rich and poor. Indeed, in the POST–CIVIL RIGHTS ERA there has been a significant strain of support for principles of SOCIALISM, including, for example, government ownership of banks, utilities, and hospitals.

Further reading: David Carroll Cochran, *The Color of Freedom: Race and Contemporary Liberalism* (Albany: State University of New York Press, 1999); Richard Seltzer and Robert C. Smith, "Race and Ideology: Measuring Liberalism and Conservatism in Black America," *Phylon* 46 (1985): 98–105.

Liberia

Liberia, a small country in West Africa, occupies a special place in African-American history and consciousness. HAITI also occupies a special place because its people were the first Africans to successfully use VIOLENCE in a revolution that displaced a European regime of OPPRESSION based on RACISM and WHITE SUPREMACY. Liberia occupies a special place because it is the only nation established by African Americans. It is therefore the most important example of the BACK-TO-AFRICA MOVEMENTS that have been such an important part of the tradition of BLACK NATIONALISM in the United States.

Liberia was established as a colony for African Americans in 1822 by the AMERICAN COLONIALIZATION SOCIETY, a racist and white-supremacist organization of white Americans who wished to rid the United States of the FREE NEGROES. The society purchased the land that became Liberia. While little more than 20,000 African Americans emigrated to Liberia, they were to impose a form of COLONIALISM that was sometimes as oppressive and brutal as that imposed by the Europeans on the peoples of Africa, including the denial of basic CIVIL RIGHTS and the imposition of a system of forced labor that at times resembled SLAVERY. The Americo-Liberians (the term used for the African-American immigrants and their descendants) dominated the indigenous tribes of Liberia from the founding of the colony (it became an independent nation—the first in postcolonial black Africa—in 1847) until the 1970s, when a series of brutal coups set in motion a civil war that lasted into the 21st century. The Americo-Liberians in many ways considered themselves "African Anglo-Saxons" because of their exposure in the United States to Western culture. They, therefore, like the Europeans who colonized

Africa, viewed the indigenous African peoples as inferior and developed a system of black-on-black oppression based on those views. Part of the legacy of that oppression is the brutal civil war that engulfed the country beginning in the 1980s, which by the end of the 20th century had killed more than 200,000 people and left more than 1 million refugees. By the late 1990s the country and its people had been so devastated that, in an ironic reversal of history, many Liberians were emigrating to the United States.

Lincoln, Abraham (1809–1865) *16th president of the United States*

Abraham Lincoln, the 16th president of the United States, is almost universally considered by American historians to be the greatest of the American presidents. He is also considered by students of African-American history to be, after LYNDON B. JOHNSON, the best or the greatest president in the cause of African-American FREEDOM, although not EQUALITY. Lincoln's greatness, however, does not derive from his being the "Great Emancipator" who freed the slaves. The EMANCIPATION PROCLAMATION, which he reluctantly issued, in fact freed few slaves, and after he issued it he still entertained notions of rescinding it in favor of a plan of gradual, compensated emancipation if the SOUTHERN STATES would agree to end the war and return to the Union. Lincoln was prepared, if necessary to maintain the Union, to allow SLAVERY to remain forever in the United States, as shown by his signing of the first proposed THIRTEENTH AMENDMENT, which allowed the Southern states to maintain slavery in perpetuity. And in a famous letter to Horace Greeley in response to the "Prayer of 20 Million" calling for freedom for the slaves, Lincoln made it clear that although he was personally opposed to slavery, he would take no action against it unless such action was necessary to preserve the Union, which he said was the "paramount" objective of the CIVIL WAR. In fact, he told Greeley in the 1862 letter that if he could save the Union "without freeing any slave [he] would do it." And as the Civil War neared its end, Lincoln told a meeting of black leaders at the White House that he did not support the INTEGRATION of blacks into American society on the basis of equality. Rather, he favored their forced migration to HAITI, LIBERIA, or some other place where he said the climate is "congenial."

Lincoln's opposition to equality was long-standing. In a debate with Stephen Douglas several years before he became president, he said, "I am not nor ever have been in favor of the social and political equality of the white and black races: that I am not in favor of making voters of the free Negroes, or jurors, or qualifying them to hold office or having them to marry with white people. . . . I as much as any other man am in favor of the superior position being assigned to the white man." Finally, Lincoln believed in WHITE SUPREMACY, remarking that he believed African Americans were "inferior in color and perhaps moral and intellectual endowment."

Yet, in spite of this, Lincoln's reputation as perhaps the greatest of the American presidents and one of the two or three greatest in the cause of African-American freedom is well deserved. It is well deserved first because he fought and won the Civil War at an enormous cost in blood and treasure. His commitment to waging and winning the war to preserve the Union was tenacious and unwavering. The result is that the United States did not become two nations, in which the Southern states might have maintained slavery well into the 20th century, thereafter evolving into a system resembling South African APARTHEID. Winning the war avoided these developments and set in motion processes inevitably leading to the end of slavery. Lincoln's tenacity at pursuing the war at virtually any cost is almost certainly a path that would not have been followed by either of his opponents in the 1860 and 1864 elections or his two immediate predecessors in the PRESIDENCY. A second reason for Lincoln's greatness is his principled opposition to slavery. Although Lincoln did not believe in CIVIL RIGHTS for blacks in America, he did believe in their NATURAL RIGHTS to freedom. As he said in

Abraham Lincoln *(Library of Congress)*

his second inaugural address, it seemed "strange that any man would ask a just God's assistance in wringing his bread from the sweat of other men's faces." This quote is illustrative of the third source of Lincoln's greatness, which is the way he used words as symbols to create a rhetoric that served the cause of freedom. He did this in his second inaugural where, while not condemning the Southern slaveholders (in the passage quoted above Lincoln began by saying "it *may* seem strange . . ." and concluded with "but let us [Northerners] judge not, lest we be judged"), he nevertheless told his countrymen that the bloody war was a terrible "woe" from God for the sin of slavery. And in the GETTYSBURG ADDRESS, Lincoln used words that, as one historian put it, "remade America." He did this by interpreting the war not merely as a war to save the Union but rather as a war to create a "new birth of freedom." Finally, Lincoln's martyrdom shortly after the war's end contributes to his greatness. That is, if he had lived to deal with the messy problems of RECONSTRUCTION that confronted his successors—ANDREW JOHNSON, ULYSSES S. GRANT, and RUTHERFORD B. HAYES—it is unlikely he would be considered so great.

Further reading: Lerone Bennett, *Forced into the Glory: Abraham Lincoln's White Dream* (Chicago: Johnson Publishing, 2000); David Donald, *Lincoln* (New York: Simon & Schuster, 1995); Benjamin Quarles, *Lincoln and the Negro* (New York: Oxford University Press, 1962).

litigation

Litigation—the filing of lawsuits in the courts—along with voting, LOBBYING, and peaceful, nonviolent, nondisruptive PROTEST are tactics used by individuals and INTEREST GROUPS to make demands or exert pressures on the POLITICAL SYSTEM in the United States. Litigation is an important form of pressure-group politics in the United States because the CONSTITUTION confers rights on individuals that can be vindicated through the JUDICIAL PROCESS if they are violated by the CONGRESS, the PRESIDENCY, or STATE AND LOCAL GOVERNMENTS. Because of the SEPARATION OF POWERS, this means that groups that lack the resources to use voting or lobbying to influence Congress, the president, and state and local governments can turn to the courts as an alternative. The separation of powers in the United States therefore provides multiple points of access to the political system, unlike in most other countries, where usually the only point of access is the parliament. African Americans have historically taken advantage of these multiple points of access to press their demands for CIVIL RIGHTS, relying sometimes primarily on lobbying and protest and relying at other times primarily on litigation.

After the FOURTEENTH AMENDMENT and the FIFTEENTH AMENDMENT were adopted during RECONSTRUC-TION, African Americans relied for a brief period on the courts to enforce their newly won rights. But this strategy soon reached a dead end as the SUPREME COURT, in the SLAUGHTERHOUSE CASES and in *PLESSY V. FERGUSON* and related civil rights cases, eviscerated the protections of the Fourteenth and Fifteenth Amendments and invalidated the civil rights laws enacted by Congress during the 1860s and 1870s. Blacks then turned to the Congress and the presidency, but these two branches were generally as unsympathetic as the Supreme Court. For a time—under the leadership of BOOKER T. WASHINGTON—blacks exerted relatively little pressure on either of the three branches of the government, although individuals like WILLIAM MONROE TROTTER did attempt to lobby the presidency.

All of this changed with the formation of the NAACP in 1909. Initially the NAACP focused primarily on lobbying, although in 1917 it won a major victory when the Supreme Court in *Buchanan v. Worley* ruled that a Louisville, Kentucky, law requiring residential SEGREGATION was unconstitutional. This was an important victory because it prevented the formal development of residential APARTHEID in the United States. But this was also a rare victory, because for the most part the Supreme Court from the 1880s until the 1940s was dominated by justices unsympathetic to civil rights. Thus, the NAACP from the 1920s to the 1940s relied mainly on lobbying the president and Congress, focusing primarily on legislation to punish LYNCHING as a federal crime. When lobbying proved ineffective, the NAACP gradually shifted its strategy to a primary focus on litigation. This strategy shift was initiated by CHARLES H. HOUSTON and later institutionalized with the formation of the LEGAL DEFENSE FUND (LDF). The LDF, under the leadership of THURGOOD MARSHALL, then developed a systematic strategy of litigation in pursuit of civil rights. In 1944 the LDF won an important victory when the Supreme Court ruled that the WHITE PRIMARY was unconstitutional. Then, in a series of cases, the LDF challenged segregation in education, ending in its historic victory in 1954 in *BROWN V. BOARD OF EDUCATION*. After *Brown*, the NAACP continued its strategy of litigation, but when its victories in the courts did not result in the dismantling of segregation or legalized RACISM, the NAACP once again turned to an emphasis on lobbying, led by CLARENCE MITCHELL.

Neither lobbying nor litigation proved effective. Thus African Americans, under the leadership of MARTIN LUTHER KING JR., turned to protest in the 1950s and 1960s. These protests resulted in passage of the CIVIL RIGHTS ACT OF 1964 and the VOTING RIGHTS ACT OF 1965. In the POST–CIVIL RIGHTS ERA, the NAACP and the LDF continued to use litigation in AFFIRMATIVE ACTION and in cases dealing with INDIVIDUAL RACISM and INSTITUTIONAL RACISM. In the late 1980s, however, litigation as a strategy to advance the cause of black EQUALITY apparently reached another dead end as the Supreme Court, for the first time since the 1940s, came under the control of conservative justices hostile to the cause of civil rights. The control of the courts by a conservative majority led Justice Thurgood Marshall to say in 1989 that the Supreme Court was engaged in a "deliberate retrenching of the civil rights agenda" and that African Americans therefore should return to lobbying as the primary means to pursue their agenda. Meanwhile, other groups hostile to civil rights turned to litigation to successfully advance an anti–civil rights agenda.

See also *ADARAND V. PENA* and *SHAW V. RENO*.

Further reading: Morgan J. Kouser, *Dead End: The Development of Nineteenth Century Litigation on Racial Discrimination* (New York: Oxford University Press, 1986); Gerald Rosenberg, *The Hollow Hope: Can the Courts Bring about Social Change?* (Chicago: University of Chicago Press, 1991); Clement Vose, "Litigation as a Form of Pressure Group Activity," *The Annals of the American Academy of Political and Social Science* 319 (1958): 20–31.

lobbying

Lobbying is a term that refers to a variety of means used by INTEREST GROUPS to influence the POLITICAL SYSTEM in the United States. Along with voting, LITIGATION, and peaceful, nonviolent PROTEST, lobbying is one of the acceptable ways to bring demands or exert pressure on the system. The right to lobby (and protest) is rooted in the CONSTITUTION's First Amendment, which guarantees the "right of the people to peaceably assemble and petition the government for redress of grievances." Although lobbying is constitutionally protected, it has not always been available to African Americans. For example, from 1836 to 1844 the House of Representatives imposed a GAG RULE prohibiting African Americans and their white allies in the ABOLITIONIST MOVEMENT from petitioning or lobbying the House to abolish SLAVERY.

Although African Americans gained the theoretical right to lobby during RECONSTRUCTION, they did not develop an effective national lobbying ORGANIZATION until the formation of the NAACP in 1909. Organization is indispensable to effective lobbying, but it is only the first step in an INTEREST GROUP becoming an effective lobbying presence in American politics. In addition to organization, effective lobbying requires other resources, including a favorable climate of PUBLIC OPINION on issues of concern to the group; knowledge and information; access to the MEDIA; money, which can be used for a variety of purposes, including hiring staff, doing research, buying political ads, and making campaign contributions to persons running for office; VOTING RIGHTS; and some REPRESENTATION in the government. The right to vote is critical because effective lobbying ultimately depends on the ability of a group to

exercise a BALANCE OF POWER in elections in which it may threaten ELECTED OFFICIALS with the loss of their jobs if they are not responsive to the group's interests. For much of their history African Americans have lacked virtually all of these resources, especially when compared with white groups hostile to their interests in FREEDOM and EQUALITY. The climate of white public opinion has generally been hostile; blacks have had less access to knowledge and information; the white-controlled media have generally been unsympathetic; blacks have had less money; and for most of their history they were denied the right to vote and have had little or no representation in CONGRESS, the BUREAUCRACY, or STATE AND LOCAL GOVERNMENT. Therefore, they could not effectively lobby. The NAACP, for example, spent its first 20 years lobbying Congress and the PRESIDENCY to pass a law making LYNCHING a federal crime, but the legislation never passed, in large part because the NAACP lacked the necessary resources. Thus, African Americans were forced to turn first to litigation and then protest in order to press their demands for CIVIL RIGHTS. The protests led by MARTIN LUTHER KING JR. led to the activation of a COALITION with whites that brought about the passage of the CIVIL RIGHTS ACT OF 1964 and the VOTING RIGHTS ACT OF 1965, legislation that effectively ended legalized RACISM and SEGREGATION.

In the POST–CIVIL RIGHTS ERA, blacks have had more resources with which to lobby, but they still are at a relative disadvantage compared with other groups. On post–civil rights era issues like BUSING and AFFIRMATIVE ACTION, the climate of white public opinion has been hostile. The media, while more sympathetic, still tend to cover the BLACK COMMUNITY in a stereotypical way and from the perspective of the dominant group. African Americans exercise the right to vote but, as a MINORITY GROUP, they are able to exercise the balance of power and determine the outcome in relatively few elections. Black representation in Congress, the bureaucracy, and state and local governments is relatively small. Blacks now have greater access to knowledge and information but, again, less than lobbying groups in the white community. Finally, lobbying in the post–civil rights era requires much more money than in the past because it has become more sophisticated in terms of use of the media, the use of polls, the Internet, and techniques of mass persuasion. Money is also much more important in terms of contributions to political campaigns. Candidates for office in the United States at the end of the 20th century were heavily dependent upon and influenced at least to some extent by wealthy individuals and organizations that contribute money to their campaigns. African Americans are especially disadvantaged in regards to money. They have relatively little wealth, and they contribute hardly anything to political campaigns. And their lobbying organizations have minuscule budgets compared with white organizations engaged in lobbying. For example, in the 1990s the budget of MADD (Mothers Against Drunk Driving) was larger than the combined budgets of the NAACP and the URBAN LEAGUE—the two major organizations that lobby for black interests—and the budget of the National Rifle Association (NRA) was three times larger than their combined budgets. The NRA and MADD lobby on single issues, guns and drunk driving, while the NAACP and the Urban League lobby on many issues related to race. This means that unless blacks can form COALITIONS with other groups, they can only be marginally effective at lobbying, which means that, as in the past, they may have to turn to other means to get the political system to address issues of concern to them.

lynching

VIOLENCE is an integral part of AFRICAN-AMERICAN POLITICS. It was employed to enslave Africans in the first place; SLAVERY itself was maintained by systematic and extraordinary violence; and violence in the form of lynching was used to overturn RECONSTRUCTION and reestablish and maintain the OPPRESSION of blacks. Lynching—the murder, often ritualistic and sadistic—of blacks by whites was rooted in RACISM and WHITE SUPREMACY.

Lynching emerged at the same time as the KU KLUX KLAN, which was responsible for many lynchings, mainly in the SOUTHERN STATES but occasionally in the NORTHERN STATES as well. It is estimated that from the 1870s to the 1960s, more than 6,000 African Americans were lynched. Often black men and boys were lynched on the false allegation that they had raped or made sexual advances toward white women. For example, in an infamous case in 1955, Emmett Till, a 14-year-old boy from Chicago, was lynched in Mississippi because he allegedly whistled at a white woman. IDA B. WELLS-BARNETT, who led the crusade against lynching in the 19th and early 20th centuries, demonstrated in her research and writings that sex was rarely a motive in lynchings. Rather, blacks were most frequently lynched because they tried to exercise their CIVIL RIGHTS by voting, owning property, or opening a business. Occasionally blacks were lynched simply because they refused to address a white man or woman as "Mister" or "Madam" or refused to yield the sidewalk to a white person.

Clearly, the purpose of lynchings was to use terror to force blacks to acquiesce in their oppression and accept their "place" as a SUBORDINATE GROUP. This purpose was emphasized by the sometimes extraordinary savagery and ritualized barbarisms of some lynchings, which demonstrated to all blacks—man, woman, or child—the awful things that could happen to them if they did not submit to their oppression. The political scientist Ira Katznelson in

Most lynching victims were African-American men, such as the one in the photograph. *(Library of Congress)*

Black Men, White Cities (1973) depicts this sometimes savage nature of lynchings:

> Most lynch victims were hanged or shot, but often other means, grotesque in their horror, were employed. The humiliations and tortures were often incredible. In Waco, Texas in 1916 Jesse Washington, a retarded adolescent, was burned at the stake in the public square while thousands watched and cheered. In South Carolina in May 1918, after three innocent men had been hanged for murder, the lynch mob "strung up" the pregnant widow of one by the ankles, doused her clothing with gasoline, and after it burned away, cut out her unborn child and trampled it under foot, then riddled her with bullets. Of the 416 blacks lynched between 1918 and 1927, forty-two were burned alive, sixteen burned after death and eight beaten to death and cut to pieces.

Sometimes lynchings were the occasions for celebrations—family affairs—with large turnouts of white men, women, and children who cheered the killings and took pieces of the bodies as souvenirs.

Under the CONSTITUTION's principle of FEDERALISM it is the responsibility of STATE AND LOCAL GOVERNMENTS to punish murder. Thus, rarely were lynchers captured or punished for their crimes, since the officials in these governments in the Southern states generally accepted lynching as part of the system of POLITICAL REPRESSION necessary to maintain the system of white domination, which was sometimes referred to as the "Southern way of life." Indeed, sometimes law-enforcement officials in the Southern states were coconspirators or participants in lynchings. Thus, African Americans waged a 50-year LOBBYING campaign to get CONGRESS and the PRESIDENCY to support legislation making lynching—generally defined as murder committed by a mob of three or more persons—a federal crime. Ida B. Wells-Barnett rose to distinction as a great African-American leader because of her antilynching work; the NAACP's first major lobbying campaign was on the issue of lynching; and "STRANGE FRUIT," one of the most famous protest songs in black MUSIC, dealt with lynching. The DYER ANTILYNCHING BILL never passed Congress due partly to use of the FILIBUSTER by Southern state senators.

Lynching effectively came to an end as a result of the success of the CIVIL RIGHTS MOVEMENT in ending the legalized oppression of blacks. In the POST–CIVIL RIGHTS ERA, however, there are occasional reports of lynchings. In 1998, for example, James Byrd, a young black man, was brutally murdered by being tied to the back of a pickup truck and dragged for several miles. Unlike in the past, however, the lynchers of Byrd were arrested, convicted, and sentenced to long prison terms or, in one case, to death.

Further reading: Philip Dray, *At the Hands of Persons Unknown: The Lynching of Black America* (New York: Random House, 2002); Ralph Ginzberg, *100 Years of Lynching* (New York: Lancer Books, 1962); Robert Zangrando, *The NAACP Crusade against Lynching, 1909–1950* (Philadelphia: Temple University Press, 1980).

M

Malcolm X (El-Hajj Malik El-Shabazz) (1925–1965)
black nationalist

BAYARD RUSTIN, a major strategist of the CIVIL RIGHTS MOVEMENT, in a 1965 article written shortly after the death of Malcom X, said, "We must resist the temptation to idealize Malcolm X, to elevate charisma to greatness." Rustin, whose IDEOLOGY was INTEGRATIONISM and SOCIALISM, was an adversary of Malcolm X, believing that Malcolm's MILITANCY and BLACK NATIONALISM had made little, if any, contribution to the African-American struggle for FREEDOM and EQUALITY. He concluded the 1965 article by writing, "White America, not the Negro people, will determine Malcolm's role in history." Rustin was an important scholar as well as strategist in the Civil Rights movement, but his assessment of Malcolm X's role in history was wrong. Malcolm's role in history was determined by blacks, not whites, and to some extent charisma was elevated to greatness.

In a 2000 poll of African-American political scientists who were asked to select the greatest African-American leaders of all time, Malcolm X ranked third on a list of 12, behind only MARTIN LUTHER KING JR. and W. E. B. DU BOIS. Participants in the poll did elevate charisma to greatness. One respondent in the poll described Malcolm as the "quintessential charismatic leader"; another wrote that "he expressed the anger that lay deep within the souls of the African American people"; another wrote that he "gave voice to the voiceless in the face of overwhelming racist oppression" and that in doing so in a militant and charismatic way, he "kept America on edge." Malcolm's significance as a charismatic leader is also reflected in the judgment of the author of the most complete biography of Malcolm X. Bruce Perry in *Malcolm: The Life of the Man Who Changed Black America* (1991) wrote, "Malcolm X fathered no legislation. He engineered no stunning Supreme Court victories or political campaigns. He scored no electoral triumphs. Yet, because of the way he articulated his followers' grievances and anger, the impact he had on the body politic was enormous."

Malcolm X was born Malcolm Little in 1925 in Omaha, Nebraska. His parents were followers of MARCUS GARVEY, and while he was a young man, the family moved to Lansing, Michigan. There Malcolm claimed that whites opposed to his father's militant nationalism burned his home and later murdered him. After his father's death the family was impoverished, and his mother eventually suffered a mental breakdown. Malcolm then dropped out of high school and moved to Boston to stay with relatives. There he began to use drugs and engage in petty crimes. At the age of 21 he was sentenced to prison for burglary. While in prison he came under the influence of ELIJAH MUHAMMAD, the spiritual leader of the NATION OF ISLAM. Subsequently he joined the group, and this brought about a major transformation in his life, as he became deeply religious. Using the prison library, he also became a self-taught scholar. When he was paroled in 1952 he moved to New York, where in 1954 he became minister of the Nation of Islam's HARLEM temple. His charisma and his oratorical and organizational abilities soon transformed the temple into one of the largest and most influential in the Nation of Islam. In recognition of Malcolm's work, Elijah Muhammad in 1957 made Malcolm his national representative. In this position he traveled throughout the United States, spreading the message of the Nation of Islam and organizing temples or mosques. By the early 1960s he had become the best-known minister in the Nation of Islam and the most influential advocate of black nationalism since Marcus Garvey during the 1920s.

Malcolm's agile mind, quick wit, and skill in manipulation of the MEDIA enhanced his stature as a national leader, and he became a frequent guest on television programs and a speaker on college campuses. His message was viewed as a powerful and militant alternative to the leadership of Martin Luther King Jr.'s more moderate LEADERSHIP. His growing national prominence, however, created jealousy, tensions, and conflicts within the hierarchy of the Nation of Islam, ultimately leading to Malcolm's suspension from the group and his repudiation of Elijah Muhammad and most of the core teachings of the Nation of Islam. The event that precipitated these developments was a statement he made in the aftermath of the assassination of President JOHN F. KENNEDY. When the president was murdered, Elijah Muhammad instructed his ministers to make no public comments about the president's death. But shortly thereafter Malcolm described the assassination as a case of "chickens coming home to roost," suggesting that the VIO-LENCE that had been used to suppress blacks and peoples of the THIRD WORLD had now been turned against the American president. For these remarks, he was indefinitely suspended as a minister and forbidden to speak in public or to the media.

Although Malcolm's remarks about the Kennedy assassination were the ostensible reason for the suspension, jealousy about his national stature and influence was the underlying reason. In addition, Malcolm had become disillusioned with Elijah Muhammad after learning that he had fathered several children by young women in the Nation of Islam, and there was concern within the group's hierarchy that Malcolm would soon reveal this information to the media. The suspension was therefore a convenient way to discipline and silence him. Malcolm, however, soon left the Nation of Islam; revealed Muhammad's sexual indiscretions; and denounced Muhammad's philosophy as racist, white supremacist, and a religious fraud (because of its departure from orthodox Islam). He then converted to orthodox Islam, made the hajj (a religious pilgrimage) to Mecca, and changed his name to El-Hajj Malik El-Shabazz. He established an orthodox Muslim temple as well as a separate political organization—the ORGANIZA-TION OF AFRO-AMERICAN UNITY (OAAU)—and attempted to play a role in the Civil Rights movement, which he had previously denounced and had been forbidden by Muhammad to take part in.

In the last year of his life he worked to build his organization by traveling throughout the United States as well as in Europe, Africa, and the Middle East. On February 14, 1965, he was gunned down in the Audubon Ballroom in Harlem as he prepared to deliver a speech at a meeting of the OAAU. Three members of the Nation of Islam were arrested, convicted, and sentenced to prison for the murder. Although there have been allegations of complicity by the FBI in the assassination, the available evidence indicates that the Nation of Islam was responsible, although there is speculation that the FBI knew of the plot to kill him and did not take action to stop it. The Nation of Islam's newspaper had carried stories and pictures suggesting he should be killed, and LOUIS FARRAKHAN—Malcolm's successor as minister of the Harlem temple and national representative of the Nation of Islam—in later years denied that the group had ordered Malcolm's death while admitting that the

Nation of Islam in general and he specifically had helped to create the climate that contributed to Malcolm's murder.

Malcolm died shortly before his 40th birthday. At the time of his death, having repudiated the teachings of the Nation of Islam, he was a man groping to find his place in AFRICAN-AMERICAN POLITICS. The last year of his life may have been the most significant in terms of his legacy as a great leader. Between 1964 and 1965, he attempted to develop a framework for a militant, secular, democratic black nationalism that would use "any means necessary," including violence, to achieve the objectives of CIVIL RIGHTS. (See "BALLOT OR THE BULLET" SPEECH.) He contributed to PAN-AFRICANISM and Third World solidarity as he traveled throughout Africa and the Middle East in an effort to establish practical, concrete linkages between the leaders of the African and African-American freedom movements. Using CITIZEN DIPLOMACY, Malcolm also attempted to internationalize the issue of civil rights by elevating it to an issue of HUMAN RIGHTS and seeking the support of African leaders for a petition to the UNITED NATIONS charging the United States with violating the UNIVERSAL DECLARATION OF HUMAN RIGHTS. He was also flirting with

Malcolm X *(Library of Congress)*

the idea of SOCIALISM as part of a broad COALITION of progressives. Hardly more than a start on any of these ideas or programs had been made at the time of his death, and at that time he had relatively few followers outside of the small cadre of individuals who left the Nation of Islam with him. However, his historical legacy is the ideas he left behind and the courageous and outspoken way he advanced those ideas in his last year. In this sense, Malcolm X is more influential in death than he was during his life.

The posthumous publication of Malcolm's autobiography had an enormous impact on the generation of young blacks who came of age in the 1960s, and the autobiography is recognized as a classic—comparable with FREDERICK DOUGLASS's autobiography—in African-American literature. The widespread availability of audio recordings of his speeches and lectures also influenced the 1960s and subsequent generations, as reflected in some of the themes and lyrics of RAP MUSIC. And within a year of his death, his ideas had a decisive impact on shaping two important developments in late-20th-century African-American politics: the BLACK POWER MOVEMENT and the BLACK PANTHER PARTY. STOKELY CARMICHAEL and the other men and women responsible for the Black Power movement and HUEY NEWTON and BOBBY SEALE, the founders of the Black Panther Party, described themselves, properly so, as the "children of Malcolm X."

Malcolm X's ideas on Pan-Africanism and Third World solidarity, along with his early opposition to the COLD WAR and the VIETNAM WAR, helped to lead SNCC and other black groups and individuals like MUHAMMAD ALI to embrace a critical outlook on United States FOREIGN POLICY. Finally, in his ideas are some of the seeds of the development of AFRICAN-AMERICAN STUDIES and AFROCENTRISM.

Further reading: George Breitman, *The Last Year of Malcolm X: The Evolution of a Revolutionary* (New York: Pathfinder Press, 1967); Malcolm X (with Alex Haley), *The Autobiography of Malcolm X* (New York: Grove Press, 1965); Bruce Perry, *Malcolm: The Life of a Man Who Changed Black America* (Barrytown, N.Y.: Station Hill Press, 1991).

Marable, Manning (1950–   ) *activist, scholar*
Manning Marable is one of the leading African-American PUBLIC INTELLECTUALS of the POST–CIVIL RIGHTS ERA. Unlike most well-known black public intellectuals of the era who tended to engage in studies of popular culture and esoteric literary analyses and criticism, Marable, a historian, is a politically engaged intellectual in the tradition of W. E. B. DU BOIS who views AFRICAN-AMERICAN STUDIES as a program of research and activism linked to a commitment for radical social change. Marable's embrace of RADICAL-

ISM is rooted in marxism and its view that RACISM and the OPPRESSION of African Americans is mainly a class problem and not a race problem and that racial EQUALITY can only be achieved as a result of a transformation of corporate CAPITALISM into a form of democratic SOCIALISM. He therefore rejects most forms of BLACK NATIONALISM as well as LIBERALISM and CONSERVATISM. This IDEOLOGY often puts him at odds with the mainstream African-American LEADERSHIP.

A member of the Democratic Socialists of America, Marable was active in the NATIONAL BLACK POLITICAL CONVENTION during its waning years and was a founding member of the BLACK RADICAL CONGRESS. Consistent with his ideology, Marable is a strong supporter of radical FEMINISM, GAY RIGHTS, and MULTICULTURALISM. Since the 1980s he has advocated the formation of a radical, multicultural THIRD PARTY, arguing that neither the DEMOCRATIC PARTY nor the REPUBLICAN PARTY can serve the interests of blacks and other oppressed peoples. Marable received his undergraduate education at Earlham College, an M.A. from the University of Wisconsin, and the Ph.D. from the University of Maryland. He has taught at numerous universities, including two HISTORICALLY BLACK COLLEGES AND UNIVERSITIES, and has written more than a dozen books. For more than 20 years he wrote "Along the Color Line," a weekly column that appeared in more than 200 black newspapers throughout the United States. In 1993 he was appointed professor and director of the Institute for Research on African American Studies at Columbia University.

March on Washington movement
Since the 1940s the African-American LEADERSHIP has used marches on Washington or the threat of such marches as a means of PROTEST in relationship to their demands for EQUALITY. In 1941 A. PHILIP RANDOLPH, head of the BROTHERHOOD OF SLEEPING CAR PORTERS, threatened a mass march of thousands of blacks on Washington unless President FRANKLIN D. ROOSEVELT took action to ban DISCRIMINATION in employment in factories manufacturing materials for World War II. In response to this threat, Roosevelt issued an executive order prohibiting discrimination in employment in the war industries.

The success of Randolph's threat in getting Roosevelt to act resulted in a kind of march-on-Washington ethos or movement among segments of the African-American leadership, who viewed such marches or the mere threat of them as potent protest weapons. So, for example, Randolph and BAYARD RUSTIN organized youth marches on Washington to protest school SEGREGATION in the 1950s. The MARCH ON WASHINGTON OF 1963, where MARTIN LUTHER KING JR. delivered his "I HAVE A DREAM" SPEECH, is an example of this movement, and it was initially planned and led by Randolph and his assistant Bayard Rustin. The appearance of success of the 1963 march led other Americans, including among others anti–VIETNAM WAR activists, women, farmers, homosexuals, mothers, and others to employ this as a strategy of protest or as a means to call attention to issues of concern to them.

See also MILLION MAN MARCH.

March on Washington of 1963

The March on Washington, which took place on August 28, 1963, was a high point in the PROTEST phase of the CIVIL RIGHTS MOVEMENT, and in a sense it marked the movement's symbolic end. A decade of mass protests and demonstrations—including SIT-INS, FREEDOM RIDES, and the BIRMINGHAM DEMONSTRATIONS, led earlier in the year by MARTIN LUTHER KING JR.—had finally forced a reluctant

Protesters at the 1963 March on Washington *(National Archives)*

President JOHN F. KENNEDY in June 1963 to propose what would become the CIVIL RIGHTS ACT OF 1964. The purpose of the march was to bring pressure on the CONGRESS to pass the president's proposed bill. As envisioned by some, the march was to have been a militant, disruptive demonstration involving mass sit-ins, the obstruction of traffic, and the blocking of access to public buildings. This alarmed President Kennedy, who feared this kind of MILITANCY by the Civil Rights movement would create a WHITE BACKLASH that would make it more difficult to pass the bill. At this point, A. PHILIP RANDOLPH, who had first suggested a march on Washington by blacks in the 1940s, adopted the idea and persuaded the other major civil rights leaders to join in its organizing and planning. Martin Luther King Jr. of the SOUTHERN CHRISTIAN LEADERSHIP CONFERENCE, ROY WILKINS of the NAACP, WHITNEY YOUNG of the URBAN LEAGUE, JAMES FARMER of the CONGRESS OF RACIAL EQUALITY, JOHN LEWIS of the STUDENT NONVIOLENT COORDINATING COMMITTEE, and DOROTHY HEIGHT of the NATIONAL COUNCIL OF NEGRO WOMEN agreed to cosponsor the march. The march was also supported by important white liberal, labor, and religious groups that constituted the civil rights COALITION. These leaders abandoned any thoughts of a militant, disruptive march, and with their assurances, President Kennedy reluctantly endorsed the march a month before it was scheduled to take place. This led MALCOLM X and other critics to charge that Kennedy had co-opted the march; Malcolm later derisively referred to it as the "Farce on Washington."

The march under the general direction of Randolph and the day-to-day planning of BAYARD RUSTIN took place, bringing 250,000 people, black and white, to the city to hear entertainment by Hollywood celebrities and speeches by the movement's leaders (except Height), white labor and religious leaders, and members of Congress including HUBERT HUMPHREY. The march, billed as a march for "jobs and FREEDOM," was more a celebration than a protest and is best remembered as the event where Dr. King delivered his "I HAVE A DREAM" SPEECH.

Marshall, Thurgood (1908–1993) *lawyer, justice of the Supreme Court*

Thurgood Marshall is one of the greatest leaders in the history of the African-American struggle for FREEDOM and EQUALITY. In a poll of African-American political scientists conducted in 2000, he was ranked sixth on a list of the 12 greatest African-American leaders of all time. Marshall's appointment as the first black justice of the SUPREME COURT would by itself make him a historically significant figure. However, Marshall's greatness as a black leader predates his appointment to the Court. Indeed, it was in recognition of his contributions to the law of CIVIL RIGHTS that led President LYNDON B. JOHNSON in 1967 to nominate him to the Supreme Court.

Marshall's significance as a leader is in his strategic development of LITIGATION as a powerful weapon of the CIVIL RIGHTS MOVEMENT. His careful development of this strategy of litigation resulted in the unanimous decision of the Supreme Court in BROWN V. BOARD OF EDUCATION. This decision, holding that SEGREGATION in public education violated the EQUAL PROTECTION CLAUSE of the CONSTITUTION'S FOURTEENTH AMENDMENT, did relatively little to end segregation in public education or anywhere else in American society. It was, however, a decision of enormous significance because in reversing the 40-year-old decision in PLESSY V. FERGUSON upholding segregation, the Court in effect placed the Constitution on the side of the Civil Rights movement. In symbolism, the *Brown* decision said that RACISM and WHITE SUPREMACY were unconstitutional, and given the significance of CONSTITUTIONALISM as a core value of the POLITICAL SYSTEM, the Court in effect said they were "un-American." This provided the movement with a potent weapon. A year after *Brown*, MARTIN LUTHER KING JR. used this weapon in the MONTGOMERY BUS BOYCOTT, which initiated the PROTEST phase of the movement. He did so by declaring that if those who favored DESEGREGATION of the buses were wrong, then "the Supreme Court of the United States is wrong; the Constitution of the United States is wrong."

Marshall was graduated from Lincoln University, a historically black university in Pennsylvania. After being turned down by the University of Maryland Law School (Marshall was born and raised in Maryland), he enrolled at HOWARD UNIVERSITY Law School. At this time CHARLES H. HOUSTON was turning Howard's law school into a training ground in civil rights law. After graduating from law school, Marshall began working for the NAACP and in 1940 became head of its LEGAL DEFENSE FUND. At this point he began to systematically implement on a case-by-case basis the strategy that led to *Brown*. Marshall was one of the most successful lawyers to argue before the Supreme Court, winning 29 of 32 cases. In 1961 President JOHN F. KENNEDY appointed Marshall to one of the circuit courts of appeal. In 1965 President Johnson named him solicitor-general, the number-three post in the JUSTICE DEPARTMENT, and in 1967 appointed him to the Supreme Court.

As a justice on the Court, Marshall continued his commitment to civil rights and CIVIL LIBERTIES, becoming one of the most unwaveringly liberal justices in the Court's history. Early in his tenure Marshall was part of a majority bloc of justices committed to LIBERALISM in jurisprudence, serving with WILLIAM BRENNAN and EARL WARREN. However, by the time his tenure came to an end in the late 1980s, the Court was controlled by conservative justices unsympathetic to his brand of liberal jurispru-

Justice Thurgood Marshall *(Collection of the Supreme Court of the United States)*

dence and to civil rights. Thus, he was frequently in the minority, and his dissenting opinions were increasingly marked by anger and bitterness as he accused his colleagues of deliberately turning back the clock on civil rights and acting as if racism was a thing of the past. Aging, angry, and in ill health, Marshall retired from the Court in 1992 and died a year later.

In a last and perhaps fitting contribution, Marshall's will declared that his court papers should be made available to the public at the time of his death. This was an unprecedented decision, since Supreme Court justices almost always kept their Court papers secret for long periods after their deaths. This last decision by Marshall upset his colleagues on the Court (the chief justice even mused about suing Marshall's estate to maintain the secrecy of the papers), but because of it, scholars of the court got an unprecedented contemporaneous look inside the Court's secret decision-making process.

See also LEADERSHIP.

Further reading: Juan Williams, *Thurgood Marshall: American Revolutionary* (New York: Times Books, 1998).

Martin, Louis (1912–1996) *journalist, political adviser*
Louis Martin, a journalist, served as an adviser on CIVIL RIGHTS to three American presidents, JOHN F. KENNEDY, LYNDON B. JOHNSON, and JIMMY CARTER. In these positions he played a role in helping Kennedy win the black vote in the 1960 election and in helping to shape the political responses of Kennedy and Johnson to the CIVIL RIGHTS MOVEMENT.

Martin was born in Savannah, Georgia, the son of a prosperous physician of mixed Cuban and black ancestry. Although he attended Fisk, a historically black university, he was graduated from the University of Michigan. In 1936 at the age of 23, he was appointed the first editor and publisher of the *Michigan Chronicle* by John Sengstacke, owner of the *Chicago Defender.* Understanding the role of the black MEDIA as one of PROTEST against RACISM and WHITE SUPREMACY, Martin turned the *Chronicle* into one of the most influential black newspapers in the United States. Martin also used the pages of the *Chronicle* to persuade blacks to abandon their loyalty to the REPUBLICAN PARTY and support FRANKLIN D. ROOSEVELT and the DEMOCRATIC PARTY. Although he was an enthusiastic supporter of Roosevelt and the NEW DEAL, he criticized Roosevelt editorially for not taking a stance for civil rights and for the DISCRIMINATION and SEGREGATION in many New Deal programs. Nevertheless, it was during the New Deal era that he developed his long attachment to the Democratic Party.

After working in the Kennedy campaign, he held staff positions at the Democratic National Committee and was the senior African-American advisor to Presidents Kennedy and Johnson. Martin was a political, not a policy, advisor. That is, he advised Kennedy and Johnson on how to deal with the BLACK COMMUNITY in terms of getting its vote rather than on legislation or public policy. In this capacity he was instrumental in encouraging the appointments of many blacks to the BUREAUCRACY, including ROBERT WEAVER as the first black member of the cabinet and THURGOOD MARSHALL as the first black solicitor-general and justice of the SUPREME COURT. In 1978, when President Carter faced increasing criticisms from the African-American LEADERSHIP and a loss of support in the polls among blacks, he brought Martin into the White House to advise him on how he could repair relations with blacks in time for his 1980 reelection campaign. After Carter's unsuccessful reelection campaign, Martin rejoined the board of the JOINT CENTER FOR POLITICAL AND ECONOMIC STUDIES, of which he had been a founding member; became the first African American on the board of directors of Riggs Bank in Washington; and was named the vice president for communications at HOWARD UNIVERSITY.

Further reading: Alex Poinsett, *Walking with Presidents: Louis Martin and the Rise of Black Political Power* (Lanham, Md.: Madison Books, 1997).

marxism

See CAPITALISM, COMMUNISM, RADICALISM, and SOCIALISM.

Mayfield, Curtis (1942–1999) *musician*

MUSIC is an integral part of African-American CULTURE, and historically in all of its forms—spirituals, blues, jazz, and rhythm and blues—it has sometimes played a role in AFRICAN-AMERICAN POLITICS. From the 1960s until his death in 1999, Curtis Mayfield and his music served as a kind of template for the role that music can play in black politics. Jerry Butler, a former colleague of Mayfield's in the musical group the Impressions said, "Curtis Mayfield's songs ushered in the Civil Rights movement." This is an exaggeration to some extent, but Nelson George in *The Death of Rhythm & Blues* writes that "Curtis Mayfield was black music's most unflagging civil rights champion."

Mayfield's songs inspired and chronicled the CIVIL RIGHTS MOVEMENT during the early 1960s and the BLACK POWER MOVEMENT of the late 1960s and the early 1970s. He had his finger on the pulse of the BLACK COMMUNITY, and if the observation that you can tell where the community is at any time by listening to its music is true, then a Mayfield discography in many ways is a musical history of black America: from his 1965 recording "Keep on Pushing" (the first rhythm and blues song with a civil rights theme to reach the top of the pop charts) to "A New World Order," his last CD recorded shortly after the MILLION MAN MARCH. (His 1969 recording "We're a Winner" was thought to be so inflammatory that it might incite RIOTS, and it was banned for a short time on several big-city black radio stations.) Many of Mayfield's songs were deeply rooted in the RELIGIOSITY of African-American culture, expressing themes of love, faith, and FREEDOM. Other songs expressed a lyrical political MILITANCY, and still others expressed Mayfield's commitment to FEMINISM or gender equality. The last of his recordings, "A New World Order," combined all of these themes as well as the sense of ALIENATION and hopelessness that appeared to him to be growing amidst the POVERTY and VIOLENCE of the late-20th-century GHETTO.

Mayfield was born in Chicago in 1942. At the age of 14 he joined Jerry Butler (later a Chicago county commissioner) to form the group that was later known as the Impressions (he became lead singer for the group after Butler left for a solo career). In 1971 he began to release solo recordings. In 1990 he was paralyzed from the neck down as a result of an accident on a concert stage. Although he continued to work, he was always in pain, and in 1999 he died of complications from the accident and diabetes.

Further recordings: *Curtis Mayfield: His Early Years with the Impressions* (Los Angeles: ABC Records, 1973); *Curtis Live*, 2 record set (New York: Buddah Records, 1971); *Superfly: Original Motion Picture Soundtrack*, written and performed by Curtis Mayfield (New York: Buddah Records, 1972); Curtis Mayfield, *A New World Order* (New York: Warner Brothers, 1996).

McCarthyism

McCarthyism is the term used to refer to allegations, generally unfounded, of disloyalty to the POLITICAL SYSTEM. It is a post–World War II phenomenon that emerged in the context of the COLD WAR conflict with the Soviet Union in which fears, real and imagined, of the threat of COMMUNISM and the influence of the COMMUNIST PARTY were used to undermine the CIVIL LIBERTIES of the American people. The term derives from the actions of Senator Joseph McCarthy of Wisconsin, who in the 1950s made repeated, mostly unsubstantiated, allegations that various individuals and organizations were communists, communist sympathizers, or in other ways disloyal to the United States. African-American leaders and organizations and white supporters of the CIVIL RIGHTS MOVEMENT were frequent targets of McCarthyite attacks. Allegations were made that the Civil Rights movement in general and specific individuals and organizations, including MARTIN LUTHER KING JR. and several of his advisers such as BAYARD RUSTIN, were Communists or "Communist dupes." Several prominent African-American leaders who were in fact sympathetic to communism and/or the Soviet Union were subject to various forms of McCarthyism-related POLITICAL REPRESSION, among them W. E. B. DU BOIS and PAUL ROBESON. The fear of McCarthyism distorted a tendency toward RADICALISM in the NAACP, leading it to embrace the anticommunist posture of the United States in the cold war and to the purging of individuals allegedly sympathetic to radical ideas. The allegations that a principal adviser to Dr. King—Stanley Levison—was a communist was the basis upon which the FBI started its long-term program of surveillance of King. Under pressure from President JOHN F. KENNEDY and his brother Robert, the attorney general, King for a time dismissed Levison but later reinstated him, saying he would not bow to McCarthyism.

After the 1960s, McCarthyism declined as a force in American politics. Senator McCarthy was eventually censured by the Senate for his unsubstantiated attacks on government officials. But in its heyday, McCarthyism helped to distort the direction of the black movement, discredited some of its leaders, and fostered suspicion and distrust within the broader civil rights COALITION.

media

The media—the mainstream white press and the more specialized black press—have played a very important role in the African-American struggle for FREEDOM and EQUALITY. During the ABOLITIONIST MOVEMENT, abolitionist newspapers and articles in the mainstream press helped to build opposition to SLAVERY by exposing readers to its inhumanity. In the aftermath of RECONSTRUCTION, journalists like IDA B. WELLS-BARNETT used the media to expose the horrors of LYNCHING. BOOKER T. WASHINGTON used his domination of most of the black media to maintain his credibility and support in the BLACK COMMUNITY, and journalists like WILLIAM MONROE TROTTER used the press to undermine support for Washington. W. E. B. DU BOIS used the pages of *The Crisis*, the NAACP's magazine, to celebrate black CULTURE and accomplishments, attack WHITE SUPREMACY, and build support in PUBLIC OPINION for the emerging CIVIL RIGHTS MOVEMENT. During the PROTEST phase of the Civil Rights movement in the 1950s and 1960s, the media—especially television—were vital in exposing the VIOLENCE and POLITICAL REPRESSION inherent in SEGREGATION in the SOUTHERN STATES. Televised pictures—of police commissioner Eugene "Bull" Connor's fire hoses and attack dogs during the BIRMINGHAM DEMONSTRATIONS and of Sheriff Jim Clark's bull whips and horses during the SELMA DEMONSTRATIONS—were major sources of pressure leading Presidents JOHN F. KENNEDY and LYNDON B. JOHNSON to propose the CIVIL RIGHTS ACT OF 1964 and the VOTING RIGHTS ACT OF 1965. Indeed, one of MARTIN LUTHER KING JR.'s skills as a leader was in the manipu-

Offices of *The Crisis* and the NAACP at 69 Fifth Avenue, New York City *(Library of Congress)*

lation of the media to show—"demonstrate"—to the world the grim realities of American racism.

The black press, from its inception with the founding of *Freedom's Journal* in 1827, has been at the forefront of protest against racial OPPRESSION, and along with the BLACK CHURCH it has been a central institution of the BLACK COMMUNITY, helping to define the nature and meaning of BLACKNESS. As GUNNAR MYRDAL wrote in *AN AMERICAN DILEMMA*, "*The press defines the Negro group to the Negroes themselves.* The individual is invited to share in the sufferings, grievances and pretensions of the millions of Negroes far outside the narrow local community. This creates a feeling of strength and solidarity. The press, more than any other institution, has created the Negro group as a social and psychological reality to the individual Negro" (emphasis by Myrdal). Of the 12 individuals identified by black political scientists as the greatest black leaders of all time, five were journalists or were responsible for the editing or publication of newspapers.

The African-American Media in Historical and Contemporary Perspectives

When John B. Russwurm and Samuel Cornish established *Freedom's Journal,* the first black newspaper, in 1827 in New York City, they wrote in its first edition, "We wish to plead our own cause. Too long have others spoken for us." This wish to plead the black cause from 1827 to the POST–CIVIL RIGHTS ERA led to the emergence of a varied, vibrant, and influential black press.

Scores of blacks established newspapers prior to the CIVIL WAR, and while most did not last, they gave voices to the black community as they helped to define it. After the Civil War and Reconstruction, hundreds of black newspapers were founded, and while most did not last long, a few flourished and became enduring and influential institutions; among them are HARLEM's *Amsterdam News,* the *Baltimore Afro-American,* the *Chicago Defender,* and the *Atlanta World.* In addition, African-American leaders, following in the tradition of FREDERICK DOUGLASS, published and edited journals, among them Ida B. Wells-Barnett and William Monroe Trotter. Then two major civil rights organizations—the NAACP and the URBAN LEAGUE—published influential journals of analysis and propaganda, *The Crisis* and *The Opportunity*. MARCUS GARVEY and his UNIVERSAL NEGRO IMPROVEMENT ASSOCIATION published a mass-circulation journal, *Negro World,* during the 1920s that espoused BLACK NATIONALISM, and A. PHILIP RANDOLPH's *The Messenger* was a journal espousing RADICALISM.

Until the end of the civil rights era, the black press was a fighting press, and because of this it was frequently subjected to various forms of political repression. But as Myrdal points out in the quotation below, the black press was more than a protest medium:

By expressing the protest, the press also magnifies it, acting like a huge sounding board. The press is also the chief agency of group control. It tells the individual how he should think and feel as an American Negro and creates a tremendous power of suggestion by implying that all other Negroes think and feel in this manner. It keeps the Negro spokesman in line. Every public figure knows he will be reported, and he has to weigh his words carefully. Both the leaders and the masses are kept under racial discipline by the press. This promotes unanimity without the aid of central direction.

In the post–civil rights era, INTEGRATION has reduced the influence of the black press as both an instrument of protest and of group solidarity and direction. It has declined as an instrument of protest because of the withering away of overt white supremacy and RACISM, which has diminished the direct targets of protest that had given purpose to the black press since the founding of its first newspaper. It has also declined as an instrument of group solidarity and direction because of the integration of all blacks, in various ways, into the mainstream of American society. Integration also has led to a decline in the quality of reporting, editing, and production for black newspapers, as they are less able to attract talented journalists, who find more-prestigious and better-paying jobs in the mainstream media. As a result of all of these factors, black newspapers are read less and therefore have less impact on the solidarity and direction of the black community. Black newspapers are also read less because the mainstream media have done a somewhat better job in the post–civil rights era of covering the internal life of the black community.

Several historically significant black newspapers, including the *Chicago Defender* and the *Michigan Chronicle,* in the late 20th century faced bankruptcy, closure, or the possibility of being sold to white investors. *Emerge,* the only national black news magazine, ceased publication in 1999 after 15 years because it could not develop a circulation base large enough to become profitable; *Essence,* a black women's magazine, was purchased by Time/Life; and BET (Black Entertainment Television), the nation's only black-owned cable outlet, was purchased by Viacom. The problems of the black media reflect a combination of factors: the effects of integration in general, the specific effects of integration on the loss of circulation and the resulting loss of ad revenues, and the reluctance of white-owned businesses to advertise in the black media to the same extent and with the same revenue as in comparable white media. And, like the mainstream media, the black press faces competition for talent, readers, and ads from the new media of the Internet, on-line news outlets, and the World Wide Web.

At the beginning of the 21st century, the black media comprise about 200 weekly newspapers, which are organized into the National Newspaper Publishers Association (NNPA), established in 1940. In general, the black weeklies serve as the voice for local African-American communities, focusing on community rather than general or national news. This focus tends to be on the internal civic, cultural, and especially religious affairs of the community. While the mainstream media cover the black community in greater depth than in the 1960s, their main focus necessarily is on general news of the society. Therefore, the local black media (including radio in the larger cities) are still useful as a vehicle of intragroup communication and solidarity. Many, although not all, of the black weeklies also serve as watchdogs on local government and attempt to continue the protest tradition. The NNPA also operates a national news wire, which distributes national and world news to the weeklies, and in 2000 the NPPA established an on-line website (www.BlackPressUSA.com), which distributes news exclusively from the black media.

In addition to the local weeklies, the black media comprise more than 200 black-oriented radio stations; two general-circulation feature magazines, the black-owned Johnson publications *Jet* and *Ebony* (the weekly *Jet* occasionally has good coverage of the national news along with celebrity features and gossip, while the monthly *Ebony* tends to focus almost exclusively on celebrities, consumerism, and showcasing the black middle class); a variety of special-interest magazines dealing with women, business, health and lifestyles, the hip-hop culture, and so on; and BET, which while white-owned, still orients its news and other programming toward blacks.

Unlike in earlier eras, no black leader publishes a newspaper. However, the NATION OF ISLAM led by LOUIS FARRAKHAN publishes *The Final Call*, which provides good coverage of national and international affairs along with the organization's propaganda (it has a large national circulation as a result of subscriptions and street-corner sales), and the NAACP continues publication of *The Crisis*. Finally, most of the major black organizations maintain websites, and there are many black on-line news outlets, including africana.com, The Black World Today (tbwt.com), and diversityinc.com. Although there is a racial "digital divide," about 36 percent of black households were connected to the Internet in 2000 compared with 54 percent of whites, 69 percent of Asian Americans, and 41 percent of Latinos.

African Americans in the Mainstream Media

Historically, the mainstream media have tended to ignore the black community or to portray it in stereotypical and biased ways. The KERNER REPORT in 1968 criticized the media's coverage of the black community, reporting that the America displayed on television and the newspapers appeared "almost totally white" and portrayed blacks as if they "do not read the newspapers or watch television, give

birth, marry, die or go to PTA meetings." The report concluded that "[by] failing to portray the Negro as a matter of routine and in the context of the total society, the news media . . . have contributed to the black-white schism in the country." The report recommended that the media provide more-detailed and balanced coverage and that it hire more black editors and reporters. In the several decades following the report, the situation in terms of coverage and the hiring of blacks has improved, but the coverage still tends to be somewhat spotty and often stereotypical.

In the early 1900s, a few blacks began to work for mainstream media, but their writing tended to be relegated to the back pages, with some newspapers even running a "black page" at the back on weekends containing coverage of blacks. It was not, however, until the pressures of the Civil Rights and BLACK POWER MOVEMENTs that the white media began to hire blacks in large numbers. An example of these pressures was an announcement by SNCC in 1967 that it would only allow blacks to cover its meetings and conferences. Also the RIOTS in the GHETTOS made it necessary to hire black reporters, because many white reporters were afraid to go into areas for fear of assault. But at the end of the 20th century, the number of blacks in the mainstream media remained relatively small. At the beginning of the 21st century, blacks constituted about 5 percent of newspaper, 10 percent of television, and 6 percent of radio news personnel. However, in the important decision-making positions of editors and producers, blacks made up less than 3 percent of the newspaper and radio/television workforces. In the 1950s and 1960s, studies of the content of the mass media showed that its routine, day-to-day coverage of blacks was predominantly negative and stereotypical, portraying blacks as poor, as criminals, or as entertainers and athletes. Studies show that this kind of coverage declined in the 1970s and 1980s but resurfaced somewhat in the 1990s.

In terms of explicitly political coverage, the principal structural motive guiding the mass media is generally the preservation of the "social order" and the core values and prevailing power relationships of the POLITICAL SYSTEM. To the extent that blacks challenge these values and power relationships, the resultant coverage of blacks is necessarily biased.

Further reading: Jannette Dates and William Barlow, eds., *Split Images: African Americans in the Mass Media* (Washington, D.C.: Howard University Press, 1993); Armistead Pride and Clint Wilson, *A History of the Black Press* (Washington, D.C.: Howard University Press, 1997); Roland Wolseley, *The Black Press, USA* (Ames: Iowa State University Press, 1990).

melting pot

"Melting pot" is the metaphor used to refer to the process involving the ASSIMILATION of immigrant European ETH-

NIC GROUPS into American society and culture. The term comes from Israel Zangwill, a poet and playwright, who in 1908 wrote a play called *The Melting Pot*. The idea, evoked at the height of immigration from Europe, was that individuals from the various nations of Europe would gradually lose their distinctive national identities and cultures and "melt" into a new American identity and culture, just as the various ores in a cauldron melt into a new alloy of steel. The melting-pot ideal has worked reasonably well in the United States, as most immigrants from Europe have assimilated into American society and culture. It has not worked, however, for African Americans because the metaphor, as it was originally used, was not intended to apply to blacks because of the IDEOLOGY of WHITE SUPREMACY. At the end of the 20th century, with an infusion of new immigrants of color from Asia and Latin America, the melting-pot ideal was tested yet again.

See also MULTICULTURALISM and WHITENESS.

Meredith, James *civil rights activist*

James Meredith was the first person of known African-American descent to be graduated from the University of Mississippi. When the SUPREME COURT ordered his admission to the university, the governor of the state sought to block it, forcing President JOHN F. KENNEDY to eventually dispatch the army to the campus to secure his admission. A RIOT by whites injured 300 persons and killed two. The event was a major incident, creating international protests and making Meredith a national figure. In 1966 he announced a 220-mile "march against fear" through Mississippi. He claimed that blacks in the state were afraid to exercise the rights conferred on them by the CIVIL RIGHTS ACT OF 1964. Therefore, a successful march by him—perhaps the most-hated (by whites) black man in Mississippi—walking alone would demonstrate to blacks that they need not fear to exercise their newly won CIVIL RIGHTS. (Along the march, Meredith planned to take blacks to register to vote and to join him in using previously segregated public accommodations.) On the second day of the march, Meredith was shot and wounded. MARTIN LUTHER KING JR. and STOKELY CARMICHAEL resumed what became known as the MEREDITH MARCH. It was on this march that the BLACK POWER MOVEMENT was first brought to the attention of the nation. After the march, Meredith moved to HARLEM and briefly considered running for CONGRESS against ADAM CLAYTON POWELL JR. After severe criticism from black leaders, he withdrew from the race and later returned to Mississippi, where he ran unsuccessfully for the U.S. Senate. Late in his career, in an ironic twist, Meredith became a bitter critic of the established black LEADERSHIP and of LIBERALISM, joining briefly the staff of North Carolina senator Jesse Helms, who was the most conservative, anti–civil rights member of the Senate.

Meredith march

In June 1966, JAMES MEREDITH began what he called a "march against fear" through his native state of Mississippi. Meredith, the first black graduate of the University of Mississippi, said that by walking alone through the state he "wanted to tear down the fear that grips the Negro in Mississippi" and encourage the 500,000 blacks in the state to register and vote. On the second day of the march, Meredith was shot and wounded. Immediately the leaders of the major civil rights PROTEST organizations—SCLC, CORE, SNCC—announced that they would complete the march to demonstrate that blacks could not be intimidated through VIOLENCE in the exercise of their newly won CIVIL RIGHTS. This march was covered extensively on national television, providing the first national forum for articulating the ideas of the BLACK POWER MOVEMENT.

militancy

"Militancy" is a concept used by political scientists to classify the political behavior of leaders, ORGANIZATIONS, and SOCIAL MOVEMENTS. Scholars of African-American LEADERSHIP have used it to distinguish and classify black leaders since the 1950s. Militancy as a type of political behavior is usually contrasted with moderation, LIBERALISM, CONSERVATISM, ACCOMMODATIONISM, or "Uncle Tomism." The comparison or contrast is based on the goals, rhetoric, and strategies or tactics of the leader or group. A militant leader or group is one that advocates goals or uses strategies or rhetoric that depart from the acceptable or conventional goals, rhetoric, and strategies espoused by the POLITICAL SYSTEM at any given time and circumstance. Militancy is therefore a relative concept. For example, when RACISM and WHITE SUPREMACY were prevailing characteristics of the political system in the United States in the early 1900s, the NAACP was initially considered a militant organization even though its goal was CIVIL RIGHTS; it used moderate or conventional strategies of LOBBYING and LITIGATION; and its rhetoric was in the language of CONSTITUTIONALISM. By the 1960s, however, the NAACP was considered moderate or conservative when compared with MARTIN LUTHER KING JR. and the SOUTHERN CHRISTIAN LEADERSHIP CONFERENCE (SCLC), because while King and the NAACP and SCLC shared the same goals and rhetoric, King's strategy had escalated to nonviolent PROTEST and CIVIL DISOBEDIENCE. But in this same period, King was also considered moderate when compared with MALCOLM X, whose goals, rhetoric, and strategies rejected civil rights, constitutionalism, and nonviolence. Later in the 1960s, the Malcolm X of 1964 would be considered moderate when compared with the BLACK PANTHER PARTY and its leaders, whose goals, rhetoric, and strategies included revolution, VIOLENCE, and SOCIALISM. In the POST–CIVIL RIGHTS ERA, where racism and white supremacy are no longer accepted as core values or characteristics of the system, militancy is defined by the degree to which a leader's or a group's goals or rhetoric challenge the basic system values of CAPITALISM, DEMOCRACY, and constitutionalism or employ disruptive protests or violence. Thus, in the post–civil rights era, LOUIS FARRAKHAN and the NATION OF ISLAM can be considered militant in some of their rhetoric and in their stated goal of a separate black nation, and MANNING MARABLE and the BLACK RADICAL CONGRESS are militant in their goals and rhetoric. However, since the demise of the Black Panther Party, no major black leader or group has embraced militancy in the form of violence or disruptive protests.

military

VIOLENCE is the most potent, if not the most desirable, source or base of POWER. It is, of course, the underlying basis of power for all POLITICAL SYSTEMS. Governments or political systems exercise this base of power by monopolizing the instruments of violence through the police and, ultimately, the military. This is why African Americans historically have sought to be a part of the U.S. military and why the government historically has been reluctant to allow their participation except when their service was indispensable to winning its wars.

In the period prior to the American revolution, the British would sometimes use blacks in the militias of the colonies to defend against attacks from Indians and the French and the Spanish, but as the whites in the colonies began to fear SLAVE REVOLTS, this practice was made unlawful in most colonies. During the Revolutionary War George Washington and the other leaders originally decided to exclude blacks, but after the British began to recruit blacks as soldiers, promising FREEDOM in exchange for their service, this policy was changed, and about 5,000 blacks—FREE NEGROES and enslaved men—served in the war. When the United States became independent, the CONGRESS in its first regulations for the militias limited service to "able bodied white males," and the law creating the marines also explicitly prohibited service by blacks. A few blacks did serve in the earliest army and navy units, but only as servants and laborers. Very few, if any, blacks fought in the War of 1812 against the British or in the 1848 Mexican-American War or in the early wars against the Indian peoples. (In the Seminole wars, many escaped slaves joined forces with the Indians against the American army.) During the CIVIL WAR President ABRAHAM LINCOLN opposed service by blacks, but the pressures of black leaders like FREDERICK DOUGLASS and, ultimately, the need to win the war led him to change his mind. Eventually, about 175,000 blacks (about 9 percent of the Union army) served in all-black units. African-American units were commanded by whites, although MARTIN R. DELANY became the first African-American field officer toward the end of the war.

Blacks were for a time part of the forces that occupied the SOUTHERN STATES during RECONSTRUCTION, but President ANDREW JOHNSON withdrew most of them because he did not believe blacks should exercise power over whites. At the end of Reconstruction the several all-black units were dispatched to the West to fight the Indians. Known as "Buffalo Soldiers," they were involved in some of the final battles leading to suppression of the Native Americans. Blacks also served in the Spanish-American War in the 1890s, but there were concerns about their fighting to suppress the rebellion against the American occupation of the Philippines, since some black leaders and MEDIA expressed support for "our Filipino brothers" in their fight against American COLONIALISM. In the two world wars, blacks again served, but they were only reluctantly allowed in combat units. However, those units that did see combat (under the command of white officers) provided gallant service, which resulted in the beginnings of change in the RACISM and WHITE SUPREMACY that had marked the military since George Washington. In 1945 the U.S. Marines admitted their first blacks, and the Army Air Corp allowed blacks to enlist—the famous Tuskegee airmen—and permitted a black officer to command them. In 1944 the U.S. Navy commissioned its first black-staffed combat ship (although it was commanded by a white officer), and in 1948 President HARRY TRUMAN issued an EXECUTIVE ORDER prohibiting SEGREGATION and DISCRIMINATION throughout the military. By the time of the Korean War, blacks were integrated into combat units, and in 1954 the last all-black units were disbanded.

The VIETNAM WAR was the first in which the military was fully desegregated. But unlike in past wars, where blacks were upset because they were often excluded from combat, in Vietnam they were disproportionately assigned to combat units and represented about 20 percent of the casualties compared with their 10 percent of the total force. The war in Vietnam was also the first opposed by important elements of the black LEADERSHIP, including MARTIN LUTHER KING JR. and MUHAMMAD ALI. In the later stages of the war in Vietnam there were tensions between black and white soldiers, as the BLACK POWER MOVEMENT began to influence the thinking of black soldiers.

In the POST–CIVIL RIGHTS ERA, large numbers of black men and women served in the military. In the 1970s President RICHARD NIXON ended the military draft in favor of an all-volunteer service. Blacks volunteered in disproportionate numbers, not because of any patriotic feelings or militaristic sentiments but mainly because they were denied equal opportunities for employment in the civilian economy. Thus, at the end of the 20th century, blacks, composing approximately 12 percent of the population, were about

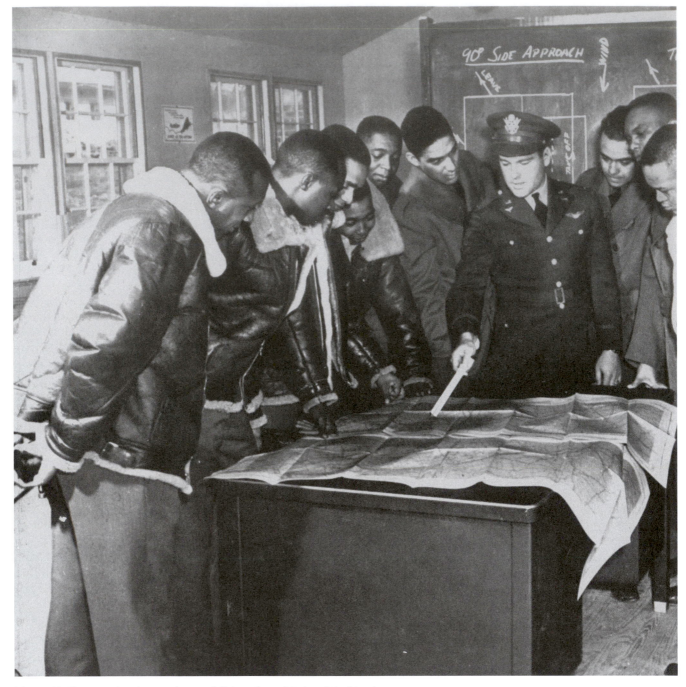

Negro Air Corps cadets in an advanced flying class (*National Archives*)

29 percent of enlisted army personnel, 18 percent of the air force, 20 percent of the navy, and 19 percent of the marines. Given the long history of the exclusion of blacks from the military, the situation at the beginning of the 21st century was a bit ironic: Blacks were disproportionately represented in the military and in its combat units, and little concern was expressed by whites about having such a large number of African Americans trained as specialists in violence.

In 1989 General COLIN POWELL became the highest-ranking officer in the military as chairman of the combined Joint Chiefs of Staff. Powell's position was symbolically significant, but it did not indicate complete INTEGRATION of the officer corps, since at the end of the century blacks constituted 12 percent of the army officer corps (compared with their 29 percent of enlisted personnel), 6 percent of the air force, and 7 percent of the navy and marines.

Further reading: Gail Buckley, *American Patriots: The Story of Blacks in the Military from the Revolution to Desert Storm* (New York: Random House, 2001); Michael Lee Lanning, *The African American Soldier: From Crispus Attucks to Colin Powell* (Secaucus, N.J.: Carol Publishers, 1997).

Milliken v. Bradley (1974)

Milliken v. Bradley (1974) was the first decision by the SUPREME COURT in which it began to back away from BUS-ING as a means to dismantle SEGREGATION in the public schools, as required by BROWN V. BOARD OF EDUCATION. In a five-to-four decision, the Court overturned the decisions of lower courts requiring the busing of pupils between the largely black Detroit school district and the districts in the largely white suburbs. The Court's majority agreed that the schools in the Detroit area were segregated, but it held that cross-district busing between the city and the suburbs was not required by the EQUAL PROTECTION CLAUSE because the suburban districts were not responsible for the segregation in the city. Justice THURGOOD MARSHALL and his dissenting colleagues argued that under the equal protection clause and prevailing principles of FEDERALISM, the state of Michigan—not the city or the suburbs—was responsible for creating the separate school districts between Detroit and its suburbs and, therefore, was also responsible for the segregation that resulted. Thus, they argued, cross-district busing was a permissible remedy if no other means could be found to accomplish the constitutional requirement that *states* operate desegregated schools. Since African Americans live disproportionately in the GHETTOS and whites largely in the suburbs, the *Milliken* case meant that school DESEGREGATION would be virtually impossible to achieve in the big cities of the United States.

See also SCHOOLS AND EDUCATION and STATE AND LOCAL GOVERNMENT.

Million Man march

On October 16, 1995, it is possible that as many as 1 million black men (and several thousand black women) marched on Washington. If these figures are accurate, that would make this march the largest in the history of the United States. (The number of marchers remains a matter of dispute.) The march was sponsored by LOUIS FARRAKHAN and the NATION OF ISLAM. Unlike other marches on Washington sponsored by blacks since A. PHILIP RANDOLPH started the MARCH ON WASHINGTON MOVEMENT in the 1940s, the Million Man march's purpose was not to make claims or bring pressures—even symbolic ones—on the POLITICAL SYSTEM. Rather, Farrakhan said the purpose of the march was moral and spiritual: a call for atonement on the part of black men for their failures to live up to their responsibilities to their families and communities and to reaffirm traditional values with respect to family, sexuality, and alcohol and drug use. Virtually all white political leaders and commentators in the MEDIA and a few prominent black leaders denounced the march because it excluded women and because it was led by Farrakhan, who was routinely described by critics as a "racist, sexist, antisemitic, homophobic demagogue." Most black leaders and a few prominent women endorsed it, and several women spoke at the march. Televised internationally, the main result of the march—if not its main purpose—was to enhance the visibility and stature of Farrakhan as a black leader. In the BLACK COMMUNITY, PUBLIC OPINION polls conducted after the march showed that Farrakhan became better known, and opinion on his standing as a leader became more favorable. Among whites, the march increased Farrakhan's visibility, but it did little to alter their overwhelmingly unfavorable view of him as a political leader.

Further reading: Joseph P. McCormick, "The Message and the Messengers: Opinions from the Million Men Who Marched," *National Political Science Review* 6 (1997): 142–64; Haki Madhubuti and Maulana Karenga, eds., *Million Man March: Day of Absence* (Chicago: Third World Press, 1996).

minority group

For social scientists, the term *minority group* does not refer to the numerical size of a group (as in smaller in number). Rather, minority group is an analytic concept that refers to POWER relationships among SUPERORDI-NATE GROUPS and SUBORDINATE GROUPS in a POLITICAL SYSTEM. Therefore, a minority group is a subordinate group, whatever its actual size, that differs from the superordinate group in RACE, ETHNICITY, GENDER, or some other salient characteristic and is subjected to OPPRESSION or DISCRIMINATION on that basis. A necessary characteristic of minority-group status is having less power to shape the values of the society and the distribution of its resources. In contrast, for social scientists a superordinate group is a majority group, no matter its numerical size, if it has the power to determine the values of the society and the distribution of its resources, especially as this power is exercised in relationship to minority groups. In the United States, African Americans are a minority group both analytically and numerically, while in South Africa the Africans are a minority group analytically although they constitute more than 80 percent of the population. Similarly, in the United States and elsewhere, women are a minority group although they are a majority of the population.

Mississippi Freedom Democratic Party

The Mississippi Freedom Democratic Party (MFDP), a COALITION of black and white Mississippi Democrats, was established in 1963 as a means to PROTEST and challenge the legitimacy of the regular all-white Mississippi Democratic Party at the 1964 DEMOCRATIC PARTY National Convention. The party was organized by ROBERT MOSES and other SNCC activists, and FANNIE LOU HAMER was its most prominent national spokesperson. At the 1964 Democratic Party convention, the MFDP challenged the seating of the regular delegation because it was constituted on the basis of RACISM and SEGREGATION, while MFDP was open to all Mississippians. The convention, under orders from President LYNDON B. JOHNSON, whom it was about to nominate, rejected the MFDP challenge, offering instead a compromise in which the regular delegation was seated and the MFDP was provided two honorary seats. In addition, party leaders promised to revise party rules to eliminate segregated state delegations at future conventions. This compromise was supported by Senator HUBERT HUMPHREY, the longtime white liberal supporter of CIVIL RIGHTS, who was about to be nominated as vice president, and MARTIN LUTHER KING JR. and the other major civil rights leaders. MFDP, however, rejected the compromise, with Hamer famously proclaiming, "We didn't come all this way for no two seats."

The failure of the convention in 1964 to support the MFDP challenge and the role of leading white liberals like Humphrey and civil rights leaders like King disillusioned the activists in SNCC, who had created MFDP and helped to heighten the growing MILITANCY in SNCC that two years later would result in the birth of the BLACK POWER MOVEMENT. The MFDP challenge did lead to Democratic Party rules changes in 1968 and 1972 prohibiting segregated delegations and requiring the adoption of AFFIRMATIVE ACTION plans to assure EQUALITY in the REPRESENTATION of women and racial minorities in all state delegations.

Mitchell, Clarence (1911–1983) civil rights activist

Clarence Mitchell became director of the Washington office of the NAACP in 1950. In this position he used LOBBYING to advance the cause of CIVIL RIGHTS until his death in 1983. Although THURGOOD MARSHALL became better known as the NAACP's chief lawyer for using LITIGATION to advance civil rights, Mitchell, as the chief lobbyist, played an important role in shaping all of the civil rights laws of the 1960s, including the CIVIL RIGHTS ACT OF 1964 and the VOTING RIGHTS ACT OF 1965. His knowledge of the legislative process and the strengths and weaknesses of both supporters and opponents of civil rights in CONGRESS led observers to refer to him as the "101st senator." Mitchell also had a close relationship with President LYN-

DON B. JOHNSON, developed during the time when Johnson was the Senate leader. This knowledge of the legislative process and the legislators was an important resource in Mitchell's effectiveness, since the NAACP's Washington office did not have a large staff or budget.

Mitchell was committed to the IDEOLOGY of INTEGRATIONISM and became a strong critic of the MILITANCY expressed by the BLACK POWER MOVEMENT of the 1960s. Mitchell was born in Baltimore, Maryland, and received his undergraduate degree from Lincoln University, a historically black university. He did graduate studies at ATLANTA UNIVERSITY and received a law degree from the University of Maryland. Prior to joining the NAACP he worked as a journalist in the black MEDIA.

Further reading: Denton Watson, *Lion in the Lobby: Clarence Mitchell and the Black Struggle for Freedom* (New York: William Morrow, 1990).

Montgomery, Isaiah T. (unknown–1908) politician

Isaiah T. Montgomery is a prototypical case of the UNCLE TOM in African-American LEADERSHIP. This is because at the 1890 Mississippi State Constitutional Convention, Montgomery, the only black delegate, supported the forces of RACISM and WHITE SUPREMACY in the adoption of various schemes that effectively deprived black Mississippians of VOTING RIGHTS as well as the other basic CIVIL RIGHTS they had exercised during RECONSTRUCTION. Anticipating the arguments made by BOOKER T. WASHINGTON five years later in the "ATLANTA COMPROMISE" ADDRESS, Montgomery said blacks were not then ready for full FREEDOM and EQUALITY and that therefore Reconstruction was a mistake. Hence, blacks should give up their civil rights, and whites should leave them alone so that they could develop their own communities separate from whites. Facing the overwhelming threat of VIOLENCE and KU KLUX KLAN terrorism, and with little prospects for protection from the governments of Mississippi or the United States, Montgomery, like Booker Washington, apparently thought he had no choice but to accept the subordination of his people. But, as the aging FREDERICK DOUGLASS remarked at the time, "He has made peace with the lion by allowing himself to be swallowed." This is because whites in Mississippi refused to allow blacks to develop their own communities. Instead, they systematically deprived them of educational and economic opportunities. For a time, Montgomery was allowed to establish and run the all-black town of Mound Bayou, Mississippi. But as it began to prosper, it was gradually destroyed by what was, in effect, a white economic boycott.

Late in life, Montgomery apparently came to regret his decision at the 1890 convention (the 1890 Mississippi Convention's constitution was widely copied throughout the

SOUTHERN STATES), but he never publicly said so, and until his death in 1908 he continued to acquiesce as the forces of racism and white supremacism intensified their OPPRESSION of Mississippi's huge black population, the largest of any state. Because he was born in SLAVERY, the date of Montgomery's birth is not known.

Montgomery bus boycott

The boycott in 1955 by African Americans of the city buses of Montgomery, Alabama, is one of the famous events of the CIVIL RIGHTS MOVEMENT. There had been bus boycotts by blacks before. Two years earlier, for example, Rev. T. J. Jamison had led an effective boycott of the buses in Baton Rouge, Louisiana. The boycott in Montgomery is famous and historically significant for two reasons. First, historians generally date the beginning of the final PROTEST phase of the Civil Rights movement to the Montgomery bus boycott. Second, the boycott resulted in the emergence of MARTIN LUTHER KING JR. as the preeminent leader of the protest phase of the movement and as the greatest or most influential leader in the history of the African-American freedom struggle.

When ROSA PARKS refused to give up her seat on a bus to a white man as required by law, she had no idea that this simple act would launch the final and most dramatic phase of the Civil Rights movement. After her arrest, E. D. Nixon, a member of the BROTHERHOOD OF SLEEPING CAR PORTERS and a former president of the local NAACP chapter, called on Montgomery's blacks to boycott the city's buses for one day. The boycott last 381 days.

To organize the boycott, the Montgomery Improvement Association was established, and Martin Luther King Jr., a young minister who had just arrived in the city to pastor one of its most influential churches, was asked to serve as its president. King's leadership of the movement at the age of 26 established him as a new leader of the Civil Rights movement. At Montgomery, King mobilized several power bases that he would employ again and again during the next years as he led the movement to a series of legislative victories that brought legal EQUALITY and FREEDOM to African Americans. These resources included size and solidarity—blacks were 75 percent of the bus riders in Montgomery, and virtually all of them supported the boycott—RELIGIOSITY, morality, and Dr. King's charisma.

At first the leaders of the boycott did not seek an end to SEGREGATION on the buses. Rather, they accepted the JIM CROW principle that blacks would sit at the back of the bus, whites the front, and the middle seats would be available on a first-come, first-serve basis. When the moderate demands were rejected by the city and when POLITICAL REPRESSION of the movement increased, the MILITANCY of blacks increased, and they finally demanded a complete end to bus segregation. LITIGATION led to a decision by the SUPREME COURT declaring such segregation a violation of the EQUAL PROTECTION CLAUSE of the FOURTEENTH AMENDMENT.

Moseley-Braun, Carol (1947–) U.S. Senator

Carol Moseley-Braun (now Moseley Braun) is one of only four blacks and the only black woman to serve in the U.S. Senate in its more than 200-year history. Elected as a Democrat from Illinois in 1992, Moseley-Braun was defeated six years later after serving a single term. As the Senate's only black and its first black woman, she enjoyed greater status than the usual beginning senator, but her six years in the Senate were not distinguished by legislative accomplishments or a major impact on the PUBLIC POLICY debate; nor did she pay special attention to issues of race or CIVIL RIGHTS. After her defeat for reelection, President BILL CLINTON appointed her ambassador to New Zealand.

See also CONGRESS.

Moses, Robert (1935–) civil rights activist

SNCC was the most self-consciously radical and democratic of the major civil rights ORGANIZATIONS of the 1960s. The organization's commitment to RADICALISM and nonauthoritarian, democratic decision-making was shaped mainly by ELLA BAKER and Robert Moses. Born in New York City and educated at Hamilton College and Harvard, Moses was a high school math teacher when he decided to join SNCC's staff as a full-time field secretary in Mississippi. A quietly charismatic, self-effacing man, Moses believed in the capacity of ordinary people to exercise leadership and helped to structure SNCC's work in Mississippi to facilitate the development of indigenous, grassroots leadership, as reflected in FANNIE LOU HAMER's emergence as a historically significant African-American leader. Moses recognized that Hamer, although poor and barely literate, had the capacity for leadership and facilitated and encouraged her growth as a leader of the MISSISSIPPI FREEDOM DEMOCRATIC PARTY, which he had helped to create. Moses himself was reluctant to occupy any position of formal leadership, and as a kind of cult of personality emerged around him, he withdrew from active participation in SNCC decision-making, explaining that he had become "too strong, too central" to the organization. In an attempt to escape from his leadership role, in 1965 Moses changed his name to Parris (his middle name).

Like many in SNCC, Moses was disillusioned and angered by the failure of the DEMOCRATIC PARTY to seat the Mississippi Freedom Democratic Party delegation at its 1964 national convention. Feeling betrayed by white liberals because of this, Moses for a time refused to associate with whites. But he also refused to join STOKELY CARMICHAEL and others in the BLACK POWER MOVEMENT in ousting whites from SNCC. Moses refused to serve in the VIETNAM WAR, claiming conscientious-objector status. When he was drafted, he fled to Canada and eventual exile in Africa, where he stayed until President JIMMY CARTER granted amnesty to Vietnam War resisters. Upon his return to the United States, he established the "Algebra Project" to teach math skills to minority students, arguing that math literacy in the 21st century was an important civil right for the economically disadvantaged in a technology-driven society. In 2000 the project was teaching math to more than 20,000 students.

Further reading: Eric Burner, *And Gently He Shall Lead Them: Robert Parris Moses and Civil Rights in Mississippi* (New York: Oxford University Press, 1994); Robert Moses and Charles Cobb, *Radical Equations: Math Literacy and Civil Rights* (Boston: Beacon Press, 2001).

Muhammad, Elijah (Elijah Poole) (1897–1975) *black nationalist*

Elijah Muhammad was one of the most remarkable Americans of the 20th century. Born Elijah Poole in rural Georgia, the son of formerly enslaved parents, Muhammad, although largely unlettered (he only completed the fourth grade) is in large part responsible for keeping the radical, separatist tradition of BLACK NATIONALISM alive in the 20th century, and he is almost single-handedly responsible for making Islam an acceptable religion in the BLACK COMMUNITY. Without Muhammad, the tradition of black nationalism would have been less influential in the 20th century, and the more than 1 million African Americans who were Muslims would probably have been Christians or nonbelievers. MALCOLM X during the period of the CIVIL RIGHTS MOVEMENT and LOUIS FARRAKHAN in the POST–CIVIL RIGHTS ERA were more effective and eloquent messengers of Islam and black nationalism than the diminutive, uncharismatic, and inarticulate Muhammad, but it was Muhammad who built the NATION OF ISLAM into the ORGANIZATION that could recruit, nurture, and sustain a Malcolm and a Farrakhan.

Poole left Georgia in 1923 after witnessing the LYNCHING of a friend. Moving to Detroit, he joined MARCUS GARVEY's organization, the UNIVERSAL NEGRO IMPROVEMENT ASSOCIATION, and later the Moorish Science Temple of America, a proto-Islamic black nationalist group founded by Noble Drew Ali. In 1931 he met W. D. Fard, the founder and leader of the Nation of Islam. Shortly thereafter, Fard made Poole his supreme minister, and Elijah Poole became Elijah Muhammad. When Fard was forced to leave Detroit by the police, Muhammad attempted to take control of the Nation of Islam, but he met opposition

(including death threats), and he left Detroit, settling eventually in the DISTRICT OF COLUMBIA. There he used the Library of Congress to read and study and to refine Fard's philosophy and theology, a philosophy and theology that were to constitute the foundations of the Nation of Islam's doctrines for the rest of the 20th century. He also traveled throughout the eastern United States spreading the Nation's message. When the Japanese attacked Pearl Harbor in 1941, Muhammad "rejoiced" in the victory of a colored nation over white America, and he not only refused to be drafted himself but instructed his followers to do so also. In 1942 he was charged with draft evasion and sedition and imprisoned for three years. Upon his release he moved to Chicago and resumed active leadership of the Nation of Islam, by now describing himself as the "Messenger of Allah." The recruitment of Malcolm X and his appointment as national spokesman was an important development because Malcolm was extraordinarily effective in recruiting members and building the organization.

By the mid-1960s the Nation of Islam was the largest and most prosperous black nationalist organization since Garvey's. It included scores of mosques and schools and numerous real estate holdings, including farms in the SOUTHERN STATES. The Nation of Islam also published a nationally circulated newspaper, *Muhammad Speaks,* and in the 1960s was considered the wealthiest black organization in the United States. And Muhammad exercised dictatorial authority over it. In 1959 he had traveled to Africa and the Middle East, including a pilgrimage to Mecca. Although the Nation of Islam's brand of Islam is radically at odds with orthodox Islam, the pilgrimage to Mecca conferred legitimacy on Muhammad as an Islamic leader.

The Nation of Islam was viewed as a possible threat to the POLITICAL SYSTEM, and J. EDGAR HOOVER and the FBI had spied on it since the 1930s. However, in the context of American politics, it was a relatively conservative organization. It condemned MARTIN LUTHER KING JR. and the CIVIL RIGHTS MOVEMENT; forbade its members to participate in American politics; and practiced and encouraged a form of petit-bourgeois CAPITALISM. The Nation of Islam never sanctioned VIOLENCE against whites or the political system, although violence was used within the Nation of Islam to settle factional disputes. (It is probable that the group's hierarchy ordered or acquiesced in the assassination of Malcolm X in part because Malcolm revealed Muhammad's numerous sexual indiscretions, which included fathering as many as a dozen children with as many as seven women.) The Nation of Islam was considered a radical organization committed to MILITANCY because of its theological condemnation of whites as "devils" and its powerful rhetorical condemnation of RACISM and WHITE SUPREMACY, but it was basically an apolitical, conservative religious organization that held that only Allah's divine intervention would bring FREEDOM and EQUALITY to African Americans, a view Muhammad expressed in his most important book, *Message to the Black Man.* This conservative, apolitical posture was one of the reasons Malcolm X left the Nation of Islam and formed an organization, the ORGANIZATION OF AFRO-AMERICAN UNITY, that would take part in the Civil Rights movement and American politics.

Elijah Muhammad died in 1975 at age 77. Shortly thereafter his son Wallace, his designated successor, repudiated his father's theological and philosophical teachings, disbanded the Nation of Islam, and transformed it into an orthodox Islamic group called the AMERICAN MUSLIM MISSION. Several years later Farrakhan—the national spokesman for the Nation of Islam at the time of Muhammad's death—reestablished the Nation of Islam on the basis of Muhammad's original teachings. In addition to the American Muslim Mission and the revitalized Nation of Islam under Farrakhan, there are several Islamic sects and factions in the black community that have their origins in the teachings of Muhammad.

Further reading: Claude A. Clegg, *An Original Man: The Life and Times of Elijah Muhammad* (New York: St. Martin's Press, 1997).

multiculturalism

The term *multiculturalism,* as used in the United States at the end of the 20th century, referred to two distinct although interrelated phenomena. *Multiculturalism* in one sense refers to the fact that the United States is becoming an increasingly multiethnic society as a result of the immigration of diverse ETHNIC GROUPS from Asia, Africa, Latin America, and the Caribbean. The second meaning of *multiculturalism* refers not to the *fact* of increased ethnic diversity but to the *question* of whether these new ethnic groups will seek to maintain their distinctive languages and cultures and thereby make the United States a genuine multicultural state, or whether these groups will follow the path of ASSIMILATIONISM of the ethnic immigrants of earlier periods of American history.

Until the 1960s immigration laws of the United States were based on principles of RACISM. Enacted in the 1920s, these laws generally excluded persons from eastern and southern Europe and the THIRD WORLD. Partly as a result of the antiracism reform climate brought about by the CIVIL RIGHTS MOVEMENT, the immigration laws were changed in 1965 to permit immigration on the basis of EQUALITY from all parts of the world. These changes in the law, the GLOBALIZATION of the economy, and the creation of refugees as a result of wars in Asia, Africa, and Latin America resulted in a massive influx of immigrants, legal and illegal. By the 2000 CENSUS, individuals from Latin America or "Hispanics" accounted for 12.5 percent of the

U.S. population of 281,421,906; Native Americans, 0.7 percent; Asian Americans 3.6 percent, African Americans, 12.5 percent, non-Hispanic whites 69.1 percent, and the new multi-racial category, 1.6 percent. (About half of the Hispanics identified themselves as white.) This represents a dramatic change from the 1960s, when blacks and whites accounted for approximately 90 percent of the population.

Although it is commonplace for social scientists and journalists to refer to Hispanics and Asian Americans as if they are single, discrete ethnic groups, they obviously are not, and to treat them as such conceals the true extent of ethnic diversity in the United States. While Latinos share a common language, they do not necessarily share a common culture, and Asian Americans do not share even a common language, let alone a culture. Thus, it is important to disaggregate or break down these artificially created groups. Among Hispanics, the largest ethnic group is Mexican American at 58.5 percent; Puerto Ricans are 9.6 percent, Cubans 3.5 percent, and persons from other Latin American countries 28.4 percent. Among Asian Americans, the breakdown is Chinese at 23.7 percent, Filipinos (classified as Asian although many speak Spanish) 18 percent, Korean 9.5 percent, Japanese 7 percent, Asian Indians 16 percent, Vietnamese 11 percent, and persons from other Asian countries 14.8 percent.

The foregoing facts about ethnic diversity do not necessarily mean that the United States will become a multicultural state. It may or may not, depending on whether these "immigrants of color" follow the path of the many diverse European ethnic groups and become "white," or whether they will follow the path of blacks and either by choice or necessity remain "colored" and maintain a relatively distinct PLURAL SOCIETY based on culture and national identities. To some extent, the answer to this question will depend on the group and its inclinations, but perhaps to a larger extent it may depend on the barriers to their becoming white, as imposed by RACISM, WHITE SUPREMACY, and ethnic DISCRIMINATION. African Americans in large part did not become white and have not become white because white Americans would not permit them to do so. Thus, the basic question about multiculturalism is whether any or all of the immigrants from the Third World will follow the path of European immigrants or the path of African Americans and embrace their version of blackness.

A related question is the consequence of this new ethnic diversity on AFRICAN-AMERICAN POLITICS. First, there is increasing ethnic diversity within the BLACK COMMUNITY in the United States. The 1990 census reported there was approximately 1.5 million foreign-born blacks (about 4 percent of the total black population) in the United States. Most are of WEST INDIAN origins, but increasing numbers are from Africa. Historically, West Indians have played an important role in African-American politics in all its manifestations—RADICALISM, BLACK NATIONALISM, and INTEGRATIONISM—as they subsumed their West Indian identities under the broader mantle of BLACKNESS. But in New York City (where almost half of the West Indian population lives) in the 1990s, West Indian leaders began to assert a distinctive West Indian or Caribbean political identity and began to compete with native-born blacks for political offices and resources. There is also competition for political office and resources between blacks and Hispanic groups in Florida, Texas, California, New York, and Illinois. Unlike blacks, Hispanic and Asian-American groups tend to be concentrated in a few states (Latinos in Texas, California, Florida, New York, New Jersey, and Illinois; Asian Americans in California, New York, and Hawaii). While there is competition and some tensions in some states and cities, at the national level, black, Hispanic, and Asian-American leaders have formed COALITIONS to emphasize the common interests of all "people of color" in fighting for CIVIL RIGHTS and educational and economic opportunities. At the beginning of the 21st century, it was not clear whether the relationship between blacks and the new immigrants would be characterized by cooperation and coalitions or competition and conflicts.

See also MELTING POT, WHITENESS.

Further reading: Yvette Alex-Assenoh and Lawrence Hanks, eds., *Black Politics and Multiracial America* (New York: New York University Press, 2000).

music

Music is an integral component of African-American CULTURE, and therefore it has always been a part of AFRICAN-AMERICAN POLITICS and a powerful agent of POLITICAL SOCIALIZATION. From the inchoate field hollers during SLAVERY to RAP MUSIC at the end of the 20th century, music has been a part of black politics. JAMES BALDWIN wrote, "It is only in his music that the Negro has been able to tell his story," and observers of African-American society have frequently noted that you can tell where black people are at any given moment by their music. The wails and moans of the enslaved Africans at camp meetings and the early churches; the "steal away" songs of runaway slaves; and the spirituals, blues, jazz, gospel, and rhythm and blues—all of these can have (as many scholars have shown) implicit political meanings, messages, or insights.

In the 20th century, artists and musicians wrote and sang music with explicitly political messages; that is, they wrote and performed PROTEST music. Sometimes this music of protest was written or performed by white artists, such as Billie Holiday's "STRANGE FRUIT," which in the 1940s protested LYNCHING, or Bob Dylan's "Blowin' in the

Billie Holiday *(Library of Congress)*

Wind," which became a mainstay for CIVIL RIGHTS activists in the 1960s. But most often, the music of protest was written and performed by black artists. Music in general and protest songs in particular were especially significant during the CIVIL RIGHTS MOVEMENT. The anthem of the movement, "WE SHALL OVERCOME," which has its origins in slavery, was according to MARTIN LUTHER KING JR. an important part of the rituals and traditions used to inspire and mobilize people to take part in a cause larger than themselves. Throughout the 1960s, music—"Freedom Songs"—as they were called, was as much a part of the movement as marches, SIT-INS, and FREEDOM RIDES. In 1963 Nina Simone's "Mississippi God Damn," recorded in the wake of the BIRMINGHAM DEMONSTRATIONS, was banned in parts of several SOUTHERN STATES; CURTIS MAYFIELD's music inspired and chronicled the Civil Rights and BLACK POWER MOVEMENTS and, to a much less significant extent, so did artists like James Brown in recordings like "Say It Loud (I'm Black and I'm Proud)"; the Temptations'

"Message to the Blackman"; Marvin Gaye's "Inner City Blues"; and Nina Simone's "Backlash Blues."

These examples of influential protest or "message" songs are not isolated examples. Rather, they reflect the symbiotic relationship between protest music and protest politics during the 1960s, which can be seen in the results of a comprehensive study conducted by Robert Walker for his dissertation research at Stanford University in 1976. Walker carried out a content analysis of all 1,100 songs that appeared in *Billboard's* (*Billboard* is the authoritative source on music sales) cumulative annual best-selling black music listings from 1946 to 1972. Walker hypothesized that the events of the 1960s had resulted in the emergence of a distinctive black consciousness and solidarity that was manifested in an increase in songs with political messages. His data showed a steady increase in "message songs" beginning after 1957, with a sustained and rapid increase occurring between 1966 and 1969, the peak years of the Black Power movement. By comparing black to white music during this same period, Walker was able to show this increase was unique to black music. And, further demonstrating the symbiotic nature of the relationship, when the protests stopped, the protest music also stopped.

The success of INTEGRATION after the Civil Rights movement resulted in the integration of popular black artists into the mainstream of the music industry. The decline or purchase by whites of independent black recording companies hastened this process, leading to the emergence of integrated or "crossover" artists, personified in the enormous crossover appeal of artists like Michael Jackson. Nelson George, a former *Billboard* African-American music critic, contends in *The Death of Rhythm & Blues* that the development of crossover artists in the POST–CIVIL RIGHTS ERA resulted in the death of the music as an authentic black cultural expression, writing that "In the twenty years since the Great Society, which marked a high point of rhythm and blues music, the community that inspired both social change and artistic creativity has become a sad shell of itself; unhappily, while the drive behind the movement for social change was the greatest inspiration for the music, the very success of the movement spelled the end of the R & B world." The death of rhythm and blues in the 1970s was followed by the emergence in the 1980s and 1990s of rap and hip-hop as authentic black music, raising troubling questions about the state of the BLACK COMMUNITY and its culture and politics.

In 2001, Patrick Milligan, Shawn Amos, and Quincy Newell produced *Say It Loud: A Celebration of Black Music in America*, a discography of 100 years of black music. The six CDs include 108 recordings, featuring gospel, blues, rhythm and blues, rock, country, and rap. The CDs are interspersed with brief excerpts from speeches and interviews by important historical figures including BOOKER T. WASHINGTON, W. E. B. DU BOIS, MARTIN LUTHER KING JR., HARRY TRUMAN, MALCOLM X, JOHN F. KENNEDY, THURGOOD MARSHALL, and LOUIS FARRAKHAN. The accompanying 72-page booklet contains photos and essays by leading cultural critics and musicologists that place the recordings in their historical and sociopolitical context.

See also MEDIA.

Further reading: Nelson George, *The Death of Rhythm & Blues* (New York: Dutton, 1989); Charles Henry, *Culture and African American Politics* (Bloomington: Indiana University Press, 1990); Leroi Jones, *Blues People* (New York: Morrow, 1963); Frank Kofsky, *Black Nationalism and the Revolution in Music* (New York: Pathfinder, 1970); *Moving On Up: Recordings from the Civil Rights Era*, prod. David Nathan (Hollywood, Calif.: The Right Stuff, 1993); Mark Anthony Neal, *What the Music Said: Black Popular Music and Black Public Culture* (New York: Routledge, 1999); Robert Walker, "Soul and Society" (Ph.D. diss., Stanford University, 1976); "Say It Loud: A Celebration of Black Music in America," prod. Patrick Milligan, Shawn Amos and Quincy Newell (Los Angeles: Rhino Entertainment, 2001).

Myrdal, Gunnar (1898–1985) *scholar*

Gunnar Myrdal was born in 1898, near Stockholm, Sweden. He received a Ph.D. in economics at Stockholm University, where he later became a professor of political economy. In 1971, he won the Nobel Prize in economics for his studies on the causes of economic underdevelopment and international economic inequality and POVERTY. He is best known in the United States, however, for his monumental study of America's "Negro problem," AN AMERICAN DILEMMA, published in two volumes in 1944. In 1937 the Carnegie Corporation invited Myrdal, then a relatively unknown scholar and member of the Swedish Parliament with no interest or experience in research on race, to come to the United States to conduct a major research project on the subject. Myrdal was selected rather than one of the many well-qualified white or African-American scholars because it was thought he would bring a tone of neutrality and objectivity to the study. Myrdal then assembled a distinguished team of black and white scholars of race, and with unlimited time and money, they examined virtually every aspect of the "Negro problem"—physiological, historical, psychological, social, cultural, economic, and political. Although Myrdal's work has been subject to extensive criticism by African-American scholars, more than 50 years after its publication it remains the most comprehensive study of race in the United States ever undertaken.

Myrdal was married to Alva Myrdal, a distinguished scholar and diplomat in her own right, who (with Alfonso

García Robles of Mexico) in 1982 won the Nobel Peace Prize. Although Myrdal won his Nobel Prize for his theoretical and empirical work on economic development, he was said to be most proud of *An American Dilemma*. At the time of his death in 1985, at age 87, he was working on a reevaluation of the conclusions in *An American Dilemma* in the light of how race relations had changed since its publication and "to express my worried thoughts about the future development." Although he finished the first draft of this reevaluation before he died, old and nearly blind, he could not complete the final revisions and thus declined to have it published.

N

NAACP (National Association for the Advancement of Colored People)

The NAACP—the National Association for the Advancement of Colored People—is the most important ORGANIZATION in AFRICAN-AMERICAN POLITICS, and historically it has been the most visible organization in the 20th-century struggle for FREEDOM and EQUALITY.

The NAACP has its historical roots in the ABOLITIONIST MOVEMENT and in the struggle for freedom and equality initiated when ABRAHAM LINCOLN issued the EMANCIPATION PROCLAMATION, setting in motion the beginnings of the end of SLAVERY. These historical links to the abolitionist movement and emancipation are clear in the names considered for the association before NAACP was chosen. Among the names considered were "New Abolition Movement," "Emancipation League," the "Lincoln Association for the Advancement of Colored People," and the "Garrison Association for the Advancement of Colored People." Moreover, there is a direct linkage between the abolitionist movement and the NAACP, since three of the latter's founders were descendants of WILLIAM LLOYD GARRISON, the leader of the abolitionist movement, including Oswald Garrison Villard, his grandson and the first chairman of the NAACP board. A final connection between the NAACP and abolitionism and emancipation is that the initial call to organize the group came in reaction to a RIOT in Springfield, Illinois, the burial place of Lincoln. This bloody riot in the "Great Emancipator's" hometown, in which eight blacks were killed and over 2,000 were forced to flee the city, outraged the small group of liberal and progressive whites, who used it as a basis to issue "the call" for a national conference to discuss "means to securing political and civil equality" for African Americans. The founding of the NAACP can also be traced historically to the NIAGARA MOVEMENT, started four years before by W. E. B. DU BOIS and WILLIAM MONROE TROTTER. This incipient movement of the TALENTED TENTH challenged the ACCOMMODATIONISM of BOOKER T. WASHINGTON and started the CIVIL RIGHTS MOVEMENT. Du Bois was among the several African Americans who signed "the call" and was the only African American among the association's early leaders. From its founding in 1909 until the end of the 20th century, the NAACP has been the most important CIVIL RIGHTS organization in the United States.

The NAACP and the Civil Rights movement, like the abolitionist movement, was an interracial COALITION organized by whites and, for its first two decades, largely led by whites. Also, like the abolitionist movement, the whites who founded the association tended to be middle- to upper-class men and women of ideas (one-third of the signers were women), Protestants, and residents of the northeast (especially New York and Boston). Although Protestants were the main organizers of the association, Jews, unlike during the abolitionist movement, were disproportionately involved. Many early founders of the association tended to adhere to the IDEOLOGY of SOCIALISM, including Mary White Ovington and William English Walling, but socialism was never the ideology of the association. Finally, although the NAACP was dedicated to fighting for the rights of blacks, in its early years the participation of prominent whites was considered indispensable. This was because liberal whites brought the money and status necessary to counterbalance the POWER of the white supremacists and racists. The prominence of whites, however, discouraged the participation of some prominent blacks, including William Monroe Trotter, who were skeptical about the depth of the commitment of whites to the interests of blacks.

Organization

From the beginning, the association embraced two contradictory organizational principles. First, it was committed to grassroots mobilization and organization at the local level. Therefore, it encouraged the formation of local branches or chapters that could carry on the work for civil rights based on local conditions. The local branches, wherever possible, would be interracial but generally headed by an African

American. Although based on local grassroots organizing and leadership, from the beginning the association attempted to maintain tight control over the branches and their activities. Branches were under the authority of the board of directors and the national office staff. Applications to establish a chapter had to be submitted in writing for board approval; membership dues (a portion of which had to be shared with the national office) were fixed by the board; and the board approved each branch's constitution or bylaws. Finally, the board, while encouraging grassroots mobilization, would not allow any deviation from the association's ideology and program as established by the board. To maintain control, the branches are required to submit regular reports, and branches that depart from established policy may face suspension.

Ideology

From its beginning the association has been committed to the philosophy of interracialism and the ideology of INTEGRATIONISM, rejecting state-imposed SEGREGATION or voluntary racial separatism as advocated by BOOKER T. WASHINGTON and some advocates of BLACK NATIONALISM. Indeed, Du Bois was ousted by the association in the 1930s because of his advocacy of voluntary segregation and SELF-HELP. The association has also always shied away from RADICALISM, viewing the American POLITICAL SYSTEM as fundamentally sound and RACISM and WHITE SUPREMACY as contrary to system values. Therefore, the association has always supported the system's core values of CAPITALISM, DEMOCRACY, and CONSTITUTIONALISM and rejected VIOLENCE, disruptive PROTEST, or CIVIL DISOBEDIENCE. Instead, the NAACP has always favored "working within the system" using its methods of LOBBYING and LITIGATION. In this sense, it has always been a conservative organization.

In its first two decades, the NAACP worked to establish itself as a presence in the BLACK COMMUNITY and to gain recognition by the black community and POWER ELITE as the legitimate representative of African-American interests in national politics. These goals were accomplished first and foremost through the pages of *The Crisis* magazine, which Du Bois, its editor, used not only to attempt to define the association's intellectual direction and publicize its activities and those of the branches, but also, in his words, to "hammer at the truth" about the nature of racism and white supremacy. That is, he sought to use the *Crisis* as a vehicle of knowledge, education, and propaganda to combat the notions of black inferiority and to shape a favorable climate of PUBLIC OPINION about blacks and civil rights. Simultaneously with Du Bois's education and propaganda, the association gained early public recognition as a result of its campaign against THE BIRTH OF A NATION, the racist movie. In its early years it also engaged in selective litiga-

tion, and in 1909 it launched its 50-year lobbying campaign against LYNCHING. Although this campaign was not successful in securing passage of the DYER ANTI-LYNCHING BILL or other federal legislation curtailing lynching, the campaign helped to build the infrastructure of the organization, sharpen its lobbying skills, and increase its visibility. In the 1930s the NAACP joined a coalition with organized labor to defeat President Herbert Hoover's nomination of John J. Parker to the SUPREME COURT because of his alleged racist and antilabor views. The widely publicized role of the NAACP in lobbying Parker's defeat crystallized its role as the leading African-American political organization.

Civil Rights Activism under Black Leadership

The NAACP was founded by whites and led by whites until the 1930s, with the exception of Du Bois, who was more of an intellectual than an organizational leader. During this period, JOEL E. SPINGARN was a key figure, but in the 1930s a gradual transition to black leadership started. By the 1940s this transition was complete with the selection of first JAMES WELDON JOHNSON and then WALTER WHITE as African-American executive directors. In 1939 it established its LEGAL DEFENSE FUND, which THURGOOD MARSHALL led until the 1960s. By the 1940s the association was black led, had a membership of nearly 400,000, had several hundred local branches, and had a strategy and program of civil rights activism involving lobbying and litigation. At this time the NAACP along with the URBAN LEAGUE was recognized, as GUNNAR MYRDAL said in AN AMERICAN DILEMMA, as "without question" the most important organization in the black freedom struggle.

Although the NAACP has been the most important organization in African-American politics at least since the 1940s, a sober analysis of its accomplishments since its founding until the end of the 20th century demonstrates that it had a limited impact on the overall achievements of the Civil Rights movement. This is because the political system tends to respond incrementally, if at all, to the conventional strategies of lobbying and litigation employed by the NAACP. The NAACP's 50-year lobbying campaign to get the CONGRESS to pass antilynching legislation was not successful, and its lobbying in the 1950s for civil rights laws resulted in the watered-down, largely symbolic Civil Rights Acts of 1957 and 1960. Similarly, its 15-year strategy of litigation, which resulted in BROWN V. BOARD OF EDUCATION, while symbolically significant, did little to end school segregation specifically or in general to alter the subordinate status of blacks. Rather, it was the strategies of protest and civil disobedience—strategies largely opposed by the NAACP—that in the 1960s resulted in legislation that effectively ended segregation and other forms of legalized racism and white supremacy.

Promotional poster for NAACP *(Library of Congress)*

The NAACP in the Post–Civil Rights Era

In the POST–CIVIL RIGHTS ERA the NAACP, like the other major civil rights organizations, found it difficult to adapt organizationally and programmatically to the new barriers to full equality for African Americans, especially those associated with INSTITUTIONAL RACISM and the so-called black UNDERCLASS. Indeed, there was scholarly consensus at the end of the 20th century that the NAACP in its organizational structure, programs, and strategies was out of touch with the complex situation of POVERTY and the multifaceted problems of the GHETTO. Criticism of the NAACP by African-American scholars is not a phenomenon of the late 20th century. In spite of or in some ways because of its recognition and visibility as the most important African-American political organization, its effectiveness has always been questioned.

In the 1930s RALPH BUNCHE and Du Bois rendered detailed critiques of the association programs and strategies. Du Bois, as one of the association's founders and early leaders, was a sympathetic but tough critic, writing in 1940 that the "crusade waged by the NAACP was one of the finest efforts of liberalism to achieve human emancipation; and much was accomplished . . . [but] by the 1930s I realized that too much in the later years the Association had attracted the higher income of colored people, who regarded it as a weapon to attack the sort of social discrimination which especially irked them; rather than an organization to improve the status and power of the whole negro group." As the Civil Rights movement approached its end in the 1960s, KENNETH CLARK, another sympathetic critic, worried whether the association was capable of dealing with the post–civil rights era problem of concentrated poverty and increased "social pathologies" of the urban ghettos. Clark wrote, "The disturbing question which must be faced is whether or not the present civil rights organizations are equipped in terms of perspective, staff and organizational structure to deal effectively with the present level of civil rights problems. And, if not, whether they are flexible enough to change." Twenty years after he wrote this, Clark woefully concluded that the NAACP had not been flexible enough, titling a 1985 essay in the *New York Times* "The NAACP: Verging on Irrelevance."

The problem of the association's relevance is related to its continued adherence to LIBERALISM in an era when the ideology is in decline; its continued reliance for financial support on white philanthropy; its continued tendency to focus on issues of concern to middle-class blacks; and its reliance on traditional lobbying and litigation strategies when these yield very little in terms of legislation or court decisions that address the problems of poverty and the ghetto. While the association has a large number of branches (more than 2,000), its membership at the end of the 20th century was only 500,000, just 100,000 more than in the 1940s, although the black population had more than doubled since then (from 14 million to 35 million). And while 2,000 is a large number of branches, they vary in their levels of programmatic activity and tend to be dominated by a middle-aged and middle- and working-class leadership and an elderly membership. (It is estimated that 75 percent of the active members are 65 or older.) The NAACP has always had trouble attracting young people. In 1936, over the initial objections of the executive director, the association established a youth council and begin to charter youth councils and college chapters. But young people, dissatisfied with the NAACP's middle-class status and conservative approach, tended to drift toward other groups such as CORE and SNCC. In the post–civil rights era, this problem continued despite the lip service of the organization's leaders to involve young people (18 to 30) in the group's membership and leadership. J. Wyatt Mondesire, the head of the 14,000-member Philadelphia branch, remarked in a 2001 interview that the situation was so bad with young people that "when I go out and speak to kids on college campuses and high schools, and I ask them what NAACP stands for, a lot of them think that I am talking about the NCAA [the National Collegiate Athletic Association]. That's how pitiful it is."

At the beginning of the 21st century, the NAACP remained the most important political organization in black America, and with its 500,000 members and 2,000 branches, it is one of the largest grassroots organizations in the United States. These local, grassroots chapters are the association's greatest strength. In every city or town, the local chapters are generally recognized as a dominant voice on black affairs, and they are usually consulted by white economic and political elites seeking advice on issues related to race. These chapters represent a potentially powerful social and political force that could be mobilized with a national strategic program and plan. But the question remains: Can the NAACP—given its history, ideology, and organizational ethos—adapt to the challenges of the 21st century and remain the most important organization in black politics?

Further reading: Charles Kellogg, *NAACP: A History of the National Association for the Advancement of Colored People* (Baltimore, Md.: Johns Hopkins University Press, 1967); Joyce B. Ross, *J. E. Spingarn and the Rise of the NAACP, 1911–1939* (New York: Atheneum, 1972); Robert C. Smith, "The NAACP in 21st Century Perspective" in *Black Political Organizations in the Post Civil Rights Era,* ed. Ollie Johnson and Karin Stanford (New Brunswick, N.J.: Rutgers State University Press, 2002); Carolyn Weldin, *Inheritors of the Spirit: Mary White Ovington and the Founding of the NAACP* (New York: John Wiley, 1998); Robert Zangrando, *The NAACP Crusade against Lynching, 1909–1950* (Philadelphia, Pa.: Temple University Press, 1980).

names controversy

The names that should be used to refer to persons of African origin in the United States have been a source of controversy since the first slaves arrived in the New World. This is because the experiences of African Americans have largely been shaped by a form of OPPRESSION that denied them the elementary FREEDOM and autonomy to maintain knowledge of their identities and languages and the POWER to claim their names.

SLAVERY in the United States was a near-total system of domination, unlike its counterparts in other times and places. It was a POWER relationship in which the Europeans monopolized virtually all bases of power. This disproportionate power of the Europeans resulted in the denial to the Africans of virtually all rights and freedoms, including the basic, elementary freedom of retaining their languages and names. Language and by implication the process of naming are therefore fundamentally political, involving power relationships within and between groups. Thus, the historical controversy about what persons of African origins should be named and who should name them is also important, because deciding on the name helps to determine the identity and parameters of a group as well as how individuals understand who they are. Therefore, the names controversy in African-American history has always been part of the larger social, cultural, and political dynamics of AFRICAN-AMERICAN POLITICS.

The Atlantic slave trade brought to the United States individuals from various tribal or ETHNIC GROUPS. Initially these individuals identified with their particular ethnic groups. That is, these individuals thought of themselves not as a RACE and not as Africans but, rather, as members of discrete ethnic groups. Over time, however, the power of the slave system destroyed these ethnic identities and replaced them with a PAN-AFRICAN identity. That is, one of the effects of slavery was to de-ethnicize or detribalize the diverse peoples of Africa, transforming them into a single people who had to forge a new identity and a new name. Initially, these diverse peoples referred to themselves as Africans. For example, the earliest institutions used African in their names, as in the African Episcopal Church or the African Free School. African as used by this earliest TALENTED TENTH of the educated elite reflected a pride in their collective ethnic heritage. Among the politically conscious Africans, it also involved an ideological orientation because it reflected a rejection of "Negro" (the Spanish word for black) and "colored," names used by Europeans to distinguish themselves as white—the opposite of black. Europeans also early on used "nigger" as a derogatory adaptation of Negro.

An early illustration of the political and ideological uses of naming is that Africans began to avoid use of African after the establishment of the AMERICAN COLONIALIZA-TION SOCIETY in 1816. This organization of wealthy whites favored sending the FREE NEGROES back to Africa. Africans who were opposed to BACK-TO-AFRICA MOVEMENTS began to avoid using African because of concerns that it encouraged the idea that they belonged in Africa. After heated debate and controversy, *African* was gradually replaced by *colored,* although many other names were in use, including Ethiopian, Abyssinian, Negro, Nubian, and Bialian. But "colored," "colored American," or "free persons of color" by the late 1830s became the preferred name among the black LEADERSHIP, whether they were integrationists or nationalists or radicals or conservatives. For example, DAVID WALKER used it in the title of his famous radical appeal published in 1829, and FREDERICK DOUGLASS used it in his speeches and writings until his death, although he also used the word *Negro.*

By the turn of the century, *colored* began to lose its appeal and *Negro* began to gain ascendancy, although as late as 1909 the NAACP included the word *colored* in its name. BOOKER T. WASHINGTON, the most influential black leader during this period, favored *Negro* and lobbied the Census Bureau to adopt it, and many of the ORGANIZATIONS of black professionals and business people adopted its usage. W. E. B. DU BOIS, the leading black intellectual at the time, used *Negro* interchangeably with *colored* and *Afro-American; Negro* was popular with the more avant-garde elements during the HARLEM RENAISSANCE; and MARCUS GARVEY used it in the name of his organization, the UNIVERSAL NEGRO IMPROVEMENT ASSOCIATION. In 1919 the *Negro Yearbook* reported that "there is increasing use of the word 'Negro' and a decreasing use of the words 'colored' and 'Afro-American' to designate us as a people. The result is that 'Negro' is more and more acquiring a dignity that it did not have in the past." This dignity was enhanced when the NAACP led a successful effort to persuade the white MEDIA to capitalize the word. From the 1920s to 1960s, *Negro* became the name of choice, but throughout this period more militant and nationalistic black leaders, including ELIJAH MUHAMMAD and ADAM CLAYTON POWELL, rejected the name, calling it a "white man's word."

In the 1950s and 1960s, MALCOLM X forcefully called for the rejection of *Negro,* labeling its use "unenlightened, and objectionable or deliberately offensive whether in speech or writing." In part as a result of the growing influence of Malcolm's ideas and the philosophy of BLACK NATIONALISM in the 1960s, the name *BLACK* was adopted as part of the overall impact of the BLACK POWER MOVEMENT. Then, in the 1980s as the result of an initiative by JESSE JACKSON, the name *AFRICAN AMERICAN* became the preferred name among intellectuals and political leaders—black and white—although it was frequently used interchangeably with black. At the end of the 20th century,

Negro and *colored* were viewed as unacceptable names, while either *black* or *African American* were acceptable.

The several name changes of African peoples since their arrival in the United States reflect shifting psychological and power relations between blacks with respect to the power of names and naming. However, they have usually reflected little change in terms of the actual material conditions of the BLACK COMMUNITY because, as Du Bois wrote in a 1928 *Crisis* essay "The Name 'Negro,'" one should not make the error of mistaking names for things: "It is not the name—it's the thing that counts."

Further reading: Ruth Grant and Marion Orr, "Language, Race, and Politics: From Black to African American," *Politics and Society* 24 (1996): 137–52; Sterling Stuckey, "Identity and Ideology: The Names Controversy," chap. 4 in *Slave Culture: Foundations of Nationalist Theory* (New York: Oxford University Press, 1987).

National Association of Colored Women's Clubs

The National Association of Colored Women's Clubs (NACWC) is one of the oldest ORGANIZATIONS in the BLACK COMMUNITY. Founded in 1896 by Josephine St. Pierre, it merged the National Federation of Afro-American Women and the National League of Colored Women. Its purpose was to unite black women in the fight against LYNCHING and against racial DISCRIMINATION in education, employment, and in public places. It also focused on issues of special concern to black women, including the VOTING RIGHTS and improvements in health care and home life. Among its early leaders were MARY CHURCH TERRELL and IDA B. WELLS-BARNETT. The women's clubs did not embrace FEMINISM as an IDEOLOGY; rather they were concerned with promoting activities that advanced the interests of the RACE as a whole.

Although the women's clubs and its leaders have not been as active in AFRICAN-AMERICAN POLITICS as the NATIONAL COUNCIL OF NEGRO WOMEN and its leaders—MARY MCLEOD BETHUNE during the NEW DEAL and DOROTHY HEIGHT during the CIVIL RIGHTS MOVEMENT—in both periods it expanded its activities and programs to deal with problems of the depression and World War II, and it provided financial support for grassroots volunteers during the CIVIL RIGHTS MOVEMENT. In the POST–CIVIL RIGHTS ERA, it focused more systematically on women's issues, such as domestic violence, rape, welfare, women's health issues, and leadership training for young women. With a national office in the DISTRICT OF COLUMBIA, at the end of the 20th century the organization reported about 40,000 members in 39 states.

Further reading: Ericka Gordon, "A Layin' on of Hands: Black Women's Community Work and the National Association of Colored Women's Clubs" in *Black Political Organizations in the Post Civil Rights Era*, ed. Ollie Johnson and Karin Stanford (New Brunswick, N.J.: Rutger State University Press, 2002).

National Baptist Convention

The National Baptist Convention is recognized as the largest and one of the most important ORGANIZATIONS in the BLACK COMMUNITY. Religious institutions are also the oldest, autonomous, continuous institutions in the community, tracing their origins to the founding of the African Methodist Episcopal Church by RICHARD ALLEN in 1787. The BLACK CHURCH is recognized as the most important organization in black America because of its long history, because of its autonomy or relative independence from the influence of whites, and because of its roots in RELIGIOSITY, one of the most important values in African-American CULTURE. The church in black America, however, is not and never has been a single, monolithic entity; rather, the church in black America is constituted by thousands of autonomous churches organized into several autonomous associations.

The most important of these associations is the National Baptist Convention, U.S.A., which is frequently referred to as the largest black organization in the world. Founded in 1880, it is the parent organization of more than 30,000 black churches with approximately 7.5 million members. The National Baptist Convention, U.S.A., is often confused with the National Baptist Convention of America, which is the second-largest black organization in America. Founded in 1891, the National Baptist Convention of America is constituted by several thousand affiliated churches and an estimated 4.5 million persons. The founding of the two associations (or conventions) of black Baptists within a decade of each other reflects the dominant religious affiliation of African Americans and the tendency toward centrifugalism in the black-church tradition. Although the first autonomous black church established by Richard Allen in 1787 was affiliated with Episcopal Methodism, historically most blacks were affiliated with a Baptist church. Episcopal Methodism has a tradition of hierarchy and centralized authority, but the Baptist tradition is democratic, which facilitates the tendency toward centrifugalism. This tendency is reflected not only in the existence of these two conventions (and a third discussed below) but also in the jealously guarded autonomy of the thousands of affiliated churches. This centrifugalism has no doctrinal or programmatic bases. That is, both conventions share the same theology and rituals, are organized in a similar fashion, and have the same basic programs that involve education and evangelical work in the United States, Africa, and the Caribbean. The existence of these two conventions is therefore largely a function of the quest of church elites for separate arenas in which they can exercise power and authority. This is understandable in a context where talented blacks were excluded from the exercise of power and authority in most arenas of the larger society, including the POLITICAL SYSTEM. This also explains the large number of black Baptist churches. In some parts of the rural south, one finds a dozen black churches serving towns with a population of 1,000 black adults or fewer.

Although some black churches and clergymen played roles in the ABOLITIONIST MOVEMENT and the CIVIL RIGHTS MOVEMENT, most black churches and the organized conventions for most of their histories have been conservative, apolitical institutions or they practiced a politics of ACCOMMODATIONISM in the tradition of BOOKER T. WASHINGTON. This kind of politics has something of a theological basis in that black religiosity is focused more on preparing individuals for their personal salvation and redemption rather than attempting to change the conditions of the world. Politics and other worldly concerns were therefore to be avoided. While the National Baptist Convention, U.S.A., and the National Baptist Convention of America were conservative, accommodationist institutions, this was particularly the case for the Baptist Convention U.S.A.

During the Civil Rights movement, the Baptist Convention U.S.A. was under the autocratic leadership of J. H. Jackson, a Chicago clergyman, who held the convention's presidency for decades based on the support of a network of rural pastors and their congregations in the SOUTHERN STATES. Jackson was one of the few members of the black LEADERSHIP to actively oppose the Civil Rights movement, and since he dominated the convention, the effect was to depress church participation in the movement, especially in the rural parts of the South. Jackson was an especially bitter rival, personally and ideologically, of MARTIN LUTHER KING JR. as his stature as the movement's leader grew. (King's father—Martin Luther King Sr.—was one of the leading clergymen in the convention.) In 1961 the rivalry between Jackson and King reached a turning point, and King withdrew from the organization and—along with a group of largely urban, well-educated preachers—formed a third Baptist convention, the Progressive Baptist Convention. This new convention now includes more than 2,000 churches and an estimated 1.9 million members. While it resembles the other conventions in doctrines, rituals, and programs, from its inception it included a program of POLITICAL PARTICIPATION and civil rights activism. Meanwhile Rev. J. H. Jackson's CONSERVATISM persisted into the POST–CIVIL RIGHTS ERA, as indicated by his endorsement of RONALD REAGAN during the 1980 presidential election. Two years later, Jackson was finally ousted as the convention president. He was replaced by T. J. Jemison, a friend of Martin Luther King Jr. and a longtime activist in the Civil Rights movement. (Jemison had led a bus boycott in Baton Rouge, Louisiana, his home town, a couple of years before the MONTGOMERY BUS BOYCOTT.) Under Jemison's leadership the convention abandoned Jackson's conservatism and began to become more actively involved in politics, encouraging its affiliate churches, for example, to hold rallies, raise money, and register voters for JESSE JACKSON's 1984 PRESIDENTIAL CAMPAIGN.

At the end of the 20th century, the three Baptist conventions were more actively involved in politics as well as economic development and social welfare activities than at any time before in their histories. However, most of the thousands of churches, while no longer conservative apolitical institutions, were still, as to be expected, mainly involved in religious matters and evangelical and missionary work.

Further reading: Eric C. Lincoln and Lawrence Mamiya, *The Black Church in America* (Durham, N.C.: Duke University Press, 1990).

National Black Election Study

The National Black Election Study (NBES) is the largest national survey of PUBLIC OPINION dealing specifically with the attitudes, beliefs, and behavior of African Americans. The NBES was conducted in 1984 and 1988 in response to JESSE JACKSON's PRESIDENTIAL CAMPAIGNS. Prior to the NBES there had been no surveys of black opinion with sample sizes large enough to permit statistically accurate generalizations about the black POPULATION or to conduct detailed intraracial analyses of opinion differences within the BLACK COMMUNITY, such as those based on gender, age, class, region, or religion. Prior to the NBES, most national surveys of opinion included too few blacks (usually fewer than 200) to permit valid and reliable generalizations about black public opinion. Thus, the NBES is a unique and innovative contribution to the study of AFRICAN-AMERICAN POLITICS. The survey was conducted by the Program for Research on Black Americans at the Institute for Social Research at the University of Michigan, which is the leading institution for the academic study of public opinion in the United States. Its Program for Research on Black Americans had conducted several surveys of black opinion, but the NBES was its first directed specifically to the study of political opinion.

The catalyst for the study was Jesse Jackson's two campaigns for president, which symbolized the heightened visibility and participation of blacks in politics. As a result, a team of black scholars at the University of Michigan led by Professor James Jackson, director of the Program for Research on Black Americans, designed the NBES and secured funding from several major American foundations.

An advisory board of leading scholars in survey research and African-American politics assisted in the design of the survey questionnaire. The NBES surveys in 1984 and 1988 were panel studies (that is, the same people were interviewed on two different occasions) in which samples of more than 1,000 blacks were interviewed before and after the November elections. The basic design and many of the questions in the NBES were modeled after the University of Michigan's National Election Study, which has been used to study national elections since 1952. However, it also contains questions of special relevance to black politics, such as measures of racial identification, consciousness, and solidarity and attitudes toward the Jackson presidential campaigns.

Dozens of scholarly papers and articles were published based on the NBES, and three major books by African-American political scientists were published: Patricia Gurin, Shirley Hatchett, and James Jackson, *Hope and Independence: Black Response to Electoral Politics* (1985); Michael Dawson, *Behind the Mule: Race and Class in American Politics* (1994); and Katherine Tate, *From Protest to Politics: The New Black Voters in American Elections* (1994). These studies made important contributions to understanding mass attitudes, beliefs, and behavior in African-American politics, and the NBES is likely to be used by scholars of black politics for a long time.

Since the first NBES was conducted, the National Opinion Research Center at the University of Chicago has routinely included large oversamples of blacks in its biannual General Social Survey, and polls by the major national news MEDIA will sometimes oversample blacks on racially salient issues such as the O. J. Simpson case (involving the murder of the white spouse and her companion by a celebrity black athlete), the RODNEY KING case, and African-American responses to the 2000 presidential election in which opinion divided sharply on racial lines. But the NBES remains the pioneering effort in the systematic study of black political attitudes and behavior.

National Black Leadership Roundtable

The National Black Leadership Roundtable (NBLR) was a COALITION of the heads of about 300 national black ORGANIZATIONS. It was formed in 1978 under the auspices of the CONGRESSIONAL BLACK CAUCUS. The purpose of the roundtable was to bring together the leaders of all the major national black organizations—religious, fraternal, professional, business, civic, labor, civil rights, and political—to develop a consensus BLACK AGENDA and a strategic plan and the resources to implement it on a long-term basis.

The leading figure in organizing NBLR and in developing the agenda and strategic plan was Walter Fauntroy, the congressman from the DISTRICT OF COLUMBIA. The group did develop an agenda and plan called *The Black Leadership Family Program for the Survival and Progress of the Black Nation*, which was published in 1982. The plan was an innovative, comprehensive program of SELF-HELP and progressive PUBLIC POLICY initiatives. But NBLR was not able to raise the funds and other resources necessary to implement it.

A principal aim of the roundtable was to create an organization completely funded by the resources of the BLACK COMMUNITY so that it might be able, unlike other black organizations, to freely pursue its agenda without having to worry about offending white patrons. While the group had some early successes in raising money, it was not able to sustain these efforts, and in 1991 it ceased operations. Although Fauntroy attempted to revive the group in 2000, the reality was that the national black LEADERSHIP at the end of the 20th century apparently lacked the wherewithal, even when it pooled its collective resources, to sustain an independent black organization pursuing an independent black agenda.

Further reading: *The Black Leadership Family Program for the Survival and Progress of the Black Nation* (Washington, D.C.: Congressional Black Caucus, 1982); Ronald Walters and Robert C. Smith, "The National Black Leadership Roundtable," in *African American Leadership* (Albany: SUNY Press, 1999).

National Black Political Convention

In 1972 the African-American LEADERSHIP for the third time in history tried to establish a grand COALITION uniting the various ideological factions of the BLACK COMMUNITY in a common political structure. The purpose of this structure was to develop a consensus BLACK AGENDA to deal with the problems confronting the community.

Like the previous conventions or congresses of this type, the 1972 convention soon collapsed as a result of rancorous conflicts over IDEOLOGY among the various factions of the leadership. The CONGRESSIONAL BLACK CAUCUS was the official convener of the 1972 convention, which met in Gary, Indiana. In its statement calling the convention, the caucus said, "It is to be held for the purpose of developing a national black agenda and the crystallization of a national black strategy for 1972 and beyond." The statement also said that the convention would be "open to all people regardless of party affiliation or ideology, to reflect the full diversity of interests of 25 million blacks." The co-conveners of the convention were AMIRI BARAKA, a leading spokesman for BLACK NATIONALISM; Congressman CHARLES DIGGS, chair of the Congressional Black Caucus; and RICHARD HATCHER, the mayor of Gary. The 3,000 delegates attending the convention represented the full diversity of black ideologies—nationalists and integrationists, conservatives and communists, and Republicans and Democrats. However, most of the leaders of the civil rights organizations were skeptical or opposed to the convention. ROY WILKINS, head of the NAACP, denounced the convention as "separatist" and "radical." The convention in fact adopted a radical, nationalist platform that was quickly disavowed by the Congressional Black Caucus, most black ELECTED OFFICIALS, and the heads of the major civil rights organizations. This led Baraka to describe members of the caucus and the other critics of the platform as UNCLE TOMS.

By the time the convention met for a second time in 1974, most of the members of the caucus (including Diggs, the co-convener) and the elected officials had dropped out, leaving this second meeting largely a gathering of nationalists and radicals. This made for greater ideological unity, but then in 1975 Baraka abruptly announced he was changing his ideology from black nationalism—specifically from CULTURAL NATIONALISM and PAN-AFRICANISM—to COMMUNISM. Shortly thereafter Baraka was dismissed from his leadership position in the convention. In 1980 the convention created a THIRD PARTY, the National Black Independent Political Party, but in 1984 this party fell apart in a dispute over whether it should endorse JESSE JACKSON for president, a position supported by the black nationalists in the party but bitterly opposed by the black marxists in the party who were associated with the white-dominated Socialist Worker Party.

See also CONVENTION MOVEMENT.

Further reading: Robert C. Smith, "The National Black Political Convention, 1972–84," in *We Have No Leaders: African Americans in the Post Civil Rights Era* (Albany: State University of New York Press, 1996).

National Conference of Black Political Scientists

The National Conference of Black Political Scientists (NCOBPS) is the professional organization devoted to the scholarly study of African-American politics in the United States. Founded in 1969, NCOBPS is an outgrowth of the 1960s BLACK POWER MOVEMENT and its concerns with RADICALISM, BLACK NATIONALISM, and independent black ORGANIZATION. It also is a reflection of the growth in the number of professional political scientists that started in the late 1960s and their disenchantment with the traditions of the discipline and the largely white American Political Science Association (APSA). Many of these young scholars viewed the traditions of the discipline and the APSA as conservative and status-quo oriented, more concerned with the maintenance of the POLITICAL SYSTEM than addressing problems of RACISM and WHITE SUPREMACY. Thus, the organizers wanted to create an organization that would in its epistemologies, the-

ories, methodologies, and pedagogies be committed to the "liberation of African people," to use the words of the groups's founding motto. Individual members of NCOBPS embrace a wide range of ideologies, but the organization institutionally from its inception has been committed to the philosophy of black power and to a radical analysis and interpretation of American society and politics. Although not racially or professionally exclusive, most of the group's members are black and academic political scientists at colleges and universities. The conference, with 150–200 members, holds an annual scholarly conference and publishes a newsletter and the journal *National Political Science Review*.

See also JONES, MACK; PRESTAGE, JEWEL.

National Council of Negro Women

The National Council of Negro Women (NCNW) is one of the leading civic ORGANIZATIONS of African-American Women. It was founded in 1935 by MARY MCLEOD BETHUNE as a "superorganization" or COALITION of black women's groups. Its purpose was to enhance the solidarity and thereby the POWER of black women in national politics. As Bethune put it "The result of such an organization will . . . make for unity of opinion among Negro women who do some thinking on public questions; it will insure greater cooperation among women in varied lines of endeavor; and it will lift the ideas not only of individual organizations but of the organizations as a group."

Although Bethune's idea of an umbrella organization (with her as its leader) was met with skepticism by MARY CHURCH TERRELL, IDA WELLS-BARNETT, and the NATIONAL ASSOCIATION OF COLORED WOMEN, Bethune's prestige and influence eventually overcame their doubts. The NCNW was somewhat successful in its advocacy and projects in its first decade or so, largely because of the presence of Bethune. But in the 1940s, Bethune was investigated by the FBI as an alleged subversive. Although the allegations were unfounded, this and other instances of POLITICAL REPRESSION diminished her and the council's status. In 1949 Bethune resigned as NCNW president. Eventually the council recovered some of its stature under the leadership of DOROTHY HEIGHT. Height, for example, during the 1950s and 1960s was recognized as the leading woman in the black LEADERSHIP establishment, but this recognition was largely symbolic because her role in the deliberations of the leadership was largely token. Lacking the clout of Bethune, Height could do little to alter the exclusionary practices of the male leaders, which were based on the prevailing SEXISM of the time. (An example of this sexism was the exclusion of Height from the list of speakers at the 1963 MARCH ON WASHINGTON.)

In the POST–CIVIL RIGHTS ERA NCNW continued its advocacy on CIVIL RIGHTS and issues of concern to women and children, but as FEMINISM began to play a larger role in American and African-American politics, the council was challenged by new female leaders and organizations for the status of the leading woman's organization in black politics. At the beginning of the 21st century the council, under new leadership, was attempting to reclaim its place as the preeminent organization of black women in politics, but its aspirations to be the superorganization of black women were no longer realistic.

See also NATIONAL POLITICAL CONGRESS OF BLACK WOMEN.

National Negro Congress

The National Negro Congress that was convened in the 1930s was the second manifestation of the Sisyphian struggle of African Americans for an organizational expression of racial solidarity in a CONVENTION MOVEMENT that would transcend divisions of IDEOLOGY. The first manifestation of this movement was in the NATIONAL NEGRO CONVENTIONS that met starting in 1830, and the last was the 1972 NATIONAL BLACK POLITICAL CONVENTION. The idea of black solidarity or unity is almost as old as the organized black FREEDOM struggle in the United States. In 1838 Rev. Lewis Woodson, who wrote under the pseudonym Augustine and who, along with MARTIN DELANY, is sometimes referred to as the "father of BLACK NATIONALISM," wrote:

> We should form an institution that will bring the most distant and detached portions of our people together, embrace their varied interests and unite their whole moral power. Our collected wisdom should be assembled, to consult on measures pertaining to the general welfare, and so direct our energies, as to do the greatest good for the greatest number. Thus, united and thus directed, every weapon that prejudice has formed against us, would be rendered powerless; and our moral elevation would be rapid, as it would be certain.

This idea of black unity in a national convention was expressed for the second time in AFRICAN-AMERICAN POLITICS in the National Negro Congress. In 1935 the Social Science Division of HOWARD UNIVERSITY led by RALPH BUNCHE held a conference of the black LEADERSHIP to discuss the situation of African Americans in the midst of the ongoing depression and the impact of the NEW DEAL in addressing the problems faced by the BLACK COMMUNITY. After the conference Bunche and several other leaders met at his home and concluded that the situation required the calling of a national congress to deal with the problems discussed at the conference and to develop a BLACK AGENDA to act on them.

The congress convened in Chicago under the leadership of A. PHILIP RANDOLPH. According to the call of the con-

vention, "Let's Build a National Negro Congress," the congress was to be a united front of all blacks without respect to ideology, and it was to develop a "minimum program of action upon which all could agree." But this was not possible because the delegates at the congress included all the various ideological factions of the black community—liberals and conservatives, Democrats and Republicans, communists and black nationalists—as well as a large contingent of white members of the COMMUNIST PARTY. The RADICALISM of the congress and the participation of whites led to opposition from many blacks. Black preachers, businessmen, professionals, and civil rights leaders (including W. E. B. DU BOIS) opposed the congress because it included communists. Black nationalists opposed it because it included whites. Historians of the congress agree that it had some success as a LOBBYING presence in Washington and was quite effective in organizing blacks at the local level around issues of jobs, housing, and police brutality. However, the ideological and racial conflicts within the congress were too great for it to survive, and the congress met only three times before it collapsed.

At the 1940 meeting, Randolph and most of the blacks who were not communists withdrew, arguing that the congress had been taken over by the Communist Party. Randolph, who in 1935 had vigorously defended the right of whites and communists to be a part of the congress now said, "The large number of white delegates at the Congress make it look like a joke. Why should a Negro Congress have white people in it? Why should Communists have a position of control? . . . The American Negro will not long follow any organization which accepts direction and control from any white organization." Randolph, after leaving the congress, went on to form the MARCH ON WASHINGTON MOVEMENT, which had some success in pressuring President FRANKLIN D. ROOSEVELT to issue an executive order banning racial DISCRIMINATION in wartime industries. This movement, unlike the congress, was not open to whites.

Further reading: Lawrence Wittner, "The National Negro Congress: A Reassessment," *American Quarterly* 22 (1968): 883–90.

National Negro Convention

The National Negro Convention, which first convened in 1830 under the leadership of RICHARD ALLEN, was the most successful of the three efforts by the African-American LEADERSHIP to form a grand COALITION uniting all the major ideological factions in the BLACK COMMUNITY. The Negro Convention, which met off and on from 1830 to 1864, was the most successful because it lasted longer than the subsequent ones in the 1930s and 1970s.

The 1830 convention, like the subsequent ones, included all the major ideological tendencies in AFRICAN-

AMERICAN POLITICS—conservatives and radicals, integrationists and nationalists, nonviolent "moral suasionists" and advocates of VIOLENCE. It attracted the leading blacks of the time, including FREDERICK DOUGLASS, MARTIN DELANY, and HENRY HIGHLAND GARNETT. These diverse personalities and ideologies were a source of the convention's strength, but they were also a source of its weakness and its ultimate collapse, because differences over IDEOLOGY made it difficult for the conventions to reach agreement on a consensus BLACK AGENDA. Delany and his followers favored emigration and BACK-TO-AFRICA MOVEMENTS. Douglass was a leader in the ABOLITIONIST MOVEMENT and favored INTEGRATIONISM. Douglass favored nonviolence and moral suasion, while Garnett called for violent SLAVE REVOLTS. In addition to these differences over ideology and strategy, there were other, continuing disagreements, including the NAMES CONTROVERSY over what the RACE should be called—African, Colored American, Negro, Oppressed Americans; debates over the merits of building separate black community institutions such as schools, newspapers, and businesses; and arguments over whether whites should be allowed to participate in the convention. (Whites were included for a time, but eventually the convention voted to exclude them on the basis of the principles of BLACK NATIONALISM.) There were also class and institutional conflicts between the middle-class black establishment of ministers, teachers, and businesspeople, who tended toward conservatism and integration, and the more radical, less-well-off persons who tended toward RADICALISM and emigration.

In 1854 the radical emmigrationists formed their own convention and began to develop plans for emigration to HAITI and other places outside of the United States. Douglass condemned the emigration convention as providing "proof to the enemies of the Negro that they were divided in thought and plans," but by 1854 the division were plain for all to see. The Negro Convention could not survive them and it dissolved, although it reconvened one last time in 1864 after the CIVIL WAR to develop plans for RECONSTRUCTION.

Further reading: Howard Bell, "National Negro Conventions of the 1840s: Moral Suasion vs. Political Action," *Journal of Negro History* 22 (1957): 247–60; Bella Gross, "The First National Negro Convention," *Journal of Negro History* 31 (1966): 435–43.

National Political Congress of Black Women

The National Political Congress of Black Women was organized in 1984. Its organizing was a product of the growing influence of FEMINISM in AFRICAN-AMERICAN POLITICS and the reaction of black women in the DEMO-CRATIC PARTY to the response of white women to JESSE JACKSON's 1984 PRESIDENTIAL CAMPAIGN. By the mid-1980s mainstream black women political leaders were fully embracing the agenda of the modern feminist movement, but many felt that the National Organization for Women (NOW) and the other largely white feminist organizations were insensitive to their concerns about RACISM and the IDEOLOGY of WHITE SUPREMACY. The perceived insensitivity of white feminist leaders to issues of concern to blacks was reinforced when the leaders of NOW and other white feminist organizations endorsed Walter Mondale rather than Jesse Jackson for the Democratic Party's presidential nomination. Since Jackson had been much more outspoken on feminist issues than Mondale, some black women felt betrayed when his candidacy was not supported by white feminist leaders, and some attributed the Mondale endorsement to racism. Therefore, shortly after the 1984 Democratic Party Convention, several prominent black female political leaders, including several members of the CONGRESSIONAL BLACK CAUCUS and former congresswoman and presidential candidate SHIRLEY CHISHOLM announced formation of the Congress for Black Women in Politics. Although most of the founders were members of the Democratic Party, the group sought to include women from the REPUBLICAN PARTY in a bipartisan COALITION.

The main purpose of the congress is to raise the visibility of black women in national politics and to focus on issues of PUBLIC POLICY that are of concern to them. Among the first initiatives of the group was a statement in support of abortion rights in 1986, one of the first such statements by an African-American women's organization. The major activity of the congress, however has been to assist black women in their campaigns for political offices and obtaining appointments in the BUREAUCRACY. But its founding president, C. Delores Tucker, also gained recognition for her campaign against the vulgar and misogynistic lyrics in some RAP MUSIC, which she claimed degraded black women.

National Urban League   See URBAN LEAGUE.

National Welfare Rights Organization

The National Welfare Rights Organization (NWRO) was formed in 1967 in order, according to its founding resolution, to promote the goals of "decent jobs with adequate pay for those who can work, and adequate income for those who cannot." NWRO, composed largely of African-American women who were welfare recipients, was the first ORGANIZATION in AFRICAN-AMERICAN POLITICS devoted exclusively to the interests of poor black women and their children. NWRO was the organizational manifestation of a SOCIAL MOVEMENT whose goal was to establish "welfare" as a right (welfare understood here as cash and related assistance to families where the head of the household is unable to work or cannot find work with adequate wages).

The movement and the organization was a direct outgrowth of the CIVIL RIGHTS MOVEMENT and the GREAT SOCIETY. After the passage of the laws in the 1960s ending legalized RACISM and SEGREGATION, the Civil Rights movement turned its attention to POVERTY among African Americans especially as is manifested in the GHETTOS. This shift in the movement's focus naturally resulted in attention to the problem of unemployment and the problem of welfare dependency among black women. The unemployment rate among blacks, particularly black males, was disproportionately high, and single black women were disproportionately recipients of welfare (officially referred to as Aid to Families with Dependent Children because the aid was provided to children defined as dependent on the basis of the absence of a working parent, usually the father). These concerns led MARTIN LUTHER KING JR. in his last years to organize a POOR PEOPLE'S CAMPAIGN, a series of PROTESTS in Washington demanding either a guaranteed job or income. These concerns also led to the emergence of the welfare rights movement and the establishment of the National Welfare Rights Organization. They also helped to shape aspects of President LYNDON B. JOHNSON's Great Society. Among the several components of the Great Society was the WAR ON POVERTY, which itself was an outgrowth of the Civil Rights movement. President Johnson and his advisers recognized that after passage of the civil rights laws, full FREEDOM and EQUALITY required an attack on poverty in the ghettos and in the rural parts of the SOUTHERN STATES. They also concluded that poor people themselves should be part of the war on poverty. Therefore, they encouraged the organizing and the participation of the poor in the various antipoverty programs.

NWRO was partly a product of these antipoverty initiatives of the federal government. Many local welfare rights chapters were organized by government-sponsored VISTA (Volunteers in Service to America) workers; Great Society-funded lawyers brought LITIGATION on behalf of the rights of welfare recipients; and NWRO in 1968 was the direct recipient of a $400,000 grant from the U.S. Department of Labor. The organization and organizing strategy of NWRO was also directly influenced by the strategic use of knowledge. In 1965 FRANCES FOX PIVEN, a white political scientist, and her colleague Richard Cloward circulated a paper among civil rights and antipoverty activists entitled "Mobilizing the Poor: How It Can Be Done." This paper, which was later published in *The Nation*, called on activists to start a movement to expand the rights of welfare recipients. Although the founders of

NWRO did not follow the exact strategy proposed by Piven and Cloward (which emphasized mobilizing the nonwelfare poor to get welfare benefits rather than organizing existing recipients), their paper and their active participation in strategy development played important roles in the formation of the organization.

Between 1967 and 1975 (when NWRO formally ceased operation), NWRO mobilized an extensive network of over 100 local chapters and more than 10,000 members, who filed lawsuits and engaged in numerous protest demonstrations at welfare offices, state legislatures, and in Washington. Most of its leaders were black women—Johnnie Tillman of California, Beulah Sanders of New York, and Annie Smart of Los Angeles—but the executive director was George Wiley, a former leader of CORE who had left that group because of his disenchantment with its embrace of the BLACK POWER MOVEMENT. In its several years NWRO was effective in increasing the number of welfare recipients and expanding benefits. It also enhanced the image of welfare recipients among themselves and was responsible for helping to establish a recipient's right to privacy. It also helped in the elimination of state residency requirements for welfare recipients and in the establishment of due process procedures for the termination of benefits. But, ironically, perhaps its major achievement was contributing to the defeat of legislation that would have guaranteed an income to poor, working families. In 1969 President RICHARD NIXON proposed abolishing welfare (AFDC) and replacing it with the Family Assistance Plan, which guaranteed a family of four an income of $1,600. The plan also required all applicants for benefits who were employable to register with local employment offices and accept either a job or job training or lose a portion of the income guaranteed by the plan. The House of Representatives passed the plan 243 to 145, and it was expected that it would also pass the Senate, which was then more liberal than the House. NWRO, however, engaged in a vigorous LOBBYING campaign against the plan because it considered the $1,600 benefit level too low and the work requirement punitive. Because of NWRO opposition, the CONGRESSIONAL BLACK CAUCUS, the URBAN LEAGUE, and other black and liberal groups who had initially supported the plan withdrew their support. In part as a result of NWRO opposition, the plan died in the Senate without ever coming to a vote. This was a bittersweet victory for NWRO because it contributed to the defeat of the first piece of legislation in American history that would have guaranteed an income or a job to all American families.

By 1975 the tide had turned against the movement for welfare rights. The government formally ended the war on poverty; energies and resources for mobilizing the poor withered away; and the climate of PUBLIC OPINION never was favorable toward welfare. Welfare recipients and welfare rights became increasingly unpopular as CONSERVATISM began to replace LIBERALISM as the dominant IDEOLOGY in American politics. In this context, in 1975 NWRO ceased operations. In 1987, after several failed attempts, the organization was reestablished as the National Welfare Rights Union (NWRU). However, it never equaled NWRO in its size or influence on PUBLIC POLICY. In 1996 President BILL CLINTON signed legislation that ended the 60-year AFDC program by limiting welfare benefits to five years and requiring all employable recipients to work. This new law in effect eliminated the limited right to welfare that had been guaranteed to poor women and their children since the NEW DEAL established the American WELFARE STATE. NWRU played hardly any role in the debate on this legislation.

The idea of welfare as a right poses a fundamental challenge to INDIVIDUALISM and classical LIBERALISM, core values of the American culture and POLITICAL SYSTEM. These values delayed the development of the American welfare state and limited its scope. Historically, the American welfare state was limited in its development during the New Deal by WHITE SUPREMACY, racism, and SEXISM. Therefore, the odds against the welfare rights movement were enormous because it was a movement of poor black women challenging core values of the culture and the political system.

Further reading: Todd Shaw, "We Refused to Lay Down Our Spears: The Persistence of Welfare Rights Activism, 1966–1976" in *Black Political Organizations in the Post Civil Rights Era*, ed. Ollie Johnson and Karin Stanford (New Brunswick, N.J.: Rutgers State University Press, 2002).

Nation of Islam (Black Muslims)

The Nation of Islam, referred to sometimes as the Black Muslims, is the most influential black nationalist ORGANIZATION in the history of the United States. Although MARCUS GARVEY's organization, the UNIVERSAL NEGRO IMPROVEMENT ASSOCIATION (UNIA) in the 1920s was larger and more influential during its heyday, with the deportation of Garvey and his subsequent death in exile, the UNIA as an effective organization collapsed. (Although UNIA influenced the development of the philosophy of BLACK NATIONALISM in the United States and elsewhere throughout the 20th century.) In contrast, the Nation of Islam has endured from its founding in the 1930s into the 21st century, exerting an important influence on AFRICAN-AMERICAN POLITICS and on the spread of Islam in the BLACK COMMUNITY.

The Nation of Islam was founded in Detroit around 1930 by Wallace D. Fard (or "Farraad"). Little is known about Fard; he may have been white or Pakistani, but in the 1930s while selling silk door to door in the Detroit GHETTO he began to teach an eclectic message that became the philosophy and theology of the Nation of Islam. The philosophy was rooted in many of the traditional tenets of black nationalism, but Fard added an important theological element that rejected Christianity and proclaimed Islam the true religion of the black man in America. The central organizing theological tenet of the Nation of Islam as taught by Fard is the "myth of Yacub," an AFROCENTRIC interpretation of the origins of man in which Yacub, a mad black scientist in rebellion against God (Allah), creates the white man out of the original black man. This grafted white man lacks humanity; he is the "human beast" or the "blue-eyed devil" whose civilization is destined to perish. Therefore, the black man should reject the doomed white devil's religion, Christianity, and embrace Islam, which Fard taught was the black man's religion by "nature." In teaching this theology, Fard relied on the Bible as well as ideas from Garvey's movement and earlier black Islamic sects, but the core of the nation's theology is rooted in this myth of Yacub.

In his brief stay in Detroit, Fard attracted a small following, established a temple, a school, a training corps for women, and the Fruit of Islam, a paramilitary unit. He also wrote two texts for the propagation of the faith, *The Secret Rituals of the Nation of Islam* and *Teachings for a Lost-Found Nation of Islam in a Mathematical Way*. And then in 1934 he disappeared. What happened to him remains a mystery. The Detroit police had investigated his possible involvement in the killing of a member of the Nation of Islam, and the forerunner of the FBI viewed him as a subversive. Therefore, his disappearance may have been related to these concerns, but it also may have been because of internal infighting within the Nation.

In any case, prior to his departure he designated ELIJAH MUHAMMAD as the temple's leader. Until his death in 1975, Muhammad led the Nation of Islam, eventually making it the most powerful black nationalist and Islamic organization in the United States. In the process of building the Nation on the foundations of Fard's teachings and writings, Muhammad defined him as a prophet or as Allah himself— the Great Mahdi of the Muslims—and February 26, Fard's birthday, is celebrated in an annual Savior's Day program. In addition to its adherence to Fard's proto-Islamic theology and his philosophy of racial separatism, the Nation of Islam enforced strict moral codes regarding sexuality, family, diet, dress, and alcohol and drug use. It also attempted to create some of the components of a nation-state, including a flag, anthem, and a militia. The longtime aspiration of the Nation of Islam was a separate, independent black nation, but this was to be achieved through the divine intervention of Allah rather than political activism. Thus, although the Nation was committed to RADICALISM, it was a rhetorical commitment.

In practice the Nation was a conservative organization, practicing ACCOMMODATIONISM, SELF-HELP, and small-scale CAPITALISM. With the help of MALCOLM X, the Nation grew rapidly during the 1950s and 1960s, with an estimated membership in 1970 of 10,000–20,000, more than 100 hundred temples or mosques, several farms, and dozens of small businesses. Its weekly newspaper was widely circulated in the black community, and its net worth was estimated at $100 million.

While the Nation of Islam in the 1960s became a prosperous organization and an effective vehicle for the spread of the philosophical tenets of black nationalism and some of the theological tenets of Islam, throughout this period it also remained a conservative organization, refraining from participation in American politics and the CIVIL RIGHTS MOVEMENT. Nevertheless, its reputation for radicalism and MILITANCY grew largely as a result of the unrelenting rhetorical attacks of Malcolm X and other ministers on whites, WHITE SUPREMACY, and RACISM. One of the reasons that Malcolm X left the Nation in 1963 was because he wanted to move beyond rhetorical militancy toward active involvement in the Civil Rights movement.

Elijah Muhammad died in 1975, leaving his son Wallace D. Muhammad as his designated successor. Within months of assuming leadership, Wallace (renamed Warith) renounced the Nation's theology; declared that neither Fard nor his father was a prophet or messenger of Allah; and fully embraced the principles of Orthodox Islam and the IDEOLOGY of INTEGRATIONISM. The Nation of Islam under Warith was renamed the World Community of Islam in the West and, later, the AMERICAN MUSLIM MISSION. Warith was eventually recognized throughout the Muslim world as a legitimate religious leader. At the end of the 20th century, Warith, by some estimates, had a following of more than 1 million.

Meanwhile, LOUIS FARRAKHAN in the late 1970s reorganized and revitalized the Nation of Islam on the bases of the traditional teachings of Fard and Muhammad. However, in the late 1980s even Farrakhan abandoned the Nation's traditional teachings on nonparticipation in American politics, and in 2000 he appeared to renounce the traditional theology of the Nation and, like Warith, to embrace Orthodox Islam. Although this signaled a major shift in doctrine and practice, it was an ambivalent one, since Farrakhan continued to describe Fard and Muhammad as messengers of Allah. Nevertheless, by 2000 there appeared to have been a major reconciliation between the factions of Islam in America led by Farrakhan and Warith Muhammad, with Warith appearing with Farrakhan as guest of honor at the Nation's 2000 Savior's Day celebration.

See also MILLION MAN MARCH.

Further reading: Eric C. Lincoln, *The Black Muslims in America* (Boston: Beacon Press, 1968); Richard B. Turner,

Islam in the African American Experience (Bloomington: Indiana University Press, 1997).

natural rights

The concept of natural rights is an idea that emerges out of the SOCIAL-CONTRACT THEORY that constitutes the philosophical basis of the DECLARATION OF INDEPENDENCE and the CONSTITUTION. The contract theory assumes the existence of a "state of nature" that preexists the formation of governments. In this prepolitical state, people are governed by the "laws of nature" and have complete FREEDOM and EQUALITY. At some point, the theory assumes that some people chose to give up some of their freedoms in exchange for the security and protection of government, but in doing so they retained their natural rights or those fundamental rights of men preexisting government. THOMAS JEFFERSON refers to these rights in the Declaration as those that are "inalienable"; that are conferred on all men by their creator and among which are "life, liberty and the pursuit of happiness."

Natural rights are distinguished from CIVIL RIGHTS. The latter may be conferred on *some* people by governments while the former are conferred on all men by God. (The reference is to men specifically.) John Dickinson, a contemporary of Jefferson's, wrote of natural rights, "we claim them from a higher source—from the king of kings, and Lord of all the earth. They are not annexed to us by parchments and seals. They are created in us by decrees of Providence, which establish the laws of nature. They are born with us; exist within us; and cannot be taken away from us by any human power without taking our lives." At a minimum, these natural rights include the right to one's life, freedom, and property. Although not just property in the narrow sense of land or wealth but, rather, as James Madison put it, "A man has property in his opinions, and in the profession and practices dictated by them. He has property very dear to him in the safety and liberty of his person. He has equal property in the free use of his facilities and free choice of the objects on which to employ them. In a word, as a man is said to have a right to his property, he may be equally said to have a property in his rights." These natural rights or freedoms are distinguished from civil rights (sometimes referred to as positive rights) such as the right to vote or hold office or the right to an education or access to places of public accommodation.

The framers of the American government in the Declaration advanced the idea of the natural rights of all men but rejected it in the social contract—the Constitution—creating the government. They did so by sanctioning SLAVERY, which in its very essence is a denial of natural rights. Indeed, they insulted the humanity of Africans by transforming them constitutionally into fractions of men and making them the property (in all senses of the word as used by Madison in the passage quoted above) of whites. It was to take the CIVIL WAR and adoption of the THIRTEENTH AMENDMENT and then the FOURTEENTH AMENDMENT before the Constitution recognized the humanity and natural rights of Africans.

The idea of natural rights was a prominent feature in AFRICAN-AMERICAN THOUGHT from its beginnings. In 1829, for example, Robert Young in *The Ethiopian Manifesto Issued in Defense of the Black Man's Right to the Scale of Universal Freedom* (one of the earliest documents in black thought) wrote of the natural rights of Africans because they were "born free of the will of God." It should be clear, however, that the recognition of the natural rights of Africans does not necessarily involve the recognition of their civil rights. ABRAHAM LINCOLN throughout his career opposed slavery because it was a violation of natural rights, but he also opposed civil rights for Africans, including the right to vote and hold office. And during the CIVIL RIGHTS MOVEMENT, some adherents of CONSERVATISM including BARRY GOLDWATER and RONALD REAGAN opposed civil rights laws, partly because they thought such laws violated the natural rights to liberty and property of those whites who believed in WHITE SUPREMACY or wished to practice RACISM.

See also THREE-FIFTHS CLAUSE.

negritude

Negritude is a literary and philosophical concept and movement that rejects INTERNAL INFERIORIZATION and seeks to establish and vindicate the values of BLACKNESS. The concept can be traced to AFRICAN-AMERICAN THOUGHT in the classical writings of MARTIN DELANY, EDWARD WILMOT BLYDEN, and W. E. B. DU BOIS. Elements of the concept were also used by MARCUS GARVEY and were part of the HARLEM RENAISSANCE. However, the term itself was first used by intellectuals in the French colonies of Africa and the Caribbean, including Léopold Senghor, Lean Damas, and Aimé Césaire. Césaire used it first in his long 1939 poem *"Cahier d'un retour au pays natal"* (translated as *Return to My Native Country*) to refer to a collective consciousness and identity of Africans created as a result of the common experience of OPPRESSION by Europeans, whether as a result of SLAVERY or COLONIALISM. Senghor, on the other hand, used it to refer to a kind of racial essentialism, arguing there was a core or essence of "blackness" that pre-existed and transcended contact with Europeans and that perhaps had a biological basis. Both formulations, however, valorize African or black culture. Both also demonstrate the significance of PAN-AFRICANISM as an IDEOLOGY and movement. This is because negritude has its roots in African-American thought and CULTURE.

In the 1960s, the concept of negritude and its use by Césaire and other WEST INDIANS influenced the development in the United States of the BLACK POWER MOVEMENT and its emphasis on the name BLACK and the vindication of blackness, as well as some of the literary output of the BLACK ARTS MOVEMENT. The negritude concept as developed by Césaire also influenced the writings of FRANTZ FANON and has some relevance to the late-20th-century debate about AFROCENTRISM in AFRICAN-AMERICAN STUDIES.

See also NAMES CONTROVERSY.

Negro national anthem

The hymn "Lift Every Voice and Sing" is generally referred to as the Negro national anthem. It was written in 1900 by JAMES WELDON JOHNSON while he was a high school principal in Jacksonville, Florida, and was set to music by his brother, J. Rosamond. It was written by Johnson for a celebration of the birthday of ABRAHAM LINCOLN at Johnson's Florida high school and was first performed by the school's choir on February 12, 1900. It is unclear why the song became so popular as to become the unofficial anthem of the BLACK COMMUNITY, but Johnson later recalled that the "school children of Jacksonville kept singing it, they went off to other schools and sang it; they became teachers and taught it to other children. Within twenty years, it was being sung all over the south. . . ."

The lyrics of the song do not mention blacks, but they evoke the sufferings of a people in the past and an optimistic sense of the future based on faith in the "God of our weary years" and the struggles for freedom of past generations. The song is therefore rooted in the values of African-American CULTURE, including race consciousness and solidarity, RELIGIOSITY, MUSIC, and FREEDOM. Since the 1920s the song has been referred to as the Negro national anthem, and it is performed at schools, churches, and social and political gatherings of African Americans. Ironically, Johnson, who was deeply committed to the IDEOLOGY of INTEGRATIONISM, did not like the reference to the song as the anthem for the race because he thought it encouraged notions of BLACK NATIONALISM.

Further reading: Julian Bond and Sandra K. Wilson, *Lift Every Voice and Sing: A Celebration of the Negro National Anthem* (New York: Random House, 2000).

New Deal

The New Deal—the set of reform programs inaugurated by FRANKLIN D. ROOSEVELT in the midst of the depression during the 1930s—represents one of the great transformations in United States history, comparable to the changes brought about by the CIVIL WAR and RECONSTRUCTION of the 1860s and the CIVIL RIGHTS MOVEMENT and the GREAT SOCIETY of the 1960s. The New Deal established the foundations of the American WELFARE STATE and modern LIBERALISM, and as a result Roosevelt is generally recognized as one of the greatest of the American presidents. However, for African Americans the legacy of Roosevelt and the New Deal is bittersweet because, from the beginning, the New Deal's programs were in their design and development shaped by RACISM and WHITE SUPREMACY and in their implementation by SEGREGATION and DISCRIMINATION. Thus, while blacks, like all Americans, benefited from the New Deal's programs for the elderly, the poor, and the unemployed and from policies to meliorate the exploitation of workers, the benefits were far less than those received by their white counterparts. This is because Roosevelt, in response to the pressures of the CONSERVATIVE COALITION in CONGRESS, allowed the Social Security Act—the cornerstone of the American welfare state—to be designed and financed on a basis that was racially discriminatory, and the basic law allowing workers to organize permitted labor unions to exclude black workers. Also, because of the pressures of the conservative coalition and because of deference to FEDERALISM, most of the New Deal's work and relief programs were segregated and administered on a racially discriminatory basis by STATE AND LOCAL GOVERNMENTS.

Both the NAACP and the URBAN LEAGUE engaged in concerted LOBBYING against these features of New Deal PUBLIC POLICY, but their efforts were insufficient against the entrenched POWER of the conservative coalition and Roosevelt's own indifference to the rights of African Americans. Most of the racist and discriminatory features of the New Deal were not changed until the 1950s and 1960s.

Further reading: Harvey Sitkoff, "The New Deal and Race Relations" in *Fifty Years Later: The New Deal Evaluated,* ed. Harvey Sitkoff (New York: Random House, 1985).

Newton, Huey (1942–1989) *activist*

Huey Newton with BOBBY SEALE in 1966 founded the BLACK PANTHER PARTY, the largest African-American revolutionary ORGANIZATION in the history of the United States. Newton, born in Monroe, Louisiana, moved to Oakland, California, at an early age. While attending Merritt College in Oakland, Newton and Seale became active in the black students association and its efforts to establish a program in AFRICAN-AMERICAN STUDIES. Increasingly skeptical about the capacity of the CIVIL RIGHTS MOVEMENT to deal with the problems of POVERTY in the GHETTOS, Newton embraced the philosophy of the BLACK POWER MOVEMENT. The writings of THIRD WORLD theorists, especially FRANTZ FANON, influenced Newton's evolving thought, and eventually he embraced the theory of INTERNAL COLONIALISM and argued that blacks should use VIOLENCE in a war of liberation.

In 1967 he was arrested and sentenced to prison for the murder of an Oakland policeman. His jailing became an international cause célèbre, and "Free Huey" rallies were held around the world. While in prison he continued to lead the party as its minister of defense. In 1969 his conviction for killing the policeman was overturned. But, by the time of his release, the party was in disarray as a result of internal infighting and corruption and external POLITICAL REPRESSION, and Newton was able to play only a marginal role in its revitalization. In 1974 he was accused of murdering a woman and fled to Cuba. Returning in 1977, he was tried twice for the murder, but the charges were dropped after two juries failed to reach verdicts. Although he continued to be a symbol of the Panthers and 1960s

Huey Newton featured in a poster for the Black Panther Party
(Library of Congress)

RADICALISM, he had only a small group of followers, and by all accounts he became increasingly isolated, paranoid, corrupt, and violent. In 1980 he received a Ph.D. from the University of California, Santa Cruz, writing a dissertation called "War against the Panthers: A Study of Repression in America." In 1985 he was arrested for embezzlement, and in 1989, addicted to alcohol and drugs, he was murdered on a dark street in Oakland, apparently in a drug deal gone bad. At the place of his death someone left a wreath that read "To Huey, for the good years." At his funeral hundreds of 1960s radicals and revolutionaries gathered, and in the funeral procession thousands marched through the streets shouting "Long live Huey P.; African people will be free."

Further reading: Hugh Pearson, *The Shadow of the Panther Party: Huey Newton and the Price of Black Power in America* (Reading, Mass.: Addison-Wesley, 1994).

Niagara movement

The Niagara movement was a gathering of a small group of male members of the TALENTED TENTH who met in 1905 in Niagara Falls at the invitation of W. E. B. DU BOIS. The purpose of the meeting was to begin to mount a challenge to BOOKER T. WASHINGTON's philosophy of ACCOMMODATIONISM, which then held sway in AFRICAN-AMERICAN POLITICS. The Niagara movement issued a manifesto, established an organization, and held three meetings between 1905 and 1908, when it was disbanded. The ORGANIZATION was small and elitist, consisting of prominent educators, clergymen, businessmen, and journalists. Its conferences were always small, devoted mainly to issuing circulars opposing SEGREGATION and calling for complete FREEDOM and EQUALITY. However, its manifesto, drafted mainly by Du Bois and WILLIAM MONROE TROTTER, can be viewed as the opening salvo of the CIVIL RIGHTS MOVEMENT. The Niagara manifesto declared, "We will not be satisfied to take one jot or title less than our manhood rights. We claim for ourselves every right that belongs to free born Americans, political, civic and social; and until we get these rights we will never cease to protest and assail the ears of America." The manifesto went on to raise specific demands for VOTING RIGHTS, an end to DISCRIMINATION in public accommodations, equal enforcement of the law, and quality education. As to how these goals were to be achieved, the manifesto said, "By voting where we may vote; by persistent unceasing agitation; by hammering at the truth; by sacrifice and hard work."

The Niagara movement as an organization was short-lived, and its successes were limited because it was an elitist group; because of differences between Du Bois and Trotter, its principal leaders; and because of efforts by Booker Washington to undermine and discredit the movement. The Niagara movement was important because it was among the first organized challenges to the dominance of Booker Washington's accommodationism and signaled the emergence of a rising tide of PROTEST and MILITANCY in African-American politics. Soon after the Niagara organization folded, the NAACP was formed and adopted as its platform the essentials of the Niagara manifesto. But, unlike Niagara, the NAACP was a much more broadly based COALITION, including among its founders both whites and women.

Nixon, Richard (1913–1993) *37th president of the United States*

Richard Nixon was the first POST–CIVIL RIGHTS ERA American president. He is also one of the most complicated and duplicitous persons ever to occupy the office. Both of these factors shaped his approach to issues of RACE during his administration. As the first post–civil rights era president, Nixon was the first to deal with a BLACK COMMUNITY that was relatively empowered and enjoyed the legal rights to FREEDOM and EQUALITY. Nixon brought to this situation a divided self, politically and personally. Nixon also confronted a country that was deeply divided as a result of the CIVIL RIGHTS MOVEMENT, the BLACK POWER MOVEMENT, the RIOTS in the GHETTOS and on college and university campuses, and the PROTESTS against the VIETNAM WAR. When he ran for president and was elected in 1968, these divisions manifested themselves in the campaign. The 1968 election was one of the closest in history, with Nixon barely defeating HUBERT HUMPHREY, the DEMOCRATIC PARTY nominee, and GEORGE WALLACE, the THIRD PARTY candidate representing the forces of RACISM and WHITE SUPREMACY. When Nixon first ran for president against JOHN F. KENNEDY in 1960, he ran as something of a racial liberal, endorsing CIVIL RIGHTS and promising to appoint the first black to the cabinet. When he ran in 1968, he campaigned as a racial conservative, using racially coded messages on crime, welfare, and BUSING to appeal to the WHITE BACKLASH in the SOUTHERN STATES and among some white voters in the NORTHERN STATES. This transformation in Nixon's racial IDEOLOGY was due mainly to the transformation in the REPUBLICAN PARTY's approach to race brought about by the nomination of BARRY GOLDWATER in 1964 and Nixon's calculation that in order to win he had to embrace the SOUTHERN STRATEGY.

Once elected (with about 10 percent black voter support), Nixon adopted policies that antagonized the black LEADERSHIP establishment. First he sought to slow down school DESEGREGATION in the Southern states and to put an end to busing for that purpose. Second, he ended the WAR ON POVERTY. Third, he nominated persons to the SUPREME COURT who were viewed by African-American leaders as anti–civil rights. And finally, he initially opposed renewal of the VOTING RIGHTS ACT OF 1965. As a result of these policies before his resignation in 1974, relations between Nixon and the leaders of black America were so rancorous that the CONGRESSIONAL BLACK CAUCUS had boycotted his State of the Union address to CONGRESS; his black appointees in the BUREAUCRACY were hinting at mass resignations; and the board chairman of the NAACP described the Nixon presidency as the first "anti-Negro" administration since WOODROW WILSON. Yet, reflecting his divided self and perhaps the divided country, Nixon also started some of the most progressive racial and social welfare reforms of any post–civil rights era president. First, he endorsed the PHILADELPHIA PLAN, drafted by ARTHUR FLETCHER, one of his black appointees to the bureaucracy, which became the basis for AFFIRMATIVE ACTION. Second, he substantially expanded funding and staff for the EQUAL EMPLOYMENT OPPORTUNITY COMMISSION and the OFFICE OF FEDERAL CONTRACT COMPLIANCE, the agencies that enforce nondiscrimination in employment. Third, he created the Office of Minority Business Enterprises to foster the development of black CAPITALISM. Fourth, he supported several programs that significantly expanded the scope of the WELFARE STATE, including the Comprehensive Employment and Training Program (CETA), which provided jobs and job training to anyone unemployed. Also, in 1974 SSI (the Supplemental Security Income Program) was created to provide income to the disabled, and Nixon supported the largest increase in social security benefits ever. Moreover, social security benefits were indexed to inflation in 1972 while Nixon was president. These programs disproportionately benefited African Americans, as expenditures on programs targeted for the poor tripled between 1969 and 1974 (Nixon's time in office). Finally, Nixon proposed a radical revision in welfare for poor families—the Family Assistance Plan—which, had it been enacted, would have guaranteed an income to all American families.

The racial strategies and PUBLIC POLICY programs of the Nixon presidency are as complicated as was the overall Nixon presidency. Nixon may have believed in white supremacy (some of his remarks recorded on the White House audio system seem to suggest this): In 1968 he pursued a subtle antiblack campaign, and in office he pursued some policies that were adverse to black interests. Yet at the end of the 20th century, on balance, his policies and programs on race and social welfare are as liberal and progressive as any pursued by any of the six post–civil rights era presidents, including BILL CLINTON and JIMMY CARTER, the two Democratic presidents.

Further reading: Herbert Parmet, *Richard Nixon and His America* (Boston: Little, Brown, 1990).

Northern states

Northern states is a term used to distinguish between those slaveholding states that seceded from the union and precipitated the CIVIL WAR and after the war imposed a rigid JIM CROW style of SEGREGATION. The term is in contrast to those states that did not secede from the Union and generally had a more flexible form of segregation after the Civil War. Thus, the Northern states include states in the North, West, and Midwest, as well as the "border states" (those slaveholding states—Missouri, Kentucky, Delaware and Maryland—that did not secede from the Union). More specifically, it refers to all the states that did not secede from the Union during the Civil War and those that subsequently became a part of the Union after the war. By contrast, the SOUTHERN STATES refers to the 11 states that seceded from the Union—South Carolina, Mississippi, Florida, Alabama, Georgia, Louisiana, Texas, Virginia, Arkansas, Tennessee, and North Carolina—and constituted themselves as the Confederate States of America.

O

Obadele, Imari A. (1930–) *black nationalist*

Imari A. Obadele is a leading advocate of the establishment of a separate, independent black nation-state within the boundaries of the United States. He is also a leading advocate of REPARATIONS. Obadele grew up in Philadelphia, Pennsylvania, where with his brother Milton Henry (Obadele's name at birth was Richard Henry) was active in local CIVIL RIGHTS groups protesting SEGREGATION in the MILITARY. He and his brother later moved to Detroit, Michigan, where they formed a local civil rights organization called the Group on Advanced Leadership (GOAL).

In 1963 GOAL invited MALCOLM X to address the group. (At this meeting Malcolm delivered one of his most important speeches: "Message to the Grassroots.") Shortly after Malcolm's assassination, GOAL changed its name to the Malcolm X Society, and its members embraced the philosophy of BLACK NATIONALISM and the idea of an independent black nation as a concrete expression of it. In 1968 the group issued what it called a Declaration of Independence and established the REPUBLIC OF NEW AFRICA (RNA), which it described as the provisional government of African Americans fighting to establish an independent nation. In 1971 Obadele became president of RNA and moved its headquarters to Jackson, Mississippi. There RNA attempted to purchase 20 acres of land to establish as the capital of its proposed new nation. In 1971 the FBI, as part of its COINTELPRO program of POLITICAL REPRESSION, conducted an early-morning raid on the Jackson offices of RNA, and in an ensuing gun battle, a Jackson police officer was killed and another officer and an FBI agent were wounded. Obadele and several other RNA leaders were sentenced to long prison terms, but as a result of PROTEST and LITIGATION he was freed after five years and resumed his leadership of RNA. But, he also decided to combine his life work of RADICALISM and MILITANCY with scholarship, enrolling at Temple University, where he earned a B.A. in 1981, a Master's in 1982, and a

Ph.D. in 1985. While continuing as RNA president, Obadele joined the political science faculty at Prairie View A & M University, a historically black university outside Houston, Texas.

A scholar of black nationalism, Obadele authored several books, including works on reparations and *Free the Land,* an autobiographical account of his work in RNA. In 1987 he formed the National Coalition of Blacks for Reparations in America (NCOBRA), a COALITION of black ORGANIZATIONS dedicated to building a mass movement for reparations. The idea of reparations for SLAVERY has long been a concern of Obadele's, as reflected by the Malcolm X Society's call in 1968 for a $400 billion dollar payment from the United States government for "slavery damages."

Office of Federal Contract Compliance

The Office of Federal Contract Compliance (OFCC) is the principal agency in the federal BUREAUCRACY responsible for the implementation and enforcement of AFFIRMATIVE ACTION programs in American businesses. The office was created by an executive order issued by LYNDON B. JOHNSON in 1965. A part of the cabinet-level Department of Labor, its responsibility is to enforce the requirement that all businesses contracting with the federal government develop an affirmative action plan to hire and promote minorities and women.

The PHILADELPHIA PLAN that established this requirement was developed by OFCC under the supervision of ARTHUR FLETCHER. If a business with a federal contract fails to develop an acceptable plan, OFCC is authorized to disqualify it from contracting for business with the federal government. However, OFCC has rarely disqualified a company, although there is evidence that many companies have not only failed to develop affirmative action plans but in some cases have engaged in actual racial DISCRIMINATION in their employment practices.

Operation PUSH

Operation PUSH is an ORGANIZATION established by JESSE JACKSON in 1971. PUSH (People United to Save Humanity) was originally Operation Breadbasket, the northern arm of MARTIN LUTHER KING JR.'s SOUTHERN CHRISTIAN LEADERSHIP CONFERENCE (SCLC). After King's death in 1968, conflicts developed between Jackson and Ralph Abernathy, King's successor as head of SCLC, and as a result Jackson quit SCLC and formed PUSH. In forming the new organization, Jackson took with him the entire Operation Breadbasket organization, including its staff, board members, and membership. Operation Breadbasket (to put "bread and money into the baskets of black people"), in its new incarnation as PUSH, relied on the strategy of economic boycotts developed earlier by LEON SULLIVAN in Philadelphia. The boycott strategy was used to negotiate agreements with businesses in order to get them to share economic opportunities with blacks, including deposits in black banks, insurance from black-owned firms, contracts with black construction companies, and the use of black advertising agencies and MEDIA.

Over the years, PUSH has reached agreements with many major American corporations, including Anheuser-Busch, General Foods, Columbia Pictures, and Toyota. In reaching these agreements, PUSH provided some stimulus to the growth of black CAPITALISM in the POST–CIVIL RIGHTS ERA. In addition to its economic activities, PUSH under Jackson's leadership also engaged in traditional CIVIL RIGHTS activities and developed SELF-HELP programs in education and other areas. After his two PRESIDENTIAL CAMPAIGNS, Jackson merged Operation PUSH with the RAINBOW COALITION, the organization he started in 1984 to advance his political program. The new organization was known as the Rainbow/PUSH Coalition.

oppression

Oppression is a word that is often used but rarely defined. In none of the many encyclopedias, dictionaries, and other reference works in the social sciences does one find an entry for oppression. The concept of oppression therefore has a murky quality, and it is often used indiscriminately and interchangeably with RACISM, DISCRIMINATION, and other types of negative behavior by one group toward another. It is also used to encapsulate the experiences of groups as diverse as women, homosexuals, African Americans, and European ETHNIC GROUPS in the United States. This usage of the concept is unsatisfactory, since the experiences of African Americans in the United States from SLAVERY to the late 20th century are clearly different and distinct from the experiences of women, gays and lesbians, and immigrants from Europe such as Jewish or Irish Americans. While each of these groups faced various forms of prejudice, discrimination, and intolerance in the United States, they were not comparable with the experiences of the Africans. Therefore, one needs a concept that distinguishes these varied group experiences. Oppression, properly defined, is that concept.

In the absence of other sources, dictionary definitions are a useful place to start in trying to come up with a working definition of oppression. Most dictionaries provide some or all of the following meanings for oppression: to weigh down, as sleep or weariness does; to weigh down in body and mind; to burden with cruel and unjust restraints; and to subject to undue burdens. While these meanings are helpful in distinguishing oppression from racism, discrimination, or other forms of intergroup bigotry or intolerance, there is obviously a lack of precision in its meaning.

Oppression, however, as suggested by the dictionaries, is a harsh, cruel, and near-total system of domination and exploitation that denies individuals in a group not merely CIVIL RIGHTS but also NATURAL RIGHTS, and not merely some freedoms (such as the right to vote or equal employment) but virtually all FREEDOM. This includes not just political freedom but cultural freedom; not just freedom in the sense of the absence of arbitrary legal or institutional restrictions, but the absence of freedom in the sense of individual autonomy—the elementary internalized sense of identity, dignity, and self-expression in language, MUSIC, and RELIGIOSITY. In this sense, oppression involves the subjugation of a group's CULTURE—its mind (in the dictionary usage) as well as its body (as in the exploitation of the labor of a group). This cultural subjugation includes interference with family formation, the stripping away of names and languages, and prohibitions on religious practices and other expressions of culture.

Systems of oppression generally are based on some IDEOLOGY that denigrates the group as inferior (such as WHITE SUPREMACY) and nearly always results in some varying degrees of INTERNAL INFERIORIZATION among some members of the oppressed group. In this sense, oppression involves a nearly unrestrained exercise of POWER by a SUPERORDINATE GROUP vis-à-vis a SUBORDINATE GROUP, that is, an unrestrained exercise of power that pushes a people down to the lowest levels of society.

See also NAMES CONTROVERSY.

organization

The creation of effective political organizations is one of the most important modes of POLITICAL PARTICIPATION in the United States. It is also an important manifestation of the POWER of INTEREST GROUPS in the American DEMOCRACY, given the prominence of PLURALISM in the United States. Political scientists generally agree that organizations are indispensable to the effective participation of individuals in U.S. politics and to the advancement of their collective or group interests. As the political scientist James Q. Wilson puts it, "If the causes represented by mass efforts are to continue to be espoused, they will continue through organizational efforts or not at all. Passions can be aroused and for the moment directed, but they can not be sustained. Organization provides continuity and predictability to social processes that would otherwise be episodic." However, while perhaps indispensable in politics in America, organization itself has a tendency to distort the interests of a group. This is because organizations and their leaders have a tendency to develop an interest in organizational maintenance, which it may pursue at the expense of the interests of the group it represents. Second, there is a marked tendency for middle- and upper-income persons to form and lead organizations, which may operate to the disadvantage of low-income and poor people. These tendencies may disadvantage the BLACK COMMUNITY in a special way, given its disproportionately high number of poor people and the domination of organizations that purport to represent their interests by the TALENTED TENTH.

Organizations have always been an abiding feature of the American CIVIC CULTURE, as noted by Tocqueville in *DEMOCRACY IN AMERICA*. And studies of the black civic culture have concluded that blacks may participate more in organizations than whites. GUNNAR MYRDAL described this phenomenon as a tendency toward "hyperorganization," which may result in severe competition for scarce resources of money and membership. The first and most enduring organization in the black community is the BLACK CHURCH, an institution rooted in the RELIGIOSITY of the CULTURE. After the church, there have been three waves of organizational formation among black Americans. The first occurred in the period before the CIVIL WAR, when a variety of black social, cultural, and educational associations were formed. The second wave of black organizational formation took place during the era of BOOKER T. WASHINGTON's leadership, when a parallel structure of black business, professional, and fraternal organizations were formed due to the exclusion of blacks because of SEGREGATION from the dominant white associations such as the American medical and bar associations. These parallel black organizations usually use the designation "National" rather than "American," as for examples the National Bar Association and the National Medical Association. The third wave of black organizing occurred in the 1960s as a by-product of the BLACK POWER MOVEMENT. Unlike those formed during the Booker Washington era, these 1960s groups were not established because blacks were excluded from the majority-dominated white organizations. Rather, blacks formed separate associations or broke away from the mainstream organizations because they wanted to pursue a BLACK AGENDA politically, economically, culturally, or professionally.

The results of these three waves of organization formation is that at the end of the 20th century the black community exhibited an extraordinarily large and diverse organizational structure. While the structure is large and diverse—or perhaps because it is large and diverse—it is difficult to bring black organizations together in a common political enterprise. Moreover, many black organizations have limited resources and are devoted mainly to narrow professional, economic, or fraternal concerns rather than political activism.

See also NATIONAL BLACK LEADERSHIP ROUNDTABLE.

Further reading: Nelson Babchuck and R. Thompson, "The Voluntary Associations of Negroes," *American Sociological Review* 27 (1962): 647–55; Ollie Johnson and Karin Stanford, eds., *Black Political Organizations in the Post Civil Rights Era* (New Brunswick, N.J.: Rutgers State University Press, 2002); *National Directory of African American Organizations, 1998–2000* (New York: Phillip Morris, 2000); James Q. Wilson, *Political Organizations* (New York: Basic Books, 1973).

Organization of Afro-American Unity

The Organization of Afro-American Unity (OAAU) is the ORGANIZATION formed in 1963 by MALCOLM X after he left the NATION OF ISLAM. The organization—modeled on the Organization of African Unity, the association of the nation-states of Africa—was envisioned as a secular COALITION devoted to political and CIVIL RIGHTS activism, in contrast to the apolitical posture of the Nation of Islam under ELIJAH MUHAMMAD's leadership. A companion religious group was also formed by Malcolm, the Muslim Mosque, Inc. At the time of Malcolm X's death in 1965, the OAAU was barely getting off the ground and had done little more than issue a statement of basic principles and hold a few rallies (Malcolm X was assassinated at one of its rallies). With very few members, it collapsed shortly after Malcolm's assassination, although Malcolm's sister Ella Collins tried for a time to keep it going as a kind of living memorial to her brother.

P

Pan-Africanism

Pan-Africanism is a historical, cultural, and political movement that asserts that there are common bonds that unite all peoples of African descent wherever they are in the world. Historically, this movement has its origins in the United States, where SLAVERY forged out of the many peoples transported to the United States a common identification and consciousness as a single African people.

Pan-Africanism as a doctrine or rudimentary IDEOLOGY emerges in the writings of EDWARD WILMOT BLYDEN and MARTIN DELANY, and its earliest expression as a political movement can be seen in the BACK-TO-AFRICA MOVEMENTS that developed in the United States in the 18th century. As it emerged, the common bonds that united African peoples were their common experiences of OPPRESSION at the hands of the European peoples. Thus, in a fundamental sense, Pan-Africanism is a reaction to RACISM and WHITE SUPREMACY. This common experience of oppression at the hands of whites created a Pan-African consciousness in Africa as well in response to COLONIALISM. Thus, Pan-Africanism as a political movement involves initiatives to unite peoples of African origins, mainly sub-Saharan "black" Africa, although in the modern era lip service is paid to the continent as a whole—against a common enemy, European racism, colonialism, and white supremacy. However, Pan-Africanism as a cultural movement transcends the bonds of oppression of blacks at the hands of whites and asserts that African peoples share a common CULTURE.

This idea of a common African culture also has its origins in the United States in the early writings of Blyden and Delany and the subsequent writings of individuals like ALEXANDER CRUMMELL and W. E. B. DU BOIS. In some versions of the cultural unity of African peoples, the idea is rooted in "racial essentialism" or the idea that there is a genetic or biological basis for the cultural distinctiveness of Africans, while in others African cultural differences are rooted in historically lived experiences in RELIGIOSITY, MUSIC, language, dance, and in other ways that express the worldview or, as Du Bois put it in the title of his famous book, *THE SOULS OF BLACK FOLK.*

Whether politically or culturally, Pan-Africanism was first expressed ideologically and institutionally in a series of Pan-African conferences organized by Du Bois and H. Sylvester Williams, the WEST INDIAN intellectual from Trinidad. The first conference met in London in 1900, and subsequent ones were held in 1919, 1923, and 1927. These conferences, gatherings of the TALENTED TENTH from the Americas and Africa, discussed the basis of Pan-Africanism consciousness and solidarity and attempted to develop strategies to meliorate the conditions of colonialism. At the end of World War II a Pan-African congress was established to push for the independence of the African colonies. Perhaps the largest Pan-African movement was led by MARCUS GARVEY in the 1920s. Garvey and his UNIVERSAL NEGRO IMPROVEMENT ASSOCIATION not only posited the cultural unity of all African peoples but proposed a visionary plan to unite all of Africa into a single nation-state, the United States of Africa. Although nothing came of Garvey's vision for a politically united Africa, his ideas constitute a major contribution to the idealogy of the movement. Garvey's ideas also influenced the approach to Pan-Africanism of MALCOLM X and STOKELY CARMICHAEL.

In the 1960s most of the peoples of Africa achieved formal independence, and in 1963 they established the Organization of African Unity (OAU) as an organization to give concrete expression to Pan-Africanism. And in 2001 the 53 member states of the OAU began discussions about the establishment of a confederacy or union of all African states, including formation of a Pan-African parliament, a common currency, a common passport, a Pan-African military force, as well as a common bank and court system. The OAU leaders also proposed dual citizenship for Africans in the diaspora. This confederation of African states would be the ultimate expression of the Pan-African idea. However, at the beginning of the 21st century, the prospects for it becoming a reality do not appear auspicious because of the uneven levels of economic and political development of the 53 nations; cultural and political differences between the nations, especially the Arab and the sub-Saharan nations; and the inevitable opportunism of African political leaders who wish to maintain the sovereignty of their countries and the trappings of privilege and power that it confers.

Meanwhile, African Americans continued to embrace the Pan-African ideal culturally and politically. Culturally, this takes the form of AFROCENTRISM and KWANZA. Politically, it takes the forms of organizations such as TRANSAFRICA and the efforts by blacks in the United States to establish linkages with blacks in Latin America (especially Brazil, which has the largest population of persons of African descent outside of Africa), Europe, and the Caribbean. These linkages frequently take the form of travel and educational and cultural exchanges. LEON SULLIVAN has continued the Du Bois practice of holding periodic summits or conferences for Africans and African Americans for purposes of building solidarity and forging common strategies to address problems of racism and neocolonialism common to all African peoples, including the problems of GLOBALIZATION, POVERTY, and the HIV-AIDS epidemic. The first "Sullivan Summit" was held in 1991 and biennially since then, usually attracting more than 5,000 delegates from Africa and the United States. After more than 200 years, Pan-Africanism maintains its vitality as one of the most important expressions of the philosophy of BLACK NATIONALISM.

See also HARLEM RENAISSANCE, NAMES CONTROVERSY, and NEGRITUDE.

Further reading: Colin Legum, *Pan Africanism* (New York: Praeger, 1965); Ronald Walters, *Pan Africanism in the African Diaspora* (Detroit, Mich.: Wayne State University Press, 1993).

Parks, Rosa (1913–   ) *civil rights activist*

Rosa Parks is one of the most famous names—an icon almost—in the modern CIVIL RIGHTS MOVEMENT. Yet, her role as an historic figure is almost accidental. On December 1, 1955, Parks refused to give her seat on a bus in Montgomery, Alabama, to a white man. After she was arrested for violating the city's law requiring SEGREGATION on its buses, the black LEADERSHIP of the city decided to use her arrest to PROTEST this form of RACISM in Montgomery. The result was the MONTGOMERY BUS BOYCOTT, which historians identify as the event that started the modern, protest phase of the Civil Rights movement. Yet, there had been bus boycotts in the SOUTHERN STATES before Montgomery, and Parks was not the first person arrested in 1955 in Montgomery for violating the city's bus segregation laws.

Rosa Parks *(Library of Congress)*

The historical significance of her arrest and the subsequent boycott lies less in the fact of her arrest and the boycott and more in the fact that Parks was selected by Montgomery's black leaders to be the symbol of the protest and that the protest was led by MARTIN LUTHER KING JR. On March 2, 1955, Claudelle Covin, a high school student, was arrested for refusing to give up her seat. However, because she had struggled, screamed, and used profanity when she was arrested, Montgomery's black leaders were reluctant to use her case as the basis for the protest, a reluctance that became outright refusal when it was learned that she was pregnant. In October 1955 Mary Louise Smith was arrested for refusing to vacate her seat. But once again E. D. Nixon, the informal leader of the city's blacks, refused to use her case as the basis for the protest because she lived in a poor, rundown part of town and her father was said to be an alcoholic. Parks's arrest constituted an acceptable test case for the protest because, unlike Covin and Smith, she was middle aged, mature, and an established member of the city's black middle class, and when she was arrested she went along quietly with barely a murmur of protest or outward indignation. Parks and her husband (Raymond) had also been active in the local CIVIL RIGHTS circles, with Mrs. Parks serving as secretary of the local NAACP chapter. Thus, Parks became a historic figure in African-American history not for the uniqueness or substance of her action but because of the class biases of Montgomery's black leadership, which made her, unlike the young pregnant Covin or the poor, uneducated Smith, an acceptable symbol of middle-class respectability. Symbolic respectability notwithstanding, however, Parks's arrest would be historically inconsequential if the boycott had not been led by Martin Luther King Jr. This is because the Montgomery bus boycott's significance is that it gave rise to King's leadership, under which a systematic strategy was developed to effectively attack segregation throughout the Southern states.

Parks was born in Tuskegee, Alabama. She attended Alabama State College, a historically black college, and subsequently became active in the Civil Rights movement. After her arrest and the success of the boycott and King's leadership, she became a movement icon, referred to as the "Mother of the Civil Rights movement." She later moved to Detroit, where she was employed by John Conyers, one of the city's black congressmen. In the later years of her life she was honored by STATE AND LOCAL GOVERNMENTS, presidents, the CONGRESS, and numerous colleges and universities.

See also BIRMINGHAM DEMONSTRATIONS, SELMA DEMONSTRATIONS.

Philadelphia Plan

The Philadelphia Plan is the informal name for the first AFFIRMATIVE ACTION plan developed by the U.S. government. It is referred to as the Philadelphia Plan because it was developed by ARTHUR FLETCHER and his colleagues in the Labor Department during RICHARD NIXON's administration to deal with problems of racial DISCRIMINATION in that city's construction industry. Once the plan was adopted for Philadelphia, it became the model for affirmative action programs throughout the United States. However, as an indicator to some extent of affirmative action's lack of success, a study by the *New York Times* (published July 9, 1995) of black employment in Philadelphia's construction industry found very little long-term progress in the employment of blacks 25 years after the Philadelphia Plan's adoption. Indeed, the *Times* described affirmative action in Philadelphia's construction industry as "something of a hollow victory."

Pierce, Samuel (1922–) *government official*

Samuel Pierce was appointed secretary of HOUSING AND URBAN DEVELOPMENT (HUD) by President RONALD REA-

GAN in 1981, becoming the third black to hold a cabinet post and the second to head HUD. Prior to his appointment by Reagan, Pierce, a graduate of Cornell University and its law school, had held a high position in the BUREAUCRACY in RICHARD NIXON's administration. An active worker for the REPUBLICAN PARTY and one of the few blacks in the POWER ELITE, Pierce was a lifelong supporter of the CIVIL RIGHTS MOVEMENT, serving, for example, on the advisory committee of the New York chapter of CORE (CONGRESS OF RACIAL EQUALITY). Pierce also ran unsuccessfully against ADAM CLAYTON POWELL to represent HARLEM in the CONGRESS.

Pierce's status as a card-carrying member of both the black LEADERSHIP and the national power elite led J. EDGAR HOOVER and the FBI, as part of the COINTELPRO program of POLITICAL REPRESSION, to focus on Pierce as the "right kind" of black leader to replace MARTIN LUTHER KING JR. once they discredited him. William Sullivan, the assistant FBI director in charge of COINTELPRO, in a 1964 memorandum wrote that once King had been "completely discredited as a fraud, demagogue and moral scoundrel . . . the Negroes will be left without a national leader of sufficiently compelling personality to steer them in the proper direction. . . . This is what could happen, but need not happen if the right kind of a national Negro leader could at this time be gradually developed so as to overshadow Dr. King and be in the position to assume the role of leadership of the Negro people when King has been completely discredited." Sullivan then suggested that Pierce was the right kind of Negro and asked Hoover's permission to quietly promote Pierce as a national leader. Hoover approved and presumably the FBI tried to promote his leadership. However, as far as it is known, Pierce was unaware of the FBI's interests.

Prior to his appointments to the bureaucracy by Nixon and Reagan, Pierce had been identified with LIBERALISM in the Republican Party. But by the time he joined Reagan's cabinet he had for the most part embraced the CONSERVATISM that had come to characterize the Republican Party since BARRY GOLDWATER's nomination in 1964. Thus, Pierce described himself as a "true believer" in the Reagan revolution. This led many African Americans in the leadership and the MEDIA to label Pierce an UNCLE TOM. This was because during his tenure as HUD secretary he rarely spoke out on issues of concern to blacks (he was referred to by CARL ROWAN as "silent Sam") and presided over dramatic reductions in HUD's budget for low- and moderate-income housing. However, unlike some other blacks in Reagan's senior level bureaucracy—notably Clarence Pendleton, chair of the CIVIL RIGHTS COMMISSION, and CLARENCE THOMAS, chair of the EQUAL EMPLOYMENT OPPORTUNITY COMMISSION—Pierce generally supported CIVIL RIGHTS, specifically the renewal of the VOTING RIGHTS ACT OF 1965 and the retention of AFFIRMATIVE ACTION. Pierce was the only member of Reagan's cabinet to serve the full eight years of Reagan's two terms. When he left office he returned to New York to practice law and serve on multiple corporate boards.

Further reading: Samuel Pierce, "The Republican Alternative" in *Black Voices in American Politics*, ed. Jeffrey Elliot (New York: Harcourt Brace Jovanovich, 1986): 117–132.

Piven, Frances Fox (1932–) *scholar*

Frances Fox Piven (with her colleague Richard Cloward) is a leading scholar of the SOCIAL MOVEMENTS of poor peoples; of PROTEST, POVERTY, and URBAN POLITICS; and of the operations of the WELFARE STATE in the United States. Piven, a white scholar born in Canada, did not situate her research in the field of AFRICAN-AMERICAN STUDIES per se, but her scholarship on protest, social movements, urban politics, poverty, the welfare state, and voting rights made major contributions to the study of AFRICAN-AMERICAN POLITICS. In addition to her scholarly work, Piven (and Cloward) was actively engaged in reform politics, helping to spark the organizing of the NATIONAL WELFARE RIGHTS ORGANIZATION and to initiate important reforms in VOTING RIGHTS.

Piven's major work on the social movements of poor people is *Poor People's Movements: Why They Succeed, Why They Fail* (1977). In it she and Cloward argue that the only POWER poor people have is their occasional capabilities to engage in large-scale disruption and destabilization of the POLITICAL SYSTEM. However, this power, they argue, is episodic and short-lived, or it results in the formation of permanent but weak and unstable ORGANIZATIONS that are easily marginalized by POLITICAL REPRESSION and CO-OPTATION. Thus, it is Piven's contention that poor people should take maximum advantage of the occasional opportunities to disrupt the system to extract maximum benefits, short- and long-term.

Piven's major work on the welfare state is *Regulating the Poor: The Functions of Public Welfare* (1971). In this work she argues that the major function of the American welfare state is to act as a mechanism of social control—to regulate the political behavior of the poor—rather than to combat poverty. Thus, she contends that poor peoples movements should at all times work to extract the largest possible welfare benefits as a means to create system instability and crisis, which might in the long run facilitate more-radical reforms. Piven's theoretical work on welfare stimulated the formation of the National Welfare Rights Organization. In 1965 she and Cloward circulated a paper to antipoverty workers and civil rights activists calling for the formation of a welfare rights movement with the express purpose of dramatically increasing the number of people on welfare. This, it was hoped, would generate a crisis in the system that would result in radical reforms along the lines of a guaranteed income. While Piven's work alone was not responsible for the rise of the welfare rights movement, it did stimulate interest and provided a rationale and direction for it.

Piven and Cloward's 1988 book *Why Americans Don't Vote* had a major impact on voter reform movements in the United States. In the book, they analyzed the results of 20th-century election reforms and concluded that they constituted part of a concerted effort to restrict voting by immigrants and blacks through a combination of the poll tax, literacy requirements, and cumbersome registration procedures. After the book's publication, Piven and Cloward became involved in a national campaign to reform the voter registration process. This resulted in the enactment by CONGRESS in 1993 of the "Motor Voter" law, which allows persons to register at motor vehicle registration and licensing offices as well as social service agencies providing housing, health, employment, and welfare benefits. It was thought that since poor people and minorities (who are less likely to register) all have some contact with some of these agencies, registration and voting among them would increase. Although there was some increases in registration and voting among these groups, it was not widespread, leading Piven and Cloward in 2000 to write *Why Americans Still Don't Vote*, in which they argued that minorities and poor people did not take advantage of the opportunities provided by the motor voter law to register and vote because the TWO-PARTY SYSTEM did not offer candidates and programs that appealed to their interests. Instead, the DEMOCRATIC PARTY and REPUBLICAN PARTY both appealed mainly to the interests of middle-class and wealthy whites.

Critics of Piven and Cloward's work contend that it tends to be polemical and driven by an IDEOLOGY of RADICALISM, but Piven is an example of a scholar who, although white, embraces what MACK H. JONES calls a system-challenging rather than a system-maintaining perspective in her studies of American politics, a perspective rooted in the perceived needs of blacks and poor people for fundamental, systemic change.

Piven was educated at the University of Chicago, where she received an undergraduate degree and a Ph.D. in political science. She began her longtime collaboration with Cloward, a sociologist, while both were on the faculty of Columbia University. She later taught at Boston College and the Graduate Center of the City University of New York.

Plessy v. Ferguson (1896)

Plessy v. Ferguson is the landmark decision of the SUPREME COURT that enshrined in the CONSTITUTION the doctrine of SEPARATE BUT EQUAL, which under the principle of FEDERALISM allowed the states to practice racial SEGREGATION in access to public institutions and places of public accommodations. The decision upheld a Louisiana law requiring separate railroad cars for blacks and whites.

Homer Ferguson, an African American although in appearance he looked white, was convicted of attempting to ride in a railroad car set aside for whites. He appealed his conviction, arguing that the Louisiana law violated the THIRTEENTH AMENDMENT and the FOURTEENTH AMENDMENT. The Court's majority rejected his claims, ruling that the law did not violate the Fourteenth Amendment's EQUAL PROTECTION CLAUSE because racial segregation was a reasonable exercise of the state's police powers to establish the "usages, customs and traditions of people and with a view to the promotion of the public peace." The Court went on to say that the equal protection clause was not "intended to abolish distinctions based on color or to enforce social, as distinguished from political equality or a commingling of the two races upon terms unsatisfactory to either." The Court concluded that the Louisiana law did not violate the Thirteenth Amendment by imposing a "badge of servitude" on blacks because the "assumption that the enforced separation of the races stamps the colored race with a badge of inferiority" was false. And the notion that it did was delusional on the part of blacks because, if there was a badge of inferiority, it had nothing to do with the law but rather existed "solely because the colored race chooses to put that construction on it." Justice John Marshall Harlan dissented, contending that the law was indeed based on the assumption that "colored citizens are so inferior and degraded that they cannot be allowed to sit in public coaches occupied by white citizens." Harlan also wrote that the Fourteenth Amendment prohibited the states from regulating "the enjoyment of civil rights solely upon the basis of race" because, he wrote, the Constitution is "color blind."

At the time the decision was handed down, its historical significance was not immediately recognized. It did not receive widespread attention in the black or white MEDIA and was viewed as far less significant than the CIVIL RIGHTS CASES OF 1883. Yet, over time, *Plessy* became better known and more historically significant than the civil rights cases because it became the constitutional basis for the adoption of an American system of APARTHEID in all of the SOUTHERN STATES, as well as many NORTHERN STATES. *Plessy* is also better known and more historically significant because it was the case the Supreme Court reversed in *BROWN V. BOARD OF EDUCATION*, setting the precedent for its attack on the constitutional bases of RACISM and WHITE SUPREMACY. In contrast, the constitutional principles of the civil rights cases of 1883 (giving private parties the constitutional right to discriminate on the basis of race in public accommodations) have not been reversed by the

Court. Indeed, those principles were reaffirmed by the Court in 2000.

See also COMMERCE CLAUSE and JIM CROW.

pluralism

Pluralism is both a theory to explain how the American DEMOCRACY operates, or should operate, and a description of the process of PUBLIC POLICY making in societies characterized by heterogeneous ORGANIZATIONS representing distinctive economic and ETHNIC GROUP interests. Pluralism is also both a theory dealing with the role of INTEREST GROUPS in American politics and a theory of the POLITICAL INCORPORATION or INTEGRATION of ethnic groups into the society and polity. However, as a theory of the American democracy, as a description of how public policy is made, and as a way to understand the role of interest groups in politics and the process of incorporating ethnic MINORITY GROUPS, pluralism has serious flaws when it is used in the study of AFRICAN-AMERICAN POLITICS.

As a theory of democracy in America, pluralism contends that POWER is held by a variety of diverse, competing, and sometimes overlapping groups and that the public policies resulting from group conflict and competition tend to serve the public good. The alternative to the theory of pluralism is the theory of the POWER ELITE, which contends that power in America is held by a small number of economic, cultural, and political institutions who exercise decisive influence on public policy issues that affect their interests. The power elite theory is related to the marxist theory, which holds that power in POLITICAL SYSTEMS dominated by CAPITALISM is always controlled by the bourgeoisie and is always exercised in an exploitative way toward the working class. Whichever theory is correct about the nature of power in the United States—pluralism or the power elite—the consequences for African-American politics are largely the same. This is because African Americans as a group historically were excluded from participation in both the power elite and in the competitive decision-making arena of pluralist politics because of RACISM and WHITE SUPREMACY. And once racism and white supremacy declined in the 1960s and African Americans became participants in the competitive pluralist arena, they had relatively few resources compared with white groups. Therefore, the system still served mainly the interests of whites. That is, pluralism as a theory views all groups—large and small, weak and powerful—and their interests as equal. This means that a smaller and less powerful group like African Americans would find it difficult to effectively compete with larger, more powerful white interest groups. This is a major defect of pluralism, recognized even by its adherents: In a system of fragmented, competitive groups in which all seek to advance their own interests, groups with fewer resources will generally tend to be less influential and effective, which means the overall pluralist system tends to be biased in favor of the interests of the wealthy and already powerful and therefore to reinforce existing inequalities in the system.

And to the extent that there is a power elite in the United States—as there almost certainly is with respect to some issues—African Americans fare no better, since for most of the nation's history blacks were excluded from it altogether, and even at the end of the 20th century their REPRESENTATION in it is minuscule. But even if African Americans became fully incorporated into the power elite, the logic of the theory suggests they would pursue the interests of the elite rather than those of African Americans as a group.

Pluralism as a theory of the incorporation of ethnic groups into American society and politics is also flawed when it comes to the African-American experience. Robert Dahl's *Who Governs?: Democracy and Power in an American City* (1961) is the seminal account of the process of the political incorporation of ethnic groups. A detailed case study of the experiences of successive waves of European immigrant groups to New Haven, Connecticut, during the 19th and 20th centuries, *Who Governs?* is generally recognized as a classic work in pluralist scholarship. In it, Dahl shows that when Irish and Italian immigrants came to New Haven, they confronted an entrenched Anglo-Saxon elite that engaged in widespread DISCRIMINATION, excluding the new immigrants from the city's political, economic, and cultural life. Initially the Irish and Italians, largely poor, organized around their ethnic identities for purposes of economic and political development. They attained upward economic mobility and ultimately were incorporated into the New Haven political system. Anglo-Saxon prejudice and discrimination slowly withered away, and gradually the Irish and Italians abandoned their ethnic group loyalties in favor of their class or socioeconomic interests. As a significant middle class developed, propensities toward RADICALISM declined, and the Irish and Italians became assimilated into New Haven's society, culture, and politics. Although Dahl's work was based on a single city, he suggested that the process he described in New Haven was true throughout the United States. It was not true, however, for African Americans. Dahl was puzzled and hard pressed to explain the situation of blacks in New Haven, mainly because his theory did not include a systematic analysis of racism and white supremacy.

Subsequent scholarship incorporating racism and white supremacy into the theory showed that pluralism is a limited theory when applied to the experiences of African Americans. The limitation derives from the fact that pluralism fails to consider the effects of racism and white supremacy, which impeded the incorporation of blacks in

a way that simple prejudice and discrimination did not impede incorporation of Italians and Irish Americans. Dianne Pinderhughes's *Race and Ethnicity in Chicago Politics: A Reexamination of Pluralist Theory* (1987) is an example of the post-Dahl scholarship on pluralism. In this detailed study comparing the experiences of blacks with Polish and Italian Americans in Chicago, she showed that economic mobility had been slower and less complete for blacks; the black middle class was smaller and its lower class much larger; white prejudice and discrimination withered away less for blacks than for other groups; class identification had not replaced race loyalties for blacks; and propensities toward radicalism remained strong in Chicago's BLACK COMMUNITY. This in spite of the fact that African Americans had been in Chicago as long or longer than the Irish and Polish Americans. All of these differences Pinderhughes attributed mainly to the impact of white supremacy and racism, which impeded black incorporation much more so than did Anglo-Saxon prejudice and discrimination impede Irish and Polish incorporation.

See also ASSIMILATION, MELTING POT, and WHITENESS.

Further reading: Robert Dahl, *Who Governs?: Democracy and Power in an American City* (New Haven, Conn.: Yale University Press, 1961); Dianne Pinderhughes, *Race and Ethnicity in Chicago Politics: A Reexamination of Pluralist Theory* (Urbana: University of Illinois Press, 1987).

plural society

A plural society is one that is segmented into two or more distinct, duplicative sets of ETHNIC GROUP institutions, except in the POLITICAL SYSTEM and the economy, where the institutions are shared. The basic determinant of a plural society is whether the groups have separate institutions while sharing a common political system (although generally the groups also share to some extent a common economy). A plural society is to be distinguished from a society characterized by PLURALISM, in which different INTEREST GROUPS compete for POWER in shaping PUBLIC POLICY. Frequently, plural societies are characterized by unequal relationships of OPPRESSION between SUPERORDINATE GROUPS and SUBORDINATE GROUPS. In the United States, the relationship between blacks and whites has always been that of a plural society, and until the 1960s CIVIL RIGHTS MOVEMENT, the relationship was characterized by white domination. However, plural societies can exist on a voluntary basis without relationships of domination and oppression. That is, in any given society, a group can reject INTEGRATION in favor of plurality. In the POST–CIVIL RIGHTS ERA, the United States continues to some extent to be a plural society segmented by ethnicity. Blacks and whites share common economic and political systems but not on an equal basis, although there are no formal or legal bases for inequality.

The primary criterion for measuring whether a society is plural or integrated is the degree of "institutional completeness" of its constituent ethnic groups. Institutional completeness is measured by the extent to which the members of a given ethnic group maintain most of their personal relations within the group and the extent to which the group maintains separate ORGANIZATIONS and institutions of various sorts, including religious, educational, fraternal, political, and cultural. Institutional completeness is also measured by the existence of ethnic MEDIA and communal and welfare organizations. Judged by these measures, the United States is a plural society with different ethnic groups exhibiting varying degrees of institutional completeness. To a considerable extent, Jews and Mormons constituted plural societies at the end of the 20th century. Recent immigrant groups or old immigrant groups with a continuing flow of new immigrants tend to constitute plural societies with high degrees of institutional completeness. This is especially the case if the group is not English-speaking. An example of the former is Vietnamese Americans and of the latter are Chinese and Mexican Americans. The BLACK COMMUNITY also constitutes a plural society, but unlike its Mormon and Jewish counterparts, black plurality remains characterized by some degree of involuntariness, and it continues to be marked by some degree of inequality in access to the economic and political systems.

See also HAROLD CRUSE, GHETTO, MINORITY GROUP, and MULTICULTURALISM.

political culture

Political culture refers to the enduring political attitudes, beliefs, and activities toward politics and government in a nation or community. The concept encompasses broadly shared values held by members of a community about government and its responsibilities, about its history and relationships to individuals in society, and about the role of individuals in the political process. The political culture constitutes the underpinnings of the POLITICAL SYSTEM, structuring the boundaries of political thinking and behavior. In large heterogeneous nations, there are certain broadly shared values that constitute the general political culture, but there are also political subcultures shaped by ETHNICITY—race, religion, language, or region. These subcultures can have distinctive values that are broadly shared within the ethnic community and that shape its members' attitudes and activities in the political process.

In the United States, RACE constitutes the basis for one of the oldest and most enduring subcultures in the United States. The BLACK COMMUNITY holds many of the values and patterns of behavior of other Americans, but it also has certain distinct values and patterns of behavior of its own. For example, African Americans share broadly the dominant CIVIL CULTURE in the United States. And notwithstanding the history of racial OPPRESSION in the United States, African Americans embrace the core values—CAPITALISM, DEMOCRACY, and CONSTITUTIONALISM—of the political system and tend to be as patriotic as other Americans. Indeed, a 1998 poll found that 84 percent of blacks compared with 91 percent of whites agreed that the United States is a "better country than most." Thus the CULTURE of the black community in general, and its political culture specifically, is American, as African Americans who travel to Africa or elsewhere quickly come to know. But there are some beliefs shared by blacks that are distinctive enough to constitute a discrete black political culture.

The first component of this culture—indeed, the prerequisite for its existence—is a conscious identification on the part of virtually all African Americans with the race or with the idea of a distinctive black community. This ethos of race identity and consciousness was reinforced by the 1960s BLACK POWER MOVEMENT, but it has been an abiding feature of black culture since its origins during SLAVERY. And while it may wax and wane, it is maintained through the various agents of POLITICAL SOCIALIZATION. A second, somewhat distinctive feature of the black political culture is the importance of RELIGIOSITY in shaping political attitudes and behavior, although this value is shared to some extent with whites in the regional subculture of the SOUTHERN STATES. A third distinctive feature of the culture is ALIENATION, manifested politically in a high degree of cynicism and distrust of the government and its officials. The political culture is also fundamentally liberal, with very few adherents of CONSERVATISM as an IDEOLOGY. Lastly, there is an ethos of EQUALITY or equalitarianism in the culture, sometimes inchoate and sometimes expressed in ideology and PUBLIC POLICY preferences. There is also a tendency in the culture to place greater emphasis on the value of charismatic styles of leadership and on political oratory and jeremiads. This cultural tendency is to some extent traceable to religiosity. MATTHEW HOLDEN JR. put this tendency in context when he wrote, "The black culture is a culture in which, relatively speaking, oratorical debating competence is far more praiseworthy. . . . Black audiences, unless very well educated, will not sit still for the sort of dullness which passes . . . in white sermons. A black preacher . . . better be a good talker." It should be emphasized, as Holden does with respect to this element, that all attributes of the black political culture are relative rather than absolute or fixed. But like the values of the general culture, they structure the nature and boundaries of political thinking and behavior in the black community.

See also BLACKNESS, LIBERALISM, PUBLIC OPINION, and SOCIALISM.

Further reading: Robert C. Smith and Richard Seltzer, *Race, Class and Culture: A Study in Afro-American Mass Opinion* (Albany: State University of New York Press, 1992).

political incorporation

Political incorporation refers to the process of incorporating or including previously excluded groups into the processes of the POLITICAL SYSTEM. In a DEMOCRACY, the process requires that the previously excluded group at a minimum be accorded the full range of opportunities for POLITICAL PARTICIPATION, including the VOTING RIGHTS; that they have at least some chance periodically to join a COALITION that will sometimes constitute the governing majority; and that this governing majority when in power will be responsive to the interests of the group with appropriate PUBLIC POLICY.

The political incorporation of African Americans occurred late in the history of the United States, roughly in the late 1960s as a result of the CIVIL RIGHTS MOVEMENT and the BLACK POWER MOVEMENT. After obtaining the right to vote, blacks soon thereafter became a part of the DEMOCRATIC PARTY coalition. Yet, even in the POST–CIVIL RIGHTS ERA, the political incorporation of African Americans remained partial or incipient, since the Democratic Party has frequently ignored or downplayed some of the basic interests of the BLACK COMMUNITY. Thus, in the post–civil rights era, blacks have had the opportunity to vote and participate in the political process, occasionally becoming a part of the governing coalition (when the Democratic Party controls the PRESIDENCY or CONGRESS). Their policy concerns are heard in the deliberations of the government but not necessarily satisfied. This is because those concerns or interests are often at odds with those of the white majority.

See also BALANCE OF POWER, JIMMY CARTER, BILL CLINTON, CO-OPTATION, INTEGRATION, and PLURALISM.

political participation

Political participation is the behavioral component—what people actually do—of the POLITICAL CULTURE. It involves a wide array of political activities that individuals may engage in to influence the POLITICAL SYSTEM. Just as African Americans have exhibited a distinctive set of attitudes toward the political system (higher levels of distrust toward government, for example), they have also exhibited somewhat distinctive modes of political participation. For example, research during the 1950s and 1960s showed that, taking into account education and other indicators of social class, blacks engaged in more social and political activities than whites, including participation in ORGANIZATIONS,

voting, and various forms of PROTEST such as picketing, marching, and boycotting. While the VOTING BEHAVIOR of blacks still exceeds that of whites when one controls for social class (that is, when one takes into account the sizeable class differences between blacks and whites and compares the rate of voting of middle-class blacks and whites and poor blacks and whites, one finds that blacks in both class categories vote more than their white counterparts), by the late 1980s black political participation no longer exceeded that of whites.

Scholars of black political participation in the 1950s and 1960s suggested that blacks "overparticipated" in certain activities because they needed to compensate for their exclusion from mainstream society or because the BLACK COMMUNITY nurtured a culture of activism during the CIVIL RIGHTS MOVEMENT. Political activism was inordinately high among African Americans during the 1950s and 1960s as blacks formed and participated in a wide array of organizations and in numerous protest activities. Participation in organizations of all kinds declined between the 1960s and 1980s among all classes of blacks, but especially among the well educated. For example, black organizational membership declined from an average of 2.5 percent in the late 1960s to 1.6 percent in the late 1980s. While organizational participation declined most sharply among well-educated middle-class blacks, it is still the case that the middle class in the black community, as in all communities, is more engaged in organizational and other forms of political participation than poor blacks. For example, research in the 1980s showed that very poor blacks in GHETTO neighborhoods were substantially less likely to engage in any social or political activities, including church activities, and that the effect of living in "deadly neighborhoods" was having a devastating impact on the political and civic cultures of the ghetto, nurturing ALIENATION and increased isolation.

With the end of the Civil Rights movement and the BLACK POWER MOVEMENT, participation in protest activities would be expected to decline. In 1966 22 percent of blacks reported participation in some kind of protest activity, but the 1984 NATIONAL BLACK ELECTION STUDY found that that proportion had declined to 15 percent. This significant decline is to be expected given the decline of movement leaders and activism and their replacement by more system-oriented leaders and systemic-type activities. Yet, at the end of the 20th century, blacks were more than twice as likely to report participating in protest activities than whites, suggesting the persistence of a kind of protest ethos in the black political culture. But along with this protest ethos, blacks tend to participate less in routine system-oriented political activities. For example Norman Nie and his colleagues in the 1990 study *Participation in America: Continuity and Change* found that blacks were less likely than whites to have worked in a political campaign (8 percent vs. 12 percent); given campaign contributions (22 percent vs. 25 percent); contacted a public official (24 percent vs. 37 percent); or to be affiliated with an organization (38 percent vs. 52 percent). Blacks, however, were somewhat more likely to report participation in informal community activities (19 percent vs. 17 percent), such as attending meetings to deal with community problems.

The BLACK CHURCH remains, as it has always been, the main arena of activism in the black community. This kind of participation, rooted in the RELIGIOSITY of the CULTURE, is reflected in higher church membership and attendance, higher participation in church organizations, and a greater likelihood to make financial contributions. While participation in church-related activities is not an explicit form of political participation, it is related, since studies show that religiosity and church attendance are associated with voting and other forms of political participation.

At the end of the 20th century, political participation in all its modes was declining among all Americans, reflecting what some scholars view as a general deterioration of the American CIVIC CULTURE.

Further reading: Lawrence Bobo and Franklin Gilliam Jr., "Race, Socio-Political Participation and Black Empowerment," *American Political Science Review* 84 (1993): 278–89; Cathy Cohen and Michael Dawson, "Neighborhood Poverty and African American Politics," *American Political Science Review* 87 (1993): 288–89; Norman Nie et al., "Race, Ethnicity and Participation," in *Participation in America: Continuity and Change* (Chicago: University of Chicago Press, 1990); Marvin Olsen, "Social and Political Participation of Blacks," *American Sociological Review* 35 (1970): 609–36.

political parties

Political parties are collections of individuals with some degree of IDEOLOGY in common who join together to contest elections, operate government, and develop PUBLIC POLICY. Political parties are closely related to INTEREST GROUPS. Both are collections of individuals who join together to influence the government and public policy, but parties are distinguishable because in a DEMOCRACY the main objective is not ideology or policy but winning elections and therefore control of the government. Thus, for parties, unlike interest groups, public policy or ideology may be subordinated to the overarching objective of winning elections.

Political scientists consider political parties indispensable to democracies because they provide mechanisms for ordinary people without wealth or status to advance their interests. To advance these interests, democracy requires at least two parties that present reasonably clear and coherent alternative policies and programs to the voters and seek, if elected, to implement those programs and policies. Political scientists in the United States refer to this as the "responsible" political party model. The United States, almost alone among the democracies of the world, has always had a TWO-PARTY SYSTEM, that is, a system where only two parties have a realistic chance of winning elections and taking part in the operation of government. And generally the two parties have not been "responsible" in presenting distinct policies and programs and successfully implementing them when elected. Rather, both parties have historically tended to present less-than-distinct policy alternatives and have only occasionally been successful in implementing the alternatives offered. This "irresponsible" nature of the American parties results from the tendency in all two-party systems for both parties to move toward the middle and the "median voter." In the United States, this tendency is reinforced by the centrifugal forces of FEDERALISM and the SEPARATION OF POWERS. Because of these centrifugal forces, autonomous state parties and presidential and congressional parties (or factions of parties) compete to win control of the PRESIDENCY, CONGRESS, and STATE AND LOCAL GOVERNMENTS in elections held at different times and places.

The consequences of these attributes of American political parties are that they have rarely been able to address issues of concern to blacks, such as SLAVERY or SEGREGATION. This is because both parties appeal to the median voter, who is white and frequently indifferent or hostile to the interests of blacks. And even when the median white voter is not hostile or indifferent to black interests, the autonomy of state parties under federalism allowed the SOUTHERN STATES to develop programs and policies adverse to blacks at the state and local level; to elect representatives to Congress independent of the national parties; and to frequently veto nominees for the presidency sympathetic to the interest of blacks. Thus, the political parties in the United States have rarely served the interests of black Americans, forcing blacks to rely more on interest groups, SOCIAL MOVEMENTS, and PROTEST to advance their interests.

See also DEMOCRATIC PARTY, REPUBLICAN PARTY, and THIRD PARTIES.

Further reading: Samuel Eldersfeld and Hanes Walton Jr., "The Party System and the Race Problem," in *Political Parties in American Society* (New York: Bedford/St. Martin's Press, 2000).

political repression

Political repression involves the application of policies and programs instituted by the elites of a POLITICAL SYSTEM in order to maintain the system's core values and its prevailing POWER relationships. All political systems wish to persist—avoid revolutionary transformations—and to avoid situations of instability or crisis that threaten the normal or routine operations or legitimacy. A major objective of a system's POWER ELITE is to maintain basic system values and institutions and to avoid or deal with threats to stability and legitimacy. The power elite also wish to maintain their disproportionate capacity to exercise power in the system. In any political system, the emergence of new groups, ideas, ideologies, organizations, and movements can occasionally threaten or appear to threaten system maintenance. When this occurs, the system responds with programs and policies of political repression, more or less severe, depending on the nature of the threat. Political repression can also be employed prophylactically to prevent the emergence of ideas, groups, or demands that might eventually pose a threat to the system.

In all political systems certain ideas or ideologies are viewed as antisystemic (that is, as contrary to the system's basic values), and consequently they are stigmatized, and persons holding them are considered "outside of the mainstream" and are discriminated against in the normal, routine processes of the system's politics. Programs and policies of political repression involve the negative sanctioning of certain individuals and groups because of their IDEOLOGY. The negative sanctions can include banning or suppressing of ideas; denial of access to the MEDIA; attempts to infiltrate, subvert, and disrupt political organizations; efforts to harass and discredit political leaders; legal or judicial repression; forced exile; and in extreme cases, violence.

For virtually all of their history in the United States, African Americans have seen their ideas, organizations, and leaders subjected to political repression. This is because for much of this history, the OPPRESSION of African Americans has been an integral part of the normal, routine operations of the political system, and RACISM and WHITE SUPREMACY have been core system values. When black leaders and organizations challenged their oppression and the values of racism and white supremacy, the system responded with policies and programs of repression. These policies have ranged from the GAG RULE of the 1830s, to efforts to harass and discredit the ABOLITIONIST MOVEMENT, to violent suppression of the SLAVE REVOLTS. As a result of the CIVIL WAR and the adoption of the RECONSTRUCTION amendments to the CONSTITUTION, racism and white supremacy formally ceased to be system values. However, the oppression of African Americans did not cease. Instead, after the abolition of SLAVERY, the oppression of blacks took on new forms with the coming of JIM CROW–style SEGREGATION. When blacks in the SOUTHERN STATES rebelled against these new forms, virtually every means of repression was employed against them by white citizens and STATE AND LOCAL GOVERNMENTS, including sometimes severe and brutal violence.

At the beginning of the 20th century, African Americans and their white allies organized the CIVIL RIGHTS MOVEMENT to PROTEST segregation and DISCRIMINATION. From its inception, the Civil Rights movement was subjected to various modes of political repression, even though this movement was simply seeking to uphold the core system value of CONSTITUTIONALISM as expressed by the FOURTEENTH AMENDMENT and the FIFTEENTH AMENDMENT. Movements of RADICALISM among blacks were also repressed throughout the 20th century, including those led by MARCUS GARVEY and ELIJAH MUHAMMAD. In the 1950s the FBI, under J. EDGAR HOOVER, developed and implemented a formal program of political repression called COINTELPRO. COINTELPRO's stated purpose was to "expose, disrupt and otherwise neutralize" black organizations and to harass and discredit black leaders, including MARTIN LUTHER KING JR., the preeminent leader of the time. In addition to challenging racism and white supremacy, some black leaders in the 20th century challenged CAPITALISM, viewing it as integral to the subordination of blacks. When such leaders as W. E. B. DU BOIS, A. PHILIP RANDOLPH, and PAUL ROBESON embraced SOCIALISM or in some cases COMMUNISM, they were politically repressed in a variety of ways because capitalism is a core system value. The BLACK PANTHER PARTY, an explicitly revolutionary organization during the 1960s, faced virtually every mode of repression including violence. But even the NAACP, a moderate, system-oriented CIVIL RIGHTS organization, was not immune to some forms of repression.

The elites of political systems would prefer to maintain their values and institutions without repression by using PUBLIC POLICY, symbolism, or CO-OPTATION. But when individuals and organizations appear to pose a continuing danger to system values or stability, political repression is routinely employed. For much of American history, the presence of African Americans has posed or appeared to pose some kind of threat to the system. Thus political repression has been an abiding feature of the African-American experience.

See also COLFAX MASSACRE, KU KLUX KLAN, LYNCHING, and RIOTS.

Further reading: Robert Goldstein, *Political Repression in Modern America* (Cambridge, Mass.: Schenkman, 1978); Stephen Tompkins, "Army Feared King, Spying on Blacks Started 75 Years Ago," *Memphis Commercial Appeal*, March 21, 1993; U.S. Congress, Senate, *Final Report of the Select Committee to Study Government Operations with Respect to Intelligence*, 94th Cong. 2nd sess., 1976, Rept. 755; Alan Wolfe, *The Seeming Side of*

Democracy: Repression in America (New York: David McKay, 1973).

political socialization

Political socialization refers to the process by which individuals acquire political attitudes, values, beliefs, and opinions. A related concept, POLITICAL CULTURE, refers to the enduring attitudes, values, and beliefs about politics and the POLITICAL SYSTEM. Political socialization deals with the process of learning and adapting to the political culture.

In 1959 the political scientist Herbert Hyman published *Political Socialization*. This book was the first scientific study of political socialization in the field of political science. Hyman's work focused on socialization as a process that begins in childhood and is generally complete by adolescence or certainly by early adulthood. The early socialization studies by Hyman and others also focused on agents or transmitters of socialization, especially the family and schools but also the church and the MEDIA. The work of Hyman established the agenda for socialization research for several decades, but by the 1980s scholars were departing from the view that socialization was complete by adolescence and questioning the centrality of the role of family and schools. The new socialization research suggests that the process is a lifelong one. That rather than ending at adolescence, the process of acquiring political attitudes and values (indeed, all attitudes and values) is rarely, if ever, fixed at a given age; rather, it is a developmental process that covers the entire life span. And while not downplaying the significance of family and school as agents of socialization, the more recent research tends to place greater emphasis on the media and on events and the environment as socialization agents. This new approach, while promising as an area of inquiry, has not stimulated a great deal of empirical work, unlike Hyman's seminal book, which resulted in a massive outpouring of socialization studies in the 1960s and 1970s. Rather, socialization studies since the 1980s—whether using Hyman's approach of focusing on children and adolescents or the new approach focusing on the entire life span—have been in short supply. Thus, we know relatively little about the political socialization process as it unfolded in the late 20th century among Americans generally and even less as it has unfolded among African Americans, since there have been even fewer studies of the socialization process in the BLACK COMMUNITY.

One thing is clear about the process in black America: It is more complicated than what takes place in white America, since it requires socialization into the dominant mainstream political culture and simultaneous socialization into the political subculture of the black community. This dual process of political socialization may involve resocialization and countersocialization. That is, black children and adults may be first socialized into the general political culture and then later resocialized to hold different attitudes and values as a result of exposure to changing environments and events, or these processes may be reversed, with initial subcultural socialization being dominant and then mainstream resocialization. With the present state of the research, these processes of socialization and resocialization are not at all clear. Also, while the same basic agents or transmitters of socialization—family, church, school, and media—may be operative in both white and black communities, they may function differently because of differences in the structures of these agents. Finally, there is a clear and discernable process of deliberate countersocialization as a result of movements of social change. However, the current state of research again leaves us in the dark on most of these matters.

The family in all likelihood is the major transmitter of attitudes and values in both white and black America, but some scholars have seen a decline or attenuation in the role of the family as an agent of socialization, the result of the changing structure (some say decay) and role of the family in the United States. While noting a decline in the role of the family, other scholars have observed a simultaneous increase in the role of the media, which has grown in size, diversity, and pervasiveness. Since the first socialization studies in the 1960s, there has been interest in the role of the black family because of the disproportionately large number of female-headed households. This difference in structure between black and white families raises the question of whether children, especially boys, develop different attitudes and values as a result of being reared in households where no father figures are present. Some of the earliest studies suggested that male children from fatherless homes exhibited less interest in politics and were less politically efficacious. However, these findings were tentative at the time, and since the 1980s there have been few systematic empirical studies, although the proportion of female-headed black families has increased dramatically since the 1970s.

Research on the school as an agent of socialization is also limited in terms of the impact of the civics curriculum and the physical environment and atmosphere of many GHETTO schools, where conditions of neglect may operate as independent agents of socialization. We do know from extensive research that the BLACK CHURCH and RELIGIOSITY are important agents of lifelong socialization, transmitting civic attitudes and participatory norms as well as working against the widespread inculcation of RADICALISM.

The media's role in political socialization is unclear. Historically, the African-American media was an important agent of socialization and resocialization, working against the negative stereotypes and negative portrayals of blacks in the mass media and inculcating a heritage of race pride and an ethos of PROTEST. More recent research is ambiguous on the role of the African-American media. Studies of the impact of the mainstream media's role in transmitting political attitudes and values are also ambiguous in their findings. Blacks of all classes, but especially poor blacks, are more exposed to television, which is believed to be the most powerful agent of media socialization. Some researchers have suggested that this television exposure limits POLITICAL PARTICIPATION and contributes to ALIENATION, because the POVERTY of so many African-American viewers means that they cannot participate in many forms of politics or take part in the conspicuous consumption that characterizes 20th-century American CAPITALISM. Other researchers see television having positive effects (providing knowledge, for example, about politics and society that would be otherwise unavailable), while still others see both positive and negative effects for television. Thus, the research is inconclusive, reflecting to some extent the difficulty of measuring the effects of media on the development of attitudes and values.

MUSIC has been shown to be an important component of the overall CULTURE of African Americans, with possibly both positive and negative consequences. Concern about the role of music in the socialization process was heightened in the late 20th century with the emergence of RAP MUSIC.

The role of the physical environment and events have also been shown to be powerful socialization agents, especially when the process is understood to be a lifelong one. From the earliest to the most recent studies, it has been shown that the conditions of poverty and danger in many ghetto neighborhoods are powerful socializing agents, providing independent learning about the negative attitudes of white society and the government toward blacks. Thus blacks, wherever they live, tend to be cynical about the government, but these attitudes are much more pronounced in high-poverty neighborhoods. Adults in these neighborhoods also tend to express more antiwhite attitudes and are somewhat more likely to embrace elements of the philosophy of BLACK NATIONALISM. Finally, the environment of the ghetto also appears to produce cynicism and distrust of the mainstream black LEADERSHIP establishment and mainstream ORGANIZATIONS such as the NAACP.

Finally, salient events and movements are also powerful agents of socialization, resocialization, and countersocialization. The CIVIL RIGHTS MOVEMENT in the 1950s and 1960s resocialized blacks into the ethos of FREEDOM and EQUALITY and transmitted an ethos of protest. The subsequent BLACK POWER MOVEMENT resocialized blacks into heightened race consciousness and solidarity and identification with BLACKNESS. The Civil Rights and Black Power movements also worked to undermine INTERNAL INFERIORIZATION. The WATTS RIOT contributed to the emergence among the 1960s generation of an ethos of MILITANCY. The videotaped beating of RODNEY KING and the subsequent acquittal of the police officers reinforced distrust and cynicism toward the CRIMINAL JUSTICE SYSTEM. And early studies suggest that the disputed 2000 election of President George W. Bush—in which there were widespread allegations of suppression of the black vote and with the SUPREME COURT finally declaring Bush as the winner in the ELECTORAL COLLEGE despite losing the popular vote to Al Gore—may have served to increase alienation and cynicism about the nature of the American DEMOCRACY.

Further reading: Paul Abramson, *The Political Socialization of Black Americans* (New York: Free Press, 1977); William Cross, "The Negro to Black Conversion Process," *Black World* 20 (July 1971): 13–27; Aldon Morris, S. Hatchett, and R. Brown, "The Civil Rights Movement and Black Political Socialization" in *Political Learning in Adulthood,* ed. Robert Siegel (Chicago: University of Chicago Press, 1989).

political system

The concept of a political system was developed in the 1960s as an abstract model designed to facilitate understanding of how governments—understood as systems that make and enforce authoritative decisions—are able to continue to exist in environments of change and instability. The model assumes that governments constitute "systems," interrelated and interacting components that constitute a whole. The model is based on two basic axioms. One is that governments as systems wish to persist; that is, the system strives to continue to govern in some fashion. To put this axiom simply: governments wish to avoid anarchy or the collapse of their authority. The second assumption is that political systems wish to avoid revolutionary or radical changes in their core values. Generally, persistence—the capacity of systems to avoid a complete collapse of authority—is rarely at issue. Most established political systems are able to continue to govern; however, political systems more commonly face threats to maintenance—the capacity to maintain their core values and institutions. In either case, the model predicts that when a political system confronts threats to its persistence or to maintenance of its core values, it will use all available options in order to survive.

The United States political system during the CIVIL WAR faced a threat to its persistence, the only time it has faced such a threat, and President ABRAHAM LINCOLN used all available options to preserve it, or as he put it, to "save the Union." Since then, the American political system has not faced a serious challenge to its persistence. But, from time to time, it has faced challenges to its stability and to the maintenance of its core values, and these challenges have frequently come from the BLACK COMMUNITY. The core values of the U.S. system are CAPITALISM, CONSTITUTIONALISM, and DEMOCRACY. Prior to the adoption of the RECONSTRUCTION amendments to the CONSTITUTION, core U.S. system values also included RACISM and WHITE SUPREMACY. Thus, from the establishment of the system in 1787 until 1868, the United States was officially or formally a racist, capitalist, constitutional democracy.

In their struggles for FREEDOM and EQUALITY, African Americans and their allies in the ABOLITIONIST MOVEMENT challenged the racism component of the system (a component embedded in the Constitution), and the system used virtually every available means, including POLITICAL REPRESSION, to maintain racism. The system continued to try to maintain racism as a core value until it was perceived that the existence of SLAVERY threatened system persistence. At this point, President Lincoln moved to destroy slavery in order to preserve the system. Once slavery was abolished and the FOURTEENTH AMENDMENT adopted, racism and white supremacy ceased to be official or formal system values, although their practices continued more or less unabated. Moreover, these practices were sanctioned by the system's value of constitutionalism, according to a series of authoritative decisions by the SUPREME COURT, most notably the CIVIL RIGHTS CASES OF 1883 and PLESSY V. FERGUSON.

At the beginning of the 20th century, African Americans, in COALITION with a few whites, started the CIVIL RIGHTS MOVEMENT. This movement, however, was perceived as a threat to system stability—not system persistence or maintenance but stability—and the maintenance of the constitutionally sanctioned practices of racism and white supremacy. Therefore the system responded with various forms of political repression. The successes of the Civil Rights movement brought an end to the formal practices of racism and white supremacy in the SOUTHERN STATES and their informal practices in the NORTHERN STATES. That is, as a result of BROWN V. BOARD OF EDUCATION and the CIVIL RIGHTS ACT OF 1964, racist practices lost their constitutional sanction, which is to say racism both as value and practice were viewed as contrary to core U.S. system values.

At this point, some leading African Americans began to view capitalism as an impediment to equality and mounted challenges. This was not a new challenge. In the 1930s and 1940s some blacks had embraced SOCIALISM and COMMUNISM, but in the 1960s and 1970s these challenges became somewhat more widespread and substantially more vocal or visible. Although they did not pose a realistic threat to the maintenance of capitalism, these challenges were, as the model predicts, repressed. In addition to these challenges to the maintenance of capitalism, a few black leaders have challenged system persistence by calling for the establish-

ment of a separate independent black nation within the boundaries of the United States. Although these challenges have never posed a serious threat to the system, they were, perhaps prophylactically, politically repressed.

The system model is a useful tool for analyzing how governments respond to challenges to their basic values and institutions. It is also useful for analyzing historically the relationship between African Americans and the U.S. government.

See also BLACK NATIONALISM.

Further reading: David Easton, *The Political System* (New York: Knopf, 1953); Robert C. Smith, "From Protest to Politics: A Framework for Analysis of Civil Rights Movement Outcomes," chap. 1 in *We Have No Leaders: African Americans in the Post Civil Rights Era* (Albany: SUNY Press, 1996).

Poor People's Campaign

The Poor People's Campaign was the last major PROTEST of the CIVIL RIGHTS MOVEMENT. It is sometimes referred to as the movement's "Waterloo" or its "Little Bighorn," referring to the places where Napoleon and Colonel George Custer, respectively, suffered decisive defeats. The Poor People's Campaign was organized by MARTIN LUTHER KING JR. in 1967, but he was murdered in April 1968, several months before the campaign was to begin in the DISTRICT OF COLUMBIA. Unlike the BIRMINGHAM DEMONSTRATIONS of 1963, which King led and which resulted in the passage of the CIVIL RIGHTS ACT OF 1964, and the SELMA DEMONSTRATIONS of 1965, which he also led and which resulted in the VOTING RIGHTS ACT OF 1965, the Poor People's Campaign achieved none of its legislative objectives. Although this campaign did not have the benefit of King's extraordinary strategic vision and charismatic authority, in all likelihood it would not have achieved its objectives even under King's leadership. This is because unlike the protests at Selma and Birmingham, which challenged RACISM and WHITE SUPREMACY, the Poor People's Campaign challenged CAPITALISM, one of the three core values of the American POLITICAL SYSTEM. Racism and white supremacy, while important practices in the United States, were—according to the SUPREME COURT in BROWN V. BOARD OF EDUCATION—not core system values. Rather the Court in *Brown* said that these practices violated another core system value, CONSTITUTIONALISM. Thus, the demonstrations at Selma and Birmingham were in one sense, as King himself frequently said, simply a challenge to the system to live up to its own values. The Poor People's Campaign, to the contrary, was a challenge to a preeminent, if not the preeminent, value of the system.

While not openly embracing SOCIALISM as the campaign's IDEOLOGY or objective, King clearly envisioned the campaign as a class-based COALITION aimed at redistribution of the nation's wealth. The campaign, also unlike the protests at Selma and Birmingham, would require a confrontation with the national POWER ELITE rather than the regional elites in the SOUTHERN STATES. JESSE JACKSON, who had initially opposed the campaign but became one of its major leaders after King's murder, was quite explicit about its radical, system-challenging objectives. Speaking at a rally during the campaign, he said, "Sometime before the night is over we are going to talk about capitalism itself. . . . People have been afraid of using the word because the alternative is supposed to be communism. Whether or not that is the alternative, capitalism is a bad system." While openly embracing RADICALISM, the campaign also, unlike the civil rights demonstrations, was targeted on the nation as a whole. That is, the target or adversary of the Civil Rights movement was mainly Southern STATE AND LOCAL GOVERNMENTS with their blatant practices of SEGREGATION. Therefore, the federal government could be called on as an ally of the movement. In contrast, the federal government was the target and putative adversary of the Poor People's Campaign. In addition, while most white Americans outside of the Southern states did not oppose the objectives of the Civil Rights movement, a 1968 Harris Poll found that only 29 percent of whites favored the Poor People's Campaign compared with 89 percent of blacks who supported it. Most of the nation's newspapers opposed the campaign, which contrasts with their support of the Civil Rights movement. Important white liberal, labor, and religious groups were part of the coalition for civil rights, but these groups were either hostile or ambivalent about the Poor People's Campaign. Putting all these factors together, it is likely that even a King-led campaign would have suffered the fate of Napoleon and Custer.

King decided to launch the Poor People's Campaign because after the CIVIL RIGHTS laws were passed, he turned his attention to the problems of POVERTY in the GHETTOS of the NORTHERN STATES. He soon came to believe that these problems could not be resolved without what he called a "massive redistribution of economic and political power." The WATTS RIOT and the subsequent RIOTS in the ghettos gave King a sense of urgency about the need for radical changes, and the ongoing BLACK POWER MOVEMENT caused him to turn increasingly to MILITANCY. This turn toward militancy was also fueled by his growing opposition to the VIETNAM WAR, which he viewed as an imperialist venture that was draining resources from the WAR ON POVERTY. These developments in 1967 led King to propose a Poor People's Campaign to the SOUTHERN CHRISTIAN LEADERSHIP CONFERENCE (SCLC) staff and board. Many of the board and staff, including Jesse Jackson and BAYARD RUSTIN, opposed the idea. Rustin, a key strategist of the Civil Rights movement who had planned the 1963 MARCH ON WASHINGTON, was adamantly opposed to the campaign. Rustin argued that although the campaign's objectives were acceptable, the strategy of protest could not be used to achieve them. Rather, Rustin argued that the objectives of the campaign should be pursued through voting, elections, and LOBBYING. King's response was that the radical objectives of the campaign could only be achieved by radical means of protest and CIVIL DISOBEDIENCE. King's views prevailed and planning for the campaign started, although without the assistance of Rustin.

The campaign's agenda included five objectives: (1) the guarantee of a meaningful job for every employable citizen, (2) a secure and adequate income for all who cannot find work or are unemployable, (3) access to land as means to income, (4) access to capital as means to full participation in the economy, and (5) recognition by law of the right of all people to participate in the design and implementation of antipoverty programs. To achieve these objectives, the campaign envisioned a multiethnic coalition of blacks, poor whites, Mexican Americans, Puerto Ricans, and Native Americans. This early version of a RAINBOW COALITION would also solicit the support of progressive, middle-class whites.

The strategy of the campaign involved three phases. First, several thousand people representing the different ETHNIC GROUPS would live in a highly visible tent city on the Washington Mall and conduct demonstrations. The second phase would involve massive civil disobedience and mass arrests, and the third envisioned a nationwide economic boycott of the nation's largest corporations and businesses. The second and third phases of the campaign were never implemented, but from May 14 to June 24, 1968, between 2,500 and 3,000 people representing the various ethnic groups came to Washington and lived in tents in an area referred to as "Resurrection City." For much of this time, heavy rains fell on the city. On June 19, a "solidarity day" brought 50,000 to a march and rally at the Lincoln Memorial. Resurrection City was closed on June 24 following two evenings of near riots. At this time no more than 300 people remained and the police, using tear gas and police dogs, easily dispersed the group, arresting nearly 200 people, including Ralph Abernathy, King's successor as head of the SCLC.

Throughout the weeks of the campaign, the protesters held daily demonstrations and meetings with government officials, but none of the objectives of the campaign were achieved. A year after the campaign RICHARD NIXON proposed a plan of welfare reform that would have guaranteed an income to all American families, but it was defeated in the CONGRESS. And for a decade following the campaign, the established black LEADERSHIP abandoned protest and pursued Bayard Rustin's strategy of lobbying to achieve the campaign's objectives of FULL EMPLOYMENT.

In 1978 the Congress enacted the HUMPHREY-HAWKINS ACT, which in its original design was supposed to guarantee a job to all Americans. But by the time it was finally passed, it was largely a symbolic gesture, having no impact on the employment or income of the unemployed and the poor.

See also NATIONAL WELFARE RIGHTS ORGANIZATION and WELFARE STATE.

Further reading: Charles Fager, *Uncertain Resurrection: The Poor People's Washington Campaign* (Grand Rapids, Mich.: William B. Eerdman, 1969).

population

In a DEMOCRACY, the size of a group's population is an important base of POWER. Other bases of power (wealth, knowledge, weapons, and so on) being the same, the larger the population of a group, the greater is its potential to exercise power. Even a relatively small group, if it is strategically located and if it exhibits solidarity or unity, can exercise the BALANCE OF POWER in some elections.

Blacks in the United States have always constituted a MINORITY GROUP in terms of population, although its proportion of the population was much larger during SLAVERY than it has been since its abolition. In the first CENSUS conducted in 1890, African Americans constituted 19 percent of the population, and at the time of the CIVIL WAR the black population was 14 percent. It then declined to as low as 9.7 percent in 1930 and then gradually increased until it stabilized at around 12 percent. In the 2000 census blacks constituted 12.5 percent of the population, or 13.9 percent if one includes those blacks who checked both black and white on the 2000 forms. For much of the country's history, blacks were the nation's largest racial minority group, but by 2000 the all-inclusive Latino or Hispanic group exceeded the percent black, and this trend of Latino growth is likely to continue well into the 21st century.

From 1790 until the GREAT MIGRATION at the beginning of the 20th century, the African-American population was concentrated in the rural areas of the SOUTHERN STATES. By 1970, the great migration of blacks from the southern region had come to an end, leaving about 53 percent of blacks in those states. Approximately 10 percent of blacks live in the western region (mainly California), 18 percent in the northeast, and 19 percent in the Midwest. This regional distribution of blacks is politically important because their presence in the large states of the northeast and Midwest means they sometimes can exercise the balance of power in the ELECTORAL COLLEGE and determine the winners in close presidential elections.

African Americans are also overwhelmingly an urban people; more than 80 percent live in large cities or their nearby suburbs, with about 20 percent of the population residing in rural areas of the southern states. About 10 percent of blacks live in suburban areas. In the POST–CIVIL RIGHTS ERA, the concentration of blacks in large cities has allowed them to dominate or exercise major influence in URBAN POLITICS, electing mayors and city council majorities in many cities. This dominance or influence is likely to decline given the growth of the Latino- and Asian-American population in many cities.

See also MULTICULTURALISM.

Further reading: U.S. Bureau of the Census, *The Social and Economic Status of the Black Population in the United States: An Historical View, 1790–1978.* Current Population Reports, Special Studies, series 23, No. 80 (Washington, D.C., n.d.); U.S. Bureau of the Census, *The Black Population of the United States: March 1994 and 1993.* Current Population Reports, series p20-480 (Washington, D.C., 1995).

populist movements (populism)

Populist movements, or populism, in the United States generally refer to SOCIAL MOVEMENTS of small farmers in the SOUTHERN STATES and the states of the Midwest and West who embraced RADICALISM in one form or another as a means to deal with the problems of POVERTY on the farms and in the cities. Its early radical reform proposals included government ownership of railroads and banks, an expanded supply of paper money, and a graduated income tax.

The populist movement first emerged in the 1890s. The historian Richard Hofstader writes that it was "the first modern political movement of practical importance in the United States to insist that the federal government has some responsibility for the common weal; indeed it was the first movement to attack seriously the problems created by industrialism." And the historian C. Vann Woodward concluded that "It is altogether probable that during the brief populist upheaval of the nineties Negroes and native whites achieved a greater comity of mind and harmony of political purpose [than] ever before or since in the south." The populist movement was the first COALITION of blacks and whites since the ABOLITIONIST MOVEMENT, but it was a short-lived coalition that was quickly undermined by RACISM and WHITE SUPREMACY.

The populist movement emerged out of the economic depression of the 1890s, when black sharecroppers and poor white farmers faced falling wages and prices and heavy taxes and debt. As a result there was an economic basis for a coalition between poor whites and blacks against the dominant economic and political elites of the Southern states. Led by Tom Watson of Georgia, who was white, the populists formed the Southern Alliance and later a THIRD

PARTY (the Populist Party). Both of these groups advocated debt relief, government ownership or regulation of railroads, and the progressive income tax. Although some white populists for a time sincerely attempted to build a biracial coalition, from the outset racism and white supremacy were stumbling blocks. For example, blacks were not allowed to join the Southern Alliance; rather, they were segregated in a separate white-led Colored Farmers Alliance. SEGREGATION was also practiced in the Populist Party leadership, even as it appealed for black votes. Eventually, the Populist Party was undermined by white supremacy as leaders of the all-white DEMOCRATIC PARTY convinced poor whites that a vote for the multiracial Populist Party was "racial treason." Thus, Hofstader concluded his study of populism by writing that this first coalition of poor whites and blacks was destroyed by fears of the "Negro bogey," fears carefully manipulated by white economic and political elites. After the populist movement collapsed, there was never another social movement of poor whites and blacks in the United States.

Further reading: Gerald Gaither, *Blacks and the Populist Revolt: Ballots and Bigotry* (Tuscaloosa: University of Alabama Press, 1977).

post–civil rights era

The post–civil rights era is the period of time in the United States beginning after the passage of the major CIVIL RIGHTS laws of the 1960s. The last of these laws, the Fair Housing Act, was passed in 1968, which was also the year of the assassination of MARTIN LUTHER KING JR. Thus, the era's beginning is also often marked by his death. The post–civil rights era also marks the end of legal RACISM and WHITE SUPREMACY in the United States as well as the end of the CIVIL RIGHTS MOVEMENT. At the start of the 21st century it constituted the longest period in history in which blacks enjoyed FREEDOM and formal EQUALITY.

poverty

Poverty is a relative concept without a fixed meaning applicable across time and space. For example, it is useful to attempt to define poverty in terms of some minimum level of adequacy required for subsistence or as some minimum level of decency in standards of living or well-being. But as a concept for empirical research, these definitions are not very helpful, since the meaning of minimum varies from society to society and within the same society over time. One way to deal with this problem is to establish a norm or standard for the entire society and then define poverty as some unacceptable deviation from the norm. But this definition of poverty also runs into the difficulty of determining the acceptable standard and then the level of deviation from it that constitutes poverty.

Fundamentally, these problems in defining and measuring poverty are resolved by politics rather than research, that is, those who have the POWER are the ones who establish or set the standards for poverty, if any are established at all. This is how the meaning and measurement of poverty was established in the United States. Until the WAR ON POVERTY was started by LYNDON B. JOHNSON in 1960, there was little interest in poverty or in defining or measuring it. In that year the BUREAUCRACY—specifically the Social Security Administration—developed an official measure of the poverty level in the United States and thereby defined the phenomenon. The measure is a crude and arbitrary one. It simply combines the cheapest cost of feeding a family for a year with an estimate of the proportion of family income used to buy food. This method of measuring poverty has been widely criticized since it was introduced, but except for minor changes (adjusting the level to rise with inflation), it has remained the definition of poverty and is widely used by scholars and policy makers concerned with the problem.

However one measures poverty, one thing is certain: It has been a widespread problem among blacks since SLAVERY. Slavery was at the roots of the creation of high levels of poverty among African Americans, since enslaved persons rarely received material goods beyond those minimally necessary for subsistence. Thus, RACISM and WHITE SUPREMACY are historically responsible for the creation and maintenance of poverty in the BLACK COMMUNITY. After slavery and until the 1960s, it was a widely accepted practice that blacks would receive those jobs—when employed at all—that paid the lowest wages. Thus, when the 1964 poverty level measure was first used, it indicated that 48 percent of all black families were poor, compared with only 15 percent of white families. Blacks were therefore more than three times as likely to be officially classified as poor than whites. Since the 1960s, the rate of officially defined poverty in the United States has declined substantially, but African-American families at the end of the 20th century were still more than three times as likely as whites to be poor: in 1993 33 percent of black families compared with 9 percent of white families. This disproportionately high rate of poverty has been the principal item on the BLACK AGENDA since the end of the CIVIL RIGHTS MOVEMENT.

The reasons for this persistently high rate of poverty and possible remedies in terms of PUBLIC POLICY were the subjects of extensive research and debate among scholars throughout much of the POST–CIVIL RIGHTS ERA, as well as arguments among policy makers. Widespread poverty in the black community was the focus of the last major PROTEST organized by MARTIN LUTHER KING JR.—the POOR PEOPLE'S CAMPAIGN—and of the formation of the

NATIONAL WELFARE RIGHTS ORGANIZATION, which was the first ORGANIZATION of poor black women in U.S. history. The problem of poverty and closing the gap between blacks and whites at the beginning of the 21st century was the last major objective in the African-American struggle for full FREEDOM and EQUALITY.

See also AFFIRMATIVE ACTION, CULTURE OF POVERTY, FULL EMPLOYMENT, HUMPHREY-HAWKINS ACT, UNDERCLASS, and WELFARE STATE.

Powell, Adam Clayton, Jr. (1908–1972) *civil rights leader, U.S. congressman*

Adam Clayton Powell Jr. was the leading African-American member of CONGRESS during the civil rights era. Elected in 1944 from HARLEM, Powell brought a style of MILITANCY and PROTEST to his work as congressman, unlike WILLIAM DAWSON, his Chicago counterpart who served at the same time. This style of protest and militancy was to some extent a product of Powell's activism prior to his election to Congress. As pastor of Harlem's largest BLACK CHURCH, Powell instituted mass marches and boycotts against DISCRIMINATION by Harlem businesses and

Adam Clayton Powell Jr. *(Library of Congress)*

the local transit authority decades before MARTIN LUTHER KING JR. used these techniques in the SOUTHERN STATES. Powell was also a militant advocate of CIVIL RIGHTS for New York City blacks. While a member of the New York City Council, he was an early advocate of QUOTAS in city employment. In Congress, again unlike Dawson, Powell demanded equal treatment for himself and his staff in the use of congressional facilities, and throughout his tenure he viewed himself as the "Congressman at large" for the entire BLACK COMMUNITY. The "Powell amendment" (requiring the cutoff of federal funds to institutions practicing racial DISCRIMINATION, which he introduced consistently throughout his tenure, was the inspiration for Title VI of the CIVIL RIGHTS ACT OF 1964.

In 1961 he became chairman of the House Education and Labor Committee. In this position he was responsible for guiding the passage of much of the WAR ON POVERTY legislation. Powell was also active outside of Congress, attending the BANDUNG CONFERENCE in 1955 (where, to the surprise of many, he defended the U.S. record on civil rights in anticipation of attacks from China and other THIRD WORLD nations) and organizing the first black power conference after the MEREDITH MARCH. (Powell saw himself as the originator of the phrase "black power," having used it as the refrain in his 1965 HOWARD UNIVERSITY commencement address.)

Powell was a flamboyant and acerbic personality. These attributes together with his militant style made him many enemies in the House, especially among racists and white supremacists from the Southern states. In 1967 he was expelled from the House on allegations of the misuse of his office budget, but a year later the SUPREME COURT in *Powell v. McCormack* ruled the expulsion unconstitutional. Although he returned to the House, his power was effectively over, since his seniority and committee chairmanship were taken away. Powell was reelected to the House in 1968, although because of a civil warrant (issued because he had refused to appear in court on charges that he had libeled a woman by describing her as a "bagwoman" for the New York police), he could appear in Harlem only on Sundays. During his last years in Congress, Powell was frequently absent, spending most of his time on the WEST INDIAN island of Bimini. In 1970 he was defeated for reelection by Charles Rangel. He died two years later.

In a survey of African-American political scientists naming the greatest black leaders of all time, Powell, the only ELECTED OFFICIAL on the list, was tied for the 10th position with FANNIE LOU HAMER. He was born in New Haven, Connecticut, the son of a prosperous preacher; educated at Colgate University (where for a time because of his light skin color he was assumed to be white); and received a master's degree from Columbia University. He authored two books, including his autobiography *Adam By Adam*.

Further reading: Charles Hamilton, *Adam Clayton Powell, Jr.: The Political Biography of an American Dilemma* (New York: Atheneum, 1991).

Powell, Colin L. (1937–   ) *government official*

In 2001 President George W. Bush appointed Colin Powell secretary of state, the most senior position in the cabinet and the fourth in line of succession to the PRESIDENCY. The secretary of state is responsible for the development and implementation of U.S. FOREIGN POLICY. Earlier, in 1989, President George H. Bush had appointed Powell chairman of the Joint Chiefs of Staff, the highest-ranking post in the MILITARY and the person who serves as the principal military adviser to the president. In naming Powell to the top military post President Bush passed over 15 more-senior generals, making Powell the first African American and the youngest chair of the Joint Chiefs in history. Still earlier, in 1987, President RONALD REAGAN had appointed Powell to the position of national security adviser to the president. The national security adviser is responsible for the coordination of diplomatic, intelligence, and military data for presentation to the president on a daily basis and is the principal "crisis manager" during periods of international conflict. Thus, in the span of little more than a decade, Powell held three of the four top positions (the other is the secretary of defense) in the foreign policy BUREAUCRACY. This was truly a remarkable development, all the more so given the historic exclusion of African Americans from the nation's diplomatic and military services.

Powell, the son of WEST INDIAN immigrants, was born in New York City and was graduated from the City College of New York, where he majored in geology while participating in the ROTC (Reserve Officers Training Corps, the university-based program for training military officers). Commissioned a second lieutenant in the army after graduation, Powell served two tours of duty during the VIETNAM WAR. In 1972 Powell, by now a lieutenant colonel, was awarded a prestigious White House fellowship. This fellowship allows young professionals to work at the highest levels of the executive branch for a year. It is at this point that Powell's rise in military and diplomatic circles began. As a White House fellow, he worked closely with Casper Weinberger, who was head of the budget office during the presidency of RICHARD NIXON. When Weinberger became secretary of defense in the Reagan administration, he named Powell his senior military aide. After six years in this position, he became deputy to National Security Advisor Frank Carlucci, and when Carlucci resigned to become secretary of defense, Powell succeeded him.

In each of his senior positions in the military and foreign-policy bureaucracies, Powell followed a pragmatic, moderate approach. Always cautious about using military force, Powell recommended the use of massive, overwhelming VIOLENCE only when this was required to win quickly and decisively, a lesson he said he learned from his experiences in Vietnam. The Persian Gulf War in 1991 illustrates Powell's approach to the use of military force. Although he opposed the initial decision to go to war to force Iraqi withdrawal from Kuwait (in favor of a prolonged economic blockade), once President Bush had made the decision to invade, Powell designed and oversaw the strategy that led to Iraq's rapid defeat. His poised and self-confident defense of the war on national television and the quick victory of the American forces made him something of a national hero and a prospective candidate for the presidency.

After serving two two-year terms as head of the Joint Chiefs, Powell resigned from the military, wrote his memoirs (entitled *My American Journey*), and announced his affiliation with the REPUBLICAN PARTY. In 1996 he briefly considered running for president. Although he eventually decided not to run, he was among the leading prospective candidates, popular with the MEDIA and among the leaders of both political parties. Polls taken at the time (1995) indicated that Powell *might* (might should be emphasized, since polls taken a year before an election are not necessarily predictive of what the outcome of a hard-fought campaign will be) have won the Republican party nomination and then defeated BILL CLINTON. Powell might have defeated Clinton in part because the polls indicated he might have received nearly half of the black vote, compared with the usual 10 percent for POST–CIVIL RIGHTS ERA Republican Party candidates. Thus, it is fair to add another historic first to Powell's list of accomplishments for an African American, which is that he is the first black person in history with a realistic chance of election to the presidency. But although he was popular among whites (more popular among whites than blacks, according to the polls) and among white media elites, politicians, and a substantial segment of the BLACK COMMUNITY—especially young blacks—his rise to prominence as a national leader was met with ambivalence and skepticism within the black LEADERSHIP establishment.

The reaction to Powell among established black leaders can be traced to his military background, his close association with Ronald Reagan, and his affiliation with the Republican Party. Powell's military background was a cause of concern because of his role in the Vietnam War, the invasions of Panama and Grenada, and the Persian Gulf War. African-American leaders in general opposed each of these wars. Powell's association with Reagan and the Republican Party in general, and Reagan in particular, was of concern because both were viewed by a majority of blacks as antiblack. Finally, some blacks expressed concern about Powell's BLACKNESS, wary that during the CIVIL RIGHTS MOVEMENT Powell was away fighting a war that was

Colin Powell *(Library of Congress)*

opposed by most blacks. RONALD WALTERS, a prominent black PUBLIC INTELLECTUAL, even went so far as to describe Powell as "un-Negro" because of his supposedly "white middle-class demeanor."

Although Powell did not run for president, he became the nation's most prominent black Republican. And while he supported the core elements of the IDEOLOGY of CONSERVATISM, Powell broke with the Republican Party by forcefully supporting AFFIRMATIVE ACTION and legalized abortion. As evidence of Powell's status as a leader able to transcend the boundaries of race, in 2000 George W. Bush reportedly asked Powell to be his vice presidential running mate. Powell declined to seek any elective office, but when Bush was elected, Powell was the first cabinet choice he announced.

Further reading: Henry Louis Gates, "Powell and the Black Elite," *The New Yorker,* September 25, 1995, 8–13; Juan William, "President Colin Powell?," *Reconstruction* 2 (1994): 57–68.

power

Power is the most widely used concept in the study of political science. Although somewhat vague and ambiguous, the concept is the key analytical tool for understanding government and politics. As Harold Lasswell and Abraham Kaplan write in their classic text *Power and Society: A Framework for Political Inquiry* (1950), "The concept of Power is perhaps the most fundamental in the whole of political science. The political process is the shaping, distribution and exercise of power." Although the concept is central to the study of politics, its definition varies. But at a minimum, scholars agree that A has power over B to the extent that A can affect B's behavior or get B to do something B otherwise was not inclined to do. Political scientists generally analyze power in terms of (1) its sources or bases, (2) the exercise or use of the source or base, and (3) the skill of the exercise in particular circumstances or situations.

With respect to AFRICAN-AMERICAN POLITICS and power, MACK H. JONES writes that "it [African-American politics] is essentially a power struggle between blacks and whites, with the latter trying to maintain their superordinate position vis a vis the former." The SUPERORDINATE GROUP–SUBORDINATE GROUP relationship is central to understanding power in African-American politics because it is this relationship that defines the phenomenon. This is because whites as the superordinate group monopolize most, if not all, of the bases of power. Although power can be derived from several bases or sources, ultimately it rests on VIOLENCE, which whites have monopolized throughout their relationship with persons of African descent. Indeed, it was the exercise of violence that facilitated the establishment of the superordinate-subordinate relationship in the first place. This asymmetrical power relationship has always characterized African-American politics and is what gives the phenomenon its abidingly fascinating quality as subject for study. This is because African-American politics has essentially been a politics without power, although the concept of politics without power is an oxymoron. African Americans do have a modicum of relative power, since while whites monopolize the bases of power, the exercise of this monopoly varies. Therefore African Americans have never been completely powerless in their relationship to whites. African-American politics is not an oxymoron, but blacks must use their relatively meager bases of power with great skill if they are to achieve their objectives of FREEDOM and EQUALITY. But no matter how skillfully they use these power bases, they generally cannot achieve their objectives—at least not fully—unless they can find allies and form COALITIONS with more powerful whites. This imperative of majority-minority coalitions is an abiding feature of African-American politics.

Power—the central concept in politics and political science—is intimately related to freedom, a central feature of African-American politics. Historically, whites have used their greater power to fashion an IDEOLOGY OF WHITE SUPREMACY that provided a rationale for them to destroy freedom for Africans in America. African Americans then developed an ideology of universal freedom as part of the rationale for their struggles to reclaim their own freedom.

See also AFRICAN-AMERICAN THOUGHT, COLONIAL-ISM, and SLAVERY.

Further reading: Robert Dahl, "The Concept of Power," *Behavioral Science* 2 (1957): 201–15; Mack Jones, "A Frame of Reference for Black Politics," in *Black Political Life in the United States,* ed. Lenneal Henderson (New York: Chandler Publishers, 1972); Ira Katznelson, "Power in the Reformulation of Race Relations Research" in *Race, Change and Urban Society,* ed. Peter Orleans and William Ellis (Beverly Hills: Sage Publications, 1971); Joseph Roucek, "Minority-Majority Relations in Their Power Aspects," *Phylon* 17 (1956): 24–30; Hanes Walton and Robert C. Smith, *American Politics and the African American Quest for Universal Freedom* (New York: Longman, 2000).

power elite

The "power elite" is a theoretical model used by social scientists to study the distribution and exercise of POWER in the United States. It is also an empirical concept that identifies and describes those individuals who hold the top positions in the institutional structures of American society.

As a theoretical model, the "power elite" concept posits that important or "critical" decisions (usually defined as those decisions related to the maintenance of the POLITICAL SYSTEM and its core values) in the United States are made by a small group—an elite—of individuals. As a model, it is contrasted with PLURALISM, which posits that in the United States, decisions are the product of the conflicting struggles of many diverse INTEREST GROUPS.

As an empirical category of individuals who can be identified and described, the power elite is largely an institutional phenomenon because, as C. Wright Mills wrote in *The Power Elite* (1956), "no one . . . can be truly powerful unless he has access to the command of major institutions, for it is over these institutional means of power that the truly powerful are, in the first instance, powerful." Mills posited that this elite was constituted by a tiny handful of individuals at the top levels of economic, military, political, and cultural institutions. Subsequent work by Thomas Dye, in a series of books entitled *Who's Running America,* identified the elite as those persons who possess the formal authority to formulate and implement PUBLIC POLICY for the federal government, and policies and programs for the major corporate, legal, educational, civic, and cultural insti-

tutions. This definition of the power elite used by Dye resulted in the identification of approximately 7,000 elite positions in three institutional sectors: (1) the corporate sector (major corporations, financial institutions, utilities, insurance, and transportation), (2) the "public interest" sector (the major national news MEDIA, educational and philanthropic institutions, the leading law firms, and civic and cultural organizations), and (3) the government sector (the top federal executive, judicial, legislative, and military officials). By far the largest number of these positions are in the two nongovernment sectors, 59 percent in the corporate, 37 percent in the public interest, and only 3 percent in the government. In all of Dye's studies, African-American REPRESENTATION in the elite was minuscule. While they constitute 12 percent of the POPULATION, they generally held substantially less than 1 percent of the elite positions. In 1990, for example, of the 7,314 elite positions identified by Dye, blacks held only 20. (Over the years, African Americans in the power elite have included PATRICIA R. HARRIS, THURGOOD MARSHALL, CLARENCE THOMAS, COLIN POWELL, SAMUEL PIERCE, and VERNON JORDAN.) This is striking evidence of the relative powerlessness of blacks in the United States.

Elite positions of power do not necessarily translate into the effective exercise of power, but they provide a *base.* That is, they give the persons holding these positions of formal authority the right to exercise power in some situations. They may not use the authority, but the point is that individuals who do not hold these elite positions are much more limited in their capabilities to exercise power. As G. William Domhoff, another leading scholar of the power elite in America, writes in *The Power Elite and the State: How Policy Is Made in America* (1990), "If a group . . . is highly overrepresented or underrepresented in relation to its proportion of the population, it can be inferred the group is relatively powerful or powerless. . . . Similarly, when it is determined that a minority group has only a small percentage of its members in leadership positions, even though it comprises 10 to 20 percent of the population, then the basic processes of power inclusion and exclusion are inferred to be at work." This is an apt description of the situation of the African-American MINORITY GROUP.

Further reading: Thomas Dye, *Who's Running America?* (Englewood Cliffs, N.J.: Prentice-Hall, 1990).

presidency

The presidency of the United States is the most powerful elected executive office in the world. This is because Article II of the CONSTITUTION vests all the "executive power" in the individual who holds the office. This "unitary" nature of the American executive contrasts with the executives in most other democracies, where the executive power is "plural" or shared among a number of persons in a cabinet. The Constitution makes the president the commander in chief of the military and the nation's chief diplomat responsible for the conduct of the nation's business with the rest of the world. The president is also required by Article II "to care that the laws be faithfully executed," making him the nation's chief law enforcement officer. He is also the chief administrative officer of the government, appointing and supervising the executive officers of the government and the BUREAUCRACY. Finally, although he is not a member of CONGRESS, the president functions as "chief legislator," recommending a legislative agenda in his annual state of the union address and other legislative proposals throughout the year. The veto is also an important part of the president's legislative role, since historically it has been very difficult for the Congress to override a veto (only about 4 percent of all presidential vetoes have been overridden). This means that little legislation can become law without the president's acquiescence. The president also in effect legislates when he issues EXECUTIVE ORDERS.

Finally, unlike in most nations, the American president is the ceremonial or symbolic chief of state as well as the chief executive. In most countries these two roles are separate, with a symbolic head of state (that is, a king or queen in England; a president in Italy or India) and a separate office of prime minister who exercises the executive power. Thus, the American presidency is an office of great majesty as well as power. The racial attitudes and policies of the American presidents therefore have always been critical in the African-American struggle for FREEDOM and EQUALITY.

At the end of the 20th century, of the 43 men who had served as president, very few have been allies of blacks in their quests for freedom and equality. HANES WALTON JR. and Robert C. Smith, in their text *American Politics and the African American Quest for Universal Freedom* (2000), classify the American presidents according to their racial attitudes and policies. Twenty-three (more than half) adhered to WHITE SUPREMACY, including ABRAHAM LINCOLN. Eighteen adhered to RACISM, supporting either SLAVERY or SEGREGATION and racial DISCRIMINATION. Twelve were neutral or ambivalent in their attitudes toward African-American freedom. Nine—Lincoln, ULYSSES GRANT, BENJAMIN HARRISON, HARRY TRUMAN, JOHN F. KENNEDY, LYNDON B. JOHNSON, RICHARD NIXON, JIMMY CARTER, and BILL CLINTON—have pursued antiracist policies in terms of emancipation of the slaves and promoting their freedom and equality in the United States. Although we classify Lincoln as an antiracist president on the basis of the CIVIL WAR and the EMANCIPATION PROCLAMATION, he was ambivalent, favoring freedom for the slaves but not racial equality and universal rights. With the exception of

Lincoln, Grant, and Harrison, all of the antiracist presidents served in the mid-20th century, most during the POST–CIVIL RIGHTS ERA.

Of the 10 greatest presidents according to a 1996 survey of American historians, six—George Washington, THOMAS JEFFERSON, Andrew Jackson, Theodore Roosevelt, WOODROW WILSON, and James Polk—pursued a racist PUBLIC POLICY; two—FRANKLIN D. ROOSEVELT and Dwight Eisenhower—were racially neutral or ambivalent in their policies; and only two of the ten—Lincoln and HARRY TRUMAN—pursued antiracist policies. In a ranking of the presidents according to their impact for good or ill on the status of blacks, the six best in order were Lyndon B. Johnson, Lincoln, John F. Kennedy, Harry Truman, Benjamin Harrison, and Richard Nixon. The five worst in order were ANDREW JOHNSON, RONALD REAGAN, Woodrow Wilson, Theodore Roosevelt, and Andrew Jackson.

In dealing with the issue of race, American presidents have been influenced by white PUBLIC OPINION, which has often been hostile to the black quest for freedom and equality, as well as the constraints of DEMOCRACY, the SEPARATION OF POWERS, FEDERALISM, and CONSTITUTIONALISM. But as Kenneth O'Reilly shows in *Nixon's Piano: Presidents and Racial Politics from Washington to Clinton* (1995), the men who have been president have not simply followed public opinion or the constraints of the POLITICAL SYSTEM; rather, all but a few worked hard to "nurture and support" racial domination.

Further reading: Kenneth O'Reilly, *Nixon's Piano: Presidents and Racial Politics from Washington to Clinton* (New York: Free Press, 1995); Richard Riley, *The Presidency and the Politics of Racial Inequality: Nation Keeping from 1831 to 1965* (New York: Columbia University Press, 1999).

presidential campaigns

Presidential campaigns are more than mere mechanisms for selecting the president. Frequently they have been mechanisms for raising issues and injecting new ideas into the political arena. Indeed, this has been the major function of THIRD PARTIES in the TWO-PARTY SYSTEM: to run candidates for president in order to place on the PUBLIC POLICY agenda issues ignored by the two major parties. It is in this context that African-American candidates have run for president.

In the 20th century, more than a dozen blacks have run for president as minor-party candidates with no realistic chances of winning, instead using their campaigns to raise issues of concern to the BLACK COMMUNITY or to serve as symbolic representatives on third-party tickets, usually parties representing some IDEOLOGY of RADICALISM. Blacks have also run for president as third-party candidates to establish or reinforce their status as political leaders. Generally, these black minor-party candidates received little attention from the black or white MEDIA and had little impact on the outcome of the elections.

In 1972 SHIRLEY CHISHOLM became the first African American to run for president by seeking the nomination of one of the two major parties. Chisholm's campaign for the nomination of the DEMOCRATIC PARTY was widely covered in the media, but her campaign had little impact on the issues debated in the campaign or on the outcome of the elections. In 1984 and 1988 JESSE JACKSON ran for the Democratic Party nomination, and in 1996 and 2000 ALAN KEYES ran for the REPUBLICAN PARTY nomination. Although Jackson received overwhelming support from the black community, his campaigns also had little impact on election outcomes, although his campaigns did raise some issues that otherwise might have been ignored. Jackson's campaigns also enhanced his status as the preeminent African-American leader and made him an important leader in the Democratic Party. Keyes's two campaigns received little voter support, did not raise new issues, and did little to enhance his status as a black leader or as a Republican Party leader.

Prestage, Jewel L. (1931–) *scholar*

Jewel L. Prestage was the first African-American woman to earn a Ph.D. in political science. Born in rural Louisiana, Prestage earned a B.A. in 1951 and then a Ph.D. in 1953 from the University of Iowa. In 1956 she joined the faculty of Southern University, the largest historically black university. As professor and chair of Southern's political science department for more than 30 years, Prestage is probably responsible for the teaching and mentoring of more African-American political scientists than any other person in the United States. Although she mentored without regard to gender, her status as the first and one of the most prominent female political scientists sparked the interest and served as a role model for many black women political scientists. She also contributed to the early development of FEMINISM in American and AFRICAN-AMERICAN POLITICS when she coedited (with Marianne Githens) *A Portrait of Marginality: The Political Behavior of the American Woman* (1977). A founder of the NATIONAL CONFERENCE OF BLACK POLITICAL SCIENTISTS, Prestage became its second president and its first woman president. She was also the first black woman president of the Southern Political Science Association and served as chair of the Louisiana advisory committee for the CIVIL RIGHTS COMMISSION. In 1989 she left Southern University after 33 years to become dean of the Benjamin Banneker College at Prairie View A & M University, the first full-honors college at a historically black college.

Proposition 209

Proposition 209 is the initiative passed by the voters of California in 1996 that prohibited AFFIRMATIVE ACTION in all STATE AND LOCAL GOVERNMENT institutions and programs. In California and many other states, citizens can by petition directly pass legislation or amendments to the state constitutions, unlike at the federal level, where the CONSTITUTION vests "all legislative powers" in the CONGRESS. The campaign for Proposition 209, officially called the Civil Rights Initiative, was led by WARD CONNERLY, an African-American businessman. The proposition prohibited the use of gender, racial, or ethnic "preferences" in the admission of students to the state colleges and universities, in the hiring and promotion of state employees, and in the award of state and local government contracts. The proposition was supported by 63 percent of white voters, 26 percent of blacks, 24 percent of Latinos, and 39 percent of Asian Americans. Sixty-one percent of men supported the proposition and 48 percent of women, but it was supported by more than two-thirds of white women.

protest

The term *protest* as used in AFRICAN-AMERICAN POLITICS has two distinct although interrelated meanings. Protest in its first meaning is contrasted with ACCOMMODATIONISM— the acceptance of the racial status quo as it exists at any given time while pursuing modest, incremental changes that do not stir up the resistance of whites. Protest in this context is simply the rejection of accommodationism in favor of strategies that challenge the racial status quo. GUNNAR MYRDAL contends that NAT TURNER and the other leaders of the SLAVE REVOLTS were the first "types of pure protest leaders" in contrast to the much more numerous UNCLE TOMS, who accepted the basic conditions of SLAVERY. However, since the revolts of the slaves were quickly and brutally crushed and often led to the intensification of POLITICAL REPRESSION, this pure type of protest was never dominant in African-American politics because of the near monopoly on VIOLENCE held by whites. The normal or routine type of protest is therefore represented by FREDERICK DOUGLASS and the ABOLITIONIST MOVEMENT. This type of protest involves nonviolent legal activities within the boundaries of the CONSTITUTION, and once established by Douglass, it became the dominant type of protest employed by the LEADERSHIP of the BLACK COMMUNITY. It was followed by W. E. B. DU BOIS and WILLIAM MONROE TROTTER and the NIAGARA MOVEMENT in their challenge to the accommodating leadership of BOOKER T. WASHINGTON and subsequently by the founders of the NAACP. In its purest and most effective form, this pattern of protest was practiced by MARTIN LUTHER KING JR. during his leadership of the CIVIL RIGHTS MOVEMENT. King's use of protest during the 1960s

Nashville police officer wielding nightstick holds African-American youth at bay during a civil rights march in Nashville, Tennessee, 1964. *(Library of Congress)*

phase of the Civil Rights movement illuminates the second meaning of protest. However, before discussing this meaning of protest, it should be understood that while the pattern established by Douglass has been the dominant or normal pattern of protest, the pure type represented by Turner never disappeared in black politics, as can be seen in the careers of individuals like DAVID WALKER, HENRY HIGHLAND GARNETT, STOKELY CARMICHAEL, HUEY NEWTON, and BOBBY SEALE.

Protest in its second meaning refers to a wide range of activities of CIVIL DISOBEDIENCE designed to provide relatively powerless groups with access and bargaining power in a POLITICAL SYSTEM. That is, INTEREST GROUPS that are relatively powerless when they use the normal routines of the political system—voting, LOBBYING, and LITIGATION—can turn to protest as extrasystemic means to influence the system to address their concerns. Michael Lipsky developed the classic model of protest in his 1968 article "Protest as a Political Resource." Lipsky writes that "The essence of protest consists of activating third parties to participate in a controversy in ways favorable to protest goals." That is, the protesters, relatively powerless, engage in dis-

ruptive acts of civil disobedience to gain the sympathy and support of more powerful groups, who in turn bring pressure on the political system on behalf of the protesters' objectives. The MEDIA play a key role in Lipsky's protest model, since the goals of protesters are to gain the attention, sympathy, and support of other groups so that they will join in a COALITION to support the PUBLIC POLICY objectives of the protesters. But Lipsky writes, "If protest tactics are not considered significant by the media or if newspaper and television reporters and editors decide to overlook protest tactics, protest organizations will not succeed. Like the tree falling unheard in the forest, there is no protest unless protest is perceived and projected." This means, Lipsky concluded, that "protest leaders must continually develop new, dramatic techniques in order to receive their lifeblood of publicity." Lipsky developed his model in part by examining the strategy of protest employed by Martin Luther King Jr. during the BIRMINGHAM DEMONSTRATIONS in 1963 and the SELMA DEMONSTRATIONS in 1965. In these protests, King used dramatic acts of civil disobedience to attract sympathetic media coverage, which gained the attention of powerful whites in the NORTHERN STATES who brought pressures on Presidents JOHN F. KENNEDY and LYNDON B. JOHNSON, which forced them to seek enactment of the CIVIL RIGHTS ACT OF 1964 and the VOTING RIGHTS ACT OF 1965. A critical factor in the success of the demonstrations at Selma and Birmingham was the violence of the police repression of the protesters. The nationally televised brutality of the police at Selma and Birmingham was indispensable in making these protests effective.

The successful use of protest by the Civil Rights movement during the 1960s led other groups to adopt protest as a strategy, including feminists, other ETHNIC GROUPS, students, gays and lesbians, farm workers, the disabled, and eventually even relatively powerful groups such as farmers and the white middle-class conservatives protesting at abortion clinics. Thus, in the POST–CIVIL RIGHTS ERA, protest tactics such as marches, picket lines, SIT-INS, and boycotts became so popular that by the end of the 20th century protest may have become a legitimate, systemic means of POLITICAL PARTICIPATION along with lobbying, litigation, and voting. The institutionalization of protest in the United States means it is to a large extent accepted as a part of the political process, which also reduces its effectiveness as a strategy because as it becomes more routine it becomes less newsworthy and receives less media coverage. This means that if African Americans or other relatively powerless groups are to use protest effectively in the 21st century, the tactics will have to be more disruptive or dramatic than those used in the 1960s. But the more disruptive the tactics used, the less likely they are to elicit the sympathy and support of others; and the greater the degree of disruption or destabilization, the greater is the likelihood of unsympathetic media coverage and a political-system response of political repression rather than public policy.

See also AFRICAN BLOOD BROTHERHOOD and BLACK PANTHER PARTY.

Further reading: Michael Lipsky, "Protest As a Political Resource," *American Political Science Review* 62 (1968): 1,144–48.

public intellectuals

The category of *public intellectuals* emerged in the early 1990s to refer to a diverse group of black scholars whose ideas transcended the narrow confines of the university and exerted influence on the broad, public discussion of issues of race and on the formulation of PUBLIC POLICY. Generally, the influence of most scholars in the United States tends to be limited to the community of scholars and students. These "academic intellectuals" do not attempt to directly influence the public debate. Rather, they confine their ideas to the routine venues of the academy: academic journals, scholarly papers, conferences, and books. The ideas of these academic intellectuals influence the public debate—to the extent that they do—indirectly and in the long run. In contrast, public intellectuals attempt to influence the public debate directly and in the short term by writing for the public as well as academic MEDIA, by appearing on television news and information programs, and by public lectures.

The tradition of the public intellectual is a long and distinguished one in the BLACK COMMUNITY, reflected in the careers of FREDERICK DOUGLASS (probably the first black public intellectual), W. E. B. DU BOIS, IDA B. WELLS-BARNETT, KENNETH CLARK, BAYARD RUSTIN, and JAMES BALDWIN. The idea of a TALENTED TENTH exercising LEADERSHIP of the black community is a variation on the notion of the public intellectual. What was new about the category of public intellectuals that emerged toward the end of the 20th century was the number of speakers and the diversity of their ideas and ideologies, and the scope of their audiences and influence. In the POST–CIVIL RIGHTS ERA, for the first time in American history, a sizable number of black intellectuals were employed at the nation's leading universities, were routinely published in the elite newspapers and magazines (the *New York Times, Washington Post, New Yorker, New Republic, Atlantic Monthly*), and invited to appear on widely heard national radio and television programs. Prior to this development, black public intellectuals were concentrated at the leading HISTORICALLY BLACK COLLEGES AND UNIVERSITIES such as HOWARD UNIVERSITY and ATLANTA UNIVERSITY, and their ideas were mainly disseminated through black media. Earlier black public intellectuals tended to be ideologically homogeneous, although there were always important voices of RADICALISM and an occasional adherent of CONSERVATISM. (Du Bois was among the radical voices, and George Schuyler, an iconoclastic writer, emerged as an advocate of conservatism in the 1950s and 1960s.)

The new category of public intellectuals is ideologically diverse, including many conservatives like Walter Williams, Shelby Steele, and THOMAS SOWELL; adherents of LIBERALISM like Henry Louis Gates, Patricia Williams, Orlando Patterson, and WILLIAM J. WILSON; radicals like MANNING MARABLE, Adolph Reed, bell hooks; and a few pragmatic adherents of BLACK NATIONALISM like HAROLD CRUSE and RONALD WALTERS. And unlike in the past, many of these individuals have directly influenced the shaping of public policy, for example, Thomas Sowell's influence on AFFIRMATIVE ACTION and William Wilson's on policies related to the UNDERCLASS. This is because many of them have direct access to the POWER ELITE, including presidents of the United States. Other public intellectuals eschew direct involvement with politics and the policy process in favor of a focus on a politics of the personal, using their ideas to encourage a kind of individual redemption based on love or other sentiments. Many of these intellectuals (Cornel West is an example) root their ideas in the writings of European thinkers (such as Foucault, Chekhov, and Habermas) and tend to reject black nationalism (referred to as "identity politics") in favor of philosophical stances on the universality of human OPPRESSION and the absurdity of the human condition in general. Still others, Ronald Walters is an example, root their work in the early tradition of AFRICAN-AMERICAN STUDIES and are actively engaged in the practice of black politics.

Knowledge is an important base of power, and at the end of the 20th century an unprecedentedly large number of black intellectuals were for the first time able to disseminate their ideas to the American public through the channels of the nation's major organs of communication.

Further reading: William Banks, *Black Intellectuals: Race and Responsibility in American Life* (New York: W. W. Norton, 1996); Jerry Watts, "Dilemmas of Black Intellectuals," *Dissent* 36 (1989): 507–34.

public opinion

Public opinion is the aggregate of the views of individuals in a society about issues of importance or of mere interest to the public. Public opinion can be about the POLITICAL SYSTEM or PUBLIC POLICY, about political leaders and ideas, or about various groups in the society. However, there is no *public* opinion in the sense of an opinion that is held by the general population; rather there are many publics that hold varying opinions on various issues. Public opinion or the opinions of various publics are important in a DEMOCRACY because, in some ways and at some times, what democratic governments do is constrained by or is a product of the opinions of the public. In democracies, public opinion manifests itself most decisively in elections, when it determines what POLITICAL PARTIES, ideas, and leaders will direct the operations of government. However, with the advent of the scientific public opinion poll or survey, public opinion in modern societies can be learned with a high degree of accuracy on a regular, routine basis.

Since the advent of public opinion polls in the early 1930s, issues related to RACE and African Americans have always been of concern to those attempting to understand the opinions of the American public. This is understandable, since issues related to race have been among the most important in the history of the United States, omnipresent and deeply divisive even before the nation was founded. The early public opinion polls on race and African Americans, however, tended to examine the opinions of only one public, the white one, ignoring the opinions of the black public. Many scholars of race opinion attribute the exclu-

sive focus on the white public to the influence of GUNNAR MYRDAL's book, *AN AMERICAN DILEMMA*. Myrdal saw the race problem in the United States as a "white problem," a problem rooted fundamentally in attitudes of RACISM and WHITE SUPREMACY held by whites. Thus, in dealing with the problem, white opinion was hegemonic, whereas black opinion was secondary, almost inconsequential. Myrdal put it this way, "In practical and political struggles of effecting changes, the views of white Americans are . . . strategic. The Negro's entire life and, consequently, also his opinions on the Negro problem are in the main considered as secondary reactions to more primary pressures from the side of the dominant majority." In other words, there was no independent black public opinion. Rather, Myrdal believed that black public opinion was not deeply rooted but instead was largely a reaction to white opinion and behavior and therefore was superficial, easily changed, and thus not worthy of study in its own right. This single-minded focus on the opinion of whites dominated research on race until the late 1970s and early 1980s, reflecting Myrdal's view that the key to solving the race problem was to change the racist and white supremacist opinions of whites.

Although a few polls and surveys of black opinion were conducted during the 1960s at the height of the PROTEST phase of the CIVIL RIGHTS MOVEMENT, they tended to be unsystematic, and they frequently used sample sizes that were too small to allow for valid generalizations. This situation began to change in the 1970s as a result of a combination of factors. The first was the emergence and growth of AFRICAN-AMERICAN STUDIES. Second, the tumultuous events of the 1960s fostered a growing interest in African-American society and politics in the traditional social science disciplines. Third, scholars began to recognize that Myrdal was wrong when he concluded that black opinion was merely a derivative, secondary, transitory reaction or response to white opinion. Rather, it was gradually accepted that black public opinion was worthy of study in its own right; that it was autonomous or independent of white opinion; and that it was as deeply rooted as white opinion. In response to these developments, survey and polling organizations began to conduct surveys specifically designed to study black public opinion. They also began to "oversample" the black population, obtaining samples of sufficient size to provide valid results as well as to study intragroup differences within the BLACK COMMUNITY. Thus the systematic study of black public opinion began in the late 1970s.

White Public Opinion

From the start of the scientific study of public opinion in the United States in the late 1930s, the numerous surveys and polls have consistently shown that the opinion of the white public generally is indifferent and uninformed about politics, political leaders, IDEOLOGY, and public policy. And on most issues it was found that the opinion of whites tended to be ad hoc, inconsistent, transitory, and often contradictory. These generalizations about white opinion held for virtually all segments of the population and for all issues, foreign and domestic, with one important exception. That exception was opinions on race. Consistently, public opinion surveys have shown that whites have fairly predictable and relatively fixed opinions on race or, more specifically, on African Americans. As Donald Kinder and Lynn Sanders put it in their 1996 book *Divided by Color: Racial Politics and Democratic Ideals,* "compared with opinion on other matters, opinions on race are coherent, more tenaciously held and more difficult to alter. . . . [White] Americans know what they think about race." What a large segment of the white public thought about race as revealed in the early polls was profoundly racist and white supremacist.

The first public opinion polls on the racial attitudes of whites were conducted sometime during the late 1930s (the exact date is not clear) by the Roper Organization. The few items that are available in the archives from these early polls show that only 13 percent of whites believed that blacks should be free to live wherever they wished; 50 percent believed that whites "should have the first chance at any job"; and 70 percent believed that blacks were less intelligent than whites. These racist and white-supremacist opinions among large segments of the white public persisted until the late 1960s. Thereafter, polls have consistently shown that very few whites express openly white-supremacist opinions (only 10 percent in a 1996 survey, for example, agreed with the statement that blacks are less intelligent than whites), and virtually all whites accept the principle of EQUALITY. (Very few whites at the end of the 20th century would agree that whites should have the first chance at any job or that blacks should not be free to live wherever they wish.) It should be emphasized, however, that this decline in racist and white-supremacist opinions may not necessarily represent a real change in attitudes. Rather, it may merely represent a change in the willingness of many whites to express such attitudes openly to survey researchers. That is, in the POST–CIVIL RIGHTS ERA, it is less socially acceptable to openly express racist and white-supremacist opinions. Thus, there is probably more racism and white supremacy in the white public than is revealed in the survey data. This does not diminish the significance of the fact that the climate of opinion on race has progressed to the extent that in the post–civil rights era whites are reluctant or ashamed to be openly racist or white supremacist, because this probably makes for a climate more conducive to dealing positively with problems of race. But although the white public is less openly racist and white supremacist than in the past, this does not nec-

essarily mean that hostility toward blacks has disappeared. Instead, most scholars of race opinion argue that what has disappeared is old-fashioned racism but not necessarily the phenomenon itself.

In the late 20th century, the old-fashioned racism has for the most part disappeared, but it has been replaced by what scholars describe as a new, more subtle form of racism that has been variously labeled as "symbolic racism," "modern racism," "racial resentment," and "laissez-faire racism." This new or modern racism is represented in attitudes among whites in which they do not say that blacks are inferior but rather that blacks lack the initiative or drive to succeed in America because they lack the commitment to core or basic American values, particularly the value of INDIVIDUALISM. For example, in a 1996 survey respondents were offered several explanations for the persistence of racial inequality. While 35 percent of whites selected DISCRIMINATION as the "main cause," 52 percent said the main cause was the "lack of individual motivation" on the part of blacks themselves, and 77 percent said that despite prejudice and discrimination, blacks could work their way up or get ahead just like other ETHNIC GROUPS—the Jews and the Irish—who had faced similar barriers in the past. This so-called new racism is also manifested in negative stereotypes about blacks held by large segments of the white public. A 1991 survey found that 47 percent of whites thought that blacks tend to be lazy, 59 percent that blacks would prefer welfare to work, and 54 percent that blacks were prone to VIOLENCE. These opinions may not constitute old-fashioned racism or white supremacy, but they are negative or hostile and constitute barriers to the acceptance by whites of blacks as equals and to their willingness to embrace INTEGRATION.

Black Public Opinion

Since the systematic study of black public opinion started in the early 1970s, scholars have been able to use survey and poll data to delineate empirically the basic elements of the black CIVIC CULTURE and how it compares with its white counterpart. These data have also been used to explore those elements of the POLITICAL CULTURE that are manifested in mass opinion and to compare and contrast black and white modes of POLITICAL PARTICIPATION. With respect to ideology, the opinion data show a strong commitment to LIBERALISM and to elements of BLACK NATIONALISM. The commitment to liberalism is reflected in black support for an activist federal government and an expanding WELFARE STATE. Specifically, African Americans are much more likely than whites to support the idea that it is the responsibility of the government to see to it that Americans have access to employment, health care, housing, and a retirement income. And although African Americans adhere to the fundamental tenets of CAPITALISM, there is also in the black public a willingness to embrace elements of SOCIALISM. A 1996 survey found, for example, that 39 percent of blacks favored government ownership of electric utilities, 59 percent favored ownership of hospitals, and 47 percent favored ownership of banks. Support for these socialist ideas was much less among whites: 17 percent for government ownership of electric utilities, 20 percent for hospitals, and 18 percent for banks. Commitment to black nationalism is manifested in support for COMMUNITY CONTROL and the ethos of BLACKNESS. And while the ultimate or extreme black nationalist idea of a separate or independent black nation is rejected by most blacks, a 1993–94 survey found that 14 percent of blacks embraced this radical idea but only 29 percent of blacks "strongly" disagreed with it. And while most blacks did not favor a separate black nation, 49 percent agreed with the statement that African Americans constituted a "nation within a nation."

African-American public opinion also exhibits a strong element of "conspiracism." Polls in the 1980s and 1990s showed large majorities of blacks indicating beliefs that the AIDS-HIV virus may have been deliberately created by the government in order to harm or destroy blacks and that the government deliberately makes sure that drugs (like crack cocaine) are widely available in the black community in order to harm black people. This conspiracism is likely a result of memories of the history of OPPRESSION and the persistence of a high degree of ALIENATION in the CULTURE.

Despite the positive impact of the Civil Rights and BLACK POWER MOVEMENTS on the psychological health of African Americans, at the end of the 20th century black public opinion still exhibited tendencies of INTERNAL INFERIORIZATION. A 1991 poll found that 43 percent of blacks believed that blacks are prone to violence and would prefer welfare to work, and an earlier 1981 poll found that a substantial minority of blacks hold negative stereotypes toward their group. In this 1981 poll, blacks were grouped according to how they answered three questions: whether blacks had less inborn ability to learn, whether blacks would rather accept welfare than work, and whether blacks lacked the motivation or willingness to pull themselves out of POVERTY. Among the respondents, 10 percent took what might be described as the "antiblack" position on all three questions, 45 percent on one or two, and 45 percent rejected all three. The poll found that these antiblack feelings were concentrated among the elderly and the poor, especially those living in the highly segregated, impoverished neighborhoods of the GHETTO.

See also NATIONAL BLACK ELECTION STUDY.

Further reading: Donald Kinder and Lynn Sanders, *Divided by Color: Racial Politics and Democratic Ideals* (Chicago: University of Chicago Press, 1996); Howard Schuman, C. Sleeth, and L. Bobo, *Racial Attitudes in America: Trends and Interpretations* (Cambridge, Mass.: Harvard University Press, 1985); Lee Sigelman and Susan Welch, *Black American Views of Racial Inequality: A Dream Deferred* (Cambridge, Mass.: Cambridge University Press, 1994); Robert C. Smith and Richard Seltzer, *Race, Class and Culture: A Study in Afro-American Mass Opinion* (Albany: State University of New York Press, 1992); Robert C. Smith and Richard Seltzer, *Contemporary Controversies and the American Racial Divide* (Boulder, Colo.: Rowman & Littlefield, 2000).

public policy

Public policy deals with government-designed and -implemented remedies to perceived societal problems. In order for a problem to be addressed with public policy, it must be perceived by those in government as one that lends itself to a politically feasible remedy by a government policy or program. Until the POST–CIVIL RIGHTS ERA, it was generally accepted that the problems of RACISM and WHITE SUPREMACY were problems that could be addressed by public policy. The challenge was for blacks in COALITIONS with whites to develop the POWER necessary to get the POLITICAL SYSTEM to develop and implement the policies. Thus, African Americans and whites struggled for public policies to end SLAVERY and then SEGREGATION and DISCRIMINATION. Once these policies were adopted in the 1860s and again in the 1960s, the persistence of racial inequality led some to argue that it did not lend itself to a public-policy remedy. Rather, it was argued by presidents like ANDREW JOHNSON in the 19th century and RONALD REAGAN in the 20th that once slavery in the 1860s and discrimination in the 1960s were made unlawful, it then became the responsibility of blacks themselves to achieve EQUALITY through SELF-HELP. Andrew Johnson stated the case for self-help rather than public policy in his veto of the bill establishing the FREEDMEN'S BUREAU when he wrote, "The idea on which slaves were assisted to freedom was that on becoming free they would be a self-sustaining population. Any legislation that shall imply they are not expected to attain a self-sustaining condition must have a tendency injurious alike to their character and prospects." The ideas of President Johnson were repeated by President Reagan in explaining his opposition to AFFIRMATIVE ACTION and the WAR ON POVERTY.

In the aftermath of RECONSTRUCTION, the idea of self-help rather than public policy as the remedy to inequality was embraced by BOOKER T. WASHINGTON. For reasons different from Washington's, the philosophy of self-help was also embraced by leading adherents of BLACK NATIONALISM, including ELIJAH MUHAMMAD and LOUIS FARRAKHAN. In the post–civil rights era, leading conservative PUBLIC INTELLECTUALS such as THOMAS SOWELL rejected public policy in favor of self-help as the path to equality. This position, however, has always been rejected by the mainstream black LEADERSHIP establishment, which tends to believe that equality can only be obtained through a combination of self-help and public policy initiatives. At the beginning of the 21st century the philosophy of self-help was ascendant over public policy as a remedy to the problems of inequality and POVERTY. However, it is probable that these problems, especially as manifested in the GHETTO, are beyond the capacities of any self-help initiatives alone to remedy.

quotas

Quotas in employment, education, housing, and access to government contracts is a concept and a PUBLIC POLICY advanced by some black leaders to achieve racial EQUALITY in the United States. The concept requires that a fixed percentage of persons of a particular RACE, ETHNIC GROUP, or gender be allocated certain resources, such as employment or admission to a school. During the NEW DEAL, some black leaders advocated quotas in the war industries and government-relief programs to assure that blacks got their "fair share" (defined as their percentage of the workforce or of those eligible for relief) of jobs and welfare benefits. In the early 1960s, HARLEM's Congressman ADAM CLAYTON POWELL demanded that blacks get 21 percent of all patronage jobs in DEMOCRATIC PARTY–controlled city governments, since they constituted 21 percent of the party's vote. Powell's demands as well as those of black leaders during the New Deal were rejected. With the advent of AFFIRMATIVE ACTION in the 1960s, some institutions adopted variants of a racial quota in the allocation of employment and university admissions, but in *BAKKE V. REGENTS OF THE UNIVERSITY OF CALIFORNIA,* the SUPREME COURT in 1978 declared that racial quotas violated the EQUAL PROTECTION CLAUSE of the FOURTEENTH AMENDMENT and the CIVIL RIGHTS ACT OF 1964. And in the Civil Rights Act of 1991 the CONGRESS also banned racial quotas.

As a means of dealing with the problems of racial DISCRIMINATION against blacks, quotas have never been acceptable in the United States, although they were used throughout much of American history to discriminate against blacks (including quotas of zero blacks in many schools and occupations). Critics contend that quotas violate the core American value of INDIVIDUALISM.

R

race

The idea of race—the concept that the peoples of the world can be divided into a few biological classifications—was widely rejected by the scientific community at the end of the 20th century. Most biologists and anthropologists now accept the view that race is a sociological construct rather than a biological basis of human classification. That is, virtually all reputable scientists at the beginning of the 21st century adhered to the view that the division of humans into three racial categories—Caucasoid, Mongoloid, and Negroid—had little, if any, biological meaning. For example, researchers on the Human Genome Project (which examined the human genome, the genetic material located in almost every cell of the body) in the 1990s concluded that the small number of genes that account for differences in skin color and hair texture do not translate into significant biological attributes unique to racial groups. In an exhaustive analysis of more than a half century of research on population genetics, Luca Cavalli-Sforza, Paolo Mennozzi, and Alberto Piazza in *The History and Geography of Human Genes* (1994) conclude that the genes for physical traits such as skin color and hair texture are insignificant as indicators of other kinds of differences between peoples. They also found that the differences or variations among individuals within one of the so-called races is so much greater than the differences among the races that the whole idea of race as a genetic phenomenon is misleading. Indeed, the research evidence is clear: There is more genetic variation within one "race" than there is between one race and another. (It is estimated that less than 10 percent of the genetic differences between individuals is accounted for by individuals' membership in the three different racial groupings.)

In 1997 the UNITED NATIONS Educational, Scientific, and Cultural Organization (UNESCO), after reviewing the scientific research, officially declared that race was useless as a tool for classifying the human population. In 1998 the American Anthropological Association concluded on the basis of a similar review that the United States CENSUS should stop collecting data on the basis of race because, it said, the concept of race was based on "pseudo-science" and that "biological sounding terms added nothing to the precision, rigor or factual information being collected to characterize the identities of the American population." (Instead of race, the American Anthropological Association recommended that the census use ETHNIC GROUP as the basis for classifying the population.)

The idea that race is a bogus concept is not, however, a late-20th-century idea. Rather, it is simply more thoroughly documented. For example, on the first page of his 1939 book *Black Folk: Then and Now*, W. E. B. DU BOIS wrote that "no scientific definition of race is possible. Especially is it difficult to say how far race is determined by a group of inherited characteristics and how far by environment." Du Bois went on to write that the most that could be said about race is that "so far as these differences are measurable they fade into one another . . . insensibly." Du Bois's views on race in 1939 were based on his broad grasp of history rather than cutting-edge scientific research, but more than a half century later his views are the views of virtually the entire scientific community. This view of race as biologically meaningless is not shared, however, by the entire scientific community. A few scholars with acceptable scientific credentials continue to view race as a biologically meaningful idea with sociological and cultural manifestations.

Researchers on the Human Genome Project and the authors of *The History and Geography of Human Genes* go to great lengths to establish the proposition that there is no scientific basis for the belief in the genetic superiority of any one population group ("race") over another. They do this because of the awareness that the classifications of the peoples of the world into three races has its origins in the era of European COLONIALISM, and that the initial classifications were part of the IDEOLOGY of WHITE SUPREMACY used to rationalize the practice of RACISM. The earliest scientific classification of humanity into races was developed by Carolus Linnaeus, a Swedish biologist and taxonomist, who in 1758 categorized the peoples of the world into four racial categories: (1) white (European), (2) red (Indians), (3) black (Africans), and (4) dark (Asians). Linnaeus contended that the Europeans were the superior race, characterized by self-reliance and industriousness, while the inferior African race was lazy and emotionally unstable. This classification scheme was modified (over the years Indians and Asians were placed in the same category) and became part of the basis for the development of various European ideologies of race superiority and inferiority and the practice of various degrees of DISCRIMINATION and OPPRESSION of nonwhite peoples. The idea of race therefore has always been more than a mere tool of scientific classification. It has virtually always been also an instrument of POWER in the subordination and exploitation of parts of humanity. This is why the renowned anthropologist Ashley Montagu called the idea of race "man's most dangerous myth," a myth that continued to find adherents at the end of the 20th century, notwithstanding the views of the established scientific community.

The U.S. government continued to use the modified Linnaeus classification in its conduct of the census of the POPULATION, contending that while it is not, perhaps, scientifically valid in a biological sense, it is still a useful sociological and political category and should be retained in order to maintain continuity in the collection of statistical data. The African-American LEADERSHIP, while recognizing the white supremacist and racist origins of the classification, also strongly supported the retention of the race classifications that have been used since the first census in 1790. In addition to its use as a sociological and political tool, the discredited Linnaeus classification is used by a few social scientists as a genetic or biological schema to buttress ideas of white supremacy and racism. In 1994 Richard Herrnstein and Charles Murray published *The Bell Curve: Intelligence and Class Structure in America,* a best-selling book that claimed there was a genetic explanation for the gap in the average "IQ" of blacks and whites. And in 1996 J. Phillipe Rushlon, a psychologist, wrote *Race, Evolution and Behavior,* which purports to show that there are genetically based differences in the brains of the three races—Europeans, Asians, and Africans—and that these differences affect IQ as well as propensities of the races toward family formation, sexual activities, and crime. While the works of Herrenstein and Murray and Rushlon and related works were condemned by the scientific establishment, the persistence of the idea of race as a biological category that partly determines behavior is not likely to disappear from the scientific research. And persistence of its use in the collection of statistical data on the population suggests that it is not likely to disappear from social and political consciousness and debate in the United States and elsewhere.

racism

Racism, VIOLENCE, and the IDEOLOGY of WHITE SUPREMACY are among the distinguishing features of the experience of African peoples in their relationships with the peoples of Europe, and they are defining attributes of AFRICAN-AMERICAN POLITICS. Racism, however, like many other important concepts in the social sciences, does not have a universally acknowledged or accepted definition. Rather, the concept is defined in different ways by social scientists, and the different definitions have important implications for the processes of PUBLIC POLICY. Scientific concepts or definitions are neither true nor false, correct nor incorrect; rather, they are more or less empirically and theoretically useful in observing and explaining phenomena. This axiom about scientific concepts is very important in research on racism, for the concept needs to be defined in a way that allows precision in empirical observation and objectivity in theoretical explanation. This is because the word *racism* is frequently used in an inflammatory way and is often confused with such related but distinct phenomena as prejudice, bigotry, and stereotypes.

The definition of racism developed by STOKELY CARMICHAEL and CHARLES HAMILTON in their book *Black Power: The Politics of Liberation in America* seems useful for purposes of empirical observation and theoretical explanation. Carmichael and Hamilton defined racism as "the predication of decisions and policies on considerations of race for the purpose of subordinating a racial group and maintaining control over it." The Carmichael and Hamilton definition does not say, as many definitions and concepts of racism do, that racism involves beliefs or attitudes about the superiority, inherent or otherwise, of a particular racial group, and that on that basis policies are implemented to subordinate and control other racial groups. Rather, it simply indicates that whenever one empirically observes decisions or policies that have the intent or effect of subordinating a racial group, that phenomenon is properly identified as racism. This way to defining racism is useful because it focuses on *behavior* and not on attitudes or beliefs. Thus, it is clearly distinguishable from such attitudinal phenomena as prejudice, stereotypical thinking, or bigotry. Individuals may be prejudiced, bigoted, or hold negative stereotypes about individuals in another group without necessarily acting in a racist manner toward those individuals. *Racism is about doing something to people on the basis of their race rather than thinking something about them.* Defining racism in this way facilitates the process of empirical research; that is, it makes racism an observable phenomenon for the researcher. Many scholars define racism as simply the belief that RACE accounts for differences in human populations and that some racial groups are superior to others. This definition makes the empirical observation of the phenomenon virtually impossible because it requires inquiry into the mind or thought processes of individuals, which is difficult to do. Moreover, these thought processes do not necessarily translate into behavior, since it is theoretically possible for an individual to believe that a racial group is inferior but not act in a negative way toward it.

Some scholars define racism by specifically linking attitudes to behavior. For example, the authoritative Oxford University reader *Racism,* edited by Martin Bulmer and John Solomos, defines racism as an ideology of racial domination or subordination based on (1) beliefs that a designated racial group is biological or culturally inferior and (2) the use of such beliefs to rationalize or prescribe the racial group's treatment in society, as well as to explain its social position and accomplishments. This definition conflates a theory or explanation of the phenomenon with its empirical observation by positing that racism exists only if a belief in racial group inferiority is used to rationalize racial group mistreatment or subordination. But again, it is theoretically possible for one group (or an individual) to mistreat or subordinate another group (or individual) without believing or rationalizing the behavior on the basis of the inferiority of the group. (Indeed, one can imagine the mistreatment or subordination of a group on the basis of a belief that it is a superior group.) The Oxford definition also makes the process of empirical observation extraordinarily difficult because it requires a two-step process, requiring first the identification and observation of the beliefs in group inferiority and then a showing that these beliefs serve as the basis for the subordinating behavior of one group by another. Again, this complicates the process of research and in principle would allow behavior that subordinates a group—but that cannot be shown to be based on a belief in the group's inferiority—not to be seen as racism. Thus, for purposes of scientific identification and observation, the Carmichael and Hamilton definition is superior because it focuses on behavior—what people or groups do—and not what they think or how they rationalize what they do.

The Carmichael and Hamilton definition is also useful because it focuses on POWER as an integral aspect of racism. For racism to exist, one racial group must have the relative power to impose its will on another less-powerful group. Without this SUPERORDINATE GROUP–SUBORDINATE GROUP relationship, racism is a mere sentiment because although group A may wish to subordinate group B, if it lacks the effective power to do so, then it remains just that—a wish. The Carmichael and Hamilton definition also facilitated the development of an important typology of racism: INDIVIDUAL RACISM, which deals with intentional acts of mistreatment or subordination, and INSTITUTIONAL RACISM, which deals with acts that may have a subordinating effect or consequence without (nec-

essarily) such an intent. This typology of racism would not be possible if the concept was linked with beliefs. In other words, institutional racism would not exist because it operates independently of conscious beliefs or attitudes.

Finally, the Carmichael and Hamilton definition is helpful for its utility in the public-policy discussion on race, especially AFFIRMATIVE ACTION. Many opponents of affirmative action, including justices of the SUPREME COURT and President RONALD REAGAN, contend that affirmative action is racism ("racism in reverse") because any taking of race into consideration for purposes of allocating benefits or resources is racism. Thus, affirmative action—although intended to remedy past racist practices against blacks or to dismantle ongoing institutional racism—is racism against whites. Therefore, racism is *any* consideration of race in public policy, whatever its purposes or rationales. The Carmichael and Hamilton definition provides a clear-cut theoretical basis for why taking race into consideration for purposes of affirmative action is not racism. By the terms of their definition, actions are racist only if their purposes are to subordinate or dominate a group. Thus, it becomes nonsensical to view affirmative action as "reverse racism," since it is unlikely that the white-dominated POLITICAL SYSTEM would use race in order to subordinate or dominate whites. However, because of its use as an intellectual rationale for affirmative action, the Carmichael and Hamilton definition was intensely controversial throughout the POST–CIVIL RIGHTS ERA.

Historically, racism was an integral feature of the American political system, a core value along with CONSTITUTIONALISM, CAPITALISM, and DEMOCRACY. Racism in the United States was historically justified on the basis of the ideology of white supremacy. Racism was constitutionally abolished as a result of the RECONSTRUCTION-era amendments to the CONSTITUTION. However, its formal, legal practice was not effectively eliminated until the adoption of the CIVIL RIGHTS laws of the 1960s, especially the CIVIL RIGHTS ACT OF 1964. Nevertheless, racism in its institutional form has continued into the 21st century. The U.S. government acknowledged the persistence of racism in a 2001 report to the UNITED NATIONS. In the first-ever such analysis, the U.S. State Department in a report prepared for the 2001 U.N. World Conference against Racism, Racial Discrimination, Xenophobia and Related Intolerance concluded that racism persisted in "subtle and elusive" forms despite "significant progress" since the 1960s. The report pointed mainly to institutional racism, including SEGREGATION in housing despite laws that prohibit it; lack of access to credit and business capital; and DISCRIMINATION in employment practices and police brutality, racial profiling, and what the report described as "startlingly high incarceration rates" of African-American men.

See also DISPARATE IMPACT and DISPARATE TREATMENT.

Further reading: Martin Bulmer and John Solomos, eds., *Racism* (New York: Oxford University Press, 1999); Joe Feagin, *Racist America: Roots, Current Realities and Future Reparations* (New York: Routledge, 2000); Frederickson, George, *Racism: A Short History* (Princeton, N. J.: Princeton University Press, 2002); Robert C. Smith, *Racism in the Post Civil Rights Era: Now You See It, Now You Don't* (Albany: State University of New York Press, 1995).

radicalism

Radicalism is a philosophy, program, or IDEOLOGY that favors fundamental changes in the social, political, economic, or cultural institutions of a society. The original Latin word means "root"; hence radicalism refers to changes that uproot basic structures of a society. Radicalism as a philosophy favors rapid implementation of fundamental or systemic changes. In the United States, radicalism involves challenges to the POLITICAL SYSTEM's core values of CAPITALISM, DEMOCRACY, and CONSTITUTIONALISM.

Until the RECONSTRUCTION era, RACISM and WHITE SUPREMACY were core system values, protected by constitutionalism. After Reconstruction, racism and white supremacy, while not system values, persisted as widespread practices. As a result, until the 1960s the BLACK COMMUNITY produced large numbers of leaders and *organization* committed to radicalism and the rapid uprooting of racism and white supremacy. Important elements of African-American LEADERSHIP in the 20th century also embraced the idea that capitalism was an impediment to EQUALITY for African Americans, and they turned to SOCIALISM or COMMUNISM as alternative solutions. Finally, a few black leaders and organizations have embraced the idea that FREEDOM and equality for African Americans could only be achieved in a separate and independent black nation-state. Their support of BLACK NATIONALISM is a further example of radicalism.

Radical Republicans

The Radical Republicans were a group of members of CONGRESS from the REPUBLICAN PARTY who, during the CIVIL WAR and RECONSTRUCTION, were committed to FREEDOM and EQUALITY for African Americans. Those ideas were radical because they were contrary to the POLITICAL SYSTEM's then-core values of CONSTITUTIONALISM, RACISM, and WHITE SUPREMACY. Full freedom and equality were opposed by ABRAHAM LINCOLN during the Civil War and by ANDREW JOHNSON during Reconstruction, as well as by white PUBLIC OPINION in the NORTHERN STATES and the SOUTHERN STATES.

Led by THADDEUS STEVENS in the House of Representatives and CHARLES SUMNER in the Senate, this minority bloc of Republicans prodded President Lincoln to issue the EMANCIPATION PROCLAMATION and to support the THIRTEENTH AMENDMENT abolishing SLAVERY. After Lincoln's death the Radical Republicans, always a minority, formed a COALITION with more moderate Republicans, and over the objections of President Andrew Johnson, they instituted a PUBLIC POLICY designed to guarantee both freedom and equality. This policy included the establishment of the FREEDMEN'S BUREAU and the passage of CIVIL RIGHTS laws, the FOURTEENTH AMENDMENT in 1868, and the FIFTEENTH AMENDMENT in 1870. Many of the Radical Republicans also favored harsh punishment for the leaders of the rebellion against the Union and a radical restructuring of the political and economic systems of the Southern states. The political restructuring included guaranteeing VOTING RIGHTS to black men and assuring their REPRESENTATION in the BUREAUCRACY and as ELECTED OFFICIALS in STATE AND LOCAL GOVERNMENT. The economic restructuring envisioned confiscation of the land of the slaveholders and dividing it among the former slaves to provide an economic foundation for freedom and equality.

Although the Radical Republicans were a minority in Congress and many of their ideas were unpopular, they were able to achieve many of their objectives through passionate persistence and legislative skill. However, their achievements were short-lived as the first WHITE BACKLASH emerged, and the COMPROMISE OF 1877 resulted in the loss of many of the rights and freedoms that were gained during their leadership.

See also FORTY ACRES AND A MULE and REPARATIONS.

Further reading: Hans Trefousse, *The Radical Republicans: Lincoln's Vanguard for Freedom* (Baton Rouge: Louisiana State University Press, 1975).

Rainbow Coalition

The Rainbow Coalition is the concept of a multiethnic COALITION developed by JESSE JACKSON during his 1984 and 1988 PRESIDENTIAL CAMPAIGNS. The Rainbow Coalition is also the name of the political ORGANIZATION started by Jackson in 1985 to pursue his political program.

The concept of a rainbow coalition of blacks, progressive whites, and "peoples of color" was first used by the White Panthers, a 1960s-era Detroit-area white student group sympathetic to the BLACK PANTHER PARTY. In 1971 the White Panthers changed their name to the Rainbow Peoples Party. In 1972 RICHARD HATCHER used the rainbow idea in his keynote address at the NATIONAL BLACK POLITICAL CONVENTION. In this address Hatcher warned that if the TWO-PARTY SYSTEM did not become responsive to the interests of blacks, then blacks would form a THIRD PARTY that would include "Chicanos, Puerto Ricans, Indians, Orientals; a wonderful kaleidoscope of colors." In his

1984 presidential campaign Jackson revived the concept of a rainbow coalition as a strategy to build a majority coalition of minorities and whites that would make it possible for him to win the PRESIDENCY. However, Jackson's hope for a majority coalition did not materialize in his 1984 or 1988 campaigns, as he did not receive a majority of the vote from any group other than African Americans. Nevertheless the idea of a multiethnic coalition of peoples of color has remained attractive to the African-American LEADERSHIP, mainly because the United States has become increasingly diverse as a result of large-scale immigration from Asia and Latin America since the 1970s. Given this ethnic diversity, the idea of a rainbow coalition is based on the assumption that because the new immigrants tend to live in POVERTY and may face DISCRIMINATION and RACISM from the white majority, there may exist objective bases for a coalition in terms of support for CIVIL RIGHTS and a more inclusive WELFARE STATE. Blacks and the leaders of Asian American and Latinos are part of a broad coalition, with the leadership LOBBYING for civil rights at the national level. However, the Jackson presidential campaigns suggest that these groups are unwilling to join in an electoral coalition to support a black candidate for president or to break with the two-party system.

The Rainbow Coalition was formally incorporated in 1985 as a national organization, with state and local chapters. The organization was envisioned as a permanent, multiethnic group devoted to progressive social change, operating not only as an electoral organization but also as a broad-based lobbying and PROTEST entity. It was also envisioned that the coalition might perhaps run its own candidates (under the DEMOCRATIC PARTY umbrella) in local and state elections. These broad visions for the coalition never materialized. Instead, it became mainly Jackson's personal organization rather than a broad-based, democratic coalition. A largely black rather than multiethnic organization, in 1995 the Rainbow Coalition was emerged with Jackson's OPERATION PUSH. The merged organization, headed by Jackson, was called the Rainbow/PUSH Coalition.

See also LEADERSHIP CONFERENCE ON CIVIL RIGHTS and MULTICULTURALISM.

Randolph, A. Philip (1889–1979) *labor and civil rights leader*

A. Philip Randolph was one of the most important African-American leaders of the 20th century. Randolph was born in Crescent City, Florida, the son of a minister who was active in the local struggle against SEGREGATION. After graduation from the Cookman Institute, a historically black college, he moved to New York City, where he soon embraced RADICALISM in the form of trade unionism and SOCIALISM. In 1917, with Chandler Owen, he founded *The Messenger*, a radical magazine that attacked LIBERALISM and the gradualism of the NAACP. In general, the magazine espoused MILITANCY in the struggle for FREEDOM and EQUALITY, and its active opposition to black participation in World War I made it one of the most radical organs in the black MEDIA. Randolph's work with the magazine and his activism in socialist politics led the forerunner of the FBI to label Randolph "the most dangerous Negro in America." A leading African American in the SOCIALIST PARTY, in 1920 he was the party's candidate for New York State comptroller. In 1925 he assumed leadership of the BROTHERHOOD OF SLEEPING CAR PORTERS, and after a decade of conflict with the Pullman Railroad Company, the brotherhood received official recognition as the union representing the black porters and maids who worked the railroads. This was the first time a union had received recognition as the bargaining agent for black workers.

Although he was viewed as a dangerous threat by the FBI and was under constant surveillance and other forms of POLITICAL REPRESSION, by the start of World War II he

A. Philip Randolph speaking at the National Press Club, 1963 *(Library of Congress)*

was recognized as the leading black in trade unionism and one of the most influential members of the black LEADERSHIP establishment. In 1936 he was elected president of the NATIONAL NEGRO CONGRESS but withdrew from the group in 1940, charging that it had been taken over by whites loyal to the COMMUNIST PARTY. In 1940 Randolph also started the MARCH ON WASHINGTON MOVEMENT, when he threatened to lead 100,000 blacks in a mass march on Washington to PROTEST unfair labor practices, DISCRIMINATION in the war industries, and segregation in the MILITARY. The threat of the march led FRANKLIN D. ROOSEVELT to issue an executive order prohibiting discrimination in war-related manufacturing. Randolph, with his longtime protégé BAYARD RUSTIN, was the principal organizer of the MARCH ON WASHINGTON OF 1963. At the 1963 march he delivered a "Tribute to Women" address in which he recognized the contributions of ROSA PARKS and other women to the CIVIL RIGHTS MOVEMENT and introduced MARTIN LUTHER KING JR. when he gave his "I HAVE A DREAM" SPEECH. In 1964 he established the A. Philip Randolph Institute, which under Rustin's leadership became an ORGANIZATION dedicated to institutionalizing Randolph's ideas on CIVIL RIGHTS and trade unionism.

As his life came to an end, Randolp was recognized as the Civil Rights movement's elder statesman, and his "dangerous" militancy and radicalism of the 1920s and 1930s were distant memories. Committed to INTEGRATIONISM, Randolph was skeptical about the BLACK POWER MOVEMENT (earlier he had been one of the most outspoken critics of MARCUS GARVEY's brand of BLACK NATIONALISM,) and at the time of his death he was viewed by many young blacks as a conservative leader, committed to ACCOMMODATIONISM.

Further reading: Daniel Davis, *Mr. Black Labor: The Story of A. Philip Randolph, Father of the Civil Rights Movement* (New York: E. P. Dutton, 1972).

rap music (hip-hop)

Rap music (sometimes referred to as hip-hop) is a musical form that emerged out of the GHETTOs of the NORTHERN STATES in the early 1970s. Although rap is not a completely new genre—its origins can be traced to the work of the "Last Poets," a 1960s group—but as a style of music that combines speaking in rhymes ("rapping"), the innovative use of record turntables, and evocative lyrics, rap represents a new and distinctive POST–CIVIL RIGHTS ERA musical form. Rap or hip-hop is also a controversial form of MUSIC, and given the centrality of music in African-American CULTURE and the influence of music as an agent of POLITICAL SOCIALIZATION in the BLACK COMMUNITY, the emergence of rap at the end of the 20th century raised complex questions about the relationship of the music to AFRICAN-AMERICAN POLITICS.

Some aspects of rap are explicitly political, rooted in a black consciousness and MILITANCY based on the general philosophy of BLACK NATIONALISM and specific doctrinal tenets of the NATION OF ISLAM and the teachings and rhetoric of ELIJAH MUHAMMAD and MALCOLM X. Some rap is also explicitly PROTEST music, using the rhymes to express discontent with the conditions of POVERTY, ALIENATION, and police repression that characterize the ghettos. But rap as a genre also includes lyrics and video images that graphically depict, sex, VIOLENCE, and the abuse of women. Indeed, variants of hip-hop are openly referred to as "thuggism" or "gangster rap," commercialized commodifications of the alleged realities of life in the ghettos. Widely publicized incidents of violence in the hip-hop community, including the murders of rival rappers Chris Wallace ("The Notorious BIG") and Tupac Shakur, suggested that thuggism and gangsterism might be integral parts of the music's culture.

These thuggish variants of rap led critics in the black community to charge that the music as a socialization agent was depoliticizing young blacks and encouraging a kind of nihilism. Critics also contend that the music fosters negative stereotypes of African Americans in the United States and throughout the world through the process of GLOBALIZATION. (According to the Recording Industry Association of America, 75 percent of the consumers of rap are white, and it is one of the dominant influences on global popular culture.) This critical view of rap was cogently expressed by Conrad Muhammad, the youth director of the Nation of Islam, who remarked, "It is no good for white America to know black America through negative images. Rappers are modern day Sambos, shining and Uncle Toming for white record executives who think that only sex and violence sell." Black adherents of FEMINISM also condemn rap for its misogyny and its frequent use of the terms "bitches" and "'ho's" to refer to black women. The founding president of the NATIONAL POLITICAL CONGRESS OF BLACK WOMEN, C. Delores Tucker, organized protests and threatened to boycott the recording companies. Rap performers and some scholars and critics defend the music by contending that thuggish and misogynistic lyrics are only a small part of the musical form, and that this small part is a realistic reflection of the grim realities of aspects of life in the ghettos.

To some extent, the controversy about rap may simply reflect a generation gap—an older generation of blacks unwilling or unable to understand and appreciate the music of the young. But it also may signal a more profound concern that the music may reflect the status of the black community at the end of the 20th century. This concern would mirror the view of those who say you can tell where the black community is at any given time by listening to its music.

Further reading: Nelson George, *Hip-Hop America* (New York: Viking Press, 1998); Tricia Rose, *Rap Music and Black Culture in Contemporary America* (Hanover, N.H.: University Press of New England, 1994).

Reagan, Ronald (1911–   ) *40th president of the United States.*
Ronald Reagan was the fourth POST–CIVIL RIGHTS ERA president. In many ways his presidency is the most important of the era because of its effect on the African-American quest for EQUALITY. Indeed, the two administrations of Reagan are among the most important in the history of the PRESIDENCY in terms of the efforts of blacks to obtain FREEDOM and equality.

Reagan was a protégé of BARRY GOLDWATER, who began the REPUBLICAN PARTY's shift to the right on issues of CIVIL RIGHTS and the WELFARE STATE. Goldwater's 1964 campaign for the presidency was not successful (he lost to LYNDON B. JOHNSON by one of the largest margins in history), but it laid the foundation for Reagan's election 16 years later and the subsequent emergence of CONSERVATISM as the dominant IDEOLOGY in the Republican Party. The dominance of conservatism in the Republican Party and its increased influence on American politics after Reagan's administrations were so decisive that some historians refer to his time in office as the "Reagan Revolution."

Reagan, an actor, started his political career as a supporter of FRANKLIN D. ROOSEVELT and the NEW DEAL, but by the 1950s he had rejected LIBERALISM and embraced a highly doctrinaire or rigid form of conservatism, which included a militant INDIVIDUALISM; opposition to the welfare state and the increasing power of the federal government; and strong support for the COLD WAR and opposition to COMMUNISM at home and abroad. In the 1950s and early 1960s Reagan abandoned his acting career and became a full-time advocate for the conservative cause. A charismatic orator, he became very popular on the conservative lecture circuit. In 1964 he received national attention when he gave a speech in support of Goldwater's PRESIDENTIAL CAMPAIGN. After Goldwater's defeat he became the most popular figure in the conservative movement, and in 1966 he was elected governor of California, although he had never run for or held public office before. In 1976 Reagan almost defeated Gerald Ford, the incumbent Republican president, for the Republican nomination. Four years later, he decisively defeated JIMMY CARTER in his bid for a second term, and in 1984 he was reelected by an overwhelming margin, carrying all of the ELECTORAL COLLEGE votes

except those of Minnesota (the home state of his opponent) and the DISTRICT OF COLUMBIA.

Reagan's presidency is important because it brought about a transformation in the context of the ideological, political, and policy debates in the United States. This contextual transformation undermined liberalism as an ideology and discredited the role of the federal government as an agent of social change. This worked to the disadvantage of the BLACK COMMUNITY, which had embraced liberalism as an ideology and strongly favored an activist role for the federal government in bringing about civil rights and other social changes in the post–civil rights era.

The civil rights legislation of the 1960s and the expansion of the welfare state as a result of the GREAT SOCIETY and the WAR ON POVERTY were the result of an activist federal government. These 1960s civil rights and Great Society initiatives in PUBLIC POLICY resulted in more progress toward freedom and equality than during any other period in American history. Reagan, however, attacked these programs throughout his public career as part of his overall stance against liberalism, the welfare state, and "big government."

Reagan's attack on liberalism in general also had a specifically racial component. First, he opposed all of the civil rights laws of the 1960s, including the CIVIL RIGHTS ACT OF 1964 and the VOTING RIGHTS ACT OF 1965. While there is no evidence that Reagan adhered to WHITE SUPREMACY, he did support RACISM. That is, he supported the right of the SOUTHERN STATES to practice racial DISCRIMINATION and SEGREGATION. He did this, he said, not because he personally favored racism but on the basis of ideological principle. That is, he argued that the efforts by the federal government to dismantle racism in the Southern states violated principles of CONSTITUTIONALISM, specifically FEDERALISM and its principle of "states rights." Rather than abandon these principles, Reagan would have allowed for the continuation of racism and segregation in those states that wished to continue the OPPRESSION of blacks. (In a symbolically significant gesture, Reagan started his 1980 campaign in Philadelphia, Mississippi, where he proclaimed "I believe in states rights." Philadelphia, Mississippi, was an important place to symbolically make this declaration because it was the place where three civil rights workers were murdered in 1964.) The second specifically racial component of Reagan's attack on liberalism involved his relentless assault on AFFIRMATIVE ACTION, which he declared to be "racism in reverse" and a violation of the principles of individualism. The third component was an attack on the black community itself. Echoing ANDREW JOHNSON a century earlier, Reagan contended that blacks were too willing to rely on welfare and "government handouts" rather than hard work and individual initiative. In doing this he helped to reframe the post–civil rights era debate on race, shifting its focus from the public policy responsibilities of government to an emphasis on the shortcomings of blacks themselves in terms of their lack of individual responsibility, "family values," and community SELF-HELP.

By the time he became president, Reagan had reconciled himself to the civil rights laws he had opposed during the 1960s (pledging to enforce them at the "point of a bayonet"), but this reconciliation led him to conclude that racism was now a thing of the past and that government policies and programs were no longer needed to address past racial injustices or present-day INSTITUTIONAL RACISM. The final racially specific component of Reagan's revolution was a concerted attempt to ignore and discredit the predominantly liberal black LEADERSHIP establishment. There was mutual animosity and hostility between the ultraconservative Reagan and the ultraliberal black leadership. Many black leaders implied or openly stated that Reagan was a racist and a white supremacist, while Reagan implied that many black leaders were "hustlers" who constantly talked about racism in order to keep their names in the MEDIA and to build support for themselves and their ORGANIZATIONs. Reagan also contended that most black leaders focused on racism while ignoring problems of crime, family breakdown, welfare dependency, and poor educational attainment in the black community. Not only did Reagan ignore black leaders (generally refusing to meet with them) and attempt to discredit them, he also set about to build an alternative, conservative black leadership group. He did this by appointing conservatives such as CLARENCE THOMAS to positions in the BUREAUCRACY; by conferring visibility and status on relatively obscure blacks by inviting them to the White House; and by facilitating the funding of new black conservative-leaning organizations and intellectuals.

The Reagan revolution in general and in terms of its racial components was quite successful. In the post–civil rights era, liberalism as the dominant ideology was discredited and to some extent displaced; the welfare state was discredited and scaled back; federalism was revitalized; affirmative action came under increasing attack; the debate on how to achieve equality shifted away from the responsibilities of government to the shortcomings of the black community; and a new black conservative leadership group was created. These accomplishments make Reagan one of the most important presidents of the post–civil rights era and, for African Americans, the president who did more than any other to slow down and to some extent reverse the efforts initiated in the 1960s to use the federal government as an instrument to achieve equality.

See also CIVIL RIGHTS COMMISSION, CIVIL RIGHTS DIVISION, COMMERCE CLAUSE, FOURTEENTH AMENDMENT, NATURAL RIGHTS, THOMAS SOWELL, and UNDERCLASS.

reapportionment   See also *BAKER V. CARR* and *SHAW V. RENO*.

Reconstruction

Reconstruction in Historiography

Reconstruction—the effort to rebuild or reconstruct the SOUTHERN STATES after the CIVIL WAR—is one of the most important eras in American history. W. E. B. DU BOIS in his magistral history of the era, *Black Reconstruction: An Essay Toward a History of the Part Which Black Folk Played in the Attempt to Reconstruct Democracy in America, 1860–1880* (1935), described Reconstruction as "the finest effort to achieve democracy for the working millions which this world had ever seen." Du Bois's book portrayed Reconstruction as an attempt by blacks to form a COALITION to create a genuine multiracial DEMOCRACY in the United States, one in which the power of working people could effectively challenge the dominance of the economic elites who controlled the politics of the Southern states before and after the Civil War. Eric Foner in his authoritative history of the era, *Reconstruction: America's Unfinished Revolution 1863–1877* (1988), published more than a half century after Du Bois, writes that in many ways Du Bois's work "anticipated the findings of modern scholarship. At the time, however it was ignored."

Du Bois's work and the lack of response to it and similar studies illustrate the important role of knowledge as a base of POWER. These works were ignored because American historians had, for the most part, deliberately and elaborately distorted the history of Reconstruction in order to justify or rationalize its end and the subsequent subordination and domination of African Americans. This rationalization of RACISM in writings on Reconstruction was based explicitly on the IDEOLOGY of WHITE SUPREMACY, and as Foner writes, it was "accorded scholarly legitimacy—to its everlasting shame—by the nation's fraternity of professional historians."

Reconstruction was an effort to grant FREEDOM and EQUALITY to African Americans, including the abolition of SLAVERY and the passage of laws and amendments to the CONSTITUTION guaranteeing CIVIL RIGHTS to all persons without respect to RACE. Reconstruction also involved the first rudimentary efforts to build a WELFARE STATE. However, Reconstruction lasted less than a decade before the former slave owners, through VIOLENCE and terrorism, were able to overthrow this effort at democracy and impose authoritarian, white supremacist rule throughout the South and in many parts of the NORTHERN STATES. The violent overthrow of Reconstruction was a betrayal of blacks and of the GETTYSBURG ADDRESS's promise of a "new birth of freedom." Thus, American historians had to rewrite history to make it appear that Reconstruction was a colossal error. In doing so, the historical profession used knowledge to give the racists and white supremacists who overthrew Reconstruction an ideological victory in the 20th century to accompany their political victory in the 19th century.

This ideological victory has its origins in the work of a group of white Southern historians at Columbia University led by William Dunning. This so-called Dunning School shaped historical writing and popular understanding of Reconstruction until the late 1950s. Beginning in the early 20th century, these scholars published books, articles, and monographs that characterized Reconstruction as a serious mistake, depicting the Reconstruction governments in the Southern states as thoroughly corrupt, inept, and inefficient. These studies also depicted blacks as totally unfit for the exercise of any kind of civil rights, including POLITICAL PARTICIPATION in the form of voting and becoming ELECTED OFFICIALS. During Reconstruction, ANDREW JOHNSON in his 1866 annual message to CONGRESS declared, "Negroes have shown less capacity for government than any other race of people. . . . [Whenever] they have been left to their own desires they have shown a constant tendency to relapse into barbarism." These sentiments were espoused by the Dunning School historians, who described blacks as "childlike" people unable to exercise freedom except under the tutelage of the white men who had enslaved them. Reconstruction was described as a "monstrous thing" and as a "horror" because it placed white men under the rule of "African savages" who had never "succeeded in subjecting passion to reason; has never therefore created a civilization of any kind." In this view, Reconstruction was rule by the savage over the civilized and was therefore clearly unacceptable. This distorted view of Reconstruction, rooted in classic white-supremacist dogma, not only dominated historical scholarship but popular culture, as it was taught in the schools and colleges, popularized in magazines and novels, and was the theme of the popular 1915 movie *THE BIRTH OF A NATION*.

This misinterpretation of Reconstruction had an enormous influence on PUBLIC OPINION and the development of race-related PUBLIC POLICY. The NAACP had to combat its influence in the pages of its magazine *The Crisis* in order to build a favorable view in the MEDIA and reshape public opinion in favor of the CIVIL RIGHTS MOVEMENT. Biographers of JOHN F. KENNEDY indicate that he was reluctant to embrace the cause of civil rights during his presidency because he had been influenced on the race issue by the Dunning School while a student at Harvard. Du Bois's *Black Reconstruction*, despite some flaws, was therefore a work of enormous importance because it eventually helped to lead to a reorientation of scholarship on Reconstruction and ultimately to the discrediting of the Dunning School. At the beginning of the book, Du Bois found it necessary to write that the book was written "as though Negroes were ordinary human beings, realizing that this attitude will seriously curtail [my] audience." And at its end, in a chapter called "The Propaganda of History," Du Bois wrote, "One fact and one fact alone explains the attitude of most writers toward Reconstruction; they can not conceive of Negroes as men."

Reconstruction in History

Historians generally divide the era of Reconstruction into two phases, Presidential Reconstruction and Congressional Reconstruction. As the Civil War came to an end, President ABRAHAM LINCOLN had no firm plans to reconstruct the South or to deal with the status of African Americans. Lincoln had argued throughout the war that the Southern states had never really left the Union and therefore, in his view, they had not lost any of their rights to govern themselves under the constitutional principle of FEDERALISM. Thus, once the Southern states had established governments loyal to the Union and accepted the THIRTEENTH AMENDMENT abolishing slavery they could return to their pre–Civil War status and manage their own affairs. As to the status of newly freed Africans, Lincoln at the time of his death was still contemplating how they could be removed from the United States. In the meantime, the fate of the freed slaves would be up to each state to decide. Lincoln, for example, encouraged Louisiana to allow blacks who had served in the army to vote, but he never indicated that he was prepared to require by law or amendment to the Constitution that all blacks (black men) be granted the right of suffrage, and he was unequivocally opposed to full social and political equality.

When Andrew Johnson succeeded Lincoln, he basically attempted to implement Lincoln's policies, which probably would have faced opposition from the RADICAL REPUBLICANS in Congress even if Lincoln had attempted to implement them. But Johnson lacked Lincoln's status and political acumen and was much more virulent in his racism and white supremacy; therefore Lincoln's policies under Johnson aroused much more intense opposition. Under Johnson, Presidential Reconstruction involved the granting of amnesty and the restoration of civil rights to most of the leaders of the rebellion. This allowed them to establish governments that denied VOTING RIGHTS to blacks and to reimpose a quasi-slavelike system of domination in the form of the BLACK CODES. Widespread violence and terrorism was employed by groups like the KU KLUX KLAN to maintain the system. Meanwhile President Johnson vetoed civil rights bills, undermined the work of the FREEDMEN'S BUREAU after it was established over his veto, and opposed adoption of the FOURTEENTH AMENDMENT. Johnson's Presidential Reconstruction came to an end after the 1866 congressional elections, which gave the REPUBLICAN PARTY the two-thirds majority needed to override

Johnson's vetoes and thereby impose Congressional Reconstruction.

Unlike Lincoln and Johnson, the Radical Republicans in Congress, led by CHARLES SUMNER and THADDEUS STEVENS, argued that the Southern states had left the Union and consequently had forfeited their rights as states and had become in effect "conquered territories." As territories rather than states Congress had full authority to govern them. Using this authority, Congress declared all the state governments created under presidential Reconstruction (except Tennessee) illegal and subject to military rule. The Southern states were then divided into five military districts. In order for these states as conquered territories to be readmitted to the Union, the Congress required that they adopt new constitutions giving blacks voting rights. The states were also required to ratify the Fourteenth Amendment. By 1870 all of the Southern states had complied and were readmitted to the Union. Blacks participated in these reconstituted STATE AND LOCAL GOVERNMENTs as voters and as elected officials. More than a dozen blacks were elected to Congress, including two to the Senate; 600 were elected to state legislatures and hundreds to local offices. Violence and intimidation by whites continued, however, and Congress responded by enacting several Enforcement Acts authorizing the president to use the army to suppress the Ku Klux Klan and similar terrorist groups. ULYSSES S. GRANT, who succeeded Johnson, for a time used the army and the newly created JUSTICE DEPARTMENT to implement the Enforcement Acts, arresting and indicting thousands of klansmen. Although most usually received suspended or light sentences, Grant's initiatives for a time resulted in sharp declines in antiblack violence. But the country eventually grew tired of the constant struggles to enforce the civil rights of African Americans, and the first WHITE BACKLASH emerged: White public opinion in the North turned against African Americans in favor of reconciliation with the white South; the SUPREME COURT in the aftermath of the COLFAX MASSACRE made it difficult for the Justice Department to implement the enforcement acts, invalidated the basic civil rights law in the CIVIL RIGHTS CASES OF 1883, and limited the protection of the Fourteenth Amendment in the SLAUGHTERHOUSE CASES; the liberal white media began to call for an end to Reconstruction; and finally the COMPROMISE OF 1877 resulted in the election of RUTHERFORD B. HAYES to the presidency.

Hayes's election signaled the end of Reconstruction because, in exchange for the disputed ELECTORAL COLLEGE votes of Louisiana and South Carolina, Hayes agreed to withdraw the remaining federal troops from the South and to a policy of noninterference in the affairs of the states. Once this was done, Southern racists and white supremacists in the state and local governments—backed by renewed Ku Klux Klan violence (including the emergence of LYNCHING)—imposed a new system of racial OPPRESSION on African Americans in the form of JIM CROW–style SEGREGATION. Upheld by the Supreme Court in PLESSY V. FERGUSON, this system of domination lasted until the 1960s. After 1877 the Republican Party—for the first time—embraced a SOUTHERN STRATEGY to appeal to white racist voters at the expense of African-American interests, and the CONSERVATIVE COALITION, which would block effective civil rights legislation until the 1960s, emerged in Congress.

Ironically, key members of the black LEADERSHIP establishment, including FREDERICK DOUGLASS and JOHN MERCER LANGSTON, perhaps the preeminent black leaders of the time, supported Hayes's policies. MARTIN R. DELANY and HENRY TURNER, founders of modern BLACK NATIONALISM, also supported Hayes, who also enjoyed the support of whites who had been leaders of the ABOLITIONIST MOVEMENT. Although most of these leaders later came to regret their support, at the time their views reflected the general disillusionment with Reconstruction and a shift in emphasis away from politics and PROTEST toward ACCOMMODATIONISM and SELF-HELP, an approach that was fully embraced by BOOKER T. WASHINGTON in the "ATLANTA COMPROMISE" ADDRESS of 1895. (It should be noted that support of Hayes's policies by Douglass, Langston, and Turner may have in part been instances of CO-OPTATION, since each was offered patronage appointments in the BUREAUCRACY.)

In the final analysis of Reconstruction, Du Bois was correct: It was one of the finest efforts to achieve democracy in the history of the United States. The Reconstruction governments in the South were the first experiments in interracial democracy in the history of the world. These governments were also among the first in the history of the United States to establish the rudiments of a WELFARE STATE. Many of them constructed hospitals, asylums, roads, and bridges and provided for the first time extensive support for SCHOOLS AND EDUCATION. Prison and tax reforms were initiated, and liberal divorce and property laws were passed that benefited women and undermined SEXISM. Many of these laws were subsequently repealed, but many were not and constitute part of the legacy of progressivism in Southern politics.

Many Reconstruction governments were, as the Dunning School historians alleged, corrupt and inefficient. But corruption and inefficiency were widespread throughout the United States during the Reconstruction era. Indeed, the Grant administration is generally viewed as one of the two most corrupt in American history. It is therefore clear that the Reconstruction experiment in democracy came to an end not merely because of corruption or inefficiency. Rather, Reconstruction also fell victim to racism and white

Radical members of the reconstructed South Carolina legislature. Fifty members were black or biracial and 13 were white. *(Library of Congress)*

supremacy. Even those whites sympathetic to blacks became unwilling to support the continued use of force against other whites to secure the freedom and equality of blacks. *The Nation*, a leading magazine of liberal opinion, reflected this first reason in an 1876 editorial, and the second reason is reflected in an interview given by President

Grant shortly after leaving office. The editorial in *The Nation* concluded that Reconstruction was a failure because it had undertaken "the insane task of making newly-emancipated [*sic*] field hands, led by barbers and barkeepers, fancy they knew as much about government and were as capable of administering it as whites." President Grant told John Russell Young in an 1879 interview (published in *Around the World with Grant*) that "the wisest thing would have been to continue for some time military rule. . . . Military rule would have been just to all, to the Negro who wanted freedom, the white man who wanted protection, the northern man who wanted union. . . . The trouble about military rule was that the people did not like it. It was not in accordance with our institutions. I am now clear that it would have been better for the north to have postponed suffrage and reconstruction state governments for ten years, and held the south in a territorial condition."

See also BROWN V. BOARD OF EDUCATION, CIVIL RIGHTS ACT OF 1964, and CIVIL RIGHTS MOVEMENT.

Further reading: W. E. B. Du Bois, *Black Reconstruction: An Essay Toward a History of the Part Which Black Folk Played in the Attempt to Reconstruct Democracy in America, 1860–1880* (1935; reprint, New York: Atheneum, 1969); Eric Foner, *Reconstruction: America's Unfinished Revolution, 1863–1877* (New York: Harper & Row, 1988); Rayford Logan, *The Betrayal of the Negro* (London: Collier Books, 1965).

religiosity

Religiosity, a faith in God, has been described as the single most important component of African-American CULTURE. This "peculiar spiritual quality" of black folk, to use W. E. B. DU BOIS's phrase, has been traced to the African heritage of blacks. This heritage from Africa was transformed in the United States into an "Africanized Christianity" in the culture that developed during SLAVERY. Africanized Christianity emerged because, for the most part, Africans in the United States were not allowed to maintain their indigenous religious beliefs and practices; rather, they were more or less forced to embrace the religion—Protestant Christianity—of the slaveholders in the SOUTHERN STATES. However, while adopting the basic tenets of Christianity, the Africans over time transformed its rituals into an Africanized Christianity that has lasted for more than 300 years.

The religious aspect of black culture is one of the foundations of the BLACK COMMUNITY and one of the things that makes African Americans a relatively distinct people. African Americans are more religious than whites, whether religiosity is measured by subjective belief in God, frequency of prayer or church attendance, or participation in religious rituals and practices. The Gallup poll in a cross-national survey comparing blacks and whites in the United States with the nations of western Europe concluded that African Americans were the "most religious people in the western world." The centrality of religiosity in the culture and community of blacks is one of the reasons that the BLACK CHURCH is the most important ORGANIZATION among African Americans and why clergymen have always been prominent in the LEADERSHIP of the group.

The pervasiveness of religiosity in the African-American experience is unquestioned. However, the impact of religiosity on AFRICAN-AMERICAN POLITICS, the POLITICAL CULTURE, and POLITICAL PARTICIPATION always has been a subject of controversy. One school of thought follows Karl Marx, who described religion as the "opium of the people," a means by which SUPERORDINATE GROUPS dominate SUBORDINATE GROUPS. Scholars who take this view see Christianity as a means by which whites exercised domination over blacks, used first during slavery and then thereafter to teach blacks to meekly accept their condition on earth while praying for a better day in heaven. In this view, religiosity fosters ACCOMMODATIONISM in African-American politics. Other scholars have seen religiosity as an inspiration to blacks in their struggle for FREEDOM, noting that freedom and deliverance are important parts of the black religious tradition. These scholars note that NAT TURNER and many other leaders of SLAVE REVOLTS were deeply religious men who were inspired to action by their faith. These scholars also point to the role of religiosity and the black church during the CIVIL RIGHTS MOVEMENT, especially that part of the movement led by MARTIN LUTHER KING JR. and the SOUTHERN CHRISTIAN LEADERSHIP CONFERENCE. In this view, religiosity is a source of MILITANCY and PROTEST in black politics.

While most of the scholarship has viewed black religiosity as more of an opiate than an inspiration for political activism, the evidence is ambiguous, probably because the role of religiosity in the political culture is ambiguous. That is, in different times and circumstances and for different people and sometimes the same people, religiosity both encourages and discourages political activism. During the Civil Rights movement, religiosity was both a force for accommodationism and protest. In the POST–CIVIL RIGHTS ERA, the evidence has consistently shown that religiosity is associated with higher levels of voting and other forms of political participation. That is, persons with higher reported levels of religiosity (measured by strength of religious beliefs, frequency of prayer, and church attendance) also report higher levels of political participation. Thus, religiosity appears to help mobilize blacks for some forms of political activism and is also a source of solidarity, but it also appears to operate as a force against RADICALISM in African-American politics.

Further reading: Frederick Harris, *Something within: Religion in African American Political Activism* (New York: Oxford University Press, 1999).

reparations

The word *reparations* refers to the idea that African Americans should be compensated for the damages inflicted on them by SLAVERY, SEGREGATION, and DISCRIMINATION. The idea first emerged after the CIVIL WAR, when there was discussion by some of the RADICAL REPUBLICANS in CONGRESS of providing reparations in the form of FORTY ACRES AND A MULE. After RECONSTRUCTION, Bishop HENRY M. TURNER raised the demand for reparations, and in the 1890s Callie House founded the National Ex-Slave Manual for Relief Bounty and Pension Association, which sought limited reparations for aging, formerly enslaved persons, their surviving spouses, caregivers, and heirs. In the 20th century, the NATION OF ISLAM, founded in the 1930s, had reparations as one of its major demands. The REPUBLIC OF NEW AFRICA in 1968 demanded payment of $400 billion in "slavery damages," and in 1987 IMARI OBADELE, a leader of the Republic of New Africa, organized the National Coalition of Blacks for Reparations in America (NCOBRA). The formation of NCOBRA brought together a COALITION of diverse groups who engaged in LOBBYING, LITIGATION, and PROTEST to mobilize black support for the reparations idea.

Beginning in 1989 Congressman John Conyers of Michigan has introduced in every CONGRESS legislation seeking to establish a commission to investigate whether the government of the United States owes a debt to the descendants of slaves. African-American supporters of reparation cite several precedents, but the one most frequently cited is the decision by Congress in 1989 to issue an apology and pay $20,000 to each Japanese American (or their survivors) who were incarcerated during World War II. Using the Japanese-American case as a precedent, NCOBRA proposed that Congress pass "An act to stimulate economic growth in the United States and compensate, in part, for the grievous wrongs of slavery and the unjust enrichment which accrued to the United States therefrom." NCOBRA included no dollar amount, but scholars have calculated that the debt owed to blacks from slavery, segregation, and discrimination is anywhere from as low as $1.6 trillion up to $24 trillion. Proposals for using the money range from giving each African-American family in the 20th century the equivalent of forty acres and a mule to the establishment of a modern-day FREEDMEN'S BUREAU that would finance such things as school construction, housing, job training, and business development in the GHETTOS.

Reparations as PUBLIC POLICY to repair the damages inflicted by the various forms of RACISM blacks have been exposed to is popular in the BLACK COMMUNITY. A 1997 poll found that 65 percent of blacks supported the idea, but white PUBLIC OPINION was overwhelmingly negative, with 88 percent expressing opposition. White opposition to the idea is as old as the idea itself. Most white leaders opposed the idea after the Civil War, and most opposed it at the end of the 20th century. (The Conyers bill, which would simply establish a commission to investigate the idea, was cosponsored by only 31 of the 435 members of the House. And the bill has never been taken up or debated.) There are undoubtedly many reasons for white opposition to reparations, but an underlying one is the legacy of WHITE SUPREMACY, which leads many whites to believe that slavery, despite its horrors, was good for Africans because it exposed them to the beneficent effects of Western civilization and culture. Indeed, most whites are opposed to even an apology for slavery. Thus, it is very unlikely, short of a POLITICAL SYSTEM crisis, that reparations will be paid to the descendants of the enslaved Africans.

Further reading: Mary F. Berry, "Reparations for Freedom, 1890–1916," *Journal of Negro History* 3 (July 1972): 219–30; Boris Bittker, *The Case for Reparations for Blacks* (New York: Random House, 1973).

representation

The idea of representation is central to the concept of DEMOCRACY in the United States. Indeed, the idea of representation is at the very root and foundation of the SOCIAL CONTRACT philosophy that is the underlying basis of the government. This was eloquently expressed by THOMAS JEFFERSON in the DECLARATION OF INDEPENDENCE when he wrote that "governments derive their just powers from the consent of the governed." The English philosopher John Stuart Mill stated the necessary relationship between democracy and representation in his 1869 treatise *Considerations on Representative Government* when he wrote, "In a really equal democracy, every or any section would be represented not disproportionately but proportionately. A majority of the electors would always have a majority of the representatives, but a minority of the electors would always have a minority of the representatives. Man for man they would be as fully represented as the majority; unless they are there is not equal government, but government of inequality and privilege . . . contrary to the principle of democracy, which professes equality as its very root and branch."

EQUALITY in representation insofar as blacks are concerned has never characterized democracy in America. Until RECONSTRUCTION, blacks were formally and officially excluded from any kind of representation, and although they were formally made eligible for representation in the 1860s during Reconstruction, it was not until the 1960s that blacks had any realistic chance for representation. Political scientists define representation in several ways, but a key aspect concerns the extent to which the institutions of government include representatives from the diverse social, economic, and ETHNIC GROUPS that constitute the society. At the end of the 20th century the institutions of the American democracy continued to reflect racial privilege and inequality. The black POPULATION in 2001 was about 12 percent of the nation, but in few institutions of government did their representation come close to this proportion. Among ELECTED OFFICIALS, blacks constituted less than 2 percent instead of 12 percent. In CONGRESS, blacks constituted 9 percent of the House but none of the 100 senators. And in the House, according to the JOINT CENTER FOR POLITICAL AND ECONOMIC STUDIES, white members of the REPUBLICAN PARTY represented 53 percent of the nation's blacks, whites in the DEMOCRATIC PARTY 20 percent, and black Democrats only 26 percent. In the BUREAUCRACY, blacks constituted about 15 percent, but at the senior policy-making level less than 5 percent. In the U.S. MILITARY, blacks are overrepresented at the enlisted level, while constituting less than 10 percent of the officer corps. Blacks were less than 2 percent of the career FOREIGN POLICY bureaucracy. In STATE AND LOCAL GOVERNMENT, blacks are less than 2 percent of elected legislators and executives, and they are an infinitesimal 0.004 percent of the POWER ELITE.

Republican Party

The Republican Party is one of the two parties that constitute the TWO-PARTY SYSTEM in the United States. Established in 1854 as a THIRD PARTY, a major objective of the party was to oppose the expansion of SLAVERY into the NORTHERN STATES and the territories. In the election of 1860, the Republican Party accomplished something extraordinary for third parties in the United States when its candidate, ABRAHAM LINCOLN, was elected to the PRESIDENCY. The election of Lincoln effectively made the Republican Party the second party in the two-party system, displacing the Whig Party, which had contested elections with the DEMOCRATIC PARTY since the 1840s.

The Republican Party and Lincoln did not oppose slavery; rather, they opposed its expansion beyond the SOUTHERN STATES. During the course of the CIVIL WAR, Lincoln reluctantly concluded that FREEDOM for the enslaved Africans was necessary to win the war. Therefore he issued the EMANCIPATION PROCLAMATION and supported the adoption of the THIRTEENTH AMENDMENT, actions that identified the party with the liberation of blacks. Consequently, it won the over-

whelming support of the BLACK COMMUNITY. The Republican Party under Lincoln was a moderate, cautious party on race issues, reluctantly favoring freedom but opposing EQUALITY and CIVIL RIGHTS. However, after Lincoln's death the party for a time was dominated by RADICAL REPUBLICANS whose goals were full equality and civil rights. During RECONSTRUCTION the Radical Republicans, led by CHARLES SUMNER and THADDEUS STEVENS, were able to accomplish their goals of adopting the FOURTEENTH AMENDMENT and a basic civil rights law. The FREEDMEN'S BUREAU, which attempted to provide land and educational, health, and other benefits to the emancipated slaves, was also supported by the Radical Republicans. These initiatives on civil rights and social welfare reinforced African-American allegiance to the Republican Party. As FREDERICK DOUGLASS put it, "The Republican Party is the deck, all else the sea."

By the late 1870s, however, a WHITE BACKLASH had developed, and in the COMPROMISE OF 1877 the Republicans under the leadership of RUTHERFORD B. HAYES effectively abandoned blacks in favor of reconciliation with Southern whites. Whites in the South then quickly disenfranchised blacks and imposed JIM CROW–style SEGREGATION. When blacks resisted, whites resorted to LYNCHING and other forms of VIOLENCE and intimidation to maintain their domination. The Republicans ignored this renewed OPPRESSION of blacks as they worked to strengthen their ties to Southern racists and white supremacists in an effort to build the CONSERVATIVE COALITION. The African-American LEADERSHIP and those blacks who could still vote continued to support the Republicans, partly because in a two-party system they had little choice, since the Democratic Party was the party of overt RACISM and WHITE SUPREMACY. Thus, from the 1880s until the 1930s the Republican Party took the black vote for granted while giving only lip service to civil rights and offering a few blacks minor patronage appointments to the BUREAUCRACY. Indeed, BENJAMIN HARRISON, who served as president from 1889 to 1893, was the last Republican president to forthrightly support civil rights for African Americans.

In the 1930s black allegiance to the Republican Party began to shift in response to FRANKLIN D. ROOSEVELT's administrations. In 1932 most blacks supported the Republican nominee, Herbert Hoover, against Roosevelt, but in 1936 more than two-thirds supported Roosevelt. This switch in party loyalties was a result of the economic benefits that flowed to the black community as a result of the NEW DEAL and the creation of the modern WELFARE STATE. Black allegiance to the Democrats was reinforced during the presidency of HARRY TRUMAN because Truman continued Roosevelt's welfare policies but also because he was the first president since Benjamin Harrison (and the first Democrat ever) to propose a civil rights reform program. Between 1936 and 1964 there was a genuine two-party system for blacks as well as whites. That is, for this brief period, both major parties competed for the black vote. The Republican Party candidate, Dwight Eisenhower, received about 40 percent of the black vote in 1952 and 1956, and in 1960 RICHARD NIXON received about 25 percent of the vote. However, after the 1964 election black attachment to the Democratic Party came to resemble its early attachment to the Republican Party. This came about as a result of the Democrats' embrace of the CIVIL RIGHTS MOVEMENT's agenda by JOHN F. KENNEDY and LYNDON B. JOHNSON and the rejection of that agenda by BARRY GOLDWATER, the Republican nominee. In addition to its embrace of civil rights, the Democrats under President Johnson significantly expanded the welfare state with the GREAT SOCIETY and the WAR ON POVERTY. Meanwhile, the Republicans once again embraced a SOUTHERN STRATEGY to appeal to the racist, anti–civil rights constituency of GEORGE WALLACE. The election of RONALD REAGAN in 1980 consolidated the Republican Party as the party of CONSERVATISM, while the Democrats became the party of LIBERALISM. This represents an important transformation in the two parties.

The Republican Party since its formation has always been the party of business, favoring a close relationship between government and business in the development of industrial CAPITALISM. It also favored a powerful activist federal government. The Democratic Party, on the other hand, historically favored FEDERALISM; a minimalist role for the federal government; the interest of small farmers and workers; and autonomy for STATE AND LOCAL GOVERNMENT. The Democrats were also agrarian, racist, and religious, while the Republicans were urban, cosmopolitan, and secular. By the end of the 20th century, the two parties had almost completely transformed themselves. The Democrats had become urban, cosmopolitan, secular, racially tolerant, and advocates of an activist federal government, while the Republicans were agrarian, religious, and advocates of federalism. Because of this transformation, one party had once again become "the deck, all else the sea" for blacks, with the Republican Party averaging a mere 10 percent of the black vote since 1964 compared with its near 90 percent when Frederick Douglass described it as the deck.

Further reading: Nancy Weiss, *Farewell to the Party of Lincoln: Black Politics in the Age of FDR* (Princeton, N.J.: Princeton University Press, 1983).

Republic of New Africa

The Republic of New Africa (RNA) is the most important POST–CIVIL RIGHTS ERA black ORGANIZATION devoted to the establishment of a separate, independent black nation-

state within the boundaries of the United States. The RNA was founded in 1968 by Gaidi and IMARI OBADELE (formerly Milton and Richard Henry), brothers who were followers of MALCOLM X. In the manifesto establishing the organization, the RNA called for the creation of an independent black nation, the Republic of New Africa, to be carved out of the five SOUTHERN STATES of Louisiana, Mississippi, Alabama, Georgia, and South Carolina. The manifesto also called for the payment of $400 billion in REPARATIONS. The RNA asserts that Africans in the United States have a right to self-determination, which should have been afforded to them after the CIVIL WAR in the form of a plebiscite. That is, the RNA contends that after the Civil War, there should have been an election in which the emancipated Africans were allowed to determine whether they wished U.S. CITIZENSHIP or an independent nation of their own. Instead, blacks were forcibly incorporated into the United States by the FOURTEENTH AMENDMENT. Thus, the first goal of the RNA is a UNITED NATIONS–supervised election among African Americans in order to determine whether they wish to form a separate nation. Assuming that the results of this election would be affirmative, the RNA would then propose to use VIOLENCE in protracted guerrilla warfare to force the government to cede the territory to create the new nation and transfer blacks in the NORTHERN STATES to the new land and the whites in the five Southern states to the remaining parts of the United States.

Most scholars consider the RNA's vision of a separate black nation to be totally unrealistic, "substantially a fantasy" in the words of RONALD WALTERS or "nothing short of romanticism" in the words of MATTHEW HOLDEN JR. This is so for several reasons. First, the idea of separating blacks into a land of their own has always been rejected by the established black LEADERSHIP, partly because they believe in INTEGRATIONISM and partly because the idea has always been supported by those whites supporting RACISM and WHITE SUPREMACY. Second, the idea probably has always been rejected by the majority of African Americans, who believe in integration in some form. At the end of the Civil War, if there had been a plebiscite, the overwhelming majority of African Americans likely would have rejected separation in favor of integration on the basis of EQUALITY. And PUBLIC OPINION polls conducted throughout the 20th century have shown support for a separate black nation never exceeding 15 percent among blacks. Third, even if the idea were supported by the BLACK COMMUNITY, it is unlikely that a successful guerrilla war against a nation with the most powerful MILITARY in the history of the world could be waged.

In spite of the unrealistic nature of the RNA's vision and its posing little, if any, threat to the POLITICAL SYSTEM, the RNA became a target for POLITICAL REPRESSION as soon as it was established. The FBI during the 1960s and 1970s made the group one of the principal targets of its COINTELPRO program, conducting surveillance, raiding its meetings, provoking violent confrontations, and harassing and jailing its leaders. Despite these efforts, the RNA survived and continued to build support for its vision of an independent nation. With several thousand members, the leaders of the RNA contend that because of the tenacity of racism and white supremacy, an independent black nation is indispensable to black FREEDOM and equality and that one day the majority of blacks will come to agree with them.

See also BLACK NATIONALISM.

Revels, Hiram R. (1822–1901) *U.S. senator*

Hiram R. Revels was the first African American elected to the CONGRESS and is one of four ever elected to the Senate. (Actually, five blacks have been elected to the Senate, including P. B. S. Pinchback, who was elected by the Louisiana legislature in 1872. The Senate, however, refused to seat him. Pinchback was also elected to the House, which also refused to seat him.) Revels, a FREE NEGRO, was born in North Carolina and received seminary training and was graduated from Knox College in Illinois. In 1845 he became an ordained minister and pastored several congregations of the Methodist Episcopal Church. During the CIVIL WAR he helped to organize a regiment of black soldiers. After the war he moved to Mississippi to become presiding elder of the Episcopal Church in Natchez. In 1868 he was elected to the Natchez city council and two years later to the U.S. Senate to fill the seat that had been vacated by Jefferson Davis when he assumed the presidency of the Confederacy.

The fact that Revels was the first African American elected to Congress—and that he was filling the seat of the man who had led the SOUTHERN STATES in rebellion against the Union—created a national sensation and made him the best-known black ELECTED OFFICIAL of the RECONSTRUCTION era. Although there was powerful opposition to seating Revels, after a three-day debate he was seated by a vote of 48 to 8. However, he served only a year and had little impact on Senate business. Revels was a conservative, cautious politician in the tradition of ACCOMMODATIONISM. Although elected as a member of the REPUBLICAN PARTY, after leaving office he allied himself with the racists and white supremacists in Mississippi's DEMOCRATIC PARTY. Revels ended his career as president of Alcorn College, a HISTORICALLY BLACK COLLEGE AND UNIVERSITY.

See also EDWARD BROOKE, BLANCHE K. BRUCE, and CAROL MOSELEY-BRAUN.

riots

VIOLENCE is an integral, defining feature of AFRICAN-AMERICAN POLITICS. Whites used violence to establish and maintain SLAVERY and subsequent forms of OPPRESSION, and blacks occasionally used violence to resist slavery and the subsequent forms of oppression such as SEGREGATION. Riots have been a major manifestation of both forms of violence, with whites rioting to oppress blacks and blacks rioting to resist oppression. In their *American Violence: A Documentary History* (1970), Richard Hoftstader and Michael Wallace classify riots as either "race riots" or "ghetto riots," the former referring to rioting by whites to oppress blacks and the latter to rioting by blacks as forms of resistance or rebellion. Race riots occurred throughout the 19th century and the first half of the 20th century, while GHETTO riots are a 20th-century phenomenon.

In 1831 whites rioted in Providence, Rhode Island, destroying much of the property in "Snowtown," a small community of FREE NEGROES, killing four, and wounding 14. In 1829 and again in 1841, there were race riots in Cincinnati, Ohio, where mobs attacked the BLACK COMMUNITY, killing and injuring dozens of blacks and in 1829 forcing more than 1,000 blacks to flee the city. In the decades before the CIVIL WAR, whites rioted dozens of times in American cities, attacking and killing free Negroes, whom they viewed as competitors for jobs, business, and housing. In 1863 during the CIVIL WAR, whites in New York City rioted over the army draft and the use of blacks as strike breakers, killing more than 100 persons, the largest number in any riot in American history. In 1866, in a riot that helped propel IDA B. WELLS-BARNETT into national LEADERSHIP, whites in Memphis, Tennessee, killed 46 blacks and burned four churches, 90 houses, and 12 schools. White riots continued into the 20th century. Indeed, a riot by whites in 1909 in Springfield, Illinois—the hometown and burial place of ABRAHAM LINCOLN—led to the call for the formation of the NAACP. In 1917 white workers in East St. Louis, Illinois, angry about job competition from blacks, rioted and killed 39 blacks. The summer of 1919 became known as "Red Summer" because there were bloody race riots in 20 cities including Chicago and the DISTRICT OF COLUMBIA. The Chicago riot was touched off when a black youngster swam past an imaginary line that separated the "white" from the "black" part of a Lake Michigan beach. Twenty-five blacks and 15 whites were killed and over 500 injured. The District of Columbia riot started as a result of a series of sensational stories in the local white MEDIA about an alleged black "sex fiend" who was attacking white women. Nine persons and more than 100 men, women, and children were injured in four days of street fights between blacks and whites. (Unlike in most of these race riots, blacks in the District armed themselves and fought their white attackers.) Perhaps the most egregious cases of white rioting occurred in Rosewood, Florida, in 1919 and in Tulsa, Oklahoma, in 1923, where not only were scores of blacks killed or injured but the prosperous black communities were completely destroyed. In Rosewood the entire black community was burned, and all the black residents were forced to flee. In Tulsa a three-day riot by an armed mob of whites destroyed Greenwood (the black section of the city), killing an estimated 300 people. In 1975 the government of Florida approved REPARATIONS for the survivors of Rosewood and their descendants, and in 1998 Oklahoma established a commission to investigate reparations for the survivors and descendants of the residents of Tulsa. These race riots by whites were based explicitly on RACISM and WHITE SUPREMACY, initiated by whites in order to maintain domination over blacks.

What Hofstader and Wallace call "ghetto riots" can also be referred to as rebellions or revolts against the oppression that characterizes the conditions of the 20th-century ghettos. As a result of the GREAT MIGRATION, by the mid-20th century a critical mass of the black POPULATION was concentrated in ghettos in the big cities of the NORTHERN STATES, places characterized by POVERTY, DISCRIMINATION, and economic exploitation. In 1935 in HARLEM, ghettoized blacks rebelled against these conditions for the first time. The Harlem riot, Hofstader and Wallace write, "marked a turning point in racial violence. Previous race riots had almost always been initiated by whites, and whites fought blacks. In this riot, there was no fighting between the two races: instead blacks attacked white property and the police who were trying to protect it." There were periodic outbursts of ghetto riots after the 1935 uprising, but the next turning point was the WATTS RIOT in 1965. The Watts riot was a turning point because of its duration (five days); because of the enormous loss of life and property; because it required use of the MILITARY to suppress it; because it led to the development of a riot IDEOLOGY; and because it presaged a series of even bloodier riots in the years that followed.

The riot ideology explicitly defined riots as a form of rebellion against racial oppression, overtly rejecting the idea that they were the actions of thugs and criminals. This ideology quickly caught on in black PUBLIC OPINION and was embraced by many elements of the black leadership establishment, including MARTIN LUTHER KING JR. This view of the Watts riot as political rather than criminal activity was also embraced by many in the academic community, in the media, and by many leading white liberal politicians (Vice President HUBERT HUMPHREY, for example, said that if he had to live in the ghetto he would likely riot). This politicized view of the riots as acts of rebellion was the explicit view of the BLACK POWER MOVEMENT, which started one year after Watts. During the late 1960s this cel-

ebration of the riots as rebellions was articulated over and over again by STOKELY CARMICHAEL and the leaders of the BLACK PANTHER PARTY. Finally, this view of the riots was given the official sanction of the government when the KERNER COMMISSION, appointed by President LYNDON B. JOHNSON, concluded that the riots were a response to "white racism." After the Watts riot there were similar outbursts every summer in most cities, large and small, in the ghettos of the Northern states. A 1967 study identified more than 250 "racial disorders" in 173 cities, resulting in 87 deaths, 2,500 injuries, and nearly 30,000 arrests. The worst riot after Watts was in Detroit, Michigan, in 1967. Lasting five days, the riot resulted in 43 deaths, 1,300 buildings burned, 2,700 businesses ransacked, and property damage exceeding $500 million. The U.S. Army and the national guard were called to suppress the rebellion, using 50-caliber machine guns to battle snipers (almost 500 black men were charged with firing rifles and shotguns at army troops).

The Detroit riot particularly alarmed authorities because they saw it as presaging urban guerrilla war and therefore as a threat to POLITICAL SYSTEM stability. As a result, the army and state and local police began to prepare for what the historian Garry Wills called "the second civil war." The army deployed special forces from Vietnam, and cities began to arm their police departments with weapons of war, including machine guns, grenades, infrared sniper scopes, and helicopters and spotter planes. J. EDGAR HOOVER and the FBI intensified POLITICAL REPRESSION of the black movement, warning in a COINTELPRO memorandum that the violence and growing RADICALISM in the black community raised the possibility of a "real Mau Mau" in America (referring to the violent rebellion by Kenyans against British COLONIALISM in the early 1950s). The ghetto riots abruptly ended in 1968 with the assassination of Martin Luther King Jr. In the days following King's death, there were riots throughout the United States, requiring the deployment of 50,000 army troops and guardsmen. For the first time since the Civil War, the army was used to protect the White House and the U.S. Capitol building.

After 1968, rioting as a routine, regular feature of black politics came to an end. There were only sporadic outbursts in the ghettos throughout the late 20th century. Like the riots of the 1960s, most of these outbursts were precipitated by allegations of police misconduct, but they tended to be isolated and did not presage a new wave of rebellions.

The riots following Watts had important consequences for African-American politics. First, they signaled a revolt by the UNDERCLASS against the conditions of the ghetto and a sharp although brief turn toward radicalism in black politics. For a short time the result of this was increased attention to the problems of poverty in black America and a renewed emphasis on PUBLIC POLICY initiatives to achieve INTEGRATION of the ghettos into mainstream society. The riots also gave impetus to programs to achieve EQUALITY, such as BUSING and AFFIRMATIVE ACTION, and greater urgency to the processes of INCORPORATION and CO-OPTATION. But the riots also fueled the emerging WHITE BACKLASH and the antiblack presidential campaigns of GEORGE WALLACE. The REPUBLICAN PARTY's adoption of a SOUTHERN STRATEGY was encouraged by the riots, and RICHARD NIXON used white resentment of the riots as a weapon in his successful 1968 campaign against Hubert Humphrey for the presidency. Thus, while the ghetto riots contributed to MILITANCY and radicalism in the black community, they contributed to the growth of CONSERVATISM among whites. Meanwhile, the underlying conditions that gave rise to ghetto riots in the 1960s remained largely unchanged at the end of the 20th century. In fact, in some ways the conditions are worse because many of the neighborhoods destroyed during the 1960s riots were not rebuilt, many businesses abandoned riot areas, and WHITE FLIGHT to the suburbs contributed to the decline of the tax base of many cities.

See also COLFAX MASSACRE, CRIMINAL JUSTICE SYSTEM, RODNEY KING, KU KLUX KLAN, LYNCHING, SLAVE REVOLTS, and URBAN POLITICS.

Further reading: Joe Feagin and Harlan Hahn, *Ghetto Revolts* (New York: Macmillan, 1973); Morris Janowitz, "Patterns of Collective Racial Violence," in *American Violence: Historical and Comparative Perspectives,* ed. Hugh David Graham and Ted Robert Gurr (New York: Bantam Books, 1969); *Report of the National Advisory Commission on Civil Disorder* (New York: Bantam Books, 1968); T.M. Tomlinson, "The Development of a Riot Ideology among Urban Negroes," *American Behavioral Scientist* 2 (1968): 17–29; Garry Wills, *The Second Civil War: Arming for Armageddon* (New York: New American Library, 1968).

Looted buildings in Newark, New Jersey, in the aftermath of July 1967 rioting *(Library of Congress)*

Robeson, Paul (1898–1976) *scholar, athlete, entertainer, human rights activist*

Paul Robeson's career is an extraordinary example of the use of knowledge and art in politics. Robeson was an extraordinarily talented individual. Robeson was born in 1898, the son of a clergyman. While at Rutgers University he became the first African-American all-American football player; at the same time, he also earned letters in three other sports—baseball, basketball, and track. In addition to his athletic abilities, Robeson had an exceptional intellect. After being elected to Phi Beta Kappa (the national honor society) and graduating from Rutgers at the top of his class, he earned a law degree from Columbia University while playing professional football on weekends. And as if that were not enough, he was an extraordinary multitalented entertainer, winning critical acclaim for his performances as a stage and movie actor, playing what some critics view as the greatest lead ever in *Othello.* He was also a successful singer, recording more than 300 songs and giving concerts throughout the world. Finally, Robeson was an exceptional linguist, mastering 13 languages.

Throughout the 1940s Robeson was probably the best-known African American in the world. Yet this extraordinarily gifted and talented man's career is also a telling example of the POLITICAL REPRESSION of a person because of his IDEOLOGY. In 1929 Robeson left the United States because, he said, he had to escape the "poison" of RACISM and WHITE SUPREMACY. In Europe, Robeson developed close relationships with European and THIRD-WORLD radicals and gradually embraced RADICALISM himself. Robeson's radicalism grew out of his opposition to COLONIALISM and his view that the GLOBALIZATION of Western CAPITALISM was generating POVERTY and inequality throughout the world. In 1935 he visited the Soviet Union and concluded that COMMUNISM was the only force that could challenge the dominance of Western racism and imperialism. When he returned to the United States in 1939 he began to use MUSIC as a tool to advance his political ideas. Unlike his earlier concerts where he mostly sang black work songs and spirituals, he now embraced an early version of MULTICULTURALISM, performing folk music from Europe, Africa, and Asia. This was part of an effort to mold a multicultural COALITION of working peoples. Robeson did not limit his performances to concert halls; he performed before diverse ETHNIC GROUPS, including Jewish garment workers, Asian-American field workers, Mexican-American miners, and black sharecroppers. These performances were integral to Robeson's CIVIL RIGHTS and HUMAN RIGHTS activism. While active in the cause of civil rights for African Americans, he viewed this focus as too narrow. Long before MALCOLM X in the 1960s, Robeson suggested that the CIVIL RIGHTS MOVEMENT broaden its agenda to include human rights. He was among the founders and the first chairman of the anticolonial COUNCIL ON AFRICAN AFFAIRS, and he advocated SOCIALISM and communism and supported the Soviet position in the COLD WAR.

Given Robeson's status as an international celebrity, his radical activism resulted in systematic political repression. The FBI and committees of CONGRESS investigated and harassed him; he was barred from stage and film work; television and radio appearances were prohibited; his trophies and awards were removed from display at Rutgers; and the State Department prohibited him from traveling abroad. When Robeson attempted to perform in an open field in Peekskill, New York, in 1949, VIOLENCE organized by local veterans groups disrupted the concert. During the height of MCCARTHYISM, the very act of owning a Robeson record could subject a government employee to investigation. Unable to work or travel and facing unrelenting repression, Robeson became an exile in his own country and went into seclusion. Living in a state of near poverty (his income dropped to $2,000 a year from more than $100,000 at the peak of his career) and abandoned by many of his friends and much of the black LEADERSHIP establishment, Robeson became a virtual nonperson. In 1958 the SUPREME COURT ruled that the State Department could not legally withhold his passport, but by this time he was too ill to travel abroad or resume his career. However, he did finish his memoirs, *Here I Stand* (1958). He died in Philadelphia in 1976.

See also BLACK ARTS MOVEMENT and HARLEM RENAISSANCE.

Further reading: Martin Duberman, *Paul Robeson* (New York: Free Press, 1976).

Robinson, Randall (1941–) *activist, author*

Randall Robinson is the founding director of TRANSAFRICA, the ORGANIZATION of African Americans founded in 1977 to influence United States FOREIGN POLICY on issues related to Africa and the Caribbean. Robinson, a native of Virginia, joined with RONALD WALTERS and others to form TransAfrica after his experiences working with Congressman CHARLES DIGGS, the CONGRESSIONAL BLACK CAUCUS's leading authority on African affairs. His work with Diggs led Robinson to recognize that black-American influence on U.S. foreign policy required the establishment of a LOBBYING group specifically focused on Africa.

A graduate of Harvard Law School, Robinson led TransAfrica from its formation in 1977 until his retirement in 2001. After TransAfrica succeeded in helping to bring about the end of COLONIALISM and APARTHEID in Africa, Robinson turned his attention to the problem of HUMAN RIGHTS and the lack of DEMOCRACY in Africa. He also joined the movement for REPARATIONS, writing *The Debt: What America Owes Blacks* in 2000. The book helped to provoke a national debate on reparations because of the attention it received in the national MEDIA and from the black LEADERSHIP establishment. His autobiography, *Defending the Spirit: A Black Life in America*, was published in 1998.

Roosevelt, Franklin D. (1882–1945) *32nd president of the United States*

Franklin D. Roosevelt is universally considered to be one of the greatest of the American presidents, usually ranked by historians with George Washington and ABRAHAM LINCOLN. Roosevelt's greatness is based on his NEW DEAL, which created the American WELFARE STATE and modern LIBERALISM, and his leadership of the alliance that defeated Fascism during World War II. Roosevelt is also the only president to serve more than two terms, elected an unprecedented four times and serving for 13 years. Yet this great American president did little during his long tenure to advance the cause of African-American FREEDOM and EQUALITY.

Roosevelt was not a racist or overtly hostile to blacks (although he did use the word *nigger* in private conversations and correspondence), but during his 13 years in office he never supported CIVIL RIGHTS legislation or the numerous bills to outlaw LYNCHING. When asked—especially by his wife Eleanor, a tireless supporter of HUMAN RIGHTS— to support such legislation, the president would usually respond, "I can't afford to take the risk." That is, Roosevelt argued that to support civil rights or antilynching legislation would risk antagonizing the powerful white members of CONGRESS from the SOUTHERN STATES who controlled many of the important committees in the House and Senate. If antagonized, these members could use their influence in the CONSERVATIVE COALITION to block his New Deal welfare programs, which (he pointed out) disproportionately benefited African Americans. Roosevelt was also aware that Southern racists and white supremacists played pivotal roles in the DEMOCRATIC PARTY nominating process and controlled an important bloc of votes in the ELECTORAL COLLEGE.

Although blacks did benefit disproportionately from the New Deal welfare programs (because they were disproportionately poor and unemployed), Roosevelt acquiesced to the establishment of the welfare state on the basis of INSTITUTIONAL RACISM, and he allowed New Deal programs to be administered on the basis of racial DISCRIMINATION. He did appoint a handful of blacks to minor posts in the BUREAUCRACY, including MARY MCLEOD BETHUNE. And in response to A. PHILIP RANDOLPH's threatened MARCH ON WASHINGTON MOVEMENT, he issued an executive order banning discrimination in employment in war industries, but he failed to vigorously enforce the order. Eleanor Roosevelt crusaded openly against RACISM and WHITE SUPREMACY, which helped to enlighten PUBLIC OPINION on issues of race during the Roosevelt era, but the president remained silent and sometimes tried to silence his wife. Thus, one of the greatest of American presidents was not so great for African Americans. As one historian concluded, "Roosevelt's commitment to the Negro was slim."

See also BLACK CABINET and PRESIDENCY.

Further reading: John Kirby, *Black Americans during the Roosevelt Era: Liberalism and Race* (Knoxville: University of Tennessee Press, 1980).

Rowan, Carl (1925–2000) *journalist, diplomat*

Carl Rowan was the leading African-American journalist of the 20th century. He also was one of the first African Americans to hold high-level posts in the FOREIGN-POLICY and diplomatic BUREAUCRACY. Rowan was one of the first black journalists to work for a major white MEDIA outlet, hired in 1951 by the *Minneapolis Tribune* as a roving correspondent. In this capacity, Rowan wrote a series of articles on the CIVIL RIGHTS MOVEMENT in the SOUTHERN STATES. He also reported from Europe, Asia, and the Middle East. His reporting from abroad brought him to the attention of JOHN F. KENNEDY, who in 1961 appointed him an assistant secretary of state. President Kennedy later appointed Rowan ambassador to Finland (the first black ambassador to a European nation). In 1964 President LYNDON B. JOHNSON appointed Rowan director of the U.S. Information Agency (USIA), the nation's international propaganda office. In this position Rowan became the first African American to sit on the National Security Council, the highest foreign-policy decision-making body. As USIA director, Rowan was personally responsible for disseminating information critical of MALCOLM X throughout the THIRD WORLD. Rowan viewed Malcolm X as a dangerous demagogue who deliberately distorted the nature of race relations in the United States. And although Rowan later came to oppose the VIETNAM WAR, he was a vociferous critic while in the government, and later as a columnist, of MARTIN LUTHER KING JR.'s opposition to the war. In 1965 Rowan left the government, returning to journalism to write a syndicated column and to broadcast nationally televised radio and television commentaries.

In the 1980s and early 1990s Rowan was the most influential African-American voice in journalism and one of the most influential persons in the national media. A member of the POWER ELITE, Rowan was passionately committed to LIBERALISM and regularly used his writings to call for a renewed WAR ON POVERTY and to support AFFIRMATIVE

ACTION. Rowan authored eight books including his memoir, *Breaking Barriers* (1991), and biographies of Martin Luther King and THURGOOD MARSHALL. He was born and raised in rural Tennessee in a family that was so poor he wrote that he would sneak onto farms and "suck hot milk from the teats of cows." He was graduated from Oberlin College and received a master's degree in journalism from the University of Minnesota.

Rustin, Bayard (1912–1987) *civil rights leader*

Bayard Rustin, a leading strategist in the CIVIL RIGHTS MOVEMENT and one of the earliest black PUBLIC INTELLECTUALS, was active in African-American movements for FREEDOM and EQUALITY from the age of 26 until his death.

The son of WEST INDIAN immigrants, Rustin attended two HISTORICALLY BLACK COLLEGES AND UNIVERSITIES and the City College of New York, but because of a lack of money and his early interests in SOCIAL MOVEMENTS, he never completed college. But Rustin was a voracious reader with a keen intellect and therefore, like HAROLD CRUSE, became a leading African-American intellectual without ever completing college. In his early 20s Rustin moved to HARLEM, where he soon joined the youth wing of the COMMUNIST PARTY. Although Rustin joined the Communist Party in his youth, its rigid, doctrinaire IDEOLOGY was too confining for Rustin's eclectic RADICALISM, and although he remained sympathetic to COMMUNISM and SOCIALISM, he soon left the Communist Party. In 1941 his work as a movement strategist began when he helped A. PHILIP RANDOLPH create the MARCH ON WASHINGTON MOVEMENT. However, he criticized Randolph when he called off the 1941 march after FRANKLIN D. ROOSEVELT issued the EXECUTIVE ORDER banning DISCRIMINATION in war industries. Rustin's radicalism embraced pacifism (he left the Communist Party partly because it supported Russia during World War II), and in 1941 he joined the Fellowship of Reconciliation (FOR), a pacifist organization committed to interracial solidarity and COALITIONS and the use of CIVIL DISOBEDIENCE. When drafted into the army, Rustin refused to serve and was sentenced to two years in prison. When released, he continued to work with FOR and joined the CONGRESS OF RACIAL EQUALITY (CORE). As a member of CORE, Rustin in 1947 participated in the first FREEDOM RIDES to PROTEST the continuing practice of SEGREGATION on interstate buses in spite of a 1946 SUPREME COURT decision declaring such segregation unlawful. In 1955 he went to Montgomery to assist MARTIN LUTHER KING JR. in planning the MONTGOMERY BUS BOYCOTT. Later, with ELLA BAKER, he helped organize the SOUTHERN CHRISTIAN LEADERSHIP CONFERENCE (SCLC). Rustin was a homosexual who had been arrested and convicted of moral charges. It is likely that if this had not been the case he would have been appointed by King to a high-level staff position in SCLC. But because of his sexual orientation he was only an informal adviser to King and SCLC. And even this informal role was opposed by WHITNEY YOUNG of the URBAN LEAGUE and ROY WILKINS of the NAACP, who viewed his sexuality, like JAMES BALDWIN's, as a potential source of embarrassment to the movement. But Rustin's intellectual and strategic talents were so valued that in spite of the objections of Young, Wilkins, and ADAM CLAYTON POWELL, he became the principal planner of the MARCH ON WASHINGTON OF 1963, although his official title was deputy to A. Philip Randolph.

Although Rustin was committed to radicalism, he was opposed to MILITANCY and BLACK NATIONALISM and the 1960s BLACK POWER MOVEMENT. This opposition was based on Rustin's unwavering commitment to INTEGRATIONISM as an ideology and pragmatism as a strategy. This commitment to pragmatism led Rustin to oppose the seating of the MISSISSIPPI FREEDOM DEMOCRATIC PARTY (MFDP) at the 1964 DEMOCRATIC PARTY Convention. Rustin's opposition to seating MFDP resulted in a bitter rivalry between Rustin and the leaders of SNCC. Thus, when STOKELY CARMICHAEL and the other leaders of SNCC launched the Black Power movement on the MEREDITH MARCH in 1966, Rustin became one of its most outspoken opponents, describing the movement as infantile, irrational, racialist, and separatist. Rustin's integrationism made him an outspoken critic of MALCOLM X, whom he viewed as a racialist demagogue. Rustin also opposed the establishment of AFRICAN-AMERICAN STUDIES and the use of QUOTAS in AFFIRMATIVE ACTION. And although he was a strong supporter of FULL EMPLOYMENT and an expanded WELFARE STATE, he refused to support Martin Luther King's POOR PEOPLE'S CAMPAIGN to achieve these objectives.

Toward the end of his life, Rustin's views were increasingly at odds with the black LEADERSHIP establishment both because of his opposition to the Black Power movement and his unwavering support of Israel in the Middle East conflict. (Most African-American leaders after the 1960s expressed some solidarity with the Palestinians and supported their right to a homeland in that part of Palestine occupied by Israel in 1967. Many also were upset by Israel's tacit alliance with the APARTHEID regime in South Africa.) As his life came to an end, however, he was recognized as a major figure in the 20th-century black freedom struggle. An accomplished intellectual (as well as a talented singer), Rustin until his death published in the leading liberal MEDIA, appeared frequently on radio and television, and became an activist in the emerging GAY RIGHTS MOVEMENT.

Further reading: Jevis Anderson, *Bayard Rustin: The Troubles I've Seen* (New York: HarperCollins, 1997).

S

Schomburg Center for Research in Black Culture

The Schomburg Center, along with HOWARD UNIVERSITY's Moorland-Spingard Research Center, is the largest repository of documents (manuscripts, books, pamphlets, letters, photographs, etc.) on the African-American experience in the United States. The library, the HARLEM branch of the New York City Public Library, is based on material initially collected by Arthur Schomburg, a WEST INDIAN immigrant. Schomburg, who was active in efforts to free Puerto Rico and Cuba from Spanish COLONIALISM, began collecting material on black history while attending college in the Virgin Islands. In 1891 he moved to New York, where he continued his anticolonialist activism and the collecting of books and documents on black history because, as he said, "History must restore what slavery took away." Schomburg died in 1898, and eventually his collection was donated to the New York Public Library and became the basis for the library's Harlem branch, becoming a major repository for documents on the African-American experience. In 1940 the library named its division on black history in Schomburg's honor. The Schomburg Center is an indispensable resource for research in all areas of AFRICAN-AMERICAN STUDIES.

schools and education

Knowledge—literacy and formal education—has always been viewed as indispensable in the African-American struggle for FREEDOM and EQUALITY. During SLAVERY, blacks at great risk often established secret groups where they could teach each other how to read and write. After the CIVIL WAR during RECONSTRUCTION, historians write that the newly freed slaves had a "seemingly unquenchable thirst for education" and displayed an "avidity for learning." At Reconstruction's end, BOOKER T. WASHINGTON, the paradigmatic representative of ACCOMMODATIONISM, and W. E. B. DU BOIS, the paradigmatic representative of PROTEST, both agreed on the centrality of education in the black struggle for freedom. Early in the development of the 20th-century CIVIL RIGHTS MOVEMENT, the NAACP focused on equality in education, believing that inequality in schooling created and perpetuated inequality in virtually all other areas of society—the economic, social, and political. BLACK NATIONALISM as a philosophy has been centrally concerned with knowledge ("true knowledge") from its earliest manifestations in the writings of MARTIN DELANY and EDWARD WILMOT BLYDEN in the 19th century to the teachings and schools established by ELIJAH MUHAMMAD and the NATION OF ISLAM to the development of AFRICAN-AMERICAN STUDIES and AFROCENTRISM in the 1960s.

This focus on the acquisition of knowledge recognizes that it is an important base of POWER, especially for an oppressed group that lacks access to other bases of power such as wealth, status, or positions of authority in government. Although education in a capitalist society is not a sufficient condition for economic or political equality, it is usually a necessary one. For this reason, a determination to acquire formal education has been one of the primary objectives in AFRICAN-AMERICAN POLITICS. Whites bent on the OPPRESSION of blacks have also understood the necessary relationships between knowledge and power and freedom and equality. Therefore, conflicts over schools and education have frequently been at the center of the struggle between the BLACK COMMUNITY and whites in the United States.

Slavery as a near-total system of domination or oppression focused attention on literacy and learning by prohibiting and severely punishing those who would teach the enslaved to read and write. Although a number of enslaved Africans did learn how to read in the secret reading groups, in general the slave system was successful in creating and perpetuating ignorance. (Over 90 percent of the adult black population in the SOUTHERN STATES was illiterate in 1860 at the start of the CIVIL WAR.) Therefore, what there was of learning and education among African Americans prior to the end of slavery was found among the small population of FREE NEGROES, who established schools and attended col-

History class, Tuskegee Institute, Tuskegee, Alabama, 1902 (*Library of Congress*)

lege in the NORTHERN STATES. At the end of the Civil War this first TALENTED TENTH joined with Northern white Christian missionaries and philanthropists and the FREEDMEN'S BUREAU to establish schools and colleges for the newly freed slaves.

Much of the research on early black schools and education focuses on the important work of white religious groups (the American Missionary Association), white philanthropic groups (the Julia Rosenwald Fund), and the Freedmen's Bureau in the establishment of schools for blacks after the Civil War. But the black community, although hindered by POVERTY, contributed significantly to the development of early black education. In all of the Southern states the BLACK CHURCH and other organizations solicited funds to establish schools. In some parts of the South, the schools organized by blacks were the first to be established in a town or village. But the black community,

and for the most part the white community, did not have the resources to establish and maintain private schools. This, under the principle of FEDERALISM, was primarily the responsibility of STATE AND LOCAL GOVERNMENT, and one of the achievements of the Reconstruction-era governments was the creation of a common school system throughout much of the South. African Americans who were a part of these governments were among the strongest advocates of the common or public school system.

The system of public education established, however, was based on principles of RACISM and WHITE SUPREMACY. After the SUPREME COURT's 1896 decision in *PLESSY V. FERGUSON*, the principle of SEPARATE BUT EQUAL was applied to schools and education. However, while the principle of separate schools for blacks and whites was strictly enforced, the principle of equality was generally ignored, often grossly so. The Supreme Court in 1899 sanctioned this gross inequality in education in CUMMINGS V. BOARD OF EDUCATION. Thus, from the establishment of systems of public education in the South in the late 19th century until the mid-20th century, there were enormous inequalities in the education of black and white children. In most Southern states, spending per pupil on blacks on average was less than one-third of the amount spent on whites. In some communities, only elementary schools were provided for blacks, while whites were provided both elementary and secondary education. In general, because of the relative poverty of the Southern states, spending on education was much less than in the Northern states; thus education spending for blacks (who lived mainly in the South) was extremely meager when compared with the national average. The BLAIR EDUCATION BILL was designed to deal with racial inequalities in education and raise the overall level of education spending. Its defeat meant that inequalities in education, including HISTORICALLY BLACK COLLEGES AND UNIVERSITIES as well as elementary and secondary schools, prevented blacks from acquiring knowledge comparable with whites, reinforcing the historic inequalities generated during slavery. These inequalities in spending manifested themselves in lower salaries for black teachers, fewer and outdated textbooks (frequently black children would be provided textbooks after they had been used for years by whites; when new, updated texts were purchased for whites, blacks would receive the used, older books), and inadequate, often dilapidated buildings and facilities. These blatant inequalities were in direct violation of the principle of separate but equal proclaimed by the Supreme Court in *Plessy v. Ferguson.*

In the 1930s the NAACP and its LEGAL DEFENSE FUND began a systematic strategy of LITIGATION challenging these inequalities. At first this campaign was limited in scope, seeking equalization in pay for black teachers. Then the campaign broadened to include full equalization in per-pupil spending, textbooks, buildings, and facilities. At first most of the Southern states resisted equalization, but as the NAACP began to win cases banning SEGREGATION in higher education, many of them—fearing the prospect of court-ordered DESEGREGATION at the elementary and secondary level—began taking steps toward equalization. (Louisiana, for example, between 1940 and 1955 increased its spending per black child from $16 to $116, bringing it from 24 to 72 percent of parity with whites.) In the meantime, however, THURGOOD MARSHALL and his colleagues in the Legal Defense Fund changed their litigation strategy and decided "to go for the whole hog" and seek repeal of the principle of separate but equal in education. The result was *BROWN V. BOARD OF EDUCATION,* the landmark 1954 decision declaring that racial segregation in education violated the EQUAL PROTECTION CLAUSE of the FOURTEENTH AMENDMENT.

In the implementation of *Brown,* however, the NAACP sought not merely an end to segregation—desegregation—but INTEGRATION, that is, the abolition of racially identifiable schools. This focus on integration was controversial within the black LEADERSHIP establishment. Some black leaders wanted to preserve traditionally black schools as long as they were equally funded, while others argued that racially separate schools were inherently unequal and that in order for black children to receive an education comparable with whites, integration was indispensable. As early as 1935, W. E. B. DU BOIS took a contrary and more sensible position: "Theoretically, the Negro needs neither segregated schools nor mixed schools. What he needs is education. What he must remember is there is no magic in either mixed schools or in segregated schools. A mixed school with poor and unsympathetic teachers, with hostile public opinion and no teaching of truth concerning black folk is bad. A segregated school with ignorant placeholders, inadequate equipment, poor salaries and wretched housing is equally bad. Other things being equal, the mixed school is the broader, more natural basis for the education of all youth. . . . But other things are seldom equal, and in that case sympathy, knowledge and truth outweigh all that mixed school can offer." And Du Bois predicted that "if any outside power forced white and colored children in the same schools, the result would be turmoil and uprising as would utterly nullify the process of education."

An outside power—the Supreme Court—did for a time try to force the mixing of black and white school children, and the results were pretty much as Du Bois predicted. In 1971 in SWANN V. MECKLENBURG, the Court ordered the BUSING of school children in order to achieve racial balance of schools or, to put it another way, eliminate racially identifiable schools. Until the Court eventually effectively abandoned busing as a PUBLIC POLICY in MILLIKEN V. BRADLEY a decade later, it did lead to turmoil and some disruption of the educational process in many cities. It also led to massive WHITE FLIGHT to private and suburban schools. And the black children who attended the mixed schools did not significantly improve their educational performance. That is, busing as a public policy failed to achieve educational equality. Moreover, even during the peak of busing's use, most school children were not bused, remaining instead in their neighborhood schools. For most whites, this meant attending schools in largely white enclaves of the cities or in the suburbs. For most blacks, it meant attending schools in the impoverished GHETTOS of the cities. The result was that 50 years after the Supreme Court declared that separate education for blacks and whites was inherently unequal and therefore incompatible with the CONSTITUTION, most black children in the South as well as in the North continued to attend schools that were separate and unequal.

The separateness is a function of the segregated housing patterns that characterize most urban areas of the United States, where blacks live mainly in central city ghettos and whites mainly in affluent urban enclaves or the suburbs. At the end of the 20th century, 40 percent of all public schools were almost exclusively white, with more than 90 percent of the students white; another 40 percent were almost exclusively minority, with 90 percent or more of the students black or Latino. The schools were unequal because of the means by which the states chose to finance education. Under the principle of federalism, public education is a responsibility of the states, which they delegate to local school districts. In delegating their responsibility for education to local school districts, the states create gross inequalities in funding the education of black and white children. This is because local school districts finance education on the basis of the value of property within their boundaries, which means that affluent districts are able to provide much more in per-pupil spending than poor districts. And since whites live disproportionately in affluent suburban districts and blacks live disproportionately in less-affluent districts, the effect is to create school systems throughout the United States that in many ways are as separate and unequal as they were prior to *Brown*.

In *San Antonio School District v. Rodriguez* (1973), the Legal Defense Fund challenged this inequality in school financing, alleging that it violated the Constitution's equal protection clause. In this case, the Texas system of financing public education was challenged because of the large disparities in per-pupil spending among the state's school districts. The wealthiest district, which was 81 percent white, taxed itself at a rate of $0.85 per $100 of assessed property value, yielding $333 per pupil (contributions from state and federal funds raised total per-pupil spending to $594). The poorest district, which was 96 percent black and Latino, taxed itself at $1.05 per $100 of assessed property value, yielding $26 per pupil (contributions from state and federal funds raised total per-pupil spending to $356). Thus, in spite of the fact that the poor minorities taxed themselves at a higher rate than the affluent whites, they were unable—even with state and federal assistance—to approach parity or equality in the education of their children. A federal district court in Texas ruled this form of school financing violated the equal protection clause. However, the Supreme Court in a 6 to 3 decision reversed this judgment. The Court majority held that education was not a "fundamental right" guaranteed by the Constitution; that PLURALISM was an important value served by locally based school districts; and that "wealth discrimination" was inherent under CAPITALISM. Thus, the majority concluded: "In sum, to the extent that the Texas system of school financing results in unequal expenditures for pupils who happen to reside in different districts, we cannot say such disparities are the product of a system that is so irrational as to be invidiously discriminating. . . . It certainly is not the product or purpose of discriminating against any group or class." The dissenting justices, led by Thurgood Marshall and WILLIAM BRENNAN, argued that the majority's judgment was a retreat from the Court's "historic commitment to equality of educational opportunity and an unsupportable acquiescence in a system which deprives children in their earliest years of the chance to reach their full potential as citizens." With respect to education, the *Rodriguez* case was as important for African Americans as the *Brown* case. *Brown* provided a symbolic commitment to racial equality in schooling, but *Rodriguez* effectively undermined this commitment in schooling by denying poor and minority communities the money to fulfill it. *Rodriguez,* as Justices Marshall and Brennan wrote, represented a retreat from *Brown*'s commitment to equality in education.

At the beginning of the 21st century, African-American education was widely seen as in a state of crisis. Most black children attended racially separate and unequal schools in which the buildings were often overcrowded, old, and in need of repair; textbooks and laboratories were outdated; and the teachers were poorly paid, often inexperienced, and incompetent. In the schools of the ghettos, the conditions were so bad that one scholar of education, Jonathan Kozol, described them as "savage." Meanwhile the educational attainments of black schoolchildren lagged well behind those of whites. In a 2000 report, the U.S. Department of Education reported that the average black 17-year-old child read only about as well as the average white 13-year-old child, and blacks (of all social classes) consistently lagged behind whites in all measures of learning, including school performance, exit examinations, and the Scholastic Aptitude Examination. Black students from families earning more than $50,000 (the solid middle class) typically did no better on these examinations than students from poor white families earning $10,000 or less. Explanations for this crisis in black education include poverty and racism; inadequate and poorly financed schools; lower expectations of teachers of the capacity of blacks to learn; biases in the tests; and a climate of anti-intellectualism in the CULTURE of the black community as reflected in the popularity of athletics and RAP MUSIC.

The schools serving mainly black neighborhoods are inadequately funded, and although the ELEMENTARY AND SECONDARY EDUCATION ACT has bridged some of the disparities in funding, it remains a major stumbling block to equality. But most students of black education agree that at the end of the 20th century, equality in educational performance requires more than simply equality in funding. It also requires, as Du Bois said in the 1930s, competent school boards, sympathetic teachers, and a curriculum concerned with teaching the truth about black folk. Many of these requirements are missing even in school districts that are reasonably well financed and where the school boards, teachers, administrators, and students are mostly black. For example, in the black-controlled school systems of Newark, Atlanta, Detroit, Gary, and the DISTRICT OF COLUMBIA—systems where African Americans have controlled the educational process for decades—the performance of black children is as bad or worse than in school districts controlled by whites. The late-20th-century crisis in black education led to varied calls for reform, including vouchers (allowing children to attend private schools with public funds), alternative charter schools, and major reform in the curriculum along the lines of Afrocentrism. None of these reforms has been embraced on a large scale. And while scholars believe that each of them alone or in combination may have some promise, a resolution of the crisis in black education is unlikely without a return to the Reconstruction-era ethos, where an "avidity for learning" and a "seemingly unquenchable thirst for education" once again become core values of the black community.

See also DISCRIMINATION, DISPARATE IMPACT, and INSTITUTIONAL RACISM.

Further reading: Henry Allen Bullock, *A History of Black Education in the South: From 1619 to the Present* (Cambridge, Mass.: Harvard University Press, 1967); Jeffrey Henig et al., *The Color of School Reform: Race, Politics and the Challenge of Urban Education* (Princeton, N.J.: Princeton University Press, 1999); Jonathan Kozol, *Savage Inequalities: Children and American Schools* (New York: Harper Perennial, 1992); John Ogbu, *Minority Education and Caste* (New York: Academic Press, 1978); Wilbur Rich *Black Mayors and School Politics: The Failure of Reform in Detroit, Gary and Newark* (New York: Garland, 1996).

SCLC See SOUTHERN CHRISTIAN LEADERSHIP CONFERENCE.

Seale, Bobby (1926–) *activist*

In 1966 Bobby Seale, with HUEY NEWTON, founded the BLACK PANTHER PARTY. Born in Dallas, Texas, Seale joined the air force after completing high school but was court-martialed and given a "bad conduct" discharge because, he said, of his resistance to RACISM by air force officers. In the early 1960s he moved to Oakland, California, and while attending Merritt College he met Newton. Shortly thereafter they established the Black Panther Party. Newton was the principal theorist and strategist of the party, although he was the minister of defense and Seale was the chairman.

But after Newton was jailed in 1968, Seale became the principal party leader and spokesman. This made him a principal target of COINTELPRO, J. EDGAR HOOVER's program of POLITICAL REPRESSION. Seale was arrested and jailed several times on charges that ranged from disturbing the peace to murder and conspiracy to murder. In 1969 Seale, along with six white VIETNAM WAR protesters, was charged with conspiracy to incite RIOTS at the 1968 DEMOCRATIC PARTY CONVENTION. During the trial in Chicago he was gagged and shackled because of his protests in the courtroom. After the Chicago trial, Seale was once again on trial in 1969 in New Haven, Connecticut, this time for kidnapping and murder. Although in each of these trials the charges were dismissed or a mistrial declared, Seale was kept in jail off and on for two years. Without his or Newton's leadership, the Black Panther Party rapidly disintegrated as a result of political repression, factionalism, and corruption. In 1973 Seale entered URBAN POLITICS by running for mayor of Oakland. Surprisingly, he came in second in a field of nine candidates, but he lost the runoff election to the incumbent mayor by a margin of 77,476 to 43,710. Although he lost, his campaign is credited with laying the groundwork for the election of the city's first black mayor in the next election. After failing to become an ELECTED OFFICIAL in Oakland, Seale moved to Philadelphia, where he wrote his memoirs, *A Lonely Rage: The Autobiography of Bobby Seale,* and a cookbook, *Barbeque'n with Bobby.* In the 1990s he occasionally lectured in Temple University's AFRICAN-AMERICAN STUDIES program.

segregation

Segregation is the practice of the enforced separation of the members of a SUBORDINATE GROUP, ETHNIC GROUP, or MINORITY GROUP from the SUPERORDINATE GROUP. In the United States this practice mainly involved the separation of whites from blacks. In 1896 in *PLESSY V. FERGUSON,* the SUPREME COURT declared that such enforced separation did not violate the CONSTITUTION. Thereafter in the SOUTHERN STATES a rigid de jure (enforced by law) system of segregation was enforced, while in the NORTHERN STATES a less rigid de facto (enforced by custom) system was imposed. In the Southern states segregation was enforced in virtually all aspects of life, while in the Northern states it was enforced mainly in housing, schools, and employment. Segregation was also enforced by the federal government in the BUREAUCRACY, the MILITARY, and in various aspects of PUBLIC POLICY. Whether de jure or de facto or whether in the North or South, the purpose of segregation was to establish and reinforce RACISM and WHITE SUPREMACY. De jure segregation was prohibited in virtually all areas of American life as a result of the CIVIL RIGHTS ACT OF 1964.

A drinking fountain on the county courthouse lawn, Halifax, North Carolina, 1938 *(Library of Congress)*

See also APARTHEID, JIM CROW, and SEPARATE BUT EQUAL.

self-help

Self-help is the concept that the BLACK COMMUNITY should rely on its own resources to achieve FREEDOM and EQUALITY. The concept is integral to the philosophy of BLACK NATIONALISM, and it has been practiced since the formation of the black community with the development of the BLACK CHURCH and related charitable, cultural and, educational institutions.

The concept of self-help, however, is controversial because it has often been used by whites and by those black leaders viewed as UNCLE TOMS to suggest that blacks should embrace ACCOMMODATIONISM and avoid PROTEST against RACISM and WHITE SUPREMACY. It has also been used to suggest that blacks should improve themselves rather than rely on PUBLIC POLICY. Self-help in this sense was at the core of the strategy of accommodationism employed by BOOKER T. WASHINGTON in the aftermath of RECONSTRUCTION. Washington suggested that blacks should have avoided protest and POLITICAL PARTICIPATION during Reconstruction and instead focused on self-help—building individual character, families, and institutions. As this strategy was articulated by Washington, it suggested that blacks as a people so soon out of SLAVERY were not ready in the 1870s and 1880s for full freedom and equality; therefore self-help was a prerequisite for equality with whites and eventually full freedom.

Although Washington's concept of self-help contributed to the development of much of the infrastructure of the modern black community—schools and colleges, businesses and MEDIA, and fraternal and professional

ORGANIZATIONS—it was rejected by W. E. B. DU BOIS and other black leaders because they saw it as accommodating racism and white supremacism and denigrating the idea of CIVIL RIGHTS. However, Du Bois and his associates did not reject the concept of self-help per se but only Washington's linking of the idea with accommodationism and the IDEOLOGY of CONSERVATISM. Du Bois wrote in *THE SOULS OF BLACK FOLK* that he "rejoiced" in Washington's program of internal community development and uplift, but insofar as it did not value VOTING RIGHTS and belittled the "emasculating effects" of SEGREGATION, he had to unceasingly protest. This tension between Du Bois and Washington over the concept of self-help continued during the CIVIL RIGHTS MOVEMENT and into the POST–CIVIL RIGHTS ERA.

Differences over the concept also divided black nationalists and adherents of INTEGRATIONISM when both MARCUS GARVEY and ELIJAH MUHAMMAD developed powerful nationalist movements based on the concept because they believed that integration and acceptance of blacks into American society was impossible. Garvey and Muhammad's concept of self-help was rejected by the leaders of the NAACP and the URBAN LEAGUE. In the post–civil rights era, self-help was embraced by elements of the BLACK POWER MOVEMENT as an alternative to integration. It was also embraced by black conservative PUBLIC INTELLECTUALS like THOMAS SOWELL and leading white conservative politicians like RICHARD NIXON and RONALD REAGAN who viewed it as an alternative to LIBERALISM.

These tensions and conflicts obscure the underlying consensus that has always existed in the black community about self-help. Blacks at all times have always embraced self-help as a necessary part of the struggle for freedom and equality. While some have viewed it as an alternative to protest and political participation, others have viewed it as in no way inconsistent with politics, protest, and public policy. Still others have viewed self-help as an alternative to integration, while others see it as in no way inconsistent with that objective. These differences, however, should not obscure the underlying consensus about the importance of self-help in the black community.

Selma demonstrations

The demonstrations organized by the STUDENT NONVIOLENT COORDINATING COMMITTEE (SNCC) and the SOUTHERN CHRISTIAN LEADERSHIP CONFERENCE (SCLC) in Selma, Alabama, in 1965 are, along with the BIRMINGHAM DEMONSTRATIONS of 1963, landmark PROTESTS in the CIVIL RIGHTS MOVEMENT. The demonstrations at Birmingham led directly to passage of the CIVIL RIGHTS ACT OF 1964, and the Selma demonstrations led directly to the passage of the VOTING RIGHTS ACT OF 1965, which for the first time since RECONSTRUCTION enforced the FIFTEENTH AMENDMENT guarantee of VOTING RIGHTS for African Americans.

In 1963 SNCC started a campaign to register blacks to vote in Selma, a small town in Alabama. After two years the campaign had registered very few blacks. Thus, SNCC called on MARTIN LUTHER KING JR. and SCLC for assistance, hoping the presence of King and his organization would bring national MEDIA attention to the campaign. King's presence did indeed bring the national media to Selma. And in a protest march on March 7, 1965, that later became known as "bloody Sunday," the media's presence resulted in a decision by President LYNDON B. JOHNSON to propose what was to become the Voting Rights Act of 1965. On that Sunday afternoon several hundred blacks led by JOHN LEWIS, the head of SNCC (King was away at a fundraising event), started a march to Montgomery, the Alabama state capital. At the Edmund Pettus Bridge they were brutally attacked by state police who used horses, whips, tear gas, and clubs. This VIOLENCE was broadcast on national television throughout the evening, leading thousands of Americans to send letters and telegrams to the president and CONGRESS urging that actions be taken to end the violence and to guarantee African-American voting rights. (In an ironic happenstance, the racist violence in Selma was shown while much of the nation was watching *Judgment at Nuremberg*, the film about Hitler's virulent racism and the Holocaust.)

President Johnson had planned to propose voting rights legislation later in the year, but as a result of the broad COALITION activated by bloody Sunday, he decided to immediately propose the legislation. In a dramatic television address several days later, Johnson closed his remarks by invoking "WE SHALL OVERCOME," the anthem of the Civil Rights movement. On March 19 the president formally sent the legislation to Congress. It was signed into law on August 6. The act not only effectively guaranteed the right of blacks in the SOUTHERN STATES to vote, it also provided procedures to increase black REPRESENTATION among ELECTED OFFICIALS. The Selma demonstrations, coming two years after the demonstrations at Birmingham, also represented the second major defeat in as many years for the forces of RACISM and WHITE SUPREMACY represented by Alabama governor GEORGE WALLACE.

Further reading: David Garrow, *Protest at Selma: Martin Luther King, Jr. and the Voting Rights Act of 1965* (New Haven, Conn.: Yale University Press, 1978).

separate but equal

"Separate but equal" is the doctrine established by the SUPREME COURT in 1896 in *PLESSY V. FERGUSON* permitting STATE AND LOCAL GOVERNMENTS to separate blacks and whites in public places. The doctrine was based on the Court's interpretation of the EQUAL PROTECTION CLAUSE of the FOURTEENTH AMENDMENT. The Court held that the clause did not prohibit racial SEGREGATION as long as the races were treated equally. Although the *Plessy* decision dealt with segregation on railroad cars, the doctrine became the basis for widespread segregation in all public places, from hospitals to cemeteries. Although the doctrine required that facilities be equal for both races, they rarely if ever were. The doctrine was reversed by the Supreme Court in the 1954 *BROWN V. BOARD OF EDUCATION* decision insofar as SCHOOLS AND EDUCATION was concerned and in all public places by the CONGRESS in the CIVIL RIGHTS ACT OF 1964.

See also JIM CROW.

separation of powers

The separation of powers is, with FEDERALISM, one of the two basic principles of government embodied in the CONSTITUTION. Both were designed to limit the POWER of government and to inhibit radical or rapid changes in PUBLIC POLICY. Both principles have advantages and disadvantages for African Americans in their struggle for FREEDOM and EQUALITY.

The separation of the powers of the government into three parts or branches (legislative, executive, and judicial) rather than concentrating them in a single person (a monarch) or place (the legislature or parliament) was viewed by the framers of the Constitution as a necessary safeguard for freedom. As James Madison wrote, "the accumulation of all powers, legislative, executive and judiciary, in the same hands . . . may justly be pronounced the very definition of tyranny." Although the principle of the separation of powers was embraced to protect freedom, as Donald Robinson shows in *Slavery in the Structure of American Politics* (1971), concerns about SLAVERY also influenced the decision to adopt the principle. This is because a divided government with little unitary and centralized power would be less likely to act against slavery. Thus, as Robinson writes, "Tensions about slavery were prominent among the forces that maintained the resolve to develop the country without strong direction from Washington." In limiting the powers of the central government, the framers at the same time limited the possibility that the government could attack the institution of slavery and later SEGREGATION.

Throughout American history the separation of powers along with federalism has more often worked to frustrate rather than facilitate the African-American struggle against OPPRESSION. Prior to the CIVIL WAR, the separation of powers allowed the Senate for a period to block actions to halt the spread of slavery, and when this failed the SUPREME COURT in the *DRED SCOTT* case interpreted the Constitu-

tion in a way that allowed the spread of slavery throughout the United States. During RECONSTRUCTION President ANDREW JOHNSON, hostile to black freedom, used the powers of the PRESIDENCY (including the veto) to block or frustrate the efforts of CONGRESS to pass laws guaranteeing black freedom and equality. When Johnson's efforts failed and CIVIL RIGHTS laws and amendments to the Constitution were enacted, the Supreme Court once again used its powers to frustrate implementation of these laws and amendments. For half of the 20th century, the separation of powers permitted senators from the SOUTHERN STATES to use the FILIBUSTER to block legislation making LYNCHING a federal crime. And until the PROTESTS of the 1960s, the Senate blocked action on most civil rights bills, despite support for such bills in PUBLIC OPINION and in the other branches of government. In other words, if the American DEMOCRACY had been organized like most Western democracies—with one democratically elected branch of government—then it is possible that actions against slavery and segregation might have been taken earlier.

On the other hand, the separation of powers sometimes has worked to the advantage of blacks by providing separate, multiple points of access to the government. Thus, when one branch of government was hostile or unsympathetic to black interests, blacks have sometimes been able to turn to another that was less hostile. For example, when President Johnson was hostile during Reconstruction, blacks turned to the RADICAL REPUBLICANS in Congress to pursue their interests. And in the mid-20th century when presidents and Congress were unsympathetic, blacks turned to LITIGATION in the Supreme Court. During the presidencies of RICHARD NIXON and RONALD REAGAN, blacks turned again to litigation in the courts and LOBBYING the Congress to block or water down actions perceived as hostile to them. And in the POST–CIVIL RIGHTS ERA as the Supreme Court became less sympathetic, blacks turned again to the Congress to overturn unfavorable Court decisions. Thus, while on balance the separation of powers has probably worked against the interests of blacks, it has also sometimes facilitated rather than frustrated the pursuit of those interests.

See also *BROWN V. BOARD OF EDUCATION*, CIVIL RIGHTS CASES OF 1883, DYER ANTILYNCHING BILL, *PLESSY V. FERGUSON*, and SLAUGHTERHOUSE CASES.

sexism

Sexism—DISCRIMINATION based on sex, especially against women by men seeking to maintain male dominance—is as integral a feature of the American DEMOCRACY and its POLITICAL SYSTEM as is RACISM. And like racism, it is deeply rooted in Western philosophy, sanctioned by an IDEOLOGY of male supremacism that is not unlike the ideology of WHITE SUPREMACY. In the SOCIAL CONTRACT THEORY that is the philosophical foundation of the American democracy, women, like blacks, were excluded from the social contract. In THOMAS JEFFERSON's draft of the DECLARATION OF INDEPENDENCE, the phrase is all "men," rather than persons, "are created equal." Although Jefferson's draft was revised many times by his colleagues in the Continental Congress, no one suggested the word *men* be changed to encompass women. And just as there were no blacks in the Congress that approved Jefferson's draft, women were also excluded. And the convention that gathered at Philadelphia to write the CONSTITUTION exclusively comprised white males. During the course of the convention, Abigail Adams, the wife of John Adams, wrote imploring him to "remember the ladies" in the new Constitution, and to "be more generous and favorable to them than [were] your ancestors. Do not put such unlimited power into the hands of husbands. Remember all men would be tyrants if they could. If particular care and attention is not paid to the ladies we are determined to foment rebellion, and will not hold ourselves bound by any such laws in which we have no voice, or representation." Adams responded to his learned wife with humor while calling attention to the OPPRESSION of blacks and Indians and their discontent. He wrote "I cannot but laugh. We have been told that our struggle has loosened the bonds of government everywhere . . . that Indians slighted their guardians and Negroes grew insolent toward their masters. But your letter was the first intimation that another tribe more numerous and powerful than all the rest were grown discontented. This is rather too coarse a complaint but you are so saucy, I won't blot it out."

Racism and sexism and their ideologies of supremacy have been integral to American politics since its beginnings, and the struggles against them have been interrelated. Women, black and white, were part of the ABOLITIONIST MOVEMENT, although this COALITION of blacks and white women broke down in conflict over adoption of the FIFTEENTH AMENDMENT. The 1960s movement for FEMINISM has its origins partly in the CIVIL RIGHTS MOVEMENT and the BLACK POWER MOVEMENT. Sexism and racism allow white men to dominate white women and black men and women; white women to dominate black men and women; and black men to dominate black women. Thus, white women have to struggle against the dominance of white men to achieve FREEDOM and EQUALITY, while black women have to struggle against the racism and white supremacy of white women and men as well as the sexism and male supremacy of black men. This triple nature of black female subordination creates tensions and conflicts within feminist movements and within African-American movements, requiring black women to consider whether racism or sexism should take priority in their struggles for freedom and equality.

Until the 1960s black women tended to give priority to the struggle against racism and white supremacy because sexism manifests itself as various forms of discrimination, invidious and benign, but racism manifested itself as a system of oppression. Thus, until the end of the 20th century, there was not the same kind of urgency in the struggle against sexism as there was in the struggle against racism. FREDERICK DOUGLASS, a passionate advocate of women's rights, put the priorities in the following way during the 19th-century debate over the ratification of the Fifteenth Amendment "when women are dragged from their houses and hung on lamp posts; when their children are torn from their arms and their brains dashed on the pavement; when they are the object of insult and outrage at every turn; when they are in danger of having their homes burnt down over their heads; when their children are not allowed to enter schools, then they will have an urgency to the ballot equal to our own." But sexism is as much a part of the ethos and traditions of the BLACK COMMUNITY and its CULTURE as it is in the larger society, rooted to some extent in the important cultural attribute of RELIGIOSITY. And while the philosophy of BLACK NATIONALISM is not sexist or supremacist in its core principles, many 20th-century black nationalists (including ELIJAH MUHAMMAD, MALCOLM X, AMIRI BARAKA, and RON KARENGA) articulated rigid sexist and supremacist doctrines. Therefore, black women have had to struggle to make the fight against sexism a part of the BLACK AGENDA, a struggle that met with little success until the POST–CIVIL RIGHTS ERA.

See also NATIONAL ASSOCIATION OF COLORED WOMEN'S CLUBS, NATIONAL COUNCIL OF NEGRO WOMEN, NATIONAL POLITICAL CONGRESS OF BLACK WOMEN, MARIA W. STEWART, and SOJOURNER TRUTH.

Further reading: Susan Okin, *Women in Western Political Thought* (Princeton, N.J.: Princeton University Press, 1979); bell hooks, *Ain't I a Woman: Black Women and Feminism* (Boston: South End Press, 1981).

Sharpton, Al (1954–) *activist, politician*
In the POST–CIVIL RIGHTS ERA, the use of PROTEST and CIVIL DISOBEDIENCE declined as most of the LEADERSHIP of the BLACK COMMUNITY embraced voting, LOBBYING, and LITIGATION as the preferred strategies to advance the BLACK AGENDA. Al Sharpton, however attempted to maintain the tradition of protest.

A protégé of JESSE JACKSON, Sharpton was born in 1954 and grew up in New York City, where at the age of four he started preaching and by 10 was touring as the "wonder-boy preacher" with Mahalia Jackson, the legendary black gospel singer. As a young preacher Sharpton met ADAM CLAYTON POWELL and became enamored of Powell's role as political leader, especially his use of RELIGIOSITY and the BLACK CHURCH. In 1969 Jesse Jackson appointed Sharpton, then age 14, as youth director of Operation Breadbasket, the operating arm of the SOUTHERN CHRISTIAN LEADERSHIP CONFERENCE in the NORTHERN STATES. As Jackson's protégé, Sharpton attended the 1972 NATIONAL BLACK POLITICAL CONVENTION. In addition to his preaching and political activism, Sharpton also worked with James Brown, the legendary black soul singer, recording a song with him and eventually becoming Brown's confidant and road manager. Thus, Sharpton has deep roots in the CULTURE of the black community in terms of religiosity and MUSIC, as well as in its established structure of leadership.

He first came to the attention of the national MEDIA as a protest leader in 1987 as a result of his involvement in the case of Tawana Brawley. In November 1987, Brawley, a 15-year-old black girl, was found in suburban New York in a plastic bag, smeared with feces, her hair yanked out, and with "KKK" scrawled on her body. She claimed that she had been kidnapped and raped by a gang of white men, one or more of them wearing police uniforms. The Brawley case became a celebrated cause in New York and to some extent throughout the nation. On the advice of Sharpton (whom the Brawley family asked to be its spokesman) and her attorneys, Brawley refused to cooperate with local police and the state attorney general in their investigation of the case, claiming they were biased. Instead, Sharpton called on the state's governor to appoint a special, independent prosecutor. The governor refused, and Brawley continued to refuse to cooperate in the investigation. Sharpton assumed a highly visible leadership role in defense of Brawley, in the course of which he made a number of inflammatory and unsubstantiated allegations, including an assertion that Brawley was attacked by a racist cult inside the local sheriff's office. Nine months after the incident, a state grand jury concluded that Brawley's story was a hoax. And in 1988 a jury in a defamation suit filed by one of the men Sharpton had accused of attacking Brawley found that Sharpton acted "with reckless disregard for the truth" and thereby defamed the man. The jury ordered Sharpton to pay $65,000 in damages, which he refused to pay, although friends of his subsequently banded together to pay the debt. Nor would he issue an apology for his behavior during the Brawley affair, saying "I did what I believed."

The Brawley case made Sharpton a recognized leader in New York City, but his demagogic behavior also made him a controversial and divisive figure. A 1988 poll found that 84 percent of white New Yorkers viewed him unfavorably, as did 55 percent of black New Yorkers. Sharpton's controversial image was further tarnished when the media reported that he had been an informant for the FBI. Sharpton denied the allegations, although he admitted to pro-

viding information to the FBI about the role of organized crime in the distribution of illegal drugs.

Despite questions about his role in the Brawley case and his relationship with the FBI, his status as a local and then a national black leader rose throughout the 1980s and 1990s. He consolidated his status as a member of the black leadership establishment by focusing on RACISM and DISCRIMINATION in the CRIMINAL JUSTICE SYSTEM, including racial profiling and police VIOLENCE against African Americans. In New York City he led days of mass demonstrations after four white police officers killed Amadaou Diallo, an unarmed West African immigrant; and later he led the protests against the brutal sodomizing of Abner Louima, an immigrant from HAITI, by New York police. After consolidating his status as a local protest leader, Sharpton, following in the paths of his mentors Adam Powell and Jesse Jackson, ran for political office. In 1992 he ran in the DEMOCRATIC PARTY primary for the United States Senate, receiving 15 percent of the vote. In 1994 he again ran for the Senate, receiving a surprising 26 percent of the vote. In 1997 he received 32 percent of the vote in the Democratic

Reverend Al Sharpton *(Hulton Archive)*

primary for New York City mayor. Although Sharpton's efforts to become an ELECTED OFFICIAL were unsuccessful, his several candidacies increased his capacity to leverage the black vote as the BALANCE OF POWER in local and state elections in New York. It also earned him grudging and reluctant acceptance into the national black leadership establishment.

Creating his own ORGANIZATION, the National Action Network, Sharpton holds weekly rallies in HARLEM to mobilize mass support for his various causes. In 2000 he served 90 days in jail for protesting the use by the United States Navy of a Puerto Rican island as a bombing range. This protest was a conscious effort by Sharpton to broaden his base beyond the black community and build a broad Jesse Jackson–style multiethnic RAINBOW COALITION. Also, like Jackson, Sharpton made forays into CITIZEN DIPLOMACY, visiting the African nation of Sudan to investigate allegations of SLAVERY and to the Middle East to meet with the leaders of Israel and Palestine. As the 20th century came to an end, Sharpton was openly seeking to compete with Jackson as the preeminent leader of the African-American community, going so far as to propose, again like Jackson, a 2004 PRESIDENTIAL CAMPAIGN as a means to enhance his national recognition and consolidate his leadership status. A 2000 poll by the JOINT CENTER FOR POLITICAL AND ECONOMIC STUDIES found that 75 percent of blacks and 44 percent of whites recognized Sharpton. This relatively high name recognition did not, however, translate into highly favorable ratings. Among blacks, 37 percent rated him favorably and 29 percent unfavorably; among whites only 10 percent rated him favorably compared with 41 percent unfavorable. (The remainder of the respondents in the poll expressed no opinion.) Nevertheless, Sharpton's organization, with a budget of more than $1 million, and his charismatic style of leadership made him a formidable force in AFRICAN-AMERICAN POLITICS at the beginning of the 21st century. In his memoir, *Go Tell It on the Mountain: The Autobiography of the Rev. Al Sharpton* (1996), Sharpton suggests that CO-OPTATION and ACCOMMODATIONISM dominate post–civil rights era black leadership and that the purpose of his leadership is to restore protest and MILITANCY to the strategies of African-American politics in the 21st century.

See also OPERATION PUSH.

Shaw v. Reno (1993)

Shaw v. Reno is an important SUPREME COURT decision dealing with the REPRESENTATION of African Americans and other ethnic MINORITY GROUPS in the CONGRESS and in the legislatures and judicial offices of STATE AND LOCAL GOVERNMENTs. The decision involved interpretation of the VOTING RIGHTS ACT OF 1965.

When the act was passed, it was initially used to simply guarantee that blacks in the SOUTHERN STATES could vote. However, in the late 1960s the Supreme Court issued a series of decisions interpreting various provisions of the act as not just guaranteeing the right to vote but also the right to cast an effective vote, one that would allow black voters to support ELECTED OFFICIALS of their choice, presumably ones of their own race. The seminal case in this series of decisions was *United Jewish Organizations v. Carey* (1977), in which the court held that the deliberate creation of majority-black legislative districts did not violate the EQUAL PROTECTION CLAUSE of the FOURTEENTH AMENDMENT. In *Shaw* the Court in effect reversed its holding in *Carey,* deciding that the deliberate creation of majority-black districts might indeed violate the equal protection clause. After the 1990 CENSUS, most of the Southern states, following the precedents established by *Carey* and the guidelines of the CIVIL RIGHTS DIVISION of the JUSTICE DEPARTMENT, created majority-black congressional districts. Twelve new black-majority districts were created, and they in turn resulted in the election of 12 new black congresspersons. In several states this was the first time an African American had been elected to Congress since RECONSTRUCTION. In North Carolina, several white voters sued, alleging that the creation of the black districts constituted "reverse discrimination" in violation of the equal protection clause. In *Shaw,* a narrow 5 to 4 majority of the Court agreed with North Carolina's whites. Writing for the majority, Justice Sandra Day O'Connor said the districts in question were so "extremely irregular on [their] face . . . that they rationally can be viewed only as an effort to segregate the races for purposes of voting." Such SEGREGATION, Justice O'Connor wrote "reinforces the perception that members of the same racial group—regardless of their age, education, economic status or the community in which they live—think alike, share the same political interests and will prefer the same candidate. We have rejected such perceptions elsewhere as impermissible racial stereotyping." Indeed, O'Connor used the word APARTHEID to refer to the districts. In his dissent, Justice John Paul Stevens pointed to the "irony" and "perversity" of using the Fourteenth Amendment, which was enacted to protect the rights of African Americans, to deny them rights and representation, writing, "If it is permissible to draw boundaries to provide adequate representation for rural voters, for union members, for Hasidic Jews, for Polish Americans or for Republicans, it necessarily follows that it is permissible to do the same thing for members of the very minority group whose history in the United States gave birth to the Equal Protection Clause. A contrary conclusion could only be described as perverse."

Following the *Shaw* decision, the lower federal courts struck down majority-black congressional and other legislative districts throughout the South. However, the Supreme Court in 2001 in *Easley v. Cromartie* clarified and to some extent retreated from the principles of *Shaw* in a way that *appears* to allow for some use of race as a factor in legislative districting. *Easley* also involved the drawing of congressional district lines in North Carolina. After the Court in *Shaw* declared the majority-black 12th congressional district in North Carolina unconstitutional, the state legislature redrew the lines to create a district with a 41 percent black population. A three-judge federal district court declared this new district unconstitutional because it had used race as the "predominant" factor in redrawing the lines. In *Easley,* a 5 to 4 majority reversed the district court, ruling that the lower court's conclusion that race was the predominant factor in drawing the lines was "clearly erroneous." Rather, Justice Stephen Breyer, writing for the majority (which included Justice O'Connor), concluded that the lines were drawn on the basis of party affiliation rather than race, and since there is a high correlation between race and party (95 percent of black voters in North Carolina typically vote for the DEMOCRATIC PARTY candidate), it was constitutionally permissible for the legislature to take race into account as a surrogate for party. Thus, Breyer concluded that race was not an illegitimate consideration in districting as long as it was not the "dominant and controlling" consideration. Justice CLARENCE THOMAS, writing for himself and the other dissenting justices, argued that the majority should not have second-guessed the conclusions of the district court on whether race or party was the predominant factor, and that even if the majority was correct in second-guessing, the lines were still unconstitutional because "it is not a defense that the Legislature may merely have drawn the district based on the stereotype that blacks are reliable Democratic voters." While the Court's narrow decision in *Easley* suggested that race could be used in the districting process, it left the situation muddled in terms of the factual determination of when the use of race is "predominant," "dominant," or "controlling."

However the Court eventually resolves the constitutional issues, the theoretical problem of how best to deal with the representation of African-American interests in the POLITICAL SYSTEM will remain. This is because the resolution of constitutional issues does not resolve the question of whether black interests are best represented by having the maximum number of constituencies with a black majority so they may elect black representatives, or whether those interests are best served by having the black POPULATION dispersed among a larger number of constituencies where, although not a majority, they are sufficiently large so as to constitute the BALANCE OF POWER. This theoretical issue has been debated by scholars and black political leaders throughout most of the POST–CIVIL RIGHTS ERA. But it became particularly contentious after the REPUBLICAN PARTY gained the majority in the House of Representatives in 1994. Although the numbers are in dispute, virtually all political scientists who have studied the 1994 election conclude that some of the Republican gains are directly attributable to the creation in 1990 of majority-black districts in the Southern states. Since black POWER in the House (in terms of committee and subcommittee assignments) depends on the Democratic Party having a majority, some observers conclude that black interests are served best by a Democratic majority and fewer blacks in the House than by having more blacks in a House controlled by a Republican majority. To some extent, resolution of this issue depends on which dimension of representation blacks wish to emphasize: descriptive or symbolic, which requires the presence of blacks themselves in legislative bodies, or the substantive dimension, which requires the presence of representatives favorable to black PUBLIC POLICY interests, whatever their race.

Further reading: David Canon, *Race, Redistricting and Representation: The Unintended Consequences of Black Majority Districts* (Chicago: University of Chicago Press, 1999); Frank Parker, *Black Votes Count* (Chapel Hill: University of North Carolina Press, 1990); Carol Swain, *Black Faces, Black Interests: The Representation of African American Interests in Congress* (Cambridge, Mass.: Harvard University Press, 1993).

sit-ins

Sit-ins and FREEDOM RIDES were two of the most innovative strategies of CIVIL DISOBEDIENCE developed during the PROTEST phase of the CIVIL RIGHTS MOVEMENT. The origins of sit-ins as a strategy of protest are usually traced to the sit-ins in Greensboro, North Carolina, in 1960. However, sit-ins as a form of CIVIL RIGHTS protest predate the Greensboro incident; for example, RONALD WALTERS, while a part of the NAACP youth council, led sit-in demonstrations in Witchita, Kansas, during the 1950s. The sit-ins, however, at Greensboro were the first to attract the attention of the national MEDIA.

On February 1, 1960, Ezell Blair, Joseph McNeil, David Richmond, and Franklin McCain—students at North Carolina A & T, a historically black college—sat down at a lunch counter at an F. W. Woolworth store and ordered coffee. Because the laws of North Carolina required SEGREGATION at lunch counters, the students were refused service. But rather than leave as ordered, they "sat down." The following day the four students returned with more than a dozen other students. Again

A group of black students, who were refused service at a luncheon counter reserved for white customers, staged a sit-down strike at the F.W. Woolworth store in Greensboro, North Carolina, 1960. *(Library of Congress)*

they were refused service, and again they sat down rather than leave. Several days later dozens of students (including some whites) joined the protest, which the national media began to refer to as the "sit-in" movement. Within two weeks the movement spread to several other SOUTHERN STATES, and hundreds of students were arrested and many were expelled from colleges and universities. This led to sympathy sit-ins by black and white students at lunch counters in NORTHERN STATES.

Although the sit-ins rarely led to DESEGREGATION of lunch counters, they sparked similar strategies of protest, including "read-ins" at segregated libraries and "pray-ins" at segregated churches. However, the significance of the sit-ins was their manifestation of a new spirit of MILITANCY in the Civil Rights movement and their leading to the establishment of a new civil rights ORGANIZATION: SNCC, the STUDENT NONVIOLENT COORDINATING COMMITTEE. This new organization, formed under the guidance of ELLA BAKER, was to play a major role in the civil rights struggle in the Southern states and in the development of the BLACK POWER MOVEMENT.

slaughterhouse cases (1873)

The slaughterhouse cases decided in 1873 were the first decisions by the SUPREME COURT interpreting the FOURTEENTH AMENDMENT. Although the cases did not involve the CIVIL RIGHTS of African Americans, the decision had a profound impact on those rights because it established the precedent that principles of FEDERALISM in the CONSTITUTION would be more important than the principles of FREEDOM and EQUALITY in the Fourteenth Amendment.

The slaughterhouse cases (three related cases were heard by the Court) involved a challenge by a group of butchers in New Orleans to a Louisiana law that gave one company a monopoly of the slaughtering of livestock in the city. The butchers claimed that the law violated several provisions of the Fourteenth Amendment, including its "privileges and immunities clause," because it took away their right as citizens to earn a living and therefore their property rights. The Court's 5 to 4 majority disagreed, holding in an opinion by Justice Samuel Miller that the Fourteenth Amendment only prohibited the states from infringing on the privileges and immunities of "national citizenship," which the Court held included only such minor rights as the right to protection on the high seas or to use of the rivers of the United States. (The Court also included among these national rights "habeas corpus," the right of a person held in custody to be brought before a judge to seek his release.) In reaching this conclusion, the Court distinguished between two types of CITIZENSHIP in the United States: "national," which is conferred by birth or naturalization, and "state," which is conferred by residency in a particular state. And while states could not deny persons their national citizenship rights, they were free under the principles of federalism to define and restrict as they wished state citizenship rights, notwithstanding the privileges and immunities clause or the amendment's DUE PROCESS CLAUSE and its EQUAL PROTECTION CLAUSE. The decision in the slaughterhouse cases dealt with the rights of butchers rather than blacks, but the Court was well aware that its decision in the case would eventually affect the rights of African Americans. Indeed, Justice Miller wrote that protection of blacks from the "oppression of those who had formerly exercised unlimited dominion over [them] . . . was at the 'foundations' of the Amendment." Sure enough, the slaughterhouse cases became a precedent for the CIVIL RIGHTS CASES OF 1883, which overturned the Civil Rights Act of 1875, and PLESSY V. FERGUSON, the 1896 case establishing the right of the states to establish racial SEGREGATION and the doctrine of SEPARATE BUT EQUAL.

slave revolts

Although the odds were overwhelmingly against them because of the monopoly of VIOLENCE and virtually all other sources of POWER held by whites, African Americans during SLAVERY early and often used various forms of violence to resist their OPPRESSION. Most often these forms of violence were unorganized, individual acts of rebellion, but according to HERBERT APTHEKER, over 250 organized slave rebellions took place before slavery came to an end.

The first recorded revolt occurred in 1526. The most daring and famous took place in 1831, led by NAT TURNER. Although the clearest short-term results of the revolts were increased POLITICAL REPRESSION of Africans—the enslaved as well as FREE NEGROES—the series of rebellions and conspiracies to revolt continued until the CIVIL WAR. A base of power or source of inspiration for these revolts was RELIGIOSITY; that is, a deep religious belief inspired many of the revolts as many enslaved persons came to believe that their fight for FREEDOM was divinely ordained. However, an absence of solidarity among the enslaved also contributed to their often speedy repression, as many of the revolts and conspiracies were betrayed by UNCLE TOMS and other blacks sympathetic to or afraid of the slave owners. The three largest and most daring revolts were led by

Gabriel Prosser in 1800, Denmark Vesey in 1822, and Nat Turner in 1831.

In 1800 Gabriel Prosser, a deeply religious 24-year-old Virginia slave, developed plans to seize the Virginia arsenal and take over the state and make it a homeland for Africans or, failing that, flee into the mountains and wage guerrilla war. Prosser secretly assembled a large supply of weapons and men (some historians estimate that he may have recruited anywhere from 2,000 to 5,000 men). On the day of the planned attack, however, Prosser was betrayed by two slaves who informed the plantation owner, who in turn informed the governor, who called out the state militia. Unaware that his plans were no longer secret, Prosser and more than 1,000 men assembled to march on Richmond, the state capital. But on that night, most of the roads and bridges to Richmond were washed away in a massive rainstorm, causing the attack to be postponed. Prosser and 34 of the leaders were captured, tried, convicted, and sentenced to death. At the trial Prosser (or one of his colleagues, the record is not clear) made a memorable speech:

> I have nothing more to offer than what General Washington would have had to offer, had he been taken by the British and put on trial by them. I have adventured my life in endeavoring to obtain the liberty of my countrymen, and I am a willing sacrifice to their cause; I beg, as a favour, that I may be immediately led to execution. I know that you have predetermined to shed my blood, why then all this mockery of trial.

In 1822 Denmark Vesey planned a rebellion in Charleston, South Carolina, similar to the one attempted by Prosser. Vesey, also deeply religious, had purchased his freedom as a young man, and by the time he was 50 began to recruit men (an estimated 500) for an attack on the Charleston arsenal, the seizure of the city, and the killing of all its white residents. However, like Prosser, Vesey's plans were also betrayed by a slave, and he and the other leaders were executed.

The most successful and most famous slave revolt was led by Nat Turner, also a deeply religious man. In 1831 Turner and 70 men in Jerusalem, Virginia, led an attack that killed 57 whites, including Turner's owner's wife and three children. Soldiers from throughout Virginia and South Carolina were called in to track down Turner and his men. It took two months to find Turner, and in the meantime whites in Virginia, Maryland, and South Carolina were in panic, with many families fleeing their homes in fear. Unable to quickly find Turner and his men, the soldiers turned on innocent blacks, slave and free, torturing and killing scores of men. Eventually, the 3,000 soldiers were called out to protect the slave owners and their families (only poor whites who owned no slaves were spared by

Turner and his men) and search for Turner. Like Prosser and Vesey, he too was tried, convicted, and hanged.

Although each of these slave revolts was quickly crushed, their significance in the African-American freedom struggle should not be dismissed or discounted, since they gave a new sense of urgency and MILITANCY to the ABOLITIONIST MOVEMENT and intensified the sectional debate between the NORTHERN STATES and the SOUTHERN STATES on the future of slavery and the Union.

See also JOHN BROWN, HAITI.

Further reading: Herbert Aptheker, *Negro Slave Revolts* (New York: International Publishers, 1963); Eugene Genovese, *From Rebellion to Revolution: Afro-American Slave Revolts in the Making of the New World* (New York: Vintage Books, 1984).

slavery

Slavery as practiced in the United States constituted a totalitarian POLITICAL SYSTEM, one in which virtually all bases of POWER were monopolized by whites in a brutal, barbarous relationship with enslaved Africans. Slavery was more than mere RACISM; more than mere inequalities in power and status between a SUPERORDINATE GROUP and a SUBORDINATE GROUP; more than mere DISCRIMINATION by a majority group against a MINORITY GROUP. Instead it was a system of OPPRESSION on a scale of barbarity and savagery unparalleled in human history, a system of oppression based on RACE that deprived enslaved black people—children, women, and the elderly included—of all HUMAN RIGHTS. It was a system consciously and systematically based on an institutionalized IDEOLOGY of WHITE SUPREMACY that justified the oppression of Africans because they were seen as cursed, inferior, debased subhumans. And it was a system created and maintained by extraordinary, nearly unrestrained VIOLENCE.

Holocaust is not an inappropriate word to describe the transatlantic slave trade and the system of plantation slavery in the SOUTHERN STATES in which millions died or were killed. In *From Slavery to Freedom,* John Hope Franklin writes that the voyage to the Americas, the so-called middle passage, was "a veritable nightmare. Overcrowding was most common. There was hardly standing room, lying or sitting room. Chained together by twos, hand and feet, the slaves had no room to move about and no freedom to exercise their bodies even in the slightest." For those lucky enough to survive the journey (or perhaps unlucky, given what the survivors were to endure; indeed, many Africans committed suicide rather than endure slavery), plantation slavery was a nightmare. After arrival in the Americas, the Africans were put through the "seasoning process," a system of dehumanization designed to transform an African

person into a slave. (The seasoning process was dramatically depicted in a scene from Alex Haley's 1977 ABC television series *Roots: The Saga of an American Family,* where Kunta Kinte, the free-spirited African boy played by Levar Burton, was repeatedly beaten until he accepted his master's slave name "Toby." In agreeing eventually to refer to himself as Toby, Kunta Kinte symbolically ceased to be an African and became an enslaved Negro. In other words, the seasoning process was complete.) Then, for most of the enslaved, day-to-day life was characterized by unrelenting, regimented work from "sunup to sundown," cultivating rice, hemp, cotton, and tobacco. Some enslaved people worked in cities or on small farms, and some worked as skilled craftsmen and mechanics. However, whether in town or on plantation, craftsman or field worker, they had no rights—sexual, social, economic, religious, cultural, or political—that their white slavers were bound to respect.

The sexual exploitation of women and children was an inherent aspect of the system. Black women and girls could be raped or coerced into sexual relations at the whim of any slaver. (THOMAS JEFFERSON in his mid-40s forced Sally Hemings, an enslaved teenager, into a sexual relationship in which he fathered at least one and perhaps several children.) Some slavers actually ran breeding farms where young girls were expected to have babies as soon as they came of age, often as young as 12. Reportedly one slave breeder's "farm" produced 300 persons starting with just two women; every time the daughter, granddaughter, or great granddaughter of the two women came of age, they had to bear children until they reached the end of fertility.

Slavery as practiced in the United States was unique, but slavery itself has existed and been generally accepted since prebiblical times. Before the transatlantic slave trade, a trans-Saharan slave trade had existed for several centuries during which Africans were transported by Muslims to Islamic countries as well as to India and China. In African societies, slavery was widespread, and in Europe the "Slavs" of eastern Europe were routinely enslaved for centuries. And SLAVERY IN WESTERN THOUGHT was embraced and celebrated by many of the leading philosophers. Thus, what distinguishes slavery in the United States is not that some persons were chattel or in servitude to others, but that the United States maintained a slave system in which the enslaved Africans were deprived of NATURAL RIGHTS and CIVIL RIGHTS and subject to totalitarian and frequently savage rule. The number of persons transported to the Americas from Africa is not known with precision, but most scholars put the number between the 1520s and 1860s at between 10 and 12 million, with millions more killed or dying of disease and deprivation on the journey or during confinement prior to the journey. The reason for the trade in the African peoples is, however, quite clear. In order to exploit the resources of the country and develop it economically, a ready supply of cheap, exploitable labor was necessary. Eventually, but only eventually, the English in North America came to believe that the cheapest and most reliable source for this labor supply was to import and enslave Africans.

Initially, the English sought to enslave the indigenous peoples, but this proved unworkable because they were not easily conquered and captured. It was also difficult to get them to adapt to the regimented routine of the plantation, and they frequently died as a result of diseases carried by the Europeans. The Americans next turned to their fellow Europeans first as possible slaves and then as indentured servants. The poor, the drunk, and homeless of England were imported, sometimes by literally rounding them up and transporting them against their will. Debtors, paupers, and prisoners were imported. Volunteer immigrants were given free passage in exchange for their labor as indentured servants. Finally, the English began to raid the prisons in search of workers. (The state of Georgia was to a large extent a prison colony, populated by accused criminals and convicts.) None of this worked, so as a last resort the English North Americans turned to Africa as the cheapest, most reliable source of labor.

The first Africans brought to the United States came not as slaves but, like their white counterparts, as indentured servants bound to labor for a fixed period and then set free. The status of white and black indentured labor began to change in the 1640s, and gradually black labor evolved to the status of slavery. This change can be seen in the case of John Punch, a black indentured servant in Virginia. In 1640 Punch, along with two white indentured servants, ran away. When they were captured, all three were punished with 30 lashes, and the two whites were given two additional years of labor while Punch was sentenced to life servitude. In 1660 Virginia, whose laws on slavery served as a model for the other Southern colonies, enacted a law saying that Negro indentured servants who ran away could be punished for life because they were "incapable of making satisfaction by addition of time." Later the law was modified so that the children of African laborers also could be punished with life servitude for the crimes of their fathers. Eventually, the laws of Virginia and each of the Southern states were rewritten to permit the enslavement of Africans and only Africans. Thus was set in motion the centuries-long holocaust of American slavery.

African societies and their leaders were willing participants in the slave trade, although it is likely that they viewed it in the comparatively benign sense that was practiced there rather than as the holocaust that it had become in the United States. Ultimately the basis of the slave trade, however, was European power, technological and military. Enslaved African labor was used to build the plantation economies of the SOUTHERN STATES producing agricultural products—hemp, tobacco, rice, and especially cotton—for sale on world markets. Significant numbers of the enslaved also worked on small farms and in the towns and cities. (The majority of slavers owned fewer than 10 persons; less

A slave auction *(Library of Congress)*

than 5 percent owned more than 100.) Slavery was not widespread in the NORTHERN STATES, but it was legal and morally acceptable in many states of the North. However, while the economy of the states of the North was not directly dependent on slave labor, it was indirectly dependent on the labor of the enslaved because of the manufacture and marketing of the products of their labor and the profits accrued from the transportation of slaves. Thus, to a considerable extent, the foundations of American CAPITALISM are built on the backs of the uncompensated labor of African Americans.

As a political system, slavery in the Southern states was a police state, where any form of overt resistance was met with swift and often brutal forms of punishment. Rebellious enslaved persons were sometimes burned alive, broken on the wheel, had their tongues or genitalia cut off, and beaten with bullwhips, among other grotesque tortures. But the Africans did resist and fight for FREEDOM. Sometimes the resistance took the form of SLAVE REVOLTS, but more often resistance took discrete forms on a day-to-day basis, including such actions as destruction of property, arson, poisoning livestock (and occasionally slavers and overseers), "laziness," and feigning madness or illness. Perhaps the most prevalent form of resistance was the simple act of running away. Running away was a decisive and potent form of resistance because it deprived the slavers of their most valuable possession—their human chattel. The practice of running away became so widespread and costly to the system that CONGRESS enacted the Fugitive Slave Act; the STATE AND LOCAL GOVERNMENTs established slave patrols; and slavers employed bounty hunters. And a new psychological disorder, "drapetomania," was discovered and catalogued. Drapetomania, according to Dr. Samuel Cartwright, a Louisiana surgeon and psychologist, was a "mental disorder" that caused slaves to run away. Apparently serious, Cartwright in 1851 published a report in a New Orleans medical journal that described drapetomania as a real malady, noting that "the cause, in most cases, that induces Negroes to run away from service, is as much a disease of the mind as any other species of mental alienation, and much more curable. With the advantage of proper medical care, strictly followed, this troublesome practice that many Negroes have of running away can be almost entirely prevented." (No evidence of a "cure" exists in the medical literature of the time.)

Slavery was formally abolished in 1865 as a result of the Civil War, with the ratification of the second proposed THIRTEENTH AMENDMENT. It is important to recognize that slavery was not abolished as a result of a recognition by the POWER ELITE or white PUBLIC OPINION that it was morally wrong and unjust. Rather, it was abolished as a pragmatic consequence of a war to preserve the union of the states rather than to conquer the evil of slavery. ABRA-HAM LINCOLN issued the EMANCIPATION PROCLAMATION, which set in motion slavery's abolition as a military necessity, to win the war and preserve the Union rather than as a moral necessity to end slavery and secure the freedom of the enslaved Africans. Indeed, Lincoln had earlier proposed—as a means to preserve the Union—what would have been, if ratified, the first Thirteenth Amendment, which would have forever allowed the Southern states to maintain slavery without federal interference. And when the existing Thirteenth Amendment was first presented to the House of Representatives in April 1864, it was defeated 95 to 66 in a House with hardly any representatives from the Southern states. This grudging, reluctant, ambivalent abolition of slavery is worth underscoring for historical reasons as well as contemporaneous ones at the start of the 21st century. Historically, it helps to explain why a new CONSTITUTION was never adopted, expunging the references to slavery and explicitly including Africans as a people in a new social contract (based explicitly on equality). In contemporary terms, it helps to explain the reluctance of the Western nations, the United States government, and the American people to unequivocally condemn the slave trade and slavery, apologize, and pay REPARATIONS.

In 2001 at the UNITED NATIONS "Conference against Racism, Discrimination, Xenophobia and Related Intolerance," African and African-American leaders proposed a resolution condemning the transatlantic slave trade as a "crime against humanity," equivalent to the Holocaust. The resolution also called for an apology and reparations. The union of European nations, the United States, and Canada opposed the resolution. These nations not only opposed an apology and reparations but only favored the conference adopting language saying that "slavery and the slave trade *are* a crime against humanity (the operative word is "are" rather than "were"). With respect to the past, the delegates from the nations that participated in slavery and the slave trade would not acknowledge that it was morally wrong at the time but only that it *should* have always been wrong. In the late 1990s Congressman Tony Hall, a white Democrat from Ohio, proposed that Congress formally apologize for slavery. The leadership of the House refused to allow Hall's resolution to come to a vote, perhaps because public opinion polls showed that two-thirds of white Americans opposed an apology. And African-American congressman John Conyers's bill to establish a commission to investigate reparations has been stalled in committee since its introduction in 1995, presumably because reparations are also opposed by more than two-thirds of white Americans.

See also *DREDD SCOTT V. SANFORD*, FUGITIVE SLAVE CLAUSE, and SOCIAL CONTRACT THEORY.

Further reading: John Hope Franklin and Loren Schweninger, *Runaway Slaves: Rebels on the Plantation*

(New York: Oxford University Press, 1999); Wilma King, *Stolen Childhood: Slave Youth in Nineteenth Century America* (Bloomington: Indiana University Press, 1998); James Melton, ed., *Bullwhip Days: The Slaves Remember* (New York: Widenfield and Nicolson, 1988); Hugh Thomas, *Slave Trade: The Story of the Atlantic Slave Trade, 1440–1870* (New York: Simon & Schuster, 1997).

slavery in Western thought

The idea of SLAVERY is widely accepted in Western thought, embraced by Aristotle, Plato, and two of the three leading philosophers of the SOCIAL CONTRACT THEORY (Hobbes, Rousseau, and Locke). Many of the men who framed the DECLARATION OF INDEPENDENCE and the CONSTITUTION were familiar with these philosophers and their writings on slavery and drew on their thought in developing the IDEOLOGY of WHITE SUPREMACY that was used to justify the enslavement of Africans.

From the time of the ancient Greeks, slave trading and slavery had been integral components of the societies of the Western world. Of the 200,000 to 300,000 persons in Plato's Athens, for example, it is estimated that 60,000 to 80,000 were slaves (approximately 30 to 40 percent of the population). For Plato, slavery in his republic was so commonplace, so unremarkable that it did not require extensive discussion, elaboration, or justification. Rather, it was in the natural order of things, as night follows day, that some persons would be slaves because in their nature, Plato said, some men lacked "logos" (reasoning abilities) and therefore needed benevolent masters to guide them; otherwise they would become "vicious" and "disorderly." Plato's most famous pupil, Aristotle, used similar arguments to justify slavery, writing that slaves should be "naturally inferior" to the slave master; thus Greeks should not be slaves, given that they were not an inferior people. Aristotle, like many others throughout history, justified slavery on the basis of war. That is, persons conquered and captured in a just war could be enslaved, but the war is just in his view only when it is waged against an inferior people who are intended by nature to be slaves but refused to submit. In an argument that anticipates justifications for slavery in the United States, Aristotle in his *Politics* wrote, "Therefore, whenever there is the same wide discrepancy between human beings as there is between soul and body or between man and beast, then those whose condition is such that their function is the use of their bodies and nothing better can be expected of them, those, I say are slaves by nature." Except for the Bible, no other philosophical source was more frequently cited than Aristotle by American slaveholders in defense of slavery.

American statesmen in their defenses of slavery also referred to the social-contract theorists, especially John Locke, the English philosopher who is often referred to as the philosophical father of the Constitution. The views of the French social-contract theorist Jean-Jacques Rousseau, however, were rejected by most of the men who drafted the Constitution because he unequivocally condemned slavery as a violation of NATURAL RIGHTS. In *The Social Contract,* Rousseau was emphatic in his belief that "no man, as we have seen, has any natural authority over his fellow man, and might, as we have seen also, makes no right." Therefore, "Any way you look at it, then, the right to enslave is nonexistent; it is not merely illegitimate, but absurd and meaningless as well." John Locke was ambiguous on the question. In his *Second Treatise of Government* he wrote "that in the state of nature all men existed in a 'state of perfect freedom' and a 'state also of perfect equality' since there being nothing more evident than that creatures of the same species and rank, promiscuously born to all the same advantages of nature, and the use of the same facilities, should also be equal one amongst another, without subordination or subjection, unless the Lord and maker of them all should, by any manifest declaration of his will, set one above another and confer on him, by evident and clear appointment, an undoubted right to dominion. . . ." Locke here, like Rousseau, seems to emphatically condemn slavery unless it is clearly or "manifestly" ordained by God. However, he made an exception in terms of war. Rousseau in the passage quoted above, in saying that might does not make right, was rejecting the idea then widespread throughout the world that prisoners of war could be justifiably enslaved. Locke, however, like Aristotle, embraced this notion, arguing that slavery could be justified on the basis of the "just war" argument. That is, for Locke, men who engaged in aggressive war surrendered their natural right to freedom and equality. Locke was not only the most influential of the philosophers in terms of the founders; he also helped to write the charter of the Carolina colonies in which black slavery was sanctioned. And his just war argument was sometimes used to justify African slavery, although African slavery clearly was not a result of war, aggressive or otherwise, between English North Americans and the peoples of Africa.

Slavery in Western thought coexists with the ideas of FREEDOM and EQUALITY. While this is paradoxical, in the last several decades of the 20th century an important body of historical research has developed suggesting a symbiotic relationship between slavery and freedom in Western culture. This scholarship suggests that the idea of freedom is inextricably linked to the idea and practice of slavery. Orlando Patterson, for example, in *Freedom in the Making of Western Culture*, writes that with respect to Europe that "it can now be said with some confidence that the idea and value of freedom was the direct product of the institution of slavery. Where there has been no slavery there has never been a trace of freedom even as a minor value." And in the United States, Patterson writes, "without the institution of slavery America in all likelihood would not . . . have come to enshrine freedom at the very top of the pantheon of values." In other words, this scholarship suggests that the idea of freedom has its origins in the struggles of slaves to become free.

Further reading: David Brion Davis, *The Problem of Slavery in Western Culture* (Ithaca, N.Y.: Cornell University Press, 1966); Orlando Patterson, *Freedom in the Making of Western Culture* (New York: Basic Books, 1991).

SNCC See STUDENT NONVIOLENT COORDINATING COMMITTEE.

social-contract theory

The CONSTITUTION can be viewed as a contract between "we the people" of the United States and the government, in which citizens decide to create a government while retaining for themselves fundamental NATURAL RIGHTS. This contract theory of government derives from the writings of Thomas Hobbes, John Locke, and Jean-Jacques Rousseau.

Each assumed the "nature" of man could be discerned; that man's nature had an impact on the "state of nature"; and that conditions in this state of nature explain both the origins and the purposes of government. For Hobbes, man's nature was guided by an instinctual will to power and domination; therefore life in the state of nature was, in his famous phrase, "a war of every man against every man" and life was "solitary, poor, nasty, brutish and short." Consequently, men desire an all-powerful government—a Leviathan—to protect them from their natural inclinations toward domination of each other. Thus, they enter into a contract or "covenant" in which they give up all of their FREEDOM in exchange for security. For Rousseau, man's nature is good, but it is corrupted by the introduction of private property, which generates inequality. Thus, for Rousseau too, an all-powerful government is necessary to create an egalitarian society. Between the authoritarian state of Hobbes and the radical egalitarian vision of Rousseau stands John Locke.

It is John Locke's moderate philosophical stance, with its emphasis on limited government and the protection of private property as the ultimate value or purpose of government, that most influenced the founders of the American government. Indeed, Locke is frequently referred to as "the philosopher of the American Revolution" with respect both to his influence on the DECLARATION OF INDEPENDENCE and the Constitution. For Locke, man's nature was

neither good nor evil; rather, men have the capacity for both. However, while there were some "suspicious, degenerate and corrupt men," life in the state of nature was by and large one of "peace, good will, mutual assistance and preservation." Why then did men in such a state decide to give up their freedom? Because, Locke wrote, "the enjoyment of the property he has in this state is very unsafe, very insecure. This makes him willing to quit this condition, which, however free is full of fears and continued danger. . . ." Thus, for Locke, "The great and chief end, therefore, of men uniting into commonwealths, and putting themselves under government is the preservation of their property, which in the state of nature there are many things wanting." Men, therefore, enter into a contract, a mutual contract, between the governed and the government, granting to the authorities those powers—but only those powers—necessary for the protection of "life, liberty and property." That is, the government is to be one of limited powers, with the people retaining the bulk of their natural rights or freedoms; as Locke put it, "he is to part with as much of his natural liberty, in providing for himself, as the good, prosperity and the safety of society shall require."

What is the place of African Americans in the Lockean social contract? In adopting Locke, the framers of the Constitution embraced the philosophical notions of limited government and natural rights but also the philosophical notions of SLAVERY and inequality. That is, Locke's philosophy provides a rationale for the denial of natural rights to some persons as well as their exclusion from the contracting process that creates government. This is because, of the three major contract theorists, Locke is the only one to accept slavery in both theory and practice. In Hobbes's philosophy, slavery is rejected not on moral grounds but rather because in his mythical state of nature all humans are roughly equal in POWER and therefore slavery is impossible. Presumably, for Hobbes, if there were systematic disparities in power between individuals or groups, slavery would be legitimate. Rousseau rejects this Hobbesian idea, arguing that "might does not make right" and that slavery is not only illegitimate but "absurd" and "meaningless" because "no man has any natural authority over his fellow man." Locke, while generally hostile to slavery, saw it as legitimate or justifiable on three grounds. First, unlike Rousseau, Locke argued that might did make right in that slavery could be justified on the basis of a "just war." That is, men who engaged in an aggressive war and lost surrendered their natural right to freedom and EQUALITY. Second, men could be enslaved if it was discerned that it was the will of God, with Locke writing that all men should be free of "subordination or subjection, unless the Lord and maker of them all should, by any manifest declaration of his will, set one above another and confer on him, by evident and clear appointment, an undoubted right to dominion. . . ." Third,

Locke's philosophy suggests that "savages"—men without the capacity to reason—might legitimately be enslaved. Each of these ideas in Locke's philosophy became a basis for justifying the enslavement of Africans.

Locke, the philosopher of freedom, was, like THOMAS JEFFERSON, a slave proprietor as one of the principal authors of the *Charter of the Carolina Colonies* in which slavery was sanctioned. (The *Charter* said, "Every freeman of Carolina shall have absolute power over his Negro slaves, of what opinion or religion soever.") The enslavement of Africans was justifiable, Locke suggests, because the enslaved Africans had been captured by other Africans in just wars and sold to European merchants. This "just war" argument, although dubious, was articulated by many proponents of slavery during the colonial era. But Locke's suggestion about slavery as the will of God and the legitimacy of enslaving savages were much more influential, eventually becoming two of the three central ideas in the IDEOLOGY of WHITE SUPREMACY used to justify RACISM and slavery. On the basis of these Lockean ideas, Africans were excluded from the convention at Philadelphia that wrote the American social contract in 1787. Instead, the "racial contract" among the white men at the Philadelphia convention defined African people as property. And since, for Locke, a principal purpose of government was the protection of property, his philosophy became a barrier to the African-American struggle for freedom and equality. This is because unlike in Rousseau's philosophy, where a principal purpose of government is to eliminate inequalities resulting from private property, for Locke government has as its principal purpose the protection of property, including property in persons.

See also LIBERALISM and SLAVERY IN WESTERN THOUGHT.

Further reading: James Farr, "So Vile and Miserable: The Problem of Slavery in Locke's Political Thought," *Political Theory* 14 (1986): 263–89; Charles Mills, *The Racial Contract* (Ithaca, N.Y.: Cornell University Press, 1997).

socialism

Socialism is an IDEOLOGY that advocates government ownership or regulation of the means of production and the distribution of goods and services in order to achieve EQUALITY. The basic aim of socialism is to replace or modify the private ownership of the economy (basic industry, finance, communications, and utilities)—an inherent aspect of CAPITALISM—with a system in which the government owns or directs the operations of the economy. The objective of government ownership or regulation is to create an egalitarian WELFARE STATE. Socialism, unlike COMMUNISM, may allow some private ownership and production for profit in the economy, but the government plays an extensive role in planning and regulating the overall economy in the interest of a more equitable distribution of income and other resources (education, housing, health care). Although these objectives are common to all socialists, the tradition of socialism is not monolithic. Socialists around the world have been especially divided on the means to achieve these objectives, whether through VIOLENCE or DEMOCRACY.

Socialism has been a powerful force in the societies and politics of Europe and the THIRD WORLD, but in the United States the tradition has had much less success, although some socialistlike programs were adopted by FRANKLIN D. ROOSEVELT during the NEW DEAL and by LYNDON B. JOHNSON with his GREAT SOCIETY. However, compared with the rest of the world, neither socialism nor the SOCIALIST PARTY has been influential in American politics. Instead, there is a substantial body of scholarship devoted to answering the question of why socialism failed in America. Among the reasons offered are the absence of a feudal past; the almost universal embrace of the principles of classical LIBERALISM; INDIVIDUALISM; the enormous wealth and prosperity of the country; CONSTITUTIONALISM; the SEPARATION OF POWERS; the TWO-PARTY SYSTEM; and the POLITICAL REPRESSION of socialist ideas and movements. Scholars have also pointed to RACE, ETHNICITY, and RACISM as factors accounting for the failure of socialism. Karl Marx and Friedrich Engels pointed to these factors in their writings, contending that racial and ethnic diversity undermined the development of working-class consciousness and solidarity in the United States by allowing the POWER ELITE to pit workers of different racial and ethnic groups against each other.

The development of the economy of the SOUTHERN STATES on the basis of SLAVERY and then SEGREGATION and the prevalence of the IDEOLOGY of WHITE SUPREMACY made the task of building a multiracial COALITION to advance the cause of socialism particularly difficult. Despite these difficulties, however, important elements of the African-American LEADERSHIP have always been committed to socialism. This commitment to socialism is in part a product of the importance of equality in AFRICAN-AMERICAN THOUGHT and because of the disproportionately high rates of POVERTY that have always characterized the BLACK COMMUNITY. Socialism as an ideology committed to equality therefore would naturally attract the allegiance of the African-American leadership. Although African-American PUBLIC OPINION is generally supportive of capitalism, one finds in it also much more support for socialism than is found in white public opinion.

See also POPULISM.

Further reading: Seymour Martin Lipset and Gary Marks, *It Didn't Happen Here: Why Socialism Failed in the United States* (New York: W. W. Norton, 2000).

Socialist Party

Third parties in the United States committed to SOCIALISM have been a feature of American politics since the beginning of the 20th century. As an IDEOLOGY committed to EQUALITY in access to basic material needs (housing, education, health care, etc.), socialism and socialist parties have always had some attraction to leaders of the BLACK COMMUNITY.

Early in his long career, W. E. B. DU BOIS, a preeminent leader of the community, affiliated himself with the Socialist Party, and many of the early founders of the NAACP were socialists, although the NAACP as an organization never embraced socialism or attempted to form a COALITION with socialist parties. This is partly because socialist parties, while committed to economic equality, were generally hostile to racial equality and in favor of SEGREGATION. For example, the Socialist Party organized in 1901 was committed to RACISM and WHITE SUPREMACY, declaring in its newspaper *Appeal to Reason* that "socialists believe in justice to the Negro; not social equality. Socialism will separate the races." And one of the party's founders, the writer Jack London, said, "I am first a white man and only then a socialist." The Socialist Party continued its embrace of racism and white supremacy until it faced competition for the allegiance of blacks from the COMMUNIST PARTY, which was committed to racial as well as economic equality. As a result, it gradually changed its position and began to recruit blacks like A. PHILIP RANDOLPH, and under the leadership of Norman Thomas in the 1930s the party began to forcefully challenge segregation and racial DISCRIMINATION. For a variety of reasons (including the structure of the TWO-PARTY SYSTEM), Socialist Party candidates have had relatively little success in becoming ELECTED OFFICIALS in the United States. Among those reasons, however, is that socialist movements and parties, like POPULISM, were distorted by racism and white supremacy, which undermined their capacity to develop working-class solidarity and a multiethnic coalition, both of which are necessary to build a SOCIAL MOVEMENT that could effectively advance the cause of socialism.

social movements

Social movements are self-conscious, organized challenges by persons seeking to change one or more of the prevailing or core values of a POLITICAL SYSTEM. Social movements always involve challenging the POWER ELITE of the system because the elite seek to maintain core or prevailing system values. Generally, although not always, social movements are organized by individuals from structurally SUBORDINATE GROUPS. Frequently, but again not always, such movements employ extrasystemic methods such as PROTEST, CIVIL DISOBEDIENCE, or VIOLENCE, although systemic methods such as voting, LOBBYING, and LITIGA-

TION may also be used. The distinguishing attribute of a social movement, however, is not its methods but its aims, which are to challenge elites who uphold core system values that disadvantage groups in a society.

For much of American history RACISM and WHITE SUPREMACY, expressed first in SLAVERY and then SEGREGATION and DISCRIMINATION, have been basic values of the system. Therefore, with the exception of BOOKER T. WASHINGTON's strategy of ACCOMMODATIONISM, African-American LEADERSHIP has been involved in social movements, beginning with the ABOLITIONIST MOVEMENT and including the CIVIL RIGHTS MOVEMENT and the BLACK POWER MOVEMENT. Some blacks have also organized or participated in movements challenging CAPITALISM, a core system value, and a few black leaders have challenged the essential existence of the system by calling for the creation of an independent black nation within the geographic boundaries of the United States. In the POST–CIVIL RIGHTS ERA, social movements have withered away in AFRICAN-AMERICAN POLITICS as a result of the INCORPORATION and CO-OPTATION of blacks into the political system. As a result, INTEREST GROUPS rather than social movements have become dominant.

See also NATION OF ISLAM and REPUBLIC OF NEW AFRICA.

Souls of Black Folk, The

The Souls of Black Folk: Essays and Sketches, W. E. B. DU BOIS's elegant little book of essays published in 1903, is one of the most important texts in AFRICAN-AMERICAN STUDIES and a seminal document in AFRICAN-AMERICAN THOUGHT. Du Bois, the preeminent African-American intellectual and one of the two or three leading American intellectuals of the 20th century, wrote 15 books (his doctoral dissertation on the suppression of the African slave trade was the first volume published in Harvard's Historical Studies series), including pioneering studies in African cultures; creative sociological research on the life of blacks in the emerging GHETTO; innovative studies of the BLACK CHURCH; and his monumental, revisionist history *Black Reconstruction: An Essay Toward a History of the Part Black Folk Played in the Attempt to Reconstruct Democracy in America, 1860–1880*.

The 14 "sketches and essays" that Du Bois published in 1903—in which he said he sought to "sketch, in vague uncertain outline, the spiritual world in which ten thousand thousand Americans live and strive"—is his master work. The publication of the book was itself an event of historical importance, signaling the emergence of Du Bois as the leading African American in the emerging CIVIL RIGHTS MOVEMENT. The book's most famous essay, "Of Mr. Booker

T. Washington and Others," sparked a major debate over IDEOLOGY in the BLACK COMMUNITY. In it, Du Bois challenged Washington's strategy of ACCOMMODATIONISM, which then held sway in the black community under the leadership of BOOKER T. WASHINGTON. This challenge, which eventually resulted in the displacement of Washington's accommodationism with Du Bois's strategy of PROTEST, forced the black community to choose sides: Are you with "Mr. Washington," or are you with "Dr. Du Bois"? The resulting debate was passionate and often bitter, involving recurring attacks and counterattacks between the Washington and Du Bois factions. Looking back on the impact of the book during this period, JAMES WELDON JOHNSON concluded that the book had "a greater effect upon and within the Negro race in America than any other single book published in this country since *Uncle Tom's Cabin.*" The book is also famous for Du Bois's famous line, "The problem of the twentieth century is the problem of the color line," which he used in essay III, "Of the Dawn of Freedom," a history of the FREEDMEN'S BUREAU. *The Souls* is also remembered for essay IV, "Of the Training of Black Men," in which Booker Washington's philosophy of agricultural and mechanical education is challenged and the rudiments of Du Bois's notion of the TALENTED TENTH is advanced for the first time. Finally, the first essay is significant for its perceptive exploration of the psychological meanings of BLACKNESS. In this essay he develops his famous concept of the divided black psyche, what he calls a feeling of "twoness—an American, a Negro, two souls, two thoughts, two unreconciled strivings, two warring ideals in one dark body . . . [who] wishes to make it possible to be both a Negro and an American, without being cursed and spit upon by his fellows, without having the doors of opportunity closed in his face."

In addition to these more famous essays, *The Souls* is important for its spiritual and lyrical essays celebrating black CULTURE, especially the culture's RELIGIOSITY and MUSIC. For example, each of the 14 essays begins with lines from a Negro spiritual, what Du Bois describes as "a bar of a Sorrow Song—some echo of the haunting melody of the only American music which welled up from black souls in the dark past." And using the metaphor of "the veil," Du Bois writes with beauty and emotion of the struggles of the blacks in the SOUTHERN STATES, about the death of his first-born son, and about the life of his mentor and hero ALEXANDER CRUMMELL. Nine of the 14 essays in *The Souls* are revised versions of articles originally published elsewhere. But when brought together with the five original essays, they fit together as an elegant, erudite celebration of the "souls" of a people who survived the horrors of SLAVERY without surrendering their humanity. In doing so, *The Souls* became an important weapon in the struggle against WHITE SUPREMACY.

Southern Christian Leadership Conference (SCLC)

The Southern Christian Leadership Conference (SCLC) is the ORGANIZATION formed in 1957 by MARTIN LUTHER KING JR. after the MONTGOMERY BUS BOYCOTT. SCLC's purpose was to use the momentum that came out of the boycott's success and King's increasing national stature to build an organization to challenge SEGREGATION and other forms of RACISM throughout the SOUTHERN STATES. The leaders of the NAACP and the URBAN LEAGUE, the traditional CIVIL RIGHTS organizations, were initially wary about the formation of a new civil rights organization but were assuaged when King and SCLC leaders and strategists (including ELLA BAKER and BAYARD RUSTIN) assured them that SCLC would not be a membership organization and would confine its activities to the Southern states. Instead of individual members, SCLC was organized essentially as a COALITION of activist black preachers. Thus, it drew its strength from the BLACK CHURCH, the most influential institution in the BLACK COMMUNITY. Initially SCLC (with Dr. King as its president) concentrated on the development of voter education and registration, but soon it developed a strategy of nonviolent PROTEST and CIVIL DISOBEDIENCE. This turn toward MILITANCY upset the leadership of the NAACP, but it became the most dynamic and successful strategy of the CIVIL RIGHTS MOVEMENT, to some extent displacing the NAACP's more moderate strategies of LOBBYING and LITIGATION. SCLC's 1963 BIRMINGHAM DEMONSTRATIONS led directly to President JOHN F. KENNEDY's decision to propose what would become the CIVIL RIGHTS ACT OF 1964. Similarly, SCLC's SELMA DEMONSTRATIONS led directly to President LYNDON B. JOHNSON's decision to propose the VOTING RIGHTS ACT OF 1965. Thus, SCLC was responsible for passage of the two cornerstone civil rights laws of the 1960s, laws that effectively ended both segregation and legalized racism and broke the back of WHITE SUPREMACY.

After its civil rights successes, SCLC turned its attention to problems of POVERTY and INSTITUTIONAL RACISM in the GHETTOS of the NORTHERN STATES. In 1967 it established Operation Breadbasket, which, under the leadership of JESSE JACKSON, organized demonstrations and consumer boycotts to push for employment opportunities for black workers and contracts for black businesses. However, King eventually came to believe that the problem of poverty was systemic, requiring fundamental reforms in CAPITALISM. Therefore, a divided SCLC board and staff reluctantly embraced King's idea of a POOR PEOPLE'S CAMPAIGN designed to guarantee FULL EMPLOYMENT or an income to all Americans. King was murdered in the midst of planning for the campaign, and under the leadership of Ralph Abernathy—his designated successor as president—SCLC was unable to achieve any of the campaign's basic reform objectives. (A decade after the campaign, under the lead-

Civil rights leaders (left to right): Martin Luther King Jr., leader of the Southern Christian Leadership Conference; Attorney General Robert Kennedy; Roy Wilkins, executive secretary of the NAACP; and Vice President Lyndon B. Johnson, after a special White House conference on civil rights, 1963 *(Library of Congress)*

ership of Congressman AUGUSTUS HAWKINS and the CONGRESSIONAL BLACK CAUCUS, the CONGRESS did enact full-employment legislation—the HUMPHREY-HAWKINS ACT—but it was more symbolism than effective PUBLIC POLICY.)

In 1965 KENNETH CLARK wrote that "SCLC is Martin Luther King," suggesting that the organization was little more than a vehicle for the expression of King's charismatic leadership and that it would inevitably decline or disappear with his departure. Whether inevitable or not, SCLC did decline after the death of its charismatic leader. The SCLC also lost some stature as a result of the decline of protest in AFRICAN-AMERICAN POLITICS and the CO-OPTATION or INCORPORATION of blacks into the POLITICAL SYSTEM. SCLC, however, did not disappear. Instead, in the POST–CIVIL RIGHTS ERA, SCLC joined the NAACP, the Urban League, and Operation PUSH as one of the four major civil rights organizations. But instead of using protest tactics, it relied mainly on lobbying and the occasional sym-

bolic rally or march. In 1999 it elected King's son, Martin Luther King III, to lead it into the 21st century.

See also NATIONAL BAPTIST CONVENTION and OPERATION PUSH.

Further reading: David Garrow, *Bearing the Cross: Martin Luther King, Jr. and the Southern Christian Leadership Conference* (New York: William Morrow, 1986); F. Carl Walton, "The Southern Christian Leadership Conference: Beyond Civil Rights," in *Black Political Organizations in the Post Civil Rights Era,* ed. Ollie Johnson and Karin Stanford (New Brunswick, N.J.: Rutgers University Press, 2002).

Southern states

The term *Southern states* refers to the region of the United States in the southern part of the country where 11 states seceded from the Union, precipitating the CIVIL WAR. The area, stretching from Virginia in the southeast to Texas in the southwest, was until the GREAT MIGRATION the place of residence of the overwhelming majority of the black POPULATION. All of the Southern states sanctioned SLAVERY prior to the Civil War; however, the states in the region (such as Maryland) that did not secede from the Union are generally grouped with the NORTHERN STATES, although these states are sometimes referred to as the "border states."

After the war the Southern states were subjected to RECONSTRUCTION. After Reconstruction's collapse, a rigid system of JIM CROW–style SEGREGATION was imposed throughout the region. While segregation was practiced in many Northern states, it was more rigid in the South because the STATE AND LOCAL GOVERNMENTS sanctioned it by law. Segregation in the South was explicitly based on the IDEOLOGY of WHITE SUPREMACY, and VIOLENCE was used more frequently to maintain it. Segregation in the Southern states came to an end in the 1960s as a result of the CIVIL RIGHTS MOVEMENT. By the end of the 20th century the Southern states resembled the states of the North in terms of the relationship between blacks and whites. That is, legalized DISCRIMINATION and INDIVIDUAL RACISM had for the most part come to an end, and the practice of INSTITUTIONAL RACISM was more or less the same in both regions. As a result, black migration from the region came to an end in the 1970s, leaving slightly more than half of the black population resident in the region.

See also BIRMINGHAM DEMONSTRATIONS, CIVIL RIGHTS ACT OF 1964, SELMA DEMONSTRATIONS, and VOTING RIGHTS ACT OF 1965.

Southern strategy

"Southern strategy" refers primarily to efforts by the REPUBLICAN PARTY to win the support of whites in the SOUTHERN STATES by distancing itself from CIVIL RIGHTS and other issues of concern to blacks. The strategy was first employed by the Republican Party in the election of RUTHERFORD B. HAYES to the PRESIDENCY in the COMPROMISE OF 1877. The strategy was employed again by the party during the 1964 election, when BARRY GOLDWATER ran for president against LYNDON B. JOHNSON. Since 1964, the strategy has been employed by all subsequent Republican presidential candidates, including RICHARD NIXON and RONALD REAGAN.

In the 1870s the Southern strategy was employed as a result of the first WHITE BACKLASH, during which whites in the Southern as well as the NORTHERN STATES grew tired of the conflicts associated with RECONSTRUCTION. As a result, leaders of the Republican Party abandoned their efforts to guarantee the FREEDOM and EQUALITY of African Americans. Although the Republican Party had abandoned the cause of civil rights, until 1964 it continued to pay lip

service to the issue. Meanwhile, the DEMOCRATIC PARTY was completely hostile to civil rights, and the Southern states, dominated by the forces of RACISM and WHITE SUPREMACY, constituted its core base of support in the ELECTORAL COLLEGE. The BLACK COMMUNITY remained loyal to the Republicans until FRANKLIN D. ROOSEVELT and the NEW DEAL during the 1930s. A majority of black voters joined the New Deal COALITION in the 1930s because of its WELFARE STATE programs rather than its stance on civil rights. This, however, put them in an uneasy alliance with Southern white supremacists and racists. This uneasy alliance lasted until the 1964 election, when Goldwater—the Republican nominee—opposed the CIVIL RIGHTS ACT OF 1964, while President Johnson—the Democratic nominee—was responsible for the act's passage. The result was that Johnson received more than 90 percent of the black vote, Goldwater less than 10 percent. But Goldwater carried five Deep South states. From this point on, the Republican Party embraced the Southern strategy.

In 1968 Kevin Phillips, a strategist in Richard Nixon's campaign, wrote *The Emerging Republican Majority,* in which he argued that the Republican Party could win a majority in the electoral college and in CONGRESS by ceding the black vote to the Democrats and appealing to the anti-civil-rights vote in the Southern states. Although Nixon adopted this strategy in 1968, it was not fully successful because GEORGE WALLACE, the openly racist and white supremacist governor of Alabama, ran as a THIRD-PARTY candidate for president and carried several Southern states. By 1972, however, with Wallace out of the picture, the strategy was successful, and Nixon carried all of the Southern states. Since 1972 the Southern states have been the core base of Republican support in the electoral college, and in 1994 the South was critical in the Republican Party's winning control of both houses of Congress.

Since 1972 the Republicans have generally received about two-thirds of the Southern white vote, while the black vote in the region is more than 90 percent Democratic. Although the black vote is cohesive in the region, it is too small to constitute the BALANCE OF POWER in most elections. While the Southern strategy is identified with the Republican Party, the Democratic Party has also employed its own variation of the strategy. Franklin Roosevelt, for example, refused to embrace the cause of civil rights because he feared losing the support of the South, and JOHN F. KENNEDY was reluctant to support civil rights legislation for the same reason. And in the POST–CIVIL RIGHTS ERA the two successful Democratic presidential candidates—JIMMY CARTER and BILL CLINTON, Southerners themselves—were successful in part because they distanced themselves from issues of concern to blacks in order to appeal to Southern whites. In doing so they won several Southern states and therefore the presidency.

Sowell, Thomas (1930–   ) *author, scholar*

Thomas Sowell, recognized as a brilliant economist, is the leading black conservative PUBLIC INTELLECTUAL of the POST–CIVIL RIGHTS ERA. Indeed, Sowell in his many books, articles, op-ed essays, lectures, and television appearances during the 1980s—more so than any other person—made the IDEOLOGY of CONSERVATISM a viable intellectual alternative to the dominant traditions of LIBERALISM and RADICALISM in AFRICAN-AMERICAN POLITICS.

Sowell was born in Gastonia, North Carolina, but grew up in HARLEM. Although he ranked near the top of his class, he dropped out of high school in order to work. After graduating from high school, Sowell briefly attended HOWARD UNIVERSITY, one of the HISTORICALLY BLACK COLLEGES AND UNIVERSITIES, but later transferred to Harvard, where he received the B.A. Subsequently, he earned an M.A. from Columbia and the Ph.D. from the University of Chicago. Sowell's earliest writings were in traditional neoclassical economics, but in 1975 he published *Race and Economics*, a widely acclaimed study of the relationship between the CULTURE of ETHNIC GROUPS and their levels of economic success. In this and subsequent works, Sowell contends that African Americans have failed to achieve EQUALITY partly because of cultural deficiencies that sustain the GHETTO and the UNDERCLASS rather than mainly because of RACISM, whether INDIVIDUAL RACISM or INSTITUTIONAL RACISM. Sowell attempts to substantiate his argument about the importance of cultural differences rather than racism in accounting for economic success by pointing to the relatively greater educational and economic attainments of WEST INDIANS, compared with black Americans. Sowell attributes the relative success of West Indians to cultural differences between native-born blacks and black West Indian immigrants. Sowell, who is strongly committed to laissez-faire CAPITALISM, also contends that elements of the WELFARE STATE, the GREAT SOCIETY, and the WAR ON POVERTY hurt rather than help blacks because they contribute to a CULTURE OF POVERTY and dependency that undermines INDIVIDUALISM and SELF-HELP, which he believes are indispensable for individuals in groups to escape POVERTY. Sowell also passionately opposes AFFIRMATIVE ACTION because he believes it undermines individual initiative on the part of blacks and the principle of individualism in American culture.

Although Sowell's writings on race were always well received in conservative intellectual circles and THINK TANKS, they did not receive widespread attention until the election of RONALD REAGAN in 1980. The Reagan administration actively recruited black conservative intellectuals and sought to give their ideas widespread attention in PUBLIC POLICY and MEDIA circles. As a result, Sowell's writings were widely publicized in the national media. In 1981

Newsweek described Sowell as the "fountain head of black conservatism" because of the way his work was beginning to shape policy debates on race and how he was viewed as a role model by young black conservatives. Sowell was frequently consulted by the Reagan administration as it developed policies on race and poverty, but he declined to accept a high-level appointment in the BUREAUCRACY, preferring to maintain his intellectual autonomy.

Although Sowell and his ideas were admired in mainstream white intellectual circles, among mainstream black intellectuals and within the black LEADERSHIP establishment—which tends to be liberal or radical—Sowell and his ideas were ignored or discredited. Sowell himself was sometimes referred to by his black critics as an UNCLE TOM, leading him to respond that the black intellectual and leadership establishments were intellectually and politically bankrupt because they were wedded to an outmoded liberalism and were captives of the DEMOCRATIC PARTY.

Early in his career Sowell taught briefly at Howard University and later at UCLA and Brandeis University. Since the 1980s he has been affiliated with the Hoover Institution, a conservative think tank at Stanford University. In addition to his scholarly writings, he writes a syndicated weekly newspaper column.

Spingarn, Joel E. (1875–1939) *civil rights activist*

Joel Elias Spingarn is one of the remarkable group of white men and women who organized the NAACP and led and sustained it during its formative years and helped to launch the CIVIL RIGHTS MOVEMENT. Spingarn, Mary White Ovington, Oswald Garrison Villard, and Spingarn's brother, Arthur—all white—organized the NAACP in 1909 and until the 1930s shaped its IDEOLOGY in the direction of LIBERALISM and laid the foundation for its becoming the most important 20th-century ORGANIZATION devoted to the cause of CIVIL RIGHTS. With the exception of W. E. B. DU BOIS, these white people were the principal leaders of the NAACP throughout its earliest years. By the time JAMES WELDON JOHNSON and WALTER WHITE, African Americans, assumed leadership, the NAACP was well established as the most effective LOBBYING and LITIGATION organization in the BLACK COMMUNITY. This was due in large measure to the work of Spingarn.

Born in New York City, Spingarn received a Ph.D. from Columbia University, where he later served as professor and chair of the Department of Comparative Literature. (He was eventually dismissed from the university in a dispute over academic freedom and free speech.) A principal organizer of the NAACP, he served as its incorporator and then in virtually every leadership role in the association—chairman, treasurer, and president—in a period that spanned nearly three decades. In 1913 he created the

NAACP's Spingarn Medal, which is awarded annually to the African American who has contributed the most to the advancement of blacks. Some critics of Spingarn and his white colleagues who founded and led the NAACP contend they distorted the direction of the Civil Rights movement by steering it away from BLACK NATIONALISM and RADICALISM toward a narrow focus on legal rights, INDIVIDUALISM, INTEGRATIONISM and liberalism. Indeed, Spingarn and the other whites in the early NAACP were committed to liberalism and integration and hostile to radicalism and black nationalism, and they used their influence to steer the organization in those directions. However, it is not clear that this was not the tendency of the black LEADERSHIP independent of the influence of Spingarn and his associates.

In addition to his work with the NAACP, Spingarn was active in the arts, philanthropy, and politics. In 1908 he was an unsuccessful REPUBLICAN PARTY candidate for CONGRESS. At his death in 1939, his brother Arthur resigned as head of the association's legal department to succeed him as president, and Joel's wife was elected to complete his term on the board of directors.

Further reading: B. Joyce Ross, *J. E. Spingarn and the Rise of the NAACP* (New York: Atheneum, 1972); Carolyn Weldin, *Inheritors of the Spirit: Mary White Ovington and the Founding of the NAACP* (New York: John Wiley & Sons, 1998).

state and local government

The principle of FEDERALISM that structures the operation of government in the United States means there is not one but multiple governments. The principle of the SEPARATION OF POWERS is also employed by many of these governments, which means there are multiple centers of power and access to these multiple governments. Historically, these multiple governments with their multiple centers of power have both harmed and helped African Americans in their struggles for FREEDOM and EQUALITY. They have harmed or disadvantaged blacks because, like federalism in general, they make it difficult to establish and implement universal or national standards for CIVIL RIGHTS. Thus, state and local governments in the SOUTHERN STATES sanctioned SLAVERY, and in the aftermath of RECONSTRUCTION, these governments engaged in racial SEGREGATION and DISCRIMINATION. These governments also used their authority to allow RIOTS, LYNCHING, and other forms of VIOLENCE perpetuated against blacks to go unpunished. As a result of the CIVIL RIGHTS MOVEMENT, the CONGRESS in the 1960s used its authority to enact laws preventing state and local governments from practicing segregation and discrimination and to punish persons using

violence against blacks. As a result, in the POST–CIVIL RIGHTS ERA this disadvantage of state and local governments diminished considerably, but until the 1960s these governments in the Southern states, and to some extent in the NORTHERN STATES, operated as mechanisms to defend RACISM and WHITE SUPREMACY. In the post–civil rights era there are national or universal standards for civil rights applicable to all governments, but there are still variations in their implementation at state and local levels.

There are more than 80,000 levels and units of government in the United States, including the federal government in Washington, the 50 state governments, 19,000 city governments, approximately 3,000 county governments, 16,000 town governments, 14,000 school districts, and about 29,000 special districts (special districts are units of government created by the states and localities to deliver specialized services, such as water, electricity, waste treatment, or transportation). Systematic data on black participation and access to these many governments are not available, mainly because it is difficult and expensive to collect such information. Thus, except for URBAN POLITICS (dealing with the larger cities) and the more visible state legislative and executive offices, social scientists know very little about blacks in state and local government.

Black participation in these levels of government started after the CIVIL WAR during Reconstruction. Approximately 1,400 African Americans held state and local offices in the Southern states during Reconstruction, including 25 state executive positions (lieutenant governor, treasurer, superintendent of education, secretary of state), and P. B. S. Pinchback, an African American, served for 40 days as governor of Louisiana after the incumbent governor was impeached. Historians suggest that Reconstruction black ELECTED OFFICIALS generally pursued progressive or liberal PUBLIC POLICY in areas of education, public health, and public works. Although a few blacks held state and local offices in the Northern states before and after Reconstruction, significant participation in these governments by blacks did not occur until the post–civil rights era. However, at the close of the 20th century this level of participation was still limited, with blacks holding then less than 2 percent of the more than 500,000 state and local offices compared with their 12 percent of the POPULATION. Beginning with the election in 1967 of CARL STOKES and RICHARD HATCHER as mayors of major American cities, blacks have been elected mayors of most of the nation's major cities. But only one black has been elected governor of one of the states, DOUGLAS WILDER in Virginia in 1989. (Thomas Bradley, the long-serving mayor of Los Angeles, was almost elected governor of California in 1982, losing by a margin of 49.3 percent to 48.1 percent, a margin of a mere 93,000 votes out of nearly 8 million.) Since the 1970s, 12 blacks have been elected to statewide executive office, including secretaries of state, five treasurers/comptrollers, one superintendent of education, two state attorneys general, and two lieutenant governors. At the beginning of the 20th century 600 blacks served in state legislatures in 44 states. In 22 of these states, these legislators formed caucuses modeled after the CONGRESSIONAL BLACK CAUCUS, and there is a national ORGANIZATION—the National Caucus of Black State Legislators—representing their collective interests. Five blacks have served in top state legislative leadership positions, as Speakers of the House in New Jersey, California, Pennsylvania, and North Carolina. In general, the research shows these black legislators frequently sponsored bills dealing with POVERTY, the CRIMINAL JUSTICE SYSTEM, and SCHOOLS AND EDUCATION, with success in getting these bills enacted varying from state to state.

Below the state level, little is known about black participation, but the guess among scholars is that the level is quite low. Using Georgia as a case study suggests that this is the case. While African Americans in 1990 were 27 percent of the state's population, they held 18 percent of state legislative seats, were just 6 percent of the state's judges, 6 percent of district attorneys, 4 percent of sheriffs, 7 percent of mayors, 12 percent of county commissioners, and 12 percent of school district superintendents.

See also CIVIL RIGHTS ACT OF 1964, COMMERCE CLAUSE, FOURTEENTH AMENDMENT, and VOTING RIGHTS ACT OF 1965.

Stewart, Maria W. (1803–1879) *African-American feminist*

The roles of women like SOJOURNER TRUTH and HARRIET TUBMAN in AFRICAN-AMERICAN POLITICS are generally well known to students of African-American history, but Maria W. Stewart is less known, although she is probably the first African-American woman to take a leadership role (although brief) in the ABOLITIONIST MOVEMENT and one of the first to embrace the cause of FEMINISM.

Maria W. Stewart was born in Boston in 1803. At age five she was orphaned and became a servant to a white clergyman, where she received an education by attending Sunday school and reading material from the clergyman's library. A deeply religious woman, Stewart was well versed in the Bible, history, and the classics and used these materials in her writing and lectures. She was also influenced by DAVID WALKER and his *Appeal*. After being widowed after only three years of marriage, Stewart began her career as an antislavery and feminist lecturer and writer. The historian Dorothy Porter describes her as "probably the earliest Negro woman lecturer and writer," and Marilyn Richardson writes that in September 1832 "Maria Stewart . . . did what no American-born woman, black or white, before her is recorded as having done. She mounted a lecture platform and raised a political argument before a 'promiscuous audience,'" that is, an audience composed of both men and women. Stewart's career as a writer and lecturer lasted little more than three years. But during that time while living in Boston, she published a political treatise and a religious pamphlet, and gave three public lectures. Her abolitionist views were deeply rooted in RELIGIOSITY, in that she viewed SLAVERY as a violation of Christian principles. She was also a "moral suasionist" in the tradition of WILLIAM LLOYD GARRISON, although like David Walker she also embraced the idea of VIOLENCE. She strongly opposed the idea of colonialization and BACK-TO-AFRICA MOVEMENTS, arguing that FREEDOM for African men and women was possible in the United States. Stewart was an ardent feminist. Not only did she urge black women to join the abolitionist movement, she encouraged the formation of black women's rights organizations and literary societies. She also supported the then-radical idea that black women should pursue an education and career outside of the home, writing, "How long shall the fair daughters of Africa be compelled to bury their minds and talents beneath a load of iron pots and kettles?"

After the CIVIL WAR Stewart became a teacher in the DISTRICT OF COLUMBIA schools and later the matron of Freedmen's Hospital. She died in 1879 at the age of 76. Shortly before her death she received a pension from her husband's service in the War of 1812, which she used to finance the publication of a new edition of her collected essays and speeches entitled *Meditations from the Pen of Mrs. Maria W. Stewart*.

Further reading: Marilyn Richardson, *Maria Stewart: America's First Black Woman Political Writer* (Bloomington: Indiana University Press, 1987).

Stevens, Thaddeus (1792–1868) *U.S. congressman*

Thaddeus Stevens in the House of Representatives and CHARLES SUMNER in the Senate were leaders of the RADICAL REPUBLICANS in CONGRESS during RECONSTRUCTION. His MILITANCY in advocacy of FREEDOM and EQUALITY for African Americans predated his leadership during Reconstruction. Elected to the House from Pennsylvania in 1848 as a member of the Whig Party, Stevens's militant speeches denouncing SLAVERY and the FUGITIVE SLAVE CLAUSE caused dissension among the Whigs, so after two terms he left the House. The formation of the REPUBLICAN PARTY led Stevens to return to the House in 1858. After the CIVIL WAR began, Stevens urged ABRAHAM LINCOLN to issue an EMANCIPATION PROCLAMATION and employ African Americans as soldiers. After the war, Stevens supported the FREEDMEN'S BUREAU, the first CIVIL RIGHTS bill enacted by Congress, and the design of the FOUR-

TEENTH AMENDMENT. Stevens viewed the leaders of the rebellion as traitors and argued that the defeated SOUTHERN STATES should be treated as "conquered provinces" and governed by the military until they could be "reconstructed" to assure freedom and equality for the blacks. Stevens also favored confiscation of the land of the large plantation owners as a form of punishment for their treasonous behavior and its division among the former slaves as a form of REPARATIONS. This idea, expressed as FORTY ACRES AND A MULE, did not win approval in Congress in part because of the passionate opposition of President ANDREW JOHNSON. This and other acts by President Johnson, which Stevens believed to be in violation of the CONSTITUTION and based on RACISM and WHITE SUPREMACY, caused Stevens to lead the efforts in the House that resulted in Johnson's impeachment. He died 10 days after the Senate failed to convict Johnson and remove him from office. Reflecting his lifelong commitment to racial equality, Stevens requested that he be buried in a racially integrated cemetery.

Thaddeus Stevens, referred to as the "scourge of the South," was a tribune of the BLACK COMMUNITY and one of the best friends it has ever had in the American government. A lawyer by training, he was educated at Dartmouth College and practiced law in Gettysburg, Pennsylvania, before his election to the Congress.

Further reading: Fawn Brodie, *Thaddeus Stevens: Scourge of the South* (New York: W. W. Norton, 1959).

Stokes, Carl (1927–1996) *politician*

Carl Stokes was the first African American elected mayor of a large American city, elected mayor of Cleveland, Ohio, in 1967. A former prosecutor and state legislator, Stokes won a narrow victory by putting together a COALITION that included virtually the entire black vote and about 20 percent of the white vote. Although the election represented a first in American politics, it represented the maturation of forces in URBAN POLITICS that would result in the election of blacks as mayors in most major American cities during the next two decades. Stokes served two two-year terms and then declined to seek reelection. In 1973 he wrote his memoirs, *Promises of Power: A Political Biography*, in which he expressed his frustrations about his inability as mayor to implement PUBLIC POLICY to deal with the problems of POVERTY in the Cleveland GHETTO. After leaving office, Stokes joined the MEDIA as a commentator on urban affairs for a local television station in New York City and then returned to Cleveland, where he served as a judge. Born in Cleveland, Stokes served in the army and was graduated from the University of Minnesota and the Cleveland-Marshall School of Law.

Further reading: William Nelson and Phillip Meranto, *Electing Black Mayors: Political Action in the Black Community* (Columbus: Ohio State University Press, 1977).

"Strange Fruit"

MUSIC, an integral part of the CULTURE of the BLACK COMMUNITY, has played an important role in AFRICAN-AMERICAN POLITICS. Often this politicized music involved explicit PROTEST themes and was written and performed by African Americans. However, "Strange Fruit," one of the earliest explicitly black protest songs, was written by Abel Meeropol, a Jewish high school teacher in New York City affiliated with the COMMUNIST PARTY. "Strange Fruit," written as a poem to protest LYNCHING, was published in 1937 in a magazine of the New York Teacher's Union. Later set to music by Meeropol, it was performed in left-wing circles, but it did not receive national attention until 1939 when it was recorded by Billie Holiday, the legendary African-American jazz singer. Holiday's recording of the song had an immediate impact, as she bitterly evoked the "strange fruit" of "southern trees" "with blood on the leaves and blood at the root" and a "black body

Thaddeus Stevens *(Library of Congress)*

swinging in southern breeze." Holiday's recording company, Columbia, refused to record the song, contending that the lyrics were too political (antilynching legislation was then being debated in CONGRESS), so it was released by Commodore, an obscure label. The song was controversial and was rarely played on radio and was difficult to find in record stores. It was rarely performed by other artists, and Holiday's performances of it sometimes resulted in protests. Although she said she wept every time she sang it, Holiday performed "Strange Fruit" until her death in 1959. After her death the song was largely forgotten. The original 1939 Commodore recording, however, is available (including on compact disc) and in 2000 a book was published about the song's history.

Further reading: David Margolick, *Strange Fruit: Billie Holiday, Cafe Society and an Early Cry for Civil Rights* (New York: Running Press, 2000).

Student Nonviolent Coordinating Committee (SNCC)

SNCC—the Student Nonviolent Coordinating Committee—was the principal ORGANIZATION of students during the CIVIL RIGHTS MOVEMENT. It was formed in 1960 as an outgrowth of the SIT-INS in Greensboro, North Carolina, by black college students.

The sit-ins in February 1960 sparked a chain reaction that led to similar acts of PROTEST and CIVIL DISOBEDIENCE by black and white students throughout the nation. This spontaneous outburst of student activism led to calls for the institutionalization of student involvement in the Civil Rights movement. Thus, three months after Greensboro, student leaders from HISTORICALLY BLACK COLLEGES AND UNIVERSITIES and elsewhere were called together by the SOUTHERN CHRISTIAN LEADERSHIP CONFERENCE (SCLC) to develop a strategy for student participation in the movement. MARTIN LUTHER KING JR. encouraged the students to organize as the youth wing of SCLC. The NAACP head, ROY WILKINS, urged affiliation with its youth councils. ELLA BAKER, however, insisted that students organize as a separate, autonomous organization. Baker's views prevailed and SNCC was organized as a biracial COALITION to "coordinate" and plan strategy for student participation in the movement. This strictly coordinating role was short-lived because by 1962 SNCC had abandoned its focus on sit-ins and moved into the rural areas of the SOUTHERN STATES, focusing on VOTING RIGHTS and protests against SEGREGATION in public facilities. By this time SNCC was composed of about 200 former college students (black and white) who had either dropped out to devote full time to the movement or had been expelled for their civil rights activism.

The period from 1962 to 1965 was the high point of CIVIL RIGHTS protests in the South. SNCC played a pivotal role in these protests. It was the movement's frontline troops in the struggle, working in the most dangerous areas of the rural South. Its leaders—JOHN LEWIS, ROBERT MOSES, and STOKELY CARMICHAEL, among others—in their dress (blue denims and overalls), manner, and methods sought conscious identification with the rural masses. Out of this grassroots organizing came an important new form of POLITICAL PARTICIPATION. By and large, the Civil Rights movement had avoided involvement in partisan politics. With SNCC's assistance, the MISSISSIPPI FREEDOM DEMOCRATIC PARTY (MFDP) was created to directly challenge in the electoral process Mississippi's DEMOCRATIC PARTY, which excluded African Americans. The MFDP provided ordinary blacks with political skills and led to the emergence of new grassroots leaders, including FANNIE LOU HAMER. The refusal of the 1964 Democratic Party Convention to seat the multiracial MFDP, in place of the all-white regular Mississippi Democratic delegation, left many in SNCC with a sense of betrayal not only by President LYNDON B. JOHNSON (who had directed the convention not to seat the MFDP) but also by white liberals like HUBERT HUMPHREY and black leaders like Martin Luther King Jr., Roy Wilkins, and BAYARD RUSTIN, who supported Johnson's decision. The MFDP experience disillusioned many SNCC workers, leading many to argue that SNCC and the Civil Rights movement generally needed to change its IDEOLOGY and strategies. In addition to the MFDP experience, some SNCC leaders were also disillusioned by the continued VIOLENCE against its members by white Southerners, which the federal government refused to punish. (The unpunished murder of Sammy Young Jr., a teenage SNCC worker, especially angered SNCC's leadership.) The VIETNAM WAR, in which blacks were being drafted and killed in disproportionately high numbers, was also opposed by SNCC's leaders, who viewed the war as an attempt to maintain COLONIALISM in the THIRD WORLD. The WATTS RIOT suggested to some in SNCC that it should refocus its work away from protesting segregation and INDIVIDUAL RACISM in the Southern states toward a concern with the problems of POVERTY and INSTITUTIONAL RACISM in the GHETTOS of the NORTHERN STATES. Finally, the martyred MALCOLM X's philosophy of BLACK NATIONALISM became increasingly influential among SNCC workers, especially after the posthumous publication of his autobiography. These developments contributed to a growing sense of MILITANCY and RADICALISM within the organization.

This turn toward militancy and radicalism was first expressed when SNCC became the first Civil Rights organization to break with the COLD WAR consensus and oppose the Vietnam War. In a 1966 position paper, SNCC urged African Americans to seek service in the Civil Rights movement as an alternative to the draft "knowing full well that it may cost them their lives as painfully as in Vietnam." The SNCC position paper, which caused a furor within the black LEADERSHIP establishment and the liberal MEDIA, said in part, "We believe the United States government has been deceptive in its concern for the freedom of the Vietnamese people, just as it has been deceptive in claiming concern for the freedom of the colored people . . . in other countries. Our work . . . has taught us that the United States government has never guaranteed the freedom of oppressed citizens, and is not yet truly determined to end the rule of terror and oppression within its own borders." (SNCC's statement led to the exclusion of Julian Bond, one of its leaders, from the Georgia legislature to which he was elected in 1966. Bond's exclusion was overturned by the SUPREME COURT.) By this time SNCC had already adopted the philosophy of black power and voted to exclude whites from the organization. In June 1966 the BLACK POWER MOVEMENT was brought to national attention on the MEREDITH MARCH. Although the Black Power movement profoundly reshaped the structure and symbolism of black politics, shortly after SNCC launched the movement it began to decline as a viable organization. Its precipitous turn toward radicalism and militancy led to the loss of white philanthropic support; factionalism and infighting increased within the organization; and the FBI intensified its program of POLITICAL REPRESSION. By 1967 SNCC was in disarray and would soon formally disband. Its members went their separate ways. Some were imprisoned or went into exile; some returned to college, where they became activists in efforts to create AFRICAN-AMERICAN STUDIES; some became ELECTED OFFICIALS; and still others joined the BLACK PANTHER PARTY and other radical organizations.

Further reading: Claybourne Carson, *In Struggle: SNCC and the Black Awakening of the 1960s* (Cambridge, Mass.: Harvard University Press, 1981).

subordinate group

A subordinate group is a less powerful group in a POWER relationship with a SUPERORDINATE GROUP in a POLITICAL SYSTEM. The subordinate group, because of the difference in power, is subject to differential treatment. The superordinate and subordinate groups are often from different ETHNIC GROUPS, and these ethnic differences usually constitute the basis for DISCRIMINATION or OPPRESSION of the subordinate by the superordinate group. In the relationship between blacks and whites in the United States, the former constitute the subordinate group and the latter the superordinate group.

See also AFRICAN-AMERICAN POLITICS and MINORITY GROUP.

Sullivan, Leon H. (1922–2001) *activist, business leader, minister*

Leon H. Sullivan, a Philadelphia clergyman, used the BLACK CHURCH to develop a strategy of economic PROTEST to deal with problems of POVERTY in the GHETTOS and foster the development of black CAPITALISM. Sullivan also embraced PAN-AFRICANISM by organizing a series of summits in Africa that brought together African and African-American leaders to discuss issues of common concern, and he was among the leaders in the United States in the struggle to dismantle APARTHEID in South Africa.

In the early 1960s Sullivan began to organize consumer boycotts of businesses in Philadelphia that did not employ black workers. This approach to dealing with employment DISCRIMINATION against blacks had been used earlier by ADAM CLAYTON POWELL in HARLEM, and Sullivan may have learned how to use it from Powell, since he served as an assistant at Powell's Harlem church. (Sullivan used the slogan "Don't buy where you can't work," which Powell used in Harlem during the 1940s.) Once Philadelphia employers agreed to hire blacks, Sullivan found that he could not find enough skilled blacks to fill the jobs. This led him in 1964 to create Opportunities Industrialization Center (OIC), an ORGANIZATION that provided job-training programs for unemployed ghetto residents. (Sullivan would often remark that "integration without preparation is frustration.") Starting in an abandoned building with only the resources of his small church, within a decade there were more than 140 OIC branches throughout the United States, Africa, and the Caribbean, financed by grants from the federal government, corporations, and foundations. Sullivan's strategy was later adopted by MARTIN LUTHER KING JR. and the SOUTHERN CHRISTIAN LEADERSHIP CONFERENCE, when they established Operation Breadbasket in Chicago under the leadership of JESSE JACKSON (Operation Breadbasket subsequently was renamed OPERATION PUSH). Meanwhile Sullivan's Philadelphia congregation, Zion Baptist, had grown from a membership of 500 to 5,000, making it the largest church in the city. Recognizing the potential of the church as an agent of economic development and SELF-HELP, Sullivan created the Zion Non-Profit Charitable Trust, which, with government and corporate contributions, financed several economic development projects, including the first black-owned shopping center. The trust also established housing and education programs for low-income persons.

In 1971 Sullivan became the first African American appointed to a major corporate board when he was named to the board of General Motors Corporation. From this position in the POWER ELITE, Sullivan—to the dismay of his colleagues—called on General Motors and other American corporations to boycott South Africa to protest apartheid. Although he was initially not successful in getting General Motors or other corporations to withdraw from South Africa, he did get many American corporations operating in South Africa to adopt the "Sullivan principles," ending SEGREGATION in their facilities and providing for EQUALITY in employment. Two years after Sullivan proposed the principles, they were adopted by General Motors and more than a dozen other U.S. corporations. Shortly thereafter, many corporations began to leave South Africa, and in 1986 CONGRESS passed the Anti-Apartheid Act (overriding RONALD REAGAN's veto), which required all U.S. corporations in South Africa to adopt the Sullivan principles. These principles were integral components of the pressures that persuaded the South African government to begin the process of dismantling apartheid. Once apartheid came to an end, Sullivan turned his attention to the problems of economic development in Africa, organizing a series of African–African-American leadership summits. He argued that in the context of GLOBALIZATION, the problems of RACISM and WHITE SUPREMACY and poverty required Pan-African solidarity and COALITIONS between the African-American LEADERSHIP and the leaders of the nations of Africa. After Sullivan's death, ANDREW YOUNG became the chair of summits, and at the 2001 summit the participants agreed to rename the gatherings the "Leon Howard Sullivan Summits."

Sullivan was born in Charleston, West Virginia, and attended West Virginia State College and Union Theological Seminary in New York City. He was ordained a Baptist minister at the age of 17.

Sumner, Charles (1811–1874) *U.S. senator*

Charles Sumner in the Senate, along with THADDEUS STEVENS in the House of Representatives, was the leader of the RADICAL REPUBLICANS in the CONGRESS during RECONSTRUCTION. Described by FREDERICK DOUGLASS as the best friend the Negro ever had in public life, Sumner in the period leading up to the CIVIL WAR and during Reconstruction was the Senate's most passionate opponent of SLAVERY and an unwavering advocate of FREEDOM and EQUALITY for African Americans. His MILITANCY on the issue was said to have been ignited when he witnessed a slave auction while a young man visiting the DISTRICT OF COLUMBIA.

Born in Boston, Sumner was graduated from Harvard Law School. As a lawyer in Boston, he was part of a landmark case on school DESEGREGATION; as the attorney in the 1850 case of *Sarah C. Roberts v. The City of Boston*, he argued before the Massachusetts Supreme Court that school SEGREGATION violated the state's constitution. Although this LITIGATION was unsuccessful, Sumner pursued a LOBBYING campaign, and in 1853 the state legislature abolished school segregation in Boston. Elected to the Senate in 1852, Sumner spent much of his first term trying to repeal the Fugitive Slave Law. In an 1856 speech, he bitterly attacked South Carolina Senator Andrew Butler for his support of slavery. Two days later Butler's nephew, Congressman Preston Brocks, entered the Senate chamber and nearly beat Sumner to death with a cane, claiming that his remarks were a libel on the SOUTHERN STATES. After a three-year recovery, Sumner returned to the Senate, and as the Civil War got underway he was the leading advocate of an EMANCIPATION PROCLAMATION because, unlike ABRAHAM LINCOLN, he viewed the war as a moral struggle to end slavery rather than simply a military struggle to maintain the United States.

Sumner made his greatest contributions to the black struggle for freedom and equality after the Civil War during Reconstruction. With Thaddeus Stevens he led the fight in Congress for the adoption of the first CIVIL RIGHTS laws and the FOURTEENTH AMENDMENT and the FIFTEENTH AMENDMENT. Sumner and Stevens also pushed for FORTY ACRES AND A MULE, introducing legislation to confiscate the slaveholders' plantations, divide them up, and give them to slaves as REPARATION and as a means to punish the slaveholders for treason. He also was the Senate's leading advocate of the impeachment and removal of ANDREW JOHNSON from the PRESIDENCY. Sumner exercised the greatest influence in Congress between 1866 and 1870, because by the time of his death in 1874 the first WHITE BACKLASH made his views on racial inequality increasingly unpopular in the REPUBLICAN PARTY. But he did not waver. At the time of his death he was fighting for passage of a civil rights law banning DISCRIMINATION in every public place in the country—from schools to churches and from cemeteries to hospitals. On his deathbed, surrounded by Frederick Douglass and other black leaders, Sumner's last words were "Take care of my civil rights bill—take care of it—you must do it."

See also FUGITIVE SLAVE CLAUSE.

Further reading: Frederick Blue, *Charles Sumner: The Conscience of the North* (New York: W. W. Norton, 1976).

superordinate group

A superordinate group is the more powerful group in a POWER relationship with a SUBORDINATE GROUP. The superordinate group, because of the differences in power, is able to subject the subordinate group to DISCRIMINATION or OPPRESSION. Superordinate and subordinate groups are often of different ETHNIC GROUPS, which may provide the basis or rationale for the differential treatment. In the relationship between whites and blacks in the United States, the former constitute the superordinate group, the latter the subordinate group.

See also AFRICAN-AMERICAN POLITICS, MINORITY GROUP.

Supreme Court

The Supreme Court is one of the three branches of the government of the United States established by the CONSTITUTION under the principle of the SEPARATION OF POWERS. Of the three branches, the Constitution is much more explicit and detailed about the powers and responsibilities of the PRESIDENCY and CONGRESS than it is about the Court. Between 1790 and 1803 the Court made few important decisions. But in 1803 in the landmark *Marbury v. Madison* case, the Court asserted that when it judges a law passed by Congress to be inconsistent with the Constitution, it is, in the opinion of Chief Justice John Marshall, "emphatically" the duty of the Supreme Court to declare it unconstitutional and unenforceable. This power of "judicial review" (that is, the power of the Court to declare null and void acts of Congress, the president, and STATE AND LOCAL GOVERNMENTS) is not explicitly conferred on the Supreme Court by the Constitution, but it is inherent in the idea of a written Constitution that limits the POWER of government and protects the NATURAL RIGHTS and CIVIL RIGHTS of the people. As Alexander Hamilton wrote in the *Federalist Paper* No. 78, "Limitations of this kind can be preserved in practice no other way than through the medium of courts of justice, whose duty it must be to declare all acts contrary to the manifest tenet of the Constitution void. Without this, all the reservations of particular rights or privileges would amount to nothing."

This power of judicial review is unique and makes the courts of the United States, unlike the courts of the rest of the world, political as well as judicial institutions with the power to decide questions of politics and PUBLIC POLICY as well as the usual judicial concerns of guilt or innocence in criminal cases or resolving civil disputes. Tocqueville recognized this, writing in *DEMOCRACY IN AMERICA*, "Scarcely any political question arises in the United States that is not resolved sooner or later into a judicial question." And Robert Dahl in his article "Decision Making in a Democracy: The Supreme Court as a Decision Maker" concluded, "To consider the Supreme Court of the United States strictly as a legal institution is to underestimate its significance in the American political system. For it is also a political institution, an institution, that is to say, for arriving at decisions on controversial questions of national policy."

As a political institution the Supreme Court has throughout most of its history been hostile to the African-American quest for FREEDOM and EQUALITY, usually upholding the IDEOLOGY of WHITE SUPREMACY and the practice of RACISM. Indeed, of the three branches of the government, the Supreme Court has been the most con-

sistently hostile. In its most infamous decision, the *DRED SCOTT* case, the Court stripped Africans in America of their natural rights, declaring they had no rights—none—except those that whites might choose to give them. (*Dred Scott* was only the second time since the precedent-setting *Marbury v. Madison* decision that the Court declared an act of Congress unconstitutional.) And when, after the CIVIL WAR, the Congress and the presidency explicitly conferred natural and civil rights on African Americans by enacting the THIRTEENTH AMENDMENT, the FOURTEENTH AMENDMENT, the FIFTEENTH AMENDMENT, and a series of civil rights laws, the Supreme Court in case after case rendered them null and void. In the cases arising out of the COLFAX MASSACRE—*United States v. Cruikshank* (1876)—the Court took away the authority of the federal government to protect blacks from VIOLENCE and LYNCHINGS. In *PLESSY V. FERGUSON* the Court gave the imprimatur of CONSTITUTIONALISM to the practice of JIM CROW–style SEGREGATION in the SOUTHERN STATES when it established the doctrine of SEPARATE BUT EQUAL. And in *CUMMINGS V. BOARD OF EDUCATION* the Court refused to enforce its own doctrine of separate but equal by allowing a school district to provide a high school for whites but not for blacks. Indeed, rather than using the Fourteenth Amendment—which Justice Edward White in the SLAUGHTERHOUSE CASES said was "so clearly a provision for the [black] race . . . that a strong case would be necessary for the application to any other"—to protect the rights of blacks, the Court until the 1940s used it to protect unfettered CAPITALISM from government regulations protecting the rights of working people. Specifically, the court used the DUE PROCESS CLAUSE of the Fourteenth Amendment to prohibit laws regulating child labor and the minimum wage.

During the Great Depression the Court attempted to block the NEW DEAL and the development of the WELFARE STATE, leading to a historic confrontation with FRANKLIN D. ROOSEVELT. This confrontation resulted in a transformation of the Court's jurisprudence from protecting the property rights of corporations to protecting the rights of MINORITY GROUPS. This concern with minorities was first expressed in 1928 in Justice Harlan Fiske Stone's famous footnote No. 4 in *United States v. Carolene Products*. In this footnote Stone developed the concept of "discrete and insular minorities" who, because of their relative powerlessness, needed special concern from the Court to protect their rights against incursions from a hostile majority. The beginnings of the New Deal transformation in the Court's jurisprudence coincided with a strategy shift in the CIVIL RIGHTS MOVEMENT from LOBBYING to LITIGATION. This shift was reflected in the establishment by the NAACP of its LEGAL DEFENSE FUND under the leadership of THURGOOD MARSHALL. The result of these two developments—the transformation of the Court's jurisprudence and the evolution of the NAACP's strategy—was a series of cases culminating in BROWN V. BOARD OF EDUCATION, which led to the gradual legal dismantling of white supremacy and racism. From the early 1950s to the middle of the 1970s the Court, first under the leadership of Chief Justice EARL WARREN and then Justice WILLIAM BRENNAN, made a remarkable historical turnabout and began to enforce provisions of law and the Constitution requiring equality for all persons, including blacks, women, and other ETHNIC GROUPS. The Court also nationalized most of the provisions of the BILL OF RIGHTS, especially those relating to the rights of persons accused of crimes, which in turn led to some reforms in the CRIMINAL JUSTICE SYSTEM.

However, this turnabout was relatively short-lived because by the late 1980s—as a result of appointments by RICHARD NIXON and RONALD REAGAN—the Court was gradually transformed again from an institution that embraced LIBERALISM to one embracing CONSERVATISM. This conservative transformation was solidified into a reliable five-person majority with the appointment of CLARENCE THOMAS by President George H. W. Bush in 1989, leading African-American observers of the Court to raise the ominous question "will the Supreme Court revert to racism."

In its 1988–89 term the Court, to some observers, including its own Justice Marshall, appeared to be reverting to racism. In this term the court in six back-to-back 5-4 decisions significantly undermined the structure of POST–CIVIL RIGHTS ERA employment-DISCRIMINATION law. The most important of the six decisions was WARDS COVE V. ANTONIO. In this case the Court set new standards for suits challenging discrimination in employment, ruling that plaintiffs in DISPARATE IMPACT cases had to identify "specific practices" that caused the discrimination. The *Wards Cove* majority also ruled that some discriminatory practices could be maintained if they served in a significant way a business's "legitimate employment goals." The dissenting justices and other critics of *Wards Cove* argued that the majority opinion reversed two decades of employment discrimination law going back to GRIGGS V. DUKE POWER and that it made it almost impossible for victims of INSTITUTIONAL RACISM to prevail in court. Justice Marshall wrote an angry dissent in the case, and in a speech at the close of the 1988–89 term he declared that "It is difficult to characterize the term's decisions as anything other than a deliberate retrenching of the civil rights agenda." In other words, Marshall suggested that the Court was reverting to racism. Consequently, he suggested that blacks should turn from a strategy of litigation in the courts to a strategy of lobbying the Congress in order to protect and advance the civil rights agenda. The black LEADERSHIP followed Marshall's suggestion and persuaded the Congress to pass, and a reluctant President George Bush to sign, the Civil Rights Act of 1991, which sought to reverse the Court's decision in *Wards Cove* and the related 1988–89 cases.

In spite of this rebuff by the Congress and the president, the Court's narrow 5-4 conservative majority continued throughout the remainder of the 20th century to reverse civil rights precedents on cases dealing with racism and civil rights. Many of these subsequent cases were decided on constitutional rather than statutory grounds, making them immune to reversal by acts of Congress (a statutory decision by the Court interprets an act of Congress and can be reversed by Congress, but a constitutional interpretation can only be reversed by amending the Constitution). With the election of a conservative REPUBLICAN PARTY majority in Congress in 1994, a reversal of Court decisions was less likely in any case. Thus, as the 21st century opened, African-American leaders openly worried that the Court was poised, as soon as the appropriate case came before it, to reverse the precedent established in BAKKE V. REGENTS OF THE UNIVERSITY OF CALIFORNIA and declare AFFIRMATIVE ACTION unconstitutional.

History suggests that the Supreme Court is fundamentally a political institution devoted to maintaining the core values of the POLITICAL SYSTEM, including constitutionalism. And because constitutionalism is a core value of the system, the Court's interpretation of the Constitution confers enormous legitimacy on its decisions. Thus, when the Court uses the language of the Constitution to decide controversial public policy issues, it legitimates the winning side in the conflict and deligitimates the side that loses. Historically, in deciding cases, the Court responds slowly but surely to PUBLIC OPINION and the long-term trends of national elections. Thus, if the Supreme Court was reverting to racism at the close of the 20th century, it is likely that it was reflecting its understanding of the "shifting winds" of public opinion and the outcomes of five of the last seven presidential elections, in which Republican candidates—perceived as hostile to civil rights and CIVIL LIBERTIES—won the elections and appointed conservative justices to the Court.

Given the pro–civil rights activism of the Court under the leadership of Chief Justice Warren during the 1950s and 1960s, blacks came to view the Court as an important defender of minority rights. But in a critical study of the Court, Girardeau Spann concludes that it is not—and for structural reasons can not be—a defender of minorities. In *Race against the Court: The Supreme Court and Minorities* (1993), Spann writes, "My argument is that, for structural reasons, the institutional role that the Court is destined to play within our constitutional scheme of government is the role of assuring the continued subordination of racial minority interests. I believe that this subordination function is inevitable; that it will be served irrespective of the Court's composition at any particular point in time; and that it will persist irrespective of the conscious motives of the individual justices." Swann's point of view is supported by historical analysis. For most of the Court's history, it has been a majoritarian, antiblack institution. The Warren Court was an anomaly.

At the beginning of the 21st century, 108 persons had served as justices of the Supreme Court. This number includes two African Americans: Thurgood Marshall and Clarence Thomas.

See also CIVIL RIGHTS CASES OF 1883, DISPARATE TREATMENT, INDIVIDUAL RACISM, and SCHOOLS AND EDUCATION.

Further reading: John R. Howard, *The Shifting Wind: The Supreme Court and Civil Rights from Reconstruction to Brown* (Albany: State University of New York Press, 1999); William Leuctenburg, *The Supreme Court Reborn: The Constitutional Revolution in the Age of Roosevelt* (New York: Oxford University Press, 1995); Girardeau Spann, *Race against the Court: The Supreme Court and Minorities* (New York: New York University Press, 1993); Eugene Walton, "Will the Supreme Court Revert to Racism?," *Black World* 21 (1972): 46–48.

Swann v. Charlotte–Mecklenburg Board of Education (1971)

Swann v. Charlotte–Mecklenburg Board of Education is the first case in which the SUPREME COURT authorized the use of BUSING to implement the *BROWN V. BOARD OF EDUCATION* decision regarding DESEGREGATION of the nation's public schools. In *Swann* the Court held that to eliminate segregated school systems, the lower courts could require school districts to assign students on the basis of race and use transportation by bus as a tool to eliminate racially identifiable schools. The principles of *Swann* initially applied only to school districts in the SOUTHERN STATES, which had practiced de jure school SEGREGATION; however, in *KEYES V. SCHOOL DISTRICT NO. 1, DENVER*, the Court applied the principles to school districts in the NORTHERN STATES where *de facto* segregation existed. The *Swann* case resulted in enormous political controversy, conflict and occasional VIOLENCE as whites resisted busing for purposes of school desegregation. As a result the Court in 1974 in *MILLKEN V. BRADLEY* set in motion a process that gradually led to an end to busing for purposes of school desegregation. The results of the end of busing was that at the beginning of the 21st century most black schoolchildren attended racially separate and unequal schools, the decision in *Brown* notwithstanding. In 2001 the 4th Circuit Court of Appeals ordered an end to race-based pupil assignments and busing in the Charlotte-Mecklenburg district.

See also DISPARATE TREATMENT, DISPARATE IMPACT, INDIVIDUAL RACISM, INSTITUTIONAL RACISM, INTEGRATION, and SCHOOLS AND EDUCATION.

T

Talented Tenth

The Talented Tenth is a concept concerned with the development of a strategy of higher education of African Americans and with the roles and responsibilities of the educated elite in the LEADERSHIP of the BLACK COMMUNITY. The phrase was first used by a white man, Henry Morehouse, but it was popularized by W. E. B. DU BOIS. Morehouse, the executive secretary of the American Baptist Home Mission Society, first used the phrase in an 1896 article challenging BOOKER T. WASHINGTON's emphasis on industrial and vocational education for blacks. Morehouse wrote that "not to make proper provision for the high education of the talented tenth man of the colored colleges is a prodigious mistake. . . . Industrial education is good for the nine . . . [but] that tenth man ought to have the best opportunities for making the most of himself for humanity and God." Du Bois used Morehouse's concept as the title of his contribution to *The Negro Problem: A Series of Articles by Representative American Negroes Today* published in 1903. The book was probably initiated by Booker Washington, who contributed an article along with several other leading clergymen, educators, and journalists. Although the volume was sponsored by Washington, Du Bois nevertheless used his article to forthrightly attack Washington's educational philosophy and his strategy of ACCOMMODATIONISM. In the opening sentence of "The Talented Tenth," Du Bois wrote, "The Negro race, like all races, is going to be saved by its exceptional men. The problem of education, then, among Negroes must first of all deal with the 'talented tenth'; it is the problem of developing the best of this race that they may guide the mass away from the contamination and death of the worst, in their own and other races."

Although Du Bois borrowed the phrase from Morehouse, the philosophy it articulates is rooted in the ideas of ALEXANDER CRUMMELL, Du Bois's mentor, who in 1877 had founded the American Negro Academy. Du Bois's notion was a self-consciously elitist concept of leadership, based on the duty of the "college-bred Negro" to provide guidance for the masses of ignorant and uneducated African Americans. Du Bois wrote that "He is, as he ought to be, the group leader, the man who sets the ideals of the community where he lives, directs its thoughts and heads its social movements." This self-consciously elitists and male notion of leadership guided the black community throughout most of the 20th century, influencing the course of higher education at places like ATLANTA UNIVERSITY and HOWARD UNIVERSITY and the development of black leadership strategies of PROTEST and SELF-HELP.

In a 1948 address to a gathering of the elite grand boule of the Sigma Pi Phi, Du Bois reexamined the thesis of the talented tenth, suggesting that he may have put too much faith in the leadership of the elite (who he said as a group might be "selfish, self-indulgent, well-to-do men, whose basic interest in solving the Negro problem was personal . . . without any real care, or certainly no arousing care, as to what became of the mass of American Negroes, or to the mass of people") and too little to the masses who, because they "know life in its bitter struggle," might more naturally produce "real, unselfish and clearsighted leadership." At this point in his career, Du Bois was disillusioned with the idea of CIVIL RIGHTS and moving toward Marxist class analysis and RADICALISM. However, he did not abandon altogether his notion of an elite leadership of blacks, calling in his 1948 address for a "Guiding Hundredth" rather than a talented tenth. This guiding hundred would avoid the pitfalls of the talented tenth by developing a BLACK AGENDA, a planned program, and a national ORGANIZATION rooted firmly in the CULTURE of African Americans.

See also HISTORICALLY BLACK COLLEGES AND UNIVERSITIES.

Terrell, Mary Church (1863–1954) *activist*

Mary Eliza Church Terrell, one of the few women among the early-20th-century TALENTED TENTH, played a leading role in organizing black women in the African-American struggle for EQUALITY.

Born in Memphis, Tennessee, to prosperous parents just as the CIVIL WAR was coming to an end, Terrell was graduated from Oberlin College in 1884. In 1886 she accepted a high school teaching position in the DISTRICT OF COLUMBIA. There she met her husband, Robert Terrell, who was later to become a judge. After traveling in Europe, Terrell returned to the United States and began a long career of activism in CIVIL RIGHTS and FEMINISM. In an 1890 speech at the National Woman Suffrage Association Convention, Terrell expressed her commitment to the cause of a black feminism by remarking that "A white woman has only one handicap to overcome—a great one true, her sex; a colored woman faces two—her sex and her race. A colored man has only one—that of race."

Terrell viewed SEXISM and RACISM as interrelated problems confronting the BLACK COMMUNITY as a community. Therefore, in 1896 she founded and became the first president of the NATIONAL ASSOCIATION OF COLORED WOMEN (NACW), an ORGANIZATION dedicated to combating racism by improving the conditions of black women. Terrell believed that the "development of black womanhood" would improve the conditions of the black community as a whole because whites would judge blacks as a whole through the "womanhood of the race." NACW attempted to build solidarity among all black women, but it was mainly an elite organization of middle-class women devoted to "uplifting the race" through SELF-HELP. Viewing the masses of black women as ignorant and to some extent lacking in moral virtues, the NACW under Terrell's leadership preached BOOKER T. WASHINGTON's "gospel of the toothbrush," developing programs to improve moral standards and provide information on child rearing and the economics of the home. The NACW also established homes for girls, the aged, and the ill.

Terrell was among the founders of the NAACP, worked with IDA B. WELLS-BARNETT in her campaigns against LYNCHING, and was the first black woman appointed to the District of Columbia Board of Education. Although her efforts were often frustrated by the WHITE SUPREMACY beliefs of some white feminists, she tried to build COALITIONS between black and white women in the struggle for VOTING RIGHTS. She wrote articles and short stories on black life and lectured in the United States and Europe (she spoke three languages). The last years of her life were devoted to PROTEST to end SEGREGATION and DISCRIMINATION in public places in the District of Columbia. At the age of 90 she walked at the head of a picket line protesting segregated restaurants. LITIGATION initiated by Terrell led to a 1953 court ruling ordering the DESEGREGATION of District of Columbia restaurants. Her autobiography, *A Colored Woman in a White World*, was published in 1940.

Mary Church Terrell *(Library of Congress)*

Further reading: Beverly Jones, *Quest for Equality: The Life and Writings of Mary Church Terrell* (Brooklyn: Carlson Publishing, 1990).

think tanks

Think tanks are ORGANIZATIONS established to bring systematic knowledge into the PUBLIC POLICY process in the United States. As organizations of scholars (and frequently former government officials) who do research and planning on policy issues, think tanks are important parts of the policy-making process. They develop ideas that shape the policy debate and, unlike university-based scholars or PUBLIC INTELLECTUALS, they sometimes serve in government or are otherwise directly linked to policy makers. Among the more important think tanks are the Brookings Institution, the American Enterprise Institute, and the Urban Institute.

The LEADERSHIP of the BLACK COMMUNITY has long recognized the importance of systematic research and knowledge in developing strategies and programs to deal with problems of RACISM and POVERTY. The URBAN

LEAGUE in 1921, with funding from the Carnegie Foundation, established a department with the goal of doing "action research" on problems confronting the black community. But, over the years, the black community has been unable to develop and sustain well-funded, autonomous think tanks or similar research institutions devoted to research on race-related issues. The Urban League's research department, for example, has waxed and waned since its establishment in 1921, depending on the whims of white philanthropy. At the beginning of the 21st century, the JOINT CENTER FOR POLITICAL STUDIES was the only think tank devoted to race-related policy research. However, it was so heavily dependent on white philanthropy that it could not pursue an autonomous research agenda. Given the importance of think tanks in the development of public policy, this means that the black community is at a disadvantage in developing ideas and research for the BLACK AGENDA and in using knowledge to influence public policy.

third parties

DEMOCRACY in the United States since the adoption of the CONSTITUTION has been characterized by a TWO-PARTY SYSTEM, but occasionally third parties have emerged to challenge the dominance of the two major parties, and frequently these parties have come about as a result of issues related to RACE. Third parties have frequently been a part of SOCIAL MOVEMENTS, seeking to PROTEST a prevailing two-party consensus on one or more issues of PUBLIC POLICY by threatening to get enough votes to become the BALANCE OF POWER in specific elections. Third parties in this sense are distinguishable from "minor parties," which, like the COMMUNIST PARTY, tend to be doctrinaire and usually do not seek to influence election outcomes.

The REPUBLICAN PARTY historically is the most successful third party because in 1856 it challenged the then-two-party consensus on SLAVERY and in 1860 displaced the Whig Party to become one of the two major parties. Those blacks in the NORTHERN STATES who could vote supported the Republican Party, and earlier some leaders of the ABOLITIONIST MOVEMENT including FREDERICK DOUGLASS had supported the antislavery Liberty and Free Soil Parties. But except for the Republican Party, third parties have not had much success. Two of the five most successful third parties in American history have been parties of RACISM and WHITE SUPREMACY, including Strom Thurmond's 1948 Dixiecrat Party challenge to the election of HARRY TRUMAN and GEORGE WALLACE's several third-party presidential campaigns during the 1960s and 1970s. The other three most-effective third-party challenges were Theodore Roosevelt's 1912 "Bull Moose" Party, which split the Republican vote and allowed WOODROW WILSON to win the

PRESIDENCY; Robert LaFollette's 1924 Progressive Party campaign; and Ross Perot's 1992 Reform Party campaign. Although neither of these third-party challenges decisively affected the outcome of specific elections, both affected the policy debate and, in the case of the Wallace campaigns, helped to encourage the Republican Party to shift its stance on CIVIL RIGHTS and embrace the SOUTHERN STRATEGY. In terms of the dynamics of the two-party system in the United States, this is the significance of third parties: not to win elections but to get enough voter support to force one or both of the major parties to adopt some or all of its policy positions.

African Americans for virtually all of their history have been dissatisfied with the positions of the two major parties because generally both have ignored their quests for FREEDOM and EQUALITY, or one party has given mere lip service to these concerns while the other has ignored them altogether. Blacks, however, have never been able to establish a viable third party in national politics that is, a party able to affect or threaten to affect the outcome of national elections. In the POST–CIVIL RIGHTS ERA several efforts were made to establish a third-political-party COALITION organized around issues of concern to blacks, the poor, and other minorities, most notably during the 1972 NATIONAL BLACK POLITICAL CONVENTION. But these efforts met with very little success because of the loyalty of the black LEADERSHIP and probably most black voters to the DEMOCRATIC PARTY and also because of the enormous difficulties of organizing a viable national third party. Some African-American leaders have affiliated with minor parties, including the Communist and the SOCIALIST PARTY, and several black or black-led third parties have been formed in the SOUTHERN STATES, the most noteworthy being the MISSISSIPPI FREEDOM DEMOCRATIC PARTY. However, as HANES WALTON JR. writes, these black parties have "disappeared almost as quickly as they have appeared."

At the end of the 20th century the Republican Party generally ignored the black vote and the Democratic Party took it for granted while ignoring many of the policy concerns of blacks or giving them only symbolic attention. Many black PUBLIC INTELLECTUALS including HAROLD CRUSE and RONALD WALTERS argued that this situation urgently required the formation of a third party, but their views found little favor among the overwhelmingly Democratic black leadership who favored ACCOMMODATIONISM with the two-party system rather than protest.

Further reading: Steven Rosenstone, R. Behr, and Edward Lazarus, *Third Parties in America* (Princeton, N.J.: Princeton University Press, 1984); Hanes Walton Jr., *The Negro in Third Party Politics* (Philadelphia, Pa.: Dorrance, 1969); ———, *Black Political Parties: A Historical Political Analysis* (New York: Free Press, 1972).

Third World

"Third World," a phrase first used in 1952 by a French demographer, refers to those countries seeking a "third way" between CAPITALISM and COMMUNISM in the context of the COLD WAR. In the context of the cold war the "First World" was constituted by those countries in western Europe and several in Asia (Japan, South Korea, Australia, the Philippines, New Zealand) allied with the United States. The "Second World" was constituted by those eastern European nations allied with the Soviet Union, and the "Third World" constituted the rest of the countries of Asia, Latin America, and Africa. The Third World therefore tends to be populated by nonwhites. It is also constituted by countries subjected to COLONIALISM by the First World nations of Europe. And the Third World tends to be constituted by poor, "developing" countries compared with the relatively affluent "developed" countries of the First and Second Worlds. Finally, virtually all Third World countries have experienced WHITE SUPREMACY and RACISM either directly through colonialism or indirectly through imperialism. Some of these common experiences were believed to constitute a basis for an international solidarity, which was first expressed at the 1955 BANDUNG CONFERENCE. In the POST–CIVIL RIGHTS ERA, there were sentiments to establish COALITIONS between African Americans and Third World peoples in the United States. When the cold war ended in the 1990s, the strategic basis for the Third World also came to an end. However, in the context of GLOBALIZATION and the persistence of POVERTY in Third World countries, there remained a basis for solidarity to meet the challenges of a kind of global APARTHEID.

See also MULTICULTURALISM and RAINBOW COALITION.

Further reading: Darryl Thomas, *The Theory and Practice of Third World Solidarity* (Westport, Conn.: Praeger, 2001).

Thirteenth Amendment, U.S. Constitution

The CONGRESS proposed two Thirteenth Amendments to the CONSTITUTION. These two amendments constitute dramatic incongruities in the African-American struggle for FREEDOM and EQUALITY, because the first Thirteenth Amendment adopted by Congress would, if ratified, have forever frozen SLAVERY into the Constitution while the second abolished slavery. The first Thirteenth Amendment was adopted by Congress near the beginning of the CIVIL WAR as a last-ditch effort to avoid war; the second was adopted near its end as the first fruit of victory at the war's end.

In 1861 as the prospects for secession by the SOUTHERN STATES increased, the Congress appointed a committee to investigate the situation and make recommendations that might avoid secession and war. Among the recommen-

dations proposed was an amendment to the Constitution that would have prohibited any other amendment to the Constitution granting Congress the authority or power to interfere in any way with slavery in any state. The text of the proposed amendment read, "no amendment shall be made to the Constitution which will authorize or give Congress the power to abolish or interfere, within any state, with the domestic institutions thereof, including that of persons held to labor or servitude by the laws of said state." This extraordinary amendment was adopted on March 2, 1861, by a Congress that was overwhelmingly composed of members from the NORTHERN STATES, since by that time representatives and senators from seven Southern states that had already seceded were not present. President ABRAHAM LINCOLN took the extraordinary and completely unnecessary step of signing the amendment (the SUPREME COURT had ruled in 1798 that the president had no role to play in the approving of amendments), the first time a president has signed a proposed amendment to the Constitution. Three states—Ohio, Illinois, and Maryland—quickly ratified the amendment, but the start of the war one month later ended any prospect of avoiding war by preserving slavery.

The second Thirteenth Amendment was proposed in April 1864, a year before the war came to an end. It passed the Senate 38 to 6, far more than the two-thirds necessary to adopt an amendment, but it was defeated in the House 95 to 66. On reconsideration, the House in January 1865 adopted the amendment 119 to 56. President Lincoln once again signed it, and it was ratified by three-fourths of the Northern states in December 1865. The Thirteenth Amendment in full reads: "Neither slavery, nor involuntary servitude, except as a punishment for crime whereof the party shall have been duly convicted, shall exist within the United States, or any place subject to their jurisdiction. Congress shall have power to enforce this article by appropriate legislation." This simple language, as ANGELA DAVIS and other 20th-century prison-reform activists point out, does not technically abolish slavery, rather it is allowed as punishment for crime if persons are "duly convicted." (Davis and other prison-reform advocates invoked this language to suggest that many African Americans in prison constitute "20th-century slaves.")

In addition to abolishing slavery, some legal commentators and justices of the Supreme Court have contended that the amendment also was intended to abolish the "badges and incidents" and "burdens and disabilities" of slavery. For example, Justice John Marshall Harlan in his dissenting opinion in *PLESSY V. FERGUSON* argued that the Thirteenth Amendment forbade SEGREGATION on railroad cars because "The arbitrary separation of citizens on the basis of race, while they are on a public highway, is a badge of servitude, wholly inconsistent with civil freedom and the equality before the law established by the Constitution." A hundred years later in *Jones v. Alfred H. Mayer Co.* (1968), a case involving racial DISCRIMINATION in the purchase of housing, Justice Potter Stewart, writing for the majority, concluded, "At the very least, the freedom that Congress is empowered to secure under the Thirteenth Amendment includes the freedom to buy whatever a white man can buy, the right to live wherever a white man can live. If Congress can not say that being a free man means at least this much, then the Thirteenth Amendment made a promise the nation can not keep." And Justice William O. Douglas in a concurring opinion added that "the true curse of slavery is not what it did to the black man, but what it has done to the white man. For the existence of the institution produced the notion that the white man was of superior character, intelligence and morality. . . . Some badges of slavery remain today. While the institution has been outlawed, it has remained in the minds and hearts of many white men. Cases which come to this court depict a spectacle of a slavery unwilling to die." This broad interpretation of the amendment to abolish any forms of racially based discrimination or disabilities, however, was largely abandoned after the tenure of Chief Justice EARL WARREN.

Thomas, Clarence (1948–) *106th justice of the U.S. Supreme Court*

Clarence Thomas was the second African American appointed to the SUPREME COURT. Thomas was nominated by President George Bush in 1991 to succeed THURGOOD MARSHALL, an NAACP lawyer and the first African American to serve on the court. Because of his adherence to the IDEOLOGY of CONSERVATISM, Thomas's appointment was widely opposed by the black LEADERSHIP establishment, including black intellectuals, the black ORGANIZATIONS of lawyers, ELECTED OFFICIALS, and the leaders of the major CIVIL RIGHTS organizations.

Some blacks used unusually harsh and vituperative language in their criticisms of Thomas, calling him an UNCLE TOM and a "hustler." RONALD WALTERS in an article in the *Washington Post* wrote that Thomas was "estranged" from his BLACKNESS, and JESSE JACKSON said he was "unworthy to shine the shoes of the hero he would replace." Thomas's appointment was also opposed by the leading CIVIL LIBERTIES organizations and by leaders of women's groups and advocates of FEMINISM, who were concerned that he would week to overturn *Roe v. Wade,* the 1972 decision creating a constitutional right to an abortion. Feminists and black leaders were also concerned about Thomas's appointment because of his opposition to AFFIRMATIVE ACTION.

In spite of this opposition, Thomas's nomination seemed assured of approval by the Senate until allegations of sexual harassment were made against him by Anita Hill. Hill, then an African-American law professor at the University of Oklahoma, alleged that while she was an employee of Thomas's at the EQUAL EMPLOYMENT OPPORTUNITY COMMISSION and the Department of Education, he sexually harassed her by using inappropriate language. Coming just before the Senate was scheduled to vote on his appointment, Hill's allegations created a huge controversy that threatened to block Senate confirmation of his nomination. But after a weekend of sensational, widely watched nationally televised hearings (in which both Thomas and Hill testified) by the Senate's Judiciary Committee, the Senate voted to confirm Thomas, although by the narrowest margin—52 to 48—in the history of Supreme Court nominees. Prior to Hill's allegations polls indicated that most Americans, black and white, did not have an opinion on whether the Senate should confirm Thomas. But those with an opinion favored confirmation by a margin of 25 to 16 percent among blacks and 29 to 12 percent among whites. After the televised hearings (88 percent of whites and 90 percent of blacks reported watching), however, PUBLIC OPINION changed dramatically. At the hearings, Hill had presented her allegations in sometimes graphic detail, while Thomas had angrily and unequivocally denied them, at one point accusing his critics of a "high-tech LYNCHING" of an "uppity nigger" who refused to adhere to the liberal orthodoxy of the black establishment. Most Americans after the hearings thought that Hill's allegations "should be taken seriously" and, if true, Thomas should not be confirmed, but most Americans also did not believe Hill. Only 34 percent of blacks and 35 percent of whites in a *New York Times* poll agreed that Hill's allegations were "probably true." Thus, as the Senate prepared to vote and with black leaders still calling for his defeat, polls indicated that 58 percent of whites and 70 percent of blacks favored his confirmation. Ironically, then, if Hill's allegations were a last-minute attempt by his critics to block his nomination, they had the opposite effect, with public support for his confirmation increasing among blacks from 25 to 70 percent and among whites from 29 to 58 percent.

As the 21st century began, Thomas had completed a decade on the Court and, as his critics feared, during this period he became perhaps its most conservative member. Thomas's conservative jurisprudence is based on "originalism," the principle that in interpreting the CONSTITUTION, justices should follow the original intent of the framers of the document and its subsequent amendments. This doctrine of originalism contrasts sharply with the liberal jurisprudence of Thurgood Marshall, EARL WARREN, and WILLIAM BRENNAN, who held that the Constitution is a living document that should be interpreted in the context of an ever-changing society. Thomas flatly rejects this kind of LIBERALISM in interpreting the Constitution, viewing it as a violation of the first principles of CONSTITUTIONALISM, which in his view requires strict adherence to original intent.

Thomas's conservative jurisprudence runs the gamut of issues. For example, he rejects the use of the COMMERCE CLAUSE as a basis for the expansion of federal power; takes a narrow view of the scope of the FOURTEENTH AMENDMENT in terms of civil liberties and civil rights; and is a strong supporter of FEDERALISM. In his years on the Court, Thomas has been a reliable member of the Court's narrow five-person majority that shifted the Court in a markedly conservative direction. In some areas he was the Court's most aggressive conservative, calling for a rollback of precedents going back to the NEW DEAL. He was also consistently hostile to abortion (voting to reverse *Roe v. Wade*), BUSING, affirmative action, and to the use of federal power. Thus, his years on the Court have only intensified the hostility of his critics in the BLACK COMMUNITY and among liberals in general. Early in his tenure on the Court, a leading black news magazine, *Emerge,* published a story on Thomas in which he was depicted on the cover as an Uncle Tom, and in a 1995 issue of *Time* magazine he was referred to as "Uncle Tom Justice." Meanwhile Thomas was a hero in conservative circles, widely feted for the courageousness of his conservative jurisprudence in the face of hostile criticisms.

Thomas was born in rural Georgia. Abandoned by his parents at the age of six, he was raised by his grandparents. Thomas attributes to his grandfather a strain of "black puritanism" that helped him to survive and prosper in the midst of the indignities of RACISM, WHITE SUPREMACY, and SEGREGATION. In *Clarence Thomas: A Biography* (2001), a sympathetic account of Thomas's life and career by conservative journalist Andrew Peyton Thomas (no relation), it is suggested that Thomas, perhaps more so than most blacks, was deeply scarred by the pains of INTERNAL INFERIORIZATION because of his dark skin color and his speech patterns. Thomas indicates that these burdens of internal inferiorization continue to have an impact even as an adult who is arguably one of the most powerful blacks in the POWER ELITE. In a December 2000 question-and-answer session with high school students, Thomas revealed that he rarely asked questions during oral arguments before the Court because, as a child attending an all-white school, other students made fun of him because of the dialect he spoke, and as a result he became "self-conscious" about his use of standard English, which caused him to become a listener rather than a talker on the Court.

Thomas attended an all-white Catholic school and the Conception Seminary with the intent of becoming a priest. However, he claims he lost his faith after the assassination of MARTIN LUTHER KING JR. and decided instead to become a lawyer. Given his subsequent passionate opposi-

tion to affirmative action, it is ironic that Thomas was admitted to Holy Cross College (where he was graduated with honors) and Yale Law School as a result of their affirmative action programs. (Thomas's critics see this as hypocrisy, pointing out that he benefited from affirmative action throughout his career—including Bush's selection of him to succeed Marshall as the court's only black—but now wishes to deny similar opportunities to others.) During his college years Thomas was known for his MILITANCY (he wore a BLACK PANTHER PARTY–style beret and hung a photo of MALCOLM X in his dormitory room) and outspoken liberalism. But he made a sharp turn to the right after college and passionately embraced conservatism. The basis for this ideological shift is not clear in the available biographical sources on Thomas. Perhaps it was because his first employment was with conservatives and members of the REPUBLICAN PARTY. Or perhaps it was because as an ambitious young man he saw more opportunities to advance as a black conservative than as a liberal. As one Thomas critic quipped, he "may have taken the right turn to the top when

Clarence Thomas *(U.S. Supreme Court)*

he saw the left lane was crowded," implying that since there are relatively few black conservatives, opportunities for advancement are greater. In any event, Thomas did advance rapidly to one of the highest positions in the POLITICAL SYSTEM, becoming a justice of the Supreme Court at age 43.

After law school Thomas worked as an assistant attorney general of Missouri for the state attorney general, John Danforth. He then worked briefly for the Monsanto Corporation before joining Danforth's staff in Washington when he was elected to the Senate. At the age of 33 he received his first appointment to the federal BUREAUCRACY, named by RONALD REAGAN as the assistant secretary of education for civil rights in 1981. In 1982 Reagan appointed him chairman of the Equal Employment Opportunity Commission, and in 1990 President Bush made him a judge of the Court of Appeals for the DISTRICT OF COLUMBIA. A year later he was appointed to the Supreme Court.

At the beginning of the 21st century, Thomas at age 53 was the Court's youngest member. Given his age and the tenure pattern of justices, it is possible he could serve for another 30 years. Whether, if he serves until he is an old man, he will continue his conservative jurisprudence is unclear. Justices of the Court have been known to change their judicial philosophies as they age or as circumstances change. Friends of Thomas contend that his doctrinaire conservatism in his first decade on the Court is only partly a result of conviction and ideology. They suggest that his conservatism is also a function of his continuing feelings of anger, bitterness, and disappointment as a result of what he calls the "plain whipping" he took during the confirmation process. Thomas's friends suggest that, with time, these feelings may wane and with them perhaps some of Justice Thomas's conservative jurisprudence.

Further reading: Scott Gerber, *First Principles: The Jurisprudence of Clarence Thomas* (New York: New York University Press, 1999); Thomas Phelps and Helen Winternitz, *Capitol Games: Clarence Thomas, Anita Hill and the Story of a Supreme Court Nomination* (New York: Hyperion, 1992).

three-fifths clause, U.S. Constitution

The three-fifths clause is the most infamous part of the CONSTITUTION insofar as black Americans are concerned. This is because it formalizes RACISM and WHITE SUPREMACY in the document, reflecting the debased, dehumanized status of African peoples in the minds of the Constitution's framers. The clause deals with how the enslaved African peoples were to be counted for purposes of taxation and REPRESENTATION in the CONGRESS.

Prior to adoption of the Sixteenth Amendment (permitting Congress to tax income directly), Congress could only lay and collect taxes on the basis of the size of a state's population. The larger a state's population, the greater was its tax burden. For this reason the SOUTHERN STATES insisted that the enslaved POPULATION should not be counted since, like horses and cows, they were property. However for purposes of representation in the House (where each state is allocated seats on the basis of the size of its population) the South wished to count the slaves as persons, although they of course could not vote. This would not only enhance the power of the South in the House but also in choosing the president, since the number of votes a state can cast for president in the ELECTORAL COLLEGE is equal to the total of its representation in the House and Senate. The NORTHERN STATES on the other hand wished to count the slaves for purposes of taxation but not representation. Hence, the great compromise. In U.S. Constitution, art. 1, sec. 4:

> Representatives and direct taxes shall be apportioned among the several states that may be included within this union, according to their respective numbers, which shall be determined by adding to the whole number of free persons, including those bound to service for a term of years and excluding Indians not taxed, three-fifths of all other persons.

The effect of this decision was to increase the Southern states's share of House seats from 41 to 46 percent. In attempting to justify or explain this compromise, James Madison (in *Federalist* No. 54) disingenuously puts his words in the mouth of a fictional Southerner:

> The Federal Constitution, therefore, decides with great propriety on the case of our slaves, when it views them in the mixed character of persons and property. . . . Let the slaves be considered, as it is in truth a peculiar one. Let the compromising expedient of the Constitution be mutually adopted which regards them as inhabitants, but as debased by servitude below the equal level of free inhabitants; which regards the slave as divested as of two fifths of the man.

But as Professor Donald Robinson in *Slavery in the Structure of American Politics* (1971) so astutely observes, "It bears repeating, however, that Madison's formula did not make blacks three-fifths of a human being. It was much worse than that. It gave slave owners a bonus in representation for their human property, while doing nothing for the status of blacks as nonpersons under the law." The clause's legal or constitutional effects were eliminated with the adoption of the FOURTEENTH AMENDMENT, but the clause remains in the amended Constitution as an ugly stain on the document and as a slur on the humanity of African Americans.

TransAfrica

TransAfrica, organized in 1977, is the principal ORGANIZATION of African Americans focusing on U.S. FOREIGN POLICY toward Africa and the Caribbean.

In the 1930s W. E. B. DU BOIS and PAUL ROBESON, among others, organized the COUNCIL OF AFRICAN AFFAIRS, which focused on U.S. policy toward Africa. The Council on African Affairs's embrace of RADICALISM and COMMUNISM in the context of the COLD WAR resulted in POLITICAL REPRESSION of the council and its leaders. The rise of MCCARTHYISM in the 1950s helped to contribute to the collapse of the council as an African-American interest organization, as it lost the support of the mainstream black LEADERSHIP establishment. Thereafter, there were several organizations of African Americans interested in African affairs—especially COLONIALISM—including the African American Institute, the Washington Task Force on Africa, and the African Liberation Support Committee. These organizations, however, were small, underfunded, and poorly staffed, and as a result they exercised little influence on CONGRESS or the foreign-policy BUREAUCRACY.

TransAfrica arose out of these earlier organizations, but it learned from their experiences and sought to establish itself as a well-funded and well-staffed organization that avoided the kind of radicalism that had resulted in the collapse of the Council on African Affairs. Indeed, TransAfrica was organized and its initial directions were established by the black leadership establishment. Specifically, it emerged out of a 1976 conference of the CONGRESSIONAL BLACK CAUCUS convened to explore ways that African Americans could influence the policy of President Gerald Ford toward white-ruled Rhodesia. The conference, under the leadership of CHARLES DIGGS and ANDREW YOUNG, brought together more than 30 national black leaders who concluded that they could do little to alter the administration's support for the white-supremacist regime in Rhodesia or its Africa policies generally. After the conference, the Congressional Black Caucus concluded that this problem could only be corrected by the establishment of a black-American organization devoted exclusively to LOBBYING on African foreign-policy issues. As a Congressional Black Caucus statement declared, "the conspicuous absence of African Americans in high level international affairs position and the general subordination, if not neglect, of African and Caribbean priorities could only be corrected by the establishment of a private advocacy organization." Thus, TransAfrica, the "Black American Lobby for Africa and the Caribbean," was born.

Since its inception until the beginning of the 21st century, the organization was led by RANDALL ROBINSON. With the support of the Congressional Black Caucus and other black leaders and organizations, Robinson quickly made TransAfrica a well-funded (with corporate, foundation, and individual contributions), well-staffed, and respected lobby on African issues. TransAfrica's rapid rise to influence was facilitated by the 1976 election of JIMMY CARTER to the PRESIDENCY, because Carter brought a concern for HUMAN RIGHTS to foreign-policy priorities, and he selected Andrew Young for a senior position in the foreign-policy bureaucracy, appointing him ambassador to the UNITED NATIONS.

Since its founding, TransAfrica's influence on U.S. foreign policy has been considerable. It worked to impose and maintain sanctions against Rhodesia until the white-ruled government agreed to yield power and negotiate the creation of the independent nation of Zimbabwe. It successfully lobbied Congress to pass an amendment ending intervention by the CIA in the Angolan civil war. And with somewhat less success, it lobbied for increased U.S. foreign assistance and trade with African and Caribbean nations. Perhaps TransAfrica's most important contribution to changing U.S. foreign policy was its role in organizing the Free South Africa movement. This movement began on Thanksgiving eve 1984 when Robinson and two other black leaders staged a SIT-IN at the South African embassy in the DISTRICT OF COLUMBIA. This demonstration sparked a series of PROTESTs, including boycotts, mass demonstrations, and a sustained lobbying campaign that eventually resulted in passage of the Comprehensive Anti-Apartheid Act of 1986. This act, which imposed economic sanctions on South Africa, was passed by Congress by overriding RONALD REAGAN's veto, and it was a contributing factor to the dismantling of APARTHEID. With the end of apartheid in South Africa and the independence of Zimbabwe and Namibia, the African continent was for the first time since the 1880s free of European colonialism and rule by white-supremacist regimes. TransAfrica subsequently turned its attention to ending military rule and bringing democracy to the black-led governments on the continent. TransAfrica also led the lobbying efforts in the early 1990s to get President BILL CLINTON's administration to intervene in HAITI to restore Jean-Bertrand Aristide, the democratically elected president, to office. And Randall Robinson went on a 27-day hunger strike to protest what he saw as RACISM in the refusal of the United States to admit Haitian refugees on the same basis as those from Cuba and other nonblack nations.

In addition to its lobbying and protest activities, TransAfrica published two quarterly journals and held annual policy conferences and periodic policy symposiums. It also conducted seminars to prepare blacks to take the foreign-service examination. In 2000 Robinson took up the cause of REPARATIONS, publishing a widely publicized book on the subject (*The Debt: What America Owes Blacks*) and attempted to mobilize elite and grassroots support for the idea.

Trotter, William Monroe (1872–1934) *Civil Rights activist*

In the first two decades of the 20th century William Monroe Trotter was, with W. E. B. DU BOIS, the most important leader of the CIVIL RIGHTS MOVEMENT. Trotter, with Du Bois, was among the first black leaders to challenge BOOKER T. WASHINGTON's strategy of ACCOMMODATIONISM, was a principal organizer of the NIAGARA MOVEMENT, and was a founder of the NAACP.

Like Du Bois, Trotter was a certified member of the TALENTED TENTH. His father, James Trotter, was a businessman and race-conscious political activist in Boston who, unlike most blacks in the post-RECONSTRUCTION era, was a member of the DEMOCRATIC PARTY. James Trotter's affiliation with the Democrats led President Grover Cleveland to appoint him to the highest position in the BUREAUCRACY then available to African Americans, Recorder of Deeds for the DISTRICT OF COLUMBIA, a post previously headed by FREDERICK DOUGLASS. The young Trotter therefore grew up in a politically conscious household in Boston, a city known for its history and tradition of LIBERALISM on issues of race. Trotter, also like Du Bois, was intellectually gifted; he was the first African American elected to Phi Beta Kappa at Harvard, where he was graduated in 1895 magna cum laude.

In 1901 Trotter founded *The Guardian,* a Boston newspaper, and immediately made it the most passionate and powerful voice in the black MEDIA opposing Booker T. Washington. In the pages of *The Guardian,* Trotter demanded full EQUALITY and denounced Washington as an UNCLE TOM and traitor to the BLACK COMMUNITY. Trotter's MILITANCY was not limited to words in his newspaper. In 1903 he was jailed for a month after disrupting a speech by Washington in a disturbance that became known as the "Boston Riot." In 1914 Trotter engaged in an angry 45-minute toe-to-toe argument in the White House with President WOODROW WILSON over Wilson's imposition of SEGREGATION in the federal bureaucracy. Although Trotter was widely criticized at the time for being insolent and insulting to the president, the spectacle of a black man forthrightly challenging a president for the practice of RACISM was a personal triumph for him, which increased his status as a national leader. Trotter attacked Wilson because he was disappointed with his stance on segregation and related issues because in 1912, in an early version of the BALANCE OF POWER strategy, Trotter had urged blacks to abandon the REPUBLICAN PARTY and support Wilson, the Democratic nominee. Thus, Trotter felt that Wilson had betrayed him and the black community.

In 1915 Trotter was a leader in organizing PROTESTs against *THE BIRTH OF A NATION,* a white-supremacist film. And in 1919 he attempted to lead a delegation to the Paris Peace Conference in order to press the victorious nations to include a clause in the peace treaty calling for the elimination in all nations of all forms of racial DISCRIMINATION. When the U.S. State Department refused to grant passports for Trotter's delegation, Trotter made the trip by hiring out as a cook on a ship heading to France. Although he was unable to influence the proceedings of the conference, Trotter was able to get his views aired in the French media, and the trip to the conference enhanced his leadership status back in the United States. Trotter's biographer, Stephen Fox, in *The Guardian of Boston,* concludes that Trotter's significance as a black leader rests on three well-publicized incidents: the encounter with Wilson in 1914, the protests against *Birth of a Nation* in 1915, and the trip to France in 1919; "Thereafter he did nothing that attracted comparable attention and his leadership position eroded."

Trotter's significance as an African-American leader did decline after 1919, but these three incidents do not do justice to Trotter's historical significance as a leader of the black community. His major significance is in neither of these incidents but rather in his militant challenge of Booker Washington's accommodationism and his articulation of protest as an alternative strategy. As a leader of the Niagara movement he attempted to put this strategy into practice, writing with Du Bois the *Niagara Manifesto,* which became the agenda of the modern Civil Rights movement. Trotter was among the few blacks in the early leadership of the NAACP. However, he broke with the association early on because his "idiosyncratic independence" was a source of tension and conflict with Du Bois and others in the emerging NAACP bureaucracy and because of his abiding skepticism about the viability of interracial COALITIONS, a reflection of his distrust of white liberals. Thus, he left the NAACP and established the all-black National Equal Rights League. The Equal Rights League never attained the status of the NAACP, in part because of its militancy, its lack of funding, and Trotter's idiosyncratic style of leadership, which was described as "austere and opinionated." But his militancy, his emphasis on race solidarity, and his support of independent black ORGANIZATIONs anticipates the 1960s BLACK POWER MOVEMENT.

The last years of Trotter's life were filled with frustrations and disappointments: his health declined; his wife, who was his close collaborator, died; old colleagues abandoned him; he was unable to continue publishing the paper; and his importance as a national leader was barely acknowledged. On his 62nd birthday, Trotter probably committed suicide by jumping from the roof of a building. Although there has never been a definitive determination of the cause of his death and it might have been accidental, the evidence strongly suggests that Trotter decided to end his life because he saw no way to effectively continue the work of his life.

Further reading: Stephen R. Fox, *The Guardian of Boston: William Monroe Trotter* (New York: Atheneum, 1970).

Truman, Harry S. (1884–1972)   *33rd president of the United States*

Harry Truman in 1948 became the first DEMOCRATIC PARTY president to propose CIVIL RIGHTS legislation and the first from either party to propose civil rights legislation in the 20th century, indeed the first since Republican president BENJAMIN HARRISON in the 1880s. Truman became president after the death of FRANKLIN D. ROOSEVELT, who had avoided taking any initiatives on civil rights for fear of antagonizing the racists and white supremacists who controlled the Democratic Party in the SOUTHERN STATES. Truman decided to take the risks that Roosevelt avoided because he recognized the BALANCE OF POWER role that the black vote might play in the 1948 election and because he saw civil rights as a COLD WAR imperative. Truman was not a racist, but he shared elements of the IDEOLOGY of WHITE SUPREMACY and occasionally referred to blacks in derogatory language. Thus, his ascension to the PRESIDENCY did not suggest he would take an aggressive position on civil rights, but at the end of his presidency WALTER WHITE, head of the NAACP, said "no occupant of the White House since the nation was born has taken so frontal or consistent a stand against racial and religious discrimination as Mr. Truman."

When Truman became president he recognized that blacks were skeptical about his commitment to LIBERALISM and compared him unfavorably with Roosevelt. Although Roosevelt had failed to act substantively on civil rights, the black LEADERSHIP had generally embraced him because of his symbolic gestures (the appointment of the BLACK CABINET and his EXECUTIVE ORDER prohibiting DISCRIMINATION in war-related industries), the racial liberalism of Eleanor Roosevelt, and the NEW DEAL's development of the WELFARE STATE. Thus Truman, like LYNDON B. JOHNSON after he succeeded JOHN F. KENNEDY, felt he had to reach out to black voters to maintain their support in the Democratic Party COALITION. Although Missouri, Truman's home state, was a border state, it (like Lyndon Johnson's Texas) shared the basic mores of the Southern states on RACE issues. This reinforced Truman's desire to establish good relations with the BLACK COMMUNITY.

Truman's first initiative on civil rights came in December 1946 when he appointed a 15-person presidential committee on civil rights. This committee, which included two blacks, was charged with determining what measures might

be necessary to "safeguard the civil rights of the people." In June 1947 Truman became the first president to address the NAACP, giving a passionate speech before the group at the Lincoln Memorial and declaring that it was the duty of the federal government to protect the civil rights of all Americans. Later, he directed the DEPARTMENT OF JUSTICE to intervene in LITIGATION before the SUPREME COURT in cases seeking to end SEGREGATION in the housing market. Truman also promised to issue executive orders prohibiting discrimination in federal employment and in the U.S. MILITARY. In taking these steps, Truman invoked the cold war, suggesting that the nation's success in the struggle against international COMMUNISM required "correcting imperfections in our practice of democracy."

These initiatives alarmed the racists and white supremacists who controlled the Democratic Party in the Southern states, and they threatened to withdraw from the party coalition. This threat caused Truman to hesitate. When the president's committee on civil rights issued its report in the fall of 1947 (calling for, among other things, abolition of the poll tax, legislation making LYNCHING a federal crime, and prohibitions on discrimination in interstate transportation), the White House downplayed its importance. The president also postponed issuing the executive orders on discrimination in federal employment and in the military. And when HUBERT HUMPHREY successfully persuaded the Democratic Party to adopt a civil rights platform, he did so over Truman's objections. The die, however, was cast; the Democratic Party's adoption of a civil rights platform—the first in its history—caused the Southern Democrats to walk out of the party convention and mount a THIRD PARTY challenge to Truman's election. (Strom Thurmond of South Carolina ran as the Dixiecrat Party presidential candidate.) This forced Truman to change his political calculations. He recognized that the votes of the white South might be lost, and facing a challenge from the racially liberal Progressive Party candidate Henry Wallace, he saw the black vote as even more crucial to his election. In addition, the prospective REPUBLICAN PARTY candidate, New York's governor Thomas Dewey, had a generally progressive record on civil rights. Thus, in a famous memorandum, Clark Clifford, Truman's chief political strategist, advised him that the black vote could be the balance of power in the election and that a strong commitment to civil rights was "the politically advantageous thing to do." Interestingly, Henry Moon, the NAACP's public relations director, published his book *Balance of Power: The Negro Vote* just as the 1948 campaign was getting underway. In it he argued that the black vote could be the margin of victory in the ELECTORAL COLLEGE in 12 NORTHERN STATES. (Walter White had an autographed copy of the book sent to Truman.)

The cumulative result of these developments was an aggressive embrace of civil rights by Truman in rhetoric and PUBLIC POLICY. In his speeches he described civil rights as a national and international imperative. In terms of public policy he reversed himself and submitted a civil rights bill to CONGRESS based on the report of his civil rights committee and issued the long-postponed executive orders banning discrimination in federal employment and in the military. These actions by Truman were directly attributable to Truman's concern about winning the election and the persistent LOBBYING of the black LEADERSHIP, especially Walter White and A. PHILIP RANDOLPH. In a stunning upset, Truman won the 1948 election, defeating the Republican, Dixiecrat, and Progressive candidates. Truman won 69 percent of the black vote, which was the decisive factor—the balance of power—in his election.

Once elected, however, Truman again reversed himself. Although he continued his rhetorical commitment to civil rights, he did not actively lobby Congress on behalf of his civil rights bills, which did not pass either house of Congress. Truman also set in motion a process that began to associate civil rights PROTEST with disloyalty or "un-Americanism," a process that helped to create a climate conducive to POLITICAL REPRESSION and that eventually ended in MCCARTHYISM. Nevertheless, Truman's executive orders, the report of his civil rights committee, and his rhetoric are part of the legacy that subsequent presidents, the Congress, and the Supreme Court used to enact the comprehensive civil rights legislation of the 1960s. A part of the Truman legacy is its demonstration of the significance of the black vote in presidential elections. On the other hand, it also revealed the significance of the SOUTHERN STRATEGY as a counterweight to the black vote.

Further reading: William C. Berman, *The Politics of Civil Rights in the Truman Administration* (Columbus: Ohio State University Press, 1970).

Truth, Sojourner (1799–1883) *abolitionist, feminist*
Sojourner Truth is one of the most famous leaders in the African-American struggle for FREEDOM and EQUALITY. She is also famous because she is one of the earliest black female leaders to unambiguously embrace FEMINISM, arguing that the struggle against SEXISM was as important as the struggle against RACISM.

Truth was born as Isabella Bomefree, an enslaved person in the state of New York. After SLAVERY was abolished in New York, she became free and joined a utopian community in Massachusetts that was committed to equality for blacks and women. RELIGIOSITY had played a role in her life since childhood, and in 1843 her deep religious convictions led her to change her name to Sojourner Truth. While at the Massachusetts commune she met FREDERICK DOUGLASS and other leaders of the ABOLITIONIST MOVEMENT.

Soon she was recruited as a lecturer on the antislavery circuit where, because of her powerful oratory, she gained a national following. However, most men in the abolitionist movement were sexist and thought it was inappropriate for women to engage in public speaking or LEADERSHIP. When Truth was challenged in 1851 by a white minister who claimed that it was God's will that women be subordinate to men, she responded with her famous "And Ain't I a Woman" speech, an iconic text in the literature of American feminism. During the CIVIL WAR Truth served as a nurse to black soldiers. She also met with three U.S. presidents, ABRAHAM LINCOLN, ANDREW JOHNSON, and ULYSSES S. GRANT. During the debate about the FIFTEENTH AMENDMENT, she broke with Frederick Douglass and most other black leaders and joined with white feminists in opposing the amendment because it gave black men the right to vote while denying it to women.

Although illiterate, she dictated her autobiography, *The Narrative of Sojourner Truth*, which was initially published during the 1850s. Truth is perhaps the most important symbolic figure in African-American feminist discourse.

See also MARIA W. STEWART.

Further reading: Nell Irvin Painter, *Sojourner Truth: A Life, a Symbol* (New York: W. W. Norton, 1996).

Tubman, Harriet (ca. 1821–1913) *abolitionist*
Harriet Tubman is a legendary figure in the history of the African-American struggle for FREEDOM because of her role in developing and implementing a systematic strategy for the escape of African Americans from SLAVERY. The fear that enslaved persons would escape from their OPPRESSION was omnipresent among the slaveholders, leading to insertion of the FUGITIVE SLAVE CLAUSE into the CONSTITUTION and acts of CONGRESS to punish runaway slaves and those who assisted or harbored them. Tubman developed an ingenious system involving the use of MUSIC as codes and an elaborate series of secret routes that between 1849 and the 1860s facilitated the escape of an estimated 300 enslaved persons on her Underground Railroad.

Tubman was born to enslaved parents in Maryland in about 1821 (the exact year is uncertain) and began her work helping runaway slaves by escaping herself in 1849. After her escape, she returned to rescue her sisters and children. Thus began the first of more than a dozen journeys into the SOUTHERN STATES to rescue enslaved people. Although she suffered from frequent seizures as a result of a beating by a slave overseer, she was nonetheless able to carry on this skilled and dangerous work partly because her deep RELIGIOSITY made her believe that her work was guided by divine providence. Southern slaveholders placed a huge bounty for her capture or death, but she eluded capture while becoming famously known as the "Moses" of her people. Tubman's work prevented her from playing an overt leadership role in the ABOLITIONIST MOVEMENT, but she was a friend of FREDERICK DOUGLASS and JOHN BROWN and even considered joining Brown in his ill-fated use of VIOLENCE at the 1859 Harpers Ferry raid (Tubman usually carried a gun). During the CIVIL WAR she continued to rescue slaves while serving as a spy and nurse in the Union army. After the war she worked with the BLACK CHURCH to establish schools for the newly freed slaves and homes for the elderly and destitute. Late in her life she was associated with the NATIONAL ASSOCIATION OF COLORED WOMEN and with white woman suffragists, who reflected her interest in FEMINISM. In the last years of her life, whites and blacks helped to raise money to support her and her charitable works. Despite her long and significant life, Tubman resisted entreaties to write a memoir.

Turner, Henry M. (1834–1915) *church leader, black nationalist*

Henry M. Turner is one of the most paradoxical personalities ever to occupy an important place in the established structure of black LEADERSHIP. A passionate advocate of BLACK NATIONALISM, with MARCUS GARVEY and MARTIN DELANY he is probably the foremost advocate of BACK-TO-AFRICA movements in U.S. history. But he also embraced a key element of the IDEOLOGY of WHITE SUPREMACY, believing that SLAVERY was God's will—a "providential institution"—to civilize African peoples. Yet he was one of the first BLACK CHURCH leaders to proclaim that God was black. Turner at one stage of his career embraced CONSERVATISM and ACCOMMODATIONISM in the tradition of BOOKER T. WASHINGTON, yet his later MILITANCY and RADICALISM anticipate the ideas of MALCOLM X and LOUIS FARRAKHAN. But the paradoxes in Turner's leadership—what one writer calls his "maddeningly inconsistent" political behavior—can be understood not as a function of Turner's personality or his proclivity for political vacillation but rather as the adaptation of a creative mind to the changing character of racial OPPRESSION during the period of his leadership. W. E. B. DU BOIS, another black leader accused of political inconsistency and ideological vacillation, once responded that African Americans face a "condition not a theory" and therefore they should embrace any ideology or strategy that at any particular time and place seemed most likely to advance the struggle for FREEDOM and EQUALITY.

Turner was born a FREE NEGRO in South Carolina in 1834. Although he was never enslaved, he was familiar with the brutalities of SLAVERY because he frequently worked with slaves. As a young man he learned how to read and

write and soon caught the attention of clergy in the largely white Methodist Episcopal Church, who recruited him as an itinerant preacher. During the 1850s he traveled throughout the SOUTHERN STATES preaching to blacks and sometime whites. The turning point in Turner's career came in 1858 when he joined the all-black African Methodist Episcopal Church (AME). Assigned to the AME congregation in Baltimore, Turner was able to receive theological training and rapidly advanced in the church hierarchy from deacon to elder to pastor of the largest AME congregation in the DISTRICT OF COLUMBIA. During the CIVIL WAR Turner gained national attention when President ABRAHAM LINCOLN named him the army's first black chaplain, an appointment that resulted in part from his friendship with RADICAL REPUBLICAN leaders like THADDEUS STEVENS and CHARLES SUMNER. After the war he moved to Georgia, where he worked briefly for the FREEDMEN'S BUREAU, but his main work was as the presiding elder of the AME church in the state and the state's leading African American in the REPUBLICAN PARTY. While recruiting thousands of blacks to the church and hundreds to the clergy, Turner became active in state and local politics. Because of his successes in recruiting blacks to the church, white Republican Party leaders asked him to organize black voters in the state. It is at this point that he embraced conservatism and accommodationism.

As a delegate to the convention that wrote Georgia's RECONSTRUCTION-era constitution, Turner consistently took the side of the large plantation owners, opposing the confiscation or sale of their lands and supporting their demands for a poll tax and a literacy requirement for VOTING RIGHTS. Turner took these positions apparently because he believed that the conservative whites who controlled the state would allow educated African-Americans to participate in the state's politics without prejudice or DISCRIMINATION. When this assumption quickly proved wrong, Turner changed his ideology and began to champion the cause of the black masses. Where once he had described his motto in politics as "Anything to please the white man," by the time he became an ELECTED OFFICIAL as a member of the state legislature he had become an advocate for LIBERALISM. During his brief time in the legislature he introduced bills for the education of all freedmen, abolition of the convict lease system, and protection of black workers from other forms of economic exploitation. Most ominously in the minds of his former white allies, Turner proposed the creation of an all-black militia to protect blacks from the then-emerging KU KLUX KLAN–style VIOLENCE and terrorism. Turner served for two years in the legislature. By the time he left in the 1870s, Reconstruction in Georgia was effectively over, undermined by the failure of the federal government to intervene to protect the CIVIL RIGHTS of blacks.

Disillusioned, angry, and bitter about the betrayal of Reconstruction, Turner returned to his church work, becoming a bishop of the AME church in 1880. For more than 20 years he served as a senior bishop, during which time he made major contributions to making the AME church one of the most important institutions in black Christiandom. Recognizing the centrality of RELIGIOSITY in African-American CULTURE and of the church in the institutional life of the BLACK COMMUNITY, Turner attempted to create a black theology based on the basic tenets of Christianity but grounded in the culture of blacks. Although Turner contended that God had ordained slavery so as to provide Africans with the beneficent effects of Christianity (the most effective means to move Africans from "barbarism to Christian civilization"), he was fully aware of the negative consequences of slavery and "white" Christianity on the development of INTERNAL INFERIOR-IZATION. Therefore, his theology proclaimed that "God is a Negro," and he emphasized those tenets of Christianity grounded in freedom and deliverance. As the senior bishop, Turner reorganized the AME bureaucracy and rituals and emphasized SCHOOLS AND EDUCATION, establishing dozens of schools and colleges throughout the Southern states. Turner insisted that these schools be black controlled because only blacks could provide the knowledge that would lead to freedom. The cornerstone of Turner's educational efforts is Morris Brown College, a HISTORICALLY BLACK COLLEGE AND UNIVERSITY that is now a part of the ATLANTA UNIVERSITY complex. Turner directed the development and growth of Morris Brown, serving for a time as its chancellor. Turner's other major church initiative was missionary work in Africa. Consistent with his theological notions about the civilizing effects of Christianity, Turner sent missionaries to Africa and traveled to the continent three times, where he established churches and schools.

In addition to his religious work in the 1880s, Turner continued his secular leadership and was recognized for a time, with FREDERICK DOUGLASS, as the preeminent leader of African Americans. Like Douglass, Turner continued to fight for equality for Africans in America and was the first national black leader to call for REPARATIONS as a means to achieve that objective. But unlike Douglass, Turner increasingly came to believe that equality was not possible for blacks and that emigration to Africa was the only path to freedom. His visits to Africa reinforced this view. But the proverbial straw that broke the camel's back was the SUPREME COURT's decision in the CIVIL RIGHTS CASES OF 1883, declaring the Civil Rights Act of 1875 unconstitutional. Turner's bitter denunciation of the decision was widely reported and hailed throughout black America. He described it as a "barbarous decision . . . that absolv[ed] the allegiance of the Negro to the United States." After this decision, Turner's advocacy of emigration to Africa became passionate and unwavering. When

he used the AME church magazine to advance his views, its control was taken away from him. Undaunted, he established his own journal, *Voice of the People,* to use the MEDIA as a vehicle to advance his broad black-nationalist agenda. This agenda put Turner increasingly at odds with the established black leadership, including both Booker Washington's accommodationist approach and Du Bois's strategy of PROTEST. The conflict between Turner and other black leaders intensified after he attempted to form COALITIONS with those white supremacists and racists who supported emigration because they wanted the United States to be a "white man's country." (For a time Turner served as honorary vice president of the AMERICAN COLONIALIZATION SOCIETY.) Like all previous and subsequent back-to-Africa programs, Turner's met with little success. It was opposed by the black leadership establishment and in all likelihood by black PUBLIC OPINION, which favored INTEGRATION. Turner, however, did not relent. In 1906 he was elected president of the Georgia Equal Rights Association, an ORGANIZATION established by the state's leading blacks. At its convention he made perhaps his most famous speech, which in a way represents the final statement of his ideology. Turner proclaimed, "I used to love . . . the grand old flag, and sing with ecstasy about the stars and stripes, but to a Negro in this country the American flag is a dirty and contemptible rag. Not a star in it can the colored man claim, for it is no longer the symbol of our own manhood rights and liberty. . . . I wish to say that hell is an improvement on the United States where the Negro is concerned."

Bishop Turner died in 1915 at the age of 81 after suffering a heart attack in Ontario, Canada, where he had gone to preside at an AME conference. In his long life he did not write his memoirs and there is, surprisingly, not yet a full-length biography of this important black leader, although the historian Edwin Redkey has compiled a useful collection of his writings, *The Writings and Speeches of Henry MacNeil Turner* (1972).

Further reading: John Dittmer, "The Education of Henry MacNeil Turner," in *Black Leaders of the Nineteenth Century,* ed. Leon Litwack and August Meier (Urbana: University of Illinois Press, 1988), 253–74; Edwin Redkey, "The Flowering of Black Nationalism: Henry MacNeil Turner and Marcus Garvey," in *Key Issues in the Afro-American Experience* Vol. II, ed. Nathan Huggins, Martin Kilson, and Daniel Fox (New York: Harcourt Brace Jovanovich, 1971), 107–24.

Turner, Nat (1800–1831) *slave rebel*

Of the stories of SLAVE REVOLTS that mark the history of SLAVERY in the United States, the one led by Nat Turner is the most famous and historically significant.

Like most who led slave rebellions, Turner was inspired by RELIGIOSITY. Turner was a religious mystic and visionary whom some enslaved persons referred to as "The Prophet." In Turner's mind, the revolt he led in 1831 in Southampton, Virginia, was inspired by a vision from God. On August 31 Turner and six other men armed with a hatchet and ax began their bloody rebellion. First, they killed Turner's owner, Joseph Travis, and his family, and then within 24 hours at least 50 other whites were killed. No white person in their path was spared except a family of poor whites who owned no slaves. Even infants were killed. When one of his men protested that children should be spared, Turner reportedly responded "nits make lice" and ordered the child killed. As the 24-hour rebellion continued, more than 50 other enslaved persons joined Turner's brigade. When the first bodies were discovered, panic spread throughout the white population and men, women, and children rushed to public buildings or fled into the Virginia swamps. POLITICAL REPRESSION and VIOLENCE against blacks in the state in the days after the revolt were widespread, and dozens of innocent blacks were tortured or killed. Turner and his men eluded capture by the military for two months, which intensified the sense of panic among whites in Virginia and many other SOUTHERN STATES. When he was captured and placed on trial, Turner pleaded not guilty, saying he did not feel guilty. He was executed by hanging on November 11th.

Although Turner's revolt lasted only 24 hours, it had an important impact on American politics. It increased the MILITANCY of the ABOLITIONIST MOVEMENT while spurring further efforts to repress the entire black POPULATION, FREE NEGROES as well as the enslaved. It also shattered the myth, widespread among whites, that enslaved Africans were docile and contented. For this reason some African

A broadside depicting Nat Turner's rebellion *(Library of Congress)*

Americans consider Turner to be one of the greatest black leaders of all time, although his contribution consisted of a single day's work.

Further reading: Herbert Aptheker, *Nat Turner's Slave Revolt* (New York: Humanities Press, 1966); Stephen Oakes, *The Fires of Jubilee: Nat Turner's Fierce Rebellion* (New York: Harper & Row, 1975).

Tuskegee Institute

Tuskegee Institute (now known as Tuskegee University) is one of the most important HISTORICALLY BLACK COLLEGES AND UNIVERSITIES. Founded in 1881 in Tuskegee, Alabama, by BOOKER T. WASHINGTON, Tuskegee is historically important because it is the paradigmatic site for the implementation of Washington's philosophy of vocational and industrial education. Tuskegee's curriculum became the model for the colleges and universities established by the SOUTHERN STATES to educate African Americans, a model that lasted until the late 1940s. The Tuskegee model for black education is contrasted with the liberal arts education model and the TALENTED TENTH concept advanced by W. E. B. DU BOIS. The sites of the Du Bois model were institutions like HOWARD UNIVERSITY and ATLANTA UNIVERSITY. Tuskegee is also historically significant because it was the site of Washington's "Tuskegee Machine." That is, the Tuskegee Institute was the place from which Washington developed ACCOMMODATIONISM as a leadership strategy and exercised his near-dictatorial POWER in the BLACK COMMUNITY until his death in 1915. After Washington's death Tuskegee gradually declined as an important site of black education and political power. In the POST–CIVIL RIGHTS ERA the university, like many other historically black universities, was in a continuous struggle to maintain its viability.

See also SCHOOLS AND EDUCATION.

Twenty-fourth Amendment, U.S. Constitution

The Twenty-fourth Amendment to the CONSTITUTION prohibits the states from requiring citizens to pay a poll tax or any other fee as qualifications to vote for president, vice president, or members of Congress. It was adopted in 1964 in part as a response to the growing influence of the CIVIL RIGHTS MOVEMENT. The poll tax (a requirement that citizens pay a small fee in order to register to vote) was among the many mechanisms adopted in many of the SOUTHERN STATES after the end of RECONSTRUCTION to deny VOTING RIGHTS to African Americans. Although the poll tax also affected poor whites, its intent and disproportionate impact was on blacks because they were more likely to live in POVERTY than whites. The amendment only prohibits the use of the poll tax in federal elections, reserving to the states, under the principle of FEDERALISM, the right to continue to use poll taxes in the election of STATE AND LOCAL GOVERNMENT officials. However, the SUPREME COURT in 1966 in *Harper v. Virginia Board of Elections* ruled that a requirement to pay a tax in any election was a violation of the EQUAL PROTECTION CLAUSE of the FOURTEENTH AMENDMENT.

See also FIFTEENTH AMENDMENT and VOTING RIGHTS ACT OF 1965.

Twenty-third Amendment, U.S. Constitution

The Twenty-third Amendment to the CONSTITUTION grants the citizens of the DISTRICT OF COLUMBIA the right to cast votes for president in the ELECTORAL COLLEGE. Adopted in 1961, the amendment provides that the District shall be entitled to the number of electoral votes as if it were a state "but in no event more than the least populous state." The District's population since the amendment's adoption has never entitled it to more than three votes (the number for the least populous states), but this clause means that even if its population increased substantially, the District could never receive full EQUALITY in choosing the president. The District since the amendment's adoption has had a majority black population, so the effect of the amendment is to provide the BLACK COMMUNITY with three of the 538 votes in the electoral college. Or, to put it another way, African-American voters control one of the 51 constituencies that elect the president. The District's black voters, like those elsewhere in the nation, are overwhelmingly affiliated with the DEMOCRATIC PARTY, and the District of Columbia has proved to be the most reliable Democratic Party constituency in the nation. Indeed, during the POST–CIVIL RIGHTS ERA it is the only constituency in the electoral college the REPUBLICAN PARTY has never won.

two-party system

A two-party system is one in which only two parties have a realistic chance of electing persons to political offices because of the structural arrangements of the POLITICAL SYSTEM and the partisan loyalties of the voters. In two-party systems THIRD PARTIES are virtually excluded from the political system, although from time to time they may emerge as instruments of PROTEST and as a means to force the two major parties to place new issues on the PUBLIC POLICY agenda. Since the adoption of the CONSTITUTION, the United States has had a two-party system. Historically, this system has been traced to the early divisions over ratification of the Constitution and a tendency toward moderation rather than RADICALISM in the POLITICAL CULTURE. Structurally, the bias of the two-party system in the United States is the "winner take all" basis of allocating voters in the ELECTORAL COLLEGE and the single-member district system of electing members of CONGRESS, especially members of the House of Representatives. These two structural features inevitably result in a system where only two parties have a realistic chance of winning office. In contrast, political systems with multiple parties use some form of proportional allocation of votes and multimember districts. Virtually all of the nations of the world practicing DEMOCRACY at the end of the 20th century have multiparty systems.

Most political scientists in the United States defend the two-party system, arguing that it avoids radicalism and encourages compromise, moderation, and stability in government. Critics of the system argue that it decreases POLITICAL PARTICIPATION, limits the range of debate on IDEOLOGY and public policy, and dilutes the REPRESENTATION of MINORITY GROUPS. Whatever the general merits of two-party versus multiparty systems, with respect to the BLACK COMMUNITY it is clear that the two-party system in the United States historically has marginalized black voters. This is because, as Paul Frymer shows in *Uneasy Alliances: Race and Party Competition in America* (1999), the two parties inevitably appeal to the "median" or "swing" voter, which in the United States has tended to be racially conservative white voters. This tendency to appeal to the median voter, who is always white and often leaning toward CONSERVATISM or RACISM, inevitably requires both of the parties to ignore or downplay issues of concern to black voters. Frymer contends that the two-party system in the United States was in part designed to keep issues of concern to blacks, primarily SLAVERY, off the public-policy agenda. Thus Frymer contends that the two-party system constitutes a "genuine" form of INSTITUTIONAL RACISM. This institutionally racist nature of the two-party system is only partly a function of the absence of multipartyism. It is also partly a function of the fact that from RECONSTRUCTION (when blacks first got the right to vote) until the start of the 21st century, the two-party system has mainly been a *one-party system* for black voters. Historically, the two-party system has worked reasonably well for white voters, offering them two relatively distinct candidates, programs, and policies from which to choose. But for blacks since they first gained VOTING RIGHTS after the CIVIL WAR, this rarely has been the case.

When blacks first began to vote during Reconstruction, FREDERICK DOUGLASS is said to have told a group of black voters that the "Republican Party is the deck, all else

the sea." What he meant was that only one of the two parties, the REPUBLICAN PARTY, was willing to offer any kind of program or policy to address black concerns. The second party, the DEMOCRATIC PARTY, was unrelentingly hostile. Since Douglass's time, except for a brief period, hardly anything has changed; one party is the deck, the other the sea, except in the POST–CIVIL RIGHTS ERA the Democratic Party is the deck. For the brief period between 1936 and 1964, African-American voters did enjoy the benefits of the two-party system, as both parties competed for the black vote with policy pledges, promises, and patronage. And the black vote, like the white vote, was split between them. For example, in 1960 the Republican nominee for president, RICHARD NIXON, received about one-third of the black vote against JOHN F. KENNEDY, the Democratic nominee. Since 1964, however, the American party system has returned to its normal status for blacks—one partyism. That is, since the 1964 nomination of BARRY GOLDWATER, the Republican Party has embraced a SOUTHERN STRATEGY, a strategy requiring Republicans to ignore the black vote and its policy concerns while going after the antiblack vote in the SOUTHERN STATES and the so-called Reagan Democrats (Democrats from white ETHNIC GROUPS who voted for RONALD REAGAN) in the NORTHERN STATES. And since the election of JIMMY CARTER in 1976, the Democratic Party has increasingly taken the black vote for granted while moving away from LIBERALISM and the policy interests of blacks. The Democratic Party can ignore the ideology and policy concerns of the black vote and appeal to the white "median" or "swing" voter because its leaders know that blacks have no alternative except to vote Democratic as the lesser of two evils or the better of two bad choices. Between 1964 and 2000 the Democrats averaged 90 percent of the black vote in the 10 presidential elections.

In 1924 WALTER WHITE of the NAACP lamented that in a two-party system the "least objectionable alternative exhausts the alternatives available to us." At the beginning of the 21st century White's lament was still correct, and given the structural and other barriers blacks would face in trying to establish a viable third party, it is likely to remain so for a long time unless there are fundamental transformations in one or both of the two parties.

See also BILL CLINTON.

Further reading: Paul Frymer, *Uneasy Alliances: Race and Party Competition in America* (Princeton, N.J.: Princeton University Press, 1999).

U

Uncle Tom

Uncle Tom is a pejorative term used to refer to a category of black LEADERSHIP that is viewed as accepting the subordinate place of African Americans in a system of racial OPPRESSION. The term is also used to refer to blacks who are viewed as traitors to the interests of the BLACK COMMUNITY or who behave in an obsequious way when dealing with whites. GUNNAR MYRDAL used Uncle Tom to refer to leaders that eschewed PROTEST in favor of an ACCOMMODATIONISM that involved a "pattern of begging and pleading to whites" in positions of POWER. The term is sometimes also used to refer to those blacks who have become leaders through CO-OPTATION. All of these uses of Uncle Tom encompass the notion that the leader is not honestly or aggressively pursuing the struggle for FREEDOM and EQUALITY. In some cases "Uncle Tomism" may be a realistic IDEOLOGY or strategy of black leaders, given the disproportionate power of whites at a particular time and place. In others, it may reflect the requirements of the position the leader holds, while in still others it may reflect cowardice or opportunism.

The origins of the term can be traced to *UNCLE TOM'S CABIN*, the 1852 antislavery novel by Harriet Beecher Stowe in which Uncle Tom, an elderly slave who, although frequently beaten by his owner, remained loyal to him. Historically, ISAIAH MONTGOMERY and BOOKER T. WASHINGTON are viewed as paradigmatic Uncle Toms. In the POST–CIVIL RIGHTS ERA the term is sometimes used to refer to those who are viewed as estranged from some aspect of BLACKNESS or who embrace CONSERVATISM. Thus, at the beginning of the 21st century CLARENCE THOMAS, the African-American justice of the SUPREME COURT, was sometimes referred to as an Uncle Tom in the MEDIA and by black intellectuals and political leaders.

Uncle Tom's Cabin

Uncle Tom's Cabin: Life among the Lowly is the 1852 novel written by Harriet Beecher Stowe, a white woman active in the ABOLITIONIST MOVEMENT. The novel, which depicts the suffering of Uncle Tom, a loyal, elderly enslaved man who dies as a result of frequent beatings, was explicitly written to influence PUBLIC OPINION on SLAVERY in the NORTHERN STATES. It had the intended effect; widely read, it is credited with leading thousands to embrace the antislavery cause. (ABRAHAM LINCOLN, on greeting Stowe at the White House, reportedly referred to her as the little lady who started the CIVIL WAR.) The novel's main character is the source of the pejorative term used to refer to an accommodating, obsequious IDEOLOGY or strategy of black LEADERSHIP.

See also ACCOMMODATIONISM.

underclass

Underclass is a term popularized in the POST–CIVIL RIGHTS ERA to refer to persons living in poverty in the GHETTOS of the United States. It was first used by GUNNAR MYRDAL in his 1963 book *The Challenge to Affluence* to categorize what he called "the unemployed and unemployable persons and families at the bottom of society." For Myrdal this group was emerging in the United States because of GLOBALIZATION and transformations in CAPITALISM that had reduced the need for unskilled labor and therefore increased the pool of unemployed and unemployable persons "who have happened to be born in regions, localities, or economic and social strata where education and training for life and work in this new America are not provided as a normal thing." However, as the concept was used by many scholars and in the MEDIA beginning in the 1980s, it became a pejorative term used to refer mainly to blacks in the ghettos—the "black underclass" or the "ghetto underclass"—who displayed a high concentration of social problems (out-of-wedlock births, crime, drug abuse, welfare dependency) that were transmitted intergenerationally. This notion of the underclass is somewhat akin to the concept of the CULTURE OF POVERTY developed by scholars

A poster for the play based on *Uncle Tom's Cabin* (*Library of Congress*)

welfare as causes. The underclass concept was also used by adherents of CONSERVATISM, especially after the election of RONALD REAGAN, to stigmatize the ghetto poor and to call for an end to welfare assistance to them.

This use of the term *underclass* by conservative intellectuals and political leaders led WILLIAM J. WILSON—a leading black PUBLIC INTELLECTUAL who, more so than any other scholar, had given academic respectability to the term—to call for its abandonment. Wilson said the term should be abandoned because it had little scientific usefulness, because it had become a "code word" for poor blacks, and because it allowed journalists to focus on "unflattering" behavior in the ghettos. Wilson defended his earlier usage of the concept by arguing that it had led to greater scientific precision in studying ghetto poverty, but its stigmatizing consequences now outweighed whatever scientific utility it might have had. The underclass concept, however, never had much scientific utility. Rather, it was mainly an ideological word used to denigrate the black poor and buttress the case for cutbacks in the welfare state. As a scientific concept, it did little to advance knowledge of poverty in advanced capitalist societies beyond the 1960s work of Myrdal and the culture-of-poverty scholars. But it did have political utility because its popular and scholarly usage helped to fuel the PUBLIC POLICY debate on welfare and eventually played a role in the process that led in 1996 to reforms that denied long-term welfare assistance to poor women and their children.

See also BILL CLINTON, NATIONAL WELFARE RIGHTS ORGANIZATION and NEW DEAL.

Further readings: Mack H. Jones, "The Black Underclass as a Systemic Phenomenon," in *Race, Politics and Economic Development*, ed. James Jennings (New York: Verso Press, 1992); John MacNicol, "In Pursuit of the Underclass," *Journal of Social Policy* 16 (1989): 289–326; Garry Ralison, "An Exploration of the Underclass Term as It Relates to African Americans," *Journal of Black Studies* 23 (1991): 186–203.

United Nations

The United Nations (UN), founded in 1945, is the major organization of the international community. It represents an attempt by the nations of the world to develop international rules of conduct, provide procedures for the peaceful settlement of disputes, and encourage cooperation among the peoples and nations of the world in dealing with social and economic problems.

From its inception the LEADERSHIP of black America and leaders of the THIRD WORLD have viewed the UN as an important organization in their struggles for FREEDOM and EQUALITY. This view of the UN's role goes back to its pre-

during the 1960s. But unlike the culture-of-poverty literature, which focused on the lack of FULL EMPLOYMENT and an inadequate WELFARE STATE as causes of the phenomenon, the underclass, literature tended to focus on cultural deficiencies of poor people and dependency on decessor, the League of Nations. At the Paris Peace Conference establishing the league, Japan—the most influential nonwhite nation at the conference—attempted to insert a clause in the league charter banning racial DISCRIMINATION. This clause was supported by W. E. B. DU BOIS, WILLIAM MONROE TROTTER, and other African-American leaders attending the conference. The clause, however, was rejected largely at the insistence of WOODROW WILSON. At the founding of the UN, Iraq and China again asked for an antidiscrimination clause, and they were again supported by black leaders including Du Bois, MARY MCLEOD BETHUNE, and WALTER WHITE. The United States, Britain, and the Soviet Union initially opposed the clause. However, they later relented and agreed to a clause guaranteeing the nations and peoples of the world freedom from discrimination on the basis of "race, language, religion or sex." But, like all other international conventions or treaties on HUMAN RIGHTS that the United States has agreed to, it included (at U.S. insistence) a provision that the ban on discrimination not be self-executing. That is, the ban could not become a basis for legal action against the United States without a comparable act of CONGRESS. African-American leaders and ORGANIZATIONS (including the NAACP, the NATIONAL COUNCIL OF NEGRO WOMEN, and the COUNCIL ON AFRICAN AFFAIRS) also joined with Third World nations to demand an end to COLONIALISM, but again the United States joined with the European powers to defeat the call for immediate independence for the nations of Africa and Asia. With the assistance of RALPH BUNCHE (a technical adviser to the U.S. delegation), the UN did create a Trusteeship Council, whose principal responsibility was to oversee administration of the colonial territories seized from Germany and Italy as well as any other areas the colonial powers might voluntarily surrender to its supervision. Finally, African-American leaders and organizations were among the strongest supporters of the UNIVERSAL DECLARATION OF HUMAN RIGHTS, adopted in 1948. And Ralph Bunche, the African-American political scientist, left the FOREIGN POLICY bureaucracy of the United States to join the newly organized UN's, eventually becoming undersecretary general, the second ranking post in the UN administrative structure.

As soon as the UN was formed, black leaders and organizations began to turn to it as a forum to attack RACISM and WHITE SUPREMACY in the United States. In 1946 the NATIONAL NEGRO CONGRESS filed a petition with the UN Social and Economic Council protesting the OPPRESSION of African Americans. The document, prepared by HERBERT APTHEKER, cited the sections of the UN charter dealing with human rights, reviewed evidence on discrimination and VIOLENCE against blacks, and called for actions to protect their rights. In 1947 Du Bois presented to the UN on behalf of the NAACP "An Appeal to the World" detailing the oppression of blacks in the SOUTHERN STATES and calling for action by the international community. The appeal was endorsed by hundreds of black organizations and several Third World leaders, including Jomo Kenyatta of Kenya and Kwame Nkrumah of Ghana. In 1955 Congressman CHARLES DIGGS wrote Undersecretary General Bunche requesting his assistance in submitting the "race" question in America to the proper agency within the United Nations. And at the time of his death in 1965, MALCOLM X was seeking support among African and Islamic nations for a petition charging the United States with violating the Universal Declaration of Human Rights. Although the UN did not act on any of these appeals, it did provide a forum for the internationalization of the CIVIL RIGHTS MOVEMENT, and in the context of the COLD WAR, these appeals for redress were a source of embarrassment and pressure on the U.S. government.

In the POST–CIVIL RIGHTS ERA, black leaders and organizations continued to use the UN as a forum to PROTEST racism in the United States. In 1969 the UN approved the "International Convention on the Elimination of All Forms of Discrimination." It allowed victims of discrimination to file complaints directly with the UN. Although the United States signed the convention, it did so with the usual reservation that it was not bound by any parts of it not consistent with the CONSTITUTION. As part of the implementation of the convention, the UN's General Assembly declared three decades to combat racism and discrimination, with international conferences to receive reports and adopt recommendations and resolutions. The United States boycotted each of the three conferences. JIMMY CARTER refused to send a delegation to the first conference in 1978; RONALD REAGAN refused to participate in the second decade conference in 1982; and the administration of George W. Bush refused to send a delegation to the 2001 conference. The United States refused to send delegations to each of the conferences because of concerns that they would pass resolutions condemning Zionism as a form of racism. In addition, at the 2001 conference Secretary of State COLIN POWELL, on behalf of the George W. Bush administration, expressed concerns about a resolution proposed by African and African-American leaders condemning SLAVERY as a "crime against humanity" and calling for REPARATIONS. Although the United States (and Israel) boycotted the conferences, the other nations of the world attended, and the conferences did serve their purpose of calling attention to racism in the context of GLOBALIZATION. The Convention on the Elimination of Racism also required each nation to submit a biannual report to the UN on its progress in eliminating racism and for the UN to issue reports on the status of discrimination in the nations of the world. After much delay, the United States in 2001 complied and issued a report declaring that while INDI-

VIDUAL RACISM and SEGREGATION had been substantially eliminated, INSTITUTIONAL RACISM continued in many areas of American life.

At the time of its founding, the UN was constituted by 51 nations, mostly European and Latin American. At the beginning of the 21st century it was constituted by 190 nations, mostly African and Asian. This gives the Third World substantial influence in the General Assembly, where each nation has one vote. However, decision-making authority in the UN is held by the 15-member Security Council, where the five permanent members (the United States, Russia, France, Britain, and China) exercise a veto (the other 10 members are elected by the General Assembly for two-year terms). Of the seven secretaries-general, two—Boutros Boutros-Ghali of Egypt and Kofi Annan of Ghana—have come from Africa. And two African Americans have served as U.S. ambassadors to the UN, including ANDREW YOUNG.

Universal Declaration of Human Rights (1948)

The Universal Declaration of Human Rights is the attempt by the international community to codify HUMAN RIGHTS, rights to which all persons of the world are entitled. Adopted in 1948 by the UNITED NATIONS General Assembly, the declaration, like the U.S. DECLARATION OF INDEPENDENCE and CONSTITUTION, encompasses NATURAL RIGHTS and CIVIL RIGHTS. But unlike the U.S. declaration and Constitution, the universal declaration goes farther to proclaim that all persons are entitled to social and economic rights, including the "right to a standard of living adequate for the health and well being of his family, including food, clothing, housing, medical care and social services." The declaration, however, is nonbinding, partly because Eleanor Roosevelt, the wife of FRANKLIN D. ROOSEVELT, advised that only a nonbinding declaration could win approval by CONGRESS. Despite its nonbinding status, the universal declaration is an important document, and in the context of GLOBALIZATION, it is a resource for human-rights activists. Since the adoption of the declaration in 1948, African-American leaders have frequently invoked its provisions in their struggles for FREEDOM and EQUALITY.

Universal Negro Improvement Association

The Universal Negro Improvement Association (UNIA) is the ORGANIZATION established by MARCUS GARVEY in the 1920s to advance his IDEOLOGY of PAN-AFRICANISM and his BACK-TO-AFRICA MOVEMENT. At its peak, UNIA—headquartered in HARLEM—was the largest and, arguably, the most influential black organization in the world. But after Garvey's deportation from the United States, UNIA rapidly declined, in large part because Garvey administered it in an autocratic manner based on charismatic rather than democratic or bureaucratic authority. Although UNIA did not survive the loss of its founding leader, remnants of the organization remained active in Harlem and other GHETTOS of the NORTHERN STATES well into the late 20th century.

Urban League

The Urban League, with the NAACP, is one of the two most important ORGANIZATIONS in the BLACK COMMUNITY concerned with issues of CIVIL RIGHTS. The Urban League, like the NAACP, emerged out of the tradition of early-20th-century LIBERALISM and progressive social reform. Established on the principles of interracial COALITIONS and INTEGRATIONISM, the Urban League was created in 1911 as a result of the merger of three other organizations: the National League for the Protection of Colored Women, the Committee for Improving Industrial Conditions among Negroes, and the Committee on Urban Conditions among Negroes.

The white liberal reformers who founded the NAACP in 1909 viewed its primary purpose as securing civil rights, narrowly defined in terms of enforcing the FIFTEENTH AMENDMENT and the EQUAL PROTECTION CLAUSE of the FOURTEENTH AMENDMENT. The founders of the Urban League viewed its primary purpose as providing social services and developing SELF-HELP programs for the black migrants from the rural parts of the SOUTHERN STATES in order to help them adjust to life in the emerging GHETTOS of the NORTHERN STATES. The principal strategies of the NAACP were LOBBYING and LITIGATION, while the principal strategies of the Urban League were scientific research on social problems and professionalized social work. Historically, therefore, the roles of the two organizations—founded two years apart—were viewed as distinct but complementary.

During the decades of the CIVIL RIGHTS MOVEMENT and in the POST–CIVIL RIGHTS ERA the two organizations continued their historically distinct roles. The Urban League worked in the ghettos; the NAACP worked in the courts and CONGRESS. Both sought FREEDOM and EQUALITY for African Americans, but by different means. They both worked to influence PUBLIC OPINION by establishing MEDIA outlets (the NAACP published *The Crisis*, the Urban League *Opportunity*). But the league also established a research department which, under the direction of the black sociologist Charles Johnson, published studies on the effects of joblessness and RACISM in producing and reproducing POVERTY and the CULTURE OF POVERTY. During the PROTEST phase of the Civil Rights movement in the 1950s and 1960s, the Urban League under WHITNEY YOUNG's leadership became more active in lobbying and it cosponsored the MARCH ON WASHINGTON OF 1963. However, the Urban League never embraced mass demonstrations, boycotts, or CIVIL DISOBEDIENCE.

The WAR ON POVERTY during the PRESIDENCY OF LYNDON B. JOHNSON provided resources to the Urban League to increase its social-service activities, and during RICHARD NIXON's administration the league entered into an informal partnership with the federal government to deliver training and employment services to ghetto residents. Although this partnership was dissolved by RONALD REAGAN, the league continued to receive government contracts to provide social services in the ghettos. In addition it developed a comprehensive "Marshall Plan" to reconstruct the ghettos. Although the plan was never given serious consideration by the Congress, it constitutes a kind of blueprint of what the black LEADERSHIP considers a realistic PUBLIC POLICY to attack the problem of concentrated urban poverty. When VERNON JORDAN became head of the Urban League in the 1970s, it became more active in encouraging voting and other forms of POLITICAL PARTICIPATION and began to develop programs to deal with problems that came to be associated with the UNDERCLASS, such as female-headed households and teenage pregnancy. Jordan also revitalized the league's research department, establishing a quarterly public-policy journal, the *Urban League Review,* and an annual report on the status of blacks.

Unlike the NAACP, the Urban League is not a membership organization. Rather, it is a professionalized reform organization with four regional offices and affiliates in about 100 cities in 30 states. It is nonpartisan and has always had close links to the POWER ELITE through the receipt of corporate grants and through the service of leading white industrialists on its board. (By tradition the chair of its board is white, the president black.) At the start of the 21st century, SCHOOLS AND EDUCATION were a primary focus of its work.

See also GREAT MIGRATION.

Further reading: Nancy Weiss, *The National Urban League* (New York: Oxford University Press, 1989).

urban politics

At the end of the 20th century, cities large and small were the geographical or spatial location for the exercise of POWER by African Americans in the POLITICAL SYSTEM. Because of the relatively small size of the black POPULATION and its distribution, it is difficult for blacks to become ELECTED OFFICIALS in most STATE AND LOCAL GOVERNMENTS. Since the adoption of the VOTING RIGHTS ACT OF 1965, blacks have achieved a significant level of representation in the House of Representatives, but it is less than their proportionate share, and even this level of REPRESENTATION is jeopardized by the SUPREME COURT's decision in *SHAW V. RENO* and subsequent cases. At the end of the 20th century, no blacks served in the Senate or as governor of one of the 50 states. This is because governors and senators are elected by majority-white electorates, and black candidates find it difficult to put together statewide biracial majority COALITIONS. Thus, in the history of the United States only two blacks—EDWARD BROOKE and CAROL MOSELEY-BRAUN—have been elected to the Senate (two others were appointed during RECONSTRUCTION), and only one black, DOUGLAS WILDER, has been elected governor of a state. But since the election of CARL STOKES and RICHARD HATCHER in 1967, blacks have been elected mayor of virtually all of the nation's big cities, and many city councils and other local governing bodies are majority black.

Black political power in the cities is a recent phenomenon, largely a product of forces that matured during the POST–CIVIL RIGHTS ERA. From the formation of post–CIVIL WAR urban black communities in the 1870s until about 1900, urban black politics in the NORTHERN STATES was characterized by considerable variability: In many cities blacks were permitted to vote, schools were integrated, public accommodations were legally open to all, and blacks were elected to office, occasionally even by predominantly white constituencies. After 1890 a new pattern emerged in urban black politics in the North. Although it was not a formal system of disenfranchisement and SEGREGATION, as in the SOUTHERN STATES, this new pattern operated almost as effectively to repress and exclude the participation of the growing black communities.

From 1900 to 1940 the urban black communities of the North as well as the South were subordinate to and manipulated by political machines—hierarchically controlled white political organization—that exchanged material benefits—services and jobs (patronage)—for votes. Although each urban political machine differed in style, in no city during this period (except for Chicago, perhaps) was the black community included in the governing process. Rather, as Martin Kilson writes, "in the years 1900–1940 the goal of the white dominated city machines toward Negroes was to neutralize and thus minimize the political clout of the Negro urban community and not infrequently to distort that community's social and political modernization." Kilson states that this goal of the machines was animated by RACISM and the ideology of WHITE SUPREMACY: "The goals of the neutralization and distortion of the position of the Negro community emanated largely from the racist perspective of the American social system. . . . Thus, the patterns of the ideology of white racism explain the extent and intensity of the city machines' policy of neutralizing and distorting the political capability of the Negro urban subsystem in the years of 1900–1940." This racist exclusion of African Americans from urban political system did not begin to change until the 1960s.

The 1960s ushered in a fundamental transformation in urban black politics. Several factors facilitated this transformation. They include: changes in the racial composition of the cities; the growth and development of the black middle class; the CIVIL RIGHTS MOVEMENT; the BLACK POWER MOVEMENT; the WAR ON POVERTY's community action programs; and the decline and eventually the collapse of the big-city political machines.

In terms of population, as a result of the GREAT MIGRATION, the BLACK COMMUNITY even in the 1950s and 1960s had considerable political strength. This strength, however, markedly increased during the post–civil rights era. As a result, in most of the large cities blacks either constituted a majority of the population or a substantial minority. The changing racial composition of America's large cities is a result of black migration from the rural South, white out-migration to the suburbs, and racial barriers to black suburbanization. Blacks also have a somewhat higher birthrate than whites. As a result of these population shifts, at the end of the 20th century more than 80 percent of blacks lived in urban areas.

In addition to population changes, the growth and diversification of the black middle class (in terms of education and professional occupations) also facilitated the development of urban black power. The Civil Rights movement and the legislation enacted in its wake, especially the VOTING RIGHTS ACT OF 1965, are important because they removed barriers to voting, particularly in the South. Similarly, the Black Power movement contributed to black urban empowerment in the cities by encouraging racial solidarity and race-group voting. The GREAT SOCIETY's war on poverty and its community-action programs with their requirements for "maximum feasible" participation of the poor were also an important factor in the early development of urban black power. A fundamental objective of the antipoverty community-action programs in the big cities was the organization and institutionalization of the black community as constituent components of the urban political regime. In effect, antipoverty agencies became a federal-government-mandated alternative to the white-dominated machines. Finally, the machines themselves began to wither away and eventually collapsed.

This combination of factors—population changes, the growth of the black middle class, the Civil Rights and Black Power movements, the War on Poverty's community-action program, and the decline of the urban machines—led in the 1960s to the emergence of urban black power to its consolidation in the 1970s and 1980s. The table below illustrates the pattern of this growth and development in urban black power between 1960 and 1990 in the nation's 25 largest cities. The data show a substantial increase in the size of the black population during this period in most of the cities. As of 1990, blacks had been elected mayor of 22 of the 25 largest cities. In most of these cities blacks constitute a majority or a substantial minority. However, blacks have also been elected mayor in several cities that have relatively small black populations, including Denver, San Francisco, Minneapolis, and Seattle.

American cities are the sites for the exercise of political power by African Americans, but this power is limited in two important ways. First, there are constitutional or legal limits, and second there are structural or economic limits. Under the CONSTITUTION's principle of FEDERALISM, urban governments do not have autonomous or independent power or authority; rather they are mere instruments of the states, who exercise exclusive power over them. This view of the exclusive power of the states vis-à-vis their cities was first expounded by John Charles Dillon, the chief justice of the Iowa Supreme Court in 1868. His view has come to be known as "Dillon's Rule." In *City of Clinton v. Cedar Rapids Missouri Railroad Company* (a case involving whether Iowa could take over the streets of Clinton in order to allow the construction of a railroad), Dillon wrote:

> The true view is that: municipal corporations owe their origin and derive their powers and rights *wholly* from the legislature. It breathes into them the breath of life, without which they can not exist. *As it creates, so it may destroy.* If it may destroy, it may abridge and control. Unless there is some constitutional limitation on the right, *the legislature might destroy by a single act, if we can suppose it capable of so great a folly and so great a wrong, sweep from its existence all of the municipal corporations in the state, and the corporations could not prevent it . . .* (emphasis added).

This sweeping view of the limits of the power of city governments was affirmed by the U.S. Supreme Court in *Trenton v. New Jersey* (1923). This means that black-led city governments can do no more than the white-dominated state governments allow them to do. City governments are also limited by the structural imperatives of CAPITALISM, which require that cities maintain a climate favorable to business and the middle class. This necessity of the city to maintain its economic viability and tax base is critical. It means that cities cannot afford to redistribute income or substantially increase taxes to provide services for the poor. As Paul Peterson argues in *City Limits* (1981), cities cannot afford to do much about POVERTY in the GHETTOS because they will lose their competitive edge as

AFRICAN-AMERICAN POPULATION IN 25 PRINCIPAL AMERICAN CITIES IN 1960–90, AND THE YEAR OF ELECTION OF BLACK MAYORS

	1960, %	1970, %	1980, %	1990, %	Year of Election Black Mayor
Atlanta, Ga.	38.3	51.3	66.2	67.1	1973
Baltimore, Md.	34.7	51.3	54.8	59.2	1984
Birmingham, Ala.	39.6	44.6	55.2	63.3	1974
Boston, Mass.	9.1	16.3	22.4	25.6	never
Chicago, Ill.*	22.9	32.7	39.8	39.1	1983
Cleveland, Ohio	21.6	38.3	43.7	46.6	1967
Dallas, Tex.	19.0	25.4	29.3	29.5	1995
Denver, Colo.	6.1	9.1	12.0	12.8	1991
Detroit, Mich.	29.0	43.0	63.0	75.7	1973
Gary, Ind.*	39.0	53.0	71.0	80.6	1967
Houston, Tex.	22.9	26.4	27.5	28.1	1997
Los Angeles, Calif.*	13.5	17.9	12.6	14.0	1973
Miami, Fla.	22.4	22.7	25.0	27.4	never
Milwaukee, Wis.	8.4	15.5	23.1	30.5	never
Minneapolis, Minn.	2.4	6.3	7.8	13.0	1993
Newark, N.J.	34.0	54.0	58.0	58.0	1970
New Orleans, La.	34.2	45.0	55.3	61.9	1977
New York, N.Y.*	14.0	21.1	25.2	28.7	1989
Oakland, Calif.	22.8	34.5	46.9	43.9	1988
Philadelphia, Pa.	26.4	24.2	37.8	39.9	1983
Richmond, Va.	34.2	42.4	52.0	55.2	1977
San Francisco, Calif.	10.0	13.4	12.7	19.9	1995
Seattle, Wash.	4.8	12.6	9.4	9.5	1989
St. Louis, Mo.	28.6	40.9	45.5	47.5	1995
Washington, D.C.	53.9	71.1	70.2	65.8	1975

*City no longer has a black mayor. Except for Cleveland and Gary (and the cities with an asterisk), all the cities that have elected black mayors have had them continuously since the first was elected.

SOURCE: City and County Data Book, Statistical Supplement (Washington, D.C.: Government Printing Office, 1967, 1977, 1983, 1993).

businesses, and the middle class will flee to the surrounding suburbs or to other cities. This competition among cities for business and highly skilled middle- and upper-class professional and managerial workers means that they must keep the cost of welfare and other social services low and thereby keep the burden of local taxes low. It is under these severe constitutional and structural limits that African-American urban governments have sought to use their power to further the African-American quest for social and economic EQUALITY. At best, the results of their efforts during the post–civil rights era have been mixed.

There are approximately 300 African-American mayors in the United States; the great majority, however, are mayors of small towns in the rural South. Others are mayors of cities where the black population is relatively small, and thus the governments are effectively in the hands of whites, such as Los Angeles, Denver, Seattle, and San Francisco. Then there are those cities that have been defined as "black urban

regimes," cities where blacks are a substantial majority of the population and where blacks control the mayor's office and a clear-cut city council majority. The governments of these cities, within their legal limits, are effectively controlled by African Americans. But in addition and corollary to having large black populations, these cities have a large percentage of poor people (mostly black). Thus they have a smaller middle-class tax base and a larger community of people in need of welfare and other social services. But these cities are reluctant to provide these services for fear of driving the middle class and businesses out.

While the election of black mayors has not made much difference in terms of needed services and material benefits for the urban poor, there are studies showing that the election of black mayors has contributed psychological benefits to African Americans. The election of a black mayor, especially for the first time, is an important psychological benefit to blacks, symbolizing their inclusion in the political system

AFRICAN-AMERICAN URBAN REGIMES AND THE PERCENT OF THE POPULATION BELOW POVERTY LEVEL YEAR OF ELECTION OF BLACK MAYOR AND 1990*

	Black Population in 1990, %	Below Poverty Level in Year of Election of Black Mayor, %		Below Poverty Level 1990, %
Atlanta, Ga.	67.1	15.9	(1973)	27.3
Baltimore, Md.	59.2	14.0	(1984)	21.7
Birmingham, Ala.	63.3	22.0	(1974)	29.7
Detroit, Mich.	75.7	18.7	(1973)	32.4
Gary, Ind.	80.6	12.3	(1967)	29.4
Newark, N.J.	58.0	18.4	(1970)	28.3
New Orleans, La.	61.9	21.6	(1977)	31.6
Oakland, Calif.	43.9	12.2	(1988)	18.8
Richmond, Va.	55.2	13.3	(1977)	20.9
Washington, D.C.	65.8	12.7	(1975)	16.9

*1970 is the first census year since the election of the first African-American mayor of a major American city. In 1995 Gary became the first black-regime city to elect a white mayor.
SOURCE: City and County Data Book, Statistical Abstract Supplement (Washington, D.C.: Government Printing Office, 1967, 1977, 1983, 1993).

at the highest level. Blacks in Chicago chanted after the election of Harold Washington, Chicago's first black mayor: "Our time has come." This sentiment has been shown to translate into higher levels of trust, support, and satisfaction with black-led city governments. The election and service of black mayors also appear to make white voters somewhat more willing to vote for other black candidates.

In addition to these symbolic, psychological benefits, studies have shown that the election of African-American mayors also results in a more equitable allocation of material benefits. In black-regime cities, black workers are more likely to find employment in city government, and black businesspeople are more likely to receive contracts to do business with the city as a result of AFFIRMATIVE ACTION programs. And scholars of big-city politics have also reported a decline in police brutality and other forms of misconduct toward African Americans, in part as a result of the election of black mayors, the appointment of black police chiefs, and the racial integration and reform of the police departments. But on the needs of the urban black poor for jobs, education, and social services, the constitutional and structural constraints have blocked any meaningful reforms. Indeed, in the face of these constraints, no black mayor has even attempted such reforms. Thus, as the table above shows, the problem of poverty has grown worse in black-regime cities since the election of black mayors.

Ironically, just as blacks were beginning to come to power in cities, the cities themselves (especially those with black regimes) began an ominous decline. Forces shaping this decline include depopulation and the disinvestment and deindustrialization associated with GLOBALIZATION; white and increasingly black middle-class flight to the sub-urbs; and a sharp decline in federal aid to the cities beginning with the PRESIDENCY of RONALD REAGAN. Given these problems, black mayors could do little to improve the conditions of the urban black poor in part because of their limited constitutional powers and their needs to accommodate the local business community. Thus, in the last 20 years in most American cities, including the black-regime ones, the conditions of the urban poor have become worse. At the start of the 21st century, there was little prospect for change in these conditions.

See also CONGRESS.

Further reading: Rufus Browning, Dale Rogers Marshall and David Tabb, *Protest Is Not Enough: The Struggle of Blacks and Hispanics for Equality in Urban Politics* (Berkeley: University of California Press, 1984); Rufus Browning, Dale Rogers, Marshall Tabb, and David Tabb, eds., *Racial Politics in American Cities* (New York: Longman, 2003); Valerie Johnson, *Black Power in the Suburbs: The Myth or Reality of African American Suburban Political Incorporation* (Albany: SUNY Press, 2002); Martin Kilson, "Political Change in the Negro Ghetto, 1990–1940s," in *Key Issues in the Afro-American Experience, Vol. 2,* ed. Nathan Huggins, Martin Kilson, and Daniel Fox (New York: Harcourt Brace Jovanovich, 1971); Adolph Reed, "The Black Urban Regime: Structural Origins and Constraints," in Power, Community and the City: Comparative Urban Research, ed. Peter Smith (New Brunswick, N.J.: Transaction Publishers, 1988); Robert C. Smith, "The Changing Shape of Urban Black Politics, 1960–1970," *The Annals of the American Academy of Political and Social Science* 439 (1978): 16–28.

V

Vietnam War

The Vietnam War—the effort of the United States to prevent by the use of military force the unification of North and South Vietnam under Communist control—was a watershed event in American and African-American politics. It was a turning point mainly because it led to a breakup of the COLD WAR consensus that the United States should use all reasonable means to stop the spread of international COMMUNISM.

At the outset of the cold war in the late 1940s, the NAACP and most of the established black LEADERSHIP and MEDIA had expressed skepticism or opposition to the cold war. This opposition or skepticism was based on a kind of THIRD WORLD solidarity that viewed the effort to stop the spread of communism as a subterfuge for the maintenance of western COLONIALISM and international practices of RACISM and WHITE SUPREMACISM. Although most black leaders were not sympathetic to the Soviet Union or communism, most probably agreed with sentiments expressed in a 1947 *Crisis* article, which said that at least the Soviet Union had never subscribed to white supremacy and that its mere presence as a force in international politics might mean that "human rights may now and then get a break." Earlier, WALTER WHITE in his 1946 address to the NAACP convention pointed to what he saw as the hypocrisy of U.S. FOREIGN POLICY, which complained loudly about the Soviet Union's denial of FREEDOM to the peoples of Eastern Europe but said nothing about and indeed supported the colonial powers in their continued denial of freedom to the colonized peoples of Africa and Asia. The 1946 NAACP convention then adopted a resolution calling for an end to colonialism and commending colonial peoples in their struggles for freedom.

As the cold war intensified after 1947, established black leaders and media abruptly changed their views and embraced the emerging cold war anticommunism consensus. Several factors account for this change. First, most black leaders were committed to CAPITALISM and DEMOC-RACY and came to see international communism as a threat to these values. Second, many came to view Soviet support for Third World anticolonialism movements as a ruse to gain control of the strategic resources of Africa and Asia. Third, white liberal elements who were a vital part of the COALITION that constituted the CIVIL RIGHTS MOVEMENT began to pressure black leaders to join the cold war consensus. Fourth, black leaders were grateful to President HARRY TRUMAN for the unprecedented CIVIL RIGHTS initiatives he had undertaken and began to see the value of the cold war as a means to leverage further support for civil rights. Finally, the CONGRESS and the president began to institute various "loyalty programs" that defined opposition to the cold war as "un-American"; and racists and white supremacists in Congress and the media attempted to link the communist challenge at home and abroad to the challenge to racism and white supremacism in the United States. Thus, some black leaders feared the Civil Rights movement would be labeled "red," a communist-inspired movement. Although this was clearly not the case, these fears were heightened with the emergence of MCCARTHY-ISM. As a result, black leaders joined the cold war consensus and ceased criticism of U.S. foreign policy. (Not only did most black leaders embrace the struggle against international communism, they also joined the struggle against domestic communism by ousting communists from their ORGANIZATIONs.) Thus, like the leaders of most INTEREST GROUPS blacks by the early 1950s were not inclined to express opposition or skepticism about the cold war. There were black leaders and organizations who dissented, including W. E. B. DU BOIS, PAUL ROBESON, and ELIJAH MUHAMMAD and the COUNCIL ON AFRICAN AFFAIRS and the NATION OF ISLAM. But they were marginalized and ostracized by mainstream leaders and institutions, black and white, and subjected to various forms of POLITICAL REPRESSION. The Vietnam War changed all of this and eventually led to a fundamental transformation in attitudes toward U.S. foreign policy in the BLACK COMMUNITY.

Like most Americans, blacks had supported the Korean War, which in many ways was a precursor to Vietnam. Like Vietnam, it was an attempt by the United States to use VIOLENCE to prevent the unification of North and South Korea under communist rule. Like Vietnam, it was also an undeclared war, waged on the initiative of the president rather than Congress. And, also like Vietnam, eventually thousands of Americans lost their lives (in Korea more than 30,000; in Vietnam more than 50,000). But here the similarities end. First, United States was able to successfully maintain the division of Korea into a communist north and noncommunist south, while Vietnam was eventually unified under communist control. Second, unlike Korea, a massive antiwar PROTEST movement developed in the course of the Vietnam War—a movement that African Americans were at the forefront of—that eventually forced the U.S. government to withdraw from the conflict. Finally, Vietnam was the first American war in which black soldiers and sailors participated in the MILITARY in a formally integrated and nondiscriminatory way.

Although President Truman had issued his EXECUTIVE ORDER banning SEGREGATION and DISCRIMINATION in the military in 1948, during the 1950s Korean War, segregated units were maintained and discrimination was widespread. In Vietnam all units were integrated, and blacks—because of the absence of EQUALITY in the society—were drafted in disproportionately high numbers. The fact that blacks served and died in Vietnam in disproportionately high numbers was one of the factors that fueled black opposition, but initially most black leaders and organizations supported the war. The Nation of Islam was opposed, as it had been to the Korean War and World War II. MALCOLM X therefore spoke out against the war from its beginning, labeling it a white man's war to suppress the aspirations of the Vietnamese for freedom. He also explicitly linked the Vietnamese struggle for freedom with the black struggle in the United States. Malcolm's views, however, were marginal, but in 1966 MUHAMMAD ALI, the heavyweight boxing champion and recent convert to the Nation of Islam, also denounced the war and refused to be drafted. Ali's status made opposition to the war a cause célèbre in the black community and fueled opposition there and on college campuses. However, when Ali denounced the war it was still supported by most black leaders, organizations, media, and PUBLIC OPINION. (A 1966 poll found that only 32 percent of blacks disapproved of the war, while 68 percent favored its continuation or expansion. Only 20 percent favored withdrawal.) In 1966 the STUDENT NONVIOLENT COORDINATING COMMITTEE (SNCC) became the first civil-rights organization to come out against the war, declaring it a racist, colonial endeavor and urging blacks to resist the draft. A year later MARTIN LUTHER KING JR. declared

his opposition and began to take an active role in the antiwar movement. King said that the war was racist, white supremacist, and based on a "morbid fear of communism." He also urged young men to resist the draft and linked the war to the black struggle for freedom. For example, he said that a government that could not secure the freedom of blacks in the SOUTHERN STATES had no business sending black boys 5,000 miles away to guarantee the "freedom" of other people. He also argued that the war was killing young, poor blacks in disproportionately high numbers; fueling RIOTS in the GHETTOS; and draining attention and resources away from the WAR ON POVERTY.

King's opposition to the war was decisive in shifting opinion in the black community. Recognized as the preeminent black leader and a heroic figure to many, King's opposition bitterly and deeply divided the black LEADERSHIP establishment. This establishment was in general loyal to President LYNDON B. JOHNSON in part because of his strong support for the CIVIL RIGHTS ACT OF 1964 and the VOTING RIGHTS ACT OF 1965. (Earlier they had supported President Truman's cold war policies because of his support for civil rights.) ROY WILKINS of the NAACP and WHITNEY YOUNG of the URBAN LEAGUE as well as BAYARD RUSTIN denounced King's stance, claiming that it undermined support for the Civil Rights movement and broke the long-held leadership consensus on the cold war. (CARL ROWAN) the syndicated columnist and radio commentator, made similar attacks on King.) But, the tide had turned. King's opposition to the war galvanized opposition to the war in the black community, leading to a precipitous shift in public opinion so that by the time RICHARD NIXON became president, opposition to the war was widespread in the black community, reflected in the media, popular MUSIC, campus demonstrations, the sermons of leading black clergymen, the formal resolutions of most black political organizations. Black opposition to the war was part of a larger antiwar movement, but black leaders were at the cutting edge of this movement.

In a sense, the eventual opposition of blacks to the war was a return to a pre–cold war concern with Third World solidarity, linking the struggles of African Americans to the struggles of colored peoples throughout the world. Once Vietnam broke the cold war consensus, virtually the entire black leadership establishment (reflecting public opinion in the black community) began to express opposition to America's wars in the Third World, whether in Africa, the Middle East, or Latin America. Throughout the POST–CIVIL RIGHTS ERA—whether it was RONALD REAGAN waging war against communism in Grenada or Nicaragua or George W. Bush waging war against Iraq—blacks have been in the forefront of dissent. Again, this likely reflects a Third World solidarity that was repressed by the cold war consensus and McCarthyism. The significance of Vietnam is that it broke that consensus, freeing African Americans to take whatever positions on American foreign policy that their history, interests, and circumstances dictated.

violence

Violence is an integral, defining feature of AFRICAN-AMERICAN POLITICS. The other attributes that distinguish African-American politics are RACISM and the IDEOLOGY of WHITE SUPREMACY. But, violence is the indispensable attribute because without violence, the European OPPRESSION of Africans through the practice of racism and the ideology of white supremacy would not have been possible. Ultimately, the phenomenon of African-American politics rests on the foundations of force—the ultimate base of political POWER. Violence in the first instance therefore is crucial in understanding the experiences of African peoples in relationship to the peoples of Europe, whether in Africa or the Americas. However, it is not just violence as a source of the base of power of oppression; rather, as FRANTZ FANON, among others, has shown, violence is an integral feature of the experiences of Africans in their relationship to Europeans. Generally, this integral violence can be classified into three types. The first is the violence of oppression, which is the violence used to subordinate and oppress Africans. The second is the violence of resistance, which is the violence employed by Africans to overturn subordination and oppression. The final type—the focus here is on physical violence rather than the kind of psychological violence expressed in some manifestations of INTERNAL INFERIORIZATION—is communal violence, which is "black on black" violence or what Fanon referred to as the phenomenon of "niggers killing niggers on Saturday night."

The first type of violence begins with European COLONIALISM and the enslavement of African peoples. Extraordinary violence was employed in these distinct but related processes of oppression. With respect to colonialism, for example, it is estimated that several million African were killed by the Belgians during the colonialization of the Congo, and by some estimates as many as 10 million Africans may have been killed during the 300 years of the Atlantic slave trade. During SLAVERY, violence in various forms—whippings, mutilations, rape, murder—was indispensable to maintenance of the system. After slavery's end, the new JIM CROW style of SEGREGATION and subordination was maintained by violence including LYNCHINGS, KU KLUX KLAN terrorism, and race RIOTS by white citizens. All of these forms of violence were state sanctioned, first formally and officially by all levels of government, then after the CIVIL WAR and RECONSTRUCTION by STATE AND LOCAL GOVERNMENTS. In the 20th century violence was frequently employed against blacks through DISCRIMINATION in the CRIMINAL JUSTICE SYSTEM, including well-documented cases of police brutality and murder, the failure to enforce the requirements of the DUE PROCESS CLAUSES of the CONSTITUTION, and the racially discriminatory application of the death penalty.

The second type of violence, resistance, manifested itself in wars and battles against European colonizers and slavers in Africa; SLAVE REVOLTS, large and small; GHETTO riots or rebellions during the 20th century; and sporadic attempts at organized violence as espoused by groups like the AFRICAN BLOOD BROTHERHOOD and the BLACK PANTHER PARTY.

The last type, communal violence, is manifested in the extraordinarily high levels of black-on-black violence that has characterized African communities ever since they came under European domination. When Fanon used the phrase "niggers killing niggers on Saturday night" he was referring to Africans killing Africans in the ghettos and rural areas of Algeria (the North African French colony), but the phrase is also commonly used in the United States. Fanon traced this type of violence to ALIENATION, internal inferiorization, and the inevitable psychological frustrations that flow from existence in systems of white oppression that are themselves maintained through violence. Fanon contends that blacks living under such systems usually cannot—because of the disproportionate power of whites—release their frustrations against whites, therefore they turn on each other. In the United States this phenomenon is referred to as "black on black" crime. Although the early data are not exact, since the beginning of the collection of statistical data, the BLACK COMMUNITY has displayed disproportionately high rates of internal violence, including child and spousal abuse. In the POST–CIVIL RIGHTS ERA, where data are somewhat more accurate, it is clear that this pattern continues. In the late 20th century the FBI reported that in any year selected, blacks were responsible for about 40 percent of the violent crime—murders, armed assaults, and rapes—committed, although they constituted little more than 12 percent of the POPULATION. Ninety percent of the victims of these crimes were usually other blacks. At the dawn of the 21st century, ironically, communal violence was probably more widespread than racist or oppressive violence and certainly more widespread than the violence of resistance.

See also COLFAX MASSACRE and RODNEY KING.

Further reading: Robert C. Smith, "Beyond Marx: Fanon and the Concept of Colonial Violence," *Black World* 27 (1973): 39–41; Robert Staples, "Violence in Black America: The Political Implications," *Black World* 28 (1974): 17–34.

voting behavior

Voting in a DEMOCRACY is not the most important or influential form of POLITICAL PARTICIPATION (political scientists generally rank it at about eighth in a list of 12, where holding political office is ranked first); however, it is the most widespread and it does ultimately determine the elites of the POLITICAL SYSTEM as well as all other ELECTED OFFICIALS.

At the inception of the United States, African Americans, whether enslaved or FREE NEGROES, were denied VOTING RIGHTS in all of the SOUTHERN STATES and in virtually all of the NORTHERN STATES. After the CIVIL WAR, black males were granted voting rights as a result of adoption of the FIFTEENTH AMENDMENT. During RECONSTRUCTION they exercised these rights, apparently at a rate equal to or greater than whites. For example, in Louisiana (which kept voter registration figures by race) in 1867, 70 percent of eligible black men were registered to vote. However, after the COMPROMISE OF 1871, the right to vote was in effect taken away from black men. So, in Louisiana by 1900, the percentage of blacks registered to vote had dropped to less than 10 percent from its high of 70 percent 30 years earlier. Voting rights were not effectively restored to Southern blacks (by now including women as a result of adoption of the Nineteenth Amendment) until adoption of the VOTING RIGHTS ACT OF 1965.

Since then, roughly 50 percent of blacks have been registered to vote, and at the end of the 20th century about 50 percent of blacks usually voted in presidential elections (where voter turnout is highest) compared with about 55 percent of whites. This race gap of five percentage points between blacks and whites has persisted through the POST–CIVIL RIGHTS ERA, reflecting in part the fact that voting in the United States is a class phenomenon in which poor people are less likely to vote than middle- and upper-income people. And since blacks are disproportionately poor (about one-third compared with 10 percent of whites), this accounts for virtually all of the gap. Indeed, given their rates of POVERTY, blacks vote at higher rates than whites. That is, middle-class blacks tend to vote at comparable rates with middle-class whites, and poor blacks at a somewhat higher rate than poor whites. Voting in America whether by blacks or whites is relatively low when compared with other industrialized democracies, where turnout is generally 70 percent or more.

Black voting behavior is shaped by gender, RELIGIOSITY, region, and age. Black women tend to vote at a higher rate than men; the more religious more so than the less religious; and the young less so than the older and elderly. In the post–civil rights era, the black vote is highly partisan, generally voting at near 90 percent for DEMOCRATIC PARTY candidates.

See also CIVIC CULTURE, POLITICAL CULTURE.

voting rights

The right to vote is the foundation of DEMOCRACY. The ELECTED OFFICIALS who direct and operate the POLITICAL SYSTEM derive their legitimacy from the right of the people to choose them in regularly scheduled elections. Yet in the American democracy there is no universal or national right to vote. Rather, under the principle of FEDERALISM, the right of persons to vote is left to the determination of the states.

Under the CONSTITUTION as originally written, individuals in the United States only had the right to vote for members of the House of Representatives, since members of the Senate were elected by the state legislatures, the president by the ELECTORAL COLLEGE, and members of the SUPREME COURT by the joint action of the president and the Senate. But the Constitution does not even establish national or federal qualifications for voting in House elections. Rather, Article I, Section 2 states that the qualifications for voting for members of the House shall be the same as "Electors for the most numerous branch of the state legislature." In other words, the qualifications for voting for members of the national CONGRESS were whatever

A cover of *Harper's Weekly* depicting blacks voting for the first time, 1867 *(Library of Congress)*

qualifications a state might use in determining who could vote in elections for the lower house of its legislature. This provision allowed each state to impose whatever barriers to voting it wished, for example, property qualifications, or even CITIZENSHIP, since not all states allowed all male citizens to vote. The Constitution was subsequently amended four times to prohibit the states from denying voting rights to black men (the FIFTEENTH AMENDMENT) and to women (the Nineteenth Amendment), for failure to pay a poll tax (the TWENTY-FOURTH AMENDMENT), and to persons 18 years or older (Twenty-sixth Amendment). But, these amendments are negative prohibitions—telling the states what they can not do—rather than positive grants of universal voting rights.

The absence of national qualifications for voting has always disadvantaged African Americans. After the Fifteenth Amendment prohibited states from denying the vote to African-American men, the SOUTHERN STATES used an extraordinary set of voter qualifications—literacy tests, poll taxes, grandfather clauses (where one was qualified to vote if one's grandfather was qualified), and the WHITE PRIMARY—to effectively disqualify blacks. Some of these qualifications were outlawed by Supreme Court decisions, but African Americans did not regain the right to vote until Congress adopted the VOTING RIGHTS ACT OF 1965. This act banned most qualifications that impeded black voting, and as a result blacks began to vote at rates comparable with whites.

In the POST–CIVIL RIGHTS ERA, the principal impediment to black voting rights is the disqualification of persons convicted of felonies. Maine and Vermont were the only states that did not disqualify felons, while 48 states and the DISTRICT OF COLUMBIA denied felons voting rights while they were incarcerated. Thirty-two states denied paroled felons voting rights, in 29 states felons lose their voting rights forever. Since blacks (especially men) are disproportionately convicted of felonies, the effect of these qualifications at the end of the 20th century was to deny voting rights to 13 percent of black men in the United States. In seven states between one-fourth and one-third of black men had lost voting rights as a result of this disqualification. In 2000 the CONGRESSIONAL BLACK CAUCUS proposed legislation to allow felons to vote in elections for Congress and president. However, many scholars argued that the legislation violated the principle of federalism and it was not acted on by the Congress.

See also CRIMINAL JUSTICE SYSTEM, VOTING BEHAVIOR.

Voting Rights Act of 1965

The Voting Rights Act of 1965 effectively guaranteed VOTING RIGHTS to African Americans for the first time since RECONSTRUCTION. The act was proposed by President LYNDON B. JOHNSON and enacted by CONGRESS in response to the SELMA DEMONSTRATIONS led by JOHN LEWIS and SNCC and MARTIN LUTHER KING JR. and the SOUTHERN CHRISTIAN LEADERSHIP CONFERENCE. With the CIVIL RIGHTS ACT OF 1964, it is the most important legislative accomplishment of the CIVIL RIGHTS MOVEMENT.

Passed pursuant to Congress's authority to enact "appropriate legislation" to enforce the FIFTEENTH AMENDMENT, the act, among other things, suspended the use of literacy and other qualifications used to discriminate against blacks and authorized the DEPARTMENT OF JUSTICE to send registrars to any state where such tests had been used and where less than 50 percent of eligible voters were registered. Section 5 of the act required approval by the Justice Department or the U.S. District Court for the DISTRICT OF COLUMBIA of any changes in voting qualifications or practices in states affected by the act. As a result of the act, by 1970 African Americans were voting at rates comparable with whites.

The act was passed as a five-year temporary measure to compel STATE AND LOCAL GOVERNMENTs in the SOUTHERN STATES to allow blacks to register and vote. It was renewed three times in the 20th century. In 1970 it was renewed for five years. In 1975 it was renewed for seven years; its coverage was extended to additional states; bilingual ballots were required; and voting-rights protections were added for other MINORITY GROUPS, including Native Americans, Latinos, and Asian Americans. In 1982 it was extended for twenty-five years (until 2007) and was amended to prohibit any change in a state's voting procedures or election laws that had a DISPARATE IMPACT on minority voting rights. This amendment to Section 2 of the act recognized that INDIVIDUAL RACISM or overt DISCRIMINATION in voting had been largely eliminated, but that INSTITUTIONAL RACISM might still be a barrier to blacks achieving equitable REPRESENTATION among ELECTED OFFICIALS. Thus, the amended Section 2 prohibited any changes in voting procedures or practices "which *result* in a denial or abridgment of the right of any citizen . . . to vote" and concluded that a violation occurs when members of a "protected class" (minority groups) "have less opportunity than other members of the electorate to participate in the political process and to elect representatives of their choice." Unlike other provisions of the act, Section 2 is not temporary and its coverage is not limited to the Southern states. Thus, it is used in LITIGATION throughout the United States as a means to compel state and local governments to create legislative districts that maximize the opportunities for minorities to win elected office. Although Section 2 explicitly prohibits QUOTAS in representation, prior to *SHAW V. RENO* the CIVIL RIGHTS DIVISION of the Justice Department and judges generally interpreted it to mean that legislative districts should be drawn in ways that would allow minorities to elect representatives in rough proportion to their share of the jurisdiction's population. This generally meant creating districts with majorities of minorities.

In *Shaw v. Reno* the SUPREME COURT declared that the deliberate use of race to create legislative districts violated the EQUAL PROTECTION CLAUSE of the FOURTEENTH AMENDMENT. Thus, at the beginning of the 21st century the status of the Voting Rights Act as a tool to enhance black representation in the POLITICAL SYSTEM was unclear, as were the prospects for its renewal in 2007. However, in more than three decades of its operation, it resulted in the extension of voting rights to millions of minority-group citizens and the election of thousands to public office.

W

Walker, David (1785–1830) abolitionist, author

David Walker is the author of one of the most influential texts in AFRICAN-AMERICAN THOUGHT, *Walker's Appeal in Four Articles; Together with a Preamble To the Colored World, But in Particular and Very Expressly to Those of the United States of America*. The document, published as a pamphlet in 1829, was a kind of manifesto for the emerging ABOLITIONIST MOVEMENT, and it is a seminal source for the philosophy of BLACK NATIONALISM. In the *Appeal*, Walker first uses RELIGIOSITY, the DECLARATION OF INDEPENDENCE, and the doctrine of NATURAL RIGHTS to condemn SLAVERY as a violation of Christian teachings, HUMAN RIGHTS, and natural law. In the second part of the work, he calls on blacks and enslaved and FREE NEGROES to use "any means necessary," including VIOLENCE, to achieve FREEDOM and EQUALITY. Walker also harshly condemned blacks who failed to stand up and fight against OPPRESSION or who betrayed those who did. Finally, the *Appeal* embraces PAN-AFRICANISM by calling on blacks to fight for the freedom of Africans everywhere.

Despite efforts by whites to suppress it, the *Appeal* was widely distributed in the NORTHERN STATES and the SOUTHERN STATES. Its message of MILITANCY and RADICALISM inspired many in the abolitionist movement, including HENRY HIGHLAND GARNETT and MARIA W. STEWART. Alarmed that the pamphlet might incite SLAVE REVOLTS, officials in many of the Southern states used various forms of POLITICAL REPRESSION to prevent its printing or distribution. It was banned from the mail; officials in Massachusetts (where Walker lived) were asked to stop its printing; Georgia imposed the death penalty on anyone found distributing it; and a $10,000 bounty was placed on Walker's life by a group of slave owners. His friends, fearing for his life, urged him to move to Canada. Walker refused, saying, "Somebody must die in this cause. I may be doomed to the stake and fire or scaffold tree, but it is not in me to falter if I can promote the work of emancipation." One year later Walker was dead, probably the victim of poi-

soning. Two years after the *Appeal*'s publication NAT TURNER, perhaps inspired by it, launched the bloodiest slave revolt in American history.

Walker was born in slavery and ran away to Pennsylvania, where he opened a clothing store. He later moved to Boston, where he wrote articles for abolitionist newspapers. The *Appeal* is his only contribution to African-American politics, but it is an important one. It influenced Henry Highland Garnett in writing his 1843 *"Address to the Slaves,"* in which he called for violent rebellion, and it shaped the thinking and rhetoric of MALCOLM X, STOKELY CARMICHAEL, and the leaders of the BLACK PANTHER PARTY when they made similar calls in the 1960s. The *Appeal* is still available in major bookstores and is often assigned in AFRICAN-AMERICAN STUDIES classes. HERBERT APTHEKER is the author of one of two major studies of Walker's life and his *Appeal*.

Further reading: Herbert Aptheker, *One Continual Cry: David Walker's Appeal to the Colored Citizens of the World, 1829–1830* (New York: Humanities Press, 1965); Charles Wiltse, *David Walker's Appeal* (New York: Hill and Wang, 1965).

Wallace, George (1919–1988) U.S. governor, white supremacist leader

Among ELECTED OFFICIALS, George Wallace was the best-known opponent of the CIVIL RIGHTS MOVEMENT during the 1960s. Although he was defeated by the movement in two historic confrontations—the BIRMINGHAM DEMONSTRATIONS and the SELMA DEMONSTRATIONS—in four presidential campaigns he exerted a major influence on the direction of POST–CIVIL RIGHTS ERA politics in the United States. Indeed, Wallace's THIRD PARTY presidential campaigns are among the most effective and influential in American history.

Wallace came to national prominence as a passionate advocate of WHITE SUPREMACY, RACISM, SEGREGATION, and DISCRIMINATION. In 1958 Wallace, then a state judge, ran for governor of Alabama on a platform that to some extent embraced POPULISM, but he was defeated by an opponent who took a more outspoken position in defense of segregation. Wallace vowed at that point that he would never again be "out-niggered" in an election. Four years later he was elected governor in one of the most openly racist campaigns in modern American history, pledging as governor to personally "stand in the school house door" to block the DESEGREGATION of any school in Alabama. At his inauguration Wallace said, "I toss the gauntlet into the dust,

and I say segregation today, segregation tomorrow, segregation forever!" One year after becoming governor Wallace kept his promise and personally stood in front of the University of Alabama's administration building to block the admission of two black students. President JOHN F. KENNEDY federalized the Alabama militia and dispatched U.S. marshals to the campus to enforce the SUPREME COURT's order requiring the desegregation of the university. Wallace's defiant stand at the university's door was broadcast live on national television, making him an overnight hero to racists and white supremacists through-

Gov. George Wallace of Alabama holding a photo he describes as showing "known agitators" in his state *(Library of Congress)*

out the nation. A year later Wallace sent the state police to Birmingham to assist local police in the violent suppression of the demonstrations led by MARTIN LUTHER KING JR. And two years later he used VIOLENCE again by sending state police to Selma, where they brutally beat JOHN LEWIS and protesters who were attempting to march to the state capital. Historically, these two confrontations with the forces of OPPRESSION led by Wallace resulted in two of the Civil Rights movement's greatest victories: The confrontation at Birmingham led directly to passage of the CIVIL RIGHTS ACT OF 1964, and the one at Selma led directly to passage of the VOTING RIGHTS ACT OF 1965. Selma and Birmingham were directly responsible for the end of segregation throughout the United States and the enforcement of black VOTING RIGHTS in the SOUTHERN STATES. Thus, in direct confrontations with Dr. King, Wallace suffered humiliating defeats. But rather than retiring from the battlefield, Wallace turned these defeats into the basis for four campaigns for the PRESIDENCY. These campaigns did not result in his election, but that was not their purpose. Rather, as he said, their purpose was to "send 'em a message," that is, to send the two major parties a message about the size and intensity of white voter resentment about FREEDOM and EQUALITY for African Americans.

Wallace first ran for president in the 1964 DEMOCRATIC PARTY primaries against LYNDON B. JOHNSON. Although he clearly had no chance to defeat the hugely popular Johnson, Wallace did send a message by running close races against Johnson surrogates in Wisconsin, Maryland, and Indiana, thereby demonstrating that there was a WHITE BACKLASH in the NORTHERN STATES as well as the states of the South. In 1968 Wallace abandoned the Democratic Party and ran as a third-party candidate against HUBERT HUMPHREY and RICHARD NIXON. In this election Wallace's vote was almost large enough to constitute the balance of power in the ELECTORAL COLLEGE, as he won several Deep South states and did well in several Northern states. A shift of relatively few votes in a few states would have given the presidency to Humphrey or allowed Wallace to play the kingmaker role. Recognizing this, Nixon and REPUBLICAN PARTY strategists accelerated their embrace of the SOUTHERN STRATEGY that had started four years before with the nomination of BARRY GOLDWATER. That is, the party abandoned its historic identification with CIVIL RIGHTS and appeals to black voters and instead went after the anti–civil rights constituency represented by the Wallace vote. In 1972 Wallace ran for president again; this time in the Democratic Party primaries, winning many of the Southern states and several in the North before he was shot (by a white man) and paralyzed from the waist down. Prior to the assassination attempt, polls indicated Wallace commanded about 20 percent of the national vote. With Wallace out of the race, Nixon won reelection by an overwhelming margin, carrying the Wallace vote throughout the nation and demonstrating the viability of the Southern strategy. In 1976 Wallace ran for president for the last time, but disabled in a wheelchair, he was defeated by JIMMY CARTER, a fellow Southerner, in the early primaries and withdrew from the race. In his 1972 and 1976 campaigns Wallace played down his racist and white-supremacist positions and claimed his opposition to civil rights was based on adherence to principles of FEDERALISM and "states rights." In these last campaigns he emphasized his opposition to BUSING and his commitment to "law and order" as a response to the RIOTS in the GHETTOS, the MILITANCY and RADICALISM of the BLACK POWER MOVEMENT and the BLACK PANTHER PARTY, and the VIETNAM WAR protests. This strategy was followed by Nixon and RONALD REAGAN as they worked to build a majority-Republican COALITION on the basis of the white backlash and the Southern strategy. This strategy was also used by Newt Gingrich as part of the basis for the election of a Republican majority in CONGRESS in 1994.

Although paralyzed, Wallace was reelected governor in 1974 and again in 1978. Indeed, Wallace was so popular among whites in Alabama that when he was ineligible to run for reelection, his wife was elected as his surrogate. As a result of the Voting Rights Act, blacks in Alabama begin to vote, and Wallace began to repudiate his early racist and white-supremacist views and reach out to black voters, who constituted a quarter of the electorate. In his last election for governor he received some support from blacks, and as he neared death, several black leaders, including JESSE JACKSON, visited him in a gesture of reconciliation. Yet Wallace will be remembered as one of the most important racist and white-supremacist politicians in American history; a symbol of resistance to black freedom and equality; and the first national leader to demonstrate the significance of the white backlash in the post–civil rights era.

Further reading: Dan Carter, *From George Wallace to Newt Gingrich: Race and the Conservative Counter-Revolution, 1963–1994* (Baton Rouge: Louisiana State University Press, 1996); Marshall Frady, *Wallace* (New York: New American Library, 1976).

Walters, Ronald (1938–) *adviser, public intellectual*
Ronald Walters is one of the leading black PUBLIC INTELLECTUALS of the POST–CIVIL RIGHTS ERA. But unlike most black public intellectuals whose activities tend to be limited to the dissemination of their scholarship in the popular MEDIA as well as traditional scholarly outlets, Walters is also an activist intellectual in the tradition of W. E. B. DU BOIS. That is, to use the title of a *Washington Post* profile, he is "a participatory pundit" (Jacqueline Trescott, "Howard Uni-

versity's Participatory Pundit," *Washington Post,* November 8, 1990).

Walters is the most influential post–civil rights era adviser and strategist for the black LEADERSHIP establishment, playing a role akin to that played by BAYARD RUSTIN during the CIVIL RIGHTS MOVEMENT. Walters's activism in the African-American struggle for FREEDOM and EQUALITY goes back to the early days of the PROTEST phase of the Civil Rights movement. Two years before the famous SIT-INS in Greensboro, North Carolina, Walters as president of the NAACP youth council of Wichita, Kansas, his home town, led what may have been the first modern sit-in at a downtown drug store. After graduating from Fisk University, a historically black university, Walters earned a Ph.D. in political science from American University and then began an extraordinary career of scholarship and activism. In the late 1960s he established the first program in AFRICAN-AMERICAN STUDIES at Brandeis University. In the early 1970s he became chairman of the political science department at HOWARD UNIVERSITY, helping to turn it into the leading academic center for the study of AFRICAN-AMERICAN POLITICS in the United States.

A prolific author, Walters has written more than 100 articles and several books, including important studies of the theory and practice of PAN-AFRICANISM, on African-American leadership, on strategies of black participation in PRESIDENTIAL CAMPAIGNS, and on the resurgence of the IDEOLOGY of CONSERVATISM as an expression of "white Nationalism." Walters, a "pragmatic black nationalist," has written extensively on how BLACK NATIONALISM, properly understood and practiced, constitutes the BLACK COMMUNITY's "unifying ideology." In addition to his scholarly writings, Walters is the leading political science interpreter of black politics in the national media, black and white. He has written articles in most of the leading newspapers of the United States and appeared on virtually all of the national television and radio news and commentary programs. His column on black politics is syndicated by the National Newspaper Publishers Association (NNPA), the ORGANIZATION of weekly newspapers. He also worked as a roving correspondent for NNPA, covering major national and international events. Lastly, he is the principal commentator on black politics for *BET News,* the only national African-American cable outlet. From these numerous media activities, he helped to shape popular interpretations of black politics. Walters is among a handful of black scholars able and willing to bridge the divide between black scholarship and black politics. This is a divide that many do not wish to bridge because they think scholars should be detached from politics, while others cannot bridge it because of the esoteric nature of their work, while still others cannot because of their critical analyses of black leadership.

Walters, while maintaining a critical perspective, has throughout the post–civil rights era been an adviser and strategist for the black leadership establishment, including the CONGRESSIONAL BLACK CAUCUS, state legislative black caucuses, the NATIONAL BLACK POLITICAL CONVENTION, and the black caucuses of both the DEMOCRATIC PARTY and the REPUBLICAN PARTY. In 1984 he was a principal strategist in JESSE JACKSON's presidential campaign. He has participated in the writing of every post–civil rights era BLACK AGENDA, from the 1972 National Black Political Convention to the MILLION MAN MARCH. In addition to his work in domestic politics and PUBLIC POLICY, he has extensive background and experience in FOREIGN POLICY. (His doctoral dissertation was on African politics and one of his books is on South Africa's development of a nuclear bomb.) As chairman of Howard's political science department, he organized and attended several conferences on Pan-Africanism in the United States and Africa, was a leader in several anti-APARTHEID organizations, and was a founder of TRANSAFRICA and chairman of the board of its affiliate organization TransAfrica Forum. A consultant to the UNITED NATIONS conferences on RACISM and DISCRIMINATION, Walters lectured throughout the United States, Asia, Africa, and Latin America on issues of race in America and in the context of GLOBALIZATION. In the early 1990s Walters left Howard to join the faculty of the University of Maryland as a senior scholar and director of the Institute on the Study of African American Leadership.

Further reading: Ronald Walters, "African American Nationalism: A Unifying Ideology," *Black World* 23 (1973): 9–27; ———, "In World Relations: The Future of Pan Africanism," *Black World* 24 (1974): 4–18.

Walton, Hanes, Jr. (1941–) *scholar*

Hanes Walton Jr. is a pioneering scholar in the development of AFRICAN-AMERICAN POLITICS as a recognized field of study in the discipline of political science. Walton received his B.A. and M.A. from ATLANTA UNIVERSITY, and in 1967 he became the first person to earn a Ph.D. in political science from HOWARD UNIVERSITY. He then joined the faculty at Savannah State, a small historically black university in Georgia. Like most small black colleges, Savannah provides relatively little support for research and requires its faculty to devote most of its time to teaching. Nevertheless, Walton in more than 20 years on the faculty produced a large and varied body of work that constitutes an essential part of the foundations of the modern study of black politics.

For a social science field of study to develop, it requires extensive bibliographic work that lays out the research that has already been done and points students toward areas requiring future research. This kind of bibliographic work is necessary to establish the theoretical and methodological boundaries of the field. After publishing his dissertation on MARTIN LUTHER KING JR., Walton undertook this tedious and time-consuming work beginning in 1973 with the publication of *The Study and Analysis of Black Politics: A Bibliography*. He then published four other bibliographic essays surveying the literature of the field. These essays start with the formative work in the field in the first decades of the 20th century and conclude with the work of its last decade. Together, the four essays provide a continuing and comprehensive overview of the development of research on African-American politics. In addition to being the "bibliophile of black politics," Walton is the author of the first undergraduate textbook in black politics, *Black Politics: A Theoretical and Structural Analysis* (1972), and the first advanced, graduate-level text, *Invisible Politics: Black Political Behavior* (1985). He is also the coauthor of a textbook in American politics, *American Politics and the African American Quest for Universal Freedom* (2000), in which the black experience is systematically integrated into the study of the subject.

After 25 years on the faculty at Savannah State, Walton in 1992 joined the faculty of the University of Michigan. In 1993 Howard University gave him its Distinguished Ph.D. Alumni Award.

Further reading: Hanes Walton, "The Recent Literature of Black Politics," *PS: Political Science and Politics* 18 (1985): 769–80; ———, "The Current Literature on Black Politics," *National Political Science Review* 1 (1989): 152–68; Hanes Walton, Leslie B. McLemore, and C. Vernon Gray, "The Pioneering Books in Black Politics and the Political Science Community," *National Political Science Review* 2 (1990): 196–218; Hanes Walton, Cheryl Miller, and Joseph McCormick, "Race and Political Science: The Dual Traditions of Race Relations Politics and African American Politics," in *Political Science and Its History: Research Programs and Political Traditions* (New York: Cambridge University Press, 1994); Hanes Walton, John Dryzek, et al., "The Literature of African American Politics: The Decade of the Nineties," *Politics and Society* 29 (2001): 453–82.

Wards Cove v. Antonio (1989)

Wards Cove v. Antonio is the most important of six decisions by the SUPREME COURT in its 1988–89 term that significantly undermined the law on employment DISCRIMINATION, making it very difficult for individuals to engage in LITIGATION against businesses whose employment practices have a discriminatory impact on blacks, women, or other MINORITY GROUP workers. (The case involved Native American cannery workers in Alaska.)

In *Wards Cove* the Court in a 5-4 decision ruled that employees had to show that a business engaged in direct discrimination or INDIVIDUAL RACISM, rather than rely on statistical or other evidence showing its practices had a DISPARATE IMPACT on minority workers or reflected a pattern of INSTITUTIONAL RACISM. In addition, the Court held that employees were required to identify specific discriminatory practices and show that the employer had no "business need" for them. It also held that some discriminatory practices could be legally justified if they served businesses' "legitimate employment goals." The four dissenting justices argued that new standards of *Wards Cove* reversed two decades of law going back to GRIGGS V. DUKE POWER and created a nearly insurmountable burden of proof for victims of employment discrimination. Justice THURGOOD MARSHALL, who was among the dissenters, later cited *Wards Cove* as evidence that the Court was deliberately retreating from enforcing CIVIL RIGHTS law. Marshall urged black LEADERSHIP to shift to LOBBYING the CONGRESS rather than litigation to protect civil rights.

As a result of black lobbying, the Congress two years later overturned *Wards Cove* by passing the Civil Rights Act of 1991, which replaced the *Wards Cove* DISPARATE TREATMENT standard with the *Griggs* disparate impact standard. But in 2001 in *Circuit City v. Adams*, the Court substantially overruled the 1991 Civil Rights Act by deciding that businesses could require employers to take complaints of job discrimination to private arbitration rather than to court. This decision essentially repealed the right of workers to sue for job discrimination because it permitted businesses to use private arbitration as an alternative to litigation.

War on Poverty

The War on Poverty was a series of programs initiated by President LYNDON B. JOHNSON as part of the GREAT SOCIETY. The Great Society included a variety of programs that expanded the WELFARE STATE created by FRANKLIN D. ROOSEVELT during the NEW DEAL. These programs included Medicare, Medicaid, legal services to the poor, and the ELEMENTARY AND SECONDARY EDUCATION ACT. While each of these programs dealt with the problem of POVERTY, generally they are not considered part of the War on Poverty but, rather, a part of a general program of reform in the tradition of American LIBERALISM. In general, they were designed to enhance the social and economic well-being of all Americans.

The programs that constituted the War on Poverty, in contrast, were designed to specifically attack the problem of poverty in the BLACK COMMUNITY in the rural areas of the SOUTHERN STATES but especially in the big-city GHETTOS. Although African-American CIVIL RIGHTS leaders and

ORGANIZATIONS were not involved in the development or design of the war, many scholars view it as a natural outgrowth of the CIVIL RIGHTS MOVEMENT. In his account of the origins of the war in *The Politics of Poverty,* John C. Donovan writes that it was a "prime example of [legislation] drafted principally for the poor Negro although public discussion of the program has seldom been completely candid in acknowledging this fact . . . but the urgent necessity of an all out attack on the pathology of the dark ghetto dictated the prime objective of the war on poverty." From a different perspective, FRANCES FOX PIVEN contends that the war was a strategy of CO-OPTATION designed to "regulate" the political behavior of poor blacks in order to avoid an outbreak of MILITANCY.

Whatever its precise origins or purposes, the War on Poverty had a major impact on the development of black URBAN POLITICS. President Johnson declared the War on Poverty in 1964 in his first State of the Union address to the CONGRESS, saying that the struggle would be long but "we shall not rest until the war is won." Yet by 1966 the war was effectively over; in John Donovan's words "the first domestic casualty of the war in Vietnam." The War on Poverty, formally known as the Economic Opportunity Act of 1964, included the following programs: Head Start, the Job Corps, the Neighborhood Youth Corps, VISTA (a kind of domestic Peace Corps), and various student work-study programs. These programs were administered by the Office of Economic Opportunity (OEO), a new agency in the BUREAUCRACY headed by Sargent Shriver, the brother-in-law of President JOHN F. KENNEDY. By creating a new office under direct presidential control and headed by a relative of the former president, Johnson intended to signal that the war was a priority item on his domestic PUBLIC POLICY agenda. However, these symbolic gestures were not matched by the outlay of funds. The initial 1964 budget for OEO was $800 million, in 1965 $1.5 billion, and in 1967 the president requested $1.5 billion. But in 1966 OEO was already funding antipoverty projects at an amount projected at nearly $2 billion. Thus, within two years the war was being underfunded, in part because of the need to shift funds to fight the VIETNAM WAR and probably because the CONSERVATIVE COALITION, which had opposed the War on Poverty from the outset, vowed to cut Johnson's request, claiming that the country could not afford "guns and butter." That is, the country could not afford to wage two wars—a domestic war on poverty and a foreign war in Vietnam. As a result, the War on Poverty came to an end before it could really begin. MARTIN LUTHER KING JR., in his first major speech opposing the Vietnam War, cited the diversion of funds from the War on Poverty as one of the main reasons for his opposition, saying, "We have not put enough money in that war [on poverty] to even fight a good skirmish."

However, it is not clear that the War on Poverty would have been sustained even without the war in Vietnam because it was widely and correctly viewed as a program for poor blacks. Therefore, unlike the other Great Society programs, which benefited the broad middle class, the War on Poverty never had broad support in PUBLIC OPINION. The REPUBLICAN PARTY had opposed it from the beginning, and when RICHARD NIXON took office in 1969, he brought the war to an end by abolishing OEO and its community-action program. Although poverty overall and black poverty specifically declined after the war started, it is difficult to attribute this decline to the programs that were specifically part of the war. Rather, other changes—the general growth in the economy during the 1960s, the decline in employment DISCRIMINATION as a result of implementation of the CIVIL RIGHTS ACT OF 1964, and the beginnings of AFFIRMATIVE ACTION—probably are more responsible for the decline.

Several War on Poverty programs were not eliminated and continued in operation into the 21st century, including Head Start, the Job Corps, and various student work programs. But the centerpiece of the war—the community-action program—was eliminated during the Nixon administration. The planners of the war saw poverty in political as well as economic terms. That is, poor blacks not only lacked money or economic resources but also POWER, political organizations, and influence in urban politics. Thus, the purpose of the community-action component of the war was to attack "political poverty." David Greenstone and Paul Peterson in their study of the War on Poverty and its origins write that the planners had as a "fundamental political objective . . . the organization and consequent institutionalization of black (and other minority groups) interests as constituent components of the urban political regime." That is, although PLURALISM was supposed to characterize urban politics, the planners of the war recognized that blacks in general and poor blacks in particular lacked access to the political process in the cities. In order to deal with this problem, the War on Poverty created community-action programs to plan and implement antipoverty strategies in local communities. The law required that the agencies administering these programs have the "maximum feasible participation" of poor people themselves. In other words, the programs were to be controlled by poor people to the extent possible. In this way, the War on Poverty sought to "mandate pluralism" in urban politics and to a somewhat lesser extent in the politics of rural areas of the South. In many cities these black-controlled community-action agencies engaged in direct confrontations with white-dominated city governments, and this was one of the reasons the Nixon administration eliminated the program, although the process of elimination started in the Johnson administration.

The community action programs were short-lived, but they had some important and long-lasting effects on the development of urban black politics. First, for a brief period they provided blacks a place of their own in the urban bureaucracy. Second, the process of selection and service on the staffs and boards of the agencies operated as agents of POLITICAL SOCIALIZATION and encouraged POLITICAL PARTICIPATION. Third, the programs provided a new mechanism for LEADERSHIP recruitment and development. In the POST–CIVIL RIGHTS ERA a large number of blacks used their work in these programs as the basis to become ELECTED OFFICIALS, including several members of the CONGRESSIONAL BLACK CAUCUS.

Further reading: John Donovan, *The Politics of Poverty* (New York: Pegasus, 1967); David Greenstone and Paul Peterson, *Race and Authority in Urban Politics: Community Participation and the War on Poverty* (New York: Russell Sage Foundation, 1973).

Warren, Earl (1891–1974) *14th chief justice of the United States*

Earl Warren, the 14th chief justice of the United States, is the person most sympathetic to the African-American quest for FREEDOM and EQUALITY of all the men who have held the post, and one of the dozen or so most sympathetic of any person to hold a position of great power in the POLITICAL SYSTEM. As chief justice, Warren used CONSTITUTIONALISM as a weapon to wage an unwavering, relentless assault on RACISM and WHITE SUPREMACY.

Warren was appointed to head the SUPREME COURT by President Dwight Eisenhower in 1953 as a political favor because, as governor of California, he had helped Eisenhower win the REPUBLICAN PARTY nomination in 1952. Warren came to the Court as a popular and progressive governor, but his record had not shown any particular concern for CIVIL LIBERTIES or CIVIL RIGHTS. On the contrary, his role in supporting the incarceration of Japanese Americans during World War II raised concerns about his commitment to these values. However, once he assumed leadership of the Court, his jurisprudence of LIBERALISM became the most remarkable in the Court's history.

Warren did not have prior experience as a judge (although he had served as local prosecutor and state attorney general), but he brought to the Court remarkable leadership skills. Those skills were immediately put to the test in the case of BROWN V. BOARD OF EDUCATION. The case had been argued the year before, and the justices were divided. However, within a year Warren was able to persuade his eight colleagues to join him in a unanimous opinion declaring that SEGREGATION and the 50-year-old doctrine of SEPARATE BUT EQUAL violated the EQUAL PROTECTION CLAUSE of the FOURTEENTH AMENDMENT. (Warren bluntly told his wavering colleagues that the only way segregation could be rationally defended was on the basis of white supremacy, and that if that was their IDEOLOGY they should be prepared to openly state it.) The *Brown* opinion was narrowly written to deal with segregation in SCHOOLS AND EDUCATION; however, Warren used it as a precedent in a series of per curiam decisions (unsigned opinions by the Court used to dispose of uncomplicated questions) to strike down segregation in all government-operated facilities. And prior to CONGRESS's passage of the CIVIL RIGHTS ACT OF 1964, Warren was searching for a case that would allow the Court to strike down segregation in privately owned public accommodations. (This would have overturned both *PLESSY V. FERGUSON* and the CIVIL RIGHTS CASES OF 1883.) Under Warren's leadership the Court quickly upheld the constitutionality of Congress's use of the COMMERCE CLAUSE to pass the 1964 act, and it also quickly approved the constitutionality of the VOTING RIGHTS ACT OF 1965. Also in the area of civil rights and RACE, the Court supported the use of SIT-INS as constitutionally protected forms of PROTEST; and in *Loving v. Virginia* (1967) the Court prohibited the states from using the principle of FEDERALISM to prohibit interracial marriages.

Warren's liberal jurisprudence extended beyond civil rights. Indeed Warren himself said his most important case was the *BAKER V. CARR* "one man, one vote" decision, because it significantly expanded DEMOCRACY in the United States. Although *Baker* did not directly deal with race, the effect of it and its progeny was to increase the REPRESENTATION of blacks among ELECTED OFFICIALS. The Warren Court also issued a series of decisions that substantially expanded the rights of persons accused of crimes. These decisions led to reforms in the CRIMINAL JUSTICE SYSTEM, which, given the disproportionate number of blacks accused of crimes, also had an impact on the BLACK COMMUNITY. Finally, the Warren Court significantly undermined the constitutional basis of POLITICAL REPRESSION, by ruling that members of the COMMUNIST PARTY and other adherents of RADICALISM had a constitutional right of association that precluded the government from repressing them merely because of their beliefs.

All of these liberal decisions led to a WHITE BACKLASH in the SOUTHERN STATES and reaction from adherents of CONSERVATISM. In the late 1950s and early 1960s "Impeach Earl Warren" billboards appeared on highways throughout the South. BARRY GOLDWATER made opposition to Warren an important part of the conservative movement. The Warren Court was a frequent target of the rhetoric of GEORGE WALLACE and other white supremacists, and RICHARD NIXON and RONALD REAGAN campaigned for president by pledging to appoint justices who would reverse many Warren Court decisions. Warren retired from the Court in 1969, and President Nixon appointed his successor, Warren Burger. Nixon and Reagan in their terms in office appointed a majority of the Court's justices, and these justices did begin a gradual retreat from Warren Court precedents in areas of civil liberties, civil rights, and the COMMERCE CLAUSE, but at the beginning of 21st century most of the landmark Warren Court precedents remained in place. President Eisenhower reportedly said that the appointment of Warren (and WILLIAM BRENNAN) was "the biggest damn fool mistake I ever made." However, many historians rank Warren as second only to John Marshall in his leadership of the Court and in his impact on American jurisprudence. For African Americans, he ranks with THADDEUS STEVENS, CHARLES SUMNER, HUBERT HUMPHREY, THURGOOD MARSHALL, LYNDON B. JOHNSON, William Brennan, and EDWARD KENNEDY as among the best friends they have had in the power structure of the U.S. government.

Further reading: Bernard Schwarz, *Superchief: Earl Warren and His Supreme Court* (New York: New York University Press, 1983).

Washington, Booker T. (1856–1915) *African-American leader, educator*

Booker T. Washington is arguably the most powerful person ever to occupy a position in the LEADERSHIP structure of the BLACK COMMUNITY. Yet of all the leaders in the history of black America, Washington's claim to that title, the historian Louis Harlan writes, "is the most often dismissed" because Washington is viewed as the paradigmatic UNCLE TOM. Of Washington's POWER in the black community, GUNNAR MYRDAL in *AN AMERICAN DILEMMA* wrote, "Washington was not only a national Negro leader, but actually held a virtual monopoly on national Negro leadership for nearly three decades." The historian Lerone Bennett in *Before the Mayflower: A History of the Negro in America* (1966) concurs, writing that Washington "wielded more political power than any other Negro in American history." But of Washington MACK H. JONES writes, "His leadership was instrumental in allowing the southern planter class to reimpose its domination after Reconstruction with minimal cost."

In a 2000 poll of African-American political scientists rating the greatest black leaders of all time, Washington ranked fifth on a list of 12. But virtually all of the political scientists who ranked him as a great leader were either negative or at best ambivalent in their assessment. One described him simply as a "villain," while still another wrote, "He was wrong about many things but who can question that for many years he was 'The man' in Afro-American life." The controversy about Washington's leadership revolves around how he adjusted to the end of RECONSTRUCTION and whether, on balance, his strategy of ACCOMMODATIONISM in the long run advanced or retarded the African-American struggle for FREEDOM and EQUALITY.

Washington was born into SLAVERY just as the CIVIL WAR approached its end. After the war he was educated for a time in schools established by the FREEDMEN'S BUREAU, but in 1872 he left his home in West Virginia to study at newly established Hampton Institute. Almost penniless (he is said to have had only $1.50), he paid his tuition by working as a janitor and with the help of Northern philanthropists. Hampton Institute emphasized vocational and agricultural training—practical knowledge—that would prepare its students for work in the postslavery economy of the SOUTHERN STATES. This educational philosophy was implemented by Washington when shortly after graduation he was asked to serve as head of TUSKEGEE INSTITUTE, a school established by the government of Alabama to educate blacks. When Tuskegee opened in 1881 (as the Tuskegee Normal School for Colored Youth) it had hardly any money. The government provided a small budget for teacher salaries but little for buildings, books, or supplies. Washington borrowed money to buy an abandoned plantation and the students built the campus.

These early SELF-HELP initiatives impressed Northern philanthropists, who began to contribute relatively large sums to Tuskegee. By the 1890s Tuskegee had an enrollment of 400 students (it started with 30) and was housed on an attractive 500-acre campus. These accomplishments gained Washington national recognition as an educational leader, and he began to lecture throughout the United States. In these lectures Washington and his educational philosophy attracted the support of influential elements of the POWER ELITE, and soon they recognized him as an emerging leader of the black community. Meanwhile, Reconstruction was coming to an end as a result of the VIOLENCE and intimidation of the KU KLUX KLAN and other white terrorist groups. The COMPROMISE OF 1877 represented the symbolic end of the Reconstruction experiment in racial DEMOCRACY, CIVIL RIGHTS, and full POLITICAL PARTICIPATION. In his 1895 "ATLANTA COMPROMISE" ADDRESS, Washington signaled to the nation that the black community was prepared to accept or accommodate for a time its exclusion from the political process, the denial of civil rights, and the onset of SEGREGATION. At the time of Washington's compromise address, his views were almost certainly supported by black PUBLIC OPINION and the overwhelming majority of black leaders, because there were really no viable alternatives. In the face of overwhelming violence from whites in the Southern states and with little prospect for protection or assistance from the federal government after the Compromise of 1877, blacks had little choice: either accommodation or extermination. (The near extermination of Native Americans may have been a lesson to African Americans.)

Booker T. Washington *(Library of Congress)*

Thus, Washington entered into a COALITION with the former slave owners and Northern businessmen that embraced the idea of limited African-American freedom and equality. That is, Washington argued that the masses of the newly freed slaves were not ready for full freedom and equality because they lacked the necessary character, education, and property. Thus, for Washington, Reconstruction was a mistake and blacks should, at least temporarily, give up their quest for civil rights. In return Washington asked the former slave owners to grant blacks NATURAL RIGHTS, personal autonomy, the right to work, and the right to develop their own community on a SEPARATE BUT EQUAL basis. In contemporary language, Washington asked for the development of a PLURAL SOCIETY. To a limited extent the white power elite kept its part of the bargain and, under Washington's leadership, the modern infrastructure of black ORGANIZATIONs and institutional life developed—separate black businesses, schools, professional associations, fraternities and sororities, and MEDIA. Washington continually emphasized self-help and the development of black business. In some

ways he can be viewed as a kind of father of black CAPITALISM, organizing in 1900 the National Business League to facilitate black entrepreneurship. The white power elite helped to consolidate Washington's power by giving him the resources to create the "Tuskegee Machine," which allowed him to exercise near dictatorial power in the black community. Bennett's vivid description of Washington's power from *Before the Mayflower* is worth quoting at length:

When Washington arrived at his office, everything of importance that had happened in Negro America in the preceding twenty-four hours was at his fingertips. Confidential reports from agents had been sorted and analyzed. Important letters—from the President and influential whites and Negroes—were ready for his perusal; . . . From his office for more than twenty years Washington practically ruled Negro America. Like a reigning monarch, he issued an annual message "To My People." He was the court of last resort on Negro appointments in America and white political appointments in the South. No Negro institution, his critics said with only slight exaggeration, could get a substantial amount of money without his approval. He made and broke men and institutions with a word or a nod of his head and his silence in the face of a request for "information" could ruin a career. He corrected messages of Presidents and said the word which made confederates and sons of confederates postmasters and federal judges.

It was this quasi-dictatorial power as much as Washington's accommodationism that eventually resulted in a backlash and a challenge to his leadership by W. E. B. DU BOIS and WILLIAM MONROE TROTTER, among others. As the 19th century ended, elements of the TALENTED TENTH began to object to Washington's accommodationism. His refusal to condemn JIM CROW and LYNCHINGS, his obsequious attitude toward whites, his argument that slavery had benefited blacks, and his frequent "darky jokes" finally led to the development of a full-fledged PROTEST movement that by the time of his death in 1915 was on the verge of displacing him as the undisputed leader of black America. Yet, at the time of his death he was still a towering figure in African-American life.

Washington's legacy is controversial and ambivalent. He was viewed by many as the quintessential Uncle Tom and by others as the "uplifter" of the race. (It is estimated that more black children were named after Washington than any other person in American history.) Washington was in the final analysis a pragmatic politician who tried to make the best deal for blacks that he could given the circumstances of overwhelming white hostility and violence and black deprivation and powerlessness. There is in Washington's thought an important strain of BLACK NATIONALISM, and his philosophy of self-help is an important component in AFRICAN-AMERICAN THOUGHT. (MARCUS GARVEY, the preeminent black nationalist leader of the 20th century, originally came to the United States to visit Washington, whose ideas he said had impressed him as a young man in Jamaica.) Washington's leadership is unique among the great leaders of black America because it embraced limited rather than universal freedom and equality. It is clear, however, that for Washington this was a temporary accommodation to the circumstances of his time. He thought—wrongly as it turned out—that through education, work, and accumulation of property, blacks could overcome RACISM and WHITE SUPREMACY and eventually "earn" full freedom and equality or what he called "full citizenship rights."

Washington was a prolific writer, and his autobiography, *Up From Slavery,* a best-seller at the time of its publication in 1900, is a classic text in AFRICAN-AMERICAN STUDIES.

Further reading: Louis Harlan, *Booker T. Washington: The Making of a Black Leader* (New York: Oxford University Press, 1972); Louis Harlan, *Booker T. Washington: The Wizard of Tuskegee* (New York: Oxford University Press, 1983).

Watts, J. C. (1956–) *U.S. congressman*

J. C. Watts is one of two members of the REPUBLICAN PARTY elected to the House of Representatives during the POST–CIVIL RIGHTS ERA. Like Gary Franks, the other black Republican elected to the House, Watts embraced the IDEOLOGY of CONSERVATISM and was elected from an overwhelmingly majority-white district.

Watts grew up in Oklahoma and played quarterback for the University of Oklahoma, where he won several championships. After playing professional football for several years, he returned to Oklahoma, where he went into business and politics. In 1990 he was elected state corporation commissioner, and in 1994 he was elected to the CONGRESS, narrowly defeating his opponent in the Republican primary but winning easily against his DEMOCRATIC PARTY opponent in the general election. Watts's district, 83 percent white, is conservative, and in Congress Watts faithfully represented its views. As the only black Republican in Congress and the only conservative in the black congressional delegation, Watts achieved status in the House. In 1999 this status led to his election as chairman of the Republican Party Conference, the fourth-ranking position in the leadership structure. Although a conservative, Watts developed good relationships with blacks in the House and with the black LEADERSHIP establishment, unlike Gary Franks, who was called an UNCLE TOM by some black congressmen. (Franks was elected from Connecticut and served from 1991 until his defeat in 1996.) Although Watts declined to join the CONGRESSIONAL BLACK CAUCUS (remarking, "I didn't come to Congress to be a black leader or a white leader, but a leader"), he worked in support of several PUBLIC POLICY issues of concern to blacks, including AFFIRMATIVE ACTION and increased funding for HISTORICALLY BLACK COLLEGES AND UNIVERSITIES. In 2002, Watts announced his retirement from Congress in order to return to private life in Oklahoma.

Watts riot

The Watts riot is one of the most important events in modern African-American political history. There had been RIOTS in the GHETTOS of the United States before, but the riot in Watts—the largely black section of Los Angeles—was different in that it signaled a major change in the character of the African-American struggle for FREEDOM and EQUALITY.

The Watts riot took place in August 1965, just two weeks after President LYNDON B. JOHNSON signed the VOTING RIGHTS ACT OF 1965. Occurring so soon after one of the CIVIL RIGHTS MOVEMENT's greatest triumphs, the riot in effect symbolized the end of that movement. From its inception with the NIAGARA MOVEMENT and the founding of the NAACP, the Civil Rights movement had focused mainly on dismantling overt INDIVIDUAL RACISM in the SOUTHERN STATES as manifested in JIM CROW–style SEGREGATION. These objectives were achieved with the passage of the CIVIL RIGHTS ACT OF 1964 and the 1965 Voting Rights Act. These historic achievements, however, had little impact on the lives of blacks in the ghettos of the NORTHERN STATES because segregation was for the most part already illegal, and blacks in those states already had VOTING RIGHTS.

The barriers to freedom and equality in the ghettos—POVERTY and INSTITUTIONAL RACISM—had been for the most part ignored by the Southern-oriented Civil Rights movement. Watts changed this, shifting the focus of the movement toward the problems of the ghetto. The Watts riot also signaled a strategy shift away from nonviolent PROTEST and CIVIL DISOBEDIENCE and toward RADICALISM and VIOLENCE. The riot in Watts was up until that point the most violent ghetto riot in American history. Over five days a 45-square-mile area was burned, millions of dollars in property was destroyed, more than 1,000 people were injured, and 34 people were killed (31 of them

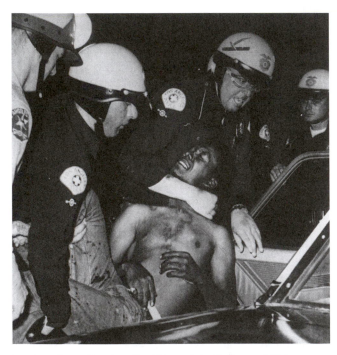

Los Angeles police hustling Watts rioter into car, 1965 (*Library of Congress*)

blacks). Three thousand police officers and as many national guard troops were used to suppress the riot, and the Watts area was occupied by the military for almost two weeks. And unlike earlier ghetto riots in HARLEM and elsewhere, after Watts a riot IDEOLOGY developed. This ideology, which gained widespread acceptance in the BLACK COMMUNITY, explicitly defined and defended the riot as a revolt or rebellion against racial OPPRESSION.

The Watts riot also set a precedent, for between 1965 and 1968 there were riots of increasing severity in virtually all the ghettos of the Northern states. These riots had a major impact on the black LEADERSHIP structure. MARTIN LUTHER KING JR. and the leaders of the NAACP and the URBAN LEAGUE condemned the riots but used them to urge the government to develop PUBLIC POLICY to address their underlying causes, which they identified as poverty and RACISM. King, while not abandoning his philosophical commitment to nonviolence, increasingly embraced militancy in his strategy and rhetoric, first by joining the VIETNAM WAR protests and then by launching the POOR PEOPLE'S CAMPAIGN. The leaders of SNCC and CORE, the other major CIVIL RIGHTS organizations, abandoned nonviolence and INTEGRATIONism and started the BLACK POWER MOVEMENT. And one year after Watts, HUEY NEWTON and BOBBY SEALE formed the BLACK PANTHER PARTY, which by 1967 was an explicitly revolutionary ORGANIZATION committed to fundamental changes in the POLITICAL SYSTEM.

Besides influencing the internal dynamics of black politics, Watts also affected the politics of the larger American society. The government responded with increased attention to the problem of ghetto poverty, including a bit more money for the WAR ON POVERTY and the beginnings of AFFIRMATIVE ACTION. The ongoing processes of CO-OPTATION and INCORPORATION of blacks into the system were also accelerated. These largely positive public policy responses occurred simultaneously with increased POLITICAL REPRESSION of the Black Power movement by the FBI and the MILITARY. Watts also accelerated the WHITE BACKLASH against the movement and helped to fuel a growing CONSERVATISM in the white electorate. Antiriot rhetoric became a staple of the presidential campaigns of GEORGE WALLACE, RICHARD NIXON, and RONALD REAGAN.

Further reading: Gerald Horne, *The Fire This Time: The Watts Uprising and the 1960s* (Charlottesville: University Press of Virginia, 1995); David Sears and John McConahay, *The Politics of Violence: The New Urban Blacks and the Watts Riot* (Boston: Houghton Mifflin, 1973).

Weaver, Robert C. (1907–1997) *government official*
Robert C. Weaver was the first African American to serve in the cabinet of an American president, appointed secre-

tary of the Department of HOUSING AND URBAN DEVELOPMENT (HUD) by President LYNDON B. JOHNSON in 1966. Weaver was first appointed to an important position in the federal BUREAUCRACY during the NEW DEAL when he served in the BLACK CABINET, appointed by President FRANKLIN D. ROOSEVELT in 1938 to serve as special assistant to the head of the Federal Housing Authority. In 1955 Weaver became the first black American to hold a state-level cabinet position when he was appointed New York's commissioner of rent. An active member of the DEMOCRATIC PARTY in New York and a former chair of the NAACP board, Weaver was appointed director of the Federal Housing and Home Finance Agency (FHHFA) in 1961 by President JOHN F. KENNEDY. When Kennedy appointed Weaver, he indicated that he intended to ask CONGRESS to make the agency a cabinet-level department and appoint Weaver its first secretary. Because this would make Weaver the first black in the cabinet, the CONSERVATIVE COALITION blocked Kennedy's plan. But it was enacted after his assassination, and Johnson—following Kennedy's pledge—named Weaver to head the new department. In his tenure as secretary, Weaver devoted most of his time to organizing the department, since it brought together FHHFA and five other agencies.

Weaver was born in the DISTRICT OF COLUMBIA and was graduated from Harvard University, where he also received a Ph.D. in economics. In addition to his work in the bureaucracy, Weaver taught at several universities. After leaving the cabinet, Weaver served briefly as president of Bernard Baruch College in New York City and then as distinguished professor of urban affairs at New York's Hunter College. A specialist in housing and labor economics, he wrote four books on these issues and served on the board of several major corporations, making him an early black member of the POWER ELITE.

welfare state

The American welfare state is less comprehensive than those of other Western democracies. It has no national health insurance system, and it does not provide comprehensive child care. But even this restricted welfare system provided less security and protection for African Americans than it did for the general population because it was designed partly on the basis of RACISM and WHITE SUPREMACY (as well as SEXISM).

The American welfare state was created in the 1930s as part of the NEW DEAL reform program of FRANKLIN D. ROOSEVELT. It was substantially expanded in the 1960s as part of the GREAT SOCIETY reform program of LYNDON B. JOHNSON. The Social Security Act and the National Labor Relations Act (both passed in 1935) and the Fair Labor Standards Act of 1938 constitute the basic foundations of

the welfare state. Each of these acts in their design and implementation resulted in DISCRIMINATION against blacks, especially black women. The expansion of the welfare state in the 1960s provided medical care for the elderly (Medicare) and the poor (Medicaid) as well as a variety of social services, including job training and legal assistance. Unlike the 1930s New Deal programs, the 1960s programs did not discriminate against blacks. On the contrary many of them, such as the WAR ON POVERTY, were specifically designed to assist blacks.

The Social Security Act created a two-tier welfare system. The first tier established a social insurance system for unemployed and retired workers. The second tier provided assistance to the blind, elderly, and children from single-parent families. The first system is viewed as an "insurance" program to which all eligible workers are entitled on the basis of their "contributions" (in the form of the social security tax). The second system is viewed as a "welfare" program for the poor because they do not make "contributions." Although the African-American LEADERSHIP strongly supported the creation of the welfare state, it just as strongly opposed the creation of the two-tier system. Opposition to the two-tier system arose because the majority of blacks were excluded from the first tier. In order to get the support of members of CONGRESS from the SOUTHERN STATES, Roosevelt agreed to exclude the self-employed, domestic servants, clergymen, and nurses from the tier-one insurance program. By excluding these categories of workers, the system excluded 60 percent of all black workers and 80 percent of black women workers while covering 70 percent of whites. This is because in the 1930s black workers were mainly farm laborers or domestic servants. The leaders of both the NAACP and the URBAN LEAGUE engaged in a concerted LOBBYING campaign, but Roosevelt would not alter the coverage because he feared the exclusion of those workers was the only way he could get a bill through a Congress dominated by the CONSERVATIVE COALITION. The NAACP and the Urban League also opposed funding the social security system on the basis of worker contributions (actually a flat tax on the covered workers and their employers), preferring instead financing on the basis of general tax revenue. Roosevelt opposed using general tax revenue because he said it would cost too much and would turn the system into "welfare" or the "dole." However, the income of many covered black workers was at that time too low to pay the social security tax. Thus, they too were in effect excluded. The second component of the New Deal welfare state—the National Labor Relations Act—also disadvantaged black workers because it permitted unions to operate "closed shops," which limited employment to members of the union. Black leaders opposed this provision because of concerns that many unions would exclude blacks. The NAACP proposed an amendment to the act that would have permitted closed shops only when a union did not restrict membership on the basis of race. But this amendment was opposed by the major unions; Roosevelt declined to support it; and it was not adopted. The final component of the welfare state—the Fair Labor Standards Act—established minimum wage and working hours and provided compensation to the unemployed, but this also disadvantaged black workers. First, like the Social Security Act, it excluded domestic and farm labor and was financed on the basis of worker "contributions." Again, black leaders opposed this system, favoring instead a system that covered all workers and was financed on the basis of income and inheritance taxes. Again, Roosevelt opposed this initiative and it was defeated. The result was the exclusion of the vast majority of black workers from wage and hour protection and unemployment compensation when they lost their jobs. Thus, each of the three components of the early welfare state were based on INSTITUTIONAL RACISM, disadvantaging black workers in general and black female workers in particular. The provision excluding domestic and farm labor was not repealed until 1952.

The exclusion of blacks from the first tier of the welfare state meant that they were relegated to the second tier, which was based on POVERTY status rather than a guaranteed entitlement. The major tier-two program was the Aid to Families with Dependent Children (AFDC) program, which provided assistance to single-parent families. Unlike the social security insurance system, which was a universal program with national standards administered by the federal government, AFDC under the principle of FEDERALISM was a joint federal-state program in which eligibility and benefit levels were determined mainly by STATE AND LOCAL GOVERNMENTS. This allowed the Southern states to manipulate eligibility and benefits in order to maintain a cheap supply of black domestic and farm labor. And since farm and domestic labor were excluded by both the Social Security and Fair Labor Standard Acts, blacks and especially black women became heavily dependent on AFDC and were often exploited by the states. Some states in the rural south would simply cut off benefits during cotton-picking season while others would sometimes deny benefits to blacks altogether. And in every Southern state AFDC benefits overall were lower for blacks than whites. Throughout the debate on the Social Security Act, black leaders warned that the exclusion of most black workers from the tier-one programs would over time make them dependent on "welfare," that is, on the tier-two AFDC program. At its outset, most AFDC recipients were white single women, but gradually black women became the major recipients, from 21 percent in 1942 to 48 percent by 1961. This change was due in part to the continuing GREAT MIGRATION of blacks to the NORTHERN STATES, where eligibility requirements were more lenient and benefit levels were more generous.

The dependency of large numbers of black single-parent mothers on AFDC led many to argue that AFDC caused out-of-wedlock births, leading to the emergence and perpetuation of an UNDERCLASS. As a result, in 1996 President BILL CLINTON signed welfare-reform legislation limiting AFDC eligibility and requiring all recipients to find employment within two years. The states were also granted increased authority over the program. Because of the disproportionate dependency of poor black women and children on the program, the Clinton legislation was opposed by virtually the entire black leadership establishment, including all except two of the 39 members of the CONGRESSIONAL BLACK CAUCUS. Interestingly, however, the legislation was supported by a majority of blacks in surveys of PUBLIC OPINION.

See also CULTURE OF POVERTY, INDIVIDUALISM, NATIONAL WELFARE RIGHTS ORGANIZATION, FRANCES FOX PIVEN, SELF-HELP, and SOCIALISM.

Further reading: Dana Hamilton and Charles Hamilton, *The Dual Agenda: Social Policies of Civil Rights Organizations from the New Deal to the Present* (New York: Columbia University Press, 1996); Linda Williams, *The Constraint of Race: Legacies of White Skin Privilege and the Politics of American Social Policy* (Albany: SUNY Press, 2002).

Wells-Barnett, Ida B. (1862–1931) *journalist, civil rights leader*

Ida B. Wells-Barnett is best known for her militant campaign against LYNCHING, but her significance as an African-American leader goes far beyond her antilynching work. Linda O. McMurry, in *To Keep the Waters Troubled: The Life of Ida B. Wells,* writes, "For several years in the 1880s, no African American except for Frederick Douglass, received more attention than Ida B. Wells. . . . When Douglass died in 1895, Wells was his logical heir apparent; they had closely collaborated on several projects. She was better known than W. E. B. Du Bois and more ideologically compatible with Douglass than Booker T. Washington—the two men who eventually became the main contenders to fill Douglass' shoes. However, Wells had a problem: She was a woman." Although SEXISM among the TALENTED TENTH from which the African-American LEADERSHIP was disproportionately drawn was certainly a factor in Wells-Barnett's failure to rise to leadership preeminence in the BLACK COMMUNITY, McMurry's observation is probably an exaggeration. For reasons having nothing to do with gender, it is not likely that she could have outpaced BOOKER T. WASHINGTON or W. E. B. DU BOIS in leadership prominence. But McMurry's observation does call attention to the fact that Wells-Barnett is one of the most important leaders in

African-American history. In a 2000 poll of African-American political scientists asking them to rank the greatest black leaders of all time, Wells-Barnett ranked eighth in a list of 12. Although the respondents who selected her referred most often to her antilynching work—"At great personal risk . . . more than anyone else she made lynching a national issue"—Wells-Barnett was a pioneering CIVIL RIGHTS leader and an early exemplar of FEMINISM in black politics.

Wells-Barnett was born during SLAVERY and grew up during RECONSTRUCTION. At age 16 she assumed responsibility for raising her five siblings after her parents died of yellow fever, while also teaching and attending Fisk University. She became active in the emerging CIVIL RIGHTS MOVEMENT as a result of LITIGATION she initiated against SEGREGATION on a Tennessee railroad car. Although she lost the case, her involvement led her to turn to the MEDIA as a means to continue the struggle against RACISM and WHITE SUPREMACY. First, she edited two Memphis newspapers and then began writing a weekly column under the pen name "Iola." This column, which was eventually published in the *New York Age* and other black weeklies, made her one of the most prominent black journalists in the United States.

Wells-Barnett started her crusade against lynching in 1892 after a RIOT in Memphis in which three of her friends were lynched. Then she did become, at great personal risk, the leading crusader against lynching, conducting investigations and writing detailed articles and pamphlets describing its horrors. *Red Record: Tabulated Statistics and Alleged Causes of Lynching in the United States* (1895) is a classic study of the phenomenon. In her work Wells-Barnett went to great lengths to expose as a myth the idea that black men were lynched because they raped white women. Rather, her work showed that most blacks were lynched because they resisted OPPRESSION, and that many of the alleged rapes were actually consensual sexual relationships. Wells-Barnett's MILITANCY in opposition to lynching made her a leader of international stature. Her work was widely read and she lectured throughout the United States and Europe. She organized antilynching societies and personally lobbied President William McKinley to make a speech against lynching. Working closely with the leading blacks of her time—Douglass, Washington, MARY CHURCH TERRELL, and WILLIAM MONROE TROTTER (she accompanied Trotter to the White House for one of his meetings with WOODROW WILSON)—she was among the founders of the NAACP and the NATIONAL ASSOCIATION OF COLORED WOMEN and was a leader in several organizations working for VOTING RIGHTS for women. In 1895 she married Ferdinand Barnett, a wealthy Chicago newspaper editor and judge. Although she relished her role as wife and mother, she did not give up her public role. In Chicago she became

the first black woman probation officer in the city's history and was involved in several SELF-HELP projects that provided social services to migrants from the SOUTHERN STATES. This self-help work anticipated the programs later developed by the URBAN LEAGUE. Finally, Wells-Barnett attempted to become an ELECTED OFFICIAL, running unsuccessfully for the Illinois state legislature, while continuing LOBBYING the president and CONGRESS for antilynching legislation.

By her own account Wells-Barnett was not an easy person to get along with. She, like her colleague William Monroe Trotter, was smart, ambitious, and headstrong. For these reasons she did not achieve formal positions of leadership in any of the black ORGANIZATIONs she was associated with. In her memoir, *Crusade for Justice: The Autobiography of Ida B. Wells-Barnett* (1970), edited and published after her death by her daughter, she is particularly bitter that she never was elected president of the National Association of Colored Women, losing first to Mary Church Terrell and then to MARY MCLEOD BETHUNE. In the memoir she portrays herself as a "lonely warrior," battling the forces of racism, white supremacy, sexism, as well as the pettiness and shortsightedness of blacks. Three years before her death at age 69, she wrote, "All at once the realization came to me that I had nothing to show for all those years of toil and labor." This was a grimly pessimistic assessment of her life's work. And it was not correct. In the long struggle for African-American FREEDOM and EQUALITY, Wells-Barnett is among the foremost leaders.

Further reading: Linda O. McMurry, *To Keep the Waters Troubled: The Life of Ida B. Wells* (New York: Oxford University Press, 1998).

"We Shall Overcome"

Although JAMES WELDON JOHNSON's "Lift Every Voice and Sing" is referred to as the NEGRO NATIONAL ANTHEM, "We Shall Overcome" was the anthem of the CIVIL RIGHTS MOVEMENT. Sung during most of the major demonstrations of the 1960s and at the 1963 MARCH ON WASHINGTON, it is among the most famous PROTEST songs in American history. The origins of the song are not known exactly, but it probably began as a work song during SLAVERY, and a modern version of it has been traced to a 1903 gospel song written by Charles Tindley. A song of faith and inspiration, Tindley's lyrics resonate with the RELIGIOSITY of black CULTURE and were sung in the BLACK CHURCH in the early years of the 20th century. As a protest song, however, "We Shall Overcome" was first used in the labor movement in the SOUTHERN STATES during the 1930s. The HIGHLANDER FOLK SCHOOL used it as part of the training for CIVIL RIGHTS and labor organizers during the 1940s, and the white folksinger Pete Seeger and a black group called the Freedom Singers sang it during tours in the 1950s. MARTIN LUTHER KING JR. became aware of "We Shall Overcome"—probably from the Highlander Folk School—and, recognizing the importance of MUSIC in the culture of African Americans and how it could be used to inspire and mobilize people, decided to begin using it at rallies and demonstrations. By the time of the 1965 BIRMINGHAM DEMONSTRATIONS it was recognized as the anthem of the movement. When after the SELMA DEMONSTRATIONS President LYNDON B. JOHNSON went before CONGRESS to propose what would become the VOTING RIGHTS ACT OF 1965, he ended by proclaiming "and we shall overcome."

From its origins as a song of enslaved workers, "We Shall Overcome" in the 21st century has become an international protest song. For example, students in China's Tiananmen Square sang the song during their 1989 protests against the Chinese government.

See also "STRANGE FRUIT."

West Indians

West Indians—immigrants and their descendants from the Caribbean—are the largest ETHNIC GROUP within the African-American POPULATION. Historically, the West Indian population has not been widely distributed throughout the United States but has tended to be concentrated in the New York City area, especially HARLEM. The diversity of the West Indian population to some extent reflects the different mechanisms of COLONIALISM imposed on the various Caribbean islands.

Until the POST–CIVIL RIGHTS ERA, West Indians did not attempt to maintain a separate political identity but identified with the broader BLACK COMMUNITY. However, they brought a distinctive ethos to the community's politics. First, they were somewhat more likely to engage in most forms of POLITICAL PARTICIPATION, including voting and running for office. Thus, New York's first black member of the ELECTORAL COLLEGE was West Indian, as was one of the first of two New York City judges. RAYMOND J. JONES, the first DEMOCRATIC PARTY leader in New York, and SHIRLEY CHISHOLM, the nation's first female member of Congress, were of West Indian origin. West Indians were also noted for their tendencies toward MILITANCY and RADICALISM in Harlem and elsewhere. In general, whether radical or not, West Indian political activism was expressed under the broad umbrella of BLACKNESS.

In the post–civil rights era this has changed to some extent, as some West Indian political leaders in New York have sought to carve out a political identity separate and distinct from African Americans. West Indians to some extent always maintained a PLURAL SOCIETY with residential enclaves, businesses, MEDIA, and voluntary associations, but beginning in the middle 1970s they also began to establish separate political organizations, run ethnic-oriented campaigns, and develop a distinct West Indian PUBLIC POLICY agenda dealing with immigration issues, FOREIGN POLICY, and appointments to the BUREAUCRACY. In 2000 a West Indian candidate used her ethnicity as an explicit basis to challenge an incumbent African-American member of CONGRESS, unlike Shirley Chisholm, who ran for Congress simply as a black American.

The 1990 CENSUS estimated that there were about 1.5 million foreign-born blacks in the United States, most from the Caribbean. Almost half of them lived in New York City, making West Indian immigrants roughly 40 percent of the city's black population. Although the recent scholarship is ambiguous, generally New York's West Indian population is somewhat more advantaged than native-born blacks, but both groups lagged behind whites.

See also AFRICAN AMERICAN and MULTICULTURALISM.

Further reading: Philip Kasinitz, *Caribbean New York: Black Immigrants and Race* (Ithaca, N.Y.: Cornell University Press, 1992); Mary Waters, *Black Identities: West Indian Immigrants Dreams and American Realities* (Cambridge, Mass.: Harvard University Press, 2000).

White, George (1852–1918) *U.S. congressman*

George White was the last African American elected to the CONGRESS during RECONSTRUCTION. Between 1869 and 1901 when White departed, 22 blacks served in the Congress (two in the Senate, 20 in the House). However, as a result of the COMPROMISE OF 1877, the VIOLENCE and intimidation of the KU KLUX KLAN, and the gradual taking of VOTING RIGHTS from blacks, by 1891 the number of blacks in Congress had declined to one. White was the last of these.

Elected to the House in 1892 from North Carolina, White served two terms and then declined to seek reelection because he said the pervasiveness of RACISM and WHITE SUPREMACY in North Carolina and in the House made it futile for a black to attempt to serve in Congress. In his four years in the House, White was largely ignored by his colleagues and got hardly anything accomplished. He did, however, make a bit of history by becoming the first member of Congress to introduce antiLYNCHING legislation. In his last days in the House White made a grimly pessimistic speech about black REPRESENTATION and DEMOCRACY in the United States. White said, "Our representation is poor. . . . Justly we are entitled to fifty-one members. . . . We are entitled to a member of the Supreme Court. We never had a member, and probably never will; but we have kept quiet. . . . We should have the recognition of a place in the president's cabinet. . . . We are entitled to thirteen senators according to justice and our numerical strength but we have none and possibly will never get one, and yet we keep quiet." In his farewell address White told his colleagues, "This Mr. Chairman is perhaps the Negro's temporary farewell to the American Congress, but let me say Phoenix-like he will rise up someday and come again. These parting words are on behalf of an outraged, heart-broken, bruised, bleeding, but God-fearing people." After White left the House another black was not elected until 1928, and another from North Carolina was not elected until 1992.

White was the last enslaved person to serve in Congress. Born in SLAVERY, White earned a law degree from HOWARD UNIVERSITY and practiced law in North Carolina before being first elected to the state legislature and then Congress. After leaving the House, White moved to Philadelphia, where he established a bank and founded an all-black town in New Jersey.

See also WILLIAM DAWSON.

White, Walter (1893–1955) *author, administrator*

Walter White served as executive secretary of the NAACP from 1931 to 1955, succeeding JAMES WELDON JOHNSON as the second African-American head of the organization. White, ironically, was an African American by choice, since in appearance he was indistinguishable from a white man. Born to a prosperous family of mixed-race origins in Atlanta, White chose to identify with blacks and BLACK-NESS. After graduating from ATLANTA UNIVERSITY, White joined the NAACP as its assistant executive secretary in 1918. Since in appearance White looked white, he, unlike other black leaders, could go into areas of the SOUTHERN STATES and gather information in white communities. Early in his work he used this ability to investigate LYNCHINGS and wrote *Rope and Faggot: A Biography of Judge Lynch* (1929), a widely read book that influenced PUBLIC OPINION in the NORTHERN STATES on lynching. When he became head of the NAACP in 1931, White reorganized the association's bureaucracy and through the force of his personality (one historian described him as a "consummate schmoozer") and his skills as an administrator, writer, and lecturer, he transformed the NAACP into a respected LOB-BYING force in Washington. White emphasized building COALITIONS with white labor, civil liberties, and religious groups, and lobbying and LITIGATION in order to achieve the objectives of the CIVIL RIGHTS MOVEMENT. These strategies and White's personality and leadership style led to repeated clashes with W. E. B. DU BOIS, who 25 years White's senior, had been his professor at Atlanta University. White was also unwavering in his commitment to LIBER-ALISM and INTEGRATIONISM, and when Du Bois used his editorship of *The Crisis,* the NAACP's magazine, to suggest

that blacks embrace elements of BLACK NATIONALISM and consciously attempt to create a PLURAL SOCIETY, he clashed with White. At the end of the bureaucratic infight-ing between Du Bois and White, Du Bois—the towering figure who had founded the NAACP and been its leading black presence for two decades—was forced out.

During his tenure, White was a formidable presence in Washington, having easy access to leading members of CONGRESS and Presidents FRANKLIN D. ROOSEVELT and HARRY TRUMAN. During the NEW DEAL he lobbied unsuc-cessfully for the creation of a WELFARE STATE that did not discriminate against blacks. He was also unsuccessful in his efforts to get Roosevelt to support antilynching legisla-tion or propose CIVIL RIGHTS reforms. He was, however, successful in helping to persuade President Truman to pro-pose both civil rights and antilynching legislation. (Truman became the first president to address an NAACP confer-ence.) White's success as the preeminent black lobbyist in the 1930s and 1940s was in part based on his skillful use of the MEDIA, writing a syndicated column, and hosting a radio program. He wrote several books including his mem-oirs, *A Man Called White* (1948). He died in 1955, a year after the LEGAL DEFENSE FUND, which he helped to estab-lish, won the landmark *BROWN V. BOARD OF EDUCATION* case. He was succeeded by his assistant and protégé ROY WILKINS. In spite of his significance as an African-Ameri-can leader, there is not a biography of White available.

white backlash

White backlash refers to the tendency of white PUBLIC OPINION, political leaders, and MEDIA to react negatively to or withdraw support from black struggles for FREEDOM and EQUALITY. It is related to GUNNAR MYRDAL's concept of ACCOMMODATIONISM. In *AN AMERICAN DILEMMA,* Myrdal argued that demands for freedom and equality for blacks had to be pursued cautiously and incrementally so as not to upset whites and stimulate their resistance. In other words, MILITANCY, PROTEST, and RADICALISM should be avoided because they would cause a white backlash. His-torically, this has tended to be the case.

The first white backlash occurred in the 1870s as a reaction to the RADICAL REPUBLICANS' program for RECONSTRUCTION. President ULYSSES S. GRANT, a sup-porter of Radical Reconstruction, was reelected to the PRESIDENCY in a landslide in 1872, but during the next two years, in the midst of a recession and revelations of scandals in the Grant administration, white public opinion in the NORTHERN STATES began to turn against Grant and the Republican Party. A major reason for this shift in opinion was Grant's support for CIVIL RIGHTS and the use of army troops in the SOUTHERN STATES to protect those rights. In 1874 the DEMOCRATIC PARTY won control of the House of

Representatives for the first time since the CIVIL WAR, leading many Republican Party leaders and liberal media to urge the party to "jettison the dead weight of Reconstruction" to avoid defeat in the 1876 presidential election. In the COMPROMISE OF 1877 the Republicans did abandon Reconstruction in reaction to the withdrawal of white voter support.

The second white backlash occurred in the 1960s in reaction to the successes of the CIVIL RIGHTS MOVEMENT, the RIOTS in the GHETTOS, and the emergence of the BLACK POWER MOVEMENT. In 1964 LYNDON B. JOHNSON was elected to the presidency in a landslide, but in the 1966 elections Johnson and the Democrats suffered substantial losses in the congressional elections. In 1968 and 1972 the Democratic candidates for president, who were longtime supporters of civil rights, were defeated by RICHARD NIXON partly on the basis of his appeal to the white backlash. In 1976 the Democratic Party nominated JIMMY CARTER for president. Carter won in part because he moderated the party's position on race-related issues in order to appeal to the white backlash.

See also SOUTHERN STRATEGY.

white flight

"White flight" is the term used to refer to the tendency of whites to flee areas and institutions once the percentage of blacks reaches a certain level. Sociologists refer to this percentage as the "tipping point," the proportion of blacks in a residential area or a school that causes whites to leave. Although the tipping point varies depending on the area and the institution, generally if a neighborhood or school becomes 30 percent black it will generate white flight. White flight is partly responsible for the high levels of SEGREGATION in housing and education.

See also BUSING, GHETTO, and SCHOOLS AND EDUCATION.

whiteness

Whiteness is an idea developed by Europeans as an integral part of the processes of the OPPRESSION of the peoples of the THIRD WORLD through COLONIALISM and SLAVERY. Like the concept of RACE, the idea of whiteness is socially constructed, that is, it has no biological meaning. Instead, it was invented by Europeans as a means to unite and create solidarity among the different peoples of Europe and to distinguish them as "whites" from nonwhites as a means to facilitate the oppression of the latter.

In the IDEOLOGY of WHITE SUPREMACY, whiteness was used to stand for civilization in contrast to "blackness," which represented backwardness and savagery. W. E. B. DU BOIS did some of the earliest studies of whiteness, first in his

1920 book of essays *Darkwater* and then in his 1935 book *Black Reconstruction.* In *Darkwater: Voices from the Veil,* Du Bois wrote that "the discovery of personal whiteness among the world's people is a very modern thing . . . The ancient world would have laughed at such a distinction . . . we have changed all that, and the world in a sudden emotional conversion has discovered that it is white and by that token, wonderful." Yet, as Du Bois skillfully demonstrated in *Black Reconstruction,* whiteness was not a laughing matter, because it was a major weapon in the hands of the POWER ELITE in their efforts to inhibit the development during RECONSTRUCTION of a biracial, working-class COALITION. For Du Bois, whiteness was a "public and psychological wage": a public wage because white workers were paid more than black workers, and a psychological wage because no matter how poor they were, whites at least had the psychic compensation of whiteness, that is, of not being part of the debased, inferior black race. This psychological benefit of whiteness also conferred sociological status, because in the system of JIM CROW–style SEGREGATION, whites could use public places (theaters, restaurants, parks) not open to blacks, and they had access to better housing and schools. For Du Bois these public and psychological wages of whiteness more than anything else made white workers forget their common class interests with blacks and accept a subordinate-class position in exchange for the privileges of whiteness.

Not only was whiteness used to undermine interracial solidarity in the SOUTHERN STATES after Reconstruction; after the GREAT MIGRATION it was employed in the NORTHERN STATES with the same purposes and effects on Irish, Italian, and other European ETHNIC GROUPS. At the outset of the immigration of these groups to the United States, whiteness was reserved for white Anglo-Saxon Protestants (the so-called WASPs), and immigrants from Ireland and southern and eastern Europe were viewed as other, inferior races. (In the 1920s they were sometimes referred to as the "Alpine" race, a race lacking in reasoning and coordinating powers.) In 1924 CONGRESS enacted a racist immigration law that excluded eastern and southern European immigrants. However, gradually as a result of ASSIMILATION, these groups "became white" and were afforded psychological and public wages similar to Southern whites. That is, while they were often exploited in the unregulated CAPITALISM of the late 19th and early 20th centuries, their pay was still somewhat higher than that of blacks, they had access to better housing and schools, and they had the psychic esteem that flowed from not being black.

Although Du Bois pioneered research on whiteness, in the POST–CIVIL RIGHTS ERA a group of young white scholars began to do "whiteness studies," in some cases seeking to establish white-studies programs modeled on AFRICAN-AMERICAN STUDIES. To some, white studies is a troubling development because it is linked to white nationalist and white supremacist movements, but the mainstream scholars of whiteness seek to do research on whiteness in order to eliminate it.

See also POPULISM and SOCIALISM.

Further reading: Theodore Allen, *The Invention of the White Race: Racial Oppression and Social Control,* Vol. 1 (New York: Verso, 1994); Noel Ignatiev, *How the Irish Became White* (New York: Routledge, 1995); David Roediger, *The Wages of Whiteness: Race and the Making of the American Working Class* (New York: Verso, 1991); Ronald Walters, *White Nationalism in the Second Reconstruction* (Detroit, Mich.: Wayne State University Press, 2002).

white primary

The white primary was one of the more important mechanisms adopted by STATE AND LOCAL GOVERNMENTs in the SOUTHERN STATES to deny VOTING RIGHTS to African Americans. These governments, using the principle of FEDERALISM, defined POLITICAL PARTIES as private, voluntary associations that could practice DISCRIMINATION in determining who could become members and therefore vote in the primary elections. The primary elections were the principal means used to select the parties' candidates for office. After the end of RECONSTRUCTION, the REPUBLICAN PARTY was effectively eliminated as a competitor in Southern politics. As a result, the party system in the South was a one-party system in which only candidates from the DEMOCRATIC PARTY had a realistic chance to become ELECTED OFFICIALS. Thus racial discrimination in the Democratic Party's primaries eliminated blacks from participation in the electoral process altogether. White primaries were used in many of the Southern states until the SUPREME COURT in *Smith v. Allwright* (1944) declared them an unconstitutional violation of the FIFTEENTH AMENDMENT. However, African Americans in most Southern states did not get the right to vote in Democratic Party primaries or other elections until the VOTING RIGHTS ACT OF 1965 was enacted.

white supremacy

White supremacy is the IDEOLOGY developed by Europeans to justify RACISM. Together with racism and VIOLENCE, white supremacy is an integral, defining feature of AFRICAN-AMERICAN POLITICS. Although some elements of the ideology are present in all places where Europeans have practice racism or COLONIALISM, white supremacy as an ideology or doctrine received its most extensive articulation, elaboration, and institutionalization in the United States. This is so in part because of the doctrine of EQUAL-ITY that animated the founding of the nation and is to this day an integral part of its POLITICAL CULTURE. That is, it is probable that without the doctrine of equality, racism would have developed in the United States with less attention to ideology and with a more uneven pattern of institutionalization. For example, many of the elements that constitute the ideology were current in Latin America and South Africa, but in those places they did not give rise to an elaborate doctrine of race supremacy. But THOMAS JEFFERSON in the DECLARATION OF INDEPENDENCE argued that all men were created equal and had NATURAL RIGHTS to FREEDOM and equality. Jefferson wrote that these rights were "inalienable," meaning they could not be surrendered or taken away. Yet at this time Jefferson personally—and the nation as a whole—practiced and sanctioned SLAVERY. How could this obvious contradiction between words and deeds be rationalized or justified? Rationally, of course, it could not be except by denying the humanity of the enslaved people. Thus at the same time that the doctrine of equality was initiated with the Declaration of Independence, the doctrine of black inferiority or subhumanity was developed and institutionalized and, finally, codified in the THREE-FIFTHS CLAUSE of the CONSTITUTION.

The ideology of white supremacy (or of black inferiority) is constituted by three core elements or beliefs: (1) the idea of the "white man's burden" to civilize the savage, (2) the idea of God's curse, and (3) the idea that there was scientific proof of black inferiority. Each of these elements has infused the ideology of white supremacy from its inception, but the first two were more influential in the 18th and 19th centuries, while the third was most influential in the 20th century.

The Euro-Americans viewed—or at least they said they did—the African peoples as inferior in their color, in their RELIGIOSITY, in their dress, in their sexual practices, and in their governance—in other words, in virtually all aspect of their CULTURE. The color black was an important part of this complex of attitudes. Long before the English ancestors of the Americans had come into contact with the black people of Africa, they had profoundly negative attitudes toward blackness in the abstract. Winthrop Jordan in *White over Black: American Attitudes toward the Negro, 1550–1812,* his monumental study of the subject, provides the following definitions of black from the 16th-century *Oxford English Dictionary:* Deeply stained with dirt, soiled, dirty, foul. . . . Having dark, deadly purposes; malignant; pertaining to or involving death, deadly; baneful, disastrous, sinister . . . iniquitous, atrocious, horrible, wicked. . . . Indicating disgrace, censure, liability to punishment." In other words, virtually every negative connotation one can imagine was associated with black. This intense meaning of blackness shaped English attitudes toward black people in a negative way. In terms of religiosity, Jordan writes, "Englishmen were ill prepared to see any legitimacy in African religious practices. Judged by Christian cosmology Negroes stood in a separate category of men." Jordan quotes one of the earliest English accounts of African culture in terms of religiosity, which said Africans "were a beastly people living without God, law, religion or commonwealth." Thus, an important part of the white man's burden was to Christianize the heathen savages. The Europeans also claimed that the Africans lived without government, which Aristotle, among others, had claimed was a just basis for enslaving people. The dress patterns of Africans (the fact that men and women wore very little apparel) and reports of alleged polygamy and infanticide were cited as further evidence of uncivilized African practices. But the alleged sexual promiscuity of Africans (especially the women) was probably the most frequently cited "evidence" of their inferiority. Indeed, a fascination with black sexuality has always been an important part of the ideology of white supremacy. In any event, these ideas about African culture became the basis for the defenders of slavery in the United States, who rationalized that slavery was good for the Africans because it brought them the benefits of Christianity and Western Civilization. (Interestingly and ironically, variations on this rationale have been embraced by important African-American thinkers, including EDWARD WILMOT BLYDEN, HENRY M. TURNER, and ALEXANDER CRUMMELL.) Ideologically, then, the institution of slavery was turned on its head in that the burden was on the slave owner rather than the enslaved, a notion captured in Rudyard Kipling's famous poem "The White Man's Burden."

The second element of the ideology is the biblical notion of God's curse. In Genesis 9:10 the story is told that after the flood, Ham had looked upon his father's nakedness as Noah lay drunk, but the other two sons covered their father without looking at him. When Noah awoke he cursed Canaan, the son of Ham, saying he would be a "servant of servants." While this story may logically imply slavery, it says nothing about the color of those to be enslaved. However, in Jewish folklore and the Talmud, the story of Noah and his sons is told in a way that specifically makes black skin a curse. There are many versions of the story in Jewish tradition, but the following makes the relevant point:

> Therefore, it must be Canaan, your first born, whom enslave. And since you have disabled me . . . doing ugle things in blackness of night, Canaan's children shall be borne ugle and black. Moreover, because you twisted your head around to see my nakedness, your grandchildren's hair shall be twisted into kinks and their eyes red; again because your lips jested at my misfortune, theirs shall swell; and because you neglected my nakedness,

you shall go naked and their male members shall be shamefully elongated.

From the justification of slavery at the founding of the Republic to defense of SEGREGATION during the CIVIL RIGHTS MOVEMENT, this notion of the curse has been a frequently invoked element of the doctrine of white supremacy and black inferiority and the consequent imperative of black subordination.

In the late 19th century and especially in the 20th century, science began to replace God and the white man's burden as the most influential component of the ideology of white supremacy. The scientific component can be divided into three categories: sociological, physiological, and psychological. The sociological analysis sought to prove black inferiority on the basis of comparative analysis of statistical data on the social organization of black and white communities in terms of such things as unemployment, housing conditions, educational attainments, family dissolutions, out-of-wedlock births, alcohol abuse, and crime. On the basis of this type of analysis (which showed that blacks fared poorly when compared with whites), sociologists concluded that blacks' moral attitudes and behavior were inferior to those of whites. The physiological approach usually dealt with brain or, more precisely, skull sizes, arguing that the average black brain was smaller than the average white brain and that there was a direct correlation among brain size, intelligence, and behavior. It was, however, the psychologists' use of the IQ test from the 1920s to the 1940s that became the most frequently cited scientific proof of black inferiority. That blacks typically performed less well on these tests was cited as evidence of a genetic deficiency on the part of blacks. By the 1940s most scientists rejected the idea that there was any scientific (sociological, physiological, or psychological) basis for a belief in black inferiority. It was one of the major contributions of GUNNAR MYRDAL, in AN AMERICAN DILEMMA, to synthesize the available evidence showing that there was no credible scientific evidence for the claim that blacks were an inferior people. In the POST–CIVIL RIGHTS ERA, modern science has dismissed the idea of RACE itself, concluding that as a biological concept it is meaningless as a basis to distinguish among the peoples of the world.

At the beginning of the 21st century, most people rejected all three elements of the ideology of white supremacy, although the consequences of each were still present in various racial stereotypes. A handful of preachers still openly espoused the doctrine of God's curse, and a few social scientists continued to attempt to prove that blacks were inferior on the basis of skull size and performance on the IQ test. And quite a few respectable scholars (including a handful of blacks) in the 21st century continued to write that African and African-American cultures were deficient or inferior. But such ideas were generally taboo in respectable intellectual and political circles in the United States.

See also INTERNAL INFERIORIZATION, SLAVERY IN WESTERN THOUGHT, and WHITENESS.

Further reading: George Frederickson, *White Supremacy: A Comparative Study in American and South African History* (New York: Oxford University Press, 1981); Winthrop Jordan, *White over Black: American Attitudes toward the Negro, 1550–1812* (Baltimore, Md.: Penguin Books, 1968); Joel Kovel, *White Racism: A Psychohistory* (New York: Vintage Books, 1971); Robert C. Smith, *Racism in the Post Civil Rights Era: Now You See It, Now You Don't* (Albany: SUNY Press, 1995); Forrest Wood, *The Arrogance of Faith: Christianity and Race in America from the Colonial Era to the Twentieth Century* (New York: Knopf, 1990).

Wilder, Douglas L. (1931–) U.S. governor

Douglas Wilder is the first African American elected governor of one of the states. He was elected governor of Virginia in 1989.

Wilder was born in Richmond, Virginia, and was graduated from Virginia Union University, a historically black university. After receiving a law degree from HOWARD UNIVERSITY, Wilder returned to Richmond to practice law. In 1969 he became the first black elected to the Virginia Legislature since RECONSTRUCTION. When Wilder first became an ELECTED OFFICIAL he embraced elements of MILITANCY and aspects of the philosophy of the BLACK POWER MOVEMENT. However, during his 16 years in the legislature his IDEOLOGY evolved, and by the time he ran for governor he had embraced elements of CONSERVATISM. In 1985 he was elected lieutenant governor, and four years later he was elected governor by the narrowest of margins (by 6,741 votes out of 1.8 million). Wilder's campaign for governor was based on the strategy of DERACIALIZATION, in which he downplayed his race and deemphasized issues such as POVERTY and AFFIRMATIVE ACTION. Given Virginia's relative small black POPULATION (19 percent) and the generally conservative bent of Virginia's white electorate, it is likely that a strategy of deracialization was the only way he could have assembled a majority COALITION. As governor, Wilder generally eschewed the LIBERALISM typical of blacks in the DEMOCRATIC PARTY in favor of moderate, conservative policies and programs. In terms of black PUBLIC POLICY concerns, Wilder supported affirmative action, increased support for the state's HISTORICALLY BLACK COLLEGES AND UNIVERSITIES, and appointed a relatively large number of blacks to the state BUREAUCRACY. In 1991 he mounted a short-lived PRESIDENTIAL CAMPAIGN but dropped out because

he received little support in the early polls and was unable to get major campaign contributions.

See also STATE AND LOCAL GOVERNMENT.

Further reading: Judson Jeffries, *Virginia's Native Son: The Election and Administration of Governor Douglas L. Wilder* (West Lafayette, Ind.: Purdue University Press, 2000).

Wilkins, Roy (1902–1981) author, administrator

Roy Wilkins was the third African American to head the NAACP. He was appointed executive director in 1955 as the successor to his mentor WALTER WHITE.

Born in St. Louis, Missouri, Wilkins was graduated from the University of Minnesota and then joined the staff of the *Kansas City Call*, a weekly black newspaper, eventually becoming its editor. Wilkins's work in the black MEDIA brought him to the attention of Walter White and W. E. B. DU BOIS, who asked him to join the national staff of the NAACP in New York. In 1931 he did, eventually becoming editor of *The Crisis*, the association's magazine, and then in 1940 becoming White's assistant director. When he succeeded White in 1955, the PROTEST phase of the CIVIL RIGHTS MOVEMENT was just getting underway, one year after the MONTGOMERY BUS BOYCOTT led by MARTIN LUTHER KING JR. Wilkins was skeptical of mass protest and CIVIL DISOBEDIENCE, favoring instead reliance on the NAACP's time-tested strategies of LOBBYING and LITIGATION. But the NAACP under his leadership reluctantly provided legal and financial support to the SIT-INS, FREEDOM RIDES, and the protests led by SNCC, CORE, and the SOUTHERN CHRISTIAN LEADERSHIP CONFERENCE (SCLC). He also reluctantly joined the 1963 MARCH ON WASHINGTON. After the CIVIL RIGHTS ACT OF 1964 and the VOTING RIGHTS ACT OF 1965 were passed as a result of the BIRMINGHAM DEMONSTRATIONS and the SELMA DEMONSTRATIONS, Wilkins urged blacks to abandon protests and work with President LYNDON B. JOHNSON to implement the new laws and strengthen the WAR ON POVERTY. However, in 1966 the black movement turned toward MILITANCY and RADICALISM, first in the BLACK POWER MOVEMENT, then in the formation of the BLACK PANTHER PARTY, and finally in opposition to the VIETNAM WAR. Wilkins opposed all of these developments: He viewed the Black Power movement as separatist and racist, the Black Panther Party as utopian and reckless, and opposition to the Vietnam War as undermining President Johnson's support for CIVIL RIGHTS. Wilkins also opposed adoption of the new name "Black" (preferring instead Negro), the POOR PEOPLE'S CAMPAIGN, the creation of AFRICAN-AMERICAN STUDIES programs, and the 1972 NATIONAL BLACK POLITICAL CONVENTION. Finally, he outspokenly supported the use of the

MILITARY to suppress the RIOTS in the GHETTOS, arguing that VIOLENCE was an unacceptable means of making demands on the POLITICAL SYSTEM.

All of these stances led some in the BLACK COMMUNITY to refer to Wilkins, the veteran leader of the Civil Rights movement, as an UNCLE TOM. Throughout his career, however, Wilkins had been committed to INTEGRATIONISM and LIBERALISM; therefore, he saw the events of the 1960s as a dangerous turn toward radicalism and BLACK NATIONALISM. Thus, he felt obligated to "stand fast" against them. In 1976, aged and in ill health, he retired as executive director. Prior to his death he completed his memoirs, *Standing Fast: The Autobiography of Roy Wilkins* (1982).

Wilson, William J. (1935–) *scholar*

William J. Wilson, a sociologist, is the scholar who made the term *UNDERCLASS* an acceptable way to refer to poor blacks in the GHETTOS. Although he later repudiated the term, Wilson—through his books, papers, articles, edited works, op-ed essays, interviews with the MEDIA, congressional testimony, and as a consultant to government, foundations, and THINK TANKS—made the underclass the dominant concept in research on POVERTY in the ghettos. His 1987 book *The Truly Disadvantaged: The Inner City, the Underclass and Public Policy* is the definitive work on the subject. Widely read and reviewed, it helped to shape PUBLIC POLICY debate on the causes and remedies for urban poverty, and it made Wilson one of the most influential black public intellectuals of the POST–CIVIL RIGHTS ERA.

An adviser to President BILL CLINTON, Wilson was among a number of scholars who urged the DEMOCRATIC PARTY to embrace a strategy of DERACIALIZATION in order to build a progressive multiethnic COALITION to address the problems of poverty. Wilson advocated deracialization because he believed that RACISM played a relatively minor role in the creation and perpetuation of ghetto poverty and that an emphasis on racism impeded the development of deracialized public policies, such as FULL EMPLOYMENT, that could address the problems of poverty. Because of his emphasis on deracialization and his downplaying of racism, many viewed Wilson's IDEOLOGY as CONSERVATISM. But, actually, he identified with the tradition of democratic SOCIALISM, favoring an expansive WELFARE STATE, including full employment, national health insurance, child care, and NEW DEAL–style job training and work programs. Although Wilson was committed to an expansive welfare state, his ideas about the underclass were used to buttress support for cutbacks in the welfare state, including the 1996 welfare reform legislation that eliminated the federal guarantee of welfare for poor women and their children. In 1990 he was elected president of the American Sociological Association, and in his inaugural address he called on scholars to stop using the term *underclass* because it had stigmatizing effects on the black poor.

Wilson received his undergraduate training at Wilberforce University, a historically black university, and the Ph.D. from Washington State University. From 1971 to 1996 he held a distinguished professorship at the University of Chicago. In 1997 he was invited to join the National Academy of Sciences, a rare honor for a social scientist. Wilson later joined the faculty at Harvard, where he was associated with the AFRICAN-AMERICAN STUDIES program.

Wilson, Woodrow (1856–1924) *28th president of the United States*

Woodrow Wilson is generally considered by historians to be one of the greatest of the American presidents. In a 1996 poll of historians, he ranked seventh, mainly because of his progressive domestic reforms and his leadership during World War I. However, for African Americans in their struggles for FREEDOM and EQUALITY, he is among the worst of the presidents. Wilson embraced the IDEOLOGY of WHITE SUPREMACY and the practice of RACISM. Indeed, he is one of the few 20th-century presidents to overtly embrace white supremacy and racism. In some ways this is ironic because Wilson in general advocated LIBERALISM and because he was the first DEMOCRATIC PARTY candidate for president to receive support from important elements of the black LEADERSHIP. Concerned that blacks were being taken for granted by the REPUBLICAN PARTY and angered by the white supremacist rhetoric and racist policies of Theodore Roosevelt, W. E. B. DU BOIS and WILLIAM MONROE TROTTER supported Wilson in his three-way race with Roosevelt and William Howard Taft. However, shortly after Wilson assumed the PRESIDENCY, Du Bois wrote him a letter that said, "You have been president of the United States for six months and what is the result. It is no exaggeration to say that every enemy of the Negro race is greatly encouraged; that every man who dreams of making the Negro race a group of menials and pariahs is alert and hopeful." And later Trotter engaged in an angry shouting match with Wilson at the White House.

Several Wilson actions and policies upset blacks. First, he endorsed the racist and white supremacist film *BIRTH OF A NATION*, describing it as "history written with lightning." Second, almost immediately upon assuming office he increased DISCRIMINATION against blacks in the BUREAUCRACY and imposed a system of rigid SEGREGATION in all federal workplaces. Third, during World War I he vigorously opposed the use of blacks in the MILITARY because he did not like the idea of armed blacks. When he relented under military necessity, blacks were segregated and generally relegated to menial service. Finally, at the Paris

Peace Conference after the war, Wilson rejected the pleas of Japan and black leaders like Du Bois and Trotter to include a ban on racial discrimination in the League of Nations Charter.

Wilson is the only president who was a political scientist, earning a Ph.D. from Johns Hopkins and serving on the faculty and as president of Princeton University prior to being elected governor of New Jersey and president.

Woodson, Carter G. (1875–1950) *scholar*

Carter G. Woodson was one of the most important figures in the early development of AFRICAN-AMERICAN STUDIES. Firmly committed to the idea that knowledge is an important base of POWER, in 1915 he helped to establish the Association for the Study of Negro Life and History, the oldest professional association of scholars of the African-American experience. Shortly thereafter he established the *Journal of Negro History,* the oldest scholarly journal for research on the history of blacks. He also created Associated Publishers, a black-owned company that published books by and about blacks. The association, the journal, and the publishing company were mainly for scholars, but Woodson was also interested in educating ordinary people,

so in 1926 he created Negro History week, which later became Negro History month, celebrated annually in February. In 1937 he established the *Negro History Bulletin,* a journal for ordinary people rather than scholars. He also prepared curriculum material and study guides in black history for high school teachers. In 1933 he published his most influential book, *The Miseducation of the Negro.*

Woodson, the son of former slaves, was born in West Virginia. He received his undergraduate education at Berea College and the Ph.D. from Harvard University. In 1919 he was named dean of the faculty at HOWARD UNIVERSITY, but he found the academic bureaucracy too constraining and left after a year to pursue independent research and scholarship. Many persons have contributed to historical understanding of the African-American experience, including EDWARD WILMOT BLYDEN, ALEXANDER CRUMMELL, W. E. B. DU BOIS, GUNNAR MYRDAL, JOHN HOPE FRANKLIN, HERBERT APTHEKER, and Arthur Schomburg, founder of the SCHOMBURG LIBRARY; but Woodson is widely considered the "Father of Black History."

Further reading: Jacqueline Goggin, *Carter G. Woodson: A Life in Black History* (Baton Rouge: Louisiana State University Press, 1993).

Y

Young, Andrew (1932–) *civil rights activist*

Andrew Young was a principal assistant to MARTIN LUTHER KING JR. during the CIVIL RIGHTS MOVEMENT. Young joined the staff of the SOUTHERN CHRISTIAN LEADERSHIP CONFERENCE (SCLC) in 1961, serving as its executive director and then executive vice president until King's death. With SCLC Young was involved in planning the BIRMINGHAM DEMONSTRATIONS, the SELMA DEMONSTRATIONS, and the POOR PEOPLE'S CAMPAIGN. Among King's half-dozen top assistants, Young was generally viewed as the moderate conciliator whose diplomatic skills often helped meliorate conflicts within SCLC and in negotiations

Andrew Young, shown here being sworn in as United States ambassador to the United Nations by Supreme Court Justice Thurgood Marshall, 1977 *(Jimmy Carter Library)*

with the movement's adversaries. After King's assassination, Young became an ELECTED OFFICIAL.

In 1972 Young was elected to CONGRESS from Atlanta, putting together a biracial COALITION in a majority-white district to become the first black elected to the Congress from Georgia since RECONSTRUCTION. In the House of Representatives, Young focused on Africa-related issues and was among the founders of TRANSAFRICA. When JIMMY CARTER ran for president in 1976, Young was his most influential supporter in the BLACK COMMUNITY, credited with helping Carter to turn out the black vote in the early DEMOCRATIC PARTY primaries. Partly as a reward for his support, Carter named Young ambassador to the UNITED NATIONS, the first African American to hold the position. At the UN and in internal Carter administration FOREIGN POLICY deliberations, Young attempted without much success to shift U.S. policy in Africa away from its COLD WAR orientation toward a concern with the internal problems of the continent and with the elimination of APARTHEID. Eventually, he was forced to resign as UN ambassador because of an unauthorized meeting he had with representatives of the Palestine Liberation Organization. He then returned to Atlanta, where he was twice elected mayor. After an unsuccessful bid for governor of Georgia, Young became an international business consultant, working to develop linkages between Africa and African-American businessmen and foster DEMOCRACY and CAPITALISM on the continent. In 2001 he succeeded LEON SULLIVAN as head of the African–African-American Summit.

Young was born in New Orleans and was graduated from HOWARD UNIVERSITY and Hartford Theological Seminary. A clergyman, in 1996 he wrote a memoir covering his years in the Civil Rights movement, *An Easy Burden: The Civil Rights Movement and the Transformation of America.*

Young, Whitney (1921–1971) *administrator*

Whitney Young served as executive director of the URBAN LEAGUE from 1961 until his death in a drowning accident in Nigeria in 1971. Under Young's leadership the Urban League, while continuing its focus on social services and SELF-HELP, became more actively involved in the CIVIL RIGHTS MOVEMENT. While the Urban League did not engage in PROTESTS or CIVIL DISOBEDIENCE, it did engage in LOBBYING and joined in sponsorship of the 1963 MARCH ON WASHINGTON, where Young delivered an address. In the late 1960s the Urban League developed what it called a domestic "Marshall Plan," a comprehensive PUBLIC POLICY strategy to deal with the problem of POVERTY in the GHETTOS. As head of the relatively moderate Urban League, an ORGANIZATION with close links to the POWER ELITE, Young was the CIVIL RIGHTS leader that President RICHARD NIXON preferred to deal with. Indeed, Nixon even considered appointing Young to the BUREAUCRACY as head of HOUSING AND URBAN DEVELOPMENT. Although he did not name him to the cabinet, beginning in 1970 the Urban League received substantial funding from the Nixon administration for its social service programs. As a measure of his respect for Young, Nixon dispatched an Air Force plane to return his body from Nigeria to the United States and attended his funeral.

Young was born in Kentucky and was graduated from Kentucky State College, a historically black college, and received a graduate degree from the University of Minnesota. From 1954 to 1961 he was dean of the ATLANTA UNIVERSITY school of social work. He authored two books, *To Be Equal* (1964) and *Beyond Racism: Building an Open Society* (1969).

Further reading: Nancy Weiss, *Whitney M. Young and the Struggle for Civil Rights* (Princeton, N.J.: Princeton University Press, 1989).

Documentary Sources in the Study of African-American Politics

The following volumes are important resources in the study of African-American politics. They include petitions, speeches, articles, pamphlets, manifestos, and excerpts from books from the colonial era to the post–civil rights era.

Aptheker, Herbert, ed. *A Documentary History of the Negro People in the United States,* Vol. 1. New York: Citadel Press, 1951.

This volume includes more than 200 documents written by blacks beginning with a slave petition in 1761 and ending with black writings on the Emancipation Proclamation. The source and historical significance of each document are explained by the editor in introductory remarks.

Aptheker, Herbert, ed. *A Documentary History of the Negro People in the United States,* Vol. 2. New York: Citadel Press, 1951.

This volume includes more than 200 documents written by blacks beginning with Reconstruction in 1865 and ending with the founding of the NAACP in 1909. The source and historical significance of the documents are explained by the editor in introductory remarks.

Baraka, Imamu Amiri. *African Congress: A Documentary of the First Modern Pan African Congress.* New York: William Morrow, 1972.

This volume includes speeches and documents from workshops at the September 1970 Congress of African Peoples held in Atlanta, Georgia. It includes speeches by most leading blacks in politics and the arts. The 70 documents are excellent sources for material on black radicalism and on the ideological conflicts within the black leadership group in the United States.

Barbour, Floyd, ed. *The Black Power Revolt.* Boston: Extending Horizon Books, 1968.

This volume includes mainly material on the origins and development of the 1960s Black Power movement, but the editor also includes historical material dating to the 1600s. Among the important historical documents included are excerpts from David Walker's *Appeal,* Henry Highland Garnett's *Address to the Slaves,* and Nat Turner's *Confessions.* More than 40 documents are included.

Bracey, John, August Meier, and Elliott Rudwick, eds. *Black Nationalism in America.* New York: Bobbs-Merrill, 1970.

This volume includes virtually all of the important documents in the development of the tradition of black nationalism in the United States. The 77 documents begin with Richard Allen's 1787 description of the founding of the black church and ends with the 1968 platform of the Black Panther Party.

Marable, Manning, and Leith Mullings, eds. *Let Nobody Turn Us Around: An African American Anthology.* Lanham, Md.: Rowman & Littlefield, 2000.

The 99 documents in this volume begin with a 1789 slave narrative and end with the 1998 manifesto of the black radical congress. It is especially valuable for its material on black feminist thought. The editors provide introductory notes on each document explaining its historical significance.

Meier, August, Elliott Rudwick, and Francis Broderick, eds. *Black Protest Thought in the Twentieth Century.* New York: Bobbs-Merrill, 1971.

The 71 documents in this volume begin with Booker T. Washington's 1895 Atlanta Exposition Address and conclude with 1967 critiques of the Black Power movement by Kenneth Clark and Bayard Rustin. The editors provide introductory remarks explaining the historical context and significance of each document.

Stuckey, Sterling. *The Ideological Origins of Black Nationalism.* Boston: Beacon Press, 1972.

Nine seminal documents in the development of the tradition of black nationalism, including David Walker's *Appeal,* Henry Highland Garnett's *Address to the Slaves,* and Martin Delany's *The Political Destiny of the Colored Race.* The editor in a long introductory essay discusses the origins and historical significance of each document and how they relate to each in the development of black nationalism.

Bibliography

Aberbach, Joel, and Jack Walker. "The Meaning of Black Power: A Comparison of White and Black Interpretations of a Political Slogan." *American Political Science Review* 64 (1970): 332–364.

Abramson, Paul. *The Political Socialization of Black Americans: Critical Evaluation of Research on Efficacy and Trust.* New York: Free Press, 1977.

Alex-Assensoh, Yvette, and Lawrence Hanks, eds. *Black and Multiracial Politics.* New York: New York University Press, 2000.

Allen, Robert. *The Reluctant Reformers: Racism and Social Reform Movements in the United States.* Washington, D.C.: Howard University Press, 1983.

Allen, Theodore. *The Invention of the White Race: Racial Oppression and Social Control.* New York: Verso, 1994.

Altshuler, Alan. *Community Control: The Black Demand for Participation in Large American Cities.* New York: Pegasus, 1970.

Amar, Akil Reed. *The Bill of Rights: Creation and Reconstruction.* New Haven, Conn.: Yale University Press, 1998.

Anderson, Jervis. *Bayard Rustin: Troubles I've Seen.* New York: HarperCollins, 1977.

Aptheker, Herbert. *Black Abolitionism: A Revolutionary Movement.* Boston: Twayne, 1989.

———. *American Negro Slave Revolts.* New York: International, 1983.

———. *Nat Turner's Slave Revolt.* New York: Humanities, 1966.

———. *One Continual Cry: David Walker's Appeal to the Colored Citizens of World.* New York: Humanities, 1965.

Babchuck, Nicholas, and Robert Thompson. "Voluntary Associations of Negroes." *American Sociological Review* 27 (1962): 647–655.

Banks, William. *Black Intellectuals: Race and Responsibility in American Life.* New York: W. W. Norton, 1996.

Beard, Charles. *An Economic Interpretation of the Constitution.* New York: Free Press, 1913, 1965.

Becker, Carl. *The Declaration of Independence: A Study in the History of an Idea.* New York: Vintage Books, 1922, 1970.

Bell, Howard. "National Negro Conventions of the Middle 1840s: Moral Suasion vs Political Action." *Journal of Negro History* 31 (1966): 435–443.

Bennett, Lerone. *Forced into Glory: Abraham Lincoln's White Dream* Chicago: Johnson Publishing, 2000.

———. *Before the Mayflower: A History of the Negro in America.* Baltimore: Penguin Books, 1966.

———. *The Negro Mood and Other Essays.* New York: Ballantine, 1964.

Berg, John. *Unequal Struggle: Class, Gender, Race and Power in the U.S. Congress.* Boulder, Colo.: Westview Press, 1994.

Berman, William. *The Politics of Civil Rights in the Truman Administration.* Columbus: Ohio State University Press, 1970.

Berry, Mary F. "Reparations for Freedom, 1890–1916." *Journal of Negro History* 37 (1972): 219–230.

Billingsly, Andrew. *Mighty Like a River: The Black Church and Social Reform.* New York: Oxford University Press, 1999.

Bittker, Boris. *The Case for Black Reparations.* New York: Random House, 1973.

Blassingame, John. *New Perspectives on Black Studies.* Urbana: University of Illinois Press, 1971.

Blauner, Robert. *Racial Oppression in America.* New York: Harper & Row, 1972.

———. "Internal Colonialism and Ghetto Revolt." *Social Problems* 16 (1969): 398–408.

Blue, Frederick. *Charles Sumner and the Conscience of the North.* New York: W. W. Norton, 1976.

Bobo, Lawrence, and Franklin Gilliam. "Race, Sociopolitical Participation and Black Empowerment." *American Political Science Review* 84 (1990): 450–462.

Bond, Julian, and Sandra Wilson. *Lift Every Voice and Sing: A Celebration of the Negro National Anthem.* New York: Random House, 2000.

Bornett, Vaughn. *The Presidency of Lyndon B. Johnson.* Lawrence: University Press of Kansas, 1995.

Bowen, William, and Derek Bok. *The Shape of the River: Long-term Consequences of Considering Race in College Admission.* Princeton, N.J.: Princeton University Press, 1998.

Bracey, John, August Meier, and Elliot Rudwick. *Black Nationalism in America.* New York: Bobbs-Merrill, 1970.

Branch, Taylor. *Parting the Waters: America in the King Years, 1954–63.* New York: Simon & Schuster, 1988.

Brauer, Carl. *John F. Kennedy and the Second Reconstruction.* New York: Columbia University Press, 1977.

Breitman, George. *The Last Year of Malcolm X: Evolution of a Revolutionary.* New York: Pathfinder, 1992.

———. *Malcolm X Speaks: Selected Speeches and Statements.* New York: Grove Press, 1965.

Brodie, Fawn. *Thaddus Stevens, Scourge of the South.* New York: W. W. Norton, 1959.

Brown, Robert. *Charles Beard and the Constitution: A Critical Analysis of an Economic Interpretation of the Constitution.* New York: W. W. Norton, 1965.

Browning, Rufus, Dale Rogers Marshall, and David Tabb. *Protest Is Not Enough: The Struggle of Blacks and Hispanics in Urban Politics.* Berkeley: University of California Press, 1984.

———, Dale Rogers, Marshall Tabb, and David Tabb, eds. *Racial Politics in American Cities.* New York: Longman, 2003.

Buckley, Gail. *American Patriots: The Story of Blacks in the Military from the Revolution to Desert Storm.* New York: Random House, 2001.

Bullock, Henry Allen. *A History of Black Education in the South: 1619 to the Present.* Cambridge, Mass.: Harvard University Press, 1967.

Bulmer, John, and John Solomos, eds. *Racism.* New York: Oxford University Press, 1999.

Bulter, John Sibley. *Entrepreneurship and Self-Help Among Black Americans.* Albany: SUNY Press, 1991.

Burner, Eric. *And Gently He Shall Lead Them: Robert Parris Moses and the Civil Rights Movement in Mississippi.* New York: Oxford University Press, 1994.

Canon, David. *Race, Redistricting and Representation: The Unintended Consequences of Black Majority Districts.* Chicago: University of Chicago Press, 1999.

Carmichael, Stokely, and Charles Hamilton. *Black Power: Politics of Liberation.* New York: Vintage Books, 1967.

Carson, Claybourne, ed. *The Autobiography of Martin Luther King, Jr.* New York: Warner Brothers, 1998.

———. *In Struggle: SNCC and the Black Awakening of the 1960s.* Cambridge, Mass.: Harvard University Press, 1981.

Carter, Dan. *From George Wallace to Newt Gingrich: Race in the Conservative Counterrevolution 1963–64.* Baton Rouge: Louisiana State University Press, 1996.

Castel, Albert. *The Presidency of Andrew Johnson.* Lawrence: University Press of Kansas, 1986.

Cochran, David. *The Color of Freedom: Race and Contemporary Liberalism.* Albany: SUNY Press, 1999.

Congressional Black Caucus. *The Black Leadership Family Program for the Survival and Progress of the Black Nation.* Washington, D.C.: Congressional Black Caucus, 1982.

Chambliss, Theresa. "The Growth and Significance of African American Elected Officials." In *From Exclusion to Inclusion: The Long Struggle for African American Political Power,* edited by Ralph Gomes and Linda Williams. Westport, Conn.: Greenwood Press, 1992.

Chisholm, Shirley. *The Good Fight.* New York: Harper & Row, 1973.

Clark, Kenneth. *Dark Ghetto: Dilemmas of Social Power.* New York: Harper & Row, 1965.

———, and Maimie Clark. "What Do Blacks Think of Themselves." *Ebony,* November, 1980, 176–182.

———. "The Civil Rights Movement: Momentum and Organization." In *The Negro American,* edited by Talcott Parsons and K. Clark. Boston: Beacon Press, 1966.

Clegg, Claude. *An Original Man: The Life and Times of Elijah Muhammad.* New York: St. Martin's Press, 1997.

Clymer, Adam. *Edward M. Kennedy: A Biography.* New York: Morrow, 1999.

Cohen, Cathy. *Beyond the Boundaries: AIDS and the Breakdown of Black Politics.* Chicago: University of Chicago Press, 1999.

———, and Michael Dawson. "Neighborhood Poverty and African American Politics." *American Political Science Review* 87 (1993): 286–302.

Cole, David. *No Equal Justice: Race and Class in American Criminal Justice System.* New York: Free Press, 1999.

Collins, Patricia Hill. *Black Feminist Thought: Knowledge, Consciousness and the Politics of Empowerment.* New York: Routledge, 1991.

Connerly, Ward. *Creating Equal: My Fight Against Racial Preferences.* San Francisco: Encounter Books, 2000.

Conti, John, and Barbara Stetson. *Challenging the Civil Rights Establishment: Profiles of a New Black Vanguard.* Westport, Conn.: Praeger, 1989.

Conyers, James, and Walter Wallace. *Black Elected Officials: A Study of Black Americans Holding Governmental Office.* New York: Russell Sage, 1976.

Crofts, Daniel. "The Black Response to the Blair Education Bill." *Journal of Southern History* 34 (1971): 41–65.

Croson, Edmund. *Black Moses: The Story of Marcus Garvey and the Universal Negro Improvement Association.* Madison: University of Wisconsin Press, 1966.

Cross, William. *Shades of Black: Diversity of African American Identity.* Philadelphia, Pa.: Temple University Press, 1991.

———. "The Negro to Black Conversion Experience." *Black World* 20 (1971): 13–27.

Cruse, Harold. *The Crisis of the Negro Intellectual.* New York: William Morrow, 1967.

———. *Plural but Equal: Blacks and Minorities in America's Plural Society.* New York: William Morrow, 1987.

Culverson, Donald. *Contesting Apartheid: 1960–1987.* Boulder, Colo.: Westview, 1999.

Curry, George, ed. *The Affirmative Action Debate.* Reading, Mass.: Addison-Wesley, 1996.

Dahl, Robert. *Who Governs: Democracy and Power in an American City.* New Haven, Conn.: Yale University Press, 1961.

———. "The Concept of Power." *Behavioral Science* 2 (1957): 201–215.

Dates, Jannette, and William Barlow, eds. *Split Images: African Americans in the Mass Media.* Washington, D.C.: Howard University Press, 1993.

Davis, Angela. *Women, Race and Class.* New York: Random House, 1981.

Davis, Daniel. *Mr. Black Labor: The Story of A. Phillip Randolph, Father of the Civil Rights Movement.* New York: E. P. Dutton, 1972.

Dawson, Michael. *Behind the Mule: Race, Class and African American Politics.* Princeton, N.J.: Princeton University Press, 1994.

———. *Black Visions: The Roots of Contemporary Black Ideologies.* Chicago: University of Chicago Press, 2001.

Dittmer, John. "The Education of Henry Macneil Turner." In *Black Leaders of the Nineteenth Century,* edited by Leon Litwack, and August Meier. Urbana: University of Illinois Press.

Donald, David. *Lincoln.* New York: Simon & Schuster, 1995.

Donovan, John. *The Politics of Poverty.* New York: Pegasus, 1967.

Drake, W. Avon, and Robert Holsworth. *Affirmative Action and the Stalled Quest for Black Progress.* Urbana: University of Illinois Press, 1996.

Dray, Philip. *At the Hands of Persons Unknown: The Lynching of Black America.* New York: Random House, 2002.

Dreyfuss, Joel, and Charles Lawrence. *The Bakke Case: The Politics of Inequality.* New York: Longman, 1979.

Duberstein, Martin. *Paul Robeson.* New York: Free Press, 1976.

Du Bois, W. E. B. *Dusk of Dawn.* New York: Harcourt Brace, 1940.

———. *Black Reconstruction.* New York: Harcourt Brace, 1935.

———. *Darkwater.* New York: Harcourt Brace, 1920.

———. *The Souls of Black Folk.* Chicago: A. C. McClurg, 1903.

Dudziak, Mary. *Cold War Civil Rights: Race and the Image of American Democracy.* Princeton, N.J.: Princeton University Press, 2000.

Dye, Thomas. *Who's Running America.* Englewood Cliffs, N.J.: Prentice Hall, 1990.

Easton, David. *The Political System.* New York: Knopf, 1953.

Edsal, Thomas, and Mary Edsal. *Chain Reaction: The Impact of Race, Rights and Taxes on American Politics.* New York: W. W. Norton, 1992.

Eisler, Kim Issac. *A Justice for All: William Brennan, Jr. and the Decisions That Transformed America.* New York: Simon & Schuster, 1993.

Eldersveld, Samuel, and Hanes Walton, Jr. *Political Parties in American Society.* New York: Bedford/St. Martin's Press, 2000.

Ellis, Joseph. *American Sphinx: The Character of Thomas Jefferson.* New York: Knopf, 1997.

Evans, Sara. *Personal Politics: The Roots of Women's Liberation in the Civil Rights Movement and the New Left.* New York: Vintage Books, 1991.

Fager, Charles. *Uncertain Resurrection: The Poor People's Campaign.* Grand Rapids, Mich.: William B. Eerdman, 1969.

Fanon, Frantz. *The Wretched of the Earth.* New York: Grove Press, 1968.

———. *Black Skin, White Masks: The Experiences of a Black Man in a White World.* New York: Grove Press, 1967.

Farr, James. "So Vile and Miserable: The Problem of Slavery in Locke's Political Thought." *Political Theory* 14 (1986): 263–289.

Feagin, Joe R. *Racist America: Roots, Current Realities and Future Reparations.* New York: Routledge, 2000.

———, and Harlan Hahn. *Ghetto Revolts.* New York: MacMillan, 1973.

Fehrenbacher, Don, and Ward McAfree. *The Slaveholding Republic: An Account of the United States Government's Relations to Slavery.* New York: Oxford University Press, 2001.

Flingstein, Neil. *Going North: Migration of Blacks and Whites from the South, 1900–1950.* New York: Academic Press, 1981.

Foner, Eric. *Reconstruction: America's Unfinished Revolution, 1863–1877.* New York: Harper & Row, 1988.

Forsythe, Dennis. "Frantz Fanon: The Marx of the Third World." *Phylon* 34 (1973): 19–34.

Fox, Stephen. *The Guardian of Boston: William Monroe Trotter.* New York: Antheneum, 1970.

Frady, Marshall. *Wallace.* New York: American Library, 1976.

———. *Jesse: The Life and Pilgrimage of Jesse Jackson.* New York: Random House, 1996.

Franklin, John Hope, and Loren Schweninger. *Runaway Slaves: Rebels on the Plantation.* New York: Oxford University Press, 1999.

———. *The Emancipation Proclamation.* New York: Doubleday, 1963.

———, and August Meier. *Black Leaders of the Twentieth Century.* Urbana: University of Illinois Press, 1982.

———. *From Slavery to Freedom: A History of Negro Americans.* New York: Knopf, 1980.

Frazier, Franklin E. *The Negro Church in America.* New York: Schocken Books, 1964.

Frederickson, George. *Racism: A Short History.* Princeton, N. J.: Princeton University Press, 2002.

———. *White Supremacy: A Comparative Study in American and South African History.* New York: Oxford University Press, 1981.

Freehling, William. "The Founding Fathers and Slavery." *American Historical Review* 77 (1972): 81–93.

Frymer, Paul. *Uneasy Alliances: Race and Party Competition in America.* Princeton, N.J.: Princeton University Press, 1999.

Gaither, Gerald. *Blacks and the Populist Revolt: Ballots and Bigotry.* Tuscaloosa: University of Alabama Press, 1977.

Gardell, Mattias. *In the Name of Elijah Muhammad: Louis Farrakhan and the Nation of Islam.* Durham, N.C.: Duke University Press, 1996.

Garrow, David. *Protest at Selma: Martin Luther King, Jr. and the Voting Rights Act.* New Haven, Conn.: Yale University Press, 1978.

———. *The FBI and Martin Luther King, Jr.* New York: Penguin Books, 1983.

———. *Bearing The Cross: Martin Luther King, Jr. and the Southern Christian Leadership Conference.* New York: William Morrow & Company, 1999.

Garvey, Amy Jacques, and E. U. Eissen-Odom. *The Philosophy and Opinions of Marcus Garvey.* London: Cass, 1977.

Gates, Henry Louis. "Powell and the Black Elite." *New Yorker,* September 25, 1995.

Genovese, Eugene. *From Rebellion to Revolution: Afro-American Slave Revolts in the Making of the New World.* New York: Vintage Books, 1984.

George, Carol. *Segregated Sabbaths: Richard Allen and the Emergence of Independent Black Churches.* New York: Oxford University Press, 1973.

George, Nelson. *Hip-Hop America.* New York: Viking Press, 1998.

———. *The Death of Rhythm and Blues.* New York: Dutton, 1989.

Gerber, Scott. *First Principles: The Jurisprudence of Clarence Thomas.* New York: New York University Press, 1999.

Gerth, H. H., and C. Wright Mills, eds. *From Max Weber.* New York: Oxford University Press, 1958.

Giddings, Paula. *When and Where I Enter: The Impact of Black Women on Race and Sex.* New York: William Morrow, 1984.

Gillette, William. *The Right to Vote: Politics and Passage of the Fifteenth Amendment.* Baltimore: Johns Hopkins University Press, 1969.

Ginzberg, Ralph. *100 Years of Lynching.* New York: Lancer Books, 1962.

Githens, Marianne, and Jewel Prestage, eds. *A Portrait of Marginality: The Political Behavior of American Women.* New York: David McKay, 1977.

Glazer, Nathan, and Daniel P. Moynihan. *Beyond the Melting Pot.* Cambridge, Mass.: MIT Press, 1963.

———, eds. *Ethnicity: Theory and Experience.* Cambridge, Mass.: Harvard University Press, 1975.

Goggins, Jacqueline. *Carter G. Woodson: A Life in Black History.* Baton Rouge: Louisiana State University Press, 1993.

Goings, Allen. "The South and the Blair Education Bill." *Mississippi Valley Historical Review* 44 (1957): 269–290.

Goldstein, Robert. *Political Repression in Modern America.* Cambridge, Mass.: Schenkman, 1978.

Gomes, Ralph, and Linda Williams. "Coalition Politics: Past, Present and Future." In *From Exclusion to Inclusion: The Long Struggle for African American Political Power,* edited by Gomes and Williams. Westport, Conn.: Praeger, 1992.

Gordon, Ericka. "A Layin' on of Hands: Black Women's Community Work and the National Association of Colored Women's Clubs." In *Black Political Organizations in the Post Civil Rights Era,* edited by Ollie Johnson and Karin Stanford. New Brunswick, N.J.: Rutgers University Press, 2002.

Gordon, Milton. *Assimilation in America: The Role of Race, Religion and National Origin.* New York: Oxford University Press, 1964.

Graham, Hugh Davis. *The Civil Rights Era: Origins and Development of National Policy.* New York: Oxford University Press, 1990.

Grant, Joanne. *Ella Baker: Freedom Bound.* New York: John Wiley, 1998.

Grant, Ruth, and Marion Orr. "Language, Race and Politics: From Black to African American." *Politics & Society* 24 (1996): 137–152.

Greeley, Andrew. *Ethnicity in the United States.* New York: John Wiley, 1974.

Green, Charles, ed. *Globalization and Survival in the Black Diaspora.* Albany: SUNY Press, 1994.

Green, Constance. *The Secret City: A History of Race Relations in the Nation's Capital.* Princeton, N.J.: Princeton University Press, 1967.

Green, Kathanne. *Affirmative Action and Principles of Justice.* New York: Greenwood Press, 1989.

Greenstone, David, and Paul Peterson. *Race and Authority in Urban Politics: Community Participation and the War on Poverty.* New York: Russell Sage Foundation, 1973.

Grendzier, Irene. *Frantz Fanon: A Critical Study.* London: Wildwood House, 1973.

Gross, Bella. "The First National Negro Convention." *Journal of Negro History* 31 (1966): 435–443.

Guinier, Lani. *The Tyranny of the Majority.* New York: Free Press, 1994.

Hamilton, Charles. *Adam Clayton Powell: The Political Biography of an American Dilemma.* New York: Atheneum, 1991.

———, and Dana Hamilton. *The Dual Agenda: Social Policies of Civil Rights Organizations from the New Deal to the Present.* New York: Columbia University Press, 1996.

———. "Full Employment As a Viable Issue." In *When the Marching Stopped: An Analysis of Black Issues in the Seventies.* New York: National Urban League, 1973.

———. "Deracialization: Examination of A Political Strategy." *First World* 1 (1977): 3–5.

Hannerz, Ulf. *Soulside: Studies in Ghetto Culture and Community.* New York: Columbia University Press, 1969.

Hargreaves, Mary. *The Presidency of John Quincy Adams.* Lawrence: University Press of Kansas, 1985.

Harlan, Louis. *Booker T. Washington: The Wizard of Tuskegee.* New York: Oxford University Press, 1983.

———. *Booker T. Washington: The Making of A Black Leader.* New York: Oxford University Press, 1972.

Harris, Charles. *Congress and the Governance of the Nation's Capital.* Washington, D.C.: Georgetown University Press, 1995.

Harris, Frederick. *Something Within: Religion in African American Political Activism.* New York: Oxford University Press, 1999.

Harris, Robert, Darlene Clark Hine, and Nellie McKay. *Three Essays: Black Studies in the United States.* New York: Ford Foundation, 1990.

Harris, William. *Keeping the Faith: A. Phillip Randolph, Milton P. Webster and the Brotherhood of Sleeping Car Porters.* Urbana: University of Illinois Press, 1977.

Henderson, Erol. *AfroCentrism and World Politics: Toward A New Paradigm.* Westport, Conn.: Praeger, 1995.

Henig, Jeffrey, et al. *The Color of School Reform: Race, Politics and the Challenge of Urban Education.* Princeton, N.J.: Princeton University Press, 1999.

Henry, Charles, ed. *Foreign Policy and the Black International Interest.* Albany: SUNY Press, 2000.

———, ed. *Ralph J. Bunche: Selected Speeches and Writings.* Ann Arbor: University of Michigan, 1995.

———. *Ralph Bunche: Model Negro or American Other?* New York: New York University Press, 1999.

———. *Culture and African American Politics.* Bloomington: Indiana University Press, 1990.

Hentoff, Nat. "The Integrationist." *The New Yorker,* August 23, 1982.

Hine, Darlene Clark, and Pero Dagbovie, eds. *African Americans and the Clinton Presidency Reconsidered.* Urbana: University of Illinois Press, 2003.

Hofstader, Richard, and Michael Wallace, eds. *American Violence: A Documentary History.* New York: Vintage Books, 1971.

Holden, Matthew. *The Politics of the Black "Nation."* New York: Chandler Publishing, 1973.

———. *The White Man's Burden.* New York: Chandler Publishing, 1973.

Holt, Rackham. *Mary McLeod Bethune.* New York: Doubleday, 1974.

hooks, bell. *Ain't I a Woman: Black Women and Feminism.* Boston: South End Press, 1981.

Horne, Gerald. *The Fire This Time: The Watts Uprising and the 1960s.* Charlottesville: University Press of Virginia, 1995.

———. *Black and Red: W. E. B. DuBois and the Afro-American Response to the Cold War.* Albany: SUNY Press, 1986.

Howard, John. *The Shifting Wind: The Supreme Court and Civil Rights From Reconstruction to Brown.* Albany: SUNY Press, 1999.

Huggins, Nathan. *The Harlem Renaissance.* New York: Oxford University Press, 1971.

Human Rights Watch. *Punishment and Prejudice: Racial Disparities in the War on Drugs.* Washington, D.C.: Human Rights Watch, 2000.

Ignatiev, Noel. *How the Irish Became White.* New York: Routledge, 1995.

Jackson, Walter. *Gunnar Myrdal and America's Conscience.* Chapel Hill: University of North Carolina Press, 1990.

Janowitz, Morris. "Patterns of Collective Racial Violence." In *American Violence: Historical and Comparative Perspectives,* edited by Hugh Davis Graham and Ted Robert Gurr. New York: Bantam Books, 1969.

Jeffries, Judson. *Virginia's Native Son: The Election and Administration of Governor L. Douglas Wilder.* West Lafayette: Indiana University Press, 2000.

Johnson, James Weldon. *Black Manhattan.* Salem, N.H.: Ayer Co. 1988.

Johnson, Ollie, and Karin Stanford, eds. *Black Political Organizations in the Post Civil Rights Era.* New Brunswick, N.J.: Rutgers State University Press, 2002.

Johnson, Valerie. *Black Power in the Suburbs: The Myth or Reality of African American Suburban Political Incorporation.* Albany: SUNY Press, 2002.

Jones, Beverly. *Quest for Equality: The Life and Writings of Mary Church Terrell.* Brooklyn, N.Y.: Carlson Publishing, 1990.

Jones, Charles. "From Protest to Black Conservatism: The Demise of the Congress of Racial Equality." In *Black Political Organizations in the Post Civil Rights Era,* edited by Ollie Johnson and Karin Stanford. New Brunswick, N.J.: Rutgers University Press, 2002.

———, ed. *The Black Panther Party Reconsidered.* Baltimore: Black Classics Press, 1998.

Jones, Howard. *Mutiny on the Amistad.* New York: Oxford University Press, 1987.

Jones, Mack. "The Black Underclass As a Systemic Phenomenon." In *Race, Politics and Economic Development,* edited by James Jennings. New York: Verso Press, 1992.

———. "Political Science and the Black Political Experience: Issues in Epistemology and Revelance." *National Political Science Review* 3 (1992): 25–40.

———. "The Political Thought of the New Black Conservatives." In *Readings in American Political Issues,* edited by Franklin Jones et al. Dubuque, Iowa: Kendall/Hunt, 1987.

———. "A Frame of Reference for Black Politics." In *Black Political Life in the United States,* edited by Lenneal Henderson. New York: Chandler Publishing, 1972.

Jordan, Winthrop. *White Over Black: American Attitudes Toward the Negro, 1550–1812.* Baltimore: Penguin Books, 1969.

Kasinitz, Philip. *Caribbean New York: Black Immigrants and the Politics of Race.* Ithaca, N.Y.: Cornell University Press, 1992.

Katznelson, Ira. "Power in the Reformulation of Race Relations Research." In *Race, Change and Urban Policy,* edited by William Ellis and Peter Orleans. Newburg Park, Calif.: Sage, 1971.

———. *Black Men, White Cities.* New York: Oxford University Press, 1973.

Kelley, Robin. *Hammer and Hoe: Alabama Communists During the Great Depression.* Chapel Hill: University of North Carolina Press, 1990.

Kellogg, Charles. *NAACP: A History of the National Association for the Advancement of Colored People.* Baltimore: Johns Hopkins, University Press, 1967.

Kennedy, Randall. *Race, Crime and Law.* New York: Pantheon, 1997.

Kilson, Martin. "Anatomy of Black Conservatism." *Transition* 59 (1993): 4–19.

———. "Political Change in the Negro Ghetto, 1900–1940s." In *Key Issues in the Afro-American Experience,* edited by Nathan Higgins, Martin Kilson, and Daniel Fox. New York: Harcourt Brace Jovanovich, 1971.

Kinder, Donald, and Lynn Sanders. *Divided by Color: Racial Politics and Democratic Ideals.* Chicago: University of Chicago Press, 1996.

King, Desmond. *Separate and Unequal: Black Americans and the U.S. Federal Government.* London: Oxford University Press, 1995.

King, Richard. *Civil Rights and the Idea of Freedom.* New York: Oxford University Press, 1992.

King, Wilma. *Stolen Childhood: Slave Youth in Nineteenth Century America.* Bloomington: Indiana University Press, 1995.

Kluger, Richard. *Simple Justice: The Story of Brown vs Board of Education.* New York: Vintage Books, 1977.

Kofsky, Frank. *Black Nationalism and the Revolution in Music.* New York: Pathfinder Press, 1970.

Kornweibel, Theodore. *Seeing Red: Federal Campaigns Against Black Militancy, 1919–1925.* Bloomington: Indiana University Press, 1998.

Kouser, Morgan J. *Dead End: The Development of Nineteenth Century Litigation on Race.* New York: Oxford University Press, 1986.

Kovel, Joel. *White Racism: A Psychohistory.* New York: Vintage Books, 1971.

Kozol, Johnathan. *Savage Inequalities: Children and American Schools.* New York: HarperPerennial, 1992.

Krenn, Michael. *The African American Voice in U.S. Foreign Policy Since World War II.* New York: Garland Publishing, 1999.

———. *Black Diplomacy: African Americans and the State Department, 1945–1969.* Armonk, N.Y.: M. E. Sharpe, 1998.

Krislov, Samuel. *The Negro in Federal Employment: The Quest for Equal Opportunity.* Minneapolis: University of Minnesota Press, 1967.

"Kwame Ture/Stokely Carmichael: A Tribute to a Life of Struggle." *Black Scholar, Special Memorial Issue* (1998): 27.

Lagemann, Ellen. *The Politics of Knowledge: The Carnegie Corporation, Philanthropy and Public Policy.* Middleton, Conn.: Wesleyan University Press, 1989.

Lansberg, Brian. *Enforcing Civil Rights: Race Discrimination and the U.S. Department of Justice.* Lawrence: University Press of Kansas, 1998.

Lasswell, Harold, and Abraham Kaplan. *Power and Society: A Framework for Political Inquiry.* New Haven, Conn.: Yale University Press, 1950.

Lee, Chana Kai. *For Freedom's Sake: The Life of Fannie Lou Hamer.* Urbana: University of Illinois Press, 2000.

Leeming, David. *James Baldwin: A Biography.* New York: Henry Holt, 1994.

Legum, Colin. *Pan Africanism.* New York: Praeger, 1965.

Lehman, Nicholas. *The Promised Land: The Great Black Migration and How It Changed America.* New York: Knopf, 1991.

Levy, Eugene. *James Weldon Johnson: Black Leader, Black Voice.* Chicago: University of Chicago Press, 1973.

Levy, Harold. *Origins of the Bill of Rights.* New Haven, Conn.: Yale University Press, 1999.

Lester, Julius. *Look Out Whitey: Black Power Gon' Get Your Mama.* New York: Dial Press, 1968.

Leuctenberg, William. *The Supreme Court Reborn: The Constitutional Revolution in the Age of Roosevelt.* New York: Oxford University Press, 1995.

Lewis, David. *W. E. B. DuBois: The Fight for Equality and the American Century, 1919–1963.* New York: Henry Holt, 2000.

———. *W. E. B. DuBois: Biography of A Race.* New York: Henry Holt, 1993.

———. *When Harlem Was in Vogue.* New York: Knopf, 1981.

Lewis, Oscar. *Four Men: An Oral History of Contemporary Cuba.* Urbana: University of Illinois Press, 1978.

———. *La Vida: A Puerto Rican Family in the Culture of Poverty in San Juan and New York.* New York: Random House, 1966.

———. *Five Families: Mexican Case Studies in the Culture of Poverty.* New York: Basic Books, 1959.

Lieberson, Stanley. *A Piece of the Pie: Black and White Immigrants Since 1880.* Berkeley: University of California Press, 1980.

Lincoln, Eric C., and Lawrence Mamiya. *The Black Church in the African American Experience.* Durham, NC: Duke University Press, 1990.

———. *The Black Muslims in America.* Boston: Beacon Press, 1961.

Lipset, Seymour Martin, and Gary Marks. *It Didn't Happen Here: Why Socialism Failed in the United States.* New York: W. W. Norton, 2000.

Lipsky, Michael. "Protest As a Political Resource." *American Political Science Review* 62 (1968): 1,144–1,158.

Litwack, Leon, and August Meier, eds. *Black Leaders of the Nineteenth Century*. Urbana: University of Illinois Press, 1988.

Loevy, Robert. *The Civil Rights Act of 1964: The Passage of the Act That Ended Racial Segregation*. Albany, N.Y.: SUNY Press, 1997.

Logan, Rayford. *Howard University: The First Hundred Years*. Washington, D.C.: Howard University, 1969.

———. *The Betrayal of the Negro: From Rutherford B. Hayes to Woodrow Wilson*. New York: Collier Books, 1965.

Lynch, Hollis. *Edward Wilmot Blyden: Pan Negro Patriot*. New York: Oxford University Press, 1967.

MacNeil, Genna Rae. *Groundwork: Charles Hamilton Houston and the Struggle for Civil Rights*. College Park: University of Maryland Press, 1983.

MacNicol, John. "In Pursuit of the Underclass." *Journal of Social Policy* 16 (1989): 326–389.

Madhubuti, Haki, and Ron Karenga. *Million Man March/Day of Absence*. Chicago: Third World Press, 1996.

Malcolm X. *The Autobiography of Malcolm X*. New York: Grove Press, 1965.

Mann, Robert. *The Walls of Jericho: Lyndon Johnson, Hubert Humphrey, Richard Russell and the Struggle for Civil Rights*. New York: Harcourt Brace, 1996.

Margolick, David. *Strange Fruit: Billie Holiday, Cafe Society and an Early Cry for Civil Rights*. New York: Running Press, 2000.

Martin, Ben L. "From Negro to Black to African American." *Political Science Quarterly* 106 (1991): 83–107.

Martin, Tony. *The Ideological and Organizational Struggles of Marcus Garvey and the Universal Negro Improvement Association*. Westport, Conn.: Greenwood Press, 1976.

Massey, Douglas, and Nancy Denton. *American Apartheid: Segregation and the Making of the Underclass*. Cambridge, Mass.: Harvard University Press, 1993.

Mauer, Mark. *Young Black Men and the Criminal Justice System*. Washington, D.C.: The Sentencing Project, 1995.

Mayer, Henry. *All on Fire: William Lloyd Garrison and the Abolition of Slavery*. New York: St. Martin's Press, 1998.

Mayer, Kenneth. *With the Stroke of a Pen: Executive Orders and Presidential Power*. Princeton, N.J.: Princeton University Press, 2001.

Mayfield, Curtis. *A New World Order*. New York: Warner Brothers, 1996.

———. *Curtis Live*. New York: Buddah Records, 1971.

———. *His Early Years With the Impressions*. Los Angeles: ABC Records, 1973.

McAdams, Douglass. *Political Process and the Development of Black Insurgency*. Chicago: University of Chicago Press, 1982.

McCormack, Donald. "Stokely Carmichael and Pan Africanism: Back to Black Power." *Journal of Politics* 35 (1973): 386–409.

McCormick, Joseph P., ed. "Symposium: The Politics of the Black 'Nation': A Twenty-five Year Perspective." *National Political Science Review* 8 (2001): 1–72.

———. "The Message and the Messengers: Opinions From the Million Man March." *National Political Science Review* 6 (1997): 142–164.

———, and Charles Jones, eds. "The Conceptualization of Deracialization: Thinking Through the Dilemma." In *Dilemmas of Black Leadership*. New York: Harper Collins, 1993.

McFeely, William. *Frederick Douglass*. New York: W. W. Norton, 1991.

McMurry, Linda. *To Keep the Waters Troubled: The Life of Ida B. Wells*. New York: Oxford University Press, 1998.

McWhorter, Diane. *Birmingham, Alabama: The Climatic Battle of the Civil Rights Revolution*. New York: Simon & Schuster, 2001.

Meier, August, and Elliott Rudwick. *CORE: A Study in the Civil Rights Movement*. New York: Oxford University Press, 1973.

———, and Francis Broderick, eds. *Black Protest Thought in the Twentieth Century*. Indianapolis, Ind.: Bobbs-Merrill, 1965.

Melton, James, ed. *Bullwhip Days: The Slaves Remember*. New York: Widenfield and Nicolson, 1988.

Miller, Jake. *The Black Presence in American Foreign Policy*. Washington, D.C.: Howard University Press, 1978.

Miller, William Lee. *Arguing About Slavery: The Great Battle in the United States Congress*. New York: Knopf, 1995.

Mills, Charles. *The Racial Contract*. Ithaca, N.Y.: Cornell University Press, 1997.

Mills, Kay. *This Little Light of Mine: The Life of Fannie Lou Hamer*. New York: Dutton, 1993.

Mills, Nicholas. *The Great School Bus Controversy*. New York: Teachers College Press, 1973.

Mills, Wright C. *The Power Elite*. New York: Oxford University Press, 1956.

Moon, Henry Lee. *Balance of Power: The Negro Vote*. New York: Doubleday, 1948.

Morris, Aldon. *The Origins of the Civil Rights Movement*. New York: Free Press, 1984.

Morris, Lorenzo. "Rise and Fall of the Two Party System." In *The Social and Political Implications of the 1984 Jesse Jackson Presidential Campaign*. Westport, Conn.: Praeger, 1990.

———. *The Social and Political Implications of the 1984 Jesse Jackson Presidential Campaign*. Westport, Conn.: Praeger, 1990.

Moses, Robert, and Charles Cobb. *Racial Equations: Math Literacy and Civil Rights*. Boston, Mass.: Beacon Press, 2001.

Moses, William. *Alexander Crummell: A Study of Civilization and Discontent*. New York: Oxford University Press, 1989.

———. *Classical Black Nationalism: From the Revolution to Marcus Garvey*. New York: New York University Press, 1996.

Moss, Alfred. *The American Negro Academy: Voice of the Talented Tenth*. Baton Rouge: Louisiana State University Press, 1981.

Moynihan, Daniel. *The Politics of a Guaranteed Income: The Nixon Administration and the Family Assistance Plan.* New York: Vintage Books, 1973.

Myrdal, Gunnar. *The Challenge of Affluence.* New York: Pantheon, 1963.

———. *An American Dilemma: The Negro Problem and Modern Democracy.* New York: Harper & Row, 1944, 1967.

Naison, Mark. *Communists in Harlem During the Depression.* New York: Grove Press, 1983.

National Directory of African American Organizations, 1988–2000. New York: Philip Morris, 2000.

Neal, Mark Anthony. *What the Music Said: Black Popular Music and Black Public Culture.* New York: Routledge, 1999.

Nelson, William. *The Fourteenth Amendment: From Political Principle to Judicial Doctrine.* Cambridge, Mass.: Harvard University Press, 1988.

Nelson, William, and Phillip Meranto. *Electing Black Mayors: Political Action in the Black Community.* Columbus: Ohio State University Press, 1977.

Newman, Michelle. *White Women's Rights: The Racial Origins of Feminism in the United States.* New York: Oxford University Press, 1999.

Nie, Norman, et al. *Participation in America: Continuity and Change.* Chicago: University of Chicago Press, 1990.

Nobles, Melissa. *Shades of Citizenship: Race and the Census in Modern Politics.* Palo Alto, Calif.: Stanford University Press, 2000.

Oakes, Stephen. *To Purge This Land With Blood: A Biography of John Brown.* Amherst: University of Massachusetts Press, 1984.

———. *The Fires of Jubilee: Nat Turner's Fierce Rebellion.* New York: Harper & Row, 1975.

Ofari, Earl. *Let Your Motto Be Resistance: The Life and Thought of Henry Highland Garnett.* Boston, Mass.: Beacon Press, 1972.

Ogbu, John. *Minority Education and Caste.* New York: Academic Press, 1978.

Okin, Susan. *Women in Western Thought.* Princeton, N.J.: Princeton University Press, 1979.

Oliver, Melvin, and Thomas Shapiro. *Black Wealth/White Wealth: A New Perspective on Racial Equality.* New York: Routledge, 1995.

Olsen, Marvin. "Social and Political Participation of Blacks." *American Sociological Review* 35 (1969): 609–696.

O'Reilly, Kenneth. *Nixon's Piano: Presidents and Racial Politics from Washington to Clinton.* New York: Free Press, 1995.

———. *Racial Matters: The FBI's Secret File on Black America, 1960–72.* New York: Carroll & Graf, 1994.

Orfield, Gary. *Dismantling Desegregation: The Quiet Reversal of Brown vs Board of Education.* New York: Norton, 1996.

———. *Must We Bus: Segregation and National Policy.* Washington, D.C.: Brookings Institution, 1978.

Osofsky, Gilbert. *Harlem: The Making of a Ghetto, 1890–1930.* New York: Harper & Row, 1966.

Painter, Nell Irvin. *Sojourner Truth: A Life, a Symbol.* New York: W. W. Norton, 1996.

Parmet, Herbert. *Richard Nixon and His America.* Boston: Little, Brown, 1990.

Patterson, Orlando. *Freedom in the Making of Western Culture.* New York: Basic Books, 1991.

Payne, Charles. *I've Got the Light of Freedom: The Organizing Tradition in the Mississippi Freedom Struggle.* Berkeley: University of California Press, 1995.

Pearson, Hugh. *The Shadow of the Panther: Huey Newton and the Price of Black Power in America.* Reading, Mass.: Addison-Wesley, 1994.

Perlstein, Rick. *Before the Storm: Barry Goldwater and the Unmaking of the American Consensus.* New York: Hill and Wang, 2001.

Perry, Bruce. *Malcolm: The Life of a Man Who Changed Black America.* Barrytown, N.Y.: Station Hill Press, 1991.

Phelps, Timothy, and Helen Winternitz. *Capitol Games: Clarence Thomas, Anita Hill and the Story of a Supreme Court Nomination.* New York: Hyperion, 1992.

Picard, Earl, ed. "Essays in Honor of Mack Jones." *National Political Science Review* 9 (2002): 4–19.

Pinderhughes, Dianne. *Race and Ethnicity in Chicago Politics.* Urbana: University of Illinois Press, 1987.

Piven, Frances Fox, and Richard Cloward. *Poor People's Movements: Why They Succeed, Why They Fail.* New York: Vintage Books, 1977.

———. *Regulating the Poor: The Functions of Social Welfare.* New York: Vintage Books, 1971.

Plummer, Brenda Gayle. *Haiti and the United States.* Athens: University of Georgia Press, 1992.

———. *Window on Freedom: Race, Civil Rights and U.S. Foreign Policy.* Chapel Hill: University of North Carolina Press, 2003.

Poinsett, Alex. *Walking With Presidents: Louis Martin and the Rise of Black Political Power.* Lanham, Md.: Madison Books, 1997.

Pride, Armistead, and Clint Wilson. *A History of the Black Press.* Washington, D.C.: Howard University Press, 1997.

Quarles, Benjamin. *Lincoln and the Negro.* New York: Oxford University Press, 1962.

———. *Black Abolitionists.* New York: Oxford University Press, 1970.

Ralison, Garry. "An Exploration of the Term Underclass as It Relates to African Americans." *Journal of Black Studies* 23 (1991): 289–306.

Redkey, Edwin. "The Flowering of Black Nationalism: Henry McNeal Turner and Marcus Garvey." In *Key Issues in the Afro-American Experience,* edited by Nathan Higgins, Martin Kilson, and Daniel Fox. New York: Harcourt Brace Jovanovich, 1971.

Reed, Adolph. *The Jesse Jackson Phenomenon.* New Haven, Conn.: Yale University Press, 1986.

———. "The Black Urban Regime: Structural Origins and Constraints." In *Power, Community and the City,* edited by Michael Smith. New Brunswick, N.J.: Transaction, 1988.

Report of the National Advisory Commission on Civil Disorders. New York: Bantam, 1968.

Rich, Wilbur. *Black Mayors and School Politics.* New York: Garland, 1996.

Richardson, Marilyn. *Maria Stewart: America's First Black Woman Political Writer.* Bloomington: Indiana University Press, 1987.

Riker, William. *Federalism: Origin, Operation and Significance.* Boston: Little, Brown, 1964.

Riley, Richard. *The Presidency and the Politics of Racial Inequality.* New York: Columbia University Press, 1999.

Roak, James. "American Black Leaders Response to Colonialism and the Cold War, 1943–1953." In *The African American Voice in U.S. Foreign Policy Since World War II,* edited by Michael Krenn. New York: Garland, 1999.

Robinson, Dean. *Black Nationalism in American Political Thought.* New York: Cambridge University Press, 2001.

Robinson, Donald. *Slavery in the Structure of American Politics.* New York: Harcourt Brace Jovanovich, 1971.

Robnet, Belinda. *How Long? How Long? African American Women in the Civil Rights Movement.* New York: Oxford University Press, 1997.

Roediger, David. *The Wages of Whiteness: Race and the Making of the American Working Class.* New York: Verso Press, 1991.

Rose, Tricia. *Rap Music and Black Culture in Contemporary America.* Hanover, N.H.: University Press of England, 1994.

Rosenberg, Gerald. *The Hollow Hope: Can the Courts Bring About Social Change?* Chicago: University of Chicago Press, 1991.

Rosenstone, Steven, Roy Behr, and Edward Lazarus. *Third Parties in America.* Princeton, N.J.: Princeton University Press, 1984.

Ross, Joyce B. *J.E. Spingarn and the Rise of the NAACP.* New York: Atheneum, 1972.

Rossiter, Clinton. *Conservatism in America.* New York: Vintage Books, 1955.

Roucek, Joseph. "Minority–Majority Relations in Their Power Aspect." *Phylon* 15 (1956): 24–30.

Russell, Kathy, Midge Wilson, and Ronald Hall. *The Color Complex: The Politics of Skin Color.* New York: Harcourt Brace Jovanovich, 1992.

Rustin, Bayard. "From Protest to Politics: The Future of the Civil Rights Movement." *Commentary* 39 (1965): 25–31.

Say It Loud: A Celebration of Black Music in America. Produced by Patrick Milligan, Shawn Amos, and Quincy Newell. Los Angeles, Rhino Entertainment, 2001.

Schlesinger, Arthur, Jr. *The Disuniting of America: Reflections on a Multicultural Society.* New York: W. W. Norton, 1991, 1998.

Schuman, Howard, Carlotta Steeth, and Lawrence Bobo. *Racial Attitudes in America: Trends and Interpretations.* Cambridge, Mass.: Harvard University Press, 1985.

Schwarz, Bernard. *Behind Bakke: Affirmative Action and the Supreme Court.* New York: New York University Press, 1988.

———. *Superchief: Earl Warren and His Supreme Court.* New York: New York University Press, 1983.

Schwarz, Michael. *Visions of a Liberated Future: Black Arts Movement Writings.* New York: Thunder Mouth Press, 1989.

Sears, David, and John McConahay. *The Politics of Violence: The New Urban Blacks and the Watts Riot.* Boston: Houghton Mifflin, 1973.

Seltzer, Richard, and Robert C. Smith. "Race and Ideology." *Phylon* 46 (1985): 98–105.

———. "Skin Color Differences in the Afro-American Community and the Differences They Make." *Journal of Black Studies* 21 (1991): 279–86.

Shaw, Todd. "We Refused to Lay Down Our Spears: The Persistence of Welfare Rights Activism, 1966–1976." In *Black Political Organizations in the Post Civil Rights Era,* edited by Ollie Johnson and Karin Stanford. New Brunswick, N.J.: Rutgers State University Press, 2002.

Sigelman, Lee, and Susan Welch. *Black Americans' Views of Racial Inequality.* Cambridge, Mass.: Cambridge University Press, 1994.

Sindler, Alan. *Bakke, Defunnis and Minority Admissions.* New York: Longman, 1978.

Singh, Robert. *The Congressional Black Caucus: Racial Politics in the U.S. Congress.* Thousand Oaks: Sage, 1998.

Sitkopf, Harvey. "The New Deal and Race Relations." In *Fifty Years Later: The New Deal Evaluated.* New York: Random House, 1985.

Skerry, Peter. *Counting on the Census: Race, Group Identity and the Evasion of Politics.* Washington, D.C.: Brookings Institution, 2000.

Skinner, Elliot. *African Americans and U.S. Foreign Policy, 1850–1924.* Washington, D.C.: Howard University Press, 1992.

Skrenty, John David. *The Ironies of Affirmative Action: Politics, Culture and Justice in America.* Chicago: University of Chicago Press, 1996.

Spann, Girardeau. *Race Against the Court: The Supreme Court and Minorities in America.* New York: New York University Press, 1993.

Spear, Alan. "The Origins of the Urban Ghetto, 1870–1915." In *Key Issues in the Afro-American Experience,* edited by Nathan Huggins, Martin Kilson, and Daniel Fox. New York: Harcourt Brace Jovanovich, 1971.

Smith, Robert C. "The NAACP in 21st Century Perspective." In *Black Political Organizations in the Post Civil Rights Era,* edited by Ollie Johnson and Kann Stanford. New Brunswick, N.J.: Rutgers University Press.

———. "Rating Black Leaders." *National Political Science Review* 8 (2001): 69–77.

———. *We Have No Leaders: African Americans in the Post Civil Rights Era.* Albany: SUNY Press, 1996.

———. *Racism in the Post Civil Rights Era: Now You See It, Now You Don't.* Albany: SUNY Press, 1995.

———. "Ideology As the Enduring Dilemma of Black Politics." In *Dilemmas of Black Politics,* edited by Georgia Persons. New York: Harper Collins, 1992.

———. "Black Appointed Officials: A Neglected Category of Political Participation Research." *Journal of Black Studies* 14 (1984): 369–388.

———. "The Changing Shape of Urban Black Politics, 1960–70." *The Annals of the American Academy of Political and Social Science* 439 (1978): 16–28.

———. "Black Power and the Transformation From Protest to Politics." *Political Science Quarterly* 96 (1981): 431–43.

———. "Beyond Marx: Fanon and the Concept of Colonial Violence." *Black World* 27 (1973): 23–33.

———, and Richard Seltzer. *Contemporary Controversies and the American Racial Divide.* Boulder, Colo.: Rowman & Littlefield, 2000.

———. *Race, Class and Culture: A Study in Afro-American Mass Opinion.* Albany: SUNY Press, 1992.

Solomon, Mark. "Black Critics of the Cold War." In *The African American Voice in U.S. Foreign Policy Since World War II,* edited by Michael Krenn. New York: Garland, 1999.

Spencer, Jon Michael. *The New Colored People: The Mixed Race Movement in America.* New York: New York University Press, 1997.

Stanford, Karin. *Beyond the Boundaries: Jesse Jackson in International Affairs.* Albany, N.Y.: SUNY Press, 1997.

Staples, Robert. "Violence and Black America: The Political Implications." *Black World* 28 (1974): 17–34.

Starks, Robert. "A Commentary and Response to Exploring the Meaning of Deracialization." *Urban Affairs Quarterly* 27 (1991): 216–222.

Stern, Mark. *Calculating Visions, Kennedy, Johnson and Civil Rights.* New Brunswick, N.J.: Rutgers University Press, 1992.

Stuckey, Sterling. *The Ideological Origins of Black Nationalism.* Boston, Mass.: Beacon Press, 1972.

———. *Slave Culture: Foundations of Nationalist Thought.* New York: Oxford University Press, 1987.

Swain, Carol. *Black Faces, Black Interests: The Representation of African American Interests in Congress.* Cambridge, Mass.: Harvard University Press, 1993.

Tate, Gayle, and Lewis Randolph, eds. *Dimensions of Black Conservatism in the United States.* New York: Palgrave, 2002.

Tate, Katherine. *From Protest to Politics: The New Black Voter.* Cambridge, Mass.: Harvard University Press, 1994.

Thomas, Darryl. *The Theory and Practice of Third World Solidarity.* Westport, Conn.: Praeger, 2001.

Thomas, Hugh. *Slave Trade: The Story of the Atlantic Slave Trade, 1440–1870.* New York: Simon & Schuster, 1997.

Thurber, Timothy. *The Politics of Equality: Hubert H. Humphrey and the African American Freedom Struggle.* New York: Columbia University Press, 1999.

Tocqueville, Alexis de. *Democracy in America,* Vol. 1. Edited by Phillips Bradley. New York: Vintage Books, 1945.

Tomlinson, T. M. "The Development of a Riot Ideology Among Urban Negroes." *American Behavioral Scientist* 2 (1968): 17–29.

Tompkins, Stephen. "Army Feared King, Secretly Watched Him, Spying Started 75 Years Ago." *Memphis Commercial Appeal,* March 21, 1993.

Trefousse, Hans. *The Radical Republicans: Lincoln's Vanguard for Freedom* Baton Rouge: Louisiana State University Press, 1975.

Turner, Richard. *Islam in the African American Experience.* Bloomington: Indiana University Press, 1997.

Tushnet, Mark. *The NAACP's Legal Strategy against Segregation, 1925–50.* Chapel Hill: University of North Carolina Press, 1987.

Ullman, Victor. *Martin R. Delany: The Beginnings of Black Nationalism.* Boston, Mass.: Beacon Press, 1971.

U.S. Bureau of the Census. *The Social and Economic Status of the Black Population in the United States: An Historical Overview, 1790–1978.* Current Population Reports, Special Studies, series 23, No. 80. Washington, D.C., 1995.

———. *The Black Population of the United States: March 1994 and 1993.* Current Population Reports, series p20–480. Washington, D.C., 1995.

U.S. Congress, Senate. *Final Report of the Select Committee to Study Government Operations with Respect to Intelligence.* 94th Cong., 2nd sess., 1976. Rept. 755.

Ungar, Sanford. *FBI: An Uncensored Look Behind the Walls.* Boston: Little, Brown, 1975.

Valentine, Charles. *Culture of Poverty: Critique and Counter-Proposals.* Chicago: University of Chicago Press, 1968.

Vose, Clement. "Litigation As a Form of Pressure Group Activity." *The Annals of the American Academy of Political and Social Science* 319 (1958): 20–43.

Walker, Robert. "Soul and Society." Doctoral dissertation, Stanford University, 1976.

Walter, John C. *The Harlem Fox: J. Raymond Jones and Tammany, 1920–1970.* Albany: SUNY Press, 1989.

Walters, Ronald. *White Nationalism in the Second Reconstruction.* Detroit, Mich.: Wayne State University Press, 2002.

———. *Pan Africanism: An Analysis of Modern Afrocentric Movements.* Detroit, Mich.: Wayne State University Press, 1993.

———. *Black Presidential Politics in America: A Strategic Approach.* Albany: SUNY Press, 1988.

———. "In World Relations: The Future of Pan Africanism." *Black World* 24 (1974): 10–15.

———. "African American Nationalism." *Black World* 22 (1973): 9–21.

Walters, Ronald, and Cedric Johnson. *Bibliography of African American Leadership.* Westport, Conn.: Greenwood Press, 2000.

Walters, Ronald, and Robert C. Smith. *African American Leadership.* Albany: SUNY Press, 1999.

Walton, Carlton F. "The Southern Christian Leadership Conference: Beyond Civil Rights." In *Black Political Organizations in the Post Civil Rights Era,* edited by Ollie Johnson and Karin Stanford. New Brunswick, N.J.: Rutgers University Press, 2002.

Walton, Eugene. "Will the Supreme Court Revert to Racism." *Black World* 21 (1972): 46–48.

Walton, Hanes, Jr., *Reelection: William Jefferson Clinton as a Native Son Presidential Candidate.* New York: Columbia University Press, 2000.

———. "Democrats and African Americans: The American Idea." In *Democrats and the American Idea,* edited by Peter Kover. Washington, D.C.: Center for National Policy Press, 1992.

———. *When the Marching Stopped: The Politics of Civil Rights Regulatory Agencies.* Albany: SUNY Press, 1988.

———. *Invisible Politics: Black Political Behavior.* Albany: SUNY Press, 1985.

———. *The Study and Analysis of Black Politics: A Bibliography.* Trenton, N.J.: Scarecrow Press, 1973.

———. *Black Politics: A Theoretical and Structural Analysis.* Philadelphia: J.B. Lippincott, 1972.

———. *Black Political Parties: A Historical and Political Analysis.* New York: Free Press, 1972.

———. *The Negro in Third Party Politics.* Philadelphia: Dorrance, 1969.

———. "The Current Literature on Black Politics." *National Political Science Review* 1 (1989): 152–168.

———. "The Recent Literature of Black Politics." *PS: Political Science and Politics* 18 (1985): 769–780.

Walton, Hanes, Jr., and Robert C. Smith. *American Politics and the African American Quest for Universal Freedom.* New York: Longman, 2000.

Walton, Hanes, Jr., Cheryl Miller, and Joseph P. McCormick. "Race and Political Science: The Dual Traditions of Race Relations Politics and African American Politics." In *Political Science and Its History: Research Programs and Political Traditions,* edited by John Dryzek et al. New York: Cambridge University Press, 1994.

Walton, Hanes, Jr., Leslie B. McLemore, and C. Vernon Gray. "The Pioneering Books in Black Politics and the Political Science Community." *National Political Science Review* 2 (1990): 196–218.

Walton, Hanes, Jr., et al. "The Literature of Black Politics: The Decade of the Nineties." *Politics and Society* 29 (2001): 453–482.

Waters, Mary. *Black Identities: West Indian Immigrant Dreams and American Realities.* Cambridge, Mass.: Harvard University Press, 2000.

Watson, Denton. *Lion in the Lobby: Clarence Mitchell's Struggles to Pass Civil Rights Laws.* New York: Morrow, 1990.

Watts, Jerry. *Amiri Baraka: The Politics and Art of a Black Intellectual.* New York: New York University Press, 2001.

———. *Heroism and the Black Intellectual: Ralph Ellison, Politics and Afro-American Intellectual Life.* Chapel Hill: University of North Carolina Press, 1994.

———. "Dilemmas of Black Intellectuals." *Dissent* 36 (1989): 507–534.

Weiss, Nancy. *Farewell to the Party of Lincoln: Black Politics in the Age of FDR.* Princeton, N.J.: Princeton University Press, 1983.

———. *Whitney M. Young and the Struggle for Civil Rights.* Princeton, N.J.: Princeton University Press, 1989.

———. *The National Urban League.* New York: Oxford University Press, 1989.

Weldin, Carolyn. *Inheritors of the Spirit: Mary White Ovington and the Founding of the NAACP.* New York: John Wiley, 1998.

Whelan, Charles, and Barbara Whelan. *The Longest Debate: The Legislative History of the 1964 Civil Rights Act.* Cabin John, Md.: Seven Locks Press, 1985.

Williams, Juan. *Thurgood Marshall: American Revolutionary.* New York: Times Books, 1998.

———. "President Colin Powell." *Reconstruction* 2 (1994): 57–68.

Williams, Linda. *The Constraint of Race: Legacies of White Skin Privilege and the Politics of American Social Policy.* Albany: SUNY Press, 2002.

Wills, Gary. *Lincoln at Gettysburg: The Words That Remade America.* New York: Touchstone, 1992.

———. *The Second Civil War: Arming for Armageddon.* New York: New American Library, 1968.

Wilson, James Q. *Political Organizations.* New York: Basic Books, 1973.

———. "Two Negro Politicians." *Midwest Political Science Review* 12 (1960): 365–379.

Wilson, William J. *The Truly DisAdvantaged: The Inner City, the Underclass and Public Policy.* Illinois: University of Chicago Press, 1987.

———. "Race Neutral Programs and the Democratic Party." *American Prospect* 1 (1990): 74–81.

Wiltse, Charles. *David Walker's Appeal.* New York: Hill & Wang, 1965.

Wittner, Lawrence. "The National Negro Congress: A Reassessment." *American Quarterly* 22 (1968): 883–901.

Wolfe, Alan. *The Seamy Side of Democracy: Repression in the United States.* New York: David McKay, 1973.

Wolters, Raymond. *Right Turn: William Bradford Reynolds, the Reagan Administration and Black Civil Rights.* New Brunswick, N.J.: Transaction, 1996.

Wood, Forrest. *The Arrogance of Faith: Christianity and Race in America from the Colonial Era to the Twentieth Century.* New York: Knopf, 1990.

Woodward, C. Vann. *Reunion and Reaction.* New York: Doubleday Anchor, 1956.

———. *The Strange Career of Jim Crow.* New York: Oxford University Press, 1966.

Zangrando, Robert. *The NAACP Crusade Against Lynching, 1909–1950.* Philadelphia: Temple University Press, 1980.

Index

Boldface page numbers denote extensive treatment of a topic. *Italic* page numbers refer to illustrations; *c* refers to the Chronology; and *m* indicates a map.